The Oxford Russian Language Program

Using teams of spec...
orators, The Oxford...
duced the world's...
authority on contemporary language.

Also available

The Oxford Colour Russian Dictionary

compiled by
Della Thompson

OXFORD UNIVERSITY PRESS

OXFORD
UNIVERSITY PRESS

Great Clarendon Street, Oxford OX2 6DP

Oxford University Press is a department of the University of Oxford.
It furthers the University's objective of excellence in research, scholarship,
and education by publishing worldwide in

Oxford New York

Auckland Cape Town Dar es Salaam Hong Kong Karachi Kuala Lumpur
Madrid Melbourne Mexico City Nairobi New Delhi Taipei Toronto
Shanghai

With offices in
Argentina Austria Brazil Chile Czech Republic France Greece Guatemala
Hungary Italy Japan South Korea Poland Portugal Singapore Switzerland
Thailand Turkey Ukraine Vietnam

British Library Cataloguing in Publication Data

Data available

Library of Congress Cataloging in Publication Data

Data available

ISBN-13: 978-0-19-860699-4
ISBN-10: 0-19-860699-0

10 9 8 7 6 5

Printed in Italy by
Legoprint S.p.A.
Lavis (TN)

Contents

Preface

The Oxford Colour Russian Dictionary is the latest addition to the
Oxford Russian Dictionary range. Colour headwords throughout make it the most useful and easy-to-use dictionary for
beginners. The word games in the centre of the dictionary
build knowledge of grammar and vocabulary, and provide
valuable practice in using your dictionary, helping you get the
best out of it.

Particular attention has been given to the provision of
inflected forms where these cause difficulty, and to showing
the stressed syllable of every Russian word as well as changes
in stress where they occur. Perfective and imperfective aspects
are distinguished and both are given wherever appropriate.

Thanks are due to Alexander and Nina Levtov for their editorial help and valuable advice on contemporary Russian
usage, and to Helen McCurdy for help with proofreading.

D. J. T.

Introduction

As an aid to easy reference all main headwords, compounds, and derivatives appear in blue.

In order to save space, related words are often grouped together in paragraphs, as are cross-references and compound entries.

The swung dash (∼) and the hyphen are also used to save space. The swung dash represents the headword preceding it in bold, or the preceding Russian word, e.g. **Georgian** *n* грузи́н, ∼ка. The hyphen is mainly used, in giving grammatical forms, to stand for part of the preceding, or (less often) following, Russian word, e.g. **приходи́ть** (-ожу́, -о́дишь).

Russian headwords are followed by inflexional information where considered necessary. So-called regular inflexions for the purpose of this dictionary are listed in the Appendices.

Where a noun ending is given but not labeled in the singular, it is the genitive ending; other cases are named; in the plural, where cases are identifiable by their endings, they are not labeled, e.g. **сестра́** (*pl* сёстры, сестёр, сёстрам). The gender of Russian nouns can usually be deduced from their endings and it is indicated only in exceptional cases (e.g. for masculine nouns in **-а**, **-я**, and **-ь**, neuter nouns in **-мя**, and all indeclinable nouns).

Verbs are labeled *impf* or *pf* to show their aspect. Where a perfective verb is formed by the addition of a prefix to the imperfective, this is shown at the headword by a light vertical stroke, e.g. про|лепета́ть. When a verb requires the use of a case other than the accusative, this is indicated, e.g. **маха́ть** *impf*, **махну́ть** *pf* + *instr* wave, brandish.

Both the comma and the ampersand (&) are used to show alternatives, e.g. **хоте́ть** + *gen*, *acc* means that the Russian verb may govern either the genitive or accusative; **сирота́** *m* & *f* orphan means that the Russian noun is treated as masculine or feminine according to the sex of the person denoted;

Cossack *n* каза́к, -а́чка represents the masculine and feminine translations of Cossack; **dilate** *vt* & *i* расширя́ть(ся) means that the Russian verb forms cover both the transitive and intransitive English verbs.

Stress

The stress of Russian words is shown by an acute accent over the vowel of the stressed syllable. The vowel **ё** has no stress-mark since it is almost always stressed. The presence of two stress-marks indicates that either of the marked syllables may be stressed.

Changes of stress in inflexion are shown, e.g.

   i) **предложи́ть** (-жу́, -жи́шь)

The absence of a stress-mark on the second person singular indicates that the stress is on the preceding syllable and that the rest of the conjugation is stressed in this way.

   ii) **нача́ть** (............; на́чал, -а́, -о)

The final form, на́чало, takes the stress of the first of the two preceding forms when these differ from each other. Forms that are not shown, here на́чали, are stressed like the last form given.

   iii) **дождь** (-дя́)

The single form given in brackets is the genitive singular and all other forms have the same stressed syllable.

   iv) **душа́** (*acc* -у; *pl* -и)

If only one case-labeled form is given in the singular, it is an exception to the regular paradigm. If only one plural form is given (the nominative), the rest follow this. In other words, in this example, the accusative singular and all the plural forms have initial stress.

   v) **скоба́** (*pl* -ы, -а́м)

In the plural, forms that are not shown (here instrumental and prepositional) are stressed like the last form given.

Proprietary terms

This dictionary includes some words which are, or are asserted to be, proprietary names or trade marks. Their inclusion does not imply that they have acquired for legal purposes a non-proprietary or general significance, nor is any other judgment implied concerning their legal status. In cases where the editor has some evidence that a word is used as a proprietary name or trade mark this is indicated by the label *propr*, but no judgment concerning the legal status of such words is made or implied thereby.

Abbreviations

abbr	abbreviation	fig	figurative
abs	absolute	fut	future (tense)
acc	accusative		
adj, adjs	adjective(s)	gen	genitive
adv, advs	adverb(s)	geog	geography
aeron	aeronautics	geol	geology
agric	agriculture	geom	geometry
anat	anatomy	gram	grammar
approx	approximate(ly)		
archaol	archaeology	hist	historical
archit	architecture		
astron	astronomy	imper	imperative
attrib	attributive	impers	impersonal
aux	auxiliary	impf	imperfective
		indecl	indeclinable
bibl	biblical	indef	indefinite
biol	biology	indet	indeterminate
bot	botany	inf	infinitive
		instr	instrumental
chem	chemistry	int	interjection
cin	cinema(tography)	interrog	interrogative
coll	colloquial		
collect	collective(ly)	ling	linguistics
comb	combination	loc	locative
comm	commerce		
comp	comparative	m	masculine
comput	computing	math	mathematics
conj, conjs	conjunction(s)	med	medicine
cul	culinary	meteorol	meteorology
		mil	military
dat	dative	mus	music
def	definite		
derog	derogatory	n	noun
det	determinate	naut	nautical
dim	diminutive	neg	negative
		neut	neuter
eccl	ecclesiastical	nn	nouns
econ	economics	nom	nominative
electr	electricity		
electron	electronics	o.s.	oneself
emph	emphatic		
esp	especially	parl	parliamentary
etc.	etcetera	part	participle
		partl	particle
f	feminine	pers	person

pf	perfective
philos	philosophy
phon	phphonetics
phot	photography
phys	physics
pl	plural
polit	political
poss	possessive
predic	predicate; predicative
pref	prefix
prep	preposition; prepositional
pres	present (tense)
pron, prons	pronoun(s)
propr	proprietary term
psych	psychology
refl	reflexive
rel	relative
relig	religion; religious
rly	railway
sb	substantive
sg	singular
sl	slang
s.o.	someone
sth	something
superl	superlative
tech	technical
tel	telephony
theat	theater
theol	theology
univ	university
usu	usually
v	verb
v aux	auxiliary verb
vbl	verbal
vi	intransitive verb
voc	vocative
vt	transitive verb
vulg	vulgar
vv	verbs
zool	zoology

A

a[1] *conj* and, but; **а (не) то** or else, otherwise.

a[2] *int* oh, ah.

абажу́р lampshade.

абба́тство abbey.

аббревиату́ра abbreviation.

абза́ц indention; paragraph.

абонеме́нт subscription, season ticket. **абоне́нт** subscriber.

абориге́н aborigine.

або́рт abortion; **де́лать** *impf*, **с~** *pf* **~** have an abortion.

абрико́с apricot.

абсолю́тно *adv* absolutely. **абсолю́тный** absolute.

абстра́ктный abstract.

абсу́рд absurdity; the absurd. **абсу́рдный** absurd.

абсце́сс abscess.

аванга́рд advanced guard; vanguard; avant-garde. **аванга́рдный** avant-garde. **аванпо́ст** outpost; forward position.

ава́нс advance (*of money*); *pl* advances, overtures. **ава́нсом** *adv* in advance, on account.

авансце́на proscenium.

авантю́ра (*derog*) adventure; venture; escapade; shady enterprise. **авантюри́ст** (*derog*) adventurer. **авантюри́стка** (*derog*) adventuress. **авантю́рный** adventurous; adventure.

авари́йный breakdown; emergency. **ава́рия** accident, crash; breakdown.

а́вгуст August. **а́вгустовский** August.

а́виа *abbr* (*of* **авиапо́чтой**) by airmail.

авиа- *abbr in comb* (*of* **авиацио́нный**) air-, aero-; aircraft; aviation. **авиали́ния** air-route, airway. **~но́сец** (**-сца**) aircraft carrier. **~по́чта** airmail.

авиацио́нный aviation; flying; aircraft. **авиа́ция** aviation; aircraft; air-force.

авока́до *neut indecl* avocado (pear).

аво́сь *adv* perhaps; **на ~** at random, on the off-chance.

австрали́ец (-и́йца), австрали́йка Australian. **австрали́йский** Australian. **Австра́лия** Australia.

австри́ец (-и́йца), австри́йка Austrian. **австри́йский** Austrian. **А́встрия** Austria.

авто- *in comb* self-; auto-; automatic; motor-. **автоба́за** motor-transport depot. **~биографи́ческий** autobiographical. **~биогра́фия** autobiography; curriculum vitae. **автобу́с** bus. **~вокза́л** bus-station. **авто́граф** autograph. **~запра́вочная ста́нция** petrol station. **~кра́т** autocrat. **~крати́ческий** autocratic. **~кра́тия** autocracy. **~магистра́ль** motorway. **~маши́на** motor vehicle. **~моби́ль** *m* car. **~но́мия** autonomy. **~но́мный** autonomous; self-contained. **~пило́т** automatic pilot. **~портре́т** self-portrait. **~ру́чка** fountain-pen. **~ста́нция** bus-station. **~стра́да** motorway.

автома́т slot-machine; automatic device, weapon, etc.; sub-machine gun; robot; **(телефо́н-)~** public call-box. **автоматиза́ция** automation. **автоматизи́ровать** *impf & pf* automate; make automatic. **автомати́ческий** automatic.

а́втор author; composer; inventor; (*fig*) architect.

авторизо́ванный authorized.

авторите́т authority. **авторите́тный** authoritative.

а́вторск|ий authors'; **~ий гонора́р** royalty; **~ое пра́во** copyright. **а́вторство** authorship.

ага́ *int* aha; yes.

аге́нт agent. **аге́нтство** agency. **агенту́ра** (network of) agents.

агита́тор agitator, propagandist; canvasser. **агитацио́нный** propaganda. **агита́ция** propaganda, agitation;

campaign. **агити́ровать** *impf* (*pf* с~) agitate, campaign; (try to) persuade, win over. **агитпу́нкт** *abbr* agitation centre.

агóния agony.

агра́рный agrarian.

агрега́т aggregate; unit.

агресси́вный aggressive. **агре́ссия** aggression. **агре́ссор** aggressor.

агроно́м agronomist. **агроно́мия** agriculture.

ад (*loc* -ý) hell.

ада́птер adapter; (*mus*) pick-up.

адвока́т lawyer. **адвокату́ра** legal profession; lawyers.

администрати́вный administrative. **администра́тор** administrator; manager. **администра́ция** administration; management.

адмира́л admiral.

а́дрес (*pl* -á) address. **адреса́т** addressee. **а́дресный** address; ~ая кни́га directory. **адресова́ть** *impf & pf* address, send.

а́дский infernal, hellish.

адъюта́нт aide-de-camp; ста́рший ~ adjutant.

ажу́рный delicate, lacy; ~ая рабо́та openwork; tracery.

аза́рт heat; excitement; fervour, ardour, passion. **аза́ртный** venturesome; heated; ~ая игра́ game of chance.

а́збука alphabet; ABC.

Азербайджа́н Azerbaijan. **азербайджа́нец** (-нца), **азербайджа́нка** Azerbaijani. **азербайджа́нский** Azerbaijani.

азиа́т, ~ка Asian. **азиа́тский** Asian, Asiatic. **А́зия** Asia.

азо́т nitrogen.

а́ист stork.

ай *int* oh; oo.

а́йсберг iceberg.

акаде́мик academician. **академи́ческий** academic. **акаде́мия** academy.

аквала́нг aqualung.

акваре́ль water-colour.

аква́риум aquarium.

акведу́к aqueduct.

акклиматизи́ровать *impf & pf* acclimatize; ~ся become acclimatized.

аккомпанеме́нт accompaniment; под ~ +*gen* to the accompaniment

of. **аккомпаниа́тор** accompanist. **аккомпани́ровать** *impf* +*dat* accompany.

аккóрд chord.

аккордеóн accordion.

аккóрдный by agreement; ~ая рабóта piece-work.

аккредити́в letter of credit. **аккредитова́ть** *impf & pf* accredit.

аккумуля́тор accumulator.

аккура́тный neat, careful; punctual; exact, thorough.

акри́л acrylic. **акри́ловый** acrylic.

акроба́т acrobat.

аксессуа́р accessory; (stage) props.

аксио́ма axiom.

акт act; deed, document; обвини́тельный ~ indictment.

актёр actor.

акти́в (*comm*) asset(s).

активиза́ция stirring up, making (more) active. **активизи́ровать** *impf & pf* make (more) active, stir up. **акти́вный** active.

акти́ровать *impf & pf* (*pf also* с~) register, record, presence or absence of; (*sl*) write off.

а́ктовый зал assembly hall.

актри́са actress.

актуа́льный topical, urgent.

аку́ла shark.

аку́стика acoustics. **акусти́ческий** acoustic.

акуше́р obstetrician. **акуше́рка** midwife.

акце́нт accent, stress. **акценти́ровать** *impf & pf* accent; accentuate.

акционе́р shareholder. **акционе́рный** joint-stock. **а́кция**[1] share; *pl* stock. **а́кция**[2] action.

а́лгебра algebra.

а́либи *neut indecl* alibi.

алиме́нты (*pl*; *gen* -ов) (*law*) maintenance.

алкоголи́зм alcoholism. **алкоголи́к** alcoholic. **алкого́ль** *m* alcohol. **алкого́льный** alcoholic.

аллего́рия allegory.

аллерги́я allergy.

алле́я avenue; path, walk.

аллига́тор alligator.

алло́ hello! (*on telephone*).

алма́з diamond.

алта́рь (-я́) *m* altar; chancel, sanctuary.

алфавит alphabet. алфавитный alphabetical.

алчный greedy, grasping.

алый scarlet.

альбом album; sketch-book.

альманах literary miscellany; almanac.

альпийский Alpine. альпинизм mountaineering. альпинист, альпинистка (mountain)climber.

альт (-á; pl -ы́) alto; viola.

альтернатива alternative. альтернативный alternative.

альтруистический altruistic.

алюминий aluminium.

амазонка Amazon; horsewoman; riding-habit.

амбар barn; storehouse, warehouse.

амбиция pride; arrogance.

амбулатория out-patients' department; surgery. амбулаторный больной sb outpatient.

Америка America. американец (-нца), американка American. американский American; US.

аминокислота amino acid.

аминь m amen.

аммиак ammonia.

амнистия amnesty.

аморальный amoral; immoral.

амортизатор shock-absorber. амортизация depreciation; shock-absorption.

ампер (gen pl ампер) ampere.

ампутация amputation. ампутировать impf & pf amputate.

амфетамин amphetamine.

амфибия amphibian.

амфитеатр amphitheatre; circle.

анализ analysis; ~ крови blood test. анализировать impf & pf analyse. аналитик analyst. аналитический analytic(al).

аналог analogue. аналогичный analogous. аналогия analogy.

ананас pineapple.

анархист, ~ка anarchist. анархический anarchic. анархия anarchy.

анатомический anatomical. анатомия anatomy.

анахронизм anachronism. анахронический anachronistic.

ангар hangar.

ангел angel. ангельский angelic.

ангина sore throat.

английск|ий English; ~ая булавка safety-pin. англичанин (pl -чане, -чан) Englishman. англичанка Englishwoman. Англия England, Britain.

анекдот anecdote, story; funny thing.

анемия anaemia.

анестезиолог anaesthetist. анестезировать impf & pf anaesthetize. анестезирующее средство anaesthetic. анестезия anaesthesia.

анкета questionnaire, form.

аннексировать impf & pf annex. аннексия annexation.

аннулировать impf & pf annul; cancel, abolish.

аномалия anomaly. аномальный anomalous.

анонимка anonymous letter. анонимный anonymous.

анонсировать impf & pf announce.

анорексия anorexia.

ансамбль m ensemble; company, troupe.

антагонизм antagonism.

Антарктика the Antarctic.

антенна antenna; aerial.

антибиотик antibiotic(s).

антидепрессант antidepressant.

антиквар antiquary; antique-dealer. антиквариат antique-shop. антикварный antiquarian; antique.

антилопа antelope.

антипатия antipathy.

антисемитизм anti-Semitism. антисемитский anti-Semitic.

антисептик antiseptic. антисептический antiseptic.

антитезис (philos) antithesis.

антитело (pl -á) antibody.

антифриз antifreeze.

античность antiquity. античный ancient, classical.

антология anthology.

антракт interval.

антрацит anthracite.

антрекот entrecôte, steak.

антрепренёр impresario.

антресоли (pl; gen -ей) mezzanine; shelf.

антрополог anthropologist. антропологический anthropological. антропология anthropology.

анфилада suite (of rooms).

анчоус anchovy.

аншла́г 'house full' notice.

апартеи́д apartheid.

апати́чный apathetic. апа́тия apathy.

апелли́ровать *impf & pf* appeal. апелляцио́нный суд Court of Appeal. апелля́ция appeal.

апельси́н orange; orange-tree. апельси́нный, апельси́новый orange.

аплоди́ровать *impf* +*dat* applaud. аплодисме́нты *m pl* applause.

апло́мб aplomb.

Апока́липсис Revelation. апокалипти́ческий apocalyptic.

апо́стол apostle.

апостро́ф apostrophe.

аппара́т apparatus; machinery, organs. аппарату́ра apparatus, gear; (*comput*) hardware. аппара́тчик operator; apparatchik.

аппе́ндикс appendix. аппендици́т appendicitis.

аппети́т appetite; прия́тного ~a! bon appétit! аппети́тный appetizing.

апре́ль *m* April. апре́льский April.

апте́ка chemist's. апте́карь *m* chemist. апте́чка medicine chest; first-aid kit.

ара́б, ара́бка Arab. ара́бский Arab, Arabic.

арави́йский Arabian.

аранжи́ровать *impf & pf* (*mus*) arrange. аранжиро́вка (*mus*) arrangement.

ара́хис peanut.

арби́тр arbitrator. арбитра́ж arbitration.

арбу́з water-melon.

аргуме́нт argument. аргумента́ция reasoning; arguments. аргументи́ровать *impf & pf* argue, (try to) prove.

аре́на arena, ring.

аре́нда lease. аренда́тор tenant. аре́ндная пла́та rent. арендова́ть *impf & pf* rent.

аре́ст arrest. арестова́ть *pf*, аресто́вывать *impf* arrest; seize, sequestrate.

аристокра́т, ~ка aristocrat. аристократи́ческий aristocratic. аристокра́тия aristocracy.

арифме́тика arithmetic. арифмети́ческий arithmetical.

а́рия aria.

а́рка arch.

А́рктика the Arctic. аркти́ческий arctic.

армату́ра fittings; reinforcement; armature. армату́рщик fitter.

арме́йский army.

Арме́ния Armenia.

а́рмия army.

армяни́н (*pl* -я́не, -я́н), армя́нка Armenian. армя́нский Armenian.

арома́т scent, aroma. арома́тный aromatic, fragrant.

арсена́л arsenal.

арте́ль artel.

арте́рия artery.

арти́куль *m* (*gram*) article.

артилле́рия artillery.

арти́ст, ~ка artiste, artist; expert. артисти́ческий artistic.

артри́т arthritis.

а́рфа harp.

арха́ический archaic.

арха́нгел archangel.

архео́лог archaeologist. археологи́ческий archaeological. археоло́гия archaeology.

архи́в archives. архиви́ст archivist. архи́вный archive, archival.

архиепи́скоп archbishop. архиере́й bishop.

архипела́г archipelago.

архите́ктор architect. архитекту́ра architecture. архитекту́рный architectural.

арши́н arshin (*71 cm.*).

асбе́ст asbestos.

асимметри́чный asymmetrical. асимметри́я asymmetry.

аске́т ascetic. аскети́зм asceticism. аскети́ческий ascetic.

асоциа́льный antisocial.

аспира́нт, ~ка post-graduate student. аспиранту́ра post-graduate course.

аспири́н aspirin.

ассамбле́я assembly.

ассигна́ция banknote.

ассимиля́ция assimilation.

ассисте́нт assistant; junior lecturer, research assistant.

ассортиме́нт assortment.

ассоциа́ция association. ассоции́ровать *impf & pf* associate.

áстма asthma. астмати́ческий asthmatic.

астро́лог astrologer. астроло́гия astrology.

астрона́вт astronaut. астроно́м astronomer. астрономи́ческий astronomical. астроно́мия astronomy.

асфа́льт asphalt.

ата́ка attack. атакова́ть impf & pf attack.

атама́н ataman (Cossack chieftain); (gang-)leader.

атеи́зм atheism. атеи́ст atheist.

ателье́ neut indecl studio; atelier.

а́тлас¹ atlas.

атла́с² satin. атла́сный satin.

атле́т athlete; strong man. атле́тика athletics. атлети́ческий athletic.

атмосфе́ра atmosphere. атмосфе́рный atmospheric.

а́том atom. а́томный atomic.

атташе́ m indecl attaché.

аттеста́т testimonial; certificate; pedigree. аттестова́ть impf & pf attest; recommend.

аттракцио́н attraction; sideshow; star turn.

ау́ int hi, cooee.

аудито́рия auditorium, lecture-room.

аукцио́н auction.

аул aul (Caucasian or Central Asian village).

ауто́псия autopsy.

афе́ра speculation, trickery. афери́ст speculator, trickster.

афи́ша placard, poster.

афори́зм aphorism.

А́фрика Africa. африка́нец (-нца), африка́нка African. африка́нский African.

аффе́кт fit of passion; temporary insanity.

ах int ah, oh. а́хать impf (pf а́хнуть) sigh; exclaim; gasp.

аэро|вокза́л air terminal. ~дина́мика aerodynamics. ~дро́м aerodrome, air-field. ~зо́ль m aerosol. ~по́рт (loc -у́) airport.

Б

б partl: see бы

ба́ба (coll) (old) woman; снéжная ~ snowman.

ба́бочка butterfly.

ба́бушка grandmother; grandma.

бага́ж (-á) luggage. бага́жник carrier; luggage-rack; boot. бага́жный ваго́н luggage-van.

баго́р (-грá) boat-hook.

багро́вый crimson, purple.

бадья́ (gen pl -дéй) tub.

бáза base; depot; basis; ~ дáнных database.

база́р market; din.

ба́зис base; basis.

байда́рка canoe.

ба́йка flannelette.

бак¹ tank, cistern.

бак² forecastle.

бакала́вр (univ) bachelor.

бакале́йный grocery. бакале́я groceries.

ба́кен buoy.

бакенба́рды (pl; gen -бáрд) side-whiskers.

баклажа́н (gen pl -ов or -жа́н) aubergine.

бакте́рия bacterium.

бал (loc -ý; pl -ы́) dance, ball.

балага́н farce.

балала́йка balalaika.

бала́нс (econ) balance.

баланси́ровать impf (pf с~) balance; keep one's balance.

балбе́с booby.

балдахи́н canopy.

балери́на ballerina. бале́т ballet.

ба́лка¹ beam, girder.

ба́лка² gully.

балко́н balcony.

балл mark (in school); degree; force; вéтер в пять ~ов wind force 5.

балла́да ballad.

балла́ст ballast.

балло́н container, carboy, cylinder; balloon tyre.

баллоти́ровать impf vote; put to the vote; ~ся stand, be a candidate (в or на+acc for).

балова́ть impf (pf из~) spoil, pamper; ~ся play about, get up to tricks; amuse o.s. баловство́ spoiling; mischief.

Балти́йское мо́ре Baltic (Sea).

бальза́м balsam; balm.

балюстра́да balustrade.

бамбу́к bamboo.

ба́мпер bumper.

банáльность banality; platitude. банáльный banal.

банáн banana.

бáнда band, gang.

бандáж (-á) truss; belt, band.

бандерóль wrapper; printed matter, book-post.

бáнджо neut indecl banjo.

бандúт bandit; gangster.

банк bank.

бáнка jar; tin.

банкéт banquet.

банкúр banker. банкнóта banknote. банкрóт bankrupt. банкрóтство bankruptcy.

бант bow.

бáня bath; bath-house.

бар bar; snack-bar.

барабáн drum. барабáнить impf drum, thump. барабáнная перепóнка ear-drum. барабáнщик drummer.

барáк wooden barrack, hut.

барáн ram; sheep. барáнина mutton.

барáнка ring-shaped roll; (steering-) wheel.

барахлó old clothes, jumble; odds and ends. барахóлка flea market.

барáшек (-шка) young ram; lamb; wing nut; catkin. барáшковый lambskin.

бáржá (gen pl барж(éй)) barge.

бáрин (pl -ре or -ры, бар) landowner; sir.

баритóн baritone.

бáрка barge.

бáрмен barman.

барóкко neut indecl baroque.

барóметр barometer.

барóн baron. баронéсса baroness.

барóчный baroque.

баррикáда barricade.

барс snow-leopard.

бáрский lordly; grand.

барсýк (-á) badger.

бархáн dune.

бáрхат (-у) velvet. бáрхатный velvet.

бáрыня landowner's wife; madam.

барыш (-á) profit. барышник dealer; (ticket) speculator.

бáрышня (gen pl -шень) young lady; miss.

барьéр barrier; hurdle.

бас (pl -ы) bass.

баскетбóл basket-ball.

баснослóвный mythical, legendary; fabulous. бáсня (gen pl -сен) fable; fabrication.

басóвый bass.

бассéйн (geog) basin; pool; reservoir.

бастовáть impf be on strike.

батальóн battalion.

батарéйка, батарéя battery; radiator.

батóн long loaf; stick, bar.

бáтька m, бáтюшка m father; priest. бáтюшки int good gracious!

бах int bang!

бахвáльство bragging.

бахромá fringe.

бац int bang! crack!

бацúлла bacillus. бациллоносúтель m carrier.

бачóк (-чкá) cistern.

башкá head.

башлык (-á) hood.

башмáк (-á) shoe; под ~óм у+gen under the thumb of.

бáшня (gen pl -шен) tower, turret.

баюкать impf (pf y~) sing lullabies (to). бáюшки-баю int hushabye!

баян accordion.

бдéние vigil. бдúтельность vigilance. бдúтельный vigilant.

бег (loc -ý; pl -á) run, running; race. бéгать indet (det бежáть) impf run. бегемóт hippopotamus.

беглéц (-á), беглянка fugitive. бéглость speed, fluency, dexterity. бéглый rapid, fluent; fleeting, cursory; sb fugitive, runaway. беговóй running; race. бегóм adv running, at the double. беготня running about; bustle. бéгство flight; escape. бегýн (-á), бегýнья (gen pl -ний) runner.

бедá (pl -ы) misfortune; disaster; trouble; ~ в том, что the trouble is (that). беднéть impf (pf о~) grow poor. бéдность poverty; the poor. бéдный (-ден, -днá, -дно) poor. беднягá m, беднúжка m & f poor thing. беднúк (-á), беднúчка poor peasant; poor man, poor woman.

бедрó (pl бёдра, -дер) thigh; hip.

бéдственный disastrous. бéдствие disaster. бéдствовать impf live in poverty.

бежáть (бегý det; indet бéгать) impf

(*pf* по~) run; flow; fly; boil over; *impf* & *pf* escape. **бе́женец** (-нца), **бе́женка** refugee.

без *prep+gen* without; ~ пяти́ (мину́т) три five (minutes) to three; ~ че́тверти a quarter to.

без-, безъ-, бес- *in comb* in-, un-; non-; -less. **без**алкого́льный non-alcoholic. ~апелляцио́нный peremptory, categorical. ~бо́жие atheism. ~бо́жный godless; shameless; outrageous. ~боле́зненный painless. ~бра́чный celibate. ~бре́жный boundless. ~ве́стный unknown; obscure. ~вку́сие lack of taste, bad taste. ~вку́сный tasteless. ~вла́стие anarchy. ~во́дный arid. ~возвра́тный irrevocable; irrecoverable. ~возме́здный free, gratis. ~во́лие lack of will. ~во́льный weak-willed. ~вре́дный harmless. ~вре́менный untimely. ~вы́ходный hopeless, desperate; uninterrupted. ~гла́зый one-eyed; eyeless. ~гра́мотный illiterate. ~грани́чный boundless, infinite. ~да́рный untalented. ~де́йственный inactive. ~де́йствие inertia, idleness; negligence. ~де́йствовать *impf* be idle, be inactive; stand idle.

безде́лица trifle. **безделу́шка** knick-knack. **безде́льник** idler; ne'er-do-well. **безде́льничать** *impf* idle, loaf.

бе́здна abyss, chasm; a huge number, a multitude.

без-. бездоказа́тельный unsubstantiated. ~до́мный homeless. ~до́нный bottomless; fathomless. ~доро́жье lack of (good) roads; season when roads are impassable. ~ду́мный unthinking. ~ду́шный heartless; inanimate; lifeless. ~жа́лостный pitiless, ruthless. ~жи́зненный lifeless. ~забо́тный carefree; careless. ~заве́тный selfless, wholehearted. ~зако́ние lawlessness; unlawful act. ~зако́нный illegal; lawless. ~засте́нчивый shameless, barefaced. ~защи́тный defenceless. ~зву́чный silent. ~зло́бный good-natured. ~ли́чный characterless; impersonal. ~лю́дный uninhabited; sparsely populated; lonely.

безме́н steelyard.

без-. безме́рный immense; excessive. ~мо́лвие silence. ~мо́лвный silent, mute. ~мяте́жный serene, placid. ~наде́жный hopeless. ~надзо́рный neglected. ~нака́занно *adv* with impunity. ~нака́занный unpunished. ~но́гий legless; one-legged. ~нра́вственный immoral.

безо *prep+gen* = **без** (*used before* весь *and* вся́кий).

безобра́зие ugliness; disgrace, scandal. **безобра́зничать** *impf* make a nuisance of o.s. **безобра́зный** ugly; disgraceful.

без-. безоговоро́чный unconditional. ~опа́сность safety; security. ~опа́сный safe; secure. ~ору́жный unarmed. ~основа́тельный groundless. ~остано́вочный unceasing; non-stop. ~отве́тный meek, unanswering; dumb. ~отве́тственный irresponsible. ~отка́зно *adv* without a hitch. ~отка́зный trouble-free, smooth-(running). ~отлага́тельный urgent. ~относи́тельно *adv+к+dat* irrespective of. ~отчётный unaccountable. ~оши́бочный unerring; correct. ~рабо́тица unemployment. ~рабо́тный unemployed. ~разли́чие indifference. ~разли́чно *adv* indifferently; it is all the same. ~разли́чный indifferent. ~рассу́дный reckless, imprudent. ~ро́дный alone in the world; without relatives. ~ро́потный uncomplaining; meek. ~рука́вка sleeveless pullover. ~ру́кий armless; one-armed. ~уда́рный unstressed. ~уде́ржный unrestrained; impetuous. ~укори́зненный irreproachable.

безу́мец (-мца) madman. **безу́мие** madness. **безу́мный** mad. **безу́мство** madness.

без-. безупре́чный irreproachable, faultless. ~усло́вно *adv* unconditionally; of course, undoubtedly. ~усло́вный unconditional, absolute; indisputable. ~успе́шный unsuccessful. ~уста́нный tireless. ~уте́шный inconsolable. ~уча́стие indifference, apathy. ~уча́стный indifferent, apathetic. ~ымя́нный nameless, anonymous; **~ымя́нный па́лец** ring-finger. **~искýсный** artless, ingenuous. **~ысхо́дный** irreparable; interminable.

бейсбо́л baseball.

бека́р (*mus*) natural.

бека́с snipe.

беко́н bacon.

Белару́с , Belarus.

беле́ть *impf* (*pf* **по~**) turn white; show white.

белизна́ whiteness. **бели́ла** (*pl*; *gen* **-и́л**) whitewash; Tippex (*propr*). **бели́ть** (**бе́лишь**) *impf* (*pf* **вы́~, на~, по~**) whitewash; whiten; bleach.

бе́лка squirrel.

беллетри́ст writer of fiction. **беллетри́стика** fiction.

бело- *in comb* white-, leuco-. **белогварде́ец** (**-е́йца**) White Guard. **~кро́вие** leukaemia. **~кýрый** fair, blonde. **~рýс, ~рýска, ~рýсский** Belorussian. **~снéжный** snow-white.

белови́к (**-á**) fair copy. **беловой** clean, fair.

бело́к (**-лкá**) white (*of egg, eye*); protein.

белошве́йка seamstress. **белошве́йный** linen.

белýга white sturgeon. **белýха** white whale.

бéл|**ый** (**бел, -á, бéло**) white; clean, blank; *sb* white person; **~ая берёза** silver birch; **~ое калéние** white heat; **~ый медвéдь** polar bear; **~ые но́чи** white nights, midnight sun.

бельги́ец, -ги́йка Belgian. **бельги́йский** Belgian. **Бéльгия** Belgium.

бельё linen; bedclothes; underclothes; washing.

бельмо́ (*pl* **-a**) cataract.

бельэта́ж first floor; dress circle.

бемо́ль *m* (*mus*) flat.

бенефи́с benefit (performance).

бензи́н petrol.

бензо- *in comb* petrol. **бензоба́к** petrol-tank. **~во́з** petrol tanker. **~запра́вочная** *sb* filling-station. **~коло́нка** petrol pump. **~прово́д** petrol pipe, fuel line.

берёг *etc.*: *see* **берéчь**

бéрег (*loc* **-ý**; *pl* **-á**) bank, shore;

coast; **на ~ý мо́ря** at the seaside. **берегово́й** coast; coastal.

бережёшь *etc.*: *see* **берéчь**. **бережли́вый** thrifty. **бéрежный** careful.

берёза birch. **Берёзка** hard-currency shop.

берéменеть *impf* (*pf* **за~**) be(come) pregnant. **берéменная** pregnant (+*instr* with). **берéменность** pregnancy; gestation.

берéт beret.

берéчь (**-регý, -режёшь; -рёг, -лá**) *impf* take care of; keep; cherish; husband; be sparing of; **~ся** take care; beware (+*gen* of).

берло́га den, lair.

берý *etc.*: *see* **брать**

бес devil, demon.

бес-: *see* **без-**

бесéда talk, conversation. **бесéдка** summer-house. **бесéдовать** *impf* talk, converse.

беси́ть (**бешý, бéсишь**) *impf* (*pf* **вз~**) enrage; **~ся** go mad; be furious.

бес-. бесконéчность infinity; endlessness. **~конéчный** endless. **~корыстие** disinterestedness. **~корыстный** disinterested. **~крáйний** boundless.

бесо́вский devilish.

бес-. беспáмятство unconsciousness. **~партийный** non-party **~перспективный** without prospects; hopeless. **~пéчность** carelessness, unconcern. **~плáтно** *adv* free. **~плáтный** free. **~пло́дие** sterility, barrenness. **~пло́дность** futility. **~пло́дный** sterile, barren; futile. **~поворо́тный** irrevocable. **~подóбный** incomparable. **~позвоно́чный** invertebrate.

беспоко́ить *impf* (*pf* **о~, по~**) disturb, bother; trouble; **~ся** worry; trouble. **беспоко́йный** anxious; troubled; fidgety. **беспоко́йство** anxiety.

бес-. бесполéзный useless. **~помóщный** helpless; feeble. **~поро́дный** mongrel, not thoroughbred. **~поря́док** (**-дка**) disorder; untidy state. **~поря́дочный** disorderly; untidy. **~посáдочный** nonstop. **~по́чвенный** groundless. **~по́шлинный** duty-free. **~пощáд-**

ный merciless. ~пра́вный without rights. ~преде́льный boundless. ~предме́тный aimless; abstract. ~препя́тственный unhindered; unimpeded. ~преры́вный continuous. ~преста́нный continual.

беспризо́рный, -ница waif, homeless child. беспризо́рный neglected; homeless; sb waif, homeless child.

бес-. бесприме́рный unparalleled. ~принци́пный unscrupulous. ~пристра́стие impartiality. ~пристра́стный impartial. ~просве́тный pitch-dark; hopeless; unrelieved. ~пу́тный dissolute. ~свя́зный incoherent. ~серде́чный heartless. ~си́лие impotence; feebleness. ~си́льный impotent, powerless. ~сла́вный inglorious. ~сле́дно adv without trace. ~слове́сный dumb; silent, meek; (theat) walk-on. ~сме́нный permanent, continuous. ~сме́ртие immortality. ~сме́ртный immortal. ~смы́сленный senseless; foolish; meaningless. ~смы́слица nonsense. ~со́вестный unscrupulous; shameless. ~созна́тельный unconscious; involuntary. ~со́нница insomnia. ~спо́рный indisputable. ~сро́чный indefinite; without a time limit. ~стра́стный impassive. ~стра́шный fearless. ~сты́дный shameless. ~та́ктный tactless.

бестолко́вщина confusion, disorder. бестолко́вый muddle-headed, stupid; incoherent.

бес-. бесфо́рменный shapeless. ~хара́ктерный weak, spineless. ~хи́тростный artless; unsophisticated. ~хозя́йственный improvident. ~цве́тный colourless. ~це́льный aimless; pointless. ~це́нный priceless. ~цено́к: за ~цено́к very cheap, for a song. ~церемо́нный unceremonious. ~челове́чный inhuman. ~че́стить (-е́щу) impf (pf о~че́стить) dishonour. ~че́стный dishonourable. ~чи́сленный innumerable, countless.

бесчу́вственный insensible; insensitive. бесчу́вствие insensibility; insensitivity.

бес-. бесшу́мный noiseless.

бето́н concrete. бето́нный concrete.

бетономеша́лка concrete-mixer. бето́нщик concrete-worker.

бечева́ tow-rope; rope. бечёвка cord, string.

бе́шенство rabies; rage. бе́шеный rabid; furious.

бешу́ etc.: see беси́ть

библе́йский biblical. библиографи́ческий bibliographical. библиогра́фия bibliography. библиоте́ка library. библиоте́карь m, -те́карша librarian. би́блия bible.

бива́к bivouac, camp.

би́вень (-вня) m tusk.

бигуди́ pl indecl curlers.

бидо́н can; churn.

бие́ние beating; beat.

бижуте́рия costume jewellery.

би́знес business. бизнесме́н businessman.

биле́т ticket; card; pass. биле́тный ticket.

биллио́н billion.

билья́рд billiards.

бино́кль m binoculars.

бинт (-а́) bandage. бинтова́ть impf (pf за~) bandage. бинто́вка bandaging.

био́граф biographer. биографи́ческий biographical. биогра́фия biography. био́лог biologist. биологи́ческий biological. биоло́гия biology. биохи́мия biochemistry.

би́ржа exchange.

би́рка name-plate; label.

бирюза́ turquoise.

бис int encore.

би́сер (no pl) beads.

бискви́т sponge cake.

би́та bat.

би́тва battle.

битко́м adv: ~ наби́т packed.

биту́м bitumen.

бить (бью, бьёшь) impf (pf за~, по~, про~, уда́рить) beat; hit; defeat; sound; thump, bang; smash; ~ в цель hit the target; ~ на+acc strive for; ~ отбо́й beat a retreat; ~ по+dat damage, wound; ~ся fight; beat; struggle; break; +instr knock, hit, strike; +над+instr struggle with, rack one's brains over.

бифште́кс beefsteak.

бич (-а́) whip, lash; scourge; homeless person. бичева́ть (-чу́ю) impf flog; castigate.

бла́го good; blessing.

бла́го- *in comb* well-, good-. Благове́щение Annunciation. ~ви́дный plausible, specious. ~воле́ние goodwill; favour. ~воспи́танный well-brought-up.

благодари́ть (-рю́) *impf* (*pf* по~) thank. благода́рность gratitude; не сто́ит благодари́ти don't mention it. благода́рный grateful. благодаря́ *prep+dat* thanks to, owing to.

бла́го-. благоде́тель *m* benefactor. ~де́тельница benefactress. ~де́тельный beneficial. ~ду́шный placid; good-humoured. ~жела́тель *m* well-wisher. ~жела́тельный well-disposed; benevolent. ~зву́чный melodious, harmonious. ~надёжный reliable. ~наме́ренный well-intentioned. ~получие well-being; happiness. ~получно *adv* all right, well; happily; safely. ~получный happy, successful; safe. ~прия́тный favourable. ~приятствовать *impf* +*dat* favour. ~разу́мие sense; prudence. ~разу́мный sensible. ~ро́дие: ва́ше ~ро́дие Your Honour. ~ро́дный noble. ~ро́дство nobility. ~скло́нность favour, good graces. ~скло́нный favourable; gracious. ~слови́ть *pf*, благословля́ть *impf* bless. ~состоя́ние prosperity. ~твори́тель *m*, -ница philanthropist. ~твори́тельный charitable, charity. ~тво́рный salutary; beneficial; wholesome. ~устро́енный well-equipped, well-planned; with all amenities.

блаже́нный blissful; simple-minded. блаже́нство bliss.

бланк form.

блат (*sl*) string-pulling; pull, influence. блатно́й criminal; soft, cushy.

бледне́ть (-е́ю) *impf* (*pf* по~) (grow) pale. бле́дность paleness, pallor. бле́дный (-ден, -дна́, -о) pale.

блеск brightness, brilliance, lustre; magnificence.

блесну́ть (-ну́, -нёшь) *pf* flash, gleam; shine. блесте́ть (-ещу́, -сти́шь *or* бле́щешь) *impf* shine; glitter.

бле́стка sparkle; sequin.

блестя́щий shining, bright; brilliant.

бле́ять (-е́ет) *impf* bleat.

ближа́йший nearest, closest; next.

бли́же *comp* of бли́зкий, бли́зко.

бли́жний near, close; neighbouring; *sb* neighbour. близ *prep+gen* near, by. бли́зкий (-зок, -изка́, -о) near; close; imminent; ~кие *sb pl* one's nearest and dearest, close relatives. бли́зко *adv* near (от+*gen* to). близне́ц (-а́) twin; *pl* Gemini. близору́кий short-sighted. бли́зость closeness, proximity.

блик patch of light; highlight.

блин (-а́) pancake.

блинда́ж (-а́) dug-out.

блиста́ть *impf* shine; sparkle.

блок block, pulley, sheave.

блока́да blockade. блоки́ровать *impf* & *pf* blockade; ~ся form a bloc.

блокно́т writing-pad, note-book.

блонди́н, блонди́нка blond(e).

блоха́ (*pl* -и, -а́м) flea.

блуд lechery. блудни́ца whore.

блужда́ть *impf* roam, wander.

блу́за, блу́зка blouse.

блю́дечко saucer; small dish. блю́до dish; course. блю́дце saucer.

боб (-а́) bean. бобо́вый bean.

бобр (-а́) beaver.

Бог (*voc* Бо́же) God; дай ~ God grant; ~ его́ зна́ет who knows? не дай ~ God forbid; Бо́же (мой)! my God! good God!; ра́ди ~а for God's sake; сла́ва ~у thank God.

богате́ть *impf* (*pf* раз~) grow rich. бога́тство wealth. бога́тый rich, wealthy; *sb* rich man. богач (-а́) rich man.

богаты́рь (-я́) *m* hero; strong man.

боги́ня goddess. Богома́терь Mother of God. богомо́лец (-льца), богомо́лка devout person; pilgrim. богомо́лье pilgrimage. богомо́льный religious, devout. Богоро́дица the Virgin Mary. богосло́в theologian. богосло́вие theology. богослуже́ние divine service. боготвори́ть *impf* idolize; deify. богоху́льство blasphemy.

бодри́ть *impf.* stimulate, invigorate; ~ся try to keep up one's spirits. бо́дрость cheerfulness, courage. бо́дрствовать be awake; stay awake; keep vigil. **бо́дрый** (бодр, -а́, -о) cheerful, bright.

боеви́к (-а́) smash hit. **боево́й** fighting, battle. **боеголо́вка** warhead. **боеприпа́сы** (pl; gen -ов) ammunition. **боеспосо́бный** battle-worthy.

бое́ц (бойца́) soldier; fighter, warrior.

Бо́же: see **Бог.** **бо́жеский** divine; just. **боже́ственный** divine. **божество́** deity; divinity. **бо́ж|ий** God's; ~ья коро́вка ladybird. **божо́к** (-жка́) idol.

бой (-ю; loc -ю́; pl -и́, -ёв) battle, action, fight; fighting; slaughtering; striking; breakage(s).

бо́йкий (бо́ек, бойка́, -о) smart, sharp; glib; lively. **бойко́т** boycott.

бо́йня (gen pl бо́ен) slaughter-house; butchery.

бок (loc -у́; pl -а́) side; flank; ~ о́ ~ side by side; на́ ~ to the side; на ~у́ on one side; по́д ~ом near by; с ~у from the side, from the flank; с ~у на́ бок from side to side.

бока́л glass; goblet.

боково́й side; lateral. **бо́ком** adv sideways.

бокс boxing. **боксёр** boxer.

болва́н blockhead. **болва́нка** pig (of iron etc.).

болга́рин (pl -га́ры), **болга́рка** Bulgarian. **болга́рский** Bulgarian. **Болга́рия** Bulgaria.

бо́лее adv more; ~ всего́ most of all; тем ~, что especially as.

боле́зненный sickly; unhealthy; painful. **боле́знь** illness, disease; abnormality.

боле́льщик, -щица fan, supporter.

боле́ть¹ (-е́ю) impf be ill, suffer. **боле́ть²** (-ли́т) impf ache, hurt.

боло́тистый marshy. **боло́то** marsh, bog.

болта́ть¹ impf stir; shake; dangle; ~ся dangle, swing; hang about.

болта́ть² impf chat, natter. **болтли́вый** talkative; indiscreet. **болтовня́** talk; chatter; gossip. **болту́н** (-а́), **болту́нья** chatterbox.

боль pain; ache. **больни́ца** hospital. **больни́чный** hospital; ~ листо́к medical certificate. **бо́льно¹** adv painfully, badly; predic+dat it hurts.

бо́льно² adv very, terribly.

больно́й (-лен, -льна́) ill, sick; diseased; sore; sb patient, invalid.

бо́льше comp of **большо́й, мно́го;** bigger, larger; greater; more; ~ не not any more, no longer; ~ того́ and what is more; adv for the most part. **большеви́к** Bolshevik. **бо́льш|ий** greater, larger; ~ей ча́стью for the most part. **большинство́** majority. **больш|о́й** big, large; great; grown-up; ~а́я бу́ква capital letter; ~о́й па́лец thumb; big toe; ~и́е sb pl grown-ups.

бо́мба bomb. **бомбардирова́ть** impf bombard; bomb. **бомбарди́ровка** bombardment, bombing. **бомбардиро́вщик** bomber. **бомбёжка** bombing. **бомби́ть** (-блю́) bomb. **бомбоубе́жище** bomb shelter.

бор (loc -у́; pl -ы́) coniferous forest.

бордо́вый wine-red.

бордю́р border.

боре́ц (-рца́) fighter; wrestler.

бо́рзый swift.

бормаши́на (dentist's) drill.

бормота́ть (-очу́, -о́чешь) impf (pf про~) mutter, mumble.

борода́ (acc бо́роду; pl бо́роды, -ро́д, -а́м) beard. **борода́вка** wart. **борода́тый** bearded.

борозда́ (pl бо́розды, -о́зд, -а́м) furrow; fissure. **борозди́ть** (-зжу́) impf (pf вз~) furrow; plough.

борона́ (acc бо́рону; pl бо́роны, -ро́н, -а́м) harrow. **борони́ть** impf (pf вз~) harrow.

боро́ться (-рю́сь, бо́решься) impf wrestle; struggle, fight.

борт (loc -у́; pl -а́, -о́в) side, ship's side; front; за ~, за ~ом overboard; на ~, на ~у́ on board. **бортпроводни́к** (-а́) air steward. **бортпроводни́ца** air hostess.

борщ (-а́) borshch (beetroot soup).

борьба́ wrestling; struggle, fight.

босико́м adv barefoot.

босни́ец (-и́йца), **босни́йка** Bosnian. **босни́йский** Bosnian. **Бо́сния** Bosnia.

босо́й (бос, -а́, -о) barefooted. **босоно́жка** sandal.

бот, бо́тик small boat.

бота́ник botanist. **бота́ника** botany.

ботани́ческий botanical.

боти́нок (-нка) *(ankle-high)* boot.

бо́цман boatswain

бо́чка barrel. **бочо́нок** (-нка) keg, small barrel.

боязли́вый timid, timorous. **боя́знь** fear; dread.

боя́рин *(pl* -я́ре, -я́р) boyar.

боя́рышник hawthorn.

боя́ться (бою́сь) *impf* +*gen* be afraid of, fear; dislike.

брак[1] marriage.

брак[2] defective goods; waste. **брако-ва́ть** *impf (pf* за~) reject.

браконьёр poacher.

бракоразво́дный divorce. **брако-сочета́ние** wedding.

брани́ть *impf (pf* вы~) scold; abuse, curse; ~**ся** *(pf* по~) swear, curse; quarrel. **бра́нн|ый** abusive; ~ое **сло́во** swear-word.

брань bad language; abuse.

брасле́т bracelet.

брасс breast stroke.

брат *(pl* -тья, -тьев) brother; comrade; mate; lay brother, monk. **брата́ться** *impf (pf* по~) fraternize. **братоуби́йство** fratricide. **бра́т-ский** brotherly, fraternal. **бра́тство** brotherhood, fraternity.

брать (беру́, -рёшь; брал, -а́, -о) *impf (pf* взять) take; hire; seize; demand, require; surmount, clear; work; +*instr* succeed by means of; ~**ся** +за+*acc* touch; seize; get down to; +за+*acc or inf* undertake; appear, come.

бра́чный marriage; mating.

бреве́нчатый log. **бревно́** *(pl* брёвна, -вен) log, beam.

бред *(loc* -у́) delirium; raving(s). **бре́дить** (-е́жу) *impf* be delirious, rave; +*instr* rave about, be infatuated with. **бредо́вый** delirious; fantastic, nonsensical.

бреду́ *etc.: see* **брести́. бре́жу** *etc.: see* **бре́дить**

брезга́ть *impf (pf* по~) +*inf or instr* be squeamish about. **брезгли́вый** squeamish.

брезе́нт tarpaulin.

бре́зжить(ся *impf* dawn; gleam faintly, glimmer.

брёл *etc.: see* **брести́.**

брело́к charm, pendant.

бремени́ть *impf (pf* о~) burden. **бре́мя** (-мени) *neut* burden; load.

бренча́ть (-чу́) *impf* strum; jingle.

брести́ (-еду́, -едёшь; брёл, -а́) *impf* stroll; drag o.s. along.

брете́ль, брете́лька shoulder strap.

брешь breach; gap.

бре́ю *etc.: see* **брить**

брига́да brigade; crew, team. **брига-ди́р** brigadier; team-leader; foreman.

бриллиа́нт, брилья́нт diamond.

брита́нец (-нца), **брита́нка** Briton. **брита́нск|ий** British; Б~ие острова́ the British Isles.

бри́тва razor. **бри́твенный** shaving.

бри́тый shaved; clean-shaven. **брить** (бре́ю) *impf (pf* по~) shave; ~**ся** shave (o.s.).

бровь *(pl* -и, -е́й) eyebrow; brow.

брод ford.

броди́ть (-ожу́, -о́дишь) *impf* wander, roam, stroll; ferment. **бродя́га** *m & f* tramp, vagrant. **бродя́ж-ничество** vagrancy. **бродя́чий** vagrant; wandering. **броже́ние** ferment, fermentation.

броне- *in comb* armoured, armour.

броневи́к (-а́) armoured car. ~**во́й** armoured. ~**но́сец** (-сца) battleship; armadillo.

бро́нза bronze; bronzes. **бро́нзовый** bronze; tanned.

брониро́ванный armoured.

брони́ровать *impf & pf (pf also* за~) reserve, book.

бронхи́т bronchitis.

бро́ня[1] reservation; commandeering.

броня́[2] armour.

броса́ть *impf,* **бро́сить** (-о́шу) *pf* throw (down); leave, desert; give up, leave off; ~**ся** throw o.s., rush; +*inf* begin; +*instr* squander; pelt one another with; ~**ся в глаза́** be striking.

бро́ский striking; garish, glaring.

бросо́к (-ска́) throw; bound, spurt.

бро́шка, брошь brooch.

брошю́ра pamphlet, brochure.

брус *(pl* -сья, -сьев) squared beam, joist; (паралле́льные) ~**ья** parallel bars.

брусни́ка red whortleberry; red whortleberries.

брусо́к (-ска́) bar; ingot.

бру́тто *indecl adj* gross.

бры́згать (-зжу *or* -га́ю) *impf*, бры́знуть (-ну) *pf* splash; sprinkle. бры́зги (брызг) *pl* spray, splashes; fragments.

брыка́ть *impf*, брыкну́ть (-ну́, -нёшь) *pf* kick.

брюзга́ *m & f* grumbler. брюзгли́вый grumbling, peevish. брюзжа́ть (-жу́) *impf* grumble.

брю́ква swede.

брю́ки (*pl*; *gen* брюк) trousers.

брюне́т dark-haired man. брюне́тка brunette.

брю́хо (*pl* -и) belly; stomach. брюшно́й abdominal; ~ тиф typhoid. бряца́ть *impf* rattle; clank, clang.

бу́бен (-бна) tambourine. бубене́ц (-нца́) small bell. бу́бны (*pl*; *gen* -бён, *dat* -бна́м) (*cards*) diamonds. бубно́вый diamond.

буго́р (-гра́) mound, hillock; bump, lump.

будди́зм Buddhism. будди́йский Buddhist. будди́ст Buddhist.

бу́дет that will do; +*inf* it's time to stop.

буди́льник alarm-clock. буди́ть (бужу́, бу́дишь) *impf* (*pf* про~, раз~) wake; arouse.

бу́дка box, booth; hut; stall.

бу́дни (*pl*; *gen* -ней) *pl* weekdays; working days; humdrum existence. бу́дний, бу́дничный weekday; everyday; humdrum.

бу́дто *conj* as if, as though; ~ (бы), (как) ~ apparently, ostensibly.

бу́ду *etc*.: *see* быть. бу́дучи being. бу́дущ|ий future; next; ~ee *sb* future. бу́дущность future. бу́дь(те): *see* быть

бужу́: *see* буди́ть

бузина́ (*bot*) elder.

буй (*pl* -и́, -ёв) buoy.

бу́йвол buffalo.

бу́йный (бу́ен, буйна́, -о) violent, turbulent; luxuriant, lush. бу́йство unruly behaviour. бу́йствовать *impf* create an uproar, behave violently.

бук beech.

бука́шка small insect.

бу́ква (*gen pl* букв) letter; ~ в бу́кву literally. буква́льно *adv* literally. буква́льный literal. буква́рь (-я́) *m* ABC. букво́ед pedant.

буке́т bouquet; aroma.

букини́ст second-hand bookseller.

бу́кля curl, ringlet.

бу́ковый beech.

букси́р tug-boat; tow-rope. букси́ровать *impf* tow.

буксова́ть *impf* spin, slip.

була́вка pin.

бу́лка roll. бу́лочная *sb* baker's. бу́лочник baker.

булы́жник cobble-stone, cobbles.

бульва́р avenue; boulevard.

бульдо́г bulldog.

бульдо́зер bulldozer.

бу́лькать *impf* gurgle.

бульо́н broth.

бум (*sport*) beam.

бума́га cotton; paper; document. бума́жка piece of paper; note. бума́жник wallet; paper-maker. бума́жн|ый cotton; paper; ~ змей kite.

бу́нкер bunker.

бунт (*pl* -ы́) rebellion; riot; mutiny. бунта́рь (-я́) *m* rebel; insurgent. бунтова́ть(ся (*impf* (*pf* вз~) rebel; riot. бунтовщи́к (-а́), -щи́ца rebel, insurgent.

бур auger.

бура́в (-а́; *pl* -а́) auger; gimlet. бура́вить (-влю) *impf* (*pf* про~) bore, drill.

бура́н snowstorm.

буреве́стник stormy petrel.

буре́ние boring, drilling.

буржуа́ *m indecl* bourgeois. буржуа́зия bourgeoisie. буржуа́зный bourgeois.

бури́льщик borer, driller. бури́ть *impf* (*pf* про~) bore, drill.

бурли́ть *impf* seethe.

бу́рный (-рен, -рна́, -о) stormy; rapid; energetic.

бурово́й boring; ~а́я вы́шка derrick; ~а́я (сква́жина) borehole; ~о́й стано́к drilling rig.

бу́рый (бур, -а́, -о) brown.

бурья́н tall weeds.

бу́ря storm.

бу́сина bead. бу́сы (*pl*; *gen* бус) beads.

бутафо́рия (*theat*) props.

бутербро́д open sandwich.

буто́н bud.

бу́тсы (*pl*; *gen* -ов) *pl* football boots.

буты́лка bottle. **буты́ль** large bottle; carboy.

буфе́т snack bar; sideboard; counter. **буфе́тчик** barman. **буфе́тчица** barmaid.

бух *int* bang, plonk. **бу́хать** *impf* (*pf* **бу́хнуть**) thump, bang; bang down; thunder, thud; blurt out.

буха́нка loaf.

бухга́лтер accountant. **бухгалте́рия** accountancy; accounts department.

бу́хнуть (**-ну**) *impf* swell.

бу́хта bay.

бушева́ть (**-шу́ю**) *impf* rage, storm.

буя́н rowdy. **буя́нить** *impf* create an uproar.

бы, **б** *partl* I. +*past tense* or *inf indicates the conditional or subjunctive.* II. (+**ни**) *forms* indef *prons and conjs.*

быва́лый experienced; former; habitual, familiar. **быва́ть** *impf* be; happen; be inclined to be; **как ни в чём не быва́ло** as if nothing had happened; **быва́ло** *partl* used to, would; **мать быва́ло ча́сто пе́ла э́ту пе́сню** my mother would often sing this song. **бы́вший** former, ex-.

бык (**-а́**) bull, ox; pier.

были́на ancient Russian epic.

бы́ло *partl* nearly, on the point of; (only) just. **был|о́й** past, bygone; **~о́е** *sb* the past. **быль** true story; fact.

быстрота́ speed. **бы́стрый** (**быстр, -а́, -о**) fast, quick.

быт (*loc* **-ý**) way of life. **бытие́** being, existence; objective reality; **кни́га Бытия́** Genesis. **бытово́й** everyday; social.

быть (*pres 3rd sg* **есть**, *pl* **суть**; *fut* **бу́ду**; *past* **был, -а́, -о**; *imper* **бу́дь(те)**) *impf* be; be situated; happen. **бытьё** way of life.

бычо́к (**-чка́**) steer.

бью *etc.: see* **бить**

бюдже́т budget.

бюллете́нь *m* bulletin; ballot-paper; doctor's certificate.

бюро́ *neut indecl* bureau; office; writing-desk. **бюрокра́т** bureaucrat. **бюрократи́зм** bureaucracy. **бюрократи́ческий** bureaucratic. **бюрокра́тия** bureaucracy; bureaucrats.

бюст bust. **бюстга́льтер** bra.

В

в, **во** *prep* I. +*acc* into, to; on; at; within; through; **быть в** take after; **в два ра́за бо́льше** twice as big; **в на́ши дни** in our day; **войти́ в дом** go into the house; **в понеде́льник** on Monday; **в течёние**+*gen* three metres high; **игра́ть в ша́хматы** play chess; **пое́хать в Москву́** go to Moscow; **сесть в ваго́н** get into the carriage; **смотре́ть в окно́** look out of the window. II. +*prep* in; at; **в двадца́том ве́ке** in the twentieth century; **в теа́тре** at the theatre; **в трёх киломе́трах от го́рода** three kilometres from the town; **в э́том году́** this year; **в январе́** in January.

ваго́н carriage, coach; **~-рестора́н** restaurant car. **ваго́нетка** truck, trolley. **вагоновожа́тый** *sb* tram-driver.

ва́жничать *impf* give o.s. airs; +*instr* plume o.s., pride o.s. on. **ва́жность** importance; pomposity. **ва́жный** (**-жен, -жна́, -о**) important; weighty; pompous.

ва́за vase, bowl.

вазели́н Vaseline (*propr*).

вака́нсия vacancy. **вака́нтный** vacant.

ва́кса (shoe-)polish.

ва́куум vacuum.

вакци́на vaccine.

вал[1] (*loc* **-ý**; *pl* **-ы́**) bank; rampart; billow, roller; barrage.

вал[2] (*loc* **-ý**; *pl* **-ы́**) shaft.

ва́ленок (**-нка**; *gen pl* **-нок**) felt boot.

вале́т knave, Jack.

ва́лик roller, cylinder.

вали́ть[1] *impf* flock, throng; **вали́(те)!** have a go!

вали́ть[2] (**-лю́, -лишь**) *impf* (*pf* **по~**, **с~**) throw down, bring down; pile up; **~ся** fall, collapse.

валово́й gross; wholesale.

валто́рна French horn.

валу́н (**-а́**) boulder.

вальс waltz. **вальси́ровать** *impf* waltz.

валю́та currency; foreign currency.

валя́ть *impf* (*pf* на~, с~) drag; roll; shape; bungle; ~ дурака́ play the fool; валя́й(те)! go ahead!; ~ся lie, lie about; roll, wallow.

вам, ва́ми: *see* вы

вампи́р vampire.

вандáл vandal. **вандали́зм** vandalism.

вани́ль vanilla.

ва́нна bath. **ва́нная** *sb* bathroom.

ва́рвар barbarian. **ва́рварский** barbaric. **ва́рварство** barbarity; vandalism.

ва́режка mitten.

варёный boiled. **варе́нье** jam. **вари́ть** (-рю́, -ришь) *impf* (*pf* с~) boil; cook; ~ся boil; cook.

вариа́нт version; option; scenario.

вас: *see* вы

василёк (-лька́) cornflower.

ва́та cotton wool; wadding.

ватерли́ния water-line. **ватерпа́с** (spirit-)level.

вати́н (sheet) wadding. **ва́тник** quilted jacket. **ва́тный** quilted, wadded.

ватру́шка cheese-cake.

ватт (*gen pl* ватт) watt.

ва́учер coupon (*exchangeable for government-issued share*).

ва́фля (*gen pl* -фель) wafer; waffle.

ва́хта (*naut*) watch. **вахтёр** janitor, porter.

ваш (-его) *m*, **ва́ша** (-ей) *f*, **ва́ше** (-его) *neut*, **ва́ши** (-их) *pl*, *pron* your, yours.

вбега́ть *impf*, **вбежа́ть** (вбегу́) *pf* run in.

вберу́ *etc.*: *see* вобрать

вбива́ть *impf of* вбить

вбира́ть *impf of* вобрать

вбить (вобью́, -бьёшь) *pf* (*impf* вбива́ть) drive in, hammer in.

вблизи́ *adv* (+от+*gen*) close (to), near by.

вбок *adv* sideways, to one side.

вброд *adv*: переходи́ть ~ ford, wade.

вва́ливать *impf*, **ввали́ть** (-лю́, -лишь) *pf* throw heavily, heave, bundle; ~ся fall heavily; sink, become sunken; burst in.

введе́ние introduction. **введу́** *etc.*: *see* ввести́

ввезти́ (-зу́, -зёшь; ввёз, -ла́) *pf* (*impf* ввози́ть) import; bring in.

вве́рить *pf* (*impf* вверя́ть) entrust, confide; ~ся +*dat* trust in, put one's faith in.

ввернуть (-ну́, -нёшь) *pf*, **вве́ртывать** *impf* screw in; insert.

вверх *adv* up, upward(s); ~дном upside down; ~ (по ле́стнице) upstairs. **вверху́** *adv* above, overhead.

вверя́ть(ся) *impf of* вве́рить(ся)

ввести́ (-еду́, -едёшь; ввёл, -á) *pf* (*impf* вводи́ть) bring in; introduce.

ввиду́ *prep*+*gen* in view of.

ввинти́ть (-нчу́) *pf*, **вви́нчивать** *impf* screw in.

ввод lead-in. **вводи́ть** (-ожу́, -о́дишь) *impf of* ввести́. **вво́дный** introductory; parenthetic.

ввожу́ *see* вводи́ть, ввози́ть

ввоз importation; import(s). **ввози́ть** (-ожу́, -о́зишь) *impf of* ввезти́

вво́лю *adv* to one's heart's content.

ввысь *adv* up, upward(s).

ввяза́ть (-яжу́, -я́жешь) *pf*, **ввя́зывать** *impf* knit in; involve; ~ся meddle, get or be mixed up (in).

вглубь *adv* & *prep*+*gen* deep (into), into the depths.

вгляде́ться (-яжу́сь) *pf*, **вгля́дываться** *impf* peer, look closely (в+*acc* at).

вгоня́ть *impf of* вогна́ть. **вда-ва́ться** (вдаю́сь, -ёшься) *impf of* вда́ться

вдави́ть (-авлю́, -а́вишь) *pf*, **вда́-вливать** *impf* press in.

вдалеке́, вдали́ *adv* in the distance, far away. **вдаль** *adv* into the distance.

вда́ться (-а́мся, -а́шься, -а́стся, -а́димся; -а́лся, -ла́сь) *pf* (*impf* вдава́ться) jut out; penetrate, go in.

вдво́е *adv* twice; double; ~ бо́льше twice as big, as much, as many. **вдвоём** *adv* (the) two together both. **вдвойне́** *adv* twice as much double; doubly.

вдева́ть *impf of* вдеть

вде́лать *pf*, **вде́лывать** *impf* set in fit in.

вдёргивать *impf*, **вдёрнуть** (-ну) *pf* в+*acc* thread through, pull through.

вдеть (-е́ну) *pf* (*impf* вдева́ть) put in, thread.

вдоба́вок *adv* in addition; besides.

вдова́ widow. вдове́ц. (-вца́) widower.

вдо́воль *adv* enough; in abundance.

вдого́нку *adv* (за+*instr*) after, in pursuit (of).

вдоль *adv* lengthwise; ~ и поперёк far and wide; in detail; *prep+gen or* по+*dat* along.

вдох breath. вдохнове́ние inspiration, вдохнове́нный inspired. вдохнови́ть (-влю́) *pf*, вдохновля́ть *impf* inspire. вдохну́ть (-ну́, -нёшь) *pf* (*impf* вдыха́ть) breathe in.

вдре́безги *adv* to smithereens.

вдруг *adv* suddenly.

вду́маться *pf*, вду́мываться *impf* ponder, meditate; +в+*acc* think over. вду́мчивый thoughtful.

вдыха́ние inhalation. вдыха́ть *impf of* вдохну́ть.

вегетариа́нец (-нца), -нка vegetarian. вегетариа́нский vegetarian.

ве́дать *impf* know; +*instr* manage, handle. ве́дение[1] authority, jurisdiction.

веде́ние[2] conducting, conduct; ~ книг book-keeping.

ве́домость (*gen pl* -е́й) list, register. ве́домственный departmental. ве́домство department.

ведро́ (*pl* вёдра, -дер) bucket; vedro (*approx 12 litres*).

веду́ *etc.: see* вести́. веду́щий leading.

ведь *partl & conj* you see, you know; isn't it? is it?

ве́дьма witch.

ве́ер (*pl* -á) fan.

ве́жливость politeness. ве́жливый polite.

везде́ *adv* everywhere.

везе́ние luck. везу́чий lucky. везти́ (-зу́, -зёшь; вёз, -ла́) *impf* (*pf* по~) convey; bring, take; *impers+dat* be lucky; ему́ не везло́ he had no luck.

век (*loc* -ý; *pl* -á) age; life, lifetime. век *adv* for ages.

ве́ко (*pl* -и, век) eyelid.

веково́й ancient, age-old.

ве́ксель (*pl* -я́, -е́й) *m* promissory note, bill (of exchange).

вёл *etc.: see* вести́

веле́ть (-лю́) *impf & pf* order; не ~ forbid.

велика́н giant. вели́кий (вели́к, -а *or* -á) great; big, large; too big; ~ пост Lent.

велико- *in comb* great. Великобрита́ния Great Britain. великоду́шие magnanimity. ~ду́шный magnanimous. ~ле́пие splendour. ~ле́пный splendid.

велича́вый stately, majestic. велича́йший greatest, supreme. вели́чественный majestic, grand. вели́чество Majesty. вели́чие greatness, grandeur. величина́ (*pl* -и́ны, -а́м) size; quantity, magnitude; value; great figure.

велосипе́д bicycle. велосипеди́ст cyclist.

вельве́т velveteen; ~ в ру́бчик corduroy.

вельмо́жа *m* grandee.

ве́на vein.

венге́рец (-рца), венге́рка Hungarian. венге́рский Hungarian. венгр Hungarian. Ве́нгрия Hungary.

венде́тта vendetta.

венери́ческий venereal.

вене́ц (-нца́) crown; wreath.

ве́ник besom; birch twigs.

вено́к (-нка́) wreath, garland.

ве́нтиль *m* valve.

вентиля́тор ventilator; extractor (fan). вентиля́ция ventilation.

венча́ние wedding; coronation. венча́ть *impf* (*pf* об~, по~, у~) crown; marry; ~ся be married, marry. ве́нчик halo; corolla; rim; ring, bolt.

ве́ра faith, belief.

вера́нда veranda.

ве́рба willow; willow branch. ве́рбн|ый; ~ое воскресе́нье Palm Sunday.

верблю́д camel.

вербова́ть *impf* (*pf* за~) recruit; win over. вербо́вка recruitment.

верёвка rope; string; cord. верёвочный rope.

верени́ца row, file, line, string.

ве́реск heather.

веретено́ (*pl* -тёна) spindle.

вереща́ть (-щу́) *impf* squeal; chirp.

ве́рить *impf* (*pf* по~) believe, have faith; +*dat or* в+*acc* trust (in), believe in.

вермише́ль vermicelli.

вернее adv rather. **верно** partl probably, I suppose. **верность** faithfulness, loyalty.

вернуть (-ну, -нёшь) pf (impf возвращать) give back, return; ~ся return.

верный (-рен, -рна, -о) faithful, loyal; true; correct; reliable.

верование belief. **веровать** impf believe. **вероисповедание** religion; denomination. **вероломный** treacherous, perfidious. **вероотступник** apostate. **веротерпимость** (religious) toleration. **вероятно** adv probably. **вероятность** probability. **вероятный** probable.

версия version.

верста (pl вёрсты) verst (1.06 km.).

верстак (-а) work-bench.

вертел (pl -а) spit, skewer. **вертеть** (-чу, -тишь) impf turn (round); twirl; ~ся turn (round), spin. **вертлявый** fidgety; flighty.

вертикаль vertical line. **вертикальный** vertical.

вертолёт helicopter.

вертушка flirt.

верующий sb believer.

верфь shipyard.

верх (loc -у; pl -и) top; summit; height; pl upper crust, top brass; high notes. **верхний** upper; top. **верховный** supreme. **верховой** riding; sb rider. **верховье** (gen pl -вьев) upper reaches. **верхолаз** steeplejack. **верхом** adv on horseback; astride. **верхушка** top, summit; apex; top brass.

верчу etc.: see **вертеть**

вершина top, summit; peak; apex. **вершить** impf +instr manage, control.

вершок vershok (4.4 cm.); smattering.

вес (loc -у; pl -а) weight.

веселить impf (pf раз~) cheer, gladden; ~ся enjoy o.s.; amuse o.s. **весело** adv merrily. **весёлый** (весел, -а, -о) merry; cheerful. **веселье** merriment.

весенний spring.

весить (вешу) impf weigh. **веский** weighty, solid.

весло (pl вёсла, -сел) oar.

весна (pl вёсны, -сен) spring.

весной adv in (the) spring. **веснушка** freckle.

вест (naut) west; west wind.

вести (веду, -дёшь; вёл, -а) impf (pf по~) lead, take; conduct; drive; run; keep; ~ behave, conduct o.s.; ~сь be the custom.

вестибюль m (entrance) hall, lobby. **вестник** herald; bulletin. **весть**[1] (gen pl -ей) news; **без вести** without trace. **весть**[2]: Бог ~ God knows.

весы (pl; gen -ов) scales, balance; Libra.

весь (всего m, вся, всей f, всё, всего neut, все, всех pl) pron all, the whole of; **всё** best; **всё хорошего!** all the best!; **всё** everything; **без всего** without anything; **все** everybody.

весьма adv very, highly.

ветвь (gen pl -ей) branch; bough.

ветер (-тра, loc -у) wind. **ветерок** (-рка) breeze.

ветеран veteran.

ветеринар vet.

ветка branch; twig.

вето neut indecl veto.

ветошь old clothes, rags.

ветреный windy; frivolous. **ветров|ой** wind; ~ое стекло windscreen. **ветряк** (-а) wind turbine; windmill.

ветхий (ветх, -а, -о) old; dilapidated; В~ завет Old Testament.

ветчина ham.

ветшать impf (pf об~) decay; become dilapidated.

веха landmark.

вечер (pl -а) evening; party. **вечеринка** party. **вечерний** evening. **вечерня** (gen pl -рен) vespers. **вечером** adv in the evening.

вечно adv for ever, eternally. **вечнозелёный** evergreen. **вечность** eternity; ages. **вечный** eternal.

вешалка peg, rack; tab, hanger. **вешать** impf (pf взвесить, повесить, свешать) hang; weigh (out); ~ся hang o.s.; weigh o.s.

вешу etc.: see **весить**

вещание broadcasting. **вещать** impf broadcast.

вещевой clothing; ~ мешок hold-all, kit-bag. **вещественный** substantial, material, real. **вещество** substance; matter. **вещь** (gen pl -ей) thing.

ве́ялка winnowing-machine. **ве́яние** winnowing; blowing; trend. **ве́ять** (ве́ю) *impf* (*pf* про~) winnow; blow; flutter.

взад *adv* backwards; ~ и вперёд back and forth.

взаи́мность reciprocity. **взаи́мный** mutual, reciprocal.

взаимо- *in comb* inter-. **взаимоде́йствие** interaction; co-operation. ~**де́йствовать** *impf* interact; cooperate. ~**отноше́ние** interrelation; *pl* relations. ~**по́мощь** mutual aid. ~**понима́ние** mutual understanding. ~**связь** interdependence, correlation.

взаймы́ *adv*: взять ~ borrow; дать ~ lend.

взаме́н *prep+gen* instead of; in return for.

взаперти́ *adv* under lock and key; in seclusion.

взба́лмошный unbalanced, eccentric.

взбега́ть *impf*, **взбежа́ть** (-егу́) *pf* run up.

взберу́сь *etc.*: *see* **взобра́ться**. **вз|беси́ть(ся** (-ешу́(сь, -е́сишь(ся) *pf*. **взбива́ть** *impf of* **взбить**. **взбира́ться** *impf of* **взобра́ться**

взби́тый whipped, beaten. **взбить** (взобью́, -бьёшь) *pf* (*impf* **взбива́ть**) beat (up), whip; shake up.

вз|борозди́ть (-зжу́) *pf*.

вз|бунтова́ться *pf*.

взбуха́ть *impf*, **взбу́хнуть** (-нет; -ух) *pf* swell (out).

взва́ливать *impf*, **взвали́ть** (-лю́, -лишь) *pf* load; +на+*acc* saddle with.

взве́сить (-е́шу) *pf* (*impf* **ве́шать**, **взве́шивать**) weigh.

взвести́ (-еду́, -едёшь; -ёл, -а́) *pf* (*impf* **взводи́ть**) lead up; raise; cock; +на+*acc* impute to.

взве́шивать *impf of* **взве́сить**

взвива́ть(ся *impf of* **взви́ть(ся**

взви́зг scream; yelp. **взви́згивать** *impf*, **взви́згнуть** (-ну) *pf* scream; yelp.

взвинти́ть (-нчу́) *pf*, **взви́нчивать** *impf* excite, work up; inflate. **взви́нченный** worked up; nervy; inflated. **взвить** (взовью́, -ёшь; -ил, -а́, -о) *pf* (*impf* **взвива́ть**) raise; ~ся rise, be hoisted; soar.

взвод[1] platoon, troop.

взвод[2] notch. **взводи́ть** (-ожу́, -о́дишь) *impf of* **взвести́**

взволно́ванный agitated; worried. **вз|волнова́ть(ся** (-ну́ю(сь) *pf*.

взгляд look; glance; opinion. **взгля́дывать** *impf*, **взгляну́ть** (-яну́, -я́нешь) *pf* look, glance.

взго́рье hillock.

вздёргивать *impf*, **вздёрнуть** (-ну) *pf* hitch up; jerk up; turn up.

вздор nonsense. **вздо́рный** cantankerous; foolish.

вздорожа́ние rise in price. **вз|дорожа́ть** *pf*.

вздох sigh. **вздохну́ть** (-ну́, -нёшь) *pf* (*impf* **вздыха́ть**) sigh.

вздра́гивать *impf* (*pf* **вздро́гнуть**) shudder, quiver.

вздремну́ть *pf* have a nap, doze.

вздро́гнуть (-ну) *pf* (*impf* **вздра́гивать**) start; wince.

вздува́ть(ся *impf of* **вздуть**[1](ся

взду́мать *pf* take it into one's head; не взду́май(те)! don't you dare!

взду́тие swelling. **взду́тый** swollen. **взду́ть**[1] (-у́ю) *pf* (*impf* **вздува́ть**) inflate; ~ся swell.

вздуть[2] *pf* thrash.

вздыха́ть *impf* (*pf* **вздохну́ть**) breathe; sigh.

взима́ть *impf* levy, collect.

взла́мывать *impf of* **взлома́ть**.

вз|леле́ять *pf*.

взлёт flight; take-off. **взлета́ть** *impf*, **взлете́ть** (-лечу́) *pf* fly (up); take off. **взлётный** take-off; **взлётно-поса́дочная полоса́** runway.

взлом breaking open, breaking in. **взлома́ть** *pf* (*impf* **взла́мывать**) break open; break up. **взло́мщик** burglar.

взлохма́ченный dishevelled.

взмах stroke, wave, flap. **взма́хивать** *impf*, **взмахну́ть** (-ну́, -нёшь) *pf* +*instr* wave, flap.

взмо́рье seaside; coastal waters.

вз|мути́ть (-учу́, -у́тишь) *pf*.

взнос payment; fee, dues.

взнузда́ть *pf*, **взну́здывать** *impf* bridle.

взобра́ться (взберу́сь, -ёшься; -а́лся, -ла́сь, -а́лось) *pf* (*impf* **взбира́ться**) climb (up).

взобью́ *etc.*: *see* **взбить**. **взовью́** *etc.*:

see **взвить**

взойти́ (-йду́, -йдёшь; -ошёл, -шла́) *pf* (*impf* **вос-, всходи́ть**) rise, go up; на+*acc* mount.

взор look, glance.

взорва́ть (-ву́, -вёшь; -а́л, -а́, -о) *pf* (*impf* **взрыва́ть**) blow up; exasperate; ~**ся** burst, explode.

взро́слый *adj & sb* adult.

взрыв explosion; outburst. **взрыва́тель** *m* fuse. **взрыва́ть** *impf*, **взрыть** (-ро́ю) *pf* (*pf also* **взорва́ть**) blow up; ~**ся** explode. **взрывно́й** explosive; blasting. **взрывча́тка** explosive. **взры́вчатый** explosive.

взъеро́шенный tousled, dishevelled. **взъеро́шивать** *impf*, **взъеро́шить** (-шу) *pf* tousle, rumple.

взыва́ть *impf of* **воззва́ть**

взыска́ние penalty; exaction. **взыска́тельный** exacting. **взыска́ть** (-ыщу́, -ы́щешь) *pf*, **взы́скивать** *impf* exact, recover; call to account.

взя́тие taking, capture. **взя́тка** bribe. **взя́точничество** bribery. **взять(ся** (возьму́(сь, -мёшь(ся; -я́л(ся, -а́(сь, -о(сь) *pf of* **брать(ся**

вибра́ция vibration. **вибри́ровать** *impf* vibrate.

вивисе́кция vivisection.

вид[1] (*loc* -у́) look; appearance; shape, form; condition; view; prospect; sight; де́лать вид pretend; име́ть в ~у́ intend; mean; bear in mind.

вид[2] kind; species.

вида́ться *impf* (*pf* по~) meet. **ви́дение**[1] sight, vision. **виде́ние**[2] vision, apparition.

ви́део *neut indecl* video (cassette) recorder; video film; video cassette. **ви́деоигра́** video game. **видеока́мера** video camera. **видеокассе́та** video cassette. **видеомагнитофо́н** video (cassette) recorder.

ви́деть (ви́жу) *impf* (*pf* у~) see; ~ во сне dream (of); ~**ся** see one another; appear. **ви́димо** *adv* evidently. **ви́димость** visibility; appearance. **ви́димый** visible; apparent, evident. **ви́дный** (-ден, -дна́, -о) visible; distinguished.

видоизмене́ние modification. **видоизмени́ть** *pf*, **видоизменя́ть** *impf* modify.

видоиска́тель *m* view-finder.

ви́жу *see* **ви́деть**

ви́за visa.

визг squeal; yelp. **визжа́ть** (-жу́) *impf* squeal, yelp, squeak.

визи́т visit. **визи́тка** business card.

викто́рина quiz.

ви́лка fork; plug. **ви́лы** (*pl*; *gen* вил) pitchfork.

вильну́ть (-ну́, -нёшь) *pf*, **виля́ть** *impf* twist and turn; prevaricate; +*instr* wag.

вина́ (*pl* ви́ны) fault, guilt; blame.

винегре́т Russian salad; medley.

вини́тельный accusative. **вини́ть** *impf* accuse; ~**ся** (*pf* по~) confess.

ви́нный wine; winy. **вино́** (*pl* -а) wine.

винова́тый guilty. **вино́вник** initiator; culprit. **вино́вный** guilty.

виногра́д vine; grapes. **виногра́дник** vineyard. **виногра́дный** grape; wine. **винокуренный заво́д** distillery.

винт (-а́) screw. **винти́ть** (-нчу́) *impf* screw up. **винто́вка** rifle. **винтово́й** screw; spiral.

виолонче́ль cello.

вира́ж (-а́) turn; bend.

виртуо́з virtuoso. **виртуо́зный** masterly.

ви́рус virus. **ви́русный** virus.

ви́селица gallows. **висе́ть** (вишу́) *impf* hang. **ви́снуть** (-ну; вис(нул)) *impf* hang; droop.

ви́ски *neut indecl* whisky.

висо́к (-ска́) temple.

висо́косный год leap-year.

вист whist.

вися́чий hanging; ~ замо́к padlock; ~ мост suspension bridge.

витами́н vitamin.

витиева́тый flowery, ornate. **вито́й** twisted, spiral. **вито́к** (-тка́) turn, coil.

витра́ж (-а́) stained-glass window. **витри́на** shop-window; showcase.

вить (вью, вьёшь; вил, -а́, -о) *impf* (*pf* с~) twist, wind, weave; ~**ся** wind, twine; curl; twist; whirl.

вихо́р (-хра́) tuft. **вихра́стый** shaggy. **вихрь** *m* whirlwind; vortex; сне́жный ~ blizzard.

ви́це- *pref* vice-. **ви́це-адмира́л** vice-admiral. ~**президе́нт** vice-president.

вицмунди́р (dress) uniform.

ВИЧ (abbr of ви́рус иммуноде-фици́та челове́ка) HIV.

вишнёвый cherry. **ви́шня** (gen pl -шен) cherry, cherries; cherry-tree.

вишу́: see висе́ть

вишь partl look, just look!

вка́лывать impf (sl) work hard; impf of вколо́ть

вка́пывать impf of вкопа́ть

вкати́ть (-ачу́, -а́тишь) pf, **вка́тывать** impf roll in; administer.

вклад deposit; contribution. **вкла́дка** supplementary sheet. **вкладно́й лист** loose leaf, insert. **вкла́дчик** depositor.

вкла́дывать impf of вложи́ть

вкле́ивать impf, **вкле́ить** pf stick in.

вкли́ниваться impf, **вклини́ться** pf edge one's way in.

включа́тель m switch. **включа́ть** impf, **включи́ть** (-чу́) pf include; switch on; plug in; ~ся в+acc join in, enter into. **включа́я** including. **включе́ние** inclusion, insertion; switching on. **включи́тельно** adv inclusive.

вкола́чивать impf, **вколоти́ть** (-очу́, -о́тишь) pf hammer in, knock in.

вколо́ть (-олю́, -о́лешь) pf (impf вка́лывать) stick (in).

вкопа́ть pf (impf вка́пывать) dig in.

вкось adv obliquely.

вкра́дчивый ingratiating. **вкра́дываться** impf, **вкра́сться** (-аду́сь, -адёшься) pf creep in; insinuate o.s.

вкра́тце adv briefly, succinctly.

вкривь adv aslant; wrongly, perversely.

вкруг = вокру́г

вкруту́ю adv hard(-boiled).

вкус taste. **вкуси́ть** (-ушу́, -у́сишь) pf, **вкуша́ть** impf taste; partake of. **вку́сный** (-сен, -сна́, -о) tasty, nice.

вла́га moisture.

влага́лище vagina.

владе́лец (-льца), **-лица** owner. **владе́ние** ownership; possession; property. **владе́тель** m, **-ница** possessor; sovereign. **владе́ть** (-е́ю) impf +instr own, possess; control.

влады́ка m master, sovereign. **влады́чество** dominion, sway.

вла́жность humidity; moisture.

вла́жный (-жен, -жна́, -о) damp, moist, humid.

вла́мываться impf of вломи́ться

вла́ствовать impf +(над+) instr rule, hold sway over. **властели́н** ruler; master. **вла́стный** imperious, commanding; empowered, competent. **власть** (gen pl -е́й) power; authority.

вле́во adv to the left (от+gen of).

влеза́ть impf, **влезть** (-зу; влез) pf climb in; get in; fit in.

влёк etc.: see влечь

влета́ть impf, **влете́ть** (-ечу́) pf fly in; rush in.

влече́ние attraction; inclination. **влечь** (-еку́, -ечёшь; влёк, -ла́) impf draw; attract; ~ за собо́й involve, entail.

влива́ть impf, **влить** (волью́, -ёшь; влил, -а́, -о) pf pour in; instil.

влия́ние influence. **влия́тельный** influential. **влия́ть** impf (pf по~) на+acc influence, affect.

вложе́ние enclosure; investment. **вложи́ть** (-ожу́, -о́жишь) pf (impf вкла́дывать) put in, insert; enclose; invest.

вломи́ться (-млю́сь, -мишься) pf (impf вла́мываться) break in.

влюби́ть (-блю́, -бишь) pf, **влюбля́ть** impf make fall in love (в+acc with); ~ся fall in love. **влюблённый** (-лён, -а́) in love; sb lover.

вма́зать (-а́жу) pf, **вма́зывать** impf cement, putty in.

вмени́ть pf, **вменя́ть** impf impute; impose. **вменя́емый** (law) responsible; sane.

вме́сте adv together; ~ с тем at the same time, also.

вмести́лище receptacle. **вмести́мость** capacity; tonnage. **вмести́тельный** capacious. **вмести́ть** (-ещу́) pf (impf вмеща́ть) hold, accommodate; put; ~ся go in.

вме́сто prep+gen instead of.

вмеша́тельство interference; intervention. **вмеша́ть** pf, **вме́шивать** impf mix in; implicate; ~ся interfere, intervene.

вмеща́ть(ся impf of вмести́ть(ся

вмиг adv in an instant.

вмина́ть impf, **вмять** (вомну́, -нёшь) pf press in, dent. **вмя́тина** dent.

внаём, внаймы́ *adv* to let; for hire.
внача́ле *adv* at first.
вне *prep+gen* outside; ~ себя́ beside o.s.
вне- *pref* extra-; outside; -less. вне-бра́чный extra-marital; illegitimate. ~вре́менный timeless. ~кла́ссный extracurricular. ~очередно́й out of turn; extraordinary. ~шта́тный freelance, casual.
внедре́ние introduction; inculcation.
внедри́ть *pf*, внедря́ть *impf* inculcate; introduce; ~ся take root.
внеза́пно *adv* suddenly. внеза́пный sudden.
вне́млю *etc.: see* внима́ть
внесе́ние bringing in; deposit.
внести́ (-су́, -сёшь; внёс, -ла́) *pf* (*impf* вноси́ть) bring in; introduce; deposit; insert.
вне́шне *adv* outwardly. вне́шний outer; external; outside; foreign. вне́шность exterior; appearance.
вниз *adv* down(wards); ~ по-да́ду down. внизу́ *adv* below; downstairs.
вника́ть *impf*, вни́кнуть (-ну; вник) *pf* +в+*acc* go carefully into, investigate thoroughly.
внима́ние attention. внима́тельный attentive. внима́ть *impf* (*pf* внять) listen to; heed.
вничью́ *adv*: око́нчиться ~ end in a draw; сыгра́ть ~ draw.
вновь *adv* anew; again.
вноси́ть (-ошу́, -о́сишь) *impf of* внести́
внук grandson; *pl* grandchildren, descendants.
вну́тренний inner; internal. вну́тренность interior; *pl* entrails; internal organs. внутри́ *adv* & *prep+gen* inside. внутрь *adv* & *prep+gen* inside, in; inwards.
внуча́та (*pl*; *gen* -ча́т) grandchildren. внуча́тый second, great-; ~ брат second cousin; ~ племя́нник great-nephew. вну́чка grand-daughter.
внуша́ть *impf*, внуши́ть (-шу́) *pf* instil; +*dat* inspire with. внуше́ние suggestion; reproof. внуши́тельный inspiring; imposing.
вня́тный distinct. внять (*no fut*; -ял, -á, -о) *pf of* внима́ть
во: *see* в
вобра́ть (вберу́, -рёшь; -а́л, -á, -о) *pf* (*impf* вбира́ть) absorb; inhale.
вобью́ *etc.: see* вбить
вовлека́ть *impf*, вовле́чь (-еку́, -ечёшь; -ёк, -екла́) *pf* draw in, involve.
во́время *adv* in time; on time.
во́все *adv* quite; ~ не not at all.
во-вторы́х *adv* secondly.
вогна́ть (вгоню́, -о́нишь; -гна́л, -á, -о) *pf* (*impf* вгоня́ть) drive in.
во́гнутый concave. вогну́ть (-ну́, -нёшь) *pf* (*impf* вгиба́ть) bend or curve inwards.
вода́ (*acc* во́ду, *gen* -ы́; *pl* -ы) water; *pl* the waters; spa.
водвори́ть *pf*, водворя́ть *impf* settle, install; establish.
води́тель *m* driver. води́ть (вожу́, во́дишь) *impf* lead; conduct; take; drive; ~ся be found; associate (with); be the custom.
во́дка vodka. во́дный water; ~ые лы́жи water-skiing; water-skis.
водо- *in comb* water; water-; hydraulic; hydro-. водобоя́знь hydrophobia. ~воро́т whirlpool; maelstrom. ~ём reservoir. ~измеще́ние displacement. ~ка́чка water-tower, pumping station. ~ла́з diver. ~ле́й Aquarius. ~непроница́емый waterproof. ~отво́дный drainage. ~па́д waterfall. ~по́й watering-place. ~прово́д water-pipe, water-main; water supply. ~прово́дчик plumber. ~разде́л watershed. ~ро́д hydrogen. водоро́сль water-plant; seaweed. ~снабже́ние water supply. ~сто́к drain, gutter. ~храни́лище reservoir.
водружа́ть *impf*, водрузи́ть (-ужу́) *pf* hoist; erect.
водяни́стый watery. водяно́й water.
воева́ть (вою́ю) *impf* wage war.
воево́да *m* voivode; commander.
воедино́ *adv* together.
военко́м military commissar.
вое́нно- *in comb* military; war-. вое́нно-возду́шный air-, air-force. вое́нно-морско́й naval. ~пле́нный *sb* prisoner of war. вое́нно-полево́й суд court-martial. ~слу́жащий *sb* serviceman.
вое́нный military; war; *sb* serviceman; ~ое положе́ние martial law;

~ый суд court-martial.

вожа́к (-а́) guide; leader. вожа́тый *sb* guide; tram-driver.

вожделе́ние desire, lust.

вождь (-я́) *m* leader, chief.

вожжа́ (*pl* -и, -е́й) rein.

вожу́ *etc.: see* води́ть, вози́ть

воз (*loc* -ý; *pl* -ы́) cart; cart-load.

возбуди́мый excitable. возбуди́тель *m* agent; instigator. возбуди́ть (-ужу́) *pf*, возбужда́ть *impf* excite, arouse; incite. возбужда́ющ|ий: ~ее сре́дство stimulant. возбужде́ние excitement. возбуждённый excited.

возвести́ть (-ещу́) *pf*, возвеща́ть *impf* proclaim.

возводи́ть (-ожу́, -о́дишь) *impf of* возвести́

возвра́т return; repayment. возврати́ть (-ащу́) *pf*, возвраща́ть *impf* (*pf also* верну́ть) return, give back; ~ся return; go back, come back. возвра́тный return; reflexive. возвраще́ние return.

возвы́сить *pf*, возвыша́ть *impf* raise; ennoble; ~ся rise. возвыше́ние rise; raised place. возвы́шенность height; loftiness. возвы́шенный high; elevated.

возгла́вить (-влю) *pf*, возглавля́ть *impf* head.

во́зглас exclamation. возгласи́ть (-ашу́) *pf*, возглаша́ть *impf* proclaim.

возгора́емый inflammable. возгора́ться *impf*, возгоре́ться (-рю́сь) *pf* flare up; be seized (with).

воздава́ть (-даю́, -даёшь) *impf*, возда́ть (-а́м, -а́шь, -а́ст, -ади́м; -а́л, -а́, -о) *pf* render.

воздвига́ть *impf*, воздви́гнуть (-ну; -дви́г) *pf* raise.

возде́йствие influence. возде́йствовать *impf & pf* +на+*acc* influence.

возде́лать *pf*, возде́лывать *impf* cultivate, till.

воздержа́ние abstinence; abstention. возде́ржанный abstemious. воздержа́ться (-жу́сь, -жишься) *pf*, возде́рживаться *impf* refrain; ab-

stain.

во́здух air. воздухонепроница́емый air-tight. возду́шн|ый air, aerial; airy; flimsy; ~ый змей kite; ~ый шар balloon.

зоззва́ние appeal. воззва́ть (-зову́, -вёшь) *pf* (*impf* взыва́ть) appeal (о+*prep* for).

воззре́ние opinion, outlook.

вози́ть (вожу́, во́зишь) *impf* convey; carry; bring, take; ~ся romp, play noisily; busy o.s.; potter about.

возлага́ть *impf of* возложи́ть

во́зле *adv & prep*+*gen* by, near; near by; past.

возложи́ть (-жу́, -жишь) *pf* (*impf* возлага́ть) lay; place.

возлю́бленный beloved; *sb* sweet-heart.

возме́здие retribution.

возмести́ть (-ещу́) *pf*, возмеща́ть *impf* compensate for; refund. возмеще́ние compensation; refund.

возмо́жно *adv* possibly; +*comp* as ... as possible. возмо́жность possibility; opportunity. возмо́жный possible.

возмужа́лый mature; grown up. возмужа́ть *pf* grow up; gain strength.

возмути́тельный disgraceful. возмути́ть (-ущу́) *pf*, возмуща́ть *impf* disturb; stir up; rouse to indignation; ~ся be indignant. возмуще́ние indignation. возмущённый (-щён, -щена́) indignant.

вознагради́ть (-ажу́) *pf*, вознагражда́ть *impf* reward. вознагражде́ние reward; fee.

возненави́деть (-и́жу) *pf* conceive a hatred for.

вознесе́ние Ascension. вознести́ (-несу́, -несёшь; -нёс, -ла́) *pf* (*impf* возноси́ть) raise, lift up; ~сь rise; ascend.

возника́ть *impf*, возни́кнуть (-нет; -ни́к) *pf* arise, spring up. возникнове́ние rise, beginning, origin.

возни́ца *m* coachman.

возноси́ть(ся (-ошу́(сь, -о́сишь(ся) *impf of* вознести́(сь. возноше́ние raising, elevation.

возня́ row, noise; bother.

возобнови́ть (-влю́) *pf*, возобновля́ть *impf* renew; restore; ~ся begin again. **возобновле́ние** renewal; revival.

возража́ть *impf*, **возрази́ть** (-ажу́) *pf* object. **возраже́ние** objection.

во́зраст age. **возраста́ние** growth, increase. **возраста́ть** *impf*, **возрасти́** (-тёт; -ро́с, -ла́) *pf* grow, increase.

возроди́ть (-ожу́) *pf*, **возрожда́ть** *impf* revive; ~ся revive. **возрожде́ние** revival; Renaissance.

возро́с *etc.*: see **возрасти́**. **возро́сший** increased.

во́зчик carter, carrier.

возьму́ *etc.*: see **взять**.

во́ин warrior; soldier. **во́инск**|**ий** military; ~ая пови́нность conscription. **вои́нственный** warlike. **вои́нствующий** militant.

вой howl(ing); wail(ing).

войду́ *etc.*: see **войти́**

во́йлок felt. **во́йлочный** felt.

война́ (*pl* -ы) war.

во́йско (*pl* -а́) army; *pl* troops, forces. **войсково́й** military.

войти́ (-йду́, -йдёшь; вошёл, -шла́) *pf* (*impf* **входи́ть**) go in, come in, enter; get in(to).

вокза́л (railway) station.

во́кмен Walkman (*propr*), personal stereo.

вокру́г *adv & prep+gen* round, around.

вол (-а́) ox, bullock.

вола́н flounce; shuttlecock.

волды́рь (-я́) *m* blister; bump.

волево́й strong-willed.

волейбо́л volleyball.

во́лей-нево́лей *adv* willy-nilly.

волк (*pl* -и, -о́в) wolf. **волкода́в** wolf-hound.

волна́ (*pl* -ы, во́лна́м) wave. **волне́ние** choppiness; agitation; emotion. **волни́стый** wavy. **волнова́ть** *impf* (*pf* вз~) disturb; agitate; excite; ~ся be disturbed; worry, be nervous. **волноло́м**, **волноре́з** breakwater. **волну́ющий** disturbing; exciting.

волоки́та red tape; rigmarole.

волокни́стый fibrous, stringy. **волокно́** (*pl* -а) fibre, filament.

волоку́ *etc.*: see **воло́чь**

во́лос (*pl* -ы, -о́с, -а́м); *pl* hair. **волоса́тый** hairy. **волосно́й** capillary.

во́лость (*pl* -и, -е́й) volost (*administrative division*).

волочи́ть (-очу́, -о́чишь) *impf* drag; ~ся drag, trail; +за+*instr* run after, court. **воло́чь** (-оку́, -очёшь; -о́к, -ла́) *impf* drag.

во́лчий wolf's; wolfish. **волчи́ха**, **волчи́ца** she-wolf.

волчо́к (-чка́) top; gyroscope.

волчо́нок (-нка; *pl* -ча́та, -ча́т) wolf cub.

волше́бник magician; wizard. **волше́бница** enchantress. **волше́бный** magic; enchanting. **волше́бство́** magic, enchantment.

вольнонаёмный civilian. **во́льность** liberty; license. **во́льный** (-лен, -льна́, -о, во́льны) free; freestyle.

вольт[1] (*gen pl* вольт) volt.

вольт[2] (*loc* -у́) vault.

вольфра́м tungsten.

во́ля will; liberty.

вомну́ *etc.*: see **вмять**

вон *adv* out; off, away.

вон *partl* there, over there.

вонза́ть *impf*, **вонзи́ть** (-нжу́) *pf* plunge, thrust.

вонь stench. **воню́чий** stinking. **воня́ть** *impf* stink.

вообража́емый imaginary. **вообража́ть** *impf*, **вообрази́ть** (-ажу́) *pf* imagine. **воображе́ние** imagination. **вообрази́мый** imaginable.

вообще́ *adv* in general; generally.

воодушеви́ть (-влю́) *pf*, **воодушевля́ть** *impf* inspire. **воодушевле́ние** inspiration; fervour.

вооружа́ть *impf*, **вооружи́ть** (-жу́) *pf* arm, equip; ~ся arm o.s.; take up arms. **вооруже́ние** arming; arms; equipment. **вооружённый** (-жён, -а́) armed; equipped.

воо́чию *adv* with one's own eyes.

во-пе́рвых *adv* first, first of all.

вопи́ть (-плю́) *impf* yell, howl. **вопию́щий** crying; scandalous.

воплоти́ть (-ощу́) *pf*, **воплоща́ть** *impf* embody. **воплоще́ние** embodiment.

вопль *m* cry, wail; howling.

вопреки́ *prep+dat* in spite of.

вопро́с question; problem. **вопроси́тельный** interrogative; questioning; ~ знак question-mark.

вор (pl -ы, -о́в) thief; criminal.
ворва́ться (-ву́сь, -вёшься; -а́лся, -ла́сь, -а́ло́сь) pf (impf **врыва́ться**) burst in.
воркотня́ grumbling.
воробе́й sparrow.
ворова́тый thievish; furtive. **ворова́ть** impf (pf с~) steal. **воро́вка** woman thief. **воровско́й** thieves'. **воровство́** stealing; theft.
во́рон raven. **воро́на** crow.
воро́нка funnel; crater.
вороно́й black.
во́рот[1] collar; neckband.
во́рот[2] winch; windlass.
воро́та (pl; gen -ро́т) gate(s); gateway; goal.
вороти́ть (-очу́, -о́тишь) pf bring back, get back; turn back; ~ся return.
воротни́к (-á) collar.
во́рох (pl -á) heap, pile; heaps.
воро́чать impf turn; move; +instr have control of; ~ся move, turn.
ворочу́(сь etc.: see **вороти́ть(ся**
вороши́ть (-шу́) impf stir up; turn (over).
ворс nap, pile.
ворча́ть (-чу́) impf grumble; growl. **ворчли́вый** peevish; grumpy.
восвоя́си adv home.
восемна́дцатый eighteenth. **восемна́дцать** eighteen. **во́семь** (-сьми́, instr -семью or -семью) eight. **во́семьдесят** eighty. **восемьсо́т** (-сьмисо́т, -ста́ми) eight hundred. **во́семью** adv eight times.
воск wax, beeswax.
воскли́кнуть (-ну) pf, **восклица́ть** impf exclaim. **восклица́ние** exclamation. **восклица́тельный** exclamatory; ~ знак exclamation mark.
восково́й wax; waxy; waxed.
воскреса́ть impf, **воскре́снуть** (-ну; -éc) pf rise from the dead; revive. **воскресе́ние** resurrection. **воскресе́нье** Sunday. **воскреси́ть** (-ешу́) pf, **воскреша́ть** impf resurrect; revive. **воскреше́ние** resurrection; revival.
воспале́ние inflammation. **воспалённый** (-лён, -á) inflamed. **воспали́ть** pf, **воспаля́ть** impf inflame; ~ся become inflamed.

воспита́ние upbringing, education. **воспи́танник**, -ница pupil. **воспи́танный** well-brought-up. **воспита́тель** m tutor; educator. **воспита́тельный** educational. **воспита́ть** pf, **воспи́тывать** impf bring up; foster; educate.
воспламени́ть pf, **воспламеня́ть** impf ignite; fire; ~ся ignite; flare up. **воспламеня́емый** inflammable.
вос|по́льзоваться pf.
воспомина́ние recollection, memory; pl memoirs; reminiscences.
вос|препя́тствовать pf.
воспрети́ть (-ещу́) pf, **воспреща́ть** impf forbid. **воспреще́ние** prohibition. **воспрещённый** (-щён, -á) prohibited.
восприи́мчивый impressionable; susceptible. **воспринима́ть** impf, **восприня́ть** (-иму́, -и́мешь; -и́нял, -á, -о) pf perceive; grasp. **восприя́тие** perception.
воспроизведе́ние reproduction. **воспроизвести́** (-еду́, -едёшь; -вёл, -á) pf, **воспроизводи́ть** (-ожу́, -о́дишь) impf reproduce. **воспроизводи́тельный** reproductive. **воспроизво́дство** reproduction.
вос|проти́виться (-влюсь) pf.
воссоедине́ние reunification. **воссоедини́ть** pf, **воссоединя́ть** impf reunite.
восстава́ть (-таю́, -таёшь) impf of **восста́ть**.
восста́ние insurrection.
восстанови́ть (-влю́, -вишь) pf (impf **восстана́вливать**) restore; reinstate; recall; ~ про́тив+gen set against. **восстановле́ние** restoration.
восста́ть (-а́ну) pf (impf **восстава́ть**) rise (up).
восто́к east.
восто́рг delight, rapture. **восторга́ться**+instr be delighted with, go into raptures over. **восто́рженный** enthusiastic.
восто́чный east, eastern; easterly; oriental.
востре́бование: до востре́бования to be called for, poste restante.
восхвали́ть (-лю́, -лишь) pf, **восхваля́ть** impf praise, extol.
восхити́тельный entrancing; de-

lightful. восхити́ть (-хищу́) pf, восхища́ть impf enrapture; ~ся +instr be enraptured by. восхище́ние delight; admiration.

восхо́д rising. восходи́ть (-ожу́, -о́дишь) impf of взойти́; ~ к+dat go back to, date from. восхожде́ние ascent. восходя́щий rising.

восше́ствие accession.

восьма́я sb eighth; octave. восьмёрка eight; figure eight; No. 8; figure of eight.

восьми- in comb eight-; octo-. восьмигра́нник octahedron. ~деся́тый eightieth. ~ле́тний eight-year; eight-year-old. ~со́тый eight-hundredth. ~уго́льник octagon. ~уго́льный octagonal.

восьмо́й eighth.

вот partl here (is), there (is); this (is); ~ и всё and that's all; ~ как! no! really? ~ та́к! that's right!; ~ что! no! not really? вот-во́т adv just, on the point of; partl that's right!

воткну́ть (-ну́, -нёшь) pf (impf втыка́ть) stick in, drive in.

вотру́ etc.: see втере́ть

воцари́ться pf, воцаря́ться impf come to the throne; set in.

вошёл etc.: see войти́

вошь (вши; gen pl вшей) louse.

вошью́ etc.: see вшить

вою́ etc.: see воева́ть

вою́ю etc.: see воева́ть

впада́ть impf, впасть (-аду́) pf flow; lapse; fall in; +в+acc verge on, approximate to. впаде́ние confluence; (river-)mouth. впа́дина cavity, hollow; socket. впа́лый sunken.

впервы́е adv for the first time.

вперёд adv forward(s), ahead; in future; in advance; идти́ ~ (of clock) be fast. впереди́ adv in front, ahead; in (the) future; prep+gen in front of, before.

впечатле́ние impression. впечатли́тельный impressionable.

вписа́ть (-ишу́, -и́шешь) pf, впи́сывать impf enter, insert; ~ся be enrolled, join.

впита́ть pf, впи́тывать impf absorb, take in; ~ся soak.

впи́хивать impf, впихну́ть (-ну́, -нёшь) pf cram in; shove.

вплавь adv (by) swimming.

вплести́ (-ету́, -етёшь; -ёл, -á) pf, вплета́ть impf plait in, intertwine; involve.

вплотну́ю adv close; in earnest. вплоть adv; ~ до+gen (right) up to.

вполго́лоса adv under one's breath.

вполне́ adv fully, entirely; quite.

впопыха́х adv hastily; in one's haste.

впо́ру adv at the right time; just right, exactly.

впосле́дствии adv subsequently.

впотьма́х adv in the dark.

впра́ве adv: быть ~ have a right.

впра́во adv to the right (от+gen of).

впредь adv in (the) future; ~ до+gen until.

впро́голодь adv half starving.

впро́чем conj however, but; though.

впры́скивание injection. впры́скивать impf, впры́снуть (-ну) pf inject.

впряга́ть impf впрячь (-ягу́, -яжёшь; -яг, -ла́) pf harness.

впуск admittance. впуска́ть impf, впусти́ть (-ущу́, -у́стишь) pf admit, let in.

впусту́ю adv to no purpose, in vain.

впущу́ etc.: see впусти́ть

враг (-а́) enemy. вражда́ enmity. вражде́бный hostile. враждова́ть be at enmity. вра́жеский enemy.

вразбро́д adv separately, disunitedly.

вразре́з adv: идти́ ~ с+instr go against.

вразуми́тельный intelligible, clear; persuasive.

врасплóх adv unawares.

враста́ть impf, врасти́ (-тёт; врос, -ла́) pf grow in; take root.

врата́рь (-я́) m goalkeeper.

врать (вру, врёшь; -ал, -á, -о) impf (pf на~, со~) lie, tell lies; talk nonsense.

врач (-á) doctor. враче́бный medical.

враща́ть impf rotate, revolve; ~ся revolve, rotate. враще́ние rotation, revolution.

вред (-á) harm; damage. вреди́тель m pest; wrecker; pl vermin. вреди́тельство wrecking, (act of) sabotage. вреди́ть (-ежу́) impf (pf по~) +dat harm; damage. вре́дный (-ден, -дна́, -о) harmful.

врéзать (-éжу) pf, вреза́ть impf cut

in; set in; (sl) +dat hit; ~ся cut (into); run (into); be engraved; fall in love.
временами adv at times. временно adv temporarily. временной temporal. временный temporary; provisional. время (-мени, pl -мена, -мён, -ам) neut time; tense; ~ года season; ~ от времени at times, from time to time; на ~ for a time; сколько времени? what is the time?; тем временем meanwhile.
вровень adv level, on a level.
вроде prep+gen like; partl such as, like; apparently.
врождённый (-дён, -а) innate.
врозь, врозь adv separately, apart.
врос etc.: see врасти. вру etc.: see врать
врун (-а), врунья liar.
вручать impf, вручить (-чу) pf hand, deliver; entrust.
вручную adv by hand.
врываться impf of ворваться
вряд (ли) adv it's not likely; hardly, scarcely.
всадить (-ажу, -адишь) pf, всаживать impf thrust in; sink in. всадник rider, horseman. всадница rider, horsewoman.
всасывать impf of всосать
всё, все see весь. всё adv always, all the time; ~ (ещё) still; conj however, nevertheless; ~ же all the same.
все- in comb all-, omni-. всевозможный of every kind; all possible. ~дозволенность permissiveness. ~мерный of every kind. ~мирный world-wide, world-wide. ~могущий omnipotent. ~народно adv publicly. ~народный national; nation-wide. ~объемлющий comprehensive, all-embracing. ~российский All-Russian. ~сильный omnipotent. ~сторонний all-round; comprehensive.
всегда always.
всего adv in all, all told; only.
вселенная sb universe.
вселить pf, вселять impf install, lodge; inspire; ~ся move in, install o.s.; be implanted.
всенощная sb night service.
всеобщий general, universal.
всерьёз adv seriously, in earnest.

всё-таки conj & partl all the same, still. всецело adv completely.
вскакивать impf of вскочить
вскачь adv at a gallop.
вскипать impf, вс|кипеть (-плю) pf boil up; flare up.
вс|кипятить(ся) (-ячу(сь)) pf
всколыхнуть (-ну, -нёшь) pf stir; stir up.
вскользь adv slightly; in passing.
вскоре adv soon, shortly after.
вскочить (-очу, -очишь) pf (impf вскакивать) jump up.
вскрикивать impf, вскрикнуть (-ну) pf shriek, scream. вскричать (-чу) pf exclaim.
вскрывать impf, вскрыть (-рою) pf open; reveal; dissect. вскрытие opening; revelation; post-mortem.
вслед adv & prep+dat after; ~ за+instr after, following. вследствие prep+gen in consequence of.
вслепую adv blindly; blindfold.
вслух adv aloud.
вслушаться pf, вслушиваться impf listen attentively.
всматриваться impf, всмотреться (-рюсь, -ришься) pf look closely.
всмятку adv soft(-boiled).
всовывать impf of всунуть
всосать (-су, -сёшь) pf (impf всасывать) suck in; absorb; imbibe.
вс|пахать (-ашу, -ашешь) pf, вспахивать impf plough up. вспашка ploughing.
вс|потеть pf.
всплеск splash. всплёскивать impf, всплеснуть (-ну, -нёшь) pf splash; ~ руками throw up one's hands.
всплывать impf, всплыть (-ыву, -ывёшь; -ыл, -а, -о) pf rise to the surface; come to light.
вспоминать impf, вспомнить pf remember; ~ся impers+dat: мне вспомнилось I remembered.
вспомогательный auxiliary.
вс|потеть pf.
вспрыгивать impf, вспрыгнуть (-ну) pf jump up.
вспухать impf, вс|пухнуть (-нет; -ух) pf swell up.
вспылить pf flare up. вспыльчивый hot-tempered.
вспыхивать impf, вспыхнуть (-ну)

pf blaze up; flare up. **вспы́шка** flash; outburst; outbreak.

вставать (-таю́, -таёшь) *impf of* встать

вста́вить (-влю) *pf*, **вставля́ть** *impf* put in, insert. **вста́вка** insertion; framing; mounting; inset. **вставно́й** inserted; set in; ~ые зу́бы false teeth.

встать (-а́ну) *pf* (*impf* вставать) get up; stand up.

встрево́женный *adj* anxious. **вс|трево́жить** (-жу) *pf*.

встрепену́ться (-ну́сь, -нёшься) *pf* rouse o.s.; start (up); beat faster.

встре́тить (-е́чу) *pf*, **встреча́ть** *impf* meet (with); ~ся meet; be found. **встре́ча** meeting. **встре́чный** coming to meet; contrary; head; counter; *sb* person met with; пе́рвый ~ the first person you meet, anybody.

встря́ска shaking; shock. **встря́хивать** *impf*, **встряхну́ть** (-ну́, -нёшь) *pf* shake (up); rouse; ~ся shake o.s.; rouse o.s.

вступа́ть *impf*, **вступи́ть** (-плю́, -пишь) *pf* +в+*acc* enter (into); join (in); +на+*acc* go up, mount; ~ся intervene; +за+*acc* stand up for. **вступи́тельный** introductory; entrance. **вступле́ние** entry, joining; introduction.

всу́нуть (-ну) *pf* (*impf* всо́вывать) put in, stick in.

всхли́пывать (-ну) *pf*, **всхли́пывать** *impf* sob.

всходи́ть (-ожу́, -о́дишь) *impf of* взойти́. **всхо́ды** (*pl; gen* -ов) (corn-) shoots.

всю: *see* весь

всю́ду *adv* everywhere.

вся: *see* весь

вся́к|ий any; every, all kinds of; ~ом слу́чае in any case; на ~ий слу́чай just in case; *pron* anyone. **вся́чески** *adv* in every possible way.

втайне *adv* secretly.

вта́лкивать *impf of* втолкну́ть. **вта́птывать** *impf of* втопта́ть. **вта́скивать** *impf*, **втащи́ть** (-щу́, -щишь) *pf* drag in.

втере́ть (вотру́, вотрёшь; втёр) *pf* (*impf* втира́ть) rub in; ~ся insinuate o.s., worm o.s.

втира́ть(ся *impf of* втере́ть(ся

вти́скивать *impf*, **вти́снуть** (-ну) *pf* squeeze in; ~ся squeeze (o.s.) in.

втихомо́лку *adv* surreptitiously.

втолкну́ть (-ну́, -нёшь) *pf* (*impf* вта́лкивать) push in.

втопта́ть (-пчу́, -пчешь) *pf* (*impf* вта́птывать) trample (in).

вторга́ться *impf*, **вто́ргнуться** (-нусь; вто́ргся, -лась) *pf* invade; intrude. **вторже́ние** invasion; intrusion.

вто́рить *impf* play or sing second part; +*dat* repeat, echo. **втори́чный** second, secondary. **вто́рник** Tuesday. **вто́р|о́й** second; ~о́е *sb* second course. **второстепе́нный** secondary, minor.

второпя́х *adv* in haste.

в-тре́тьих *adv* thirdly. **втро́е** *adv* three times. **втроём** *adv* three (together). **втро́йне** *adv* three times as much.

вту́лка plug.

втыка́ть *impf of* воткну́ть **втя́гивать** *impf*, **втяну́ть** (-ну́, -нешь) *pf* draw in; ~ся +в+*acc* enter; get used to.

вуа́ль veil.

вуз *abbr* (*of* вы́сшее уче́бное заведе́ние) higher educational establishment; college.

вулка́н volcano.

вульга́рный vulgar.

вундерки́нд infant prodigy.

вход entrance; entry. **входи́ть** (-ожу́, -о́дишь) *impf of* войти́. **входно́й** entrance.

вхолосту́ю *adv* idle, free.

вцепи́ться (-плю́сь, -пишься) *pf*, **вцепля́ться** *impf* +в+*acc* clutch, catch hold of.

вчера́ *adv* yesterday. **вчера́шний** yesterday's.

вчерне́ *adv* in rough.

вче́тверо *adv* four times. **вчетверо́м** *adv* four (together).

вши *etc*.: *see* вошь

вшива́ть *impf of* вшить

вши́вый lousy.

вширь *adv* in breadth; widely.

вшить (вошью́, -ьёшь) *pf* (*impf* вшива́ть) sew in.

въе́дливый corrosive; caustic.

въезд entry; entrance. **въезжа́ть** *impf*, **въе́хать** (-е́ду, -е́дешь) *pf*

(+в+*acc*) ride in(to); drive in(to); crash into.

вы (вас, вам, ва́ми, вас) *pron* you.

выбега́ть *impf*, **вы́бежать** (-егу, -ежишь) *pf* run out.

вы́|белить *pf*.

вы́беру *etc.*: *see* **вы́брать**. **выбива́ть(ся** *impf of* **вы́бить(ся**. **выбира́ть(ся** *impf of* **вы́брать(ся**

вы́бить (-бью) *pf* (*impf* **выбива́ть**) knock out; dislodge; ~**ся** get out; break loose; come out; ~**ся из сил** exhaust o.s.

вы́бор choice; selection; *pl* election(s). **вы́борный** elective; electoral. **вы́борочный** selective.

вы́|бранить *pf*. **выбра́сывать(ся** *impf of* **вы́бросить(ся**

вы́брать (-беру) *pf* (*impf* **выбира́ть**) choose; elect; take out; ~**ся** get out.

выбрива́ть *impf*, **вы́брить** (-рею) *pf* shave.

вы́бросить (-ошу) *pf* (*impf* **выбра́сывать**) throw out; throw away; ~**ся** throw o.s. out, leap out.

выбыва́ть *impf*, **вы́быть** (-буду) *pf* из+*gen* leave, quit.

выва́ливать *impf*, **вы́валить** *pf* throw out; pour out; ~**ся** tumble out.

вы́везти (-зу, -ез) *pf* (*impf* **вывози́ть**) take, bring, out; export; rescue.

вы́верить *pf* (*impf* **выверя́ть**) adjust, regulate.

вы́вернуть (-ну) *pf*, **вывёртывать** *impf* turn inside out; unscrew; wrench.

выверя́ть *impf of* **вы́верить**

вы́весить (-ешу) *pf* (*impf* **выве́шивать**) weigh; hang out. **вы́веска** sign; pretext.

вы́вести (-еду, -ел) *pf* (*impf* **выводи́ть**) lead, bring, take, out; drive out; remove; exterminate; deduce; hatch; grow, breed; erect; depict; draw; ~**сь** go out of use; become extinct; hatch out.

выве́тривание airing.

выве́шивать *impf of* **вы́весить**

вы́вих dislocation. **вывихивать** *impf*, **вы́вихнуть** (-ну) *pf* dislocate.

вы́вод conclusion; withdrawal. **выводи́ть(ся** (-ожу(сь, -о́дишь(ся) *impf of* **вы́вести(сь**. **вы́водок** (-дка) brood; litter.

вывожу́ *see* **выводи́ть, вывози́ть**

вы́воз export; removal. **вывози́ть** (-ожу́, -о́зишь) *impf of* **вы́везти**. **вывозно́й** export.

вы́гадать *pf*, **выга́дывать** *impf* gain, save.

вы́гиб curve. **выгиба́ть** *impf of* **вы́гнуть**

вы́гладить (-ажу) *pf*.

вы́глядеть (-яжу) *impf* look, look like. **выгля́дывать** *impf*, **вы́глянуть** (-ну) *pf* look out; peep out.

вы́гнать (-гоню) *pf* (*impf* **выгоня́ть**) drive out; distil.

вы́гнутый curved, convex. **вы́гнуть** (-ну) *pf* (*impf* **выгиба́ть**) bend, arch.

выгова́ривать *impf*, **вы́говорить** *pf* pronounce, speak; ~**ся** speak out. **вы́говор** pronunciation; reprimand.

вы́года advantage; gain. **вы́годный** advantageous; profitable.

вы́гон pasture; common. **выгоня́ть** *impf of* **вы́гнать**

выгора́ть *impf*, **вы́гореть** (-рит) *pf* burn down; fade.

вы́|гравировать *pf*.

выгружа́ть *impf*, **вы́грузить** (-ужу) *pf* unload; disembark. **вы́грузка** unloading; disembarkation.

выдава́ть (-даю́, -даёшь) *impf*, **вы́дать** (-ам, -ашь, -аст, -адим) *pf* give (out); issue; betray; extradite; +за+*acc* pass off as; ~**ся** protrude; stand out; present itself. **вы́дача** issue; payment; extradition. **выдаю́щийся** prominent.

выдвига́ть *impf*, **вы́двинуть** (-ну) *pf* move out; pull out; put forward, nominate; ~**ся** move forward, move out; come out; get on (in the world). **выдвиже́ние** nomination; promotion.

выделе́ние secretion; excretion; isolation; apportionment. **вы́делить** *pf*, **выделя́ть** *impf* pick out; detach; allot; secrete; excrete; isolate; ~ **курси́вом** italicize; ~**ся** stand out, be noted (+*instr* for).

выдёргивать *impf of* **вы́дернуть**

вы́держанный consistent; self-possessed; firm; matured, seasoned. **вы́держать** (-жу) *pf*, **выде́рживать** *impf* bear; endure; contain o.s.; pass (*exam*); sustain. **вы́держка**[1] endurance; self-possession; exposure.

вы́держка[2] excerpt.

вы́дернуть pf (impf выдёргивать) pull out.

вы́дохнуть (-ну) pf (impf выдыха́ть) breathe out; ~ся have lost fragrance or smell; be past one's best.

вы́дра otter.

вы́|драть (-деру) pf. вы́|дрессировать pf.

выдува́ть impf of вы́дуть

вы́думанный made-up, fabricated. вы́думать pf, выду́мывать impf invent; fabricate. вы́думка invention; device; inventiveness.

вы́дуть (impf also выдува́ть) blow; blow out.

выдыха́ние exhalation. выдыха́ть(ся impf of вы́дохнуть(ся

вы́езд departure; exit. вы́ездн|ой exit; ~ая се́ссия суда́ assizes. выезжа́ть impf of вы́ехать

вы́емка taking out; excavation; hollow.

вы́ехать (-еду) pf (impf выезжа́ть) go out, depart; drive out, ride out; move (away).

вы́жать (-жму, -жмешь) pf (impf выжима́ть) squeeze out; wring out.

вы́жечь (-жгу) pf (impf выжига́ть) burn out; cauterize.

выжива́ние survival. выжива́ть impf of вы́жить

выжига́ть impf of вы́жечь

выжида́тельный waiting; temporizing.

выжима́ть impf of вы́жать

вы́жить (-иву) pf (impf выжива́ть) survive; hound out; ~ из ума́ become senile.

вы́звать (-зову) pf (impf вызыва́ть) call (out); send for; challenge; provoke; ~ся volunteer.

выздора́вливать impf, вы́здороветь (-ею) pf recover. выздоровле́ние recovery; convalescence.

вы́зов call; summons; challenge.

вы́золоченный gilt.

вызу́бривать impf, вы́|зубрить pf learn by heart.

вызыва́ть(ся impf of вы́звать(ся. вызыва́ющий defiant; provocative.

вы́играть pf, выи́грывать impf win; gain. вы́игрыш win; gain; prize. вы́игрышный winning; lottery; advantageous.

вы́йти (-йду; -шел, -шла) pf (impf выходи́ть) go out; come out; get out; appear; turn out; be used up; have expired; ~ в свет appear; ~ за́муж (за+acc) marry; ~ из себя́ lose one's temper.

выка́лывать impf of вы́колоть.

выка́пывать impf of вы́копать

выка́рмливать impf of вы́кормить

выка́чать pf, выка́чивать impf pump out.

выки́дывать impf, вы́кинуть pf throw out, reject; put out; miscarry, abort; ~ флаг hoist a flag. вы́кидыш miscarriage, abortion.

вы́кладка laying out; lay-out; facing; kit; computation; calculation. выкла́дывать impf of вы́ложить

выключа́тель m switch. выключа́ть impf, вы́ключить (-чу) pf turn off, switch off; remove, exclude.

выкола́чивать impf, вы́колотить (-лочу) pf knock out, beat out; beat; extort, wring out.

вы́колоть (-лю) pf (impf выка́лывать) put out; gouge out; tattoo.

вы́копать pf (impf also выка́пывать) dig; dig up, dig out; exhume; unearth.

вы́кормить (-млю) pf (impf выка́рмливать) rear, bring up.

вы́корчевать (-чую) pf, выкорчёвывать impf uproot, root out; eradicate.

выкра́ивать impf of вы́кроить

вы́|красить (-ашу) pf, выкра́шивать impf paint; dye.

выкри́кивать impf, вы́крикнуть (-ну) pf cry out; yell.

вы́кроить pf (impf выкра́ивать) cut out; find (time etc.). вы́кройка pattern.

вы́крутить (-учу) pf, выкру́чивать impf unscrew; twist; ~ся extricate o.s.

вы́куп ransom; redemption.

вы́|купать[1] pf.

выкупа́ть[2] impf, вы́купить (-плю) pf ransom, redeem.

вы́лазка sally, sortie; excursion.

выла́мывать impf of вы́ломать

вылеза́ть impf, вы́лезти (-зу; -лез) pf climb out; come out.

вы́|лепить (-плю) pf.

вы́лет flight; take-off. вылета́ть

impf, вы́лететь (-ечу) *pf* fly out; take off.

выле́чивать *impf*, вы́лечить (-чу) *pf* cure; ~ся recover, be cured.

вылива́ть(ся *pf of* вы́лить(ся

вы́линять *pf*.

вы́лить (-лью) *pf* (*impf* вылива́ть) pour out; cast, found; ~ся flow (out); be expressed.

вы́ложить (-жу) *pf* (*impf* выкла́дывать) lay out.

вы́ломать *pf*, вы́ломить (-млю) *pf* (*impf* выла́мывать) break open.

вы́лупиться (-плюсь) *pf*, вылупля́ться *impf* hatch (out).

вы́лью *etc.: see* вы́лить

вы́|мазать (-мажу) *pf*, выма́зывать *impf* smear, dirty.

выма́нивать *impf*, вы́манить *pf* entice, lure.

вымере́ть (-мрет; -мер) *pf* (*impf* вымира́ть) die out; become extinct. вы́мерший extinct.

вы́мести (-ету) *pf*, вымета́ть *impf* sweep (out).

вымога́тельство blackmail, extortion. вымога́ть *impf* extort.

вымока́ть *impf*, вы́мокнуть (-ну; -ок) *pf* be drenched; soak; rot.

вы́молвить (-влю) *pf* say, utter.

вы́|мостить (-ощу) *pf*. вы́мою *etc.: see* вы́мыть

вы́мпел pennant.

вы́мрет *see* вы́мереть. вымыва́ть(ся *impf of* вы́мыть(ся

вы́мысел (-сла) invention, fabrication; fantasy.

вы́|мыть (-мою) *pf* (*impf also* вымыва́ть) wash; wash out, off; wash away; ~ся wash o.s.

вы́мышленный fictitious.

вы́мя (-мени) *neut* udder.

вына́шивать *impf of* вы́носить[2]

вы́нести (-су; -нес) *pf* (*impf* выноси́ть[1]) carry out, take out; carry away; endure.

вынима́ть(ся *impf of* вы́нуть(ся

вы́нос carrying out. выноси́ть[1] (-ошу, -о́сишь) *impf of* вы́нести. выноси́ть[2] *pf* (*impf* вына́шивать) bear; nurture. вы́носка carrying out; removal; footnote. выно́сливость endurance; hardiness.

вы́нудить (-ужу) *pf*, вынужда́ть *impf* force, compel. вы́нужденный

forced.

вы́нуть (-ну) *pf* (*impf* вынима́ть) take out.

вы́пад attack; lunge. выпада́ть *impf of* вы́пасть

выпа́ливать *impf*, вы́парить evaporate; steam.

выпа́рывать *impf of* вы́пороть[2]

вы́пасть (-аду; -ал) *pf* (*impf* выпада́ть) fall out; fall; occur, turn out; lunge.

выпека́ть *impf*, вы́печь (-еку; -ек) *pf* bake.

выпива́ть *impf of* вы́пить; enjoy a drink. вы́пивка drinking bout; drinks.

выпи́ливать *impf*, вы́пилить *pf* saw, cut out.

вы́писать (-ишу) *pf*, выпи́сывать *impf* copy out; write out; order; subscribe to; send for; ~ из больни́цы discharge from hospital; ~ся be discharged. вы́писка writing out; extract; ordering, subscription; discharge.

вы́|пить (-пью) *pf* (*impf also* выпива́ть) drink; drink up.

вы́плавить (-влю) *pf*, выплавля́ть *impf* smelt. вы́плавка smelting; smelted metal.

вы́платить (-ачу) *pf*, выпла́чивать *impf* pay (out); pay off.

выплёвывать *impf of* вы́плюнуть

выплыва́ть *impf*, вы́плыть (-ыву) *pf* swim out, sail out; emerge; crop up.

вы́плюнуть (-ну) *pf* (*impf* выплёвывать) spit out.

выполза́ть *impf*, вы́ползти (-зу; -олз) *pf* crawl out.

выполне́ние execution, carrying out; fulfilment. вы́полнить *pf*, выполня́ть *impf* execute, carry out; fulfil.

вы́|полоскать (-ощу) *pf*.

вы́|полоть (-лю) *pf* (*impf also* выпа́лывать) weed out; weed.

вы́|пороть[1] (-рю) *pf*.

вы́пороть[2] (-рю) *pf* (*impf* выпа́рывать) rip out, rip up.

вы́|потрошить (-шу) *pf*.

вы́правка bearing; correction.

выпра́шивать *impf of* вы́просить; solicit.

выпрова́живать *impf*, вы́проводить (-ожу) *pf* send packing.

вы́просить (-ошу) *pf* (*impf* выпра́шивать) (ask for and) get.

выпряга́ть *impf of* выпрячь

вы́прямить (-млю) *pf,* выпрямля́ть *impf* straighten (out); rectify; ~ся become straight; draw o.s. up.

вы́прячь (-ягу; -яг) *pf* (*impf* выпряга́ть) unharness.

вы́пуклый protuberant; bulging; convex.

вы́пуск output; issue; discharge; part, instalment; final-year students; omission. выпуска́ть *impf,* вы́пустить (-ущу) *pf* let out; issue; produce; omit. выпускни́к (-а́) -ица́ final-year student. выпускн|о́й discharge; exhaust; ~о́й экза́мен finals, final examination.

вы́путать *pf,* выпу́тывать *impf* disentangle; ~ся extricate o.s.

вы́пью *etc.: see* вы́пить

выраба́тывать *impf,* вы́работать *pf* work out; work up; draw up; produce, make; earn. вы́работка manufacture; production; working out; drawing up; output; make.

выра́внивать(ся *impf of* вы́ровнять(ся

выража́ть *impf,* вы́разить (-ажу) *pf* express; ~ся express o.s. выраже́ние expression. вырази́тельный expressive.

выраста́ть *impf,* вы́расти (-ту; -рос) *pf* grow, grow up. вы́растить (-ащу) *pf,* выра́щивать *impf* bring up; breed; cultivate.

вы́рвать¹ (-ву) *pf* (*impf* вырыва́ть²) pull out, tear out; extort; ~ся break loose, break free; escape; shoot.

вы́рвать² (-ву) *pf.*

вы́рез cut; décolletage. вы́резать (-ежу) *pf,* выреза́ть *impf,* вырезы́вать *impf* cut (out); engrave. вы́резка cutting out, excision; cutting; fillet.

вы́ровнять *pf* (*impf* выра́внивать) level; straighten (out); draw up; ~ся become level; equalize; catch up.

вы́родиться *pf,* вырожда́ться *impf* degenerate. вы́родок (-дка) black sheep. вырожде́ние degeneration.

вы́ронить *pf* drop.

вы́рос *etc.: see* вы́расти

вы́рою *etc.: see* вы́рыть

выруба́ть *impf,* вы́рубить (-блю) *pf* cut down; cut (out); carve (out). вы́рубка cutting down; hewing out.

вы́|ругать(ся *pf.*

выру́ливать *impf,* вы́|рулить *pf* taxi.

выруча́ть *impf,* вы́ручить (-чу) *pf* rescue; help out; gain; make. вы́ручка rescue; gain; proceeds; earnings.

вырыва́ть¹ *impf,* вы́рыть (-рою) *pf* dig up, unearth.

вырыва́ть²(ся *impf of* вы́рвать(ся

вы́садить (-ажу) *pf,* выса́живать *impf* set down; put ashore; transplant; smash; ~ся alight; disembark. вы́садка disembarkation; landing; transplanting.

выса́сывать *impf of* вы́сосать

вы́свободить (-божу) *pf,* высвобожда́ть *impf* free; release.

высека́ть *impf of* вы́сечь²

выселе́ние eviction. вы́селить *pf,* выселя́ть *impf* evict; evacuate; move; ~ся move, remove.

вы́|сечь¹ (-еку -сек) *pf.* вы́сечь² (-еку; -сек) (*impf* высека́ть) cut (out); carve.

вы́сидеть (-ижу) *pf,* выси́живать *impf* sit out; stay; hatch.

вы́ситься *impf* rise, tower.

выска́бливать *impf of* вы́скоблить

вы́сказать (-ажу) *pf,* выска́зывать *impf* express; state; ~ся speak out вы́сказывание utterance; pronouncement

выска́кивать *impf of* вы́скочить

вы́скоблить *pf* (*impf* выска́бливать) scrape out; erase; remove.

вы́скочить (-чу) *pf* (*impf* выска́кивать) jump out; spring out; ~ с+*instr* come out with. вы́скочка upstart.

вы́слать (вы́шлю) *pf* (*impf* высыла́ть) send (out); exile; deport.

вы́следить (-ежу) *pf,* высле́живать *impf* trace; shadow.

выслу́живать *impf,* вы́служить (-жу) *pf* qualify for; serve (out); ~ся gain promotion; curry favour.

вы́слушать *pf,* выслу́шивать *impf* hear out; sound; listen to.

высме́ивать *impf,* вы́смеять (-ею) *pf* ridicule.

вы́|сморкать(ся *pf.* высо́вывать-(ся *impf of* вы́сунуть(ся

высо́кий (-о́к, -а́, -око́) high; tall; lofty; elevated.

высоко- in comb high-, highly. высокоблагоро́дие (your) Honour, Worship. ~во́льтный high-tension. ~го́рный mountain. ~ка́чественный high-quality. ~квалифици́рованный highly qualified. ~ме́рие haughtiness. ~ме́рный haughty. ~па́рный high-flown; bombastic. ~часто́тный high-frequency.

высо́сать (-осу) pf (impf выса́сывать) suck out.

высота́ (pl -ы) height, altitude. высо́тный high-altitude; high-rise.

вы́|сохнуть (-ну; -ох) pf (impf also высыха́ть) dry (out); dry up; wither (away).

вы́спаться (-плюсь, -пишься) pf (impf высыпа́ться²) have a good sleep.

вы́ставить (-влю) pf, выставля́ть impf display, exhibit; post; put forward; set down; take out; +instr represent as; ~ся show off. вы́ставка exhibition.

выста́ивать impf of вы́стоять

вы́|стегать pf. вы́|стирать pf.

вы́стоять (-ою) pf (impf выста́ивать) stand; stand one's ground.

вы́страдать pf suffer; gain through suffering.

выстра́ивать(ся impf of вы́строить(ся

вы́стрел shot; report. вы́стрелить pf shoot, fire.

вы́|строгать pf.

вы́строить pf (impf выстра́ивать) build; draw up, order, arrange; form up. ~ся form up.

вы́ступ protuberance, projection. выступа́ть impf, вы́ступить (-плю) pf come forward; come out; perform; speak; +из+gen go beyond. выступле́ние appearance, performance; speech; setting out.

вы́сунуть (-ну) pf (impf высо́вывать) put out, thrust out; ~ся show o.s.; thrust o.s. forward.

вы́|сушить(ся (-шу(сь) pf.

вы́сший highest; high; higher.

высыла́ть impf of вы́слать. вы́сылка sending, dispatch; expulsion, exile.

вы́сыпать (-плю) pf, высыпа́ть impf pour out; spill; ~ся¹ pour out; spill.

высыпа́ться² impf of вы́спаться

высыха́ть impf of вы́сохнуть

высь height; summit.

выта́лкивать impf of вы́толкать, вы́толкнуть. выта́скивать impf of вы́тащить. выта́чивать impf of вы́точить

вы́|тащить (-щу) pf (impf also выта́скивать) drag out; pull out.

вы́|твердить (-ржу) pf.

вытека́ть impf (pf вы́течь); ~ из+gen flow from, out of; result from.

вы́тереть (-тру; -тер) pf (impf вытира́ть) wipe (up); dry; wear out.

вы́терпеть (-плю) pf endure.

вы́тертый threadbare.

вы́теснить pf, вытесня́ть impf force out; oust; displace.

вы́течь (-чет; -ек) pf (impf вытека́ть) flow out, run out.

вытира́ть impf of вы́тереть

вы́толкать pf, вы́толкнуть (-ну) pf (impf выта́лкивать) throw out; push out.

вы́точенный turned. вы́|точить (-чу) pf (impf also выта́чивать) turn; sharpen; gnaw through.

вы́|травить (-влю) pf, вытравля́ть impf, вытравля́ть impf exterminate, destroy; remove; etch; trample down, damage.

вытрезви́тель m detoxification centre. вы́трезвить(ся (-влю(сь) pf, вытрезвля́ть(ся impf sober up.

вы́тру etc.: see вы́тереть

вы́|трясти (-су; -яс) pf shake out.

вытря́хивать impf, вы́тряхнуть (-ну) pf shake out.

выть (во́ю) impf howl; wail.

вытя́гивать impf, вы́тянуть (-ну) pf stretch (out); extend; extract; endure; ~ся stretch, stretch out, stretch o.s.; shoot up; draw o.s. up. вы́тяжка drawing out, extraction; extract.

вы́|утюжить (-жу) pf.

выу́чивать impf, вы́учить (-чу) pf learn; teach; ~ся +dat or inf learn.

выха́живать impf of вы́ходить²

вы́хватить (-ачу) pf, выхва́тывать impf snatch out, up, away; pull out.

вы́хлоп exhaust. выхлопно́й exhaust, discharge.

вы́ход going out; departure; way out,

exit; vent; appearance; yield; ~ замуж marriage. выходец (-дца) emigrant; immigrant. выходить[1] (-ожу, -одишь) impf of выйти; +на+acc look out on.

выходить[2] (-ожу) pf (impf выхаживать) nurse; rear, bring up.

выходка trick; prank.

выходн|ой exit; going-out, outgoing; discharge; ~ой день day off; ~ой sb person off duty; day off. выхожу etc.: see выходить[1]. выхожу etc.: see выходить[2]

выцвести (-ветет) pf, выцветать impf fade. выцветший faded.

вычёркивать impf, вычеркнуть (-ну) pf cross out.

вычерпать pf, вычёрпывать impf bale out.

вычесть (-чту; -чел, -чла) pf (impf вычитать) subtract. вычет deduction. вычисление calculation. вычислитель m calculator. вычислительн|ый calculating, computing; ~ая машина computer. вычислить pf, вычислять impf calculate, compute.

вы|чистить (-ищу) pf (impf also вычищать) clean, clean up. вычитание subtraction. вычитать impf of вычесть

вычищать impf of вычистить. вычту etc.: see вычесть

вышибáл|а m chucker-out. вышибáть impf, вышибить (-бу; -иб) pf knock out; chuck out.

вышивáние embroidery, needlework. вышивáть impf of вышить. вышивка embroidery.

вышинá height.

вышить (-шью) pf (impf вышивáть) embroider. вышитый embroidered.

вышка tower; (буровáя) ~ derrick.

вышлю etc.: see выслать. вышью etc.: see вышить

выявить (-влю) pf, выявлять impf reveal; make known; expose; ~ся come to light, be revealed.

выяснéние elucidation; explanation. выяснить pf, выяснять impf elucidate; explain; ~ся become clear; turn out.

Вьетнáм Vietnam. вьетнáмец, -мка Vietnamese. вьетнáмский Vietnamese.

вью etc.: see вить

вьюга snow-storm, blizzard.

вьюнóк (-нкá) bindweed.

вьючн|ый pack; ~ое живóтное beast of burden.

вьющийся climbing; curly.

вяжу etc.: see вязáть. вяжущий binding; astringent.

вяз elm.

вязáние knitting, crocheting; binding, tying. вязáнка[1] knitted garment. вязáнка[2] bundle. вязаный knitted, crocheted. вязáнье knitting; crochet(-work). вязáть (вяжу, вяжешь) impf (pf с~) tie, bind; knit, crochet; be astringent; ~ся accord; tally. вязка tying; knitting, crocheting; bunch.

вязкий (-зок, -зкá, -о) viscous; sticky; boggy. вязнуть (-ну; вяз(нул), -зла) impf (pf за~, у~) stick, get stuck.

вязовый elm.

вязь ligature; arabesque.

вяленый dried; sun-cured.

вялый limp; sluggish; slack. вянуть (-ну; вял) impf (pf за~, у~) fade, wither; flag.

Г

г. abbr (of год) year; (of гóрод) city; (of господин) Mr.

г abbr (of грамм) gram.

га abbr (of гектáр) hectare.

гáвань harbour.

гагáчий пух eiderdown.

гад reptile; repulsive person; pl. vermin.

гадáлка fortune-teller. гадáние fortune-telling; guess-work. гадáть impf (pf по~) tell fortunes; guess.

гáдина reptile; repulsive person; pl. vermin. гáдить (гáжу) impf (pf на~) +в+prep, на+acc, prep foul, dirty, defile. гáдкий (-док, -дкá, -о) nasty, vile, repulsive. гáдость filth, muck; dirty trick; pl filthy expressions.

гадюка adder, viper; repulsive person.

гаечный ключ spanner, wrench.

газ¹ gauze.

газ² gas; wind; дать ~ step on the gas; сбавить ~ reduce speed.

газета newspaper. газетчик journalist; newspaper-seller.

газированный aerated. газовый gas.

газон lawn. газонокосилка lawn-mower.

газопровод gas pipeline; gas-main.

гайка nut; female screw.

галактика galaxy.

галантерейный магазин haberdasher's. галантерея haberdashery.

галантный gallant.

галерея gallery. галёрка gallery, gods.

галифе indecl pl riding-breeches.

галка jackdaw.

галлюцинация hallucination.

галоп gallop.

галочка tick.

галстук tie; neckerchief.

галушка dumpling.

галька pebble; pebbles, shingle.

гам din, uproar.

гамак (-á) hammock.

гамма scale; gamut; range.

гангрена gangrene.

гангстер gangster.

гантель dumb-bell.

гараж (-á) garage.

гарантировать impf & pf guarantee. гарантия guarantee.

гардероб wardrobe; cloakroom. гардеробщик, -щица cloakroom attendant.

гардина curtain.

гармонизировать impf & pf harmonize.

гармоника accordion, concertina. гармонический, гармоничный harmonious. гармония harmony; concord. гармонь accordion, concertina.

гарнизон garrison.

гарнир garnish; vegetables.

гарнитур set; suite.

гарь burning; cinders.

гаситель m extinguisher; suppressor. гасить (гашу, гасишь) impf (pf за~, по~) extinguish; suppress. гаснуть (-ну; гас) impf (pf за~, по~, у~) be extinguished, go out; grow feeble.

гастроли f pl tour; guest-appearance, performance. гастролировать impf (be on) tour.

гастроном gourmet; provision shop. гастрономический gastronomic; provision. гастрономия gastronomy; provisions; delicatessen.

гауптвахта guardroom.

гашиш hashish.

гвардеец (-ейца) guardsman. гвардейский guards'. гвардия Guards.

гвоздик tack. гвоздика pink(s), carnation(s); cloves. гвоздики (-ов) pl stilettos. гвоздь (-я; pl -и, -ей) m nail; tack; crux; highlight, hit.

гг. abbr (of годы) years.

где adv where; ~ бы ни wherever. где-либо adv anywhere. где-нибудь adv somewhere; anywhere. где-то adv somewhere.

гектар hectare.

гелий helium.

гемоглобин haemoglobin.

геморрой haemorrhoids. гемофилия haemophilia.

ген gene.

генезис origin, genesis.

генерал general. генеральн|ый general; ~ая репетиция dress rehearsal.

генератор generator.

генерация generation; oscillation.

генетика genetics. генетический genetic.

гениальный brilliant. гений genius.

гео- in comb geo-. географ geographer. ~графический geographical. ~графия geography. геолог geologist. ~логический geological. ~логия geology. ~метрический geometric. ~метрия geometry.

георгин dahlia.

геофизика geophysics.

гепард cheetah.

гепатит hepatitis.

герань geranium.

герб arms, coat of arms. гербов|ый heraldic; ~ая печать official stamp.

геркулес Hercules; rolled oats.

германец (-нца) ancient German. Германия Germany. германский Germanic.

гермафродит hermaphrodite.

герметичный hermetic; hermetically sealed; air-tight.

героизм heroism. **геройня** heroine. **геройческий** heroic. **герой** hero. **геройский** heroic.

герц (*gen pl* герц) hertz.

герцог duke. **герцогиня** duchess.

г-жа *abbr* (*of* госпожа) Mrs.; Miss.

гиацинт hyacinth.

гибель death; destruction, ruin; loss; wreck; downfall. **гибельный** disastrous, fatal.

гибкий (-бок, -бка, -бко) flexible, adaptable, versatile; supple. **гибкость** flexibility; suppleness.

гибнуть (-ну; гиб(нул)) *impf* (*pf* по~) perish.

гибрид hybrid.

гигант giant. **гигантский** gigantic.

гигиена hygiene. **гигиенический, -ичный** hygienic, sanitary.

гид guide.

гидравлический hydraulic.

гидро- *pref* hydro-. **~электростанция** hydro-electric power-station.

гиена hyena.

гильза cartridge-case; sleeve; (cigarette-)wrapper.

гимн hymn.

гимназия grammar school, high school.

гимнаст gymnast. **гимнастика** gymnastics. **гимнастический** gymnastic.

гинеколог gynaecologist. **гинекология** gynaecology.

гипербола hyperbole.

гипноз hypnosis. **гипнотизёр** hypnotist. **гипнотизировать** *impf* (*pf* за~) hypnotize. **гипнотический** hypnotic.

гипотеза hypothesis. **гипотетический** hypothetical.

гиппопотам hippopotamus.

гипс gypsum, plaster (of Paris); plaster cast. **гипсовый** plaster.

гирлянда garland.

гиря weight.

гистерэктомия hysterectomy.

гитара guitar.

гл. *abbr* (*of* глава) chapter.

глав- *abbr in comb* head, chief, main. **глава** (*pl* -ы) head; chief; chapter; cupola. **главарь** (-я) *m* leader, ringleader. **главк** central directorate. **главнокомандующий** *sb* commander-in-chief. **главный** chief, main; ~ым образом chiefly, mainly,

for the most part; ~ое *sb* the main thing; the essentials.

глагол verb.

гладить (-ажу) *impf* (*pf* вы~, по~) stroke; iron. **гладкий** smooth; plain. **гладко** *adv* smoothly. **гладь** smooth surface.

глаз (*loc* -ý; *pl* -á, глаз) eye; в ~á to one's face; за ~á+*gen* behind the back of; смотреть во все ~á be all eyes.

глазированный glazed; glossy; iced; glacé.

глазница eye-socket. **глазной** eye; optic; ~ врач oculist. **глазок** (-зка) peephole.

глазунья fried eggs.

глазурь glaze; syrup; icing.

гланды (гланд) *pl* tonsils.

гласность publicity; glasnost, openness. **гласный** public; vowel; *sb* vowel.

глина clay. **глинистый** clayey. **глиняный** clay; earthenware; clayey.

глиссер speed-boat.

глист (*intestinal*) worm.

глицерин glycerine.

глобус globe.

глотать *impf* swallow. **глотка** gullet; throat. **глоток** (-тка) gulp; mouthful.

глохнуть (-ну; глох) *impf* (*pf* за~, о~) become deaf; die away, subside; grow wild.

глубина (*pl* -ы) depth; heart, interior. **глубокий** (-ок, -á, -óкó) deep; profound; late, advanced, extreme. **глубокомыслие** profundity. **глубокоуважаемый** (*in formal letters*) dear.

глумиться (-млюсь) *impf* mock, jeer (над+*instr* at). **глумление** mockery.

глупеть (-ею) *impf* (*pf* по~) grow stupid. **глупец** (-пца) fool. **глупость** stupidity. **глупый** (глуп, -á, -о) stupid.

глухарь (-я) *m* capercaillie. **глухой** (глух, -á, -о) deaf; muffled; obscure, vague; dense; wild; remote; deserted; sealed; blank; ~ой, ~áя *sb* deaf man, woman. **глухонемой** deaf and dumb; *sb* deaf mute. **глухота** deafness. **глушитель** *m* silencer. **глушить** (-шу) *impf* (*pf* за~, о~) stun; muffle; dull; jam; extinguish; stifle;

suppress. **глушь** backwoods.

глы́ба clod; lump, block.

глюко́за glucose.

гляде́ть (-жу́) *impf* (*pf* по~, гля́нуть) look, gaze, peer; ~ **в о́ба** be on one's guard; (того́ и) **гляди́** it looks as if; I'm afraid; **гля́дя** по+*dat* depending on.

гля́нец (-нца) gloss, lustre; polish.

гля́нуть (-ну) *pf* (*impf* гляде́ть) glance.

гм *int* hm!

г-н *abbr* (*of* господи́н) Mr.

гнать (гоню́, го́нишь; гнал, -а́, -о) *impf* drive; urge (on); hunt, chase; persecute; distil; ~**ся** за+*instr* pursue.

гнев anger, rage. **гне́ваться** *impf* (*pf* раз~) be angry. **гне́вный** angry.

гнедо́й bay.

гнездо́ (*pl* гнёзда) nest.

гнёт weight; oppression. **гнету́щий** oppressive.

гни́да nit.

гние́ние decay, putrefaction, rot. **гнило́й** (-и́л, -а́, -о) rotten; muggy. **гнить** (-и́ю, -и́ёшь; -ил, -а́, -о) *impf* (*pf* с~) rot. **гное́ние** suppuration, discharge matter. **гной** pus. **гно́йник** abscess; ulcer. **гно́йный** purulent.

гну́сный (-сен, -сна́, -о) vile, foul.

гнуть (гну, гнёшь) *impf* (*pf* со~) bend; aim at; ~**ся** bend; stoop.

гнуша́ться *impf* (*pf* по~) disdain; +*gen* or *instr* shun; abhor.

гобеле́н tapestry.

гобо́й oboe.

гове́ть (-е́ю) *impf* fast.

говно́ (*vulg*) shit.

говори́ть *impf* (*pf* по~, сказа́ть) speak, talk; say; tell; ~**ся**: **как говори́тся** as one says.

говя́дина beef. **говя́жий** beef.

го́гот cackle; loud laughter. **гогота́ть** (-очу́, -о́чешь) *impf* cackle; roar with laughter.

год (*loc* -у́; *pl* -ы́ *or* -а́, *gen* -о́в *or* лет) year. **года́ми** *adv* for years (on end).

годи́ться (-жу́сь) *impf* be fit, suitable; serve.

годи́чный a year's; annual.

го́дный (-ден, -дна́, -о, -ы *or* -ы́) fit, suitable; valid.

годова́лый one-year-old. **годово́й**

annual. **годовщи́на** anniversary.

гожу́сь *etc.*: *see* годи́ться

гол goal.

голени́ще (boot-)top. **го́лень** shin.

голла́ндец (-дца) Dutchman. **Голла́ндия** Holland. **голла́ндка** Dutchwoman; tiled stove. **голла́ндский** Dutch.

голова́ (*acc* го́лову; *pl* го́ловы, -о́в, -а́м) head. **голова́стик** tadpole. **голо́вка** head; cap, nose, tip. **головн|о́й** head; leading; ~**а́я боль** headache; ~**о́й мозг** cerebrum; ~**о́й убо́р** headgear, headdress. **головокруже́ние** giddiness, dizziness. **головоло́мка** puzzle. **головоре́з** cut-throat; rascal.

го́лод hunger; famine; acute shortage. **голода́ние** starvation; fasting. **голода́ть** *impf* go hungry, starve; fast. **голо́дный** (голо́ден, -дна́, -о, -ы *or* -ы́) hungry. **голодо́вка** hunger-strike.

гололёд, гололе́дица (period of) black ice.

го́лос (*pl* -а́) voice; part; vote. **голоси́ть** (-ошу́) *impf* sing loudly; cry; wail.

голосло́вный unsubstantiated, unfounded.

голосова́ние voting; poll. **голосова́ть** *impf* (*pf* про~) vote; vote on.

голу́бка pigeon; (my) dear, darling. **голубо́й** light blue. **голу́бчик** my dear (fellow); darling. **го́лубь** *m* pigeon, dove. **голубя́тня** (*gen pl* -тен) dovecote, pigeon-loft.

го́лый (гол, -а́, -ло) naked, bare.

гомоге́нный homogeneous.

го́мон hubbub.

гомосексуали́ст homosexual. **гомосексуа́льный** homosexual.

гондо́ла gondola.

гоне́ние persecution. **го́нка** race; dashing; haste.

гонора́р fee.

го́ночный racing.

гонча́р (-а́) potter.

го́нщик racer. **гоню́** *etc.*: *see* гнать. **гоня́ть** *impf* drive; send on errands; ~**ся** за+*instr* chase, hunt.

гора́ (*acc* го́ру; *pl* го́ры, -а́м) mountain; hill; **в го́ру** uphill; **под го́ру** downhill.

гора́здо *adv* much, far, by far.

горб (-á, loc -ý) hump; bulge. гор-
бáтый hunchbacked. го́рбить (-блю)
impf (pf c~) arch, hunch; ~ся stoop.
горбу́н (-á) m, горбу́нья (gen pl
-ний) hunchback. горбу́шка (gen pl
-шек) crust (of loaf).

горди́ться (-ржу́сь) impf put on airs;
+instr be proud of. го́рдость pride.
го́рдый (горд, -á, -о, го́рды) proud.
горды́ня arrogance.

го́ре grief, sorrow; trouble. горевáть
(-рю́ю) impf grieve.

горéлка burner. горéлый burnt.
горéние burning, combustion; enthusiasm.

го́рестный sad; mournful. го́ресть
sorrow; pl misfortunes.

горéть (-рю́) impf (pf c~) burn.

горéц (-рца) mountain-dweller.

го́речь bitterness; bitter taste.

горизóнт horizon. горизонтáль horizontal. горизонтáльный horizontal.

гори́стый mountainous, hilly. го́рка
hill; hillock; steep climb.

го́рло throat; neck. горловóй
throat; guttural; raucous. го́рлышко
neck.

гормóн hormone.

горн¹ furnace, forge.

горн² bugle.

го́рничная sb maid, chambermaid.

горнорабóчий sb miner.

горностáй ermine.

го́рный mountain; mountainous; mineral; mining. горня́к (-á) miner.

го́род (pl -á) town; city. городóк
(-дкá) small town. городскóй urban; city; municipal. горожáнин (pl
-áне, -áн) m, -жáнка town-dweller.

гороскóп horoscope.

горóх pea, peas. горóшек (-шка)
spots, spotted pattern; душистый ~
sweet peas; зелёный ~ green peas.
горóшина pea.

горсовéт abbr (of городскóй совéт)
city soviet, town soviet.

горсть (gen pl -éй) handful.

гортáнный guttural. гортáнь larynx.

горчи́ца mustard. горчи́чник mustard plaster.

горшóк (-шкá) flowerpot; pot; potty;
chamber-pot.

го́рький (-рькá, -о) bitter.

горю́чий combustible; ~ее sb fuel.
горя́чий (-ря́ч, -á) hot; passionate;
ardent.

горячи́ться (-чу́сь) impf (pf раз~)
get excited. горя́чка fever; feverish
haste. горя́чность zeal.

гос- abbr in comb (of госудáрственный) state.

го́спиталь m (military) hospital.

го́споди int good heavens! госпо-
ди́н (pl -одá, -óд, -áм) master; gentleman; Mr; pl ladies and gentlemen.
госпóдство supremacy. госпóд-
ствовать impf hold sway; prevail.
Госпóдь (Гóспода, voc Гóсподи) m
God, the Lord. госпожá lady; Mrs.

гостеприи́мный hospitable. госте-
прии́мство hospitality. гости́ная sb
drawing-room, sitting-room. гости́-
ница hotel. гости́ть (гощу́) impf
stay, be on a visit. гость (gen pl -éй)
m, гóстья (gen pl -ий) guest, visitor.

госудáрственный State, public.
госудáрство State. госудáрыня
госудáрь m sovereign; Your Majesty.

готи́ческий Gothic.

готóвить (-влю) impf (pf c~) prepare; ~ся prepare (o.s.); be at hand.
готóвность readiness, willingness.
готóвый ready.

гофрирóванный corrugated; waved;
pleated.

грабёж robbery; pillage. граби́тель
m robber. граби́тельский predatory; exorbitant. грáбить (-блю)
impf (pf o~) rob, pillage.

грáбли (-бель or -блей) pl rake.

гравёр, гравирóвщик engraver.

грáвий gravel. гравирóвать impf
(pf вы~) engrave; etch. гравирóвка
engraving.

гравитацио́нный gravitational.

гравю́ра engraving, print; etching.

град¹ city, town.

град² hail; volley. грáдина hailstone.

грáдус degree. грáдусник thermometer.

граждани́н (pl грáждане, -дан),
граждáнка citizen. граждáнский
civil; civic; civilian. граждáнство
citizenship.

грамзáпись (gramophone) recording.

грамм gram.

граммáтика grammar. граммати́-
ческий grammatical.

грáмота reading and writing; official
document; deed. грáмотность

literacy. гра́мотный literate; competent.

грампласти́нка (gramophone) record.

грана́т pomegranate; garnet. грана́та shell, grenade.

грандио́зный grandiose.

гранёный cut, faceted; cut-glass.

грани́т granite.

грани́ца border; boundary; limit; за грани́цей, за грани́цу abroad. грани́чить impf border.

грань border, verge; side, facet.

граф count; earl.

графа́ column. гра́фик graph; chart; schedule; graphic artist. гра́фика drawing; script.

графи́н carafe; decanter.

графи́ня countess.

графи́т graphite.

графи́ческий graphic.

графлёный ruled.

гра́фство county.

грацио́зный graceful. гра́ция grace.

грач (-а́) rook.

гребёнка comb. гре́бень (-бня) m comb; crest. гребе́ц (-бца́) rower, oarsman. гребно́й rowing. гребу́ etc.: see грести́

грёза day-dream, dream. гре́зить (-е́жу) impf dream.

грек Greek.

гре́лка hot-water bottle.

греме́ть impf (pf про~) thunder; roar; rattle; resound. грему́чая змея́ rattlesnake.

грести́ (-ебу́, -ебёшь; грёб, -бла́) impf row; rake.

греть (-е́ю) impf warm, heat; ~ся warm o.s., bask.

грех (-а́) sin. грехо́вный sinful. грехопаде́ние the Fall; fall.

Гре́ция Greece. гре́цкий оре́х walnut. греча́нка Greek. гре́ческий Greek, Grecian.

гре́чиха buckwheat. гре́чневый buckwheat.

греши́ть (-шу́) impf (pf по~, со~) sin. гре́шник, -ница sinner. гре́шный (-шен, -шна́, -о) sinful.

гриб (-а́) mushroom. грибно́й mushroom.

гри́ва mane.

гри́венник ten-copeck piece.

грим make-up; grease-paint.

гримирова́ть impf (pf за~) make

up; +instr make up as.

грипп flu.

гриф neck (of violin etc.).

гри́фель m pencil lead.

гроб (loc -ý; pl -ы́ or -á) coffin; grave. гробни́ца tomb. гробово́й coffin; deathly. гробовщи́к (-а́) coffin-maker; undertaker.

гроза́ (pl -ы) (thunder-)storm.

гроздь (pl -ди or -дья, -де́й or -дьев) cluster, bunch.

грози́ть(ся (-ожу́(сь) impf (pf по~, при~) threaten. гро́зный (-зен, -зна́, -о) menacing; terrible; severe.

гром (pl -ы, -о́в) thunder.

грома́да mass; bulk, pile. грома́дный huge, colossal.

громи́ть (-млю́) impf destroy; smash, rout.

гро́мкий (-мок, -мка́, -о) loud; famous; notorious; fine-sounding. гро́мко adv loud(ly); aloud. громкоговори́тель m loud-speaker. громово́й thunder; thunderous; crushing. громогла́сный loud; public.

громозди́ть (-зжу́) impf (pf за~) pile up; ~ся tower; clamber up. громо́здкий cumbersome.

гро́мче comp of гро́мкий, гро́мко

гроссме́йстер grand master.

гроте́скный grotesque.

гро́хот crash, din.

грохота́ть (-очу́, -о́чешь) impf (pf про~) crash; rumble; roar.

грош (-а́) half-copeck piece; farthing. грошо́вый cheap; trifling.

грубе́ть (-е́ю) impf (pf за~, о~, по~) grow coarse. груби́ть (-блю́) impf (pf на~) be rude. грубия́н boor. гру́бость rudeness; coarseness; rude remark. гру́бый (груб, -á, -о) coarse; rude.

гру́да heap, pile.

груди́на breastbone. груди́нка brisket; breast. грудно́й breast, chest; pectoral. грудь (-й or -и, instr -ю, loc -й; pl -и, -е́й) breast; chest.

груз load; burden.

грузи́н (gen pl -и́н), грузи́нка Georgian. грузи́нский Georgian.

грузи́ть (-ужу́, -у́зишь) impf (pf за~, на~, по~) load, lade, freight; ~ся load, take on cargo.

Гру́зия Georgia.

гру́зный (-зен, -зна́, -о) weighty;

bulky. **грузови́к** lorry, truck.
грузово́й goods, cargo. **гру́зчик**
stevedore; loader.
грунт ground, soil; priming. **грунто-
ва́ть** *impf* (*pf* за∼) prime.
грунтово́й soil, earth; priming.
гру́ппа group. **группирова́ть** *impf*
(*pf* с∼) group; ∼ся group, form
groups. **группиро́вка** grouping.
группово́й group; team.
грусти́ть (-ущу́) *impf* grieve, mourn;
+по+*dat* pine for. **гру́стный** (-тен,
-тна́, -о) sad. **грусть** sadness.
гру́ша pear.
гры́жа hernia, rupture.
грызть (-зу́, -зёшь; грыз) *impf* (*pf*
раз∼) gnaw; nag; ∼ся fight; squabble. **грызу́н** (-á) rodent.
гряда́ (*pl* -ы, -áм) ridge; bed; row,
series; bank. **гря́дка** (flower-)bed.
гряду́щий approaching; future.
гря́зный (-зен, -зна́, -о) muddy; dirty.
грязь (*loc* -и́) mud; dirt, filth; *pl*
mud-cure.
гря́нуть (-ну) *pf* ring out, crash out;
strike up.
губа́ (*pl* -ы, -áм) lip; *pl* pincers.
губерна́тор governor. **губе́рния**
province. **губе́рнский** provincial.
губи́тельный ruinous; pernicious.
губи́ть (-блю́, -бишь) *impf* (*pf* по∼)
ruin; spoil.
гу́бка sponge.
губна́я пома́да lipstick.
гу́бчатый porous, spongy.
гуверна́нтка governess. **гувернёр**
tutor.
гуде́ть (гужу́) *impf* (*pf* про∼) hum;
drone; buzz; hoot. **гудо́к** (-дка́)
hooter, siren, horn, whistle; hoot.
гудро́н tar. **гудро́нный** tar, tarred.
гул rumble. **гу́лкий** (-лок, -лка́, -о)
resonant; booming.
гуля́нье (*gen pl* -ний) walk; fête; outdoor party. **гуля́ть** *impf* (*pf* по∼)
stroll; go for a walk; have a good
time.
гуманита́рный of the humanities;
humane. **гума́нный** humane.
гумно́ (*pl* -а, -мен *or* -мён, -ам)
threshing-floor; barn.
гурт (-á) herd; flock. **гуртовщи́к**
(-á) herdsman. **гурто́м** *adv* wholesale; en masse.
гуса́к (-á) gander.

гу́сеница caterpillar; (caterpillar)
track. **гу́сеничный** caterpillar.
гусёнок (-нка; *pl* -ся́та, -ся́т) gosling.
гуси́н|**ый** goose; ∼ая ко́жа goose-
flesh.
густе́ть (-éет) *impf* (*pf* за∼) thicken.
густо́й (густ, -á, -о) thick, dense;
rich. **густота́** thickness, density; rich-
ness.
гусы́ня goose. **гусь** (*pl* -и, -éй) *m*
goose. **гусько́м** *adv* in single file.
гута́лин shoe-polish.
гу́ща grounds, sediment; thicket;
thick. **гу́ще** *comp* of густо́й.
ГЭС *abbr* (*of* гидроэлектроста́нция)
hydro-electric power station.

Д

д. *abbr* (*of* дере́вня) village; (*of* дом)
house.
да *conj* and; but.
да *partl* yes; really? well; +*3rd pers
of* v, may, let; да здра́вствует...!
long live...!
дава́ть (даю́, -ёшь) *impf* of дать;
дава́й(те) let us, let's; come on; ∼ся
yield; come easy.
дави́ть (-влю́, -вишь) *impf* (*pf* за∼,
по∼, раз∼, у∼) press; squeeze;
crush; oppress; ∼ся choke; hang o.s.
да́вка crushing; crush. **давле́ние**
pressure.
да́вний ancient; of long standing.
давно́ *adv* long ago; for a long time.
да́вность antiquity; remoteness;
long standing. **давны́м-давно́** *adv*
long long ago.
дади́м *etc.*: *see* дать. **даю́** *etc.*: *see*
дава́ть
да́же *adv* even.
да́лее *adv* further; и так ∼ and so
on, etc. **далёкий** (-ёк, -á, -ёко) distant, remote; far. **далеко́** *adv*
far; far off; by a long way; ∼ за long
after; ∼ не far from. **даль** (*loc* -и́)
distance. **дальне́йший** further.
да́льний distant, remote; long; ∼
Восто́к the Far East. **дально-
зо́ркий** long-sighted. **да́льность**
distance; range. **да́льше** *adv* further;
then, next; longer.
дам *etc.*: *see* дать
да́ма lady; partner; queen.

дáмба dike; dam.

дáмский ladies'.

Дáния Denmark.

дáнные *sb pl* data; facts. **дáнный** given, present. **дань** tribute; debt.

дантúст dentist.

дар (*pl* -ы́) gift. **дарúть** (-рю́, -ришь) *impf* (*pf* по~) +*dat* give, make a present.

дарованúе talent. **дарова́ть** *impf & pf* grant, confer. **дарови́тый** gifted. **дарово́й** free (of charge). **да́ром** *adv* free, gratis; in vain.

дáта date.

дáтельный dative.

датúровать *impf & pf* date.

дáтский Danish. **датчáнин** (*pl* -áне, -áн), **датчáнка** Dane.

дать (дам, дашь, даст, дади́м; дал, -á, дáло) *pf* (*impf* дава́ть) give; grant; let; ~ взаймы́ lend; ~ся *pf of* дава́ться

дáча dacha; на дáче in the country. **дáчник** (holiday) visitor.

два *m & neut*, **две** *f* (двух, -ум, -умя́, -ух) two. **двадцатилéтний** twenty-year; twenty-year-old. **двáдцатый** twent!eth; ~ые гóды the twenties. **двáдцать** (-и, *instr* -ью) twenty. **двáжды** *adv* twice; double. **двенáдцатый** twelfth. **двенáдцать** twelve.

дверь (*loc* -и́; *pl* -и, -éй, *instr* -я́ми or -ьми́) door.

двéсти (двухсóт, -умстáм, -умястáми, -ухстáх) two hundred.

двúгатель *m* engine, motor; motive force. **двúгать** (-аю or -и́жу) *impf*, **двúнуть** (-ну) *pf* move; set in motion; advance; ~ся move; advance; get started. **движéние** movement; motion; exercise; traffic. **двúжимость** chattels; personal property. **двúжимый** movable; moved. **двúжущий** moving.

двóе (-и́х) two; two pairs. **двое-** *in comb* two-; double(-). **двоебóрье** biathlon. **~жéнец** (-нца) bigamist. **~жéнство** bigamy. **~тóчие** colon.

двоúться *impf* divide in two; appear double; у негó двоúлось в глазáх he saw double. **двóйка** two; figure 2; No. 2. **двойнúк** (-á) double. **двойнóй** double,

twofold; binary. **двóйня** (*gen pl* -óен) twins. **двóйственный** two-faced; dual.

двор (-á) yard; courtyard; homestead; court. **дворéц** (-рцá) palace. **двóрник** yard caretaker; windscreen-wiper. **дворня́** servants. **дворóвый** yard, courtyard; **дворóвый** house-serf. **дворянúн** (*pl* -я́не, -я́н), **дворя́нка** member of the nobility or gentry. **дворя́нство** nobility, gentry.

двоюрóдн|ый; ~ый брат, ~ая сестрá (first) cousin; ~ый дя́дя, ~ая тётка first cousin once removed.

двоя́кий double; two-fold.

дву-, двух- *in comb* two-; bi-; double. **двубóртный** double-breasted. **~лúчный** two-faced. **~нóгий** two-legged. **~ру́чный** two-handed; two-handled. **~ру́шник** double-dealer. **~смы́сленный** ambiguous. **~(х)-спáльный** double. **~сторо́нний** double-sided; two-way; bilateral. **~х-годúчный** two-year. **~хлéтний** two-year; two-year-old; biennial. **~хмéстный** two-seater; two-berth. **~хмотóрный** twin-engined. **~хсот-лéтие** bicentenary. **~хсóтый** two-hundredth. **~хтáктный** two-stroke. **~хэтáжный** two-storey. **~язы́чный** bilingual.

дебáты (-ов) *pl* debate.

дéбет debit. **дебетова́ть** *impf & pf* debit.

дебúт yield, output.

дéбри (-ей) *pl* jungle; thickets; the wilds.

дебю́т début.

дéва maid, maiden; Virgo.

девальвáция devaluation.

девáться *impf of* дéться

девúз motto; device.

девúца spinster; girl. **дéвич|ий** girl-ish, maidenly; ~ья фамúлия maiden name. **дéвка** wench, lass; tart. **дéвочка** (little) girl. **дéвственник, -ица** virgin. **дéвственный** virgin; innocent. **дéвушка** girl. **девчóнка** girl.

девянóсто ninety. **девянóстый** ninetieth. **девя́тка** nine; figure 9; No. 9. **девятнáдцатый** nineteenth. **девятнáдцать** nineteen. **девя́тый** ninth. **дéвять** (-и́, *instr* -ью́) nine. **девятьсóт** (-тисóт, -тистáм, -тьюста́ми, -тиста́х) nine hundred.

дегенери́ровать *impf & pf* degenerate.

дёготь (-гтя) tar.

дегуста́ция tasting.

дед grandfather; grandad. **де́душка** grandfather; grandad.

дееприча́стие adverbial participle.

дежу́рить *impf* be on duty. **дежу́рный** on duty; *sb* person on duty. **дежу́рство** (being on) duty.

дезерти́р deserter. **дезерти́ровать** *impf & pf* desert.

дезинфе́кция disinfection. **дезинфици́ровать** *impf & pf* disinfect.

дезодора́нт deodorant; air-freshener.

дезориента́ция disorientation. **дезориенти́ровать** *impf & pf* disorient; ~**ся** lose one's bearings.

де́йственный efficacious; effective. **де́йствие** action; operation; effect; act. **действи́тельно** *adv* really; indeed. **действи́тельность** reality; validity; efficacy. **действи́тельный** actual; valid; efficacious; active. **де́йствовать** *impf* (*pf* по~) affect, have an effect; act; work. **де́йствующий** active; in force; working; ~**ее лицо́** character; ~**ие ли́ца** cast.

декабри́ст Decembrist. **декабрь** (-я́) *m* December. **дека́брьский** December.

дека́да ten-day period *or* festival.

дека́н dean. **декана́т** office of dean.

деклама́ция recitation, declamation. **деклами́ровать** *impf* (*pf* про~) recite, declaim.

деклара́ция declaration.

де́ланный artificial, affected. **де́лать** *impf* (*pf* с~) make; do; ~ **вид** pretend; ~**ся** become; happen.

делега́т delegate. **делега́ция** delegation; group.

дележ (-á), **делёжка** sharing; partition. **деле́ние** division; point (*on a scale*).

делец (-льца́) smart operator.

делика́тный delicate.

дели́мое *sb* dividend. **дели́мость** divisibility. **дели́тель** *m* divisor.

дели́ть (-лю́, -лишь) *impf* (*pf* по~, раз~) divide; share; ~ **шесть на́ три** divide six by three; ~**ся** divide; be divisible; +*instr* share.

де́ло (*pl* -á) business: affair: matter; deed; thing; case; **в са́мом де́ле** really, indeed; ~ **в том** the point is; **как (ва́ши) дела́?** how are things?; **на са́мом де́ле** in actual fact; **по де́лу, по дела́м** on business. **делови́тый** business-like, efficient. **делово́й** business-like; business. **де́льный** efficient; sensible.

де́льта delta.

дельфи́н dolphin.

демаго́г demagogue.

демобилиза́ция demobilization. **демобилизова́ть** *impf & pf* demobilize.

демокра́т democrat. **демократиза́ция** democratization. **демократизи́ровать** *impf & pf* democratize. **демократи́ческий** democratic. **демокра́тия** democracy.

де́мон demon.

демонстра́ция demonstration. **демонстри́ровать** *impf & pf* demonstrate.

де́нежный monetary; money; ~ **перево́д** money order.

денусь *etc.: see* де́ться

день (дня) *m* day; afternoon; **днём** in the afternoon; **на днях** the other day; one of these days; **че́рез** ~ every other day.

де́ньги (-нег, -ьга́м) *pl* money.

департа́мент department.

депо́ *neut indecl* depot.

депорта́ция deportation. **депорти́ровать** *impf & pf* deport.

депута́т deputy; delegate.

дёргать *impf* (*pf* дёрнуть) pull, tug; pester; ~**ся** twitch; jerk.

дереве́нский village; rural. **дере́вня** (*pl* -и, -ве́нь, -вня́м) village; the country. **де́рево** (*pl* -е́вья, -ьев) tree; wood. **деревя́нный** wood; wooden.

держа́ва power. **держа́ть** (-жу́, -жишь) *impf* hold; support; keep; ~ **пари́** bet; ~ **себя́** behave; ~**ся** hold; be held up; hold o.s.; hold out; +*gen* keep to.

дерза́ние daring. **дерза́ть** *impf*, **дерзну́ть** (-ну́, -нёшь) *pf* dare.

дёрзкий impudent; daring. **дёрзость** impertinence; daring.

дёрн turf.

дёрнуть(ся (-ну(сь)) *pf of* **дёргать(ся**

деру́ *etc.: see* **драть**

деса́нт landing; landing force.

де́скать *partl indicating reported speech.*

десна́ (*pl* дёсны, -сен) gum.

де́спот despot.

десятиле́тие decade; tenth anniversary. **десятиле́тка** ten-year (*secondary*) school. **десятиле́тний** ten-year; ten-year-old. **деся́тичный** decimal. **деся́тка** ten; figure 10; No. 10; tenner (*10-rouble note*). **деся́ток** (-тка) ten; decade. **деся́тый** tenth. **де́сять** (-и, *instr* -ью) ten.

детдо́м children's home. **детса́д** kindergarten.

дета́ль detail; part, component. **дета́льный** detailed; minute.

детекти́в detective story.

детёныш young animal; *pl* young. **де́ти** (-те́й, -тям, -тьми́, -тях) *pl* children. **де́тская** *sb* nursery. **де́тский** children's; childish. **де́тство** childhood.

де́ться (де́нусь) *pf* (*impf* дева́ться) get to. disappear to.

дефе́кт defect.

дефи́с hyphen.

дефици́т deficit; shortage. **дефици́тный** scarce.

дешеве́ть (-е́ет) *impf* (*pf* по~) fall in price. **деше́вле** *comp of* дёшево. **дешёвый**. **дёшево** *adv* cheap, cheaply. **дешёвый** (дёшев, -а́, -о) cheap; empty, worthless.

де́ятель *m*: госуда́рственный ~ statesman; обще́ственный ~ public figure. **де́ятельность** activity; work. **де́ятельный** active, energetic.

джаз jazz.

дже́мпер pullover.

джентельме́н gentleman.

джинсо́вый denim. **джи́нсы** (-ов) *pl* jeans.

джо́йстик joystick.

джу́нгли (-ей) *pl* jungle.

диабе́т diabetes.

диа́гноз diagnosis.

диагона́ль diagonal

диагра́мма diagram.

диале́кт dialect. **диале́ктика** dialectics.

диало́г dialogue.

диа́метр diameter.

диапазо́н range; band.

диапозити́в slide, transparency.

диафра́гма diaphragm.

дива́н sofa; divan.

диверса́нт saboteur. **диве́рсия** sabotage.

диви́зия division.

диви́ться (-влю́сь) *impf* (*pf* по~) marvel (at + *dat*).

ди́вный marvellous. **ди́во** wonder, marvel.

дида́ктика didactics.

дие́з (*mus*) sharp.

дие́та diet. **диети́ческий** dietetic.

ди́зель *m* diesel; diesel engine. **ди́зельный** diesel.

дизентери́я dysentery.

дика́рь (-я́) *m*, **дика́рка** savage. **ди́кий** wild; savage; queer; preposterous. **дикобра́з** porcupine. **дикорасту́щий** wild. **ди́кость** wildness, savagery; absurdity.

дикта́нт dictation. **дикта́тор** dictator. **диктату́ра** dictatorship.

диктова́ть *impf* (*pf* про~) dictate. **ди́ктор** announcer. **ди́кция** diction.

диле́мма dilemma.

дилета́нт dilettante.

дина́мика dynamics.

динами́т dynamite.

динами́ческий dynamic.

дина́стия dynasty.

диноза́вр dinosaur.

дипло́м diploma; degree; degree work. **диплома́т** diplomat. **диплома́тический** diplomatic.

директи́ва instructions; directives.

дире́ктор (*pl* ~а́) director; principal. **дире́кция** management.

дирижа́бль *m* airship, dirigible.

дирижёр conductor. **дирижи́ровать** *impf* +*instr* conduct.

диск disc, disk; dial; discus.

ди́скант treble.

дискоте́ка discotheque.

дискре́тный discrete; digital.

дискримина́ция discrimination.

диску́ссия discussion, debate.

диспансе́р clinic.

диспе́тчер controller.

дису́т public debate.

диссерта́ция dissertation, thesis.

дистанцио́нный distance, distant,

remote; remote-control. **диста́нция**
distance; range; region.
дисципли́на discipline.
дитя́ (-я́ти; pl де́ти, -е́й) neut child;
baby.
дифтери́т diptheria.
дифто́нг diphthong.
диффама́ция libel.
дичь game.
длина́ length. **дли́нный** (-нен, -нна́,
-о) long. **дли́тельность** duration.
дли́тельный long, protracted.
дли́ться impf (pf про~) last.
для prep+gen for; for the sake of; ~
того́, что́бы... in order to.
днева́льный sb orderly, man on
duty. **дневни́к** (-а́) diary, journal.
дневно́й daily. **днём** adv in the
day time; in the afternoon. **дни** etc.:
see **день**
дни́ще bottom.
ДНК abbr (of дезоксирибонукле-
и́новая кислота́) DNA.
дно (дна; pl до́нья, -ьев) bottom.
до prep+gen (up) to; as far as; until;
before; to the point of; до на́шей
э́ры BC; до сих пор till now; до
тех пор till then; before; до того́,
как before; до того́, что to such an
extent that; to the point where; мне
не до I'm not in the mood for.
доба́вить (-влю) pf, **добавля́ть**
impf (+acc or gen) add. **доба́вка** addition; second helping. **добавле́ние**
addition; supplement; extra. **доба́-
вочный** additional.
добега́ть impf, **добежа́ть** (-егу́) pf
+до+gen run to, as far as; reach.
добива́ть impf, **доби́ть** (-бью, -бьёшь)
pf finish (off); ~ся+gen get; obtain;
~ся своего́ get one's way.
добира́ться impf of **добра́ться**
до́блесть valour.
добра́ться (-беру́сь, -ёшься; -а́лся,
-ла́сь, -а́ло́сь) pf (impf добира́ться)
+до+gen get to, reach.
добро́ good; э́то не к добру́ it is a
bad sign.
добро- in comb good-, well-. **добро-
во́лец** (-льца) volunteer. ~**во́льно**
adv voluntarily. ~**во́льный** voluntary. ~**де́тель** virtue. ~**де́тельный**
virtuous. ~**душие** good nature.
~**душный** good-natured. ~**жела́-
тельный** benevolent. ~**ка́чест-**

венный of good quality; benign.
~**со́вестный** conscientious.
доброта́ goodness, kindness. **доб-
ро́тный** of good quality. **до́брый**
(добр, -а́, -о, до́бры) good; kind;
бу́дьте добры́+imper please; would
you be kind enough to.
добыва́ть impf, **добы́ть** (-бу́ду;
до́был, -а́, -о) pf get, obtain; procure;
mine. **добы́ча** output; mining; booty.
добью etc.: see **добить**. **доведу́** etc.:
see **довести́**
довезти́ (-езу́, -езёшь, -вёз, -ла́) pf
(impf **довози́ть**) take (to), carry (to),
drive (to).
дове́ренность warrant; power of attorney. **дове́ренный** trusted; sb
agent, proxy. **дове́рие** trust, confidence. **дове́рить** pf (impf до-
веря́ть) entrust; ~ся +dat trust in;
confide in.
до́верху adv to the top.
дове́рчивый trustful, credulous.
доверя́ть impf of **дове́рить**; (+dat)
to trust.
дове́сок (-ска) makeweight.
довести́ (-еду́, -едёшь; -вёл, -а́) pf,
доводи́ть (-ожу́, -о́дишь) impf lead,
take (to); bring, drive (to). **до́вод**
argument, reason.
дово́енный pre-war.
довози́ть (-ожу́, -о́зишь) impf of
довезти́
дово́льно adv enough; quite, fairly.
дово́льный satisfied; pleased. **до-
во́льствие** contentment. **дово́ль-
ствоваться** impf (pf у~) be content.
догада́ться pf, **дога́дываться** impf
guess; suspect. **дога́дка** surmise, conjecture. **дога́дливый** quick-witted.
до́гма dogma.
догна́ть (-гоню́, -го́нишь; -гна́л, -а́, -о)
pf (impf догоня́ть) catch up (with).
догова́риваться impf, **догово-
ри́ться** pf come to an agreement; arrange. **догово́р** (pl -ы́ or -а́, -о́в)
agreement; contract; treaty. **дого-
во́рный** contractual; agreed.
догоня́ть impf of **догна́ть**
догора́ть impf, **догоре́ть** (-ри́т) pf
burn out, burn down
дое́ду etc.: see **дое́хать**. **доезжа́ть**
impf of **дое́хать**
дое́хать (-е́ду) pf (impf доезжа́ть)

+до+gen reach, arrive at.

дожда́ться (-ду́сь, -дёшься; -а́лся, -ла́сь, -а́лось) pf +gen wait for, wait until.

дождеви́к (-а́) raincoat. дождево́й rain(y). дождли́вый rainy. дождь (-я́) m rain; ~ идёт it is raining.

дожива́ть impf, дожи́ть (-иву́, -ивёшь; до́жил, -а́, -о) pf live out; spend.

дожида́ться impf +gen wait for.

до́за dose.

дозво́лить pf, дозволя́ть impf permit.

дозвони́ться pf get through, reach by telephone.

дозо́р patrol.

дозрева́ть impf, дозре́ть (-е́ет) pf ripen.

доистори́ческий prehistoric.

дойти́ impf (pf по~) milk.

дойти́ (дойду́, -дёшь; дошёл, -шла́) pf (impf доходи́ть) +до+gen reach; get through to.

док dock.

доказа́тельный conclusive. доказа́тельство proof, evidence. доказа́ть (-ажу́) pf, дока́зывать impf demonstrate, prove.

докати́ться (-ачу́сь, -а́тишься) pf, дока́тываться impf roll; boom; +до+gen sink into.

докла́д report; lecture. докладна́я (запи́ска) report; memo. докла́дчик speaker, lecturer. докла́дывать impf of доложи́ть

до́красна adv to red heat; to redness.

до́ктор (pl -а́) doctor. до́кторский doctoral. до́кторша woman doctor; doctor's wife.

доктри́на doctrine.

докуме́нт document; deed. документа́льный documentary. документа́ция documentation; documents.

долби́ть (-блю́) impf hollow; chisel; repeat; swot up.

долг (loc -у́; pl -и́) duty; debt; взять в ~ borrow; дать в ~ lend.

до́лгий (до́лог, -лга́, -о) long. до́лго adv long, (for) a long time. долгове́чный lasting; durable. долгожд́анный long-awaited. долгоигра́ющая пласти́нка LP.

долголе́тие longevity. долго

ле́тний of many years; long-standing. долгосро́чный long-term.

долгота́ (pl -ы) length; longitude.

долево́й lengthwise. до́лее adv longer.

должа́ть impf (pf за~) borrow.

до́лжен (-жна́) predic+dat in debt to; +inf obliged, bound; likely; must, have to, ought to; должно́ быть probably. должни́к (-а́), -ни́ца debtor. до́лжное sb due. должностно́й official. до́лжность (gen pl -е́й) post, office; duties. до́лжный due, fitting.

доли́на valley.

до́ллар dollar.

доложи́ть¹ (-ожу́, -о́жишь) pf (impf докла́дывать) add.

доложи́ть² (-ожу́, -о́жишь) pf (impf докла́дывать) +acc or o+prep report; announce.

доло́й adv away, off; +acc down with!

долото́ (pl -а) chisel.

до́лька segment; clove.

до́льше adv longer.

до́ля (gen pl -е́й) portion; share; lot, fate.

дом (loc -у́; pl -а́) house; home. до́ма adv at home. дома́шн|ий house; home; domestic; home-made; ~яя хозя́йка housewife.

до́менн|ый blast-furnace; ~ая печь blast-furnace.

домини́ровать impf dominate, predominate.

домкра́т jack.

до́мна blast-furnace.

домовладе́лец (-льца), -ли́ца houseowner; landlord. домово́дство housekeeping; domestic science. домо́вый house; household; housing.

домога́тельство solicitation; bid. домога́ться impf +gen solicit, bid for.

домо́й adv home, homewards. домохозя́йка housewife. домрабо́тница domestic servant, maid.

доне́льзя adv in the extreme.

донесе́ние dispatch, report. донести́ (-су́, -сёшь; -нёс, -сла́) pf (impf доноси́ть) report, announce; +dat inform; +на+acc inform against; ~сь be heard; +до+gen reach.

до́низу adv to the bottom; све́рху ~ from top to bottom.

до́нор donor.

доно́с denunciation, information. доноси́ть(ся -ношу́(сь, -но́сишь(ся) *impf of* донести́(сь

доно́счик informer.

донско́й Don.

доны́не *adv* hitherto.

до́нья *etc.: see* дно

до н.э. *abbr (of* до на́шей э́ры) BC.

допла́та additional payment, excess fare. доплати́ть (-ачу́, -а́тишь) *pf*, допла́чивать *impf* pay in addition; pay the rest.

допо́длинно *adv* for certain. допо́длинный authentic, genuine.

дополне́ние supplement, addition; (*gram*) object. дополни́тельно *adv* in addition. дополни́тельный supplementary, additional. допо́лнить *pf*, дополня́ть *impf* supplement.

допра́шивать *impf*, допроси́ть (-ошу́, -о́сишь) *pf* interrogate. допро́с interrogation.

до́пуск right of entry, admittance. допуска́ть *impf*, допусти́ть (-ущу́, -у́стишь) *pf* admit; permit; tolerate; suppose. допусти́мый permissible, acceptable. допуще́ние assumption.

дореволюцио́нный pre-revolutionary.

доро́га road; way; journey; route: по доро́ге on the way.

до́рого *adv* dear, dearly. дорогови́зна high prices. дорого́й (до́рог, -а́, -о) dear.

доро́дный portly.

дорожа́ть *impf* (*pf* вз~, по~) rise in price, go up. доро́же *comp of* до́рого, дорого́й. дорожи́ть (-жу́) *impf* +*instr* value.

доро́жка path; track; lane; runway; strip, runner, stair-carpet. доро́жный road; highway; travelling.

доса́да annoyance. досади́ть (-ажу́) *pf*, досажда́ть *impf* +*dat* annoy. доса́дный annoying. досадова́ть be annoyed (на+*acc* with).

доска́ (*acc* до́ску; *pl* -и, -со́к, -ска́м) board; slab; plaque.

досло́вный literal; word-for-word.

досмо́тр inspection.

доспе́хи *pl* armour.

досро́чный ahead of time, early.

доставáть(ся (-таю́(сь, -ёшь(ся) *impf of* доста́ть(ся

доста́вить (-влю) *pf*, доставля́ть *impf* deliver; supply; cause, give. доста́вка delivery.

доста́ну *etc.: see* доста́ть

доста́ток (-тка) sufficiency; prosperity. доста́точно *adv* enough, sufficiently. доста́точный sufficient; adequate.

доста́ть (-а́ну) *pf* (*impf* доставáть) take (out); get, obtain; +*gen or* до+*gen* touch; reach; *impers* suffice; ~ся+*dat* be inherited by; fall to the lot of: ему́ доста́нется he'll catch it.

достига́ть *impf*, дости́гнуть, дости́чь (-и́гну; -стиг) *pf* +*gen* reach, achieve; +*gen or* до+*gen* reach. достиже́ние achievement.

достове́рный reliable, trustworthy; authentic.

досто́инство dignity; merit; value. досто́йный deserved; suitable; worthy; +*gen* worthy of.

достопримеча́тельность sight, notable place.

достоя́ние property.

до́ступ access. досту́пный accessible; approachable; reasonable; available.

досу́г leisure, (spare) time. досу́жий leisure; idle.

до́сыта *adv* to satiety.

досье́ *neut indecl* dossier.

досяга́емый attainable.

дота́ция grant, subsidy.

дотла́ utterly; to the ground.

дотра́гиваться *impf*, дотро́нуться (-нусь) *pf* +до+*gen* touch.

дотя́гивать *impf*, дотяну́ть (-яну́, -я́нешь) *pf* draw, drag, stretch out; hold out; live; put off; ~ся stretch; reach; drag on.

до́хлый dead; sickly. до́хнуть[1] (-нет; дох) (*pf* из~, по~, с~) die; kick the bucket.

дохну́ть[2] (-ну́, -нёшь) *pf* draw a breath.

дохо́д income; revenue. доходи́ть (-ожу́, -о́дишь) *impf of* дойти́. дохо́дный profitable. дохо́дчивый intelligible.

доце́нт reader, senior lecturer.

до́чиста *adv* clean; completely.

до́чка daughter. дочь (-чери, *instr* -черью; *pl* -чери, -чере́й, *instr* -черьми́) daughter.

дошёл etc.: see **дойти**

дошкольник, **-ница** child under school age. **дошкольный** pre-school.

дощатый plank, board. **дощечка** small plank, board; plaque.

доярка milkmaid.

драгоценность jewel; treasure; pl jewellery; valuables. **драгоценный** precious.

дразнить (-ню, -нишь) impf tease.

драка fight.

дракон dragon.

драма drama. **драматический** dramatic. **драматург** playwright. **драматургия** dramatic art; plays.

драп thick woollen cloth.

драпировка draping; curtain; hangings. **драпировщик** upholsterer.

драть (деру, -рёшь; драл, -á, -о) impf (pf вы~, за~, со~) tear (up); irritate; make off; flog; ~ся fight.

дребезги pl; в ~ to smithereens. **дребезжать** (-жит) impf jingle, tinkle.

древесина wood; timber. **древесный** wood; ~ уголь charcoal.

древко (-и, -ов) pole, staff; shaft.

древнегреческий ancient Greek. **древнееврейский** Hebrew. **древнерусский** Old Russian. **древний** ancient; aged. **древность** antiquity.

дрейф drift; leeway. **дрейфовать** impf drift.

дремать (-млю, -млешь) impf doze; slumber. **дремота** drowsiness.

дремучий dense.

дрессированный trained; performing. **дрессировать** impf (pf вы~) train; school. **дрессировка** training. **дрессировщик** trainer.

дробить (-блю) impf (pf раз~) break up, smash; crush; ~ся break to pieces, smash. **дробовик** (-á) shot-gun. **дробь** (small) shot; drumming; fraction. **дробный** fractional.

дрова (дров) pl firewood.

дрогнуть (-ну) pf, **дрожать** (-жу) impf tremble; shiver; quiver.

дрожжи (-ей) pl yeast.

дрожь shivering, trembling.

дрозд (-á) thrush.

дротик javelin, dart.

дроссель m throttle, choke.

друг[1] (pl -узья, -зей) friend. **друг**[2]:

~ дру́га (дру́гу) each other, one another. **друго́й** other, another; different; на ~ день (the) next day. **дру́жба** friendship. **дружелюбный**, **дру́жеский**, **дру́жественный** friendly. **дружи́ть** (-жу́, -у́жи́шь) impf be friends; ~ся (pf по~ся) make friends. **дру́жный** (-жен, -жна́, -о) amicable; harmonious; simultaneous, concerted.

дря́блый (дрябл, -á, -о) flabby.

дря́зги (-зг) pl squabbles.

дрянно́й worthless; good-for-nothing. **дрянь** rubbish.

дряхле́ть (-ею) impf (pf o~) become decrepit. **дря́хлый** (-хл, -лá, -о) decrepit, senile.

дуб (pl -ы́) oak; blockhead. **дуби́на** club, cudgel; blockhead. **дуби́нка** truncheon, baton.

дублёнка sheepskin coat.

дублёр understudy. **дублика́т** duplicate. **дубли́ровать** duplicate; understudy; dub.

дубо́вый oak; coarse; clumsy.

дуга́ (pl -и) arc; arch.

ду́дка pipe, fife.

ду́ло muzzle; barrel.

ду́ма thought; Duma; council. **ду́мать** impf (pf по~) think; +inf think of, intend. **ду́маться** impf (impers +dat) seem.

дунове́ние puff, breath. **ду́нуть** (-ну) pf of **дуть**

дупло́ (pl -а, -пел) hollow; hole; cavity.

ду́ра, **дура́к** (-á) fool. **дура́чить** (-чу) impf (pf o~) fool, dupe; ~ся play the fool.

дуре́ть (-ею) impf (pf o~) grow stupid.

дурма́н narcotic; intoxicant. **дурма́нить** impf (pf o~) stupefy.

дурно́й (-рен, -рнá, -о) bad, evil; ugly; мне ду́рно I feel faint, sick. **дурнота́** faintness; nausea.

ду́тый hollow; inflated. **дуть** (дýю) impf (pf вы́~, по~, ду́нуть) blow; ду́ет there is a draught. **дутьё** glass-blowing. **ду́ться** (дýюсь) impf pout; sulk.

дух spirit; spirits; heart; mind; breath; ghost; smell; в ~е in a good mood; не в моём ~е not to my taste; ни слу́ху ни ~у no news, not a word.

душ**и́** (-**о́в**) *pl* scent, perfume. Д**у́хов**
день Whit Monday. духов**е́нство**
clergy. духов**и́дец** (-**дца**) clairvoyant; medium. дух**о́вка** oven. дух**о́в-**
ный spiritual; ecclesiastical. духов**о́й**
wind. духот**а́** stuffiness, closeness.
душ shower(-bath).
душ**а́** (*acc* -**у**, *pl* -**и**) soul; heart; feeling; spirit; inspiration; **в душе́** inwardly; at heart; **от всей души́** with
all one's heart.
душев**а́я** *sb* shower-room.
душевнобольн**о́й** mentally ill, insane; *sb* mental patient; lunatic.
душ**е́вный** mental; sincere, cordial.
душ**и́стый** fragrant; ~ **горо́шек**
sweet pea(s).
душ**и́ть** (-**у́**, -**шишь**) *impf* (*pf* за~)
strangle; stifle, smother.
душ**и́ться** (-**шу́сь**, -**шишься**) *impf* (*pf*
на~) use, put on, perfume.
д**у́шный** (-**шен**, -**шна́**, -**о**) stuffy, close.
ду**э́ль** duel.
ду**э́т** duet.
д**ы́бом** *adv* on end; **у меня́ во́лосы**
вста́ли ~ my hair stood on end.
дыб**ы́**: **станови́ться на** ~ rear; resist.
дым (*loc* -**у́**; *pl* -**ы́**) smoke. дым**и́ть**
(-**млю́**) *impf* (*pf* на~) smoke; ~**ся**
smoke, steam; billow. д**ы́мный**
smoky. дымов**о́й** smoke;
~**а́я труба́** flue, chimney. дым**о́к**
(-**мка́**) puff of smoke. дымох**о́д** flue.
д**ы́ня** melon.
дыр**а́** (*pl* -**ы**), д**ы́рка** (*gen pl* -**рок**)
hole; gap.
дых**а́ние** breathing; breath. дых**а́-**
тельный respiratory; breathing;
~**ое го́рло** windpipe. дыш**а́ть** (-**шу́**,
-**шишь**) *impf* breathe.
дь**я́вол** devil. дь**я́вольский** devilish, diabolical.
дь**я́кон** (*pl* -**а́**) deacon.
д**ю́жина** dozen.
дюйм inch.
д**ю́на** dune.
д**я́дя** (*gen pl* -**ей**) *m* uncle.
д**я́тел** (-**тла**) woodpecker.

E

ева́нгелие gospel; the Gospels.
евангели́ческий evangelical.

евре́й, евре́йка Jew; Hebrew.
евре́йский Jewish.
Евро́па Europe. европе́ец (-е́йца)
European. европе́йский European.
Еги́пет Egypt. еги́петский Egyptian. египтя́нин (*pl* -я́не, -я́н),
египтя́нка Egyptian.
его́ *see* он, оно́; *pron* his; its.
еда́ food; meal.
едва́ *adv* & *conj* hardly; just; scarcely;
~ ли hardly; ~ (ли) не almost, all
but.
еди́м *etc.*: *see* есть¹
едине́ние unity. едини́ца (figure)
one; unity; unit; individual. еди-
ни́чный single; individual.
едино- *in comb* mono-, uni-; one; co-.
единобра́чие monogamy. ~вла́-
стие autocracy. ~вре́менно *adv*
only once; simultaneously. ~гла́сие,
~ду́шие unanimity. ~гла́сный,
~ду́шный unanimous. ~кро́вный
брат half-brother. ~мы́слие like-
mindedness; agreement. ~мы́шлен-
ник like-minded person. ~утро́б-
ный брат half-brother.
еди́нственно *adv* only, solely.
еди́нственный only, sole. еди́н-
ство unity. еди́ный one; single;
united.
е́дкий (е́док, едка́, -о) caustic; pungent.
едо́к (-а́) mouth, head; eater.
е́ду *etc.*: *see* е́хать
её *see* она́; *pron* her, hers; its.
ёж (ежа́) hedgehog.
еже- *in comb* every; -ly ежего́дник
annual, year-book. ~го́дный annual. ~дне́вный daily. ~ме́сячник,
~ме́сячный monthly. ~неде́ль-
ник, ~неде́льный weekly.
ежеви́ка (*no pl*; *usu collect*) blackberry; blackberries; blackberry bush.
ёжели *conj* if.
ёжиться (ёжусь) *impf* (*pf* съ~) huddle up; shrink away.
езда́ ride, riding; drive, driving; journey. е́здить (е́зжу) *impf* go; ride,
drive; ~ верхо́м ride. ездо́к (-а́)
rider.
ей *see* она́
ей-бо́гу *int* really! truly!
ел *etc.*: *see* есть¹
е́ле *adv* scarcely; only just. е́ле-е́ле
emphatic variant of е́ле

ёлка fir-tree; spruce; Christmas tree. **ёлочка** herring-bone pattern. **ёлочный** Christmas-tree. **ель** fir-tree; spruce.

ем etc.: see **есть**[1]

ёмкий capacious. **ёмкость** capacity.

ему́ see **он, оно́**

епи́скоп bishop.

е́ресь heresy. **ерети́к** (-á) heretic. **ерети́ческий** heretical.

ёрзать impf fidget.

еро́шить (-шу) impf (pf взъ~) ruffle, rumple.

ерунда́ nonsense.

е́сли conj if; ~ бы if only; ~ бы не but for, if it were not for; ~ не unless.

ест see **есть**[1]

есте́ственно adv naturally. **есте́ственный** natural. **естество́** nature; essence. **естествозна́ние** (natural) science.

есть[1] (ем, ешь, ест, еди́м; ел) impf (pf съ~) eat; corrode, eat away.

есть[2] see **быть**; is, are; there is there are; у меня́ ~ I have.

ефре́йтор lance-corporal.

е́хать (е́ду) impf (pf по~) go; ride, drive; travel; ~ верхо́м ride.

ехи́дный malicious, spiteful.

ешь see **есть**[1]

ещё adv still; yet; (some) more; any more; yet, further; again; +comp still, yet even; всё ~ still; ~ бы! of course! oh yes! can you ask?; ~ не, нет ~ not yet; ~ раз once more, again; пока́ ~ for the present, for the time being.

е́ю see **она́**

Ж

ж conj: see **же**

жа́ба toad.

жа́бра (gen pl -бр) gill.

жа́воронок (-нка) lark.

жа́дничать impf be greedy; be mean. **жа́дность** greed; meanness. **жа́дный** (-ден, -дна́, -о) greedy; avid; mean.

жа́жда thirst; +gen thirst, craving for. **жа́ждать** (-ду) impf thirst, yearn.

жаке́т, жаке́тка jacket.

жале́ть (-е́ю) impf (pf по~) pity, feel sorry for; regret; +acc or gen grudge.

жа́лить impf (pf у~) sting, bite. **жа́лкий** (-лок, -лка́, -о) pitiful. **жа́лко** predic: see **жаль**.

жа́ло sting.

жа́лоба complaint. **жа́лобный** plaintive.

жа́лованье salary. **жа́ловать** impf (pf по~) +acc or dat of person, instr or acc of thing grant, bestow on; ~ся complain (на+acc of, about).

жа́лостливый compassionate. **жа́лостный** piteous; compassionate. **жа́лость** pity. **жаль, жа́лко** predic, impers (it is) a pity; +dat it grieves; +gen grudge; как ~ what a pity; мне ~ его́ I'm sorry for him.

жалюзи́ neut indecl Venetian blind.

жанр genre.

жар (loc -ý) heat; heat of the day; fever; (high) temperature; ardour. **жара́** heat; hot weather.

жарго́н slang.

жа́реный roast; grilled; fried. **жа́рить** impf (pf за~, из~) roast; grill; fry; scorch, burn; ~ся roast, fry. **жа́рк|ий** (-рок, -рка́, -о) hot; passionate; -óе sb. roast (meat). **жаро́вня** (gen pl -вен) brazier. **жар-пти́ца** Firebird. **жа́рче** comp of **жа́ркий**

жа́тва harvest. **жать**[1] (жну, жнёшь) impf (pf с~) reap, cut.

жать[2] (жму, жмёшь) impf press, squeeze; pinch; oppress.

жва́чка chewing, rumination; cud; chewing-gum. **жва́чн|ый** ruminant; -ое sb ruminant.

жгу etc.: see **жечь**

жгут (-á) plait; tourniquet.

жгу́чий burning. **жёг** etc.: see **жечь**

ждать (жду, ждёшь; -ал, -á, -о) impf +gen wait (for); expect.

же, ж conj but; and; however; also; partl giving emphasis or expressing identity; мне же ка́жется it seems to me, however; сего́дня же this very day; что же ты де́лаешь? what on earth are you doing?

жева́тельная рези́нка chewing-gum. **жева́ть** (жую, жуёшь) impf chew; ruminate.

жезл (-á) rod; staff.

жела́ние wish, desire. **жела́нный** longed-for; beloved. **жела́тельный** desirable; advisable. **жела́ть** impf (*pf* по∼) +*gen* wish for, desire; want. желе́ *neut indecl* jelly.

железа́ (*pl* же́лезы, -ле́з, -за́м) gland; *pl* tonsils.

железнодоро́жник railwayman. железнодоро́жный railway. желе́зн|ый iron; ∼ая доро́га railway. желе́зо iron.

железобето́н reinforced concrete.

жёлоб (*pl* -а́) gutter. желобо́к (-бка́) groove, channel, flute.

желте́ть (-е́ю) *impf* (*pf* по∼) turn yellow; be yellow. желто́к (-тка́) yolk. желту́ха jaundice. жёлтый (жёлт, -а́, жёлто) yellow.

желу́док (-дка) stomach. желу́дочный stomach; gastric.

жёлудь (*gen pl* -е́й) *m* acorn.

жёлчный bilious; gall; irritable. жёлчь bile, gall.

жема́ниться *impf* mince, put on airs. жема́нный mincing, affected. жема́нство affectedness.

жемчуг (*pl* -а́) pearl(s). жемчу́жина pearl. жемчу́жный pearl(y).

жена́ (*pl* жёны) wife. жена́тый married.

жени́ть (-ню́, -нишь) *impf* & *pf* (*pf also* по∼) marry. жени́тьба marriage. жени́ться (-ню́сь, -нишься) *impf* & *pf* (+на+*prep*) marry, get married (to). жени́х (-а́) fiancé; bridegroom. же́нский woman's; feminine; female. же́нственный womanly, feminine. же́нщина woman.

жердь (*gen pl* -е́й) pole; stake.

жеребёнок (-нка; *pl* -бя́та, -бя́т) foal. жеребе́ц (-бца́) stallion.

жеребьёвка casting of lots.

жерло́ (*pl* -а) muzzle; crater.

жёрнов (*pl* -а́, -о́в) millstone.

же́ртва sacrifice; victim. же́ртвенный sacrificial. же́ртвовать *impf* (*pf* по∼) present, make a donation (of); +*instr* sacrifice.

жест gesture. жестикули́ровать *impf* gesticulate.

жёсткий (-ток, -тка́, -о) hard; tough; rigid, strict.

жесто́кий (-то́к, -а́, -о) cruel; severe. жесто́кость cruelty.

жесть tin(-plate). жестяно́й tin.

жето́н medal; counter; token.

жечь (жгу, жжёшь; жёг, жгла) *impf*

(*pf* с∼) burn; ∼ся burn, sting; burn o.s.

живи́тельный invigorating. жи́вность poultry, fowl. жив|о́й (жив, -а́, -о) living, alive; lively; vivid; brisk; animated; poignant; bright; на ∼ую ни́тку hastily, anyhow; шить на ∼ую ни́тку tack. живопи́сец (-сца) painter. живопи́сный picturesque. жи́вопись painting. жи́вость liveliness.

живо́т (-а́) abdomen; stomach. животново́дство animal husbandry. живо́тное *sb* animal. живо́тный animal.

живу́ *etc.: see* жить. живу́чий hardy. живьём *adv* alive.

жи́дк|ий (-док, -дка́, -о) liquid; watery; weak; sparse; ∼ий криста́лл liquid crystal. жи́дкость liquid, fluid; wateriness, weakness. жи́жа sludge; slush; liquid. жи́же *comp of* жи́дкий

жи́зненный life, of life; vital; living; ∼ у́ровень standard of living. жизнеописа́ние biography. жизнера́достный cheerful. жизнеспосо́бный capable of living; viable. жизнь life.

жи́ла vein; tendon, sinew.

жиле́т, жиле́тка waistcoat.

жиле́ц (-льца́), жили́ца lodger; tenant; inhabitant.

жили́ще dwelling, abode. жили́щный housing; living.

жи́лка vein; fibre; streak.

жил|о́й dwelling; habitable; ∼о́й дом dwelling house; block of flats; ∼ая пло́щадь, жилпло́щадь floor-space; housing, accommodation. жильё habitation; dwelling.

жир (*loc* -у́; *pl* -ы́) fat; grease. жире́ть (-ре́ю) *impf* (*pf* о∼, раз∼) grow fat. жи́рный (-рен, -рна́, -о) fatty; greasy; rich. жирово́й fatty; fat.

жира́ф giraffe.

жите́йский worldly; everyday. жи́тель *m* inhabitant; dweller. жи́тельство residence. жи́тница granary. жи́то corn, cereal. жить (живу́, -вёшь; жил, -а́, -о) *impf* live. житьё life; existence; habitation.

жму *etc.: see* жать²

жму́риться *impf* (*pf* за∼) screw up one's eyes, frown.

жнивьё (*pl* -ья, -ьев) stubble (-field).

жну *etc.: see* жать[1]

жокей jockey.

жонглёр juggler.

жрать (жру, жрёшь; -ал, -а́, -о) guzzle.

жре́бий lot; fate, destiny; ~ бро́шен the die is cast.

жрец priest. **жри́ца** priestess.

жужжа́ть (-жжу́) hum, buzz, drone; whiz(z).

жук (-а́) beetle.

жу́лик petty thief; cheat. **жу́льничать** *impf* (*pf* с~) cheat.

жура́вль (-я́) *m* crane.

жури́ть *impf* reprove.

журна́л magazine, periodical. **журнали́ст** journalist. **журнали́стика** journalism.

журча́ние babble; murmur. **журча́ть** (-чи́т) *impf* babble, murmur.

жу́ткий (-ток, -тка́, -о) uncanny; terrible, terrifying. **жу́тко** *adv* terrifyingly; terribly, awfully.

жую́ *etc.: see* жева́ть

жюри́ *neut indecl* judges.

З

за *prep* I. +*acc* (*indicating motion or action*) *or instr* (*indicating rest or state*) behind; beyond; across, the other side of; at; to; **за́ город, за́ городом** out of town; **за рубежо́м** abroad; **сесть за роя́ль** sit down at the piano; **сиде́ть за роя́лем** be at the piano; **за́ угол, за угло́м** round the corner. II. +*acc* after; over; during, in the space of; by; for; to; **за ва́ше здоро́вье!** your health!; **вести́ за́ руку** lead by the hand; **далеко́ за́ полночь** long after midnight; **за два дня до+**gen two days before; **за три киломе́тра от дере́вни** three kilometres from the village; **плати́ть за биле́т** pay for a ticket; **за после́днее вре́мя** lately. III. +*instr* after; for; because of; at; during; for; **год за го́дом** year after year; **идти́ за молоко́м** go for milk; **за обе́дом** at dinner.

заба́ва amusement; game; fun. **забавля́ть** *impf* amuse; ~ся amuse o.s. **заба́вный** amusing, funny.

забастова́ть *pf* strike; go on strike. **забасто́вка** strike. **забасто́вщик** striker.

забве́ние oblivion.

забе́г heat, race. **забега́ть** *impf*, **забежа́ть** (-егу́) *pf* run up; +к+*dat* drop in on; ~ вперёд run ahead; anticipate.

за|бере́менеть (-ею) *pf* become pregnant.

заберу́ *etc.: see* забра́ть

забива́ние jamming. **забива́ть(ся** *impf of* заби́ть(ся[1]

забинтова́ть *pf*, **забинто́вывать** *impf* bandage.

заби́тый downtrodden. **заби́ть**[1] (-бью, -бьёшь) *pf* (*impf* забива́ть) drive in, hammer in; score; seal, block up; obstruct; choke; jam; cram; beat up; beat; ~ся hide, take refuge; become cluttered *or* clogged; +в+*acc* get into, penetrate. **за|би́ть**[2] *pf* begin to beat. **забия́ка** *m & f* squabbler; bully.

заблаговре́менно *adv* in good time; well in advance. **заблаговре́менный** timely.

заблесте́ть (-ещу́, -ести́шь *or* -е́щешь) *pf* begin to shine, glitter, glow.

заблуди́ться (-ужу́сь, -у́дишься) *pf* get lost. **заблу́дший** lost, stray. **заблужда́ться** *impf* be mistaken. **заблужде́ние** error; delusion.

забо́й (pit-)face.

заболева́емость sickness rate. **заболева́ние** sickness, illness; falling ill. **заболева́ть**[1] *impf*, **заболе́ть**[1] (-е́ю) *pf* fall ill; +*instr* go down with. **заболева́ть**[2] *impf*, **заболе́ть**[2] (-ли́т) *pf* (begin to) ache, hurt.

забо́р[1] fence.

забо́р[2] taking away; obtaining on credit.

забо́та concern; care; trouble(s). **забо́тить** (-о́чу) *impf* (*pf* о~) trouble, worry; ~ся *impf* (*pf* по~) worry; take care (о+*prep* of); take trouble; care. **забо́тливый** solicitous, thoughtful.

за|бракова́ть *pf*.

забра́сывать *impf of* заброса́ть, **забро́сить**

забра́ть (-беру́, -берёшь; -а́л, -а́, -о)

pf (*impf* забира́ть) take; take away; seize; appropriate; ~ся climb; get to, into.

забреда́ть *impf*, забрести́ (-еду́, -еде́шь; -ёл, -а́) *pf* stray, wander; drop in.

за|брони́ровать *pf*.

заброса́ть *pf* (*impf* забра́сывать) fill up; bespatter, deluge. забро́сить (-о́шу) *pf* (*impf* забра́сывать) throw; abandon; neglect. забро́шенный neglected; deserted.

забры́згать *pf*, забры́згивать *impf* splash, bespatter.

забыва́ть *impf*, забы́ть (-бу́ду) *pf* forget; ~ся doze off; lose consciousness; forget o.s. забы́вчивый forgetful. забытьё oblivion; drowsiness.

забью́ *etc.*: see забить

зава́ливать *impf*, завали́ть (-лю́, -лишь) *pf* block up; pile; cram; overload; knock down; make a mess of; ~ся fall; collapse; tip up.

зава́ривать *impf*, завари́ть (-арю́, -а́ришь) *pf* make; brew; weld. зава́рка brewing; brew; welding.

заведе́ние establishment. заве́довать *impf* +*instr* manage.

заве́домо *adv* wittingly. заве́домый notorious, undoubted.

заведу́ *etc.*: see завести́

заве́дующий *sb* (+*instr*) manager; head.

завезти́ (-зу́, -зёшь; -ёз, -ла́) *pf* (*impf* завози́ть) convey, deliver.

за|вербова́ть *pf*.

завери́тель *m* witness. заве́рить *pf* (*impf* заверя́ть) assure; certify; witness.

заверну́ть (-ну́, -нёшь) *pf* (*impf* завёртывать, завора́чивать) wrap, wrap up; roll up; screw tight, screw up; turn (off); drop in, call in.

заверте́ться (-рчу́сь, -ртишься) *pf* begin to turn *or* spin; lose one's head.

завёртывать *impf* of заверну́ть

заверша́ть *impf*, заверши́ть (-шу́) *pf* complete, conclude. заверше́ние completion; end.

заверя́ть *impf* of заве́рить

заве́са veil, screen. заве́сить (-е́шу) *pf* (*impf* заве́шивать) curtain (off).

завести́ (-еду́, -ёшь; -вёл, -а́) *pf* (*impf* заводи́ть) take, bring; drop

off; start up; acquire; introduce; wind (up), crank; ~сь be; appear; be established; start.

заве́т behest, bidding, ordinance; Testament. заве́тный cherished; secret.

заве́шивать *impf* of заве́сить

завеща́ние will, testament. завеща́ть bequeath.

завзя́тый inveterate, out-and-out.

завива́ть(ся *impf* of зави́ть(ся. зави́вка waving; curling; wave.

зави́дно *impers*+*dat*: мне ~ I feel envious. зави́дный enviable. зави́довать *impf* (*pf* по~) +*dat* envy.

завинти́ть (-нчу́) *pf*, зави́нчивать *impf* screw up.

зави́сеть (-и́шу) *impf* +от+*gen* depend on. зави́симость dependence; в зави́симости от depending on; subject to. зави́симый dependent.

зави́стливый envious. за́висть envy.

завито́й (за́вит, -а́, -о) curled, waved. завито́к (-тка́) curl, lock; flourish. зави́ть (-вью́, -вьёшь; -и́л, -а́, -о) *pf* (*impf* завива́ть) curl, wave; ~ся curl, wave, twine; have one's hair curled.

завладева́ть *impf*, завладе́ть (-е́ю) *pf* +*instr* take possession of; seize.

завлека́тельный alluring; fascinating. завлека́ть *impf*, завле́чь (-еку́, -ечёшь: -лёк, -ла́) *pf* lure; fascinate.

заво́д[1] factory; works; studfarm.

заво́д[2] winding mechanism. заводи́ть(ся (-ожу́(сь, -о́дишь(ся) *impf* of завести́(сь. заводно́й clockwork; winding, cranking.

заводско́й factory, factory; *sb* factory worker. заво́дчик factory owner.

за́водь backwater.

завоева́ние winning; conquest; achievement. завоева́тель *m* conqueror. завоева́ть (-ою́ю) *pf*, завоёвывать *impf* conquer; win, gain; try to get.

завожу́ *etc.*: see завести́, завози́ть

заво́з delivery; carriage. завози́ть (-ожу́, -о́зишь) *impf* of завезти́

завора́чивать *impf* of заверну́ть. заворо́т turn, turning; sharp bend.

завою́ *etc.*: see завы́ть

завсегда́ *adv* always. завсегда́тай habitué, frequenter.

за́втра tomorrow. за́втрак breakfast; lunch. за́втракать impf (pf по~) have breakfast; have lunch. за́втрашний tomorrow's; ~ день tomorrow.

завыва́ть impf, завы́ть (-во́ю) pf (begin to) howl.

завяза́ть (-яжу́, -я́жешь) pf (impf завя́зывать) tie, tie up; start; ~ся start; arise; (of fruit) set. завя́зка string, lace; start; opening.

за|вя́знуть (-ну; -я́з) pf. завя́зывать(ся impf of завяза́ть(ся

за|вя́нуть (-ну; -я́л) pf.

загада́ть pf, зага́дывать impf think of; plan ahead; guess at the future; ~ зага́дку ask a riddle. зага́дка riddle; enigma. зага́дочный enigmatic, mysterious.

зага́р sunburn, tan.

за|гаси́ть (-ашу́, -а́сишь) pf. за|га́снуть (-ну) pf.

загво́здка snag; difficulty.

заги́б fold; exaggeration. загиба́ть impf of загну́ть

за|гипнотизи́ровать pf.

загла́вие title; heading. загла́вный title; ~ая бу́ква capital letter.

загла́дить (-а́жу) pf, загла́живать impf iron, iron out; make up for; expiate; ~ся iron out, become smooth; fade.

за|гло́хнуть (-ну; -гло́х) pf.

заглуша́ть impf, за|глуши́ть (-шу́) pf drown, muffle; jam; suppress, stifle; alleviate.

загляде́нье lovely sight загляде́ться (-яжу́сь) pf, загля́дываться impf на+acc stare at; be lost in admiration of. загля́дывать impf, загляну́ть (-ну́, -нешь) pf peep; drop in.

загна́ть (-гоню́, -го́нишь; -а́л, -а́, -о) pf (impf загоня́ть) drive in, drive home; drive; exhaust.

загнива́ние decay; suppuration. загнива́ть impf, загни́ть (-ию́, -иёшь; -и́л, -а́, -о) pf rot; decay; fester.

загну́ть (-ну́, -нёшь) pf (impf загиба́ть) turn up, turn down; bend.

загова́ривать impf, заговори́ть pf begin to speak; tire out with talk; cast a spell over; protect with a charm (от+gen against). за́говор plot; spell. загово́рщик conspirator.

заголо́вок (-вка) title; heading; headline.

заго́н enclosure, pen; driving in. загоня́ть[1] impf of загна́ть. загоня́ть[2] pf tire out; work to death.

загора́живать impf of загороди́ть

загора́ть impf, загоре́ть (-рю́) pf become sunburnt; ~ся catch fire; blaze; impers+dat want very much. загоре́лый sunburnt.

загороди́ть (-рожу́, -ро́дишь) pf (impf загора́живать) enclose, fence in; obstruct. загоро́дка fence, enclosure.

за́городный suburban; country.

загота́вливать impf, заготовля́ть impf, загото́вить (-влю) pf lay in (a stock of); store; prepare. загото́вка (State) procurement, purchase; laying in.

загради́ть (-ажу́) pf, загражда́ть impf block, obstruct; bar. загражде́ние obstruction; barrier.

грани́ца abroad, foreign parts. заграни́чный foreign.

загреба́ть impf, загрести́ (-ебу́, -ебёшь; -ёб, -ла́) pf rake up, gather; rake in.

загри́вок (-вка) withers; nape (of the neck).

за|гримирова́ть pf.

загромозжда́ть impf, загромозди́ть (-зжу́) pf block up, encumber; cram.

загружа́ть impf, за|грузи́ть (-ужу́, -у́зишь) pf load; feed; ~ся +instr load up with, take on. загру́зка loading, feeding; charge, load, capacity.

за|грунтова́ть pf.

загрусти́ть (-ущу́) pf grow sad.

загрязне́ние pollution. за|грязни́ть pf, загрязня́ть impf soil; pollute; ~ся become dirty.

загс abbr (of отде́л) за́писи а́ктов гражда́нского состоя́ния) registry office.

загуби́ть (-блю́, -бишь) pf ruin; squander, waste.

загуля́ть pf, загу́ливать impf take to drink.

за|густе́ть pf.

зад (loc -у́; pl -ы́) back; hindquarters; buttocks; ~ом наперёд back to front.

задава́ть(ся (-даю́(сь) impf of зада́ть(ся

задави́ть (-влю́, -вишь) pf crush; run over.

задади́м etc., зада́м etc.: see зада́ть

зада́ние task, job.

зада́тки (-тков) pl abilities, promise.

зада́ток (-тка) deposit, advance.

зада́ть (-а́м, -а́шь, -а́ст, -ади́м; за́дал, -а́, -о) pf (impf задава́ть) set; give; ~ вопро́с ask a question; ~ся turn out well; succeed; ~ся мы́слью, це́лью make up one's mind. зада́ча problem; task.

задвига́ть impf, задви́нуть (-ну) pf bolt; bar; push; ~ся shut; slide. задви́жка bolt; catch.

задво́рки (-рок) pl back yard; backwoods.

задева́ть impf of заде́ть

заде́лать pf, заде́лывать impf do up; block up, close up.

заде́ну etc.: see заде́ть. задёргивать impf of задёрнуть

задержа́ть (-жу́, -жишь) pf, заде́рживать impf delay; withhold; arrest; ~ся stay too long; be delayed. заде́ржка delay.

задёрнуть (-ну) pf (impf задёргивать) pull; draw.

задеру́ etc.: see задра́ть

заде́ть (-е́ну) pf (impf задева́ть) brush (against), graze; offend; catch (against).

задира m & f bully; trouble-maker. задира́ть impf of задра́ть

за́дн|ий back, rear; дать ~ий ход reverse; ~яя мысль ulterior motive; ~ий план background; ~ий прохо́д anus. за́дник back; backdrop.

задо́лго adv +до+gen long before.

за|должа́ть pf. задо́лженность debts.

задо́р fervour. задо́рный provocative; fervent.

задохну́ться (-ну́сь, -нёшься; -о́хся or -у́лся) pf (impf задыха́ться) suffocate; choke; pant.

за|дра́ть (-деру́, -дерёшь; -а́л, -а́, -о) pf (impf also задира́ть) tear to pieces, kill; lift up; break; provoke, insult.

задрема́ть (-млю́, -млешь) pf doze off.

задрожа́ть (-жу́) pf begin to tremble.

задува́ть impf of заду́ть

заду́мать pf, заду́мывать impf plan; intend; think of; ~ся become thoughtful; meditate. заду́мчивость reverie. заду́мчивый pensive.

заду́ть (-у́ю) pf (impf задува́ть) blow out; begin to blow.

задуше́вный sincere; intimate.

за|души́ть (-ушу́, -у́шишь) pf.

задыха́ться impf of задохну́ться

заеда́ть impf of зае́сть

зае́зд calling in; lap, heat. зае́здить (-зжу) pf override; wear out. заезжа́ть impf of зае́хать. зае́зженный hackneyed; worn out. зае́зжий visiting.

заём (за́йма) loan.

зае́сть (-е́м, -е́шь, -е́ст, -еди́м) pf (impf заеда́ть) torment; jam; entangle.

зае́хать (-е́ду) pf (impf заезжа́ть) call in; enter, ride in, drive in; reach; +за+acc go past; +за+instr call for, fetch.

за|жа́рить(ся pf.

зажа́ть (-жму́, -жмёшь) pf (impf зажима́ть) squeeze; grip; suppress.

заже́чь (-жгу́, -жжёшь; -жёг, -жгла́) pf (impf зажига́ть) set fire to; kindle; light; ~ся catch fire.

зажива́ть impf of зажи́ть. заживи́ть (-влю́) pf, заживля́ть impf heal. за́живо adv alive.

зажига́лка lighter. зажига́ние ignition. зажига́тельный inflammatory; incendiary. зажига́ть(ся impf of заже́чь(ся

зажи́м clamp; terminal; suppression. зажима́ть impf of зажа́ть. зажи́мный tight-fisted.

зажи́точный prosperous. зажи́ть (-иву́, -ивёшь; -ил, -а́, -о) pf (impf зажива́ть) heal; begin to live.

зажму́ etc.: see зажа́ть. за|жму́риться pf.

зазвене́ть (-и́т) pf begin to ring.

зазелене́ть (-е́ет) pf turn green.

заземле́ние earthing; earth. заземли́ть pf, заземля́ть impf earth.

зазнава́ться (-наю́сь, -наёшься) impf, зазна́ться pf give o.s. airs.

зазу́брина notch.

за|зубри́ть (-рю, -у́бри́шь) pf.

заи́грывать impf flirt.

за́йка m & f stammerer. заика́ние stammer. заика́ться impf, заикну́ться (-ну́сь, -нёшься) pf stammer, stutter; +о+prep mention.

заи́мствование borrowing. заи́мствовать impf & pf (pf also по~) borrow.

заинтересо́ванный interested. за-
интересова́ть *pf*, заинтересо́-
вывать *impf* interest; ~ся +*instr*
become interested in.

за́искивать *impf* ingratiate o.s.

зайду́ *etc.*: *see* зайти́. займу́ *etc.*: *see*
заня́ть

зайти́ (-йду́, -йдёшь; зашёл, -шла́) *pf*
(*impf* заходи́ть) call; drop in; set;
+в+*acc* reach; +за+*acc* go behind,
turn; +за+*instr* call for, fetch.

за́йчик little hare (*esp. as endearment*); reflection of sunlight. за́йчи-
ха doe hare.

закаба́лить *pf*, закабаля́ть *impf*
enslave.

закады́чный intimate, bosom.

зака́з order; на ~ to order. заказа́ть
(-ажу́, -а́жешь) *pf*, зака́зывать *impf*
order; book. заказн|о́й made to or-
der; ~о́е (письмо́) registered letter.
зака́зчик customer, client.

зака́л temper; cast. зака́ливать
impf, закали́ть (-лю́) *pf* (*impf also*
закаля́ть) temper; harden. зака́лка
tempering, hardening.

зака́лывать *impf of* заколо́ть. зака-
ля́ть *impf of* закали́ть. зака́н-
чивать(ся *impf of* зако́нчить(ся

зака́пать (-аю), зака́пывать[1] *impf* begin to drip; rain; spot.

зака́пывать[2] *impf of* закопа́ть

зака́т sunset. заката́ть *pf*, зака́-
тывать[1] *impf* begin to roll; roll up;
roll out. закати́ть (-ачу́, -а́тишь) *pf*,
зака́тывать[2] *impf* roll; ~ся roll;
set.

заква́ска ferment; leaven.

закида́ть *pf*, заки́дывать[1] *impf*
shower; bespatter.

заки́дывать[2] *impf*, заки́нуть (-ну)
pf throw (out, away).

закипа́ть *impf*, закипе́ть (-пи́т) *pf*
begin to boil.

закиса́ть *impf*, заки́снуть (-ну; -и́с,
-ла) *pf* turn sour; become apathetic.
за́кись oxide.

закла́д pawn; pledge; bet; би́ться об
~ bet; в ~е in pawn. закла́дка laying; bookmark. закладно́й pawn.
закла́дывать *impf of* заложи́ть

закле́ивать *impf*, закле́ить *pf* glue
up.

за|клейми́ть (-млю́) *pf*.

заклепа́ть *pf*, заклёпывать *impf*

rivet. заклёпка rivet; riveting.

заклина́ние incantation; spell. за-
клина́ть *impf* invoke; entreat.

заключа́ть *impf*, заключи́ть (-чу́)
pf conclude; enter into; contain; confine. заключа́ться consist; lie, be.
заключе́ние conclusion; decision;
confinement. заключённый *sb* prisoner. заключи́тельный final, concluding.

закля́тие pledge. закля́тый sworn.

закова́ть (-кую́, -куёшь) *pf*, зако́-
вывать *impf* chain; shackle.

закола́чивать *impf of* заколоти́ть

заколдо́ванный bewitched; ~ круг
vicious circle. заколдова́ть *pf* bewitch; lay a spell on.

зако́лка hair-grip; hair-slide.

заколоти́ть (-лочу́, -ло́тишь) *pf*
(*impf* закола́чивать) board up;
knock in; knock insensible.

за|коло́ть (-олю́, -о́лешь) *pf* (*impf
also* зака́лывать) stab; pin up;
(*impers*) у меня́ заколо́ло в боку́ I
have a stitch.

зако́н law. законорождённый legitimate. зако́нность legality. за-
ко́нный legal; legitimate.

зако́но- *in comb* law, legal. законо-
ве́дение law, jurisprudence. ~да́-
тельный legislative. ~да́тельство
legislation. ~ме́рность regularity,
normality. ~ме́рный regular, natural. ~прое́кт bill.

за|консерви́ровать *pf*. за|кон-
спекти́ровать *pf*.

зако́нченность completeness. за-
ко́нченный finished; accomplished.
зако́нчить (-чу) *pf* (*impf* закан-
чивать) end, finish; ~ся end, finish.

закопа́ть *pf* (*impf* зака́пывать[2]) begin to dig; bury.

закопте́лый sooty, smutty. за|копт-
те́ть (-ти́т) *pf*. за|копти́ть (-пчу́) *pf*.

закорене́лый deep-rooted; inveterate.

закосне́лый incorrigible.

закоу́лок (-лка) alley; nook.

закочене́лый numb with cold.
за|кочене́ть (-е́ю) *pf*.

закра́дываться *impf of* закра́сться

закра́сить (-а́шу) *pf* (*impf* закра́-
шивать) paint over.

закра́сться (-аду́сь, -адёшься) *pf*
(*impf* закра́дываться) steal in,

creep in.

закра́шивать *impf of* закра́сить

закрепи́тель *m* fixative. **закрепи́ть** (-плю́) *pf*, **закрепля́ть** *impf* fasten; fix; consolidate; +за +*instr* assign to; ~ за собо́й secure.

закрепости́ть (-ощу́) *pf*, **закрепоща́ть** *impf* enslave. **закрепоще́ние** enslavement; slavery, serfdom.

закрича́ть (-чу́) *pf* cry out; begin to shout.

закро́йщик cutter.

закро́ю *etc.: see* закры́ть

закругле́ние rounding; curve. **закругли́ть** (-лю́) *pf*, **закругля́ть** *impf* make round; round off; ~ся become round; round off.

закружи́ться (-ужу́сь, -у́жи́шься) *pf* begin to whirl *or* go round.

за|крути́ть (-учу́, -у́тишь) *pf*, **закру́чивать** *impf* twist, twirl; wind round; turn; screw in; turn the head of; ~ся twist, twirl, whirl; wind round.

закрыва́ть *impf*, **закры́ть** (-ро́ю) *pf* close, shut; turn off; close down; cover; ~ся close, shut; end; close down; cover o.s.; shelter. **закры́тие** closing; shutting; closing down; shelter. **закры́тый** closed, shut; private.

закули́сный behind the scenes; backstage.

закупа́ть *impf*, **закупи́ть** (-плю́, -пишь) *pf* buy up; stock up with. **заку́пка** purchase.

заку́поривать *impf*, **заку́порить** *pf* cork; stop up; coop up. **заку́порка** corking; thrombosis.

заку́почный purchase. **заку́пщик** buyer.

заку́ривать *impf*, **закури́ть** (-рю́, -ришь) *pf* light up; begin to smoke.

закуси́ть (-ушу́, -у́сишь) *pf*, **заку́сывать** *impf* have a snack; bite. **заку́ска** hors-d'oeuvre; snack. **заку́сочная** *sb* snack-bar.

за|ку́тать (-а́ю), **заку́тывать** *impf* wrap up; ~ся wrap o.s. up.

зал hall; ~ ожида́ния waiting-room.

залега́ть *impf of* залечь

за|ледене́ть (-е́ю) *pf*.

залежа́лый stale, long unused. **залежа́ться** (-жу́сь) *pf*, **залёживаться** *impf* lie too long; find no market; become stale. **за́лежь** de-

posit, seam; stale goods.

залеза́ть *impf*, **зале́зть** (-зу; -ез) *pf* climb, climb up; get in; creep in.

за|лепи́ть (-плю́, -пишь) *pf*, **залепля́ть** *impf* paste over; glue up.

залета́ть *impf*, **залете́ть** (-ечу́) *pf* fly; +в +*acc* fly into.

зале́чивать *impf*, **залечи́ть** (-чу́, -чишь) *pf* heal, cure; ~ся heal (up).

зале́чь (-ля́гу, -ля́жешь; залёг, -ла́) *pf* (*impf* залега́ть) lie down; lie low; lie, be deposited.

зали́в bay; gulf. **залива́ть** *impf*, **зали́ть** (-лью́, -льёшь; за́лил, -а́, -о) *pf* flood, inundate; spill on; extinguish; spread; ~ся be flooded; pour, spill; +*instr* break into.

зало́г deposit; pledge; security, mortgage; token; voice. **заложи́ть** (-жу́, -жишь) *pf* (*impf* закла́дывать) lay; put; mislay; pile up; pawn, mortgage; harness; lay in. **зало́жник** hostage.

залп volley, salvo; ~ом without pausing for breath.

залью́ *etc.: see* зали́ть. **заля́гу** *etc.: see* зале́чь

зам *abbr* (*of* замести́тель) assistant, deputy, deputy. **зам-** *abbr in comb* (*of* замести́тель) assistant, deputy, vice-.

за|ма́зать (-а́жу) *pf*, **зама́зывать** *impf* paint over; putty; smear; soil; ~ся get dirty. **зама́зка** putty; puttying.

зама́лчивать *impf of* замолча́ть

зама́нивать *impf*, **замани́ть** (-ню́, -нишь) *pf* entice; decoy. **зама́нчивый** tempting.

за|маринова́ть *pf*.

за|маскирова́ть *pf*, **замаскиро́вывать** *impf* mask; disguise; ~ся disguise o.s.

зама́х threatening gesture. **зама́хиваться** *impf*, **замахну́ться** (-ну́сь, -нёшься) *pf* +*instr* raise threateningly.

зама́чивать *impf of* замочи́ть

замедле́ние slowing down, deceleration; delay. **заме́длить** *pf*, **замедля́ть** *impf* slow down; slacken; delay; ~ся slow down.

замёл *etc.: see* замести́

заме́на substitution; substitute. **замени́мый** replaceable. **замени́тель** *m* (+*gen*) substitute (for). **замени́ть** (-ню́, -нишь) *pf*, **заменя́ть** *impf* re-

place; be a substitute for.
замере́ть (-мру́, -мрёшь; за́мер, -ла́, -о) *pf* (*impf* замира́ть) stand still; freeze; die away.
замерза́ние freezing. **замерза́ть** *impf*, **за|мёрзнуть** (-ну) *pf* freeze (up); freeze to death.
заме́рить *pf* (*impf* замеря́ть) measure, gauge.
замеси́ть (-ешу́, -е́сишь) *pf* (*impf* заме́шивать[2]) knead.
замести́ (-ету́, -ете́шь; -мёл, -а́) *pf* (*impf* замета́ть) sweep up; cover.
замести́тель *m* substitute; assistant, deputy, vice-. **замести́ть** (-ещу́) *pf* (*impf* замеща́ть) replace; deputize for.
замета́ть[1] *pf of* замести́
заме́тить (-е́чу) *pf* (*impf* замеча́ть) notice; note; remark. **заме́тка** mark; note. **заме́тный** noticeable; outstanding.
замеча́ние remark; reprimand. **замеча́тельный** remarkable; splendid.
замеча́ть *impf of* заме́тить
замеша́тельство confusion; embarrassment. **замеша́ть** *pf*, **заме́шивать**[1] *impf* mix up, entangle. **заме́шивать**[2] *impf of* замеси́ть
замеща́ть *impf of* замести́ть. **замеще́ние** substitution; filling.
зами́нка hitch; hesitation.
замира́ть *impf of* замере́ть
за́мкнутый reserved; closed, exclusive. **замкну́ть** (-ну́, -нёшь) *pf* (*impf* замыка́ть) lock; close; ~ся close; shut o.s. up; become reserved.
замо́к[1] (-мка́) castle.
замо́к[2] (-мка́) lock; padlock; clasp.
замолка́ть *impf*, **замо́лкнуть** (-ну; -мо́лк) *pf* fall silent; stop.
замолча́ть (-чу́) *pf* (*impf* зама́лчивать) fall silent; cease corresponding; hush up.
замора́живать *impf*, **заморо́зить** (-ро́жу) *pf* freeze. **заморо́женный** frozen; iced. **за́морозки** (-ов) *pl* (slight) frosts.
замо́рский overseas.
за|мочи́ть (-чу́, -чишь) *pf* (*impf also* зама́чивать) wet; soak; ret.
замо́чная сква́жина keyhole.
замру́ *etc.*: *see* замере́ть
за́муж *adv*: вы́йти ~ (за+*acc*) marry. **за́мужем** *adv* married (за+*instr* to).

за|му́чить (-чу) *pf* torment; wear out; bore to tears. **за|му́читься** (-чусь) *pf*.
за́мша suede.
замыка́ние locking; short circuit. **замыка́ть(ся** *impf of* замкну́ть(ся
за́мысел (-сла) project, plan. **за|мы́слить** *pf*, **замышля́ть** *impf* plan; contemplate.
за́навес, **занаве́ска** curtain.
занести́ (-су́, -сёшь; -ёс, -ла́) *pf* (*impf* заноси́ть) bring; note down; (*impers*) cover with snow etc.; (*impers*) skid.
занима́ть *impf* (*pf* заня́ть) occupy; interest; engage; borrow; ~ся +*instr* be occupied with; work at; study.
зано́за splinter. **занози́ть** (-ожу́) *pf* get a splinter in.
зано́с snow-drift; skid. **заноси́ть** (-ошу́, -о́сишь) *impf of* занести́.
зано́счивый arrogant.
заня́тие occupation; *pl* studies.
занято́й busy. **за́нятый** (-нят, -á, -о) occupied; taken; engaged. **заня́ть(ся** (займу́(сь, -мёшь(ся; за́нял(ся, -á(сь, -о(сь) *pf of* занима́ть(ся
заодно́ *adv* in concert; at one; at the same time.
заостри́ть *pf*, **заостря́ть** *impf* sharpen; emphasize.
зао́чник, **-ница** student taking correspondence course; external student. **зао́чно** *adv* in one's absence; by correspondence course. **зао́чный курс** correspondence course.
за́пад west. **за́падный** west, western; westerly.
западня́ (*gen pl* -не́й) trap; pitfall, snare.
за|пакова́ть *pf*, **запако́вывать** *impf* pack; wrap up.
запа́л ignition; fuse. **запа́ливать** *impf*, **запали́ть** *pf* light, kindle; set fire to. **запа́льная свеча́** (spark-)plug.
запа́с reserve; supply; hem. **запаса́ть** *impf*, **запасти́** (-су́, -сёшь; -áс, -лá) *pf* stock, store; lay in a stock of; ~ся +*instr* provide o.s. with; stock up with. **запасно́й** *sb* reservist. **запасно́й**, **запа́сный** spare; reserve; ~ вы́ход emergency exit.
за́пах smell.
запа́хивать *impf*, **запахну́ть**[2] (-ну́, -нёшь) *pf* wrap up.
запа́хнуть[1] (-ну; -áх) *pf* begin to smell.

за|па́чкать pf.

запека́ть(ся impf of запе́чь(ся. запеку́ etc.: see запе́чь

за|пелена́ть pf.

запере́ть (-пру́, -прёшь; за́пер, -ла́, -ло) pf (impf запира́ть) lock; lock in; bar; ~ся lock o.s. in.

запеча́тать pf, запеча́тывать impf seal. запечатлева́ть impf, запечатле́ть (-е́ю) pf imprint, engrave.

запе́чь (-еку́, -ечёшь; -пёк, -ла́) pf (impf запека́ть) bake; ~ся bake; become parched; clot, coagulate.

запива́ть impf of запи́ть

запина́ться impf of запну́ться. запи́нка nesitation.

запира́ть(ся impf of запере́ть(ся

записа́ть (-ишу́, -и́шешь) pf, запи́сывать impf note; take down; record; enter; ~ся register, enrol (в+acc at, in). запи́ска note. запи́сн|о́й note; inveterate; ~ая кни́жка notebook. за́пись recording; registration; record.

запи́ть (-пью́, -пьёшь; за́пи́л, -а́, -о) pf (impf запива́ть) begin drinking; wash down (with).

запиха́ть pf, запи́хивать impf, запихну́ть (-ну́, -нёшь) pf push in, cram in.

запишу́ etc.: see записа́ть

запла́кать (-а́чу) pf begin to cry.

за|плани́ровать pf.

запла́та patch.

за|плати́ть (-ачу́, -а́тишь) pf pay (за+acc for).

запла́чу etc.: see запла́кать. запла́чу see заплати́ть

заплести́ (-ету́, -етёшь; -ёл, -а́) pf, заплета́ть impf plait.

за|пломбирова́ть pf.

заплы́в heat, round. заплыва́ть impf, заплы́ть (-ыву́, -ывёшь; -ы́л, -а́, -о) pf swim in, sail in; swim out, sail out; be bloated.

запну́ться (-ну́сь, -нёшься) pf (impf запина́ться) hesitate; stumble.

запове́дник reserve; preserve; госуда́рственный ~ national park. запове́дный prohibited. за́поведь precept; commandment.

заподо́зривать impf, заподо́зрить pf suspect (в+prep of).

запозда́лый belated; delayed. запозда́ть pf (impf запа́здывать)

be late.

запо́й hard drinking.

заполза́ть impf, заползти́ pf (-зу́, -зёшь; -о́лз, -зла́) creep, crawl.

запо́лнить pf, заполня́ть impf fill (in, up).

запомина́ть impf, запо́мнить pf remember; memorize; ~ся stay in one's mind.

запо́нка cuff-link; stud.

запо́р bolt; lock; constipation.

за|поте́ть (-е́ет) pf mist over.

запою́ etc.: see запе́ть

запра́вить (-влю) pf, заправля́ть impf tuck in; prepare; refuel; season, dress; mix in; ~ся refuel. запра́вка refuelling; seasoning, dressing.

запра́шивать impf of запроси́ть

запре́т prohibition, ban. запрети́ть (-ещу́) pf, запреща́ть impf prohibit, ban. запре́тный forbidden. запреще́ние prohibition.

за|программи́ровать pf.

запро́с inquiry; overcharging; pl needs. запроси́ть (-ошу́, -о́сишь) pf (impf запра́шивать) inquire.

за́просто adv without ceremony.

запрошу́ etc.: see запроси́ть. запру́ etc.: see запере́ть

запру́да dam, weir; mill-pond.

запряга́ть impf, запря́чь (-ягу́, -яжёшь; -я́г, -ла́) pf harness; yoke.

запуга́ть pf, запу́гивать impf cow, intimidate.

за́пуск launching. запуска́ть impf, запусти́ть (-ущу́, -у́стишь) pf thrust (in); start; launch; (+acc or instr) fling; neglect. запусте́лый neglected; desolate. запусте́ние neglect; desolation.

за|пу́тать pf, запу́тывать impf tangle; confuse; ~ся get tangled; get involved.

запущу́ etc.: see запусти́ть

запча́сть (gen pl -е́й) abbr (of запасна́я часть) spare part.

запыха́ться pf be out of breath.

запью́ etc.: see запи́ть

запя́стье wrist.

запята́я sb comma.

за|пятна́ть pf.

зараба́тывать impf, зарабо́тать pf earn; start (up). заработн|ый: ~ая пла́та wages; pay. за́работок (-тка) earnings.

заража́ть impf, **зарази́ть** (-ажу́) pf infect; ~ся +instr be infected with, catch. **зара́за** infection. **зарази́тельный** infectious. **зара́зный** infectious.

зара́нее adv in good time; in advance.

зараста́ть impf, **зарасти́** (-ту́, -тёшь; -ро́с, -ла́) pf be overgrown; heal. **за́рево** glow.

за|регистри́ровать(ся pf.

за|ре́зать (-е́жу) pf kill, knife; slaughter.

зарека́ться impf of заре́чься

зарекомендова́ть pf: ~ себя́ +instr show o.s. to be.

заре́чься (-еку́сь, -ечёшься; -ёкся, -екла́сь) pf (impf зарека́ться) +inf renounce.

за|ржа́веть (-еет) pf.

зарисо́вка sketching; sketch.

зароди́ть (-ожу́) pf, **зарожда́ть** impf generate; ~ся be born; arise. **заро́дыш** foetus; embryo. **зарожде́ние** conception; origin.

заро́к vow, pledge.

заро́с etc.: see зарасти́

зарою́ etc.: see зары́ть

зарпла́та abbr (of за́работная пла́та) wages; pay.

заруба́ть impf of заруби́ть

зарубе́жный foreign.

заруби́ть (-блю́, -бишь) pf (impf заруба́ть) kill, cut down; notch. **зару́бка** notch.

заруча́ться impf, **заручи́ться** (-чу́сь) pf +instr secure.

зарыва́ть impf, **зары́ть** (-ро́ю) pf bury.

заря́ (pl зо́ри, зорь) dawn; sunset.

заря́д charge; supply. **заряди́ть** (-яжу́, -я́дишь) pf, **заряжа́ть** impf load; charge; stoke; ~ся be loaded; be charged. **заря́дка** loading; charging; exercises.

заса́да ambush. **засади́ть** (-ажу́, -а́дишь) pf, **заса́живать** impf plant; drive; set (за+acc to); ~ (в тюрьму́) put in prison. **заса́живаться** impf of засе́сть

заса́ливать impf of засоли́ть

засвети́ть (-ечу́, -е́тишь) pf light; ~ся light up.

за|свиде́тельствовать pf.

засе́в sowing; seed; sown area.

засева́ть impf of засе́ять

заседа́ние meeting; session. **заседа́ть** impf sit, be in session.

засе́ивать impf of засе́ять. **засе́к** etc.: see засе́чь. **засека́ть** impf of засе́чь

засекре́тить (-ре́чу) pf, **засекре́чивать** impf classify as secret; clear, give access to secret material.

засеку́ etc.: see засе́чь. **засёл** etc.: see засе́сть

заселе́ние settlement. **засели́ть** pf, **заселя́ть** impf settle; colonize; populate.

засе́сть (-ся́ду; -сёл) pf (impf заса́живаться) sit down; sit tight; settle; lodge in.

засе́чь (-еку́, -ечёшь; -ёк, -ла́) pf (impf засека́ть) flog to death; notch.

засе́ять (-е́ю) pf (impf засева́ть, засе́ивать) sow.

заси́лье dominance, sway.

заслони́ть pf, **заслоня́ть** impf cover, screen; push into the background. **засло́нка** (furnace, oven) door.

заслу́га merit, desert; service. **заслу́женный** deserved, merited; Honoured; time-honoured. **заслу́живать** impf, **заслужи́ть** (-ужу́, -у́жишь) pf deserve; earn; +gen be worthy of.

засмея́ться (-ею́сь, -еёшься) begin to laugh.

заснима́ть impf of засня́ть

засну́ть (-ну́, -нёшь) pf (impf засыпа́ть) fall asleep.

засня́ть (-ниму́, -и́мешь; -я́л, -а́, -о) pf (impf заснима́ть) photograph.

засо́в bolt, bar.

засо́вывать impf of засу́нуть

засо́л salting, pickling. **засоли́ть** (-олю́, -о́лишь) pf (impf заса́ливать) salt, pickle.

засоре́ние littering; contamination; obstruction. **засори́ть** pf, **засоря́ть** impf litter; get dirt into; clog.

за|со́хнуть (-ну; -со́х) pf (impf also засыха́ть) dry (up); wither.

заста́ва gate; outpost.

застава́ть (-таю́, -таёшь) impf of заста́ть

заста́вить (-влю) pf, **заставля́ть** impf make; compel.

заста́иваться impf of застоя́ться.

застáну *etc.*: *see* застáть

застáть (-áну) *pf* (*impf* заставáть) find; catch.

застёгивать *impf*, застегнýть (-нý, -нёшь) *pf* fasten, do up. застёжка fastening; clasp, buckle; ~-мóлния zip.

застеклúть *pf*, застеклять *impf* glaze.

застéнок (-нка) torture chamber.

застéнчивый shy.

застигáть *impf*, застúгнуть, застúчь (-úгну; -úг) *pf* catch; take unawares.

застúчь *see* застигнуть

застóй stagnation. застóйный stagnant.

за|стóпориться *pf*.

застояться (-úтся) *pf* (*impf* застáиваться) stagnate; stand too long.

застрáивать *impf of* застрóить

застрахóванный insured. за|страховáть, застрахóвывать *impf* insure.

застревáть *impf of* застрять

застрелúть (-елю́, -éлишь) *pf* shoot (dead); ~ся shoot o.s.

застрóить (-óю) *pf* (*impf* застрáивать) build over, on, up. застрóйка building.

застрять (-яну) *pf* (*impf* застревáть) stick; get stuck.

застýп spade.

заступáться *impf*, заступúться (-плю́сь, -пишься) *pf* +за+*acc* stand up for. застýпник defender. застýпничество protection; intercession.

застывáть *impf*, застыть (-ы́ну) *pf* harden, set; become stiff; freeze; be petrified.

засýнуть (-ну) *pf* (*impf* засóвывать) thrust in, push in.

зáсуха drought.

засыпáть[1] (-плю) *pf*, засыпáть *impf* fill up; strew.

засыпáть[2] *impf of* заснýть

засыхáть *impf of* засóхнуть.

засýдду *etc.*: *see* засéсться

затаённый (-ён, -енá) secret; repressed. затáивать *impf*, затаúть *pf* suppress; conceal; harbour; ~ дыхáние hold one's breath.

затáпливать *impf of* затопúть.

затáптывать *impf of* затоптáть

затáскивать *impf*, затащúть (-щý, -щишь) *pf* drag in; drag off; drag away.

затвердевáть *impf*, за|твердéть (-éет) *pf* become hard; set. затвердéние hardening; callus.

затвóр bolt; lock; shutter; flood-gate. затворúть (-рю́, -ришь) *pf*, затворять *impf* shut, close; ~ся shut o.s. up, lock o.s. in. затвóрник hermit, recluse.

затевáть *impf of* затéять

затёк *etc.*: *see* затéчь. затекáть *impf of* затéчь

затéм *adv* then, next; ~ что because.

затемнéние darkening, obscuring; blacking out; black-out. затемнúть *pf*, затемнять *impf* darken, obscure; black out.

затéривать *impf*, затерять *pf* lose, mislay; ~ся be lost; be mislaid; be forgotten.

затéчь (-ечёт, -екýт; -тёк, -клá) *pf* (*impf* затекáть) pour, flow; swell up; become numb.

затéя undertaking, venture; escapade; joke. затéять *pf* (*impf* затевáть) undertake, venture.

затихáть *impf*, затúхнуть (-ну; -тúх) *pf* die down, abate; fade. затúшье calm; lull.

заткнýть (-нý, -нёшь) *pf* (*impf* затыкáть) stop up; plug, thrust.

затмевáть *impf*, затмúть (-мúшь) *pf* darken; eclipse; overshadow. затмéние eclipse.

затó *conj* but then, but on the other hand.

затонýть (-óнет) *pf* sink, be submerged.

затопúть[1] (-плю́, -пишь) *pf* (*impf* затáпливать) light; turn on the heating.

затопúть[2] (-плю́, -пишь) *pf*, затоплять *impf* flood, submerge; sink.

затоптáть (-пчý, -пчешь) *pf* (*impf* затáптывать) trample (down).

затóр obstruction, jam; congestion.

за|тормозúть (-ожý) *pf*.

заточáть *impf*, заточúть (-чý) *pf* incarcerate. заточéние incarceration.

затрáгивать *impf of* затрóнуть

затрáта expense; outlay. затрáтить (-áчу) *pf*, затрáчивать *impf* spend.

затрёбовать *pf* request, require; ask for.

затро́нуть (-ну) *pf* (*impf* затра́гивать) affect; touch (on).

затрудне́ние difficulty. затрудни́тельный difficult. затрудни́ть *pf*, затрудня́ть *impf* trouble; make difficult; hamper; ∼ся +*inf or instr* find difficulty in.

за|тупи́ться (-пится) *pf*.

за|туши́ть (-шу́, -шишь) *pf* extinguish; suppress.

за́тхлый musty, mouldy; stuffy.

затыка́ть *impf of* заткну́ть

заты́лок (-лка) back of the head; scrag-end.

затя́гивать *impf*, затяну́ть (-ну́, -нешь) *pf* tighten; cover; close, heal; spin out; ∼ся be covered; close; be delayed; drag on; inhale. затя́жка inhaling; prolongation; delaying, putting off; lagging. затяжно́й long-drawn-out.

заурядный ordinary; mediocre.

зау́треня morning service.

зау́чивать *impf*, заучи́ть (-чу́, -чишь) *pf* learn by heart.

за|фарширо́ва́ть *pf*. за|фикси́ровать *pf*. за|фрахтова́ть *pf*.

захва́т seizure, capture. захвати́ть (-ачу́, -а́тишь) *pf*, захва́тывать *impf* take; seize; thrill. захва́тнический aggressive. захва́тчик aggressor. захва́тывающий gripping.

захлебну́ться (-ну́сь, -нёшься) *pf*, захлёбываться *impf* choke (от+*gen* with).

захлестну́ть (-ну́, -нёшь) *pf*, захлёстывать *impf* flow over, swamp, overwhelm.

захло́пнуть (-ну) *pf*, захло́пывать *impf* slam, bang; ∼ся slam (to).

захо́д sunset; calling in. заходи́ть (-ожу́, -о́дишь) *impf of* зайти́

захолу́стный remote, provincial. захолу́стье backwoods.

за|хорони́ть (-ню́, -нишь) *pf*. за|хоте́ть(ся (-очу́(сь, -о́чешь(ся, -оти́м(ся) *pf*.

зацвести́ (-етёт; -вёл, -а́) *pf*, зацвета́ть *impf* come into bloom.

зацепи́ть (-плю́, -пишь) *pf*, зацепля́ть *impf* hook; engage; sting; catch (за+*acc* on); ∼ся за+*acc* catch on; catch hold of.

зачасту́ю *adv* often.

зача́тие conception. зача́ток (-тка) embryo; rudiment; germ. зача́точный rudimentary. зача́ть (-чну́, -чнёшь; -ча́л, -а́, -о) *pf* (*impf* зачина́ть) conceive.

зачёл *etc.: see* заче́сть

зачём *adv* why; what for. зачём-то *adv* for some reason.

заче́ркивать *impf*, зачеркну́ть (-ну́, -нёшь) *pf* cross out.

зачерпну́ть (-ну́, -нёшь) *pf*, заче́рпывать *impf* scoop up; draw up.

за|черстве́ть (-éет) *pf*.

заче́сть (-чту, -чтёшь; -чёл, -чла́) *pf* (*impf* зачи́тывать) take into account, reckon as credit. зачёт test; получи́ть, сдать ∼ no+*dat* pass a test in; поста́вить ∼ no+*dat* pass in. зачётная кни́жка (student's) record book.

зачина́ть *impf of* зача́ть. зачи́нщик instigator.

зачи́слить *pf*, зачисля́ть *impf* include; enter; enlist; ∼ся join, enter.

зачи́тывать *impf of* заче́сть. зачту́ *etc.: see* заче́сть. зашёл *etc.: see* зайти́

зашива́ть *impf*, заши́ть (-шью́, -шьёшь) *pf* sew up.

за|шифрова́ть *pf*, зашифро́вывать *impf* encipher, encode.

за|шнурова́ть *pf*, зашнуро́вывать *impf* lace up.

за|шпаклева́ть (-лю́ю) *pf*. за|штопать *pf*. за|штрихова́ть *pf*. зашью́ *etc.: see* заши́ть

защи́та defence; protection. защити́ть (-ищу́) *pf*, защища́ть *impf* defend, protect. защи́тник defender. защи́тный protective.

заяви́ть (-влю́, -вишь) *pf*, заявля́ть *impf* announce, declare; ∼ся turn up. зая́вка claim; demand. заявле́ние statement; application.

за́яц (за́йца) hare; stowaway; éхать за́йцем travel without a ticket.

зва́ние rank; title. зва́ный invited; ∼ обéд banquet, dinner. зва́тельный vocative. звать (зову́, -вёшь; звал, -á, -о) *impf* (*pf* по∼) call; ask, invite; как вас зову́т? what is your name?; ∼ся be called.

звезда́ (*pl* звёзды) star. звёздный star; starry; starlit; stellar. звёз-

дочка little star; asterisk.
звене́ть (-ню́) *impf* ring; +*instr* jingle, clink.
звено́ (*pl* звенья, -ьев) link; team, section; unit; component. **звеньево́й** *sb* section leader.
звери́нец (-нца) menagerie. **зверово́дство** fur farming. **зве́рский** brutal; terrific. **зве́рство** atrocity. **зве́рствовать** *impf* commit atrocities. **зверь** (*pl* -и, -е́й) *m* wild animal.
звон ringing (sound); peal, chink, clink. **звони́ть** *impf* (*pf* по~) ring; ring up; ~ кому́-нибудь (по телефо́ну) ring s.o. up. **зво́нкий** (-нок, -нка́, -о) ringing, clear. **звоно́к** (-нка́) bell; (*telephone*) call.
звук sound.
зву́ко- *in comb* sound. **звукоза́пись** (sound) recording. **~изоля́ция** sound-proofing. **~непроница́емый** sound-proof. **~сни́матель** *m* pickup.
звуково́й sound; audio; acoustic. **звуча́ние** sound(ing); vibration. **звуча́ть** (-чи́т) *impf* (*pf* про~) be heard; sound. **зву́чный** (-чен, -чна́, -о) sonorous.
зда́ние building.
здесь *adv* here. **зде́шний** local; не ~ a stranger here.
здоро́ваться *impf* (*pf* по~) exchange greetings. **здо́рово** *adv* splendidly; very (much); well done!; great! **здоро́вый** healthy, strong; well; wholesome, sound. **здоро́вье** health; за ва́ше ~! your health! как ва́ше ~? how are you? **здра́вница** sanatorium.
здравомы́слящий sensible, judicious. **здравоохране́ние** public health.
здра́вствовать *impf* be healthy; prosper. **здра́вствуй(те)** how do you do?; hello! **да здра́вствует!** long live! **здра́вый** sensible; ~ смысл common sense.
зе́бра zebra.
зева́ть *impf*, **зевну́ть** (-ну́, -нёшь) *pf* yawn; gape; (*pf also* про~) miss, let slip, lose. **зево́к** (-вка́), **зево́та** yawn.
зелене́ть (-е́ет) *impf* (*pf* по~) turn green; show green. **зелёный** (зе́лен,

-а́, -о) green; ~ лук spring onions. **зе́лень** green; greenery; greens.
земе́льный land.
земле- *in comb* land; earth. **землевладе́лец** (-льца) landowner. **~де́лец** (-льца) farmer. **~де́лие** farming, agriculture. **~де́льческий** agricultural. **~ко́п** navvy. **~ро́йный** excavating. **~трясе́ние** earthquake.
земля́ (*acc* -ю; *pl* -и, земе́ль, -ям) earth; land; soil. **земля́к** (-а́) fellow-countryman. **земляни́ка** (*no pl; usu collect*) wild strawberry; wild strawberries. **земля́нка** dug-out; mud hut. **земляно́й** earthen; earth; earthy. **земля́чка** country-woman. **земно́й** earthly; terrestrial; ground; mundane; ~ шар the globe.
зени́т zenith. **зени́тный** zenith; anti-aircraft.
зе́ркало (*pl* -а́) mirror. **зерка́льный** mirror; smooth; plate-glass.
зерни́стый grainy. **зерно́** (*pl* зёрна, зёрен) grain; seed; kernel; core; кофе в зёрнах coffee beans. **зерново́й** grain. **зерновы́е** *sb pl* cereals. **зернохрани́лище** granary.
зигза́г zigzag.
зима́ (*acc* -у, *pl* -ы) winter. **зи́мний** winter, wintry. **зимова́ть** *impf* (*pf* пере~, про~) spend the winter; hibernate. **зимо́вка** wintering; hibernation. **зимо́вье** winter quarters. **зимо́й** *adv* in winter.
зия́ть *impf* gape, yawn.
злак grass; cereal.
злить (злю) *impf* (*pf* обо~, о~, разо~) anger; irritate; ~ся be angry, be in a bad temper; rage. **зло** (*gen pl* зол) evil; harm; misfortune; malice.
зло- *in comb* evil, harm, malice. **злове́щий** ominous. **~во́ние** stink. **~во́нный** stinking. **~ка́чественный** malignant; pernicious. **~па́мятный** rancorous, unforgiving. **~ра́дный** malevolent, gloating. **~сло́вие** malicious gossip. **~умы́шленник** malefactor; plotter. **~язы́чный** slanderous.
зло́ба spite; anger; ~ дня topic of the day, latest news. **зло́бный** malicious. **злободне́вный** topical. **злоде́й** villain. **злоде́йский** villainous. **злоде́йство** villainy; crime, evil

deed. **злодея́ние** crime, evil deed.
злой (зол, зла) evil; wicked; malicious; vicious; bad-tempered; severe.
зло́стный malicious; intentional.
злость malice; fury.
злоупотреби́ть (-блю́) *pf*, **злоупотребля́ть** *impf* +*instr* abuse.
злоупотребле́ние +*instr* abuse of.
змеи́ный snake; cunning. **змей** snake; dragon; kite. **змея́** (*pl* -и) snake.
знак sign; mark; symbol.
знако́мить (-млю) *impf* (*pf* о~, по~) acquaint; introduce; ~ся become acquainted; get to know; +c+*instr* meet, make the acquaintance of. **знако́мство** acquaintance; (circle of) acquaintances. **знако́мый** familiar; быть ~ым c+*instr* be acquainted with, know; ~ый, ~ая *sb* acquaintance.
знамена́тель *m* denominator. **знамена́тельный** significant. **знаме́ние** sign. **знамени́тость** celebrity. **знамени́тый** celebrated, famous. **зна́мя** (-мени; *pl* -мёна) *neut* banner; flag.
зна́ние knowledge.
зна́тный (-тен, -тна́, -о) distinguished; aristocratic; splendid. **знато́к** (-а́) expert; connoisseur. **знать** *impf* know; дать ~ inform, let know.
значе́ние meaning; significance; importance. **зна́чит** so then; that means. **значи́тельный** considerable; important; significant. **зна́чить** (-чу) *impf* mean; signify; be of importance; ~ся be mentioned, appear. **значо́к** (-чка́) badge; mark.
зна́ющий expert; learned.
зноби́ть *impf*, *impers*+*acc*: меня́, *etc*., **зноби́т** I feel shivery.
зной intense heat. **зно́йный** hot; burning.
зов call, summons. **зову́** *etc.: see* **звать**
зо́дчество architecture. **зо́дчий** *sb* architect.
зол *see* **зло, злой**
зола́ ashes, cinders.
золо́вка sister-in-law (*husband's sister*).
золоти́стый golden. **зо́лото** gold. **золото́й** gold; golden.
золочёный gilt, gilded.

зо́на zone; region.
зонд probe. **зонди́ровать** *impf* sound, probe.
зонт (-а́), **зо́нтик** umbrella.
зоо́лог zoologist. **зоологи́ческий** zoological. **зооло́гия** zoology. **зоопа́рк** zoo. **зоотехник** livestock specialist.
зо́ри *etc.: see* **заря́**
зо́ркий (-рок, -рка́, -о) sharp-sighted; perspicacious.
зрачо́к (-чка́) pupil (*of the eye*).
зре́лище sight; spectacle.
зре́лость ripeness; maturity; **аттеста́т зре́лости** school-leaving certificate. **зре́лый** (зрел, -а́, -о) ripe, mature.
зре́ние (eye)sight, vision; **то́чка зре́ния** point of view.
зреть (-е́ю) *impf* (*pf* co~) ripen; mature.
зри́мый visible.
зри́тель *m* spectator, observer; *pl* audience. **зри́тельный** visual; optic; ~ зал hall, auditorium.
зря *adv* in vain.
зуб (*pl* -ы *or* -бья, -о́в *or* -бьев) tooth; cog. **зуби́ло** chisel. **зубно́й** dental; tooth; ~ врач dentist. **зубовраче́бный** dentists', dental; ~ кабине́т dental surgery. **зубочи́стка** toothpick.
зубр (European) bison; die-hard.
зубри́ть (-рю́, зубри́шь) *impf* (*pf* вы~, за~) cram.
зубча́тый toothed; serrated.
зуд itch. **зуде́ть** (-и́т) itch.
зы́бкий (-бок, -бка́, -о) unsteady, shaky; vacillating. **зыбь** (*gen pl* -е́й) ripple, rippling.
зюйд (*naut*) south; south wind.
зя́блик chaffinch.
зя́бнуть (-ну; зяб) *impf* suffer from cold, feel the cold.
зябь land ploughed in autumn for spring sowing.
зять (*pl* -тья́, -тьёв) son-in-law; brother-in-law (*sister's husband or husband's sister's husband*).

И, Й

и *conj* and; even; too; (*with neg*) either; и... и both ... and.

йбо *conj* for.

йва willow.

иглá (*pl* -ы) needle; thorn; spine; quill. **иглоукáлывание** acupuncture.

игнорúровать *impf & pf* ignore.

йго yoke.

игóлка needle.

игóрный gaming, gambling. **игрá** (*pl* -ы) play, playing; game; hand; turn; ~ слов pun. **игрáльн|ый** playing; ~ые кóсти dice. **игрáть** *impf* (*pf* сыгрáть) play; act; ~ в+*acc* play (*game*); ~ на+*prep* play (*an instrument*). **игрúвый** playful. **игрóк** (-á) player; gambler. **игрýшка** toy.

идеáл ideal. **идеалúзм** idealism. **идеáльный** ideal.

идéйный high-principled; acting on principle; ideological.

идеологúческий ideological. **идеолóгия** ideology.

идёт *etc.*: *see* идтú

идéя idea; concept.

идúллия idyll.

идиóт idiot.

йдол idol.

идтú (идý, идёшь; шёл, шла) *impf* (*pf* пойтú) go; come; run, work; pass; go on, be in progress; be on; fall; +(к+)*dat* suit.

иерéй priest.

иждивéнец (-нца), -вéнка dependant. **иждивéние** maintenance; на иждивéнии at the expense of.

из, изо *prep*+*gen* from, out of, of.

избá (*pl* -ы) izba (*hut*).

избáвить (-влю) *pf*, **избавля́ть** *impf* save, deliver; ~ся be saved, escape; ~ся от get rid of; get out of.

избалóванный spoilt.

избегáть *impf*, **избéгнуть** (-ну; -бéг(нул)) *pf*, **избежáть** (-егу́) *pf* +*gen* or *inf* avoid; escape, evade.

изберý *etc.*: *see* избрáть

избивáть *impf* of избúть. **избиéние** slaughter, massacre; beating, beating-up.

избирáтель *m*, ~ница elector, voter. **избирáтельный** electoral; election. **избирáть** *impf* of избрáть

избúтый trite, hackneyed. **избúть** (изобью́, -бьёшь) *pf* (*impf* избивáть) beat unmercifully, beat up; massacre.

йзбранн|ый selected; select; ~ые *sb*

pl the élite. **избрáть** (-берý, -берёшь; -áл, -á, -о) *pf* (*impf* избирáть) elect; choose.

избы́ток (-тка) surplus; abundance. **избы́точный** surplus; abundant.

йзверг monster. **изверже́ние** eruption; expulsion; excretion.

извернýться (-нýсь, -нёшься) *pf* (*impf* изворáчиваться) dodge, be evasive.

извéстие news; information; *pl* proceedings. **известúть** (-ещý) *pf* (*impf* извещáть) inform, notify.

извéстка lime.

извéстно it is (well) known; of course, certainly. **извéстность** fame, reputation. **извéстный** known; well-known, famous; notorious; certain.

известня́к (-á) limestone. **йзвесть** lime.

извещáть *impf* of известúть. **извеще́ние** notification; advice.

извивáться *impf* coil; writhe; twist, wind; meander. **извúлина** bend, twist. **извúлистый** winding; meandering.

извинéние excuse; apology. **извинúть** *pf*, **извиня́ть** *impf* excuse; извинúте excuse me, (I'm) sorry; ~ся apologise; excuse o.s.

извúться (изовью́сь, -вьёшься; -úлся, -áсь, -ось) *pf* coil; writhe.

извлекáть *impf*, **извлéчь** (-екý, -ечёшь; -ёк, -лá) *pf* extract; derive, elicit.

извнé *adv* from outside.

извóзчик cabman; carrier.

изворáчиваться *impf* of извернýться. **извóрот** bend, twist; *pl* tricks, wiles. **извóротливый** resourceful; shrewd.

извратúть (-ащý) *pf*, **извращáть** *impf* distort; pervert. **извраще́ние** perversion; distortion. **извращённый** perverted, unnatural.

изгúб bend, twist. **изгибáть(ся** *impf* of изогнýть(ся

изгнáние banishment; exile. **изгнáнник** exile. **изгнáть** (-гоню́, -гóнишь; -áл, -á, -о) *pf* (*impf* изгоня́ть) banish; exile.

изголóвье bed-head.

изголодáться be famished, starve; +по+*dat* yearn for.

изгоню́ *etc.*: *see* изгнáть. **изгоня́ть**

impf of изгна́ть
и́згородь fence, hedge.
изгота́вливать *impf*, **изгото́вить** (-влю) *pf*, **изготовля́ть** *impf* make, manufacture; ~ся get ready. **изгото-вле́ние** making, manufacture.
издава́ть (-даю́, -даёшь) *impf of* изда́ть
и́здавна *adv* from time immemorial; for a very long time.
издади́м *etc.: see* изда́ть
издалека́, и́здали *advs* from afar.
изда́ние publication; edition; promulgation. **изда́тель** *m* publisher. **изда́тельство** publishing house. **изда́ть** (-а́м, -а́шь, -а́ст, -ади́м; -а́л, -á, -о) *pf* (*impf* издава́ть) publish; promulgate; produce; emit; ~ся be published.
издева́тельство mockery; taunt. **изде-ва́ться** *impf* (+над+*instr*) mock (at).
изде́лие work; make; article; *pl* wares.
изде́ржки (-жек) *pl* expenses; costs; cost.
издо́хнуть *pf.*
из|жа́рить(ся *pf.*
изжо́га heartburn.
из-за *prep*+*gen* from behind; because of.
излага́ть *impf of* изложи́ть
излече́ние treatment; recovery; cure. **излечи́ть** (-чу́, -чишь) cure; ~ся be cured; ~от+*gen* rid o.s. of.
изли́шек (-шка) surplus; excess. **изли́шество** excess; over-indulgence. **изли́шний** (-шен, -шня) superfluous.
изложе́ние exposition; account. **изло-жи́ть** (-жу́, -жишь) *pf* (*impf* изла-га́ть) expound; set forth; word.
изло́м break, fracture; sharp bend. **излома́ть** *pf* break; smash; wear out; warp.
излуча́ть *impf* radiate, emit. **излу-че́ние** radiation; emanation.
из|ма́зать (-а́жу) *pf* dirty, smear all over; use up; ~ся get dirty, smear o.s. all over.
изме́на betrayal; treason; infidelity. **измене́ние** change, alteration; inflection. **измени́ть**[1] (-ню́, -нишь) *pf* (*impf* изменя́ть[1]) change, alter; ~ся change.

измени́ть[2] (-ню́, -нишь) *pf* (*impf* изменя́ть[2]) +*dat* betray; be unfaithful to. **изме́нник, -ица** traitor.
изменя́емый variable. **изме-ня́ть**[1,2]**(ся** *impf of* измени́ть[1,2]**(ся**
измере́ние measurement, measuring. **изме́рить** *pf*, **измеря́ть** *impf* measure, gauge.
измождённый (-ён, -á) worn out.
из|му́чить (-чу) *pf* torment; tire out, exhaust; ~ся be exhausted. **изму́-ченный** worn out.
измышле́ние fabrication, invention.
измя́тый crumpled, creased; haggard, jaded. **из|мя́ть(ся** (измну́(сь, -нёшь(ся) *pf.*
изна́нка wrong side; seamy side.
из|наси́ловать *pf* rape, assault.
изна́шивание wear (and tear). **изна́-шивать(ся** *impf of* износи́ть(ся
изне́женный pampered; delicate; effeminate.
изнемога́ть *impf*, **изнемо́чь** (-огу́, -о́жешь; -о́г, -лá) *pf* be exhausted. **изнеможе́ние** exhaustion.
изно́с wear; wear and tear; deterioration. **износи́ть** (-ошу́, -о́сишь) *pf* (*impf* изна́шивать) wear out; ~ся wear out; be used up. **изно́шенный** worn out; threadbare.
изнуре́ние exhaustion. **изнурённый** (-ён, -ена́) exhausted; worn out; jaded. **изнури́тельный** exhausting. **изнутри́** *adv* from inside, from within.
изо *see* из
изоби́лие abundance, plenty. **изоби́ловать** *impf* +*instr* abound in, be rich in. **изоби́льный** abundant.
изоблича́ть *impf*, **изобличи́ть** (-чу́) *pf* expose; show. **изобличе́ние** exposure; conviction.
изобража́ть *impf*, **изобрази́ть** (-ажу́) *pf* represent, depict, portray (+*instr* as); ~ из себя́+*acc* make o.s. out to be. **изображе́ние** image; representation; portrayal. **изобрази́-тельный** graphic; decorative; ~ые иску́сства fine arts.
изобрести́ (-ету́, -ете́шь; -ёл, -á) *pf*, **изобрета́ть** *pf* invent; devise. **изобре́татель** *m* inventor. **изобре-та́тельный** inventive. **изобре́те-ние** invention.
изобью́ *etc.: see* изби́ть. **изовью́сь** *etc.: see* изви́ться

изо́гнутый bent, curved; winding.
изогну́ть(ся (-ну́(сь, -нёшь(ся) pf
(impf изгиба́ть(ся) bend, curve.

изоли́ровать impf & pf isolate; insulate. изоля́тор insulator; isolation ward; solitary confinement cell. изоля́ция isolation; quarantine; insulation.

изомну́(сь etc.: see измя́ть

изо́рванный tattered, torn. изорва́ть (-ву́, -вёшь; -а́л, -а́, -о) pf tear, tear to pieces; ~ся be in tatters.

изощрённый (-рён, -а́) refined; keen. изощри́ться pf, изощря́ться impf acquire refinement; excel.

из-под prep+gen from under.

Изра́иль m Israel. изра́ильский Israeli.

из|расхо́довать(ся pf.

и́зредка adv now and then.

изре́зать (-е́жу) pf cut up.

изрече́ние dictum, saying.

изры́ть (-ро́ю) pf dig up, plough up. изры́тый pitted.

изря́дно adv fairly, pretty. изря́дный fair, handsome; fairly large.

изуве́чить (-чу) pf maim, mutilate.

изуми́тельный amazing. изуми́ть (-млю́) pf, изумля́ть impf amaze; ~ся be amazed. изумле́ние amazement.

изумру́д emerald.

изуро́дованный maimed; disfigured. из|уро́довать pf.

изуча́ть impf, изучи́ть (-чу́, -чишь) pf learn, study. изуче́ние study.

изъе́здить (-зжу) pf travel all over; wear out.

изъяви́ть (-влю́, -вишь) pf, изъявля́ть impf express.

изъя́н defect, flaw.

изъя́тие withdrawal; removal; exception. изъя́ть (изыму́, -мешь) pf. изыма́ть impf withdraw.

изыска́ние investigation, research; prospecting; survey. изы́сканный refined. изыска́ть (-ыщу́, -ыщешь) pf, изы́скивать impf search out; (try to) find.

изю́м raisins.

изя́щество elegance, grace. изя́щный elegant, graceful.

ика́ть impf, икну́ть (-ну́, -нёшь) pf hiccup.

ико́на icon.

ико́та hiccup, hiccups.

икра́[1] (hard) roe; caviare.

икра́[2] (pl -ы) calf (of leg).

ил silt; sludge.

и́ли conj or; ~... ~ either ... or.

и́листый muddy, silty.

иллюзиони́ст illusionist. иллю́зия illusion.

иллюмина́тор porthole. иллюмина́ция illumination.

иллюстра́ция illustration. иллюстри́ровать impf & pf illustrate.

им see он, они́, оно́

им. abbr (of и́мени) named after.

и́мени etc.: see и́мя

име́ние estate.

имени́ны (-и́н) pl name-day (party). имени́тельный nominative. и́менно adv namely; exactly, precisely; вот ~! exactly!

име́ть (-е́ю) impf have; ~ де́ло c+instr have dealings with, have to do with; ~ ме́сто take place; ~ся be; be available.

и́ми see они́

имита́ция imitation. имити́ровать impf imitate.

иммигра́нт, ~ка immigrant.

импера́тор emperor. импера́торский imperial. императри́ца empress. империали́зм imperialism. империали́ст imperialist. империалисти́ческий imperialist(ic). импе́рия empire.

и́мпорт import. импорти́ровать impf & pf import. и́мпортный import(ed).

импровиза́ция improvisation. импровизи́ровать impf & pf improvise.

и́мпульс impulse.

иму́щество property.

и́мя (и́мени; pl имена́, -ён) neut name; first name; noun; ~ прилага́тельное adjective; ~ существи́тельное noun; ~ числи́тельное numeral.

и́наче adv differently, otherwise; так и́ли ~ in any event; conj otherwise, or else.

инвали́д disabled person; invalid. инвали́дность disablement, disability.

инвента́рь (-я́) m stock; equipment; inventory.

инде́ец (-е́йца) (American) Indian. инде́йка (gen pl -е́ек) turkey(-hen).

индейский (American) Indian.
йндекс index; code.
индианка Indian; American Indian.
индеец (-йца) Indian.
индивидуализм individualism. индивидуальность individuality. индивидуальный individual. индивидуум individual.
индийский Indian. Йндия India. индус, индуска Hindu. индусский Hindu.
индустриализация industrialization. индустриализировать impf & pf industrialize. индустриальный industrial. индустрия industry.
индюк, индюшка turkey.
йней hoar-frost.
инертность inertia; sluggishness. инерция inertia.
инженер engineer; ~-механик mechanical engineer; ~-строитель m civil engineer.
инжир fig.
инициал initial.
инициатива initiative. инициатор initiator.
инквизиция inquisition.
инкрустация inlaid work, inlay.
инкубатор incubator.
ино- in comb other, different; hetero-. иногородний of, from, another town. ~родец (-дца) non-Russian. ~родный foreign. ~сказательный allegorical. ~странец (-нца), ~странка (gen pl -нок) foreigner. ~странный foreign. ~язычный speaking, of, another language; foreign.
иногда adv sometimes.
иной different; other; some; ~ раз sometimes.
инок monk. инокиня nun.
инотдел foreign department.
инсектицид insecticide.
инспектор inspector. инспекция inspection; inspectorate.
инстанция instance.
инстинкт instinct. инстинктивный instinctive.
институт institute.
инструктор instructor. инструкция instructions.
инструмент instrument; tool.
инсулин insulin.
инсценировка dramatization, adap-

tation; pretence.
интеграция integration.
интеллект intellect. интеллектуальный intellectual.
интеллигент intellectual. интеллигентный cultured, educated. интеллигенция intelligentsia.
интенсивность intensity. интенсивный intensive.
интервал interval.
интервенция intervention.
интервью neut indecl interview.
интерес interest. интересный interesting. интересовать impf interest; ~ся be interested (+instr in).
интернат boarding-school.
интернациональный international.
интернировать impf & pf intern.
интерпретация interpretation. интерпретировать impf & pf interpret.
интерьер interior.
интимный intimate.
интонация intonation.
интрига intrigue; plot. интриговать impf, (pf за~) intrigue.
интуиция intuition.
инфаркт infarct; coronary (thrombosis), heart attack.
инфекционный infectious. инфекция infection.
инфляция inflation.
информация information.
инфракрасный infra-red.
иод etc.: see йод
ион ion.
ипохондрик hypochondriac. ипохондрия hypochondria.
ипподром racecourse.
Ирак Iraq. иракец (-кца) Iraqi. иракский Iraqi.
Иран Iran. иранец (-нца), иранка Iranian. иранский Iranian.
ирландец (-дца) Irishman. Ирландия Ireland. ирландка Irishwoman. ирландский Irish.
иронический ironic. ирония irony.
ирригация irrigation.
иск suit, action.
искажать impf, исказить (-ажу) pf distort, pervert; misrepresent. искажение distortion, perversion.
искалеченный crippled, maimed. искалечить (-чу) pf cripple, maim; break.

искать (ищу, ищешь) *impf* (+*acc* or *gen*) seek, look for.

исключать *impf*, **исключить** (-чу) *pf* exclude; eliminate; expel. **исключая** *prep*+*gen* except. **исключение** exception; exclusion; expulsion; elimination; **за исключением** +*gen* with the exception of. **исключительно** *adv* exceptionally; exclusively. **исключительный** exceptional; exclusive.

исконный primordial.

ископаемое *sb* mineral; fossil. **ископаемый** fossilized, fossil.

искоренить *pf*, **искоренять** *impf* eradicate.

искоса *adv* askance; sidelong.

искра spark.

искренний sincere. **искренность** sincerity.

искривление bend; distortion, warping.

искупать¹(ся *pf*.

искупать² *impf*, **искупить** (-плю, -пишь) *pf* atone for; make up for. **искупление** redemption, atonement.

искусить (-ушу) *pf of* искушать

искусный skilful; expert. **искусственный** artificial; feigned. **искусство** art; skill. **искусствовед** art historian.

искушать *impf* (*pf* искусить) tempt; seduce. **искушение** temptation, seduction.

испанец (-нца) Spaniard. **Испания** Spain. **испанка** Spanish woman. **испанский** Spanish.

испарение evaporation; *pl* fumes. **испариться** *pf*, **испаряться** *impf* evaporate.

испачкать *pf*. **испечь** (-еку, -ечёшь) *pf*.

исповедовать *impf* & *pf* confess; profess; ~ся confess; make one's confession; +в +*prep* unburden o.s. of. **исповедь** confession.

исподтишка *adv* in an underhand way; on the quiet.

исполин giant. **исполинский** gigantic.

исполком *abbr* (*of* исполнительный комитет) executive committee.

исполнение fulfilment, execution. **исполнитель** *m*, ~ница executor; performer. **исполнительный** executive. **исполнить** *pf*, **исполнять** *impf* carry out, execute; fulfil; perform; ~ся be fulfilled.

использование utilization. **использовать** *impf* & *pf* make (good) use of, utilize.

испортить(ся (-рчу(сь) *pf*. **испорченный** depraved; spoiled; rotten.

исправительный correctional; corrective. **исправить** (-влю) *pf*, **исправлять** *impf* rectify, correct; mend; reform; ~ся improve, reform. **исправление** repairing; improvement; correction. **исправленный** improved, corrected; revised; reformed. **исправный** in good order; punctual; meticulous.

испробовать *pf*.

испуг fright. **испугать**(ся *pf*.

испускать *impf*, **испустить** (-ущу, -устишь) *pf* emit, let out.

испытание test, trial; ordeal. **испытать** *pf*, **испытывать** *impf* test; try; experience.

исследование investigation; research. **исследователь** *m* researcher; investigator. **исследовательский** research. **исследовать** *impf* & *pf* investigate, examine; research into.

истаскать *pf*, **истаскиваться** *impf* wear out; be worn out.

истекать *impf of* истечь. **истёкший** past.

истерика hysterics. **истерический** hysterical. **истерия** hysteria.

истечение outflow; expiry. **истечь** (-ечёт; -тёк, -ла) *pf* (*impf* истекать) elapse; expire.

истина truth. **истинный** true.

истлевать *impf*, **истлеть** (-ею) *pf* rot, decay; be reduced to ashes.

исток source.

истолковать *pf*, **истолковывать** *impf* interpret; comment on.

истолочь (-лку, -лчёшь; -лок, -лкла) *pf*.

истома languor.

исторгать *impf*, **исторгнуть** (-ну, -орг) *pf* throw out.

историк historian. **исторический** historical; historic. **история** history; story; incident.

источник spring; source.

истощать *impf*, **истощить** (-щу) *pf*

exhaust; emaciate. **истоще́ние** emaciation; exhaustion.

ис|тра́тить (-а́чу) *pf*.

истреби́тель *m* destroyer; fighter. **истреби́ть** (-блю́) *pf*, **истребля́ть** *impf* destroy; exterminate.

ис|тупи́ться (-пится) *pf*.

истяза́ние torture. **истяза́ть** *impf* torture.

исхо́д outcome; end; Exodus. **исходи́ть** (-ожу́, -о́дишь) *impf* (+из or от+*gen*) issue (from), come (from); proceed (from). **исхо́дный** initial; departure.

исхуда́лый undernourished, emaciated.

исцеле́ние healing; recovery. **исцели́ть** *pf*, **исцеля́ть** *impf* heal, cure.

исчеза́ть *impf*, **исче́знуть** (-ну; -е́з) *pf* disappear, vanish. **исчезнове́ние** disappearance.

исче́рпать *pf*, **исче́рпывать** *impf* exhaust; conclude. **исче́рпывающий** exhaustive.

исчисле́ние calculation; calculus.

ита́к *conj* thus; so then.

Ита́лия Italy. **италья́нец** (-нца), **италья́нка** Italian. **италья́нский** Italian.

ИТА́Р-ТА́СС *abbr* (*of* Информацио́нное телегра́фное аге́нтство Росси́и; *see* ТАСС) ITAR-Tass.

и т.д. *abbr* (*of* и так да́лее) etc., and so on.

ито́г sum; total; result. **ито́го** *adv* in all, altogether.

и т.п. *abbr* (*of* и тому́ подо́бное) etc., and so on.

иуде́й, **иуде́йка** Jew. **иуде́йский** Judaic.

их their, theirs; *see* они́.

иша́к (-а́) donkey.

ище́йка bloodhound; police dog.

ищу́ *etc.*: *see* иска́ть

ию́ль *m* July. **ию́льский** July.

ию́нь *m* June. **ию́ньский** June.

йо́га yoga.

йод iodine.

йо́та iota.

К

к, **ко** *prep*+*dat* to, towards; by; for;

on; on the occasion of; **к пе́рвому января́** by the first of January; **к тому́ вре́мени** by then; **к тому́ же** besides, moreover; **к чему́?** what for?

-ка *partl modifying force of imper or expressing decision or intention*; **да́йте-ка пройти́** let me pass, please; **скажи́-ка мне** do tell me.

каба́к (-а́) tavern.

кабала́ servitude.

каба́н (-а́) wild boar.

кабаре́ *neut indecl* cabaret.

кабачо́к (-чка́) marrow.

ка́бель *m* cable. **ка́бельтов** cable, hawser.

каби́на cabin; booth; cockpit; cubicle; cab. **кабине́т** study; surgery; room; office; Cabinet.

каблу́к (-а́) heel.

кабота́ж coastal shipping. **кабота́жный** coastal.

кабы́ if.

кавале́р knight; partner, gentleman. **кавалери́йский** cavalry. **кавалери́ст** cavalryman. **кавале́рия** cavalry.

ка́верзный tricky.

Кавка́з the Caucasus. **кавка́зец** (-зца), **кавка́зка** Caucasian. **кавка́зский** Caucasian.

кавы́чки (-чек) *pl* inverted commas, quotation marks.

каде́т cadet. **каде́тский ко́рпус** military school.

кадр frame, still; close-up; cadre; *pl* establishment; staff; personnel; specialists. **ка́дровый** (*mil*) regular; skilled, trained.

кады́к (-а́) Adam's apple.

каждодне́вный daily, everyday. **ка́ждый** each, every; *sb* everybody.

ка́жется *etc.*: *see* каза́ться

каза́к (-а́; *pl* -áки́, -áко́в), **каза́чка** Cossack.

каза́рма barracks.

каза́ться (кажу́сь, ка́жешься) *impf* (*pf* по~) seem, appear; *impers* **ка́жется**, **каза́лось** apparently; **каза́лось бы** it would seem; +*dat*: **мне ка́жется** it seems to me; I think.

Казахста́н Kazakhstan. **каза́чий** Cossack.

каземáт casemate.

казённый State; government; fiscal;

public; formal; banal, conventional. казна́ Exchequer, Treasury; public purse; the State. казначе́й treasurer, bursar; paymaster.

казино́ *neut indecl* casino.

казни́ть *impf & pf* execute; punish; castigate. казнь execution.

кайма́ (*gen pl* каём) border, edging.

как *adv* how; what; вот ~! you don't say!; ~ вы ду́маете? what do you think?; ~ его́ зову́т? what is his name?; ~ наtrýрально, of course; ~ же так? how is that?; ~ ни however. как *conj* as; like; when; since; +*neg* but, except, than; в то вре́мя ~ while, whereas; ~ мо́жно, нельзя́+*comp* as ... as possible; ~ мо́жно скоре́е as soon as possible; ~ нельзя́ лу́чше as well as possible; ~ то́лько as soon as, when; ме́жду тем, ~ while, whereas. как бу́дто *conj* as if; *partl* apparently. как бы how; as if; как бы... не what if, supposing; как бы... ни however. ка́к-либо *adv* somehow. ка́к-нибудь *adv* somehow; anyhow. как раз *adv* just, exactly. как-то *adv* somehow; once.

кака́о *neut indecl* cocoa.

како́в (-á, -ó, -ы́) *pron* what, what sort (of); ~ он? what is he like?; ~ он собо́й? what does he look like?; пого́да-то какова́! what weather! каково́ *adv* how what; какой *pron* what; (such) as; which; ~... ни whatever, whichever. како́й-либо, како́й-нибудь *prons* some; any; only. како́й-то *pron* some; a; a kind of.

как раз, как-то *see* как

ка́ктус cactus.

кал faeces, excrement.

каламбу́р pun.

кале́ка *m & f* cripple.

календа́рь (-я́) *m* calendar.

кале́ние incandescence.

кале́чить (-чу) *impf* (*pf* ис~, по~) cripple, maim; ~ся become a cripple.

кали́бр calibre; bore; gauge.

ка́лий potassium.

кали́тка (wicket-)gate.

каллигра́фия calligraphy.

кало́рия calorie.

кало́ша galosh.

ка́лька tracing-paper; tracing.

калькуля́ция calculation.

кальсо́ны (-н) *pl* long johns.

ка́льций calcium.

ка́мбала flat-fish; plaice; flounder.

камени́стый stony, rocky. каменно-у́гольный coal; ~ бассе́йн coalfield. ка́менный stone; rock; stony; hard, immovable; ~ век Stone Age; ~ у́голь coal. каменоло́мня (*gen pl* -мен) quarry. ка́менщик (stone) mason; bricklayer. ка́мень (-мня; *pl* -мни, -мне́й) *m* stone.

ка́мера chamber; cell; camera; inner tube, (football) bladder; ~ хране́ния cloak-room, left-luggage office. ка́мерный chamber. камерто́н tuning-fork.

ками́н fireplace; fire.

камко́рдер camcorder.

камо́рка closet, very small room.

кампа́ния campaign; cruise.

камы́ш (-á) reed, rush; cane.

кана́ва ditch; gutter.

Кана́да Canada. кана́дец (-дца), кана́дка Canadian. кана́дский Canadian.

кана́л canal; channel. канализа́ция sewerage (system).

канаре́йка canary.

кана́т rope; cable.

канва́ canvas; groundwork; outline, design.

кандалы́ (-о́в) *pl* shackles.

кандида́т candidate; ~ нау́к person with higher degree. кандидату́ра candidature.

кани́кулы (-ул) *pl* vacation; holidays.

кани́стра can, canister.

канони́ческий canon(ical).

кано́э *neut indecl* canoe.

кант edging; bead. кантова́ть *impf*; «не ~» 'this way up'.

кану́н eve.

ка́нуть (-ну) *pf* drop, sink; как в во́ду ~ vanish into thin air.

канцеля́рия office. канцеля́рский office; clerical. канцеля́рщина redtape.

ка́нцлер chancellor.

ка́пать (-аю *or* -плю) *impf* (*pf* ка́пнуть, на~) drip, drop; trickle; +*instr* spill.

капе́лла choir; chapel.

ка́пелька small drop; a little; ~ росы́ dew-drop.

капельме́йстер conductor; bandmaster.

капилля́р capillary.

капита́л capital. капитали́зм capitalism. капитали́ст capitalist. капиталисти́ческий capitalist. капита́льный capital; main, fundamental; major.

капита́н captain; skipper.

капитули́ровать *impf* & *pf* capitulate. капитуля́ция capitulation.

капка́н trap.

ка́пля (*gen pl* -пель) drop; bit, scrap. ка́пнуть (-ну) *pf of* ка́пать

капо́т hood, cowl, cowling; bonnet; house-coat.

капри́з caprice. капри́зничать *impf* play up. капри́зный capricious.

капу́ста cabbage.

капюшо́н hood.

ка́ра punishment.

кара́бкаться *impf* (*pf* вс~) clamber.

карава́н caravan; convoy.

кара́кули *f pl* scribble.

караме́ль caramel; caramels.

каранда́ш (-á) pencil.

каранти́н quarantine.

кара́т carat.

кара́тельный punitive. кара́ть *impf* (*pf* по~) punish.

карау́л guard; watch; ~! help! карау́лить *impf* guard; lie in wait for. карау́льный guard; *sb* sentry, sentinel, guard.

карбюра́тор carburettor.

каре́та carriage, coach.

ка́рий brown; hazel.

карикату́ра caricature; cartoon.

карка́с frame; framework.

ка́ркать *impf*, ка́ркнуть (-ну) *pf* caw, croak.

ка́рлик, ка́рлица dwarf; pygmy. ка́рликовый dwarf; pygmy.

карма́н pocket. карма́нник pickpocket. карма́нный *adj* pocket.

карни́з cornice; ledge.

карп carp.

ка́рта map; (playing-)card.

карта́вить (-влю) *impf* burr.

картёжник gambler.

карте́чь case-shot, grape-shot.

карти́на picture; scene. карти́нка picture; illustration. карти́нный picturesque; picture.

карто́н cardboard. карто́нка cardboard box.

картоте́ка card-index.

карто́фель *m* potatoes; potato(-plant). карто́фельный potato; ~ое пюре́ mashed potatoes.

ка́рточка card; season ticket; photo. ка́рточный card.

карто́шка potatoes; potato.

карусе́ль merry-go-round.

ка́рцер cell, lock-up.

карье́р¹ full gallop.

карье́р² quarry; sand-pit.

карье́ра career. карьери́ст careerist.

каса́ние contact. каса́тельная *sb* tangent. каса́ться *impf* (*pf* косну́ться) +*gen or* до+*gen* touch; touch on; concern; что каса́ется as regards.

ка́ска helmet.

каска́д cascade.

каспи́йский Caspian.

ка́сса till; cash-box; booking-office; box-office; cash-desk; cash.

кассе́та cassette. кассе́тный магнитофо́н cassette recorder.

касси́р, касси́рша cashier.

кастра́т eunuch. кастра́ция castration. кастри́ровать *impf* & *pf* castrate, geld.

кастрю́ля saucepan.

катало́г catalogue.

ката́ние rolling; driving; ~ верхо́м riding; ~ на конька́х skating.

катапу́льта catapult. катапульти́ровать(ся *impf* & *pf* catapult.

ката́р catarrh.

катара́кта cataract.

катастро́фа catastrophe. катастрофи́ческий catastrophic.

ката́ть *impf* (*pf* вы~, с~) roll; (take for a) drive; ~ся roll, roll about; go for a drive; ~ся верхо́м ride, go riding; ~ся на конька́х skate, go skating.

категори́ческий categorical. катего́рия category.

ка́тер (*pl* -á) cutter; launch.

кати́ть (-ачу́, -а́тишь) *impf* bowl along, rip, tear; ~ся rush, tear; flow, stream, roll; кати́сь, кати́тесь get out! clear off! като́к (-тка́) skating-rink; roller.

като́лик, католи́чка Catholic. католи́ческий Catholic.

ка́торга penal servitude, hard labour. ка́торжник convict. ка́торжн|ый penal; ~ые работы hard labour; drudgery.

катушка reel, bobbin; spool; coil.

каучук rubber.

кафе *neut indecl* café.

кафедра pulpit; rostrum; chair; department.

кафель *m* Dutch tile.

качалка rocking-chair. качание rocking, swinging; pumping. качать *impf* (*pf* качнуть) +*acc or instr* rock, swing; shake; ~ся rock, swing; roll; reel. качели (-ей) *pl* swing.

качественный qualitative; highquality. качество quality; в качестве+*gen* as, in the capacity of.

качка rocking; tossing.

качнуть(ся (-ну(сь, -нёшь(ся) *pf of* качать(ся. качу *etc.: see* катить

каша gruel, porridge; mess. заварить кашу stir up trouble.

кашель (-шля) cough. кашлянуть (-ну) *pf*, кашлять *impf* (have a) cough.

каштан chestnut. каштановый chestnut.

каюта cabin, stateroom.

кающийся penitent. каяться (каюсь) *impf* (*pf* по~, рас~) repent; confess; каюсь I (must) confess.

кв. *abbr* (*of* квадратный) square; (*of* квартира) flat.

квадрат square; quad; в квадрате squared; возвести в ~ square. квадратный square; quadratic.

квакать *impf*, квакнуть (-ну) *pf* croak.

квалификация qualification. квалифицированный qualified, skilled.

квант, кванта quantum. квантовый quantum.

квартал block; quarter. квартальный quarterly.

квартет quartet.

квартира flat; apartment(s); quarters. квартирант, -рантка lodger; tenant. квартирная плата, квартплата rent.

кварц quartz.

квас (*pl* ~ы) kvass. квасить (-ашу) *impf* sour; pickle. квашеная капуста sauerkraut.

кверху *adv* up, upwards.

квит, квиты quits.

квитанция receipt. квиток (-тка) ticket, check.

КГБ *abbr* (*of* Комитет государственной безопасности) KGB.

кегля skittle.

кедр cedar.

кеды (-ов) *pl* trainers.

кекс (fruit-)cake.

келья (*gen pl* -лий) cell.

кем *see* кто

кемпинг campsite.

кенгуру *m indecl* kangaroo.

кепка cloth cap.

керамика ceramics.

керосин paraffin. керосин|ый: ~ая икра red caviare.

керосинка paraffin stove.

кета Siberian salmon. кетов|ый: ~ая икра red caviare.

кефир kefir, yoghurt.

кибернетика cybernetics.

кивать *impf*, кивнуть (-ну, -нёшь) *pf* (головой) nod (one's head); (+на+*acc*) motion (to). кивок (-вка) nod.

кидать *impf* (*pf* кинуть) throw, fling; ~ся fling o.s.; rush; +*instr* throw.

кий (-я; *pl* -и, -ёв) (*billiard*) cue.

кил|ёвой keel; ~ая качка pitching.

кило *neut indecl* kilo. киловатт kilowatt. килограмм kilogram. километр kilometre.

киль *m* keel; fin. кильватер wake.

килька sprat.

кинжал dagger.

кино *neut indecl* cinema.

кино- *in comb* film-, cine-. киноаппарат cinecamera. ~артист, ~артистка film actor, actress. ~журнал news-reel. ~зал cinema; auditorium. ~звезда film-star. ~зритель *m* film-goer. ~картина film. ~оператор camera-man. ~плёнка film. ~режиссёр film director. ~театр cinema. ~хроника news-reel.

кинуть(ся (-ну(сь) *pf of* кидать(ся

киоск kiosk, stall.

кипа pile, stack; bale.

кипарис cypress.

кипение boiling. кипеть (-плю) *impf* (*pf* вс~) boil, seethe.

кипучий boiling, seething; ebullient. кипятильник kettle, boiler. кипятить (-ячу) *impf* (*pf* вс~) boil; ~ся boil; get excited. кипяток (-тка) boiling water. **кипячёный** boiled.

Кирги́зия Kirghizia.

кирка́ pick(axe).

кирпи́ч (-á) brick; bricks. **кирпи́ч-ный** brick; brick-red.

кисе́ль *m* kissel, blancmange.

кисе́т tobacco-pouch.

кисея́ muslin.

кислоро́д oxygen. **кислота́** (*pl* -ы) acid; acidity. **кисло́тный** acid. **кислый** sour; acid. **ки́снуть** (-ну; кис) *impf* (*pf* про~) turn sour.

ки́сточка brush; tassel. **кисть** (*gen pl* -е́й) cluster, bunch; brush; tassel; hand.

кит (-á) whale.

кита́ец (-а́йца; *pl* -цы, -цев) Chinese. **Кита́й** China. **кита́йский** Chinese.

китая́нка Chinese (woman).

китобо́й whaler. **китобо́й** whale.

кичи́ться (-чу́сь) *impf* plume o.s.; strut. **кичли́вость** conceit. **кичли́вый** conceited.

кише́ть (-ши́т) *impf* swarm, teem.

кише́чник bowels, intestines. **кише́чный** intestinal. **кишка́** gut, intestine; hose.

клавеси́н harpsichord. **клавиату́ра** keyboard. **кла́виша** key. **кла́вишный**: ~ **инструме́нт** keyboard instrument.

клад treasure.

кла́дбище cemetery, graveyard.

кла́дка laying; masonry. **кладова́я** *sb* pantry; store-room. **кладовщи́к** (-á) storeman. **кладу́** *etc.*: *see* **класть**

кла́няться *impf* (*pf* **поклони́ться**) +*dat* bow to; greet.

кла́пан valve; vent.

кларне́т clarinet.

класс class; class-room. **кла́ссик** classic. **кла́ссика** the classics. **классифици́ровать** *impf & pf* classify. **класси́ческий** classical. **кла́ссный** class; first-class. **кла́ссовый** class.

класть (-аду́, -адёшь; -ал) *impf* (*pf* **положи́ть, сложи́ть**) lay; put.

клева́ть (клюю, клюёшь) *impf* (*pf* **клю́нуть**) peck; bite.

кле́вер (*pl* -á) clover.

клевета́ slander; libel. **клевета́ть** (-ещу́, -ещешь) *impf* (*pf* на~) +на+*acc* slander; libel. **клеветни́к** (-á), -ни́ца slanderer. **клеветни́ческий** slanderous; libellous.

клеёнка oilcloth. **кле́ить** *impf* (*pf* с~) glue; stick; ~ся stick; become sticky. **клей** (*loc* -ю́; *pl* -и́) glue, adhesive. **кле́йкий** sticky.

клейми́ть (-млю́) *impf* (*pf* за~) brand; stamp; stigmatize. **клеймо́** (*pl* -а) brand; stamp; mark.

кле́йстер paste.

клён maple.

клепа́ть *impf* rivet.

кле́тка cage; check; cell. **кле́точка** cellule. **кле́точный** cellular. **клетча́тка** cellulose. **кле́тчатый** checked.

клёш flare.

клешня́ (*gen pl* -е́й) claw.

кле́щи (-е́й) *pl* pincers, tongs.

клие́нт client. **клиенту́ра** clientèle.

кли́зма enema.

клик cry, call. **кли́кать** (-и́чу) *impf*, **кли́кнуть** (-ну) *pf* call.

кли́макс menopause.

кли́мат climate. **климати́ческий** climatic.

клин (*pl* -нья, -ньев) wedge. **клино́к** (-нка́) blade.

кли́ника clinic. **клини́ческий** clinical.

кли́пс clip-on ear-ring.

клич call. **кли́чка** name; nickname. **кли́чу** *etc.*: *see* **кли́кать**

клок (-á; *pl* -о́чья, -ьев *or* -и́, -о́в) rag, shred; tuft.

кло́кот bubbling; gurgling. **клокота́ть** (-о́чет) *impf* bubble; gurgle; boil up.

клони́ть (-ню́, -нишь) *impf* bend; incline; +к+*dat* drive at; ~ся bow, bend; +к+*dat* near, approach.

клоп (-á) bug.

кло́ун clown.

клочо́к (-чка́) scrap, shred. **кло́чья** *etc.*: *see* **клок**

клуб[1] club.

клуб[2] (*pl* -ы́) puff; cloud.

клу́бень (-бня) *m* tuber.

клуби́ться *impf* swirl; curl.

клубни́ка (*no pl; usu collect*) strawberry; strawberries.

клубо́к (-бка́) ball; tangle.

клу́мба (flower-)bed.

клык (-á) fang; tusk; canine (*tooth*).

клюв beak.

клю́ква cranberry; cranberries.

клю́нуть (-ну) *pf of* **клева́ть**

ключ[1] (-á) key; clue; keystone; clef;

wrench, spanner.
ключ[2] (-á) spring; source.
ключево́й key. **ключи́ца** collarbone.
клю́шка (hockey) stick; (golf-)club.
клюю́ etc.: see **клева́ть**
кля́кса blot, smudge.
кляну́ etc.: see **клясть**
кля́нчить (-чу) impf (pf вы́~) beg.
кляп gag.
клясть (-яну́, -янёшь; -ял, -á, -о) impf curse; (pf по~ся) swear, vow. **кля́тва** oath, vow. **кля́твенный** on oath.
кни́га book.
книго- in comb book, biblio-. **книгове́дение**[1] bibliography. **~ве́дение**[2] book-keeping. **~изда́тель** m publisher. **~люб** bibliophile, book-lover. **~храни́лище** library; book-stack. **кни́жечка** booklet. **кни́жка** book; note-book; bank-book. **кни́жный** book; bookish.
кни́зу adv downwards.
кно́пка drawing-pin; press-stud; (push-)button, knob.
княги́ня princess. **кня́жество** principality. **княжна́** (gen pl -жо́н) princess. **князь** (pl -зья́, -зе́й) m prince.
ко see **к** prep.
коали́ция coalition.
кобура́ holster.
кобы́ла mare; (vaulting-)horse.
ко́ваный forged; wrought; terse.
кова́рный insidious, crafty; perfidious. **кова́рство** insidiousness, craftiness; perfidy.
кова́ть (кую́, -ёшь) impf (pf под~) forge; hammer; shoe.
ковёр (-вра́) carpet; rug; mat.
кове́ркать impf (pf ис~) distort, mangle, ruin.
ко́вка forging; shoeing.
коври́жка honeycake, gingerbread.
ко́врик rug; mat.
ковче́г ark.
ковш (-á) scoop, ladle.
ковы́ль m feather-grass.
ковыля́ть impf hobble.
ковырну́ть (-ну́, -нёшь) pf, **ковыря́ть** impf dig into; tinker; ~в+prep pick (at); ~ся rummage; tinker.
когда́ adv when; ~ (бы) ни whenever; conj when; while; as; if. **когда́-**

-либо, когда́-нибудь advs some time; ever. **когда́-то** adv once; formerly; some time.
кого́ see **кто**
ко́готь (-гтя; pl -гти, -гте́й) m claw; talon.
код code.
коде́ин codeine.
ко́декс code.
ко́е-где́ adv here and there. **ко́е-ка́к** adv anyhow; somehow (or other). **ко́е-како́й** pron some. **ко́е-кто́** pron somebody; some people. **ко́ечто́** (-чего́) pron something; a little.
ко́жа skin; leather; peel. **ко́жанка** leather jacket. **ко́жаный** leather. **коже́венный** leather; tanning. **ко́жный** skin. **кожура́** rind, peel, skin.
коза́ (pl -ы) goat, nanny-goat. **козёл** (-зла́) billy-goat. **козеро́г** ibex; Capricorn. **ко́зий** goat; ~ пух angora.
козлёнок (-нка; pl -ля́та, -ля́т) kid. **ко́злы** (-зел) pl coach driver's seat; trestle(s); saw-horse.
ко́зни (-ей) pl machinations.
козырёк (-рька́) peak.
козырно́й trump. **козырну́ть** (-ну́, -нёшь) pf, **козыря́ть** impf lead trumps; trump; play one's trump card; salute. **ко́зырь** (pl -и, -е́й) m trump.
ко́йка (gen pl ко́ек) berth, bunk; bed.
кока́ин cocaine.
ко́ка-ко́ла Coca-Cola (propr).
коке́тка coquette. **коке́тство** coquetry.
коклю́ш whooping-cough.
ко́кон cocoon.
коко́с coconut.
кокс coke.
кокте́йль m cocktail.
кол (-á; pl -лья, -ьев) stake, picket.
ко́лба retort.
колбаса́ (pl -ы) sausage.
колго́тки (-ток) pl tights.
колдова́ть impf practise witchcraft. **колдовство́** sorcery. **колду́н** (-á) sorcerer, magician. **колду́нья** (gen pl -ний) witch, sorceress.
коле́бание oscillation; variation; hesitation. **колеба́ть** (-е́блю) impf (pf по~) shake; ~ся oscillate; fluctuate; hesitate.
коле́но (pl -и, -ей, -ям) knee; (in pl) lap. **коле́нчатый** crank, cranked; bent; ~ вал crankshaft.

колесни́ца chariot. **колесо́** (*pl* -ёса) wheel.

колея́ rut; track, gauge.

ко́лика (*usu pl*) colic; stitch.

коли́чественн|**ый** quantitative; ~ое **числи́тельное** cardinal number. **коли́чество** quantity; number.

колле́га *m* & *f* colleague. **колле́гия** board; college.

коллекти́в collective. **коллективиза́ция** collectivization. **коллекти́вный** collective. **коллекционе́р** collector. **колле́кция** collection.

колли́зия clash, conflict.

коло́да block; pack (*of cards*).

коло́дец (-дца) well.

ко́локол (*pl* -а́, -о́в) bell. **коло́кольный** bell. **колоко́льня** belltower. **колоко́льчик** small bell; bluebell.

колониали́зм colonialism. **колониа́льный** colonial. **колониза́тор** colonizer. **колониза́ция** colonization. **колонизова́ть** *impf* & *pf* colonize. **коло́ния** colony.

коло́нка (*street*) water fountain; stand-pipe; column; бензи́новая ~ petrol pump. **коло́нна** column.

колори́т colouring, colour. **колори́тный** colourful, graphic.

ко́лос (-о́сья, -ьев) ear. **колоси́ться** *impf* form ears.

колосса́льный huge; terrific.

колоти́ть (-очу́, -о́тишь) *impf* (*pf* по~) beat; pound; thrash; smash; ~ся pound, thump; shake.

коло́ть[1] (-лю́, -лешь) *impf* (*pf* рас~) break, chop.

коло́ть[2] (-лю́, -лешь) *impf* (*pf* за~, кольну́ть) prick; stab; sting; slaughter; ~ся prick.

колпа́к (-а́) cap; hood, cowl.

колхо́з *abbr* (*of* **колекти́вное хозя́йство**) kolkhoz, collective farm. **колхо́зник**, ~**ица** kolkhoz member. **колхо́зный** kolkhoz.

колыбе́ль cradle.

колыха́ть (-ы́шу) *impf*, **колыхну́ть** (-ну́, -нёшь) *pf* sway, rock; ~ся sway; flutter.

кольну́ть (-ну́, -нёшь) *pf of* **коло́ть**

кольцо́ (*pl* -а, -ле́ц, -льцам) ring.

колю́ч|**ий** prickly; sharp; ~ая про́волока barbed wire. **колю́чка** prickle; thorn.

коля́ска carriage; pram; side-car.

ком (*pl* -мья, -мьев) lump; ball.

ком *see* **кто**

кома́нда command; order; detachment; crew; team. **команди́р** commander. **командирова́ть** *impf* & *pf* post, send on a mission. **командиро́вка** posting; mission, business trip. **командиро́вочные** *sb pl* travelling expenses. **кома́ндование** command. **кома́ндовать** *impf* (*pf* с~) give orders; be in command; +*instr* command. **кома́ндующий** *sb* commander.

кома́р (-а́) mosquito.

комба́йн combine harvester.

комбина́т industrial complex. **комбина́ция** combination; manoeuvre; slip. **комбинезо́н** overalls, boiler suit; dungarees. **комбини́ровать** *impf* (*pf* с~) combine.

коме́дия comedy.

коменда́нт commandant; manager; warden. **комендату́ра** commandant's office.

коме́та comet.

ко́мик comic actor; comedian. **ко́микс** comic, comic strip.

комисса́р commissar.

комиссионе́р (commission-)agent, broker. **комиссио́нн**|**ый** commission; ~ый **магази́н** second-hand shop; ~ые *sb pl* commission. **коми́ссия** commission; committee.

комите́т committee.

коми́ческий comic; comical. **коми́чный** comical, funny.

ко́мкать *impf* (*pf* с~) crumple.

коммента́рий commentary; *pl* comment. **коммента́тор** commentator. **комменти́ровать** *impf* & *pf* comment (on).

коммерса́нт merchant; businessman. **комме́рция** commerce. **комме́рческий** commercial.

коммивояжёр commercial traveller.

комму́на commune. **коммуна́льный** communal; municipal. **коммуни́зм** communism.

коммуника́ция communication.

коммуни́ст, ~**ка** communist. **коммунисти́ческий** communist.

коммута́тор switchboard.

коммюнике́ *neut indecl* communiqué.

ко́мната room. **ко́мнатный** room; indoor.

комо́д chest of drawers.

комо́к (-мка́) lump.

компа́кт-ди́ск compact disc. **компа́ктный** compact.

компа́ния company. **компаньо́н**, ~ка companion; partner.

компа́ртия Communist Party.

ко́мпас compass.

компенса́ция compensation. **компенси́ровать** *impf & pf* compensate.

ко́мплекс complex. **ко́мплексный** complex, compound; composite; combined. **компле́кт** (complete) set; complement; kit. **комплектова́ть** *impf* (*pf* с~, у~) complete; bring up to strength. **компле́кция** build; constitution.

комплиме́нт compliment.

компози́тор composer. **компози́ция** composition.

компоне́нт component.

компо́ст compost.

компо́стер punch. **компости́ровать** *impf* (*pf* про~) punch.

компо́т stewed fruit.

компре́ссор compressor.

компромети́ровать *impf* (*pf* с~) compromise. **компроми́сс** compromise.

компью́тер computer.

комсомо́л Komsomol. **комсомо́лец** (-льца), -лка Komsomol member. **комсомо́льский** Komsomol.

кому́ *see* кто

комфо́рт comfort.

конве́йер conveyor.

конве́рт envelope; sleeve.

конво́йр escort. **конво́йровать** *impf* escort. **конво́й** escort, convoy.

конгре́сс congress.

конденса́тор condenser.

конди́терская *sb* confectioner's, cake shop.

кондиционе́р air-conditioner. **кондицио́нный** air-conditioning.

конду́ктор (*pl* -а́), -торша conductor; guard.

конево́дство horse-breeding. **конёк** (-нька́) *dim of* конь; hobby(-horse).

коне́ц (-нца́) end; **в конце́ концо́в** in the end, after all. **коне́чно** *adv* of course. **коне́чность** extremity. **ко-**

не́чный final, last; ultimate; finite.

кони́ческий conic, conical.

конкре́тный concrete.

конкуре́нт competitor. **конкуре́нция** competition. **конкури́ровать** *impf* compete. **ко́нкурс** competition; contest.

ко́нница cavalry. **ко́нный** horse; mounted; equestrian; ~ заво́д stud.

конопля́ hemp.

консервати́вный conservative. **консерва́тор** Conservative.

консервато́рия conservatoire.

консерви́ровать *impf & pf* (*pf also* за~) preserve; can, bottle. **консе́рвн|ый** preserving; ~ая ба́нка tin; ~ый нож tin-opener. **консерво-откры́ватель** *m* tin-opener. **консе́рвы** (-ов) *pl* tinned goods.

конси́лиум consultation.

конспе́кт synopsis, summary. **конспекти́ровать** *impf* (*pf* за~, про~) make an abstract of.

конспирати́вный secret, clandestine. **конспира́ция** security.

констата́ция ascertaining; establishment. **констати́ровать** *impf & pf* ascertain; establish.

конституцио́нный constitutional. **конститу́ция** constitution.

констру́ировать *impf & pf* (*pf also* с~) construct; design. **констру́кти́вный** structural; constructional; constructive. **констру́ктор** designer, constructor. **констру́кция** construction; design.

ко́нсул consul.

консульта́ция consultation; advice; clinic; tutorial. **консульти́ровать** *impf* (*pf* про~) advise; +c+*instr* consult; ~ся obtain advice; +c+*instr* consult.

конта́кт contact. **конта́ктные ли́нзы** *f pl* contact lenses.

конте́йнер container.

конте́кст context.

контине́нт continent.

конто́ра office. **конто́рский** office.

контраба́нда contraband. **контрабанди́ст** smuggler.

контраба́с double-bass.

контраге́нт contractor. **контра́кт** contract.

контра́льто *neut/fem indecl* contralto (*voice/person*).

контрама́рка complimentary ticket.
контрапу́нкт counterpoint.
контра́ст contrast.
контрибу́ция indemnity.
контрнаступле́ние counter-offensive.
контролёр inspector; ticket-collector. контроли́ровать *impf* (*pf* про~) check; inspect. контро́ль *m* control; check; inspection. контро́льн|ый control; ~ая рабо́та test.
контрразве́дка counter-intelligence; security service. контрреволю́ция counter-revolution.
конту́зия bruising; shell-shock.
ко́нтур contour, outline; circuit.
конура́ kennel.
ко́нус cone.
конфедера́ция confederation.
конфере́нция conference.
конфе́та sweet.
конфискова́ть *impf* & *pf* confiscate.
конфли́кт conflict.
конфо́рка ring (*on stove*).
конфу́з discomfort, embarrassment. конфу́зить (-у́жу) (*pf* с~) confuse, embarrass; ~ся feel embarrassed.
концентра́т concentrate. концентрацио́нный concentration. конце́нтрация concentration. концентри́ровать(ся *impf* (*pf* с~) concentrate.
конце́пция conception.
конце́рт concert; concerto. концертме́йстер leader; soloist. конце́ртный concert.
концла́герь *abbr* (*of* концентрацио́нный ла́герь) concentration camp.
конча́ть *impf*, ко́нчить *pf* finish; end; +*inf* stop; ~ся end, finish; expire. ко́нчик tip. кончи́на decease.
конь (-я́; *pl* -и, -е́й) *m* horse; knight. коньки́ (-о́в) *pl* skates; ~ на ро́ликах roller skates. конькобе́жец (-жца) skater.
конья́к (-а́) cognac.
ко́нюх groom, stable-boy. коню́шня (*gen pl* -шен) stable.
кооперати́в cooperative. кооперати́вный cooperative. коопера́ция cooperation.
координа́та coordinate. координа́ция coordination.

копа́ть *impf* (*pf* копну́ть, вы́~) dig; dig up, dig out; ~ся rummage.
копе́йка copeck.
ко́пи (-ей) *pl* mines.
копи́лка money-box.
копи́рка carbon paper. копирова́льный copying. копи́ровать *impf* (*pf* с~) copy; imitate.
копи́ть (-плю́, -пишь) *impf* (*pf* на~) save (up); accumulate; ~ся accumulate.
ко́пия copy.
копна́ (*pl* -ы, -пён) shock, stook.
копну́ть (-ну́, -нёшь) *pf of* копа́ть
ко́поть soot.
копте́ть (-пчу́) *impf* swot; vegetate.
копти́ть (-пчу́) *impf* (*pf* за~, на~) smoke, cure; blacken with smoke. копче́ние smoking; smoked foods. копчёный smoked.
копы́то hoof.
копьё (*pl* -я, -пий) spear, lance.
кора́ bark, rind; cortex; crust.
кора́бельный ship; naval. кораблевожде́ние navigation. кораблекруше́ние shipwreck. кораблестрое́ние shipbuilding. кора́бль (-я́) *m* ship, vessel; nave.
кора́лл coral.
коре́йский Korean. Коре́я Korea.
корена́стый thickset. корени́ться *impf* be rooted. коренно́й radical, fundamental; native. ко́рень (-рня; *pl* -и, -е́й) *m* root. корешо́к (-шка́) root(let); spine; counterfoil.
корзи́на, корзи́нка basket.
коридо́р corridor.
кори́ца cinnamon.
кори́чневый brown.
ко́рка crust; rind, peel.
корм (*loc* -у́; *pl* -а́) fodder.
корма́ stern.
корми́лец (-льца) bread-winner. корми́ть (-млю́, -мишь) *impf* (*pf* на~, по~, про~) feed; ~ся feed; +*instr* live on, make a living by. кормле́ние feeding. кормово́й[1] fodder.
кормово́й[2] stern.
корнево́й root; radical. корнепло́ды (-ов) root-crops.
коро́бить (-блю) *impf* (*pf* по~) warp; jar upon; ~ся (*pf also* с~ся) warp.
коро́бка box.

коро́ва cow.

короле́ва queen. короле́вский royal. короле́вство kingdom. коро́ль (-я́) *m* king.

коромы́сло yoke; beam; rocking shaft.

коро́на crown.

коронаротромбо́з coronary (thrombosis).

коро́нка crown. короно́ва́ть *impf & pf* crown.

коро́ткий (ко́роток, -тка́, ко́ротко́, ко́ротки́) short; intimate. коро́тко *adv* briefly; intimately. коротково́лновый short-wave. коро́че *comp of* коро́ткий, ко́ротко

корпора́ция corporation.

ко́рпус (*pl* -ы, -ов *or* -а́, -о́в) corps; services; building; hull; housing; case; body.

корректи́ровать *impf* (*pf* про~, с~) correct, edit. корре́ктный correct, proper. корре́ктор (*pl* -а́) proof-reader. корректу́ра proofreading; proof.

корреспонде́нт correspondent. корреспонде́нция correspondence.

корро́зия corrosion.

корру́пция corruption.

корт (tennis-)court.

корте́ж cortège; motorcade.

ко́ртик dirk.

ко́рточки (-чек) *pl*; сиде́ть на ко́рточках squat.

корчева́ть (-чу́ю) *impf* root out.

ко́рчить (-чу) *impf* (*pf* с~) contort; *impers* convulse; ~ из себя́ pose as; ~ся writhe.

ко́ршун kite.

коры́стный mercenary. коры́сть avarice; profit.

коры́то trough; wash-tub.

корь measles.

коса́[1] (*acc* -у; *pl* -ы) plait, tress.

коса́[2] (*acc* ко́су; *pl* -ы) spit.

коса́[3] (*acc* ко́су; *pl* -ы) scythe.

ко́свенный indirect.

коси́лка mowing-machine, mower. коси́ть[1] (кошу́, ко́сишь) *impf* (*pf* с~) cut; mow (down).

коси́ть[2] (кошу́) *impf* (*pf* по~, с~) squint; be crooked; ~ся slant; look sideways; look askance.

косме́тика cosmetics, make-up.

косми́ческий cosmic; space. космо-

дро́м spacecraft launching-site. космона́вт, -на́втка cosmonaut, astronaut. ко́смос cosmos; (outer) space.

косноязы́чный tongue-tied.

косну́ться (-ну́сь, -нёшься) *pf of* каса́ться

косогла́зие squint. косо́й (кос, -а́, -о) slanting; oblique; sidelong; squinting, cross-eyed.

костёр (-тра́) bonfire; camp-fire.

костля́вый bony. ко́сточка (small) bone; stone.

косты́ль (-я́) *m* crutch.

кость (*loc* и́; *pl* -и, -е́й) bone; die.

костю́м clothes; suit. костюмиро́ванный fancy-dress.

костяно́й bone; ivory.

косы́нка (*triangular*) head-scarf, shawl.

кот (-а́) tom-cat.

котёл (-тла́) boiler; copper, cauldron. котело́к (-лка́) pot; mess-tin; bowler (hat). коте́льная *sb* boiler-room, -house.

котёнок (-нка; *pl* -тя́та, -тя́т) kitten. ко́тик fur-seal; sealskin.

котле́та rissole; burger; отбивна́я ~ chop.

котлова́н foundation pit, trench.

кото́мка knapsack.

кото́рый *pron* which, what; who; that; ~ час? what time is it?

котя́та *etc.: see* котёнок

ко́фе *m indecl* coffee. кофева́рка percolator. кофе́ин caffeine.

ко́фта, ко́фточка blouse, top.

коча́н (-а́ *or* -чна́) (cabbage-)head.

кочева́ть (-чу́ю) *impf* be a nomad; wander; migrate. коче́вник nomad. кочево́й nomadic.

кочега́р stoker, fireman. кочега́рка stokehold, stokehole.

коченѐть *impf* (*pf* за~, о~) grow numb.

кочерга́ (*gen pl* -рёг) poker.

ко́чка hummock.

кошелёк (-лька́) purse.

ко́шка cat.

кошма́р nightmare. кошма́рный nightmarish.

кошу́ *etc.: see* коси́ть

кощу́нство blasphemy.

коэффицие́нт coefficient.

КП *abbr* (*of* Коммунисти́ческая па́ртия) Communist Party. КПСС *abbr* (*of* Коммунисти́ческая па́ртия

Сове́тского Сою́за) Communist Party of the Soviet Union, CPSU.

краб crab.

кра́деный stolen. **краду́** etc.: see **красть**

кра́жа theft; ~ со взло́мом burglary.

край (loc -ю́; pl -я́, -ёв) edge; brink; land; region. **кра́йне** adv extremely. **кра́йний** extreme; last; outside, wing; по кра́йней ме́ре at least. **кра́йность** extreme; extremity.

крал etc.: see **красть**

кран tap; crane.

крапи́ва nettle.

краса́вец (-вца) handsome man. **краса́вица** beauty. **краси́вый** beautiful; handsome.

краси́тель m dye. **кра́сить** (-а́шу) impf (pf вы́~, о~, по~) paint; colour; dye; stain; ~ся (pf на~) make-up. **кра́ска** paint, dye; colour.

красне́ть (-е́ю) impf (pf по~) blush; redden; show red.

красноарме́ец (-е́йца) Red Army man. **красноарме́йский** Red Army. **красноречи́вый** eloquent.

краснота́ redness. **красну́ха** German measles. **кра́сный** (-сен, -сна́, -о) red; beautiful; fine; ~ое де́рево mahogany; ~ая сморо́дина (no pl; usu collect) redcurrant; redcurrants; ~ая строка́ (first line of) new paragraph.

красова́ться impf impress by one's beauty; show off. **красота́** (pl -ы) beauty. **кра́сочный** paint; ink; colourful.

красть (-аду́, -аде́шь; крал) impf (pf у~) steal; ~ся creep.

кра́тер crater.

кра́ткий (-ток, -тка́, -о) short; brief. **кратковре́менный** brief; transitory. **кратко́срочный** short-term.

кра́тное sb multiple.

кратча́йший superl of **кра́ткий**. **кра́тче** comp of **кра́ткий**, **кра́тко**

крах crash; failure.

крахма́л starch. **крахма́лить** impf (pf на~) starch.

кра́ше comp of **краси́вый**, **краси́во**

кра́шеный painted; coloured; dyed; made up. **кра́шу** etc.: see **кра́сить**

креве́тка shrimp; prawn.

креди́т credit. **креди́тный** credit. **кредитоспосо́бный** solvent.

кре́йсер (pl -а́, -о́в) cruiser.

крем cream.

кремато́рий crematorium.

креме́нь (-мня́) m flint.

кремль (-я́) m citadel; Kremlin.

кре́мний silicon.

кре́мовый cream.

крен list, heel; bank. **крени́ться** impf (pf на~) heel over, list; bank.

крепи́ть (-плю́) impf strengthen; support; make fast; constipate; ~ся hold out. **кре́пкий** (-пок, -пка́, -о) strong; firm; ~ие напи́тки spirits. **крепле́ние** strengthening; fastening.

кре́пнуть (-ну; -еп) impf (pf о~) get stronger.

крепостни́чество serfdom. **крепостно́й** serf; ~ое пра́во serfdom; ~о́й sb serf.

кре́пость fortress; strength. **кре́пче** comp of **кре́пкий**, **кре́пко**

кре́сло (gen pl -сел) arm-chair; stall.

крест (-а́) cross. **крести́ны** (-и́н) pl christening. **крести́ть** (крещу́, -е́стишь) impf & pf (pf also о~, пере~) christen; make sign of the cross over; ~ся cross o.s.; be christened. **крест-на́крест** adv crosswise. **кре́стник, кре́стница** godchild. **крёстный** ~ая (мать) godmother; ~ый оте́ц godfather. **кресто́но́сец** (-сца) crusader. **крестоно́сец** (-сца) crusader.

крестья́нин (pl -я́не, -я́н), **крестья́нка** peasant. **крестья́нский** peasant. **крестья́нство** peasantry.

креще́ние christening; Epiphany. **крещёный** (-ён, -ена́) baptized; sb Christian. **крещу́** etc.: see **крести́ть**

крива́я sb curve. **кривизна́** crookedness; curvature. **криви́ть** (-влю́) impf (pf по~, с~) bend, distort; ~ душо́й go against one's conscience; ~ся become crooked or bent; make a wry face. **кривля́ться** impf give o.s. airs.

криво́й (крив, -а́, -о) crooked; curved; one-eyed.

кри́зис crisis.

крик cry, shout.

крике́т cricket.

кри́кнуть (-ну) pf of **крича́ть**

кримина́льный criminal.

криста́лл crystal. **кристалли́ческий** crystal.

крите́рий criterion.

кри́тик critic. **кри́тика** criticism; critique. **критикова́ть** *impf* criticize. **крити́ческий** critical.

крича́ть (-чу́) *impf* (*pf* **кри́кнуть**) cry, shout.

кров roof; shelter.

крова́вый bloody.

крова́тка, крова́ть bed.

кровено́сный blood-; circulatory.

кро́вля (*gen pl* -вель) roof.

кро́вный blood; thoroughbred; vital, intimate.

крово- *in comb* blood. **кровожа́дный** bloodthirsty. ~**изли́я́ние** haemorrhage. ~**обраще́ние** circulation. ~**проли́тие** bloodshed. ~**проли́тный** bloody. ~**смеше́ние** incest. ~**тече́ние** bleeding; haemorrhage. ~**точи́ть** (-чи́т) *impf* bleed.

кровь (*loc* -и́) blood. **кровяно́й** blood.

кро́и́ть (крою́) *impf* (*pf* **с**~) cut (out). **кро́йка** cutting out.

крокоди́л crocodile.

кро́лик rabbit.

кроль *m* crawl(-stroke).

кроль́чи́ха she-rabbit, doe.

кро́ме *prep+gen* except; besides; ~ того́ besides, moreover.

кро́мка edge.

кро́на crown; top.

кронште́йн bracket; corbel.

кропотли́вый painstaking; laborious.

кросс cross-country race.

кроссво́рд crossword (puzzle).

крот (-á) mole.

кро́ткий (-ток, -тка́, -тко) meek, gentle. **кро́тость** gentleness; mildness.

кро́хотный, кро́шечный tiny. **кро́шка** crumb; a bit.

круг (*loc* -ý; *pl* -и́) circle; circuit; sphere. **круглосу́точный** round-the-clock. **кру́глый** (кругл, -á, -о) round; complete; ~ год all the year round. **кругово́й** circular; all-round. **кругозо́р** prospect; outlook. **круго́м** *adv* around; *prep+gen* round. **кругосве́тный** round-the-world.

кружевно́й lace; lacy. **кру́жево** (*pl* -á, -ев, -áм) lace.

кружи́ть (-ужу́, -у́жи́шь) *impf* whirl, spin round; ~**ся** whirl, spin round.

кру́жка mug.

кружо́к (-жка́) circle, group.

круи́з cruise.

крупа́ (*pl* -ы) groats; sleet. **крупи́ца** grain.

кру́пный large, big; great; coarse; ~ый план close-up.

крутизна́ steepness.

крути́ть (-учу́, -у́тишь) *impf* (*pf* **за**~, **с**~) twist, twirl; roll; turn, wind; ~**ся** turn, spin; whirl.

круто́й (крут, -á, -о) steep; sudden; sharp; severe; drastic. **кру́ча** steep slope. **кру́че** *comp of* **круто́й, кру́то**

кручу́ etc.: see **крути́ть**

круше́ние crash; ruin; collapse.

крыжо́вник gooseberries; gooseberry bush.

крыла́тый winged. **крыло́** (*pl* -лья, -льев) wing; vane; mudguard.

крыльцо́ (*pl* -а, -ле́ц, -ца́м) porch; (front, back) steps.

Крым the Crimea. **кры́мский** Crimean.

кры́са rat.

крыть (кро́ю) *impf* cover; roof; trump; ~**ся** be, lie; be concealed. **кры́ша** roof. **кры́шка** lid.

крюк (-á; *pl* -ки́, -ко́в *or* -ю́чья, -чьев) hook; detour. **крючо́к** (-чка́) hook.

кря́ду *adv* in succession.

кряж ridge.

кря́кать *impf*, **кря́кнуть** (-ну) *pf* quack.

кряхте́ть (-хчу́) *impf* groan.

кста́ти *adv* to the point; opportunely; at the same time; by the way.

кто (кого́, кому́, кем, ком) *pron* who; anyone; ~ (бы) ни whoever. **кто́-либо, кто́-нибудь** *prons* anyone; someone. **кто́-то** *pron* someone.

куб (*pl* -ы́) cube; boiler; в ~е cubed. **ку́бик** brick, block.

куби́нский Cuban.

куби́ческий cubic; cube.

ку́бок (-бка) goblet; cup.

кубоме́тр cubic metre.

кувши́н jug; pitcher. **кувши́нка** water-lily.

кувырка́ться *impf*, **кувыркну́ться** (-ну́сь) *pf* turn somersaults. **кувырко́м** *adv* head over heels; topsy-turvy.

куда́ *adv* where (to); what for; +*comp* much, far; ~ (бы) ни wherever. **куда́-либо, куда́-нибудь** *adv* anywhere, somewhere. **куда́-то** *adv* somewhere.

ку́дри (-е́й) *pl* curls. **кудря́вый** curly; florid.

кузне́ц (-а́) blacksmith. **кузне́чик** grasshopper. **ку́зница** forge, smithy.

ку́зов (*pl* -а́) basket; body.

ку́кла doll; puppet. **ку́колка** dolly; chrysalis. **ку́кольный** doll's; puppet.

кукуру́за maize.

куку́шка cuckoo.

кула́к (-а́) fist; kulak. **кула́цкий** kulak. **кула́чный** fist.

кулёк (-лька́) bag.

кули́к (-а́) sandpiper.

кулина́рия cookery. **кулина́рный** culinary.

кули́сы (-йс) wings; **за кули́сами** behind the scenes.

кули́ч (-а́) Easter cake.

кулуа́ры (-ов) *pl* lobby.

кульмина́ция culmination.

культ cult. **культиви́ровать** *impf* cultivate.

культу́ра culture; standard; cultivation. **культури́зм** body-building. **культу́рно** *adv* in a civilized manner. **культу́рный** cultured; cultivated; cultural.

куми́р idol.

кумы́с koumiss (*fermented mare's milk*).

куни́ца marten.

купа́льный bathing. **купа́льня** bathing-place. **купа́ть** *impf* (*pf* вы́-, ис~) bathe; bath; ~ся bathe; take a bath.

купе́ *neut indecl* compartment.

купе́ц (-пца́) merchant. **купе́ческий** merchant. **купи́ть** (-плю́, -пишь) *pf* (*impf* покупа́ть) buy.

ку́пол (*pl* -а́) cupola, dome.

купо́н coupon.

купоро́с vitriol.

купчи́ха merchant's wife; female merchant.

кура́нты (-ов) *pl* chiming clock; chimes.

курга́н barrow; tumulus.

куре́ние smoking. **кури́льщик, -щица** smoker.

кури́ный hen's; chicken's.

кури́ть (-рю́, -ришь) *impf* (*pf* по~) smoke; ~ся burn; smoke.

ку́рица (*pl* ку́ры, кур) hen, chicken.

куро́к (-рка́) cocking-piece; **взвести́** ~ cock a gun; **спусти́ть** ~ pull the trigger.

куропа́тка partridge.

куро́рт health-resort; spa.

курс course; policy; year; exchange rate. **курса́нт** student.

курси́в italics.

курси́ровать *impf* ply.

ку́ртка jacket.

курча́вый curly(-headed).

ку́ры *etc.: see* ку́рица

курьёз a funny thing **курьёзный** curious.

курье́р messenger; courier. **курье́рский** express.

куря́тник hen-house.

куря́щий *sb* smoker.

куса́ть *impf* bite; sting; ~ся bite.

кусо́к (-ска́) piece; lump. **кусо́чек** (-чка) piece.

куст (-а́) bush, shrub. **куста́рник** bush(es), shrub(s).

куста́рн|ый hand-made; handicrafts; primitive; ~ая промы́шленность cottage industry. **куста́рь** (-я́) *m* craftsman.

ку́тать *impf* (*pf* за~) wrap up; ~ся muffle o.s. up.

кути́ть (кучу́, ку́тишь) *impf*, **кутну́ть** (-ну́, -нёшь) *pf* carouse; go on a binge.

куха́рка cook. **ку́хня** (*gen pl* -хонь) kitchen; cuisine. **ку́хонный** kitchen.

ку́ча heap; heaps.

ку́чер (*pl* -а́) coachman.

ку́чка small heap *or* group.

кучу́ *see* кути́ть

куша́к (-а́) sash; girdle.

ку́шанье food; dish. **ку́шать** *impf* (*pf* по~, с~) eat.

куше́тка couch.

кую́ *etc.: see* кова́ть

Л

лабора́нт, -а́нтка laboratory assistant. **лаборато́рия** laboratory.

ла́ва lava.

лави́на avalanche.

ла́вка bench; shop. **ла́вочка** small shop.

лавр bay tree, laurel.

ла́герный camp. **ла́герь** (*pl* -я́ *or* -и,

-ей *or* -ей) *m* camp; campsite.
лад (*loc* -ý; *pl* -ы́, -о́в) harmony; manner, way; stop, fret.
ла́дан incense.
ла́дить (ла́жу) *impf* get on, be on good terms. ла́дно *adv* all right; very well! ла́дный fine, excellent; harmonious.
ладо́нь palm.
ладья́ rook, castle; boat.
ла́жу *etc.: see* ла́дить, ла́зить
лазаре́т field hospital; sick-bay.
ла́зать *see* ла́зить. лазе́йка hole; loop-hole.
ла́зер laser.
ла́зить (ла́жу) ла́зать *impf* climb, clamber.
лазу́рный sky-blue, azure. лазу́рь azure.
лазу́тчик scout; spy.
лай bark, barking. ла́йка[1] (Siberian) husky, laika.
ла́йка[2] kid. ла́йковый kid; kidskin.
ла́йнер liner; airliner.
лак varnish, lacquer.
лака́ть *impf* (*pf* вы́~) lap.
лаке́й footman, man-servant; lackey.
лакирова́ть *impf* (*pf* от~) varnish, lacquer.
ла́кмус litmus.
ла́ковый varnished, lacquered.
ла́комиться (-млюсь) *impf* (*pf* по~) +*instr* treat o.s. to. ла́комка *m & f* gourmand. ла́комство delicacy. ла́комый dainty, tasty; +до fond of.
лakoни́чный laconic.
ла́мпа lamp; valve, tube. лампа́да icon-lamp. ла́мпочка lamp; bulb.
ландша́фт landscape.
ла́ндыш lily of the valley.
лань fallow deer; doe.
ла́па paw; tenon.
ла́поть (-птя; *pl* -и, -е́й) *m* bast shoe.
ла́почка pet, sweetie.
лапша́ noodles; noodle soup.
ларёк (-рька́) stall. ларь (-я́) *m* chest; bin.
ла́ска[1] caress.
ла́ска[2] weasel.
ласка́ть *impf* caress, fondle; ~ся +к+*dat* make up to; fawn upon. ла́сковый affectionate, tender.
ла́сточка swallow.
латве́ц (-и́йца), -и́йка Latvian. латви́йский Latvian. Ла́твия

Latvia.
лати́нский Latin.
лату́нь brass.
ла́ты (лат) *pl* armour.
латы́нь Latin.
латы́ш, латы́шка Latvian, Lett. латы́шский Latvian, Lettish.
лауреа́т prize-winner.
ла́цкан lapel.
лачу́га hovel, shack.
ла́ять (ла́ю) *impf* bark.
лба *etc.: see* лоб
лгать (лгу, лжёшь; лгал, -а́, -о) *impf* (*pf* на~, со~) lie; tell lies; +на+*acc* slander. лгун (-а́), лгу́нья liar.
лебеди́ный swan. лебёдка swan, pen; winch. ле́бедь (*pl* -и, -е́й) *m* swan, cob.
лев (льва) lion.
левобере́жный left-bank. левша́ (*gen pl* -е́й) *m & f* left-hander. ле́вый *adj* left; left-hand; left-wing.
лёг *etc.: see* лечь
лега́льный legal.
леге́нда legend. легенда́рный legendary.
лёгк|ий (-гок, -гка́, лёгки́) light; easy; slight, mild; ~ая атле́тика field and track events. легко́ *adv* easily, lightly, slightly.
легко- *in comb* light; easy, easily. легкове́рный credulous. ~ве́с light-weight. ~мы́сленный thoughtless; flippant, frivolous, superficial. ~мы́слие flippancy, frivolity.
легков|о́й: ~а́я маши́на (private) car. лёгкое *sb* lung. лёгкость lightness; easiness. ле́гче *comp of* лёгкий, легко́
лёд (льда, *loc* -у́) ice. ледене́ть (-е́ю) *impf* (*pf* за~, о~) freeze; grow numb with cold. леденец (-нца́) fruit-drop. леденя́щий chilling, icy.
ле́ди *f indecl* lady.
ле́дник[1] ice-box; refrigerator van. ледни́к[2] (-а́) glacier. леднико́вый glacial; ~ пери́од Ice Age. ледо́вый ice. ледоко́л ice-breaker. ледяно́й icy; ice.
лежа́ть (-жу́) *impf* lie; be, be situated. лежа́чий lying (down).
ле́звие (cutting) edge; razor-blade.
лезть (-зу; лез) *impf* (*pf* по~) climb, clamber, crawl; get, go; fall out.
лейбори́ст Labourite.

ле́йка watering-can.

лейтена́нт lieutenant.

лека́рство medicine.

ле́ксика vocabulary. **лексико́н** lexicon; vocabulary.

ле́ктор lecturer. **ле́кция** lecture.

леле́ять (-е́ю) *impf* (*pf* вз~) cherish, foster.

лён (льна) flax.

лени́вый lazy.

ленингра́дский (of) Leningrad. **ле́нинский** (of) Lenin; Leninist.

лени́ться (-ню́сь, -нишься) *impf* (*pf* по~) be lazy; +*inf* be too lazy to.

ле́нта ribbon; band; tape.

ленти́й, -я́йка lazy-bones. **лень** laziness.

лепесто́к (-тка́) petal.

ле́пет babble; prattle. **лепета́ть** (-ечу́, -е́чешь) *impf* (*pf* про~) babble, prattle.

лепёшка scone; tablet, pastille.

лепи́ть (-плю́, -пишь) *impf* (*pf* вы́~, за~, с~) model, fashion; mould; ~ся cling; crawl. **ле́пка** modelling. **лепно́й** modelled, moulded.

лес (*loc* -у́; *pl* -а́) forest, wood; *pl* scaffolding.

леса́ (*pl* ле́сы) fishing-line.

лесни́к (-а́) forester. **лесни́чий** *sb* forestry officer; forest warden. **лесно́й** forest.

лесо- *in comb* forest, forestry; timber wood. **лесово́дство** forestry. ~**загото́вка** logging. ~**пи́лка**, ~**пи́льня** (*gen pl* -лен) sawmill. ~**ру́б** woodcutter.

ле́стница stairs, staircase; ladder.

ле́стный flattering. **лесть** flattery.

лёт (*loc* -у́) flight, flying.

лета́ (лет) *pl* years; age; **ско́лько вам лет?** how old are you?

лета́тельный flying. **лета́ть** *impf*, **лете́ть** (лечу́) *impf* (*pf* полете́ть) fly; rush; fall.

ле́тний summer.

лётный flying, flight.

ле́то (*pl* -а́) summer; *pl* years. **ле́том** *adv* in summer.

ле́топись chronicle.

летосчисле́ние chronology.

лету́ч|ий flying; passing; brief; volatile; ~**ая мышь** bat. **лётчик, -чица** pilot.

лече́бница clinic. **лече́бный** medical; medicinal. **лече́ние** (medical) treatment. **лечи́ть** (-чу́, -чишь) *impf* treat (**от** for); ~**ся** be given, have treatment (**от** for).

лечу́ *etc.*: *see* **лете́ть, лечи́ть**

лечь (ля́гу, ля́жешь; лёг, -ла́) *pf* (*impf* ложи́ться) lie, lie down; go to bed.

лещ (-а́) bream.

лжесвиде́тельство false witness.

лжец (-а́) liar. **лжи́вый** lying; deceitful.

ли, ль *interrog partl & conj* whether, if; **ли,... ли** whether ... or; **ра́но ли, по́здно ли** sooner or later.

либера́л liberal. **либера́льный** liberal.

ли́бо *conj* or; ~**...** ~ either ... or.

ли́вень (-вня) *m* heavy shower, downpour.

ливре́я livery.

ли́га league.

ли́дер leader. **лиди́ровать** *impf & pf* be in the lead.

лиза́ть (лижу́, -е́шь) *impf*, **лизну́ть** (-ну́, -нёшь) *pf* lick.

ликвида́ция liquidation; abolition. **ликвиди́ровать** *impf & pf* liquidate; abolish.

ликёр liqueur.

ликова́ние rejoicing. **ликова́ть** *impf* rejoice.

ли́лия lily.

лило́вый lilac, violet.

лима́н estuary.

лими́т limit.

лимо́н lemon. **лимона́д** lemonade; squash. **лимо́нный** lemon.

ли́мфа lymph.

лингви́ст linguist. **лингви́стика** linguistics. **лингвисти́ческий** linguistic.

лине́йка ruler; line. **лине́йный** linear; ~ **кора́бль** battleship.

ли́нза lens.

ли́ния line.

лино́леум lino(leum).

линя́ть *impf* (*pf* вы́~, по~, с~) fade; moult.

ли́па lime tree.

ли́пкий (-пок, -пка́, -о) sticky. **ли́пнуть** (-ну; лип) *impf* stick.

ли́повый lime.

ли́ра lyre. **ли́рик** lyric poet. **ли́рика** lyric poetry. **лири́ческий** lyric; lyrical.

лиса́ (*pl* -ы),-си́ца fox.

лист (-а́; *pl* -ы́ *or* -ья, -ов *or* -ьев) leaf; sheet; page; form; игра́ть с ~а́ play at sight. листа́ть *impf* leaf through. листва́ foliage. ли́ственница larch. ли́ственный deciduous.

листо́вка leaflet. листово́й sheet, plate; leaf. листо́к (-тка́) *dim of* лист; leaflet; form, pro-forma.

Литва́ Lithuania.

лите́йный founding, casting.

литера́тор man of letters. литерату́ра literature. литерату́рный literary.

лито́вец (-вца), лито́вка Lithuanian. лито́вский Lithuanian.

лито́й cast.

литр litre.

лить (лью, льёшь; лил, -а́, -о) *impf* (*pf* с~) pour; shed; cast, mould. литьё founding, casting, moulding; castings, mouldings. ли́ться (льётся; ли́лся, -а́сь, ли́ло́сь) *impf* flow; pour.

лиф bodice. ли́фчик bra.

лифт lift.

лихо́й[1] (лих, -а́, -о) dashing, spirited. лихо́й[2] (лих, -а́, -о, ли́хи́) evil.

лихора́дка fever. лихора́дочный feverish.

лицево́й facial; exterior; front.

лицеме́р hypocrite. лицеме́рие hypocrisy. лицеме́рный hypocritical.

лицо́ (*pl* -а) face; exterior; right side; person; быть к лицу́ +*dat* suit, befit. личи́нка larva, grub; maggot. ли́чно *adv* personally, in person. ли́чность personality; person. ли́чный personal; private; ~ соста́в staff, personnel.

лиша́й lichen; herpes; shingles. лиша́йник lichen.

лиша́ть(ся *impf of* лиши́ть(ся

лише́ние deprivation; privation. лишённый (-ён, -ена́) +*gen* lacking in, devoid of. лиши́ть (-шу́) *pf* (*impf* лиша́ть) +*gen* deprive of; ~ся +*gen* lose, be deprived of. ли́шний superfluous; unnecessary; spare; ~ раз once more; с ~им odd, and more.

лишь *adv* only; *conj* as soon as; ~ бы if only, provided that.

лоб (лба, *loc* лбу) forehead.

ло́бзик fret-saw.

лови́ть (-влю́, -вишь) *impf* (*pf* пойма́ть) catch, try to catch.

ло́вкий (-вок, -вка́, -о) adroit; cunning. ло́вкость adroitness; cunning.

ло́вля (*gen pl* -вель) catching, hunting; fishing-ground. лову́шка trap.

ло́вче *comp of* ло́вкий

логари́фм logarithm.

ло́гика logic. логи́ческий, логи́чный logical.

ло́говище, ло́гово den, lair.

ло́дка boat.

лоды́рничать *impf* loaf, idle about. ло́дырь *m* loafer, idler.

ло́жа box; (masonic) lodge.

ложби́на hollow.

ло́же couch; bed.

ложи́ться (-жу́сь) *impf of* лечь

ло́жка spoon.

ло́жный false. ложь (лжи) lie, falsehood.

лоза́ (*pl* -ы) vine.

ло́зунг slogan, catchword.

лока́тор radar *or* sonar apparatus.

локомоти́в locomotive.

ло́кон lock, curl.

ло́коть (-ктя; *pl* -и, -е́й) *m* elbow.

лом (*pl* -ы, -о́в) crowbar; scrap, waste. лома́ный broken. лома́ть *impf* (*pf* по~, с~) break; cause to ache; ~ся break; crack; put on airs; be obstinate.

ломба́рд pawnshop.

ло́мберный стол card-table.

ломи́ть (ло́мит) *impf* break; break through, rush; *impers* cause to ache; ~ся be (near to) breaking. ло́мка breaking; *pl* quarry. ло́мкий (-мок, -мка́, -о) fragile, brittle.

ломо́ть (-мтя́; *pl* -мти́) *m* large slice; hunk; chunk. ло́мтик slice.

ло́но bosom, lap.

ло́пасть (*pl* -и, -е́й) blade; fan, vane; paddle.

лопа́та spade; shovel. лопа́тка shoulder-blade; shovel; trowel.

ло́паться *impf*, ло́пнуть (-ну) *pf* burst; split; break; fail; crash.

лопу́х (-а́) burdock.

лорд lord.

лоси́на elk-skin, chamois leather; elk-meat.

лоск lustre, shine.

лоску́т (-а́; *pl* -ы́ *or* -ья, -о́в *or* -ьев) rag, shred, scrap.

лосни́ться *impf* be glossy, shine.

ло́сось *m* salmon.

лось (*pl* -и, -éй) *m* elk.
лосьóн lotion; aftershave; cream.
лот lead, plummet.
лотерéя lottery, raffle.
лотóк (-ткá) hawker's stand *or* tray; chute; gutter; trough.
лохмáтый shaggy; dishevelled.
лохмóтья (-ьев) *pl* rags.
лóцман pilot.
лошадúный horse; equine. **лóшадь** (*pl* -и, -éй, *instr* -дьмú *or* -дя́ми) horse.
лощёный glossy, polished.
лощúна hollow, depression.
лоя́льный fair, honest; loyal.
лубóк (-бкá) splint; popular print.
луг (*loc* -ý; *pl* -á) meadow.
лýжа puddle.
лужáйка lawn, glade.
лужёный tin-plated.
лук[1] onions.
лук[2] bow.
лукáвить (-влю) *impf* (*pf* с~) be cunning. **лукáвство** craftiness. **лукáвый** crafty, cunning.
лýковица onion; bulb.
лунá (*pl* -ы) moon. **лунáтик** sleep-walker.
лýнка hole; socket.
лýнный moon; lunar.
лýпа magnifying-glass.
лупúть (-плю, -пишь) *impf* (*pf* от~) flog.
луч (-á) ray; beam. **лучевóй** ray, beam; radial; radiation. **лучезáрный** radiant.
лучúна splinter.
лýчше better; ~ всегó, ~ всех best of all. **лýчш|ий** better; best; в ~ем слýчае at best; всегó ~его! all the best!
лыжа ski. **лыжник** skier. **лыжный спорт** skiing. **лыжня́** ski-track.
лыко bast.
лысéть (-éю) *impf* (*pf* об~, по~) grow bald. **лысина** bald spot; blaze. **лысый** (лыс, -á, -о) bald.
ль *see* ли
льва *etc.: see* лев. **львúный** lion, lion's. **львúца** lioness.
льгóта privilege; advantage. **льгóтный** privileged; favourable.
льда *etc.: see* лёд. **льдúна** block of ice; ice-floe.
льна *etc.: see* лён. **льновóдство** flax-growing.
льнýть (-ну, -нёшь) *impf* (*pf* при~) +к+*dat* cling to; have a weakness for; make up to.
льняно́й flax, flaxen; linen; linseed.
льстéц (-á) flatterer. **льстúвый** flattering; smooth-tongued. **льстúть** (льщу) *impf* (*pf* по~) +*dat* flatter.
лью *etc.: see* пить
любéзность courtesy; kindness; compliment. **любéзн|ый** courteous; obliging; kind; бýдьте ~ы be so kind (as to).
любúмец (-мца), -**мица** pet, favourite. **любúмый** beloved; favourite.
любúтель *m*, -**ница** lover; amateur. **любúтельский** amateur. **любúть** (-блю, -бишь) *impf* love; like.
любовáться *impf* (*pf* по~) +*instr* or на+*acc* admire.
любóвник lover. **любóвница** mistress. **любóвный** love-; loving. **любóвь** (-бвú, *instr* -бóвью) love.
любознáтельный inquisitive.
любóй any; either; *sb* anyone.
любопы́тный curious; inquisitive. **любопы́тство** curiosity.
любя́щий loving.
лю́ди (-éй, -ям, -дьмú, -ях) *pl* people. **лю́дный** populous; crowded. **людоéд** cannibal; ogre. **людскóй** human.
люк hatch(way); trap; manhole.
лю́лька cradle.
люминесцéнтный luminescent. **люминесцéнция** luminescence.
лю́стра chandelier.
лю́тня (*gen pl* -ен) lute.
лю́тый (лют, -á, -о) ferocious.
лягáть *impf*, **лягнýть** (-ну́, -нёшь) *pf* kick; ~ся kick.
ля́гу *etc.: see* печь
лягýшка frog.
ля́жка thigh, haunch.
ля́згать *impf* clank; +*instr* rattle.
ля́мка strap; тянýть ля́мку toil.

M

мавзолéй mausoleum.
мавр, **мавритáнка** Moor. **мавритáнский** Moorish.
магазúн shop.
магúстр (holder of) master's degree.

магистра́ль main; main line, main road.

маги́ческий magic(al). **ма́гия** magic.

магнети́зм magnetism.

ма́гний magnesium.

магни́т magnet. **магни́тный** magnetic. **магнитофо́н** tape-recorder.

мада́м f indecl madam, madame.

мажо́р major (key); cheerful mood. **мажо́рный** major; cheerful.

ма́зать (**ма́жу**) impf (pf вы~, за~, из~, на~, по~, про~) oil, grease; smear, spread; soil; ~ся get dirty; make up. **мазо́к** (-зка́) touch, dab; smear. **мазу́т** fuel oil. **мазь** ointment; grease.

маи́с maize.

май May. **ма́йский** May.

ма́йка T-shirt.

майо́р major.

мак poppy, poppy-seeds.

макаро́ны (-н) pl macaroni.

мака́ть impf (pf макну́ть) dip.

маке́т model; dummy.

макну́ть (-ну́, -нёшь) pf of мака́ть

макре́ль mackerel.

максима́льный maximum. **ма́ксимум** maximum; at most.

макулату́ра waste paper; pulp literature.

маку́шка top; crown.

мал etc.: see ма́лый

малахи́т malachite.

мале́йший least, slightest. **ма́ленький** little; small.

мали́на (no pl; usu collect) raspberry; raspberries; raspberry-bush. **мали́новый** raspberry.

ма́ло adv little, few; not enough; ~ того́ moreover; ~ того́ что... not only ....

мало- in comb (too) little. **малова́жный** of little importance. ~вероя́тный unlikely. ~гра́мотный semi-literate; crude. ~ду́шный faint-hearted. ~иму́щий needy. ~кро́вие anaemia. ~ле́тний young; juvenile; minor. ~о́пытный inexperienced. ~чи́сленный small (in number), few.

мало-ма́льски adv in the slightest degree; at all. **мало-пома́лу** adv little by little.

ма́л|ый (мал, -а́) little, (too) small; са́мое ~ое at the least; sb fellow;

lad. **малы́ш** (-а́) kiddy; little boy. **ма́льчик** boy. **мальчи́шка** m urchin, boy. **мальчуга́н** little boy. **малю́тка** m & f baby, little one.

маля́р (-а́) painter, decorator.

маляри́я malaria.

ма́ма mother, mummy. **мама́ша** mummy. **ма́мин** mother's.

ма́монт mammoth.

мандари́н mandarin, tangerine.

манда́т warrant; mandate.

манёвр manoeuvre; shunting. **маневри́ровать** impf (pf с~) manoeuvre; shunt; +instr make good use of.

мане́ж riding-school.

манеке́н dummy; mannequin. **манеке́нщик, -щица** model.

мане́ра manner; style. **мане́рный** affected.

манже́та cuff.

маникю́р manicure.

манипули́ровать impf manipulate. **манипуля́ция** manipulation; machination.

мани́ть (-ню́, -нишь) impf (pf по~) beckon; attract; lure.

манифе́ст manifesto. **манифеста́ция** demonstration.

мани́шка (false) shirt-front.

ма́ния mania; ~ вели́чия megalomania.

ма́нная ка́ша semolina.

мано́метр pressure-gauge.

ма́нтия cloak; robe, gown.

мануфакту́ра manufacture; textiles.

манья́к maniac.

марафо́нский бег marathon.

ма́рганец (-нца) manganese.

маргари́н margarine.

маргари́тка daisy.

марино́ванный pickled. **маринова́ть** impf (pf за~) pickle; put off.

марионе́тка puppet.

ма́рка stamp; counter; brand; trademark; grade; reputation.

ма́ркий easily soiled.

маркси́зм Marxism. **маркси́ст** Marxist. **маркси́стский** Marxist.

ма́рлевый gauze. **ма́рля** gauze; cheesecloth.

мармела́д fruit jellies.

ма́рочный high-quality.

Марс Mars.

март March. **ма́ртовский** March. **марты́шка** marmoset; monkey.

марш march.

ма́ршал marshal.

марширова́ть *impf* march.

маршру́т route, itinerary.

ма́ска mask. маскара́д masked ball; masquerade. маскирова́ть *impf (pf* за~) disguise; camouflage. маски-ро́вка disguise; camouflage.

Ма́сленица Shrovetide. маслёнка butter-dish; oil-can. масли́на olive.

ма́сло (*pl* -á, ма́сел, -слáм) butter; oil; oil paints. маслобо́йка churn. маслобо́йня (*gen pl* -бен), масло-заво́д dairy. масляни́стый oily. ма́сляный oil.

ма́сса mass; a lot, lots.

масса́ж massage. масси́ровать *impf & pf* massage.

масси́в massif; expanse, tract. мас-си́вный massive.

ма́ссовый mass.

ма́стер (*pl* -á), мастери́ца foreman, forewoman; (master) craftsman; expert. мастери́ть *impf (pf* с~) make, build. мастерска́я *sb* workshop. мастерско́й masterly. мастерство́ craft; skill.

масти́ка mastic; putty; floor-polish.

масти́тый venerable.

масть (*pl* -и, -éй) colour; suit.

масшта́б scale.

мат¹ checkmate.

мат² mat.

мат³ foul language.

матема́тик mathematician. матема́-тика mathematics. математи́че-ский mathematical.

материа́л material. материали́зм materialism. материалисти́ческий materialist. материа́льный mater-ial.

матери́к (-á) continent; mainland. материко́вый continental.

матери́нский maternal, motherly. матери́нство maternity.

мате́рия material; pus; topic.

ма́тка womb; female.

ма́товый matt; frosted.

матра́с, матра́ц mattress.

матрёшка Russian doll.

ма́трица matrix; die, mould.

матро́с sailor, seaman.

матч match.

мать (ма́тери, *instr* -рью; *pl* -тери, -рей) mother.

ма́фия Mafia.

max swing, stroke. маха́ть (машу́, ма́шешь) *impf*, махну́ть (-ну́, -нёшь) *pf* +*instr* wave; brandish; wag; flap; go; rush.

махина́ция machinations.

махови́к (-á) fly-wheel.

махро́вый dyed-in-the-wool; terry.

ма́чеха stepmother.

ма́чта mast.

маши́на machine; car. машина́ль-ный mechanical. маши́ни́ст oper-ator; engine-driver; scene-shifter. ма-ши́ни́стка typist; ~-стенографи́ст-ка shorthand-typist. маши́нка machine; typewriter; sewing-machine. машинопи́сный typewritten. ма-ши́нопись typing; typescript. маши-нострое́ние mechanical engineer-ing.

мая́к (-á) lighthouse; beacon.

ма́ятник pendulum. ма́яться *impf* toil; suffer; languish.

мгла haze; gloom.

мгнове́ние instant, moment. мгно-ве́нный instantaneous, momentary.

ме́бель furniture. меблиро́ванный furnished. меблиро́вка furnishing; furniture.

мегава́тт (*gen pl* -а́тт) megawatt. ме-го́м megohm. мегато́нна megaton.

мёд (*loc* -ý; *pl* -ы́) honey.

меда́ль medal. медальо́н medal-lion.

медве́дица she-bear. медве́дь *m* bear. медве́жий bear('s). медве-жо́нок (-нка; *pl* -жа́та, -жа́т) bear cub.

ме́дик medical student; doctor. медикаме́нты (-ов) *pl* medicines. медици́на medicine. медици́нский medical.

ме́дленный slow. медли́тельный sluggish; slow. ме́длить *impf* linger; be slow.

ме́дный copper; brass.

медо́вый honey; ~ ме́сяц honey-moon.

медосмо́тр medical examination, check-up. медпу́нкт first aid post. медсестра́ (*pl* -сёстры, -сестёр, -сёстрам) nurse.

меду́за jellyfish.

медь copper.

меж *prep* +*instr* between.

меж- *in comb* inter-.

межа́ (*pl* -и, меж, -а́м) boundary.

междоме́тие interjection.

ме́жду *prep*+*instr* between; among; ~ про́чим incidentally, by the way; ~ тем meanwhile; ~ тем, как while.

между- *in comb* inter-. **междугоро́дный** inter-city. **~наро́дный** international.

межконтинента́льный intercontinental. **межплане́тный** interplanetary.

мезони́н attic (storey); mezzanine (floor).

Ме́ксика Mexico.

мел (*loc* -у́) chalk.

мёл *etc.*: *see* мести́

меланхо́лия melancholy.

меле́ть (-е́ет) *impf* (*pf* об~) grow shallow.

ме́лкий (-лок, -лка́, -о) small; shallow; fine; petty. **ме́лко** *adv* fine, small. **мелкобуржуа́зный** petty bourgeois. **мелково́дный** shallow.

мелоди́чный melodious, melodic. **мело́дия** melody.

ме́лочный petty. **ме́лочь** (*pl* -и, -е́й) small items; (small) change; *pl* trifles, trivialities.

мель (*loc* -и́) shoal; bank; на мели́ aground.

мелька́ть *impf*, **мелькну́ть** (-ну́, -нёшь) *pf* be glimpsed fleetingly. **ме́льком** *adv* in passing; fleetingly.

ме́льник miller. **ме́льница** mill.

мельча́йший *superl* of ме́лкий. **ме́льче** *comp* of ме́лкий, ме́лко.

мелюзга́ small fry.

мелю́ *etc.*: *see* моло́ть

мембра́на membrane; diaphragm.

мемора́ндум memorandum.

мемуа́ры (-ов) *pl* memoirs.

ме́на exchange, barter.

ме́неджер manager.

ме́нее *adv* less; тем не ~ none the less.

мензу́рка measuring-glass.

меново́й exchange; barter.

менуэ́т minuet.

ме́ньше smaller; less. **меньшеви́к** (-а́) Menshevik. **ме́ньший** lesser, smaller; younger. **меньшинство́** minority.

меню́ *neut indecl* menu.

меня́ *see* я *pron*

меня́ть *impf* (*pf* об~, по~) change; exchange; ~ся change; +*instr* exchange.

ме́ра measure.

мере́щиться (-щусь) *impf* (*pf* по~) seem, appear.

мерза́вец (-вца) swine, bastard.

ме́рзкий (-зок, -зка́, -о) disgusting.

мерзлота́: ве́чная ~ permafrost. **мёрзнуть** (-ну; мёрз) *impf* (*pf* за~) freeze.

ме́рзость vileness; abomination.

меридиа́н meridian.

мери́ло standard, criterion.

ме́рин gelding.

ме́рить *impf* (*pf* по~, с~) measure; try on. **ме́рка** measure.

ме́рный measured; rhythmical. **меропри́ятие** measure.

мертве́ть (-е́ю) *impf* (*pf* о~, по~) grow numb; be benumbed. **мертве́ц** (-а́) corpse, dead man. **мёртвый** (мёртв, -а́, мёртво́) dead.

мерца́ть *impf* twinkle; flicker.

меси́ть (мешу́, ме́сишь) *impf* (*pf* с~) knead.

ме́сса Mass.

места́ми *adv* here and there. **месте́чко** (*pl* -и, -чек) small town.

мести́ (мету́, -тёшь; мёл, -а́) *impf* sweep; whirl.

ме́стность locality; area. **ме́стный** local; locative. **-ме́стный** *in comb* -berth, -seater. **ме́сто** (*pl* -а́) place; site; seat; room; job. **местожи́тельство** (place of) residence. **местоиме́ние** pronoun. **местонахожде́ние** location, whereabouts. **месторожде́ние** deposit; layer.

месть vengeance, revenge.

ме́сяц month; moon. **ме́сячный** monthly; *sb pl* period.

мета́лл metal. **металли́ческий** metal, metallic. **металлу́ргия** metallurgy.

мета́н methane.

мета́ние throwing, flinging. **мета́ть**[1] (мечу́, ме́чешь) *impf* (*pf* метну́ть) throw, fling; ~ся rush about; toss (and turn).

мета́ть[2] *impf* (*pf* на~, с~) tack.

метафи́зика metaphysics.

мета́фора metaphor.

метёлка panicle.

метéль snow-storm.

метеóр meteor. **метеорúт** meteorite. **метеорóлог** meteorologist. **метеорологúческий** meteorological. **метеоролóгия** meteorology.

метеосвóдка weather report. **метеостáнция** weather-station.

мéтить[1] (мéчу) impf (pf на~, по~) mark.

мéтить[2] (мéчу) impf (pf на~) aim; mean.

мéтка marking, mark.

мéткий (-ток, -ткá, -о) well-aimed, accurate.

метлá (pl мётлы, -тел) broom.

метнýть (-нý, -нёшь) pf of **метáть**[1]

мéтод method. **метóдика** method(s); methodology. **метóдичный** methodical. **методолóгия** methodology.

метр metre.

мéтрика birth certificate. **метрúческий**[1]: ~ое свидéтельство birth certificate.

метрúческий[2] metric; metrical.

метрó neut indecl, **метрополитéн** Metro; underground.

метý etc.: see **местú**

мех[1] (loc -ý; pl -á) fur.

мех[2] (pl -и́) wine-skin, water-skin; pl bellows.

механизáция mechanization. **механúзм** mechanism; gear(ing). **механик** mechanic. **механика** mechanics; trick; knack. **механúческий** mechanical; mechanistic.

меховóй fur.

меч (-á) sword.

мéченый marked.

мечéть mosque.

мечтá (day-)dream. **мечтáтельный** dreamy. **мечтáть** impf dream.

мéчу etc.: see **мéтить**. **мечý** etc.: see **метáть**

мешáлка mixer.

мешáть[1] impf (pf по~) +dat hinder; prevent; disturb.

мешáть[2] impf (pf по~, с~) stir; mix; mix up; ~ся (в+acc) interfere (in), meddle (with).

мешóк (-шкá) bag; sack. **мешковúна** sacking, hessian.

мещанúн (pl -áне, -áн) petty bourgeois; Philistine. **мещáнский** bourgeois, narrow-minded; Philistine. **ме-**

щáнство petty bourgeoisie; philistinism, narrow-mindedness.

миг moment, instant.

мигáть impf, **мигнýть** (-нý, -нёшь) pf blink; wink, twinkle.

мúгом adv in a flash.

мигрáция migration.

мигрéнь migraine.

мизантрóп misanthrope.

мизúнец (-нца) little finger; little toe.

микрóб microbe.

микроволнóвая печь microwave oven.

микрóн micron.

микроорганúзм micro-organism.

микроскóп microscope. **микроскопúческий** microscopic.

микросхéма microchip.

микрофóн (gen pl -н) microphone.

мúксер (cul) mixer, blender.

микстýра medicine, mixture.

мúленький pretty; nice; sweet; dear.

милитарúзм militarism.

милиционéр militiaman, policeman.

милúция militia, police force.

миллиáрд billion, a thousand million. **миллимéтр** millimetre. **миллиóн** million. **миллионéр** millionaire.

милосéрдие mercy, charity. **милосéрдный** merciful, charitable.

мúлостивый gracious, kind. **мúлостыня** alms. **мúлость** favour, grace.

мúлый (мил, -á, -о) nice; kind; sweet; dear.

мúля mile.

мúмика (facial) expression; mimicry.

мúмо adv & prep +gen by, past.

мимолётный fleeting. **мимохóдом** adv in passing.

мúна[1] mine; bomb.

мúна[2] expression, mien.

миндáль (-я́) m almond(-tree); almonds.

минерáл mineral. **минералóгия** mineralogy. **минерáльный** mineral.

миниатюра miniature. **миниатюрный** miniature; tiny.

минимáльный minimum. **мúнимум** minimum.

министéрство ministry. **минúстр** minister.

миновáть impf & pf pass; impers+dat escape.

миномёт mortar. **миноносец** (-сца)

torpedo-boat.

мино́р minor (key); melancholy.

мину́вш|ий past; ~ee sb the past.

ми́нус minus.

мину́та minute. мину́тный minute; momentary.

мину́ть (-нешь; ми́нул) pf pass.

мир¹ (pl -ы́) world.

мир² peace.

мира́ж mirage.

мири́ть impf (pf по~, при~) reconcile; ~ся be reconciled. ми́рный peace; peaceful.

мировоззре́ние (world-)outlook; philosophy. мирово́й world. мироздание universe.

миролюби́вый peace-loving.

ми́ска basin, bowl.

мисс f indecl Miss.

миссионе́р missionary.

ми́ссия mission.

ми́стер Mr.

ми́стика mysticism.

мистифика́ция hoax, leg-pull.

ми́тинг mass meeting; rally.

митрополи́т metropolitan.

миф myth. мифи́ческий mythical. мифологи́ческий mythological. мифоло́гия mythology.

ми́чман warrant officer.

мише́нь target.

ми́шка (Teddy) bear.

младе́нец (-нца) baby; infant. мла́дший younger; youngest; junior.

млекопита́ющие sb pl mammals. Мле́чный Путь Milky Way.

мне see я pron

мне́ние opinion.

мни́мый imaginary; sham. мни́тельный hypochondriac; mistrustful.

мнить (мню) impf think.

мно́гие sb pl many (people); ~ое sb much, a great deal. мно́го adv+gen much; many; на ~ by far.

много- in comb many-, poly-, multi-, multiple-. многобо́рье combined event. ~гра́нный polyhedral; manysided. ~де́тный having many children. ~жёнство polygamy. ~значи́тельный significant. ~кра́тный repeated; frequentative. ~ле́тний lasting, living, many years; of many years' standing; perennial. ~лю́дный crowded. ~национа́льный multi-national. ~обеща́ющий prom-

ising. ~обра́зие diversity. ~сло́вный verbose. ~сторо́нний multilateral; many-sided; versatile. ~то́чие dots, omission points. ~уважа́емый respected; Dear. ~уго́льный polygonal. ~цве́тный multi-coloured; multiflorous. ~чи́сленный numerous. ~эта́жный many-storeyed. ~язы́чный polyglot.

мно́жественный plural. мно́жество great number. мно́жить (-жу) impf (pf y~) multiply; increase.

мной etc.: see я pron. мну etc.: see мять

мобилиза́ция mobilization. мобилизова́ть impf & pf mobilize.

мог etc.: see мочь

моги́ла grave. моги́льный (of the) grave; sepulchral.

могу́ etc.: see мочь. могу́чий mighty. могу́щественный powerful. могу́щество power, might.

мо́да fashion.

модели́ровать impf & pf design. моде́ль model; pattern. модельер fashion designer. моде́льный model; fashionable.

модернизи́ровать impf & pf modernize.

мо́дный (-ден, -дна́, -о) fashionable; fashion.

мо́жет see мочь

можжеве́льник juniper.

мо́жно one may, one can; it is permissible; it is possible; как ~+comp as ... as possible; как ~ скоре́е as soon as possible.

моза́ика mosaic; jigsaw.

мозг (loc -ý; pl -и́) brain; marrow. мозгово́й cerebral.

мозо́ль corn; callus.

мой (моего́) m, моя́ (мое́й) f, моё (моего́) neut, мой (-и́х) pl pron my; mine; по-мо́ему in my opinion; in my way.

мо́йка washing.

мо́кнуть (-ну; мок) impf get wet; soak. мокро́та phlegm. мо́крый wet, damp.

мол (loc -ý) mole, pier.

молва́ rumour, talk.

моле́бен (-бна) church service.

моле́кула molecule. молекуля́рный molecular.

моли́тва prayer. моли́ть (-лю́, -лишь) *impf* pray; beg; ~ся (*pf* по~ся) pray.

моллю́ск mollusc.

молниено́сный lightning. мо́лния lightning; zip(-fastener).

молодёжь youth, young people. молоде́ть (-е́ю) *impf* (*pf* по~) get younger, look younger. молоде́ц (-дца́) fine fellow *or* girl; ~! well done! молодожёны (-ов) *pl* newly-weds. молодо́й (мо́лод, -á, -о) young. мо́лодость youth. моло́же *comp* of молодо́й

молоко́ milk.

мо́лот hammer. молоти́ть (-очу́, -о́тишь) *impf* (*pf* с~) thresh; hammer. молото́к (-тка́) hammer. мо́лотый ground. моло́ть (мелю́, ме́лешь) *impf* (*pf* с~) grind, mill.

моло́чная *sb* dairy. моло́чный milk; dairy; milky.

мо́лча *adv* silently, in silence. молчали́вый silent, taciturn; tacit. молча́ние silence. молча́ть (-чу́) *impf* be *or* keep silent.

моль moth.

мольба́ entreaty.

мольбе́рт easel.

моме́нт moment; feature. момента́льно *adv* instantly. момента́льный instantaneous.

мона́рх monarch. монархи́ст monarchist.

монасты́рь (-я́) *m* monastery; convent. мона́х monk. мона́хиня nun.

монго́л, ~ка Mongol.

моне́та coin.

моногра́фия monograph.

моноли́тный monolithic.

моноло́г monologue.

монопо́лия monopoly.

моното́нный monotonous.

монта́ж (-á) assembling; mounting; editing. монта́жник rigger, fitter. монтёр fitter, mechanic. монти́ровать *impf* (*pf* с~) mount; install, fit; edit.

монуме́нт monument. монумента́льный monumental.

мора́ль moral; morals, ethics. мора́льный moral; ethical.

морг morgue.

морга́ть *impf*, моргну́ть (-ну́, -нёшь) *pf* blink; wink.

мо́рда snout, muzzle; (ugly) mug.

мо́ре (*pl* -я́, -éй) sea.

морепла́вание navigation. морепла́ватель *m* seafarer. морехо́дный nautical.

морж (-á), моржи́ха walrus.

Мо́рзе *indecl* Morse; áзбука ~ Morse code.

мори́ть *impf* (*pf* у~) exhaust; ~ го́лодом starve.

морко́вка carrot. морко́вь carrots.

моро́женое *sb* ice-cream. моро́женый frozen, chilled. моро́з frost; *pl* intensely cold weather. моро́зилка freezer compartment; freezer. моро́зильник deep-freeze. моро́зить (-óжу) freeze. моро́зный frosty.

мороси́ть *impf* drizzle.

морск|о́й sea; maritime; marine, nautical; ~áя сви́нка guinea-pig; ~о́й флот navy, fleet.

морфи́й morphine.

морщи́на wrinkle; crease. мо́рщить (-щу) *impf* (*pf* на~, по~, с~) wrinkle; pucker; ~ся knit one's brow; wince; crease, wrinkle.

моря́к (-á) sailor, seaman.

москви́ч (-á), ~ка Muscovite. моско́вский (of) Moscow.

мост (мостá, *loc* -ý; *pl* -ы́) bridge. мо́стик bridge. мости́ть (-ощу́) *impf* (*pf* вы́~) pave. мостки́ (-о́в) *pl* planked footway. мостова́я *sb* roadway; pavement. мостово́й bridge.

мота́ть[1] *impf* (*pf* мотну́ть, на~) wind, reel.

мота́ть[2] *impf* (*pf* про~) squander.

мота́ться *impf* dangle; wander; rush about.

моти́в motive; reason; tune; motif. мотиви́ровать *impf* & *pf* give reasons for, justify. мотивиро́вка reason(s); justification.

мотну́ть (-ну́, -нёшь) *pf* of мота́ть

мото- *in comb* motor-, engine-. мотого́нки (-нок) *pl* motor-cycle races. ~пе́д moped. ~пехо́та motorized infantry. ~ро́ллер (motor-)scooter. ~ци́кл motor cycle.

мото́к (-тка́) skein, hank.

мото́р motor, engine. мотори́ст motor-mechanic. мото́рный motor; engine.

моты́га hoe, mattock.

мотылёк (-лька́) butterfly, moth.

мох (мха or мо́ха, loc мху, pl мхи, мхов) moss. мохна́тый hairy, shaggy.

моча́ urine.

моча́лка loofah.

мочево́й пузы́рь bladder. мочи́ть (-чу́, -чишь) impf (pf за~, на~) wet, moisten; soak; ~ся (pf по~ся) urinate.

мо́чка ear lobe.

мочь (могу́, мо́жешь; мог, -ла́) impf (pf с~) be able; мо́жет (быть) perhaps.

моше́нник rogue. моше́нничать impf (pf с~) cheat, swindle. моше́н-нический rascally.

мо́шка midge. мошкара́ (swarm of) midges.

мо́щность power; capacity. мо́щный (-щен, -щна́, -о) powerful.

мощу́ etc.: see мости́ть

мощь power.

мо́ю etc.: see мыть. мо́ющий washing; detergent.

мрак darkness, gloom. мракобе́с obscurantist.

мра́мор marble. мра́морный marble.

мра́чный dark; gloomy.

мсти́тельный vindictive. мстить (мщу) impf (pf ото~) take vengeance on; +за+acc avenge.

мудре́ц (-а́) sage, wise man. му́д-рость wisdom. му́дрый (-др, -а́, -о) wise, sage.

муж (pl -жья́ or -и́) husband. мужа́ть impf grow up; mature; ~ся take courage. мужеподо́бный mannish; masculine. му́жественный manly, steadfast. му́жество courage.

мужи́к (-а́) peasant; fellow.

мужско́й masculine; male. мужчи́на m man.

му́за muse.

музе́й museum.

му́зыка music. музыка́льный musical. музыка́нт musician.

му́ка[1] torment.

мука́[2] flour.

мультиплика́ция, мультфи́льм cartoon film.

му́мия mummy.

мунди́р (full-dress) uniform.

мундштук (-а́) mouthpiece; cigar-ette-holder.

муниципа́льный municipal.

мураве́й (-вья́) ant. мураве́йник ant-hill.

мурлы́кать (-ы́чу or -каю) impf purr.

муска́т nutmeg.

му́скул muscle. му́скульный mus-cular.

му́сор refuse; rubbish. му́сорный я́щик dustbin.

мусульма́нин (pl -ма́не, -ма́н), -а́нка Muslim.

мути́ть (мучу́, му́тишь) impf (pf вз~) make muddy; stir up, upset. му́тный (-тен, -тна́, -о) turbid, troubled; dull. муть sediment; murk.

му́ха fly.

муче́ние torment, torture. му́ченик, му́ченица martyr. мучи́тельный agonizing. му́чить (-чу) impf (pf за~, из~) torment; harass; ~ся tor-ment o.s.; suffer agonies.

мучно́й flour, meal; starchy.

мха etc.: see мох

мчать (мчу) impf rush along, whirl along; ~ся rush.

мщу etc.: see мстить

мы (нас, нам, на́ми, нас) pron we; мы с ва́ми you and I.

мы́лить impf (pf на~) soap; ~ся wash o.s. мы́ло (pl -а́) soap. мы́льница soap-dish. мы́льный soap, soapy.

мыс cape, promontory.

мы́сленный mental. мы́слимый conceivable. мысли́тель m thinker. мы́слить impf think; conceive. мысль thought; idea. мы́слящий thinking.

мыть (мо́ю) impf (pf вы́~, по~) wash; ~ся wash (o.s.).

мыча́ть (-чу́) impf (pf про~) low, moo; bellow; mumble.

мышело́вка mousetrap.

мы́шечный muscular.

мышле́ние thinking, thought.

мы́шца muscle.

мышь (gen pl -е́й) mouse.

мэр mayor. мэ́рия town hall.

мя́гкий (-гок, -гка́, -о) soft; mild; ~ знак soft sign, the letter ь. мя́гче comp of мя́гкий, мя́гко. мя́коть fleshy part; flesh; pulp.

мяси́стый fleshy; meaty. мясни́к (-а́) butcher. мясно́й meat. мя́со meat;

flesh. мясору́бка mincer.

мя́та mint; peppermint.

мяте́ж (-á) mutiny, revolt. мя-те́жник mutineer, rebel. мяте́жный rebellious; restless.

мя́тный mint, peppermint.

мять (мну, мнёшь) impf (pf из~, раз~, с~) work up; knead; crumple; ~ся become crumpled; crush (easily).

мяу́кать impf miaow.

мяч (-á), мя́чик ball.

Н

на[1] prep I. +acc on; on to, to, into; at; till, until; for; by. II. +prep on, upon; in; at.

на[2] partl here; here you are.

наба́вить (-влю) pf, набавля́ть impf add (to), increase.

наба́т alarm-bell.

набе́г raid, foray.

набекре́нь adv aslant.

на|бели́ть (-éлишь) pf. на́бело adv without corrections.

на́бережная sb embankment, quay.

наберу́ etc.: see набра́ть

набива́ть(ся impf of наби́ть(ся. наби́вка stuffing, padding; (textile) printing.

набира́ть(ся impf of набра́ть(ся

наби́тый packed, stuffed; crowded. наби́ть (-бью, -бьёшь) pf (impf набива́ть) stuff, pack, fill; smash; print; hammer, drive; ~ся crowd in.

наблюда́тель m observer. наблюда́тельный observant; observation. наблюда́ть impf observe, watch; +за+instr look after; supervise. наблюде́ние observation; supervision.

на́божный devout, pious.

набо́к adv on one side, crooked.

наболе́вший sore, painful.

набо́р recruiting; collection; set; typesetting.

набра́сывать(ся impf of наброса́ть, набро́сить(ся

набра́ть (-беру́, -берёшь; -а́л, -á, -о) pf (impf набира́ть) gather; enlist; compose, set up; ~ но́мер dial a number; ~ся assemble, collect; +gen find, acquire, pick up; ~ся сме́лости

pluck up courage.

набрести́ (-еду́, -дёшь; -ёл, -ела́) pf +на+acc come across.

наброса́ть pf (impf набра́сывать) throw (down); sketch; jot down. набро́сить (-óшу) pf (impf набра́сывать) throw; ~ся throw o.s.; ~ся на attack. набро́сок (-ска) sketch, draft.

набуха́ть impf, набу́хнуть (-нет; -ýх) pf swell.

набью́ etc.: see наби́ть

наважде́ние delusion.

нава́ливать impf, навали́ть (-лю́, -лишь) pf heap, pile up; load; ~ся; +на+acc fall (up)on.

наведе́ние laying (on); placing.

наведу́ etc.: see навести́

наве́к, наве́ки adv for ever.

навёл etc.: see навести́

наве́рно, наве́рное adv probably. наверняка́ adv certainly, for sure.

наверста́ть pf, навёрстывать impf make up for.

наве́рх adv up(wards); upstairs. наверху́ adv above; upstairs.

наве́с awning.

наве́сить (-éшу) pf (impf наве́шивать) hang (up). навесно́й hanging.

навести́ (-еду́, -едёшь; -вёл, -á) pf (impf наводи́ть) direct; aim; cover (with), spread; introduce, bring; make.

навести́ть (-ещу́) pf (impf навеща́ть) visit.

наве́шать pf, наве́шивать[1] impf hang (out); weigh out.

наве́шивать[2] impf of наве́сить. навеща́ть impf of навести́ть

на́взничь adv backwards, on one's back.

навзры́д adv: пла́кать ~ sob.

навига́ция navigation.

нависа́ть impf, нави́снуть (-нет; -ви́с) pf overhang, hang (over); threaten. нави́сший beetling.

навлека́ть impf, навле́чь (-еку́, -ечёшь; -ёк, -ла́) pf bring, draw; incur.

наводи́ть (-ожу́, -о́дишь) impf of навести́; наводя́щий вопро́с leading question. наво́дка aiming; applying.

наводне́ние flood. наводни́ть pf,

наводня́ть *impf* flood; inundate.

навóз dung, manure.

нáволочка pillowcase.

на|врáть (-рý, -рёшь; -áл, -á, -о) *pf* tell lies, romance; talk nonsense; +в+*prep* make mistake(s) in.

навреди́ть (-ежý) *pf* +*dat* harm.

навсегдá *adv* for ever.

навстрéчу *adv* to meet; идти́ ~ go to meet; meet halfway.

навы́ворот *adv* inside out; back to front.

нáвык experience, skill.

навы́нос *adv* to take away.

навы́пуск *adv* worn outside.

навью́чивать *impf*, на|вью́чить (-чу) *pf* load.

навязáть (-яжý, -я́жешь) *pf*, навя́зывать *impf* tie, fasten; thrust, foist; ~ся thrust o.s. навя́зчивый importunate; obsessive.

на|гáдить (-áжу) *pf*.

нагáн revolver.

нагибáть(ся *impf of* нагнýть(ся

нагишóм *adv* stark naked.

наглéц (-á) impudent fellow. нáглость impudence. нáглый (нагл, -á, -о) impudent.

нагля́дный clear, graphic; visual.

нагнáть (-гоню́, -гóнишь; -áл, -á, -о) *pf* (*impf* нагоня́ть) overtake, catch up (with); inspire, arouse.

нагнести́ (-етý, -етёшь) *pf*, нагнетáть *impf* compress; supercharge.

нагноéние suppuration. нагнои́ться *pf* suppurate.

нагнýть (-нý, -нёшь) *pf* (*impf* нагибáть) bend; ~ся bend, stoop.

нагова́ривать *impf*, наговори́ть *pf* slander; talk a lot (of); record.

нагóй (наг, -á, -о) naked, bare.

нáголо *adv* naked, bare.

нагоня́ть *impf of* нагнáть

нагорáть *impf*, нагорéть (-ри́т) *pf* be consumed; *impers*+*dat* to be scolded.

нагóрный upland, mountain; mountainous.

наготá nakedness, nudity.

награ́бить (-блю) *pf* amass by dishonest means.

награ́да reward; decoration; prize. награди́ть (-ажу́) *pf*, награждáть *impf* reward; decorate; award prize to.

нагревáтельный heating. нагре-

вáть *impf*, нагрéть (-éю) *pf* warm, heat; ~ся get hot, warm up.

нагромождáть *impf*, на|громозди́ть (-зжý) *pf* heap up, pile up. нагромождéние heaping up; conglomeration.

на|груби́ть (-блю́) *pf*.

нагружáть *impf*, на|грузи́ть (-ужý, -ýзишь) *pf* load; ~ся load o.s. нагрýзка loading; load; work; commitments.

нагря́нуть (-ну) *pf* appear unexpectedly.

над, надо *prep*+*instr* over, above; on, at.

надави́ть (-влю́, -вишь) *pf*, надáвливать *impf* press; squeeze out; crush.

надбáвка addition, increase.

надвигáть *impf*, надви́нуть (-ну) *pf* move, pull, push; ~ся approach.

нáдвое *adv* in two.

надгрóбие epitaph. надгрóбный (on or over a) grave.

надевáть *impf of* надéть

надéжда hope. надёжность reliability. надёжный reliable.

надéл allotment.

надели́ть (-лю́, -ли́шь) *pf*, наделя́ть *impf* endow, provide.

надéть (-éну) *pf* (*impf* надевáть) put on.

надéяться (-éюсь) *impf* (*pf* по~) hope; rely.

надзирáтель *m* overseer, supervisor. надзирáть *impf* +за+*instr* supervise, oversee. надзóр supervision; surveillance.

надлáмывать(ся *impf of* над|ломи́ть(ся

надлежáщий fitting, proper, appropriate. надлежи́т (-жáло) *impers* (+*dat*) it is necessary, required.

надлóм break; crack; breakdown. надломи́ть (-млю́, -мишь) *pf* (*impf* надлáмывать) break; crack; breakdown; ~ся break, crack, break down. надлóмленный broken.

надмéнный haughty, arrogant.

нáдо[1] (+*dat*) it is necessary; I (*etc.*) must, ought to; I (*etc.*) need. нáдобность necessity, need.

нáдо[2]: *see* над.

надоедáть *impf*, надоéсть (-éм, -éшь,

-ёст, -еди́м) *pf* +*dat* bore, pester.
надоедли́вый boring, tiresome.
надо́лго *adv* for a long time.
надорва́ть (-ву́, -вёшь; -а́л, -а́, -о)
pf (*impf* надрыва́ть) tear; strain;
~ся tear; overstrain o.s.
на́дпись inscription.
надре́з cut, incision. **надре́зать**
(-е́жу) *pf*, **надреза́ть** *impf*, **над-
ре́зывать** *impf* make an incision in.
надруга́тельство outrage. **надру-
га́ться** *pf* +*над*+*instr* outrage, insult.
надры́в tear; strain; breakdown; outburst. **надрыва́ть(ся** *impf of* надо-
рва́ть(ся. **надры́вный** hysterical;
heartrending.
надста́вить (-влю) *pf*, **надста-
вля́ть** *impf* lengthen.
надстра́ивать *impf*, **надстро́ить**
(-о́ю) *pf* build on top; extend upwards. **надстро́йка** building upwards; superstructure.
надува́тельство swindle. **наду-
ва́ть(ся** *impf. of* наду́ть(ся. на-
ду́вно́й** pneumatic, inflatable.
наду́манный far-fetched.
наду́тый swollen; haughty; sulky.
наду́ть (-у́ю) *pf* (*impf* надува́ть) inflate; swindle; ~ся swell up; sulk.
на|души́ть(ся (-шу́(сь, -шишь(ся) *pf*.
наеда́ться *impf of* нае́сться
наедине́ *adv* privately, alone.
нае́зд flying visit; raid. **нае́здник,
-ица** rider. **наезжа́ть** *impf of*
нае́здить, нае́хать; pay occasional
visits.
наём (на́йма) hire; renting; **взять в
~ rent; сдать в ~ let. наёмник** hire-
ling; mercenary. **наёмный** hired,
rented.
нае́сться (-е́мся, -е́шься, -е́стся,
-еди́мся) *pf* (*impf* наеда́ться) eat
one's fill; stuff o.s.
нае́хать (-е́ду) *pf* (*impf* наезжа́ть)
arrive unexpectedly; +*на*+*acc* run
into, collide with.
нажа́ть (-жму́, -жмёшь) *pf* (*impf*
нажима́ть) press; put pressure (on).
наждак (-а́) emery. **нажда́чная
бума́га** emery paper.
нажи́ва profit, gain.
нажива́ть(ся *impf of* нажи́ть(ся
нажи́м pressure; clamp. **нажима́ть**
impf of нажа́ть.
нажи́ть (-иву́, -ивёшь; на́жил, -а́, -о)

pf (*impf* нажива́ть) acquire; contract, incur; ~ся (-жи́лся, -а́сь) get
rich.
нажму́ *etc.: see* **нажа́ть**
наза́втра *adv* (the) next day.
наза́д *adv* back(wards); (тому́) ~
ago.
назва́ние name; title. **назва́ть** (-зову́,
-зовёшь; -а́л, -а́, -о) *pf* (*impf* назы-
ва́ть) call, name; ~ся be called.
назе́мный ground, surface.
на́зло́ *adv* out of spite; to spite.
назнача́ть *impf*, **назна́чить** (-чу)
pf appoint; fix, set; prescribe. **назна-
че́ние** appointment; fixing, setting;
prescription.
назову́ *etc.: see* **назва́ть**
назо́йливый importunate.
назрева́ть *impf*, **назре́ть** (-е́ет) *pf*
ripen, mature; become imminent.
называ́емый: так ~ so-called. **на-
зыва́ть(ся** *impf of* назва́ть(ся.
наибо́лее *adv* (the) most. **наибо́ль-
ший** greatest, biggest.
наи́вный naive.
наивы́сший highest.
наигра́ть *pf*, **наи́грывать** *impf* win;
play, pick out.
наизна́нку *adv* inside out.
наизу́сть *adv* by heart.
наилу́чший best.
наименова́ние name; title.
наи́скось *adv* obliquely.
найму́ *etc.: see* **наня́ть**
найти́ (-йду́, -йдёшь; нашёл, -шла́,
-шло́) *pf* (*impf* находи́ть) find; ~сь
be found; be, be situated.
наказа́ние punishment. **наказа́ть**
(-ажу́, -а́жешь) *pf*, **нака́зывать**
impf punish.
нака́л incandescence. **нака́ливать**
impf, **накали́ть** *pf*, **нака́ливать** *impf*
heat; make red-hot; strain, make
tense; ~ся glow, become incandescent; become strained.
нака́лывать(ся *impf of* наколо́ть-
(ся
накану́не *adv* the day before.
нака́пливать(ся *impf of* накопи́ть-
(ся
накача́ть *pf*, **нака́чивать** *impf*
pump (up).
наки́дка cloak, cape; extra charge.
наки́нуть (-ну) *pf*, **наки́дывать**
impf throw; throw on; ~ся throw

o.s.; ~ся на attack.
на́кипь scum; scale.
накладна́я sb invoice. накладн|о́й laid on; false; ~ые расхо́ды overheads. накла́дывать impf of наложи́ть
на|клевета́ть (-ещу́, -е́щешь) pf.
накле́ивать impf, накле́ить pf stick on. накле́йка sticking (on, up); label.
накло́н slope, incline. наклоне́ние inclination; mood. наклони́ть (-ню́, -нишь) pf, наклоня́ть impf incline, bend; ~ся stoop, bend. накло́нный inclined, sloping.
нако́лка pinning; (pinned-on) ornament for hair; tattoo. наколо́ть[1] (-лю́, -лешь) pf (impf нака́лывать) prick; pin; ~ся prick o.s.
наколо́ть[2] (-лю́, -лешь) pf (impf нака́лывать) chop.
наконе́ц adv at last. наконе́чник tip, point.
на|копи́ть (-плю́, -пишь) pf, накопля́ть impf (impf also нака́пливать) accumulate; ~ся accumulate. накопле́ние accumulation.
на|копти́ть (-пчу́) pf. на|корми́ть (-млю́, -мишь) pf.
на|кра́сить (-а́шу) pf paint; make up. на|кра́ситься (-а́шусь) pf.
на|крахма́лить pf.
на|крени́ть pf. накрени́ться (-ни́тся) pf, накреня́ться impf tilt; list.
на|кричать (-чу́) pf (+на+acc) shout (at).
накро́ю etc.: see накры́ть
накрыва́ть impf, накры́ть (-ро́ю) pf cover; catch; ~ (на) стол lay the table; ~ся cover o.s.
накури́ть (-рю́, -ришь) pf fill with smoke.
налага́ть impf of наложи́ть
нала́дить (-а́жу) pf, нала́живать impf regulate, adjust; repair; organize; ~ся come right; get going.
на|лга́ть (-лгу́, -лжёшь; -а́л, -а́, -о) pf.
нале́во adv to the left.
налёг etc.: see нале́чь. налега́ть impf of нале́чь
налегке́ adv lightly dressed; without luggage.
налёт raid; flight; thin coating.
налета́ть[1] pf have flown. налета́ть[2] impf, налете́ть (-лечу́) pf

swoop down; come flying; spring up.
нале́чь (-ля́гу, -ля́жешь; -лёг, -ла́) pf (impf налега́ть) lean, apply one's weight, lie; apply o.s.
налжёшь etc.: see налга́ть
налива́ть(ся impf of нали́ть(ся.
нали́вка fruit liqueur.
нали́ть (-лью́, -льёшь; на́лил, -а́, -о) pf (impf налива́ть) pour (out), fill; ~ся (-и́лся, -а́сь, -и́лось) pour in; ripen.
налицо́ adv present; available.
нали́чие presence. нали́чн|ый on hand; cash; ~ые (де́ньги) ready money.
нало́г tax. налогоплате́льщик taxpayer. наложенн|ый; ~ым платежо́м C.O.D. наложи́ть (-жу́, -жишь) pf (impf накла́дывать, налага́ть) lay (in, on), put (in, on); apply; impose.
налью́ etc.: see нали́ть
наля́гу etc.: see нале́чь
нам etc.: see мы
на|ма́зать (-а́жу) pf, нама́зывать impf oil, grease; smear, spread.
нама́тывать impf of намота́ть.
нама́чивать impf of намочи́ть
намёк hint. намека́ть impf, намекну́ть (-ну́, -нёшь) pf hint.
намерева́ться impf +inf intend to.
наме́рен predic: я ~(a)+inf I intend to. наме́рение intention. наме́ренный intentional.
на|ме́тать pf. на|ме́тить[1] (-е́чу) pf.
наме́тить[2] (-е́чу) pf (impf намеча́ть) plan; outline; nominate; ~ся be outlined, take shape.
намно́го adv much, far.
намока́ть impf, намо́кнуть (-ну) pf get wet.
намо́рдник muzzle.
на|мо́рщить(ся (-щу(сь) pf.
на|мота́ть pf (impf also нама́тывать) wind, reel.
на|мочи́ть (-очу́, -о́чишь) pf (impf also нама́чивать) wet; soak; splash; spill.
намы́ливать impf, на|мы́лить pf soap.
нанести́ (-су́, -сёшь; -ёс, -ла́) pf (impf наноси́ть) carry, bring; draw, plot; inflict.
на|низа́ть (-ижу́, -и́жешь) pf, нани́зывать impf string, thread.

нанима́тель *m* tenant; employer.

нанима́ть(ся *impf of* наня́ть(ся

наноси́ть (-ошу́, -о́сишь) *impf of* нанести́

наня́ть (найму́, -мёшь; на́нял, -а́, -о) *pf* (*impf* **нанима́ть**) hire; rent; ~ся get a job.

наоборо́т *adv* on the contrary; back to front; the other, the wrong, way (round); vice versa.

на́отмашь *adv* violently.

наотре́з *adv* flatly, point-blank.

напада́ть *impf of* напа́сть. **напада́ющий** *sb* forward. **нападе́ние** attack; forwards.

напа́рник co-driver, (work)mate.

напа́сть (-аду́, -адёшь; -а́л) *pf* (*impf* **напада́ть**) на+*acc* attack; descend on; seize; come upon. **напа́сть** misfortune.

напе́в tune. **напева́ть** *impf of* напе́ть

наперебо́й *adv* interrupting, vying with, one another.

наперёд *adv* in advance.

напереко́р *adv*+*dat* in defiance of, counter to.

наперсток (-тка) thimble.

напе́ть (-пою́, -поёшь) *pf* (*impf* **напева́ть**) sing; hum, croon.

на|печа́тать(ся *pf.* **напива́ться** *impf of* напи́ться

напи́льник file.

на|писа́ть (-ишу́, -и́шешь) *pf.*

напи́ток (-тка) drink. **напи́ться** (-пью́сь, -пьёшься; -и́лся, -а́сь, -и́лось) *pf* (*impf* **напива́ться**) quench one's thirst; drink; get drunk.

напиха́ть *pf*, **напи́хивать** *impf* cram, stuff.

на|плева́ть (-люю́, -люёшь) *pf*; ~! to hell with it! who cares?

наплы́в influx; accumulation; canker. **наплюю́** *etc.*: *see* наплева́ть

напова́л outright.

наподо́бие *prep*+*gen* like, not unlike.

на|пои́ть (-ою́, -о́ишь) *pf.*

напока́з *adv* for show.

наполни́тель *m* filler. **напо́лнить(ся** *pf*, **наполня́ть(ся** *impf* fill. **наполови́ну** *adv* half.

напомина́ние reminder. **напомина́ть** *impf*, **напо́мнить** *pf* (+*dat*) remind.

напо́р pressure. **напо́ристый** energetic, pushing.

напосле́док *adv* in the end; after all.

напою́ *etc.*: *see* напе́ть, напои́ть

напр. *abbr* (*of* **наприме́р**) e.g., for example.

напра́вить (-влю) *pf*, **направля́ть** *impf* direct; send; sharpen; ~ся make (for), go (towards). **направле́ние** direction; trend; order. **напра́вленный** purposeful.

напра́во *adv* to the right.

напра́сно *adv* in vain, for nothing; unjustly, mistakenly.

напра́шиваться *impf of* напроси́ться

наприме́р for example.

на|прока́зничать *pf.*

напрока́т *adv* for, on, hire.

напролёт *adv* through, without a break.

напроло́м *adv* straight, regardless of obstacles.

напроси́ться (-ошу́сь, -о́сишься) *pf* (*impf* **напра́шиваться**) thrust o.s.; suggest itself; ~ на ask for, invite.

напро́тив *adv* opposite; on the contrary. **напро́тив** *prep*+*gen* opposite.

напряга́ть(ся *impf of* напря́чь(ся. **напряже́ние** tension; exertion; voltage. **напряжённый** tense; intense; intensive.

напрями́к *adv* straight (out).

напря́чь (-ягу́, -яжёшь; -я́г, -ла́) *pf* (*impf* **напряга́ть**) strain; ~ся strain o.s.

на|пуга́ть(ся *pf.* **на|пу́дриться** *pf.*

напуска́ть *impf*, **напусти́ть** (-ущу́, -у́стишь) *pf* let in; let loose; ~ся +на+*acc* fly at, go for.

напу́тать *pf* +в+*prep* make a mess of.

на|пыли́ть *pf.*

напью́сь *etc.*: *see* напи́ться

нара́вне *adv* level; equally.

нараспа́шку *adv* unbuttoned.

нараста́ние growth, accumulation. **нараста́ть** *impf*, **нарасти́** (-тёт; -ро́с, -ла́) *pf* grow; increase.

нарасхва́т *adv* very quickly, like hot cakes.

нарва́ть[1] (-ву́, -вёшь; -а́л, -а́, -о) *pf* (*impf* **нарыва́ть**) pick; tear up.

нарва́ть[2] (-вёт; -а́л, -а́, -о) *pf* (*impf* **нарыва́ть**) gather.

нарва́ться (-ву́сь, -вёшься; -а́лся, -ала́сь, -а́ло́сь) *pf* (*impf* **нарыва́ться**) +на+*acc* run into, run up against.

наре́зать (-е́жу) pf, **нареза́ть** impf cut (up), slice, carve; thread, rifle.

наре́чие[1] dialect.

наре́чие[2] adverb.

на|рисова́ть pf.

нарко́з narcosis. **наркома́н, -ма́нка** drug addict. **наркома́ния** drug addiction. **нарко́тик** narcotic.

наро́д people. **наро́дность** nationality; national character. **наро́дный** national; folk; popular; people's.

наро́с etc.: see **нарасти́**

наро́чно adv on purpose, deliberately. **наро́чный** sb courier.

нару́жность exterior. **нару́жный** external, outward. **нару́жу** adv outside.

нару́чник handcuff. **нару́чный** wrist.

наруше́ние breach; infringement. **нару|ши́тель** m transgressor. **нару|ши́ть** (-шу) pf, **наруша́ть** impf break; disturb, infringe, violate.

нарци́сс narcissus; daffodil.

на́ры (нар) pl plank-bed.

нары́в abscess, boil. **нарыва́ть(ся** impf of **нарва́ть(ся**

наря́д[1] order, warrant.

наря́д[2] attire; dress. **наряди́ть** (-яжу́) pf (impf наряжа́ть) dress (up); ~ся dress up. **наря́дный** well-dressed.

наряду́ adv alike, equally; side by side.

наряжа́ть(ся impf of **наряди́ть(ся.** **нас** see **мы**

насади́ть (-ажу́, -а́дишь) pf, **насажда́ть** impf (impf also **наса́живать**) plant; propagate; implant. **наса́дка** setting, fixing. **насажде́ние** planting; plantation; propagation. **наса́живать** impf of **насади́ть**

насеко́мое sb insect.

населе́ние population. **населённость** density of population. **населённый** populated; ~ пункт settlement; built-up area. **насели́ть** pf, **населя́ть** impf settle, people.

наси́лие violence, force. **наси́ловать** impf (pf из~) coerce; rape. **наси́лу** adv with difficulty. **наси́льник** aggressor; rapist; violator. **наси́льно** adv by force. **наси́льственный** violent, forcible.

наска́кивать impf of **наскочи́ть**

наскво́зь adv through, throughout.

наско́лько adv how much?, how far?; as far as.

на́скоро adv hastily.

наскочи́ть (-очу́, -о́чишь) pf (impf **наска́кивать**) +на+acc run into, collide with; fly at.

наску́чить (-чу) pf bore.

наслади́ться (-ажу́сь) pf, **наслажда́ться** impf (+instr) enjoy, take pleasure. **наслажде́ние** pleasure, enjoyment.

насле́дие legacy; heritage. **на|следи́ть** (-ежу́) pf. **насле́дник** heir; successor. **насле́дница** heiress. **насле́дный** next in succession. **насле́довать** impf & pf (pf also у~) inherit, succeed to. **насле́дственность** heredity. **насле́дственный** hereditary, inherited. **насле́дство** inheritance; heritage.

на́смерть adv to (the) death.

на|смеши́ть (-шу́) pf **насме́шка** mockery; gibe. **насме́шливый** mocking.

на́сморк runny nose; cold.

на|сори́ть pf.

насо́с pump.

на́спех adv hastily.

на|спле́тничать pf. **настава́ть** (-таёт) impf of **наста́ть**

наставле́ние exhortation; directions, manual.

наста́вник tutor, mentor.

наста́ивать[1] impf of **настоя́ть**[1]. **наста́ивать**[2](ся impf of **настоя́ть**[2](ся

наста́ть (-а́нет) pf (impf **настава́ть**) come, begin, set in.

на́стежь adv wide (open).

настелю́ etc.: see **настла́ть**

настига́ть impf, **насти́гнуть, насти́чь** (-и́гну; -и́г) pf catch up with, overtake.

насти́л flooring, planking. **настила́ть** impf of **настла́ть**

насти́чь see **настига́ть**

настла́ть (-телю́, -те́лешь) pf (impf **настила́ть**) lay, spread.

насто́йка liqueur, cordial.

насто́йчивый persistent; urgent.

насто́лько adv so, so much.

насто́льный table, desk; reference.

настора́живать impf, **насторо|жи́ть** (-жу́) pf set; prick up; ~ся prick up one's ears. **насторо́жен-**

ный (-ен, -енна) guarded; alert.
настоя́тельный insistent; urgent.
настоя́ть¹ (-ою́) pf (impf наста́ивать¹) insist.
настоя́ть² (-ою́) pf (impf наста́ивать²) brew; ~ся draw, stand.
настоя́щее sb the present. настоя́щий (the) present, this; real, genuine.
настра́ивать(ся impf of настро́ить(ся
настри́чь (-игу́, -ижёшь; -йг) pf shear, clip.
настрое́ние mood. настро́ить (-о́ю) pf (impf настра́ивать) tune (in); dispose; ~ся dispose o.s. настро́йка tuning. настро́йщик tuner.
на|строчи́ть (-чу́) pf.
наступа́тельный offensive. наступа́ть¹ impf of наступи́ть¹
наступа́ть² impf of наступи́ть². наступа́ющий¹ coming.
наступа́ющий² sb attacker.
наступи́ть¹ (-плю́, -пишь) pf (impf наступа́ть¹) tread; attack; advance.
наступи́ть² (-у́пит) pf (impf наступа́ть²) come, set in. наступле́ние¹ coming.
наступле́ние² offensive, attack.
насу́питься (-плюсь) pf, насу́пливаться impf frown.
на́сухо adv dry. насуши́ть (-шу́, -шишь) pf dry.
насу́щный urgent, vital; хлеб ~ daily bread.
насчёт prep+gen about, concerning; as regards. насчита́ть pf, насчи́тывать impf count; hold; ~ся +gen number.
насы́пать (-плю) pf, насыпа́ть impf pour in, on; fill; spread; heap up. на́сыпь embankment.
насы́тить (-ы́щу) pf, насыща́ть impf satiate; saturate; ~ся be full; be saturated.
ната́лкивать(ся impf of натолкну́ть(ся. ната́пливать impf of натопи́ть
натаска́ть pf, ната́скивать impf train; coach, cram; bring in, lay in.
натвори́ть pf do, get up to.
натере́ть (-тру́, -трёшь; -тёр) pf (impf натира́ть) rub on, in; polish; chafe; grate; ~ся rub o.s.
на́тиск onslaught.

наткну́ться (-ну́сь, -нёшься) pf (impf натыка́ться) +на+acc run into; strike, stumble on.
натолкну́ть (-ну́, -нёшь) pf (impf ната́лкивать) push; lead; ~ся run against, across.
натопи́ть (-плю́, -пишь) pf (impf ната́пливать) heat (up); stoke up; melt.
на|точи́ть (-чу́, -чишь) pf.
натоща́к adv on an empty stomach.
натрави́ть (-влю́, -вишь) pf, натра́вливать impf, натравля́ть impf set (on); stir up.
на|трениро́вать(ся pf.
на́трий sodium.
нату́ра nature. натура́льный natural; genuine. нату́рщик, -щица artist's model.
натыка́ть(ся impf of наткну́ть(ся
натюрмо́рт still life.
натя́гивать impf, натяну́ть (-ну́, -нешь) pf stretch; draw; pull (on); ~ся stretch. натя́нутость tension. натя́нутый tight; strained.
науга́д adv at random.
нау́ка science; learning.
нау́тро adv (the) next morning.
на|учи́ть (-чу́, -чишь) pf.
нау́чный scientific; ~ая фанта́стика science fiction.
нау́шник ear-flap; ear-phone; informer.
нафтали́н naphthalene.
наха́л, -ха́лка impudent creature. наха́льный impudent. наха́льство impudence.
нахвата́ть pf, нахва́тывать impf pick up, get hold of; ~ся +gen pick up.
нахле́бник hanger-on.
нахлы́нуть (-нет) pf well up; surge; gush.
на|хму́рить(ся pf.
находи́ть(ся (-ожу́(сь, -о́дишь(ся) impf of найти́(сь. нахо́дка find. нахо́дчивый resourceful, quickwitted.
наце́ливать impf, на|це́лить pf aim; ~ся (take) aim.
наце́нка extra, addition; additional charge.
наци́зм Nazism. национализа́ция nationalization. национализи́ровать impf & pf nationalize.

национали́зм nationalism. **националисти́ческий** nationalist(ic). **национа́льность** nationality; ethnic group. **национа́льный** national. **наци́ст,** -ка Nazi. **на́ция** nation. **нацме́н,** -ме́нка *abbr* member of national minority.

нача́ло beginning; origin; principle, basis. **нача́льник** head, chief; boss. **нача́льный** initial; primary. **нача́льство** the authorities; command. **нача́ть** (-чну́, -чнёшь; на́чал, -а́, -о) *pf* (*impf* **начина́ть**) begin; ~ся begin.

начерта́ть *pf* trace, inscribe. **на|черти́ть** (-рчу́, -ртишь) *pf*.

начина́ние undertaking. **начина́ть(ся** *impf of* нача́ть(ся. **начина́ющий** *sb* beginner.

начини́ть *pf*, **начиня́ть** *impf* stuff, fill. **начи́нка** stuffing, filling.

начи́стить (-и́щу) *pf* (*impf* **начища́ть**) clean. **на́чисто** *adv* clean; flatly, decidedly; openly, frankly. **начистоту́** *adv* openly, frankly.

начи́танность learning; wide reading. **начи́танный** well-read.

начища́ть *impf of* начи́стить

наш (-его) *m*, **на́ша** (-ей) *f*, **на́ше** (-его) *neut*, **на́ши** (-их) *pl*, *pron* our, ours.

наша́тырный спирт ammonia. **наша́тырь** (-я́) *m* sal-ammoniac; ammonia.

нашёл *etc.: see* найти́

наше́ствие invasion.

нашива́ть *impf*, **наши́ть** (-шью́, -шьёшь) *pf* sew on. **наши́вка** stripe, chevron; tab.

нашлёпать *impf* slap.

нашуме́ть (-млю́) *pf* make a din; cause a sensation.

нашью́ *etc.: see* наши́ть

нащу́пать *pf*, **нащу́пывать** *impf* grope for.

на|электризова́ть *pf*.

наяву́ *adv* awake; in reality.

не *partl* not

не- *pref* un-, in-, non-, mis-, dis-; -less; not. **неаккура́тный** careless; untidy; unpunctual. **небезразли́чный** not indifferent. **небезызве́стный** not unknown; notorious; well-known.

небеса́ *etc.: see* не́бо[2]. **небе́сный** heavenly; celestial.

не-. неблагода́рный ungrateful;

thankless. **неблагонадёжный** unreliable. **неблагополу́чный** unsuccessful, bad, unfavourable. **неблагоприя́тный** unfavourable. **неблагоразу́мный** imprudent. **неблагоро́дный** ignoble, base.

нёбо[1] palate.

не́бо[2] (*pl* -беса́, -бе́с) sky; heaven.

не-. небога́тый of modest means, modest. **небольшо́й** small, not great; с небольши́м a little over.

небосво́д firmament. **небоскло́н** horizon. **небоскрёб** skyscraper.

небо́сь *adv* I dare say; probably.

не-. небре́жный careless. **небыва́лый** unprecedented; fantastic. **небыли́ца** fable, cock-and-bull story. **небытие́** non-existence. **небью́щийся** unbreakable. **нева́жно** *adv* not too well, indifferently. **нева́жный** unimportant; indifferent. **невдалеке́** *adv* not far away. **неве́дение** ignorance. **неве́домый** unknown; mysterious. **неве́жа** *m* & *f* boor, lout. **неве́жда** *m* & *f* ignoramus. **неве́жественный** ignorant. **неве́жество** ignorance. **неве́жливый** rude. **невели́кий** (-и́к, -а́, -и́ко́) small. **неве́рие** unbelief, atheism; scepticism. **неве́рный** (-рен, -рна́, -о) incorrect, wrong; inaccurate, unsteady; unfaithful. **невероя́тный** improbable; incredible. **неве́рующий** unbelieving; *sb* atheist. **неве́сомый** weightless; imponderable.

неве́ста fiancée; bride. **неве́стка** daughter-in-law; brother's wife, sister-in-law.

не-. невзго́да adversity. **невзира́я на** *prep+acc* regardless of. **невзнача́й** *adv* by chance. **невзра́чный** unattractive, plain. **неви́данный** unprecedented, unheard-of. **неви́димый** invisible. **неви́нность** innocence. **неви́нный, невино́вный** innocent. **невменя́емый** irresponsible. **невмеша́тельство** non-intervention; non-interference. **невмоготу́, невмо́чь** *adv* unbearable, too much (for). **невнима́тельный** inattentive, thoughtless.

нево́д seine(-net).

не-. невозврати́мый, невозвра́тный irrevocable, irrecoverable. **не-**

возмо́жный impossible. **невозму-
ти́мый** imperturbable.

нево́льник, -ница slave. **нево́ль-
ный** involuntary; unintentional;
forced. **нево́ля** captivity; necessity.

не-. невообрази́мый unimaginable,
inconceivable. **невооружённ\|ый**
unarmed; ~ным гла́зом with the
naked eye. **невоспи́танный** ill-bred,
bad-mannered. **невоспламеня́ю-
щийся** non-flammable. **невоспри-
и́мчивый** unreceptive; immune.

невралги́я neuralgia.

невреди́мый safe, unharmed.

невро́з neurosis. **неврологи́ческий**
neurological. **невроти́ческий** neurotic.

не-. невы́годный disadvantageous;
unprofitable. **невы́держанный**
lacking self-control; unmatured. **не-
выноси́мый** unbearable. **невыпол-
ни́мый** impracticable. **невысо́кий**
(-со́к, -а́, -о́ко) low; short.

не́га luxury; bliss.

негати́вный negative.

не́где adv (there is) nowhere.

не-. неги́бкий (-бок, -бка́, -о) inflexible, stiff. **негла́сный** secret. **не-
глубо́кий** (-бо́к, -а́, -о) shallow. **не-
глу́пый** (-у́п, -а́, -о) sensible, quite
intelligent. **него́дный** (-ден, -дна́,
-о) unfit, unsuitable; worthless. **не-
годова́ние** indignation. **негодо-
ва́ть** impf be indignant. **негодя́й**
scoundrel. **негостеприи́мный** inhospitable.

негр Negro, black man.

негра́мотность illiteracy. **негра́-
мотный** illiterate.

негритя́нка Negress, black woman.
негритя́нский Negro.

не-. негро́мкий (-мок, -мка́, -о)
quiet. **неда́вний** recent. **неда́вно**
adv recently. **недалёкий** (-ёк, -а́,
-ёко) near; short; not far, dull-
witted. **недалеко́** adv not far, near.
неда́ром adv not for nothing, not
without reason. **недви́жимость** real
estate. **недви́жимый** immovable.
недвусмы́сленный unequivocal.
недействи́тельный ineffective;
invalid. **недели́мый** indivisible.
неде́льный of a week, week's.
неде́ля week.

не-. недёшево adv dear(ly).

недоброжела́тель m ill-wisher.
недоброжела́тельность hostility.
недоброка́чественный of poor
quality. **недобросо́вестный** unscrupulous; careless. **недо́брый** (-бр,
-бра́, -о) unkind; bad. **недове́рие**
distrust. **недове́рчивый** distrustful
недово́льный dissatisfied. **недо-
во́льство** dissatisfaction. **недоеда́-
ние** malnutrition. **недоеда́ть** impf
be undernourished.

не-. недо́лгий (-лог, -лга́, -о) short,
brief. **недо́лго** adv not long. **недо-
лгове́чный** short-lived. **недомо-
га́ние** indisposition. **недомога́ть**
impf be unwell. **недомы́слие**
thoughtlessness. **недоно́шенный**
premature. **недооце́нивать** impf,
недооцени́ть (-ню́, -нишь) pf underestimate; underrate. **недооце́нка**
underestimation. **недопусти́мый**
inadmissible, intolerable. **недоразу-
ме́ние** misunderstanding. **недо-
рого́й** (-до́рог, -а́, -о) inexpensive.
недосмотре́ть (-рю́,-ришь) pf overlook. **недоспа́ть** (-плю́; -а́л, -а́, -о)
pf (impf **недосыпа́ть**) not have
enough sleep.

недостава́ть (-таёт) impf, **недо-
ста́ть** (-а́нет) pf impers be missing,
be lacking. **недоста́ток** (-тка) shortage, deficiency. **недоста́точный** in-
sufficient, inadequate. **недоста́ча**
lack, shortage.

не-. недостижи́мый unattainable.
недосто́йный unworthy, **недо-
сту́пный** inaccessible. **недо-
счита́ться** pf, **недосчи́тываться**
impf miss, find missing, be short (of).
недосыпа́ть impf of **недоспа́ть**.
недосяга́емый unattainable.

недоумева́ть impf be at a loss, be
bewildered. **недоуме́ние** bewilderment.

не-. недоу́чка m & f half-educated
person. **недочёт** deficit; defect.
не́дра (недр) pl depths, heart, bowels.
не-. недру́г enemy. **недружелю́б-
ный** unfriendly.

неду́г illness, disease.

недурно́й not bad; not bad-looking.

не-. неесте́ственный unnatural. **не-
жда́нный** unexpected. **нежела́ние**
unwillingness. **нежела́тельный** undesirable.

не́жели than.

нежена́тый unmarried.

не́женка *m & f* mollycoddle.

нежило́й uninhabited; uninhabitable.

не́житься (-жусь) *impf* luxuriate, bask. **не́жность** tenderness; *pl* endearments. **не́жный** tender; affectionate.

не-. **незабве́нный** unforgettable. **незабу́дка** forget-me-not. **незабыва́емый** unforgettable. **незави́симость** independence. **незави́симый** independent. **незадо́лго** *adv* not long. **незаконорождённый** illegitimate. **незако́нный** illegal, illicit; illegitimate. **незако́нченный** unfinished. **незамени́мый** irreplaceable. **незамерза́ющий** ice-free; anti-freeze. **незаме́тный** imperceptible. **незаму́жняя** unmarried. **незапа́мятный** immemorial. **незаслу́женный** unmerited. **незауря́дный** uncommon, outstanding.

не́зачем *adv* there is no need.

не-. **незащищённый** unprotected. **незва́ный** uninvited. **нездоро́виться** *impf, impers* +dat: мне нездоро́вится I don't feel well. **нездоро́вый** unhealthy. **нездоро́вье** ill health. **незнако́мец** (-мца) stranger. **незнако́мка** stranger. **незнако́мый** unknown, unfamiliar. **незна́ние** ignorance. **незначи́тельный** insignificant. **незре́лый** unripe, immature. **незри́мый** invisible. **незы́блемый** unshakable, firm. **неизбе́жность** inevitability. **неизбе́жный** inevitable. **неизве́данный** unknown.

неизве́стность uncertainty; ignorance; obscurity. **неизве́стный** unknown; *sb* stranger.

не-. **неизлечи́мый** incurable. **неизме́нный** unchanged, unchanging; devoted. **неизменя́емый** unalterable. **неизмери́мый** immeasurable, immense. **неизу́ченный** unstudied; unexplored. **неиму́щий** poor. **неинтере́сный** uninteresting. **неи́скренний** insincere. **неискушённый** inexperienced, unsophisticated. **неисполни́мый** impracticable. **неисправи́мый** incorrigible; irreparable. **неиспра́вный** out of order, defective; careless. **неиссле́дованный** unexplored. **неиссяка́емый** inexhaustible. **нейстовство** fury, frenzy; atrocity. **нейстовый** furious, frenzied, uncontrolled. **неисчерпа́емый** inexhaustible. **неисчисли́мый** innumerable.

нейло́н, нейло́новый nylon.

нейро́н neuron.

нейтрализа́ция neutralization. **нейтрализова́ть** *impf & pf* neutralize. **нейтралите́т** neutrality. **нейтра́льный** neutral. **нейтро́н** neutron.

неквалифици́рованный unskilled.

не́кий *pron* a certain, some.

не́когда[1] *adv* once, formerly.

не́когда[2] *adv* there is no time; мне ~ I have no time.

не́кого (не́кому, не́кем, не́ о ком) *pron* there is nobody.

некомпете́нтный not competent, unqualified.

не́котор|ый *pron* some; ~ые *sb pl* some (people).

некраси́вый plain, ugly; not nice.

некроло́г obituary.

некста́ти *adv* at the wrong time, out of place.

не́кто *pron* somebody; a certain.

не́куда *adv* there is nowhere.

не-. **некульту́рный** uncivilized, uncultured. **некуря́щий** *sb* nonsmoker. **нела́дный** wrong. **нелега́льный** illegal. **нелёгкий** not easy; heavy. **неле́пость** absurdity; nonsense. **неле́пый** absurd. **нело́вкий** awkward. **нело́вкость** awkwardness.

нельзя́ *adv* it is impossible; it is not allowed.

не-. **нелюби́мый** unloved. **нелюди́мый** unsociable. **нема́ло** *adv* quite a lot (of). **нема́лый** considerable. **неме́дленно** *adv* immediately. **неме́дленный** immediate.

неме́ть (-е́ю) *impf* (*pf* о~) become dumb. **не́мец** (-мца) German. **неме́цкий** German.

немину́емый inevitable.

не́мка German woman.

немно́гие *sb pl* (a) few. **немно́го** *adv* a little; some; a few. **немно́жко** *adv* a little.

немо́й (нем, -а́, -о) dumb, mute, silent. **немота́** dumbness.

немощный feeble.

немыслимый unthinkable.

ненавидеть (-йжу) *impf* hate. ненавистный hated; hateful. ненависть hatred.

не-. ненаглядный beloved. ненадёжный unreliable. ненадолго for a short time. ненастье bad weather. ненасытный insatiable. ненормальный abnormal. ненужный unnecessary, unneeded. необдуманный thoughtless, hasty. необеспеченный without means, unprovided for. необитаемый uninhabited. необозримый boundless, immense. необоснованный unfounded, groundless. необработанный uncultivated; crude; unpolished. необразованный uneducated.

необходимость necessity. необходимый necessary.

не-. необъяснимый inexplicable. необъятный immense. необыкновенный unusual. необычайный extraordinary. необычный unusual. необязательный optional. неограниченный unlimited. неоднократный repeated. неодобрительный disapproving. неодушевлённый inanimate.

неожиданность unexpectedness. неожиданный unexpected, sudden.

неоклассицизм neoclassicism.

не-. неоконченный unfinished. неоплаченный unpaid. неоправданный unjustified. неопределённый indefinite; infinitive; vague. неопровержимый irrefutable. неопубликованный unpublished. неопытный inexperienced. неорганический inorganic. неоспоримый incontestable. неосторожный careless. неосуществимый impracticable. неотвратимый inevitable.

неоткуда *adv* there is nowhere.

не-. неотложный urgent. неотразимый irresistible. неотступный persistent. неотъемлемый inalienable. неофициальный unofficial. неохота reluctance. неохотно *adv* reluctantly. неоценимый inestimable, invaluable. непартийный nonparty; unbefitting a member of the (Communist) Party. непереводимый untranslatable. непереходный intransitive. неплатёжеспособный insolvent.

не-. неплохо *adv* not badly, quite well. неплохой not bad, quite good. непобедимый invincible. неповиновение insubordination. неповоротливый clumsy. неповторимый inimitable, unique. непогода bad weather. непогрешимый infallible. неподалёку *adv* not far (away). неподвижный motionless, immovable; fixed. неподдельный genuine; sincere. неподкупный incorruptible. неподражаемый inimitable. неподходящий unsuitable, inappropriate. непоколебимый unshakable, steadfast. непокорный recalcitrant, unruly.

не-. неполадки (-док) *pl* defects. неполноценность; комплекс неполноценности inferiority complex. неполноценный defective; inadequate. неполный incomplete; not (a) full. непомерный excessive. непонимание incomprehension, lack of understanding. непонятный incomprehensible. непоправимый irreparable. непорядок (-дка) disorder. непорядочный dishonourable. непоседа *m & f* fidget. непосильный beyond one's strength. непоследовательный inconsistent. непослушание disobedience. непослушный disobedient. непосредственный immediate; spontaneous. непостижимый incomprehensible. непостоянный inconstant, changeable. непохожий unlike; different.

не-. неправда untruth. неправдоподобный improbable. неправильно *adv* wrong. неправильный irregular; wrong. неправый wrong. непрактичный unpractical. непревзойдённый unsurpassed. непредвиденный unforeseen. непредубеждённый unprejudiced. непредусмотренный unforeseen. непредусмотрительный short-sighted. непреклонный inflexible; adamant. непреложный immutable.

не-. непременно *adv* without fail. непременный indispensable. непреодолимый insuperable. непререкаемый unquestionable. непре-

ры́вно adv continuously. **непре-ры́вный** continuous. **непреста́н-ный** incessant. **неприве́тливый** unfriendly; bleak. **непривлека́тель-ный** unattractive. **непривы́чный** unaccustomed. **непригля́дный** un-attractive. **неприго́дный** unfit, use-less. **неприе́млемый** unacceptable. **неприкоснове́нность** inviolability, immunity. **неприкоснове́нный** in-violable; reserve. **неприли́чный** in-decent. **непримири́мый** irreconcil-able. **непринуждённый** uncon-strained; relaxed. **неприспосо́блен-ный** unadapted; maladjusted. **не-присто́йный** obscene. **непристу́п-ный** inaccessible. **непритяза́тель-ный, неприхотли́вый** unpreten-tious, simple. **неприя́зненный** hos-tile, inimical. **неприя́знь** hostility. **неприя́тель** m enemy. **неприя́-тельский** enemy. **неприя́тность** unpleasantness; trouble. **неприя́т-ный** unpleasant.

не-. непрове́ренный unverified. **непрогля́дный** pitch-dark. **непро-е́зжий** impassable. **непрозра́чный** opaque. **непроизводи́тельный** un-productive. **непроизво́льный** in-voluntary. **непромока́емый** water-proof. **непроница́емый** impene-trable. **непрости́тельный** unfor-givable. **непроходи́мый** impass-able. **непро́чный** (-чен, -чна́ -о) fragile, flimsy.

не прочь predic not averse.

не-. непро́шеный uninvited, unsoli-cited. **нераworkinǵспосо́бный** dis-abled. **нераboт** ~ день day off. **нера́венство** inequality. **нерав-номе́рный** uneven. **нера́вный** un-equal. **неради́вый** lackadaisical. **неразбери́ха** muddle. **неразбо́р-чивый** not fastidious; illegible. **не-развито́й** (-ра́звит, -а́, -о) undevel-oped; backward. **неразгово́рчивый** taciturn. **неразделённый:** ~ая лю-бо́вь unrequited love. **неразличи́-мый** indistinguishable. **неразлу́ч-ный** inseparable. **неразреши́мый** un-solved; forbidden. **неразреши́мый** insoluble. **неразры́вный** indissol-uble. **неразу́мный** unwise; unrea-sonable. **нераствори́мый** insoluble. **нерв** nerve. **не́рвничать** impf fret,

be nervous. **нервнобольно́й** sb neurotic. **не́рвный** (-вен, -вна́, -о) nervous; nerve; irritable. **нерво́з-ный** nervy, irritable.

не-. нереа́льный unreal; unrealistic. **нере́дкий** (-док, -дка́, -о) not infre-quent, not uncommon. **нереши́-тельность** indecision. **нереши́-тельный** indecisive, irresolute. **не-ржаве́ющая сталь** stainless steel. **неро́вный** (-вен, -вна́, -о) uneven, rough; irregular. **неруши́мый** inviol-able.

неря́ха m & f sloven. **неря́шливый** slovenly.

не-. несбы́точный unrealizable. **несваре́ние желу́дка** indigestion. **несве́жий** (-еж, -á) not fresh; tainted; weary. **несвоевре́менный** ill-timed; overdue. **несво́йствен-ный** not characteristic. **несгора́е-мый** fireproof. **несерьёзный** not serious.

несессе́р case.

несимметри́чный asymmetrical.

несвя́зный incoherent; awkward. **несклоня́емый** indeclinable.

не́сколько (-их) pron some, several; adv somewhat.

не-. несконча́емый interminable. **нескро́мный** (-мен, -мна́, -о) im-modest; indiscreet. **несло́жный** sim-ple. **неслы́ханный** unprecedented. **неслы́шный** inaudible. **несме́тный** countless, incalculable. **несмолка́е-мый** ceaseless.

несмотря́ на prep+acc in spite of. **не-. несно́сный** intolerable. **несо-блюде́ние** non-observance. **несо-вершенноле́тний** under-age; sb mi-nor. **несоверше́нный** imperfect, in-complete: imperfective. **несове́р-ше́нство** imperfection. **несовме-сти́мый** incompatible. **несогла́сие** disagreement. **несогласо́ванный** uncoordinated. **несозна́тельный** ir-responsible. **несоизмери́мый** in-commensurable. **несокруши́мый** indestructible. **несомне́нный** un-doubted, unquestionable. **несооб-ра́зный** incongruous. **несоотве́т-ствие** disparity. **несостоя́тельный** insolvent; of modest means; unten-able. **неспе́лый** unripe. **неспоко́й-ный** restless; uneasy. **неспосо́бный**

not bright; incapable. **несправедли́вость** injustice. **несправедли́вый** unjust, unfair; incorrect. **несравне́нный** (-е́нен, -е́нна) incomparable. **несравни́мый** incomparable. **нестерпи́мый** unbearable.

нести́ (-су́, -сёшь; нёс, -ла́) *impf* (*pf* по~, с~) carry; bear; bring, take; suffer; incur; lay; ~**сь** rush, fly; float, be carried.

не-. **нето́йкий** unstable. **несуще́ственный** immaterial, inessential.

несу́ *etc.*: *see* нести́

несхо́дный unlike, dissimilar.

несчастли́вый unfortunate, unlucky; unhappy. **несча́стный** unhappy, unfortunate; ~ **слу́чай** accident. **несча́стье** misfortune; **к несча́стью** unfortunately.

несчётный innumerable.

нет *partl* no, not; nothing. **нет, не́ту** there is not, there are not.

не-. **нетакти́чный** tactless. **нетвёрдый** (-ёрд, -а́, -о) unsteady, shaky. **нетерпели́вый** impatient. **нетерпе́ние** impatience. **нетерпи́мый** intolerable, intolerant. **неторопли́вый** leisurely. **нето́чный** (-чен, -чна́, -о) inaccurate, inexact. **нетре́звый** drunk. **нетро́нутый** untouched; chaste, virginal. **нетрудово́й дохо́д** unearned income. **нетрудоспосо́бность** disability.

не́тто *indecl adj* & *adv* net(t).

не́ту *see* нет

не-. **неубеди́тельный** unconvincing. **неуваже́ние** disrespect. **неуве́ренность** uncertainty. **неуве́ренный** uncertain. **неувяда́емый, неувяда́ющий** unfading. **неугомо́нный** indefatigable. **неуда́ча** failure. **неуда́чливый** unlucky. **неуда́чник, -ница** unlucky person, failure. **неуда́чный** unsuccessful, unfortunate. **неудержи́мый** irrepressible. **неудо́бный** uncomfortable; inconvenient; embarrassing. **неудо́бство** discomfort; inconvenience; embarrassment. **неудовлетворе́ние** dissatisfaction. **неудовлетворённый** dissatisfied. **неудовлетвори́тельный** unsatisfactory. **неудово́льствие** displeasure.

неуже́ли? *partl* really?

не-. **неузнава́емый** unrecognizable. **неукло́нный** steady; undeviating. **неуклю́жий** clumsy. **неулови́мый** elusive; subtle. **неуме́лый** inept; clumsy. **неуме́ренный** immoderate. **неуме́стный** inappropriate; irrelevant. **неумоли́мый** implacable, inexorable. **неумы́шленный** unintentional.

не-. **неупла́та** non-payment. **неуравнове́шенный** unbalanced. **неурожа́й** bad harvest. **неуро́чный** untimely, inopportune. **неуря́дица** disorder, mess. **неуспева́емость** poor progress. **неусто́йка** forfeit. **неусто́йчивый** unstable; unsteady. **неусту́пчивый** unyielding. **неуте́шный** inconsolable. **неутоли́мый** unquenchable. **неутоми́мый** tireless. **неу́ч** ignoramus. **неучти́вый** discourteous. **неуязви́мый** invulnerable.

нефри́т jade.

нефте- *in comb* oil, petroleum. **нефтено́сный** oil-bearing. ~**перего́нный заво́д** oil refinery. ~**прово́д** (oil) pipeline. ~**проду́кты** (-ов) *pl* petroleum products.

нефть oil, petroleum. **нефтяно́й** oil, petroleum.

не-. **нехва́тка** shortage. **нехорошо́** *adv* badly. **нехоро́ший** (-о́ш, -а́) bad; ~**о́** it is bad, it is wrong. **нехотя** *adv* unwillingly; unintentionally. **нецелесообра́зный** inexpedient; pointless. **нецензу́рный** unprintable. **неча́янный** unexpected; accidental.

не́чего (не́чему, -чем, не́ о чем) *pron* (*with separable pref*) (there is) nothing.

нечелове́ческий inhuman, superhuman.

нече́стный dishonest, unfair.

нечётный odd.

нечистопло́тный dirty; slovenly; unscrupulous. **нечистота́** (*pl* -о́ты, -о́т) dirtiness, filth; *pl* sewage. **нечи́стый** (-и́ст, -а́, -о) dirty, unclean; impure; unclear. **нечи́сть** evil spirits; scum.

нечленоразде́льный inarticulate.

не́что *pron* something.

не-. **неэконо́мный** uneconomical. **неэффекти́вный** ineffective; inefficient. **нея́вка** failure to appear. **не-**

я́ркий dim, faint; dull, subdued. **неясный** (-сен, -сна́, -о) not clear; vague.

ни *partl* not a; **ни оди́н (одна́, одно́)** not a single; (*with prons and pronominal advs*) -ever; **кто...** ни whoever. **ни** *conj*: **ни... ни** neither ... nor; **ни то ни сё** neither one thing nor the other.

ни́ва cornfield, field.

нивели́р level.

нигде́ *adv* nowhere.

нидерла́ндец (-дца; *gen pl* -дцев) Dutchman. **нидерла́ндка** Dutchwoman. **нидерла́ндский** Dutch. **Нидерла́нды** (-ов) *pl* the Netherlands.

ни́же *adj* lower, humbler; *adv* below; *prep+gen* below, beneath. **нижесле́дующий** following. **ни́жн|ий** lower, under-; **~ее бельё** underclothes; **~ий эта́ж** ground floor. **низ** (*loc* -у́; *pl* -ы́) bottom; *pl* lower classes; low notes.

низа́ть (нижу́, ни́жешь) *impf* (*pf* на~) string, thread.

низверга́ть *impf*, **низве́ргнуть** (-ну; -е́рг) *pf* throw down, overthrow; **~ся** crash down; be overthrown. **низверже́ние** overthrow.

низи́на low-lying place. **ни́зкий** (-зок, -зка́, -о) low; base, mean. **низкопокло́нство** servility. **низкопро́бный** base; low-grade. **низкоро́слый** undersized. **низкосо́ртный** low-grade.

ни́зменность lowland; baseness. **ни́зменный** low-lying; base.

низо́вье (*gen pl* -ьев) the lower reaches. **ни́зость** baseness, meanness. **ни́зш|ий** lower, lowest; **~ее образова́ние** primary education.

ника́к *adv* in no way. **никако́й** *pron* no; no ... whatever

ни́кель *m* nickel.

нике́м *see* никто́. **никогда́** *adv* never. **никто́** (-кого́, -кому́, -ке́м, ни о ко́м) *pron* (*with separable pref*) nobody, no one. **никуда́** nowhere. **никчёмный** useless. **нима́ло** *adv* not in the least.

нимб halo, nimbus.

ни́мфа nymph; pupa.

ниотку́да *adv* from nowhere.

нипочём *adv* it is nothing; dirt cheap; in no circumstances.

ниско́лько *adv* not at all.

ниспроверга́ть *impf*, **ниспрове́ргнуть** (-ну; -е́рг) *pf* overthrow. **ниспроверже́ние** overthrow.

нисходя́щий descending.

ни́тка thread; string; **до ни́тки** to the skin; **на живу́ю ни́тку** hastily, anyhow. **ни́точка** thread. **нить** thread; filament.

ничего́ *etc*.: *see* ничто́. **ничего́** *adv* all right; it doesn't matter, never mind; *as indecl adj* not bad, pretty good. **ниче́й** (-чья́, -чьё) *pron* nobody's; **ничья́ земля́** no man's land. **ничья́** *sb* draw; tie.

ничко́м *adv* face down, prone.

ничто́ (-чего́, -чему́, -че́м, ни о чём) *pron* (*with separable pref*) nothing. **ничто́жество** nonentity, nobody. **ничто́жный** insignificant; worthless.

ничу́ть *adv* not a bit.

ничье́ *etc*.: *see* ничей

ни́ша niche, recess.

ни́щенка beggar-woman. **ни́щенский** beggarly. **нищета́** poverty. **ни́щий** (нищ, -а́, -е) destitute, poor; *sb* beggar.

но *conj* but; still

нова́тор innovator. **нова́торский** innovative. **нова́торство** innovation. **Но́вая Зела́ндия** New Zealand.

нове́йший newest, latest.

нове́лла short story.

но́венький brand-new.

новизна́ novelty; newness. **нови́нка** novelty. **новичо́к** (-чка́) novice.

ново- *in comb* new(ly). **новобра́нец** (-нца) new recruit. **~бра́чный** *sb* newly-wed. **~введе́ние** innovation. **~го́дний** new year's. **~зела́ндец** (- дца; *gen pl* -дцев), **~зела́ндка** New-Zealander. **~зела́ндский** New Zealand. **~лу́ние** new moon. **~при́бывший** newly-arrived; *sb* newcomer. **~рождённый** newborn. **~сёл** new settler. **~се́лье** new home; housewarming. **новостро́йка** new building.

но́вость news; novelty. **но́вшество** innovation, novelty. **но́вый** (нов, -а́, -о) new; modern; **~ год** New Year's Day.

нога́ (*acc* но́гу; *pl* но́ги, ног, нога́м) foot, leg.

но́готь (-гтя; *pl* -и) *m* finger-nail, toe-nail.

нож (-а́) knife.

но́жка small foot or leg; leg; stem, stalk.

но́жницы (-иц) *pl* scissors, shears.

но́жны (-жен) *pl* sheath, scabbard.

ножо́вка saw, hacksaw.

ноздря́ (*pl* -и, -е́й) nostril.

нока́ут knock-out. **нокаути́ровать** *impf & pf* knock out.

нолево́й, нулево́й zero. **ноль** (-я́), **нуль** (-я́) *m* nought, zero, nil.

номенклату́ра nomenclature; top positions in government.

но́мер (*pl* -а́) number; size; (hotel-) room; item; trick. **номеро́к** (-рка́) tag; label, ticket.

номина́л face value. **номина́льный** nominal.

нора́ (*pl* -ы) burrow, hole.

Норве́гия Norway. **норве́жец** (-жца), **норве́жка** Norwegian. **норве́жский** Norwegian.

норд (*naut*) north; north wind.

но́рка mink.

но́рма standard, norm; rate. **нормализа́ция** standardization. **норма́льно** all right, OK. **норма́льный** normal; standard. **норми́рование, нормиро́вка** regulation; rate-fixing; rationing. **норми́ровать** *impf & pf* regulate, standardize; ration.

нос (*loc* -у́; *pl* -ы́) nose; beak; bow, prow. **но́сик** (*small*) nose; spout.

носи́лки (-лок) *pl* stretcher; litter. **носи́льщик** porter. **носи́тель** *m*, **~ница** (*fig*) bearer; (*med*) carrier. **носи́ть** (-ошу́, -о́сишь) *impf* carry, bear; wear; **~ся** rush, tear along, fly; float, be carried; wear. **но́ска** carrying, wearing. **но́ский** hard-wearing.

носово́й nose; nasal; **~ плато́к** (pocket) handkerchief. **носо́к** (-ска́) little nose; toe; sock. **носоро́г** rhinoceros.

но́та note; *pl* music. **нота́ция** notation; lecture, reprimand.

нота́риус notary.

ночева́ть (-чу́ю) *impf* (*pf* пере~) spend the night. **ночёвка** spending the night; passing the night. **ночле́г** place to spend the night. **ночле́жка** doss-house. **ночни́к** (-а́) night-light. **ночн|о́й** night, nocturnal; **~а́я руба́шка** nightdress; **~о́й горшо́к** potty; chamber-pot. **ночь** (*loc* -и́; *gen pl* -е́й) night. **но́чью** *adv* at night.

но́ша burden. **но́шеный** worn; second-hand.

но́ю *etc*.: *see* ныть

ноя́брь (-я́) *m* November. **ноя́брьский** November.

нрав disposition, temper; *pl* customs, ways. **нра́виться** (-влюсь) *impf* (*pf* по~) +*dat* please; **мне нра́вится** I like. **нра́вственность** morality, morals. **нра́вственный** moral.

ну *int & partl* well, well then.

ну́дный tedious.

нужда́ (*pl* -ы) need. **нужда́ться** *impf* be in need; +в+*prep* need, require. **ну́жн|ый** (-жен, -жна́, -о, ну́жны́) necessary; **~о** it is necessary; +*dat* I, *etc*., must, ought to, need.

нулево́й, нуль *see* нолево́й, ноль

нумера́ция numeration; numbering. **нумерова́ть** *impf* (*pf* про~) number.

нутро́ inside, interior; instinct(s).

ны́не *adv* now; today. **ны́нешний** present; today's. **ны́нче** *adv* today; now.

нырну́ть (-ну́, -нёшь) *pf*, **ныря́ть** *impf* dive.

ныть (но́ю) *impf* ache; whine. **нытьё** whining.

н.э. *abbr* (*of* на́шей э́ры) AD.

нюх scent; flair. **ню́хать** *impf* (*pf* по~) smell, sniff.

ня́нчить (-чу) *impf* nurse, look after; **~ся** с+*instr* nurse; fuss over. **ня́нька** nanny. **ня́ня** (*children's*) nurse, nanny.

О

о, об, обо *prep* I. +*prep* of, about, concerning. II. +*acc* against; on, upon.

о *int* oh!

оа́зис oasis.

об *see o prep.*

о́ба (обо́их) *m & neut*, **о́бе** (обе́их) *f* both.

обалдева́ть *impf*, **обалде́ть** (-е́ю) *pf* go crazy; become dulled; be stunned.

обанкро́титься (-о́чусь) *pf* go bankrupt.

обая́ние fascination, charm. обая́тельный fascinating, charming.

обва́л fall(ing); crumbling; collapse; caving-in; landslide; (снежный) ~ avalanche. обвали́ть (-лю́, -лишь) pf (impf обва́ливать) cause to fall or collapse; crumble; heap round; ~ся collapse, cave in; crumble.

обваля́ть pf (impf обва́ливать) roll. обва́ривать impf, обвари́ть (-рю́, -ришь) pf pour boiling water over; scald; ~ся scald o.s.

обведу́ etc.: see обвести́. обвёл etc.: see обвести́. об|венча́ть(ся pf.

обверну́ть (-ну́, -нёшь) pf, обвёртывать impf wrap, wrap up.

обве́с short weight. обве́сить (-ёшу) pf (impf обве́шивать) cheat in weighing.

обвести́ (-еду́, -едёшь; -ёл, -ела́) pf (impf обводи́ть) lead round, take round; encircle; surround; outline; dodge.

обве́тренный weather-beaten.

обветша́лый decrepit. об|ветша́ть pf.

обве́шивать impf of обве́сить.

обвива́ть(ся impf of обви́ть(ся pf.

обвине́ние charge, accusation; prosecution. обвини́тель m accuser; prosecutor. обвини́тельный accusatory; ~ акт indictment; ~ пригово́р verdict of guilty. обвини́ть pf, обвиня́ть impf prosecute, indict; +в+prep accuse of, charge with. обвиня́емый sb the accused; defendant.

обви́ть (обовью́, обовьёшь; обви́л, -а́, -о) pf (impf обвива́ть) wind round; ~ся wind round.

обводи́ть (-ожу́, -о́дишь) impf of обвести́

обвора́живать impf, обворожи́ть (-жу́) pf charm, enchant. обворожи́тельный charming, enchanting.

обвяза́ть (-яжу́, -я́жешь) pf, обвя́зывать impf tie round; ~ся +instr tie round o.s.

обго́н passing. обгоня́ть impf of обогна́ть

обгора́ть impf, обгоре́ть (-рю́) pf be burnt, be scorched. обгоре́лый burnt, charred, scorched.

обде́лать pf (impf обде́лывать) fin-ish; polish, set; manage, arrange.

обдели́ть (-лю́, -лишь) pf (impf обделя́ть) +instr do out of one's (fair) share of.

обде́лывать impf of обде́лать. обделя́ть impf of обдели́ть

обдеру́ etc.: see ободра́ть. обди-ра́ть impf of ободра́ть

обду́манный deliberate, well-considered. обду́мать pf, обду́мывать impf consider, think over.

о́бе: see о́ба. обега́ть impf of обежа́ть. обегу́ etc.: see обежа́ть

обе́д dinner, lunch. обе́дать impf (pf по~) have dinner, dine. обе́денный dinner.

обедне́вший impoverished. обедне́ние impoverishment. о|бедне́ть (-е́ю) pf.

обе́дня (gen pl -ден) mass.

обежа́ть (-егу́) pf (impf обега́ть) run round; run past; outrun.

обезбо́ливание anaesthetization. обезбо́ливать impf, обезбо́лить pf anaesthetize.

обезвре́дить (-е́жу) pf, обезвре́живать impf render harmless.

обездо́ленный unfortunate, hapless.

обеззара́живающий disinfectant.

обезли́ченный depersonalized; robbed of individuality.

обезобра́живать impf, о|безобра́зить (-а́жу) pf disfigure.

обезопа́сить (-а́шу) pf secure.

обезору́живать impf, обезору́жить (-жу) pf disarm.

обезу́меть (-ею) pf lose one's senses, lose one's head.

обезья́на monkey; ape.

обели́ть (-лю́, обеля́ть impf vindicate; clear of blame.

оберега́ть impf, обере́чь (-егу́, -ежёшь; -рёг, -ла́) pf guard; protect.

оберну́ть (-ну́, -нёшь) pf, обёртывать impf (impf also обора́чивать) twist; wrap up; turn; ~ся turn (round); turn into; +instr or в+acc turn into. обёртка wrapper; (dust-) jacket, cover. обёрточный wrapping.

оберу́ etc.: see обобра́ть

обескура́живать impf, обескура́жить (-жу) pf discourage; dishearten.

обескро́вить (-влю) pf, обескро́вливать impf drain of blood, bleed white; render lifeless.

обеспечение securing, guaranteeing; ensuring; provision; guarantee; security. обеспеченность security; +instr provision of. обеспеченный well-to-do; well provided for. обеспечивать impf, обеспечить (-чу) pf provide for; secure; ensure; protect; +instr provide with.

о|беспокоить(ся pf.

обессилеть (-ею) pf grow weak, lose one's strength. обессиливать impf, обессилить pf weaken.

о|бесславить (-влю) pf.

обессмертить (-рчу) pf immortalize.

обесценение depreciation. обесценивать impf, обесценить pf depreciate; cheapen; ~ся depreciate.

о|бесчестить (-ещу) pf.

обет vow, promise. обетованный promised. обещание promise. обещать impf & pf (pf also по~) promise.

обжалование appeal. обжаловать pf appeal against.

обжечь (обожгу, обожжёшь; обжёг, обожгла) pf, обжигать impf burn; scorch; bake; ~ся burn o.s.; burn one's fingers.

обжора m & f glutton. обжорство gluttony.

обзавестись (-едусь, -едёшься; -вёлся, -лась) pf, обзаводиться (-ожусь, -одишься) impf +instr provide o.s. with; acquire.

обзову etc.: see обозвать

обзор survey, review.

обзывать impf of обозвать

обивать impf of обить. обивка upholstering; upholstery.

обида offence, insult; nuisance. обидеть (-ижу) pf, обижать impf offend; hurt; wound; ~ся take offence; feel hurt. обидный offensive; annoying. обидчивый touchy. обиженный offended.

обилие abundance. обильный abundant.

обирать impf of обобрать

обитаемый inhabited. обитатель m inhabitant. обитать impf live.

обить (обобью, -ьёшь) pf (impf обивать) upholster; knock off.

обиход custom, (general) use, practice. обиходный everyday.

обкладывать(ся impf of обложить(ся

обкрадывать impf of обокрасть.

облава raid; cordon, cordoning off.

облагаемый taxable. облагать(ся impf of обложить(ся; ~ся налогом be liable to tax.

обладание possession. обладатель m possessor. обладать impf +instr possess.

облако (pl -á, -ób) cloud.

обламывать(ся impf of обломать(ся, обломить(ся

областной regional. область (gen pl -ей) region; field, sphere.

облачность cloudiness. облачный cloudy.

облёг etc.: see облечь. облегать impf of облечь

облегчать impf, облегчить (-чу) pf lighten; relieve; alleviate; facilitate. облегчение relief.

обледенелый ice-covered. обледенение icing over. обледенеть (-ёет) pf become covered with ice.

облезлый shabby; mangy.

облекать(ся impf of облечь[2](ся. облеку etc.: see облечь[2]

облепить (-плю, -пишь) pf, облеплять impf stick to, cling to; throng round; plaster.

облетать impf, облететь (-лечу) pf fly (round); spread (all over); fall.

облечь[1] (-ляжет; -лёг, -ла) pf (impf облегать) cover, envelop; fit tightly.

облечь[2] (-еку, -ечёшь; -ёк, -кла) pf (impf облекать) clothe, invest; ~ся clothe o.s.; +gen take the form of.

обливать(ся impf of облить(ся

облигация bond.

облизать (-ижу, -ижешь) pf, облизывать impf lick (all over); ~ся smack one's lips.

облик look, appearance.

облитый (облит, -á, -о) covered, enveloped. облить (оболью, -льёшь; облил, -ила, -о) pf (impf обливать) pour, sluice, spill; ~ся sponge down, take a shower; pour over o.s.

облицевать (-цую) pf, облицовывать impf face. облицовка facing; lining.

обличать impf, обличить (-чу) pf expose; reveal; point to. обличение exposure, denunciation. обличительный denunciatory.

обложе́ние taxation; assessment.

обложи́ть (-жу́, -жишь) pf (impf обкла́дывать, облага́ть) edge; face; cover; surround; assess; круго́м обложи́ло (не́бо) the sky is completely overcast; ~ нало́гом tax; ~ся +instr surround o.s. with. обло́жка (dust-) cover; folder.

облока́чиваться impf, облокоти́ться (-очу́сь, -о́тишься) pf на+acc lean one's elbows on.

обло́мать pf (impf обла́мывать) break off; ~ся break off. обломи́ться (-ломится) pf (impf обла́мываться) break off. обло́мок (-мка) fragment.

облу́пленный chipped.

облучи́ть (-чу́) pf, облуча́ть impf irradiate. облуче́ние irradiation.

об|лысе́ть (-е́ю) pf.

обля́жет etc.: see обле́чь[1]

обма́зать (-а́жу) pf, обма́зывать impf coat; putty; besmear; ~ся +instr get covered with.

обма́кивать impf, обмакну́ть (-ну́, -нёшь) pf dip.

обма́н deceit; illusion; ~ зре́ния optical illusion. обма́нный deceitful. обману́ть (-ну́, -нешь) pf, обма́нывать impf deceive; cheat; ~ся be deceived. обма́нчивый deceptive. обма́нщик deceiver; fraud.

обма́тывать(ся impf of обмота́ть(ся

обма́хивать impf, обмахну́ть (-ну́, -нёшь) pf brush off; fan; ~ся fan o.s.

обмёл etc.: see обмести́

обмеле́ние shallowing. об|меле́ть (-е́ет) pf become shallow.

обме́н exchange; barter; в ~ за+acc in exchange for; ~ веще́ств metabolism. обме́нивать impf, обмени́ть (-ню́, -нишь) pf, об|меня́ть pf exchange; ~ся +instr exchange. обме́нный exchange.

обме́р measurement; false measure.

обмере́ть (обомру́, -рёшь; о́бмер, -ла́, -ло) pf (impf обмира́ть) faint; ~ от у́жаса be horror-struck.

обме́ривать impf, обме́рить (-еет) pf measure; cheat in measuring.

обмести́ (-ету́, -ете́шь; -мёл, -мела́, -а́) pf, обмета́ть[1] impf sweep off, dust.

обмета́ть[2] (-ечу́ or -а́ю, -ече́шь or

-а́ешь) pf (impf обмётывать) oversew.

обмету́ etc.: see обмести́. обмётывать impf of обмета́ть. обмира́ть impf of обмере́ть.

обмо́лвиться (-влюсь) pf make a slip of the tongue; +instr say, utter. обмо́лвка slip of the tongue.

обморо́женный frost-bitten.

о́бморок fainting-fit, swoon.

обмота́ть pf (impf обма́тывать) wind round; ~ся +instr wrap o.s. in. обмо́тка winding; pl puttees.

обмо́ю etc.: see обмы́ть

обмундирова́ние fitting out (with uniform); uniform. обмундирова́ть pf, обмундиро́вывать impf fit out (with uniform).

обмыва́ть impf, обмы́ть (-мо́ю) pf bathe, wash; ~ся wash, bathe.

обмяка́ть impf, обмя́кнуть (-ну; -мя́к) pf become soft or flabby.

обнадёживать impf, обнадёжить (-жу) pf reassure.

обнажа́ть impf, обнажи́ть (-жу́) pf bare, uncover; reveal. обнажённый (-ён, -ена́) naked, bare; nude.

обнаро́довать impf & pf promulgate.

обнаруже́ние revealing; discovery; detection. обнару́живать impf, обнару́жить (-жу) pf display; reveal; discover; ~ся come to light.

обнести́ (-су́, -сёшь; -нёс, -ла́) pf (impf обноси́ть) enclose; +instr serve round; pass over, leave out.

обнима́ть(ся impf of обня́ть(ся. обниму́ etc.: see обня́ть

обнища́ние impoverishment.

обнови́ть (-влю́) pf, обновля́ть impf renovate; renew. обно́вка new acquisition; new garment. обновле́ние renovation, renewal.

обноси́ть (-ошу́, -о́сишь) impf of обнести́; ~ся pf have worn out one's clothes.

обня́ть (-ниму́, -ни́мешь; о́бнял, -а́, -о) pf (impf обнима́ть) embrace; clasp; ~ся embrace; hug one another.

обо see o or prep.

обобра́ть (оберу́, -рёшь; обобра́л, -а́, -о) pf (impf обира́ть) rob; pick.

обобща́ть impf, обобщи́ть (-щу́) pf generalize. обобще́ние generalization. обобществи́ть (-влю́) pf, обобществля́ть *impf* socialize; collectivize. обобществле́ние socialization; collectivization.

обобью́ *etc.*: see обить. обовью́ *etc.*: see обви́ть

обогати́ть (-ащу́) *pf*, обогаща́ть *impf* enrich; ~ся become rich; enrich o.s. обогаще́ние enrichment.

обогна́ть (обгоню́, -о́нишь; обогна́л, -а́, -о) *pf* (*impf* обгоня́ть) pass; outstrip.

обогну́ть (-ну́, -нёшь) *pf* (*impf* огиба́ть) round; bend round.

обогрева́тель *m* heater. обогрева́ть *impf*, обогре́ть (-е́ю) *pf* heat, warm; ~ся warm up.

о́бод (*pl* -о́дья, -ьев) rim. ободо́к (-дка́) thin rim, narrow border.

обо́дранный ragged. ободра́ть (обдеру́, -рёшь; -а́л, -а́, -о) *pf* (*impf* обдира́ть) skin, flay; peel; fleece.

ободре́ние encouragement, reassurance. ободри́тельный encouraging, reassuring. ободри́ть *pf*, ободря́ть *impf* encourage, reassure; ~ся cheer up, take heart.

обожа́ть *impf* adore.

обожгу́ *etc.*: see обже́чь

обожестви́ть (-влю́) *pf*, обожествля́ть *impf* deify.

обожжённый (-ён, -ена́) burnt, scorched.

обо́з string of vehicles; transport.

обозва́ть (обзову́, -вёшь; -а́л, -а́, -о) *pf* (*impf* обзыва́ть) call; call names.

обозлённый (-ён, -а́) angered; embittered. обо|зли́ть, о|зли́ть *pf* anger; embitter; ~ся get angry.

обозна́ться *pf* mistake s.o. for s.o. else.

обознача́ть *impf*, обозна́чить (-чу) *pf* mean; mark; ~ся appear, reveal o.s. обозначе́ние sign, symbol.

обозрева́тель *m* reviewer; columnist. обозрева́ть *impf*, обозре́ть (-рю́) *pf* survey. обозре́ние survey; review; revue. обозри́мый visible.

обо́и (-ев) *pl* wallpaper.

обо́йма (*gen pl* -о́йм) cartridge clip.

обойти́ (-йду́, -йдёшь; -ошёл, -ошла́) *pf* (*impf* обходи́ть) go round; pass; avoid; pass over; ~сь manage, make do; +*instr* treat.

обокра́сть (обкраду́, -дёшь) *pf* (*impf* обкра́дывать) rob.

оболо́чка casing; membrane; cover, envelope, jacket; shell.

обольсти́тель *m* seducer. обольсти́тельный seductive. обольсти́ть (-льщу́) *pf*, обольща́ть *impf* seduce. обольще́ние seduction; delusion.

оболью́ *etc.*: see обли́ть

обомру́ *etc.*: see обмере́ть

обоня́ние (sense of) smell. обоня́тельный olfactory.

обопру́ *etc.*: see опере́ть

обора́чивать(ся *impf of* оберну́ть(ся, оборо́тить(ся

обо́рванный torn, ragged. оборва́ть (-ву́, -вёшь; -а́л, -а́, -о) *pf* (*impf* обрыва́ть) tear off; break; snap; cut short; ~ся break; snap; fall; stop suddenly.

обо́рка frill, flounce.

оборо́на defence. оборони́тельный defensive. обороня́ть *impf* defend; ~ся defend o.s. оборо́нный defence, defensive.

оборо́т turn; revolution; circulation; turnover; back; ~ ре́чи (turn of) phrase; смотри́ на ~е P.T.O. обороти́ть (-рочу́, -ро́тишь) *pf* (*impf* обора́чивать) turn; ~ся turn (round); +*instr* or в+*acc* turn into. оборо́тный circulating; reverse; ~ капита́л working capital.

обору́дование equipping; equipment. обору́довать *impf & pf* equip.

обоснова́ние basing; basis, ground. обосно́ванный well-founded. обоснова́ть, обосно́вывать *impf* ground, base; substantiate; ~ся settle down.

обосо́бленный isolated, solitary.

обостре́ние aggravation. обострённый keen; strained; sharp, pointed. обостри́ть *pf*, обостря́ть *impf* sharpen; strain; aggravate; ~ся become strained; be aggravated; become acute.

оботру́ *etc.*: see обтере́ть

обо́чина verge; shoulder, edge.

обошёл *etc.*: see обойти́. обошью́ *etc.*: see обши́ть

обою́дный mutual, reciprocal.

обраба́тывать *impf*, обрабо́тать *pf* till, cultivate; work, work up; treat, process. обрабо́тка working (up); processing; cultivation.

об|ра́довать(ся pf.

о́браз shape, form; image; manner; way; icon; гла́вным ~ом mainly; таки́м ~ом thus. образе́ц (-зца́) model; pattern; sample. о́бразный graphic; figurative. образова́ние formation; education. образо́ванный educated. образова́тельный educational. образова́ть impf & pf, образо́вывать impf form; ~ся form; arise; turn out well.

образу́мить (-млю) pf bring to reason; ~ся see reason.

образцо́вый model. о́бразчик specimen, sample.

обра́мить (-млю) pf, обрамля́ть impf frame.

обраста́ть impf, обрасти́ (-ту́, -тёшь; -ро́с, -ла́) pf be overgrown.

обрати́мый reversible, convertible. обрати́ть (-ащу́) pf, обраща́ть impf turn; convert; ~ внима́ние на+acc pay or draw attention to; ~ся turn; appeal; apply; address; +в+acc turn into; +c+instr treat; handle. обра́тно adv back; backwards; conversely; ~ пропорциона́льный inversely proportional. обра́тный reverse; return; opposite; inverse. обраще́ние appeal, address; conversion; (+c+instr) treatment (of); handling (of); use (of).

обре́з edge; sawn-off gun; в ~+gen only just enough. обре́зать (-е́жу) pf, обреза́ть impf cut (off); clip, trim; pare; prune; circumcise; ~ся cut o.s. обре́зок (-зка) scrap; pl ends; clippings.

обрека́ть impf of обре́чь. обреку́ etc.: see обре́чь. обрёл etc.: see обрести́

обремени́тельный onerous. о|бремени́ть pf, обременя́ть impf burden.

обрести́ (-ету́, -етёшь; -рёл, -а́) pf, обрета́ть impf find.

обрече́ние doom. обречённый doomed. обре́чь (-еку́, -ечёшь; -ёк, -ла́) pf (impf обрека́ть) doom.

обрисова́ть pf, обрисо́вывать impf outline, depict; ~ся appear (in outline).

оброни́ть (-ню́, -нишь) pf drop; let drop.

обро́с etc.: see обрасти́.

обруба́ть impf, обруби́ть (-блю́, -бишь) pf chop off; cut off. обру́бок (-бка) stump.

об|руга́ть pf.

о́бруч (pl -и, -е́й) hoop. обруча́льный engagement; ~ое кольцо́ betrothal ring, wedding ring. обруча́ть impf, обручи́ть (-чу́) betroth; ~ся +с+instr become engaged to. обруче́ние engagement.

обру́шивать impf, об|ру́шить (-шу) pf bring down; ~ся come down, collapse.

о́брыв precipice. обрыва́ть(ся impf of оборва́ть(ся. обры́вок (-вка) scrap; snatch.

обры́згать pf, обры́згивать impf splash; sprinkle.

обрю́зглый flabby.

обря́д rite, ceremony.

обсервато́рия observatory.

обслу́живание service; maintenance. обслу́живать impf, обслужи́ть (-жу́, -жишь) pf serve; service; operate.

обсле́дование inspection. обсле́дователь m inspector. обсле́довать impf & pf inspect.

обсо́хнуть (-ну, -ох) pf (impf обсыха́ть) dry (off).

обста́вить (-влю) pf, обставля́ть impf surround; furnish; arrange. обстано́вка furniture; situation, conditions; set.

обстоя́тельный thorough, reliable; detailed. обстоя́тельство circumstance. обстоя́ть (-ои́т) impf be; go; как обстои́т де́ло? how is it going?

обстре́л firing; fire; под ~ом under fire. обстре́ливать impf, обстреля́ть pf fire at; bombard.

обступа́ть impf, обступи́ть (-у́пит) pf surround.

обсуди́ть (-ужу́, -у́дишь) pf, обсужда́ть impf discuss. обсужде́ние discussion.

обсчита́ть pf, обсчи́тывать impf shortchange; ~ся miscount, miscalculate.

обсыпа́ть (-плю) pf, обсыпа́ть impf strew; sprinkle.

обсыха́ть impf of обсо́хнуть. обта́чивать impf of обточи́ть

обтека́емый streamlined.

обтере́ть (оботру́, -трёшь; обтёр) pf (impf обтира́ть) wipe; rub; ~ся dry o.s.; sponge down.

о(б)теса́ть (-ешу́, -ешешь) pf, о(б)тёсывать impf rough-hew; teach good manners to; trim.

обтира́ние sponge-down. обтира́ть(ся pf of обтере́ть(ся

обточи́ть (-чу́, -чишь) pf обта́чивать) grind; machine.

обтрёпанный frayed; shabby.

обтя́гивать impf, обтяну́ть (-ну́, -нешь) pf cover; fit close. обтя́жка cover; skin; в обтя́жку close-fitting.

обува́ть(ся impf of обу́ть(ся. обувь footwear; boots, shoes.

обу́гливать impf, обу́глить pf char; carbonize; ~ся char, become charred.

обу́за burden.

обузда́ть pf, обу́здывать impf bridle, curb.

обурева́ть impf grip; possess.

обусло́вить (-влю) pf, обусло́вливать impf cause; +instr make conditional on; ~ся +instr be conditional on; depend on.

обу́тый shod. обу́ть (-у́ю) pf (impf обува́ть) put shoes on; ~ся put on one's shoes.

обу́х butt, back.

обуча́ть impf, обу́чить (-чу́, -чишь) pf teach; train; ~ся +dat or inf learn. обуче́ние teaching; training.

обхва́т girth; в ~е in circumference. обхвати́ть (-ачу́, -а́тишь) pf, обхва́тывать impf embrace; clasp.

обхо́д round(s); roundabout way; by-pass. обходи́тельный courteous; pleasant. обходи́ть(ся (-ожу́(сь, -о́дишь(ся) impf of обойти́(сь. обхо́дный roundabout.

обша́ривать impf, обша́рить pf rummage through, ransack.

обшива́ть impf pf of обши́ть. обши́вка edging; trimming; boarding, panelling; plating.

обши́рный extensive; vast.

обши́ть (обошью́, -шьёшь) pf (impf обшива́ть) edge; trim; make outfit(s) for; plank.

обшла́г (-а́; pl -а́, -о́в) cuff.

обща́ться impf associate.

обще- in comb common(ly), general(ly). общедосту́пный mod-

erate in price; popular. ~житие hostel. ~изве́стный generally known. ~наро́дный national, public. ~образова́тельный of general education. ~при́нятый generally accepted. ~сою́зный All-Union. ~челове́ческий common to all mankind; universal.

обще́ние contact; social intercourse. обще́ственность (the) public; public opinion; community. обще́ственный social, public; voluntary. обще́ство society; company.

о́бщ|ий general; common; в ~ем on the whole, in general. о́бщина community; commune.

об|щипа́ть (-плю́, -плешь) pf.

общи́тельный sociable. о́бщность community.

объеда́ть(ся impf of объе́сть(ся

объедине́ние unification; merger; union, association. объединённый (-ён, -а́) united. объедини́тельный unifying. объедини́ть pf, объединя́ть impf unite; join; combine; ~ся unite.

объе́дки (-ов) pl leftovers, scraps.

объе́зд riding round; detour.

объе́здить (-зжу, -здишь) pf (impf объезжа́ть) travel over; break in.

объезжа́ть impf of объе́здить, объе́хать

объе́кт object; objective; establishment, works. объекти́в lens. объекти́вность objectivity. объекти́вный objective.

объём volume; scope. объёмный by volume, volumetric.

объе́сть (-е́м, -е́шь, -е́ст, -еди́м) pf (impf объеда́ть) gnaw (round), nibble; ~ся overeat.

объе́хать (-е́ду) pf (impf объезжа́ть) drive or go round; go past; travel over.

объяви́ть (-влю́, -вишь) pf, объявля́ть impf declare, announce; ~ся turn up; +instr declare o.s. объявле́ние declaration, announcement; advertisement.

объясне́ние explanation. объясни́мый explainable. объясни́ть pf, объясня́ть impf explain; ~ся be explained; make o.s. understood; +c+instr have it out with.

объя́тие embrace.

обыва́тель *m* Philistine. обыва́тельский narrow-minded.

обыгра́ть *pf*, обы́грывать *impf* beat (*in a game*).

обы́денный ordinary; everyday.

обыкнове́ние habit. обыкнове́нно *adv* usually. обыкнове́нный usual; ordinary.

о́быск search. обыска́ть (-ыщу́, -ы́щешь) *pf*, обы́скивать *impf* search.

обы́чай custom; usage. обы́чно *adv* usually. обы́чный usual.

обя́занность duty; responsibility. обя́занный (+*inf*) obliged; +*dat* indebted to (+*instr* for). обяза́тельно *adv* without fail. обяза́тельный obligatory. обяза́тельство obligation; commitment. обяза́ть (-яжу́, -я́жешь) *pf*, обя́зывать *impf* bind; commit; oblige; ~ся pledge o.s., undertake.

ова́л oval. ова́льный oval.

ова́ция ovation.

овдове́ть (-е́ю) *pf* become a widow, widower.

овёс (овса́) oats.

ове́чка *dim of* овца́; harmless person.

овладева́ть *impf*, овладе́ть (-е́ю) *pf* +*instr* seize; capture; master.

о́вод (*pl* -ы *or* -á) gadfly.

о́вощ (*pl* -и, -е́й) vegetable. овощно́й vegetable.

овра́г ravine, gully.

овся́нка oatmeal; porridge. овся́ный oat, oatmeal.

овца́ (*pl* -ы, ове́ц, о́вцам) sheep; ewe. овча́рка sheep-dog. овчи́на sheepskin.

ога́рок (-рка) candle-end.

огиба́ть *impf of* обогну́ть

оглавле́ние table of contents.

огласи́ть (-ашу́) *pf*, оглаша́ть *impf* announce; fill (with sound); ~ся resound. огла́ска publicity. оглаше́ние publication.

огло́бля (*gen pl* -бель) shaft.

о|гло́хнуть (-ну; -о́х) *pf*.

оглуша́ть *impf*, о|глуши́ть (-шу́) *pf* deafen; stun. оглуши́тельный deafening.

огляде́ть (-яжу́) *pf*, огля́дывать *impf*, огляну́ть (-ну́, -нешь) *pf* look round; look over; ~ся look round; look back. огля́дка looking back.

огнево́й fire; fiery. о́гненный fiery. огнеопа́сный inflammable. огнеприпа́сы (-ов) *pl* ammunition. огнесто́йкий fire-proof. огнестре́льный: ~ое ору́жие firearm(s). огнетуши́тель *m* fire-extinguisher. огнеупо́рный fire-resistant.

ого́ *int* oho!

огова́ривать *impf*, оговори́ть *pf* slander; stipulate (for); ~ся make a proviso; make a slip (of the tongue). огово́р slander. огово́рка reservation, proviso; slip of the tongue.

оголённый bare, nude. оголи́ть *pf* (*impf* оголя́ть) bare; strip; ~ся strip o.s.; become exposed.

оголя́ть(ся *impf of* оголи́ть(ся

огонёк (-нька́) (*small*) light; zest. ого́нь (огня́) *m* fire; light.

огора́живать *impf*, огороди́ть (-рожу́, -ро́ди́шь) *pf* fence in, enclose; ~ся fence o.s. in. огоро́д kitchen-garden. огоро́дный kitchen-garden.

огорча́ть *impf*, огорчи́ть (-чу́) *pf* grieve, pain; ~ся grieve, be distressed. огорче́ние grief; chagrin.

о|гра́бить (-блю) *pf*. ограбле́ние robbery; burglary.

огра́да fence. огради́ть (-ажу́) *pf*, огражда́ть *impf* guard, protect.

ограниче́ние limitation, restriction. ограни́ченный limited. ограни́чивать *impf*, ограни́чить (-чу) *pf* limit, restrict; ~ся +*instr* limit or confine o.s. to; be limited to.

огро́мный huge; enormous.

о|грубе́ть (-е́ю) *pf*.

огры́зок (-зка) bit, end; stub.

огуре́ц (-рца́) cucumber.

ода́лживать *impf of* одолжи́ть

одарённый gifted. ода́ривать *impf*, одари́ть *pf*, одаря́ть *impf* give presents to; +*instr* endow with.

одева́ть(ся *impf of* оде́ть(ся

оде́жда clothes; clothing.

одеколо́н eau-de-Cologne.

оделя́ть *pf*, оделя́ть *impf* (+*instr*) present (with); endow (with).

оде́ну *etc.*: *see* оде́ть. одёргивать *impf of* одёрнуть

о|деревене́ть (-е́ю) *pf*.

одержа́ть (-жу́, -жишь) *pf*, оде́рживать *impf* gain. одержи́мый possessed.

одёрнуть (-ну) *pf* (*impf* одёргивать) pull down, straighten.

одéтый dressed; clothed. **одéть** (-éну) *pf* (*impf* одевáть) dress; clothe; ~ся dress (o.s.). одеяло blanket. одеяние garb, attire.

одúн (одногó), **однá** (однóй), **однó** (одногó); *pl* одни (одних) one; a, an; a certain; alone; only; nothing but; same; однó и то же the same thing; одúн на одúн in private; одúн раз once; однúм слóвом in a word; по одному one by one.

одинáковый identical, the same, equal.

одúннадцатый eleventh. **одúннадцать** eleven.

одинóкий solitary; lonely; single. **одинóчество** solitude; loneliness. **одинóчка** *m & f* (one) person alone. **одинóчный** individual; one-man; single; ~ое заключéние solitary confinement.

одичáлый wild.

однáжды *adv* once; one day; once upon a time.

однáко *conj* however.

одно- *in comb* single, one; uni-, mono-, homo-. **однобóкий** one-sided. ~**врéменно** *adv* simultaneously, at the same time. ~**врéменный** simultaneous. ~**звýчный** monotonous. ~**знáчащий** synonymous. ~**знáчный** synonymous; one-digit. ~**имéнный** of the same name. ~**клáссник** classmate. ~**клéточный** unicellular. ~**крáтный** single. ~**лéтний** one-year; annual. ~**мéстный** single-seater. ~**обрáзие**, ~**обрáзность** monotony. ~**обрáзный** monotonous. ~**рóдность** homogeneity, uniformity. ~**рóдный** homogeneous; similar. ~**стóронний** one-sided; unilateral; one-way. ~**фамúлец** (-льца) person of the same surname. ~**цвéтный** one-colour; monochrome. ~**этáжный** one-storeyed.

одобрéние approval. **одобрúтельный** approving. **одóбрить** *pf*, **одобрять** *impf* approve (of).

одолевáть *impf*, **одолéть** (-éю) *pf* overcome.

одолжáть *impf*, **одолжúть** (-жý) *pf* +*y*+*gen* borrow from. **одолжéние** favour.

о|дряхлéть (-éю) *pf*.

одувáнчик dandelion.

одýматься *pf*, **одýмываться** *impf* change one's mind.

одурéлый stupid. **о|дурéть** (-éю) *pf*.

одурмáнивать *impf*, **о|дурмáнить** *pf* stupefy. **одурять** *impf* stupefy.

одухотворённый inspired; spiritual. **одухотворúть** *pf*, **одухотворять** *impf* inspire.

одушевúть (-влю) *pf*, **одушевлять** *impf* animate. **одушевлéние** animation.

одышка shortness of breath.

ожерéлье necklace.

ожесточáть *impf*, **ожесточúть** (-чý) *pf* embitter, harden. **ожесточéние** bitterness. **ожесточённый** bitter; hard.

оживáть *impf of* ожúть

оживúть (-влю) *pf*, **оживлять** *impf* revive; enliven; ~ся become animated. **оживлéние** animation; reviving; enlivening. **оживлённый** animated, lively.

ожидáние expectation; waiting. **ожидáть** *impf* +*gen* wait for; expect.

ожирéние obesity. **о|жирéть** (-éю) *pf*.

ожúть (-ивý, -ивёшь; óжил, -á, -о) *pf* (*impf* оживáть) come to life, revive.

ожóг burn, scald.

озабóченность preoccupation; anxiety. **озабóченный** preoccupied; anxious.

озаглáвить (-лю) *pf*, **озаглáвливать** *impf* entitle; head. **озадáчивать** *impf*, **озадáчить** (-чу) *pf* perplex, puzzle.

озарúть *pf*, **озарять** *impf* light up, illuminate; ~ся light up.

оздоровúтельный бег jogging. **оздоровлéние** sanitation.

озеленúть *pf*, **озеленять** *impf* plant (*with trees etc.*).

óзеро (*pl* озёра) lake.

озúмые *sb* winter crops. **озúмый** winter. **óзимь** winter crop.

озирáться *impf* look round; look back.

о|злúть(ся: *see* **обозлúть(ся**

о|злóбить (-блю) *pf*, **озлоблять** *impf* embitter; ~ся grow bitter. **озлоблéние** bitterness, animosity.

озлобленный embittered.

о|знакомить (-млю) *pf*, ознакомлять *impf* c+*instr* acquaint with; ~ся c+*instr* familiarize o.s. with.

ознаменовать *pf*, ознаменовывать *impf* mark; celebrate.

означать *impf* mean, signify.

озноб shivering, chill.

озон ozone.

озорник (-á) mischief-maker. озорной naughty, mischievous. озорство mischief.

озябнуть (-ну; озяб) *pf* be cold, be freezing.

ой *int* oh.

оказать (-ажу, -ажешь) *pf* (*impf* оказывать) render, provide, show; ~ся turn out, prove; find o.s., be found.

оказия unexpected event, funny thing.

оказывать(ся *impf of* оказать(ся

окаменелость fossil. окаменелый fossilized; petrified. о|каменеть (-éю) *pf*.

окантовка mount.

оканчивать(ся *impf of* окончить(ся. окапывать(ся *impf of* окопать(ся

окаянный damned, cursed.

океан ocean. океанский ocean; oceanic.

окидывать *impf*, окинуть (-ну) *pf*; ~ взглядом take in at a glance, glance over.

окисел (-сла) oxide. окисление oxidation. окись oxide.

оккупант invader. оккупация occupation. оккупировать *impf & pf* occupy.

оклад salary scale; (basic) pay.

оклеветать (-ещу, -ещешь) *pf* slander.

оклеивать *impf*, оклеить *pf* cover; paste over; ~ обоями paper.

окно (*pl* окна) window.

око (*pl* очи, очей) eye.

оковы (оков) *pl* fetters.

околдовать *pf*, околдовывать *impf* bewitch.

около *adv & prep*+*gen* by; close (to), near; around; about.

окольный roundabout.

оконный window.

окончание end; conclusion, termination; ending. окончательный

final. окончить (-чу) *pf* (*impf* оканчивать) finish, end; ~ся finish, end.

окоп trench. окопать *pf* (*impf* окапывать) dig round; ~ся entrench o.s., dig in. окопный trench.

окорок (*pl* -á, -óв) ham, gammon.

окоченелый stiff with cold. о|коченеть (-éю) *pf*.

окошечко, окошко (*small*) window.

окраина outskirts, outlying districts.

о|красить (-áшу) *pf*, окрашивать *impf* paint, colour; dye. окраска painting; colouring; dyeing; colouration.

о|крепнуть (-ну) *pf*. о|крестить(ся (-ещу(сь, -éстишь(ся) *pf*.

окрестность environs. окрестный neighbouring.

окрик hail; shout. окрикивать *impf*, окрикнуть (-ну) *pf* hail, call, shout to.

окровавленный blood-stained.

округ (*pl* ~á) district. округа neighbourhood. округлить *pf*, округлять *impf* round; round off. округлый rounded. окружать *impf*, окружить (-жу) *pf* surround; encircle. окружающ|ий surrounding; ~ее *sb* environment; ~ие *sb pl* associates. окружение encirclement; environment. окружной district. окружность circumference.

окрылить *pf*, окрылять *impf* inspire, encourage.

октава octave.

октан octane.

октябрь (-á) *m* October. октябрьский October.

окулист oculist.

окунать *impf*, окунуть (-ну, -нёшь) *pf* dip; ~ся dip; plunge; become absorbed.

окунь (*pl* -и, -éй) *m* perch.

окупать *impf*, окупить (-плю, -пишь) *pf* compensate, repay; ~ся be repaid, pay for itself.

окурок (-рка) cigarette-end.

окутать *pf*, окутывать *impf* wrap up; shroud, cloak.

окучивать *impf*, окучить (-чу) *pf* earth up.

оладья (*gen pl* -ий) fritter; dropscone.

оледенелый frozen. о|леденеть (-éю) *pf*. .

оле́ний deer, deer's; reindeer.
оле́нина venison. оле́нь *m* deer; reindeer.
оли́ва olive. оли́вковый olive; olive-coloured.
олига́рхия oligarchy.
олимпиа́да olympiad; Olympics. олимпи́йск|ий Olympic; Olympian; ~ие и́гры Olympic games.
оли́фа drying oil (*e.g. linseed oil*).
олицетворе́ние personification; embodiment. олицетвори́ть *pf*, олицетворя́ть *impf* personify, embody.
о́лово tin. оловя́нный tin.
ом ohm.
ома́р lobster.
омерзе́ние loathing. омерзи́тельный loathsome.
омертве́лый stiff, numb; necrotic. о|мертве́ть (-е́ю) *pf*.
омле́т omelette.
омоложе́ние rejuvenation.
омо́ним homonym.
омо́ю *etc.: see* омы́ть
омрача́ть *impf*, омрачи́ть (-чу́) *pf* darken, cloud.
о́мут whirlpool; maelstrom.
омыва́ть *impf*, омы́ть (омо́ю) *pf* wash; ~ся be washed.
он (его́, ему́, им, о нём) *pron* he. она́ (её, ей, ей (е́ю), о ней) *pron* she.
онда́тра musk-rat.
онеме́лый numb. о|неме́ть (-е́ю) *pf*.
они́ (их, им, и́ми, о них) *pron* they. оно́ (его́, ему́, им, о нём) *pron* it; this, that.
опада́ть *impf of* опа́сть.
опа́здывать *impf of* опозда́ть
опа́ла disgrace.
о|пали́ть *pf*.
опа́ловый opal.
опа́лубка casing.
опаса́ться *impf +gen* fear; avoid, keep off. опасе́ние fear; apprehension.
опа́сность danger; peril. опа́сный dangerous.
опа́сть (-аде́т) *pf* (*impf* опада́ть) fall, fall off; subside.
опе́ка guardianship; trusteeship. опека́емый *sb* ward. опека́ть *impf* be guardian of; take care of. опеку́н (-а́), -у́нша guardian; tutor; trustee.
о́пера opera.
операти́вный efficient; operative,

surgical; operation(s), operational.
опера́тор operator; cameraman.
операцио́нн|ый operating; ~ая *sb* operating theatre. опера́ция operation.
опереди́ть (-режу́) *pf*, опережа́ть *impf* outstrip, leave behind.
опере́ние plumage.
опере́тта, -е́тка operetta.
опере́ть (обопру́, -прёшь; опёр, -ла́) *pf* (*impf* опира́ть) +о+*acc* lean against; ~ся на *or* о+*acc* lean on, lean against.
опери́ровать *impf & pf* operate on; operate, act; +*instr* use.
о́перный opera; operatic.
о|печа́лить(ся *pf*.
опеча́тать *pf* (*impf* опеча́тывать) seal up.
опеча́тка misprint.
опеча́тывать *impf of* опеча́тать
опеши́ть (-шу́) *pf* be taken aback.
опи́лки (-лок) *pl* sawdust; filings.
опира́ть(ся *impf of* опере́ть(ся
описа́ние description. описа́тельный descriptive. описа́ть (-ишу́, -и́шешь) *pf*, опи́сывать *impf* describe; ~ся make a slip of the pen. опи́ска slip of the pen. о́пись inventory.
о́пиум opium.
опла́кать (-а́чу) *pf*, опла́кивать *impf* mourn for; bewail.
опла́та payment. оплати́ть (-ачу́, -а́тишь) *pf*, опла́чивать *impf* pay (for).
оплачу́ *etc.: see* опла́кать. оплачу́ *etc.: see* оплати́ть
оплеу́ха slap in the face.
оплодотвори́ть *pf*, оплодотворя́ть *impf* impregnate; fertilize.
о|пломбирова́ть *pf*.
опло́т stronghold, bulwark.
опло́шность blunder, mistake.
оповести́ть (-ещу́) *pf*, оповеща́ть *impf* notify. оповеще́ние notification.
опозда́вший *sb* late-comer. опозда́ние lateness; delay. опозда́ть *pf* (*impf* опа́здывать) be late; +на+*acc* miss.
опознава́тельный distinguishing; ~ знак landmark. опознава́ть (-наю́, -наёшь) *impf*, опозна́ть *pf* identify. опозна́ние identification.

о|позо́рить(ся *pf.*

ополза́ть *impf*, оползти́ (-зёт; -о́лз, -ла́) *pf* slip, slide. о́ползень (-зня) *m* landslide.

ополче́ние militia.

опо́мниться *pf* come to one's senses.

опо́р: во весь ∼ at full speed.

опо́ра support; pier; то́чка опо́ры fulcrum, foothold.

опора́живать *impf of* опоро́жнить

опо́рный support, supporting, supported; bearing.

опоро́жнить *pf*, опорожня́ть *impf* (*impf also* опора́жнивать) empty.

о|поро́чить (-чу) *pf.*

опохмели́ться *pf*, опохмеля́ться *impf* take a hair of the dog that bit you.

опо́шлить *pf*, опошля́ть *impf* vulgarize, debase.

опоя́сать (-я́шу) *pf*, опоя́сывать *impf* gird; girdle.

оппозицио́нный opposition. оппози́ция opposition.

оппортуни́зм opportunism.

опра́ва setting, mounting; spectacle frames.

оправда́ние justification; excuse; acquittal. оправда́тельный пригово́р verdict of not guilty. оправда́ть *pf*, опра́вдывать *impf* justify; excuse; acquit; ∼ся justify o.s.; be justified.

опра́вить (-влю) *pf*, оправля́ть *impf* set right, adjust; mount; ∼ся put one's dress in order; recover; +от+*gen* get over.

опра́шивать *impf of* опроси́ть

определе́ние definition; determination; decision. определённый definite; certain. определи́мый definable. определи́ть, определя́ть *impf* define; determine; appoint; ∼ся be formed; be determined; find one's position.

опроверга́ть *impf*, опрове́ргнуть (-ну; -ве́рг) *pf* refute, disprove. опроверже́ние refutation; denial.

опроки́дывать *impf*, опроки́нуть (-ну) *pf* overturn; topple; ∼ся overturn; capsize.

опроме́тчивый rash, hasty.

опро́с (cross-)examination; (opinion) poll. опроси́ть (-ошу́, -о́сишь) *pf* (*impf* опра́шивать) question; (cross-)

examine. опро́сный лист questionnaire.

опры́скать *pf*, опры́скивать *impf* sprinkle; spray.

опря́тный neat, tidy.

о́птик optician. о́птика optics. опти́ческий optic, optical.

оптима́льный optimal. оптими́зм optimism. оптими́ст optimist. оптимисти́ческий optimistic.

опто́вый wholesale. о́птом *adv* wholesale.

опубликова́ние publication; promulgation. о|публикова́ть *pf*, опубли́ковывать *impf* publish; promulgate.

опуска́ть(ся *impf of* опусти́ть(ся

опусте́лый deserted. о|пусте́ть (-е́ет) *pf.*

опусти́ть (-ущу́, -у́стишь) *pf* (*impf* опуска́ть) lower; let down; turn down; omit; post; ∼ся lower o.s.; sink; fall; go down; go to pieces.

опустоша́ть *impf*, опустоши́ть (-шу́) *pf* devastate. опустоше́ние devastation. опустоши́тельный devastating.

опу́тать *pf*, опу́тывать *impf* entangle; ensnare.

опуха́ть *impf*, о|пу́хнуть (-ну; опу́х) *pf* swell, swell up. о́пухоль swelling, tumour.

опу́шка edge of a forest; trimming.

опущу́ *etc.: see* опусти́ть

опыле́ние pollination. опыли́ть *pf*, опыля́ть *impf* pollinate.

о́пыт experience; experiment. о́пытный experienced; experimental.

опьяне́ние intoxication. опьяне́ть (-е́ю) *pf*, о|пьяни́ть *pf*, опьяня́ть *impf* intoxicate, make drunk.

опя́ть *adv* again.

ора́ва crowd, horde.

ора́кул oracle.

орангута́нг orangutan.

ора́нжевый orange. оранжере́я greenhouse, conservatory.

ора́тор orator. орато́рия oratorio.

ора́ть (ору́, орёшь) *impf* yell.

орби́та orbit; (eye-)socket.

о́рган[1] organ; body. орга́н[2] (*mus*) organ. организа́тор organizer. организацио́нный organization(al). организа́ция organization. органи́зм organism. организо́ванный organized. **организова́ть** *impf & pf* (*pf also* **с~**) organize; **~ся** be organized; organize. **органи́ческий** organic.

óргия orgy.

орда́ (*pl* **-ы**) horde.

óрден (*pl* **-á**) order.

óрдер (*pl* **-á**) order; warrant; writ.

ордина́та ordinate.

ордина́тор house-surgeon.

орёл (орла́) eagle; ~ **и́ли ре́шка?** heads or tails?

орео́л halo.

оре́х nut, nuts; walnut. **оре́ховый** nut; walnut. **оре́шник** hazel; hazel-thicket.

оригина́л original; eccentric. **оригина́льный** original.

ориента́ция orientation. **ориенти́р** landmark; reference point. **ориенти́роваться** *impf & pf* orient o.s.; **+на**+*acc* head for; aim at. **ориенти́ровка** orientation. **ориенти́ровочный** reference; tentative; approximate.

орке́стр orchestra.

орли́ный eagle; aquiline.

орна́мент ornament; ornamental design.

о|робе́ть (**-е́ю**) *pf.*

ороси́тельный irrigation. **ороси́ть** (**-ошу́**) *pf,* **ороша́ть** *impf* irrigate. **ороше́ние** irrigation; **поля́ ороше́ния** sewage farm.

ору́ *etc.: see* **ора́ть**

ору́дие instrument; tool; gun. **ору́дийный** gun. **ору́довать** *impf* +*instr* handle; run. **оруже́йный** arms; gun. **ору́жие** arm, arms; weapons.

орфографи́ческий orthographic(al). **орфогра́фия** orthography, spelling.

оса́ (*pl* **-ы**) wasp.

оса́да siege. **осади́ть**[1] (**-ажу́**) *pf* (*impf* **осажда́ть**) besiege.

осади́ть[2] (**-ажу́, -а́дишь**) *pf* (*impf* **оса́живать**) check; force back; rein in; take down a peg.

оса́дка siege.

оса́док (**-дка**) sediment; fall-out; aftertaste; *pl* precipitation, fall-out. **оса́дочный** sedimentary.

осажда́ть *impf of* **осади́ть**[1]

оса́живать *impf of* **осади́ть**[2]. **осажу́** *see* **осади́ть**[1,2]

оса́нка carriage, bearing.

осва́ивать(ся *impf of* **осво́ить(ся**

осведоми́тельный informative; information. **осве́домить** (**-млю**) *pf,* **осведомля́ть** *impf* inform; **~ся** о+*prep* inquire about, ask after. **осведомле́ние** notification. **осведомлённый** well-informed, knowledgeable.

освежа́ть *impf,* **освежи́ть** (**-жу́**) *pf* refresh; air. **освежи́тельный** refreshing.

освети́тельный illuminating. **освети́ть** (**-ещу́**) *pf,* **освеща́ть** *impf* light up; illuminate; throw light on; **~ся** light up. **освеще́ние** lighting, illumination. **освещённый** (**-ён, -а́**) lit.

о|свиде́тельствовать *pf.*

освиста́ть (**-ищу́, -и́щешь**) *pf,* **осви́стывать** *impf* hiss (off); boo.

освободи́тель *m* liberator. **освободи́тельный** liberation, emancipation. **освободи́ть** (**-ожу́**) *pf,* **освобожда́ть** *impf* liberate; free; dismiss; vacate; empty; **~ся** free o.s.; become free. **освобожде́ние** liberation; release; emancipation; vacation. **освобождённый** (**-ён, -á**) freed, free; exempt.

освое́ние mastery; opening up. **осво́ить** *pf* (*impf* **осва́ивать**) master; become familiar with; **~ся** familiarize o.s.

освящённый (**-ён, -ена́**) consecrated; sanctified; ~ **века́ми** time-honoured.

оседа́ть *impf of* **осе́сть**

о|седла́ть *pf,* **осёдлывать** *impf* saddle.

осёдлый settled.

осека́ться *impf of* **осе́чься**

осёл (**-сла́**) donkey; ass.

осело́к (**-лка́**) touchstone; whetstone.

осени́ть *pf* (*impf* **осеня́ть**) overshadow; dawn upon.

осе́нний autumn(al). **óсень** autumn. **óсенью** *adv* in autumn.

осеня́ть *impf of* **осени́ть**

осе́сть (**осяду; осёл**) *pf* (*impf* **оседа́ть**) settle; subside.

осётр (**-á**) sturgeon. **осетри́на** sturgeon.

осе́чка misfire. **осе́чься** (**-еку́сь, -ечёшься; -ёкся, -екла́сь**) *pf* (*impf* **осека́ться**) stop short.

оси́ливать *impf,* **оси́лить** *pf* overpower; master.

оси́на aspen.

о|си́пнуть (-ну; оси́п) *pf* get hoarse.

осироте́лый orphaned. **осироте́ть** (-е́ю) *pf* be orphaned.

оска́ливать *impf*, **о|ска́лить** *pf*; ~ зу́бы, ~ся bare one's teeth.

о|сканда́лить(ся *pf*.

оскверни́ть *pf*, **оскверня́ть** *impf* profane; defile.

оско́лок (-лка) splinter; fragment.

оско́мина bitter taste (in the mouth); наби́ть оско́мину set the teeth on edge.

оскорби́тельный insulting, abusive. **оскорби́ть** (-блю́) *pf*, **оскорбля́ть** *impf* insult; offend; ~ся take offence. **оскорбле́ние** insult. **оскорблён-ный** (-ён, -а́) insulted.

ослабева́ть *impf*, **о|слабе́ть** (-е́ю) *pf* weaken; slacken. **осла́бить** (-блю) *pf*, **ослабля́ть** *impf* weaken; slacken. **ослабле́ние** weakening; slackening; relaxation.

ослепи́тельный blinding, dazzling. **ослепи́ть** (-плю́) *pf*, **ослепля́ть** *impf* blind, dazzle. **ослепле́ние** blinding; dazzling; blindness. **о|слеп-ну́ть** (-ну; -éп) *pf*.

осли́ный donkey; asinine. **осли́ца** she-ass.

осложне́ние complication. **осложни́ть** *pf*, **осложня́ть** *impf* complicate; ~ся become complicated.

ослы́шаться (-шусь) *pf* mishear.

осма́тривать(ся *impf of* **осмотре́ть-(ся. осме́ивать** *impf of* **осмея́ть**

о|смеле́ть (-е́ю) *pf*. **осме́ливаться** *impf*, **осме́литься** *pf* dare; venture.

осмея́ть (-ею́, -еёшь) *pf* (*impf* осме́-ивать) ridicule.

осмо́тр examination, inspection. **осмотре́ть** (-рю́, -ришь) *pf* (*impf* осма́тривать) examine, inspect; look round; ~ся look round. **осмо-три́тельный** circumspect.

осмы́сленный sensible, intelligent. **осмы́сливать** *impf*, **осмы́слить** *pf*, **осмысля́ть** *impf* interpret; com-prehend.

оснасти́ть (-ащу́) *pf*, **оснаща́ть** *impf* fit out, equip. **осна́стка** rigging. **оснаще́ние** fitting out; equipment.

осно́ва base, basis, foundation; *pl* fundamentals; stem (*of a word*).

основа́ние founding, foundation; base; basis; reason; на како́м осно-ва́нии? on what grounds? **основа́-тель** *m* founder. **основа́тельный** well-founded; solid; thorough. **осно-ва́ть** *pf*, **осно́вывать** *impf* found; base; ~ся settle; be founded, be based. **основно́й** fundamental, basic; main; в основно́м in the main, on the whole. **основополо́жник** founder.

осо́ба person. **осо́бенно** *adv* espe-cially. **осо́бенность** peculiarity; в осо́бенности in particular. **осо́бен-ный** special, particular, peculiar. **особня́к** (-а́) private residence; de-tached house. **особняко́м** *adv* by o.s. **осо́бо** *adv* apart; especially. **осо́бый** special; particular.

осознава́ть (-наю́, -наёшь) *impf*, **осозна́ть** *pf* realize.

осо́ка sedge.

о́спа smallpox; pock-marks.

оспа́ривать *impf*, **оспо́рить** *pf* dis-pute; contest.

о|срами́ть(ся (-млю́(сь) *pf*. **оста-ва́ться** (-таю́сь, -таёшься) *impf of* **оста́ться**

ост (*naut*) east; east wind.

оста́вить (-влю) *pf*, **оставля́ть** *impf* leave; abandon; reserve.

остальн|о́й the rest of; ~о́е *sb* the rest; ~ы́е *sb pl* the others.

остана́вливать(ся *impf of* **останов-и́ть(ся**

оста́нки (-ов) *pl* remains.

останови́ть (-влю́, -вишь) *pf* (*impf* остана́вливать) stop; restrain; ~ся stop, halt; stay; +на+*prep* dwell on; settle on. **остано́вка** stop.

оста́ток (-тка) remainder; rest; resi-due; *pl* remains; leftovers. **оста́ться** (-а́нусь) *pf* (*impf* остава́ться) re-main; stay; *impers* it remains, it is necessary; нам не остаётся ничего́ друго́го, как we have no choice but.

остекли́ть *pf*, **остекля́ть** *impf* glaze.

остервене́ть *pf* become enraged.

остерега́ть *impf*, **остере́чь** (-регу́, -режёшь; -рёг, -ла́) *pf* warn; ~ся (+*gen*) beware (of).

о́стов frame, framework; skeleton.

о|столбене́ть (-е́ю) *pf*.

осторо́жно *adv* carefully; ~! look

out! осторо́жность care, caution. осторо́жный careful, cautious.

остри́гать(ся *impf of* остри́чь(ся

острие́ point; spike; (cutting) edge. остри́ть[1] *impf* sharpen. остри́ть[2] *impf (pf c~)* be witty.

о|стри́чь (-игу́, -ижёшь; -и́г) *pf (impf also* остри́гать) cut, clip; ~ся have one's hair cut.

о́стров (*pl* -а́) island. островок (-вка́) islet; ~ безопа́сности (traffic) island.

острота́[1] witticism, joke. острота́[2] sharpness; keenness; pungency.

остроу́мие wit. остроу́мный witty.

о́стрый (остр, -а́, -о) sharp; pointed; acute; keen. остря́к (-а́) wit.

о|студи́ть (-ужу́, -у́дишь) *pf*, остужа́ть *impf* cool.

оступа́ться *impf*, оступи́ться (-плюсь, -пишься) *pf* stumble.

остыва́ть *impf*, осты́ть (-ы́ну) *pf* get cold; cool down.

осуди́ть (-ужу́, -у́дишь) *pf*, осужда́ть *impf* condemn; convict. осужде́ние condemnation; conviction. осуждённый (-ён, -а́) condemned, convicted; *sb* convict.

осу́нуться (-нусь) *pf* grow thin, become drawn.

осуша́ть *impf*, осуши́ть (-шу́, -шишь) *pf* drain; dry. осуше́ние drainage.

осуществи́мый feasible. осуществи́ть (-влю́) *pf*, осуществля́ть *impf* realize, bring about; accomplish; ~ся be fulfilled, come true. осуществле́ние realization; accomplishment.

осчастли́вить (-влю) *pf*, осчастли́вливать *impf* make happy.

осыпа́ть (-плю) *pf*, осыпа́ть *impf* strew; shower; ~ся crumble; fall. о́сыпь scree.

ось (*gen pl* -е́й) axis; axle.

осьмино́г octopus.

ося́ду *etc.: see* осе́сть

осяза́емый tangible. осяза́ние touch. осяза́тельный tactile; tangible. осяза́ть *impf* feel.

от, ото *prep+gen* from; of; against.

ота́пливать *impf of* отопи́ть

ота́ра flock (*of sheep*).

отба́вить (-влю) *pf*, отбавля́ть *impf* pour off; хоть отбавля́й more than enough.

отбега́ть *impf*, отбежа́ть (-егу́) *pf*

run off.

отберу́ *etc.: see* отобра́ть

отбива́ть(ся *impf of* отби́ть(ся

отбивна́я котле́та cutlet, chop.

отбира́ть *impf of* отобра́ть

отби́ть (отобью́, -ёшь) *pf (impf* отбива́ть) beat (off), repel; win over; break off; ~ся break off; drop behind; +от+gen defend o.s. against.

о́тблеск reflection.

отбо́й repelling; retreat; ringing off; бить ~ beat a retreat; дать ~ ring off.

отбо́йный молото́к (-тка́) pneumatic drill.

отбо́р selection. отбо́рный choice, select(ed).

отбра́сывать *impf*, отбро́сить (-о́шу) *pf* throw off *or* away; hurl back; reject; ~ тень cast a shadow. отбро́сы (-ов) *pl* garbage.

отбыва́ть *impf*, отбы́ть (-бу́ду; о́тбыл, -а́, -о) *pf* depart; serve (*a sentence*).

отва́га courage, bravery.

отва́живаться *impf*, отва́житься (-жусь) *pf* dare. отва́жный courageous.

отва́л dump, slag-heap; casting off; до ~а to satiety. отва́ливать *impf*, отвали́ть (-лю́, -лишь) *pf* push aside; cast off; fork out.

отва́р broth; decoction. отва́ривать *impf*, отвари́ть (-рю́, -ришь) *pf* boil. отварно́й boiled.

отве́дать *pf (impf* отве́дывать) taste, try.

отведу́ *etc.: see* отвести́

отве́дывать *impf of* отве́дать

отвезти́ (-зу́, -зёшь; -вёз, -ла́) *pf (impf* отвози́ть) take *or* cart away.

отвёл *etc.: see* отвести́

отверга́ть *impf*, отве́ргнуть (-ну; -ве́рг) *pf* reject; repudiate.

отве́рженный outcast.

отверну́ть (-ну́, -нёшь) *pf (impf* отвёртывать, отвора́чивать) turn aside; turn down; turn on; unscrew; screw off; ~ся turn away; come unscrewed.

отве́рстие opening; hole.

отверте́ть (-рчу́, -ртишь) *pf (impf* отвёртывать) unscrew; twist off; ~ся come unscrewed; get off. отвёртка screwdriver.

отвёртывать(ся *impf of* отвернуть(ся, отвертеть(ся

отвес plumb; vertical slope. отвесить (-ешу) *pf* (*impf* отвешивать) weigh out. отвесный perpendicular, sheer.

отвести (-еду, -едёшь; -вёл, -á) *pf* (*impf* отводить) lead, take; draw *or* take aside; deflect; draw off; reject; allot.

ответ answer.

ответвиться *pf*, ответвляться *impf* branch off. ответвление branch, offshoot.

ответить (-éчу) *pf*, отвечать *impf* answer; +на+*acc* reply to; +за+*acc* answer for. ответный in reply, return. ответственность responsibility. ответственный responsible. ответчик defendant.

отвешивать *impf of* отвесить. отвешу *etc.: see* отвесить

отвинтить (-нчу) *pf*, отвинчивать *impf* unscrew.

отвисать *impf*, отвиснуть (-нет; -ис) *pf* hang down, sag. отвислый hanging, baggy.

отвлекать (-еку, -ечёшь; -влёк, -лá) *pf* distract, divert; ~ся be distracted. отвлечённый abstract.

отвод taking aside; diversion; leading, taking; rejection; allotment. отводить (-ожу, -одишь) *impf of* отвести.

отвоевать (-оюю) *pf*, отвоёвывать *impf* win back; spend in fighting.

отвозить (-ожу, -озишь) *impf of* отвезти. отворачивать(ся *impf of* отвернуть(ся

отворить (-рю, -ришь) *pf* (*impf* отворять) open; ~ся open.

отворять(ся *impf of* отворить(ся. отворю *etc.: see* отвоевать

отвратительный disgusting. отвращение disgust, repugnance.

отвыкать *impf*, отвыкнуть (-ну; -вык) *pf* +от *or* inf lose the habit of; grow out of.

отвязать (-яжу, -яжешь) *pf*, отвязывать *impf* untie, unfasten; ~ся come untied, come loose; +от+*gen* get rid of; leave alone.

отгадать *pf*, отгадывать *impf* guess. отгадка answer.

отгибать(ся *impf of* отогнуть(ся

отгладить (-ажу) *pf*, отглаживать *impf* iron (out).

отговаривать *impf*, отговорить *pf* dissuade; ~ся +instr plead. отговорка excuse, pretext.

отголосок (-ска) echo.

отгонять *impf of* отогнать

отгораживать *impf*, отгородить (-ожу, -одишь) *pf* fence off; partition off; ~ся shut o.s. off.

отдавать(ся[1] (-даю(сь) *impf of* отдать(ся. отдавать[2] (-аёт) *impf impers+instr* taste of; smell of; smack of; от него отдаёт водкой he reeks of vodka.

отдаление removal; distance. отдалённый remote. отдалить *pf*, отдалять *impf* remove; estrange; postpone; ~ся move away; digress.

отдать (-ам, -ашь, -аст, -адим; отдал, -á, -о) *pf* (*impf* отдавать[1]) give back, return; give; give up; give away; recoil; cast off; ~ся give o.s. (up); resound. отдача return; payment; casting off; efficiency; output; recoil.

отдел department; section.

отделать *pf* (*impf* отделывать) finish, put the finishing touches to; trim; ~ся +от+*gen* get rid of; +instr get off with.

отделение separation; department; compartment; section. отделить (-елю, -елишь) *pf* (*impf* отделять) separate; detach; ~ся separate; detach o.s.; get detached.

отделка finishing; finish, decoration. отделывать(ся *impf of* отделать(ся

отдельно separately; apart. отдельный separate. отделять(ся *impf of* отделить(ся

отдёргивать *impf*, отдёрнуть (-ну) *pf* draw *or* pull aside *or* back.

отдеру *etc.: see* отодрать. отдирать *impf of* отодрать

отдохнуть (-ну, -нёшь) *pf* (*impf* отдыхать) rest.

отдушина air-hole, vent.

отдых rest. отдыхать *impf* (*pf* отдохнуть) rest; be on holiday.

отдышаться (-шусь, -шишься) *pf* recover one's breath.

отекать *impf of* отечь. о|телиться (-елится) *pf*.

отéль *m* hotel.

отесáть *etc.: see* обтесáть

отéц (отцá) father. отéческий fatherly, paternal. отéчественный home, native. отéчество native land, fatherland.

отéчь (-екý, -ечёшь; отёк, -лá) *pf* (*impf* отекáть) swell (up).

отживáть *impf*, отжить (-ивý, -ивёшь; óтжил, -á, -о) *pf* become obsolete *or* outmoded. отживший obsolete; outmoded.

óтзвук echo.

óтзыв[1] opinion; reference; review; response. отзыв[2] recall. отзывáть-(ся *impf of* отозвáть(ся. отзыв́-чивый responsive.

откáз refusal; repudiation; failure; natural. отказáть (-ажý, -áжешь) *pf*, откáзывать *impf* break down; (+*dat* в+*prep*) refuse, deny (*s.o. sth*); ~ся (+от+*gen or* +*inf*) refuse; turn down; renounce, give up.

откáлывать(ся *impf of* отколóть-(ся. откáпывать *impf of* откопáть.

откáрмливать *impf of* откормить

откатить (-ачý, -áтишь) *pf*, откá-тывать *impf* roll away; ~ся roll away *or* back; be forced back.

откачáть *pf*, откáчивать *impf* pump out; give artificial respiration to.

откáшливаться *impf*, откá-шляться *pf* clear one's throat.

откиднóй folding, collapsible. откú-дывать *impf*, откúнуть (-ну) *pf* fold back; throw aside.

откладывать *impf of* отложить

отклéивать *impf*, отклéить (-éю) *pf* unstick; ~ся come unstuck.

óтклик response; comment; echo. откликáться *impf*, отклúкнуться (-нусь) *pf* answer, respond.

отклонéние deviation; declining, refusal; deflection. отклонить (-ню, -нишь) *pf*, отклонять *impf* deflect; decline; ~ся deviate; diverge.

отключáть *impf*, отключить (-чý) *pf* cut off, disconnect.

отколотить (-очý, -óтишь) *pf* knock off; beat up.

отколóть (-лю, -лешь) *pf* (*impf* откáлывать) break off; chop off; unpin; ~ся break off; come unpinned; break away.

откопáть *pf* (*impf* откáпывать) dig up; exhume.

откормить (-млю, -мишь) *pf* (*impf* откáрмливать) fatten.

откóс slope.

открепить (-плю) *pf*, открепля́ть *impf* unfasten; ~ся become unfastened.

откровéние revelation. откровéн-ный frank; outspoken; unconcealed. открóю *etc.: see* открыть

открутить (-учý, -ýтишь) *pf*, от-крýчивать *impf* unscrew, unscrew.

открывáть *impf*, открыть (-рóю) *pf* open; reveal; discover; turn on; ~ся open; come to light, be revealed. открытие discovery; revelation; opening. открытка postcard; card. открыто openly. открытый open.

откýда *adv* from where; from which; how; ~ ни возьмись from out of nowhere. откýда-либо, -нибудь from somewhere or other. откýда-то from somewhere.

откýпоривать *impf*, откýпорить *pf* uncork.

откусить (-ушý, -ýсишь) *pf*, откý-сывать *impf* bite off.

отлагáтельство delay. отлагáть *impf of* отложить

от|лакировáть *pf*. отлáмывать *impf of* отломáть, отломить

отлепить (-плю, -пишь) *pf* unstick, take off; ~ся come unstuck, come off.

отлёт flying away; departure. отле-тáть *impf*, отлетéть (-лечý) *pf*, fly, fly away, fly off; rebound.

отлúв ebb, ebb-tide; tint; play of colours. отливáть *impf*, отлить (отолью; óтлил, -á, -о) *pf* pour off; pump out; cast, found; (*no pf*) +*instr* be shot with. отлúвка casting; moulding.

отличáть *impf*, отличить (-чý) *pf* distinguish; ~ся distinguish o.s.; differ; +*instr* be notable for. отлúчие difference; distinction; знак отлúчия order, decoration; с отлúчием with honours. отлúчник outstanding student, worker, etc. отличúтельный distinctive; distinguishing. отлúч-ный different; excellent.

отлóгий sloping.

отложéние sediment; deposit. от-ложить (-ожý, -óжишь) *pf* (*impf* отклáдывать, отлагáть) put aside; postpone; deposit.

отломáть, отломúть (-млю́, -мишь) *pf* (*impf* **отлáмывать**) break off.

от|лупúть *pf*.

отлучáть *impf*, **отлучúть** (-чý) *pf* (от цéркви) excommunicate; ~**ся** absent o.s. **отлýчка** absence.

отлы́нивать *impf* +от+*gen* shirk.

отмáхивать *impf*, **отмахнýться** (-нýсь, -нёшься) *pf* от+*gen* brush off; brush aside.

отмежевáться (-жýюсь) *pf*, **отмежёвываться** *impf* от+*gen* dissociate o.s. from.

óтмель (sand-)bank.

отмéна abolition; cancellation. **отменúть** (-ню́, -нишь) *pf*, **отменя́ть** *impf* repeal; abolish; cancel.

отмерéть (отомрёт; óтмер, -лá, -ло) *pf* (*impf* **отмирáть**) die off; die out.

отмéривать *impf*, **отмéрить** *pf*, **отмеря́ть** *impf* measure off.

отместú (-етý, -етёшь; -ёл, -á) *pf* (*impf* **отметáть**) sweep aside.

отметáть *impf of* **отместú**

отмéтить (-éчу) *pf*, **отмечáть** *impf* mark, note; celebrate; ~**ся** sign one's name; sign out. **отмéтка** note; mark.

отмирáть *impf of* **отмерéть**

отморáживать *impf*, **отморóзить** (-óжу) *pf* injure by frost-bite. **отморóжение** frost-bite. **отморóженный** frost-bitten.

отмóю *etc.: see* **отмы́ть**

отмывáть *impf*, **отмы́ть** (-мóю) *pf* wash clean; wash off; ~**ся** wash o.s. clean; come out.

отмыкáть *impf of* **отомкнýть**

отмы́чка master key.

отнестú (-сý, -сёшь; -нёс, -лá) *pf* (*impf* **относúть**) take; carry away; ascribe, attribute; ~**сь** к+*dat* treat; regard; apply to; concern, have to do with.

отнимáть(ся *impf of* **отня́ть(ся**

относúтельно *adv* relatively; *prep* +*gen* concerning. **относúтельность** relativity. **относúтельный** relative.

относúть(ся (-ошý(сь, -óсишь(ся) *impf of* **отнестú(сь. отношéние** attitude; relation; respect; ratio; в отношéнии+*gen*, по отношéнию к+*dat* with regard to; в прямóм (обрáтном) отношéнии in direct (in-

verse) ratio.

отны́не *adv* henceforth.

отню́дь not at all.

отня́тие taking away; amputation. **отня́ть** (-нимý, -нимешь; óтнял, -á, -о) *pf* (*impf* **отнимáть**) take (away); amputate; ~ от грудú wean; ~**ся** be paralysed.

ото: *see* **от**

отображáть *impf*, **отобразúть** (-ажý) *pf* reflect; represent. **отображéние** reflection; representation.

отобрáть (отберý, -рёшь; отобрáл, -á, -о) *pf* (*impf* **отбирáть**) take (away); select.

отобью́ *etc.: see* **отбúть**

отовсю́ду *adv* from everywhere.

отогнáть (отгоню́, -óнишь; отогнáл, -á, -о) *pf* (*impf* **отгоня́ть**) drive away, off.

отогнýть (-нý, -нёшь) *pf* (*impf* **отгибáть**) bend back; ~**ся** bend.

отогревáть *impf*, **отогрéть** (-éю) *pf* warm.

отодвигáть *impf*, **отодвúнуть** (-ну) *pf* move aside; put off.

отодрáть (отдерý, -рёшь; отодрáл, -á, -о) *pf* (*impf* **отдирáть**) tear off, rip off.

отож(д)ествúть (-влю́) *pf*, **отож(д)ествля́ть** *impf* identify.

отозвáть (отзовý, -вёшь; отозвáл, -á, -о)*pf* (*impf* **отзывáть**) take aside; recall; ~**ся** на+*acc* answer; на+*acc* or *prep* tell on; have an affect on.

отойтú (-йдý, -йдёшь; отошёл, -шлá) *pf* (*impf* **отходúть**) move away; depart; withdraw; digress; come out; recover.

отолью́ *etc.: see* **отлúть. отомрёт** *etc.: see* **отмерéть. ото|мстúть** (-мщý) *pf*.

отомкнýть (-нý, -нёшь) *pf* (*impf* **отмыкáть**) unlock, unbolt.

отопúтельный heating. **отопúть** (-плю́, -пишь) *pf* (*impf* **отáпливать**) heat. **отоплéние** heating.

отопрý *etc.: see* **отперéть. отопью́** *etc.: see* **отпúть**

отóрванный cut off, isolated. **оторвáть** (-вý, -вёшь) *pf* (*impf* **отрывáть**) tear off; tear away; ~**ся** come off, be torn off; be cut off, lose touch; break away; tear o.s. away; ~**ся** от землú take off.

оторопéть (-éю) *pf* be struck dumb.

отосла́ть (-ошлю́, -ошлёшь) *pf* (*impf* отсыла́ть) send (off); send back; +к+*dat* refer to.

отоспа́ться (-сплю́сь, -а́лся, -ала́сь, -ось) *pf* (*impf* отсыпа́ться) catch up on one's sleep.

отошёл *etc.*: *see* отойти́. отошлю́ *etc.*: *see* отосла́ть

отпада́ть *impf of* отпа́сть.

от|пари́ровать *pf.* отпа́рывать *impf of* отпоро́ть

отпа́сть (-адёт) *pf* (*impf* отпада́ть) fall off; fall away; pass.

отпева́ние funeral service.

отпере́ть (отопру́, -прёшь; о́тпер, -ла́, -ло) *pf* (*impf* отпира́ть) unlock; ~ся open; +от+*gen* deny; disown.

от|печа́тать *pf*, отпеча́тывать *impf* print (off); type (out); imprint. отпеча́ток (-тка) imprint, print.

отпива́ть *impf of* отпи́ть

отпи́ливать *impf*, отпили́ть (-лю́, -лишь) *pf* saw off.

от|пира́тельство denial. отпира́ть(ся *impf of* отпере́ть(ся

отпи́ть (отопью́, -пьёшь; о́тпи́л, -а́, -о) *pf* (*impf* отпива́ть) take a sip of.

отпи́хивать *impf*, отпихну́ть (-ну́, -нёшь) *pf* push off; shove aside.

отплати́ть (-ачу́, -а́тишь) *pf*, отпла́чивать *impf* +*dat* pay back.

отплыва́ть *impf*, отплы́ть (-ыву́, -ывёшь; -ы́л, -а́, -о) *pf* (set) sail; swim off. отплы́тие sailing, departure.

о́тповедь rebuke.

отползáть *impf*, отползти́ (-зу́, -зёшь; -о́лз, -ла́) *pf* crawl away.

от|полирова́ть *pf.* от|полоска́ть (-ощу́) *pf.*

отпо́р repulse; rebuff.

отпоро́ть (-рю́, -решь) *pf* (*impf* отпа́рывать) rip off.

отправи́тель *m* sender. отпра́вить (-влю) *pf*, отправля́ть *impf* send, dispatch; ~ся set off, start. отпра́вка dispatch. отправле́ние sending; departure; performance. отправн|о́й: ~о́й пункт, ~а́я то́чка starting-point.

от|пра́здновать *pf.*

отпра́шиваться *impf*, отпроси́ться (-ошу́сь, -о́сишься) *pf* ask for leave, get leave.

отпры́гивать *impf*, отпры́гнуть (-ну) *pf* jump *or* spring back *or* aside.

о́тпрыск offshoot, scion.

отпряга́ть *impf of* отпря́чь

отпря́нуть (-ну) *pf* recoil, start back.

отпря́чь (-ягу́, -яжёшь; -я́г, -ла́) *pf* (*impf* отпряга́ть) unharness.

отпу́гивать *impf*, отпугну́ть (-ну́, -нёшь) *pf* frighten off.

о́тпуск (*pl* -á) leave, holiday(s). отпуска́ть *impf*, отпусти́ть (-ущу́, -у́стишь) *pf* let go, let off; set free; release; slacken; (let) grow; allot; remit. отпускни́к (-á) person on leave. отпускно́й holiday; leave. отпуще́ние remission; козёл отпуще́ния scapegoat.

отраба́тывать *impf*, отрабо́тать *pf* work off; master. отрабо́танный worked out; waste, spent, exhaust.

отра́ва poison. отрави́ть (-влю́, -вишь) *pf*, отравля́ть *impf* poison.

отра́да joy, delight. отра́дный gratifying, pleasing.

отража́тель *m* reflector; scanner. отража́ть *impf*, отрази́ть (-ажу́) *pf* reflect; repulse; ~ся be reflected; +на+*prep* affect. отраже́ние reflection; repulse.

о́трасль branch.

отраста́ть *impf*, отрасти́ (-тёт; отро́с, -ла́) *pf* grow. отрасти́ть (-ащу́) *pf*, отра́щивать *impf* (let) grow.

от|реаги́ровать *pf.* от|регули́ровать *pf.* от|редакти́ровать *pf.*

отре́з cut; length. отре́зать (-е́жу) *pf*, отреза́ть *impf* cut off; snap.

о|трезве́ть (-е́ю) *pf.* отрезви́ть (-влю́, -ви́шь) *pf*, отрезвля́ть *impf* sober; ~ся sober up.

отре́зок (-зка) piece; section; segment.

отрека́ться *impf of* отре́чься

от|рекомендова́ть(ся *pf.* отрёкся *etc.*: *see* отре́чься. от|ремонти́ровать *pf.* от|репети́ровать *pf.*

отре́пье, отре́пья (-ьев) *pl* rags.

от|реставри́ровать *pf.*

отрече́ние renunciation; ~ от престо́ла abdication. отре́чься (-еку́сь, -ечёшься) *pf* (*impf* отрека́ться) renounce.

отреша́ться *impf*, отреши́ться (-шу́сь) *pf* renounce; get rid of.

отрица́ние denial; negation. отрица́тельный negative. отрица́ть *impf* deny.

отро́с etc.: see отрасти́. отро́сток (-тка) shoot, sprout; appendix. о́трочество adolescence.

отруба́ть impf of отруби́ть

о́труби (-ей) pl bran.

отруби́ть (-блю́, -бишь) pf (impf отруба́ть) chop off; snap back.

от|руга́ть pf.

отры́в tearing off; alienation, isolation; ~e от+gen out of touch with; ~ (от земли́) take-off. отрыва́ть(ся impf of оторва́ть(ся. отры́вистый staccato; disjointed. отрывно́й tear-off. отры́вок (-вка) fragment, excerpt. отры́вочный fragmentary, scrappy.

отры́жка belch; throw-back.

от|ры́ть (-ро́ю) pf.

отря́д detachment; order.

отря́хивать impf, отряхну́ть (-ну́, -нёшь) pf shake down or off.

от|салютова́ть pf.

отса́сывание suction. отса́сывать impf of отсоса́ть

отсве́чивать impf be reflected; +instr shine with.

отсе́в sifting, selection; dropping out. отсе́ва́ть(ся, отсе́ивать(ся impf of отсе́ять(ся

отсе́к compartment. отсека́ть impf, отсе́чь (-еку́, -ечёшь; -сёк, -ла́) pf chop off.

отсе́ять (-е́ю) pf (impf отсева́ть, отсе́ивать) sift, screen; eliminate; ~ся drop out.

отсиде́ть (-ижу́) pf, отси́живать impf make numb by sitting; sit through; serve out.

отска́кивать impf, отскочи́ть (-чу́, -чишь) pf jump aside or away; rebound; come off.

отслу́живать impf, отслужи́ть (-жу́, -жишь) pf serve one's time; be worn out.

отсоса́ть (-осу́, -осёшь) pf (impf отса́сывать) suck off, draw off.

отсо́хнуть (-ну) pf (impf отсыха́ть) wither.

отсро́чивать impf, отсро́чить pf postpone, defer. отсро́чка postponement, deferment.

отстава́ние lag; lagging behind. отстава́ть (-таю́, -аёшь) impf of отста́ть

отста́вить (-влю) pf, отставля́ть impf set or put aside. отста́вка resignation; retirement; в отста́вке retired; вы́йти в отста́вку resign, retire. отставно́й retired.

отста́ивать(ся impf of отстоя́ть(ся

отста́лость backwardness. отста́лый backward. отста́ть (-а́ну) pf (impf отстава́ть) fall behind; lag behind; become detached; lose touch; break (off); be slow. отстаю́щий sb backward pupil.

от|стега́ть pf.

отстёгивать impf, отстегну́ть (-ну́, -нёшь) pf unfasten, undo; ~ся come unfastened or undone.

отстоя́ть¹ (-ою́) pf (impf отста́ивать) defend; stand up for. отстоя́ть² (-ои́т) impf на+acc be ... distant (от+gen from). отстоя́ться pf (impf отста́иваться) settle; become stabilized.

отстра́ивать(ся impf of отстро́ить(ся

отстране́ние pushing aside; dismissal. отстрани́ть pf, отстраня́ть impf push aside; remove; suspend; ~ся move away; keep aloof; ~ся от dodge.

отстре́ливаться impf, отстреля́ться pf fire back.

отстрига́ть impf, отстри́чь (-игу́, -ижёшь; -риг) pf cut off.

отстро́ить pf (impf отстра́ивать) finish building; build up.

отступа́ть impf, отступи́ть (-плю́, -пишь) pf step back; recede; retreat; back down; ~ от+gen give up; deviate from; ~ся от+gen give up; go back on. отступле́ние retreat; deviation; digression. отступни́|о́й: ~ы́е де́ньги, ~о́е sb indemnity, compensation. отступя́ adv (farther) off, away (от+gen from).

отсу́тствие absence; lack. отсу́тствовать impf be absent. отсу́тствующий absent; sb absentee.

отсчита́ть pf, отсчи́тывать impf count off.

отсыла́ть impf of отосла́ть

отсы́па́ть (-плю) pf, отсыпа́ть impf pour out; measure off.

отсыпа́ться impf of отоспа́ться

отсыре́лый damp. от|сыре́ть (-е́ет) pf.

отсыха́ть impf of отсо́хнуть

отсю́да *adv* from here; hence.

отта́ивать *impf of* отта́ять

отта́лкивать *impf of* оттолкну́ть. отта́лкивающий repulsive, repellent.

отта́чивать *impf of* отточи́ть

отта́ять (-а́ю) *pf* (*impf* отта́ивать) thaw out.

отте́нок (-нка) shade, nuance; tint.

о́ттепель thaw.

оттесни́ть *pf*, оттесня́ть *impf* drive back; push aside.

о́ттиск impression; off-print, reprint.

оттого́ *adv* that is why; ~, что because.

оттолкну́ть (-ну́, -нёшь) *pf* (*impf* отта́лкивать) push away; antagonize; ~ся push off.

оттопы́ренный protruding. оттопы́ривать *impf*, оттопы́рить *pf* stick out; ~ся protrude; bulge.

отточи́ть (-чу́, -чишь) *pf* (*impf* отта́чивать) sharpen.

отту́да *adv* from there.

оття́гивать *impf*, оттяну́ть (-ну́, -нешь) *pf* draw out; draw off; delay. оття́жка delay.

отупе́ние stupefaction. о|тупе́ть (-е́ю) *pf* sink into torpor.

от|утю́жить (-жу) *pf*.

отуча́ть *impf*, отучи́ть (-чу́, -чишь) *pf* break (of); ~ся break o.s. (of).

отха́ркать *pf*, отха́ркивать *impf* expectorate.

отхвати́ть (-чу́, -тишь) *pf*, отхва́тывать *impf* snip or chop off.

отхлебну́ть (-ну́, -нёшь) *pf*, отхлёбывать *impf* sip, take a sip of.

отхлы́нуть (-нет) *pf* flood or rush back.

отхо́д departure; withdrawal. отходи́ть (-ожу́, -о́дишь) *impf of* отойти́. отхо́ды (-ов) *pl* waste.

отцвести́ (-ету́, -етёшь; -ёл, -а́) *pf*, отцвета́ть *impf* finish blossoming, fade.

отцепи́ть (-плю́, -пишь) *pf*, отцепля́ть *impf* unhook; uncouple.

отцо́вский father's; paternal.

отча́иваться *impf of* отча́яться

отча́ливать *impf*, отча́лить *pf* cast off.

отча́сти *adv* partly.

отча́яние despair. отча́янный desperate. отча́яться (-а́юсь) *pf* (*impf* отча́иваться) despair.

отчего́ *adv* why. отчего́-либо, -нибудь *adv* for some reason or other. отчего́-то *adv* for some reason.

от|чека́нить *pf*.

о́тчество patronymic.

отчёт account; отда́ть себе́ ~ в+*prep* be aware of, realize. отчётливый distinct; clear. отчётность bookkeeping; accounts. отчётный *adj*: ~ год financial year, current year; ~ докла́д report.

отчи́зна native land. о́тчий paternal. о́тчим step-father.

отчисле́ние deduction; dismissal. отчи́слить *pf*, отчисля́ть *impf* deduct; dismiss.

отчита́ть *pf*, отчи́тывать *impf* tell off; ~ся report back.

отчужде́ние alienation; estrangement.

отшатну́ться (-ну́сь, -нёшься) *pf*, отша́тываться *impf* start back, recoil; ~от+*gen* give up, forsake.

отшвы́ривать *impf*, отшвырну́ть (-ну́, -нёшь) *pf* fling away; throw off.

отше́льник hermit; recluse.

от|шлёпать *pf* spank.

от|шлифова́ть *pf*. от|штукату́рить *pf*.

отщепе́нец (-нца) renegade.

отъе́зд departure. отъезжа́ть *impf*, отъе́хать (-е́ду) *pf* drive off, go off. отъя́вленный inveterate.

отыгра́ть *pf*, оты́грывать *impf* win back; ~ся win back what one has lost.

отыска́ть (-ыщу́, -ы́щешь) *pf*, оты́скивать *impf* find; look for; ~ся turn up, appear.

отяготи́ть (-ощу́) *pf*, отягоща́ть *impf* burden.

офице́р officer. офице́рский officer's, officers'.

официа́льный official.

официа́нт waiter. официа́нтка waitress.

официо́з semi-official organ. официо́зный semi-official.

оформи́тель *m* designer; stage-painter. офо́рмить (-млю) *pf*, оформля́ть *impf* design; put into shape; make official; process; ~ся take shape; go through the formalities. оформле́ние design; mounting, staging; processing.

ox *int* ок! ah!

оха́пка armful.

о|**характеризова́ть** *pf.*

о́хать *impf* (*pf* о́хнуть) moan; sigh.

охва́т scope; inclusion; outflanking. **охвати́ть** (-ачу́, -а́тишь) *pf*, **охва́тывать** *impf* envelop; seize; comprehend.

охладева́ть *impf*, **охладе́ть** (-е́ю) *pf* grow cold. **охлади́ть** (-ажу́) *pf*, **охлажда́ть** *impf* cool; ~ся become cool, cool down. **охлажде́ние** cooling; coolness.

о|**хмеле́ть** (-е́ю) *pf.* **о́хнуть** (-ну) *pf* of **о́хать**.

охо́та[1] hunt, hunting; chase.

охо́та[2] wish, desire.

охо́титься (-о́чусь) *impf* hunt. **охо́тник**[1] hunter.

охо́тник[2] volunteer; enthusiast.

охо́тничий hunting.

охо́тно *adv* willingly, gladly.

о́хра ochre.

охра́на guarding; protection; guard. **охрани́ть** *pf*, **охраня́ть** *impf* guard, protect.

охри́плый, **охри́пший** hoarse. **о**|**хри́пнуть** (-ну; охри́п) *pf* become hoarse.

о|**цара́пать**(**ся** *pf.*

оце́нивать *impf*, **оцени́ть** (-ню́, -нишь) *pf* estimate; appraise. **оце́нка** estimation; appraisal; estimate. **оце́нщик** valuer.

о|**цепене́ть** (-е́ю) *pf.*

оцепи́ть (-плю́, -пишь) *pf*, **оцепля́ть** *impf* surround; cordon off.

оча́г (-а́) hearth; centre; breeding ground; hotbed.

очарова́ние charm, fascination. **очарова́тельный** charming. **очарова́ть** *pf*, **очаро́вывать** *impf* charm, fascinate.

очеви́дец (-дца) eye-witness. **очеви́дно** *adv* obviously, evidently. **очеви́дный** obvious.

о́чень *adv* very; very much.

очередно́й next in turn; usual, regular; routine. **о́чередь** (*gen pl* -е́й) turn; queue.

о́черк essay, sketch.

о|**черни́ть** *pf.*

о|**черстве́ть** (-е́ю) *pf.*

очерта́ние outline(s), contour(s).

очерти́ть (-рчу́, -ртишь) *pf*, **оче́рчивать** *impf*: see outline.

о́чи *etc.*: see **о́ко**

очисти́тельный cleansing. **о**|**чи́стить** (-и́щу) *pf*, **очища́ть** *impf* clean; refine; clear; peel; ~ся clear o.s.; become clear (от+*gen* of). **очи́стка** cleaning; purification; clearance. **очи́стки** (-ов) *pl* peelings. **очище́ние** cleaning; purification.

очки́ (-о́в) *pl* spectacles. **очко́** (*gen pl* -о́в) pip; point. **очко́вая змея́** cobra.

очну́ться (-ну́сь, -нёшься) *pf* wake up; regain consciousness.

о́чн|**ый**: ~ое обуче́ние classroom instruction; ~ая ста́вка confrontation.

очути́ться (-у́тишься) *pf* find o.s.

оше́йник collar.

ошеломи́тельный stunning. **ошеломи́ть** (-млю́) *pf*, **ошеломля́ть** *impf* stun.

ошиба́ться *impf*, **ошиби́ться** (-бу́сь, -бёшься; -и́бся) *pf* be mistaken, make a mistake; be wrong. **оши́бка** mistake; error. **оши́бочный** erroneous.

ошпа́ривать *impf*, **о**|**шпа́рить** *pf* scald.

о|**штрафова́ть** *pf.* **о**|**штукату́рить** *pf.*

още́тиниваться *impf*, **о**|**щети́ниться** *pf* bristle (up).

о|**щипа́ть** (-плю́, -плешь) *pf*, **ощи́пывать** *impf* pluck.

ощу́пать *pf*, **ощу́пывать** *impf* feel; grope about. **о́щупь**: на ~ to the touch; by touch. **о́щупью** *adv* gropingly; by touch.

ощути́мый, **ощути́тельный** perceptible; appreciable. **ощути́ть** (-ущу́) *pf*, **ощуща́ть** *impf* feel, sense. **ощуще́ние** sensation; feeling.

П

па *neut indecl* dance step.

павильо́н pavilion; film studio.

павли́н peacock.

па́водок (-дка) (sudden) flood.

па́вший fallen.

па́губный pernicious, ruinous.

па́даль carrion.

па́дать *impf* (*pf* пасть, упа́сть) fall; ~ ду́хом lose heart. **паде́ж** (-а́) case.

паде́ние fall; degradation; incidence.

па́дкий на+*acc or* до+*gen* having a weakness for.

па́дчерица step-daughter.

паёк (пайка́) ration.

па́зуха bosom; sinus; axil.

пай (*pl* -и́, -ёв) share. па́йщик shareholder.

паке́т package; packet; paper bag.

Пакиста́н Pakistan. пакиста́нец (-нца), -а́нка Pakistani. пакиста́нский Pakistani.

па́кля tow; oakum.

пакова́ть *impf* (*pf* за~, у~) pack.

па́костный dirty, mean. па́кость dirty trick; obscenity.

пакт pact.

пала́та chamber, house. пала́тка tent; stall, booth.

пала́ч (-а́) executioner.

па́лец (-льца) finger; toe.

палиса́дник (*small*) front garden.

палиса́ндр rosewood.

пали́тра palette.

пали́ть¹ *impf* (*pf* о~, с~) burn; scorch.

пали́ть² *impf* (*pf* вы́~, пальну́ть) fire, shoot.

па́лка stick; walking-stick.

пало́мник pilgrim. пало́мничество pilgrimage.

па́лочка stick; bacillus; wand; baton.

па́луба deck.

пальба́ fire.

па́льма palm(-tree). па́льмовый palm.

пальну́ть (-ну́, -нёшь) *pf of* пали́ть

пальто́ *neut indecl* (over)coat.

паля́щий burning, scorching.

па́мятник monument; memorial. па́мятный memorable; memorial. па́мять memory; consciousness; на ~ as a keepsake.

панаце́я panacea.

пане́ль footpath; panel(ling), wainscot(ing). пане́льный panelling.

па́ника panic. панике́р alarmist.

панихи́да requiem.

пани́ческий panic; panicky.

панно́ *neut indecl* panel.

панора́ма panorama.

пансио́н boarding-house; board and lodging. пансиона́т holiday hotel. пансионе́р boarder; guest.

пантало́ны (-о́н) *pl* knickers.

панте́ра panther.

пантоми́ма mime.

па́нцирь *m* armour, coat of mail.

па́па¹ *m* pope.

па́па² *m*, папа́ша *m* daddy.

па́паха tall fur cap.

папиро́са (*Russian*) cigarette.

па́пка file; folder.

па́поротник fern.

пар¹ (*loc* -у́; *pl* -ы́) steam.

пар² (*loc* -у́; *pl* -ы́) fallow.

па́ра pair; couple; (two-piece) suit.

пара́граф paragraph.

пара́д parade; review. пара́дный parade; gala; main, front; ~ая фо́рма full dress (uniform).

парадо́кс paradox. парадокса́льный paradoxical.

парази́т parasite.

парализова́ть *impf & pf* paralyse. парали́ч (-а́) paralysis.

паралле́ль parallel. паралле́льный parallel.

пара́метр parameter.

парано́йя paranoia.

парашю́т parachute.

паре́ние soaring.

па́рень (-рня; *gen pl* -рне́й) *m* lad; fellow.

пари́ *neut indecl* bet; держа́ть ~ bet, lay a bet.

пари́к (-а́) wig. парикма́хер hairdresser. парикма́херская *sb* hairdresser's.

пари́ровать *impf & pf* (*pf also* от~) parry, counter.

парите́т parity.

пари́ть¹ *impf* soar, hover.

па́рить² *impf* steam; stew; *impers* па́рит it is sultry; ~ся (*pf* по~ся) steam, sweat; stew.

парк park; depot; stock.

парке́т parquet.

парла́мент parliament. парламента́рный parliamentarian. парламенте́р envoy; bearer of flag of truce. парла́ментский parliamentary; ~ зако́н Act of Parliament.

парни́к (-а́) hotbed; seed-bed. парнико́|вый *adj*: ~ые расте́ния hot-house plants.

парни́шка *m* boy, lad.

парно́й fresh; steamy.

па́рный (forming a) pair; twin.

паро- *in comb* steam-. парово́з

(steam-)engine, locomotive. ~обра́зный vaporous. ~хо́д steamer; steamship. ~хо́дство steamship-line.

парово́й steam; steamed.

паро́дия parody.

паро́ль m password.

паро́м ferry(-boat).

парт- *abbr in comb* Party. партбиле́т Party (membership) card. ~ко́м Party committee. ~организа́ция Party organization.

па́рта (*school*) desk.

партёр stalls; pit.

партиза́н (*gen pl* -а́н) partisan; guerilla. партиза́нский partisan, guerilla; unplanned.

парти́йный party; Party; *sb* Party member.

партиту́ра (*mus*) score.

па́ртия party; group; batch; game, set; part.

партнёр partner.

па́рус (*pl* -а́, -о́в) sail. паруси́на canvas. па́русник sailing vessel. па́русный sail; ~ спорт sailing.

парфюме́рия perfumes.

парча́ (*gen pl* -е́й) brocade. парчо́вый brocade.

па́сека apiary, beehive.

пасётся *see* пасти́сь

па́сквиль m lampoon; libel.

па́смурный overcast; gloomy.

па́спорт (*pl* -а́) passport.

пасса́ж passage; arcade.

пассажи́р passenger.

пасси́вный passive.

па́ста paste.

па́стбище pasture.

па́ства flock.

пасте́ль pastel.

пастерна́к parsnip.

пасти́ (-су́, -сёшь; пас, -ла́) *impf* graze; tend.

пасти́сь (-сётся; па́сся, -ла́сь) *impf* graze. пасту́х (-а́) shepherd. па́стырь m pastor.

пасть[1] mouth; jaws.

пасть[2] (паду́, -дёшь; пал) *pf of* па́дать

Па́сха Easter; Passover.

па́сынок (-нка) stepson, stepchild.

пат stalemate.

пате́нт patent.

патети́ческий passionate.

па́тока treacle; syrup.

патоло́гия pathology.

патриа́рх patriarch.

патрио́т patriot. патриоти́зм patriotism. патриоти́ческий patriotic.

патро́н cartridge; chuck; lamp-socket.

патру́ль (-я́) m patrol.

па́уза pause; (*also mus*) rest.

пау́к (-а́) spider. паути́на cobweb; gossamer; web.

па́фос zeal, enthusiasm.

пах (*loc* -у́) groin.

па́харь m ploughman. паха́ть (пашу́, па́шешь) *impf* (*pf* вс~) plough.

па́хнуть[1] (-ну; пах) *impf* smell (+*instr* of).

пахну́ть[2] (-нёт) *pf* puff, blow.

па́хота ploughing. па́хотный arable.

паху́чий odorous, strong-smelling.

пацие́нт, ~ка patient.

пацифи́зм pacificism. пацифи́ст pacifist.

па́чка bundle; packet, pack; tutu.

па́чкать *impf* (*pf* за~, ис~) dirty, soil, stain.

пашу́ *etc.*: *see* паха́ть. па́шня (*gen pl* -шен) ploughed field.

паште́т pâté.

пая́льная ла́мпа blow-lamp. пая́льник soldering iron. пая́ть (-я́ю) *impf* solder.

пая́ц clown, buffoon.

певе́ц (-вца́), певи́ца singer. певу́чий melodious. пе́вчий singing; *sb* chorister.

пе́гий piebald.

педаго́г teacher; pedagogue. педаго́гика pedagogy. педагоги́ческий pedagogical; educational; ~ институ́т (teachers') training college.

педа́ль pedal.

педиа́тр paediatrician. педиатри́ческий paediatric.

пейза́ж landscape; scenery.

пёк *see* печь. пека́рный baking. пека́рня (*gen pl* -рен) bakery. пе́карь (*pl* -я́, -е́й) m baker. пе́кло scorching heat; hell-fire. пеку́ *etc.*: *see* печь

пелена́ (*gen pl* -лён) shroud. пелена́ть *impf* (*pf* за~) swaddle; put a nappy on.

пе́ленг bearing. пеленгова́ть *impf* & *pf* take the bearings of.

пелёнка nappy.

пельме́нь m meat dumpling.

пéна foam; scum; froth.

пенáл pencil-case.

пéние singing.

пéнистый foamy; frothy. пéниться *impf* (*pf* вс~) foam.

пéнка skin. пеноплáст plastic foam.

пеницилли́н penicillin.

пенсионéр, пенсионéрка pensioner. пенсиóнный pensionable. пéнсия pension.

пень (пня) *m* stump, stub.

пенькá hemp.

пéпел (-пла) ash, ashes. пéпельница ashtray.

пéрвейший the first; first-class. пéрвенец (-нца) first-born. пéрвенство first place; championship. пéрвенствовать *impf* take first place; take priority. пéрви́чный primary.

перво- *in comb* first; prime. первобы́тный primitive; primeval. ~истóчник source; origin. ~клáссный first-class. ~ку́рсник first-year student. ~начáльный original; primary. ~сóртный best-quality; first-class. ~степéнный paramount.

пéрвое *sb* first course. пéрвый first; former.

пергáмент parchment.

перебегáть *impf*, перебежáть (-бегу́) *pf* cross, run across; desert. перебéжчик deserter; turncoat.

переберу́ *etc.: see* перебрáть

перебивáть(ся *impf of* переби́ть(ся

перебирáть(ся *impf of* перебрáть(ся

переби́ть (-бью, -бьёшь) *pf* (*impf* перебивáть) interrupt; slaughter; beat; break; re-upholster; ~ся break; make ends meet. перебóй interruption; stoppage; irregularity.

перебóрка sorting out; partition; bulkhead.

переборóть (-рю́, -решь) *pf* overcome.

переборщи́ть (-щу́) *pf* go too far; overdo it.

перебрáсывать(ся *impf of* переброси́ть(ся

перебрáть (-беру́, -берёшь; -áл, -á, -о) *pf* (*impf* перебирáть) sort out; look through; turn over in one's mind; finger; ~ся get over, cross; move.

переброси́ть (-óшу) *pf* (*impf* перебрáсывать) throw over; transfer; ~ся fling o.s.; spread. перебрóска transfer.

перебью́ *etc.: see* переби́ть

перевáл crossing; pass. перевáливать *impf*, перевали́ть (-лю́, -лишь) *pf* transfer, shift; cross, pass.

перевáривать *impf*, перевари́ть (-рю́, -ришь) *pf* reheat; overcook; digest; tolerate.

переведу́ *etc.: see* перевести́

перевезти́ (-зу́, -зёшь; -вёз, -лá) *pf* (*impf* перевози́ть) take across; transport; (re)move.

перевернýть (-нý, -нёшь) *pf*, перевёртывать *impf* (*impf also* переворáчивать) turn (over); upset; turn inside out; ~ся turn (over).

перевéс preponderance; advantage. перевéсить (-éшу) *pf* (*impf* перевéшивать) re-weigh; outweigh; tip the scales; hang elsewhere.

перевести́ (-веду́, -ведёшь; -вёл, -á) *pf* (*impf* переводи́ть) take across; transfer, move, shift; translate; convert; ~сь be transferred; run out; become extinct.

перевéшивать *impf of* перевéсить, перевирáть *impf of* переврáть

перевóд transfer, move, shift; translation; conversion; waste. переводи́ть(ся (-ожу́(сь, -óдишь(ся) *impf of* перевести́(сь. переводнóй: ~áя бумáга carbon paper; ~áя карти́нка transfer. перевóдный transfer; translated. перевóдчик, ~ица translator; interpreter.

перевóз transporting; ferry. перевози́ть (-ожу́, -óзишь) *impf of* перевезти́. перевóзка conveyance. перевóзчик ferryman; removal man.

перевооружáть *impf*, перевооружи́ть (-жу́) *pf* rearm; ~ся rearm. перевооружéние rearmament.

перевоплоти́ть (-лощу́) *pf*, перевоплощáть *impf* reincarnate; ~ся be reincarnated. перевоплощéние reincarnation.

переворáчивать(ся *impf of* перевернýть(ся. переворóт revolution; overturn; cataclysm; госудáрственный ~ coup d'état.

перевоспитáние re-education. перевоспитáть *pf*, перевоспи́тывать *impf* re-educate.

перевра́ть (-ру́, -рёшь; -а́л, -а́, -о) *pf* (*impf* перевира́ть) garble; misquote.

перевыполне́ние over-fulfilment. **перевы́полнить** *pf*, **перевыполня́ть** *impf* over-fulfil.

перевяза́ть (-яжу́, -я́жешь) *pf*, перевя́зывать *impf* bandage; tie up; re-tie. перевя́зка dressing, bandage.

переги́б bend; excess, extreme. **перегиба́ть(ся** *impf of* перегну́ть(ся

перегля́дываться *impf*, переглянуться (-ну́сь, -нешься) *pf* exchange glances.

перегна́ть (-гоню́, -го́нишь; -а́л, -а́, -о) *pf* (*impf* перегоня́ть) outdistance; surpass; drive; distil.

перегно́й humus.

перегну́ть (-ну́, -нёшь) *pf* (*impf* перегиба́ть) bend; ~ па́лку go too far; ~ся bend; lean over.

перегова́ривать *impf*, переговори́ть *pf* talk; out-talk; ~ся (c+*instr*) exchange remarks (with). перегово́ры (-ов) *pl* negotiations, parley. перегово́рный *adj*: ~ пункт public call-boxes; trunk-call office.

перего́н driving; stage. перего́нка distillation. перего́нный distilling, distillation. перегоню́ *etc.*: *see* перегна́ть. перегоня́ть *impf of* перегна́ть

перегора́живать *impf of* перегороди́ть

перегора́ть *impf*, перегоре́ть (-ри́т) *pf* burn out, fuse.

перегороди́ть (-рожу́, -ро́дишь) *pf* (*impf* перегора́живать) partition off; block. перегоро́дка partition.

перегре́в overheating. перегрева́ть *impf*, перегре́ть (-е́ю) *pf* overheat; ~ся overheat.

перегружа́ть *impf*, перегрузи́ть (-ужу́, -у́зишь) *pf* overload; transfer. перегру́зка overload; transfer.

перегрыза́ть *impf*, перегры́зть (-зу́, -зёшь; -гры́з) *pf* gnaw through.

пе́ред, **пе́редо**, **пред**, **пре́до** *prep+instr* before; in front of; compared to. перёд (пе́реда; *pl* -а́) front, forepart.

передава́ть (-даю́, -даёшь) *impf*, переда́ть (-а́м, -а́шь, -а́ст, -ади́м; пе́редал, -а́, -о) *pf* pass, hand, hand over; transfer; hand down; make over; tell; communicate; convey; give too much; ~ся pass; be transmitted; be communicated; be inherited. переда́тчик transmitter. переда́ча passing; transmission; communication; transfer; broadcast; drive; gear, gearing.

передвига́ть *impf*, передви́нуть (-ну) *pf* move, shift; ~ся move, shift. передвиже́ние movement; transportation. передви́жка movement; *in comb* travelling; itinerant. передвижно́й movable, mobile.

переде́лать *pf*, переде́лывать *impf* alter; refashion. переде́лка alteration.

передёргивать(ся *impf of* передёрнуть(ся

передержа́ть (-жу́, -жишь) *pf*, переде́рживать *impf* overdo; overcook; overexpose.

передёрнуть (-ну) *pf* (*impf* передёргивать) pull aside *or* across; cheat; distort; ~ся wince.

пере́дний front; ~ план foreground. пере́дник apron. пере́дняя *sb* (entrance) hall, lobby. передо: *see* пе́ред. передови́к (-а́) exemplary worker. передови́ца leading article. передово́й advanced; foremost; leading.

передохну́ть (-ну́, -нёшь) *pf* pause for breath.

передра́знивать *impf*, передразни́ть (-ню́, -нишь) *pf* mimic.

переду́мать *pf*, переду́мывать *impf* change one's mind.

переды́шка respite.

перее́зд crossing; move. переезжа́ть *impf*, перее́хать (-е́ду) *pf* cross; run over, knock down; move (house).

пережа́ривать *impf*, пережа́рить *pf* overdo, overcook.

пережда́ть (-жду́, -ждёшь; -а́л, -а́, -о) *pf* (*impf* пережида́ть) wait for the end of.

пережёвывать *impf* chew; repeat over and over again.

пережива́ние experience. пережива́ть *impf of* пережи́ть

пережида́ть *impf of* пережда́ть

пережито́е *sb* the past. пережи́ток (-тка) survival; vestige. пережи́ть

(-иву́, -ивёшь; пе́режи́л, -а́, -о) pf
(impf пережива́ть) experience; go
through; endure; outlive.

перезаряди́ть (-яжу́, -яди́шь) pf,
перезаряжа́ть impf recharge, re-
load.

перезва́нивать impf, перезвони́ть
pf +dat ring back.

пере|зимова́ть pf.

перезре́лый overripe.

переигра́ть pf, переи́грывать impf
play again; overact.

переизбира́ть impf, переизбра́ть
(-беру́, -берёшь; -бра́л, -а́, -о) pf re-
elect. переизбра́ние re-election.

переизбира́ть (-даю́, -даёшь) impf,
переизда́ть (-а́м, -а́шь, -а́ст, -ади́м;
-а́л, -а́, -о) pf republish, reprint.
переизда́ние republication; new
edition.

переименова́ть pf, переимено́вы-
вать impf rename.

перейму́ etc.: see переня́ть

перейти́ (-йду́, -йдёшь; перешёл,
-шла́) pf (impf переходи́ть) cross;
pass; turn (в+acc to, into).

перекантова́ть pf transfer (a load).

перека́пывать impf of перекопа́ть

перека́тывать (-чу́, -тишь) pf, пере-
ка́тывать impf roll; ~ся roll.

перека́чать pf, перека́чивать impf
pump (across).

переквалифици́роваться impf &
pf retrain.

переки́дывать impf, переки́нуть
(-ну) pf throw over; ~ся leap.

переки́сь peroxide.

перекла́дина cross-beam; joist; horizontal bar.

перекла́дывать impf of перело-
жи́ть

перекли́чка roll-call.

переключа́тель m switch. пере-
ключа́ть impf, переключи́ть (-чу́)
pf switch (over); ~ся switch (over).

перекова́ть (-кую́, -куёшь) pf, пере-
ко́вывать impf re-shoe; re-forge.

перекопа́ть pf (impf перека́пы-
вать) dig (all of); dig again.

перекоси́ть (-ошу́, -о́сишь) pf warp;
distort; ~ся warp; become distorted.

перекочева́ть (-чу́ю) pf, переко-
чёвывать impf migrate.

переко́шенный distorted, twisted.

перекра́ивать impf of перекро́ить

перекра́сить (-а́шу) pf, перекра́-
шивать impf (re-)paint; (re-)dye;
~ся change colour; turn one's coat.

пере|крести́ть (-ещу́, -е́стишь) pf,
перекре́щивать impf cross; ~ся
cross, intersect; cross o.s. пере-
кре́стный cross; ~ый допро́с
cross-examination; ~ый ого́нь cross-
fire; ~ая ссы́лка cross-reference.

перекрёсток (-тка) cross-roads,
crossing.

перекри́кивать impf, перекрича́ть
(-чу́) pf shout down.

перекро́ить (-ою́) pf (impf пере-
кра́ивать) cut out again; reshape.

перекрыва́ть impf, перекры́ть
(-ро́ю) pf re-cover; exceed. пере-
кры́тие ceiling.

перекую́ etc.: see перекова́ть

перекупа́ть impf, перекупи́ть
(-плю́, -пишь) pf buy up; buy by out-
bidding s.o. переку́пщик second-
hand dealer.

перекуси́ть (-ушу́, -у́сишь) pf, пере-
ку́сывать impf bite through; have a
snack.

перелага́ть impf of переложи́ть

перела́мывать impf of переломи́ть

перелеза́ть impf, переле́зть (-зу;
-ез) pf climb over.

переле́сок (-ска) copse.

перелёт migration; flight. переле-
та́ть impf, перелете́ть (-лечу́) pf
fly over. перелётный migratory.

перелива́ние decanting; transfusion.
перелива́ть impf of перели́ть.
перелива́ться impf of перели́ться;
gleam; modulate.

перелиста́ть pf, перели́стывать
impf leaf through.

перели́ть (-лью́, -льёшь; -и́л, -а́, -о)
pf (impf перелива́ть) pour; decant;
let overflow; transfuse. перели́ться
(-льётся; -и́лся, -ила́сь, -и́ло́сь)
pf (impf перелива́ться) flow; overflow.

перелицева́ть (-цу́ю) pf, пере-
лицо́вывать impf turn; have turned.

переложе́ние arrangement. пере-
ложи́ть (-жу́, -жишь) pf (impf пере-
кла́дывать, перелага́ть) put elsewhere; shift; transfer; interlay; put in
too much; set; arrange; transpose.

перело́м breaking; fracture; turning-
point; crisis; sudden change.

перелома́ть *pf* break; ~ся break, be broken. переломи́ть (-млю́, -мишь) *pf* (*impf* перела́мывать) break in two; master. перело́мный critical.

перелью́ *etc.*: see перели́ть

перема́нивать *impf*, перемани́ть (-ню́, -нишь) *pf* win over; entice.

перемежа́ться *impf* alternate.

переме́на change; break. перемени́ть (-ню́, -нишь) *pf*, переменя́ть *impf* change; ~ся change. переме́нный variable; ~ ток alternating current. переме́нчивый changeable.

перемести́ть (-мещу́) *pf* (*impf* перемеща́ть) move; transfer; ~ся move.

перемеша́ть *pf*, переме́шивать *impf* mix; mix up; shuffle; ~ся get mixed (up).

перемеща́ть(ся *impf of* перемести́ть(ся. перемеще́ние transference; displacement. перемещённый displaced; ~ые ли́ца displaced persons.

переми́рие armistice, truce.

перемыва́ть *impf*, перемы́ть (-мо́ю) *pf* wash (up) again.

перенапряга́ть *impf*, перенапря́чь (-ягу́, -яжёшь: -яг, -ла́) *pf* overstrain.

перенаселе́ние overpopulation. перенаселённый (-лён, -а́) overpopulated; overcrowded.

перенести́ (-су́, -сёшь; -нёс, -ла́) *pf* (*impf* переноси́ть) carry, move, take; transfer; take over; postpone; endure, bear; ~сь be carried; be carried away.

перенима́ть *impf of* переня́ть

перено́с transfer; word division; знак ~а end-of-line hyphen. переноси́мый endurable. переноси́ть(ся (-ошу́(сь, -о́сишь(ся) *impf of* перенести́(сь

перено́сица bridge (*of the nose*).

перено́ска carrying over; transporting; carriage. перено́сный portable; figurative. перено́счик carrier.

пере|ночева́ть (-чу́ю) *pf*. переношу́ *etc.*: see переноси́ть

переня́ть (-ейму́, -еймёшь; пе́ренял, -а́, -о) *pf* (*impf* перенима́ть) imitate; adopt.

переобору́довать *impf & pf* re-equip.

переобува́ться *impf*, переобу́ться (-у́юсь, -у́ешься) *pf* change one's shoes.

переодева́ться *impf*, переоде́ться (-е́нусь) *pf* change (one's clothes).

переосвиде́тельствовать *impf & pf* re-examine.

переоце́нивать *impf*, переоцени́ть (-ню́, -нишь) *pf* overestimate; revalue. переоце́нка overestimation; revaluation.

перепа́чкать *pf* make dirty; ~ся get dirty.

пе́репел (*pl* -а́) quail.

перепелена́ть *pf* change (*a baby*).

перепеча́тать *pf*, перепеча́тывать *impf* reprint. перепеча́тка reprint.

перепи́ливать *impf*, перепили́ть (-лю́, -лишь) *pf* saw in two.

переписа́ть (-ишу́, -и́шешь) *pf*, перепи́сывать *impf* copy; re-write; make a list of. перепи́ска copying; correspondence. перепи́сываться *impf* correspond. пе́репись census.

перепла́вить (-влю) *pf*, переплавля́ть *impf* smelt.

переплати́ть (-ачу́, -а́тишь) *pf*, перепла́чивать *impf* overpay.

переплести́ (-лету́, -летёшь; -лёл, -а́) *pf*, переплета́ть *impf* bind; interlace, intertwine; re-plait; ~ся interlace, interweave; get mixed up. переплёт binding. переплётчик bookbinder.

переплыва́ть *impf*, переплы́ть (-ыву́, -ывёшь; -ы́л, -а́, -о) *pf* swim or sail across.

переподгото́вка further training; refresher course.

переполза́ть *impf*, переползти́ (-зу́, -зёшь; -о́лз, -ла́) *pf* crawl or creep across.

переполне́ние overfilling; overcrowding. перепо́лненный overcrowded; too full. перепо́лнить *pf*, переполня́ть *impf* overfill; overcrowd.

переполо́х commotion.

перепо́нка membrane; web.

перепра́ва crossing; ford. перепра́вить (-влю) *pf*, переправля́ть *impf* convey; take across; forward; ~ся cross, get across.

перепродава́ть (-даю́, -даёшь) *impf*, перепрода́ть (-а́м, -а́шь, -а́ст, -ади́м; -про́дал, -а́, -о) *pf* re-sell. перепрода́жа re-sale.

перепроизво́дство overproduction.

перепры́гивать *impf*, перепры́гнуть (-ну) *pf* jump (over).

перепуга́ть *pf* frighten, scare; ~ся get a fright.

пере|пу́тать *pf*, перепу́тывать *impf* tangle; confuse, mix up.

перепу́тье cross-roads.

перераба́тывать *impf*, перерабо́тать *pf* convert; treat; re-make; recast; process; work overtime; overwork; ~ся overwork. перерабо́тка processing; reworking; overtime work.

перераспределе́ние redistribution. перераспредели́ть *pf*, перераспределя́ть *impf* redistribute.

перераста́ние outgrowing; escalation; development (into). перераста́ть *impf*, перерасти́ (-ту́, -тёшь; -ро́с, -ла́) *pf* outgrow; develop.

перерасхо́д over-expenditure; overdraft. перерасхо́довать *impf & pf* expend too much of.

перерасчёт recalculation.

перерва́ть (-ву́, -вёшь; -а́л, -а́, -о) *pf* (*impf* перерыва́ть) break, tear asunder; ~ся break, come apart.

перере́зать (-е́жу) *pf*, перереза́ть *impf*, перере́зывать *impf* cut; cut off; kill.

перероди́ть (-ожу́) *pf*, перерожда́ть *impf* regenerate; ~ся be reborn; be regenerated; degenerate. перерожде́ние regeneration; degeneration.

перерос *etc.*: *see* перерасти. перерою *etc.*: *see* перерыть

переруба́ть *impf*, переруби́ть (-блю́, -бишь) *pf* chop in two.

переры́в break; interruption; interval.

перерыва́ть¹(ся *impf of* перерва́ть(ся

перерыва́ть² *impf of* перерыть, переры́ть (-ро́ю) *pf* dig up; rummage through.

пересади́ть (-ажу́, -а́дишь) *pf*, переса́живать *impf* transplant; graft; seat somewhere else. переса́дка transplantation; grafting; change.

переса́живаться *impf of* пересе́сть. переса́ливать *impf of* пересоли́ть

пересдава́ть (-даю́сь) *impf*, пересда́ть (-а́м, -а́шь, -а́ст, -ади́м; -да́л, -а́, -о) *pf* sublet; re-sit.

пересека́ть(ся *impf of* пересе́чь(ся переселе́нец (-нца) settler; immigrant. переселе́ние migration; im-

migration, resettlement; moving. пересели́ть *pf*, переселя́ть *impf* move; ~ся move; migrate.

пересе́сть (-ся́ду) *pf* (*impf* переса́живаться) change one's seat; change (*trains etc.*).

пересече́ние crossing, intersection. пересе́чь (-секу́, -сечёшь; -сёк, -ла́) *pf* (*impf* пересека́ть) cross; intersect; ~ся cross, intersect.

переси́ливать *impf*, переси́лить *pf* overpower.

переска́з (re)telling; exposition. пересказа́ть (-ажу́, -а́жешь) *pf*, переска́зывать *impf* retell.

переска́кивать *impf*, перескочи́ть (-чу́, -чишь) *pf* jump *or* skip (over).

пересла́ть (-ешлю́, -шлёшь) *pf* (*impf* пересыла́ть) send; forward.

пересма́тривать *impf*, пересмотре́ть (-трю́, -тришь) *pf* look over; reconsider. пересмо́тр revision; reconsideration; review.

пересоли́ть (-олю́, -о́ли́шь) *pf* (*impf* переса́ливать) over-salt; overdo it.

пересо́хнуть (-нет; -о́х) *pf* (*impf* пересыха́ть) dry up, become parched.

переспа́ть (-плю́; -а́л, -а́, -о) *pf* oversleep; spend the night.

переспе́лый overripe.

переспра́шивать *impf*, переспроси́ть (-ошу́, -о́сишь) *pf* ask again.

переставать (-таю́, -таёшь) *impf of* переста́ть

переста́вить (-влю) *pf*, переставля́ть *impf* move; re-arrange; transpose. перестано́вка rearrangement; transposition.

переста́ть (-а́ну) *pf* (*impf* переставать) stop, cease.

пострада́ть *pf* have suffered.

перестра́ивать(ся *impf of* перестро́ить(ся

перестрахо́вка re-insurance; overcautiousness.

перестре́лка exchange of fire. перестреля́ть *pf* shoot (down).

перестро́ить *pf* (*impf* перестра́ивать) rebuild; reorganize; retune; ~ся re-form; reorganize o.s.; switch over (на+*acc* to). перестро́йка reconstruction; reorganization; retuning; perestroika.

переступа́ть *impf*, переступи́ть

(-плю́, -пишь) pf step over; cross; overstep.

пересчита́ть pf, **пересчи́тывать** impf (pf also **перече́сть**) re-count; count.

пересыла́ть impf of **пересла́ть**. **пересы́лка** sending, forwarding.

пересыпа́ть impf, **пересы́пать** (-плю, -плешь) pf pour; sprinkle; pour too much.

пересыха́ть impf of **пересо́хнуть**. **переся́ду** etc.: see **пересе́сть**. **перета́пливать** impf of **перетопи́ть**

перета́скивать impf, **перетащи́ть** (-щу́, -щишь) pf drag (over, through); move.

перетере́ть (-тру́, -трёшь; -тёр) pf, **перетира́ть** impf wear out, wear down; grind; wipe; ~ся wear out or through.

перетопи́ть (-плю́, -пишь) pf (impf **перета́пливать**) melt.

перетру́ etc.: see **перетере́ть**

перетя́гивать impf, **перетяну́ть** (-ну́, -нешь) pf pull, draw; win over; outweigh.

переубеди́ть pf, **переубежда́ть** impf make change one's mind.

переу́лок (-лка) side street, alley, lane.

переустро́йство reconstruction, reorganization.

переутоми́ть (-млю́) pf, **переутомля́ть** impf overtire; ~ся overtire o.s. **переутомле́ние** overwork.

переучёт stock-taking.

переу́чивать impf, **переучи́ть** (-чу́, -чишь) pf teach again.

перефрази́ровать impf & pf paraphrase.

перехвати́ть (-ачу́, -а́тишь) pf, **перехва́тывать** impf intercept; snatch a bite (of); borrow.

перехитри́ть pf outwit.

перехо́д transition; crossing; conversion. **переходи́ть** (-ожу́, -о́дишь) impf of **перейти́**. **перехо́дный** transitional; transitive. **переходя́щий** transient; intermittent; brought forward.

пе́рец (-рца) pepper.

перечёл etc.: see **перече́сть**

пе́речень (-чня) m list, enumeration.

перечёркивать impf, **перечеркну́ть** (-ну́, -нёшь) pf cross out, cancel.

перече́сть (-чту́, -чтёшь; -чёл, -чла́) pf: see **пересчита́ть, перечита́ть**

перечисле́ние enumeration; transfer. **перечи́слить** pf, **перечисля́ть** impf enumerate; transfer.

перечита́ть pf, **перечи́тывать** impf (pf also **перече́сть**) re-read.

пере́чить (-чу) impf contradict; cross, go against.

пе́речница pepper-pot.

перечту́ etc.: see **перече́сть**. **пере́чу** etc.: see **пере́чить**

переша́гивать impf, **перешагну́ть** (-ну́, -нёшь) pf step over.

переше́ек (-е́йка) isthmus, neck.

перешёл etc.: see **перейти́**

переши́вать impf, **переши́ть** (-шью, -шьёшь) pf alter; have altered.

перешлю́ etc.: see **пересла́ть**

переэкзамено́вка pf, **переэкзамено́вывать** impf re-examine; ~ся retake an exam.

пери́ла (-и́л) pl railing(s); banisters.

пери́на feather-bed.

пери́од period. **перио́дика** periodicals. **периоди́ческий** periodical; recurring.

пе́ристый feathery; cirrus.

периферия periphery.

перламу́тр mother-of-pearl. **перламу́тровый** mother-of-pearl. **перло́вый**: ~ая крупа́ pearl barley.

перма́не́нт perm. **перма́не́нтный** permanent.

перна́тый feathered. **перна́тые** sb pl birds. **перо́** (pl пе́рья, -ьев) feather; pen. **перочи́нный нож, но́жик** penknife.

перпендикуля́рный perpendicular.

перро́н platform.

перс Persian. **перси́дский** Persian. **пе́рсик** peach.

персия́нка Persian woman.

персо́на person; со́бственной персо́ной in person. **персона́ж** character; personage. **персона́л** personnel, staff. **персона́льный** personal.

перспекти́ва perspective; vista; prospect. **перспекти́вный** perspective; long-term; promising.

пе́рстень (-тня) m ring.

перфокáрта punched card.

пéрхоть dandruff.

перчáтка glove.

пéрчить (-чу) impf (pf по~) pepper.

пёс (пса) dog.

пéсенник song-book; (choral) singer; song-writer. пéсенный song; of songs.

песéц (-сцá) (polar) fox.

песнь (gen pl -ей) song; canto. пéсня (gen pl -сен) song.

песóк (-скá) sand. песóчный sand; sandy.

пессими́зм pessimism. пессими́ст pessimist. пессимисти́ческий pessimistic.

пестротá diversity of colours; diversity. пёстрый variegated; diverse; colourful.

песчáник sandstone. песчáный sandy. песчи́нка grain of sand.

петербýргский (of) St Petersburg.

пети́ция petition.

петли́ца buttonhole; tab. пéтля (gen pl -тель) loop; noose; buttonhole; stitch; hinge.

петрýшка¹ parsley.

петрýшка² m Punch; f Punch-and-Judy show.

петýх (-á) cock. петушóк (-шкá) cockerel.

петь (пою, поёшь) impf (pf про~, с~) sing.

пехóта infantry, foot. пехоти́нец (-нца) infantryman. пехóтный infantry.

печáлить impf (pf о~) sadden; ~ся grieve, be sad. печáль sorrow. печáльный sad.

печáтать impf (pf на~, от~) print; ~ся write, be published; be at the printer's. печáтн|ый printing; printer's; printed; ~ые бýквы block capitals; ~ый станóк printing-press. печáть seal, stamp; print; printing; press.

печéние baking.

печёнка liver.

печёный baked.

пéчень liver.

печéнье pastry; biscuit. пéчка stove.

печнóй stove; oven; kiln. печь (loc -и́, gen pl -éй) stove; oven; kiln. печь (пекý, -чёшь; пёк, -лá) impf (pf ис~) bake; ~ся bake.

пешехóд pedestrian. пешехóдный pedestrian; foot-. пéший pedestrian; foot. пéшка pawn. пешкóм adv on foot.

пещéра cave. пещéрный cave; ~ человéк cave-dweller.

пиани́но neut indecl (upright) piano. пиани́ст, ~ка pianist.

пивнáя sb pub. пивнóй beer. пи́во beer. пивовáр brewer.

пигмéй pygmy.

пиджáк (-á) jacket.

пижáма pyjamas.

пижóн dandy.

пик peak; часы́ пик rush-hour.

пи́ка lance.

пикáнтный piquant; spicy.

пикáп pick-up (van).

пикé neut indecl dive.

пикéт picket. пикéтчик picketer.

пи́ки (пик) pl (cards) spades.

пики́ровать impf & pf (pf also с~) dive.

пики́ровщик, пики́рующий бомбарди́ровщик dive-bomber.

пикни́к (-á) picnic.

пи́кнуть (-ну) pf squeak; make a sound.

пи́ковый of spades.

пилá (pl -ы) saw; nagger. пилёный sawed, sawn. пили́ть (-лю, -лишь) impf saw; nag (at). пи́лка sawing; fret-saw; nail-file.

пилóт pilot.

пилóтка forage-cap.

пилоти́ровать impf pilot.

пилю́ля pill.

пинáть impf (pf пнуть) kick. пинóк (-нкá) kick.

пингви́н penguin.

пинцéт tweezers.

пиóн peony.

пионéр pioneer. пионéрский pioneer.

пипéтка pipette.

пир (loc -ý; pl -ы́) feast, banquet. пировáть impf feast.

пирами́да pyramid.

пирáт pirate.

пирóг (-á) pie. пирóжное sb cake, pastry. пирожóк (-жкá) pasty.

пирс pier.

пируэ́т pirouette.

пи́ршество feast; celebration.

пи́саный handwritten. писáрь (pl

-я) *m* clerk. писа́тель *m*, писа́тельница writer, author. писа́ть (пишу́, пи́шешь) *impf* (*pf* на~) write; paint; ~ ма́слом paint in oils; ~ся be spelt.

писк squeak, chirp. писќли́вый squeaky. пи́скнуть (-ну) *pf of* пища́ть

пистоле́т pistol; gun; ~-пулемёт sub-machine gun.

писто́н (percussion-)cap; piston.

писчебума́жный stationery. пи́счая бума́га writing paper. пи́сьменно *adv* in writing. пи́сьменность literature. пи́сьменный writing, written. письмо́ (*pl* -а, -сем) letter.

пита́ние nourishment; feeding. пита́тельный nutritious; alimentary; feed. пита́ть *impf* feed; nourish; supply; ~ся be fed, eat; +*instr* feed on.

пито́мец (-мца) charge; pupil; alumnus. пито́мник nursery.

пить (пью, пьёшь; пил, -а́, -о) *impf* (*pf* вы~) drink. питьё (*pl* -тья́, -те́й, -тья́м) drinking; drink. питьево́й drinkable; drinking.

пиха́ть *impf*, пихну́ть (-ну́, -нёшь) *pf* push, shove.

пи́хта (silver) fir.

пи́чкать *impf* (*pf* на~) stuff.

пи́шущий writing; ~ая маши́нка typewriter.

пи́ща food.

пища́ть (-щу́) *impf* (*pf* пи́скнуть) squeak; cheep.

пищеваре́ние digestion. пищево́д oesophagus, gullet. пищево́й food.

пия́вка leech.

пла́вание swimming; sailing; voyage. пла́вательный swimming; ~ бассе́йн swimming-pool. пла́вать *impf* swim; float; sail. плавба́за depot ship, factory ship.

пла́вильный melting, smelting. пла́вильня foundry. пла́вить (-влю) *impf* (*pf* рас~) melt, smelt; ~ся melt. пла́вка fusing; melting.

пла́вки (-вок) *pl* bathing trunks.

пла́вкий fusible; fuse. плавле́ние melting.

плавни́к (-а́) fin; flipper. пла́вный smooth, flowing; liquid. плаву́чий floating.

плагиа́т plagiarism. плагиа́тор plagiarist.

пла́зма plasma.

плака́т poster; placard.

пла́кать (-а́чу) *impf* cry, weep; ~ся complain, lament; +на+*acc* complain of; bemoan.

пла́кса cry-baby. плакси́вый whining. пла́кучий weeping.

пла́менный flaming; ardent. пла́мя (-мени) *neut* flame; blaze.

план plan.

планёр glider. планери́зм gliding. планери́ст glider-pilot.

плане́та planet. плане́тный planetary.

плани́рование[1] planning.

плани́рование[2] gliding; glide.

плани́ровать[1] *impf* (*pf* за~) plan.

плани́ровать[2] *impf* (*pf* с~) glide (down).

пла́нка lath, slat.

пла́новый planned, systematic; planning. планоме́рный systematic, planned.

планта́ция plantation.

пласт (-а́) layer; stratum. пласти́на plate. пласти́нка plate; (*gramophone*) record.

пласти́ческий, пласти́чный plastic. пластма́сса plastic. пластма́ссовый plastic.

пла́стырь *m* plaster.

пла́та pay; charge; fee. платёж (-а́) payment. платёжеспосо́бный solvent. платёжный pay.

пла́тина platinum. пла́тиновый platinum.

плати́ть (-ачу́, -а́тишь) *impf* (*pf* за~, у~) pay; ~ся (*pf* по~ся) за+*acc* pay for. пла́тный paid; requiring payment.

плато́к (-тка́) shawl; head-scarf; handkerchief.

платони́ческий platonic.

платфо́рма platform; truck.

пла́тье (*gen pl* -ьев) clothes, clothing; dress; gown. платяно́й clothes.

плафо́н ceiling; lamp shade.

плацда́рм bridgehead, beach-head; base; springboard.

плацка́рта reserved-seat ticket.

плач weeping. плаче́вный lamentable. пла́чу *etc.: see* пла́кать

плачу́ *etc.: see* плати́ть

плашмя́ *adv* flat, prone.

плащ (-а́) cloak; raincoat.

плебе́й plebeian.

плева́тельница spittoon. **плева́ть** (плюю́, плюёшь) *impf* (*pf* на~, плю́нуть) spit; *inf+dat*: мне ~ I don't give a damn (на+*acc* about); ~ся spit. **плево́к** (-вка́) spit, spittle.

плеври́т pleurisy.

плед rug; plaid.

плёл *etc.*: *see* плести́

племенно́й tribal; pedigree. **пле́мя** (-мени; *pl* -мена́, -мён) *neut* tribe. **племя́нник** nephew. **племя́нница** niece.

плен (*loc* -у́) captivity.

плена́рный plenary.

плени́тельный captivating. **плени́ть** *pf* (*impf* пленя́ть) captivate; ~ся be captivated.

плёнка film; tape; pellicle.

пле́нник prisoner. **пле́нный** captive.

пле́нум plenary session.

пленя́ть(ся *impf of* плени́ть(ся

пле́сень (-ени) mould.

плеск splash, lapping. **плеска́ть** (-ещу́, -е́щешь) *impf* (*pf* плесну́ть) splash; lap; ~ся splash; lap.

пле́сневеть (-еет) *impf* (*pf* за~) go mouldy, grow musty.

плесну́ть (-ну́, -нёшь) *pf of* плеска́ть

плести́ (-ету́, -етёшь; плёл, -а́) *impf* (*pf* с~) plait; weave; ~сь trudge along. **плете́ние** plaiting; wicker-work. **плетёный** wattled; wicker. **плете́нь** (-тня́) *m* wattle fencing. **плётка, плеть** (*gen pl* -е́й) lash.

пле́чико (*pl* -и, -ов) shoulder-strap; *pl* coat-hanger. **плечи́стый** broad-shouldered. **плечо́** (*pl* -и, -а́м) shoulder.

плеши́вый bald. **плеши́на, плешь** bald patch.

плещу́ *etc.*: *see* плеска́ть

пли́нтус plinth; skirting-board.

плис velveteen.

плиссирова́ть *impf* pleat.

плита́ (*pl* -ы) slab; flag-(stone); stove, cooker; моги́льная ~ gravestone. **пли́тка** tile; (thin) slab; stove, cooker; ~ шокола́да bar of chocolate. **пли́точный** tiled.

плове́ц (-вца́), **пловчи́ха** swimmer. **плову́чий** floating; buoyant.

плод (-а́) fruit. **плоди́ть** (-ожу́) *impf* (*pf* рас~) produce, procreate; ~ся propagate.

плодо- *in comb* fruit-. **плодови́тый** fruitful, prolific; fertile. **~во́дство** fruit-growing. **~но́сный** fruit-bearing, fruitful. **~овощно́й** fruit and vegetable. **~ро́дный** fertile. **~тво́рный** fruitful.

пло́мба seal; filling. **пломбирова́ть** *impf* (*pf* за~, о~) fill; seal.

пло́ский (-сок, -ска́, -о) flat; trivial. **плоско-** *in comb* flat. **плоского́рье** plateau. **~гу́бцы** (-ев) *pl* pliers. **~до́нный** flat-bottomed.

пло́скость (*gen pl* -е́й) flatness; plane; platitude.

плот (-а́) raft.

плоти́на dam; weir; dyke.

пло́тник carpenter.

пло́тность solidity; density. **пло́тный** (-тен, -тна́, -о) thick; compact; dense; solid, strong; hearty.

плотоя́дный carnivorous. **плоть** flesh.

плохо́й bad; poor.

площа́дка area, (sports) ground, court, playground; site; landing; platform. **пло́щадь** (*gen pl* -е́й) area; space; square.

плуг (*pl* -и́) plough.

плут (-а́) cheat, swindler; rogue. **плутова́тый** cunning. **плутовско́й** roguish; picaresque.

плуто́ний plutonium.

плыть (-ыву́, -ывёшь; плыл, -а́, -о) *impf* swim; float; sail.

плюну́ть (-ну) *pf of* плева́ть

плюс plus; advantage.

плюш plush.

плющ (-а́) ivy.

плюю́ *etc.*: *see* плева́ть

пляж beach.

пляса́ть (-яшу́, -я́шешь) *impf* (*pf* с~) dance. **пля́ска** dance; dancing.

пневмати́ческий pneumatic.

пневмони́я pneumonia.

пну́ть (пну, пнёшь) *pf of* пина́ть

пня *etc.*: *see* пень

по *prep* I. +*dat* on; along; round, about; by; over; according to; in accordance with; for; in; at; by (reason of); on account of; from; по понеде́льникам on Mondays; по профе́ссии by profession; по ра́дио over the radio. II. +*dat or acc* of cardinal number, forms distributive number: по два, по дво́е in twos, two by two; по пять рубле́й шту́ка at five roubles each. **III.** +*acc* to, up to; for, to get; идти́ по во́ду go to get water; по пе́рвое сентября́ up to (and including) 1st September. **IV.** +*prep* on, (immediately) after; по прибы́тии on arrival.

по- *pref* **I.** *in comb* +*dat of adjs, or with advs in* -и, *indicates manner, use of a named language, or accordance with the opinion or wish of:* говори́ть по-ру́сски speak Russian; жить по-ста́рому live in the old style; по-мо́ему in my opinion. **II.** *in comb with adjs and nns, indicates situation along or near a thing:* помо́рье seaboard, coastal region. **III.** *in comb with comp of adjs indicates a smaller degree of comparison:* поме́ньше a little less.

поба́иваться *impf* be rather afraid.
побе́г[1] flight; escape.
побе́г[2] shoot; sucker.
побегу́шки: быть на побегу́шках run errands.
побе́да victory. **победи́тель** *m* victor; winner. **победи́ть** *pf* (*impf* **побежда́ть**) conquer; win. **побе́дный, победоно́сный** victorious, triumphant.
по|бежа́ть *pf*.
побежда́ть *impf of* победи́ть
по|беле́ть (-е́ю) *pf*. **по|бели́ть** *pf*. **побе́лка** whitewashing.
побере́жный coastal. **побере́жье** (sea-)coast.
по|беспоко́ить(ся *pf*.
побира́ться *impf* beg; live by begging.
по|би́ть (-бью́(сь, -бьёшь(ся) *pf*.
по|благодари́ть *pf*.
побла́жка indulgence.
по|бледне́ть (-е́ю) *pf*.
поблёскивать *impf* gleam.
побли́зости *adv* nearby.
побо́и (-ев) *pl* beating. **побо́ище** slaughter; bloody battle.
побо́рник champion, advocate. **по|боро́ть** (-рю́, -решь) *pf* overcome.
побо́чный secondary; done on the side; ~ проду́кт by-product.
по|брани́ться *pf*.
по|брата́ться *pf*. **побрати́м** twin town.
по|брезга́ть *pf*. **по|бри́ть(ся** (-бре́ю(сь) *pf*.

побуди́тельный stimulating. **побуди́ть** (-ужу́) *pf*, **побужда́ть** *impf* induce, prompt. **побужде́ние** motive; inducement.
побыва́ть *pf* have been, have visited; look in, visit. **побы́вка** leave. **по|бы́ть** (-бу́ду, -дешь; по́был, -а́, -о) *pf* stay (for a short time).
по|вади́ться (-а́жусь) *pf* get into the habit (of). **пова́дка** habit.
по|вали́ть(ся (-лю́(сь, -лишь(ся) *pf*.
пова́льно *adv* without exception. **пова́льный** general, mass.
по́вар (*pl* -а́) cook, chef. **пова́ренный** culinary; cookery, cooking.
по-ва́шему *adv* in your opinion.
пове́дать *pf* disclose; relate.
поведе́ние behaviour.
поведу́ *etc.: see* повести́. **по|везти́** (-зу́, -зёшь; -вёз, -ла́) *pf*. **повёл** *etc.: see* повести́
повелева́ть *impf* rule (over); +*dat* command. **повеле́ние** command. **повели́тельный** imperious; imperative.
по|венча́ть(ся *pf*.
поверга́ть *impf*, **пове́ргнуть** (-ну; -ве́рг) *pf* throw down; plunge.
пове́ренная *sb* confidante. **пове́ренный** *sb* attorney; confidant; ~ в дела́х chargé d'affaires. **по|ве́рить**[1].
пове́рить[2] *pf* (*impf* **поверя́ть**) check; confide. **пове́рка** check; roll-call.
поверну́ть (-ну́, -нёшь) *pf*, **повёртывать** *impf* (*impf also* **повора́чивать**) turn; ~ся turn.
пове́рх *prep*+*gen* over. **пове́рхностный** surface, superficial. **пове́рхность** surface.
пове́рье (*gen pl* -ий) popular belief, superstition. **поверя́ть** *impf of* пове́рить[2]
пове́са playboy.
по|весели́ть(ся (-е́ю) *pf*.
повесели́ть *pf* cheer (up), amuse; ~ся have fun.
по|ве́сить(ся (-ве́шу(сь) *pf of* ве́шать(ся
повествова́ние narrative, narration. **повествова́тельный** narrative. **повествова́ть** *impf* +*o*+*prep* narrate, relate.
по|вести́ (-еду́, -едёшь; -вёл, -а́) *pf*

(*impf* поводить) +*instr* move.

повестка notice; summons; ~ (дня) agenda.

повесть (*gen pl* -ей) story, tale.

поветрие epidemic; craze.

повешу *etc.*: *see* повесить. по|вздорить *pf*.

повзрослеть (-ею) *pf* grow up.

по|видать(ся *pf*.

по-видимому apparently.

повидло jam.

по|виниться *pf*.

повинность duty, obligation; воинская ~ conscription. повинный guilty.

повиноваться *impf* & *pf* obey. повиновение obedience.

повисать *impf*, по|виснуть (-ну; -вис) *pf* hang (on); hang down, droop.

повлечь (-еку, -ечёшь; -ёк, -ла) *pf* (за собой) entail, bring in its train.

по|влиять *pf*.

повод[1] occasion, cause; по ~у+*gen* as regards, concerning.

повод[2] (*loc* -у; *pl* -бдья, -ьев) rein; быть на ~у у+*gen* be under the thumb of. поводить (-ожу, -одишь) *impf of* повести. поводок (-дка) leash. поводырь (-я) *m* guide.

повозка cart; vehicle.

поворачивать(ся *impf of* повернуть(ся, поворотить(ся; поворачивайся, -айтесь! get a move on!

поворот turn, turning; bend; turningpoint. поворотить(ся (-рочу(сь, -ротишь(ся) *pf* (*impf* поворачивать(ся) turn. поворотливый agile, nimble; manoeuvrable. поворотный turning; rotary; revolving.

по|вредить (-ежу) *pf*, повреждать *impf* damage; injure; ~ся be damaged; be injured. повреждение damage, injury.

повременить *pf* wait a little; +c+*instr* delay over.

повседневный daily; everyday.

повсеместно *adv* everywhere. повсеместный universal, general.

повстанец (-нца) rebel, insurgent. повстанческий rebel; insurgent.

повсюду *adv* everywhere.

повторение repetition. повторить *pf*, повторять *impf* repeat; ~ся repeat o.s.; be repeated; recur. повторный repeated.

повысить (-ышу) *pf*, повышать *impf* raise, heighten; ~ся rise. повышение rise; promotion. повышенный heightened, high.

повязать (-яжу, -яжешь) *pf*, повязывать *impf* tie. повязка band; bandage.

по|гадать *pf*.

поганка toadstool. поганый foul; unclean.

погасать *impf*, по|гаснуть (-ну) *pf* go out, be extinguished. по|гасить (-ашу, -асишь) *pf*. погашать *impf* liquidate, cancel. погашенный used, cancelled, cashed.

погибать *impf*, по|гибнуть (-ну; -гиб) *pf* perish; be lost. погибель ruin. погибший lost; ruined; killed.

по|гладить (-ажу) *pf*.

поглотить (-ощу, -отишь) *pf*, поглощать *impf* swallow up; absorb. поглощение absorption.

по|глупеть (-ею) *pf*.

по|глядеть (-яжу) *pf*. поглядывать *impf* glance (from time to time); +за+*instr* keep an eye on.

погнать (-гоню, -гонишь; -гнал, -а, -о) *pf* drive; ~ся за+*instr* run after; start in pursuit of.

по|гнуть(ся (-ну(сь, -нёшь(ся) *pf*. по|гнушаться *pf*.

поговорить *pf* have a talk.

поговорка saying, proverb.

погода weather.

погодить (-ожу) *pf* wait a little; немного погодя a little later.

поголовно *adv* one and all. поголовный general; capitation. поголовье number.

погон (*gen pl* -он) shoulder-strap. погонщик driver. погоню *etc.*: *see* погнать. погоня pursuit, chase. погонять *impf* urge on, drive.

погорячиться (-чусь) *pf* get worked up.

погост graveyard.

пограничник frontier guard. пограничный frontier.

погреб (*pl* -а) cellar. погребальный funeral. погребать *impf of* погрести. погребение burial.

погремушка rattle.

погрести[1] (-ебу, -ебёшь; -ёб, -ла) *pf* (*impf* погребать) bury.

погрести́[2] (-ебу́, -ебёшь; -рёб, -ла́) pf row for a while.

погре́ть (-е́ю) pf warm; ~ся warm o.s.

по|греши́ть (-шу́) pf sin; err. погре́шность error, mistake.

по|грози́ть(ся (-ожу́(сь) pf. по|грубе́ть (-е́ю) pf.

погружа́ть impf, по|грузи́ть (-ужу́, -у́зи́шь) pf load; ship; dip, plunge, immerse; ~ся sink, plunge; dive; be plunged, absorbed. погруже́ние submergence; immersion; dive. погру́зка loading; shipment.

погряза́ть impf, по|гря́знуть (-ну; -я́з) pf be bogged down; wallow.

по|губи́ть (-блю́, -бишь) pf. по|гуля́ть pf.

под, подо prep I. +acc or instr under; near, close to; взять под ру́ку+acc take the arm of; ~ ви́дом+gen under the guise of; под гору downhill; ~ Москво́й in the environs of Moscow. II. +instr occupied by, used as; (meant, implied) by; in, with; говя́дина ~ хре́ном beef with horse-radish. III. +acc towards; to (the accompaniment of); in imitation of; on; for, to serve as; ему́ ~ пятьдеся́т (лет) he is getting on for fifty.

подава́ть(ся (-даю́(сь, -даёшь(ся) impf of пода́ть(ся

подави́ть (-влю́, -вишь) pf, подавля́ть impf suppress; depress; overwhelm. по|дави́ться (-влю́сь, -вишься) pf. подавле́ние suppression; repression. пода́вленность depression. пода́вленный suppressed; depressed. подавля́ющий overwhelming.

пода́вно adv all the more.

пода́гра gout.

пода́льше adv a little further.

по|дари́ть (-рю́, -ришь) pf. пода́рок (-рка) present.

пода́тливый pliant, pliable. по́дать (gen pl -е́й) tax. пода́ть (-а́м, -а́шь, -а́ст, -ади́м; по́дал, -а́, -о) pf (impf подава́ть) serve; give; put, move, turn; put forward, present, hand in; ~ся give way; yield; +на+acc set out for. пода́ча giving, presenting; serve; feed, supply. пода́чка handout, crumb. подаю́ etc.: see

подава́ть. подая́ние alms.

подбега́ть impf, подбежа́ть (-егу́) pf come running (up).

подберу́ etc.: see подобра́ть. подбира́ть(ся impf of подобра́ть(ся

подби́ть (-добью́, -добьёшь) pf (impf подбива́ть) line; re-sole; bruise; put out of action; incite.

подбодри́ть pf, подбодря́ть impf cheer up, encourage; ~ся cheer up, take heart.

подбо́р selection, assortment.

подборо́док (-дка) chin.

подбоче́нившись adv with hands on hips.

подбра́сывать impf, подбро́сить (-ро́шу) pf throw up.

подва́л cellar; basement. подва́льный basement, cellar.

подведу́ etc.: see подвести́

подвезти́ (-зу́, -зёшь; -вёз, -ла́) pf (impf подвози́ть) bring, take; give a lift.

подвене́чный wedding.

подверга́ть impf, подве́ргнуть (-ну; -ве́рг) pf subject; expose; ~ся +dat undergo. подве́рженный subject, liable.

подверну́ть (-ну́, -нёшь) pf, подвёртывать impf turn up; tuck under; sprain; tighten; ~ся be sprained; be turned up; be tucked under.

подве́сить (-е́шу) pf (impf подве́шивать) hang up, suspend. подвесно́й hanging, suspended.

подвести́ (-еду́, -едёшь; -вёл, -а́) pf (impf подводи́ть) lead up, bring up; place (under); bring under, subsume; let down; ~ ито́ги reckon up; sum up.

подве́шивать impf of подве́сить

по́двиг exploit, feat.

подвига́ть(ся impf of подви́нуть(ся подви́жник religious ascetic; champion.

подвижно́й mobile; ~ соста́в rolling-stock. подви́жность mobility. подви́жный mobile; lively; agile.

подвиза́ться impf (в or на+prep) work (in).

подви́нуть (-ну) pf (impf подвига́ть) move; push; advance; ~ся move; advance.

подвла́стный +dat subject to; under

the control of.
подво́да cart. подводи́ть (-ожу́, -о́дишь) *impf of* подвести́
подво́дный submarine; underwater; ~ая скала́ reef.
подво́з transport; supply. подвози́ть (-ожу́, -о́зишь) *impf of* подвезти́
подворо́тня (*gen pl* -тен) gateway.
подво́х trick.
подвы́пивший tipsy.
подвяза́ть (-яжу́, -я́жешь) *pf*, подвя́зывать *impf* tie up. подвя́зка garter; suspender.
подгиба́ть *impf of* подогну́ть
подгляде́ть (-яжу́) *pf*, подгля́дывать *impf* peep; spy.
подгова́ривать *impf*, подговори́ть *pf* incite.
подгоню́ *etc.: see* подогна́ть. подго́ня́ть *impf of* подогна́ть
подгора́ть *impf*, подгоре́ть (-ри́т) *pf* get a bit burnt. подгоре́лый slightly burnt.
подготови́тельный preparatory. подгото́вить (-влю) *pf*, подготовля́ть *impf* prepare; ~ся prepare, get ready. подгото́вка preparation, training.
поддава́ться (-даю́сь, -даёшься) *impf of* подда́ться
подда́кивать *impf* agree, assent.
по́дданный *sb* subject; citizen. по́дданство citizenship. подда́ться (-а́мся, -а́шься, -а́стся, -ади́мся; -а́лся, -ла́сь) *pf* (*impf* поддава́ться) yield, give way.
подде́лать *pf*, подде́лывать *impf* counterfeit; forge. подде́лка falsification; forgery; imitation. подде́льный false, counterfeit.
поддержа́ть (-жу́, -жишь) *pf*, подде́рживать *impf* support; maintain. подде́ржка support.
по|де́йствовать *pf*.
поде́лать *pf* do; ничего́ не поде́лаешь it can't be helped.
по|дели́ть(ся (-лю́(сь, -лишь(ся) *pf*.
поде́лка *pl* small (hand-made) articles.
подело́м *adv*: ~ ему́ (*etc.*) it serves him (*etc.*) right.
подённый by the day. подённщик, -ица day-labourer.
подёргиваться *impf* twitch.
подёржанный second-hand.

подёрнуть (-нет) *pf* cover.
подеру́ *etc.: see* подра́ть. по|дешеве́ть (-е́ет) *pf*.
поджа́ривать(ся *impf*, поджа́рить(ся *pf* fry, roast, grill; toast. поджа́ристый brown(ed).
поджа́рый lean, wiry.
поджа́ть (-дожму́, -дожмёшь) *pf* (*impf* поджима́ть) draw in, draw under; ~ гу́бы purse one's lips.
подже́чь (-дожгу́, -ожжёшь; -жёг, -дожгла́) *pf*, поджига́ть *impf* set fire to; burn. поджига́тель *m* arsonist; instigator.
поджида́ть *impf* (+*gen*) wait (for).
поджима́ть *impf of* поджа́ть
поджо́г arson.
подзаголо́вок (-вка) subtitle, subheading.
подземе́лье (*gen pl* -лий) cave; dungeon. подзе́мный underground.
подзову́ *etc.: see* подозва́ть
подзо́рная труба́ telescope.
подзыва́ть *impf of* подозва́ть
по|диви́ться (-влю́сь) *pf*.
подка́пывать(ся *impf of* подкопа́ть(ся
подкара́уливать *impf*, подкара́улить *pf* be on the watch (for).
подкати́ть (-ачу́, -а́тишь) *pf*, подка́тывать *impf* roll up, drive up; roll.
подка́шивать(ся *impf of* подкоси́ть(ся
подки́дывать *impf*, подки́нуть (-ну) *pf* throw up. подки́дыш foundling.
подкла́дка lining. подкла́дывать *impf of* подложи́ть
подкле́ивать *impf*, подкле́ить *pf* glue (up); mend.
подко́ва (horse-)shoe. под|кова́ть (-кую́, -ёшь) *pf*, подко́вывать *impf* shoe.
подко́жный hypodermic.
подкоми́ссия, подкомите́т subcommittee.
подко́п undermining; underground passage. подкопа́ть *pf* (*impf* подка́пывать) undermine; ~ся под+*acc* undermine; burrow under.
подкоси́ть (-ошу́, -о́сишь) *pf* (*impf* подка́шивать) cut down; ~ся give way.

подкра́дываться *impf of* подкра́сться

подкра́сить (-а́шу) *pf* (*impf* подкра́шивать) touch up; ~ся make up lightly.

подкра́сться (-аду́сь, -адёшься) *pf* (*impf* подкра́дываться) sneak up.

подкра́шивать(ся *impf of* подкра́сить(ся. подкра́шу *etc.: see* подкра́сить

подкрепи́ть (-плю́) *pf*, подкрепля́ть *impf* reinforce; support; corroborate; fortify; ~ся fortify o.s. подкрепле́ние confirmation; sustenance; reinforcement.

подкрути́ть (-учу́, -у́тишь) *pf* (*impf* подкру́чивать) tighten up.

по́дкуп bribery. подкупа́ть *impf*, подкупи́ть (-плю́, -пишь) *pf* bribe; win over.

подла́диться (-а́жусь) *pf*, подла́живаться *impf* +к+*dat* adapt o.s. to; make up to.

подла́мываться *impf of* подломи́ться

по́дле *prep*+*gen* by the side of, beside.

подлежа́ть (-жу́) *impf* +*dat* be subject to; не подлежи́т сомне́нию it is beyond doubt. подлежа́щее *sb* subject. подлежа́щий+*dat* subject to.

подлеза́ть *impf*, подле́зть (-зу; -е́з) *pf* crawl (under).

подле́сок (-ска) undergrowth.

подле́ц (-а́) scoundrel.

подлива́ть *impf of* подли́ть. подли́вка sauce, dressing; gravy.

подли́за *m & f* toady. подлиза́ться (-ижу́сь, -и́жешься) *pf*, подли́зываться *impf* +к+*dat* suck up to.

по́длинник original. по́длинно *adv* really. по́длинный genuine; authentic; original; real.

подли́ть (-долью́, -дольёшь; по́дли́л, -а́, -о) *pf* (*impf* подлива́ть) pour; add.

подло́г forgery.

подло́дка submarine.

подложи́ть (-жу́, -жишь) *pf* (*impf* подкла́дывать) add; +под+*acc* lay under; line.

подло́жный false, spurious; counterfeit, forged.

подлоко́тник arm (*of chair*).

подломи́ться (-о́мится) *pf* (*impf*

подла́мываться) break; give way.

по́длость meanness, baseness; mean trick. по́длый (подл, -а́, -о) mean, base.

подма́зать (-а́жу) *pf*, подма́зывать *impf* grease; bribe.

подмасте́рье (*gen pl* -ьев) *m* apprentice.

подме́н, подме́на replacement. подме́нивать *impf*, подмени́ть (-ню́, -нишь) *pf*, подменя́ть *impf* replace.

подмести́ (-ету́, -етёшь; -мёл, -а́) *pf*, подмета́ть[1] *impf* sweep.

подмета́ть[2] *pf* (*impf* подмётывать) tack.

подме́тить (-е́чу) *pf* (*impf* подмеча́ть) notice.

подмётка sole.

подмётывать *impf of* подмета́ть[2]. подмеча́ть *impf of* подме́тить

подмеша́ть *pf*, подме́шивать *impf* mix in, stir in.

подми́гивать *impf*, подмигну́ть (-ну́, -нёшь) *pf* +*dat* wink at.

подмо́га help.

подмока́ть *impf*, подмо́кнуть (-нет; -мо́к) *pf* get damp, get wet.

подмора́живать *impf*, подморо́зить *pf* freeze.

подмоско́вный (situated) near Moscow.

подмо́стки (-ов) *pl* scaffolding; stage.

подмо́ченный damp; tarnished.

подмыва́ть *impf*, подмы́ть (-о́ю) *pf* wash; wash away; его́ так и подмыва́ет he feels an urge (to).

подмы́шка armpit.

поднево́льный dependent; forced.

поднести́ (-су́, -сёшь; -ёс, -ла́) *pf* (*impf* подноси́ть) present; take, bring.

поднима́ть(ся *impf of* подня́ть(ся

поднови́ть (-влю́) *pf*, подновля́ть *impf* renew, renovate.

подного́тная *sb* ins and outs.

подно́жие foot; pedestal. подно́жка running-board. подно́жный корм pasture.

подно́с tray. подноси́ть (-ошу́, -о́сишь) *impf of* поднести́. подноше́ние giving; present.

подня́тие raising. подня́ть (-ниму́, -ни́мешь; по́днял, -а́, -о) *pf* (*impf* поднима́ть, подыма́ть) raise; lift (up); rouse; ~ся rise; go up.

подо *see* под

подоба́ть *impf* befit, become. подоба́ющий proper.

подо́бие likeness; similarity. подо́бный like, similar; и тому́ ~ое and so on, and such like; ничего́ ~ого! nothing of the sort!

подобостра́стие servility. подобостра́стный servile.

подобра́ть (-дберу́, -дберёшь; -брал, -а́, -о) *pf* (*impf* подбира́ть) pick up; tuck up, put up; pick; ~ся steal up.

подобью́ *etc.: see* подби́ть

подогна́ть (-дгоню́, -дго́нишь; -гна́л, -а́, -о) *pf* (*impf* подгоня́ть) drive; urge on; adjust.

подогну́ть (-ну́, -нёшь) *pf* (*impf* подгиба́ть) tuck in; bend under.

подогрева́ть *impf*, подогре́ть (-е́ю) *pf* warm up.

пододвига́ть *impf*, пододви́нуть (-ну) *pf* move up.

пододея́льник blanket cover; top sheet.

подожгу́ *etc.: see* подже́чь

подожда́ть (-ду́, -дёшь; -а́л, -а́, -о) *pf* wait (+*gen or acc* for).

подожму́ *etc.: see* поджа́ть

подозва́ть (-дзову́, -дзовёшь; -а́л, -а́, -о) *pf* (*impf* подзыва́ть) call to; beckon.

подозрева́емый suspected; suspect. подозрева́ть *impf* suspect. подозре́ние suspicion. подозри́тельный suspicious.

по|до́ить (-ою́, -о́ишь) *pf*.

подойти́ (-йду́, -йдёшь; -ошёл, -шла́) *pf* (*impf* подходи́ть) approach; come up; +*dat* suit, fit.

подоко́нник window-sill.

подо́л hem.

подо́лгу *adv* for ages; for hours (*etc.*) on end.

подолью́ *etc.: see* подли́ть

подо́нки (-ов) *pl* dregs; scum.

подоплёка underlying cause.

подопру́ *etc.: see* подпере́ть

подо́пытный experimental.

подорва́ть (-рву́, -рвёшь; -а́л, -а́, -о) *pf* (*impf* подрыва́ть) undermine; blow up.

по|дорожа́ть *pf*.

подоро́жник plantain. подоро́жный roadside.

подосла́ть (-ошлю́, -ошлёшь) *pf* (*impf* подсыла́ть) send (secretly).

подоспева́ть *impf*, подоспе́ть (-е́ю) *pf* arrive, appear (in time).

подостла́ть (-дстелю́, -дсте́лешь) *pf* (*impf* подстила́ть) lay under.

подотде́л section, subdivision.

подотру́ *etc.: see* подтере́ть

подотчётный accountable.

по|до́хнуть (-ну) *pf* (*impf also* поды́хать).

подохо́дный нало́г income-tax.

подо́шва sole; foot.

подошёл *etc.: see* подойти́. подошлю́ *etc.: see* подосла́ть подошью́ *etc.: see* подши́ть.

подпада́ть *impf*, подпа́сть (-аду́, -адёшь; -а́л) *pf* под+*acc* fall under.

подпева́ть *impf* (+*dat*) sing along (with).

подпере́ть (-допру́; -пёр) *pf* (*impf* подпира́ть) prop up.

подпи́ливать *impf*, подпили́ть (-лю́, -лишь) *pf* saw; saw a little off.

подпира́ть *impf of* подпере́ть

подписа́ние signing. подписа́ть (-ишу́, -и́шешь) *pf*, подпи́сывать *impf* sign; ~ся sign; subscribe. подпи́ска subscription. подписно́й subscription. подпи́счик subscriber. по́дпись signature.

подплыва́ть *impf*, подплы́ть (-ыву́, -ывёшь; -плы́л, -а́, -о) *pf* к+*dat* swim or sail up to.

подполза́ть *impf*, подползти́ (-зу́, -зёшь; -по́лз, -ла́) *pf* creep up (к+*dat* to); +под+*acc* crawl under.

подполко́вник lieutenant-colonel.

подпо́лье cellar; underground. подпо́льный underfloor; underground.

подпо́ра, подпо́рка prop, support.

подпо́чва subsoil.

подпра́вить (-влю) *pf*, подправля́ть *impf* touch up, adjust.

подпры́гивать *impf*, подпры́гнуть (-ну) *pf* jump up (and down).

подпуска́ть *impf*, подпусти́ть (-ущу́, -у́стишь) *pf* allow to approach.

подраба́тывать *impf*, подрабо́тать *pf* earn on the side; work up.

подра́внивать *impf of* подровня́ть

подража́ние imitation. подража́ть *impf* imitate.

подразделе́ние subdivision. подраздели́ть *pf*, подразделя́ть *impf* subdivide.

подразумева́ть *impf* imply, mean; ~ся be meant, be understood.

подраста́ть *impf*, **подрасти́** (-ту́, -тёшь; -ро́с, -ла́) *pf* grow.

по|дра́ть(ся (-деру́(сь, -дерёшь(ся, -а́л(ся, -а́(сь, -о́(сь *or* -о́(сь) *pf*.

подре́зать (-е́жу) *pf*, **подреза́ть** *impf* cut; clip, trim.

подро́бно *adv* in detail. **подро́бность** detail. **подро́бный** detailed.

подровня́ть *pf* (*impf* подра́внивать) level, even; trim.

подро́с *etc.*: *see* подрасти́. **подро́сток** (-тка) adolescent; youth.

подро́ю *etc.*: *see* подры́ть

подруба́ть *impf*, **подруби́ть** (-блю́, -бишь) *pf* chop down; cut short(er).

подруба́ть[2] *impf*, **подруби́ть** (-блю́, -бишь) *pf* hem.

подру́га friend. **по-дру́жески** *adv* in a friendly way. **по|дружи́ться** (-жу́сь) *pf*.

по-друго́му *adv* in a different way.

подру́чный at hand; improvised; *sb* assistant.

подры́в undermining; injury.

подрыва́ть[1] *impf of* подорва́ть

подрыва́ть[2] *impf*, **подры́ть** (-ро́ю) *pf* undermine, sap. **подрывно́й** blasting, demolition; subversive.

подря́д[1] *adv* in succession.

подря́д[2] contract. **подря́дчик** contractor.

подса́живаться *impf of* подсе́сть

подса́ливать *impf of* подсоли́ть

подсве́чник candlestick.

подсе́сть (-ся́ду; -се́л) *pf* (*impf* подса́живаться) sit down (к+*dat* near).

подсказа́ть (-ажу́, -а́жешь) *pf*, **подска́зывать** *impf* prompt; suggest. **подска́зка** prompting.

подска́кивать *impf*, **подскочи́ть** (-чу́, -чишь) *pf* jump (up); soar; come running.

подсласти́ть (-ащу́) *pf*, **подсла́щивать** *impf* sweeten.

подсле́дственный under investigation.

подслу́шать *pf*, **подслу́шивать** *impf* overhear; eavesdrop, listen.

подсма́тривать *impf*, **подсмотре́ть** (-рю́, -ришь) *pf* spy (on).

подсне́жник snowdrop.

подсо́бный subsidiary; auxiliary.

подсо́вывать *impf of* подсу́нуть

подсозна́ние subconscious (mind). **подсозна́тельный** subconscious.

подсоли́ть (-со́лишь) *pf* (*impf* подса́ливать) add salt to.

подсо́лнечник sunflower. **подсо́лнечный** sunflower.

подсо́хнуть (-ну) *pf* (*impf* подсыха́ть) dry out a little.

подспо́рье help.

подста́вить (-влю) *pf*, **подставля́ть** *impf* put (under); bring up; expose; ~ но́жку к+*dat* trip up. **подста́вка** stand; support. **подставно́й** false.

подстака́нник glass-holder.

подстелю́ *etc.*: *see* подостла́ть

подстерега́ть *impf*, **подстере́чь** (-егу́, -ежёшь; -рёг, -ла́) *pf* lie in wait for.

подстила́ть *impf of* подостла́ть. **подсти́лка** litter.

подстра́ивать *impf of* подстро́ить

подстрека́тель *m* instigator. **подстрека́тельство** instigation. **подстрека́ть** *impf*, **подстрекну́ть** (-ну́, -нёшь) *pf* instigate, incite.

подстре́ливать *impf*, **подстрели́ть** (-лю́, -лишь) *pf* wound.

подстрига́ть *impf*, **подстри́чь** (-игу́, -ижёшь; -и́г) *pf* cut; clip, trim; ~ся have a hair-cut.

подстро́ить *pf* (*impf* подстра́ивать) build on; cook up.

подстро́чн|ый literal; ~ое примеча́ние footnote.

по́дступ approach. **подступа́ть** *impf*, **подступи́ть** (-плю́, -пишь) *pf* approach; ~ся к+*dat* approach.

подсуди́мый *sb* defendant; the accused. **подсу́дный**+*dat* under the jurisdiction of.

подсу́нуть (-ну) *pf* (*impf* подсо́вывать) put, shove; palm off.

подсчёт calculation; count. **подсчита́ть** *pf*, **подсчи́тывать** count (up); calculate.

подсыла́ть *impf of* подосла́ть.

подсыха́ть *impf of* подсо́хнуть.

подся́ду *etc.*: *see* подсе́сть. **подта́лкивать** *impf of* подтолкну́ть

подта́скивать *impf of* подтащи́ть

подтасова́ть *pf*, **подтасо́вывать** *impf* shuffle unfairly; juggle with.

подта́чивать *impf of* подточи́ть

подтащи́ть (-щу́, -щишь) pf (impf **подта́скивать**) drag up.

подтверди́ть (-ржу́) pf, **подтвержда́ть** impf confirm; corroborate. **подтвержде́ние** confirmation, corroboration.

подтёк bruise. **подтека́ть** impf of **подте́чь**; leak.

подтере́ть (-дотру́, -дотрёшь; подтёр) pf (impf **подтира́ть**) wipe (up).

подте́чь (-ечёт; -тёк, -ла́) pf (impf **подтека́ть**) под+acc flow under.

подтира́ть impf of **подтере́ть**

подтолкну́ть (-ну́, -нёшь) pf (impf **подта́лкивать**) push; urge on.

подто́чивать impf of **подточи́ть**

подточи́ть (-чу́, -чишь) pf (impf **подта́чивать**) sharpen; eat away; undermine.

подтру́нивать impf, **подтруни́ть** pf над+instr tease.

подтя́гивать impf, **подтяну́ть** (-ну́, -нешь) pf tighten; pull up; move up; ~ся tighten one's belt etc.; move up; pull o.s. together. **подтя́жки** (-жек) pl braces, suspenders. **подтя́нутый** smart.

по|ду́мать pf think (for a while). **поду́мывать** impf+inf or o+prep think about.

по|ду́ть (-у́ю) pf.

поду́шка pillow; cushion.

подхали́м m toady. **подхали́мство** grovelling.

подхвати́ть (-ачу́, -а́тишь) pf, **подхва́тывать** impf catch (up), pick up, take up.

подхлестну́ть (-ну́, -нёшь) pf, **подхлёстывать** impf whip up.

подхо́д approach. **подходи́ть** (-ожу́, -о́дишь) impf of **подойти́. подходя́щий** suitable.

подцепи́ть (-плю́, -пишь) pf, **подцепля́ть** impf hook on; pick up.

подча́с adv sometimes.

подчёркивать impf, **подчеркну́ть** (-ну́, -нёшь) pf underline; emphasize.

подчине́ние subordination; submission. **подчинённый** subordinate. **подчини́ть** pf, **подчиня́ть** impf subordinate, subject; ~ся +dat submit to.

подшива́ть impf of **подши́ть. подши́вка** hemming; lining; soling.

подши́пник bearing.

подши́ть (-дошью́, -дошьёшь) pf (impf **подшива́ть**) hem, line; sole.

подшути́ть (-учу́, -у́тишь) pf, **подшу́чивать** impf над+instr mock; play a trick on.

подъе́ду etc.: see **подъе́хать**

подъе́зд entrance, doorway; approach. **подъезжа́ть** impf of **подъе́хать**

подъём lifting; raising; ascent; climb; enthusiasm; instep; reveille. **подъёмник** lift, elevator, hoist. **подъёмный** lifting; ~ кран crane; ~ мост drawbridge.

подъе́хать (-е́ду) pf (impf **подъезжа́ть**) drive up.

подыма́ть(ся impf of **подня́ть(ся**

подыска́ть (-ыщу́, -ы́щешь) pf, **поды́скивать** impf seek (out).

подыто́живать impf, **подыто́жить** (-жу) pf sum up.

подыха́ть impf of **подо́хнуть**

подыша́ть (-шу́, -шишь) pf breathe.

поеда́ть impf of **пое́сть**

поеди́нок (-нка) duel.

по́езд (pl -а́) train. **пое́здка** trip.

пое́сть (-е́м, -е́шь, -е́ст, -еди́м; -е́л) pf (impf **поеда́ть**) eat, eat up; have a bite to eat.

по|е́хать (-е́ду) pf go; set off.

по|жале́ть (-е́ю) pf.

по|жа́ловать(ся pf. **пожа́луй** adv perhaps. **пожа́луйста** partl please; you're welcome.

пожа́р fire. **пожа́рище** scene of a fire. **пожа́рник, пожа́рный** sb fireman. **пожа́рный** fire; ~ая кома́нда fire-brigade; ~ая ле́стница fire-escape; ~ая маши́на fire-engine.

пожа́тие handshake. **пожа́ть**[1] (-жму́, -жмёшь) pf (impf **пожима́ть**) press; ~ ру́ку+dat shake hands with; ~ плеча́ми shrug one's shoulders.

пожа́ть[2] (-жну́, -жнёшь) pf (impf **пожина́ть**) reap.

пожела́ние wish, desire. **по|жела́ть** pf.

по|желте́ть (-е́ю) pf.

по|жени́ть (-ню́, -нишь) pf. **пожени́ться** (-же́нимся) pf get married.

поже́ртвование donation. **по|же́ртвовать** pf.

пожива́ть impf live; как (вы) пожива́ете? how are you (getting on)? **пожи́зненный** life(long). **пожило́й** elderly.

пожима́ть *impf of* пожа́ть[1]. пожина́ть *impf of* пожа́ть[2]. пожира́ть *impf of* пожра́ть

пожи́тки (-ов) *pl* belongings.

пожи́ть (-иву́, -ивёшь; по́жил, -а́, -о) *pf.* live for a while; stay.

пожму́ *etc.: see* пожа́ть[1]. пожну́ *etc.: see* пожа́ть[2]

пожра́ть (-ру́, -рёшь; -а́л, -а́, -о) *pf* (*impf* пожира́ть) devour.

по́за pose.

по|забо́титься (-о́чусь) *pf.*

позабыва́ть *impf*, позабы́ть (-у́ду) *pf* forget all about.

по|зави́довать *pf.* по|за́втракать *pf.*

позавчера́ *adv* the day before yesterday.

позади́ *adv & prep+gen* behind.

по|заи́мствовать *pf.*

позапро́шлый before last.

по|зва́ть (-зову́, -зовёшь; -а́л, -а́, -о) *pf.*

позволе́ние permission. позволи́тельный permissible. позво́лить *pf*, позволя́ть *impf +dat or acc* allow, permit; позво́ль(те) allow me; excuse me.

по|звони́ть *pf.*

позвоно́к (-нка́) vertebra. позвоно́чник spine. позвоно́чный spinal; vertebrate; ~ые *sb pl* vertebrates.

поздне́е *adv* later. по́здний late; по́здно it is late.

по|здоро́ваться *pf.* поздра́вить (-влю) *pf*, поздравля́ть *impf*+*instr* congratulate on. поздравле́ние congratulation.

по|зелене́ть (-е́ет) *pf.*

по́зже *adv* later (on).

пози́ровать *impf* pose.

позити́в positive. позити́вный positive.

пози́ция position.

познава́тельный cognitive. познава́ть (-наю́, -наёшь) *impf of* позна́ть по|знако́мить(ся) (-млю(сь)) *pf.*

позна́ние cognition. позна́ть *pf* (*impf* познава́ть) get to know.

позоло́та gilding. по|золоти́ть (-лочу́) *pf.*

позо́р shame, disgrace. позо́рить *impf* (*pf* о~) disgrace; ~ся disgrace o.s. позо́рный shameful.

позы́в urge; inclination.

поигра́ть *pf* play (for a while).

поимённо *adv* by name.

пои́мка capture.

поинтересова́ться *pf* be curious.

поиска́ть (-ищу́, -и́щешь) *pf* look for. по́иски (-ов) *pl* search.

пои́стине *adv* indeed.

пои́ть (пою́, по́ишь) *impf* (*pf* на~) give something to drink; water.

пойду́ *etc.: see* пойти́

пойло swill.

пойма́ть *pf of* лови́ть. пойму́ *etc.: see* поня́ть

пойти́ (-йду́, -йдёшь; пошёл, -шла́) *pf of* идти́, ходи́ть; go, walk; begin to walk; +*inf* begin; пошёл! off you go! I'm off; пошёл вон! be off!

пока́ *adv* for the present; cheerio; ~ что in the meanwhile. пока́ *conj* while; ~ не until.

пока́з showing, demonstration. показа́ние testimony, evidence; reading. показа́тель *m* index. показа́тельный significant; model; demonstration. показа́ть (-ажу́, -а́жешь) *pf*, пока́зывать *impf* show. пока́за́ться (-ажу́сь, -а́жешься) *pf*, пока́зываться *impf* show o.s.; appear. показно́й for show; ostentatious. показу́ха show.

по|кале́чить(ся) (-чу(сь)) *pf.*

пока́мест *adv & conj* for the present; while; meanwhile.

по|кара́ть *pf.*

покати́ть (-чу́, -тишь) *pf* start (rolling); ~ся start rolling.

пока́тый sloping; slanting.

покача́ть *pf* rock, swing; ~ голово́й shake one's head. пока́чивать rock slightly; ~ся rock; stagger. покачну́ть (-ну́, -нёшь) shake; rock; ~ся sway, totter, lurch.

пока́шливать *impf* have a slight cough.

покая́ние confession; repentance. по|ка́яться *pf.*

поквита́ться *pf* be quits; get even.

покида́ть *impf*, поки́нуть (-ну) *pf* leave; abandon. поки́нутый deserted.

покла́дая: не ~ рук untiringly.

покла́дистый complaisant, obliging. покло́н bow; greeting; regards. поклоне́ние worship. поклони́ться

(-ню́сь, -ни́шься) *pf of* кла́няться.
покло́нник admirer; worshipper.
поклоня́ться *impf* +*dat* worship.
по|кля́сться (-яну́сь, -нёшься; -я́лся, -ла́сь) *pf.*
поко́иться *impf* rest, repose. поко́й rest, peace; room. поко́йник, -ица the deceased. поко́йный calm, quiet; deceased.
по|колеба́ть(ся (-е́блю(сь) *pf.*
поколе́ние generation.
по|колоти́ть(ся (-очу́(сь, -о́тишь(ся) *pf.*
поко́нчить (-чу) *pf* c+*instr* finish; put an end to; ~ с собо́й commit suicide.
покоре́ние conquest. покори́ть *pf (impf* покоря́ть) subdue; conquer; ~ся submit.
по|корми́ть(ся (-млю́(сь, -мишь(ся) *pf.*
поко́рный humble; submissive, obedient.
по|коро́бить(ся (-блю(сь) *pf.*
покоря́ть(ся *impf of* покори́ть(ся
поко́с mowing; meadow(-land).
покоси́вшийся rickety, ramshackle.
по|коси́ть(ся (-ошу́(сь) *pf.*
по|кра́сить (-а́шу) *pf.* покра́ска painting, colouring.
по|красне́ть (-е́ю) *pf.* по|криви́ть(ся (-влю́(сь) *pf.*
покро́в cover. покрови́тель *m*, покрови́тельница patron; sponsor. покрови́тельственный protective; patronizing. покрови́тельство protection, patronage. покрови́тельствовать *impf* +*dat* protect, patronize.
покро́й cut.
покроши́ть (-шу́, -шишь) *pf* crumble; chop.
покрути́ть (-учу́, -у́тишь) *pf* twist.
покрыва́ло cover; bedspread; veil. покрыва́ть *impf,* по|кры́ть (-ро́ю) *pf* cover; ~ся cover o.s.; get covered. покры́тие covering; surfacing; payment. покры́шка cover; tyre.
покупа́тель *m* buyer; customer. по|купа́ть *impf of* купи́ть. поку́пка purchase. покупно́й bought, purchased; purchase.
по|кури́ть (-рю́, -ришь) *pf* have a smoke.
по|ку́шать *pf.*

покуше́ние +на+*acc* attempted assassination of.
пол¹ (*loc* -у́; *pl* -ы́) floor.
пол² sex.
пол- *in comb with n in gen, in oblique cases usu* полу-, half.
пола́ (*pl* -ы) flap; из-под полы́ on the sly.
полага́ть *impf* suppose, think. полага́ться *impf of* положи́ться; полага́ется *impers* one is supposed to; +*dat* it is due to.
по|ла́комить(ся (-млю(сь) *pf.*
полго́да (полуго́да) *m* half a year.
по́лдень (-дня *or* -лу́дня) *m* noon. полдне́вный *adj.*
по́ле (*pl* -я́, -е́й) field; ground; margin; brim. полев|о́й field; ~ы́е цветы́ wild flowers.
полежа́ть (-жу́) *pf* lie down for a while.
поле́зн|ый useful; helpful; good, wholesome; ~ая нагру́зка payload.
по|ле́зть (-зу; -ле́з) *pf.*
полемизи́ровать *impf* debate, engage in controversy. поле́мика controversy; polemics. полеми́ческий polemical.
по|лени́ться (-ню́сь, -нишься) *pf.*
поле́но (*pl* -е́нья, -ьев) log.
полёт flight. по|лете́ть (-лечу́) *pf.*
по́лзать *indet impf,* ползти́ (-зу́, -зёшь; полз, -ла́) *det impf* crawl, creep; ooze; fray. ползу́чий creeping.
поли- *in comb* poly-.
полива́ть(ся *impf of* поли́ть(ся. поли́вка watering.
полига́мия polygamy.
полигло́т polyglot.
полиграфи́ческий printing. полиграфи́я printing.
полиго́н range.
поликли́ника polyclinic.
полиме́р polymer.
полиня́лый faded. по|линя́ть *pf.*
полиомиели́т poliomyelitis.
полирова́льный polishing. полирова́ть *impf (pf* от~) polish. полиро́вка polishing; polish. полиро́вщик polisher.
полит- *abbr in comb (of* полити́ческий) political. политбюро́ *neut indecl* Politburo. ~заключённый *sb* political prisoner.
политехни́ческий polytechnic.

поли́тик politician. **поли́тика** policy; politics. **полити́ческий** political.

поли́ть (-лью́, -льёшь; по́лил, -а́, -о) pf (impf **полива́ть**) pour over; water; ~**ся** +instr pour over o.s.

полице́йский police; sb policeman. **поли́ция** police.

поли́чн|ое sb: с ~ым red-handed.

полк (-а́, loc -у́) regiment.

по́лка shelf; berth.

полко́вник colonel. **полково́дец** (-дца) commander; general. **полково́й** regimental.

пол-ли́тра half a litre.

полне́ть (-е́ю) impf (pf **по**~) put on weight.

по́лно adv that's enough! stop it!

полно- in comb full; completely. **полнолу́ние** full moon. ~**метра́жный** full-length. ~**пра́вный** enjoying full rights; competent. ~**це́нный** of full value.

полномо́чие (usu pl) authority, power. **полномо́чный** plenipotentiary.

по́лностью adv in full; completely. **полнота́** completeness; corpulence.

по́лночь (-л(у́)ночи) midnight.

по́лный (-лон, -лна́, по́лно) full; complete; plump.

полови́к (-а́) mat, matting.

полови́на half; два с полови́ной two and a half; ~ **шесто́го** half-past five. **полови́нка** half.

полови́ца floor-board.

полово́дье high water.

полово́й[1] floor.

полово́й[2] sexual.

поло́гий gently sloping.

положе́ние position; situation; status; regulations; thesis; provisions. **поло́женный** agreed; determined. **поло́жим** let us assume; suppose. **положи́тельный** positive. **положи́ть** (-жу́, -жишь) pf (impf **класть**) put; lay (down); ~**ся** (impf **полага́ться**) rely.

по́лоз (pl -о́зья, -ьев) runner.

по|лома́ть(ся pf. **поло́мка** breakage.

полоса́ (acc по́лосу, pl по́лосы, -по́с, -а́м) stripe; strip; band; region; belt; period. **полоса́тый** striped.

полоска́ть (-ощу́, -о́щешь) impf (pf

вы~, от~, про~) rinse; ~ **го́рло** gargle; ~**ся** paddle; flap.

по́лость[1] (gen pl -е́й) cavity.

по́лость[2] (gen pl -е́й) travelling rug.

полоте́нце (gen pl -нец) towel.

полотёр floor-polisher.

полотни́ще width; panel. **полотно́** (pl -а, -тен) linen; canvas. **полотня́ный** linen.

поло́ть (-лю́, -лешь) impf (pf вы~) weed.

полощу́ etc.: see **полоска́ть**

полти́нник fifty copecks.

полтора́ (-у́тора) m & neut, **полторы́** (-у́тора) f one and a half. **полтора́ста** (полу́т-) a hundred and fifty.

полу-[1] see **пол-**

полу-[2] in comb half-, semi-, demi-. **полуботи́нок** (-нка; gen pl -нок) shoe. ~**го́дие** half a year. ~**годи́чный** six months', lasting six months. ~**годова́лый** six-month-old. ~**годово́й** half-yearly, six-monthly. ~**гра́мотный** semi-literate. ~**защи́тник** half-back. ~**круг** semicircle. ~**кру́глый** semicircular. ~**ме́сяц** crescent (moon). ~**мра́к** semi-darkness. ~**но́чный** midnight. ~**о́стров** peninsula. ~**откры́тый** ajar. ~**проводни́к** semi-conductor, transistor. ~**ста́нок** (-нка) halt. ~**тьма́** semi-darkness. ~**фабрика́т** semi-finished product, convenience food. ~**фина́л** semi-final. ~**часово́й** half-hourly. ~**ша́рие** hemisphere. ~**шу́бок** (-бка) sheepskin coat.

полу́денный midday.

получа́тель m recipient. **получа́ть** impf, **получи́ть** (-чу́, -чишь) pf get, receive, obtain; ~**ся** come, turn up; turn out; из э́того ничего́ не получи́лось nothing came of it. **получе́ние** receipt. **полу́чка** receipt; pay(-packet).

полу́чше adv a little better.

полчаса́ (получа́са) m half an hour.

по́лчище horde.

по́лый hollow; flood.

по|лысе́ть (-е́ю) pf.

по́льза use; benefit, profit; в по́льзу+gen in favour of, on behalf of. **по́льзование** use. **по́льзоваться** impf (pf вос~) +instr make use of, utilize; profit by; enjoy.

по́лька Pole; polka. по́льский Polish; sb polonaise.

по|льсти́ть(ся (-льщу́(сь) pf. польщу́ etc. see польти́ть

По́льша Poland.

полюби́ть (-блю́, -бишь) pf come to like; fall in love with.

по|любова́ться (-бу́юсь) pf.

полюбо́вный amicable.

по|любопы́тствовать pf.

по́люс pole.

поля́к Pole.

поля́на glade, clearing.

поляриза́ция polarization. поля́рник polar explorer. поля́рн|ый polar; ~ая звезда́ pole-star.

пом- abbr in comb (of помо́щник) assistant. ~на́ч assistant chief, assistant head.

пома́да pomade; lipstick.

пома́зание anointment. по|ма́зать(ся (-а́жу(сь) pf. помазо́к (-зка́) small brush.

помале́ньку adv gradually; gently; modestly; so-so.

пома́лкивать impf hold one's tongue.

по|мани́ть (-ню́, -нишь) pf.

пома́рка blot; pencil mark; correction.

по|ма́слить pf.

помаха́ть (-машу́, -ма́шешь) pf, пома́хивать impf +instr wave; wag.

по|ме́длить pf +c+instr delay.

поме́ньше a little smaller; a little less.

по|меня́ть(ся pf.

помере́ть (-мру́, -мрёшь; -мер, -ла́, -ло) pf (impf помира́ть) die.

по|мере́щиться (-щусь) pf. по|ме́рить pf.

помертве́лый deathly pale. по|мертве́ть (-е́ю) pf.

помести́ть (-ещу́) pf (impf помеща́ть) accommodate; place, locate; invest; ~ся lodge; find room. поме́стье (gen pl -тий, -тьям) estate.

по́месь cross(-breed), hybrid.

помёт dung; droppings; litter, brood.

поме́та, поме́тка mark, note. по|ме́тить (-е́чу) pf (impf also помеча́ть) mark; date; ~ га́лочкой tick.

поме́ха hindrance; obstacle; pl interference.

помеча́ть impf of поме́тить

поме́шанный mad; sb lunatic. поме́ша́тельство madness; craze. по|меша́ть pf. помеша́ться pf go mad.

помеща́ть impf of помести́ть. помеща́ться impf of помести́ться; be (situated); be accommodated, find room. помеще́ние premises; apartment, room, lodging; location; investment. поме́щик landowner.

помидо́р tomato.

поми́лование forgiveness. поми́ловать pf forgive.

поми́мо prep+gen apart from; besides; without the knowledge of.

помина́ть impf of помяну́ть; не ~ ли́хом remember kindly. поми́нки (-нок) pl funeral repast.

помира́ть impf of помере́ть.

по́мнить impf remember.

помога́ть impf of помо́чь.

по-мо́ему adv in my opinion.

помо́и (-ев) pl slops. помо́йка (gen pl -о́ек) rubbish dump. помо́йный slop.

помо́л grinding.

помо́лвка betrothal.

по|моли́ться (-лю́сь, -лишься) pf. по|молоде́ть (-е́ю) pf.

помолча́ть (-чу́) pf be silent for a time.

помо́рье: see по- II.

по|мо́рщиться (-щусь) pf.

помо́ст dais; rostrum.

по|мочи́ться (-чу́сь, -чишься) pf.

помо́чь (-огу́, -о́жешь; -о́г, -ла́) pf (impf помога́ть) (+dat) help. помо́щник, помо́щница assistant. по́мощь help; на ~! help!

помо́ю etc.: see помы́ть

по́мпа pump.

помутне́ние dimness, clouding.

помча́ться (-чу́сь) pf rush; dart off.

помыка́ть impf +instr order about.

по́мысел (-сла) intention; thought.

по|мы́ть(ся (-мо́ю(сь) pf.

помяну́ть (-ну́, -нешь) pf (impf помина́ть) mention; pray for.

помя́тый crumpled. по|мя́ться (-мнётся) pf.

по|наде́яться (-е́юсь) pf count, rely.

пона́добиться (-блюсь) pf be or become necessary; е́сли пона́добится if necessary.

понапра́сну *adv* in vain.

понаслы́шке *adv* by hearsay.

по-настоя́щему *adv* properly, truly.

поначалу *adv* at first.

понево́ле *adv* willynilly; against one's will.

понеде́льник Monday.

понемно́гу, понемно́жку *adv* little by little.

по|нести́(сь (-су́(сь, -сёшь(ся; -нёс(ся, -ла́(сь) *pf*.

понижа́ть *impf*, пони́зить (-и́жу) *pf* lower; reduce; ~ся fall, drop, go down. пониже́ние fall; lowering; reduction.

поника́ть *impf*, по|ни́кнуть (-ну; -ник) *pf* droop, wilt.

понима́ние understanding. понима́ть *impf of* поня́ть

по-но́вому *adv* in a new fashion.

поно́с diarrhoea.

поноси́ть[1] (-ошу́, -о́сишь) *pf* carry; wear.

поноси́ть[2] (-ошу́, -о́сишь) *impf* abuse (*verbally*).

поно́шенный worn; threadbare.

по|нра́виться (-влюсь) *pf*.

понто́н pontoon.

пону́дить (-у́жу) *pf*, понужда́ть *impf* compel.

понука́ть *impf* urge on.

пону́рить *pf*: ~ го́лову hang one's head. пону́рый downcast.

по|ню́хать *pf*. поню́шка: ~ табаку́ pinch of snuff.

поня́тие concept; notion, idea. поня́тливый bright, quick. поня́тный understandable, comprehensible; clear; ~о naturally; ~о? (do you) see? поня́ть (пойму́, -мёшь; по́нял, -а́, -о) *pf* (*impf* понима́ть) understand; realize.

по|обе́дать *pf*. по|обеща́ть *pf*.

поо́даль *adv* at some distance.

поодино́чке *adv* one by one.

поочерёдно *adv* in turn.

поощре́ние encouragement. поощри́ть *pf*, поощря́ть *impf* encourage.

поп (-а́) priest.

попада́ние hit. попада́ть(ся *impf of* попа́сть(ся

попадья́ priest's wife.

попа́ло: *see* попа́сть. по|па́риться *pf*.

попа́рно *adv* in pairs, two by two.

попа́сть (-аду́, -адёшь; -а́л) *pf* (*impf* попада́ть) в+*acc* hit; get (in)to, find o.s. in; +на+*acc* hit upon, come on; не туда́ ~ get the wrong number; ~ся be caught; find o.s.; turn up; meet. попадётся anything. попа́ло *with prons & advs*: где ~ anywhere; как ~ anyhow; что ~ the first thing to hand.

попере́к *adv & prep*+*gen* across.

попереме́нно *adv* in turns.

попере́чник diameter. попере́чный transverse, diametrical, cross; ~ый разре́з, ~ое сече́ние cross-section.

поперхну́ться (-ну́сь, -нёшься) *pf* choke.

по|пе́рчить (-чу) *pf*.

попече́ние care; charge; на попече́нии+*gen* in the care of. попечи́тель *m* guardian, trustee.

попира́ть *impf* (*pf* попра́ть) trample on; flout.

попи́ть (-пью́, -пьёшь; по́пил, -ла, по́пило) *pf* have a drink.

поплаво́к (-вка́) float.

попла́кать (-а́чу) *pf* cry a little.

по|плати́ться (-чу́сь, -тишься) *pf*.

поплы́ть (-ыву́, -ывёшь; -ы́л, -ыла́, -о) *pf* start swimming.

попо́йка drinking-bout.

попола́м *adv* in two, in half; half-and-half.

поползнове́ние half a mind; pretension(s).

пополне́ние replenishment; reinforcement. по|полне́ть (-е́ю) *pf*. попо́лнить (-ню), пополня́ть *impf* replenish; re-stock; reinforce.

пополу́дни *adv* in the afternoon; p.m.

попо́на horse-cloth.

по|по́тчевать (-чую) *pf*.

поправи́мый rectifiable. попра́вить (-влю) *pf*, поправля́ть *impf* repair; correct, put right; set straight; ~ся correct o.s.; get better, recover; improve. попра́вка correction; repair; adjustment; recovery.

попра́ть *pf of* попира́ть

по-пре́жнему *adv* as before.

попрёк reproach. попрека́ть *impf*, попрекну́ть (-ну́, -нёшь) *pf* reproach.

по́прище field; walk of life.

по|про́бовать *pf*. по|проси́ть(ся

(-ошу́(сь, -о́сишь(ся) pf.

по́просту adv simply; without ceremony.

попроша́йка m & f cadger. попроша́йничать impf cadge.

попроща́ться pf (+c+instr) say goodbye (to).

попры́гать pf jump, hop.

попуга́й parrot.

популя́рность popularity. популя́рный popular.

попусти́тельство connivance.

по-пусто́му, по́пусту adv in vain.

попу́тно adv at the same time; in passing. попу́тный passing. попу́тчик fellow-traveller.

попыта́ться pf. попы́тка attempt. попя́титься (-я́чусь) pf. попя́тный backward; идти́ на ~ go back on one's word.

по́ра¹ pore.

пора́² (acc -у; pl -ы, пор, -а́м) time; it is time; до каки́х пор? till when?; до сих пор till now; с каки́х пор? since when?

порабо́тать pf do some work. поработи́ть (-ощу́) pf, порабоща́ть impf enslave. порабоще́ние enslavement.

поравня́ться pf come alongside.

по|ра́довать(ся pf.

поража́ть impf, по|рази́ть (-ажу́) pf hit; strike; defeat; affect; astonish; ~ся be astounded. пораже́ние defeat. порази́тельный striking; astonishing.

по-ра́зному adv differently.

пора́нить pf wound; injure.

порва́ть (-ву́, -вёшь; -ва́л, -а́, -о) pf (impf порыва́ть) tear (up); break, break off; ~ся tear; break (off).

по|реде́ть (-е́ет) pf.

поре́з cut. поре́зать (-е́жу) pf cut; ~ся cut o.s.

поре́й leek.

по|рекомендова́ть pf. по|ржа́веть (-еет) pf.

по́ристый porous.

порица́ние censure; blame. порица́ть impf blame; censure.

по́рка flogging.

по́ровну adv equally.

поро́г threshold; rapids.

поро́да breed, race, species. поро́дистый thoroughbred. породи́ть

(-ожу́) pf (impf порожда́ть) give birth to; give rise to.

по|родни́ть(ся pf. поро́дный pedigree.

порожда́ть impf of породи́ть

поро́жний empty.

по́рознь adv separately, apart.

поро́й, поро́ю adv at times.

поро́к vice; defect.

поросёнок (-нка; pl -ся́та, -ся́т) piglet.

по́росль shoots; young wood.

поро́ть¹ (-рю́, -решь) impf (pf вы́~) thrash; whip.

поро́ть² (-рю́, -решь) impf (pf рас~) undo, unpick; ~ся come unstitched.

по́рох (pl ~а́) gunpowder, powder. порохово́й powder.

поро́чить (-чу) impf (pf о~) discredit; smear. поро́чный vicious, depraved; faulty.

пороши́ть (-ши́т) impf snow slightly.

порошо́к (-шка́) powder.

порт (loc -у́; pl -ы, -о́в) port.

портати́вный portable.

портве́йн port (wine).

по́ртик portico.

по́ртить (-чу) impf (pf ис~) spoil; corrupt; ~ся deteriorate; go bad.

портни́ха dressmaker. портно́вский tailor's. портно́й sb tailor.

порто́вый port.

портре́т portrait.

портсига́р cigarette-case.

португа́лец (-льца), -лка Portuguese. Португа́лия Portugal. португа́льский Portuguese.

портфе́ль m brief-case; portfolio.

портье́ра curtain(s), portière.

портя́нка foot-binding.

поруга́ние desecration; humiliation. поруга́нный desecrated; outraged.

поруга́ть pf scold, swear at; ~ся swear; fall out.

пору́ка bail; guarantee; surety; на пору́ки on bail.

по-ру́сски adv (in) Russian.

поруча́ть impf of поручи́ть. поруче́ние assignment; errand; message.

по́ручень (-чня) m handrail.

поручи́тельство guarantee; bail.

поручи́ть (-чу́, -чишь) pf (impf поруча́ть) entrust; instruct.

поручи́ться (-чу́сь, -чишься) pf of руча́ться

порха́ть *impf*, порхну́ть (-ну́, -нёшь) *pf* flutter, flit.

по́рция portion; helping.

по́рча spoiling; damage; curse.

по́ршень (-шня) *m* piston.

поры́в[1] gust; rush; fit

поры́в[2] breaking. порыва́ть(ся[1] *impf of* порва́ть(ся

порыва́ться[2] *impf* make jerky movements; endeavour. поры́вистый gusty; jerky; impetuous; fitful.

поря́дковый ordinal. поря́док (-дка) order; sequence; manner, way; procedure; всё в поря́дке everything is alright; ~ дня agenda, order of the day. поря́дочный decent; honest; respectable; fair, considerable.

посади́ть (-ажу́, -а́дишь) *pf of* сади́ть, сажа́ть. поса́дка planting; embarkation; boarding; landing. поса́дочный planting; landing.

посажу́ *etc.*: *see* посади́ть. по|сва́тать(ся *pf.* по|свежеть (-е́ет) *pf.* по|свети́ть (-ечу́, -е́тишь) *pf.* по|светле́ть (-е́ет) *pf.* посви́стывать *impf* whistle.

по-сво́ему *adv* (in) one's own way.

посвяти́ть (-ящу́) *pf*, посвяща́ть *impf* devote; dedicate; let in; ordain. посвяще́ние dedication; initiation; ordination.

посе́в sowing; crops. посевн|о́й sowing; ~а́я пло́щадь area under crops.

по|седе́ть (-е́ю) *pf.*

поселе́нец (-нца) settler; exile. поселе́ние settlement; exile. по|сели́ть *pf*, поселя́ть *impf* settle; lodge; arouse; ~ся settle, take up residence. посёлок (-лка) settlement; housing estate.

посеребрённый (-рён, -а́) silverplated. по|серебри́ть *pf.*

посереди́не *adv* & *prep+gen* in the middle (of).

посети́тель *m* visitor. посети́ть (-ещу́) *pf* (*impf* посеща́ть) visit; attend.

по|се́товать *pf.*

посеща́емость attendance. посеща́ть *impf of* посети́ть. посеще́ние visit.

по|се́ять (-е́ю) *pf.*

посиде́ть (-ижу́) *pf* sit (for a while).

поси́льный within one's powers; feasible.

посине́лый gone blue. по|сине́ть (-е́ю) *pf.*

по|скака́ть (-ачу́, -а́чешь) *pf.*

поскользну́ться (-ну́сь, -нёшься) *pf* slip.

поско́льку *conj* as far as, (in) so far as.

по|скро́мничать *pf.* по|скупи́ться (-плю́сь) *pf.*

посла́нец (-нца) messenger, envoy. посла́ние message; epistle. посла́нник envoy, minister. посла́ть (-шлю́, -шлёшь) *pf* (*impf* посыла́ть) send.

по́сле *adv* & *prep+gen* after; afterwards.

после- *in comb* post-; after-. послевое́нный post-war. ~за́втра *adv* the day after tomorrow. ~родово́й post-natal. ~сло́вие epilogue; concluding remarks.

после́дний last; recent; latest; latter. после́дователь *m* follower. после́довательность sequence; consistency. после́довательный consecutive; consistent. по|сле́довать *pf.* после́дствие consequence. после́дующий subsequent; consequent.

посло́вица proverb, saying.

по|служи́ть (-жу́, -жишь) *pf.* послужно́й service.

послуша́ние obedience. по|слу́шать(ся *pf.* послу́шный obedient.

по|слы́шаться (-шится) *pf.*

посма́тривать *impf* look from time to time.

посме́иваться *impf* chuckle.

посме́ртный posthumous.

по|сме́ть (-е́ю) *pf.*

посме́яние ridicule. посмея́ться (-ею́сь, -еёшься) *pf* laugh; +над+*instr* laugh at.

по|смотре́ть(ся (-рю́(сь, -ришь(ся) *pf.*

посо́бие aid; allowance; benefit; textbook. посо́бник accomplice.

по|сове́товать(ся *pf.* по|соде́йствовать *pf.*

посо́л (-сла́) ambassador.

по|соли́ть (-олю́, -о́лишь) *pf.*

посо́льство embassy.

поспа́ть (-плю́; -а́л, -а́, -о) *pf* sleep; have a nap.

поспева́ть[1] *impf*, по|спе́ть[1] (-е́ет) *pf* ripen.

поспева́ть[2] *impf*, поспе́ть[2] (-е́ю) *pf*

have time; be in time (к+*dat*, на+*acc* for); +за+*instr* keep up with.

по|спеши́ть (-шу́) *pf*. поспе́шный hasty, hurried.

по|спо́рить *pf*. по|спосо́бствовать *pf*.

посрами́ть (-млю́) *pf*, посрамля́ть *impf* disgrace.

посреди́, посреди́не *adv & prep*+*gen* in the middle (of). посре́дник mediator. посре́дничество mediation. посре́дственный mediocre. по-сре́дством *prep*+*gen* by means of.

по|ссо́рить(ся *pf*.

пост[1] (-á, *loc* -ý) post.

пост[2] (-á, *loc* -ý) fast(ing).

по|ста́вить[1] (-влю) *pf*.

по|ста́вить[2] (-влю) *pf*, поставля́ть *impf* supply. поста́вка delivery. поставщи́к (-á) supplier.

постаме́нт pedestal.

постанови́ть (-влю́, -вишь) *pf* (*impf* постановля́ть) decree; decide. постано́вка production; arrangement; putting, placing.

постановле́ние decree; decision. постановля́ть *impf of* постанови́ть

постано́вщик producer; (film) director.

по|стара́ться *pf*.

по|старе́ть (-е́ю) *pf*. по-ста́рому *adv* as before.

посте́ль bed. постелю́ *etc.*: see по-стла́ть

постепе́нный gradual.

по|стесня́ться *pf*.

постига́ть *impf of* пости́чь. пости́г-нуть: see пости́чь. постиже́ние comprehension, grasp. постижи́-мый comprehensible.

постила́ть *impf of* постла́ть

постира́ть *pf* do some washing.

пости́ться (-щу́сь) *impf* fast.

пости́чь, пости́гнуть (-и́гну, -и́г(нул)) *pf* (*impf* постига́ть) comprehend, grasp; befall.

по|стла́ть (-стелю́, -сте́лешь) *pf* (*impf also* постила́ть) spread; make (bed).

по́стн|ый lenten; lean; glum; ~ое ма́сло vegetable oil.

постово́й on point duty.

посто́й billeting.

постольку: ~, поско́льку *conj* to

that extent, insofar as.

по|сторони́ться (-ню́сь, -ни́шься) *pf*.

посторо́нний strange; foreign; extraneous, outside; *sb* stranger, outsider.

постоя́нный permanent; constant; continual; ~ый ток direct current. постоя́нство constancy.

по|стоя́ть (-ою́) *pf* stand (for a while); +за+*acc* stand up for.

пострада́вший *sb* victim. по|страда́ть *pf*.

пострига́ться *impf*, постри́чься (-игу́сь, -ижёшься, -игся) *pf* take monastic vows; get one's hair cut.

построе́ние construction; building; formation. по|стро́ить(ся (-ро́ю(сь) *pf*. постро́йка building.

постскри́птум postscript.

постули́ровать *impf & pf* postulate.

поступа́тельный forward. поступа́ть *impf*, поступи́ть (-плю́, -пишь) *pf* act; do; be received; +в *or* на+*acc* enter, join; +с+*instr* treat; ~ся +*instr* waive, forgo. поступле́ние entering, joining; receipt. посту́пок (-пка) act, deed. по́ступь gait; step.

по|стуча́ть(ся (-чу́(сь) *pf*.

по|стыди́ться (-ыжу́сь) *pf*. посты́д-ный shameful.

посу́да crockery; dishes. посу́дный china; dish.

по|сули́ть *pf*.

посчастли́виться *pf impers* (+*dat*) be lucky; ей посчастли́вилось +*inf* she had the luck to.

посчита́ть *pf* count (up). по|счита́ться *pf*.

посыла́ть *impf of* посла́ть. по-сы́лка sending; parcel; errand; premise. посы́льный *sb* messenger.

посыпа́ть (-плю, -плешь) *pf*, по-сыпа́ть *impf* strew. посыпа́ться (-плется) *pf* begin to fall; rain down.

посяга́тельство encroachment; infringement. посяга́ть *impf*, посягну́ть (-ну́, -нёшь) *pf* encroach, infringe.

пот (*loc* -ý; *pl* -ы́) sweat.

потайно́й secret.

потака́ть *impf* +*dat* indulge.

потасо́вка brawl.

пота́ш (-á) potash.

по-тво́ему *adv* in your opinion.

потво́рствовать *impf* (+*dat*) be indulgent (towards), pander (to).

потёк damp patch.

потёмки (-мок) *pl* darkness. **по|темнеть** (-еет) *pf*.

потенциа́л potential. **потенциа́льный** potential.

по|тепле́ть (-е́ет) *pf*.

потерпе́вший *sb* victim. **по|терпе́ть** (-плю́, -пишь) *pf*.

потеря loss; waste; *pl* casualties. **по|теря́ть(ся** *pf*.

по|тесни́ть *pf*. **по|тесни́ться** *pf* sit closer, squeeze up.

поте́ть (-е́ю) *impf* (*pf* вс~, за~) sweat; mist over.

поте́ха fun. **по|те́шить(ся** (-шу(сь) *pf*. **поте́шный** amusing.

поте́чь (-чёт, -тёк, -ла́) *pf* begin to flow.

потира́ть *impf* rub.

потихо́ньку *adv* softly; secretly; slowly.

по́тный (-тен, -тна́, -тно) sweaty.

пото́к stream; torrent; flood.

потоло́к (-лка́) ceiling.

по|толсте́ть (-е́ю) *pf*.

пото́м *adv* later (on); then. **пото́мок** (-мка) descendant. **пото́мство** posterity.

потому́ *adv* that is why; ~ что *conj* because.

по|тону́ть (-ну́, -нешь) *pf*. **пото́п** flood, deluge. **по|топи́ть** (-плю́, -пишь) *pf*, **потопля́ть** *impf* sink.

по|топта́ть (-пчу́, -пчешь) *pf*. **по|торопи́ть(ся** (-плю́(сь, -пишь(ся) *pf*.

пото́чный continuous; production-line.

по|тра́тить (-а́чу) *pf*.

потреби́тель *m* consumer, user. **потреби́тельский** consumer; consumers'. **потреби́ть** (-блю́) *pf*, **потребля́ть** *impf* consume. **потребле́ние** consumption. **потре́бность** need, requirement. **по|тре́бовать(ся** *pf*.

по|трево́жить(ся (-жу(сь) *pf*.

потрёпанный shabby; tattered. **по|трепа́ть(ся** (-плю́(сь, -плешь(ся) *pf*.

по|тре́скаться *pf*. **потре́скивать** *impf* crackle.

потро́гать *pf* touch, feel, finger.

потроха́ (-о́в) *pl* giblets. **потроши́ть** (-шу́) *impf* (*pf* вы́~) disembowel, clean.

потруди́ться (-ужу́сь, -у́дишься) *pf* do some work; take the trouble.

потряса́ть *impf*, **потрясти́** (-су́, -сёшь; -я́с, -ла́) *pf* shake; rock; stagger; +*acc or instr* brandish, shake. **потряса́ющий** staggering, tremendous. **потрясе́ние** shock.

поту́ги *f pl* vain attempts; **родовы́е** ~ labour.

по|тупи́ть (-плю́) *pf*, **потупля́ть** *impf* lower; ~ся look down.

по|тускне́ть (-е́ет) *pf*.

потусторо́нний мир the next world.

потуха́ть *impf*, **по|ту́хнуть** (-нет, -ух) *pf* go out; die out. **поту́хший** extinct; lifeless.

по|туши́ть (-шу́, -шишь) *pf*.

по́тчевать (-чую) *impf* (*pf* по~) +*instr* treat to.

потя́гиваться *impf*, **по|тяну́ться** (-ну́сь, -нешься) *pf* stretch o.s. **по|тяну́ть** (-ну́, -нешь) *pf*.

по|у́жинать *pf*. **по|уме́ть** (-е́ю) *pf*.

поуча́ть *impf* preach at.

поучи́тельный instructive.

поха́бный obscene.

похвала́ praise. **по|хвали́ть(ся** (-лю́(сь, -лишь(ся) *pf*. **похва́льный** laudable; laudatory.

по|хва́стать(ся *pf*.

похити́тель *m* kidnapper; abductor; thief. **похи́тить** (-и́щу) *pf*, **похища́ть** *impf* kidnap; abduct; steal. **похище́ние** theft; kidnapping; abduction.

похлёбка broth, soup.

по|хло́пать *pf* slap; clap.

по|хлопота́ть (-очу́, -о́чешь) *pf*.

похме́лье hangover.

похо́д campaign; march; hike; excursion.

по|хода́тайствовать *pf*.

походи́ть (-ожу́, -о́дишь) *impf* на+*acc* resemble.

похо́дка gait, walk. **похо́дный** mobile; field; marching. **похожде́ние** adventure.

похо́жий alike; ~ на like.

похолода́ние drop in temperature. **по|холоде́ть** (-ню, -нишь) *pf*. **похоро́нный** funeral. **по́хороны** (-ро́н) *pl* funeral.

по|хороше́ть (-е́ю) *pf*.

по́хоть lust.

по|худе́ть (-е́ю) *pf*.

по|целова́ть(ся pf. поцелу́й kiss.

поча́ток (-тка) ear; (corn) cob.

по́чва soil; ground; basis. по́чвенный soil; ~ покро́в top-soil.

почём adv how much; how; ~ знать? who can tell?; ~ я зна́ю? how should I know?

почему́ adv why. почему́-либо, -нибудь advs for some reason or other. почему́-то adv for some reason.

по́черк hand(writing).

почерне́лый blackened, darkened. по|черне́ть (-е́ю) pf.

почерпну́ть (-ну́, -нёшь) pf draw, scoop up; glean.

по|черстве́ть (-е́ю) pf. по|чеса́ть(ся (-ешу́(сь, -е́шешь(ся pf.

поче́сть honour. почёт honour; respect. почётный of honour; honourable; honorary.

по́чечный renal; kidney.

почива́ть impf of почи́ть

почи́н initiative.

по|чини́ть (-ню́, -нишь) pf, починя́ть impf repair, mend. почи́нка repair.

по|чи́стить(ся (-и́щу(сь) pf.

почита́ть[1] impf honour; revere.

почита́ть[2] pf read for a while.

почи́ть (-и́ю, -и́ешь) pf (impf почива́ть) rest; pass away; ~ на ла́врах rest on one's laurels.

по́чка[1] bud.

по́чка[2] kidney.

по́чта post, mail; post-office. почтальо́н postman. почта́мт (main) post-office.

почте́ние respect. почте́нный venerable; considerable.

почти́ adv almost.

почти́тельный respectful. почти́ть (-чту́) pf honour.

почто́в|ый postal; ~ая ка́рточка postcard; ~ый перево́д postal order; ~ый я́щик letter-box.

по|чу́вствовать pf.

по|чу́диться (-ишься) pf.

пошатну́ть (-ну́, -нёшь) pf shake; ~ся shake; stagger.

по|шевели́ть(ся (-елю́(сь, -е́лишь(ся) pf. пошёл etc.: see пойти́

поши́вочный sewing.

по́шлина duty.

по́шлость vulgarity; banality. по́шлый vulgar; banal.

пошту́чный by the piece.

по|шути́ть (-учу́, -у́тишь) pf.

поща́да mercy. по|щади́ть (-ажу́) pf.

по|щекота́ть (-очу́, -о́чешь) pf.

пощёчина slap in the face.

по|щу́пать pf.

поэ́зия poetry. поэ́ма poem. поэ́т poet. поэти́ческий poetic.

поэ́тому adv therefore.

пою́ etc.: see петь, пои́ть

появи́ться (-влю́сь, -вишься) pf, появля́ться impf appear. появле́ние appearance.

по́яс (pl -а́) belt; girdle; waist-band; waist; zone.

поясне́ние explanation. поясни́тельный explanatory. поясни́ть pf (impf поясня́ть) explain, elucidate.

поясни́ца small of the back. поясно́й waist; to the waist; zonal.

поясня́ть impf of поясни́ть

пра- pref first; great-. праба́бушка great-grandmother.

пра́вда (the) truth. правди́вый true; truthful. правдоподо́бный likely; plausible. пра́ведный righteous; just.

пра́вило rule; principle.

пра́вильн|ый right, correct; regular; ~о! that's right!

прави́тель m ruler. прави́тельственный government(al). прави́тельство government. пра́вить[1] (-влю) +instr rule, govern; drive.

пра́вить[2] (-влю) impf correct. пра́вка correcting.

правле́ние board; administration; government.

пра́в|внук, ~внучка great-grandson, -granddaughter.

пра́во[1] (pl -а́) law; right; (води́тельские) права́ driving licence; в права́х+gen in the capacity of, as.

пра́во[2] adv really.

пра́во-[1] in comb law; right. правове́рный orthodox. ~ме́рный lawful, rightful. ~мо́чный competent. ~наруше́ние infringement of the law, offence. ~наруши́тель m offender, delinquent. ~писа́ние spelling, orthography. ~сла́вный orthodox; sb member of the Orthodox Church. ~суди́е justice.

пра́во-[2] in comb right, right-hand. правосторо́нний right; right-hand.

правово́й legal.

правота́ rightness; innocence.

пра́вый[1] right; right-hand; right-wing.

пра́вый[2] (прав, -а́, -о) right, correct; just.

пра́вящий ruling.

пра́дед great-grandfather; pl ancestors. праде́душка m great-grand-father.

пра́здник (public) holiday. пра́здничный festive. пра́зднование celebration. пра́здновать impf (pf от~) celebrate. пра́здность idleness. пра́здный idle; useless.

пра́ктика practice; practical work. практикова́ть impf practise; ~ся (pf на~ся) be practised; +в+prep practise. практи́ческий, практи́чный practical.

пра́отец (-тца) forefather.

пра́порщик ensign.

прапра́дед great-great-grandfather. прароди́тель m forefather.

прах dust; remains.

пра́чечная sb laundry. пра́чка laundress.

пребыва́ние stay. пребыва́ть impf be; reside.

превзойти́ (-йду́, -йдёшь; -ошёл, -шла́) pf (impf превосходи́ть) surpass; excel.

превозмога́ть impf, превозмо́чь (-огу́, -о́жешь; -о́г, -ла́) pf overcome.

превознести́ (-су́, -сёшь; -ёс, -ла́) pf, превозноси́ть (-ошу́, -о́сишь) impf extol, praise.

превосходи́тельство Excellency. превосходи́ть (-ожу́, -о́дишь) impf of превзойти́. превосхо́дный superlative; superb, excellent. превосхо́дство superiority. превосходя́щий superior.

преврати́ть (-ащу́) pf, превраща́ть impf convert, turn, reduce; ~ся turn, change. превра́тный wrong; changeful. превраще́ние transformation.

превы́сить (-ы́шу) pf, превыша́ть impf exceed. превыше́ние exceeding, excess.

прегра́да obstacle; barrier. прегради́ть (-ажу́) pf, прегражда́ть impf bar, block.

пред prep+instr: see пе́ред

предава́ть(ся (-даю́(сь, -даёшь(ся

impf of преда́ть(ся

преда́ние legend; tradition; handing over, committal. пре́данность devotion. пре́данный devoted. преда́тель m, ~ница betrayer, traitor. преда́тельский treacherous. преда́тельство treachery. преда́ть (-а́м, -а́шь, -а́ст, -ади́м; про́дал, -а́, -о) pf (impf предава́ть) hand over, commit; betray; ~ся abandon o.s.; give way, indulge.

предаю́ etc.: see предава́ть

предвари́тельный preliminary; prior. предвари́ть pf, предваря́ть impf forestall, anticipate.

предве́стник forerunner; harbinger. предвеща́ть impf portend; augur.

предвзя́тый preconceived; biased.

предви́деть (-и́жу) impf foresee.

предвкуси́ть (-ушу́, -у́сишь) pf, предвкуша́ть impf look forward to.

предводи́тель m leader. предводи́тельствовать impf +instr lead.

предвое́нный pre-war.

предвосхи́тить (-и́щу) pf, предвосхища́ть impf anticipate.

предвы́борный (pre-)election.

предго́рье foothills.

преддве́рие threshold.

преде́л limit; bound. преде́льный boundary; maximum; utmost.

предзнаменова́ние omen, augury.

предисло́вие preface.

предлага́ть impf of предложи́ть. предло́г[1] pretext.

предло́г[2] preposition.

предложе́ние[1] sentence; clause.

предложе́ние[2] offer; proposition; proposal; motion; suggestion; supply. предложи́ть (-жу́, -жишь) pf (impf предлага́ть) offer; propose; suggest; order.

предло́жный prepositional.

предме́стье suburb.

предме́т object; subject.

предназнача́ть impf, предназна́чить (-чу) pf destine, intend; earmark.

преднаме́ренный premeditated.

пре́до: see пе́ред

пре́док (-дка) ancestor.

предопределе́ние predetermination. предопредели́ть pf, предопределя́ть impf predetermine, predestine.

предоста́вить (-влю) *pf*, предоставля́ть *impf* grant; leave; give.

предостерега́ть *impf*, предостере́чь (-егу́, -ежёшь; -ёг, -ла́) *pf* warn. предостереже́ние warning. предосторо́жность precaution.

предосуди́тельный reprehensible.

предотврати́ть (-ащу́) *pf*, предотвраща́ть *impf* avert, prevent.

предохране́ние protection; preservation. предохрани́тель *m* guard; safety device, safety-catch; fuse. предохрани́тельный preservative; preventive; safety. предохрани́ть *pf*, предохраня́ть *impf* preserve, protect.

предписа́ние order; *pl* directions, instructions. предписа́ть (-ишу́, -и́шешь) *pf*, предпи́сывать *impf* order, direct; prescribe.

предпле́чье forearm.

предполага́емый supposed. предполага́ется *impers* it is proposed. предполага́ть *impf*, предположи́ть (-жу́, -о́жишь) *pf* suppose, assume. предположе́ние supposition, assumption. предположи́тельный conjectural; hypothetical.

предпосле́дний penultimate, last-but-one.

предпосы́лка precondition; premise.

предпоче́сть (-чту́, -чтёшь; -чёл, -чла́) *pf*, предпочита́ть *impf* prefer. предпочте́ние preference. предпочти́тельный preferable.

предприи́мчивый enterprising.

предпринима́тель *m* owner; entrepreneur; employer. предпринима́тельство: свобо́дное ~ free enterprise. предпринима́ть *impf*, предприня́ть (-иму́, -и́мешь; -и́нял, -á, -о) *pf* undertake. предприя́тие undertaking, enterprise.

предрасположе́ние predisposition.

предрассу́док (-дка) prejudice.

предрека́ть *impf*, предре́чь (-еку́, -ечёшь; -рёк, -ла́) *pf* foretell.

предреша́ть *impf*, предреши́ть (-шу́) *pf* decide beforehand; predetermine.

председа́тель *m* chairman.

предсказа́ние prediction. предсказа́ть (-ажу́, -а́жешь) *pf*, предска́зывать *impf* predict, prophesy.

предсме́ртный dying.

представа́ть (-таю́, -таёшь) *impf of* предста́ть

представи́тель *m* representative. представи́тельный representative; imposing. представи́тельство representation.

предста́вить (-влю) *pf*, представля́ть *impf* present; submit; introduce; represent; ~ себе́ imagine; ~ся present itself, occur; seem; introduce o.s.; +*instr* pretend to be. представле́ние presentation; performance; idea, notion.

предста́ть (-а́ну) *pf* (*impf* представа́ть) appear.

предстоя́ть (-ои́т) *impf* be in prospect, lie ahead. предстоя́щий forthcoming; imminent.

предте́ча *m & f* forerunner, precursor.

предубежде́ние prejudice.

предуга́дать *pf*, предуга́дывать *impf* guess; foresee.

предупреди́тельный preventive; warning; courteous, obliging. предупреди́ть (-ежу́) *pf*, предупрежда́ть *impf* warn; give notice; prevent; anticipate. предупрежде́ние notice; warning; prevention.

предусма́тривать *impf*, предусмотре́ть (-рю́, -ришь) *pf* envisage, foresee; provide for. предусмотри́тельный prudent; far-sighted.

предчу́вствие presentiment; foreboding. предчу́вствовать *impf* have a presentiment (about).

предше́ственник predecessor. предше́ствовать *impf* +*dat* precede.

предъяви́тель *m* bearer. предъяви́ть (-влю́, -вишь) *pf*, предъявля́ть *impf* show, produce; bring (*lawsuit*); ~ пра́во на+*acc* lay claim to.

предыду́щий previous.

прее́мник successor. прее́мственность succession; continuity.

пре́жде *adv* first; formerly; *prep*+*gen* before; ~ всего́ first of all; first and foremost; ~ чем *conj* before. преждевре́менный premature. пре́жний previous, former.

презерва́тив condom.

президе́нт president. президе́нтский presidential. прези́диум presidium.

презира́ть *impf* despise. презре́ние contempt. презре́нный contemptible. презри́тельный scornful.

преиму́щественно *adv* mainly, chiefly, principally. преиму́щественный main, primary; preferential. преиму́щество advantage; preference; по преиму́ществу for the most part.

преиспо́дняя *sb* the underworld.

прейскура́нт price list, catalogue.

преклоне́ние admiration. преклони́ть *pf*, преклоня́ть *impf* bow, bend; ~ся bow down; +*dat* or перед+*instr* admire, worship. прекло́нный: ~ во́зраст old age.

прекра́сный beautiful; fine; excellent.

прекрати́ть (-ащу́) *pf*, прекраща́ть *impf* stop, discontinue; ~ся cease, end. прекраще́ние halt; cessation.

преле́стный delightful. пре́лесть charm, delight.

преломи́ть (-млю́, -мишь) *pf*, преломля́ть *impf* refract. преломле́ние refraction.

прельсти́ть (-льщу́) *pf*, прельща́ть *impf* entice; ~ся be attracted; fall (+*instr* for).

прелюбодея́ние adultery.

прелю́дия prelude.

премину́ть (-ну) *pf with neg* not fail.

премирова́ть *impf* & *pf* award a prize to; give a bonus. пре́мия prize; bonus; premium.

премье́р prime minister; lead(ing actor). премье́ра première. премье́р-мини́стр prime minister. премье́рша leading lady.

пренебрега́ть *impf*, пренебре́чь (-егу́, -ежёшь; -ёг, -ла́) *pf* +*instr* scorn; neglect. пренебреже́ние scorn; neglect. пренебрежи́тельный scornful.

пре́ния (-ий) *pl* debate.

преоблада́ние predominance. преоблада́ть *impf* predominate; prevail.

преобража́ть *impf*, преобрази́ть (-ажу́) *pf* transform. преображе́ние transformation; Transfiguration. преобразова́ние transformation; reform. преобразова́ть *pf*, преобразо́вывать *impf* transform; reform, reorganize.

преодолева́ть *impf*, преодоле́ть (-е́ю) *pf* overcome.

препара́т preparation.

препина́ние: зна́ки препина́ния punctuation marks.

препира́тельство altercation, wrangling.

преподава́ние teaching. преподава́тель *m*, ~ница teacher. преподава́тельский teaching. преподава́ть (-даю́, -даёшь) *impf* teach.

преподнести́ (-су́, -сёшь; -ёс, -ла́) *pf*, преподноси́ть (-ошу́, -о́сишь) *pf* present, give.

препроводи́ть (-вожу́, -во́дишь) *pf*, препровожда́ть *impf* send, forward.

препя́тствие obstacle; hurdle. препя́тствовать *impf* (*pf* вос~) +*dat* hinder.

прерва́ть (-ву́, -вёшь; -а́л, -а́, -о) *pf* (*impf* прерыва́ть) interrupt; break off; ~ся be interrupted; break.

пререка́ние argument. пререка́ться *impf* argue.

прерыва́ть(ся *impf of* прерва́ть(ся

пресека́ть *impf*, пресе́чь (-еку́, -ечёшь; -ёк, -екла́) *pf* stop; put an end to; ~ся stop; break.

пресле́дование pursuit; persecution; prosecution. пресле́довать *impf* pursue; haunt; persecute; prosecute.

пресло́вутый notorious.

пресмыка́ться *impf* grovel. пресмыка́ющееся *sb* reptile.

пресново́дный freshwater. пре́сный fresh; unleavened; insipid; bland.

пресс press. пре́сса the press. пресс-конфере́нция press-conference.

престаре́лый aged.

прести́ж prestige.

престо́л throne.

преступле́ние crime. престу́пник criminal. престу́пность criminality; crime, delinquency. престу́пный criminal.

пресы́титься (-ы́щусь) *pf*, пресыща́ться *impf* be satiated. пресыще́ние surfeit, satiety.

претвори́ть *pf*, претворя́ть *impf* (в+*acc*) turn, change, convert; ~ в жизнь realize, carry out.

претенде́нт claimant; candidate; pretender. претендова́ть *impf* на+*acc* lay claim to; have pretensions to. прете́нзия claim; pretension; быть в прете́нзии на+*acc* have a grudge, a grievance, against.

претерпева́ть *impf*, претерпе́ть (-плю́, -пишь) *pf* undergo; suffer.

преть (пре́ет) *impf* (*pf* co~) rot.

преувеличе́ние exaggeration. преувели́чивать *impf*, преувели́чить (-чу) *pf* exaggerate.

преуменьша́ть *impf*, преуме́ньшить (-ньшу) *pf* underestimate; understate.

преуспева́ть *impf*, преуспе́ть (-е́ю) *pf* be successful; thrive.

преходя́щий transient.

прецеде́нт precedent.

при *prep* +*prep* by, at; in the presence of; attached to, affiliated to; with; about; on; in the time of; under; during; when, in case of; ~ всём том for all that.

приба́вить (-влю) *pf*, прибавля́ть add; increase; ~ся increase; rise; wax; день приба́вился the days are getting longer. приба́вка addition; increase. прибавле́ние addition; supplement, appendix. приба́вочный additional; surplus.

Приба́лтика the Baltic States.

прибау́тка humorous saying.

прибега́ть[1] *impf of* прибежа́ть

прибега́ть[2] *impf*, прибе́гнуть (-ну; -бе́г) *pf* +к+*dat* resort to.

прибежа́ть (-егу́) *pf* (*impf* прибега́ть) come running.

прибе́жище refuge.

прибега́ть *impf*, прибере́чь (-егу́, -ежёшь; -ёг, -ла́) *pf* save (up), reserve.

прибе́ру *etc.: see* прибра́ть. прибива́ть *impf of* приби́ть. прибира́ть *impf of* прибра́ть

приби́ть (-бью, -бьёшь) *pf* (*impf* прибива́ть) nail; flatten; drive.

приближа́ть *impf*, прибли́зить (-и́жу) *pf* bring *or* move nearer; ~ся approach; draw nearer. приближе́ние approach. приблизи́тельный approximate.

прибо́й surf, breakers.

прибо́р instrument, device, apparatus; set. прибо́рная доска́ instrument panel; dashboard.

прибра́ть (-беру́, -берёшь; -а́л, -а́, -о) *pf* (*impf* прибира́ть) tidy (up); put away.

прибре́жный coastal; offshore.

прибыва́ть *impf*, прибы́ть (-бу́ду; при́был, -а́, -о) *pf* arrive; increase, grow; rise; wax. прибыль profit, gain; increase, rise. прибыльный profitable. прибы́тие arrival.

прибью́ *etc.: see* прибы́ть

прива́л halt.

прива́ривать *impf*, привари́ть (-рю́, -ришь) *pf* weld on.

приватиза́ция privatization. приватизи́ровать *impf* & *pf* privatize.

приведу́ *etc.: see* привести́

привезти́ (-зу́, -зёшь; -ёз, -ла́) (*impf* привози́ть) bring.

привере́дливый pernickety.

приве́рженец (-нца) adherent. приве́рженный devoted.

приве́сить (-е́шу) *pf* (*impf* приве́шивать) hang up, suspend.

привести́ (-еду́, -едёшь; -ёл, -а́) *pf* (*impf* приводи́ть) bring; lead; take; reduce; cite; put in(to), set.

приве́т greeting(s); regards; hi! приве́тливый friendly; affable. приве́тствие greeting; speech of welcome. приве́тствовать *impf* & *pf* greet, salute; welcome.

приве́шивать *impf of* приве́сить

привива́ть(ся *impf of* приви́ть(ся. приви́вка inoculation.

привиде́ние ghost; apparition. приви́деться *pf: see* ви́деться

привилегиро́ванный privileged. привиле́гия privilege.

привинти́ть (-нчу́) *pf*, приви́нчивать *impf* screw on.

приви́ть (-вью, -вьёшь; -и́л, -а́, -о) *pf* (*impf* привива́ть) inoculate; graft; inculcate; foster; ~ся take; become established.

при́вкус after-taste; smack.

привлека́тельный attractive. привлека́ть *impf*, привле́чь (-еку́, -ечёшь; -ёк, -ла́) *pf* attract; draw; draw in, win over; (*law*) have up; ~ к суду́ sue. привлече́ние attraction.

приво́д drive, gear. приводи́ть (-ожу́, -о́дишь) *impf of* привести́. приводно́й driving.

привожу́ *etc.: see* приводи́ть, привози́ть

приво́з bringing; importation; load. **привози́ть** (-ожу́, -о́зишь) *impf* of **привезти́. привозно́й, приво́зный** imported.

приво́льный free.

привстава́ть (-таю́, -таёшь) *impf*, **привста́ть** (-а́ну) *pf* half-rise; rise.

привыка́ть *impf*, **привы́кнуть** (-ну; -ык) *pf* get accustomed. **привы́чка** habit. **привы́чный** habitual, usual.

привью *etc.*: *see* **приви́ть**

привя́занность attachment; affection. **привяза́ть** (-яжу́, -я́жешь) *pf*, **привя́зывать** *impf* attach; tie; bind; ~**ся** become attached; attach o.s.; +**к**+*dat* pester. **привя́зчивый** annoying; affectionate. **при́вязь** tie; lead, leash; tether.

пригиба́ть *impf* of **пригну́ть**

приглаша́ть (-ашу́) *pf*, **приглаша́ть** *impf* invite. **приглаше́ние** invitation.

пригляде́ться (-яжу́сь) *pf*, **пригля́дываться** *impf* look closely; +**к**+*dat* scrutinize: get used to.

пригна́ть (-гоню́, -го́нишь; -а́л, -а́, -о) *pf* (*impf* **пригоня́ть**) bring in; fit, adjust.

пригну́ть (-ну́, -нёшь) *pf* (*impf* **пригиба́ть**) bend down.

пригова́ривать[1] *impf* keep saying.

пригова́ривать[2] *impf*, **приговори́ть** *pf* sentence, condemn. **пригово́р** verdict, sentence.

пригоди́ться (-ожу́сь) *pf* prove useful. **приго́дный** fit, suitable.

пригоня́ть *impf* of **пригна́ть**

пригора́ть *impf*, **пригоре́ть** (-ри́т) *pf* be burnt.

при́город suburb. **при́городный** suburban.

приго́рок (-рка) hillock.

при́горшня (*gen pl* -ей) handful.

приготови́тельный preparatory. **пригото́вить** (-влю) *pf*, **приготовля́ть** *impf* prepare; ~**ся** prepare. **приготовле́ние** preparation.

пригрева́ть *impf*, **пригре́ть** (-е́ю) *pf* warm; cherish.

при|грози́ть (-ожу́) *pf*.

придава́ть (-даю́, -даёшь) *impf*, **прида́ть** (-а́м, -а́шь, -а́ст, -ади́м; при́дал, -а́, -о) *pf* add; give; attach. **прида́ча** adding; addition; **в прида́чу** into the bargain.

придави́ть (-влю́, -вишь) *pf*, **прида́вливать** *impf* press (down).

прида́ное *sb* dowry. **прида́ток** (-тка) appendage.

придвига́ть *impf*, **придви́нуть** (-ну) *pf* move up, draw up; ~**ся** move up, draw near.

придво́рный court.

приде́лать *pf*, **приде́лывать** *impf* attach.

приде́рживаться *impf* hold on; hold; +**gen** keep to.

придеру́сь *etc.*: *see* **придра́ться**. **придира́ться** *impf* of **придра́ться**. **приди́рка** quibble; fault-finding. **приди́рчивый** fault-finding.

придоро́жный roadside.

придра́ться (-деру́сь, -дерёшься; -а́лся, -а́сь, -а́ло́сь) *pf* (*impf* **придира́ться**) find fault.

приду́ *etc.*: *see* **прийти́**

приду́мать *pf*, **приду́мывать** *impf* think up, invent.

прие́ду *etc.*: *see* **прие́хать. прие́зд** arrival. **приезжа́ть** *impf* of **прие́хать. прие́зжий** newly arrived; *sb* newcomer.

приём receiving; reception; surgery; welcome; admittance; dose; go; movement; method, way; trick. **прие́млемый** acceptable. **приёмная** *sb* waiting-room; reception room. **приёмник** (radio) receiver. **приёмный** receiving; reception; entrance; foster, adopted.

прие́хать (-е́ду) *pf* (*impf* **приезжа́ть**) arrive, come.

прижа́ть (-жму́, -жмёшь) *pf* (*impf* **прижима́ть**) press; clasp; ~**ся** nestle up.

прижечь (-жгу́, -жжёшь; -жёг, -жгла́) *pf* (*impf* **прижига́ть**) cauterize.

прижива́ться *impf* of **прижи́ться**

прижига́ние cauterization. **прижига́ть** *impf* of **прижечь**

прижима́ть(ся *impf* of **прижа́ть(ся**

прижи́ться (-иву́сь, -ивёшься; -жи́лся, -а́сь) *pf* (*impf* **прижива́ться**) become acclimatized.

прижму́ *etc.*: *see* **прижа́ть**

приз (*pl* -ы́) prize.

призва́ние vocation. **призва́ть** (-зову́, -зовёшь; -а́л, -а́, -о) *pf* (*impf* **призыва́ть**) call; call upon; call up.

призе́мистый stocky, squat.

приземле́ние landing. приземли́ться *pf*, приземля́ться *impf* land.

призёр prizewinner.

при́зма prism.

признава́ть (-наю́, -наёшь) *impf*, призна́ть *pf* recognize; admit; ~ся confess. при́знак sign, symptom; indication. призна́ние confession, declaration; acknowledgement; recognition. при́знанный acknowledged, recognized. призна́тельный grateful.

призову́ *etc.*: *see* призва́ть

при́зрак spectre, ghost. при́зрачный ghostly; illusory, imagined.

призы́в call, appeal; slogan; call-up. призыва́ть *impf of* призва́ть. призывно́й conscription.

при́иск mine.

прийти́ (приду́, -дёшь; пришёл, -шла́) *pf* (*impf* приходи́ть) come; arrive; ~ в себя́ regain consciousness; ~сь +по+*dat* fit; suit; +на+*acc* fall on; *impers*+*dat* have to; happen (to), fall to the lot (of).

прика́з order, command. приказа́ние order, command. приказа́ть (-ажу́, -а́жешь) *pf*, прика́зывать *impf* order, command.

прика́лывать *impf of* приколо́ть. прикаса́ться *impf of* прикосну́ться

прика́нчивать *impf of* прико́нчить

прикати́ть (-ачу́, -а́тишь) *pf*, прика́тывать *impf* roll up.

прики́дывать *impf*, прики́нуть (-ну) *pf* throw in, add; weigh; estimate; ~ся +*instr* pretend (to be).

прикла́д[1] butt.

прикла́д[2] trimmings. прикладно́й applied. прикла́дывать(ся *impf of* приложи́ть(ся

прикле́ивать *impf*, прикле́ить *pf* stick; glue.

приключа́ться *impf*, приключи́ться *pf* happen, occur. приключе́ние adventure. приключе́нческий adventure.

прико́вывать (-кую́, -куёшь) *pf*, прико́вывать *impf* chain; rivet.

прикола́чивать *impf*, приколоти́ть (-очу́, -о́тишь) *pf* nail.

приколо́ть (-лю́, -лешь) *pf* (*impf* прика́лывать) pin; stab.

прикомандирова́ть *pf*, прикомандиро́вывать *impf* attach.

прико́нчить (-чу) *pf* (*impf* прика́нчивать) use up; finish off.

прикоснове́ние touch; concern. прикосну́ться (-ну́сь, -нёшься) *pf* (*impf* прикаса́ться) к+*dat* touch.

прикрепи́ть (-плю́) *pf*, прикрепля́ть *impf* fasten, attach. прикрепле́ние fastening; registration.

прикрыва́ть *impf*, прикры́ть (-ро́ю) *pf* cover; screen; shelter. прикры́тие cover; escort.

прику́ривать *impf*, прикури́ть (-рю́, -ришь) *pf* get a light.

прикуси́ть (-ушу́, -у́сишь) *pf*, прику́сывать *impf* bite.

прила́вок (-вка) counter.

прилага́тельное *sb* adjective. прилага́ть *impf of* приложи́ть

прила́дить (-а́жу) *pf*, прила́живать *impf* fit, adjust.

приласка́ть *pf* caress, pet; ~ся snuggle up.

прилега́ть *impf* (*pf* приле́чь) к+*dat* fit; adjoin. прилега́ющий close-fitting; adjoining, adjacent.

приле́жный diligent.

прилепи́ть(ся (-плю́(сь, -пишь(ся) *pf*, прилепля́ть(ся *impf* stick.

прилёт arrival. прилета́ть *impf*, прилете́ть (-ечу́) *pf* arrive, fly in; come flying.

приле́чь (-ля́гу, -ля́жешь; -ёг, -гла́) *pf* (*impf* прилега́ть) lie down.

прили́в flow, flood; rising tide; surge. прилива́ть *impf of* прили́ть. прили́вный tidal.

прилипа́ть *impf*, прили́пнуть (-нет; -ли́п) *pf* stick.

прили́ть (-лью́т; -и́л, -а́, -о) *pf* (*impf* прилива́ть) flow; rush.

прили́чие decency. прили́чный decent.

приложе́ние application; enclosure; supplement; appendix. приложи́ть (-жу́, -жишь) *pf* (*impf* прикла́дывать, прилага́ть) put; apply; affix; add; enclose; ~ся take aim; +*instr* put, apply; +к+*dat* kiss.

прилью́т *etc.*: *see* прили́ть. прильну́ть (-ну́, -нёшь) *pf*. приля́гу *etc.*: *see* приле́чь

прима́нивать *impf*, примани́ть (-ню́, -нишь) *pf* lure; entice. прима́нка bait, lure.

примене́ние application; use. **при|мени́ть** (-ню́, -нишь) *pf*, **применя́ть** *impf* apply; use; ~ся adapt o.s., conform.

приме́р example.

при|ме́рить *pf* (*impf also* **примеря́ть**) try on. **приме́рка** fitting.

приме́рно *adv* approximately. **приме́рный** exemplary; approximate.

примеря́ть *impf of* **приме́рить**

при́месь admixture.

приме́та sign, token. **приме́тный** perceptible; conspicuous.

примеча́ние note, footnote; *pl* comments. **примеча́тельный** notable.

примеша́ть *pf*, **приме́шивать** *impf* add, mix in.

примина́ть *impf of* **примя́ть**

примире́ние reconciliation. **примири́тельный** conciliatory. **при|мири́ть** *pf*, **примиря́ть** *impf* reconcile; conciliate; ~ся be reconciled.

примити́вный primitive.

примкну́ть (-ну́, -нёшь) *pf* (*impf* **примыка́ть**) join; fix, attach.

примну́ *etc.: see* **примя́ть**

примо́рский seaside; maritime. **примо́рье** seaside.

примо́чка wash, lotion.

приму́ *etc.: see* **приня́ть**

примча́ться (-чу́сь) *pf* come tearing along.

примыка́ть *impf of* **примкну́ть**; +к+*dat* adjoin. **примыка́ющий** affiliated.

примя́ть (-мну́, -мнёшь) *pf* (*impf* **примина́ть**) crush; trample down.

принадлежа́ть (-жу́) *impf* belong. **принадле́жность** belonging; membership; *pl* accessories; equipment.

принести́ (-су́, -сёшь) *pf* (*impf* **приноси́ть**) bring; fetch.

принижа́ть *impf*, **прини́зить** (-и́жу) *pf* humiliate; belittle.

принима́ть(ся) *impf of* **приня́ть(ся)**

приноси́ть (-ошу́, -о́сишь) *impf of* **принести́**. **приноше́ние** gift, offering.

при́нтер (*comput*) printer.

принуди́тельный compulsory. **прину́дить** (-у́жу) *pf*, **принужда́ть** *impf* compel. **принужде́ние** compulsion, coercion. **принуждённый** constrained, forced.

принц prince. **принце́сса** princess.

при́нцип principle. **принципиа́льно** *adv* on principle; in principle. **принципиа́льный** of principle; general.

приня́тие taking; acceptance; admission. **при́нято** it is accepted; it is usual; не ~ it is not done. **приня́ть** (-иму́, -и́мешь; при́нял, -а́, -о) *pf* (*impf* **принима́ть**) take; accept; take over; receive; +за+*acc* take for; ~ уча́стие take part; ~ся begin; take; take root; ~ за рабо́ту set to work.

приободри́ть *pf*, **приободря́ть** *impf* cheer up; ~ся cheer up.

приобрести́ (-ету́, -етёшь; -рёл, -а́) *pf*, **приобрета́ть** *impf* acquire. **приобрете́ние** acquisition.

приобща́ть *impf*, **приобщи́ть** (-щу́) *pf* join, attach, unite; ~ся к+*dat* join in.

приорите́т priority.

приостана́вливать *impf*, **приостанови́ть** (-влю́, -вишь) *pf* stop, suspend; ~ся stop. **приостано́вка** halt, suspension.

приоткрыва́ть *impf*, **приоткры́ть** (-ро́ю) *pf* open slightly.

припа́док (-дка) fit; attack.

припа́сы (-ов) *pl* stores, supplies.

припе́в refrain.

приписа́ть (-ишу́, -и́шешь) *pf*, **припи́сывать** *impf* add; attribute. **припи́ска** postscript; codicil.

припло́д offspring; increase.

приплыва́ть *impf*, **приплы́ть** (-ыву́, -ывёшь; -ы́л, -а́, -о) *pf* swim up; sail up.

приплю́снуть (-ну) *pf*, **приплю́щивать** *impf* flatten.

приподнима́ть *impf*, **приподня́ть** (-ниму́, -ни́мешь; -о́днял, -а́, -о) *pf* raise (a little); ~ся raise o.s. (a little).

припо́й solder.

приполза́ть *impf*, **приползти́** (-зу́, -зёшь; -по́лз, -ла́) *pf* creep up, crawl up.

припомина́ть *impf*, **припо́мнить** *pf* recollect.

припра́ва seasoning, flavouring. **припра́вить** (-влю) *pf*, **приправля́ть** *impf* season, flavour.

припря́тать (-я́чу) *pf*, **припря́тывать** *impf* secrete, put by.

припу́гивать *impf*, **припугну́ть** (-ну́, -нёшь) *pf* scare.

прирабатывать *impf*, приработать *pf* earn ... extra. приработок (-тка) additional earnings.

приравнивать *impf*, приравнять *pf* equate (with к+*dat*).

прирастать *impf*, прирасти (-тёт; -рос, -ла) *pf* adhere; take; increase; accrue.

природа nature. природный natural; by birth; innate. прирождённый innate; born.

прирос *etc.*: *see* прирасти. прирост increase.

приручать *impf*, приручить (-чу) *pf* tame; domesticate.

присаживаться *impf of* присесть

присваивать *impf*, присвоить *pf* appropriate; award.

приседать *impf*, присесть (-сяду) *pf* (*impf also* присаживаться) sit down, take a seat.

прискакать (-ачу, -ачешь) *pf* come galloping.

прискорбный sorrowful.

прислать (-ишлю, -ишлёшь) *pf* (*impf* присылать) send.

прислонить(ся (-оню(сь, -онишь(ся) *pf*, прислонять(ся *impf* lean, rest.

прислуга servant; crew. прислуживать *impf* (к+*dat*) wait (on), attend. прислушиваться *impf* listen; +к+*dat* listen to; heed.

присматривать *impf*, присмотреть (-рю, -ришь) *pf* +за+*instr* look after, keep an eye on; ~ся (к+*dat*) look closely (at). присмотр supervision.

присниться *pf*.

присоединение joining; addition; annexation. присоединить *pf*, присоединять *impf* join; add; annex; ~ся к+*dat* join; subscribe to (*an opinion*).

приспособить (-блю) *pf*, приспособлять *impf* fit, adjust, adapt; ~ся adapt o.s. приспособление adaptation; device; appliance. приспособляемость adaptability.

приставать (-таю, -таёшь) *impf of* пристать

приставить (-влю) *pf* (*impf* приставлять) к+*dat* place, set, *or* lean against; add; appoint to look after. приставка prefix.

приставлять *impf of* приставить

пристальный intent.

пристанище refuge, shelter.

пристань (*gen pl* -ей) landing-stage; pier; wharf.

пристать (-ану) *pf* (*impf* приставать) stick, adhere (к+*dat* to); pester.

пристёгивать *impf*, пристегнуть (-ну, -нёшь) *pf* fasten.

пристойный decent, proper.

пристраивать(ся *impf of* пристроить(ся

пристрастие predilection, passion; bias. пристрастный biased.

пристреливать *impf*, пристрелить *pf* shoot (down).

пристроить (-ою) *pf* (*impf* пристраивать) add, build on; fix up; ~ся be fixed up, get a place. пристройка annexe, extension.

приступ assault; fit, attack. приступать *impf*, приступить (-плю, -пишь) *pf* к+*dat* set about, start.

пристыдить (-ыжу) *pf*.

пристыковаться *pf*.

присудить (-ужу, -удишь) *pf*, присуждать *impf* sentence, condemn; award; confer. присуждение awarding; conferment.

присутствие presence. присутствовать *impf* be present, attend. присутствующие *sb pl* those present.

присущий inherent; characteristic.

присылать *impf of* прислать

присяга oath. присягать *impf*, присягнуть (-ну, -нёшь) *pf* swear.

присяду *etc.*: *see* присесть

присяжный *sb* juror.

притаиться *pf* hide.

притаптывать *impf of* притоптать

притаскивать *impf*, притащить (-ащу, -ащишь) *pf* bring, drag, haul; ~ся drag o.s.

притвориться *pf*, притворяться *impf* +*instr* pretend to be. притворный pretended, feigned. притворство pretence, sham. притворщик sham; hypocrite.

притекать *impf of* притечь

притеснение oppression. притеснить *pf*, притеснять *impf* oppress.

притечь (-ечёт, -екут; -ёк, -ла) *pf* (*impf* притекать) pour in.

притихать *impf*, притихнуть (-ну; -их) *pf* quiet down.

приток tributary; influx.

притолока lintel.

притом *conj* (and) besides.

притон den, haunt.

притоптать (-пчу́, -пчешь) *pf* (*impf* **притаптывать**) trample down.

приторный sickly-sweet, luscious, cloying.

притрагиваться *impf*, **притронуться** (-нусь) *pf* touch.

притупить (-плю, -пишь) *pf*, **притуплять** *impf* blunt, dull; deaden; ~ся become blunt *or* dull.

притча parable.

притягательный attractive, magnetic. **притягивать** *impf of* **притянуть**

притяжательный possessive.

притяжение attraction.

притязание claim, pretension. **притязательный** demanding.

притянутый far-fetched. **притянуть** (-ну́, -нешь) *pf* (*impf* **притягивать**) attract; drag (up).

приурочивать *impf*, **приурочить** (-чу) *pf* к+*dat* time for.

приусадебный: ~ участок individual plot (*in kolkhoz*).

приучать *impf*, **приучить** (-чу́, -чишь) *pf* train, school.

прихлебатель *m* sponger.

приход coming, arrival; receipts; parish. **приходить(ся** (-ожу(сь, -одишь(ся) *impf of* **прийти(сь**. **приходный** receipt. **приходящий** non-resident; ~ больной outpatient.

прихожанин (*pl* -áне, -áн), -áнка parishioner.

прихожая *sb* hall, lobby.

прихотливый capricious; fanciful; intricate. **прихоть** whim, caprice.

прихрамывать limp (slightly).

прицел sight; aiming. **прицеливаться** *impf*, **прицелиться** *pf* take aim.

прицениваться *impf*, **прицениться** (-нюсь, -нишься) *pf* (к+*dat*) ask the price (of).

прицеп trailer. **прицепить** (-плю, -пишь) *pf*, **прицеплять** *impf* hitch, hook on; ~ся к+*dat* stick to, cling to. **прицепка** hitching, hooking on; quibble. **прицепной**: ~ вагон trailer.

причал mooring; mooring line. **причаливать** *impf*, **причалить** *pf*

moor.

причастие[1] participle. **причастие**[2] communion. **причастить** (-ащу́) *pf* (*impf* **причащать**) give communion to; ~ся receive communion.

причастный[1] participial. **причастный**[2] concerned; privy.

причащать *impf of* **причастить**

причём *conj* moreover, and.

причесать (-ешу́, -ешешь) *pf*, **причёсывать** *impf* comb; do the hair (of); ~ся do one's hair, have one's hair done. **причёска** hair-do; hair-cut.

причина cause; reason. **причинить** *pf*, **причинять** *impf* cause.

причислить *pf*, **причислять** *impf* number, rank (к+*dat* among); add on.

причитание lamentation. **причитать** *impf* lament.

причитаться *impf* be due.

причмокивать *impf*, **причмокнуть** (-ну) *pf* smack one's lips.

причуда caprice, whim.

при|чудиться *pf*.

причудливый odd; fantastic; whimsical.

при|швартовать *pf*. **пришёл** *etc.*: *see* **прийти**

пришелец (-льца) newcomer.

пришествие coming; advent.

пришивать *impf*, **пришить** (-шью, -шьёшь) *pf* sew on.

пришлю *etc.*: *see* **прислать**

пришпиливать *impf*, **пришпилить** *pf* pin on.

пришпоривать *impf*, **пришпорить** *pf* spur (on).

прищемить (-млю) *pf*, **прищемлять** *impf* pinch.

прищепка clothes-peg.

прищуриваться *impf*, **прищуриться** *pf* screw up one's eyes.

приют shelter, refuge. **приютить** (-ючу́) *pf* shelter; ~ся take shelter.

приятель *m*, **приятельница** friend. **приятельский** friendly. **приятный** nice, pleasant.

про *prep+acc* about; for; ~ себя to o.s.

про|анализировать *pf*.

проба trial, test; hallmark; sample.

пробег run; race. **пробегать** *impf*, **пробежать** (-егу́) *pf* run; cover; run past.

пробе́л blank, gap; flaw.

пробер́у etc.: see пробрáть. про|
бивáть(ся impf of пробúть(ся.
пробирáть(ся impf of пробрáть(ся.
пробúрка test-tube. пробúровать
impf test, assay.

про|бúть (-бью, -бьёшь) pf (impf also
пробивáть) make a hole in; pierce;
punch; ~ся force, make, one's way.

пробка cork; stopper; fuse; (traffic)
jam, congestion. пробковый cork.

пробле́ма problem.

про́блеск flash; gleam, ray.

про́бный trial, test; ~ кáмень touchstone. пробовать impf (pf ис~,
по~) try; attempt.

пробóина hole.

пробóр parting.

про|бормотáть (-очу́, -о́чешь) pf.

пробрáть (-беру́, -берёшь; -áл, -á,
-о) pf (impf пробирáть) penetrate;
scold; ~ся make or force one's way.

пробу́ду etc.: see пробы́ть

про|буди́ть (-ужу́, -у́дишь) pf, про-
буждáть impf wake (up); arouse;
~ся wake up. пробужде́ние awak-
ening.

про|бурáвить (-влю) pf, пробу-
рáвливать impf bore (through),
drill.

про|бури́ть pf.

пробы́ть (-бу́ду; про́бы́л, -á, -о) pf
stay; be.

пробью́ etc.: see пробúть

провáл failure; downfall; gap. про-
вáливать impf, провали́ть (-лю́,
-лишь) pf bring down; ruin; reject,
fail; ~ся collapse; fall in; fail; disappear.

прове́дать pf, прове́дывать impf
call on; learn.

проведе́ние conducting; construction; installation.

провезти́ (-зу́, -зёшь; -ёз, -лá) pf
(impf провози́ть) convey, transport.

прове́рить pf, проверя́ть impf
check; test. прове́рка checking,
check; testing.

про|вести́ (-еду́, -едёшь; -ёл, -á) pf
(impf also проводи́ть) lead, take;
build; install; carry out; conduct; pass;
draw; spend; +instr pass over.

прове́тривать impf, прове́трить pf
air.

про|ве́ять (-е́ю) pf.

провиде́ние Providence.

прови́зия provisions.

провини́ться pf be guilty; do wrong.

провинциáльный provincial. про-
ви́нция province; the provinces.

про́вод (pl -á) wire, lead, line. про-
води́мость conductivity. прово-
ди́ть[1] (-ожу́, -о́дишь) impf of про-
вести́; conduct.

проводи́ть[2] (-ожу́, -о́дишь) pf (impf
провожáть) accompany; see off.

прово́дка leading, taking; building,
installation; wiring, wires.

проводни́к[1] (-á) guide; conductor.

проводни́к[2] (-á) conductor; bearer;
transmitter.

про́воды (-ов) pl send-off. про-
вожáтый sb guide, escort. провожáть impf of проводи́ть

провóз conveyance, transport.

провозгласи́ть (-ашу́) pf, провоз-
глашáть impf proclaim; propose.
провозглаше́ние proclamation.

провози́ть (-ожу́, -о́зишь) impf of
провезти́

провокáтор agent provocateur. про-
вокáция provocation.

про́волока wire. про́волочный
wire.

провóрный quick; agile. провóр-
ство quickness; agility.

провоци́ровать impf & pf (pf с~)
provoke.

прогадáть pf, прогáдывать impf
miscalculate.

прогáлина glade; space.

прогибáть(ся impf of прогну́ть(ся

прогла́тывать impf, проглоти́ть
(-очу́, -о́тишь) pf swallow.

проглядéть (-яжу́) pf, прогля́ды-
вать[1] impf overlook; look through.

проглянýть (-я́нет) pf, прогля́-
дывать[2] impf show, peep through,
appear.

прогнáть (-гоню́, -гóнишь; -áл, -á, -о)
pf (impf прогоня́ть) drive away;
banish; drive; sack.

прогнивáть impf, прогни́ть (-ниёт;
-и́л, -á, -о) pf rot through.

прогнóз prognosis; (weather) forecast.

прогнýть (-нý, -нёшь) pf (impf про-
гибáть) cause to sag; ~ся sag, bend.

проговáривать impf, проговори́ть
pf say, utter; talk; ~ся let the cat

out of the bag.

проголода́ться *pf* get hungry.

про|голосова́ть *pf*.

прого́н purlin; girder; stairwell.

прогоня́ть *impf of* прогна́ть

прогора́ть *impf*, **прогоре́ть** (-рю́) *pf* burn (through); burn out; go bankrupt.

прого́рклый rancid, rank.

програ́мма programme; syllabus. **программи́ровать** *impf* (*pf* за~) programme.

прогрева́ть *impf*, **прогре́ть** (-е́ю) *pf* heat; warm up; ~ся warm up.

про|греме́ть (-млю) *pf*. **про|грохота́ть** (-очу́, -о́чешь) *pf*.

прогре́сс progress. **прогресси́вный** progressive. **прогресси́ровать** *impf* progress.

прогрыза́ть *impf*, **прогры́зть** (-зу́, -зёшь; -ы́з) *pf* gnaw through.

про|гуде́ть (-гужу́) *pf*.

прогу́л truancy; absenteeism. **прогу́ливать** *impf*, **прогуля́ть** *pf* play truant, be absent, (from); miss; take for a walk; ~ся take a walk. **прогу́лка** walk, stroll; outing. **прогу́льщик** absentee, truant.

продава́ть (-даю́, -даёшь) *impf*, **прода́ть** (-а́м, -а́шь, -а́ст, -ади́м; про́дал, -а́, -о) *pf* sell. **продава́ться** (-даётся) *impf* be for sale; sell. **продаве́ц** (-вца́) seller, vendor; salesman. **продавщи́ца** seller, vendor; saleswoman. **прода́жа** sale. **прода́жный** for sale; corrupt.

продвига́ть *impf*, **продви́нуть** (-ну) *pf* move on, push forward; advance; ~ся advance; move forward; push on. **продвиже́ние** advancement.

продева́ть *impf of* проде́ть

про|деклами́ровать *impf*.

проде́лать *pf*, **проде́лывать** *impf* do, perform, make. **проде́лка** trick; prank.

продемонстри́ровать *pf* demonstrate, show.

продёргивать *impf of* продёрнуть

продержа́ть (-жу́, -жишь) *pf* hold; keep; ~ся hold out.

продёрнуть (-ну, -нешь) *pf* (*impf* продёргивать) pass, run; criticize severely.

проде́ть (-е́ну) *pf* (*impf* продева́ть) pass; ~ ни́тку в иго́лку thread a

needle.

продешеви́ть (-влю́) *pf* sell too cheap.

про|диктова́ть *pf*.

продлева́ть *impf*, **продли́ть** *pf* prolong. **продле́ние** extension. **про|дли́ться** *pf*.

продма́г grocery. **продово́льственный** food. **продово́льствие** food; provisions.

продолгова́тый oblong.

продолжа́тель *m* continuer. **продолжа́ть** *impf*, **продо́лжить** (-жу) *pf* continue; prolong; ~ся continue, last, go on. **продолже́ние** continuation; sequel; **в** ~+*gen* in the course of. **продолжи́тельность** duration. **продолжи́тельный** long; prolonged.

продо́льный longitudinal.

продро́гнуть (-ну; -о́г) *pf* be chilled to the bone.

продтова́ры (-ов) *pl* food products.

продува́ть *impf* проду́ть

проду́кт product; *pl* food-stuffs. **продукти́вность** productivity. **продукти́вный** productive. **проду́ктовый** food. **проду́кция** production.

проду́манный well thought-out; considered. **проду́мать** *pf*, **проду́мывать** *impf* think over; think out.

проду́ть (-у́ю, -у́ешь) *pf* (*impf* продува́ть) blow through.

продыря́вить (-влю) *pf* make a hole in.

проеда́ть *impf of* прое́сть. **прое́ду** *etc.: see* прое́хать

прое́зд passage, thoroughfare; trip. **прое́здить** (-зжу) *pf* (*impf* прое́зжа́ть) spend travelling. **прое́здно́й** travelling; ~о́й биле́т ticket; ~а́я пла́та fare; ~ы́е *sb pl* travelling expenses. **проезжа́ть** *impf of* прое́здить, прое́хать. **прое́зжий** passing (by); *sb* passer-by.

прое́кт project, plan, design; draft. **проекти́ровать** *impf* (*pf* с~) project; plan. **прое́ктный** planning; planned. **прое́ктор** projector.

проекцио́нный фона́рь *m* projector. **прое́кция** projection.

прое́сть (-е́м, -е́шь, -е́ст, -еди́м; -е́л) *pf* (*impf* проеда́ть) eat through, corrode; spend on food.

проéхать (-éду) pf (impf проезжáть) pass, ride, drive (by, through); cover.

прожáренный (cul) well-done.

прожевáть (-жую, -жуёшь) pf, прожёвывать impf chew well.

прожéктор (pl -ы or -á) searchlight.

прожéчь (-жгу, -жжёшь; -жёг, -жглá) pf (impf прожигáть) burn (through).

проживáть impf of прожи́ть. прожигáть impf of прожéчь

прожи́точный ми́нимум living wage. прожи́ть (-иву́, -ивёшь; про́жил, -á, -о) pf (impf прожива́ть) live; spend.

прожóрливый gluttonous.

прóза prose. прозаи́ческий prose; prosaic.

прозва́ние, прóзвище nickname. прозва́ть (-зову́, -зовёшь; -áл, -á, -о) pf (impf прозыва́ть) nickname, name.

про|звуча́ть pf.

про|зева́ть pf. про|зимова́ть pf. прозову́ etc.: see прозва́ть

прозорли́вый perspicacious.

прозра́чный transparent.

прозрева́ть impf, прозре́ть pf regain one's sight; see clearly. прозре́ние recovery of sight; insight. прозыва́ть impf of прозва́ть

прозяба́ние vegetation. прозяба́ть impf vegetate.

проигра́ть pf, прои́грывать impf lose; play; ~ся gamble away all one's money. прои́грыватель m recordplayer. прóигрыш loss.

произведéние work; production; product. произвести́ (-еду́, -едёшь; -ёл, -á) pf, производи́ть (-ожу́, -óдишь) impf make; carry out; produce; +в+acc/nom pl promote to (the rank of). производи́тель m producer. производи́тельность productivity. производи́тельный productive. произво́дный derivative. произво́дственный industrial; production. произво́дство production. произво́л arbitrariness; arbitrary rule. произво́льный arbitrary.

произнести́ (-су́, -сёшь; -ёс, -лá) pf, произноси́ть (-ошу́, -óсишь) impf pronounce; utter. произноше́ние pronunciation.

произойти́ (-ойдёт; -ошёл, -шлá) pf (impf происходи́ть) happen, occur;

result; be descended.

произраста́ть impf, произрасти́ (-тý; -тёшь; -рос, -лá) pf sprout; grow.

прóиски (-ов) pl intrigues.

проистека́ть impf, происте́чь (-ечёт; -ёк, -лá) pf spring, result.

происходи́ть (-ожу́, -óдишь) impf of произойти́. происхожде́ние origin; birth.

происше́ствие event, incident.

пройдóха m & f sly person.

пройти́ (-йду́, -йдёшь; -ошёл, -шлá) pf (impf проходи́ть) pass; go; go past; cover; study; get through; ~сь (impf проха́живаться) take a stroll.

прок use, benefit.

прокажённый sb leper. прокáза[1] leprosy.

прокáза[2] mischief, prank. прокáзничать impf (pf на~) be up to mischief. прокáзник prankster.

прокáлывать impf of проколóть

прокáпывать impf of прокопáть

прокáт hire.

прокати́ться (-ачу́сь, -áтишься) pf roll; go for a drive.

прокáтный rolling; rolled.

прокипяти́ть (-ячý) pf boil (thoroughly).

прокиса́ть impf, про|ки́снуть (-нет) pf turn (sour).

проклáдка laying; construction; washer; packing. проклáдывать impf of проложи́ть

прокламáция leaflet.

проклина́ть impf, прокля́сть (-янý, -янёшь; -óклял, -á, -о) pf curse, damn. прокля́тие curse; damnation. прокля́тый (-ят, -á, -о) damned.

прокóл puncture.

проколóть (-лю́, -лешь) pf (impf прокáлывать) prick, pierce.

прокомменти́ровать pf comment (upon).

про|компости́ровать pf. про|конспекти́ровать pf. про|консульти́ровать(ся pf. про|контроли́ровать) pf.

прокопáть pf (impf прокáпывать) dig, dig through.

прокóрм nourishment, sustenance. про|корми́ть(ся (-млю́(сь, -мишь(ся) pf.

про|корректи́ровать pf.

прокрáдываться impf, прокрáсть-

ся (-адусь, -адёшься) *pf* steal in.
прокуратура office of public prosecutor. прокурор public prosecutor.
прокусить (-ушу, -усишь) *pf*, прокусывать *impf* bite through.
прокутить (-учу, -утишь) *pf*, прокучивать *impf* squander; go on a binge.
пролагать *impf of* проложить
проламывать *impf of* проломать
пролегать *impf* lie, run.
пролезать *impf*, пролезть (-зу; -лез) *pf* get through, climb through.
про|лепетать (-ечу, -ечешь) *pf*.
пролёт span; stairwell; flight.
пролетариат proletariat. пролетарий proletarian. пролетарский proletarian.
пролетать *impf*, пролететь (-ечу) *pf* fly; cover; fly by, past, through.
пролив strait. проливать *impf*, пролить (-лью, -льёшь; -олил, -а, -о) *pf* spill, shed; ~ся be spilt.
пролог prologue.
проложить (-жу, -жишь) *pf* (*impf* прокладывать, пролагать) lay; build; interlay.
пролом breach, break. проломать, проломить (-млю, -мишь) *pf* (*impf* проламывать) break (through).
пролью *etc.: see* пролить
про|мазать (-ажу) *pf*. проматывать(ся *impf of* промотать(ся
промах miss; slip, blunder. промахиваться *impf*, промахнуться (-нусь, -нёшься) *pf* miss; make a blunder.
промачивать *impf of* промочить
промедление delay. промедлить *pf* delay; procrastinate.
промежуток (-тка) interval; space. промежуточный intermediate
промелькнуть (-ну, -нёшь) *pf* flash (past, by).
променивать *impf*, променять *pf* exchange.
промерзать *impf*, промёрзнуть (-ну; -ёрз) *pf* freeze through. промёрзлый frozen.
промокать *impf*, промокнуть (-ну; -мок) *pf* get soaked; let water in.
промолвить (-влю) *pf* say, utter.
промолчать (-чу) *pf* keep silent.
про|мотать *pf* (*impf also* проматывать) squander.

промочить (-чу, -чишь) *pf* (*impf* промачивать) soak, drench.
промою *etc.: see* промыть
промтовары (-ов) *pl* manufactured goods.
промчаться (-чусь) *pf* rush by.
промывать *impf of* промыть
промысел (-сла) trade, business; *pl* works. промысловый producers'; business; game.
промыть (-мою) *pf* (*impf* промывать) wash (thoroughly); bathe; ~ мозги+*dat* brain-wash.
про|мычать (-чу) *pf*.
промышленник industrialist. промышленность industry. промышленный industrial.
пронести (-су, -сёшь; -ёс, -ла) *pf* (*impf* проносить) carry (past, through); pass (over); ~сь rush past, through; scud (past); fly; spread.
пронзать *impf*, пронзить (-нжу) *pf* pierce, transfix. пронзительный piercing.
пронизать (-ижу, -ижешь) *pf*, пронизывать *impf* pierce; permeate.
проникать *impf*, проникнуть (-ну; -ик) *pf* penetrate; percolate; ~ся be imbued. проникновение penetration; feeling. проникновенный heartfelt.
проницаемый permeable. проницательный perspicacious.
проносить(ся (-ошу(сь, -осишь(ся) *impf of* пронести(сь. про|нумеровать *pf*.
пронюхать (-аю), пронюхивать *impf* smell out, get wind of.
прообраз prototype.
пропаганда propaganda. пропагандист propagandist.
пропадать *impf of* пропасть. пропажа loss.
пропалывать *impf of* прополоть
пропасть precipice; abyss; lots of.
пропасть (-аду, -адёшь) *pf* (*impf* пропадать) be missing; be lost; disappear; be done for, die; be wasted. пропащий lost; hopeless.
пропекать(ся *impf of* пропечь(ся. про|петь (-пою, -поёшь) *pf*.
пропечь (-еку, -ечёшь; -ёк, -ла) *pf* (*impf* пропекать) bake thoroughly; ~ся get baked through.
пропивать *impf of* пропить

прописа́ть (-ишу́, -и́шешь) pf, про-
пи́сывать impf prescribe; register;
~ся register. пропи́ска registration;
residence permit. пропискн|о́й: ~а́я
бу́ква capital letter; ~а́я и́стина truism. про́писью adv in words.

пропита́ние subsistence, sustenance.
пропита́ть pf, пропи́тывать impf
impregnate, saturate.

пропи́ть (-пью́, -пьёшь; -о́пи́л, -а́, -о)
pf (impf пропива́ть) spend on drink.

проплыва́ть impf, проплы́ть (-ыву́,
-ывёшь; -ы́л, -а́, -о) pf swim, sail, or
float past or through.

пропове́дник preacher; advocate.
пропове́довать impf preach; advocate. про́поведь sermon; advocacy.

пропpolза́ть impf, проползти́ (-зу́,
-зёшь; -по́лз, -ла́) pf crawl, creep.

пропо́лка weeding. прополо́ть (-лю́,
-лешь) pf (impf пропа́лывать) weed.

про|полоска́ть (-ощу́, -о́щешь) pf.

пропорциона́льный proportional,
proportionate. пропо́рция proportion.

про́пуск (pl -а́ or -и, -о́в or -ов) pass,
permit; password; admission; omission; non-attendance; blank, gap.
пропуска́ть impf, пропусти́ть (-ущу́,
-у́стишь) pf let pass; let in; pass; leave
out; miss. пропускн|о́й: ~а́я
спосо́бность capacity.

пропью́ etc.: see пропи́ть

прора́б works superintendent.

прораба́тывать impf, проработа́ть
pf work (through, at); study; pick
holes in.

прораста́ние germination; sprouting.
прораста́ть impf, прорасти́ (-тёт;
-ро́с, -ла́) pf germinate, sprout.

прорва́ть (-ву́, -вёшь; -а́л, -а́, -о) pf
(impf прорыва́ть) break through;
~ся burst open; break through.

про|реаги́ровать pf.

проре́дить (-ежу́) pf, проре́живать
impf thin out.

проре́з cut; slit, notch. про|ре́зать
(-е́жу) pf, прореза́ть impf (impf
also проре́зывать) cut through; ~ся
be cut, come through.

проре́зывать(ся impf of про-
ре́зать(ся. про|репети́ровать pf.

проре́ха tear, slit; flies; deficiency.

про|рецензи́ровать pf.

проро́к prophet.

пророни́ть pf utter.

проро́с etc.: see прорасти́

проро́ческий prophetic. проро́че-
ство prophecy.

проро́ю etc.: see проры́ть

проруба́ть impf, проруби́ть (-блю́,
-бишь) pf cut or hack through.
про́рубь ice-hole.

проры́в break; break-through; hitch.
прорыва́ть¹(ся impf of про-
рва́ть(ся

прорыва́ть² impf, проры́ть (-ро́ю)
pf dig through; ~ся dig one's way
through.

проса́чиваться impf of просо-
чи́ться

просве́рливать impf, просверли́ть
(-лю́) pf drill, bore; perforate.

просве́т (clear) space; shaft of light;
ray of hope; opening. просвети́-
тельный educational. просвети́ть¹
(-ещу́) pf (impf просвеща́ть) enlighten.

просвети́ть² (-ечу́, -е́тишь) pf (impf
просве́чивать) X-ray.

просветле́ние brightening (up); lu-
cidity. про|светле́ть (-е́ет) pf.

просве́чивание radioscopy. про-
све́чивать impf of просвети́ть; be
translucent; be visible.

просвеща́ть impf of просвети́ть.
просвеще́ние enlightenment.

просви́ра communion bread.

про́седь streak(s) of grey.

просе́ивать impf of просе́ять

просе́ка cutting, ride.

просёлок (-лка) country road.

просе́ять (-е́ю) pf (impf просе́и-
вать) sift.

про|сигнализи́ровать pf.

просиде́ть (-ижу́) pf, проси́живать
impf sit.

проси́тельный pleading. проси́ть
(-ошу́, -о́сишь) impf (pf по~) ask;
beg; invite; ~ся ask; apply.

проска́кивать impf of проскочи́ть

проска́льзывать impf, прасколь-
зну́ть (-ну́, -нёшь) pf slip, creep.

проскочи́ть (-чу́, -чишь) pf (impf
проска́кивать) rush by; slip through;
creep in.

просла́вить (-влю) pf, просла-
вля́ть impf glorify; make famous;
~ся become famous. просла́влен-
ный renowned.

проследи́ть (-ежу́) pf, **просле́живать** impf track (down); trace.

прослези́ться (-ежу́сь) pf shed a few tears.

просло́йка layer, stratum.

прослужи́ть (-жу́, -жишь) pf serve (for a certain time).

про|слу́шать pf, **прослу́шивать** impf hear; listen to; miss, not catch.

про|слы́ть (-ыву́, -ывёшь; -ыл, -а́, -о) pf.

просма́тривать impf, **просмотре́ть** (-рю́, -ришь) pf look over; overlook. **просмо́тр** survey; view, viewing; examination.

просну́ться (-ну́сь, -нёшься) pf (impf **просыпа́ться**) wake up.

про́со millet.

просо́вывать(ся impf of **просу́нуть(ся**

про|со́хнуть (-ну; -о́х) pf (impf also **просыха́ть**) dry out.

просочи́ться (-и́тся) pf (impf **проса́чиваться**) percolate; seep (out); leak (out).

проспа́ть (-плю́; -а́л, -а́, -о) pf (impf **просыпа́ть**) sleep (through); oversleep.

проспе́кт avenue.

про|спряга́ть pf.

просро́ченный overdue; expired. **просро́чить** (-чу) pf allow to run out; be behind with; overstay. **просро́чка** delay; expiry of time limit.

проста́ивать impf of **простоя́ть**

проста́к (-а́) simpleton.

просте́нок (-нка) pier (between windows).

простере́ться (-трётся; -тёрся) pf, **простира́ться** impf extend.

прости́тельный pardonable, excusable. **прости́ть** (-ощу́) pf (impf **проща́ть**) forgive; excuse; ~ся (c+instr) say goodbye (to).

проститу́тка prostitute. **проститу́ция** prostitution.

про́сто adv simply.

простоволо́сый bare-headed. **просто́душный** simple-hearted; ingenuous.

просто́й¹ downtime.

прост|о́й² simple; plain; mere; ~ым гла́зом with the naked eye; ~о́е число́ prime number.

простоква́ша thick sour milk.

про́сто-на́просто adv simply.

простонаро́дный of the common people.

просто́р spaciousness; space. **просто́рный** spacious.

просторе́чие popular speech. **простосерде́чный** simple-hearted.

простота́ simplicity.

простоя́ть (-ою́) pf (impf **проста́ивать**) stand (idle).

простра́нный extensive, vast. **простра́нственный** spatial. **простра́нство** space.

простре́л lumbago. **простре́ливать** impf, **прострели́ть** (-лю́, -лишь) pf shoot through.

про|строчи́ть (-очу́, -о́чишь) pf.

просту́да cold. **простуди́ться** (-ужу́сь, -у́дишься) pf, **простужа́ться** impf catch (a) cold.

проступа́ть impf, **проступи́ть** (-ит) pf appear.

просту́пок (-пка) misdemeanour.

простыня́ (pl про́стыни, -ы́нь, -я́м) sheet.

просты́ть (-ы́ну) pf get cold.

просу́нуть (-ну) pf (impf **просо́вывать**) push, thrust.

просу́шивать impf, **просуши́ть** (-шу́, -шишь) pf dry out; ~ся (get) dry.

просуществова́ть pf exist; endure.

просчёт error. **просчита́ться** pf, **просчи́тываться** impf miscalculate.

просы́пать (-плю) pf, **просыпа́ть¹** impf spill; ~ся get spilt.

просыпа́ть² impf of **проспа́ть**. **просыпа́ться** impf of **просну́ться**. **просыха́ть** impf of **просо́хнуть**

про́сьба request.

прота́лкивать impf of **протолкну́ть**.

прота́пливать impf of **протопи́ть**

прота́птывать impf of **протопта́ть**

прота́скивать impf, **протащи́ть** (-щу́, -щишь) pf drag, push (through).

проте́з artificial limb, prosthesis; зубно́й ~ denture.

протеи́н protein.

протека́ть impf of **проте́чь**

проте́кция patronage.

протере́ть (-тру́, -трёшь; -тёр) pf (impf **протира́ть**) wipe (over); wear (through).

протест protest. **протеста́нт**, ~ка Protestant. **протестова́ть** impf & pf protest.

проте́чь (-ечёт; -тёк, -ла́) *pf* (*impf* протека́ть) flow; leak; seep; pass; take its course.

про́тив *prep+gen* against; opposite; contrary to, as against.

про́тивень (-вня) *m* baking-tray; meat-pan.

проти́виться (-влюсь) *impf* (*pf* вос~) +*dat* oppose; resist. проти́вник opponent; the enemy. проти́вный¹ opposite; contrary. проти́вный² nasty, disgusting.

противо- *in comb* anti-, contra-, counter-. противове́с counterbalance. ~возду́шный anti-aircraft. ~га́з gas-mask. ~де́йствие opposition. ~де́йствовать *impf* +*dat* oppose, counteract. ~есте́ственный unnatural. ~зако́нный illegal. ~зача́точный contraceptive. ~поло́жность opposition; contrast. ~поло́жный opposite; contrary. ~поста́вить (-влю) *pf*, ~поставля́ть *impf* oppose; contrast. ~речи́вый contradictory; conflicting. ~ре́чие contradiction. ~ре́чить (-чу) *impf* +*dat* contradict. ~стоя́ть (-ою́) *impf* +*dat* resist, withstand. ~та́нковый anti-tank. ~я́дие antidote.

протира́ть *impf of* протере́ть

проти́скивать *impf*, проти́снуть (-ну) *pf* force, squeeze (through), into).

протки́нуть (-ну́, -нёшь) *pf* (*impf* протыка́ть) pierce; skewer.

протоко́л minutes; report; protocol.

протолкну́ть (-ну́, -нёшь) *pf* (*impf* прота́лкивать) push through.

прото́н proton.

протопи́ть (-плю́, -пишь) *pf* (*impf* прота́пливать) heat (thoroughly).

протопта́ть (-пчу́, -пчешь) *pf* (*impf* прота́птывать) tread; wear out.

проторённый beaten, well-trodden.

прототи́п prototype.

прото́чный flowing, running.

про|тра́лить *pf*. протру́ *etc.*: *see* протере́ть. про|труби́ть (-блю́) *pf*.

протрезви́ться (-влюсь) *pf*, протрезвля́ться *impf* sober up.

протуха́ть *impf*, проту́хнуть (-нет; -у́х) *pf* become rotten; go bad.

протыка́ть *impf of* проткну́ть

протя́гивать *impf*, протяну́ть (-ну́, -нешь) *pf* stretch; extend; hold out;

~ся stretch out; extend; last. протяже́ние extent, stretch; period. протя́жный long-drawn-out; drawling.

проу́чивать *impf*, проучи́ть (-чу́, -чишь) *pf* study; teach a lesson.

профа́н ignoramus.

профана́ция profanation.

профессиона́л professional. профессиона́льный professional; occupational. профе́ссия profession. профе́ссор (*pl* -а́) professor.

профила́ктика prophylaxis; preventive measures.

про́филь *m* profile; type.

про|фильтрова́ть *pf*.

профсою́з trade-union.

проха́живаться *impf of* пройти́сь

прохво́ст scoundrel.

прохла́да coolness. прохлади́тельный refreshing, cooling. прохла́дный cool, chilly.

прохо́д passage; gangway, aisle; duct. проходи́мец (-мца) rogue. проходи́мый passable. проходи́ть (-ожу́, -о́дишь) *impf of* пройти́. проходно́й entrance; communicating. проходя́щий passing. прохо́жий passing, in transit; *sb* passer-by.

процвета́ние prosperity. процвета́ть *impf* prosper, flourish.

процеди́ть (-ежу́, -е́дишь) *pf* (*impf* проце́живать) filter, strain.

процеду́ра procedure; (*usu in pl*) treatment.

проце́живать *pf of* процеди́ть

проце́нт percentage; per cent; interest.

проце́сс process; trial; legal proceedings. проце́ссия procession.

про|цити́ровать *pf*.

прочёска screening; combing.

проче́сть (-чту́, -чтёшь; -чёл, -чла́) *pf of* чита́ть

про́чий other.

прочи́стить (-и́щу) *pf* (*impf* прочища́ть) clean; clear.

про|чита́ть *pf*, прочи́тывать *impf* read (through).

прочища́ть *impf of* прочи́стить

про́чность firmness, stability, durability. про́чный (-чен, -чна́, -о) firm, sound, solid; durable.

прочте́ние reading. прочту́ *etc.*: *see* прочте́сть

прочу́вствовать *pf* feel deeply;

experience, go through.

прочь adv away, off; averse to.

прошёдший past; last. **прошёл** etc.: see **пройти**

прошёние application, petition.

прошептать (-пчу, -пчешь) pf whisper.

прошёствие: по прошёствии +gen after.

прошивать impf, **прошить** (-шью, -шьёшь) pf sew, stitch.

прошлогодний last year's. **прошлый** past; last; ~oe sb the past.

про|шнуровать pf. **про|штудировать** pf. **прошью** etc.: see **прошить**

прощай(те) goodbye. **прощальный** parting; farewell. **прощание** farewell; parting. **прощать(ся** impf of **простить(ся**

прóще simpler, plainer.

прощёние forgiveness, pardon.

прощупать pf, **прощупывать** impf feel.

про|экзаменовать pf.

проявитель m developer. **проявить** (-влю, -вишь) pf, **проявлять** impf show, display; develop; ~ся reveal itself. **проявление** display; manifestation; developing.

проясниться pf, **проясняться** impf clear, clear up.

пруд (-а, loc -ý) pond. **прудить** (-ужу, -ýдишь) impf (pf за~) dam.

пружина spring. **пружинистый** springy. **пружинный** spring.

прусский Prussian.

прут (-а or -á; pl -тья) twig.

прыгать impf, **прыгнуть** (-ну) pf jump, leap; bounce; ~ с шестом pole-vault. **прыгун** (-á), **прыгунья** (gen pl -ний) jumper. **прыжóк** (-жка) jump; leap; **прыжки** jumping; прыжки в воду diving; ~ в высоту high jump; ~ в длину long jump.

прыскать impf, **прыснуть** (-ну) pf spurt; sprinkle; burst out laughing. **прыть** speed; energy.

прыщ (-á), **прыщик** pimple.

прядильный spinning. **прядильня** (gen pl -лен) (spinning-)mill. **прядильщик** spinner. **пряду** etc.: see **прясть. прядь** lock; strand. **пряжа** yarn, thread.

пряжка buckle, clasp.

прялка distaff; spinning-wheel.

прямая sb straight line. **прямо** adv straight; straight on; frankly; really.

прямодушие directness, straightforwardness. ~**душный** direct, straightforward.

прямой (-ям, -á, -о) straight; upright, erect; through; direct; straightforward; real.

прямолинейный rectilinear; straightforward. **прямоугольник** rectangle. **прямоугольный** rectangular.

пряник spice cake. **пряность** spice. **пряный** spicy; heady.

прясть (-яду, -ядёшь; -ял, -ялá, -о) impf (pf с~) spin.

прятать (-ячу) impf (pf с~) hide; ~ся hide. **прятки** (-ток) pl hide-and-seek.

пса etc.: see **пёс**

псалóм (-лмá) psalm. **псалтырь** Psalter.

псевдоним pseudonym.

псих madman, lunatic. **психиатрия** psychiatry. **психика** psyche; psychology. **психический** mental, psychical.

психоанализ psychoanalysis. **психоз** psychosis. **психолог** psychologist. **психологический** psychological. **психология** psychology. **психопат** psychopath. **психопатический** psychopathic. **психосоматический** psychosomatic. **психотерапевт** psychotherapist. **психотерапия** psychotherapy. **психотический** psychotic.

птенец (-нцá) nestling; fledgeling. **птица** bird. **птицеферма** poultry-farm. **птичий** bird, bird's; poultry. **птичка** bird; tick.

публика public; audience. **публикация** publication; notice, advertisement. **публиковать** impf (pf о~) publish. **публицистика** writing on current affairs. **публичность** publicity. **публичный** public; ~ дом brothel.

пугало scarecrow. **пугать** impf (pf ис~, на~) frighten; scare; ~ся (+gen) be frightened (of). **пугач** (-á) toy pistol. **пугливый** fearful.

пуговица button.

пуд (pl -ы) pood (= 16.38 kg). **пудовой, пудóвый** one pood in weight.

пу́дель *m* poodle.

пу́динг blancmange.

пу́дра powder. **пу́дреница** powder compact. **пу́дреный** powdered. **пу́дриться** *impf (pf* на∼) powder one's face.

пуза́тый pot-bellied.

пузырёк (-рька́) vial; bubble. **пузы́рь** (-я́) *m* bubble; blister; bladder.

пук (*pl* -и́) bunch, bundle; tuft.

пу́кать *impf*, **пу́кнуть** *pf* fart.

пулемёт machine-gun. **пулемётчик** machine-gunner. **пуленепробива́емый** bullet-proof.

пульвериза́тор atomizer; spray.

пульс pulse. **пульса́р** pulsar. **пульси́ровать** *impf* pulsate.

пульт desk, stand; control panel.

пу́ля bullet.

пункт point; spot; post; item. **пункти́р** dotted line. **пункти́рный** dotted, broken.

пунктуа́льный punctual.

пунктуа́ция punctuation.

пунцо́вый crimson.

пуп (-а́) navel. **пупови́на** umbilical cord. **пупо́к** (-пка́) navel; gizzard.

пурга́ blizzard.

пурита́нин (*pl* -та́не, -та́н), -**а́нка** Puritan.

пурпу́р purple, crimson. **пурпу́р|ный**, ∼**овый** purple.

пуск starting (up). **пуска́й** *see* пусть. **пуска́ть(ся** *impf of* пусти́ть(ся. **пусково́й** starting.

пусте́ть (-е́ет) *impf (pf* о∼) empty; become deserted.

пусти́ть (пущу́, пу́стишь) *pf (impf* пуска́ть) let go; let in; let; start; send; set in motion; throw; put forth; ∼**ся** set out; start.

пустова́ть *impf* be *or* stand empty. **пусто́й** (-ст, -а́, -о) empty; uninhabited; idle; shallow. **пустота́** (*pl* -ы) emptiness; void; vacuum; futility. **пустоте́лый** hollow.

пусты́нный uninhabited; deserted; desert. **пусты́ня** desert. **пусты́рь** (-я́) *m* waste land; vacant plot.

пусты́шка blank; hollow object; dummy.

пусть, пуска́й *partl* let; all right; though, even if.

пустя́к (-а́) trifle. **пустяко́вый** trivial.

пу́таница muddle, confusion. **пу́таный** muddled, confused. **пу́тать** *impf (pf* за∼, пере∼, с∼) tangle; confuse; mix up; ∼**ся** get confused *or* mixed up.

путёвка pass; place on a group tour. **путеводи́тель** *m* guide, guide-book. **путево́й** travelling; road. **путём** *prep+gen* by means of. **путеше́ственник** traveller. **путеше́ствие** journey; voyage. **путеше́ствовать** *impf* travel; voyage.

пу́ты (пут) *pl* shackles.

путь (-и́, *instr* -ём, *prep* -и́) way; track; path; course; journey; voyage; means; в пути́ en route, on one's way.

пух (*loc* -у́) down; fluff.

пу́хлый (-хл, -а́, -о) plump. **пу́хнуть** (-ну; пух) *impf (pf* вс∼, о∼) swell.

пухови́к (-а́) feather-bed. **пухо́вка** powder-puff. **пухо́вый** downy.

пучи́на abyss; the deep.

пучо́к (-чка́) bunch, bundle.

пу́шечный gun, cannon.

пуши́нка bit of fluff. **пуши́стый** fluffy.

пу́шка gun, cannon.

пушни́на furs, pelts. **пушно́й** fur; fur-bearing.

пу́ще *adv* more; ∼ всего́ most of all.

пущу́ *etc.: see* пусти́ть

пчела́ (*pl* -ёлы) bee. **пчели́ный** bee, bees'. **пчелово́д** bee-keeper. **пче́льник** apiary.

пшени́ца wheat. **пшени́чный** wheat(en).

пшённый millet. **пшено́** millet.

пыл (*loc* -у́) heat, ardour. **пыла́ть** *impf* blaze; burn.

пылесо́с vacuum cleaner. **пылесо́сить** *impf* vacuum (-clean).

пыли́нка speck of dust. **пыли́ть** *impf (pf* за∼, на∼) raise a dust; cover with dust; ∼**ся** get dusty.

пы́лкий ardent; fervent.

пыль (*loc* -и́) dust. **пы́льный** (-лен, -льна́, -о) dusty. **пыльца́** pollen.

пыре́й couch grass.

пырну́ть (-ну́, -нёшь) *pf* jab.

пыта́ть *impf* torture. **пыта́ться** *impf (pf* по∼) try. **пы́тка** torture, torment. **пытли́вый** inquisitive.

пыхте́ть (-хчу́) *impf* puff, pant.

пы́шка bun.

пы́шность splendour. **пы́шный**

(-шен, -шна́, -шно) splendid; lush.
пьедеста́л pedestal.
пье́са play; piece.
пью *etc.*: *see* пить
пьяне́ть (-е́ю) *impf* (*pf* о~) get drunk. **пьяни́ть** *impf* (*pf* о~) intoxicate, make drunk. **пья́ница** *m & f* drunkard. **пья́нство** drunkenness. **пья́нствовать** *impf* drink heavily. **пья́ный** drunk.
пюпи́тр lectern; stand.
пюре́ *neut indecl* purée.
пядь (*gen pl* -éй) span; ни пя́ди not an inch.
пя́льцы (-лец) *pl* embroidery frame.
пята́ (*pl* -ы, -а́м) heel.
пята́к (-а́), **пятачо́к** (-чка́) five-copeck piece. **пятёрка** five; figure 5; No. 5; fiver (5-*rouble note*).
пяти- *in comb* five; penta-. **пяти-бо́рье** pentathlon. ~**десятиле́тие** fifty years; fiftieth anniversary, birthday. П~**деся́тница** Pentecost. ~**деся́тый** fiftieth; ~**деся́тые го́ды** the fifties. ~**коне́чный** five-pointed. ~**ле́тие** five years; fifth anniversary. ~**ле́тка** five-year plan. ~**со́тый** five-hundredth. ~**уго́льник** pentagon. ~**уго́льный** pentagonal.
пя́титься (пя́чусь) *impf* (*pf* по~) move backwards; back.
пя́тка heel.
пятна́дцатый fifteenth. **пятна́дцать** fifteen.
пятна́ть *impf* (*pf* за~) spot, stain. **пятна́шки** (-шек) *pl* tag. **пятни́стый** spotted.
пя́тница Friday.
пятно́ (*pl* -а, -тен) stain; spot; blot; роди́мое ~ birth-mark.
пя́тый fifth. **пять** (-й, *instr* -ью) five. **пятьдеся́т** (-и́десяти, *instr* -ью-деся́тью) fifty. **пятьсо́т** (-тисо́т, -тиста́м) five hundred. **пя́тью** *adv* five times.

Р

раб (-а́), **раба́** slave. **рабовладе́лец** (-льца) slave-owner. **раболе́пие** servility. **раболе́пный** servile. **рабо-ле́пствовать** cringe, fawn.
рабо́та work; job; functioning. **рабо́-тать** *impf* work; function; be open;

~ над+*instr* work on. **рабо́тник,** -**ица** worker. **работоспосо́бность** capacity for work, efficiency. **рабо-тоспосо́бный** able-bodied, hard-working. **рабо́тящий** hardworking.
рабо́чий *sb* worker. **рабо́чий** worker's; -working; ~**ая си́ла** man-power.
ра́бский slave; servile. **ра́бство** slavery. **рабы́ня** female slave.
равви́н rabbi.
ра́венство equality. **равне́ние** alignment. **равни́на** plain.
равно́ *adv* alike; equally; ~ как as well as. **равно́** *predic*: *see* ра́вный
равно- *in comb* equi-, iso-. **рав-нобе́дренный** isosceles. ~**ве́сие** equilibrium; balance. ~**де́нствие** equinox. ~**ду́шие** indifference. ~**ду́шный** indifferent. ~**ме́рный** even; uniform. ~**пра́вие** equality of rights. ~**пра́вный** having equal rights. ~**си́льный** of equal strength; equal, equivalent, tantamount. ~**сто-ро́нний** equilateral. ~**це́нный** of equal value; equivalent.
ра́вный (-вен, -вна́) equal. **равно́** *predic* make(s), equal; всё ~ о́ (it is) all the same. **равня́ть** *impf* (*pf* c~) make even; treat equally; +c+*instr* compare with, treat as equal to; ~**ся** compete, compare; be equal; be tantamount.
рад (-а, -о) *predic* glad.
рада́р radar.
ра́ди *prep*+*gen* for the sake of.
радиа́тор radiator. **радиа́ция** radiation.
ра́дий radium.
радика́льный radical.
ра́дио *neut indecl* radio.
радио- *in comb* radio-; radioactive. **радиоакти́вный** radioactive. ~**ве-ща́ние** broadcasting. ~**волна́** radio-wave. ~**гра́мма** radio-telegram. **ра-дио́лог** radiologist. ~**ло́гия** radiology. ~**лока́тор** radar (set). ~**лю-би́тель** *m* radio amateur, ham. ~**мая́к** (-а́) radio beacon. ~**переда́тчик** transmitter. ~**переда́ча** broadcast. ~**приёмник** radio (set). ~**связь** radio communication. ~**слу́шатель** *m* listener. ~**ста́нция** radio station. ~**электро́ника** radio-electronics.

радио́ла radiogram.

ради́ровать *impf & pf* radio. **ра-**
ди́ст radio operator.

ра́диус radius.

ра́довать *impf* (*pf* об~, по~) gladden, make happy; ~**ся** be glad, rejoice. **ра́достный** joyful. **ра́дость**
gladness, joy.

ра́дуга rainbow. **ра́дужн|ый** irides-
cent; cheerful; ~**ая оболо́чка** iris.

раду́шие cordiality. **раду́шный** cordial.

ражу́ *etc.: see* **рази́ть**

раз (*pl* -**ы́**, раз) time, occasion; one;
ещё ~ (once) again; как ~ just, exactly; не ~ more than once; ни ~**у**
not once. **раз** *adv* once, one day. **раз**
conj if; since.

разба́вить (-влю) *pf*, **разбавля́ть**
impf dilute.

разба́заривать *impf*, **разбаза́рить**
pf squander.

разба́лтывать(ся *impf of* **разбол-**
та́ть(ся

разбе́г running start. **разбега́ться**
impf, **разбежа́ться** (-егу́сь) *pf* take
a run, run up; scatter.

разберу́ *etc.: see* **разобра́ть**

разбива́ть(ся *impf of* **разби́ть(ся.**
разби́вка laying out; spacing (out).

разбинтова́ть *pf*, **разбинто́вывать**
impf unbandage.

разбира́тельство investigation.
разбира́ть *impf of* **разобра́ть**; ~**ся**
impf of **разобра́ться**

разби́ть (-зобью́, -зобьёшь) *pf* (*impf*
разбива́ть) break; smash; divide
(up); damage; defeat; mark out; space
(out); ~**ся** break, get broken; hurt
o.s. **разби́тый** broken; jaded.

раз|богате́ть (-е́ю) *pf*.

разбо́й robbery. **разбо́йник** robber.
разбо́йничий robber.

разболе́ться[1] (-ли́тся) *pf* begin to
ache badly.

разболе́ться[2] (-е́юсь) *pf* become ill.

разболта́ть[1] *pf* (*impf* **разба́лты-**
вать) divulge, give away.

разболта́ть[2] *pf* (*impf* **разба́лты-**
вать) shake up; loosen; ~**ся** work
loose; get out of hand.

разбомби́ть (-блю́) *pf* bomb, destroy
by bombing.

разбо́р analysis; critique; discrimination; investigation. **разбо́рка** sorting

out; dismantling. **разбо́рный** collapsible. **разбо́рчивый** legible; dis-
criminating.

разбра́сывать *impf of* **разброса́ть**

разбреда́ться *impf*, **разбрести́сь**
(-едётся; -ёлся, -ла́сь) *pf* disperse;
straggle. **разбро́д** disorder.

разбро́санный scattered; disconnected, incoherent. **разброса́ть** *pf*
(*impf* **разбра́сывать**) throw about;
scatter.

раз|буди́ть (-ужу́, -у́дишь) *pf*.

разбуха́ть *impf*, **разбу́хнуть** (-нет;
-бу́х) *pf* swell.

разбушева́ться (-шу́юсь) *pf* fly into
a rage; blow up; rage.

разва́л breakdown, collapse. **разва́-**
ливать *impf*, **развали́ть** (-лю́, -лишь)
pf pull down; mess up; ~**ся** collapse;
go to pieces; tumble down; sprawl.
разва́лина ruin; wreck.

ра́зве *partl* really?; ~ (то́лько), ~
(что) except that, only.

развева́ться *impf* fly, flutter.

разве́дать *pf* (*impf* **разве́дывать**)
find out; reconnoitre.

разведе́ние breeding; cultivation.

разведён|ный divorced; ~**ый**, ~**ая**
sb divorcee.

разве́дка intelligence (service); reconnaissance; prospecting. **разве́-**
дочный prospecting, exploratory.

разведу́ *etc.: see* **развести́**

разве́дчик intelligence officer; scout;
prospector. **разве́дывать** *impf of*
разве́дать

развезти́ (-зу́, -зёшь; -ёз, -ла́) *pf*
(*impf* **развози́ть**) convey, transport;
deliver.

развева́ть(ся *impf of* **разве́ять(ся.**
развёл *etc.: see* **развести́**

развенча́ть *pf*, **развенчивать** *impf*
dethrone; debunk.

развёрнутый extensive, all-out; detailed. **разверну́ть** (-ну́, -нёшь) *pf*
(*impf* **развёртывать, развора́чи-**
вать) unfold, unwrap; unroll; unfurl;
deploy; expand; develop; turn; scan;
display; ~**ся** unfold, unroll, come un-
wrapped; deploy; develop; spread;
turn.

разве́рстка allotment, apportionment.

развёртывать(ся *impf of* **разверну́ть(ся**

раз|веселить pf cheer up, amuse; ~ся cheer up.

развесить[1] (-ешу) pf (impf развешивать) spread; hang (out).

развесить[2] (-ешу) pf (impf развешивать) weigh out. **развеска** weighing. **развесной** sold by weight.

развести (-еду, -едёшь; -ёл, -а) pf (impf разводить) take; separate; divorce; dilute; dissolve; start; breed; cultivate; ~сь get divorced; breed, multiply.

разветвиться (-ится) pf, разветвляться impf branch; fork. **разветвление** branching, forking; branch; fork.

развешать pf, развешивать impf hang.

развешивать impf of развесить, развешать. **развешу** etc.: see развесить

развеять (-ею) pf (impf развеивать) scatter, disperse; dispel; ~ся disperse; be dispelled.

развивать(ся impf of развить(ся

развилка fork.

развинтить (-нчу) pf, развинчивать impf unscrew.

развитие development. **развитой** (развит, -á, -о) developed; mature. **развить** (-зовью; -зовьёшь; -ил, -á, -о) pf (impf развивать) develop; unwind; ~ся develop.

развлекать impf, развлечь (-еку, -ечёшь; -ёк, -ла) pf entertain, amuse; ~ся have a good time; amuse o.s. **развлечение** entertainment, amusement.

развод divorce. **разводить(ся** (-ожу(сь, -одишь(ся) impf of развести(сь. **разводка** separation. **разводной**: ~ ключ adjustable spanner; ~ мост drawbridge.

развозить (-ожу, -озишь) impf of развезти

разволноваться pf get excited, be agitated.

разворачивать(ся impf of развернуть(ся

разворовать pf, разворовывать impf loot; steal.

разворот U-turn; turn; development. **разврат** depravity, corruption. **развратить** (-ащу) pf. **развращать** impf corrupt; deprave. **разврат-** ничать impf lead a depraved life. **развратный** debauched, corrupt. **развращённый** (-ён, -á) corrupt.

развязать (-яжу, -яжешь) pf, развязывать impf untie; unleash; ~ся come untied; ~ся c+instr rid o.s. of. **развязка** dénouement; outcome. **развязный** overfamiliar.

разгадать pf, разгадывать impf solve, guess, interpret. **разгадка** solution.

разгар height, climax.

разгибать(ся impf of разогнуть(ся

разглагольствовать impf hold forth.

разгладить (-ажу) pf, разглаживать impf smooth out; iron (out).

разгласить (-ашу) pf, разглашать impf divulge; +о+prep trumpet. **разглашение** disclosure.

разглядеть (-яжу) pf, разглядывать impf make out, discern.

разгневать pf anger. **раз|гневаться** pf.

разговаривать impf talk, converse. **разговор** conversation. **разговорник** phrase-book. **разговорный** colloquial. **разговорчивый** talkative.

разгон dispersal; running start; distance. **разгонять(ся** impf of разогнать(ся

разгораживать impf of разгородить

разгораться impf, разгореться (-рюсь) pf flare up.

разгородить (-ожу, -одишь) pf (impf разгораживать) partition off.

раз|горячить(ся (-чу(сь) pf.

разграбить (-блю) pf plunder, loot. **разграбление** plunder, looting.

разграничение demarcation; differentiation. **разграничивать** impf, разграничить (-чу) pf delimit; differentiate.

разгребать impf, разгрести (-ебу, -ебёшь; -ёб, -ла) pf rake or shovel (away).

разгром crushing defeat; devastation; havoc. **разгромить** (-млю) pf rout, defeat.

разгружать(ся impf, разгрузить (-ужу, -узишь) pf unload; relieve; ~ся unload; be relieved. **разгрузка** unloading; relief.

разгрыза́ть *impf*, **раз|гры́зть** (-зу́, -зёшь; -ыз) *pf* crack.

разгу́л revelry; outburst. **разгу́ливать** *impf* stroll about. **разгу́ливаться** *impf*, **разгуля́ться** *pf* spread o.s.; become wide awake; clear up. **разгу́льный** rowdy, rakish.

раздава́ть(ся (-даю́(сь, -даёшь(ся) *impf of* **разда́ть(ся**

раз|дави́ть (-влю́, -вишь; *pf*. **разда́вливать** *impf* crush; run over.

разда́ть (-а́м, -а́шь, -а́ст, -ади́м; ро́з*or* разда́л, -а́, -о) *pf* (*impf* **раздава́ть**) distribute, give out; ~ся be heard; resound; ring out; make way; expand; put on weight. **разда́ча** distribution. **раздаю́** *etc.*: *see* **раздава́ть**

раздва́ивать(ся *impf of* **раздво́ить(ся**

раздвига́ть *impf*, **раздви́нуть** (-ну) *pf* move apart; ~ся move apart. **раздвижно́й** expanding; sliding.

раздвое́ние division; split; ~ ли́чности split personality. **раздво́енный** forked; cloven; split. **раздво́ить** (-ою́) *pf* (*impf* **раздва́ивать**) divide into two; bisect; ~ся fork; split.

раздева́лка cloakroom. **раздева́ть(ся** *impf of* **разде́ть(ся**

разде́л division; section.

разде́латься *pf* +*c*+*instr* finish with; settle accounts with.

разделе́ние division. **разде́лимый** divisible. **раз|дели́ть** (-лю́, -лишь) *pf*, **разделя́ть** *impf* divide; separate; share; ~ся divide; be divided; be divisible; separate. **разде́льный** separate.

разде́ну *etc.*: *see* **разде́ть. раздеру́** *etc.*: *see* **разодра́ть**

разде́ть (-е́ну) *pf* (*impf* **раздева́ть**) undress; ~ся undress; take off one's coat.

раздира́ть *impf of* **разодра́ть**

раздобыва́ть *impf*, **раздобы́ть** (-бу́ду) *pf* get, get hold of.

раздо́лье expanse; liberty. **раздо́льный** free.

раздо́р discord.

раздоса́довать *pf* vex.

раздража́ть *impf*, **раздражи́ть** (-жу́) *pf* irritate; annoy; ~ся get annoyed. **раздраже́ние** irritation. **раздражи́тельный** irritable.

раз|дроби́ть (-блю́) *pf*, **раздробля́ть** *impf* break; smash to pieces.

раздува́ть(ся *impf of* **разду́ть(ся**

разду́мать *pf*, **разду́мывать** *impf* change one's mind; ponder. **разду́мье** meditation; thought.

разду́ть (-у́ю) *pf* (*impf* **раздува́ть**) blow; fan; exaggerate; whip up; swell; ~ся swell.

разева́ть *impf of* **рази́нуть**

разжа́лобить (-блю) *pf* move (to pity).

разжа́ловать *pf* demote.

разжа́ть (-зожму́, -мёшь) *pf* (*impf* **разжима́ть**) unclasp; open; release.

разжева́ть (-жую́, -жуёшь) *pf*, **разжёвывать** *impf* chew.

разже́чь (-зожгу́, -зожжёшь; -жёг, -зожгла́) *pf*, **разжига́ть** *impf* kindle; rouse.

разжима́ть *impf of* **разжа́ть**.

раз|жире́ть (-е́ю) *pf*.

рази́нуть (-ну) *pf* (*impf* **разева́ть**) open; ~ рот gape. **рази́ня** *m* & *f* scatter-brain.

рази́тельный striking. **рази́ть** (ражу́) *impf* (*pf* **по~**) strike.

разлага́ть(ся *impf of* **разложи́ть(ся**

разла́д discord; disorder.

разла́мывать(ся *impf of* **разлома́ть(ся, разломи́ть(ся. разлёгся** *etc.*: *see* **разле́чься**

разлеза́ться *impf*, **разле́зться** (-зется; -ле́зся) *pf* come to pieces; fall apart.

разлета́ться *impf*, **разлете́ться** (-лечу́сь) *pf* fly away; scatter; shatter; rush.

разле́чься (-ля́гусь, -ля́жется, -гла́сь) *pf* stretch out.

разли́в bottling; flood; overflow. **разлива́ть** *impf*, **разли́ть** (-золью́, -зольёшь; -и́л, -а́, -о) *pf* pour out; spill; flood (with); ~ся spill; overflow; spread. **разливно́й** draught.

различа́ть *impf*, **различи́ть** (-чу́) *pf* distinguish; discern; ~ся differ. **разли́чие** distinction; difference. **различи́тельный** distinctive, distinguishing. **разли́чный** different.

разложе́ние decomposition; decay; disintegration. **разложи́ть** (-жу́, -жишь) *pf* (*impf* **разлага́ть, раскла́дывать**) put away; spread (out); distribute; break down; decompose;

resolve; corrupt; ~ся decompose; become demoralized; be corrupted; disintegrate, go to pieces.

разло́м breaking; break. разлома́ть, разломи́ть (-млю, -мишь) pf (impf разла́мывать) break to pieces; pull down; ~ся break to pieces.

разлу́ка separation. разлуча́ть impf, разлучи́ть (-чу́) pf separate, part; ~ся separate, part.

разлюби́ть (-блю́, -бишь) pf stop loving or liking.

разля́гусь etc.: see разле́чься

разма́зать (-а́жу) pf, разма́зывать impf spread, smear.

размалывать impf of размоло́ть

разма́тывать impf of размота́ть

разма́х sweep; swing; span; scope. разма́хивать impf +instr swing; brandish. разма́хиваться impf, размахну́ться (-ну́сь, -нёшься) pf swing one's arm. разма́шистый sweeping.

размежева́ние demarcation, delimitation. размежева́ть (-жу́ю) pf, размежёвывать impf delimit.

размёл etc.: see размести́

размельча́ть impf, раз|мельчи́ть (-чу́) pf crush, pulverize.

размелю́ etc.: see размоло́ть

разме́н exchange. разме́нивать impf, разменя́ть pf change; ~ся +instr exchange; dissipate. разме́нная моне́та (small) change.

разме́р size; measurement; amount; scale, extent; pl proportions. разме́ренный measured. разме́рить pf, размеря́ть impf measure.

размести́ (-ету́, -етёшь; -мёл, -а́) pf (impf размета́ть) sweep clear; sweep away.

размести́ть (-ещу́) pf (impf размеща́ть) place, accommodate; distribute; ~ся take one's seat.

размета́ть impf of размести́

разме́тить (-е́чу) pf, размеча́ть impf mark.

размеша́ть pf, разме́шивать impf stir (in).

размеща́ть(ся impf of размести́ть(ся. размеще́ние placing; accommodation; distribution. размещу́ etc.: see размести́ть

размина́ть(ся impf of размя́ть(ся

разми́нка limbering up.

размину́ться (-ну́сь, -нёшься) pf pass; +c+instr pass; miss.

размножа́ть impf, размно́жить (-жу) pf multiply, duplicate; breed; ~ся multiply; breed.

размозжи́ть (-жу́) pf smash.

размо́лвка tiff.

размоло́ть (-мелю́, -ме́лешь) pf (impf разма́лывать) grind.

размора́живать impf, разморо́зить (-о́жу) pf unfreeze, defrost; ~ся unfreeze; defrost.

размота́ть pf (impf разма́тывать) unwind.

размыва́ть impf, размы́ть (-о́ет) pf wash away; erode.

размыка́ть impf of разомкну́ть

размышле́ние reflection; meditation. размышля́ть impf reflect, ponder.

размягча́ть impf, размягчи́ть (-чу́) pf soften; ~ся soften.

размяка́ть impf, размя́кнуть (-ну; -мя́к) pf soften.

раз|мя́ть (-зомну́, -зомнёшь) pf (impf also размина́ть) knead; mash; ~ся stretch one's legs; limber up.

разна́шивать impf of разноси́ть

разнести́ (-су́, -сёшь; -ёс, -ла́) pf (impf разноси́ть) carry; deliver; spread; note down; smash; scold; scatter; impers make puffy, swell.

разнима́ть impf of разня́ть

ра́зниться impf differ. ра́зница difference.

разно- in comb different, vari-, hetero-. разнобо́й lack of co-ordination; difference. ~ви́дность variety. ~гла́сие disagreement; discrepancy. ~обра́зие variety, diversity. ~обра́зный various, diverse. ~речи́вый contradictory. ~ро́дный heterogeneous. ~сторо́нний many-sided; versatile. ~цве́тный variegated. ~шёрстный of different colours; ill-assorted.

разноси́ть[1] (-ошу́, -о́сишь) pf (impf разна́шивать) wear in.

разноси́ть[2] (-ошу́, -о́сишь) impf of разнести́. разно́ска delivery.

ра́зность difference.

разно́счик pedlar.

разношу́ etc.: see разноси́ть

разну́зданный unbridled.

ра́зн|ый different; various; ~ое sb

various things.

разню́хать pf, **разню́хивать** impf smell out.

разня́ть (-ниму́, -ни́мешь; ро́з- or разня́л, -а́, -о) pf (impf **разнима́ть**) take to pieces; separate.

разоблача́ть impf, **разоблачи́ть** (-чу́) pf expose. **разоблаче́ние** exposure.

разобра́ть (-зберу́, -рёшь; -а́л, -а́, -о) pf (impf **разбира́ть**) take to pieces; buy up; sort out; investigate; analyse; understand; ~ся sort things out; +в+prep investigate, look into; understand.

разобща́ть impf, **разобщи́ть** (-щу́) pf separate; estrange, alienate.

разобью́ etc.: see **разби́ть. разовью́** etc.: see **разви́ть**

ра́зовый single.

разгоня́ть (-згоню́, -о́нишь; -гна́л, -а́, -о) pf (impf **разгоня́ть**) scatter; disperse; dispel; drive fast; ~ся gather speed.

разогну́ть (-ну́, -нёшь) pf (impf **разгиба́ть**) unbend, straighten; ~ся straighten up.

разогрева́ть impf, **разогре́ть** (-е́ю) pf warm up.

разоде́ть(ся (-е́ну(сь) pf dress up.

разодра́ть (-здеру́, -рёшь; -а́л, -а́, -о) pf (impf **раздира́ть**) tear (up); lacerate.

разожгу́ etc.: see **разже́чь. разожму́** etc.: see **разжа́ть**

разо|зли́ть pf.

разойти́сь (-йду́сь, -йдёшься; -ошёлся, -ошла́сь) pf (impf **расходи́ться**) disperse; diverge; radiate; differ; conflict; part; be spent; be sold out.

разолью́ etc.: see **разли́ть**

ра́зом adv at once, at one go.

разомкну́ть (-ну, -нёшь) pf (impf **размыка́ть**) open; break.

разомну́ etc.: see **размя́ть**

разорва́ть (-ву́, -вёшь; -а́л, -а́, -о) pf (impf **разрыва́ть**) tear; break (off); blow up; ~ся tear; break; explode.

разоре́ние ruin; destruction. **разори́тельный** ruinous; wasteful. **разори́ть** pf (impf **разоря́ть**) ruin; destroy; ~ся ruin o.s.

разоружа́ть impf, **разоружи́ть** (-жу́) pf disarm; ~ся disarm. **разоруже́ние** disarmament.

разоря́ть(ся impf of **разори́ть(ся**

разосла́ть (-ошлю́, -ошлёшь) pf (impf **рассыла́ть**) distribute, circulate.

разостла́ть, расстели́ть (-сстелю́, -те́лешь) pf (impf **расстила́ть**) spread (out); lay; ~ся spread.

разотру́ etc.: see **растере́ть**

разочарова́ние disappointment.

разочарова́ть pf, **разочаро́вывать** impf disappoint; ~ся be disappointed.

разочту́ etc.: see **расче́сть. разошёлся** etc.: see **разойти́сь. разошлю́** etc.: see **разосла́ть. разошью́** etc.: see **расши́ть**

разраба́тывать impf, **разрабо́тать** pf cultivate; work, exploit; work out; develop. **разрабо́тка** cultivation; working out; mining; quarry.

разража́ться impf, **разрази́ться** (-ажу́сь) pf break out; burst out.

разраста́ться impf, **разрасти́сь** (-тётся; -ро́сся, -ла́сь) pf grow; spread.

разрежённый (-ён, -а́) rarefied.

разре́з cut; section; point of view. **разреза́ть** (-е́жу) pf, **разреза́ть** impf cut; slit.

разреша́ть impf, **разреши́ть** (-шу́) pf (+dat) allow; solve; settle; ~ся be allowed; be solved; be settled. **разреше́ние** permission; permit; solution; settlement. **разреши́мый** solvable.

разро́зненный uncoordinated; odd; incomplete.

разро́сся etc.: see **разрасти́сь. разро́ю** etc.: see **разры́ть**

разруба́ть impf, **разруби́ть** (-блю́, -бишь) pf cut; chop up.

разру́ха ruin, collapse. **разруша́ть** impf, **разру́шить** (-шу) pf destroy; demolish; ruin; ~ся go to ruin, collapse. **разруше́ние** destruction. **разруши́тельный** destructive.

разры́в break; gap; rupture; burst. **разрыва́ть**[1]**(ся** impf of **разорва́ть(ся**

разрыва́ть[2] impf of **разры́ть**

разрывно́й explosive.

разрыда́ться pf burst into tears.

разры́ть (-ро́ю) pf (impf **разрыва́ть**) dig (up).

раз|рыхли́ть pf, **разрыхля́ть** impf loosen; hoe.

разря́д[1] category; class.

разря́д[2] discharge. разряди́ть (-яжу́, -я́дишь) pf (impf разряжа́ть) unload; discharge; space out; ~ся run down; clear, ease. разря́дка spacing (out); discharging; unloading; relieving.

разряжа́ть(ся impf of разряди́ть(ся

разубеди́ть (-ежу́) pf, разубежда́ть impf dissuade; ~ся change one's mind.

разува́ться impf of разу́ться

разуве́рить pf, разуверя́ть impf dissuade, undeceive; ~ся (в+prep) lose faith (in).

разузнава́ть (-наю́, -наёшь) impf, разузна́ть pf (try to) find out.

разукра́сить (-а́шу) pf, разукра́шивать impf adorn, embellish.

ра́зум reason; intellect. разуме́ться (-е́ется) impf be understood; be meant; (само́ собо́й) разуме́ется of course; it goes without saying. разу́мный rational, intelligent; sensible; reasonable; wise.

разу́ться (-у́юсь) pf (impf разува́ться) take off one's shoes.

разу́чивать impf, разучи́ть (-чу́, -чишь) pf learn (up). разучи́ться impf, разучи́ться (-чу́сь, -чишься) pf forget (how to).

разъеда́ть impf of разъе́сть

разъедини́ть pf, разъединя́ть impf separate; disconnect.

разъе́дусь etc.: see разъе́хаться

разъе́зд departure; siding (track); mounted patrol; pl travel; journeys. разъездно́й travelling. разъезжа́ть impf drive or ride about; travel; ~ся impf of разъе́хаться

разъе́сть (-е́ст, -едя́т; -е́л) pf (impf разъеда́ть) eat away; corrode.

разъе́хаться (-е́дусь) pf (impf разъезжа́ться) depart; separate; pass (one another); miss one another.

разъярённый (-ён, -а́) furious. разъяри́ть pf, разъяря́ть impf infuriate; ~ся get furious.

разъясне́ние explanation; interpretation. разъясни́тельный explanatory. разъясни́ть pf, разъясня́ть impf explain; interpret; ~ся become clear, be cleared up.

разыгра́ть pf, разы́грывать impf perform; draw; raffle; play a trick on;

~ся get up; run high.

разыска́ть (-ыщу́, -ы́щешь) pf find. разы́скивать impf search for.

рай (loc -ю́) paradise; garden of Eden.

райко́м district committee.

райо́н region. райо́нный district.

ра́йский heavenly.

рак crayfish; cancer; Cancer.

раке́та[1], раке́тка racket.

раке́та[2] rocket; missile; flare.

ра́ковина shell; sink.

ра́ковый cancer; cancerous.

раку́шка cockle-shell, mussel.

ра́ма frame. ра́мка frame; pl framework.

ра́мпа footlights.

ра́на wound. ране́ние wounding; wound. ра́неный wounded; injured.

ранг rank.

ра́нец (-нца) knapsack; satchel.

ра́нить impf & pf wound; injure.

ра́нний early. ра́но adv early. ра́ньше adv earlier; before; formerly.

папи́ра foil.

ра́порт report. рапортова́ть impf & pf report.

ра́са race. раси́зм racism. раси́стский racist.

раска́иваться impf of раска́яться

раскалённый (-ён, -а́) scorching; incandescent. раскали́ть pf (impf раскаля́ть) make red-hot; ~ся become red-hot. раска́лывать(ся impf of расколо́ть(ся. раскаля́ть(ся impf of раскали́ть(ся. раска́пывать impf of раскопа́ть

раска́т roll, peal. раската́ть pf, раска́тывать impf roll (out), smooth out, level; drive or ride (about). раска́тистый rolling, booming. раскати́ться (-ачу́сь, -а́тишься) pf, раска́тываться impf gather speed; roll away; peal, boom.

раскача́ть pf, раска́чивать impf swing; rock; ~ся swing, rock.

раска́яние repentance. рас|ка́яться pf (impf also раска́иваться) repent.

расквита́ться pf settle accounts.

раски́дывать impf, раски́нуть (-ну) pf stretch (out); spread; pitch; ~ся spread out; sprawl.

раскладно́й folding. раскладу́шка camp-bed. раскла́дывать impf of разложи́ть расклáняться *pf* bow; take leave.

расклéивать *impf*, расклéить *pf* unstick; stick (up); ~ся come unstuck.

раскóл split; schism. рас|колóть (-лю́, -лешь) *pf* (*impf also* раскáлывать) split; break; disrupt; ~ся split. раскóльник dissenter.

раскопáть *pf* (*impf* раскáпывать) dig up, unearth, excavate. раскóпки (-пок) *pl* excavations.

раскóсый slanting.

раскрáивать *impf of* раскрóить

раскрáсить (-áшу) *pf*, *impf* раскрáшивать paint, colour.

раскрепости́ть (-ощу́) *pf*, раскрепощáть *impf* liberate. раскрепощéние emancipation.

раскритиковáть *pf* criticize harshly.

раскрои́ть *pf* (*impf* раскрáивать) cut out.

раскрóю *etc.*: *see* раскры́ть

раскрути́ть (-учу́, -у́тишь) *pf*, раскрýчивать *impf* untwist; ~ся come untwisted.

раскрывáть *impf*, раскры́ть (-рóю) *pf* open; expose; reveal; discover; ~ся open; uncover o.s.; come to light.

раскупáть *impf*, раскупи́ть (-у́пит) *pf* buy up.

раскýпоривать *impf*, раскýпорить *pf* uncork, open.

раскуси́ть (-ушу́, -ýсишь) *pf*, раскýсывать *impf* bite through; see through.

рáсовый racial.

распáд disintegration; collapse. распадáться *impf of* распáсться

распаковáть *pf*, распакóвывать *impf* unpack.

распáрывать(ся *impf of* распорóть(ся

распáсться (-адётся) *pf* (*impf* распадáться) disintegrate, fall to pieces.

распахáть (-ашý, -áшешь) *pf*, распáхивать[1] *impf* plough up.

распáхивать[2] *impf*, распахнýть (-нý, -нёшь) *pf* throw open; ~ся fly open, swing open.

распашóнка baby's vest.

распевáть *impf* sing.

распечáтать *pf*, распечáтывать *impf* open; unseal.

распи́ливать *impf*, распили́ть (-лю́,

-лишь) *pf* saw up.

распинáть *impf of* распя́ть

расписáние time-table. расписáть (-ишý, -и́шешь) *pf*, распи́сывать *impf* enter; assign; paint; ~ся register one's marriage; +в+*prep* sign for; acknowledge. распи́ска receipt. расписнóй painted, decorated.

распихáть *pf*, распи́хивать *impf* push, shove, stuff.

рас|плáвить (-влю) *pf*, расплавля́ть *impf* melt, fuse. расплáвленный molten.

расплáкаться (-áчусь) *pf* burst into tears.

распластáть *pf*, распластывать *impf* spread; flatten; split; ~ся sprawl.

расплáта payment; retribution. расплати́ться (-ачýсь, -áтишься) *pf*, расплáчиваться *impf* (+с+*instr*) pay off; get even; +за+*acc* pay for.

расплескáть(ся (-ещý(сь, -éщешь(ся) *pf*, расплёскивать(ся *impf* spill.

расплести́ (-етý, -етёшь; -ёл, -á) *pf*, расплетáть *impf* unplait; untwist.

рас|плоди́ть(ся (-ожý(сь) *pf*

расплывáться *impf*, расплы́ться (-ывётся; -ы́лся, -áсь) *pf* run. расплы́вчатый indistinct; vague.

расплющивать *impf*, расплю́щить (-щу) *pf* flatten out, hammer out.

распнý *etc.*: *see* распя́ть

распознавáть (-наю́, -наёшь) *impf*, распознáть *pf* recognize, identify; diagnose.

располагáть *impf* (*pf* расположи́ть) +*instr* have at one's disposal. располагáться *impf of* расположи́ться

расползáться *impf*, расползти́сь (-зётся; -óлзся, -злáсь) *pf* crawl (away); give at the seams.

расположéние disposition; arrangement; situation; tendency; liking; mood. располóженный disposed, inclined. расположи́ть (-жý, -жишь) *pf* (*impf* располагáть) dispose; set out; win over; ~ся settle down.

распóрка cross-bar, strut.

рас|порóть (-рю́, -решь) *pf* (*impf also* распáрывать) unpick, rip; ~ся rip, come undone.

распоряди́тель *m* manager. распоряди́тельный capable; efficient.

распоряди́ться (-яжу́сь) *pf*, **распоряжа́ться** *impf* order, give orders; see; +*instr* manage, deal with.

распоря́док (-дка) order; routine. **распоряже́ние** order; instruction; disposal, command.

распра́ва violence; reprisal.

распра́вить (-влю) *pf*, **расправля́ть** *impf* straighten; smooth out; spread.

распра́виться (-влюсь) *pf*, **расправля́ться** *impf* c+*instr* deal with severely; make short work of.

распределе́ние distribution; allocation. **распредели́тель** *m* distributor. **распредели́тельный** distributive, distributing; ~ щит switchboard. **распредели́ть** *pf*, **распределя́ть** *impf* distribute; allocate.

распродава́ть (-даю́, -даёшь) *impf*, **распрода́ть** (-а́м, -а́шь, -а́ст, -ади́м; -о́дал, -а́, -о) *pf* sell off; sell out. **распрода́жа** (clearance) sale.

распростёртый outstretched; prostrate.

распростране́ние spreading; dissemination. **распространённый** (-ён, -а́) widespread, prevalent. **распространи́ть** *pf*, **распространя́ть** *impf* spread; ~ся spread.

ра́спря (*gen pl* -ей) quarrel.

распряга́ть *impf*, **распря́чь** (-ягу́, -яжёшь; -я́г, -ла́) *pf* unharness.

распрями́ться *pf*, **распрямля́ться** *impf* straighten up.

распуска́ть *impf*, **распусти́ть** (-ущу́, -у́стишь) *pf* dismiss; dissolve; let out; relax; let get out of hand; melt; spread; ~ся open; come loose; dissolve; melt; get out of hand; let o.s. go.

распу́тать *pf* (*impf* **распу́тывать**) untangle; unravel.

распу́тица season of bad roads.

распу́тный dissolute. **распу́тство** debauchery.

распу́тывать *impf of* **распу́тать**

распу́тье crossroads.

распуха́ть *impf*, **распу́хнуть** (-ну; -у́х) *pf* swell (up).

распу́щенный undisciplined; spoilt; dissolute.

распыли́тель *m* spray, atomizer. **распыли́ть** *pf*, **распыля́ть** *impf* spray; pulverize; disperse.

распя́тие crucifixion; crucifix. **распя́ть** (-пну́, -пнёшь) *pf* (*impf* **распина́ть**) crucify.

расса́да seedlings. **рассади́ть** (-ажу́, -а́дишь) *pf*, **расса́живать** *impf* plant out; seat; separate, seat separately.

расса́живаться *impf of* **рассе́сться**. **рассы́паться** *impf of* **рассы́паться**

рассвести́ (-етёт; -ело́) *pf*, **рассвета́ть** *impf* dawn. **рассве́т** dawn.

рас|свирипе́ть (-ею) *pf*.

рассе́дла́ть *pf* unsaddle.

рассе́ивание dispersal, scattering. **рассе́ивать(ся** *impf of* **рассе́ять(ся**

рассека́ть *impf of* **рассе́чь**

рассе́ние settling, resettlement; separation.

рассе́лина cleft, fissure.

рассели́ть *pf*, **расселя́ть** *impf* settle, resettle; separate.

рас|серди́ть(ся (-жу́(сь, -рдишь(ся) *pf*.

рассе́сться (-ся́дусь) *pf* (*impf* **расса́живаться**) take seats; sprawl.

рассе́чь (-еку́, -ечёшь; -ёк, -ла́) *pf* (*impf* **рассека́ть**) cut (through); cleave.

рассе́янность absent-mindedness; dispersion. **рассе́янный** absent-minded; diffused; scattered. **рассе́ять** (-е́ю) *pf* (*impf* **рассе́ивать**) disperse, scatter; dispel; ~ся disperse, scatter; clear; divert o.s.

расска́з story; account. **рассказа́ть** (-ажу́, -а́жешь) *pf*, **расска́зывать** *impf* tell, recount. **расска́зчик** story-teller, narrator.

рассла́бить (-блю) *pf*, **расслабля́ть** *impf* weaken.

рассла́ивать(ся *impf of* **расслои́ть(ся**

рассле́дование investigation, examination; inquiry; произвести́ ~+*gen* hold an inquiry into. **рассле́довать** *impf & pf* investigate, look into, hold an inquiry into.

расслои́ть *pf* (*impf* **рассла́ивать**) divide into layers; ~ся become stratified; flake off.

расслы́шать (-шу) *pf* catch.

рассма́тривать *impf of* **рассмотре́ть**; examine; consider.

рас|смеши́ть (-шу́) *pf*.

рассмея́ться (-ею́сь, -еёшься) *pf*

burst out laughing.

рассмотре́ние examination; consideration. **рассмотре́ть** (-рю́, -ришь) *pf* (*impf* **рассма́тривать**) examine, consider; discern, make out.

рассова́ть (-сую́, -суёшь) *pf*, **рассо́вывать** *impf* по+*dat* shove into.

рассо́л brine; pickle.

рассо́риться *pf* с+*instr* fall out with. **рас|сортирова́ть** *pf*, **рассорти-ро́вывать** *impf* sort out.

рассоса́ться (-сётся) *pf* (*impf* **расса́сываться**) resolve.

рассо́хнуться (-нется; -о́хся) *pf* (*impf* **рассыха́ться**) crack.

расспра́шивать *impf*, **расспроси́ть** (-ошу́, -о́сишь) *pf* question; make inquiries of.

рассро́чить (-чу) *pf* spread (over a period). **рассро́чка** instalment.

расстава́ние parting. **расстава́ться** (-таю́сь, -таёшься) *impf of* **расста́ться**

расста́вить (-влю) *pf*, **расставля́ть** *impf* place, arrange; move apart. **расстано́вка** arrangement; pause.

расста́ться (-а́нусь) *pf* (*impf* **расстава́ться**) part, separate.

расстёгивать *impf*, **расстегну́ть** (-ну́, -нёшь) *pf* undo, unfasten; ~ся come undone; unfasten.

расстели́ть(ся, *etc.*: *see* **разо-стла́ть(ся. расстила́ть(ся, -а́ю(сь** *impf of* **разостла́ть(ся**

расстоя́ние distance.

расстра́ивать(ся *impf of* **расстро́-ить(ся**

расстре́л execution by firing squad. **расстре́ливать** *impf*, **расстреля́ть** *pf* shoot.

расстро́енный disordered; upset; out of tune. **расстро́ить** *pf* (*impf* **расстра́ивать**) upset; thwart; disturb; throw into confusion; put out of tune; ~ся be upset; get out of tune; fall into confusion; fall through. **расстро́йство** upset; disarray; confusion; frustration.

расступа́ться *impf*, **расступи́ться** (-у́пится) *pf* part, make way.

рассуди́тельный reasonable; sensible. **рассуди́ть** (-ужу́, -у́дишь) *pf* judge; think; decide. **рассу́док** (-дка) reason; intellect. **рассужда́ть** *impf* reason; +о+*prep* discuss. **рассу-**

жде́ние reasoning; discussion; argument.

рассую́ *etc.*: *see* **рассова́ть**

рассчи́танный deliberate; intended. **рассчита́ть** *pf*, **рассчи́тывать** *impf*, **расче́сть** (разочту́, -тёшь; расчёл, разочла́) *pf* calculate; count; depend; ~ся settle accounts.

рассыла́ть *impf of* **разосла́ть. рас-сы́лка** distribution. **рассы́льный** *sb* delivery man.

рассы́пать (-плю) *pf*, **рассыпа́ть** *impf* spill; scatter; ~ся spill, scatter; spread out; crumble. **рассы́пчатый** friable; crumbly.

рассыха́ться *impf of* **рассо́хнуться. рассяду́сь** *etc.*: *see* **рассе́сться.**

раста́лкивать *impf of* **растолка́ть. раста́пливать(ся** *impf of* **растопи́ть(ся**

раста́скать *pf*, **раста́скивать** *impf*, **растащи́ть** (-щу́, -щишь) *pf* pilfer, filch.

растащи́ть *see* **раста́скать. рас|та́-ять** (-а́ю) *pf*.

раство́р[2] opening, span. **раство́р**[1] solution; mortar. **раствори́мый** soluble. **раствори́тель** *m* solvent. **раствори́ть**[1] *pf* (*impf* **растворя́ть**) dissolve; ~ся dissolve. **раствори́ть**[2] (-рю́, -ришь) *pf* (*impf* **растворя́ть**) open; ~ся open. **растворя́ть(ся** *impf of* **раство-ри́ть(ся. растека́ться** *impf of* **расте́чься**

расте́ние plant.

растере́ть (разотру́, -трёшь; растёр) *pf* (*impf* **растира́ть**) grind; spread; rub; massage.

растерза́ть *pf*, **расте́рзывать** *impf* tear to pieces.

растерянность confusion, dismay. **расте́рянный** confused, dismayed. **растеря́ть** *pf* lose; ~ся get lost; lose one's head.

расте́чься (-ечётся, -еку́тся; -тёкся, -лась) *pf* (*impf* **растека́ться**) run; spread.

расти́ (-ту́, -тёшь; рос, -ла́) *impf* grow; grow up.

растира́ние grinding; rubbing, massage. **растира́ть(ся** *impf of* **расте-ре́ть(ся**

расти́тельность vegetation; hair. **расти́тельный** vegetable. **расти́ть**

(ращу́) *impf* bring up; train; grow.

растлева́ть *impf*, **растли́ть** *pf* seduce; corrupt.

растолка́ть *pf* (*impf* **раста́лкивать**) push apart; shake.

растолкова́ть *pf*, **растолко́вывать** *impf* explain.

рас|толо́чь (-лку́, -лчёшь; -ло́к, -лкла́) *pf*.

растолсте́ть (-е́ю) *pf* put on weight.

растопи́ть[1] (-плю́, -пишь) *pf* (*impf* **раста́пливать**) melt; thaw; ~ся melt.

растопи́ть[2] (-плю́, -пишь) *pf* (*impf* **раста́пливать**) light, kindle; ~ся begin to burn.

растопта́ть (-пчу́, -пчешь) *pf* trample, stamp on.

расторга́ть *impf*, **расто́ргнуть** (-ну; -о́рг) *pf* annul, dissolve. **расторже́ние** annulment, dissolution.

расторо́пный quick; efficient.

расточа́ть *impf*, **расточи́ть** (-чу́) *pf* squander, dissipate. **расточи́тельный** extravagant, wasteful.

растра́вить (-влю́, -вишь) *pf*, **растравля́ть** *impf* irritate.

растра́та spending; waste; embezzlement. **растра́тить** (-а́чу) *pf*, **растра́чивать** *impf* spend; waste; embezzle.

растрёпанный dishevelled; tattered. **рас|трепа́ть** (-плю́, -плешь) *pf* disarrange; tatter.

растре́скаться *pf*, **растре́скиваться** *impf* crack, chap.

растро́гать *pf* move, touch; ~ся be moved.

расту́щий growing.

растя́гивать *impf*, **растяну́ть** (-ну́, -нешь) *pf* stretch (out); strain, sprain; drag out; ~ся stretch; drag on; sprawl. **растяже́ние** tension; strain, sprain. **растяжи́мый** tensile; stretchable. **растя́нутый** stretched; long-winded.

рас|фасова́ть *pf*.

расформирова́ть *pf*, **расформиро́вывать** *impf* break up; disband.

расха́живать *impf* walk about; pace up and down.

расхва́ливать *impf*, **расхвали́ть** (-лю́, -лишь) *pf* lavish praises on.

расхвата́ть *pf*, **расхва́тывать** *impf* seize on, buy up.

расхити́тель *m* embezzler. **расхи́тить** (-и́щу) *pf*, **расхища́ть** *impf* steal, misappropriate. **расхище́ние** misappropriation.

расхля́банный loose; lax.

расхо́д expenditure; consumption; *pl* expenses, outlay. **расходи́ться** (-ожу́сь, -о́дишься) *impf* of **разойти́сь**. **расхо́дование** expense, expenditure. **расхо́довать** (*pf* из~) spend; consume. **расхожде́ние** divergence.

расхола́живать *impf*, **расхолоди́ть** (-ожу́) *pf* damp the ardour of.

расхоте́ть (-очу́, -о́чешь, -оти́м) *pf* no longer want.

расхохота́ться (-очу́сь, -о́чешься) *pf* burst out laughing.

расцара́пать *pf* scratch (all over).

расцвести́ (-ету́, -етёшь; -ёл, -а́) *pf*, **расцвета́ть** *impf* blossom; flourish. **расцве́т** blossoming (out); flowering, heyday.

расцве́тка colours; colouring.

расце́нивать *impf*, **расцени́ть** (-ню́, -нишь) *pf* estimate, value; consider. **расце́нка** valuation; price; (wage-)rate.

расцепи́ть (-плю́, -пишь) *pf*, **расцепля́ть** *impf* uncouple, unhook.

расчеса́ть (-ешу́, -е́шешь) *pf* (*impf* **расчёсывать**) comb; scratch. **расчёска** comb.

расче́сть *etc.: see* **рассчита́ть**. **расчёсывать** *impf of* **расчеса́ть**

расчёт[1] calculation; estimate; gain; settlement. **расчётливый** thrifty; careful. **расчётный** calculation; pay; accounts; calculated.

расчи́стить (-и́щу) *pf*, **расчища́ть** *impf* clear; ~ся clear. **расчи́стка** clearing.

рас|члени́ть *pf*, **расчленя́ть** *impf* dismember; divide.

расшата́ть *pf*, **расша́тывать** *impf* shake loose, make rickety; impair.

расшевели́ть (-лю́, -éлишь) *pf* stir; rouse.

расшиба́ть *impf*, **расшиби́ть** (-бу́, -бёшь; -и́б) *pf* smash to pieces; hurt; stub; ~ся hurt o.s.

расшива́ть *impf of* **расши́ть**

расшире́ние widening; expansion; dilation, dilatation. **расши́рить** *pf*, **расширя́ть** *impf* widen; enlarge;

expand; ~ся broaden, widen; expand, dilate.

расши́ть (разошью́, -шьёшь) *pf* (*impf* **расшива́ть**) embroider; unpick.

расшифрова́ть *pf*, **расшифро́вывать** *impf* decipher.

расшнурова́ть *pf*, **расшнуро́вывать** *impf* unlace.

расще́лина crevice.

расщепи́ть (-плю́) *pf*, **расщепля́ть** *impf* split; ~ся split. **расщепле́ние** splitting; fission.

ратифици́ровать *impf* & *pf* ratify.

рать army, battle.

ра́унд round.

рафини́рованный refined.

рацио́н ration.

рационализа́ция rationalization. **рационализи́ровать** *impf* & *pf* rationalize. **рациона́льный** rational; efficient.

ра́ция walkie-talkie.

рвану́ться (-ну́сь, -нёшься) *pf* dart, dash.

рва́ный torn; lacerated. **рвать**[1] (рву, рвёшь; рвал, -á, -о) *impf* tear (out); pull out; pick; blow up; break off; ~ся break; tear; burst, explode; be bursting.

рвать[2] (рвёт; рва́ло) *impf* (*pf* **вы́~**) *impers*+*acc* vomit.

рвач (-á) self-seeker.

рве́ние zeal.

рво́та vomiting.

реабилита́ция rehabilitation. **реабилити́ровать** *impf* & *pf* rehabilitate.

реаги́ровать *impf* (*pf* **от~**, **про~**) react.

реакти́в reagent. **реакти́вный** reactive; jet-propelled. **реа́ктор** reactor. **реакционе́р** reactionary. **реакцио́нный** reactionary. **реа́кция** reaction.

реализа́ция realization. **реали́зм** realism. **реализова́ть** *impf* & *pf* realize. **реали́ст** realist. **реалисти́ческий** realistic.

реа́льность reality; practicability. **реа́льный** real; practicable.

ребёнок (-нка; *pl* ребя́та, -я́т *and* де́ти, -е́й) child; infant.

ребро́ (*pl* рёбра, -бер) rib; edge.

ребя́та (-я́т) *pl* children; guys; lads. **ребя́ческий** child's; childish. **ребя́чество** childishness. **ребя́читься**

(-чусь) *impf* be childish.

рёв roar; howl.

рева́нш revenge; return match.

reveráнс curtsey.

реве́ть (-ву́, -вёшь) *impf* roar; bellow; howl.

ревизио́нный inspection; auditing. **реви́зия** inspection; audit; revision. **ревизо́р** inspector.

ревмати́зм rheumatism.

ревни́вый jealous. **ревнова́ть** *impf* (*pf* **при~**) be jealous. **ре́вностный** zealous. **ре́вность** jealousy.

револьве́р revolver.

революционе́р revolutionary. **революцио́нный** revolutionary. **револю́ция** revolution.

рега́та regatta.

ре́гби *neut indecl* rugby.

ре́гент regent.

регио́н region. **региона́льный** regional.

регистра́тор registrar. **регистрату́ра** registry. **регистра́ция** registration. **регистри́ровать** *impf* & *pf* (*pf also* **за~**) register, record; ~ся register; register one's marriage.

регла́мент standing orders; time-limit. **регламента́ция** regulation. **регламенти́ровать** *impf* & *pf* regulate.

регресси́ровать *impf* regress.

регули́ровать *impf* (*pf* **от~**, **у~**) regulate; adjust. **регулиро́вщик** traffic controller. **регуля́рный** regular. **регуля́тор** regulator.

редакти́ровать *impf* (*pf* **от~**) edit. **реда́ктор** editor. **реда́кторский** editorial. **редакцио́нный** editorial, editing. **реда́кция** editorial staff; editorial office; editing.

реде́ть (-е́ет) *impf* (*pf* **по~**) thin (out).

реди́с radishes. **реди́ска** radish.

ре́дкий (-док, -дка́, -о) thin; sparse; rare. **ре́дко** *adv* sparsely; rarely, seldom. **ре́дкость** rarity.

редколле́гия editorial board.

рее́стр register.

режи́м régime; routine; procedure; ·regimen; conditions.

режиссёр-(постано́вщик) producer; director.

ре́жущий cutting, sharp. **ре́зать** (ре́жу) *impf* (*pf* **за~**, **про~**, **с~**) cut;

engrave; kill, slaughter.

резви́ться (-влю́сь) *impf* gambol, play. **ре́звый** frisky, playful.

резе́рв reserve. **резе́рвный** reserve; back-up.

резервуа́р reservoir.

резе́ц (-зца́) cutter; chisel; incisor.

резиде́нция residence.

рези́на rubber. **рези́нка** rubber; elastic band. **рези́новый** rubber.

ре́зкий sharp; harsh; abrupt; shrill. **резно́й** carved. **резня́** carnage.

резолю́ция resolution.

резона́нс resonance; response.

результа́т result.

резьба́ carving, fretwork.

резюме́ *neut indecl* résumé.

рейд¹ roads, roadstead.

рейд² raid.

ре́йка lath, rod.

рейс trip; voyage; flight.

рейту́зы (-у́з) *pl* leggings; riding breeches.

река́ (*acc* ре́ку, *pl* -и, -ре́кам) river.

ре́квием requiem.

реквизи́т props.

рекла́ма advertising, advertisement. **реклами́ровать** *impf* & *pf* advertise. **рекла́мный** publicity.

рекоменда́тельный of recommendation. **рекоменда́ция** recommendation; reference. **рекомендова́ть** *impf* & *pf* (*pf also* от~, по~) recommend; ~ся introduce o.s.; be advisable.

реконструи́ровать *impf* & *pf* reconstruct. **реконстру́кция** reconstruction.

реко́рд record. **реко́рдный** record, record-breaking. **рекордсме́н, -е́нка** record-holder.

ре́ктор principal (*of university*).

реле́ (*electr*) *neut indecl* relay.

религио́зный religious. **рели́гия** religion.

рели́квия relic.

релье́ф relief. **релье́фный** relief; raised, bold.

рельс rail.

рема́рка stage direction.

реме́нь (-мня́) *m* strap; belt.

реме́сленник artisan, craftsman. **реме́сленный** handicraft; mechanical. **ремесло́** (*pl* -ёсла, -ёсел) craft; trade.

ремо́нт repair(s); maintenance. **ремонти́ровать** *impf* & *pf* (*pf also* от~) repair; recondition. **ремо́нтный** repair.

ре́нта rent; income. **рента́бельный** paying, profitable.

рентге́н X-rays. **рентге́новский** X-ray. **рентгено́лог** radiologist. **рентгеноло́гия** radiology.

реорганиза́ция reorganization. **реорганизова́ть** *impf* & *pf* reorganize.

ре́па turnip.

репатрии́ровать *impf* & *pf* repatriate.

репертуа́р repertoire.

репети́ровать *impf* (*pf* от~, про~, с~) rehearse; coach. **репети́тор** coach. **репети́ция** rehearsal.

ре́плика retort; cue.

репорта́ж report; reporting. **репортёр** reporter.

репре́ссия repression.

репроду́ктор loud-speaker. **репроду́кция** reproduction.

репута́ция reputation.

респу́блика republic. **республика́нский** republican.

рессо́ра spring.

реставра́ция restoration. **реставри́ровать** *impf* & *pf* (*pf also* от~) restore.

рестора́н restaurant.

ресу́рс resort; *pl* resources.

ретрансля́тор (radio-)relay.

рефера́т synopsis, abstract; paper, essay.

рефере́ндум referendum.

рефле́кс reflex. **рефле́ктор** reflector.

рефо́рма reform. **реформи́ровать** *impf* & *pf* reform.

рефрижера́тор refrigerator.

рецензи́ровать *impf* (*pf* про~) review. **реце́нзия** review.

реце́пт prescription; recipe.

рециди́в relapse. **рецидиви́ст** recidivist.

речево́й speech; vocal.

ре́чка river. **речно́й** river.

речь (*gen pl* -е́й) speech.

реша́ть(ся *impf of* реши́ть(ся. **реша́ющий** decisive, deciding. **реше́ние** decision; solution.

решётка grating; grille, railing; lattice; trellis; fender, (fire)guard; (fire-)

grate; tail. **решето́** (*pl* -ёта) sieve. **решётчатый** lattice, latticed.

решймость resoluteness; resolve. **решйтельно** *adv* resolutely; definitely; absolutely. **решйтельность** determination. **решйтельный** definite; decisive. **решйть** (-шу́) *pf* (*impf* **реша́ть**) decide; solve; ~**ся** make up one's mind.

ржа́веть (-еет) *impf* (*pf* за~, по~) rust. **ржа́вчина** rust. **ржа́вый** rusty. **ржано́й** rye.

ржать (ржу, ржёшь) *impf* neigh.

рймлянин (*pl* -яне, -ян), **рймлянка** Roman. **рймский** Roman.

ринг boxing ring.

ри́нуться (-нусь) *pf* rush, dart.

рис rice.

риск risk. **риско́ванный** risky; risqué. **рискова́ть** *impf* run risks; +*instr* or *inf* risk.

рисова́ние drawing. **рисова́ть** *impf* (*pf* на~) draw; paint, depict; ~**ся** be silhouetted; appear; pose.

рисовый rice.

рису́нок (-нка) drawing; figure; pattern, design.

ритм rhythm. **ритми́ческий**, **ритми́чный** rhythmic.

ритуа́л ritual.

риф reef.

ри́фма rhyme. **рифмова́ть** *impf* rhyme; ~**ся** rhyme.

робе́ть (-е́ю) *impf* (*pf* о~) be timid. **ро́бкий** (-бок, -бка́, -о) timid, shy. **ро́бость** shyness.

ро́бот robot.

ров (рва, *loc* -у́) ditch.

рове́сник coeval. **ро́вно** *adv* evenly; exactly; absolutely. **ро́вный** flat; even; level; equable; exact; equal. **ровня́ть** *impf* (*pf* с~) even, level.

рог (*pl* -а́, -о́в) horn; antler. **рога́тка** catapult. **рога́тый** horned. **рого́вица** cornea. **роговой** horn; horny; horn-rimmed.

рого́жа bast mat(ting).

род (*loc* -у́; *pl* -ы́) family, kin, clan; birth, origin, stock; generation; genus; sort, kind. **роди́льный** maternity. **ро́дина** native land; homeland.

ро́динка birth-mark. **роди́тели** (-ей) *pl* parents. **роди́тельный** genitive; case. **роди́тельский** parental. **роди́ть** (рожу́, -йл, -йла́, -о) *impf* &

pf (*impf also* рожа́ть, рожда́ть) give birth to; ~**ся** be born.

родни́к (-а́) spring.

родни́ть (*pf* по~) make related, link; ~**ся** become related. **родно́й** native; home; ~**о́й брат** brother; ~**ые** *sb pl* relatives. **родня́** relative(s); kinsfolk. **родово́й** tribal; ancestral; generic; gender. **родонача́льник** ancestor; father. **родосло́вный** genealogical; ~**ая** *sb* genealogy, pedigree. **ро́дственник** relative. **ро́дственный** related. **родство́** relationship, kinship. **ро́ды** (-ов) *pl* childbirth; labour.

рожа́ (ugly) mug.

рожа́ть, **рожда́ть(ся** *impf of* **роди́ть(ся**. **рожда́емость** birthrate. **рожде́ние** birth. **рожде́ственский** Christmas. **Рождество́** Christmas.

рожь (ржи) rye.

ро́за rose.

ро́зга (*gen pl* -зог) birch.

ро́здал *etc.*: *see* **разда́ть**

розе́тка electric socket; rosette.

ро́зница retail; в ~у retail. **ро́зничный** retail. **рознь** difference; dissension.

ро́знял *etc.*: *see* **разня́ть**

ро́зовый pink.

ро́зыгрыш draw; drawn game.

ро́зыск search; inquiry.

рои́ться swarm. **рой** (*loc* -ю́; *pl* -и́, -ёв) swarm.

рок fate.

рокиро́вка castling.

рок-му́зыка rock music.

роково́й fateful; fatal.

ро́кот roar, rumble. **рокота́ть** (-о́чет) *impf* roar, rumble.

ро́лик roller; castor; *pl* roller skates.

роль (*gen pl* -е́й) role.

ром rum.

рома́н novel; romance. **романи́ст** novelist.

рома́нс (*mus*) romance.

рома́нтик romantic. **рома́нтика** romance. **романти́ческий**, **романти́чный** romantic.

рома́шка camomile.

ромб rhombus.

роня́ть *impf* (*pf* урони́ть) drop.

ро́пот murmur, grumble. **ропта́ть** (-пщу́, -пщешь) *impf* murmur, grumble.

рос *etc.*: *see* расти́

роса́ (*pl* -ы) dew. роси́стый dewy.

роско́шный luxurious; luxuriant. ро́скошь luxury; luxuriance.

ро́слый strapping.

ро́спись painting(s), mural(s).

ро́спуск dismissal; disbandment.

росси́йский Russian. Росси́я Russia.

ро́ссыпи *f pl* deposit.

рост growth; increase; height, stature.

ро́стбиф roast beef.

ростовщи́к (-а́) usurer, money-lender.

росто́к (-тка́) sprout, shoot.

ро́счерк flourish.

рот (рта, *loc* рту) mouth.

ро́та company.

рота́тор duplicator.

ро́тный company; *sb* company commander.

ротозе́й, -зе́йка gaper, rubberneck; scatter-brain.

ро́ща grove.

ро́ю *etc.*: *see* рыть

роя́ль *m* (grand) piano.

ртуть mercury.

руба́нок (-нка) plane.

руба́ха, руба́шка shirt.

рубе́ж (-а́) boundary, border(line); line; за ~о́м abroad.

рубе́ц (-бца́) scar; weal; hem; tripe.

руби́н ruby. руби́новый ruby; ruby-coloured.

руби́ть (-блю́, -бишь) *impf* (*pf* с~) fell; hew, chop; mince; build (of logs).

рубище rags.

ру́бка[1] felling; chopping; mincing.

ру́бка[2] deck house; боева́я ~ conning-tower; рулева́я ~ wheelhouse.

рублёвка one-rouble note. рублёвый (one-)rouble.

ру́бленый minced, chopped; of logs.

рубль (-я́) *m* rouble.

ру́брика rubric, heading.

рубча́тый ribbed. ру́бчик scar; rib.

ру́гань abuse, swearing. руга́тельный abusive. руга́тельство oath, swear-word. руга́ть *impf* (*pf* вы~, об~, от~) curse, swear at; abuse; ~ся curse, swear; swear at one another.

руда́ (*pl* -ы) ore. рудни́к (-а́) mine, pit. рудни́чный mine, pit; ~ газ fire-damp. рудоко́п miner.

ружейный rifle, gun. ружьё (*pl* -ья, -жей, -ьям) gun, rifle.

руи́на *usu pl* ruin.

рука́ (*acc* -у, *pl* -и, рук, -а́м) hand; arm; идти́ по́д руку с+*instr* walk arm in arm with; под руко́й at hand; руко́й пода́ть a stone's throw away; это мне на́ руку that suits me.

рука́в (-а́; *pl* -а́, -о́в) sleeve. рукави́ца mitten; gauntlet.

руководи́тель *m* leader; manager; instructor; guide. руководи́ть (-ожу́) *impf* +*instr* lead; guide; direct, manage. руково́дство leadership; guidance; direction; guide; handbook, manual; leaders. руково́дствоваться+*instr* follow; be guided by.

руководя́щий leading; guiding.

рукоде́лие needlework.

рукомо́йник washstand.

рукопа́шный hand-to-hand.

рукопи́сный manuscript. ру́копись manuscript.

рукоплеска́ние applause. рукоплеска́ть (-ещу́, -ещешь) *impf* +*dat* applaud.

рукопожа́тие handshake.

рукоя́тка handle.

рулево́й steering; *sb* helmsman.

руле́тка tape-measure; roulette.

рули́ть *impf* (*pf* вы~) taxi.

руль (-я́) *m* rudder; helm; (steering-)wheel; handlebar.

румы́н (*gen pl* -ы́н), ~ка Romanian. Румы́ния Romania. румы́нский Romanian.

румя́на (-я́н) *pl* rouge. румя́нец (-нца) (high) colour; flush; blush. румя́ный rosy, ruddy.

ру́пор megaphone; mouthpiece.

руса́к (-а́) hare.

руса́лка mermaid.

русифици́ровать *impf* & *pf* Russify.

ру́сло river-bed, channel; course.

ру́сский Russian; *sb* Russian.

ру́сый light brown.

Русь (*hist*)Russia.

рути́на routine.

ру́хлядь junk.

ру́хнуть (-ну) *pf* crash down.

руча́тельство guarantee. руча́ться *impf* (*pf* поручи́ться) +за+*acc* vouch for, guarantee.

руче́й (-чья́) brook.

ру́чка handle; (door-)knob; (chair-)arm. ручн|о́й hand; arm; manual;

tame; ~ые часы́ wrist-watch.

рýшить (-у) *impf* (*pf* об~) pull down;
~ся collapse.

ры́ба fish. рыба́к (-á) fisherman.
рыба́лка fishing. рыба́цкий, ры-
ба́чий fishing. ры́бий fish; fishy; ~
жир cod-liver oil. ры́бный fish.
рыбо́лов fisherman. рыболо́вный
fishing.

рыво́к (-вка́) jerk.

рыда́ние sobbing. рыда́ть *impf* sob.

ры́жий (рыж, -á, -е) red, red-haired;
chestnut.

ры́ло snout; mug.

ры́нок (-нка) market; market-place.
ры́ночный market.

рыса́к (-á) trotter.

рысь¹ (*loc* -и́) trot; ~ю, на рыся́х at
a trot.

рысь² lynx.

ры́твина rut, groove. ры́ть(ся
(ро́ю(сь) *impf* (*pf* вы́~, от~) dig;
rummage.

рыхли́ть *impf* (*pf* вз~, раз~) loosen.
ры́хлый (-л, -á, -о) friable; loose.

ры́царский chivalrous. ры́царь *m*
knight.

рыча́г (-á) lever.

рыча́ть (-чý) *impf* growl, snarl.

рья́ный zealous.

рюкза́к rucksack.

рю́мка wineglass.

ряби́на¹ rowan, mountain ash.

ряби́на² pit, pock. ряби́ть (-и́т) *impf*
ripple; *impers*: у меня́ ряби́т в
глаза́х I am dazzled. ря́бый pock-
marked. ря́бчик hazel hen, hazel
grouse. рябь ripples; dazzle.

ря́вкать *impf*, ря́вкнуть (-ну) *pf*
bellow, roar.

ряд (*loc* -ý; *pl* -ы́) row; line; file, rank;
series; number. ря́довой ordinary;
common; ~ соста́в rank and file; *sb*
private. ря́дом *adv* alongside; close
by; +с+*instr* next to.

ря́са cassock.

C

с, со *prep* I. +*gen* from; since; off;
for, with; on; by; с ра́дости for joy;
с утра́ since morning. II. +*acc* about;
the size of; с неде́лю for about a
week. III. +*instr* with; and; мы с

ва́ми you and I; что с ва́ми? what
is the matter?

са́бля (*gen pl* -бель) sabre.

сабота́ж sabotage. саботи́ровать
impf & *pf* sabotage.

са́ван shroud; blanket.

с|агити́ровать *pf*.

сад (*loc* -ý; *pl* -ы́) garden. сади́ть
(сажу́, са́дишь) *impf* (*pf* по~) plant.
сади́ться (сажу́сь) *impf* of сесть.
садо́вник, -ница gardener. садо-
во́дство gardening; horticulture.
садо́вый garden; cultivated.

сади́зм sadism. сади́ст sadist. са-
ди́стский sadistic.

са́жа soot.

сажа́ть *impf* (*pf* посади́ть) plant;
seat; set, put. са́женец (-нца) seedling; sapling.

са́жень (*pl* -и, -жен *or* -же́ней)
sazhen (*2.13 metres*).

сажу́ *etc.*: *see* сади́ть

са́йка roll.

с|акти́ровать *pf*.

сала́зки (-зок) *pl* toboggan.

сала́т lettuce; salad.

са́ло fat, lard; suet; tallow.

сало́н salon; saloon.

салфе́тка napkin.

са́льный greasy; tallow; obscene.

салю́т salute. салютова́ть *impf* &
pf (*pf also* от~) +*dat* salute.

сам (-ого́) *m*, сама́ (-о́й, *acc* -оё) *f*,
само́ (-ого́) *neut*, са́ми (-и́х) *pl*, *pron*
-self, -selves; myself, *etc.*, ourselves,
etc.; ~ по себе́ in itself; by o.s.; ~
собо́й of itself, of its own accord; ~б
собо́й (разуме́ется) of course; it
goes without saying.

са́мбо *neut indecl abbr* (*of* самоза-
щи́та без ору́жия) unarmed combat.

саме́ц (-мца́) male. са́мка female.

само- *in comb* self-, auto-. само-
бы́тный original, distinctive. ~вну-
ше́ние auto-suggestion. ~возгора́-
ние spontaneous combustion. ~во́ль-
ный wilful; unauthorized. ~де́ль-
ный home-made. ~держа́вие autocracy. ~держа́вный autocratic.
~де́ятельность amateur work;
amateur performance; initiative.
~дово́льный self-satisfied. ~дýр
petty tyrant. ~ду́рство high-
handedness. ~забве́ние selflessness.
~забве́нный selfless. ~защи́та

self-defence. ~зва́нец (-нца) impostor, pretender. ~ка́т scooter. ~кри́тика self-criticism. ~люби́вый proud; touchy. ~лю́бие pride, self-esteem. ~мне́ние conceit, self-importance. ~надёянный presumptuous. ~облада́ние self-control. ~обма́н self-deception. ~оборо́на self-defence. ~образова́ние self-education. ~обслу́живание self-service. ~определе́ние self-determination. ~отве́рженность selflessness. ~отве́рженный selfless. ~поже́ртвование self-sacrifice. ~ро́док (-дка) nugget; person with natural talent. ~сва́л tip-up lorry. ~созна́ние (self-)consciousness. ~сохране́ние self-preservation. ~стоя́тельность independence. ~стоя́тельный independent. ~суд lynch law, mob law. ~тёк drift. ~тёком adv by gravity; of its own accord. ~убийственный suicidal. ~убийство suicide. ~убийца m & f suicide. ~уваже́ние self-respect. ~уве́ренность self-confidence. ~уве́ренный self-confident. ~униже́ние self-abasement. ~управле́ние self-government. ~управля́ющий self-governing. ~упра́вный arbitrary. ~учи́тель m self-instructor, manual. ~у́чка m & f self-taught person. ~хо́дный self-propelled. ~чу́вствие general state; как ва́ше ~чу́вствие? how do you feel?

самова́р samovar.

самого́н home-made vodka.

самолёт aeroplane.

самоцве́т semi-precious stone.

са́мый pron very, (the) right; (the) same; (the) most.

сан dignity, office.

санато́рий sanatorium.

санда́лия sandal.

са́ни (-е́й) pl sledge, sleigh.

санита́р medical orderly; stretcher-bearer. санита́рия sanitation. санита́рка nurse. санита́рн|ый medical; health; sanitary; ~ая маши́на ambulance; ~ый у́зел = санузел.

са́нки (-нок) pl sledge; toboggan.

санкциони́ровать impf & pf sanction. са́нкция sanction.

сано́вник dignitary.

санпу́нкт medical centre.

санскри́т Sanskrit.

санте́хник plumber.

сантиме́тр centimetre; tape-measure.

сану́зел (-зла́) sanitary arrangements; WC.

санча́сть (gen pl -е́й) medical unit.

сапёр sapper.

сапо́г(-а́; gen pl -о́г) boot. сапо́жник shoemaker; cobbler. сапо́жный shoe.

сапфи́р sapphire.

сара́й shed; barn.

саранча́ locust(s).

сарафа́н sarafan; pinafore dress.

сарде́лька small fat sausage.

сарди́на sardine.

сарка́зм sarcasm. саркасти́ческий sarcastic.

сатана́ m Satan. сатани́нский satanic.

сателли́т satellite.

сати́н sateen.

сати́ра satire. сати́рик satirist. сати́рический satirical.

Сау́довская Ара́вия Saudi Arabia.

сафья́н morocco. сафья́новый morocco.

са́хар sugar. саха́рин saccharine. са́харистый sugary. са́харница sugar-basin. са́харн|ый sugar; sugary; ~ый заво́д sugar-refinery; ~ый песо́к granulated sugar; ~ая пу́дра castor sugar; ~ая свёкла sugar-beet.

сачо́к (-чка́) net.

сба́вить (-влю) pf, сбавля́ть impf take off; reduce.

с|баланси́ровать pf.

сбе́гать[1] pf run; +за+instr run for. сбега́ть[2] impf, сбежа́ть (-егу́) pf run down (from); run away; disappear; ~ся come running.

сберега́тельная ка́сса savings bank. сберега́ть impf, сбере́чь (-егу́, -ежёшь; -ёг, -ла́) pf save; save up; preserve. сбереже́ние economy; saving; savings. сберка́сса savings bank.

сбива́ть impf, с|бить (собью́, -бьёшь) pf bring down, knock down; knock off; distract; wear down; knock together; churn; whip, whisk; ~ся be dislodged; slip; go wrong; be confused; ~ся с пути́ lose one's way; ~ся с ног be run off one's feet. сби́вчивый confused; inconsistent.

сближа́ть *impf*, сбли́зить (-йжу) *pf* bring (closer) together, draw together; ~ся draw together; become good friends. сближе́ние rapprochement; closing in.

сбо́ку *adv* from one side; on one side.

сбор collection; duty; fee, toll; takings; gathering. сбо́рище crowd, mob. сбо́рка assembling, assembly; gather. сбо́рник collection. сбо́рный assembly; mixed, combined; prefabricated; detachable. сбо́рочный assembly. сбо́рщик collector; assembler.

сбра́сывать(ся *impf of* сбро́сить(ся

сбрива́ть *impf*, сбрить (сбре́ю) *pf* shave off.

сброд riff-raff.

сброс fault, break. сбро́сить (-о́шу) *pf* (*impf* сбра́сывать) throw down, drop; throw off; shed; discard.

сбру́я (*collect*) (riding) tack.

сбыва́ть *impf*, сбыть (сбу́ду; сбыл, -а́, -о) *pf* sell, market; get rid of; ~ся come true, be realized. сбыт (*no pl*) sale; market.

св. *abbr* (*of* свято́й) Saint.

сва́дебный wedding. сва́дьба (*gen pl* -деб) wedding.

сва́ливать *impf*, с|вали́ть (-лю́, -лишь) *pf* throw down; overthrow; pile up; ~ся fall (down), collapse. сва́лка dump; scuffle.

с|вали́ть *pf*.

сва́ривать *impf*, с|вари́ть (-рю́, -ришь) *pf* boil; cook; weld. сва́рка welding.

сварли́вый cantankerous.

сварно́й welded. сва́рочный welding. сва́рщик welder.

сва́стика swastika.

сва́тать *impf* (*pf* по~, со~) propose as a husband or wife; propose to; ~ся к+*dat or* за+*acc* propose to.

сва́я pile.

све́дение piece of information; knowledge; *pl* information, intelligence; knowledge. све́дущий knowledgeable; versed.

сведу́ *etc.*: *see* свести́

свежезаморо́женный fresh-frozen; chilled. све́жесть freshness. свеже́ть (-е́ет) *impf* (*pf* по~) become cooler, freshen. све́жий (-еж, -а́) fresh; new.

свезти́ (-зу́, -зёшь; свёз, -ла́) *pf* (*impf* свози́ть) take; bring *or* take down *or* away.

свёкла beet, beetroot.

свёкор (-кра) father-in-law. свекро́вь mother-in-law.

свёл *etc.*: *see* свести́

сверга́ть *impf*, све́ргнуть (-ну; сверг) *pf* throw down, overthrow. сверже́ние overthrow.

све́рить *pf* (*impf* сверя́ть) collate.

сверка́ть *impf* sparkle, twinkle; glitter; gleam. сверкну́ть (-ну́, -нёшь) *pf* flash.

сверли́льный drill, drilling; boring. сверли́ть *impf* (*pf* про~) drill; bore (through); nag. сверло́ drill. сверля́щий gnawing, piercing.

сверну́ть (-ну́, -нёшь) *pf* (*impf* свёртывать, свора́чивать) roll (up); turn; curtail, cut down; ~ ше́ю+*dat* wring the neck of; ~ся roll up, curl up; curdle, coagulate; contract.

све́рстник contemporary.

свёрток (-тка) package, bundle. свёртывание rolling (up); curdling, coagulation; curtailment, cuts. свёртывать(ся *impf of* сверну́ть(ся

сверх *prep*+*gen* over, above, on top of; beyond; in addition to; ~ того́ moreover.

сверх- *in comb* super-, over-, hyper-. сверхзвуково́й supersonic. ~пла́новый over and above the plan. ~при́быль excess profit. ~проводни́к (-а́) superconductor. ~секре́тный top secret. ~уро́чный overtime. ~уро́чные *sb pl* overtime. ~челове́к superman. ~челове́ческий superhuman. ~ъесте́ственный supernatural.

све́рху *adv* from above; ~ до́низу from top to bottom.

сверчо́к (-чка́) cricket.

сверше́ние achievement.

сверя́ть *impf of* све́рить

све́сить (-е́шу) *pf* (*impf* све́шивать) let down, lower; ~ся hang over, lean over.

свести́ (-еду́, -еде́шь; -ёл, -а́) *pf* (*impf* своди́ть) take; take down; take away; remove; bring together; reduce, bring; cramp.

свет[1] light; daybreak.

свет[2] world; society.

светать impf impers dawn. светило luminary. светить (-ечу, -етишь) impf (pf по~) shine; +dat light; light the way for; ~ся shine, gleam. светлеть (-ёет) impf (pf по~, про~) brighten (up); grow lighter. светлость brightness; Grace. светлый light; bright; joyous. светлячок (-чка) glow-worm.

свето- in comb light, photo-. светонепроницаемый light-proof. ~фильтр light filter. ~фор traffic light(s).

световой light; luminous; ~ день daylight hours.

светопреставление end of the world.

светский fashionable; refined; secular.

светящийся luminous, fluorescent. свеча (pl -и, -ей) candle; (spark-)plug. свечение luminescence, fluorescence. свечка candle. свечу etc.: see светить

с|вешать pf. свешивать(ся impf of свесить(ся. свивать impf of свить свидание meeting; appointment; до свидания! goodbye!

свидетель m, -ница witness. свидетельство evidence; testimony; certificate. свидетельствовать impf (pf за~, о~) give evidence, testify; be evidence (of); witness.

свинарник pigsty.

свинец (-нца) lead.

свинина pork. свинка mumps. свиной pig; pork. свинство despicable act; outrage; squalor.

свинцовый lead; leaden.

свинья (pl -и, -ей, -ям) pig, swine.

свирель (reed-)pipe.

свирепеть (-ею) impf (pf рас~) grow savage; become violent. свирепствовать impf rage; be rife. свирепый fierce, ferocious.

свисать impf, свиснуть (-ну; -ис) pf hang down, dangle; trail.

свист whistle; whistling. свистать (-ищу, -ищешь) impf whistle. свистеть (-ищу) impf, свистнуть (-ну) pf whistle; hiss. свисток (-тка) whistle.

свита suite; retinue.

свитер sweater.

свиток (-тка) roll, scroll. с|вить

(совью, совьёшь; -ил, -á, -о) pf (impf also свивать) twist, wind; ~ся roll up.

свихнуться (-нусь, -нёшься) impf go mad; go astray.

свищ (-á) flaw; (knot-)hole; fistula.

свищу etc.: see свистать, свистеть

свобода freedom. свободно adv freely; easily; fluently; loose(ly). свободный free; easy; vacant; spare; loose; flowing. свободолюбивый freedom-loving. свободомыслие free-thinking.

свод code; collection; arch, vault.

сводить (-ожу, -одишь) impf of свести

сводка summary; report. сводный composite; step-.

сводчатый arched, vaulted.

своеволие self-will, wilfulness. своевольный wilful.

своевременно adv in good time; opportunely. своевременный timely, opportune.

своенравие capriciousness. своенравный wilful, capricious.

своеобразие originality; peculiarity. своеобразный original; peculiar.

свожу etc.: see сводить, свозить.

свозить (-ожу, -озишь) impf of свезти

свой (своего) m, своя (своей) f, своё (своего) neut, свои (своих) pl, pron one's (own); my, his, her, its; our, your, their. свойственный peculiar, characteristic. свойство property, attribute, characteristic.

сволочь swine; riff-raff.

свора leash; pack.

сворачивать impf of свернуть, своротить. с|воровать pf.

своротить (-очу, -отишь) pf (impf сворачивать) dislodge, shift; turn; twist.

свояк brother-in-law (husband of wife's sister). свояченица sister-in-law (wife's sister).

свыкаться impf, свыкнуться (-нусь; -ыкся) pf get used.

свысока adv haughtily. свыше adv from above. свыше prep+gen over; beyond.

связанный constrained; combined; bound; coupled. с|вязать (-яжу, -яжешь) pf, связывать impf tie, bind; connect; ~ся get in touch; get involved. **связи́ст**, **-и́стка** signaller; worker in communication services. **свя́зка** sheaf, bundle; ligament. **свя́зный** connected, coherent. **связь** (loc **-и́**) connection; link, bond; liaison; communication(s).

святи́лище sanctuary. **свя́тки** (**-ток**) pl Christmas-tide. **свя́то** adv piously; religiously. **свят|о́й** (**-ят**, **-а́**, **-о**) holy; ~о́й, ~а́я sb saint. **святы́ня** sacred object or place. **свяще́нник** priest. **свяще́нный** sacred.

сгиб bend. **сгиба́ть** impf of **согну́ть сгла́дить** (**-а́жу**) pf, **сгла́живать** impf smooth out; smooth over, soften.

сгла́зить (**-а́жу**) pf put the evil eye on.

сгнива́ть impf, **с|гни́ть** (**-ию́**, **-иёшь**; **-ил**, **-а́**, **-о**) pf rot.

с|гнои́ться pf.

сгова́риваться impf, **сговори́ться** pf come to an arrangement; arrange. **сго́вор** agreement. **сгово́рчивый** compliant.

сгоня́ть impf of **согна́ть**

сгора́ние combustion; **дви́гатель вну́треннего сгора́ния** internal-combustion engine. **сгора́ть** impf of **сгоре́ть**

с|горбить(ся) (**-блю(сь)**) pf.

с|горе́ть (**-рю́**) pf (impf also **сгора́ть**) burn down; be burnt down; be used up; burn; burn o.s. out. **сгоряча́** adv in the heat of the moment.

с|гото́вить(ся) (**-влю(сь)**) pf.

сгреба́ть impf, **сгрести́** (**-ебу́**, **-ебёшь**; **-ёб**, **-ла́**) pf rake up, rake together.

сгружа́ть impf, **сгрузи́ть** (**-ужу́**, **-у́зишь**) pf unload.

с|группирова́ть(ся) pf.

сгусти́ть (**-ущу́**) pf, **сгуща́ть** impf thicken; condense; ~ся thicken; condense; clot. **сгу́сток** (**-тка**) clot. **сгуще́ние** thickening, condensation; clotting.

сдава́ть (**сдаю́**, **сдаёшь**) impf of **сдать**; ~ **экза́мен** take an examination; ~ся impf of **сда́ться**

сдави́ть (**-влю́**, **-вишь**) pf, **сда́вливать** impf squeeze.

сдать (**-ам**, **-ашь**, **-аст**, **-ади́м**; **-ал**, **-а́**, **-о**) pf (impf **сдава́ть**) hand over; pass; let, hire out; surrender, give up;

deal; ~ся surrender, yield. **сда́ча** handing over; hiring out; surrender; change; deal.

сдвиг displacement; fault; change, improvement. **сдвига́ть** impf, **сдви́нуть** (**-ну**) pf shift, move; move together; ~ся move, budge; come together.

с|де́лать(ся) pf. **сде́лка** transaction; deal, bargain. **сде́льн|ый** piece-work; ~ая рабо́та piece-work. **сде́льщина** piece-work.

сдёргивать impf of **сдёрнуть**

сде́ржанный restrained, reserved. **сдержа́ть** (**-жу́**, **-жишь**) pf, **сде́рживать** impf hold back; restrain; keep.

сдёрнуть (**-ну**) pf (impf **сдёргивать**) pull off.

сдеру́ etc.: see **содра́ть**. **сдира́ть** impf of **содра́ть**

сдо́ба shortening; fancy bread, bun(s). **сдо́бный** (**-бен**, **-бна́**, **-о**) rich, short.

с|до́хнуть (**-нет**; **сдох**) pf die; kick the bucket.

сдружи́ться (**-жу́сь**) pf become friends.

сдува́ть impf, **сду́нуть** (**-ну**) pf, **сдуть** (**-у́ю**) pf blow away or off.

сеа́нс performance; showing; sitting.

себесто́имость prime cost; cost (price).

себя́ (dat & prep **себе́**, instr **собо́й** or **собо́ю**) refl pron oneself; myself, yourself, himself, etc.; **ничего́ себе́** not bad; **собо́й** -looking, in appearance.

себялю́бие selfishness.

сев sowing.

се́вер north. **се́верный** north, northern; northerly. **се́веро-восто́к** north-east. **се́веро-восто́чный** north-east(ern). **се́веро-за́пад** north-west. **се́веро-за́падный** north-west(ern). **северя́нин** (pl **-я́не**, **-я́н**) northerner.

севооборо́т crop rotation.

сего́ see **сей**. **сего́дня** adv today. **сего́дняшний** of today, today's.

седе́ть (**-е́ю**) impf (pf **по~**) turn grey. **седина́** (pl **-ы**) grey hair(s).

седла́ть impf (pf **о~**) saddle. **седло́** (pl **сёдла**, **-дел**) saddle.

седоборо́дый grey-bearded. **седо-воло́сый** grey-haired. **седо́й** (**сед**, **-а́**, **-о**) grey(-haired).

седо́к (**-а́**) passenger; rider.

седьмой seventh.

сезон season. **сезонный** seasonal.

сей (**сего**) *m*, **сия** (**сей**) *f*, **сие** (**сего**) *neut*, **сии** (**сих**) *pl*, *pron* this; these; **сию минуту** at once, instantly.

сейсмический seismic.

сейф safe.

сейчас *adv* (just) now; soon; immediately.

сёк *etc.*: *see* **сечь**

секрет secret.

секретариат secretariat.

секретарский secretarial. **секретарь, секретарь** (-**я**) *m* secretary. **секретный** secret.

секс sex. **сексуальный** sexual; sexy.

секстет sextet.

секта sect. **сектант** sectarian.

сектор sector.

секу *etc.*: *see* **сечь**

секуляризация secularization.

секунда second. **секундант** second. **секундный** second. **секундомер** stop-watch.

секционный sectional. **секция** section.

селёдка herring.

селезёнка spleen.

селезень (-**зня**) *m* drake.

селекция breeding.

селение settlement, village.

селитра saltpetre, nitre.

селить(ся *impf* (*pf* по~) settle. **село** (*pl* сёла) village.

сельдерей celery.

сельдь (*pl* -**и**, -**ей**) herring.

сельский rural; village; ~**ое хозяйство** agriculture. **сельскохозяйственный** agricultural.

сельсовет village soviet.

семантика semantics. **семантический** semantic.

семафор semaphore; signal.

сёмга (smoked) salmon.

семейный family; domestic. **семейство** family.

семени *etc.*: *see* **семя**

семенить *impf* mince.

семениться *impf* seed. **семенник** (-**á**) testicle; seed-vessel. **семенной** seed; seminal.

семёрка seven; figure 7; No. 7. **семеро** (-**ых**) seven.

семёстр term, semester.

сёмечко (*pl* -**и**) seed; *pl* sunflower seeds.

семидесятилетие seventy years; seventieth anniversary, birthday. **семидесятый** seventieth; ~**ые годы** the seventies. **семилётка** seven-year school. **семилётний** seven-year; seven-year-old.

семинар seminar. **семинария** seminary.

семисотый seven-hundredth. **семнадцатый** seventeenth. **семнадцать** seventeen. **семь** (-**ми**, -**мью**) seven. **семьдесят** (-**мидесяти**, -**мьюдесятью**) seventy. **семьсот** (-**мисот**, *instr* -**мьюстами**) seven hundred. **семью** *adv* seven times.

семья (*pl* -**и**, -**ей**, -**ям**) family. **семьянин** family man.

семя (-**мени**; *pl* -**менá**, -**мян**, -**менáм**) seed; semen, sperm.

сенат senate. **сенатор** senator.

сени (-**ей**) *pl* (entrance-)hall.

сено hay. **сеновал** hayloft. **сенокос** haymaking; hayfield. **сенокосилка** mowing-machine.

сенсационный sensational. **сенсация** sensation.

сентенция maxim.

сентиментальный sentimental.

сентябрь (-**я**) *m* September. **сентябрьский** September.

сепсис sepsis.

сера sulphur; ear-wax.

серб, ~ка Serb. **Сербия** Serbia. **сербский** Serb(ian). **сербскохорватский** Serbo-Croat(ian).

сервант sideboard.

сервиз service, set. **сервировать** *impf* & *pf* serve; lay (a table). **сервировка** laying; table lay-out.

сердечник core. **сердечность** cordiality; warmth. **сердечный** heart; cardiac; cordial; warm(-hearted). **сердитый** angry. **сердить** (-**ржу**, -**рдишь**) *impf* (*pf* рас~) anger; ~**ся** be angry. **сердобольный** tender-hearted. **сердце** (*pl* -**á**, -**дéц**) heart; **в сердцах** in anger; **от всего сердца** from the bottom of one's heart. **сердцебиение** palpitation. **сердцевидный** heart-shaped. **сердцевина** core, pith, heart.

серебрёный silver-plated. **серебристый** silvery. **серебрить** *impf* (*pf* по~) silver, silver-plate; ~**ся** become

silvery. серебро́ silver. серебря́-
ный silver.

середи́на middle.

серёжка earring; catkin.

серена́да serenade.

се́ренький grey; dull.

сержа́нт sergeant.

серийный serial; mass. се́рия series;
part.

се́рный sulphur; sulphuric.

сероглазый grey-eyed.

се́рость uncouthness; ignorance.

серп (-á) sickle; ∼ луны́ crescent
moon.

серпанти́н streamer.

сертифика́т certificate.

се́рый (сер, -á, -о) grey; dull; uneducated.

серьга́ (pl -и, -рёг) earring.

серьёзность seriousness. серьёзный serious.

се́ссия session.

сестра́ (pl сёстры, сестёр, сёстрам)
sister.

сесть (ся́ду) pf (impf сади́ться) sit
down; land; set; shrink; +на+acc
board, get on.

се́тка net, netting; (luggage-)rack;
string bag; grid.

се́товать impf (pf по∼) complain.

сетча́тка retina. сеть (loc -и́; pl -и,
-éй) net; network.

сече́ние section. сечь (секу́, сечёшь;
сёк) impf (pf вы́∼) cut to pieces;
flog; ∼ся split.

се́ялка seed drill. се́ять (се́ю) impf
(pf по∼) sow.

сжа́литься pf take pity (над+instr)
on.

сжа́тие pressure; grasp, grip; compression. сжа́тый compressed; compact; concise.

с|жать[1] (сожму́, -нёшь) pf.

сжать[2] (сожму́, -мёшь) pf (impf
сжима́ть) squeeze; compress; grip;
clench; ∼ся tighten, clench; shrink,
contract.

с|жечь (сожгу́, сожжёшь; сжёг,
сожгла́) pf (impf сжига́ть) burn
(down); cremate.

сжива́ться impf of сжи́ться

сжига́ть impf of сжечь

сжима́ть(ся impf of сжать[2](ся

сжи́ться (-иву́сь, -ивёшься; -и́лся,
-áсь) pf (impf сжива́ться) с+instr

get used to.

с|жу́льничать pf.

сза́ди adv from behind; behind. сза́-
ди prep+gen behind.

сзыва́ть impf of созва́ть

сиби́рский Siberian. Сиби́рь Siberia. сибиря́к (-á), сибиря́чка Siberian.

сига́ра cigar. сигаре́та cigarette.

сигна́л signal. сигнализа́ция signal-
ling. сигнализи́ровать impf & pf
(pf also про∼) signal. сигна́льный
signal. сигна́льщик signal-man.

сиде́лка sick-nurse. сиде́ние sitting.
сиде́нье seat. сиде́ть (-ижу́) impf
sit; be; fit. сидя́чий sitting; sedentary.

сиé etc.: see сей

си́зый (сиз, -á, -о) (blue-)grey.

сий see сей

си́ла strength; force; power; в си́лу
+gen on the strength of, because of;
не по ∼ам beyond one's powers;
си́лой by force. сила́ч (-á) strong
man. си́литься impf try, make efforts. силово́й power; of force.

сило́к (-лка́) noose, snare.

си́лос silo; silage.

силуэ́т silhouette.

си́льно adv strongly, violently; very
much, greatly. си́льный (-лен or
-лён, -льна́, -о) strong; powerful; intense, hard.

симбио́з symbiosis.

си́мвол symbol. символизи́ровать
impf symbolize. символи́зм symbolism. символи́ческий symbolic.

симметри́я symmetry.

симпатизи́ровать impf +dat like,
sympathize with. симпати́чный
likeable, nice. симпа́тия liking; sympathy.

симпо́зиум symposium.

симпто́м symptom.

симули́ровать impf & pf simulate,
feign. симуля́нт malingerer, sham.
симуля́ция simulation, pretence.

симфо́ния symphony.

синаго́га synagogue.

синева́ blue. синева́тый bluish.
синегла́зый blue-eyed. сине́ть
(-éю) impf (pf по∼) turn blue; show
blue. си́ний (синь, -н i, -не) (dark)
blue.

сини́ца titmouse.

синод synod. синоним synonym. синтаксис syntax.

синтез synthesis. синтезировать *impf & pf* synthesize. синтетический synthetic.

синус sine; sinus.

синхронизировать *impf & pf* synchronize.

синь¹ blue. синь² *see* синий. синька blueing; blue-print. синяк (-á) bruise.

сионизм Zionism.

сиплый hoarse, husky. сипнуть (-ну; сип) *impf* (*pf* о~) become hoarse, husky.

сирена siren; hooter.

сиреневый lilac(-coloured). сирень lilac.

Сирия Syria.

сироп syrup.

сирота (*pl* -ы) *m & f* orphan. сиротливый lonely. сиротский orphan's, orphans'.

система system. систематизировать *impf & pf* systematize. систематический, систематичный systematic.

ситец (-тца) (printed) cotton; chintz.

сито sieve.

ситуация situation.

ситцевый print, chintz.

сифилис syphilis.

сифон siphon.

сия *see* сей

сияние radiance. сиять *impf* shine, beam.

сказ tale. сказание story, legend. сказать (-ажу, -ажешь) *pf* (*impf* говорить) say; speak; tell. сказаться (-ажусь, -ажешься) *pf*, сказываться *impf* tell (on); declare o.s. сказитель *m* story-teller. сказка (fairy-)tale; fib. сказочный fairytale; fantastic. сказуемое *sb* predicate.

скакалка skipping-rope. скакать (-ачу, -ачешь) *impf* (*pf* по~) skip, jump; gallop. скаковой race, racing.

скала (*pl* -ы) rock face; cliff. скалистый rocky.

скалить *impf* (*pf* о~); ~ зубы bare one's teeth; grin; ~ся bare one's teeth.

скалка rolling-pin.

скалолаз rock-climber.

скалывать *impf of* сколоть

скальп scalp.

скальпель *m* scalpel.

скамеечка footstool; small bench. скамейка bench. скамья (*pl* скамьи, -ей) bench; ~ подсудимых dock.

скандал scandal; brawl, rowdy scene. скандалист trouble-maker. скандалиться *impf* (*pf* о~) disgrace o.s. скандальный scandalous.

скандинавский Scandinavian.

скандировать *impf & pf* declaim.

скапливать(ся *impf of* скопить(ся

скарб goods and chattels.

скаредный stingy.

скарлатина scarlet fever.

скат slope; pitch.

скатать *pf* (*impf* скатывать) roll (up).

скатерть (*pl* -и, -ей) table-cloth.

скатить (-ачу, -áтишь) *pf*, скатывать¹ *impf* roll down; ~ся roll down; slip, slide. скатывать² *impf of* скатать

скафандр diving-suit; space-suit.

скачка gallop, galloping. скачки (-чек) *pl* horse-race; races. скачок (-чка) jump, leap.

скашивать *impf of* скосить

скважина slit, chink; well.

сквер public garden.

скверно badly; bad. сквернословить (-влю) *impf* use foul language. скверный foul; bad.

сквозить *impf* be transparent; show through; сквозит *impers* there is a draught. сквозной through; transparent. сквозняк (-á) draught. сквозь *prep+gen* through.

скворец (-рца) starling.

скелет skeleton.

скептик sceptic. скептицизм scepticism. скептический sceptical.

скетч sketch.

скидка reduction. скидывать *impf*, скинуть (-ну) *pf* throw off *or* down; knock off.

скипетр sceptre.

скипидар turpentine.

скирд (-á; *pl* -ы), скирда (*pl* -ы, -áм) stack, rick.

скисать *impf*, скиснуть (-ну; скис) *pf* go sour.

скиталец (-льца) wanderer. скитаться *impf* wander.

скиф Scythian.

склад[1] depot; store.

склад[2] mould; turn; logical connection; ~ умá mentality.

склáдка fold; pleat; crease; wrinkle.

склáдно adv smoothly.

складнóй folding, collapsible.

склáдный (-ден, -дна, -о) well-knit, well-built; smooth, coherent.

склáдчина: в склáдчину by clubbing together. склáдывать(ся impf of сложи́ть(ся

скле́ивать impf, скле́ить pf stick together; ~ся stick together.

склеп (burial) vault, crypt.

склепáть pf, склёпывать impf rivet. склёпка riveting.

склерóз sclerosis.

склóка squabble.

склон slope; на ~е лет in one's declining years. склонéние inclination; declension. склони́ть (-ню́, -нишь) pf, склоня́ть impf incline; bow; win over; decline; ~ся bend, bow; yield; be declined. склóнность inclination; tendency. склóнный (-нен, -ннá, -нно) inclined, disposed. склоня́емый declinable.

склянка phial; bottle; (naut) bell.

скобá (pl -ы, -áм) cramp, clamp, staple.

скóбка dim of скобá; bracket; pl parenthesis, parentheses.

скобли́ть (-облю́, -óблишь) impf scrape, plane.

скóванность constraint. скóванный constrained; bound. сковáть (скую́, скуёшь) pf (impf скóвывать) forge; chain; fetter; pin down, hold, contain.

сковородá (pl скóвороды, -рóд, -áм) сковорóдка frying-pan.

скóвывать impf of сковáть

сколáчивать impf, сколоти́ть (-очý, -óтишь) pf knock together.

сколóть (-лю́, -лешь) pf (impf скáлывать) chop off; pin together.

скольжéние sliding, slipping; glide. скользи́ть (-льжý) impf, скользнýть (-нý, -нёшь) pf slide; slip; glide. скóльзкий (-зок, -зкá, -о) slippery. скользя́щий sliding.

скóлько adv how much; how many; as far as.

с|комáндовать pf. с|комбини́ровать pf. с|кóмкать pf. с|комплектовáть pf. с|компромети́ровать pf. с|конструи́ровать pf.

сконфýженный embarrassed, confused, disconcerted. с|конфýзить(ся (-ýжу(сь) pf.

с|концентри́ровать pf.

скончáться pf pass away, die.

с|копи́ровать pf.

скопи́ть (-плю́, -пишь) pf (impf скáпливать) save (up); amass; ~ся accumulate. скоплéние accumulation; crowd.

скóпом adv in a crowd, en masse.

скорбéть (-блю́) impf grieve. скóрбный sorrowful. скорбь (pl -и, -éй) sorrow.

скорéе, скорéй comp of скóро, скóрый; adv rather, sooner; как мóжно ~ as soon as possible; ~ всегó most likely.

скорлупá (pl -ы) shell.

скорня́к (-á) furrier.

скóро adv quickly; soon.

скоро- in comb quick-, fast-. скоровáрка pressure-cooker. ~говóрка patter; tongue-twister. скóропись cursive; shorthand. ~пóртящийся perishable. ~постижный sudden. ~спéлый early; fast-ripening; premature; hasty. ~сшивáтель m binder, file. ~тéчный transient, short-lived.

скоростнóй high-speed. скóрость (gen pl -éй) speed; gear.

скорпиóн scorpion; Scorpio.

с|корректи́ровать pf. с|кóрчить(ся (-чу(сь) pf.

скóрый (скор, -á, -о) quick, fast; near; forthcoming; ~ая пóмощь first-aid; ambulance.

с|коси́ть[1] (-ошý, -óсишь) pf (impf also скáшивать) mow.

с|коси́ть[2] (-ошý) pf (impf also скáшивать) squint; cut on the cross.

скот (-á), скоти́на cattle; livestock; beast. скóтный cattle.

ското- in comb cattle. скотобóйня (gen pl -óен) slaughter-house. ~вóд cattle-breeder. ~вóдство cattle-raising.

скóтский cattle; brutish. скóтство brutish condition; brutality.

с|крáсить (-áшу) pf, скрáшивать impf smooth over; relieve.

скребо́к (-бка́) scraper. **скребу́** etc.: see **скрести́**

скре́жет grating; gnashing. **скреже-та́ть** (-ещу́, -е́щешь) impf grate; +instr gnash.

скре́па clamp, brace; counter-signature.

скрепи́ть (-плю́) pf, **скрепля́ть** impf fasten (together), make fast; clamp; countersign, ratify; **скрепя́ се́рдце** reluctantly. **скре́пка** paperclip. **скрепле́ние** fastening; clamping; tie, clamp.

скрести́ (-ебу́, -ебёшь; -ёб, -ла́) impf scrape; scratch; ~**сь** scratch.

скрести́ть (-ещу́) pf, **скре́щивать** impf cross; interbreed. **скреще́ние** crossing. **скре́щивание** crossing; interbreeding.

с|криви́ть(ся (-влю́(сь) pf.

скрип squeak, creak. **скрипа́ч** (-а́) violinist. **скрипе́ть** (-плю́) impf, **скри́пнуть** (-ну) pf squeak, creak; scratch. **скрипи́чный** violin; ~ **ключ** treble clef. **скри́пка** violin. **скри-пу́чий** squeaky, creaking.

с|крои́ть pf.

скро́мничать impf (pf по~) be (too) modest. **скро́мность** modesty. **скро́мный** (-мен, -мна́, -о) modest.

скро́ю etc.: see **скрыть**. **скрою́** etc.: see **скрои́ть**

скрупулёзный scrupulous.

с|крути́ть (-учу́, -у́тишь) pf, **скру́-чивать** impf twist; roll; tie up.

скрыва́ть impf, **скрыть** (-о́ю) pf hide, conceal; ~**ся** hide, go into hiding, be hidden; steal away; disappear. **скры́тничать** impf be secretive. **скры́тный** secretive. **скры́тый** secret, hidden; latent.

скря́га m & f miser.

ску́дный (-ден, -дна́, -о) scanty; meagre. **ску́дость** scarcity, paucity.

ску́ка boredom.

скула́ (pl -ы) cheek-bone. **скула́-стый** with high cheek-bones.

скули́ть impf whine, whimper.

ску́льптор sculptor. **скульпту́ра** sculpture.

скунс skunk.

скумбрия mackerel.

скупа́ть impf of **скупи́ть**

скупе́ц (-пца́) miser.

скупи́ть (-плю́, -пишь) pf (impf ску-

па́ть) buy (up).

скупи́ться (-плю́сь) impf (pf по~) be stingy; skimp; be sparing (of +на+acc).

ску́пка buying (up).

ску́по adv sparingly. **скупо́й** (-п, -а́, -о) stingy, meagre. **ску́пость** stinginess.

ску́пщик buyer(-up).

ску́тер (pl -а́) outboard speed-boat.

скуча́ть impf be bored; +по+dat or prep miss, yearn for.

ску́ченность density, overcrowding. **ску́ченный** dense, overcrowded. **ску́чить** (-чу) pf crowd (together); ~**ся** cluster; crowd together.

ску́чный (-чен, -чна́, -о) boring; мне **ску́чно** I'm bored.

с|ку́шать pf. **скую́** etc.: see **скова́ть**

слабе́ть (-е́ю) impf (pf о~) weaken, grow weak. **слаби́тельн|ый** laxative; ~**ое** sb laxative. **сла́бить** impf impers: его́ **сла́бит** he has diarrhoea.

слабо- in comb weak, feeble, slight. **слабово́лие** weakness of will. ~**во́льный** weak-willed. ~**не́рв-ный** nervy, nervous. ~**ра́звитый** under-developed. ~**у́мие** feeble-mindedness. ~**у́мный** feeble-minded. **сла́бость** weakness. **сла́бый** (-б, -а́, -о) weak.

сла́ва glory; fame; **на сла́ву** wonderfully well. **сла́вить** (-влю) impf glorify, sing the praises of; ~**ся** (+instr) be famous (for). **сла́вный** glorious, renowned; nice.

славяни́н (pl -я́не, -я́н), **славя́нка** Slav. **славянофи́л** Slavophil(e). **славя́нский** Slav, Slavonic.

слага́емое sb component, term, member. **слага́ть** impf of **сложи́ть**

сла́дить (-а́жу) pf c+instr cope with, handle; arrange.

сла́дк|ий (-док, -дка́, -о) sweet; ~**ое** sb sweet course. **сладостра́стник** voluptuary. **сладостра́стный** voluptuous. **сла́дость** joy; sweetness; pl sweets.

сла́женность harmony. **сла́жен-ный** co-ordinated, harmonious.

сла́мывать impf of **сломи́ть**

сла́нец (-нца) shale, slate.

сласте́на m & f person with a sweet tooth. **сласть** (pl -и, -е́й) delight; pl sweets, sweet things.

слать (шлю, шлёшь) *impf* send.

слаща́вый sugary, sickly-sweet. **сла́-ще** *comp of* **сла́дкий**

сле́ва *adv* from *or* on the left; ~ напра́во from left to right.

слёг *etc.: see* **слечь**

слегка́ *adv* slightly; lightly.

след (следа́, *dat* -у, *loc* -ý; *pl* -ы́) track; footprint; trace. **следи́ть**[1] (-ежу́) *impf* +за+*instr* watch; keep up with; look after; keep an eye on. **следи́ть**[2] (-ежу́) *impf* (*pf* на~) leave footprints. **сле́дование** movement. **сле́дователь** *m* investigator. **сле́довательно** *adv* consequently. **сле́довать** *impf* (*pf* по~) I. +*dat or* за+*instr* follow; go, be bound; II. *impers* (+*dat*) ought; be owing, be owed; вам сле́дует +*inf* you ought to; как сле́дует properly; as it should be; ско́лько с меня́ сле́дует? how much do I owe (you)? **сле́дом** *adv* (за+*instr*) immediately after, close behind. **сле́дственный** investigation, inquiry. **сле́дствие**[1] consequence. **сле́дствие**[2] investigation. **сле́дующий** following, next. **слёжка** shadowing.

слеза́ (*pl* -ёзы; -а́м) tear.

слеза́ть *impf of* **слезть**

слези́ться (-и́тся) *impf* water. **слезли́вый** tearful. **слёзный** tear; tearful. **слезоточи́вый** watering; ~ газ tear-gas.

слезть (-зу; слез) *pf* (*impf* **слеза́ть**) climb *or* get down; dismount; get off; come off.

слепе́нь (-пня́) *m* horse-fly.

слепе́ц (-пца́) blind man. **слепи́ть**[1] *impf* blind; dazzle.

с|лепи́ть[2] (-плю́, -пишь) *pf* stick together.

слепну́ть (-ну; слеп) *impf* (*pf* о~) go blind. **сле́по** *adv* blindly. **слеп|о́й** (-п, -а́, -о) blind; ~ые *sb pl* the blind.

слепо́к (-пка) cast.

слепота́ blindness.

сле́сарь (*pl* -я́ *or* -и) *m* metalworker; locksmith.

слёт gathering; rally. **слета́ть** *impf*, **слете́ть** (-ечу́) *pf* fly down *or* away; fall down *or* off; ~ся fly together; congregate.

слечь (сля́гу, -я́жешь; слёг, -ла́) *pf*

take to one's bed.

сли́ва plum; plum-tree.

слива́ть(ся *impf of* **слить(ся. сли́в-ки** (-вок) *pl* cream. **сли́вочн|ый** cream; creamy; ~ое ма́сло butter; ~ое моро́женое dairy ice-cream.

сли́зистый slimy. **слизня́к** (-а́) slug. **слизь** mucus; slime.

с|линя́ть *pf*.

слипа́ться *impf*, **сли́пнуться** (-нет-ся; -и́пся) *pf* stick together.

сли́тно *adv* together, as one word. **сли́-ток** (-тка) ingot, bar. **с|лить** (солью́, -ьёшь; -и́л, -а́, -о) *pf* (*impf also* **слива́ть**) pour, pour out *or* off; fuse, amalgamate; ~ся flow together; blend; merge.

слича́ть *impf*, **сличи́ть** (-чу́) *pf* collate; check. **сличе́ние** collation, checking.

сли́шком *adv* too; too much.

слия́ние confluence; merging; merger.

слова́к, -а́чка Slovak. **слова́цкий** Slovak.

слова́рный lexical; dictionary. **слова́рь** (-я́) *m* dictionary; vocabulary. **слове́сность** literature; philology. **слове́сный** verbal, oral. **сло́вно** *conj* as if; like, as. **сло́во** (*pl* -а́) word; одни́м ~м in a word. **сло́вом** *adv* in a word. **словообразова́ние** word-formation. **словоохо́тливый** talkative. **словосочета́ние** word combination, phrase. **словоупотребле́ние** usage.

слог[1] style.

слог[2] (*pl* -и, -о́в) syllable.

слоёный flaky.

сложе́ние composition; addition; build, constitution. **сложи́ть** (-жу́, -жишь) *pf* (*impf* **класть, скла́дывать, слага́ть**) put *or* lay (together); pile, stack; add, add up; fold (up); compose; take off, put down; lay down; ~ся turn out; take shape; arise; club together. **сло́жность** complication; complexity. **сло́жный** (-жен, -жна́, -о) complicated; complex; compound.

сло́истый stratified; flaky. **слой** (*pl* -и́, -ёв) layer; stratum.

слом demolition, pulling down. **с|лома́ть(ся** *pf*. **сломи́ть** (-млю́, -мишь) *pf* (*impf* **сла́мывать**) break (off); overcome; сломя́ го́лову at breakneck speed; ~ся break.

слон (-á) elephant; bishop. слони́ха she-elephant. слоно́в|ый elephant; ~ая кость ivory.

слоня́ться *impf* loiter, mooch (about).

слуга́ (*pl* -и) *m* (man)servant. слу-жáнка servant, maid. слу́жащий *sb* employee. слу́жба service; work. служе́бный office; official; auxiliary; secondary. служе́ние service, serving. служи́ть (-жу́, -жишь) *impf* (*pf* по~) serve; work.

с|лука́вить (-влю) *pf*.

слух hearing; ear; rumour; по ~у by ear. слухово́й acoustic, auditory, aural; ~о́й аппара́т hearing aid; ~о́е окно́ dormer (window).

слу́чай incident, event; case; opportunity; chance; ни в ко́ем слу́чае in no circumstances. случа́йно *adv* by chance, accidentally; by any chance. случа́йность chance. случа́йный accidental; chance; incidental. случа́ться *impf*, случи́ться *pf* happen.

слу́шание listening; hearing. слу́шатель *m* listener; student; *pl* audience. слу́шать *impf* (*pf* по~, про~) listen (to); hear; attend lectures on; (я) слу́шаю! hello!; very well; ~ся +*gen* obey, listen to.

слыть (-ву́, -вёшь; -ыл, -á, -о) *impf* (*pf* про~) have the reputation (+*instr or* за+*acc* for).

слыха́ть *impf*, слы́шать (-шу) *impf* (*pf* у~) hear; sense. слы́шаться (-шится) *impf* (*pf* по~) be heard. слы́шимость audibility. слы́ши-мый audible. слы́шный audible.

слюда́ mica.

слюна́ (*pl* -и, -éй) saliva; spit; *pl* spittle. слюня́вый dribbling.

сля́гу *etc.: see* слечь

сля́коть slush.

см. *abbr* (*of* смотри́) see, vide.

сма́зать (-а́жу) *pf*, сма́зывать *impf* lubricate; grease; slur over. сма́зка lubrication; greasing; grease. сма́-зочный lubricating.

смак relish. смакова́ть *impf* relish; savour.

с|маневри́ровать *pf*.

сма́нивать *impf*, смани́ть (-ню́, -нишь) *pf* entice.

с|мастери́ть *pf*. сма́тывать *impf of* смота́ть

сма́хивать *impf*, смахну́ть (-ну́, -нёшь) *pf* brush away *or* off.

сма́чивать *impf of* смочи́ть

сме́жный adjacent.

смека́лка native wit.

смёл *etc.: see* смести́

смеле́ть (-е́ю) *impf* (*pf* о~) grow bolder. сме́лость boldness, courage. сме́лый bold, courageous. смель-ча́к (-á) daredevil.

смелю́ *etc.: see* смоло́ть

сме́на changing; change; replacement(s); relief; shift. смени́ть (-ню́, -нишь) *pf*, сменя́ть[1] *impf* change; replace; relieve; ~ся hand over; be relieved; take turns; +*instr* give place to. сме́нный shift; changeable. сме́нщик relief; *pl* new shift. сменя́ть[2] *pf* exchange.

с|ме́рить *pf*.

смерка́ться *impf*, сме́ркнуться (-нется) *pf* get dark.

смерте́льный mortal, fatal, death; extreme. сме́ртность mortality. сме́ртный mortal; death; deadly, extreme. смерть (*gen pl* -éй) death.

смерч whirlwind; waterspout; sandstorm.

смеси́тельный mixing. с|меси́ть (- ешу́, -е́сишь) *pf*.

смести́ (-ету́, -етёшь; -ёл, -á) *pf* (*impf* смета́ть) sweep off, away.

смести́ть (-ещу́) *pf* (*impf* смеща́ть) displace; remove.

смесь mixture; medley.

сме́та estimate.

смета́на sour cream.

с|мета́ть[1] *pf* (*impf also* смётывать) tack (together).

смета́ть[2] *impf of* смести́

сметли́вый quick. sharp.

смету́ *etc.: see* смести́. смётывать *impf of* смета́ть

сметь (-е́ю) *impf* (*pf* по~) dare.

смех laughter; laugh. смехотво́р-ный laughable.

сме́шанный mixed; combined. с|ме-ша́ть *pf*, сме́шивать *impf* mix; blend; confuse; ~ся mix, (inter)-blend; get mixed-up. смеше́ние mixture; mixing up.

смеши́ть (-шу́) *impf* (*pf* на~, рас~) make laugh. смешли́вый given to laughing. смешно́й funny; ridiculous.

смешу́ *etc.*: *see* смеси́ть, смеши́ть

смеща́ть(ся *impf of* смести́ть(ся.
смеще́ние displacement, removal.
смещу́ *etc.*: *see* смести́ть

смея́ться (-е́юсь, -е́ёшься) *impf*
laugh (at +над+*instr*).

смире́ние humility, meekness. сми-
ре́нный humble, meek. смири́-
тельн|ый: ~ая руба́шка strait-
jacket. смири́ть *pf*, смиря́ть *impf*
restrain, subdue; ~ся submit; resign
o.s. сми́рно *adv* quietly; ~! attention! сми́рный quiet; submissive.

смогу́ *etc.*: *see* смочь

смола́ (*pl* -ы) resin; pitch, tar; rosin.
смоли́стый resinous.

с|молкать *impf*, смо́лкнуть (-ну;
-олк) *pf* fall silent.

смо́лоду *adv* from one's youth.

с|молоти́ть (-очу́, -о́тишь) *pf*. с|мо-
ло́ть (смелю́, сме́лешь) *pf*.

смоляно́й pitch, tar, resin.

с|монти́ровать *pf*.

сморка́ть *impf* (*pf* вы́~) blow; ~ся
blow one's nose.

сморо́дина (*no pl*; *usu collect*) cur-
rant; currants; currant-bush.

смо́рщенный wrinkled. с|мо́рщить-
(ся (-щу(сь) *pf*.

смота́ть *pf* (*impf* сма́тывать) wind,
reel.

смотр (*loc* -ý; *pl* -о́тры) review, inspection. смотре́ть (-рю́, -ришь)
impf (*pf* по~) look (at на+*acc*); see;
watch; look through; examine;
+за+*instr* look after; +в+*acc*, на+*acc*
look on to; +*instr* look (like);
смотри́(те)! take care!; смотря́ it de-
pends; смотря́ по+*dat* depending on;
~ся look at o.s. смотрово́й observation, inspection.

смочи́ть (-чу́, -чишь) *pf* (*impf* сма́-
чивать) moisten.

с|мочь (-огу́, -о́жешь; смог, -ла́) *pf*.

с|моше́нничать *pf*. смою́ *etc.*: *see*
смыть

смрад stench. смра́дный stinking.

сму́глый (-гл, -á, -о) dark-complex-
ioned, swarthy.

смути́ть (-ущу́) *pf*, смуща́ть *impf*
embarrass, confuse; ~ся be embarrassed, be confused. сму́тный vague;
dim; troubled. смуще́ние embarrassment, confusion. смущённый
(-ён, -á) embarrassed, confused.

смыва́ть *impf of* смыть

смыка́ть(ся *impf of* сомкну́ть(ся

смысл sense; meaning. смы́слить
impf understand. смыслово́й semantic.

смыть (смо́ю) *pf* (*impf* смыва́ть)
wash off, away.

смычо́к (-чка́) bow.

смышлёный clever.

смягча́ть *impf*, смягчи́ть (-чу́) *pf*
soften; alleviate; ~ся soften; relent;
grow mild.

смяте́ние confusion; commotion.

с|мять(ся (сомну́(сь, -нёшь(ся) *pf*.

снабди́ть (-бжу́) *pf*, снабжа́ть *impf*
+*instr* supply with. снабже́ние supply, supplying.

сна́йпер sniper.

снару́жи *adv* on *or* from (the) outside.

снаря́д projectile, missile; shell; contrivance; tackle, gear. снаряди́ть
(-жу́) *pf*, снаряжа́ть *impf* equip,
fit out. снаряже́ние equipment,
outfit.

снасть (*gen pl* -е́й) tackle; *pl* rigging.

снача́ла *adv* at first; all over again.

сна́шивать *impf of* сноси́ть

СНГ *abbr* (*of* Содру́жество не-
зави́симых госуда́рств) CIS.

снег (*loc* -ý; *pl* -á) snow.

снеги́рь (-я́) bullfinch.

снегово́й snow. снегопа́д snowfall.
Снегу́рочка Snow Maiden. сне́жин-
ка snow-flake. сне́жный snow(y);
~ая ба́ба snowman. снежо́к (-жка́)
light snow; snowball.

снести́[1] (-су́, -сёшь; -ёс, -ла́) *pf* (*impf*
сноси́ть) take; bring together; bring
or fetch down; carry away; blow off;
demolish; endure; ~сь communicate
(с+*instr* with).

с|нести́[2](сь (-су́(сь, -сёшь(ся; снёс-
(ся, -сла́(сь) *pf*.

снижа́ть *impf*, сни́зить (-и́жу) *pf*
lower; bring down; reduce; ~ся come
down; fall. сниже́ние lowering; loss
of height.

снизойти́ (-йду́, -йдёшь; -ошёл, -шла́)
pf (*impf* снисходи́ть) condescend.

сни́зу *adv* from below.

снима́ть(ся *impf of* снять(ся.
сни́мок (-мка) photograph. сниму́
etc.: *see* снять

сниска́ть (-ищу́, -и́щешь) *pf*, сни́-
скивать *impf* gain, win.

снисходи́тельность condescension; leniency. снисходи́тельный condescending; lenient. снисходи́ть (-ожу́, -о́дишь) impf of снизойти́. снисхожде́ние indulgence, leniency.

сни́ться impf (pf при~) impers+dat dream.

сноби́зм snobbery.

сно́ва adv again, anew.

снова́ть (сную́, снуёшь) impf rush about.

сновиде́ние dream.

сноп (-а́) sheaf.

сноро́вка knack, skill.

снос demolition; drift; wear. сноси́ть[1] (-ошу́, -о́сишь) pf (impf сна́шивать) wear out. сноси́ть[2](ся (-ошу́(сь, -о́сишь(ся) impf of снести́(сь. сно́ска footnote. сно́сно adv tolerably, so-so. сно́сный tolerable; fair.

снотво́рный soporific.

сноха́ (pl -и) daughter-in-law.

сноше́ние intercourse; relations; dealings.

сношу́ etc.: see сноси́ть

сня́тие taking down; removal; making. снять (сниму́, -и́мешь; -ял, -а́, -о) pf (impf снима́ть) take off; take down; gather in; remove; rent; take; make; photograph; ~ся come off; move off; be photographed.

со see с prep.

со- pref co-, joint. соа́втор co-author.

соба́ка dog. соба́чий dog's; canine. соба́чка little dog; trigger.

соберу́ etc.: see собра́ть

собе́с abbr (of социа́льное обеспе́чение) social security (department).

собесе́дник interlocutor, companion. собесе́дование conversation.

собира́тель m collector. собира́ть(ся impf of собра́ть(ся

собла́зн temptation. соблазни́тель m, ~ница tempter; seducer. соблазни́тельный tempting; seductive. соблазни́ть pf, соблазня́ть impf tempt; seduce.

соблюда́ть impf, co|блюсти́ (-юду́, -дёшь; -юл, -а́) pf observe; keep (to). соблюде́ние observance; maintenance.

собо́й, собо́ю see себя́

соболе́знование sympathy, condolence(s). соболе́зновать impf +dat sympathize or commiserate with.

со́боль (pl -и or -я́) m sable.

собо́р cathedral; council, synod. собо́рный cathedral.

собра́ние meeting; assembly; collection. со́бранный collected; concentrated.

собра́т (pl -ья, -ьев) colleague.

собра́ть (-беру́, -берёшь; -а́л, -а́, -о) pf (impf собира́ть) gather; collect; ~ся gather; prepare; intend, be going; +c+instr collect.

со́бственник owner, proprietor. со́бственнический proprietary; proprietorial. со́бственно adv: ~ (говоря́) strictly speaking, as a matter of fact. собственнору́чно adv personally, with one's own hand. со́бственность property; ownership. со́бственный (one's) own; proper; true; и́мя ~ое proper name; ~ой персо́ной in person.

собы́тие event.

собью́ etc.: see сбить

сова́ (pl -ы) owl.

сова́ть (сую́, -ёшь) impf (pf су́нуть) thrust, shove; ~ся push, push in; butt in.

соверша́ть impf, соверши́ть (-шу́) pf accomplish; carry out; commit; complete; ~ся happen; be accomplished. соверше́ние accomplishment; perpetration. соверше́нно adv perfectly; absolutely, completely. совершенноле́тие majority. совершенноле́тний of age. соверше́нный[1] perfect; absolute, complete. соверше́нный[2] perfective. соверше́нство perfection. соверше́нствовать perfecting; improvement. соверше́нствовать (pf у~) perfect; improve; ~ся в+instr perfect o.s. in; improve.

со́вестливый conscientious. со́вестно impers+dat be ashamed. со́весть conscience.

сове́т advice, counsel; opinion; council; soviet, Soviet. сове́тник adviser. сове́товать impf (pf по~) advise; ~ся c+instr consult, ask advice of. совето́лог Kremlinologist. сове́т|ский Soviet; ~ая власть the Soviet regime; ~ий Сою́з the Soviet Union. **сове́тчик** adviser.

совещáние conference. **совещáтельный** consultative, deliberative. **совещáться** impf deliberate; consult.

совладáть pf c+instr control, cope with.

совмести́мый compatible. **совмести́тель** m person holding more than one office. **совмести́ть** (-ещý) pf, **совмещáть** impf combine; ~ся coincide; be combined, combine. **совме́стно** jointly. **совме́стный** joint, combined.

сово́к (-вкá) shovel; scoop; dust-pan.

совокупи́ться (-плю́сь) pf, **совокупля́ться** impf copulate. **совокупле́ние** copulation. **совокýпно** adv jointly. **совокýпность** aggregate, sum total.

совпадáть impf, **совпáсть** (-адёт) pf coincide; agree, tally. **совпаде́ние** coincidence.

соврати́ть (-ащý) pf (impf **совращáть**) pervert, seduce.

со|врáть (-врý, -врёшь; -áл, -á, -о) pf.

совращáть(ся impf of **соврати́ть(ся**. **совраще́ние** perverting, seduction.

совреме́нник contemporary. **совреме́нность** the present (time); contemporaneity. **совреме́нный** contemporary; modern.

соврý etc.: see **соврáть**

совсе́м adv quite; entirely.

совхо́з State farm.

совью́ etc.: see **свить**

соглáсие consent; assent; agreement; harmony. **согласи́ться** (-ашýсь) pf (impf **соглашáться**) consent; agree. **соглáсно** adv in accord, in harmony; prep+dat in accordance with. **соглáсн|ый**[1] agreeable (to); in agreement; harmonious. **соглáсный**[2] consonant(al); sb consonant.

согласовáние co-ordination; agreement. **согласо́ванность** co-ordination. **согласовáть** pf, **согласо́вывать** impf co-ordinate; make agree; ~ся conform; agree.

соглашáться impf of **согласи́ться**. **соглаше́ние** agreement. **соглашý** etc.: see **согласи́ть**

согнáть (сгоню́, сго́нишь; -áл, -á, -о)

pf (impf **сгоня́ть**) drive away; drive together.

со|гнýть (-нý, -нёшь) pf (impf also **сгибáть**) bend, curve; ~ся bend (down).

согревáть impf, **согре́ть** (-е́ю) pf warm, heat; ~ся get warm; warm o.s.

со|греши́ть (-шý) pf.

со́да soda.

соде́йствие assistance. **соде́йствовать** impf & pf (pf also по~) +dat assist; promote; contribute to.

содержáние maintenance, upkeep; content(s); pay. **содержáтельный** rich in content; pithy. **содержáть** (-жý, -жишь) impf keep; maintain; contain; ~ся be kept; be maintained; be; be contained. **содержи́мое** sb contents.

со|дрáть (сдерý, -рёшь; -áл, -á, -о) pf (impf also **сдирáть**) tear off, strip off; fleece.

содрогáние shudder. **содрогáться** impf, **содрогнýться** (-нýсь, -нёшься) pf shudder.

содрýжество concord; commonwealth.

соедине́ние joining, combination; joint; compound; formation. **Соединённое Короле́вство** United Kingdom. **Соединённые Штáты (Амéрики)** m pl United States (of America). **соединённый** (-ён, -á) united, joint. **соедини́тельный** connective, connecting. **соедини́ть** pf, **соединя́ть** impf join, unite; connect; combine; ~ся join, unite; combine.

сожале́ние regret; pity; к сожале́нию unfortunately. **сожале́ть** (-е́ю) impf regret, deplore.

сожгý etc.: see **сжечь**. **сожже́ние** burning; cremation.

сожи́тель m, ~ница room-mate, flat-mate; lover. **сожи́тельство** cohabitation.

сожмý etc.: see **сжать**[2]. **сожнý** etc.: see **сжать**[1]. **созвáниваться** impf of **созвони́ться**

созвáть (-зовý, -зовёшь; -áл, -á, -о) pf (impf **сзывáть, созывáть**) call together; call; invite.

созве́здие constellation.

созвони́ться pf (impf **созвáниваться**) ring up; speak on the telephone.

созвучие accord; assonance. созвучный harmonious; +dat in keeping with.

создавать (-даю, -даёшь) impf, создать (-ам, -ашь, -аст, -адим; создал, -а, -о) pf create; establish; ~ся be created; arise, spring up. создание creation; work; creature. создатель m creator; originator.

созерцание contemplation. созерцательный contemplative. созерцать impf contemplate.

созидание creation. созидательный creative.

сознавать (-наю, -наёшь) impf, сознать pf be conscious of, realize; acknowledge; ~ся confess. сознание consciousness; acknowledgement; confession. сознательность awareness, consciousness. сознательный conscious; deliberate.

созову etc.: see созвать

созревать impf, со|зреть (-ею) pf ripen, mature.

созыв summoning, calling. созывать impf of созвать

соизмеримый commensurable.

соискание competition. соискатель m, ~ница competitor, candidate.

сойти (-йду, -йдёшь; сошёл, -шла) pf (impf сходить) go or come down; get off; leave; come off; pass, go off; ~ с ума go mad, go out of one's mind; ~сь meet; gather; become friends; become intimate; agree.

сок (loc -у) juice.

сокол falcon.

сократить (-ащу) pf, сокращать impf shorten; abbreviate; reduce; ~ся grow shorter; decrease; contract. сокращение shortening; abridgement; abbreviation; reduction.

сокровенный secret; innermost. сокровище treasure. сокровищница treasure-house.

сокрушать impf, сокрушить (-шу) pf shatter; smash; distress; ~ся grieve, be distressed. сокрушение smashing; grief. сокрушённый (-ён, -á) grief-stricken. сокрушительный shattering.

сокрытие concealment.

со|лгать (-лгу, -лжёшь; -ал, -á, -о) pf.

солдат (gen pl -ат) soldier. солдат-

ский soldier's.

соление salting; pickling. солёный (солон, -á, -о) salt(y); salted; pickled. соленье salted food(s); pickles.

солидарность solidarity. солидный solid; strong; reliable; respectable; sizeable.

солист, солистка soloist.

солить (-лю, солишь) impf (pf по~) salt; pickle.

солнечный sun; solar; sunny; ~ свет sunlight; sunshine; ~ удар sunstroke. солнце sun. солнцепёк: на ~е in the sun. солнцестояние solstice.

соло neut indecl solo; adv solo.

соловей (-вья) nightingale.

солод malt.

солодковый liquorice.

солома straw; thatch. соломенный straw; thatch. соломинка straw.

солон etc.: see солёный. солонина corned beef. солонка salt-cellar. солончак (-á) saline soil; pl salt marshes. соль (pl -и, -ей) salt.

сольный solo.

солью etc.: see слить

соляной, соляный salt, saline. соляная кислота hydrochloric acid.

сомкнутый close. сомкнуть (-ну, -нёшь) pf (impf смыкать) close; close.

сомневаться impf doubt, have doubts. сомнение doubt. сомнительный doubtful.

сому etc.: see смять

сон (сна) sleep; dream. сонливость sleepiness; somnolence. сонливый sleepy. сонный sleepy; sleeping.

соната sonata.

сонет sonnet.

соображать impf, сообразить (-ажу) pf consider, think out; weigh; understand. соображение consideration; understanding; notion. сообразительный quick-witted.

сообразный c+instr conforming to, in keeping with.

сообща adv together. сообщать impf, сообщить (-щу) pf communicate, report, announce; impart; +dat inform. сообщение communication; report; announcement. сообщество association. сообщник accomplice.

соорудить (-ужу) pf, сооружать impf build, erect. сооружение building; structure.

соответственно *adv* accordingly, correspondingly; *prep+dat* according to, in accordance with. **соответственный** corresponding. **соответствие** accordance, correspondence. **соответствовать** *impf* correspond, conform. **соответствующий** corresponding; suitable.

соотечественник fellow-countryman.

соотношение correlation.

соперник rival. **соперничать** *impf* compete, vie. **соперничество** rivalry.

сопеть (-плю) *impf* wheeze; snuffle.

сопка hill, mound.

сопливый snotty.

сопоставить (-влю) *pf*, **сопоставлять** *impf* compare. **сопоставление** comparison.

сопредельный contiguous.

со|преть *pf*.

соприкасаться *impf*, **соприкоснуться** (-нусь, -нёшься) *pf* adjoin; come into contact. **соприкосновение** contact.

сопроводительный accompanying. **сопроводить** (-ожу) *pf*, **сопровождать** *impf* accompany; escort. **сопровождение** accompaniment; escort.

сопротивление resistance. **сопротивляться** *impf+dat* resist, oppose.

сопутствовать *impf* +*dat* accompany.

сопьюсь *etc.*: *see* **спиться**

сор litter, rubbish.

соразмерить *pf*, **соразмерять** *impf* balance, match. **соразмерный** proportionate, commensurate.

соратник comrade-in-arms.

сорвать (-ву, -вёшь; -ал, -а, -о) *pf* (*impf* **срывать**) tear off, away, down; break off; pick; get; break; ruin, spoil; vent; ~ся break away, break loose; fall, come down; fall through.

с|организовать *pf*.

соревнование competition; contest. **соревноваться** *impf* compete.

сорить *impf* (*pf* **на~**) +*acc or instr* litter; throw about. **сорный** rubbish, refuse; ~ая трава weed(s). **сорняк** (-á) weed.

сорок (-á) forty.

сорока magpie.

сороков|ой fortieth; ~ые годы the forties.

сорочка shirt; blouse; shift.

сорт (*pl* -á) grade, quality; sort. **сортировать** *impf* (*pf* рас~) sort. grade. **сортировка** sorting. **сортировочн|ый** sorting; ~ая *sb* marshalling-yard. **сортировщик** sorter. **сортный** high quality.

сосать (-су, -сёшь) *impf* suck.

со|сватать *pf*.

сосед (*pl* -и), **соседка** neighbour. **соседний** neighbouring; adjacent, next. **соседский** neighbours'. **соседство** neighbourhood. **соси́ска** frankfurter, sausage.

соска (*baby's*) dummy.

соскакивать *impf* of **соскочить**

соскальзывать *impf*, **соскользнуть** (-ну, -нёшь) *pf* slide down, slide off.

соскочить (-чу, -чишь) *pf* (*impf* **соскакивать**) jump off or down; come off.

соскучиться (-чусь) *pf* get bored; ~ по+*dat* miss.

сослагательный subjunctive.

сослать (сошлю, -лёшь) *pf* (*impf* **ссылать**) exile, deport; ~ся на+*acc* refer to; cite; plead, allege.

сословие estate; class.

сослуживец (-вца) colleague.

сосна (*pl* -ы, -сен) pine(-tree). **сосновый** pine; deal.

сосок (-ска) nipple, teat.

сосредоточенный concentrated. **сосредоточивать** *impf*, **сосредоточить** (-чу) *pf* concentrate; focus; ~ся concentrate.

состав composition; structure; compound; staff; strength; train; в ~е +*gen* consisting of. **составитель** *m* compiler. **составить** (-влю) *pf*, **составлять** *impf* put together; make (up); draw up; compile; be, constitute; total; ~ся form, be formed. **составной** compound; component, constituent.

со|старить(ся *pf*.

состояние state, condition; fortune. **состоятельный** well-to-do; well-grounded. **состоять** (-ою) *impf* be; +из+*gen* consist of; +в+*prep* consist in, be. **состояться** (-ойтся) *pf* take place.

состради́ние compassion. **сострада́тельный** compassionate.

с|**остри́ть** pf. **со**|**стря́пать** pf.

со|**стыкова́ть** pf, **состыко́вывать** impf dock; **~ся** dock.

состяза́ние competition, contest. **состяза́ться** impf compete.

сосу́д vessel.

сосу́лька icicle.

сосуществова́ние co-existence.

со|**счита́ть** pf. **сот** see **сто**.

сотворе́ние creation. **со**|**твори́ть** pf.

со|**тка́ть** (-ку́, -кёшь, -а́л, -ала́, -о) pf.

со́тня (gen pl -тен) a hundred.

сотру́ etc.: see **стере́ть**

сотру́дник collaborator; colleague; employee. **сотру́дничать** impf collaborate; **+в+prep** contribute to. **сотру́дничество** collaboration.

сотряса́ть impf, **сотрясти́** (-су́, -сёшь, -я́с, -ла́) pf shake; **~ся** tremble. **сотрясе́ние** shaking; concussion.

со́ты (-ов) pl honeycomb.

со́тый hundredth.

соумы́шленник accomplice.

со́ус sauce; gravy; dressing.

соуча́стие participation; complicity. **соуча́стник** participant; accomplice.

софа́ (pl -ы) sofa.

соха́ (pl -и) (wooden) plough.

со́хнуть (-ну) impf (pf вы́~, за~, про~) (get) dry; wither.

сохране́ние preservation; conservation; (safe)keeping; retention. **со**|**храни́ть** pf, **сохраня́ть** impf preserve, keep; **~ся** remain (intact); last out; be well preserved. **сохра́нный** safe.

социа́л-демокра́т Social Democrat. **социа́л-демократи́ческий** Social Democratic. **социали́зм** socialism. **социали́ст** socialist. **социалисти́ческий** socialist. **социа́льный** social; **~ое обеспе́чение** social security. **социо́лог** sociologist. **социоло́гия** sociology.

соцреали́зм socialist realism.

сочета́ние combination. **сочета́ть** impf & pf combine; **~ся** combine; harmonize; match.

сочине́ние composition; work. **со**|**чини́ть** pf, **сочиня́ть** impf compose; write; make up.

сочи́ться (-и́тся) impf ooze (out), trickle; **~ кро́вью** bleed.

со́чный (-чен, -чна́, -о) juicy; rich.

сочту́ etc.: see **счесть**

сочу́вствие sympathy. **сочу́вствовать** impf **+dat** sympathize with.

сошёл etc.: see **сойти́**. **сошлю́** etc.: see **сосла́ть**. **сошью́** etc.: see **сшить**

сощу́ривать impf, **со**|**щу́рить** pf screw up, narrow; **~ся** screw up one's eyes; narrow.

сою́з[1] union; alliance; league. **сою́з**[2] conjunction. **сою́зник** ally. **сою́зный** allied; Union.

спад recession; abatement. **спада́ть** impf of **спасть**

спазм spasm.

спа́ивать impf of **спая́ть**, **спои́ть**

спа́йка soldered joint; solidarity, cohesion.

с|**пали́ть** pf.

спа́льн|**ый** sleeping; **~ый ваго́н** sleeping car; **~ое ме́сто** berth. **спа́льня** (gen pl -лен) bedroom.

спа́ржа asparagus.

спартакиа́да sports meeting.

спаса́тельный rescue; **~ жиле́т** life jacket; **~ круг** lifebuoy; **~ по́яс** lifebelt. **спаса́ть(ся** impf of **спасти́(сь**. **спасе́ние** rescue, escape; salvation. **спаси́бо** thank you. **спаси́тель** m rescuer; saviour. **спаси́тельный** saving; salutary.

спасти́ (-су́, -сёшь, спас, -ла́) pf (impf **спаса́ть**) save; rescue; **~сь** escape; be saved.

спасть (-адёт) pf (impf **спада́ть**) fall (down); abate.

спать (сплю; -ал, -а́, -о) impf sleep; **лечь ~** go to bed.

спа́янность cohesion, unity. **спа́янный** united. **спая́ть** pf (impf **спа́ивать**) solder, weld; unite.

спекта́кль m performance; show.

спектр spectrum.

спекули́ровать impf speculate. **спекуля́нт** speculator, profiteer. **спекуля́ция** speculation; profiteering.

спе́лый ripe.

сперва́ adv at first; first.

спе́реди adv in front, from the front; prep+gen (from) in front of.

спёртый close, stuffy.

спеси́вый arrogant, haughty. **спесь** arrogance, haughtiness.

спеть[1] (-е́ет) impf (pf по~) ripen.

с|**петь**[2] (спою́, споёшь) pf.

спец- *abbr in comb* (*of* специ-
а́льный) special. спецко́р special
correspondent. ~оде́жда protective
clothing; overalls.

специализа́ция specialization. спе-
циализи́роваться *impf & pf* specialize. специали́ст, ~ка specialist,
expert. специа́льность speciality;
profession. специа́льный special;
specialist.

специ́фика specific character. спе-
цифи́ческий specific.

спе́ция spice.

спецо́вка protective clothing; over-
all(s).

спеши́ть (-шу́) *impf* (*pf* по~) hurry,
be in a hurry; be fast.

спе́шка hurry, haste. спе́шный urgent.

спива́ться *impf of* спи́ться

СПИД *abbr* (*of* синдро́м приобре-
тённого имму́нного дефици́та)
Aids.

с|пики́ровать *pf*.

спи́ливать *impf*, спили́ть (-лю́,
-лишь) *pf* saw down, off.

спина́ (*acc* -у, *pl* -ы) back. спи́нка
back. спинно́й spinal; ~ мозг
spinal cord.

спира́ль spiral.

спирт alcohol, spirit(s). спиртн|о́й
alcoholic; ~о́е *sb* alcohol. спирто́в-
ка spirit-stove. спиртово́й spirit, alcoholic.

списа́ть (-ишу́, -и́шешь) *pf*, спи́сы-
вать *impf* copy; ~ся exchange letters. спи́сок (-ска) list; record.

спи́ться (сопью́сь, -ьёшься; -и́лся,
-а́сь) *pf* (*impf* спива́ться) take to
drink.

спи́хивать *impf*, спихну́ть (-ну́,
-нёшь) *pf* push aside, down.

спи́ца knitting-needle; spoke.

спи́чечн|ый match; ~ая коро́бка
match-box. спи́чка match.

спишу́ *etc.: see* списа́ть

сплав[1] floating. сплав[2] alloy. спла́-
вить[1] (-влю) *pf*, сплавля́ть[1] *impf*
float; raft; get rid of. сплавить[2]
(-влю) *pf*, сплавля́ть[2] *impf* alloy;
~ся fuse.

с|плани́ровать *pf*. спла́чивать(ся
impf of сплоти́ть(ся. спле́вывать
impf of сплю́нуть

с|плести́ (-ету́, -етёшь; -ёл, -а́) *pf*,

сплета́ть *impf* weave; plait; interlace. сплете́ние interlacing; plexus.
спле́тник, -ница gossip, scandal-
monger. сплетни́чать *impf* (*pf* на~)
gossip. спле́тня (*gen pl* -тен) gossip, scandal.

сплоти́ть (-очу́) *pf* (*impf* спла́чи-
вать) join; unite, rally; ~ся unite,
rally; close ranks. сплоче́ние unit-
ing. сплочённость cohesion, unity.
сплочённый (-ён, -а́) united; firm;
unbroken.

сплошно́й solid; complete; continuous;
utter. сплошь *adv* all over; completely; ~ да ря́дом pretty often.

сплю́ *see* спать

сплю́нуть (-ну) *pf* (*impf* сплёвы-
вать) spit; spit out.

сплю́щивать *impf*, сплю́щить (-щу)
pf flatten; ~ся become flat.

с|пляса́ть (-яшу́, -я́шешь) *pf*.

сподви́жник comrade-in-arms.

спои́ть (-ою́, -о́ишь) *pf* (*impf* спа́-
ивать) make a drunkard of.

споко́йн|ый quiet; calm; ~ой но́чи
good night! споко́йствие quiet;
calm, serenity.

спола́скивать *impf of* сполосну́ть

сполза́ть *impf*, сползти́ (-зу́, -зёшь;
-олз, -ла́) *pf* climb down; slip (down);
fall away.

сполна́ *adv* in full.

сполосну́ть (-ну́, -нёшь) *pf* (*impf*
спола́скивать) rinse.

спо́нсор sponsor, backer.

спор argument; controversy; dispute.
спо́рить *impf* (*pf* по~) argue; dispute; debate. спо́рный debatable,
questionable; disputed; moot.

спо́ра spore.

спорт sport. спорти́вный sports; ~
зал gymnasium. спортсме́н, ~ка
athlete, player.

спо́соб way, method; таки́м ~ом in
this way. спосо́бность ability, aptitude; capacity. спосо́бный able;
clever; capable. спосо́бствовать
impf (*pf* по~) +*dat* assist; further.

споткну́ться (-ну́сь, -нёшься) *pf*,
спотыка́ться *impf* stumble.

спохвати́ться (-ачу́сь, -а́тишься) *pf*,
спохва́тываться *impf* remember
suddenly.

спою́ *etc.: see* спеть, спои́ть

спра́ва *adv* from *or* on the right.

справедли́вость justice; fairness; truth. справедли́вый just; fair; justified.

справля́ть (-вля́ю) pf, справля́ть impf celebrate. спра́виться¹ (-влюсь) pf, справля́ться impf c+instr cope with, manage. спра́виться² (-влюсь) pf, справля́ться impf inquire; +в+prep consult. спра́вка information; reference; certificate; наводи́ть спра́вку make inquiries. спра́вочник reference-book, directory. спра́вочный inquiry, information.

спра́шивать (ся impf of спроси́ть (ся

спринт sprint. спри́нтер sprinter.

с|провоци́ровать pf. с|проекти́ровать pf.

спрос demand; asking; без ~у without permission. спроси́ть (-ошу́, -о́сишь) pf (impf спра́шивать) ask (for); inquire; ~ся ask permission.

спрут octopus.

спры́гивать impf, спры́гнуть (-ну) pf jump off, jump down.

спры́скивать impf, спры́снуть (-ну) pf sprinkle.

спряга́ть impf (pf про~) conjugate. спряже́ние conjugation.

с|прясть (-яду́, -ядёшь; -ял, -яла́, -о) pf. с|пря́тать (ся (-я́чу(сь) pf)

спу́гивать impf, спугну́ть (-ну́, -нёшь) pf frighten off.

спуск lowering; descent; slope. спуска́ть impf, спусти́ть (-ущу́, -у́стишь) pf let down, lower; let go, release; let out; send out; go down; forgive; squander; ~ кора́бль launch a ship; ~ куро́к pull the trigger; ~ пе́тлю drop a stitch; ~ся go down, descend. спускно́й drain. спусково́й trigger. спустя́ prep+acc after; later.

с|пу́тать (ся pf.

спу́тник satellite, sputnik; (travelling) companion.

спущу́ etc.: see спусти́ть

спя́чка hibernation; sleepiness.

ср. abbr (of сравни́) cf.

сраба́тывать impf, срабо́тать pf make; work, operate.

сравне́ние comparison; simile. сра́внивать impf of сравни́ть, сравня́ть. сравни́мый comparable. сравни́тельно adv comparatively. сравни́тельный comparative. срав-

ни́ть pf (impf сра́внивать) compare; ~ся c+instr compare with. сравня́ть pf (impf also сра́внивать) make even, equal; level.

сража́ть impf, срази́ть (-ажу́) pf strike down; overwhelm, crush; ~ся fight. сраже́ние battle.

сра́зу adv at once.

срам shame. срами́ть (-млю́) impf (pf o~) shame; ~ся cover o.s. with shame. срамота́ shame.

сраста́ние growing together. сраста́ться impf, срасти́сь (-тётся; сро́сся, -ла́сь) pf grow together; knit.

среда́¹ (pl -ы) environment, surroundings; medium. среда́² (acc -у; pl -ы, -а́м or -ам) Wednesday. среди́ prep+gen among; in the middle of; ~ бе́ла дня in broad daylight. средиземномо́рский Mediterranean. сре́дне adv so-so. средневеко́вый medieval. средневеко́вье the Middle Ages. сре́дний middle; medium; mean; average; middling; secondary; neuter; ~ee sb mean, average. средото́чие focus. сре́дство means; remedy.

срез cut; section; slice. с|ре́зать (-е́жу) pf, среза́ть impf cut off; slice; fail; ~ся fail.

с|репети́ровать pf.

срисова́ть pf, срисо́вывать impf copy.

с|ровня́ть pf.

сродство́ affinity.

срок date; term; time, period; в ~, к ~у in time, to time.

сро́сся etc.: see срасти́сь

сро́чно adv urgently. сро́чность urgency. сро́чный urgent; for a fixed period.

сро́ю etc.: see срыть

сруб felling; framework. сруба́ть impf, сруби́ть (-блю́, -бишь) pf cut down; build (of logs).

срыв disruption; breakdown; ruining. срыва́ть¹ impf of сорва́ть

срыва́ть² impf, срыть (сро́ю) pf raze to the ground.

сря́ду adv running.

сса́дина scratch. сса́дить (-ажу́, -а́дишь) pf, сса́живать impf set down; help down; turn off.

ссо́ра quarrel. ссо́рить impf (pf по~) cause to quarrel; ~ся quarrel.

СССР *abbr* (*of* Сою́з Сове́тских Социалисти́ческих Респу́блик) USSR.

ссу́да loan. **ссуди́ть** (-ужу́, -у́дишь) *pf*, **ссужа́ть** *impf* lend, loan.

ссыла́ть(ся *impf of* **сосла́ть(ся. ссы́лка**[1] exile. **ссы́лка**[2] reference. **ссы́льный, ссы́льная** *sb* exile.

ссыпа́ть (-плю) *pf*, **ссыпа́ть** *impf* pour.

стабилиза́тор stabilizer; tail-plane. **стабилизи́ровать(ся** *impf* & *pf* stabilize. **стаби́льность** stability. **стаби́льный** stable, firm.

ста́вень (-вня; *gen pl* -вней) *m*, **ста́вня** (*gen pl* -вен) shutter.

ста́вить (-влю) *impf* (*pf* по~) put, place, set; stand; station; erect; install; apply; present, stage. **ста́вка**[1] rate; stake. **ста́вка**[2] headquarters.

ста́вня *see* **ста́вень**

стадио́н stadium.

ста́дия stage.

ста́дность herd instinct. **ста́дный** gregarious. **ста́до** (*pl* -а́) herd, flock.

стаж length of service; probation. **стажёр** probationer; student on a special non-degree course. **стажиро́вка** period of training.

стака́н glass.

сталелите́йный steel-founding; ~ заво́д steel foundry. **сталеплави́льный** steel-making; ~ заво́д steel works. **сталепрока́тный** (steel-)rolling; ~ стан rolling-mill.

ста́лкивать(ся *impf of* **столкну́ть(ся**

ста́ло быть *conj* consequently. **сталь** steel. **стально́й** steel.

стаме́ска chisel.

стан[1] figure, torso.

стан[2] camp.

стан[3] mill.

станда́рт standard. **станда́ртный** standard.

стани́ца Cossack village.

станкостро́ение machine-tool engineering.

станови́ться (-влю́сь, -вишься) *impf of* **стать**[2]

стано́к (-нка́) machine tool, machine.

ста́ну *etc.*: *see* **стать**[2]

станцио́нный station. **ста́нция** station.

ста́пель (*pl* -я́) *m* stocks.

ста́птывать(ся *impf of* **стопта́ть(ся**

стара́ние effort. **стара́тельность** diligence. **стара́тельный** diligent. **стара́ться** *impf* (*pf* по~) try.

старе́ть *impf* (*pf* по~, у~) grow old. **ста́рец** (-рца) elder, (*venerable*) old man. **стари́к** (-а́) old man. **старина́** antiquity, olden times; antique(s); old fellow. **стари́нный** ancient; old; antique. **ста́рить** *impf* (*pf* со~) age, make old; ~ся age, grow old.

старо- in *comb* old. **старове́р** Old Believer. **~жи́л** old resident. **~мо́дный** old-fashioned. **~славя́нский** Old Slavonic.

ста́роста head; monitor; church-warden. **ста́рость** old age.

старт start; на ~! on your marks! **ста́ртер** starter. **стартова́ть** *impf* & *pf* start. **ста́ртовый** starting.

стару́ха, стару́шка old woman. **ста́рческий** old man's; senile. **ста́рше** *comp of* **ста́рый. ста́рш|ий** oldest, eldest; senior; head; ~ие *sb pl* (one's) elders; ~ий *sb* chief; man in charge. **старшина́** *m* sergeant-major; petty officer; leader, senior representative. **ста́рый** (-ар, -а́, -о) old. **старьё** old things, junk.

ста́скивать *impf of* **стащи́ть**

с|тасова́ть *pf*.

стати́ст extra.

стати́стика statistics. **статисти́ческий** statistical.

ста́тный stately.

ста́тский civil, civilian.

ста́тус status. **ста́тус-кво́** *neut indecl* status quo.

статуэ́тка statuette.

ста́туя statue.

стать[1] (-а́ну) *pf* (*impf* станови́ться) stand; take up position; stop; cost; begin; +*instr* become; +c+*instr* become of; не ~ *impers*+*gen* cease to be; disappear; его́ не ста́ло he is no more; ~ на коле́ни kneel.

стать[2] physique, build.

ста́ться (-а́нется) *pf* happen.

статья́ (*gen pl* -е́й) article; clause; item; matter.

стациона́р permanent establishment; hospital. **стациона́рный** stationary; permanent; ~ больно́й in-patient.

ста́чечник striker. **ста́чка** strike.

с|тащи́ть (-щу́, -щишь) *pf* (*impf also*

стáскивать) drag off, pull off.

стáя flock; school, shoal; pack.

ствол (-á) trunk; barrel.

ствóрка leaf, fold.

стéбель (-бля; gen pl -блéй) m stem, stalk.

стёган|ый quilted; ~ое одея́ло quilt. стегáть¹ impf (pf вы́~) quilt.

стегáть² impf, стегнýть (-нý) pf (pf also от~) whip, lash.

стежóк (-жкá) stitch.

стезя́ path, way.

стёк etc.: see стечь. стекáть(ся impf of стечь(ся

стеклó (pl -ёкла, -кол) glass; lens; (window-)pane.

стекло- in comb glass. стекловолокнó glass fibre. ~очисти́тель m windscreen-wiper. ~рéз glass-cutter. ~ткáнь fibreglass.

стекля́нный glass; glassy. стекóльщик glazier.

стели́ть see стлать

стелла́ж (-á) shelves, shelving.

стéлька insole.

стелю́ etc.: see стлать

с|темнéть (-éет) pf.

стенá (acc -у, gen -ы́, -ам) wall. стенгазéта wall newspaper.

стенд stand.

стéнка wall; side. стенно́й wall.

стеногра́мма shorthand record. стенóграф, стенографи́ст, ~ка стенographer. стенографи́ровать impf & pf take down in shorthand. стенографи́ческий shorthand. стенография shorthand.

стенокарди́я angina.

степéнный staid; middle-aged.

стéпень (gen pl -éй) degree; extent; power.

степно́й steppe. степь (loc -и́; gen pl -éй) steppe.

стервя́тник vulture.

стерегý etc.: see стерéчь

стéрео indecl adj stereo. стéрео- in comb stereo. стереоти́п stereotype. стереоти́пный stereotype(d). стереофони́ческий stereo(phonic). ~фóния stereo(phony).

стерéть (сотрý, сотрёшь; стёр) pf (impf стира́ть¹) wipe off, rub out, rub sore; ~ся rub off; wear down; be effaced.

стерéчь (-регý, -режёшь; -ёг, -лá) impf guard; watch for.

стéржень (-жня) m pivot; rod; core.

стерилизова́ть impf & pf sterilize. стери́льный sterile.

стéрлинг sterling.

стéрлядь (gen pl -éй) sterlet.

стерпéть (-плю́, -пишь) pf bear, endure.

стёртый worn, effaced.

стеснéние constraint. стесни́тельный shy; inconvenient. с|тесни́ть pf, стесня́ть impf constrain; hamper; inhibit. с|тесни́ться pf, стесня́ться impf (pf also по~) +inf feel too shy (to), be ashamed to.

стечéние confluence; gathering; combination. стечь (-чёт; -ёк, -лá) pf (impf стекáть) flow down; ~ся flow together; gather.

стилисти́ческий stylistic. стиль m style. сти́льный stylish; period.

сти́мул stimulus, incentive. стимули́ровать impf & pf stimulate.

стира́льный washing.

стира́ть¹(ся impf of стерéть(ся

стира́ть² impf (pf вы́~) wash, launder; ~ся wash. сти́рка washing, wash, laundering.

сти́скивать impf, сти́снуть (-ну) pf squeeze; clench; hug.

стих (-á) verse; line; pl poetry. стиха́ть impf of сти́хнуть

стихи́йный elemental; spontaneous. стихи́я element.

сти́хнуть (-ну; стих) pf (impf стиха́ть) subside; calm down.

стихотворéние poem. стихотво́рный in verse form.

стлать, стели́ть (стелю́, стéлешь) impf (pf по~) spread; ~ постéль make a bed; ~ся spread; creep.

сто (стá; gen pl сот) a hundred.

стог (loc -е & -ý; pl -á) stack, rick.

стóимость cost; value. стóить impf cost; be worth(while); deserve.

стой see стоя́ть

стóйка counter, bar; prop; upright; strut. стóйкий firm; stable; steadfast. стóйкость firmness, stability; steadfastness. стóйло stall. стоймя́ adv upright.

сток flow; drainage; drain, gutter; sewer.

стол (-á) table; desk; cuisine.

столб (-á) post, pole, pillar, column.

столбене́ть (-е́ю) *impf* (*pf* о~) be rooted to the ground. столбня́к (-á) stupor; tetanus.

столе́тие century; centenary. столе́тний hundred-year-old; of a hundred years.

столи́ца capital; metropolis. столи́чный (of the) capital.

столкнове́ние collision; clash. столкну́ть (-ну́, -нёшь) *pf* (*impf* ста́лкивать) push off, away; cause to collide; bring together; ~ся collide, clash; +c+*instr* run into.

столо́вая dining-room; canteen. столо́вый table.

столп (-á) pillar.

столпи́ться *pf* crowd.

столь *adv* so. сто́лько *adv* so much, so many.

столя́р (-á) joiner, carpenter. столя́рный joiner's.

стомато́лог dentist.

стометро́вка (the) hundred metres.

стон groan. стона́ть (-ну́, -нешь) *impf* groan.

стоп! *int* stop!

стопа́[1] foot.

стопа́[2] (*pl* -ы́) ream; pile.

сто́пка[1] pile.

сто́пка[2] small glass.

сто́пор stop, catch. сто́пориться *impf* (*pf* за~) come to a stop.

стопроце́нтный hundred-per-cent.

стоп-сигна́л brake-light.

стопта́ть (-пчу́, -пчешь) *pf* (*impf* ста́птывать) wear down; ~ся wear down.

с|торгова́ть(ся *pf*.

сто́рож (*pl* -á) watchman, guard. сторожево́й watch; patrol-. сторожи́ть (-жу́) *impf* guard, watch (over).

сторона́ (*acc* сто́рону, *pl* сто́роны, -ро́н, -áм) side; direction; hand; face; part; land; в сто́рону aside; с мое́й стороны́ for my part; с одно́й стороны́ on the one hand. сторони́ться (-ню́сь, -нишься) *impf* (*pf* по~) stand aside; +*gen* avoid. сторо́нник supporter, advocate.

сто́чный sewage, drainage.

стоя́нка stop; parking; stopping place, parking space; stand; rank. стоя́ть (-ою́) *impf* (*pf* по~) stand; be; stay; stop; have stopped; +за+*acc*

stand up for; ~ на коле́нях kneel.

стоя́чий standing; upright; stagnant.

сто́ящий deserving; worthwhile.

стр. *abbr* (of страни́ца) page.

страда́ (*pl* -ды) (hard work at) harvest time.

страда́лец (-льца) sufferer. страда́ние suffering. страда́тельный passive. страда́ть (-áю *or* -áжду) *impf* (*pf* по~) suffer; ~ за +*gen* feel for.

стра́жа guard, watch; под стра́жей under arrest, in custody; стоя́ть на стра́же +*gen* guard.

страна́ (*pl* -ы) country; land; ~ све́та cardinal point.

страни́ца page.

стра́нник, стра́нница wanderer.

стра́нно *adv* strangely. стра́нность strangeness; eccentricity. стра́нн|ый (-áнен, -анна́, -о) strange.

стра́нствие wandering. стра́нствовать *impf* wander.

Страстн|о́й of Holy Week; ~ая пя́тница Good Friday.

стра́стный (-тен, -тна́, -о) passionate. страсть[1] (*gen pl* -éй) passion. страсть[2] *adv* awfully, frightfully.

стратеги́ческий strategic(al). страте́гия strategy.

стратосфе́ра stratosphere.

стра́ус ostrich.

страх fear.

страхова́ние insurance; ~ жи́зни life insurance. страхова́ть *impf* (*pf* за~) insure (от+*gen* against); ~ся insure o.s. страхо́вка insurance.

страши́ться (-шу́сь) *impf* +*gen* be afraid of. стра́шно *adv* awfully. стра́шный (-шен, -шна́, -о) terrible, awful.

стрекоза́ (*pl* -ы) dragonfly.

стрекота́ть (-очу́, -о́чешь) *impf* chirr.

стрела́ (*pl* -ы) arrow; shaft; boom. стре́лка pointer; hand; needle; arrow; spit; points. стрелко́вый rifle; shooting; infantry. стрело́к (-лка́) shot; rifleman, gunner. стре́лочник points-man. стрельба́ (*pl* -ы) shooting, firing. стре́льчатый lancet; arched. стреля́ть *impf* shoot; fire; ~ся shoot o.s.; fight a duel.

стремгла́в *adv* headlong.

стреми́тельный swift; impetuous.

стреми́ться (-млю́сь) *impf* strive. стремле́ние striving, aspiration. стремни́на rapid(s).

стре́мя (-мени, *pl* -мена́, -мя́н, -а́м) *neut* stirrup. стремя́нка step-ladder.

стресс stress.

стри́женый short; short-haired, cropped; shorn. стри́жка hair-cut; shearing. стричь (-игу́, -ижёшь; -иг) *impf* (*pf* о∼) cut, clip; cut the hair of; shear; ∼ся have one's hair cut.

строга́ть *impf* (*pf* вы́∼) plane, shave. стро́гий strict; severe. стро́гость strictness.

строево́й combatant; line; drill. строе́ние building; structure; composition.

строжа́йший, стро́же *superl* & *comp* of стро́гий

строи́тель *m* builder. строи́тельный building, construction. строи́тельство building, construction; building site. стро́ить *impf* (*pf* по∼) build; construct; make; base; draw up; ∼ся be built, be under construction; draw up; стро́йся! fall in! строй (*loc* -ю́; *pl* -и́ *or* -и́, -ёв *or* -ёв) system; régime; structure; pitch; formation. стро́йка building; building-site. стро́йность proportion; harmony; balance, order. стро́йный (-о́ен, -о́йна́, -о) harmonious, orderly, well-proportioned, shapely.

строка́ (*acc* -о́ку́; *pl* -и, -а́м) line; кра́сная ∼ new paragraph.

строп, стро́па sling; shroud line. стропи́ло rafter, beam. стропти́вый refractory. строфа́ (*pl* -ы, -а́м) stanza. строчи́ть (-чу́, -о́чи́шь) *impf* (*pf* на∼, про∼) stitch; scribble, dash off. стро́чка stitch; line. стро́ю *etc.*: *see* стро́ить

струга́ть *impf* (*pf* вы́∼) plane. стру́жка shaving. струи́ться *impf* stream. структу́ра structure. струна́ (*pl* -ы) string. стру́нный stringed. струп (*pl* -пья, -пьев) scab. с|тру́сить (-у́шу) *pf*. стручо́к (-чка́) pod. струя́ (*pl* -и, -уй) jet, spurt, stream. стря́пать *impf* (*pf* со∼) cook; concoct. стряпня́ cooking.

стря́хивать *impf*, стряхну́ть (-ну́, -нёшь) *pf* shake off.

студени́стый jelly-like.

студе́нт, студе́нтка student. студе́нческий student.

сту́день (-дня) *m* jelly; aspic.

студи́ть (-ужу́, -у́дишь) *impf* (*pf* о∼) cool.

сту́дия studio.

сту́жа severe cold, hard frost.

стук knock; clatter. сту́кать *impf*, сту́кнуть (-ну) *pf* knock; bang; strike; ∼ся knock (o.s.), bang. стука́ч (-а́) informer.

стул (*pl* -лья, -льев) chair. стульча́к (-а́) (*lavatory*) seat. сту́льчик stool.

сту́па mortar.

ступа́ть *impf*, ступи́ть (-плю́, -пишь) *pf* step; tread. ступе́нчатый stepped, graded. ступе́нь (*gen pl* -éней) step, rung; stage, grade. ступе́нька step. ступня́ foot; sole.

стуча́ть (-чу́) *impf* (*pf* по∼) knock; chatter; pound; ∼ся knock in +*acc* knock at.

стушева́ться (-шу́юсь) *pf*, стушёвываться *impf* efface o.s.

стыд (-а́) shame. стыди́ть (-ыжу́) *impf* (*pf* при∼) put to shame; ∼ся (*pf* по∼ся) be ashamed. стыдли́вый bashful. стыдн|ый shameful; ∼о! shame! ∼о *impers*+*dat* ему́ ∼о he is ashamed; как тебе́ не ∼о! you ought to be ashamed of yourself!

стык joint; junction. стыкова́ть *impf* (*pf* со∼) join end to end; ∼ся (*pf* при∼ся) dock. стыко́вка docking.

сты́нуть, стыть (-ы́ну; стыл) *impf* cool; get cold.

сты́чка skirmish; squabble.

стюарде́сса stewardess.

стя́гивать *impf*, стяну́ть (-ну́, -нешь) *pf* tighten; pull together; assemble; pull off; steal; ∼ся tighten; assemble.

стяжа́тель (-я) *m* money-grubber. стяжа́ть *impf* & *pf* gain, win.

суббо́та Saturday.

субсиди́ровать *impf* & *pf* subsidize. субси́дия subsidy.

субъе́кт subject; ego; person; character, type. субъекти́вный subjective.

сувени́р souvenir.

суверените́т sovereignty. **суверéнный** sovereign.

суглинок (-нка) loam.

сугроб snowdrift.

сугубо adv especially.

суд (-á) court; trial; verdict.

судá etc.: see суд, су́дно[1]

судáк (-á) pike-perch.

суде́бный judicial; legal; forensic. **суде́йский** judge's, referee's, umpire's. **суди́мость** previous convictions. **суди́ть** (сужу́, су́дишь) impf judge; try; referee, umpire; foreordain; ~ся go to law.

су́дно[1] (pl -дá, -óв) vessel, craft.

су́дно[2] (gen pl -ден) bed-pan.

судово́й ship's; marine.

судомо́йка kitchen-maid; scullery.

судопроизво́дство legal proceedings.

су́дорога cramp, convulsion. **су́дорожный** convulsive.

судострое́ние shipbuilding. **судострои́тельный** shipbuilding. **судохо́дный** navigable; shipping.

судьба́ (pl -ы, -деб) fate, destiny.

судья́ (pl -и, -éй, -ям) m judge; referee; umpire.

суеве́рие superstition. **суеве́рный** superstitious.

суета́ bustle, fuss. **суети́ться** (-ечу́сь) impf bustle, fuss. **суетли́вый** fussy, bustling.

сужде́ние opinion; judgement.

суже́ние narrowing; constriction. **су́живать** impf, **су́зить** (-у́жу) pf narrow, contract; ~ся narrow; taper.

сук (-á, loc -ý; pl су́чья, -ьев or -и, -óв) bough.

су́ка bitch. **су́кин** adj: ~ сын son of a bitch.

сукно́ (pl -a, -кон) cloth; положи́ть под ~ shelve. **суко́нный** cloth; clumsy, crude.

сули́ть impf (pf по~) promise.

султа́н plume.

сумасбро́д, сумасбро́дка nutcase. **сумасбро́дный** wild, mad. **сумасбро́дство** wild behaviour. **сумасше́дший** mad; ~ий sb, ~ая sb lunatic. **сумасше́ствие** madness.

сумато́ха turmoil; bustle.

сумбу́р confusion. **сумбу́рный** confused.

су́меречный twilight. **су́мерки** (-рек) pl twilight, dusk.

суме́ть (-éю) pf +inf be able to, manage to.

су́мка bag.

су́мма sum. **сумма́рный** summary; total. **сумми́ровать** impf & pf add up; summarize.

су́мрак twilight; murk. **су́мрачный** gloomy.

су́мчатый marsupial.

сунду́к (-á) trunk, chest.

су́нуть(ся (-ну(сь) pf of сова́ть(ся

суп (pl -ы́) soup.

суперма́ркет supermarket.

суперобло́жка dust-jacket.

супру́г husband, spouse; pl husband and wife, (married) couple. **супру́га** wife, spouse. **супру́жеский** conjugal. **супру́жество** matrimony.

сургу́ч (-á) sealing-wax.

сурди́нка mute; под сурди́нку on the sly.

суро́вость severity, sternness. **суро́вый** severe, stern; bleak; unbleached.

суро́к (-рка́) marmot.

суррога́т substitute.

су́слик ground-squirrel.

суста́в joint, articulation.

су́тки (-ток) pl twenty-four hours; a day.

сутоло́ка commotion.

су́точн|ый daily; round-the-clock; ~ые sb pl per diem allowance.

суту́литься impf stoop. **суту́лый** round-shouldered.

суть essence, main point.

суфлёр prompter. **суфли́ровать** impf +dat prompt.

су́ффикс suffix.

суха́рь (-я́) m rusk; pl bread-crumbs.

су́хо adv drily; coldly.

сухожи́лие tendon.

сухо́й (сух, -á, -о) dry; cold. **сухопу́тный** land. **су́хость** dryness; coldness. **сухоща́вый** lean, skinny.

сучкова́тый knotty; gnarled. **сучо́к** (-чка́) twig; knot.

су́ша (dry) land. **су́ше** comp of сухо́й. **сушёный** dried. **суши́лка** dryer; drying-room. **суши́ть** (-шу́, -шишь) impf (pf вы́~) dry, dry out, up; ~ся (get) dry.

суще́ственный essential, vital. **существи́тельное** sb noun. **су́щест-**

вó being, creature; essence. **существ-**
овáние existence. **существовáть**
impf exist. **сýщий** absolute, downright. **сýщность** essence.

сую *etc.*: *see* совáть. с|фабриковáть
pf. с|фальши́вить (-влю) *pf*.
с|фантази́ровать *pf*.

сфéра sphere. **сфери́ческий** spherical.

сфинкс sphinx.

с|формировáть(ся *pf*. с|формо-
вáть *pf*. с|формули́ровать *pf*.
с|фотографи́ровать(ся *pf*.

схвати́ть (-ачý, -áтишь) *pf*, **схвáты-**
вать (*impf also* хватáть) seize;
catch; grasp; **~ся** snatch, catch; grapple. **схвáтка** skirmish; *pl* contrac-
tions.

схéма diagram; outline, plan; circuit.
схемати́ческий schematic; sketchy.
схемати́чный sketchy.

с|хитри́ть *pf*.

схлы́нуть (-нет) *pf* (break and) flow
back; subside.

сход coming off; descent; gathering.
сходи́ть[1](ся (-ожý(сь, -óдишь(ся)
impf of сойти́(сь. **сходи́ть**[2] (-ожý,
-óдишь) *pf* go; +за+*instr* go to fetch.
схóдка gathering, meeting. **схóд-**
ный (-ден, -днá, -о) similar; reasonable. **схóдня** (*gen pl* -ей) (*usu pl*)
gang-plank. **схóдство** similarity.

с|хорони́ть(ся (-ню́(сь, -нишь(ся) *pf*.
с|цеди́ть (-ежý, -éдишь) *pf*, **сцé-ж-**
ивать *impf* strain off, decant.

сцéна stage; scene. **сценáрий** scenario; script. **сценари́ст** script-writer.
сцени́ческий stage.

сцепи́ть (-плю́, -пишь) *pf*, **сцепля́ть**
impf couple; **~ся** be coupled; grapple. **сцéпка** coupling. **сцеплéние**
coupling; clutch.

счастли́вец (-вца), **счастли́вчик**
lucky man. **счастли́вица** lucky
woman. **счастли́вый** (-áив) happy;
happy; lucky; **~о!** all the best!; **~ого**
пути́ bon voyage. **счáстье** happiness; good fortune.

счесть(ся (сочтý(сь, -тёшь(ся; счёл-
(ся, сочлá(сь) *pf of* считáть(ся. **счёт**
(*loc* -ý; *pl* -á) bill; account; counting,
calculation; score; expense. **счётный**
calculating; accounts. **счетовóд** bookkeeper, accountant. **счётчик** counter; meter. **счёты** (-ов) *pl* abacus.

счи́стить (-и́щу) *pf* (*impf* **счищáть**)
clean off; clear away.

счита́ть *impf* (*pf* **со~**, **счесть**) count;
reckon; consider; **~ся** (*pf also*
по~ся) settle account; be considered; +с+*instr* take into consideration; reckon with.

счища́ть *impf of* **счи́стить**

США *pl indecl abbr* (*of* **Соединённые**
Штáты Амéрики) USA.

сшибáть *impf*, **сшиби́ть** (-бý, -бёшь;
сшиб) *pf* strike, hit, knock (off); **~ с**
ног knock down; **~ся** collide; come
to blows.

сшивáть *impf*, **с|шить** (сошью́, -ьёшь)
pf sew (together).

съедáть *impf of* **съесть**. **съедóб-**
ный edible; nice.

съéду *etc.*: *see* **съéхать**

съёживаться *impf*, **съ|ёжиться**
(-жусь) *pf* shrivel, shrink.

съезд congress; conference; arrival.
съéздить (-зжу) *pf* go, drive, travel.
съезжáть(ся *impf of* **съéхать(ся**.
съел *etc.*: *see* **съесть**

съёмка removal; survey, surveying;
shooting. **съёмный** detachable, re-
movable. **съёмщик**, **съёмщица** tenant; surveyor.

съестнóй food; **~óе** *sb* food (sup-
plies). **съ|есть** (-ем, -ешь, -ест, -ед-
и́м; съел) *pf* (*impf also* **съедáть**) eat.

съéхать (-éду) *pf* (*impf* **съезжáть**)
go down; come down; move; **~ся**
meet; assemble.

съ|язви́ть (-влю́) *pf*.

сы́воротка whey; serum.

сыгрáть *pf of* игрáть; **~ся** play
(well) together.

сын (*pl* сыновья́, -éй *or* -ы́, -óв) son.
сынóвний filial. **сынóк** (-нкá) little son; sonny.

сы́пать (-плю) *impf* pour; pour forth;
~ся fall; pour out; rain down; fray.
сыпнóй тиф typhus. **сыпýчий** friable; free-flowing; shifting. **сыпь**
rash, eruption.

сыр (*loc* -ý; *pl* -ы́) cheese.

сырéть (-éю) *impf* (*pf* **от~**) become
damp.

сырéц (-рцá) raw product.

сыр|óй (сыр, -á, -о) damp; raw; un-
cooked; unboiled; unfinished; unripe.
сы́рость dampness. **сырьё** raw
material(s).

сыска́ть (сыщу́, сы́щешь) *pf* find.
сы́тный (-тен, -тна́, -о) filling. **сы́тость** satiety. **сы́тый** (сыт, -á, -о) full.
сыч (-á) little owl.
сы́щик detective.
с|эконо́мить (-млю) *pf*.
сэр sir.
сюда́ *adv* here, hither.
сюже́т subject; plot; topic. **сюже́тный** subject; having a theme.
сюи́та suite.
сюрпри́з surprise.
сюрреали́зм surrealism. **сюрреали́стический** surrealist.
сюрту́к (-á) frock-coat.
сяк *adv*: *see* **так**. **сям** *adv*: *see* **там**

Т

та *see* **тот**
таба́к (-á) tobacco. **табаке́рка** snuff-box. **таба́чный** tobacco.
та́бель (-я; *pl* -и, -ей *or* -я́, -ей) *m* table, list. **та́бельный** table; time.
табле́тка tablet.
табли́ца table; ~ умноже́ния multiplication table.
та́бор (gipsy) camp.
табу́н (-á) herd.
табуре́т, табуре́тка stool.
тавро́ (*pl* -а, -áм) brand.
тавтоло́гия tautology.
таджи́к, -и́чка Tadzhik.
Таджикиста́н Tadzhikistan.
таёжный taiga.
таз (*loc* -ý; *pl* -ы́) basin; pelvis. **тазобе́дренный** hip. **та́зовый** pelvic.
таи́нственный mysterious; secret.
таи́ть *impf* hide, harbour; ~ся hide; lurk.
Тайва́нь *m* Taiwan.
тайга́ taiga.
тайко́м *adv* secretly, surreptitiously; ~ от+*gen* behind the back of.
тайм half; period of play.
та́йна secret; mystery. **тайни́к** (-á) hiding-place; *pl* recesses. **та́йный** secret; privy.
тайфу́н typhoon.
так *adv* so; like this; as it should be; just like that; и ~ и сяк as it is; и ~ да́лее and so on; ~ и сяк this way and that; не ~ wrong; ~ же in the same way; ~ же... как as ... as; ~ и есть I thought so!; ~ ему́ и на́до serves him right; ~ и́ли ина́че one way or another; ~ себе́ so-so. **так** *conj* then; so; ~ как as, since.
такела́ж rigging.
та́кже *adv* also, too, as well.
тако́в *m* (-á *f*, -ó *neut*, -ы́ *pl*) *pron* such.
так|о́й *pron* such (a); в ~о́м слу́чае in that case; кто он ~о́й? who is he?; ~о́й же the same; ~и́м о́бразом in this way; что это ~о́е? what is this? **тако́й-то** *pron* so-and-so; such-and-such.
та́кса fixed *or* statutory price; tariff.
таксёр taxi-driver. **такси́** *neut indecl* taxi. **такси́ст** taxi-driver. **таксопа́рк** taxi depot.
такт time; bar; beat; tact.
та́к-таки after all, really.
та́ктика tactics. **такти́ческий** tactical.
такти́чность tact. **такти́чный** tactful.
та́ктов|ый time, timing; ~ая черта́ bar-line.
тала́нт talent. **тала́нтливый** talented.
талисма́н talisman.
та́лия waist.
тало́н, тало́нчик coupon.
та́лый thawed, melted.
тальк talc; talcum powder.
там *adv* there; ~ и сям here and there; ~ же in the same place; ibid.
тамада́ *m* toast-master.
та́мбур[1] tambour; lobby; platform. **та́мбур**[2] chain-stitch.
тамо́женник customs official. **тамо́женный** customs. **тамо́жня** custom-house.
та́мошний of that place, local.
тампо́н tampon.
та́нгенс tangent.
та́нго *neut indecl* tango.
та́нец (-нца) dance; dancing.
тани́н tannin.
танк tank. **та́нкер** tanker. **танки́ст** member of a tank crew. **та́нковый** tank, armoured.
танцева́льный dancing; ~ ве́чер dance. **танцева́ть** (-цу́ю) *impf* dance. **танцо́вщик, танцо́вщица** (ballet) dancer. **танцо́р, танцо́рка** dancer.
та́пка, та́почка slipper.

тápa packing; tare.

таракáн cockroach.

тарáн battering-ram.

тарáнтул tarantula.

тарéлка plate; cymbal; satellite dish.

тарúф tariff.

таскáть *impf* drag, lug; carry; pull; take; pull out; swipe; wear; ~ся drag; hang about.

тасовáть *impf* (*pf* с~) shuffle.

ТАСС *abbr* (*of* Телегрáфное агéнтство Совéтского Сою́за) Tass (Telegraph Agency of the Soviet Union).

татáрин, татáрка Tatar.

татуирóвка tattooing, tattoo.

тафтá taffeta.

тахтá ottoman.

тáчка wheelbarrow.

тащúть (-щý, -щишь) *impf* (*pf* вы́~, с~) pull; drag, lug; carry; take; pull out; swipe; ~ся drag o.s. along; drag.

тáять (тáю) *impf* (*pf* рас~) melt; thaw; dwindle.

тварь creature(s); wretch.

твердéть (-éет) *impf* (*pf* за~) harden, become hard. твердúть (-ржý) *impf* (*pf* вы́~) repeat, say again and again; memorize. твердолóбый thick-skulled; diehard. твёрдый *adj* firm; solid; steadfast; ~ знак hard sign, ъ; ~ое тéло solid. твердýня stronghold.

твой (-егó) *m*, твоя́ (-éй) *f*, твоё (-егó) *neut*, твои́ (-úх) *pl* your, yours.

творéние creation, work; creature. творéц (-рцá) creator. творúтельный instrumental. творúть *impf* (*pf* со~) create; do; make; ~ся happen.

творóг (-á) curds; cottage cheese.

твóрческий creative. твóрчество creation; creative work; works.

те *see* тот

т.е. *abbr* (*of* то есть) that is, i.e.

теáтр theatre. театрáльный theatre; theatrical.

тебя́ *etc.: see* ты

тéзис thesis.

тёзка *m* & *f* namesake.

тёк *see* течь

текст text; libretto, lyrics.

текстúль *m* textiles. текстúльный textile.

текстýра texture.

текýчий fluid; unstable. текýщий current; routine.

теле- *in comb* tele-; television. телеателье́ *neut indecl* television maintenance workshop. ~ви́дение television. ~визио́нный television. ~ви́зор television (set). ~гра́мма telegram. ~гра́ф telegraph (office). ~графи́ровать *impf* & *pf* telegraph. ~гра́фный telegraph(ic). ~зри́тель *m* (television) viewer. ~объекти́в telephoto lens. ~пати́ческий telepathic. ~па́тия telepathy. ~ско́п telescope. ~ста́нция television station. ~сту́дия television studio. ~фо́н (telephone); (telephone) number; (по)звони́ть по ~фо́ну *+dat* ring up. ~фо́н-автома́т public telephone, call-box. ~фони́ст (tele-)phone) operator. ~фо́нный telephone; ~фо́нная кни́га telephone directory; ~фо́нная ста́нция telephone exchange; ~фо́нная тру́бка receiver. ~фо́н-отве́тчик answering machine. ~фотогра́фия telephotography. ~це́нтр television centre.

телéга cart, wagon. телéжка small cart; trolley.

телёнок (-нка; *pl* -я́та, -я́т) calf.

телéсн|ый bodily; corporal; ~ого цвéта flesh-coloured.

Телéц (-льцá) Taurus.

телúться *impf* (*pf* о~) calve. тёлка heifer.

тéло (*pl* -á) body. телогрéйка padded jacket. телосложéние build. телохранúтель *m* bodyguard.

телята *etc.: see* телёнок. телятина veal. телячий calf; veal.

тем *conj* (*so* much) the; ~ лýчше so much the better; ~ не мéнее nevertheless.

тем *see* тот, тьма

тéма subject; theme. темáтика subject-matter; themes. темати́ческий subject; thematic.

тембр timbre.

темнéть (-éет) *impf* (*pf* по~, с~) become dark. темнúца dungeon. темнó *predic* it is dark. темнокóжий dark-skinned, swarthy. тёмно-сúний dark blue. темнотá darkness. тёмный dark.

темп tempo; rate.

темперáмент temperament. темперáментный temperamental.

температу́ра temperature.

те́мя (-мени) *neut* crown, top of the head.

тенде́нция tendency; bias.

тенево́й, тени́стый shady.

те́ннис tennis. **тенниси́ст, -и́стка** tennis-player. **те́ннисн|ый** tennis; **~ая площа́дка** tennis-court.

те́нор (*pl* -á) tenor.

тент awning.

тень (*loc* -и́; *pl* -и, -е́й) shade; shadow; phantom; ghost; particle, vestige, atom; suspicion; **те́ни для век** *pl* eyeshadow.

тео́лог theologian. **теологи́ческий** theological. **теоло́гия** theology.

теоре́ма theorem. **теоре́тик** theoretician. **теорети́ческий** theoretical. **тео́рия** theory.

тепе́решн|ий present. **тепе́рь** *adv* now; today.

тепле́ть (-е́ет) *impf* (*pf* по~) get warm. **те́плиться** (-ится) *impf* flicker; glimmer. **тепли́ца** greenhouse, conservatory. **тепли́чный** hothouse. **тепло́** heat; warmth. **тепло́** *adv* warmly; *predic* it is warm. **тепло-** *in comb* heat; thermal; thermo-. **теплово́з** diesel locomotive. **~ёмкость** thermal capacity. **~кро́вный** warm-blooded. **~обме́н** heat exchange. **~прово́дный** heat-conducting. **~сто́йкий** heat-resistant. **~хо́д** motor ship. **~центра́ль** heat and power station. **теплово́й** heat; thermal. **теплота́** heat; warmth. **тёплый** (-пел, -пла́, -пло́) warm.

терапе́вт therapeutist. **терапи́я** therapy.

тереби́ть (-блю́) *impf* pull (at); pester.

тере́ть (тру, трёшь; тёр) *impf* rub; grate; **~ся** rub o.s.; **~ся о́коло+**gen hang about, hang around; **~ся среди́** +gen mix with.

терза́ть *impf* tear to pieces; torment; **~ся** +instr suffer; be a prey to.

тёрка grater.

те́рмин term. **терминоло́гия** terminology.

терми́ческий thermic, thermal. **термо́метр** thermometer. **те́рмос** thermos (flask). **термоста́т** thermostat. **термоя́дерный** thermonuclear.

терно́вник sloe, blackthorn. **терни́стый** thorny.

терпели́вый patient. **терпе́ние** patience. **терпе́ть** (-плю́, -пишь) *impf* (*pf* по~) suffer; bear, endure. **терпе́ться** (-ится) *impf* impers+dat: **ему́ не те́рпится** +inf he is impatient to. **терпи́мость** tolerance. **терпи́мый** tolerant; tolerable.

те́рпкий (-пок, -пка́, -о) astringent; tart.

терра́са terrace.

территориа́льный territorial. **террито́рия** territory.

терро́р terror. **террори́зировать** *impf & pf* terrorize. **террори́ст** terrorist.

тёртый grated; experienced.

терье́р terrier.

теря́ть *impf* (*pf* по~, у~) lose; shed; **~ся** get lost; disappear; fail, decline; become flustered.

тёс boards, planks. **теса́ть** (тешу́, тёшешь) *impf* cut, hew.

тесёмка ribbon, braid.

тесни́ть *impf* (*pf* по~, с~) crowd; squeeze, constrict; be too tight; **~ся** press through; move up; crowd, jostle. **теснота́** crowded state; crush. **те́сн|ый** crowded; (too) tight; close; compact; **~о** it is crowded.

тесо́вый board, plank.

тест test.

те́сто dough; pastry.

тесть *m* father-in-law.

тесьма́ ribbon, braid.

те́терев (*pl* -á) black grouse. **те́тёрка** grey hen.

тётка aunt.

тетра́дка, тетра́дь exercise book.

тётя (*gen pl* -ей) aunt.

тех- *abbr in comb* (*of* техни́ческий) technical.

те́хник technician. **те́хника** technical equipment; technology; technique. **те́хникум** technical college. **техни́ческ|ий** technical; **~ие усло́вия** specifications. **техно́лог** technologist. **технологи́ческий** technological. **техноло́гия** technology. **техперсона́л** technical personnel.

тече́ние flow; course; current, stream; trend.

течь[1] (-чёт; тёк, -ла́) *impf* flow; stream; leak. **течь**[2] leak.

те́шить (-шу) *impf* (*pf* по~) amuse; gratify; ~ся (+*instr*) amuse o.s. (with).

тешу́ *etc.*: *see* **теса́ть**

тёща mother-in-law.

тигр tiger. **тигри́ца** tigress.

тик¹ tic.

тик² teak.

ти́на slime, mud.

тип type. **типи́чный** typical. **типо-во́й** standard; model. **типогра́фия** printing-house, press. **типогра́ф-ский** typographical.

тир shooting-range, -gallery. **тира́ж** (-а́) draw; circulation; edition.

тира́н tyrant. **тира́нить** *impf* tyrannize. **тирани́ческий** tyrannical. **тира́ния** tyranny.

тире́ *neut indecl* dash.

ти́скать *impf*, **ти́снуть** (-ну) *pf* press, squeeze. **тиски́** (-о́в) *pl* vice; **в тиска́х** +*gen* in the grip of. **тисне́ние** stamping; imprint; design. **тиснёный** stamped.

тита́н¹ titanian.

тита́н² boiler.

тита́н³ titan.

титр title, sub-title.

ти́тул title; title-page. **ти́тульный** title.

тиф (*loc* -у́) typhus.

ти́хий (тих, -а́, -о) quiet; silent; calm; slow. **тихоокеа́нский** Pacific. **ти́ше** *comp* of **ти́хий**, **ти́хо**; **ти́ше!** quiet! **тишина́** quiet, silence.

т. к. *abbr* (*of* **так как**) as, since.

тка́ный woven. **ткань** fabric, cloth; tissue. **ткать** (тку, ткёшь; -ал, -а́ла, -о) *impf* (*pf* со~) weave. **тка́цкий** weaving; ~ **стано́к** loom. **ткач**, **ткачи́ха** weaver.

ткнуть(ся (-у(сь, -ёшь(ся) *pf of* **ты́-кать(ся**

тле́ние decay; smouldering. **тлеть** (-е́ет) *impf* rot, decay; smoulder; ~ся smoulder.

тля aphis.

тмин caraway(-seeds).

то *pron* that; **а не то́** or else, otherwise; (**да) и то́** and even then, and that; **то́ есть** that is (to say); **то и де́ло** every now and then. **то** *conj* then; **не то...**, **не то** to either ... or; half ..., half; **то...**, **то** now ..., now; **то ли...**, **то ли** whether ... or.

-то *partl* just, exactly; **в то́м-то и де́ло** that's just it.

тобо́й *see* **ты**

това́р goods; commodity.

това́рищ comrade; friend; colleague. **това́рищеский** comradely; friendly. **това́рищество** comradeship; company; association.

това́рный goods; commodity.

товаро- *in comb* commodity; goods. **товарообме́н** barter. ~**оборо́т** (sales) turnover. ~**отправи́тель** *m* consignor. ~**получа́тель** *m* consignee.

тогда́ *adv* then; ~ **как** whereas. **тогда́шний** of that time.

того́ *see* **тот**

тожде́ственный identical. **то́ж-де́ство** identity.

то́же *adv* also, too.

ток (*pl* -и) current.

тока́рный turning; ~ **стано́к** lathe. **то́карь** (*pl* -я́, -е́й *or* -и, -е́й) *m* turner, lathe operator.

токси́ческий toxic.

толк sense; use; **бе́з** ~у senselessly; **знать** ~ **в**+*prep* know well; **сбить с** ~у confuse; **с** ~ом intelligently.

толка́ть *impf* (*pf* **толкну́ть**) push, shove; jog; ~ся jostle.

то́лки (-ов) *pl* rumours, gossip.

толкну́ть(ся (-ну́(сь, -нёшь(ся) *pf of* **толка́ть(ся**

толкова́ние interpretation; *pl* commentary. **толкова́ть** *impf* interpret; explain; talk. **толко́вый** intelligent; clear; ~ **слова́рь** defining dictionary. **то́лком** *adv* plainly; seriously.

толкотня́ crush, squash.

толку́ *etc.*: *see* **толо́чь**

толку́чка crush, squash; second-hand market.

толокно́ oatmeal.

толо́чь (-лку́, -лчёшь; -ло́к, -лкла́) *impf* (*pf* ис~, рас~) pound, crush.

толпа́ (*pl* -ы) crowd. **толпи́ться** *impf* crowd; throng.

толсте́ть (-е́ю) *impf* (*pf* по~) grow fat; put on weight. **толстоко́жий** thick-skinned; pachydermatous. **то́л-стый** (-á, -о) fat; thick. **толстя́к** (-á) fat man *or* boy.

толчёный crushed; ground. **толчёт** *etc.*: *see* **толо́чь**

толчея́ crush, squash.

толчо́к (-чка́) push, shove; (*sport*) put; jolt; shock, tremor.

то́лща thickness; thick. то́лще *comp of* то́лстый. толщина́ thickness; fatness.

толь *m* roofing felt.

то́лько *adv* only, merely; ~ что (only) just; *conj* only, but; (как) ~, (лишь) ~ as soon as; ~ бы if only.

том (*pl* ~а́) volume. то́мик small volume.

тома́т tomato. тома́тный tomato.

томи́тельный tedious, wearing; agonizing. томи́ть (-млю́) *impf* (*pf* ис~) tire; torment; ~ся languish; be tormented. томле́ние languor. то́мный (-мен, -мна́, -о) languid, languorous.

тон (*pl* -а́ *or* -ы, -о́в) tone; note; shade; form. тона́льность key.

то́ненький thin; slim. то́нкий (-нок, -нка́, -о) thin; slim; fine; refined; subtle; keen. то́нкость thinness; slimness; fineness; subtlety.

то́нна ton.

тонне́ль *see* тунне́ль

то́нус tone.

тону́ть (-ну́, -нешь) *impf* (*pf* по~, у~) sink; drown.

то́ньше *comp of* то́нкий

то́пать (*pf* то́пнуть) stamp.

топи́ть¹ (-плю́, -пишь) *impf* (*pf* по~, у~) sink; drown; ruin; ~ся drown o.s.

топи́ть² (-плю́, -пишь) *impf* stoke; heat; melt (down); ~ся burn; melt. то́пка stoking; heating; melting (down); furnace.

то́пкий boggy, marshy.

то́пливный fuel. то́пливо fuel.

то́пнуть (-ну) *pf of* то́пать

топографи́ческий topographical. топогра́фия topography.

то́поль (*pl* -я́ *or* -и) *m* poplar.

топо́р (-а́) axe. топо́рик hatchet. топо́рище axe-handle. топо́рный axe; clumsy, crude.

то́пот tramp; clatter. топта́ть (-пчу́, -пчешь) *impf* (*pf* по~) trample (down); ~ся stamp; ~ся на ме́сте mark time.

топча́н (-а́) trestle-bed.

топь bog, marsh.

торг (*loc* -у́; *pl* -и́) trading; bargaining; *pl* auction. торгова́ть *impf* (*pf* с~) trade; ~ся bargain, haggle. торго́вец (-вца) merchant; tradesman. торго́вка market-woman; stallholder. торго́вля trade. торго́вый trade, commercial; merchant. торгпре́д *abbr* trade representative.

торе́ц (-рца́) butt-end; wooden paving-block.

торже́ственный solemn; ceremonial. торжество́ celebration; triumph. торжествова́ть *impf* celebrate; triumph.

торможе́ние braking. то́рмоз (*pl* -а́ *or* -ы) brake. тормози́ть (-ожу́) *impf* (*pf* за~) brake; hamper.

тормоши́ть (-шу́) *impf* pester; bother.

торопи́ть (-плю́, -пишь) *impf* (*pf* по~) hurry; hasten; ~ся hurry. торопли́вый hasty.

торпе́да torpedo.

торс torso.

торт cake.

торф peat. торфяно́й peat.

торча́ть (-чу́) *impf* stick out; protrude; hang about.

торше́р standard lamp.

тоска́ melancholy; boredom; nostalgia; ~ по+*dat* longing for. тоскли́вый melancholy; depressed; dreary. тоскова́ть *impf* be melancholy, depressed; long; ~ по+*dat* miss.

тост toast.

тот *m* (та *f*, то *neut*, те *pl*) *pron* that; the former; the other; the one; the same; the right; и ~ и друго́й both; к тому́ же moreover; не ~ the wrong; ни ~ ни друго́й neither; тот, кто the one who, the person who. то́тчас *adv* immediately.

тоталитари́зм totalitarianism. тоталита́рный totalitarian.

тота́льный total.

точи́лка sharpener; pencil-sharpener. точи́ло whetstone, grindstone. точи́льный grinding, sharpening; ~ ка́мень whetstone, grindstone. точи́льщик (knife-)grinder. точи́ть (-чу́, -чишь) *impf* (*pf* вы́~, на~) sharpen; hone; turn; eat away; gnaw at.

то́чка spot; dot; full stop; point; ~ зре́ния point of view; ~ с запято́й semicolon. то́чно¹ *adv* exactly, precisely; punctually. то́чно² *conj* as though, as if. то́чность punctuality; precision; accuracy; в то́чности exactly, precisely. то́чный (-чен, -чна́, -о) exact, precise; accurate; punctual. то́чь-в-то́чь *adv* exactly; word for word.

тошни́ть *impf impers*: меня́ тошни́т I feel sick. тошнота́ nausea. тошнотво́рный sickening, nauseating.

то́щий (тощ, -а́, -е) gaunt, emaciated; skinny; empty; poor.

трава́ (*pl* -ы) grass; herb. трави́нка blade of grass.

трави́ть (-влю, -вишь) *impf* (*pf* вы́~, за~) poison; exterminate, destroy; etch; hunt; torment; badger. . травле́ние extermination; etching. тра́вля hunting; persecution; badgering.

тра́вма trauma, injury.

травоя́дный herbivorous. травяни́стый, травяно́й grass; herbaceous; grassy.

траге́дия tragedy. тра́гик tragedian. траги́ческий, траги́чный tragic.

традицио́нный traditional. тради́ция tradition.

траекто́рия trajectory.

тракта́т treatise; treaty.

тракти́р inn, tavern.

трактова́ть *impf* interpret; treat, discuss. тракто́вка treatment; interpretation.

тра́ктор tractor. тракори́ст tractor driver.

трал trawl. тра́лить *impf* (*pf* про~) trawl; sweep. тра́льщик trawler; mine-sweeper.

трамбова́ть *impf* (*pf* у~) ram, tamp.

трамва́й tram. трамва́йный tram.

трампли́н spring-board; ski-jump.

транзи́стор transistor; transistor radio.

транзи́тный transit.

транс trance.

трансатланти́ческий transatlantic.

трансли́ровать *impf & pf* broadcast, transmit. трансляцио́нный transmission; broadcasting. трансля́ция broadcast, transmission.

тра́нспорт transport; consignment. транспортёр conveyor. транспорти́р protractor. транспорти́ровать *impf & pf* transport. тра́нспортный transport.

трансформа́тор transformer.

транше́я trench.

трап ladder.

тра́пеза meal.

трапе́ция trapezium; trapeze.

тра́сса line, course, direction; route, road.

тра́та expenditure; waste. тра́тить (-а́чу) *impf* (*pf* ис~, по~) spend, expend; waste.

тра́улер trawler.

тра́ур mourning. тра́урный mourning; funeral; mournful.

трафаре́т stencil; stereotype; cliché. трафаре́тный stencilled; conventional, stereotyped.

тра́чу *etc.*: *see* тра́тить

тре́бование demand; request; requirement; requisition; order; *pl* needs. тре́бовательный demanding. тре́бовать *impf* (*pf* по~) summon; +*gen* demand, require; need; ~ся be needed, be required.

трево́га alarm; anxiety. трево́жить (-жу) *impf* (*pf* вс~, по~) alarm; disturb; worry; ~ся worry, be anxious; trouble o.s. трево́жный worried, anxious; alarming; alarm.

тре́звенник teetotaller. трезве́ть (-е́ю) *impf* (*pf* о~) sober up.

трезво́н peal (*of bells*); rumours; row.

тре́звость sobriety. тре́звый (-зв, -а́, -о) sober; teetotal.

тре́йлер trailer.

трель trill; warble.

тре́нер trainer, coach.

тре́ние friction.

трениро́вать *impf* (*pf* на~) train, coach; ~ся be in training. трениро́вка training, coaching. трениро́вочный training.

трепа́ть (-плю, -плешь) *impf* (*pf* ис~, по~, рас~) blow about; dishevel; wear out; pat; ~ся fray; wear out; flutter. тре́пет trembling; trepidation. трепета́ть (-ещу́, -е́щешь) *impf* tremble; flicker; palpitate. тре́петный trembling; flickering; palpitating; timid.

треск crack; crackle; fuss.

треска́ cod.

тре́скаться¹ *impf* (*pf* по~) crack; chap.

тре́скаться² *impf of* тре́снуться

тре́снуть (-нет) *pf* snap, crackle;

crack; chap; bang; ~ся (*impf* тре́-
скаться) +*instr* bang.
трест trust.
тре́т|ий (-ья, -ье) third; ~ье *sb* sweet
(course).
трети́ровать *impf* slight.
треть (*gen pl* -е́й) third. **тре́тье** *etc.*:
see тре́тий. **треуго́льник** triangle.
треуго́льный triangular.
тре́фы (треф) *pl* clubs.
трёх- in *comb* three-, tri-. **трёх-
годи́чный** three-year. ~**голо́сый**
three-part. ~**гра́нный** three-edged;
trihedral. ~**колёсный** three-wheeled.
~**ле́тний** three-year; three-year old.
~**ме́рный** three-dimensional. ~**ме́-
сячный** three-month; quarterly;
three-month-old. ~**по́лне** three-field
system. ~**со́тый** three-hundredth.
~**сторо́нний** three-sided; trilateral;
tripartite. ~**эта́жный** three-storeyed.
треща́ть (-щу́) *impf* crack; crackle;
creak; chirr; crack up; chatter.
тре́щина crack, split; fissure; chap.
три (трёх, -ём, -емя́, -ёх) three.
трибу́на platform, rostrum; stand.
трибуна́л tribunal.
тригономе́трия trigonometry.
тридцатиле́тний thirty-year; thirty-
year old. **тридца́тый** thirtieth. **три́д-
цать** (-и́, *instr* -ью́) thirty. **три́жды**
adv three times; thrice.
трико́ *neut indecl* tricot; tights; knickers. **трикота́ж** knitted fabric; knitwear. **трикота́жный** jersey, tricot;
knitted.
трина́дцатый thirteenth. **трина́д-
цать** thirteen. **трио́ль** triplet.
три́ппер gonorrhoea.
три́ста (трёхсо́т, -ёмста́м, -емяста́ми,
-ёхста́х) three hundred.
трито́н *zool* triton.
триу́мф triumph.
тро́гательный touching, moving.
тро́гать(ся *impf of* тро́нуть(ся
тро́е (-и́х) *pl* three. **трое́бо́рье**
triathlon. **троекра́тный** thrice-re-
peated. **Тро́ица** Trinity; **тро́ица**
trio. **Тро́ицын день** Whit Sunday.
тро́йка three; figure 3; troika; No.
3; three-piece suit. **тройно́й** triple;
treble; three-ply. **тро́йственный**
triple; tripartite.
тролле́йбус trolley-bus.
тромб blood clot.

тромбо́н trombone.
трон throne.
тро́нуть (-ну) *pf* (*impf* тро́гать)
touch; disturb; affect; ~ся start, set
out; be touched; be affected.
тропа́ path.
тро́пик tropic.
тропи́нка path.
тропи́ческий tropical.
трос rope, cable.
тростни́к (-а́) reed, rush. **тро́сточ-
ка, трость** (*gen pl* ~е́й) cane, walking-stick.
тротуа́р pavement.
трофе́й trophy; *pl* spoils (*of war*);
booty.
трою́родн|ый: ~ый брат, ~ая
сестра́ second cousin.
тру *etc.*: *see* тере́ть
труба́ (*pl* -ы) pipe; chimney; funnel;
trumpet; tube. **труба́ч** (-а́) trumpeter; trumpet-player. **труби́ть** (-блю́)
impf (*pf* про~) blow, sound; blare.
тру́бка tube; pipe; (*telephone*) receiver. **трубопрово́д** (-а) pipe-line;
piping; manifold. **трубочи́ст** chimney-
sweep. **тру́бочный** pipe. **тру́бча-
тый** tubular.
труд (-а́) labour; work; effort; с ~о́м
with difficulty. **труди́ться** (-ужу́сь,
-у́дишься) *impf* toil, labour; work;
trouble. **тру́дно** *predic* it is difficult.
тру́дность difficulty. **тру́дный** (-ден,
-дна́, -о) difficult; hard.
трудо- in *comb* labour, work. **тру-
доде́нь** (-дня́) *m* work-day (*unit*).
~**ёмкий** labour-intensive. ~**люби́-
вый** industrious. ~**лю́бие** industry.
~**спосо́бность** ability to work.
~**спосо́бный** able-bodied; capable
of working.
трудово́й work; working; earned;
hard-earned. **трудя́щ|ийся** working;
~**иеся** *sb* pl the workers. **тру́-
женик, тру́женица** toiler.
труп corpse; carcass.
тру́ппа troupe, company.
трус coward.
трусы́ (-о́в) *pl* shorts; trunks; pants.
труси́ть[1] (-у́шу) *impf* trot, jog along.
труси́ть[2] (-у́шу) *impf* (*pf* с~) be a
coward; lose one's nerve; be afraid.
труси́ха coward. **трусли́вый** cowardly. **тру́сость** cowardice.
трусы́ (-о́в) *pl* shorts; trunks; pants.

труха́ dust; trash.

тру́шу *etc.: see* **труси́ть**[1], **тру́сить**[2]

трущо́ба slum; godforsaken hole.

трюк stunt; trick.

трюм hold.

трюмо́ *neut indecl* pier-glass.

трю́фель (*gen pl* **-ле́й**) *m* truffle.

тря́пка rag; spineless creature; *pl* clothes. **тряпьё** rags; clothes.

тряси́на quagmire. **тряски́** shaking, jolting. **трясти́** (**-су́**, **-сёшь**; **-яс**, **-ла́**) *impf*, **тряхну́ть** (**-ну́**, **-нёшь**) *pf* (*pf also* **вы~**) shake; shake out; jolt; **~сь** shake; tremble, shiver; jolt.

тсс *int* sh! hush!

туале́т dress; toilet. **туале́тный** toilet.

туберкулёз tuberculosis.

ту́го *adv* tight(ly), taut; with difficulty. **туго́й** (**туг**, **-а́**, **-о**) tight; taut; tightly filled; difficult.

туда́ *adv* there, thither; that way; to the right place; **ни ~ ни сюда́** neither one way nor the other; **~ и обра́тно** there and back.

ту́же *comp of* **ту́го**, **туго́й**

тужу́рка (double-breasted) jacket.

туз (**-а́**, *acc* **-а́**) ace; bigwig.

тузе́мец (**-мца**), **-мка** native.

ту́ловище trunk; torso.

тулу́п sheepskin coat.

тума́н fog; mist; haze. **тума́нить** *impf* (*pf* **за~**) dim, obscure; **~ся** grow misty; be befogged. **тума́нность** fog, mist; nebula; obscurity. **тума́нный** foggy; misty; hazy; obscure, vague.

ту́мба post; bollard; pedestal. **ту́мбочка** bedside table.

ту́ндра tundra.

тунея́дец (**-дца**) sponger.

туни́ка tunic.

тунне́ль *m*, **тонне́ль** *m* tunnel.

тупе́ть (**-е́ю**) *impf* (*pf* **о~**) become blunt; grow dull. **тупи́к** (**-а́**) cul-de-sac, dead end; impasse; **поста́вить в ~** stump, nonplus. **тупи́ться** (**-пится**) *impf* (*pf* **за~**, **ис~**) become blunt.

тупи́ца *m & f* blockhead, dimwit.

тупо́й (**туп**, **-а́**, **-о**) blunt; obtuse; dull; vacant, stupid. **ту́пость** bluntness; vacancy; dullness, slowness.

тур turn; round.

тура́ rook, castle.

турба́за holiday village, campsite.

турби́на turbine.

туре́цкий Turkish; **~ бараба́н** bass drum.

тури́зм tourism. **тури́ст**, **-и́стка** tourist. **тури́ст(иче)ский** tourist.

туркме́н (*gen pl* **-ме́н**), **~ка** Turkmen. **Туркмениста́н** Turkmenistan.

турне́ *neut indecl* tour.

турне́пс swede.

турни́р tournament.

ту́рок (**-рка**) Turk. **турча́нка** Turkish woman. **Ту́рция** Turkey.

ту́склый dim, dull; lacklustre. **тускне́ть** (**-е́ет**) *impf* (*pf* **по~**) grow dim.

тут *adv* here; now; **~ же** there and then.

ту́фля shoe.

ту́хлый (**-хл**, **-а́**, **-о**) rotten, bad. **ту́хнуть**[1] (**-нет**; **тух**) go bad.

ту́хнуть[2] (**-нет**; **тух**) *impf* (*pf* **по~**) go out.

ту́ча cloud; storm-cloud.

ту́чный (**-чен**, **-чна́**, **-чно**) fat; rich, fertile.

туш flourish.

ту́ша carcass.

тушева́ть (**-шу́ю**) *impf* (*pf* **за~**) shade. **тушёный** stewed. **туши́ть**[1] (**-шу́**, **-шишь**) *impf* (*pf* **с~**) stew.

туши́ть[2] (**-шу́**, **-шишь**) *impf* (*pf* **за~**, **по~**) extinguish.

тушу́ю *etc.: see* **тушева́ть**. **тушь** Indian ink; **~** (**для ресни́ц**) mascara.

тща́тельность care. **тща́тельный** careful; painstaking.

тщеду́шный feeble, frail.

тщесла́вие vanity, vainglory. **тщесла́вный** vain. **тщета́** vanity. **тще́тный** vain, futile.

ты (**тебя́**, **тебе́**, **тобо́й**, **тебе́**) you; thou; **быть на ты** c+*instr* be on intimate terms with.

ты́кать (**ты́чу**) *impf* (*pf* **ткнуть**) poke; prod; stick.

ты́ква pumpkin; gourd.

тыл (*loc* **-у́**; *pl* **-ы**) back; rear. **ты́льный** back; rear.

тын paling; palisade.

ты́сяча (*instr* **-ей** *or* **-ью**) thousand. **тысячеле́тие** millennium; thousandth anniversary. **ты́сячный** thousandth; of (many) thousands.

тычи́нка stamen.

тьма[1] dark, darkness.

тьма[2] host, multitude.

тюбете́йка skull-cap.

тю́бик tube.

тюк (-á) bale, package.

тюле́нь *m* seal.

тюльпа́н tulip.

тюре́мный prison. **тюре́мщик** gaoler. **тюрьма́** (*pl* -ы, -рем) prison, gaol.

тюфя́к (-á) mattress.

тя́га traction; thrust; draught; attraction; craving. **тяга́ться** *impf* vie, contend. **тяга́ч** (-á) tractor.

тя́гостный burdensome; painful. **тя́гость** burden. **тяготе́ние** gravity, gravitation; bent, inclination. **тяготе́ть** (-е́ю) *impf* gravitate; be attracted; ~ **над** hang over. **тяготи́ть** (-ощу́) *impf* be a burden on; oppress. **тягу́чий** malleable, ductile; viscous; slow.

тя́жба lawsuit; competition.

тяжело́ *adv* heavily; seriously. **тяжело́** *predic* it is hard; it is painful. **тяжелоатле́т** weight-lifter. **тяжелове́с** heavyweight. **тяжелове́сный** heavy; ponderous. **тяжёлый** (-ёл, -á) heavy; hard; serious; painful. **тя́жесть** gravity; weight; heaviness; severity. **тя́жкий** heavy; severe; grave.

тяну́ть (-ну́, -нешь) *impf* (*pf* по~) pull; draw; drag; drag out; weigh; *impers* attract; be tight; ~**ся** stretch; extend; stretch out; stretch o.s.; drag on; crawl; drift; move along one after another; last out; reach.

тяну́чка toffee.

У

у *prep+gen* by; at; with; from, of; belonging to; **у меня́ (есть)** I have; **у нас** at our place; in our country.

уба́вить (-влю) *pf*, **убавля́ть** *impf* reduce, diminish.

у|ба́юкать *pf*, **убаю́кивать** *impf* lull (to sleep).

убега́ть *impf of* **убежа́ть**

убеди́тельный convincing; earnest. **убеди́ть** (-и́шь) *pf* (*impf* **убежда́ть**) convince; persuade; ~**ся** be convinced; make certain.

убежа́ть (-егу́) *pf* (*impf* **убега́ть**) run away; escape; boil over.

убежда́ть(ся *impf of* **убеди́ть(ся**.

убежде́ние persuasion; conviction, belief. **убеждённость** conviction. **убеждённый** (-ён, -á) convinced; staunch.

убе́жище refuge, asylum; shelter.

уберега́ть *impf*, **убере́чь** (-регу́, -режёшь; -рёг, -гла́) *pf* protect, preserve; ~**ся от+gen** protect o.s. against.

уберу́ *etc.: see* **убра́ть**

убива́ть(ся *impf of* **уби́ть(ся. уби́йственный** deadly; murderous; killing. **уби́йство** murder. **уби́йца** *m & f* murderer.

убира́ть(ся *impf of* **убра́ть(ся; убира́йся!** clear off!

уби́тый killed; crushed; *sb* dead man. **уби́ть** (убью́, -ьёшь) *pf* (*impf* **убива́ть**) kill; murder; ~**ся** hurt o.s.

убо́гий wretched. **убо́жество** poverty; squalor.

убо́й slaughter.

убо́р dress, attire.

убо́рка harvesting; clearing up. **убо́рная** *sb* lavatory; dressing-room. **убо́рочный** harvesting; ~**ая маши́на** harvester. **убо́рщик, убо́рщица** cleaner. **убра́нство** furniture. **убра́ть** (уберу́, -рёшь; -а́л, -á, -о) *pf* (*impf* **убира́ть**) remove; take away; put away; harvest; clear up; decorate; ~ **посте́ль** make a bed; ~ **со стола́** clear the table; ~**ся** tidy up, clean up; clear off.

убыва́ть *impf*, **убы́ть** (убу́ду; у́был, -á, -о) *pf* diminish; subside; wane; leave. **у́быль** diminution; casualties. **убы́ток** (-тка) loss; *pl* damages. **убы́точный** unprofitable.

убью́ *etc.: see* **уби́ть**

уважа́емый respected; dear. **уважа́ть** *impf* respect. **уваже́ние** respect; **с ~м** yours sincerely. **уважи́тельный** valid; respectful.

уве́домить (-млю) *pf*, **уведомля́ть** *impf* inform. **уведомле́ние** notification.

уведу́ *etc.: see* **увести́**

увезти́ (-зу́, -зёшь; увёз, -ла́) *pf* (*impf* **увози́ть**) take (away); steal; abduct.

увекове́чивать *impf*, **увекове́чить** (-чу) *pf* immortalize; perpetuate.

увёл *etc.: see* **увести́**

увеличе́ние increase; magnification; enlargement. **увели́чивать** *impf*,

увели́чить (-чу) *pf* increase; magnify; enlarge; ~ся increase, grow.
увеличи́тель *m* enlarger. увеличи́тельный magnifying; enlarging; ~ое стекло́ magnifying glass.
у|венча́ть *pf*, увенчивать *impf* crown; ~ся be crowned.
уве́ренность confidence; certainty. уве́ренный confident; sure; certain. уве́рить *pf* (*impf* уверя́ть) assure; convince; ~ся satisfy o.s.; be convinced.
уверну́ться (-ну́сь, -нёшься) *pf*, увёртываться *impf* от+*gen* evade. увёртка dodge, evasion; subterfuge; *pl* wiles. увёртливый evasive, shifty.
увертю́ра overture.
уверя́ть(ся *impf of* уве́рить(ся
увеселе́ние amusement, entertainment. увесели́тельный entertainment; pleasure. увеселя́ть *impf* amuse, entertain.
уве́систый weighty.
увести́ (-еду́, -едёшь; -ёл, -а́) *pf* (*impf* уводи́ть) take (away); walk off with.
уве́чить (-чу) *impf* maim, cripple. уве́чный maimed, crippled; *sb* cripple. уве́чье maiming; injury.
уве́шать *pf*, уве́шивать *impf* hang (+*instr* with).
увеща́ть *impf*, увещева́ть *impf* exhort, admonish.
у|ви́дать *pf see.* у|ви́деть(ся (-и́жу-сь) *pf*.
уви́ливать *impf*, увильну́ть (-ну́, -нёшь) *pf* от+*gen* dodge; evade.
увлажни́ть *pf*, увлажня́ть *impf* moisten.
увлека́тельный fascinating. увлека́ть *impf*, увле́чь (-еку́, -ечёшь; -ёк, -ла́) *pf* carry away; fascinate; ~ся be carried away; become mad (+*instr* about). увлече́ние animation; passion; crush.
уво́д withdrawal; stealing. уводи́ть (-ожу́, -о́дишь) *impf of* увести́
увози́ть (-ожу́, -о́дишь) *impf of* увезти́
уво́лить *pf*, увольня́ть *impf* discharge, dismiss; retire; ~ся be discharged, retire. увольне́ние discharge, dismissal.
увы́ *int* alas!
увяда́ть *impf of* увя́нуть. увя́дший

withered.
увяза́ть[1] *impf of* увя́знуть
увяза́ть[2] (-яжу́, -я́жешь) *pf* (*impf* увя́зывать) tie up; pack up; co-ordinate; ~ся pack; tag along. увя́зка tying up; co-ordination.
у|вя́знуть (-ну; -я́з) *pf* (*impf also* увяза́ть) get bogged down.
увя́зывать(ся *impf of* увяза́ть(ся
у|вя́нуть (-ну) *pf* (*impf also* увяда́ть) fade, wither.
угада́ть *pf*, уга́дывать *impf* guess.
уга́р carbon monoxide (poisoning); ecstasy. уга́рный газ carbon monoxide.
угаса́ть *impf*, у|га́снуть (-нет; -ас) *pf* go out; die down.
угле- *in comb* coal; charcoal; carbon. углево́д carbohydrate. ~водоро́д hydrocarbon. ~добы́ча coal extraction. ~кислота́ carbonic acid; carbon dioxide. ~ки́слый carbonate (of). ~ро́д carbon.
углово́й corner; angular.
углуби́ть (-блю́) *pf*, углубля́ть *impf* deepen; ~ся deepen; delve deeply; become absorbed. углубле́ние depression, dip; deepening. углублённый deepened; profound; absorbed.
угна́ть (угоню́, -о́нишь; -а́л, -а́, -о) *pf* (*impf* угоня́ть) drive away; despatch; steal; ~ся за+*instr* keep pace with.
угнета́тель *m* oppressor. угнета́ть *impf* oppress, depress. угнете́ние oppression; depression. угнетённый oppressed; depressed.
угова́ривать *impf*, уговори́ть *pf* persuade; ~ся arrange, agree. угово́р persuasion; agreement.
уго́да: в уго́ду +*dat* to please.
угоди́ть (-ожу́) *pf*, угожда́ть *impf* fall; get; bang; (+*dat*) hit; +*dat* or на+*acc* please. угодли́вый obsequious. уго́дно *predic*+*dat*: как вам ~ as you wish; что вам ~? what would you like?; *partl* кто ~ anyone (you like); что ~ anything (you like).
уго́дье (*gen pl* -ий) land.
у́гол (угла́, *loc* -у́) corner; angle.
уголо́вник criminal. уголо́вный criminal.
уголо́к (-лка́, *loc* -у́) corner.
у́голь (у́гля; *pl* у́гли, -ей *or* -е́й) *m* coal; charcoal.

уго́льник set square.

у́гольный coal; carbon(ic).

угомони́ть *pf* calm down; **~ся** calm down.

уго́н driving away; stealing. **угоня́ть** *impf of* угна́ть

угора́ть *impf*, **угоре́ть** (-рю́) *pf* get carbon monoxide poisoning; be mad. **угоре́лый** mad; possessed.

у́горь[1] (угря́) *m* eel.

у́горь[2] (угря́) *m* blackhead.

угости́ть (-ощу́) *pf*, **угоща́ть** *impf* entertain; treat. **угоще́ние** entertaining, treating; refreshments.

угрожа́ть *impf* threaten. **угро́за** threat, menace.

угро́зыск *abbr* criminal investigation department.

угрызе́ние pangs.

угрю́мый sullen, morose.

удава́ться (удаётся) *impf of* уда́ться

у|дави́ть(ся (-влю́(сь, -вишь(ся) *pf*. **уда́вка** running-knot, half hitch.

удале́ние removal; sending away; moving off. **удали́ть** *pf* (*impf* удаля́ть) remove; send away; move away; **~ся** move off, away; retire.

удало́й, уда́лый (-а́л, -а́, -о) daring, bold. **у́даль, удальство́** daring, boldness.

удаля́ть(ся *impf of* удали́ть(ся

уда́р blow; stroke; attack; kick; thrust; seizure; bolt. **ударе́ние** accent; stress; emphasis. **уда́рить** *pf*, **ударя́ть** *impf* (*impf also* бить) strike; hit; beat; **~ся** strike, hit; +в+*acc* break into; burst into. **уда́рник, -ница** shock-worker. **уда́рный** percussion; shock; stressed; urgent.

уда́ться (-а́стся, -аду́тся; -а́лся, -ла́сь) *pf* (*impf* удава́ться) succeed, be a success; *impers* +*dat* +*inf* succeed, manage; мне удало́сь найти́ рабо́ту I managed to find a job. **уда́ча** good luck; success. **уда́чный** successful; felicitous.

удва́ивать *impf*, **удво́ить** (-ю) *pf* double, redouble. **удвое́ние** (re)-doubling.

уде́л lot, destiny.

удели́ть *pf* (*impf* уделя́ть) spare, give.

уделя́ть *impf of* удели́ть

удержа́ние deduction; retention; keeping. **удержа́ть** (-жу́, -жишь) *pf*, **уде́рживать** *impf* hold (on to); retain; restrain; suppress; deduct; **~ся** hold out; stand firm; refrain (from).

удеру́ *etc.: see* удра́ть

удешеви́ть (-влю́) *pf*, **удешевля́ть** *impf* reduce the price of.

удиви́тельный surprising; amazing; wonderful. **удиви́ть** (-влю́) *pf*, **удивля́ть** *impf* surprise, amaze; **~ся** be surprised, be amazed. **удивле́ние** surprise, amazement.

удила́ (-и́л) *pl* bit.

уди́лище fishing-rod.

удира́ть *impf of* удра́ть

уди́ть (ужу́, у́дишь) *impf* fish for; **~ ры́бу** fish; **~ся** bite.

удлине́ние lengthening; extension. **удлини́ть** *pf*, **удлиня́ть** *impf* lengthen; extend; **~ся** become longer; be extended.

удо́бно *adv* comfortably; conveniently. **удо́бный** comfortable; convenient.

удовари́мый digestible.

удобре́ние fertilization; fertilizer. **удо́брить** *pf*, **удобря́ть** *impf* fertilize.

удо́бство comfort; convenience.

удовлетворе́ние satisfaction; gratification. **удовлетворённый** (-рён, -á) satisfied. **удовлетвори́тельный** satisfactory. **удовлетвори́ть** *pf*, **удовлетворя́ть** *impf* satisfy; +*dat* meet; +*instr* supply with; **~ся** be satisfied.

удово́льствие pleasure. **у|дово́льствоваться** *pf*.

удо́й milk-yield; milking.

удоста́ивать(ся *impf of* удосто́ить(ся

удостовере́ние certification; certificate; **~ ли́чности** identity card. **удостове́рить** *pf*, **удостоверя́ть** *impf* certify, witness; **~ся** make sure (в+*prep* of), assure o.s.

удосто́ить *pf* (*impf* удоста́ивать) make an award to; +*gen* award; +*instr* favour with; **~ся** +*gen* be awarded; be favoured with.

у́дочка (fishing-)rod.

удра́ть (удеру́, -ёшь; удра́л, -á, -о) *pf* (*impf* удира́ть) make off.

удруча́ть *impf*, **удручи́ть** (-чу́) *pf* depress. **удручённый** (-чён, -á) depressed.

удуша́ть *impf*, удуши́ть (-шу́, -шишь) *pf* stifle, suffocate. удуше́ние suffocation. **уду́шливый** stifling. **уду́шье** asthma; asphyxia.

уедине́ние solitude; seclusion. **уеди-нённый** secluded; lonely. **уедини́ться** *pf*, **уединя́ться** *impf* seclude o.s.

уе́зд uyezd, District.

уезжа́ть *impf*, **уе́хать** (уе́ду) *pf* go away, depart.

уж[1] (-á) grass-snake.

уж[2]: *see* уже́[2]. уж[3], уже́[3] *partl* indeed; really.

у|жа́лить *pf*.

у́жас horror, terror; *predic* it is awful. **ужаса́ть** *impf*, **ужасну́ть** (-ну́, -нёшь) *pf* horrify; ~ся be horrified, be terrified. **ужа́сно** *adv* terribly; awfully. **ужа́сный** awful, terrible.

у́же[1] *comp of* у́зкий

уже́[2], уж[2] *adv* already; ~ не no longer. уже́[3]: *see* уж[3]

уже́ние fishing.

ужива́ться *impf of* ужи́ться. **ужи́вчивый** easy to get on with.

ужи́мка grimace.

у́жин supper. **у́жинать** *impf* (*pf* по~) have supper.

ужи́ться (-иву́сь, -ивёшься; -и́лся, -ла́сь) *pf* (*impf* ужива́ться) get on.

ужу́ *see* уди́ть

узако́нивать *impf*, **узако́нить** *pf* legalize.

узбе́к, -е́чка Uzbek. **Узбекиста́н** Uzbekistan.

узда́ (*pl* -ы) bridle.

у́зел (узла́) knot; junction; centre; node; bundle.

у́зкий (у́зок, узка́, -о) narrow; tight; narrow-minded. **узкоколе́йка** narrow-gauge railway.

узлова́тый knotty. **узлов|о́й** junction; main, key; ~а́я ста́нция junction.

узнава́ть (-наю́, -наёшь) *impf*, **узна́ть** *pf* recognize; get to know; find out.

у́зник, **у́зница** prisoner.

узо́р pattern, design. **узо́рчатый** patterned.

у́зость narrowness; tightness.

узурпа́тор usurper. **узурпи́ровать** *impf* & *pf* usurp.

у́зы (уз) *pl* bonds, ties.

уйду́ *etc.*: *see* уйти́.

у́йма lots (of).

уйму́ *etc.*: *see* уня́ть

уйти́ (уйду́, -дёшь; ушёл, ушла́) *pf* (*impf* уходи́ть) go away, leave, depart; escape; retire; bury o.s.; be used up; pass away.

ука́з decree; edict. **указа́ние** indication; instruction. **ука́занный** appointed, stated. **указа́тель** *m* indicator; gauge; index; directory. **указа́тельный** indicating; demonstrative; ~ па́лец index finger. **указа́ть** (-ажу́, -а́жешь) *pf*, **ука́зывать** *impf* show; indicate; point; point out. **ука́зка** pointer; orders.

ука́лывать *impf of* уколо́ть

уката́ть *pf*, **ука́тывать**[1] *impf* roll; flatten; wear out. **укати́ть** (-ачу́, -а́тишь) *pf*, **ука́тывать**[2] *impf* roll away; drive off; ~ся roll away.

укача́ть *pf*, **ука́чивать** *impf* rock to sleep; make sick.

укла́д structure; style; organization. **укла́дка** packing; stacking; laying; setting. **укла́дчик** packer; layer. **укла́дывать(ся)**[1] *impf of* уложи́ть(ся

укла́дываться[2] *impf of* уле́чься

укло́н slope; incline; gradient; bias; deviation. **уклоне́ние** deviation; digression. **уклони́ться** *pf*, **уклоня́ться** *impf* deviate; +от+*gen* turn (off, aside); avoid; evade. **укло́нчивый** evasive.

уклю́чина rowlock.

уко́л prick; injection; thrust. **уколо́ть** (-лю́, -лешь) *pf* (*impf* ука́лывать) prick; wound.

у|комплектова́ть *pf*, **укомплекто́вывать** *impf* complete; bring up to (full) strength; man; +*instr* equip with.

уко́р reproach.

укора́чивать *impf of* укороти́ть

укорени́ть *pf*, **укореня́ть** *impf* implant, inculcate; ~ся take root.

укори́зна reproach. **укори́зненный** reproachful. **укори́ть** *pf* (*impf* укоря́ть) reproach (в+*prep* with).

укороти́ть (-очу́) *pf* (*impf* укора́чивать) shorten.

укоря́ть *impf of* укори́ть

уко́с (hay-)crop.

укра́дкой *adv* stealthily. **украду́** *etc.*: *see* укра́сть

Украи́на Ukraine. **украи́нец** (-нца), **украи́нка** Ukrainian. **украи́нский** Ukrainian.

украси́ть (-а́шу) *pf* (*impf* **украша́ть**) adorn, decorate; ~ся be decorated; adorn o.s.

у|кра́сть (-аду́, -дёшь) *pf.*

украша́ть(ся *impf of* **украси́ть(ся.** **украше́ние** decoration; adornment.

укрепи́ть (-плю́) *pf*, **укрепля́ть** *impf* strengthen; fix; fortify; ~ся become stronger; fortify one's position. **укрепле́ние** strengthening; reinforcement; fortification.

укро́мный secluded, cosy.

укро́п dill.

укроти́тель *m* (animal-)tamer. **укроти́ть** (-ощу́) *pf*, **укроща́ть** *impf* tame; curb; ~ся become tame; calm down. **укроще́ние** taming.

укро́ю *etc.: see* **укры́ть**

укрупне́ние enlargement; amalgamation. **укрупни́ть** *pf*, **укрупня́ть** *impf* enlarge; amalgamate.

укрыва́тель *m* harbourer. **укрыва́тельство** harbouring; receiving. **укрыва́ть** *impf*, **укры́ть** (-ро́ю) *pf* cover; conceal, harbour; shelter; receive; ~ся cover o.s.; take cover. **укры́тие** cover; shelter.

у́ксус vinegar.

уку́с bite; sting. **укуси́ть** (-ушу́, -у́сишь) *pf* bite; sting.

уку́тать *pf*, **уку́тывать** *impf* wrap up; ~ся wrap o.s. up.

укушу́ *etc.: see* **укуси́ть**

ул. *abbr* (*of* **у́лица**) street, road.

ула́вливать *impf of* **улови́ть**

ула́дить (-а́жу) *pf*, **ула́живать** *impf* settle, arrange.

у́лей (у́лья) (bee)hive.

улета́ть *impf*, **улете́ть** (-лечу́) *pf* fly (away). **улету́чиваться**, *impf*, **улету́читься** (-чусь) *pf* evaporate; vanish.

уле́чься (уля́гусь, -я́жешься) улёгся, -гла́сь) *pf* (*impf* **укла́дываться**) lie down; settle; subside.

ули́ка clue; evidence.

ули́тка snail.

у́лица street; **на у́лице** in the street; outside.

улича́ть *impf*, **уличи́ть** (-чу́) *pf* establish the guilt of.

у́личный street.

уло́в catch. **улови́мый** perceptible; audible. **улови́ть** (-влю́, -вишь) *pf* (*impf* **ула́вливать**) catch; seize. **уло́вка** trick, ruse.

уложе́ние code. **уложи́ть** (-жу́, -жишь) *pf* (*impf* **укла́дывать**) lay; pack; pile; ~ спать put to bed; ~ся pack (up); fit in.

улуча́ть *impf*, **улучи́ть** (-чу́) *pf* find, seize.

улучша́ть *impf*, **улу́чшить** (-шу) *pf* improve; better; ~ся improve; get better. **улучше́ние** improvement.

улыба́ться *impf*, **улыбну́ться** (-ну́сь, -нёшься) *pf* smile. **улы́бка** smile.

ультима́тум ultimatum.

ультра- *in comb* ultra-. **ультразвуково́й** supersonic. ~**фиоле́товый** ultra-violet.

уля́гусь *etc.: see* **уле́чься**

ум (-а́) mind, intellect; head; **сойти́ с** ~а́ go mad.

умали́ть *pf* (*impf* **умаля́ть**) belittle.

умалишённый mad; *sb* lunatic.

ума́лчивать *impf of* **умолча́ть**

умаля́ть *impf of* **умали́ть**

уме́лец (-льца) skilled craftsman. **уме́лый** able, skilful. **уме́ние** ability, skill.

уменьша́ть *impf*, **уме́ньшить** (-шу) *pf* reduce, diminish, decrease; ~ся diminish, decrease; abate. **уменьше́ние** decrease, reduction; abatement. **уменьши́тельный** diminutive.

уме́ренность moderation. **уме́ренный** moderate; temperate.

умере́ть (умру́, -рёшь; у́мер, -ла́, -о) *pf* (*impf* **умира́ть**) die.

уме́рить *pf* (*impf* **умеря́ть**) moderate; restrain.

умертви́ть (-рщвлю́, -ртви́шь) *pf*, **умерщвля́ть** *impf* kill, destroy; mortify. **у́мерший** dead; *sb* the deceased. **умерщвле́ние** killing, destruction; mortification.

умеря́ть *impf of* **уме́рить**

умести́ть (-ещу́) *pf* (*impf* **умеща́ть**) fit in, find room for; ~ся fit in. **уме́стный** appropriate; pertinent; timely.

уме́ть (-е́ю) *impf* be able, know how.

умеща́ть(ся *impf of* **умести́ть(ся**

умиле́ние tenderness; emotion. **умили́ть** *pf*, **умиля́ть** *impf* move, touch; ~ся be moved.

умира́ние dying. умира́ть *impf of* умере́ть. умира́ющий dying; *sb* dying person.

умиротворе́ние pacification; appeasement. умиротвори́ть *pf*, умиротворя́ть *impf* pacify; appease.

умне́ть (-е́ю) *impf* (*pf* по~) grow wiser. у́мница good girl; *m* & *f* clever person.

умножа́ть *impf*, у|мно́жить (-жу) *pf* multiply; increase; ~ся increase, multiply. умноже́ние multiplication; increase. умножи́тель *m* multiplier.

у́мный (умён, умна́, у́мно́) clever, wise, intelligent. умозаключе́ние deduction; conclusion.

умоли́ть *pf* (*impf* умоля́ть) move by entreaties.

умолка́ть *impf*, умо́лкнуть (-ну; -о́лк) *pf* fall silent; stop. умолча́ть (-чу́) *pf* (*impf* ума́лчивать) fail to mention; hush up.

умоля́ть *impf of* умоли́ть; beg, entreat.

умопомеша́тельство derangement. умори́тельный incredibly funny, killing. у|мори́ть *pf* kill; exhaust.

умо́ю *etc.: see* умы́ть. умру́ *etc.: see* умере́ть

у́мственный mental, intellectual. умудри́ть *pf*, умудря́ть *impf* make wiser; ~ся contrive.

умыва́льная *sb* wash-room. умыва́льник wash-stand, wash-basin. умыва́ть(ся *impf of* умы́ть(ся

у́мысел (-сла) design, intention. умы́ть (умо́ю) *pf* (*impf* умыва́ть) wash; ~ся wash (o.s.).

умы́шленный intentional.

у|насле́довать *pf*.

унести́ (-су́, -сёшь; -ёс, -ла́) *pf* (*impf* уноси́ть) take away; carry off, make off with; ~сь speed away; fly by; be carried (away).

универма́г *abbr* department store. универса́льн|ый universal; all-round; versatile; all-purpose; ~ магази́н department store; ~ое сре́дство panacea. универса́м *abbr* supermarket.

университе́т university. университе́тский university.

унижа́ть *impf*, уни́зить (-и́жу) *pf* humiliate; ~ся humble o.s.; stoop.

униже́ние humiliation. уни́женный humble. унизи́тельный humiliating.

уника́льный unique.

унима́ть(ся *impf of* уня́ть(ся

унисо́н unison.

унита́з lavatory pan.

унифици́ровать *impf* & *pf* standardize.

уничижи́тельный pejorative.

уничтожа́ть *impf*, уничто́жить (-жу) *pf* destroy, annihilate; abolish; do away with. уничтоже́ние destruction, annihilation; abolition.

уноси́ть(ся (-ошу́(сь, -о́сишь(ся) *impf of* унести́(сь

у́нция ounce.

уныва́ть *impf* be dejected. уны́лый dejected; doleful, cheerless. уны́ние dejection, despondency.

уня́ть (уйму́, -мёшь; -я́л, -а́, -о) *pf* (*impf* унима́ть) calm, soothe; ~ся calm down.

упа́док (-дка) decline; decay; ~ ду́ха depression. упа́дочнический decadent. упа́дочный depressive; decadent. упаду́ *etc.: see* упа́сть

у|накова́ть *pf*, упако́вывать *impf* pack (up). упако́вка packing; wrapping. упако́вщик packer.

упа́сть (-аду́, -адёшь) *pf of* па́дать

упере́ть (упру́, -рёшь; -ёр) *pf*, упира́ть *impf* rest, lean; ~ на+*acc* stress; ~ся rest, lean; resist; +в+*acc* come up against.

упи́танный well-fed; fattened.

упла́та payment. у|плати́ть (-ачу́, -а́тишь) *pf*, упла́чивать *impf* pay.

уплотне́ние compression; condensation; consolidation; sealing. уплотни́ть *pf*, уплотня́ть *impf* condense; compress; pack more into.

уплыва́ть *impf*, уплы́ть (-ыву́, -ывёшь; -ы́л, -а́, -о) *pf* swim *or* sail away; pass.

упова́ть *impf* +на+*acc* put one's trust in.

уподо́биться (-блюсь) *pf*, уподобля́ться *impf* +*dat* become like.

упое́ние ecstasy, rapture. упои́тельный intoxicating, ravishing.

уполза́ть *impf*, уползти́ (-зу́, -зёшь; -о́лз, -зла́) *pf* creep away, crawl away.

уполномо́ченный *sb* (authorized)

agent, representative; proxy. уполно-
мо́чивать, уполномо́чить *impf*, уполномо́чить (-чу) *pf* authorize, empower.

упомина́ние mention. упомина́ть *impf*, упомяну́ть (-ну́, -нешь) *pf* mention, refer to.

упо́р prop, support; в ~ point-blank; сде́лать ~ на+*acc* or *prep* lay stress on. упо́рный stubborn; persistent. упо́рство stubbornness; persistence. упо́рствовать *impf* be stubborn; persist (в+*prep* in).

упоря́дочивать *impf*, упоря́дочить (-чу) *pf* regulate, put in order.

употреби́тельный (widely-)used; common. употреби́ть (-блю́) *pf*, употребля́ть *impf* use. употребле́ние use; usage.

упра́ва justice.

управдо́м *abbr* manager (*of block of flats*). упра́виться (-влюсь) *pf*, управля́ться *impf* cope, manage; +c+*instr* deal with. управле́ние management; administration; direction; control; driving, steering; government. управля́емый снаря́д guided missile. управля́ть *impf* +*instr* manage, direct, run; govern; be in charge of; operate; drive. управля́ющий *sb* manager.

упражне́ние exercise. упражня́ть *impf* exercise, train; ~ся practise, train.

упраздни́ть *pf*, упраздня́ть *impf* abolish.

упра́шивать *impf of* упроси́ть

упрёк reproach. упрека́ть *impf*, упрекну́ть (-ну́, -нёшь) *pf* reproach. упроси́ть (-ошу́, -о́сишь) *pf* (*impf* упра́шивать) entreat; prevail upon.

упрости́ть (-ощу́) *pf* (*impf* упроща́ть) (over-)simplify.

упро́чивать *impf*, упро́чить (-чу) *pf* strengthen, consolidate; ~ся be firmly established.

упрошу́ *etc.*: *see* упроси́ть

упроща́ть *impf of* упрости́ть. упро́щённый (-щён, -а́) (over-)simplified.

упру́ *etc.*: *see* упере́ть

упру́гий elastic; springy. упру́гость elasticity; spring. упру́же *comp of* упру́гий

упря́жка harness; team. упряжно́й draught. у́пряжь harness.

упря́миться (-млюсь) *impf* be obstinate; persist. упря́мство obstinacy. упря́мый obstinate; persistent.

упуска́ть *impf*, упусти́ть (-ущу́, -у́стишь) *pf* let go, let slip; miss. упуще́ние omission; slip; negligence.

ура́ *int* hurrah!

уравне́ние equalization; equation. ура́внивать *impf*, уравня́ть *pf* equalize. уравни́тельный equalizing, levelling. уравнове́сить (-е́шу) *pf*, уравнове́шивать *impf* balance; counterbalance. уравнове́шенность composure. уравнове́шенный balanced, composed.

урага́н hurricane; storm.

ура́льский Ural.

ура́н uranium; Uranus. ура́новый uranium.

урва́ть (-ву́, -вёшь) (-а́л, -а́, -о) *pf* (*impf* урыва́ть) snatch.

урегули́рование regulation; settlement. у|регули́ровать *pf*.

уре́зать (-е́жу) *pf*, уреза́ть, уре́зывать *impf* cut off; shorten; reduce.

у́рка *m & f* (*sl*) lag, convict.

у́рна urn; litter-bin.

у́ровень (-вня) *m* level; standard.

уро́д freak, monster.

уроди́ться (-ожу́сь) *pf* ripen; grow.

уро́дливость deformity; ugliness. уро́дливый deformed; ugly; bad. уро́довать *impf* (*pf* из~) disfigure; distort. уро́дство disfigurement; ugliness.

урожа́й harvest; crop; abundance. урожа́йность yield; productivity. урожа́йный productive, high-yield.

урождённый *née*. уроже́нец (-нца), уроже́нка native. урожу́сь *see* уроди́ться

уро́к lesson.

уро́н losses; damage. урони́ть (-ню́, -нишь) *pf of* роня́ть

урча́ть (-чу́) *impf* rumble.

урыва́ть *impf of* урва́ть. уры́вками *adv* in snatches, by fits and starts.

ус (*pl* -ы́) whisker; tendril; *pl* moustache.

усади́ть (-ажу́, -а́дишь) *pf*, уса́живать *impf* seat, offer a seat; plant. уса́дьба (*gen pl* -деб *or* -дьб) country estate; farmstead. уса́живаться *impf of* усе́сться

уса́тый moustached; whiskered.

усва́ивать *impf*, усво́ить *pf* master; assimilate; adopt. усвое́ние mastering; assimilation; adoption.

усе́рдие zeal; diligence. усе́рдный zealous; diligent.

усе́сться (уся́дусь; -е́лся) *pf* (*impf* уса́живаться) take a seat; settle down (to).

усиде́ть (-ижу́) *pf* remain seated; hold down a job. уси́дчивый assiduous.

у́сик tendril; runner; antenna; *pl* small moustache.

усиле́ние strengthening; reinforcement; intensification; amplification. уси́ленный intensified, increased; earnest. уси́ливать *impf*, уси́лить *pf* intensify; increase; amplify; strengthen, reinforce; ~ся increase, intensify; become stronger. уси́лие effort. усили́тель *m* amplifier; booster.

ускака́ть (-ачу́, -а́чешь) *pf* skip off; gallop off.

ускольза́ть *impf*, ускользну́ть (-ну́, -нёшь) *pf* slip off; steal away; escape.

ускоре́ние acceleration. ускоре́нный accelerated; rapid; crash. ускори́тель accelerator. уско́рить (-рю) *pf*, ускоря́ть *impf* quicken; accelerate; hasten; ~ся accelerate, be accelerated; quicken.

усло́вие condition. усло́виться (-влюсь) *pf*, усло́вливаться, усла́вливаться *impf* agree; arrange. усло́вленный agreed, fixed. усло́вность convention. усло́вный conditional; conditioned; conventional; agreed; relative.

усложне́ние complication. усложни́ть *pf*, усложня́ть *impf* complicate; ~ся become complicated.

услу́га service; good turn. услу́жливый obliging.

услыха́ть (-ы́шу) *pf*, у|слы́шать (-ы́шу) *pf* hear; sense; scent.

усма́тривать *impf of* усмотре́ть

усмеха́ться *impf*, усмехну́ться (-ну́сь, -нёшься) *pf* smile; grin; smirk. усме́шка smile; grin; sneer.

усмире́ние pacification; suppression. усмири́ть *pf*, усмиря́ть *impf* pacify; calm; suppress.

усмотре́ние discretion, judgement. усмотре́ть (-рю́, -ришь) *pf* (*impf*

усма́тривать) perceive; see; regard; +за+*instr* keep an eye on.

усну́ть (-ну́, -нёшь) *pf* go to sleep.

усоверше́нствование advanced studies; improvement, refinement. у|соверше́нствовать(ся *pf*.

усомни́ться *pf* doubt.

успева́емость progress. успева́ть *impf*, успе́ть (-е́ю) *pf* have time; manage; succeed. успе́х success; progress. успе́шный successful.

успока́ивать *impf*, успоко́ить *pf* calm, quiet, soothe; ~ся calm down; abate. успока́ивающий calming, sedative. успокое́ние calming, soothing; calm; peace. успокои́тель|ный calming; reassuring; ~ое *sb* sedative, tranquillizer.

уста́ (-т, -та́м) *pl* mouth.

уста́в regulations, statutes; charter.

устава́ть (-таю́, -ёшь) *impf of* уста́ть; не устава́я incessantly.

уста́вить (-влю) *pf*, уставля́ть *impf* set, arrange; cover, fill; direct; ~ся find room, go in; stare.

уста́лость tiredness. уста́лый tired.

устана́вливать *impf*, установи́ть (-влю́, -вишь) *pf* put, set up; install; set; establish; fix; ~ся be established; set in. устано́вка putting, setting up; installation; setting; plant, unit; directions. устано́вленный establishment. устано́вленный established, prescribed.

уста́ну *etc.: see* уста́ть

устарева́ть *impf*, у|старе́ть (-е́ю) *pf* become obsolete; become antiquated. устаре́лый obsolete; antiquated, out-of-date.

уста́ть (-а́ну) *pf* (*impf* устава́ть) get tired.

устила́ть *impf*, устла́ть (-телю́, -те́лешь) *pf* cover; pave.

у́стный oral, verbal.

усто́й abutment; foundation; support. усто́йчивость stability, steadiness. усто́йчивый stable, steady. усто́я́ть (-ою́) *pf* keep one's balance; stand firm; ~ся settle; become fixed.

устра́ивать(ся *impf of* устро́ить(ся

устране́ние removal, elimination. устрани́ть *pf*, устраня́ть *impf* remove; eliminate; ~ся resign, retire.

устраша́ть *impf*, устраши́ть (-шу́) *pf* frighten; ~ся be frightened.

устреми́ть (-млю́) *pf*, **устремля́ть** *impf* direct, fix; ~**ся** rush; be directed; concentrate. **устремле́ние** rush; aspiration.

у́стрица oyster.

устро́итель *m*, ~**ница** organizer. **устро́ить** *pf* (*impf* **устра́ивать**) arrange, organize; make; cause; settle, put in order; place, fix up; get; suit; ~**ся** work out; manage; settle down; be found, get fixed up. **устро́йство** arrangement; construction; mechanism, device; system.

усту́п shelf, ledge. **уступа́ть** *impf*, **уступи́ть** (-плю́, -пишь) *pf* yield; give up; ~ **доро́гу** make way. **усту́пка** concession. **усту́пчивый** pliable; compliant.

устыди́ться (-ыжу́сь) *pf* (+*gen*) be ashamed (of).

у́стье (*gen pl* -ьев) mouth; estuary.

усугуби́ть (-у́блю́) *pf*, **усугубля́ть** *impf* increase; aggravate.

усы́ *see* **ус**

усынови́ть (-влю́) *pf*, **усыновля́ть** *impf* adopt. **усыновле́ние** adoption.

усыпа́ть (-плю) *pf*, **усыпа́ть** *impf* strew, scatter.

усыпи́тельный soporific. **усыпи́ть** (-плю́) *pf*, **усыпля́ть** *impf* put to sleep; lull; weaken.

уся́дусь *etc.*: *see* **усе́сться**

ута́ивать *impf*, **утаи́ть** *pf* conceal; keep secret.

ута́птывать *impf of* **утопта́ть**

ута́скивать *impf*, **утащи́ть** (-щу́, -щишь) *pf* drag off.

у́тварь utensils.

утверди́тельный affirmative. **утверди́ть** (-ржу́) *pf*, **утвержда́ть** *impf* confirm; approve; ratify; establish; assert; ~**ся** gain a foothold; become established; be confirmed. **утвержде́ние** approval; confirmation; ratification; assertion; establishment.

утека́ть *impf of* **уте́чь**

утёнок (-нка; *pl* утя́та, -я́т) duckling.

утепли́ть *pf*, **утепля́ть** *impf* warm.

утере́ть (утру́, -рёшь; утёр) *pf* (*impf* **утира́ть**) wipe (off, dry).

утерпе́ть (-плю́, -пишь) *pf* restrain o.s.

утёс cliff, crag.

уте́чка leak, leakage; escape; loss. **уте́чь** (-еку́, -ечёшь; утёк, -ла́) *pf*

(*impf* **утека́ть**) leak, escape; pass.

утеша́ть *impf*, **уте́шить** (-шу) *pf* console; ~**ся** console o.s. **утеше́ние** consolation. **утеши́тельный** comforting.

утилизи́ровать *impf & pf* utilize.

ути́ль *m*, **утильсырьё** scrap.

утиный duck, duck's.

утира́ть(ся *impf of* **утере́ть(ся**

утиха́ть *impf*, **ути́хнуть** (-ну; -и́х) *pf* abate, subside; calm down.

у́тка duck; canard.

уткну́ть (-ну́, -нёшь) *pf* bury; fix; ~**ся** bury o.s.

утоли́ть *pf* (*impf* **утоля́ть**) quench; satisfy; relieve.

утолще́ние thickening; bulge.

утоля́ть *impf of* **утоли́ть**

утоми́тельный tedious; tiring. **утоми́ть** (-млю́) *pf*, **утомля́ть** *impf* tire, fatigue; ~**ся** get tired. **утомле́ние** weariness. **утомлённый** weary.

у|тону́ть (-ну́, -нешь) *pf* drown, be drowned; sink.

утончённый refined.

у|то́пить(ся (-плю́(сь, -пишь(ся) *pf*. **уто́пленник** drowned man.

утопи́ческий utopian. **уто́пия** Utopia.

утопта́ть (-пчу́, -пчешь) *pf* (*impf* **ута́птывать**) trample down.

уточне́ние more precise definition; amplification. **уточни́ть** *pf*, **уточня́ть** *impf* define more precisely; amplify.

утра́ивать *impf of* **утро́ить**

у|трамбова́ть *pf*, **утрамбо́вывать** *impf* ram, tamp; ~**ся** become flat.

утра́та loss. **утра́тить** (-а́чу) *pf*, **утра́чивать** *impf* lose.

у́тренний morning. **у́тренник** morning performance; early-morning frost. **утри́ровать** *impf & pf* exaggerate.

у́тро (-а *or* -á, -y *or* -ý, *pl* -а, -ам *or* -áм) morning.

утро́ба womb; belly.

утро́ить *pf* (*impf* **утра́ивать**) triple, treble.

утру́ *etc.*: *see* **утере́ть**, **у́тро**

утружда́ть *impf* trouble, tire.

утю́г (-á) iron. **утю́жить** (-жу) *impf* (*pf* **вы́~**, **от~**) iron.

ух *int* oh, ooh, ah.

уха́ fish soup.

уха́б pot-hole. **уха́бистый** bumpy.

уха́живать *impf* за+*instr* tend; look after; court.

ухвати́ть (-ачу́, -а́тишь) *pf*, ухва́-тывать *impf* seize; grasp; ~ся за+*acc* grasp, lay hold of; set to; seize; jump at. ухва́тка grip; skill; trick; manner.

ухитри́ться *pf*, ухитря́ться *impf* manage, contrive. ухищре́ние device, trick.

ухмы́лка smirk. ухмыльну́ться (-ну́сь, -нёшься) *pf*, ухмыля́ться *impf* smirk.

у́хо (*pl* у́ши, уше́й) ear; ear-flap.

ухо́д¹ +за+*instr* care of; tending, looking after.

ухо́д² leaving, departure. уходи́ть (-ожу́, -о́дишь) *impf of* уйти́

ухудша́ть *impf*, уху́дшить (-шу) *pf* make worse; ~ся get worse. ухудше́ние deterioration.

уцеле́ть (-е́ю) *pf* remain intact; survive.

уце́нивать *impf*, уцени́ть (-ню́, -нишь) *pf* reduce the price of.

уцепи́ть (-плю́, -пишь) *pf* catch hold of, seize; ~ся за+*acc* catch hold of, seize; jump at.

уча́ствовать *impf* take part; hold shares. уча́ствующий *sb* participant. уча́стие participation; share; sympathy.

участи́ть (-ащу́) *pf* (*impf* учаща́ть) make more frequent; ~ся become more frequent, quicken.

уча́стливый sympathetic. уча́стник participant. уча́сток (-тка) plot; part, section; sector; district; field, sphere. уча́сть lot, fate.

учаща́ть(ся *impf of* участи́ть(ся

уча́щийся *sb* student; pupil. уче́ба studies; course; training. уче́бник text-book. уче́бный educational; school; training. уче́ние learning; studies; apprenticeship; teaching; doctrine; exercise.

учени́к (-á), учени́ца pupil; apprentice; disciple. учени́ческий pupil's(s'); apprentice('s); unskilled; crude. уче́ность learning, erudition. учёный learned; scholarly; academic; scientific; ~ая сте́пень (*university*) degree; ~ый *sb* scholar; scientist.

уче́сть (учту́, -тёшь; учёл, учла́) *pf* (*impf* учи́тывать) take stock of; take into account; discount. учёт stock-taking; calculation; taking into account; registration; discount. без ~а +*gen* disregarding; взять на ~ register. учётный registration; discount.

учи́лище (*specialist*) school.

у|чини́ть *pf*, учиня́ть *impf* make; carry out; commit.

учи́тель (*pl* -я́) *m*, учи́тельница teacher. учи́тельск|ий teacher's, teachers'; ~ая *sb* staff-room.

учи́тывать *impf of* уче́сть

учи́ть (учу́, у́чишь) *impf* (*pf* вы́~, на~, об~) teach; be a teacher; learn; ~ся be a student; +*dat or inf* learn, study.

учреди́тельный constituent. учреди́ть (-ежу́) *pf*, учрежда́ть *impf* found, establish. учрежде́ние founding; establishment; institution.

учти́вый civil, courteous.

учту́ *etc.*: *see* уче́сть

уша́нка hat with ear-flaps.

ушёл *etc.*: *see* уйти́. у́ши *etc.*: *see* у́хо

уши́б injury; bruise. ушиба́ть *impf*, ушиби́ть (-бу́, -бёшь; уши́б) *pf* injure; bruise; hurt; ~ся hurt o.s.

ушко́ (*pl* -и́, -о́в) eye; tab.

ушно́й ear, aural.

уще́лье ravine, gorge, canyon.

ущеми́ть (-млю́) *pf*, ущемля́ть *impf* pinch, jam; limit; encroach on; hurt. ущемле́ние pinching, jamming; limitation; hurting.

уще́рб detriment; loss; damage; prejudice. уще́рбный waning.

ущипну́ть (-ну́, -нёшь) *pf of* щипа́ть

Уэ́льс Wales. уэ́льский Welsh.

ую́т cosiness, comfort. ую́тный cosy, comfortable.

язви́мый vulnerable. язви́ть (-влю́) *pf*, уязвля́ть *impf* wound, hurt.

ясни́ть *pf*, ясня́ть *impf* understand, make out.

Ф

фа́брика factory. фабрика́нт manufacturer. фабрика́т finished product, manufactured product. фабрикова́ть *impf* (*pf* с~) fabricate, forge. фабри́чн|ый factory; manufacturing; factory-made; ~ая ма́рка, ~ое клеймо́ trade-mark.

фа́була plot, story.

фаго́т bassoon.

фа́за phase; stage.

фаза́н pheasant.

фа́зис phase.

файл (*comput*) file.

фа́кел torch, flare.

факс fax.

факси́миле *neut indecl* facsimile.

факт fact; **соверши́вшийся ~** fait accompli. **факти́чески** *adv* in fact; virtually. **факти́ческий** actual; real; virtual.

фа́ктор factor.

факту́ра texture; style, execution.

факультати́вный optional. **факульте́т** faculty, department.

фа́лда tail (*of coat*).

фальсифика́тор falsifier, forger. **фальсифика́ция** falsification; adulteration; forgery. **фальсифици́ровать** *impf & pf* falsify; forge; adulterate. **фальши́вить** (**-влю**) *impf* (*pf* **c~**) be a hypocrite; sing *or* play out of tune. **фальши́вка** forged document. **фальши́вый** false; spurious; forged; artificial; out of tune. **фальшь** deception; falseness.

фами́лия surname. **фамилья́рничать** be over-familiar. **фамилья́рность** (over-)familiarity. **фамилья́рный** (over-)familiar; unceremonious.

фанати́зм fanaticism. **фана́тик** fanatic.

фане́ра veneer; plywood.

фантазёр dreamer, visionary. **фантази́ровать** *impf* (*pf* **c~**) dream; make up, dream up; improvise. **фанта́зия** fantasy; fancy; imagination; whim. **фанта́стика** fiction, fantasy. **фантасти́ческий, фантасти́чный** fantastic.

фа́ра headlight.

фарао́н pharaoh; faro.

фарва́тер fairway, channel.

фармазо́н freemason.

фармаце́вт pharmacist.

фарс farce.

фа́ртук apron.

фарфо́р china; porcelain. **фарфо́ровый** china.

фарцо́вщик currency speculator.

фарш stuffing; minced meat. **фарширова́ть** *impf* (*pf* **за~**) stuff.

фаса́д façade.

фасова́ть *impf* (*pf* **рас~**) package.

фасо́ль kidney bean(s), French bean(s); haricot beans.

фасо́н cut; fashion; style; manner. **фасо́нный** shaped.

фата́ veil.

фатали́зм fatalism. **фата́льный** fatal.

фаши́зм Fascism. **фаши́ст** Fascist. **фаши́стский** Fascist.

фая́нс faience, pottery.

февра́ль (**-я́**) *m* February. **февра́льский** February.

федера́льный federal. **федера́ция** federation.

феери́ческий fairy-tale.

фейерве́рк firework(s).

фе́льдшер (*pl* **-а́**) **, -ши́ца** (*partly-qualified*) medical assistant.

фельето́н feuilleton, feature.

фемини́зм feminism. **феминисти́ческий, фемини́стский** feminist.

фен (hair-)dryer.

фено́мен phenomenon. **феномена́льный** phenomenal.

феода́л feudal lord. **феодали́зм** feudalism. **феода́льный** feudal.

ферзь (**-я́**) *m* queen.

фе́рма[1] farm.

фе́рма[2] girder, truss.

ферма́та (*mus*) pause.

ферме́нт ferment.

фе́рмер farmer.

фестива́ль *m* festival.

фетр felt. **фе́тровый** felt.

фехтова́льщик, -щица fencer. **фехтова́ние** fencing. **фехтова́ть** *impf* fence.

фе́я fairy.

фиа́лка violet.

фиа́ско *neut indecl* fiasco.

фи́бра fibre.

фигля́р buffoon.

фигу́ра figure; court-card; (chess) piece. **фигура́льный** figurative, metaphorical. **фигури́ровать** *impf* figure, appear. **фигури́ст, -и́стка** figure-skater. **фигу́рка** figurine, statuette; figure. **фигу́рный** figured; **~ое ката́ние** figure-skating.

фи́зик physicist. **фи́зика** physics. **физио́лог** physiologist. **физиологи́ческий** physiological. **физиоло́гия** physiology. **физионо́мия** physi-

ognomy; face, expression. **физио-
тера́пeвт** physiotherapist. **физи́-
ческий** physical; physics. **физкуль-
ту́ра** *abbr* P.E., gymnastics. **физ-
культу́рный** *abbr* gymnastic; athletic; ~ **зал** gymnasium.

фикса́ж fixer. **фикса́ция** fixing.
фикси́ровать *impf* & *pf* (*pf also*
за~) fix; record.

фикти́вный fictitious. ~ **брак** marriage of convenience. **фи́кция** fiction.

филантро́п philanthropist. **филан-
тро́пия** philanthropy.

филармо́ния philharmonic society;
concert hall.

филатели́ст philatelist.

филе́ *neut indecl* sirloin; fillet.

филиа́л branch.

фили́стер philistine.

фило́лог philologist. **филологи́че-
ский** philological. **филоло́гия** philology.

фило́соф philosopher. **филосо́фия**
philosophy. **филосо́фский** philosophical.

фильм film. **фильмоско́п** projector.

фильтр filter. **фильтрова́ть** *impf*
(*pf* **про~**) filter.

фина́л finale; final. **фина́льный**
final.

финанси́ровать *impf* & *pf* finance.
фина́нсовый financial. **фина́нсы**
(-ов) *pl* finance, finances.

фи́ник date.

фи́ниш finish; finishing post.

фи́нка Finn. **Финля́ндия** Finland.
финля́ндский Finnish. **финн** Finn.
фи́нский Finnish.

фиоле́товый violet.

фи́рма firm; company. **фи́рменное
блю́до** speciality of the house.

фисгармо́ния harmonium.

фити́ль (-я́) *m* wick; fuse.

флаг flag. **фла́гман** flagship.

флако́н bottle, flask.

фланг flank; wing.

фране́ль flannel.

флегмати́чный phlegmatic.

фле́йта flute.

фле́ксия inflexion. **флекти́вный**
inflected.

фли́гель (*pl* -я́) *m* wing; annexe.

флирт flirtation. **флиртова́ть** *impf*
flirt.

флома́стер felt-tip pen.

фло́ра flora.

флот fleet. **фло́тский** naval.

флю́гер (*pl* -á) weather-vane.

флюоресце́нтный fluorescent.

флюс[1] gumboil, abscess.

флюс[2] (*pl* -ы́) flux.

фля́га flask; churn. **фля́жка** flask.

фойе́ *neut indecl* foyer.

фо́кус[1] trick.

фо́кус[2] focus. **фокуси́ровать** *impf*
focus.

фо́кусник conjurer, juggler.

фолиа́нт folio.

фольга́ foil.

фолькло́р folklore.

фон background.

фона́рик small lamp; torch. **фона́р-
ный** lamp; ~ **столб** lamp-post. **фо-
на́рь** (-я́) *m* lantern; lamp; light.

фонд fund; stock; reserves.

фоне́тика phonetics. **фонети́че-
ский** phonetic.

фонта́н fountain.

форе́ль trout.

фо́рма form; shape; mould, cast; uniform. **форма́льность** formality.
форма́льный formal. **форма́т** format. **форма́ция** structure; stage; formation; mentality. **фо́рменный** uniform; proper, regular. **формирова́-
ние** forming; unit, formation. **фор-
мирова́ть** *impf* (*pf* **с~**) form; organize; ~**ся** form, develop. **формова́ть**
impf (*pf* **с~**) form, shape; mould,
cast.

фо́рмула formula. **формули́ровать**
impf & *pf* (*pf also* **с~**) formulate.
формулиро́вка formulation; wording; formula. **формуля́р** log-book;
library card.

форси́ровать *impf* & *pf* force; speed
up.

форсу́нка sprayer; injector.

фортепья́но *neut indecl* piano.

фо́рточка small hinged (window-)
pane.

форту́на fortune.

фо́рум forum.

фо́сфор phosphorus.

фо́то *neut indecl* photo(graph).

фото- *in comb* photo-, photo-electric.
фотоаппара́т camera. ~**бума́га**
photographic paper. ~**гени́чный**
photogenic. **фото́граф** photographer.

~графи́ровать *impf* (*pf* с~) photograph. **~графи́роваться** be photographed, have one's photograph taken. **~графи́ческий** photographic. **~гра́фия** photography; photograph; photographer's studio. **~ко́пия** photocopy. **~люби́тель** *m* amateur photographer. **~объекти́в** (camera) lens. **~репортёр** press photographer. **~хро́ника** news in pictures. **~элеме́нт** photoelectric cell.

фрагме́нт fragment.

фра́за sentence; phrase. **фразеоло́гия** phraseology.

фрак tail-coat, tails.

фракцио́нный fractional; factional. **фра́кция** fraction; faction.

франк franc.

франкмасо́н Freemason.

франт dandy.

Фра́нция France. **францу́женка** Frenchwoman. **францу́з** Frenchman. **францу́зский** French.

фрахт freight. **фрахтова́ть** *impf* (*pf* за~) charter.

фрега́т frigate.

фрезеро́вщик milling machine operator.

фре́ска fresco.

фронт (*pl* -ы́, -о́в) front. **фронтови́к** (-а́) front-line soldier. **фронтово́й** front(-line).

фронто́н pediment.

фрукт fruit. **фрукто́вый** fruit; ~ сад orchard.

фтор fluorine. **фто́ристый** fluorine; fluoride. ~ **ка́льций** calcium fluoride.

фу *int* ugh! oh!

фуга́нок (-нка) smoothing-plane.

фуга́с landmine. **фуга́сный** high-explosive.

фунда́мент foundation. **фундамента́льный** solid, sound; main; basic.

функциона́льный functional. **функциони́ровать** *impf* function. **фу́нкция** function.

фунт pound.

фура́ж (-а́) forage, fodder. **фура́жка** peaked cap, forage-cap.

фурго́н van; caravan.

фут foot; foot-rule. **футбо́л** football. **футболи́ст** footballer. **футбо́лка** football jersey, sports shirt. **футбо́льный** football; ~ **мяч** football.

футля́р case, container.

футури́зм futurism.

фуфа́йка jersey; sweater.

фы́ркать *impf*, **фы́ркнуть** (-ну) *pf* snort.

фюзеля́ж fuselage.

X

хала́т dressing-gown. **хала́тный** careless, negligent.

халту́ра pot-boiler; hackwork; money made on the side. **халту́рщик** hack.

хам boor, lout. **ха́мский** boorish, loutish. **ха́мство** boorishness, loutishness.

хамелео́н chameleon.

хан khan.

хандра́ depression. **хандри́ть** *impf* be depressed.

ханжа́ hypocrite. **ха́нжеский** sanctimonious, hypocritical.

хао́с chaos. **хаоти́чный** chaotic.

хара́ктер character. **характеризова́ть** *impf & pf* (*pf also* о~) describe; characterize; ~ся be characterized. **характери́стика** reference; description. **хара́ктерный** characteristic; distinctive; character.

ха́ркать *impf*, **ха́ркнуть** (-ну) *pf* spit.

ха́ртия charter.

ха́та peasant hut.

хвала́ praise. **хвале́бный** laudatory. **хвалёный** highly-praised. **хвали́ть** (-лю́, -лишь) *impf* (*pf* по~) praise; ~ся boast.

хва́стать(ся *impf* (*pf* по~) boast. **хвастли́вый** boastful. **хвастовство́** boasting. **хвасту́н** (-а́) boaster.

хвата́ть[1] *impf*, **хвати́ть** (-ачу́, -а́тишь) *pf* (*pf also* схвати́ть) snatch, seize; grab; ~ся remember; +gen realize the absence of; +за+acc snatch at, clutch at; take up.

хвата́ть[2] *impf*, **хвати́ть** (-а́тит) *pf*, *impers* (+gen) suffice, be enough; last out; вре́мени не хвата́ло there was not enough time; у нас не хвата́ет де́нег we haven't enough money; хва́тит! that will do!; э́того ещё не хвата́ло! that's all we needed! **хва́тка** grasp, grip; method; skill.

хво́йн|ый coniferous; ~ые *sb pl* conifers.

хвора́ть *impf* be ill.

хво́рост brushwood; (*pastry*) straws. хворости́на stick, switch.

хвост (-á) tail; tail-end. хво́стик tail. хвостово́й tail.

хво́я needle(s); (*coniferous*) branch(es).

херуви́м cherub.

хиба́р(к)а shack, hovel.

хи́жина shack, hut.

хи́лый (-л, -á, -о) sickly.

химе́ра chimera.

хи́мик chemist. химика́т chemical. хими́ческий chemical. хи́мия chemistry.

химчи́стка dry-cleaning; dry-cleaner's.

хи́на, хини́н quinine.

хиру́рг surgeon. хирурги́ческий surgical. хирурги́я surgery.

хитре́ц (-á) cunning person. хитри́ть *impf* (*pf* с~) use cunning, be crafty. хи́трость cunning; ruse; skill; intricacy. хи́трый (-тёр, -тра́, -о) cunning; skilful; intricate.

хихи́кать *impf*, хихи́кнуть (-ну) *pf* giggle, snigger.

хище́ние theft; embezzlement. хи́щник predator, bird or beast of prey. хи́щнический predatory. хи́щный predatory; rapacious; ~ые пти́цы birds of prey.

хладнокро́вие coolness, composure. хладнокро́вный cool, composed.

хлам rubbish.

хлеб (*pl* -ы, -ов *or* -á, -ов) bread; loaf; grain. хлеба́ть *impf*, хлебну́ть (-ну́, -нёшь) *pf* gulp down. хле́бный bread; baker's; grain. хлебозаво́д bakery. хлебопека́рня (*gen pl* -рен) bakery.

хлев (*loc* -ý; *pl* -á) cow-shed.

хлеста́ть (-ещу́, -е́щешь) *impf*, хлестну́ть (-ну́, -нёшь) *pf* lash; whip.

хлоп *int* bang! хло́пать *impf* (*pf* хло́пнуть) bang; slap; ~ (в ладо́ши) clap.

хлопково́дство cotton-growing. хло́пковый cotton.

хло́пнуть (-ну) *pf of* хло́пать

хлопо́к¹ (-пка́) clap.

хло́пок² (-пка) cotton.

хлопота́ть (-очу́, -о́чешь) *impf* (*pf* по~) busy o.s.; bustle about; take trouble; +о+*prep* or за+*acc* petition for. хлопотли́вый troublesome; exacting; busy, bustling. хло́поты (-о́т) *pl* trouble; efforts.

хлопчатобума́жный cotton.

хло́пья (-ьев) *pl* flakes.

хлор chlorine. хло́ристый, хло́рный chlorine; chloride. хло́рка bleach. хлорофи́лл chlorophyll. хлорофо́рм chloroform.

хлы́нуть (-нет) *pf* gush, pour.

хлыст (-á) whip, switch.

хмеле́ть (-е́ю) *impf* (*pf* за~, о~) get tipsy. хмель (-ю) *m* hop, hops; drunkenness; во хмелю́ tipsy. хмельно́й (-лён, -льна́) drunk; intoxicating.

хму́рить *impf* (*pf* на~): ~ бро́ви knit one's brows; ~ся frown; become gloomy; be overcast. хму́рый (-ур, -á, -о) gloomy; overcast.

хны́кать (-ычу or -аю) *impf* whimper, snivel.

хо́бби *neut indecl* hobby.

хо́бот trunk. хобото́к (-тка́) proboscis.

ход (*loc* -ý; *pl* -ы, -ов *or* -á, -ов) motion; going; speed; course; operation; stroke; move; manoeuvre; entrance; passage; в ~ý in demand; дать за́дний ~ reverse; дать ~ set in motion; на ~ý in transit, on the move; in motion; in operation; по́лным ~ом at full speed; пусти́ть в ~ start, set in motion; три часа́ ~y three hours' journey.

хода́тайство petitioning; application. хода́тайствовать *impf* (*pf* по~) petition, apply.

ходи́ть (хожу́, хо́дишь) *impf* walk; go; run; pass, go round; lead, play; move; +в+*prep* wear; +за+*instr* look after. хо́дкий (-док, -дка́, -о) fast; marketable; popular. ходьба́ walking; walk. ходя́чий walking; able to walk; popular; current.

хозрасчёт *abbr* (*of* хозя́йственный расчёт) self-financing system.

хозя́ин (*pl* -я́ева, -я́ев) owner, proprietor; master; boss; landlord; host; хозя́ева по́ля home team. хозя́йка owner; mistress; hostess; landlady. хозя́йничать *impf* keep house; be in charge; lord it. хозя́йственник financial manager. хозя́йственный economic; household; economical. хозя́йство economy; housekeeping;

equipment; farm; **дома́шнее** ~ housekeeping; **се́льское** ~ agriculture.

хокке́ист (ice-)hockey-player. **хокке́й** hockey, ice-hockey.

холе́ра cholera.

холестери́н cholesterol.

холл hall, vestibule.

холм (-á) hill. **холми́стый** hilly.

хо́лод (pl -á, -óв) cold; coldness; cold weather. **холоди́льник** refrigerator. **хо́лодно** adv coldly; coldness; **холодн|ый** (хо́лоден, -дна́, -о) cold; inadequate, thin; ~**ое ору́жие** cold steel.

холо́п serf.

холосто́й (хо́лост, -á) unmarried, single; bachelor; idle; blank. **холостя́к** (-á) bachelor.

холст (-á) canvas; linen.

холу́й (-луя́) m lackey.

хому́т (-á) (horse-)collar; burden.

хомя́к (-á) hamster.

хор (pl хо́ры) choir; chorus.

хорва́т, ~**ка** Croat. **Хорва́тия** Croatia. **хорва́тский** Croatian.

хорёк (-рька́) polecat.

хореографи́ческий choreographic. **хореогра́фия** choreography.

хори́ст member of a choir or chorus.

хорони́ть (-ню́, -нишь) impf (pf за~, по~, с~) bury.

хоро́шенький pretty; nice. **хоро́шенько** adv properly, thoroughly. **хороше́ть** (-е́ю) impf (pf по~) grow prettier. **хоро́ший** (-óш, -á, -о) good; nice; pretty, nice-looking; **хорошо́** predic it is good; it is nice. **хорошо́** adv well; nicely; all right! good.

хо́ры (хор or -ов) pl gallery.

хоте́ть (хочу́, хо́чешь, хоти́м) impf (pf за~) wish; +gen, acc want; ~ **пить** be thirsty; **наприме́р**; ~ **бы** if only, for example; ~ **сказа́ть** mean; ~**ся** impers +dat want; **мне хоте́лось бы** I should like; **мне хо́чется** I want.

хоть conj although; even if; partl at least, if only; for example; ~ **бы** if only. **хотя́** conj although; ~ **бы** even if; if only.

хо́хот loud laugh(ter). **хохота́ть** (-очу́, -о́чешь) impf laugh loudly.

хочу́ etc.: see **хоте́ть**

храбре́ц (-á) brave man. **храбри́ться** make a show of bravery; pluck up courage. **хра́брость** brav-

ery. **хра́брый** brave.

храм temple, church.

хране́ние keeping; storage; **ка́мера хране́ния** cloakroom, left-luggage office. **храни́лище** storehouse, depository. **храни́тель** m keeper, custodian; curator. **храни́ть** impf keep; preserve; ~**ся** be, be kept.

храпе́ть (-плю́) impf snore; snort.

хребе́т (-бта́) spine; (mountain) range; ridge.

хрен horseradish.

хрестома́тия reader.

хрип wheeze. **хрипе́ть** (-плю́) impf wheeze. **хри́плый** (-пл, -á, -о) hoarse. **хри́пнуть** (-ну; хрип) impf (pf о~) become hoarse. **хрипота́** hoarseness.

христиани́н (pl -а́не, -а́н), **христиа́нка** Christian. **христиа́нский** Christian. **христиа́нство** Christianity. **Христо́с** (-иста́) Christ.

хром chromium; chrome.

хромати́ческий chromatic.

хрома́ть impf limp; be poor. **хромо́й** (хром, -á, -о) lame; sb lame person.

хромосо́ма chromosome.

хромота́ lameness.

хро́ник chronic invalid. **хро́ника** chronicle; news items; newsreel. **хрони́ческий** chronic.

хронологи́ческий chronological. **хроноло́гия** chronology.

хру́пкий (-пок, -пка́, -о) fragile; frail. **хру́пкость** fragility; frailness.

хруст crunch; crackle.

хруста́ль (-я́) m cut glass; crystal. **хруста́льный** cut-glass; crystal; crystal-clear.

хрусте́ть (-ущу́) impf, **хру́стнуть** (-ну) pf crunch; crackle.

хрю́кать impf, **хрю́кнуть** (-ну) pf grunt.

хрящ (-á) cartilage, gristle. **хряще**в**о́й** cartilaginous, gristly.

худе́ть (-е́ю) impf (pf по~) grow thin.

ху́до harm; evil. **ху́до** adv ill, badly. **худоба́** thinness.

худо́жественный art, arts; artistic; ~ **фильм** feature film. **худо́жник** artist.[1]

худо́й[1] (худ, -á, -о) thin, lean.

худо́й[2] (худ, -á, -о) bad; full of holes; worn; **ему́ ху́до** he feels bad.

худоща́вый thin, lean.

ху́дший *superl of* **худо́й**, **плохо́й** (the) worst. **ху́же** *comp of* **худо́й**, **ху́до**, **плохо́й**, **пло́хо** worse.

хула́ abuse, criticism.

хулига́н hooligan. **хулига́нить** *impf* behave like a hooligan. **хулига́нство** hooliganism.

ху́нта junta.

ху́тор (*pl* -á) farm; small village.

Ц

ца́пля (*gen pl* -пель) heron.

цара́пать *impf*, **цара́пнуть** (-ну) *pf* (*pf also* на~, о~) scratch; scribble; ~ся scratch; scratch one another. **цара́пина** scratch.

цари́зм tsarism. **цари́ть** *impf* reign, prevail. **цари́ца** tsarina; queen. **ца́рский** tsar's; royal; tsarist; regal. **ца́рство** kingdom; realm; reign. **ца́рствование** reign. **ца́рствовать** *impf* reign. **царь** (-я́) *m* tsar; king.

цвести́ (-ету́, -ете́шь; -ёл, -á) *impf* flower, blossom; flourish.

цвет[1] (*pl* -á) colour; ~ лица́ complexion.

цвет[2] (*loc* -у́; *pl* -ы́) flower; prime; в цвету́ in blossom. **цветни́к** (-á) flower-bed, flower-garden.

цвет|**о́й** coloured; colour; non-ferrous; ~**ая капу́ста** cauliflower; ~**ое стекло́** stained glass.

цветово́й colour; ~**ая слепота́** colour-blindness.

цвето́к (-тка́; *pl* цветы́ *or* цветки́, -óв) flower. **цвето́чный** flower.

цвету́щий flowering; prosperous.

цеди́ть (цежу́, це́дишь) *impf* strain, filter.

целе́бный curative, healing.

целево́й earmarked for a specific purpose. **целенапра́вленный** purposeful. **целесообра́зный** expedient. **целеустремлённый** (-ён, -ённа *or* -ена́) purposeful.

целико́м *adv* whole; entirely.

целина́ virgin lands, virgin soil. **цели́нн**|**ый** virgin; ~**ые зе́мли** virgin lands.

цели́тельный healing, medicinal.

це́лить(ся *impf* (*pf* на~) aim, take aim.

целлофа́н cellophane.

целова́ть *impf* (*pf* по~) kiss; ~ся kiss.

це́лое *sb* whole; integer. **целому́дренный** chaste. **целому́дрие** chastity. **це́лостность** integrity. **це́лый** (цел, -á, -o) whole; safe, intact.

цель target; aim, object, goal.

це́льный (-лен, -льна́, -o) of one piece, solid; whole; integral; single. **це́льность** wholeness.

цеме́нт cement. **цементи́ровать** *impf & pf* cement. **цеме́нтный** cement.

цена́ (*acc* -у; *pl* -ы) price, cost; worth.

цензь qualification. **це́нзор** censor. **цензу́ра** censorship.

цени́тель *m* judge, connoisseur. **цени́ть** (-ню́, -нишь) *impf* value; appreciate. **це́нность** value; price; *pl* valuables; values. **це́нный** valuable.

цент cent. **це́нтнер** centner (*100kg*).

центр centre. **централиза́ция** centralization. **централизова́ть** *impf & pf* centralize. **центра́льный** central.

центробе́жный centrifugal.

цепене́ть (-е́ю) *impf* (*pf* o~) freeze; become rigid. **це́пкий** tenacious; prehensile; sticky; obstinate. **це́пкость** tenacity. **цепля́ться** *impf* за+*acc* clutch at; cling to.

цепно́й chain. **цепо́чка** chain; file. **цепь** (*loc* -и́; *gen pl* -éй) chain; series; circuit.

церемо́ниться *impf* (*pf* по~) stand on ceremony. **церемо́ния** ceremony. **церковнославя́нский** Church Slavonic. **церко́вный** church; ecclesiastical. **це́рковь** (-кви; *gen pl* -éй) church.

цех (*loc* -у́; *pl* -и *or* -á) shop; section; guild.

цивилиза́ция civilization. **цивилизо́ванный** civilized. **цивилизова́ть** *impf & pf* civilize.

циге́йка beaver lamb.

цикл cycle.

цико́рий chicory.

цили́ндр cylinder; top hat. **цилиндри́ческий** cylindrical.

цимба́лы (-áл) *pl* cymbals.

цинга́ scurvy.

цини́зм cynicism. **ци́ник** cynic. **цини́чный** cynical.

цинк zinc. **ци́нковый** zinc.

цино́вка mat.

цирк circus.

циркули́ровать *impf* circulate. **ци́ркуль** *m* (pair of) compasses; dividers. **циркуля́р** circular. **циркуля́ция** circulation.

цисте́рна cistern, tank.

цитаде́ль citadel.

цита́та quotation. **цити́ровать** *impf* (*pf* про~) quote.

ци́трус citrus. **ци́трусов|ый** citrous; ~ые *sb pl* citrus plants.

цифербла́т dial, face.

ци́фра figure; number, numeral. **цифрово́й** numerical, digital.

цо́коль *m* socle, plinth.

цыга́н (*pl* -е, -а́н *or* -ы, -ов), **цыга́нка** gipsy. **цыга́нский** gipsy.

цыплёнок (-нка *pl* -ля́та, -ля́т) chicken; chick.

цы́почки: на ~, на цы́почках on tiptoe.

Ч

чаба́н (-а́) shepherd.

чад (*loc* -у́) fumes, smoke.

чадра́ yashmak.

чай (*pl* -и́, -ёв) tea. **чаевы́е** (-ы́х) *sb pl* tip.

ча́йка (*gen pl* ча́ек) (sea-)gull.

ча́йная *sb* tea-shop. **ча́йник** teapot; kettle. **ча́йный** tea. **чайхана́** teahouse.

чалма́ turban.

чан (*loc* -у́, *pl* -ы́) vat, tub.

чарова́ть *impf* bewitch; charm.

час (*with numerals* -а́, *loc* -у́, *pl* -ы́) hour; *pl* guard-duty; кото́рый час? what's the time?; ~ one o'clock; в два ~а́ at two o'clock; стоя́ть на ~а́х stand guard; ~ы́ пик rush-hour.

часо́вня (*gen pl* -вен) chapel. **часово́й** *sb* sentry. **часово́й** clock, watch; of one hour, hour-long. **часовщи́к** (-а́) watchmaker.

части́ца small part; particle. **части́чно** *adv* partly, partially. **части́чный** partial.

ча́стник private trader.

ча́стность detail; в ча́стности in particular. **ча́стный** private; personal; particular, individual.

ча́сто *adv* often; close, thickly. **частоко́л** paling, palisade. **частота́** (*pl* -ы)

frequency. **часто́тный** frequency.

часту́шка ditty. **ча́стый** (част, -а́, -о) frequent; close (together); dense; close-woven; rapid.

часть (*gen pl* -е́й) part; department; field; unit.

часы́ (-о́в) *pl* clock, watch.

ча́хлый stunted; sickly, puny. **чахо́тка** consumption.

ча́ша bowl; chalice; ~ весо́в scale, pan. **ча́шка** cup; scale, pan.

ча́ща thicket.

ча́ще *comp of* ча́сто, ча́стый; ~ всего́ most often, mostly.

ча́яние expectation; hope. **ча́ять** (ча́ю) *impf* hope, expect.

чва́нство conceit, arrogance.

чего́ *see* что

чей *m*, **чья** *f*, **чьё** *neut*, **чьи** *pl pron* whose. **чей-либо**, **чей-нибудь** anyone's. **чей-то** someone's.

чек cheque; bill; receipt.

чека́нить *impf* (*pf* вы~, от~) mint, coin; stamp, engrave; enunciate. **чека́нка** coinage, minting. **чека́нный** stamping, engraving; stamped, engraved; precise, expressive.

чёлка fringe; forelock.

чёлн (-а́; *pl* чёлны) dug-out (canoe); boat. **челно́к** (-а́) dug-out (canoe); shuttle.

челове́к (*pl* лю́ди; *with numerals*, *gen* -ве́к, -а́м) man, person.

челове́ко- *in comb* man-, anthropo-. **человеколюби́вый** philanthropy. **~лю́бие** philanthropy. **~ненави́стнический** misanthropic. **человеко-ча́с** (-ы́) man-hour.

челове́чек (-чка) little man. **челове́ческий** human; humane. **челове́чество** mankind. **челове́чность** humaneness. **челове́чный** humane.

че́люсть jaw(-bone); dentures, false teeth.

чем, **чём** *see* что. **чем** *conj* than; ~..., тем...+*comp* the more ..., the more.

чемода́н suitcase.

чемпио́н, ~ка champion, title-holder. **чемпиона́т** championship.

чему́ *see* что

чепуха́ nonsense; trifle.

че́пчик cap; bonnet.

че́рви (-е́й), **че́рвы** (черв) *pl* hearts. **черво́нн|ый** of hearts; ~ое зо́лото pure gold.

червь (-я́; *pl* -и, -е́й) *m* worm; bug. червя́к (-а́) worm.

черда́к (-а́) attic, loft.

черёд (-а́, *loc* -ý) turn; идти́ свои́м ~о́м take its course. чередова́ние alternation. чередова́ть *impf* alternate; ~ся alternate, take turns.

че́рез, чрез *prep+acc* across; over; through; via; in; after; every other.

черёмуха bird cherry.

черено́к (-нка́) handle; graft, cutting. че́реп (*pl* -á) skull.

черепа́ха tortoise; turtle; tortoise-shell. черепа́ховый tortoise; turtle; tortoiseshell. черепа́ший tortoise, turtle; very slow. черепи́ца tile. черепи́чный tile; tiled. черепо́к (-пка́) potsherd, fragment of pottery.

чересчу́р *adv* too; too much.

чере́шневый cherry. чере́шня (*gen pl* -шен) cherry(-tree).

черке́с, черке́шенка Circassian.

черкну́ть (-ну́, -нёшь) *pf* scrape; leave a mark on; scribble.

черне́ть (-е́ю) *impf* (*pf* по~) turn black; show black. черни́ка (*no pl*; *usu collect*) bilberry; bilberries. черни́ла (-и́л) *pl* ink. черни́льный ink. черни́ть (*pf* о~) blacken; slander. черно- *in comb* black; unskilled; rough. чёрно-бе́лый black-and-white. ~бу́рый dark-brown; ~бу́рая лиса́ silver fox. ~воло́сый black-haired. ~гла́зый black-eyed. ~зём chernozem, black earth. ~ко́жий black; *sb* black. ~мо́рский Black-Sea. ~рабо́чий *sb* unskilled worker, labourer. ~сли́в prunes. ~сморо́динный blackcurrant.

чернови́к (-а́) rough copy, draft. черново́й rough; draft. чернота́ blackness; darkness. чёрн|ый (-рен, -рна́) black; back; unskilled; ferrous; gloomy; *sb* (*derog*) black person; ~ая сморо́дина (*no pl*; *usu collect*) black-currant(s).

черпа́к (-а́) scoop. че́рпать *impf*, черпну́ть (-ну́, -нёшь) *pf* draw; scoop; extract.

черстве́ть (-е́ю) *impf* (*pf* за~, о~, по~) get stale; become hardened. чёрствый (чёрств, -á, -о) stale; hard.

чёрт (*pl* че́рти, -е́й) devil.

черта́ line; boundary; trait, characteristic. чертёж (-á) drawing; blueprint, plan. чертёжник draughtsman. чертёжный drawing. черти́ть (-рчу́, -ртишь) *impf* (*pf* на~) draw.

чёртов *adj* devil's; devilish. черто́вский devilish.

чертополо́х thistle.

чёрточка line; hyphen. черче́ние drawing. черчу́ *etc.*: *see* черти́ть

чеса́ть (чешу́, -шешь) *impf* (*pf* по~) scratch; comb; card; ~ся scratch o.s.; itch; comb one's hair.

чесно́к (-á) garlic.

че́ствование celebration. че́ствовать *impf* celebrate; honour. че́стность honesty. че́стный (-тен, -тна́, -о) honest. честолюби́вый ambitious. честолю́бие ambition. честь (*loc* -и́) honour; отда́ть ~ +*dat* salute. чета́ pair, couple.

четве́рг (-а́) Thursday. четверё́ньки: на ~, на четверё́ньках on hands and knees. четвё́рка four; figure 4; No. 4. че́тверо (-ы́х) four. четвероно́г|ий four-legged; ~ое *sb* quadruped. четверости́шие quatrain. четвё́ртый fourth. че́тверть (*gen pl* -е́й) quarter; quarter of an hour; без че́тверти час a quarter to one. четверть-фина́л quarter-final.

чё́ткий (-ток, -тка́, -о) precise; clear-cut; clear; distinct. чё́ткость precision; clarity; distinctness.

чё́тный even.

четы́ре (-рёх, -рьмя́, -рёх) four. четы́реста (-рёхсо́т, -ьмяста́ми, -ёхста́х) four hundred.

четырёх- *in comb* four-, tetra-. четырёхкра́тный fourfold. ~ме́стный four-seater. ~со́тый four-hundredth. ~уго́льник quadrangle. ~уго́льный quadrangular. четы́рнадцатый fourteenth. четы́рнадцать fourteen.

чех Czech.

чехо́л (-хла́) cover, case.

чечеви́ца lentil; lens.

че́шка (-шек), че́шский Czech.

чешу́ *etc.*: *see* чеса́ть

чешу́йка scale. чешуя́ scales.

чиж (-а́) siskin.

чин (*pl* -ы́) rank.

чини́ть[1] (-ню́, -нишь) *impf* (*pf* по~) repair, mend.

чини́ть[2] *impf* (*pf* y~) carry out; cause; ~ **препя́тствия** +*dat* put obstacles in the way of.

чино́вник civil servant; official.

чип (micro)chip.

чи́псы (-ов) *pl* (potato) crisps.

чири́кать *impf*, **чири́кнуть** (-ну) *pf* chirp.

чи́ркать *impf*, **чи́ркнуть** (-ну) *pf* +*instr* strike.

чи́сленность numbers; strength. **чи́сленный** numerical. **числи́тель** *m* numerator. **числи́тельное** *sb* numeral. **чи́слить** *impf* count, reckon; ~ся be; +*instr* be reckoned. **число́** (*pl* -а, -сел) number; date, day; **в числе́** +*gen* among; **в том числе́** including; **еди́нственное** ~ singular; **мно́жественное** ~ plural. **числово́й** numerical.

чисти́лище purgatory.

чи́стильщик cleaner. **чи́стить** (чи́щу) *impf* (*pf* вы́~, о~, по~) clean; peel; clear. **чи́стка** cleaning; purge. **чи́сто** *adv* cleanly, clean; purely; completely. **чистово́й** fair, clean. **чистокро́вный** thoroughbred. **чистописа́ние** calligraphy. **чистопло́тный** clean; decent. **чистосерде́чный** frank, sincere. **чистота́** cleanness; neatness; purity. **чи́стый** clean; neat; pure; complete. **чита́емый** widely-read, popular. **чита́льный** reading. **чита́тель** *m* reader. **чита́ть** *impf* (*pf* про~, прочесть) read; recite; ~ **ле́кции** lecture; ~ся be legible; be discernible. **чи́тка** reading.

чиха́ть *impf*, **чихну́ть** (-ну́, -нёшь) *pf* sneeze.

чи́ще *comp of* **чи́сто, чи́стый**

чи́щу *etc.*: *see* **чи́стить**

член member; limb; term; part; article. **члени́ть** *impf* (*pf* рас~) articulate. **член-корреспонде́нт** corresponding member, associate. **членоразде́льный** articulate. **чле́нский** membership. **чле́нство** membership.

чмо́кать *impf*, **чмо́кнуть** (-ну) *pf* smack; squelch; kiss noisily; ~ **губа́ми** smack one's lips.

чо́каться *impf*, **чо́кнуться** (-нусь) *pf* clink glasses.

чо́порный prim; stand-offish.

чрева́тый +*instr* fraught with. **чре́во** belly, womb. **чревовеща́тель** *m* ventriloquist. **чревоуго́дие** gluttony.

чрез *see* **че́рез. чрезвыча́йный** extraordinary; extreme; ~ое положе́ние state of emergency. **чрезме́рный** excessive.

чте́ние reading. **чтец** (-а́) reader; reciter.

чтить (чту) *impf* honour.

что, чего́, чему́, чем, о чём *pron* what?; how?; why?; how much?; which, what, who; anything; **в чём де́ло?** what is the matter? **для чего́?** what ... for? why?; ~ **ему́ до э́того?** what does it matter to him?; ~ **с тобо́й?** what's the matter (with you)?; ~ **за** what? what sort of?; what (a) ..!; **что** *conj* that. **что (бы) ни** *pron* whatever, no matter what.

чтоб, что́бы *conj* in order (to), so as; that; to. **что́-либо, что́-нибудь** *prons* anything. **что́-то**[1] *pron* something. **что́-то**[2] *adv* somewhat, slightly; somehow, for some reason.

чу́вственность sensuality. **чувстви́тельность** sensitivity; perceptibility; sentimentality. **чувстви́тельный** sensitive; perceptible; sentimental. **чу́вство** feeling; sense; senses; **прийти́ в** ~ come round. **чу́вствовать** *impf* (*pf* по~) feel; realize; appreciate; ~ся be perceptible; make itself felt.

чугу́н (-а́) cast iron. **чугу́нный** cast-iron.

чуда́к (-а́), **чуда́чка** eccentric, crank. **чуда́чество** eccentricity.

чудеса́ *etc.*: *see* **чу́до. чуде́сный** miraculous; wonderful.

чу́диться (-ишься) *impf* (*pf* по~, при~) seem.

чу́дно *adv* wonderfully; wonderful! **чудно́й** (-дён, -дна́) odd, strange. **чу́дный** wonderful; magical. **чу́до** (*pl* -деса́) miracle; wonder. **чудо́вище** monster. **чудо́вищный** monstrous. **чудоде́йственный** miracle-working; miraculous. **чу́дом** *adv* miraculously. **чудотво́рный** miracle-working, miraculous.

чужби́на foreign land. **чужда́ться** *impf* +*gen* avoid; stand aloof from. **чу́ждый** (-жд, -а́, -о) alien (to); +*gen* free from, devoid of. **чужезе́мец** (-мца), **-зе́мка** foreigner. **чужезе́м-**

ный foreign. **чужо́й** someone else's, others'; strange, alien; foreign.

чула́н store-room; larder.

чуло́к (-лка́; gen pl -ло́к) stocking.

чума́ plague.

чума́зый dirty.

чурба́н block. **чу́рка** block, lump.

чу́ткий (-ток, -тка́, -о) keen; sensitive; sympathetic; delicate. **чу́ткость** keenness; delicacy.

чу́точка: ни чу́точки not in the least; **чу́точку** a little (bit).

чу́тче comp of чу́ткий

чуть adv hardly; just; very slightly; ~ не almost; ~-чуть a tiny bit.

чутьё scent; flair.

чу́чело stuffed animal, stuffed bird; scarecrow.

чушь nonsense.

чу́ять (чу́ю) impf scent; sense.

чьё etc.: see чей

Ш

ша́баш sabbath.

шабло́н template; mould, stencil; cliché. **шабло́нный** stencil; trite; stereotyped.

шаг (with numerals -а́, loc -у́; pl -и́) step; footstep; pace. **шага́ть** impf, **шагну́ть** (-ну́, -нёшь) pf step; stride; pace; make progress. **ша́гом** adv at walking pace.

ша́йба washer; puck.

ша́йка¹ tub.

ша́йка² gang, band.

шака́л jackal.

шала́ш (-а́) cabin, hut.

шали́ть impf be naughty; play up. **шаловли́вый** mischievous, playful. **ша́лость** prank; pl mischief. **шалу́н** (-а́), **шалу́нья** (gen pl -ний) naughty child.

шаль shawl.

шально́й mad, crazy.

ша́мкать impf mumble.

шампа́нское sb champagne.

шампиньо́н field mushroom.

шампу́нь m shampoo.

шанс chance.

шанта́ж (-а́) blackmail. **шантажи́ровать** impf blackmail.

ша́пка hat; banner headline. **ша́почка** hat.

шар (with numerals -а́; pl -ы́) sphere; ball; balloon.

шара́хать impf, **шара́хнуть** (-ну) hit; ~ся dash; shy.

шарж caricature.

ша́рик ball; corpuscle. **ша́риков|ый:** ~ая (а́вто)ру́чка ball-point pen; ~ый подши́пник ball-bearing. **шарикоподши́пник** ball-bearing.

ша́рить impf grope; sweep.

ша́ркать impf, **ша́ркнуть** (-ну) pf shuffle; scrape.

шарлата́н charlatan.

шарма́нка barrel-organ. **шарма́нщик** organ-grinder.

шарни́р hinge, joint.

шарова́ры (-а́р) pl (wide) trousers.

шарови́дный spherical. **шарово́й** ball; globular. **шарообра́зный** spherical.

шарф scarf.

шасси́ neut indecl chassis.

шата́ть impf rock, shake; impers +acc его́ шата́ет he is reeling; ~ся sway; reel, stagger; come loose, be loose; be unsteady; loaf about.

шатёр (-тра́) tent; marquee.

ша́ткий unsteady; shaky.

шату́н (-а́) connecting-rod.

ша́фер (pl -а́) best man.

шах check; и мат checkmate. **шахмати́ст** chess-player. **ша́хматы** (-ат) pl chess; chessmen.

ша́хта mine, pit; shaft. **шахтёр** miner. **шахтёрский** miner's; mining.

ша́шка¹ draught; pl draughts.

ша́шка² sabre.

шашлы́к (-а́) kebab; barbecue.

шва etc.: see шов

шва́бра mop.

шваль rubbish; riff-raff.

шварто́в mooring-line; pl moorings. **швартова́ть** impf (pf при~) moor; ~ся moor.

швед, ~ка Swede. **шве́дский** Swedish.

шве́йн|ый sewing; ~ая маши́на sewing-machine.

швейца́р porter, doorman.

швейца́рец (-рца), **-ца́рка** Swiss. Швейца́рия Switzerland. **швейца́рский** Swiss.

Шве́ция Sweden.

швея́ seamstress.

швырну́ть (-ну́, -нёшь) pf, **швыря́ть**

impf throw, fling; ~ся +*instr* throw (about); treat carelessly.

шевели́ть (-елю́, -е́лишь) *impf*, шевельну́ть (-ну́, -нёшь) *pf* (*pf also* по~) (+*instr*) move, stir; ~ся move, stir.

шеде́вр masterpiece.

ше́йка (*gen pl* ше́ек) neck.

шёл *see* идти́

ше́лест rustle. шелесте́ть (-сти́шь) *impf* rustle.

шёлк (*loc* -ý, *pl* -á) silk. шелкови́стый silky. шелкови́ца mulberry (-tree). шелкови́чный mulberry; ~ червь silkworm. шёлковый silk.

шелохну́ть (-ну́, -нёшь) *pf* stir, agitate; ~ся stir, move.

шелуха́ skin; peelings; pod. шелуши́ть (-шу́) peel; shell; ~ся peel (off), flake off.

шепеля́вить (-влю) *impf* lisp. шепеля́вый lisping.

шепну́ть (-ну́, -нёшь) *pf*, шепта́ть (-пчу́, -пчешь) *impf* whisper; ~ся whisper (together). шёпот whisper. шёпотом *adv* in a whisper.

шере́нга rank; file.

шерохова́тый rough; uneven.

шерсть wool; hair, coat. шерстяно́й wool(len).

шерша́вый rough.

шест (-á) pole; staff.

ше́ствие procession. ше́ствовать process; march.

шестёрка six; figure 6; No. 6.

шестерня́ (*gen pl* -рён) gear-wheel, cogwheel.

ше́стеро (-ы́х) six.

шести- *in comb* six-, hexa-, sex(i)-. шестигра́нник hexahedron. ~дне́вка six-day (*working*) week. ~деся́тый sixtieth. ~ме́сячный six-month; six-month-old. ~со́тый six-hundredth. ~уго́льник hexagon.

шестнадцатиле́тний sixteen-year; sixteen-year-old. шестна́дцатый sixteenth. шестна́дцать sixteen. шесто́й sixth. шесть (-и́, *instr* -ью́) six. шестьдеся́т (-и́десяти, *instr* -ью́десятью) sixty. шестьсо́т (-исо́т, -иста́м, -ьюста́ми, -иста́х) six hundred. ше́стью *adv* six times.

шеф boss, chief; patron, sponsor. шеф-по́вар chef. ше́фство patronage, adoption. ше́фствовать *impf*

+над+*instr* adopt; sponsor.

ше́я neck.

ши́ворот collar.

шика́рный chic, smart; splendid.

ши́ло (*pl* -ья, -ьев) awl.

шимпанзе́ *m indecl* chimpanzee.

ши́на tyre; splint.

шине́ль overcoat.

шинкова́ть *impf* shred, chop.

ши́нный tyre.

шип (-á) thorn, spike, crampon; pin; tenon.

шипе́ние hissing; sizzling. шипе́ть (-плю́) *impf* hiss; sizzle; fizz.

шипо́вник dog-rose.

шипу́чий sparkling; fizzy. шипу́чка fizzy drink. шипя́щий sibilant.

ши́ре *comp of* широ́кий, широко́. ширина́ width; gauge. ши́рить *impf* extend, expand; ~ся spread, extend.

ши́рма screen.

широ́к|ий (-о́к, -á, -о́ко́) wide, broad; това́ры ~ого потребле́ния consumer goods. широко́ *adv* wide, widely, broadly.

широко- *in comb* wide-, broad-. широковеща́ние broadcasting. ~веща́тельный broadcasting. ~экра́нный wide-screen.

широта́ (*pl* -ы) width, breadth; latitude. широ́тный of latitude; latitudinal. широча́йший *superl of* широ́кий. ширпотре́б *abbr* consumption; consumer goods. ширь (wide) expanse.

шить (шью, шьёшь) *impf* (*pf* с~) sew; make; embroider. шитьё sewing; embroidery.

ши́фер slate.

шифр cipher, code; shelf-mark. шифро́ванный in cipher, coded. шифрова́ть *impf* (*pf* за~) encipher. шифро́вка enciphering; coded communication.

ши́шка cone; bump; lump; (*sl*) big shot.

шкала́ (*pl* -ы) scale; dial.

шкату́лка box, casket, case.

шкаф (*loc* -ý; *pl* -ы́) cupboard; wardrobe. шка́фчик cupboard, locker.

шквал squall.

шкив (*pl* -ы́) pulley.

шко́ла school. шко́льник schoolboy. шко́льница schoolgirl. шко́льный school.

шку́ра skin, hide, pelt. шку́рка skin; rind; emery paper, sandpaper.

шла *see* идти́

шлагба́ум barrier.

шлак slag; dross; clinker. шлако-бло́к breeze-block.

шланг hose.

шлейф train.

шлем helmet.

шлёпать *impf*, шлёпнуть (-ну) *pf* smack, spank; shuffle; tramp; ~ся fall flat, plop down.

шли *see* идти́

шлифова́льный polishing; grinding. шлифова́ть *impf* (*pf* от~) polish; grind. шлифо́вка polishing.

шло *see* идти́. шлю *etc.*: *see* слать

шлюз lock, sluice.

шлю́пка boat.

шля́па hat. шля́пка hat; head.

шмель (-я́) *m* bumble-bee.

шмон *sl* search, frisking.

шмы́гать *impf*, шмы́гнуть (-ыгну́, -ыгнёшь) *pf* dart, rush; +*instr* rub, brush; ~ но́сом sniff.

шни́цель *m* schnitzel.

шнур (-а́) cord; lace; flex, cable. шнурова́ть *impf* (*pf* за~, про~) lace up; tie. шнуро́к (-рка́) lace.

шов (шва) seam; stitch; joint.

шовини́зм chauvinism. шовини́ст chauvinist. шовинисти́ческий chauvinistic.

шок shock. шоки́ровать *impf* shock.

шокола́д chocolate. шокола́дка chocolate, bar of chocolate. шокола́дный chocolate.

шо́рох rustle.

шо́рты (шорт) *pl* shorts.

шо́ры (шор) *pl* blinkers.

шоссе́ *neut indecl* highway.

шотла́ндец (-дца) Scotsman, Scot. Шотла́ндия Scotland. шотла́ндка[1] Scotswoman. шотла́ндка[2] tartan. шотла́ндский Scottish, Scots.

шофёр driver; chauffeur. шофёрский driver's; driving.

шпа́га sword.

шпага́т cord; twine; string; splits.

шпаклева́ть (-лю́ю) *impf* (*pf* за~) caulk; fill, putty. шпаклёвка filling, puttying; putty.

шпа́ла sleeper.

шпана́ (*sl*) hooligan(s); riff-raff.

шпарга́лка crib.

шпа́рить *impf* (*pf* о~) scald.

шпат spar.

шпиль *m* spire; capstan. шпи́лька hairpin; hat-pin; tack; stiletto heel.

шпина́т spinach.

шпингале́т (vertical) bolt; catch, latch.

шпио́н spy. шпиона́ж espionage. шпио́нить *impf* spy (за+*instr* on). шпио́нский spy's; espionage.

шпо́ра spur.

шприц syringe.

шпро́та sprat.

шпу́лька spool, bobbin.

шрам scar.

шрапне́ль shrapnel.

шрифт (*pl* -ы́) type, print.

шт. *abbr* (*of* шту́ка) item, piece.

штаб (*pl* -ы́) staff; headquarters.

шта́бель (*pl* -я́) *m* stack.

штабно́й staff; headquarters.

штамп die, punch; stamp; cliché. штампо́ванный punched, stamped, pressed; trite; hackneyed.

шта́нга bar, rod, beam; weight. штангист weight-lifter.

штани́шки (-шек) *pl* (*child's*) shorts. штаны́ (-о́в) trousers.

штат[1] State.

штат[2], шта́ты (-ов) *pl* staff, establishment.

штати́в tripod, base, stand.

шта́тный staff; established.

шта́тск|ий civilian; ~ое (пла́тье) civilian clothes; ~ий *sb* civilian.

ште́мпель (*pl* -я́) *m* stamp; почто́вый ~ postmark.

ште́псель (*pl* -я́) *m* plug, socket.

штиль *m* calm.

штифт (-а́) pin, dowel.

што́льня (*gen pl* -лен) gallery.

што́пать *impf* (*pf* за~) darn. што́пка darning; darning wool.

што́пор corkscrew; spin.

што́ра blind.

шторм gale.

штраф fine. штрафно́й penal; penalty. штрафова́ть *impf* (*pf* о~) fine.

штрих (-а́) stroke; feature. штрихова́ть *impf* (*pf* за~) shade, hatch.

штуди́ровать *impf* (*pf* про~) study.

шту́ка item, one; piece; trick.

штукату́р plasterer. штукату́рить *impf* (*pf* от~, о~) plaster. штукату́рка plastering; plaster.

штурва́л (steering-)wheel, helm.

штурм storm, assault.

шту́рман (*pl* -ы *or* -á) navigator.

штурмова́ть *impf* storm, assault. штурмов|о́й assault; storming; ~áя авиáция ground-attack aircraft. штурмовщи́на rushed work.

шту́чный piece, by the piece.

штык (-á) bayonet.

штырь (-я́) *m* pintle, pin.

шýба fur coat.

шýлер (*pl* -á) card-sharper.

шум noise; uproar, racket; stir. шумéть (-млю́) *impf* make a noise; row; make a fuss. шýмный (-мен, -мнá, -о) noisy; loud; sensational.

шумов|о́й sound; ~ы́е эффéкты sound effects. шумо́к (-мкá) noise; под ~ on the quiet.

шýрин brother-in-law (*wife's brother*).

шурф prospecting shaft.

шуршáть (-шý) *impf* rustle.

шýстрый (-тёр, -трá, -о) smart, bright, sharp.

шут (-á) fool; jester. шути́ть (-чý, -ти́шь) *impf* (*pf* по~) joke; play, trifle; +*над*+*instr* make fun of. шýтка joke, jest. шутли́вый humorous; joking, light-hearted. шýточный comic; joking. шутя́ *adv* for fun, in jest; easily.

шушýкаться *impf* whisper together.

шхýна schooner.

шью *etc.*: *see* шить

Щ

щавéль (-я́) *m* sorrel.

щади́ть (щажý) *impf* (*pf* по~) spare.

щебёнка, щéбень (-бня) *m* crushed stone, ballast; road-metal.

щéбет twitter, chirp. щебетáть (-ечý, -éчешь) *impf* twitter, chirp.

щегóл (-глá) goldfinch.

щёголь *m* dandy, fop. щегольнýть (-нý, -нёшь) *pf*, щеголя́ть *impf* dress fashionably; strut about; +*instr* show off, flaunt. щегольско́й foppish.

щéдрость generosity. щéдрый (-др, -á, -о) generous; liberal.

щекá (*acc* щёку; *pl* щёки, -áм) cheek.

щекóлда latch, catch.

щекотáть (-очý, -óчешь) *impf* (*pf* по~) tickle. щекóтка tickling, tickle. щекотли́вый ticklish, delicate.

щёлкать *impf*, щёлкнуть (-ну) *pf* crack; flick; trill; +*instr* click, snap, pop.

щёлок bleach. щелочнóй alkaline. щёлочь (*gen pl* -éй) alkali.

щелчóк (-чкá) flick; slight; blow.

щель (*gen pl* -éй) crack; chink; slit; crevice; slit trench.

щеми́ть (-млю́) *impf* constrict; ache; oppress.

щенóк (-нкá; *pl* -нки́, -óв *or* -ня́та, -я́т) pup; cub.

щепá (*pl* -ы, -áм), щéпка splinter, chip; kindling.

щепети́льный punctilious.

щéпка *see* щепá

щепóтка, щéпоть pinch.

щети́на bristle; stubble. щети́нистый bristly. щети́ниться *impf* (*pf* о~) bristle. щётка brush; fetlock.

щи (щей *or* щец, щам, щáми) *pl* shchi, cabbage soup.

щи́колотка ankle.

щипáть (-плю́, -плешь) *impf*, щипнýть (-ну, -нёшь) *pf* (*pf also* об~, о~, ущипнýть) pinch, nip; sting, bite; burn; pluck; nibble; ~ся pinch. щипкóм *adv* pizzicato. щипóк (-пкá) pinch, nip. щипцы́ (-óв) *pl* tongs, pincers, pliers; forceps.

щит (-á) shield; screen; sluice-gate; (tortoise-)shell; board; panel. щитови́дный thyroid. щитóк (-ткá) dashboard.

щýка pike.

щуп probe. щýпальце (*gen pl* -лец) tentacle; antenna. щýпать *impf* (*pf* по~) feel, touch.

щýплый (-пл, -á, -о) weak, puny.

щýрить *impf* (*pf* со~) screw up, narrow; ~ся screw up one's eyes; narrow.

Э

эбéновый ebony.

эвакуáция evacuation. эвакуи́рованный *sb* evacuee. эвакуи́ровать *impf* & *pf* evacuate.

эвкали́пт eucalyptus.

эволюциони́ровать *impf* & *pf* evolve. эволюцио́нный evolutionary. эволю́ция evolution.

эги́да aegis.

эгои́зм egoism, selfishness. эгои́ст, ~ка egoist. эгоисти́ческий, эгои-

сти́чный egoistic, selfish.

эй *int* hi! hey!

эйфори́я euphoria.

эква́тор equator.

эквивале́нт equivalent.

экзальта́ция exaltation.

экза́мен examination; **вы́держать, сдать** ~ pass an examination. **экзамена́тор** examiner. **экзаменова́ть** *impf* (*pf* **про**~) examine; ~**ся** take an examination.

экзеку́ция (corporal) punishment.

экзе́ма eczema.

экземпля́р specimen; copy.

экзистенциали́зм existentialism.

экзоти́ческий exotic.

э́кий what (a).

экипа́ж[1] carriage.

экипа́ж[2] crew. **экипирова́ть** *impf & pf* equip. **экипиро́вка** equipping; equipment.

эклекти́зм eclecticism.

экле́р éclair.

экологи́ческий ecological. **эколо́гия** ecology.

эконо́мика economics; economy. **экономи́ст** economist. **эконо́мить** (-млю) *impf* (*pf* **с**~) use sparingly; save; economize. **экономи́ческий** economic; economical. **экономи́чный** economical. **эконо́мия** economy; saving. **эконо́мка** housekeeper. **эконо́мный** economical; thrifty.

экра́н screen. **экраниза́ция** filming; film version.

экскава́тор excavator.

экскурса́нт tourist. **экскурсио́нный** excursion. **экску́рсия** (conducted) tour; excursion. **экскурсово́д** guide.

экспанси́вный effusive.

экспатриа́нт expatriate. **экспатрии́ровать** *impf & pf* expatriate.

экспеди́ция expedition; dispatch; forwarding office.

экспериме́нт experiment. **эксперимента́льный** experimental. **эксперименти́ровать** *impf* experiment.

экспе́рт expert. **эксперти́за** (expert) examination; commission of experts.

эксплуата́тор exploiter. **эксплуатацио́нный** operating. **эксплуата́ция** exploitation; operation. **эксплуати́ровать** *impf* exploit; operate, run.

экспози́ция lay-out; exposition; ex-

posure. **экспона́т** exhibit. **экспоно́метр** exposure meter.

э́кспорт export. **экспорти́ровать** *impf & pf* export. **э́кспортный** export.

экспре́сс express (*train etc.*).

экспро́мт impromptu. **экспро́мтом** *adv* impromptu.

экспроприа́ция expropriation. **экспроприи́ровать** *impf & pf* expropriate.

экста́з ectasy.

экстравага́нтный eccentric, bizarre.

экстра́кт extract.

экстреми́ст extremist. **экстреми́стский** extremist.

э́кстренный urgent; emergency; special.

эксцентри́чный eccentric.

эксце́сс excess.

эласти́чный elastic; supple.

элева́тор grain elevator; hoist.

элега́нтный elegant, smart.

эле́гия elegy.

электризова́ть *impf* (*pf* **на**~) electrify. **эле́ктрик** electrician. **электрифика́ция** electrification. **электрифици́ровать** *impf & pf* electrify. **электри́ческий** electric(al). **электри́чество** electricity. **электри́чка** electric train.

электро- *in comb* electro-, electric, electrical. **~во́з** electric locomotive. **~дви́гатель** *m* electric motor. **электро́лиз** electrolysis. **~магни́тный** electromagnetic. **~монтёр** electrician. **~одея́ло** electric blanket. **~по́езд** electric train. **~прибо́р** electrical appliance. **~про́вод** (*pl* -а́) electric cable. **~прово́дка** electric wiring. **~ста́нция** power-station. **~те́хник** electrical engineer. **~те́хника** electrical engineering. **~шо́к** electric-shock treatment. **~эне́ргия** electrical energy.

электро́д electrode.

электро́н electron. **электро́ника** electronics.

электро́нный electron; electronic.

элеме́нт element; cell; character. **элемента́рный** elementary.

эли́та élite.

э́ллипс elipse.

эма́левый enamel. **эмалирова́ть**

impf enamel. **эма́ль** enamel.

эмансипа́ция emancipation.

эмба́рго *neut indecl* embargo.

эмбле́ма emblem.

эмбрио́н embryo.

эмигра́нт emigrant, émigré. **эмигра́ция** emigration. **эмигри́ровать** *impf & pf* emigrate.

эмоциона́льный emotional. **эмо́ция** emotion.

эмпири́ческий empirical.

эму́льсия emulsion.

э́ндшпиль *m* end-game.

энерге́тика power engineering. **энергети́ческий** energy. **энерги́чный** energetic. **эне́ргия** energy.

энтомоло́гия entomology.

энтузиа́зм enthusiasm. **энтузиа́ст** enthusiast.

энциклопеди́ческий encyclopaedic. **энциклопе́дия** encyclopaedia.

эпигра́мма epigram. **эпи́граф** epigraph.

эпиде́мия epidemic.

эпизо́д episode. **эпизоди́ческий** episodic; sporadic.

эпиле́псия epilepsy. **эпиле́птик** epileptic.

эпило́г epilogue. **эпита́фия** epitaph. **эпи́тет** epithet. **эпице́нтр** epicentre.

эпопе́я epic.

эпо́ха epoch, era.

э́ра era; **до на́шей э́ры** BC; **на́шей э́ры** AD.

эре́кция erection.

эро́зия erosion.

эроти́зм eroticism. **эро́тика** sensuality. **эроти́ческий, эроти́чный** erotic, sensual.

эруди́ция erudition.

эска́дра (*naut*) squadron. **эскадри́лья** (*gen pl* -лий) (*aeron*) squadron. **эскадро́н** (*mil*) squadron. **эскадро́нный** squadron.

эскала́тор escalator. **эскала́ция** escalation.

эски́з sketch; draft. **эски́зный** sketch; draft.

эскимо́с, эскимо́ска Eskimo.

эско́рт escort.

эсми́нец (-нца) *abbr* (*of* эска́дренный миноно́сец) destroyer.

эссе́нция essence.

эстака́да trestle bridge; overpass; pier, boom.

эста́мп print, engraving, plate.

эстафе́та relay race; baton.

эсте́тика aesthetics. **эстети́ческий** aesthetic.

эсто́нец (-нца), **эсто́нка** Estonian. **Эсто́ния** Estonia. **эсто́нский** Estonian.

эстра́да stage, platform; variety. **эстра́дный** stage; variety; ~ **конце́рт** variety show.

эта́ж (-а́) storey, floor. **этаже́рка** shelves.

э́так *adv* so, thus; about. **э́такий** such (a), what (a).

этало́н standard.

эта́п stage; halting-place.

э́тика ethics.

этике́т etiquette.

этике́тка label.

эти́л ethyl.

этимоло́гия etymology.

эти́ческий, эти́чный ethical.

этни́ческий ethnic. **этногра́фия** ethnography.

э́то *partl* this (is), that (is), it (is).

э́тот *m*, **э́та** *f*, **э́то** *neut*, **э́ти** *pl pron* this, these.

этю́д study, sketch; étude.

эфеме́рный ephemeral.

эфио́п, ~ка Ethiopian. **эфио́пский** Ethiopian.

эфи́р ether; air. **эфи́рный** ethereal; ether, ester.

эффе́кт effect. **эффекти́вность** effectiveness. **эффекти́вный** effective. **эффе́ктный** effective; striking.

эх *int* eh! oh!

э́хо echo.

эшафо́т scaffold.

эшело́н echelon; special train.

Ю

юбиле́й anniversary; jubilee. **юбиле́йный** jubilee.

ю́бка skirt. **ю́бочка** short skirt.

ювели́р jeweller. **ювели́рный** jeweller's, jewellery; fine, intricate.

юг south; **на ~е** in the south. **ю́говосто́к** south-east. **ю́го-за́пад** south-west. **югосла́в, ~ка** Yugoslav. **Югосла́вия** Yugoslavia. **югосла́вский** Yugoslav.

юдофо́б anti-Semite. **юдофо́бство**

anti-Semitism.

южа́нин (pl -а́не, -а́н), южа́нка southerner. ю́жный south, southern; southerly.

юла́ top; fidget. юли́ть impf fidget.

ю́мор humour. юмори́ст humourist.

юмористи́ческий humorous.

ю́ность youth. ю́ноша (gen pl -шей) m youth. ю́ношеский youthful. ю́ношество youth; young people. ю́ный (юн, -а́, -о) young; youthful.

юпи́тер floodlight.

юриди́ческий legal, juridical. юрисконсу́льт legal adviser. юри́ст lawyer.

ю́ркий (-рок, -рка́, -рко) quick-moving, brisk; smart.

юро́дивый crazy.

ю́рта yurt, nomad's tent.

юсти́ция justice.

юти́ться (ючу́сь) impf huddle (together).

Я

я (меня́, мне, мной (-о́ю), (обо) мне) pron I.

я́беда m & f, tell-tale; informer.

я́блоко (pl -и, -ок) apple; глазно́е ~ eyeball. я́блоневый, я́блочный apple. я́блоня apple-tree.

яви́ться (явлю́сь, яви́шься) pf, явля́ться impf appear; arise; +instr be, serve as. я́вка appearance, attendance; secret rendez-vous. явле́ние phenomenon; appearance; occurrence; scene. я́вный obvious; overt. я́вственный clear. я́вствовать be clear, be obvious.

ягнёнок (-нка; pl -ня́та, -я́т) lamb.

я́года berry; berries.

я́годица buttock(s).

ягуа́р jaguar.

яд poison; venom.

я́дерный nuclear.

ядови́тый poisonous; venomous.

я́дрёный healthy; bracing; juicy.

ядро́ (pl -а, я́дер) kernel, core; nucleus; (cannon-)ball; shot.

я́зва ulcer, sore. я́звенн|ый ulcerous; ~ая боле́знь ulcers. язви́тельный

caustic, sarcastic. язви́ть (-влю́) impf (pf съ~) be sarcastic.

язы́к (-а́) tongue; clapper; language. языкове́д linguist. языкове́дение, языкозна́ние linguistics. языково́й linguistic. язы́ковый tongue; lingual. язычко́вый reed. язы́чник heathen, pagan. язычо́к (-чка́) tongue; reed; catch.

яи́чко (pl -и, -чек) egg; testicle. яи́чник ovary. яи́чница fried eggs. яйцо́ (pl я́йца, яи́ц) egg; ovum.

я́кобы conj as if; partl supposedly.

я́корн|ый anchor; ~ая стоя́нка anchorage. я́корь (pl -я́) m anchor.

я́лик skiff.

я́ма pit, hole.

ямщи́к (-а́) coachman.

янва́рский January. янва́рь (-я́) m January.

янта́рный amber. янта́рь (-я́) m amber.

япо́нец (-нца), япо́нка Japanese. Япо́ния Japan. япо́нский Japanese.

ярд yard.

я́ркий (я́рок, ярка́, -о) bright; colourful, striking.

ярлы́к (-а́) label; tag.

я́рмарка fair.

ярмо́ (pl -а) yoke.

ярово́й spring.

я́ростный furious, fierce. я́рость fury.

я́рче comp of я́ркий

я́рый fervent; furious; violent.

я́сень m ash(-tree).

я́сли (-ей) pl manger; crèche, day nursery.

ясне́ть (-е́ет) impf become clear, clear. я́сно adv clearly. яснови́дение clairvoyance. яснови́дец (-дца), яснови́дица clairvoyant. я́сность clarity; clearness. я́сный (я́сен, ясна́, -о) clear; bright; fine.

я́ства (яств) pl victuals.

я́стреб (pl -а́) hawk.

я́хта yacht.

яче́йка cell.

ячме́нь[1] (-я́) m barley.

ячме́нь[2] (-я́) m stye.

я́щерица lizard.

я́щик box; drawer.

Test yourself with word games

This section contains a number of short exercises that will help you to use the dictionary more effectively. The answers to all the exercises are given at the end of the section.

1 Identifying Russian nouns and adjectives

Here is an extract from a Russian advertisement for a restaurant. See if you can find ten different nouns and eight different adjectives and make two lists. In each case, give the form of the word as it is found in the dictionary, i.e. the nominative singular of nouns and the nominative masculine singular of adjectives.

РУ́ССКИЙ РЕСТОРА́Н

Большо́й вы́бор ру́сских, англи́йских и интернациона́льных блюд

Прия́тная и дру́жеская атмосфе́ра

Высо́кий у́ровень обслу́живания

Конце́рт популя́рной му́зыки в пя́тницу и суббо́ту

---

2 Checking the gender of Russian nouns

Here are some English nouns that appear in the English–Russian half of the dictionary. Find out what their Russian equivalents are and make three separate lists, masculine nouns, feminine nouns, and neuter nouns.

book	club	door	England
February	grandfather	hobby	ice
journey	kitchen	life	meat
newspaper	opinion	passport	raincoat
square	tree	wine	word

3 Pronouns

What are the English equivalents of these Russian pronouns?

personal pronouns	interrogative pronouns	demonstrative pronouns	possessive pronouns
я	кто	этот	мой
он	что	тот	твой
мы	какой	эти	ваш

4 Recognizing Russian verbs

Underline the verb in each of the following sentences

Он работает на фабрике.

В прошлом году мы ездили во Францию.

Она думала об отпуске.

Они оставили свои вещи у меня.

Не беспокойтесь!

Сколько стоит билет?

Она ничего не боится.

5 Find the verb

Some words in English can be both nouns and verbs, e.g. race. Find the following words in the English–Russian half of the dictionary and then give the Russian for the verb only; give both the imperfective and perfective infinitives where both exist:

dance	demand	fly	force
hand	hold	hope	interest
jump	love	name	phone
plan	reply	request	respect
shout	smile	trade	wave

6 Which part of speech?

Use your dictionary to help you to arrange these words in separate lists according to their part of speech (noun, adjective, adverb, etc.):

автобус	быстрый	вы	где
да	éсли	ждать	здрáвствуй
из	кáк-нибудь	лéтом	мéжду
но	онá	принимáть	роя́ль
срáзу	Тýрция	у	францýзский
хотя́	целовáть	четы́ре	шути́ть
щётка	электри́ческий	юбка	я

7 Plural of nouns

Use the tables at the back of the dictionary to help you find the nominative plural of the following nouns:

автобус	англичáнин	бáбушка	боти́нок
враг	гóлос	гость	день
дéрево	женá	живóтное	здáние
идéя	и́мя	кафé	кни́жный магази́н
лицó	мужчи́на	недéля	одея́ло
платóк	прáздник	разговóр	сестрá
столéтие	толпá	трамвáй	у́лица
учёный	фами́лия	цветóк	я́блоко

8 Translating phrasal verbs

Use the dictionary to find the correct translation for the following English sentences:

She's given up smoking.

We went back home.

He hung the picture up.

They let him in.

He's moved away.

He put a sweater on.

She ran out of money.

We sat down.

They all stood up.

He took off his coat.

She woke up late.

9 Male or female?

Some nouns have both male and female forms in Russian. This is particularly true of words that denote a person's occupation or nationality, e.g.:

учи́тель/учи́тельница = a teacher

Find out the meaning of the following Russian words by looking them up in the Russian–English half of the dictionary. Then look up the English word in the English–Russian half in order to find out the feminine equivalent:

америка́нец	вегетариа́нец	иностра́нец
не́мец	преподава́тель	продаве́ц
перево́дчик	секрета́рь	сосе́д
студе́нт	учени́к	япо́нец

10 Which meaning?

Some words have more than one meaning and it is important to check that you have chosen the right one. We have given you one meaning of the Russian words listed below. Use your dictionary to find another one.

блю́до	• = dish	• =
ви́лка	• = fork	• =
води́ть	• = to take	• =
дере́вня	• = village	• =
заходи́ть	• = to call in	• =
ка́рта	• = map	• =
купа́ться	• = to bathe	• =
ла́мпочка	• = lamp	• =
ме́рить	• = to measure	• =
мо́лния	• = lightning	• =

ничего́	• = it doesn't matter	• =
носи́ть	• = to carry	• =
опа́здывать	• = to be late	• =
пе́ред	• = in front of	• =
ра́ковина	• = sink	• =
слеза́ть	• = to climb down	• =
сто́ить	• = to cost	• =
сыро́й	• = damp	• =
тень	• = shade	• =
я́щик	• = box	• =

11 Russian reflexive verbs

Use your dictionary to find the Russian equivalents of the following English sentences:

The concert begins at seven o'clock.

He quickly got changed.

She returned late.

It's getting colder.

We quarrel a lot.

What happened to him?

We washed and dressed.

The war's coming to an end.

12 Imperfective/perfective

Most Russian verbs have an imperfective and a perfective form. Use the dictionary to find the perfective infinitives of the following verbs:

выбира́ть	выходи́ть	гляде́ть	гото́вить
объясня́ть	писа́ть	плати́ть	покупа́ть
помога́ть	хоте́ть		

13 Indeterminate/determinate

Some Russian verbs have two imperfective forms, indeterminate and determinate. Use the English–Russian half of the dictionary to find out the two imperfective forms of the Russian equivalents of the following verbs:

to carry (*by hand*)

to carry (*by transport*)

to chase

to fly

to go (*on foot*)

to go (*by transport*)

to run

to swim

Answers

1 Nouns:
ресторáн, вы́бор, блю́до, атмосфéра, у́ровень, обслу́живание, концéрт, мýзыка, пя́тница, суббóта

Adjectives:
рýсский, большóй, англи́йский, интернационáльный, прия́тный, дрýжеский, высóкий, популя́рный

2 Masculine nouns:
клуб, феврáль, дéдушка, лёд, пáспорт, плащ

Feminine nouns:
кни́га, дверь, Áнглия, кýхня, жизнь, газéта, плóщадь

Neuter nouns:
хóбби, путешéствие, мя́со, мнéние, дéрево, винó, слóво

3

personal pronouns	interrogative pronouns	demonstrative pronouns	possessive pronouns
I	who	this	mine
he	what	that	yours
we	which	these	yours

4 Verbs:

рабóтает, éздили, дýмала, остáвили, беспокóйтесь, стóит, бойтся

5 Russian verbs:

танцевáть, трéбовать/потрéбовать, летáть/летéть/полетéть, заставля́ть/застáвить, передавáть/передáть, держáть, надéяться/ понадéяться, интересовáть, прыгать/прыгнуть, любить, называ́ть/ назвáть, звони́ть/позвони́ть, плани́ровать/заплани́ровать, отвечáть/отвéтить, проси́ть/попроси́ть, уважáть, кричáть/ кри́кнуть, улыбáться/улыбнýться, торговáть, махáть/махнýть

6 Nouns: автóбус, роя́ль, Тýрция, щётка, ю́бка
  Adjectives: быстрый, францýзский, электри́ческий
  Verbs: ждать, принимáть, целовáть, шути́ть
  Adverbs: где, кáк-нибудь, лéтом, срáзу
  Pronouns: вы, онá, я
  Prepositions: из, мéжду, у
  Conjunctions: éсли, но, хотя́
  Exclamation: здрáвствуй
  Number: четы́ре
  Particle: да

7 Nominative plural of nouns:

автóбусы, англичáне, бáбушки, боти́нки, враги́, голосá, гóсти, дни, дерéвья, жёны, живóтные, здáния, идéи, именá, кафé, кни́жные магази́ны, ли́ца, мужчи́ны, недéли, одея́ла, платки́, прáздники, разговóры, сёстры, столéтия, тóлпы, трамвáи, ýлицы, учёные, фами́лии, цветы́, я́блоки

8 Онá брóсила кури́ть.
  Мы вернýлись домóй.
  Он повéсил карти́ну.
  Они́ впусти́ли егó.
  Он уéхал.
  Он надéл сви́тер.
  У неё кóнчились дéньги.
  Мы сéли.
  Они́ все встáли.
  Он снял пальтó.
  Онá проснýлась пóздно.

9 Feminine equivalents:

америкáнка, вегетариáнка, иностра́нка, нéмка, перевóдчица, преподавáтельница, продавщи́ца, секретáрша, сосéдка, студéнтка, учени́ца, япóнка.

10 | блюдо | • = dish | • = course
| ви́лка | • = fork | • = plug
| води́ть | • = to take | • = to drive
| дере́вня | • = village | • = the country(side)
| заходи́ть | • = to call in | • = to set
| ка́рта | • = map | • = (playing) card
| купа́ться | • = to bathe | • = to have a bath
| ла́мпочка | • = lamp | • = bulb
| ме́рить | • = to measure | • = to try on
| мо́лния | • = lightning | • = zip(per)
| ничего́ | • = it doesn't matter | • = all right
| носи́ть | • = to carry | • = to wear
| опа́здывать | • = to be late | • = to miss
| пе́ред | • = in front of | • = before
| ра́ковина | • = sink | • = shell
| слеза́ть | • = to climb down | • = to climb off
| сто́ить | • = to cost | • = to be worth
| сыро́й | • = damp | • = raw
| тень | • = shade | • = shadow
| я́щик | • = box | • = drawer

11 Конце́рт начина́ется в семь часо́в.

Он бы́стро переоде́лся.

Она́ верну́лась по́здно.

Стано́вится холодне́е.

Мы мно́го ссо́римся

Что с ним случи́лось?

Мы умы́лись и оде́лись.

Война́ конча́ется.

12 Perfective infinitives:

вы́брать, вы́йти, погляде́ть, пригото́вить, объясни́ть, написа́ть, заплати́ть, купи́ть, помо́чь, захоте́ть.

13 носи́ть/нести́

вози́ть/везти́

гоня́ться/гна́ться

лета́ть/лете́ть

ходи́ть/идти́

е́здить/е́хать

бе́гать/бежа́ть

пла́вать/плыть

A

a, an *indef article, not usu translated;* **twice a week** два раза в неделю.

aback *adv:* **take ~** озадачивать *impf,* озадачить *pf.*

abacus *n* счёты *m pl.*

abandon *vt* покидать *impf,* покинуть *pf; (give up)* отказываться *impf,* отказаться *pf* от+*gen;* **~ o.s. to** предаваться *impf,* предаться *pf* +*dat.* **abandoned** *adj* покинутый; *(profligate)* распутный.

abase *vt* унижать *impf,* унизить *pf.* **abasement** *n* унижение.

abate *vi* затихать *impf,* затихнуть *pf.*

abattoir *n* скотобойня.

abbey *n* аббатство.

abbreviate *vt* сокращать *impf,* сократить *pf.* **abbreviation** *n* сокращение.

abdicate *vi* отрекаться *impf,* отречься *pf* от престола. **abdication** *n* отречение (от престола).

abdomen *n* брюшная полость. **abdominal** *adj* брюшной.

abduct *vt* похищать *impf,* похитить *pf.* **abduction** *n* похищение.

aberration *n (mental)* помутнение рассудка.

abet *vt* подстрекать *impf,* подстрекнуть *pf* (к совершению преступления *etc.*).

abhor *vt* ненавидеть *impf.* **abhorrence** *n* отвращение. **abhorrent** *adj* отвратительный.

abide *vt (tolerate)* выносить *impf,* вынести *pf;* **~ by** *(rules etc.)* следовать *impf,* по~ *pf.* **ability** *n* способность.

abject *adj (wretched)* жалкий; *(humble)* униженный; **~ poverty** крайняя нищета.

ablaze *predic* охваченный огнём.

able *adj* способный, умелый; **be ~ to** мочь *impf,* с~ *pf; (know how to)* уметь *impf,* с~ *pf.*

abnormal *adj* ненормальный. **abnormality** *n* ненормальность.

aboard *adv* на борт(у); *(train)* в поезд(е).

abode *n* жилище; **of no fixed ~** без постоянного местожительства.

abolish *vt* отменять *impf,* отменить *pf.* **abolition** *n* отмена.

abominable *adj* отвратительный. **abomination** *n* мерзость.

aboriginal *adj* коренной; *n* абориген, коренной житель *m.* **aborigine** *n* абориген, коренной житель *m.*

abort *vi (med)* выкидывать *impf,* выкинуть *pf; vt (terminate)* прекращать *impf,* прекратить *pf.* **abortion** *n* аборт; **have an ~** делать *impf,* с~ *pf* аборт. **abortive** *adj* безуспешный.

abound *vi* быть в изобилии; **~ in** изобиловать *impf* +*instr.*

about *adv & prep (approximately)* около+*gen; (concerning)* о+*prep,* насчёт+*gen; (up and down)* по+*dat; (in the vicinity)* кругом; **be ~ to** собираться *impf,* собраться *pf* +*inf.*

above *adv* наверху; *(higher up)* выше; **from ~** сверху; свыше; *prep* над+*instr; (more than)* свыше+*gen.* **above-board** *adj* честный. **above-mentioned** *adj* вышеупомянутый.

abrasion *n* истирание; *(wound)* ссадина. **abrasive** *adj* абразивный; *(manner)* колючий; *n* абразивный материал.

abreast *adv* в ряд; **keep ~ of** идти в ногу с+*instr.*

abridge *vt* сокращать *impf,* сократить *pf.* **abridgement** *n* сокращение.

abroad *adv* за границей, за границу; **from ~** из-за границы.

abrupt *adj (steep)* крутой; *(sudden)* внезапный; *(curt)* резкий.

abscess *n* абсцесс.

abscond *vi* скрываться *impf,* скрыться *pf.*

absence *n* отсутствие. **absent** *adj* отсутствующий; **be ~** отсутствовать *impf*; *vt*: ~ o.s. отлуча́ться *impf*, отлучи́ться *pf*. **absentee** *n* отсу́тствующий *sb*. **absenteeism** *n* прогу́л. **absent-minded** *adj* рассе́янный.

absolute *adj* абсолю́тный; (*complete*) по́лный, соверше́нный.

absolution *n* отпуще́ние грехо́в. **absolve** *vt* проща́ть *impf*, прости́ть *pf*.

absorb *vt* впи́тывать *impf*, впита́ть *pf*. **absorbed** *adj* поглощённый. **absorbent** *adj* вса́сывающий. **absorption** *n* впи́тывание; (*mental*) погружённость.

abstain *vi* возде́рживаться *impf*, воздержа́ться *pf* (from от+*gen*). **abstemious** *adj* возде́ржанный. **abstention** *n* воздержа́ние; (*person*) воздержа́вшийся *sb*. **abstinence** *n* воздержа́ние.

abstract *adj* абстра́ктный, отвлечённый; *n* рефера́т.

absurd *adj* абсу́рдный. **absurdity** *n* абсу́рд.

abundance *n* оби́лие. **abundant** *adj* оби́льный.

abuse *vt* (*insult*) руга́ть *impf*, вы́~, об~, от~ *pf*; (*misuse*) злоупотребля́ть *impf*, злоупотреби́ть *pf*; *n* (*curses*) ру́гань, руга́тельства *neut pl*; (*misuse*) злоупотребле́ние. **abusive** *adj* оскорби́тельный, руга́тельный.

abut *vi* примыка́ть *impf* (on к+*dat*).

abysmal *adj* (*extreme*) безграни́чный; (*bad*) ужа́сный. **abyss** *n* бе́здна.

academic *adj* академи́ческий. **academician** *n* акаде́мик. **academy** *n* акаде́мия.

accede *vi* вступа́ть *impf*, вступи́ть *pf* (to в, на+*acc*); (*assent*) соглаша́ться *impf*, согласи́ться *pf*.

accelerate *vt & i* ускоря́ть(ся) *impf*, уско́рить(ся) *pf*; (*motoring*) дава́ть *impf*, дать *pf* газ. **acceleration** *n* ускоре́ние. **accelerator** *n* ускори́тель *m*; (*pedal*) акселера́тор.

accent *n* акце́нт; (*stress*) ударе́ние; *vt* де́лать *impf*, с~ *pf* ударе́ние на+*acc*. **accentuate** *vt* акценти́ровать *impf & pf*.

accept *vt* принима́ть *impf*, приня́ть *pf*. **acceptable** *adj* прие́млемый. **acceptance** *n* приня́тие.

access *n* до́ступ. **accessible** *adj* досту́пный. **accession** *n* вступле́ние (на престо́л). **accessories** *n* принадле́жности *f pl*. **accessory** *n* (*accomplice*) соуча́стник, -ица.

accident *n* (*chance*) случа́йность; (*mishap*) несча́стный слу́чай; (*crash*) ава́рия; by ~ случа́йно. **accidental** *adj* случа́йный.

acclaim *vt* (*praise*) восхваля́ть *impf*, восхвали́ть *pf*; *n* восхвале́ние.

acclimatization *n* акклиматиза́ция. **acclimatize** *vt* акклиматизи́ровать *impf & pf*.

accommodate *vt* помеща́ть *impf*, помести́ть *pf*; (*hold*) вмеща́ть *impf*, вмести́ть *pf*. **accommodating** *adj* услу́жливый. **accommodation** *n* (*hotel*) но́мер; (*home*) жильё.

accompaniment *n* сопровожде́ние; (*mus*) аккомпанеме́нт. **accompanist** *n* аккомпаниа́тор. **accompany** *vt* сопровожда́ть *impf*, сопроводи́ть *pf*; (*escort*) провожа́ть *impf*, проводи́ть *pf*; (*mus*) аккомпани́ровать *impf*+*dat*.

accomplice *n* соуча́стник, -ица.

accomplish *vt* соверша́ть *impf*, соверши́ть *pf*. **accomplished** *adj* зако́нченный. **accomplishment** *n* выполне́ние; (*skill*) соверше́нство.

accord *n* согла́сие; of one's own ~ доброво́льно; of its own ~ сам собо́й, сам по себе́. **accordance** *n*: in ~ with в соотве́тствии с+*instr*, согла́сно+*dat*. **according** *adv*: ~ to по+*dat*, ~ to him по его́ слова́м. **accordingly** *adv* соотве́тственно.

accordion *n* аккордео́н.

accost *vt* пристава́ть *impf*, приста́ть *pf* к+*dat*.

account *n* (*comm*) счёт; (*report*) отчёт; (*description*) описа́ние; on no ~ ни в ко́ем слу́чае; on ~ в счёт причита́ющейся су́ммы; on ~ of из-за+*gen*, по причи́не+*gen*; take into ~ принима́ть *impf*, приня́ть *pf* в расчёт; *vi*: ~ for объясня́ть *impf*, объясни́ть *pf*. **accountable** *adj* отве́тственный.

accountancy *n* бухгалте́рия. **accountant** *n* бухга́лтер.

accrue *vi* нараста́ть *impf*, нарасти́ *pf*.

accumulate *vt & i* нака́пливать(ся)

impf, копи́ть(ся) *impf,* на~ *pf.* accumulation *n* накопле́ние. accumulator *n* аккумуля́тор.
accuracy *n* то́чность. accurate *adj* то́чный.
accusation *n* обвине́ние. accusative *adj* (*n*) вини́тельный (паде́ж). accuse *vt* обвиня́ть *impf,* обвини́ть *pf* (of в+*prep*); the ~d обвиня́емый *sb.*
accustom *vt* приуча́ть *impf,* приучи́ть *pf* (to к+*dat*). accustomed *adj* привы́чный; be, get ~ привыка́ть *impf,* привы́кнуть *pf* (to к+*dat*).
ace *n* туз; (*pilot*) ас.
ache *n* боль; *vi* боле́ть *impf.*
achieve *vt* достига́ть *impf,* дости́чь & дости́гнуть *pf* +*gen.* achievement *n* достиже́ние.
acid *n* кислота́; *adj* ки́слый; ~ rain кисло́тный дождь. acidity *n* кислота́.
acknowledge *vt* признава́ть *impf,* призна́ть *pf;* (~ receipt of) подтвержда́ть *impf,* подтверди́ть *pf* получе́ние+*gen.* acknowledgement *n* призна́ние; подтвержде́ние.
acne *n* прыщи́ *m pl.*
acorn *n* жёлудь *m.*
acoustic *adj* акусти́ческий. acoustics *n pl* аку́стика.
acquaint *vt* знако́мить *impf,* по~ *pf.* acquaintance *n* знако́мство; (*person*) знако́мый *sb.* acquainted *adj* знако́мый.
acquiesce *vi* соглаша́ться *impf,* согласи́ться *pf.* acquiescence *n* согла́сие.
acquire *vt* приобрета́ть *impf,* приобрести́ *pf.* acquisition *n* приобрете́ние. acquisitive *adj* стяжа́тельский.
acquit *vt* опра́вдывать *impf,* оправда́ть *pf;* ~ o.s. вести́ *impf* себя́. acquittal *n* оправда́ние.
acre *n* акр.
acrid *adj* е́дкий.
acrimonious *adj* язви́тельный.
acrobat *n* акроба́т. acrobatic *adj* акробати́ческий.
across *adv* & *prep* че́рез+*acc;* (*athwart*) поперёк (+*gen*); (to, on, other side) на ту сто́рону (+*gen*), на той стороне́ (+*gen*); (*crosswise*) крест-на́крест.
acrylic *n* акри́л; *adj* акри́ловый.
act *n* (*deed*) акт, посту́пок; (*law*)

акт, зако́н; (*of play*) де́йствие; (*item*) но́мер; *vi* поступа́ть *impf,* поступи́ть *pf;* де́йствовать *impf,* по~ *pf;* *vt* игра́ть *impf,* сыгра́ть *pf.* acting *n* игра́; (*profession*) актёрство; *adj* исполня́ющий обя́занности+*gen.* action *n* де́йствие, посту́пок; (*law*) иск, проце́сс; (*battle*) бой; ~ replay повто́р; be out of ~ не рабо́тать *impf.* activate *vt* приводи́ть *impf,* привести́ *pf* в де́йствие. active *adj* акти́вный; ~ service действи́тельная слу́жба; ~ voice действи́тельный зало́г. activity *n* де́ятельность. actor *n* актёр. actress *n* актри́са.
actual *adj* действи́тельный. actuality *n* действи́тельность. actually *adv* на са́мом де́ле, факти́чески.
acumen *n* проница́тельность.
acupuncture *n* иглоука́лывание.
acute *adj* о́стрый.
AD *abbr* н.э. (на́шей э́ры).
adamant *adj* непрекло́нный.
adapt *vt* приспособля́ть *impf,* приспосо́бить *pf;* (*theat*) инсцени́ровать *impf* & *pf;* ~ o.s. приспособля́ться *impf,* приспосо́биться *pf.* adaptable *adj* приспособля́ющийся. adaptation *n* приспособле́ние; (*theat*) инсцениро́вка. adapter *n* ада́птер.
add *vt* прибавля́ть *impf,* приба́вить *pf;* (*say*) добавля́ть *impf,* доба́вить *pf;* ~ together скла́дывать *impf,* сложи́ть *pf;* ~ up сумми́ровать *impf* & *pf;* ~ up to составля́ть *impf,* соста́вить *pf;* (*fig*) своди́ться *impf,* свести́сь *pf* к+*dat.* addenda *n* приложе́ния *pl.*
adder *n* гадю́ка.
addict *n* наркома́н, ~ка. addicted *adj:* be ~ to быть рабо́м+*gen;* become ~ to пристраща́ться *pf* к+*dat.* addiction *n* (*passion*) пристра́стие; (*to drugs*) наркома́ния.
addition *n* прибавле́ние; дополне́ние; (*math*) сложе́ние; in ~ вдоба́вок, кро́ме того́. additional *adj* доба́вочный. additive *n* доба́вка.
address *n* а́дрес; (*speech*) речь; ~ book записна́я кни́жка; *vt* адресова́ть *impf* & *pf;* (*speak to*) обраща́ться *impf,* обрати́ться *pf* к+*dat;* ~ a meeting выступа́ть *impf,* вы́ступить *pf* на собра́нии. addressee

n адреса́т.

adept *adj* све́дущий; *n* ма́стер.

adequate *adj* доста́точный.

adhere *vi* прилипа́ть *impf*, прили́пнуть *pf* (**to** к+*dat*); (*fig*) приде́рживаться *impf* +*gen*. **adherence** *n* приве́рженность. **adherent** *n* приве́рженец. **adhesive** *adj* ли́пкий; *n* кле́йкое вещество́.

ad hoc *adj* специа́льный.

ad infinitum *adv* до бесконе́чности.

adjacent *adj* сме́жный.

adjective *n* (и́мя) прилага́тельное.

adjoin *vt* прилега́ть *impf* к+*dat*.

adjourn *vt* откла́дывать *impf*, отложи́ть *pf*; *vi* объявля́ть *impf*, объяви́ть *pf* переры́в; (*move*) переходи́ть *impf*, перейти́ *pf*.

adjudicate *vi* выноси́ть *impf*, вы́нести *pf* реше́ние (**in** по+*dat*); суди́ть *impf*.

adjust *vt & i* приспособля́ть(ся) *impf*, приспосо́бить(ся) *pf*; *vt* пригоня́ть *impf*, пригна́ть *impf pf*; (*regulate*) регули́ровать *impf*, от~ *pf*. **adjustable** *adj* регули́руемый. **adjustment** *n* регули́рование, подго́нка.

ad lib *vt & i* импровизи́ровать *impf*, сымпровизи́ровать *pf*.

administer *vt* (*manage*) управля́ть *impf* +*instr*; (*give*) дава́ть *impf*, дать *pf*. **administration** *n* управле́ние; (*government*) прави́тельство. **administrative** *adj* администрати́вный. **administrator** *n* администра́тор.

admirable *adj* похва́льный.

admiral *n* адмира́л.

admiration *n* восхище́ние. **admire** *vt* (*look at*) любова́ться *impf*, по~ *pf* +*instr*, на+*acc*; (*respect*) восхища́ться *impf*, восхити́ться *pf* +*instr*. **admirer** *n* покло́нник.

admissible *adj* допусти́мый. **admission** *n* (*access*) до́ступ; (*entry*) вход; (*confession*) призна́ние. **admit** *vt* (*allow in*) впуска́ть *impf*, впусти́ть *pf*; (*confess*) признава́ть *impf*, призна́ть *pf*. **admittance** *n* до́ступ. **admittedly** *adv* призна́ться.

admixture *n* при́месь.

adolescence *n* о́трочество. **adolescent** *adj* подро́стковый; *n* подро́сток.

adopt *vt* (*child*) усыновля́ть *impf*, усынови́ть *pf*; (*thing*) усва́ивать *impf*, усво́ить *pf*; (*accept*) принима́ть *impf*, приня́ть *pf*. **adoptive** *adj* приёмный. **adoption** *n* усыновле́ние; приня́тие.

adorable *adj* преле́стный. **adoration** *n* обожа́ние. **adore** *vt* обожа́ть *impf*.

adorn *vt* украша́ть *impf*, укра́сить *pf*. **adornment** *n* украше́ние.

adrenalin *n* адренали́н.

adroit *adj* ло́вкий.

adulation *n* преклоне́ние.

adult *adj & n* взро́слый (*sb*).

adulterate *vt* фальсифици́ровать *impf & pf*.

adultery *n* супру́жеская изме́на.

advance *n* (*going forward*) продвиже́ние (вперёд); (*progress*) прогре́сс; (*mil*) наступле́ние; (*of pay etc.*) ава́нс; **in ~** зара́нее; *pl* (*overtures*) ава́нсы *m pl*; *vi* (*go forward*) продвига́ться *impf*, продви́нуться *pf* вперёд; идти́ *impf* вперёд; (*mil*) наступа́ть *impf*; *vt* продвига́ть *impf*, продви́нуть *pf*; (*put forward*) выдвига́ть *impf*, вы́двинуть *pf*. **advanced** *adj* (*modern*) передово́й. **advancement** *n* продвиже́ние.

advantage *n* преиму́щество; (*profit*) вы́года, по́льза; **take ~ of** по́льзоваться *impf*, вос~ *pf* +*instr*. **advantageous** *adj* вы́годный.

adventure *n* приключе́ние. **adventurer** *n* иска́тель *m* приключе́ний. **adventurous** *adj* предприи́мчивый.

adverb *n* наре́чие.

adversary *n* проти́вник. **adverse** *adj* неблагоприя́тный. **adversity** *n* несча́стье.

advertise *vt* (*publicize*) реклами́ровать *impf & pf*; *vt & i* (**~ for**) дава́ть *impf*, дать *pf* объявле́ние о+*prep*. **advertisement** *n* объявле́ние, рекла́ма.

advice *n* сове́т. **advisable** *adj* жела́тельный. **advise** *vt* сове́товать *impf*, по~ *pf* +*dat* & *inf*; (*notify*) уведомля́ть *impf*, уве́домить *pf*. **advisedly** *adv* наме́ренно. **adviser** *n* сове́тник. **advisory** *adj* совеща́тельный.

advocate *n* (*supporter*) сторо́нник; *vt* выступа́ть *impf*, вы́ступить *pf* за+*acc*; (*advise*) сове́товать *impf*, по~ *pf*.

aegis *n* эги́да.

aerial *n* анте́нна; *adj* возду́шный.

aerobics *n* аэро́бика.

aerodrome *n* аэродро́м. **aerodynamics** *n* аэродина́мика. **aeroplane** *n* самолёт. **aerosol** *n* аэрозо́ль *m*.

aesthetic *adj* эстети́ческий. **aesthetics** *n pl* эсте́тика.

afar *adv*: from ~ издалека́.

affable *adj* приве́тливый.

affair *n* (*business*) де́ло; (*love*) рома́н.

affect *vt* влия́ть *impf*, по~ *pf* на+*acc*; (*touch*) тро́гать *impf*, тро́нуть *pf*; (*concern*) затра́гивать *impf*, затро́нуть *pf*; **affectation** *n* жема́нство.

affected *adj* жема́нный. **affection** *n* привя́занность. **affectionate** *adj* не́жный.

affiliated *adj* свя́занный (to с+*instr*).

affinity *n* (*relationship*) родство́; (*resemblance*) схо́дство; (*attraction*) влече́ние.

affirm *vt* утвержда́ть *impf*. **affirmation** *n* утвержде́ние. **affirmative** *adj* утверди́тельный.

affix *vt* прикрепля́ть *impf*, прикрепи́ть *pf*.

afflict *vt* постига́ть *impf*, пости́чь *pf*; be **afflicted with** страда́ть *impf* +*instr*. **affliction** *n* боле́знь.

affluence *n* бога́тство. **affluent** *adj* бога́тый.

afford *vt* позволя́ть *impf*, позво́лить *pf* себе́; (*supply*) предоставля́ть *impf*, предоста́вить *pf*.

affront *n* оскорбле́ние; *vt* оскорбля́ть *impf*, оскорби́ть *pf*.

afield *adv*: far ~ далеко́; farther ~ да́льше.

afloat *adv & predic* на воде́.

afoot *predic*: be ~ гото́виться *impf*.

aforesaid *adj* вышеупомя́нутый.

afraid *predic*: be ~ боя́ться *impf*.

afresh *adv* сно́ва.

Africa *n* А́фрика. **African** *n* африка́нец, -ка́нка; *adj* африка́нский.

after *adv* пото́м; *prep* по́сле+*gen*; (*time*) че́рез+*acc*; (*behind*) за+*acc*, *instr*; ~ all в конце́ концо́в; *conj* по́сле того́, как.

aftermath *n* после́дствия *neut pl*.

afternoon *n* втора́я полови́на дня; in the ~ днём. **aftershave** *n* лосьо́н по́сле бритья́. **afterthought** *n* запозда́лая мысль.

afterwards *adv* пото́м.

again *adv* опя́ть; (*once more*) ещё раз; (*anew*) сно́ва.

against *prep* (*opposing*) про́тив+*gen*; (*touching*) к+*dat*; (*hitting*) о+*acc*.

age *n* во́зраст; (*era*) век, эпо́ха; *vt* ста́рить *impf*, со~ *pf*; *vi* старе́ть *impf*, по~ *pf*. **aged** *adj* преста-ре́лый.

agency *n* аге́нтство. **agenda** *n* пове́стка дня. **agent** *n* аге́нт.

aggravate *vt* ухудша́ть *impf*, уху́дшить *pf*; (*annoy*) раздража́ть *impf*, раздражи́ть *pf*.

aggregate *adj* совоку́пный; *n* совоку́пность.

aggression *n* агре́ссия. **aggressive** *adj* агресси́вный. **aggressor** *n* агре́ссор.

aggrieved *adj* оби́женный.

aghast *predic* в у́жасе (at от+*gen*).

agile *adj* прово́рный. **agility** *n* прово́рство.

agitate *vt* волнова́ть *impf*, вз~ *pf*; *vi* агити́ровать *impf*. **agitation** *n* волне́ние; агита́ция.

agnostic *n* агно́стик. **agnosticism** *n* агностици́зм.

ago *adv* (*тому́*) наза́д; long ~ давно́.

agonize *vi* му́читься *impf*. **agonizing** *adj* мучи́тельный. **agony** *n* аго́ния.

agrarian *adj* агра́рный.

agree *vi* соглаша́ться *impf*, согласи́ться *pf*; (*arrange*) догова́риваться *impf*, договори́ться *pf*. **agreeable** *adj* (*pleasant*) прия́тный. **agreement** *n* согла́сие; (*treaty*) соглаше́ние; in ~ согла́сен (-сна).

agricultural *adj* сельскохозя́йственный. **agriculture** *n* се́льское хозя́йство.

aground *predic* на мели́; *adv*: run ~ сади́ться *impf*, сесть *pf* на мель.

ahead *adv* (*forward*) вперёд; (*in front*) впереди́; ~ of time досро́чно.

aid *vt* помога́ть *impf*, помо́чь *pf* +*dat*; *n* по́мощь; (*teaching*) посо́бие; in ~ of в по́льзу+*gen*.

Aids *n* СПИД.

ailing *adj* (*ill*) больно́й.

ailment *n* неду́г.

aim *n* цель, наме́рение; take ~ прице́ливаться *impf*, прице́литься *pf* (at в+*acc*); *vi* це́литься *impf*, на~ *pf* (at в+*acc*); (*also fig*) ме́тить *impf*, на~ pf (at в+acc); vt нацеливать impf, нацелить pf; (also fig) наводить impf, навести pf. **aimless** adj бесцельный.

air n воздух; (look) вид; **by** ~ самолётом; **on the** ~ в эфире; attrib воздушный; vt (ventilate) проветривать impf, проветрить pf; (make known) выставлять impf, выставить pf напоказ. **air-conditioning** n кондиционирование воздуха. **aircraft** n самолёт. **aircraft-carrier** n авианосец. **airfield** n аэродром. **air force** n ВВС (военно-воздушные силы) pl. **air hostess** n стюардесса. **airless** adj душный. **airlift** n воздушные перевозки f pl; vt перевозить impf, перевезти pf по воздуху. **airline** n авиалиния. **airlock** n воздушная пробка. **airman** n авиа-(почта). **airman** n лётчик. **airport** n аэропорт. **air raid** n воздушный налёт. **airship** n дирижабль m. **airstrip** n взлётно-посадочная полоса. **airtight** adj герметичный. **air traffic controller** n диспетчер. **airwaves** n pl радиоволны f pl.

aisle n боковой неф; (passage) проход.

ajar predic приоткрытый.

akin predic (similar) похожий; **be** ~ **to** быть сродни к+dat.

alabaster n алебастр.

alacrity n быстрота.

alarm n тревога; vt тревожить impf, вс~ pf; ~ **clock** будильник. **alarming** adj тревожный. **alarmist** n паникёр; adj паникёрский.

alas int увы!

album n альбом.

alcohol n алкоголь m, спирт; спиртные напитки m pl. **alcoholic** adj алкогольный; n алкоголик, -ичка.

alcove n альков.

alert adj бдительный; n тревога; vt предупреждать impf, предупредить pf.

algebra n алгебра.

alias adv иначе (называемый); n кличка, вымышленное имя neut.

alibi n алиби neut indecl.

alien n иностранец, -нка; adj иностранный; ~ **to** чуждый +dat. **alienate** vt отчуждать impf. **alienation** n отчуждение.

alight[1] vi сходить impf, сойти pf; (bird) садиться impf, сесть pf.

alight[2] predic: **be** ~ гореть impf; (shine) сиять impf.

align vt выравнивать impf, выровнять pf. **alignment** n выравнивание.

alike predic похож; adv одинаково.

alimentary adj: ~ **canal** пищеварительный канал.

alimony n алименты m pl.

alive predic жив, в живых.

alkali n щёлочь. **alkaline** adj щелочной.

all adj весь; n всё, pl все; adv совсем, совершенно; ~ **along** всё время; ~ **right** хорошо, ладно; (not bad) так себе; неплохо; ~ **the same** всё равно; **in** ~ — всего; **two** ~ по два; **not at** ~ нисколько.

allay vt успокаивать impf, успокоить pf.

allegation n утверждение. **allege** vt утверждать impf. **allegedly** adv якобы.

allegiance adv верность.

allegorical adj аллегорический. **allegory** n аллегория.

allergic adj аллергический; **be** ~ **to** иметь аллергию к+dat. **allergy** n аллергия.

alleviate vt облегчать impf, облегчить pf. **alleviation** n облегчение.

alley n переулок.

alliance n союз. **allied** adj союзный.

alligator n аллигатор.

allocate vt (distribute) распределять impf, распределить pf; (allot) выделять impf, выделить pf. **allocation** n распределение; выделение.

allot vt выделять impf, выделить pf; (distribute) распределять impf, распределить pf. **allotment** n выделение; (land) участок.

allow vt разрешать impf, разрешить pf; (let happen; concede) допускать impf, допустить pf; ~ **for** учитывать impf, учесть pf. **allowance** n (financial) пособие; (deduction, also fig) скидка; **make** ~(s) **for** учитывать impf, учесть pf.

alloy n сплав.

all-round adj разносторонний.

allude vi ссылаться impf, сослаться pf (**to** на+acc).

allure vt заманивать impf, заманить

pf. **allure(ment)** *n* приманка. **alluring** *adj* заманчивый.

allusion *n* ссылка.

ally *n* союзник; *vt* соединять *impf*, соединить *pf*; ~ **oneself with** вступать *impf*, вступить *pf* в союз с+*instr*.

almighty *adj* всемогущий.

almond *n* (*tree*; *pl collect*) миндаль *m*; (*nut*) миндальный орех.

almost *adv* почти, едва не.

alms *n pl* милостыня.

aloft *adv* наверх(-у́).

alone *predic* один; (*lonely*) одинок; *adv* только; **leave** ~ оставлять *impf*, оставить *pf* в покое; **let** ~ не говоря уже о+*prep*.

along *prep* по+*dat*, (*position*) вдоль +*gen*; *adv* (*onward*) дальше; **all** ~ всё время; ~ **with** вместе с+*instr*. **alongside** *adv* & *prep* рядом (с+*instr*).

aloof *predic* & *adv* (*distant*) сдержанный; (*apart*) в стороне.

aloud *adv* вслух.

alphabet *n* алфавит. **alphabetical** *adj* алфавитный.

alpine *adj* альпийский.

already *adv* уже.

also *adv* также, тоже.

altar *n* алтарь *m*.

alter *vt* (*modify*) переделывать *impf*, переделать *pf*; *vt* & *i* (*change*) изменять(ся) *impf*, изменить(ся) *pf*. **alteration** *n* переделка; изменение.

alternate *adj* чередующийся; *vt* & *i* чередовать(ся) *impf*; **alternating current** переменный ток; **on** ~ **days** через день. **alternation** *n* чередование. **alternative** *n* альтернатива; *adj* альтернативный.

although *conj* хотя.

altitude *n* высота.

alto *n* альт.

altogether *adv* (*fully*) совсем; (*in total*) всего.

altruistic *adj* альтруистический.

aluminium *n* алюминий.

always *adv* всегда; (*constantly*) постоянно.

Alzheimer's disease *n* болезнь Альцгеймера.

a.m. *abbr* (*morning*) утра; (*night*) ночи.

amalgamate *vt* & *i* сливать(ся) *impf*,

слить(ся) *pf*; (*chem*) амальгамировать(ся) *impf* & *pf*. **amalgamation** *n* слияние; (*chem*) амальгамирование.

amass *vt* копить *impf*, на~ *pf*.

amateur *n* любитель *m*, ~ница; *adj* любительский. **amateurish** *adj* дилетантский.

amaze *vt* изумлять *impf*, изумить *pf*. **amazement** *n* изумление. **amazing** *adj* изумительный.

ambassador *n* посол.

amber *n* янтарь *m*.

ambience *n* среда; атмосфера.

ambiguity *n* двусмысленность. **ambiguous** *adj* двусмысленный.

ambition *n* (*quality*) честолюбие; (*aim*) мечта. **ambitious** *adj* честолюбивый.

amble *vi* ходить *indet*, идти *det* неторопливым шагом.

ambulance *n* машина скорой помощи.

ambush *n* засада; *vt* нападать *impf*, напасть *pf* из засады на+*acc*.

ameliorate *vt* & *i* улучшать(ся) *impf*, улучшить(ся) *pf*. **amelioration** *n* улучшение.

amen *int* аминь!

amenable *adj* сговорчивый (**to** +*dat*)

amend *vt* (*correct*) исправлять *impf*, исправить *pf*; (*change*) вносить *impf*, внести *pf* поправки в+*acc*. **amendment** *n* поправка, исправление. **amends** *n pl*: **make** ~ **for** заглаживать *impf*, загладить *pf*.

amenities *n pl* удобства *neut pl*.

America *n* Америка. **American** *adj* американский; *n* американец, -нка. **Americanism** *n* американизм.

amiable *adj* любезный. **amicable** *adj* дружелюбный.

amid(st) *prep* среди+*gen*.

amino acid *n* аминокислота́.

amiss *adv* неладный; **take** ~ обижаться *impf*, обидеться *pf* на+*acc*.

ammonia *n* аммиак; (*liquid* ~) нашатырный спирт.

ammunition *n* боеприпасы *m pl*.

amnesia *n* амнезия.

amnesty *n* амнистия.

among(st) *prep* (*amidst*) среди+*gen*, (*between*) между+*instr*.

amoral *adj* аморальный.

amorous *adj* влюбчивый.

amorphous adj бесфо́рменный.

amortization n амортиза́ция.

amount n коли́чество; vi: ~ to составля́ть impf, соста́вить pf; (be equivalent to) быть равноси́льным+dat.

ampere n ампе́р.

amphetamine n амфетами́н.

amphibian n амфи́бия. **amphibious** adj земново́дный; (mil) пла́вающий.

amphitheatre n амфитеа́тр.

ample adj доста́точный. **amplification** n усиле́ние. **amplifier** n усили́тель m. **amplify** vt уси́ливать impf, уси́лить pf. **amply** adv доста́точно.

amputate vt ампути́ровать impf & pf. **amputation** n ампута́ция.

amuse vt забавля́ть impf; развлека́ть impf, развле́чь pf. **amusement** n заба́ва, развлече́ние; pl аттракцио́ны m pl. **amusing** adj заба́вный; (funny) смешно́й.

anachronism n анахрони́зм. **anachronistic** adj анахрони́ческий.

anaemia n анеми́я. **anaemic** adj анеми́чный.

anaesthesia n анестези́я. **anaesthetic** n обезбо́ливающее сре́дство. **anaesthetist** n анестезио́лог. **anaesthetize** vt анестези́ровать impf & pf.

anagram n анагра́мма.

analogous adj аналоги́чный. **analogue** n ана́лог. **analogy** n анало́гия.

analyse vt анализи́ровать impf & pf. **analysis** n ана́лиз. **analyst** n анали́тик, психоанали́тик. **analytical** adj аналити́ческий.

anarchic adj анархи́ческий. **anarchist** n анархи́ст, ~ка; adj анархи́стский. **anarchy** n ана́рхия.

anathema n ана́фема.

anatomical adj анатоми́ческий. **anatomy** n анато́мия.

ancestor n пре́док. **ancestry** n происхожде́ние.

anchor n я́корь m; vt ста́вить impf, по~ pf на я́корь; vi станови́ться impf, стать pf на я́корь. **anchorage** n я́корная стоя́нка.

anchovy n анчо́ус.

ancient adj дре́вний, стари́нный.

and conj и, (but) а; c+instr; you ~ I

мы с ва́ми; my wife ~ I мы с жено́й.

anecdote n анекдо́т.

anew adv сно́ва.

angel n а́нгел. **angelic** adj а́нгельский.

anger n гнев; vt серди́ть impf, рас~ pf.

angina n стенокарди́я.

angle[1] n у́гол; (fig) то́чка зре́ния.

angle[2] vi уди́ть impf ры́бу. **angler** n рыболо́в.

angry adj серди́тый.

anguish n страда́ние, му́ка. **anguished** adj отча́янный.

angular adj углово́й; (sharp) углова́тый.

animal n живо́тное sb; adj живо́тный. **animate** adj живо́й. **animated** adj оживлённый; ~ **cartoon** мультфи́льм. **animation** n оживле́ние.

animosity n вражде́бность.

ankle n лоды́жка.

annals n pl ле́топись.

annex vt аннекси́ровать impf & pf. **annexation** n анне́ксия. **annexe** n пристро́йка.

annihilate vt уничтожа́ть impf, уничто́жить pf. **annihilation** n уничтоже́ние.

anniversary n годовщи́на.

annotate vt комменти́ровать impf & pf. **annotated** adj снабжённый коммента́риями. **annotation** n анно-та́ция.

announce vt объявля́ть impf, объяви́ть pf; заявля́ть impf, заяви́ть pf; (radio) сообща́ть impf, сообщи́ть pf. **announcement** n объявле́ние; сообще́ние. **announcer** n ди́ктор.

annoy vt досажда́ть impf, досади́ть pf; раздража́ть impf, раздражи́ть pf. **annoyance** n доса́да. **annoying** adj доса́дный.

annual adj ежего́дный, (of a given year) годово́й; n (book) ежего́дник; (bot) одноле́тник. **annually** adv ежего́дно. **annuity** n (ежего́дная) ре́нта.

annul vt аннули́ровать impf & pf. **annulment** n аннули́рование.

anoint vt пома́зывать impf, пома́зать pf.

anomalous adj анома́льный. **anomaly** n анома́лия.

anonymous adj анони́мный. **ano-**

nymity *n* анони́мность.
anorak *n* ку́ртка.
anorexia *n* аноре́ксия.
another *adj, pron* друго́й; ~ **one** ещё (оди́н); **in** ~ **ten years** ещё че́рез де́сять лет.
answer *n* отве́т; *vt* отвеча́ть *impf*, отве́тить *pf* (*person*) +*dat*, (*question*) на+*acc*; ~ **the door** отворя́ть *impf*, отвори́ть *pf* дверь; ~ **the phone** подходи́ть *impf*, подойти́ *pf* к телефо́ну. **answerable** *adj* отве́тственный. **answering machine** *n* телефо́н-отве́тчик.
ant *n* мураве́й.
antagonism *n* антагони́зм. **antagonistic** *adj* антагонисти́ческий. **antagonize** *vt* настра́ивать *impf*, настро́ить *pf* про́тив себя́.
Antarctic *n* Анта́рктика.
antelope *n* антило́па.
antenna *n* у́сик; (*also radio*) анте́нна.
anthem *n* гимн.
anthology *n* антоло́гия.
anthracite *n* антраци́т.
anthropological *adj* антропологи́ческий. **anthropologist** *n* антропо́лог. **anthropology** антрополо́гия.
anti-aircraft *adj* зени́тный. **antibiotic** *n* антибио́тик. **antibody** *n* антите́ло. **anticlimax** *n* разочарова́ние. **anticlockwise** *adj & adv* про́тив часово́й стре́лки. **antidepressant** *n* антидепресса́нт. **antidote** *n* противоя́дие. **antifreeze** *n* антифри́з.
antipathy *n* антипа́тия. **anti-Semitic** *adj* антисеми́тский. **anti-Semitism** *n* антисемити́зм. **antiseptic** *adj* антисепти́ческий; *n* антисе́птик. **antisocial** *adj* асоциа́льный. **antitank** *adj* противота́нковый. **antithesis** *n* противополо́жность; (*philos*) антите́зис.
anticipate *vt* ожида́ть *impf* +*gen*; (*with pleasure*) предвкуша́ть *impf*, предвкуси́ть *pf*; (*forestall*) предупрежда́ть *impf*, предупреди́ть *pf*. **anticipation** *n* ожида́ние; предвкуше́ние; предупрежде́ние.
antics *n* вы́ходки *f pl*.
antiquarian *adj* антиква́рный. **antiquated** *adj* устаре́лый. **antique** *adj* стари́нный; *n* антиква́рная вещь; ~ **shop** антиква́рный магази́н. **antiquity** *n* дре́вность.

antler *n* оле́ний рог.
anus *n* за́дний прохо́д.
anvil *n* накова́льня.
anxiety *n* беспоко́йство. **anxious** *adj* беспоко́йный; **be** ~ беспоко́иться *impf*; тревожиться *impf*.
any *adj, pron* (*some*) како́й-нибудь; ско́лько-нибудь; (*every*) вся́кий, любо́й; (*anybody*) кто́-нибудь, (*anything*) что́-нибудь; (*with neg*) ника́кой, ни оди́н; ниско́лько; никто́, ничто́; *adv* ско́лько-нибудь; (*with neg*) ниско́лько, ничу́ть. **anybody**, **anyone** *pron* кто́-нибудь; (*everybody*) вся́кий, любо́й; (*with neg*) никто́. **anyhow** *adv* ка́к-нибудь; ко́е-ка́к; (*with neg*) ника́к; *conj* во вся́ком слу́чае; всё равно́. **anyone** *see* **anybody. anything** *pron* что́-нибудь; всё (что уго́дно); (*with neg*) ничего́. **anyway** *adv* во вся́ком слу́чае; как бы то ни́ было. **anywhere** *adv* где/куда́ уго́дно; (*with neg, interrog*) где́-нибудь, куда́-нибудь.
apart *adv* (*aside*) в стороне́, в сто́рону; (*separately*) врозь; (*distant*) друг от дру́га; (*into pieces*) на ча́сти; ~ **from** кро́ме+*gen*.
apartheid *n* апарте́ид.
apartment *n* (*flat*) кварти́ра.
apathetic *adj* апати́чный. **apathy** *n* апа́тия.
ape *n* обезья́на; *vt* обезья́нничать *impf*, c~ *pf* c+*gen*.
aperture *n* отве́рстие.
apex *n* верши́на.
aphorism *n* афори́зм.
apiece *adv* (*per person*) на ка́ждого; (*per thing*) за шту́ку; (*amount*) по+*dat or acc with numbers*.
aplomb *n* апло́мб.
Apocalypse *n* Апока́липсис. **apocalyptic** *adj* апокалипти́ческий.
apologetic *adj* извиня́ющийся; **be** ~ извиня́ться *impf*. **apologize** *vi* извиня́ться *impf*, извини́ться *pf* (**to** пе́ред+*instr*; **for** за+*acc*). **apology** *n* извине́ние.
apostle *n* апо́стол.
apostrophe *n* апостро́ф.
appal *vi* ужаса́ть *impf*, ужасну́ть *pf*. **appalling** *adj* ужа́сный.
apparatus *n* аппара́т; прибо́р; (*gymnastic*) гимнасти́ческие снаря́ды *m pl*.

apparel *n* одея́ние.

apparent *adj* (*seeming*) ви́димый; (*manifest*) очеви́дный. **apparently** *adv* ка́жется, по-ви́димому.

apparition *n* виде́ние.

appeal *n* (*request*) призы́в, обраще́ние; (*law*) апелля́ция, обжа́лование; (*attraction*) привлека́тельность; ~ court апелляцио́нный суд; *vi* (*request*) взыва́ть *impf*, воззва́ть *pf* (to к+*dat*; for о+*prep*); обраща́ться *impf*, обрати́ться *pf* (с призы́вом); (*law*) апелли́ровать *impf* & *pf*; ~ to (*attract*) привлека́ть *impf*, привле́чь *pf*.

appear *vi* появля́ться *impf*, появи́ться *pf*; (*in public*) выступа́ть *impf*, вы́ступить *pf*; (*seem*) каза́ться *impf*, по~ *pf*. **appearance** *n* появле́ние; выступле́ние; (*aspect*) вид.

appease *vt* умиротворя́ть *impf*, умиротвори́ть *pf*.

append *vt* прилага́ть *impf*, приложи́ть *pf*. **appendicitis** *n* аппендици́т. **appendix** *n* приложе́ние; (*anat*) аппе́ндикс.

appertain *vi*: ~ to относи́ться *impf* +*dat*.

appetite *n* аппети́т. **appetizing** *adj* аппети́тный.

applaud *vt* аплоди́ровать *impf* +*dat*. **applause** *n* аплодисме́нты *m pl*.

apple *n* я́блоко; *adj* я́блочный; ~ tree я́блоня.

appliance *n* прибо́р. **applicable** *adj* примени́мый. **applicant** *n* кандида́т. **application** *n* (*use*) примене́ние; (*putting on*) наложе́ние; (*request*) заявле́ние. **applied** *adj* прикладно́й. **apply** *vt* (*use*) применя́ть *impf*, примени́ть *pf*; (*put on*) накла́дывать *impf*, наложи́ть *pf*; *vi* (*request*) обраща́ться *impf*, обрати́ться *pf* (to к+*dat*; for за+*acc*); ~ for (*job*) подава́ть *impf*, пода́ть *pf* заявле́ние на+*acc*; ~ to относи́ться *impf* к+*dat*.

appoint *vt* назнача́ть *impf*, назна́чить *pf*. **appointment** *n* назначе́ние; (*job*) до́лжность; (*meeting*) свида́ние.

apposite *adj* уме́стный.

appraise *vt* оце́нивать *impf*, оцени́ть *pf*.

appreciable *adj* заме́тный; (*consid-erable*) значи́тельный. **appreciate** *vt* цени́ть *impf*; (*understand*) понима́ть *impf*, поня́ть *pf*; *vi* повыша́ться *impf*, повы́ситься *pf* в цене́. **appreciation** *n* (*estimation*) оце́нка; (*gratitude*) призна́тельность; (*rise in value*) повыше́ние цены́. **appreciative** *adj* призна́тельный (of за+*acc*).

apprehension *n* (*fear*) опасе́ние. **apprehensive** *adj* опаса́ющийся.

apprentice *n* учени́к; *vt* отдава́ть *impf*, отда́ть *pf* в уче́ние. **apprenticeship** *n* учени́чество.

approach *vt* & *i* подходи́ть *impf*, подойти́ *pf* (к+*dat*); приближа́ться *impf*, прибли́зиться *pf* (к+*dat*); *vt* (*apply to*) обраща́ться *impf*, обрати́ться *pf* к+*dat*; *n* приближе́ние; подхо́д; подъе́зд; (*access*) по́дступ.

approbation *n* одобре́ние.

appropriate *adj* подходя́щий; *vt* присва́ивать *impf*, присво́ить *pf*. **appropriation** *n* присвое́ние.

approval *n* одобре́ние; **on** ~ на про́бу. **approve** *vt* утвержда́ть *impf*, утверди́ть *pf*; *vt* & *i* (~ of) одобря́ть *impf*, одо́брить *pf*.

approximate *adj* приблизи́тельный; *vi* приближа́ться *impf* (to к+*dat*). **approximation** *n* приближе́ние.

apricot *n* абрико́с.

April *n* апре́ль *m*; *adj* апре́льский.

apron *n* пере́дник.

apropos *adv*: ~ of по по́воду+*gen*.

apt *adj* (*suitable*) уда́чный; (*inclined*) скло́нный. **aptitude** *n* спосо́бность.

aqualung *n* аквала́нг. **aquarium** *n* аква́риум. **Aquarius** *n* Водоле́й. **aquatic** *adj* водяно́й; (*of sport*) во́дный. **aqueduct** *n* акведу́к.

aquiline *adj* орли́ный.

Arab *n* ара́б, ~ка; *adj* ара́бский. **Arabian** *adj* арави́йский. **Arabic** *adj* ара́бский.

arable *adj* па́хотный.

arbitrary *adj* произво́льный. **arbitrate** *vi* де́йствовать *impf* в ка́честве трете́йского судьи́. **arbitration** *n* арбитра́ж, трете́йское реше́ние. **arbitrator** *n* арби́тр, трете́йский судья́ *m*.

arc *n* дуга́. **arcade** *n* арка́да, (*shops*) пасса́ж.

arch[1] *n* а́рка, свод; (*of foot*) свод стопы́; *vt* & *i* выгиба́ть(ся) *impf*, выгнуть(ся) *pf*.

arch² *adj* игривый.

archaeological *adj* археологический. **archaeologist** *n* археолог.

archaeology *n* археология.

archaic *adj* архаический.

archangel *n* архангел.

archbishop *n* архиепископ.

arched *adj* сводчатый.

arch-enemy *n* заклятый враг.

archer *n* стрелок из лука. **archery** *n* стрельба из лука.

archipelago *n* архипелаг.

architect *n* архитектор. **architectural** *adj* архитектурный. **architecture** *n* архитектура.

archive(s) *n* архив.

archway *n* сводчатый проход.

Arctic *adj* арктический; *n* Арктика.

ardent *adj* горячий. **ardour** *n* пыл.

arduous *adj* трудный.

area *n* (*extent*) площадь; (*region*) район; (*sphere*) область.

arena *n* арена.

argue *vt* (*maintain*) утверждать *impf*; доказывать *impf*; *vi* спорить *impf*, по~ *pf*. **argument** *n* (*dispute*) спор; (*reason*) довод. **argumentative** *adj* любящий спорить.

aria *n* ария.

arid *adj* сухой.

Aries *n* Овен.

arise *vi* возникать *impf*, возникнуть *pf*.

aristocracy *n* аристократия. **aristocrat** *n* аристократ, ~ка. **aristocratic** *adj* аристократический.

arithmetic *n* арифметика. **arithmetical** *adj* арифметический.

ark *n* (Ноев) ковчег.

arm¹ *n* (*of body*) рука; (*of chair*) ручка; ~ **in** ~ под руку; **at** ~'**s length** (*fig*) на почтительном расстоянии; **with open** ~**s** с распростёртыми объятиями.

arm² *n pl* (*weapons*) оружие; *pl* (*coat of* ~**s**) герб; *vt* вооружать *impf*, вооружить *pf*. **armaments** *n pl* вооружение.

armchair *n* кресло.

Armenia *n* Армения. **Armenian** *n* армянин, армянка; *adj* армянский.

armistice *n* перемирие.

armour *n* (*for body*) доспехи *m pl*; (*for vehicles; fig*) броня. **armoured**

adj бронированный; (*vehicles etc.*) бронетанковый, броне-; ~ **car** броневик. **armoury** *n* арсенал.

armpit *n* подмышка.

army *n* армия; *adj* армейский.

aroma *n* аромат. **aromatic** *adj* ароматичный.

around *adv* кругом; *prep* вокруг+*gen*; **all** ~ повсюду.

arouse *vt* (*wake up*) будить *impf*, раз~ *pf*; (*stimulate*) возбуждать *impf*, возбудить *pf*.

arrange *vt* расставлять *impf*, расставить *pf*; (*plan*) устраивать *impf*, устроить *pf*; (*mus*) аранжировать *impf & pf*; *vi*: **to** ~ договариваться *impf*, договориться *pf +inf*. **arrangement** *n* расположение; устройство; (*agreement*) соглашение; (*mus*) аранжировка; *pl* приготовления *neut pl*.

array *vt* выставлять *impf*, выставить *pf*; *n* (*dress*) наряд; (*display*) коллекция.

arrears *n pl* задолженность.

arrest *vt* арестовывать *impf*, арестовать *pf*; *n* арест.

arrival *n* прибытие, приезд; (*new* ~) вновь прибывший *sb*. **arrive** *vi* прибывать *impf*, прибыть *pf*; приезжать *impf*, приехать *pf*.

arrogance *n* высокомерие. **arrogant** *adj* высокомерный.

arrow *n* стрела; (*pointer*) стрелка.

arsenal *n* арсенал.

arsenic *n* мышьяк.

arson *n* поджог.

art *n* искусство; *pl* гуманитарные науки *f pl*; *adj* художественный.

arterial *adj*: ~ **road** магистраль. **artery** *n* артерия.

artful *adj* хитрый.

arthritis *n* артрит.

article *n* (*literary*) статья; (*clause*) пункт; (*thing*) предмет; (*gram*) артикль *m*.

articulate *vt* произносить *impf*, произнести *pf*; (*express*) выражать *impf*, выразить *pf*; *adj* (*of speech*) членораздельный; **be** ~ чётко выражать *impf* свои мысли. **articulated lorry** *n* грузовой автомобиль с прицепом.

artifice *n* хитрость. **artificial** *adj* искусственный.

artillery *n* артиллерия.

artisan n ремесленник.

artist n художник. **artiste** n артист, ~ка. **artistic** adj художественный.

artless adj простодушный.

as adv как; conj (when) когда; в то время как; (because) так как; (manner) как; (though, however) как ни; rel pron который; что; **as ...
as** так (же)... как; **as for,** to относительно+gen; что касается +gen; **as if** как будто; **as it were** как бы; так сказать; **as soon as** как только; **as well** также; тоже.

asbestos n асбест.

ascend vt (go up) подниматься impf, подняться pf по+dat; (throne) восходить impf, взойти pf на+acc; vi возноситься impf, вознестись pf. **ascendancy** n власть. **Ascension** n (eccl) Вознесение. **ascent** n восхождение (**of** на+acc).

ascertain vt устанавливать impf, установить pf.

ascetic adj аскетический; n аскет. **asceticism** n аскетизм.

ascribe vt приписывать impf, приписать pf (**to** +dat).

ash[1] n (tree) ясень m.

ash[2], **ashes** n зола, пепел; (human remains) прах. **ashtray** n пепельница.

ashamed predic: **he is** ~ ему стыдно; **be, feel,** ~ **of** стыдиться impf, по~ pf +gen.

ashen adj (pale) мёртвенно-бледный.

ashore adv на берег(у).

Asia n Азия. **Asian, Asiatic** adj азиатский; n азиат, ~ка.

aside adv в сторону.

ask vt & i (enquire of) спрашивать impf, спросить pf; (request) просить impf, по~ pf (**for** acc, gen, o+prep); (invite) приглашать impf, пригласить pf; (demand) требовать impf +gen (**of** от+gen); ~ **after** осведомляться impf, осведомиться pf o+prep; ~ **a question** задавать impf, задать pf вопрос.

askance adv косо.

askew adv криво.

asleep predic & adv: **be** ~ спать impf; **fall** ~ засыпать impf, заснуть pf.

asparagus n спаржа.

aspect n вид; (side) сторона.

aspersion n клевета.

asphalt n асфальт.

asphyxiate vt удушать impf, удушить.

aspiration n стремление. **aspire** vi стремиться impf (**to** к+dat).

aspirin n аспирин; (tablet) таблетка аспирина.

ass n осёл.

assail vt нападать impf, напасть pf на+acc; (with questions) забрасывать impf, забросать pf вопросами. **assailant** n нападающий sb.

assassin n убийца m & f. **assassinate** vt убивать impf, убить pf. **assassination** n убийство.

assault n нападение; (mil) штурм; ~ **and battery** оскорбление действием; vt нападать impf, напасть pf .па+acc.

assemblage n сборка. **assemble** vt & i собирать(ся) impf, собрать(ся) pf. **assembly** n собрание; (of machine) сборка.

assent vi соглашаться impf, согласиться pf (**to** на+acc); n согласие.

assert vt утверждать impf; ~ **o.s.** отстаивать impf, отстоять pf свои права. **assertion** n утверждение. **assertive** adj настойчивый.

assess vt (amount) определять impf, определить pf; (value) оценивать impf, оценить pf. **assessment** n определение; оценка.

asset n ценное качество; (comm; also pl) актив.

assiduous adj прилежный.

assign vt (appoint) назначать impf, назначить pf; (allot) отводить impf, отвести pf. **assignation** n свидание. **assignment** n (task) задание; (mission) командировка.

assimilate vt усваивать impf, усвоить pf. **assimilation** n усвоение.

assist vt помогать impf, помочь pf +dat. **assistance** n помощь. **assistant** n помощник, ассистент.

associate vt ассоциировать impf & pf; vi общаться impf (**with** c+instr); n коллега m & f. **association** n общество, ассоциация.

assorted adj разный. **assortment** n ассортимент.

assuage vt (calm) успокаивать impf,

успоко́ить pf; (alleviate) смягча́ть impf, смягчи́ть pf.

assume vt (take on) принима́ть impf, приня́ть pf; (suppose) предполага́ть impf, предположи́ть pf; ~d name вы́мышленное и́мя neut; let us ~ допу́стим. **assumption** n (taking on) приня́тие на себе́; (supposition) предположе́ние.

assurance n заве́рение; (self-~) самоуве́ренность; (insurance) страхова́ние. **assure** vt уверя́ть impf, уве́рить pf.

asterisk n звёздочка.

asthma n а́стма. **asthmatic** adj астмати́ческий.

astonish vt удивля́ть impf, удиви́ть pf. **astonishing** adj удиви́тельный. **astonishment** n удивле́ние.

astound vt изумля́ть impf, изуми́ть pf. **astounding** adj изуми́тельный.

astray adv: go ~ сбива́ться impf, сби́ться pf с пути́; lead ~ сбива́ть impf, сбить pf с пути́.

astride prep верхо́м на+prep.

astringent adj вя́жущий; те́рпкий.

astrologer n астро́лог. **astrology** n астроло́гия. **astronaut** n астрона́вт. **astronomer** n астроно́м. **astronomical** adj астрономи́ческий. **astronomy** n астроно́мия.

astute adj проница́тельный.

asunder adv (apart) врозь; (in pieces) на ча́сти.

asylum n сумасше́дший дом; (refuge) убе́жище.

asymmetrical adj асимметри́чный. **asymmetry** n асимметри́я.

at prep (position) на+prep, в+prep, у+gen: at a concert на конце́рте; at the cinema в кино́; at the window у окна́; (time) в+acc: at two o'clock в два часа́; на+acc: at Easter на Па́сху; (price) по+dat: at 5p a pound по пяти́ пе́нсов за фунт; (speed): at 60 mph со ско́ростью шестьдеся́т миль в час; ~ first снача́ла, сперва́; ~ home до́ма; ~ last наконе́ц; ~ least по кра́йней ме́ре; ~ that на том; (moreover) к тому́ же.

atheism n атеи́зм. **atheist** n атеи́ст, ~ка.

athlete n спортсме́н, ~ка. **athletic** adj атлети́ческий. **athletics** n (лёгкая) атле́тика.

atlas n а́тлас.

atmosphere n атмосфе́ра. **atmospheric** adj атмосфе́рный.

atom n а́том; ~ **bomb** а́томная бо́мба. **atomic** adj а́томный.

atone vi искупа́ть impf, искупи́ть pf (for +acc). **atonement** n искупле́ние.

atrocious adj ужа́сный. **atrocity** n зве́рство.

attach vt (fasten) прикрепля́ть impf, прикрепи́ть pf; (append) прилага́ть impf, приложи́ть pf; (attribute) придава́ть impf, прида́ть pf; **attached to** (devoted) привя́занный к+dat. **attaché** n атташе́ m indecl. **attachment** n прикрепле́ние; привя́занность; (tech) принадле́жность.

attack vt напада́ть impf, напа́сть pf на+acc; n нападе́ние; (of illness) припа́док.

attain vt достига́ть impf, дости́чь & дости́гнуть pf +gen. **attainment** n достиже́ние.

attempt vt пыта́ться impf, по~ pf +inf; n попы́тка.

attend vt & i (be present at) прису́тствовать impf (на+prep); vt (accompany) сопровожда́ть impf, сопроводи́ть pf; (go to regularly) посеща́ть impf, посети́ть pf; ~ to занима́ться impf, заня́ться pf. **attendance** n (presence) прису́тствие; (number) посеща́емость. **attendant** adj сопровожда́ющий; n дежу́рный sb; (escort) провожа́тый sb.

attention n внима́ние; pay ~ обраща́ть impf, обрати́ть pf внима́ние (to на+acc); int (mil) сми́рно! **attentive** adj внима́тельный; (solicitous) забо́тливый.

attest vt & i (also ~ to) заверя́ть impf, заве́рить pf; свиде́тельствовать impf, за~ pf (o+prep).

attic n черда́к.

attire vt наряжа́ть impf, наряди́ть pf; n наря́д.

attitude n (posture) по́за; (opinion) отноше́ние (towards к+dat).

attorney n пове́ренный sb; **power of** ~ дове́ренность.

attract vt привлека́ть impf, привле́чь pf. **attraction** n привлека́тельность; (entertainment) аттракцио́н. **attractive** adj привлека́тельный.

attribute vt припи́сывать impf, приписа́ть pf; n (quality) сво́йство. **attribution** n припи́сывание. **attributive** adj атрибути́вный.

attrition n: war of ~ война́ на истоще́ние.

aubergine n баклажа́н.

auburn adj тёмно-ры́жий.

auction n аукцио́н; vt продава́ть impf, прода́ть pf с аукцио́на. **auctioneer** n аукциони́ст.

audacious adj (bold) сме́лый; (impudent) де́рзкий. **audacity** n сме́лость; де́рзость.

audible adj слы́шный. **audience** n пу́блика, аудито́рия; (listeners) слу́шатели m pl, (viewers, spectators) зри́тели m pl; (interview) аудие́нция. **audit** n прове́рка счето́в, реви́зия; vt проверя́ть impf, прове́рить pf (счета́+gen). **audition** n про́ба; vt устра́ивать impf, устро́ить pf про́бу+gen. **auditor** n ревизо́р. **auditorium** n зри́тельный зал.

augment n увели́чивать impf, увели́чить pf.

augur vt & i предвеща́ть impf.

August n а́вгуст; adj а́вгустовский. **august** adj вели́чественный.

aunt n тётя, тётка.

au pair n дома́ботница иностра́нного происхожде́ния.

aura n орео́л.

auspices n pl покрови́тельство. **auspicious** adj благоприя́тный.

austere adj стро́гий. **austerity** n стро́гость.

Australia n Австра́лия. **Australian** n австрали́ец, -и́йка; adj австрали́йский.

Austria n А́встрия. **Austrian** n австри́ец, -и́йка; adj австри́йский.

authentic adj по́длинный. **authenticate** vt устана́вливать impf, установи́ть pf по́длинность+gen. **authenticity** n по́длинность.

author, authoress n а́втор.

authoritarian adj авторита́рный. **authoritative** adj авторите́тный. **authority** n (power) власть, полномо́чие; (weight; expert) авторите́т; (source) авторите́тный исто́чник.

authorization n уполномо́чивание; (permission) разреше́ние. **authorize** vt (action) разреша́ть impf, раз-

реши́ть pf; (person) уполномо́чивать impf, уполномо́чить pf.

authorship n а́вторство.

autobiographical adj автобиографи́ческий. **autobiography** n автобиогра́фия. **autocracy** n автокра́тия. **autocrat** n автокра́т. **autocratic** adj автократи́ческий. **autograph** n авто́граф. **automatic** adj автомати́ческий. **automation** n автоматиза́ция. **automaton** n автома́т. **automobile** n автомоби́ль m. **autonomous** adj автоно́мный. **autonomy** n автоно́мия. **autopilot** n автопило́т. **autopsy** n вскры́тие; аутпси́я.

autumn n о́сень. **autumn(al)** adj осе́нний.

auxiliary adj вспомога́тельный; n помо́щник, -ица.

avail n: to no ~ напра́сно; vt: ~ o.s. of по́льзоваться impf, вос~ pf +instr. **available** adj досту́пный, нали́чный.

avalanche n лави́на.

avant-garde n аванга́рд; adj аванга́рдный.

avarice n жа́дность. **avaricious** adj жа́дный.

avenge vt мстить impf, ото~ pf за+acc. **avenger** n мсти́тель m.

avenue n (of trees) алле́я; (wide street) проспе́кт; (means) путь m.

average n сре́днее число́, сре́днее sb; on ~ в сре́днем; adj сре́дний; vt де́лать impf в сре́днем; vi & i: ~ (out at) составля́ть impf, соста́вить pf в сре́днем.

averse adj: not ~ to не прочь+inf, не про́тив+gen. **aversion** n отвраще́ние. **avert** vt (ward off) предотвраща́ть impf, предотврати́ть pf; (turn away) отводи́ть impf, отвести́ pf.

aviary n пти́чник.

aviation n авиа́ция.

avid adj жа́дный; (keen) стра́стный.

avocado n авока́до neut indecl.

avoid vt избега́ть impf, избежа́ть pf +gen; (evade) уклоня́ться impf, уклони́ться pf от+gen. **avoidance** n избежа́ние, уклоне́ние.

avowal n призна́ние. **avowed** adj при́знанный.

await vt ждать impf +gen.

awake predic: be ~ не спать impf.

awake(n) vt пробужда́ть impf, пробуди́ть pf; vi просыпа́ться impf, просну́ться pf.

award vt присужда́ть impf, присуди́ть pf (person dat, thing acc); награжда́ть impf, награди́ть pf (person acc, thing instr); n награ́да.

aware predic: be ~ of сознава́ть impf; знать impf. **awareness** n созна́ние.

away adv прочь; be ~ отсу́тствовать impf; far ~ (from) далеко́ (от+gen); 5 miles ~ в пяти́ ми́лях отсю́да; ~ game игра́ на чужо́м по́ле.

awe n благогове́йный страх.

awful adj ужа́сный. **awfully** adv ужа́сно.

awhile adv не́которое вре́мя.

awkward adj нело́вкий. **awkwardness** n нело́вкость.

awning n наве́с, тент.

awry adv ко́со.

axe n топо́р; vt уре́зывать, уреза́ть impf, уре́зать pf.

axiom n аксио́ма. **axiomatic** adj аксиомати́ческий.

axis, axle n ось.

ay int да!; n (in vote) го́лос "за".

Azerbaijan n Азербайджа́н. **Azerbaijani** n азербайджа́нец (-нца), -а́нка; adj азербайджа́нский.

azure n лазу́рь; adj лазу́рный.

B

BA abbr (univ) бакала́вр.

babble n (voices) болтовня́; (water) журча́ние; vi болта́ть impf; (water) журча́ть impf.

baboon n павиа́н.

baby n младе́нец; ~-sit присма́тривать за детьми́ в отсу́тствие роди́телей; ~-sitter приходя́щая ня́ня. **babyish** adj ребя́ческий.

bachelor n холостя́к; (univ) бакала́вр.

bacillus n баци́лла.

back n (of body) спина́; (rear) за́дняя часть; (reverse) оборо́т; (of seat) спи́нка; (sport) защи́тник; adj за́дний; vt (support) подде́рживать impf, поддержа́ть pf; (car) отодвига́ть impf, отодви́нуть pf; (horse) ста́вить impf, по~ pf на+acc; (finance) финанси́ровать impf & pf; vi ото

дви́гаться impf, отодви́нуться pf; **backed out of the garage** вы́ехал за́дом из гаража́; ~ **down** уступа́ть impf, уступи́ть pf; ~ **out** уклоня́ться impf, уклони́ться pf (of от+gen); ~ **up** (support) подде́рживать impf, поддержа́ть pf; (confirm) подкрепля́ть impf, подкрепи́ть pf. **backbiting** n спле́тня. **backbone** n позвоно́чник; (support) гла́вная опо́ра; (firmness) твёрдость хара́ктера. **backcloth, backdrop** n за́дник; (fig) фон. **backer** n спо́нсор; (supporter) сторо́нник. **backfire** vi дава́ть impf, дать pf отсе́чку. **background** n фон, за́дний план; (person's) происхожде́ние. **backhand(er)** n уда́р сле́ва. **backhanded** adj (fig) сомни́тельный. **backhander** n (bribe) взя́тка. **backing** n подде́ржка. **backlash** n реа́кция. **backlog** n задо́лженность. **backside** n зад. **backstage** adv за кули́сами; adj закули́сный. **backstroke** n пла́вание на спине́. **backup** n подде́ржка; (copy) резе́рвная ко́пия; adj вспомога́тельный. **backward** adj отста́лый. **backward(s)** adv наза́д. **backwater** n заво́дь. **back yard** n за́дний двор.

bacon n беко́н.

bacterium n бакте́рия.

bad adj плохо́й; (food etc.) испо́рченный; (language) гру́бый; ~-**mannered** невоспи́танный; ~ **taste** безвку́сица; ~-**tempered** раздражи́тельный.

badge n значо́к.

badger n барсу́к; vt трави́ть impf, за~ pf.

badly adv пло́хо; (very much) о́чень.

badminton n бадминто́н.

baffle vt озада́чивать impf, озада́чить pf.

bag n (handbag) су́мка; (plastic ~, sack, under eyes) мешо́к; (paper ~) бума́жный паке́т; pl (luggage) бага́ж.

baggage n бага́ж.

baggy adj мешкова́тый.

bagpipe n волы́нка.

bail[1] n (security) поручи́тельство; **release on** ~ отпуска́ть impf, отпусти́ть pf на пору́ки; vt (~ **out**) брать impf, взять pf на пору́ки; (help)

выруча́ть *impf*, вы́ручить *pf*.
bail², **bale²** *vt* выче́рпывать *impf*,
вы́черпнуть *pf* (во́ду из+*gen*); ~ **out**
vi выбра́сываться *impf*, вы́бро-
ситься *pf* с парашю́том.
bailiff *n* суде́бный исполни́тель.
bait *n* нажи́вка; прима́нка (*also fig*);
vt (*torment*) трави́ть *impf*, за~ *pf*.
bake *vt & i* пе́чь(ся) *impf*, ис~ *pf*.
baker *n* пе́карь *m*, бу́лочник. **bakery** *n* пека́рня; (*shop*) бу́лочная *sb*.
balalaika *n* балала́йка.
balance *n* (*scales*) весы́ *m pl*; (*equilibrium*) равнове́сие; (*econ*) бала́нс;
(*remainder*) оста́ток; ~ **sheet** ба-
ла́нс; *vt* (*make equal*) уравнове́ши-
вать *impf*, уравнове́сить *pf*; *vt & i*
(*econ*; *hold steady*) баланси́ровать
impf, с~ *pf*.
balcony *n* балко́н.
bald *adj* лы́сый; ~ **patch** лы́сина.
balding *adj* лысе́ющий. **baldness** *n*
плеши́вость.
bale¹ *n* (*bundle*) ки́па.
bale² *see* **bail²**
balk *vi* арта́читься *impf*, за~ *pf*; she
balked the price цена́ её испуга́ла.
ball¹ *n* (*in games*) мяч; (*sphere*; *billiards*) шар; (*wool*) клубо́к; ~**-bear-
ing** шарикоподши́пник; ~**-point
(pen)** ша́риковая ру́чка.
ball² *n* (*dance*) бал.
ballad *n* балла́да.
ballast *n* балла́ст.
ballerina *n* балери́на.
ballet *n* бале́т. **ballet-dancer** *n* ар-
ти́ст, ~ка, бале́та.
balloon *n* возду́шный шар.
ballot *n* голосова́ние. **ballot-paper**
n избира́тельный бюллете́нь *m*; *vt*
держа́ть *impf* голосова́ние между
+*instr*.
balm *n* бальза́м. **balmy** *adj* (*soft*)
мя́гкий.
Baltic *n* Балти́йское мо́ре; ~ **States**
прибалти́йские госуда́рства, При-
ба́лтика.
balustrade *n* балюстра́да.
bamboo *n* бамбу́к.
bamboozle *vt* надува́ть *impf*, наду́ть
pf.
ban *n* запре́т; *vt* запреща́ть *impf*,
запрети́ть *pf*.
banal *adj* бана́льный. **banality** *n*
бана́льность.

banana *n* бана́н.
band *n* (*stripe*, *strip*) полоса́; (*braid*,
tape) тесьма́; (*category*) катего́рия;
(*of people*) гру́ппа; (*gang*) ба́нда;
(*mus*) орке́стр; (*radio*) диапазо́н; *vi*:
~ **together** объединя́ться *impf*,
объедини́ться *pf*.
bandage *n* бинт; *vt* бинтова́ть *impf*,
за~ *pf*.
bandit *n* банди́т.
bandstand *n* эстра́да для орке́стра.
bandwagon *n*: jump on the ~ по́ль-
зоваться *impf*, вос~ *pf* благо-
прия́тными обстоя́тельствами.
bandy-legged *adj* кривоно́гий.
bane *n* отра́ва.
bang *n* (*blow*) уда́р; (*noise*) стук; (*of
gun*) вы́стрел; *vt* (*strike*) ударя́ть
impf, уда́рить *pf*; *vi* хло́пать *impf*,
хло́пнуть *pf*; (*slam shut*) захло́-
пываться *impf*, захло́пнуться *pf*; ~
one's head ударя́ться *impf*, уда́-
риться *pf* голово́й; ~ **the door**
хло́пать *impf*, хло́пнуть *pf* две́рью.
bangle *n* брасле́т.
banish *vt* изгоня́ть *impf*, изгна́ть *pf*.
banister *n* пери́ла *neut pl*.
banjo *n* ба́нджо *neut indecl*.
bank¹ *n* (*of river*) бе́рег; (*of earth*)
вал; *vt* сгреба́ть *impf*, сгрести́ *pf* в
ку́чу; *vi* (*aeron*) накреня́ться *impf*,
накрени́ться *pf*.
bank² *n* (*econ*) банк; ~ **account** счёт
в ба́нке; ~ **holiday** устано́вленный
пра́здник; *vi* (*keep money*) держа́ть
impf де́ньги (в ба́нке); *vt* (*put in* ~)
класть *impf*, положи́ть *pf* в банк;
~ **on** полага́ться *impf*, положи́ться
pf на+*acc*. **banker** *n* банки́р. **banknote** *n* банкно́та.
bankrupt *n* банкро́т; *adj* обанкро́-
тившийся; *vt* доводи́ть *impf*, до-
вести́ *pf* до банкро́тства. **bankruptcy** *n* банкро́тство.
banner *n* зна́мя *neut*.
banquet *n* банке́т, пир.
banter *n* подшу́чивание.
baptism *n* креще́ние. **baptize** *vt* кре-
сти́ть *impf*, о~ *pf*.
bar *n* (*beam*) брус; (*of cage*) решётка; (*of chocolate*) пли́тка; (*of
soap*) кусо́к; (*barrier*) прегра́да;
(*law*) адвокату́ра; (*counter*) сто́йка;
(*room*) бар; (*mus*) такт; *vt* (*obstruct*)
прегражда́ть *impf*, прегради́ть *pf*;

(*prohibit*) запреща́ть *impf*, запрети́ть *pf*.

barbarian *n* ва́рвар. **barbaric, barbarous** *adj* ва́рварский.

barbecue *n* (*party*) шашлы́к; *vt* жа́рить *impf*, за~ *pf* на ве́ртеле.

barbed wire *n* колю́чая про́волока.

barber *n* парикма́хер; ~'s **shop** парикма́херская *sb*.

bar code *n* маркиро́вка.

bard *n* бард.

bare *adj* (*naked*) го́лый; (*empty*) пусто́й; (*small*) минима́льный; *vt* обнажа́ть *impf*, обнажи́ть *pf*; ~ one's teeth ска́лить *impf*, о~ *pf* зу́бы. **barefaced** *adj* на́глый. **barefoot** *adj* босо́й. **barely** *adv* едва́.

bargain *n* (*deal*) сде́лка; (*good buy*) вы́годная сде́лка; *vi* торгова́ться *impf*, с~ *pf*; ~ **for, on** (*expect*) ожида́ть *impf* +*gen*.

barge *n* ба́ржа́; *vi*: ~ **into** (*room etc.*) вырыва́ться *impf*, ворва́ться *pf* в+*acc*.

baritone *n* барито́н.

bark[1] *n* (*of dog*) лай; *vi* ла́ять *impf*.

bark[2] *n* (*of tree*) кора́.

barley *n* ячме́нь *m*.

barmaid *n* буфе́тчица. **barman** *n* буфе́тчик.

barmy *adj* тро́нутый.

barn *n* амба́р.

barometer *n* баро́метр.

baron *n* баро́н. **baroness** *n* бароне́сса.

baroque *n* баро́кко *neut indecl*; *adj* баро́чный.

barrack[1] *n* каза́рма.

barrack[2] *vt* осви́стывать *impf*, освиста́ть *pf*.

barrage *n* (*in river*) запру́да; (*gunfire*) огнево́й вал; (*fig*) град.

barrel *n* бо́чка; (*of gun*) ду́ло.

barren *adj* беспло́дный.

barricade *n* баррика́да; *vt* баррикади́ровать *impf*, за~ *pf*.

barrier *n* барье́р.

barring *prep* исключа́я.

barrister *n* адвока́т.

barrow *n* теле́жка.

barter *n* товарообме́н; *vi* обме́ниваться *impf*, обменя́ться *pf* това́рами.

base[1] *adj* ни́зкий; (*metal*) неблагоро́дный.

base[2] *n* осно́ва; (*also mil*) ба́за; *vt* осно́вывать *impf*, основа́ть *pf*. **baseball** *n* бейсбо́л. **baseless** *adj* необосно́ванный. **basement** *n* подва́л.

bash *vt* тре́снуть *pf*; *n*: **have a** ~! попро́бу(йте)!

bashful *adj* засте́нчивый.

basic *adj* основно́й. **basically** *adv* в осно́вном.

basin *n* таз; (*geog*) бассе́йн.

basis *n* осно́ва, ба́зис.

bask *vi* гре́ться *impf*; (*fig*) наслажда́ться *impf*, наслади́ться *pf* (**in** +*instr*).

basket *n* корзи́на. **basketball** *n* баскетбо́л.

bass *n* бас; *adj* басо́вый.

bassoon *n* фаго́т.

bastard *n* (*sl*) негодя́й.

baste *vt* (*cul*) полива́ть *impf*, поли́ть *pf* жи́ром.

bastion *n* бастио́н.

bat[1] *n* (*zool*) летучая мышь.

bat[2] *n* (*sport*) бита́; *vi* бить *impf*, по~ *pf* по мячу́.

bat[3] *vt*: **he didn't** ~ **an eyelid** он и гла́зом не моргну́л.

batch *n* па́чка; (*of loaves*) вы́печка.

bated *adj*: **with** ~ **breath** затаи́в дыха́ние.

bath *n* (*vessel*) ва́нна; *pl* пла́вательный бассе́йн; **have a bath** принима́ть *impf*, приня́ть *pf* ва́нну; *vt* купа́ть *impf*, вы́~, ис~ *pf*. **bathe** *vi* купа́ться *impf*, вы́~, ис~ *pf*; *vt* омыва́ть *impf*, омы́ть *pf*. **bather** *n* купа́льщик, -ица. **bath-house** *n* ба́ня. **bathing** *n*: ~ **cap** купа́льная ша́почка; ~ **costume** купа́льный костю́м. **bathroom** *n* ва́нная *sb*.

baton *n* (*staff of office*) жезл; (*sport*) эстафе́та; (*mus*) (дирижёрская) па́лочка.

battalion *n* баталье́н.

batten *n* ре́йка.

batter *n* взби́тое те́сто; *vt* колоти́ть *impf*, по~ *pf*.

battery *n* батаре́я.

battle *n* би́тва; (*fig*) борьба́; *vi* боро́ться *impf*. **battlefield** *n* по́ле бо́я. **battlement** *n* зубча́тая стена́. **battleship** *n* лине́йный кора́бль *m*.

bawdy *adj* непристо́йный.

bawl *vi* ора́ть *impf*.

bay[1] n (bot) лавр; adj лавро́вый.

bay[2] n (geog) зали́в.

bay[3] n (recess) пролёт; ~ **window** фона́рь m.

bay[4] vi (bark) ла́ять impf; (howl) выть impf.

bay[5] adj (colour) гнедо́й.

bayonet n штык.

bazaar n база́р.

BC abbr до н.э. (до на́шей э́ры).

be[1] v 1. быть: usually omitted in pres: **he is a teacher** он учи́тель. 2. (exist) существова́ть impf. 3. (frequentative) быва́ть impf. 4. (~ situated) находи́ться impf; (stand) стоя́ть impf; (lie) лежа́ть impf. 5. (in general definitions) явля́ться impf +instr: **Moscow is the capital of Russia** столи́цей Росси́и явля́ется го́род Москва́. 6.: **there is, are** име́ется, име́ются; (emph) есть.

be[2] v aux 1. be+inf, expressing duty, plan: до́лжен+inf. 2. be+past participle passive, expressing passive: быть+past participle passive in short form: **it was done** бы́ло сде́лано; impers construction of 3 pl+acc: **I was beaten** меня́ би́ли; reflexive construction: **music was heard** слы́шалась му́зыка. 3. be+pres participle active, expressing continuous tenses: imperfective aspect: **I am reading** я чита́ю.

beach n пляж.

beacon n мая́к, сигна́льный ого́нь m.

bead n бу́сина; (drop) ка́пля; pl бу́сы f pl.

beak n клюв.

beaker n (child's) ча́шка с но́сиком; (chem) мензу́рка.

beam n ба́лка; (ray) луч; vi (shine) сия́ть impf.

bean n фасо́ль, боб.

bear[1] n медве́дь m.

bear[2] vt (carry) носи́ть indet, нести́ det, по~ pf; (endure) терпе́ть impf; (child) роди́ть impf & pf; ~ **out** подтвержда́ть impf, подтверди́ть pf; ~ **up** держа́ться impf. **bearable** adj терпи́мый.

beard n борода́. **bearded** adj борода́тый.

bearer n носи́тель m; (of cheque) предъяви́тель m; (of letter) пода́тель m.

bearing n (deportment) оса́нка; (relation) отноше́ние; (position) пе́ленг; (tech) подши́пник; **get one's ~s** ориенти́роваться impf & pf; **lose one's ~s** потеря́ть pf ориентиро́вку.

beast n живо́тное sb; (fig) скоти́на m & f. **beastly** adj (coll) проти́вный.

beat n бой; (round) обхо́д; (mus) такт; vt бить impf, по~ pf; (cul) взбива́ть impf, взбить pf; vi би́ться impf, ~ **off** отбива́ть impf, отби́ть pf; ~ **up** избива́ть impf, изби́ть pf. **beating** n битьё; (defeat) пораже́ние; (of heart) бие́ние.

beautiful adj краси́вый. **beautify** vt украша́ть impf укра́сить pf. **beauty** n красота́; (person) краса́вица.

beaver n бобр.

because conj потому́, что; так как; adv: ~ **of** из-за+gen.

beckon vt мани́ть impf, по~ pf к себе́.

become vi станови́ться impf, стать pf +instr; ~ **of** ста́ться pf с+instr. **becoming** adj (dress) иду́щий к лицу́ +dat.

bed n крова́ть, посте́ль; (garden) гря́дка; (sea) дно; (river) ру́сло; (geol) пласт; **go to ~** ложи́ться impf, лечь pf спать; **make the ~** стели́ть impf, по~ pf посте́ль. **bed and breakfast** n (hotel) ма́ленькая гости́ница. **bedclothes** n pl, **bedding** n посте́льное бельё. **bedridden** adj прико́ванный к посте́ли. **bedroom** n спа́льня. **bedside table** n ту́мбочка. **bedsitter** n однoко́мнатная кварти́ра. **bedspread** n покрыва́ло. **bedtime** n вре́мя neut ложи́ться спать.

bedevil vt му́чить impf, за~ pf.

bedlam n бедла́м.

bedraggled adj растрёпанный.

bee n пчела́. **beehive** n у́лей.

beech n бук.

beef n говя́дина. **beefburger** n котле́та.

beer n пи́во.

beetle n жук.

beetroot n свёкла.

befall vt & i случа́ться impf, случи́ться pf (+dat).

befit vt подходи́ть impf, подойти́ pf +dat.

before adv ра́ньше; prep пе́ред+instr,

до+*gen*; *conj* до того как; пре́жде чем; (*rather than*) скоре́е чем; **the day ~ yesterday** позавчера́. **beforehand** *adv* зара́нее.

befriend *vt* дружи́ться *impf*, по~ *pf* с+*instr*.

beg *vt* (*ask*) о́чень проси́ть *impf*, по~ *pf* (*person*+*acc*; *thing*+*acc* or *gen*); *vi* ни́щенствовать *impf*; (*of dog*) служи́ть *impf*; **~ for** проси́ть *impf*, по~ *pf* +*acc* or *gen*; **~ pardon** проси́ть *impf* проще́ния.

beggar *n* ни́щий *sb*.

begin *vt* (& *i*) начина́ть(ся) *impf*, нача́ть(ся) *pf*. **beginner** *n* начина́ющий *sb*. **beginning** *n* нача́ло.

begrudge *vt* (*give reluctantly*) жале́ть *impf*, по~ *pf* o+*prep*.

beguile *vt* (*charm*) очаро́вывать *impf*, очарова́ть *pf*; (*seduce, delude*) обольща́ть *impf*, обольсти́ть *pf*.

behalf *n*: **on ~ of** от и́мени+*gen*; (*in interest of*) в по́льзу+*gen*.

behave *vi* вести́ *impf* себя́. **behaviour** *n* поведе́ние.

behest *n* заве́т.

behind *adv*, *prep* сза́ди (+*gen*), позади́ (+*gen*), за (+*acc*, *instr*); *n* зад; **be, fall, ~** отстава́ть *impf*, отста́ть *pf*.

behold *vt* смотре́ть *impf*, по~ *pf*. **beholden** *predic*: **~ to** обя́зан+*dat*.

beige *adj* бе́жевый.

being *n* (*existence*) бытие́; (*creature*) существо́.

Belarus *n* Белару́сь.

belated *adj* запозда́лый.

belch *vi* рыга́ть *impf*, рыгну́ть *pf*; *vt* изверга́ть *impf*, изве́ргнуть *pf*.

beleaguer *vt* осажда́ть *impf*, осади́ть *pf*.

belfry *n* колоко́льня.

Belgian *n* белги́ец, -ги́йка; *adj* бельги́йский. **Belgium** *n* Бе́льгия.

belie *vt* противоре́чить *impf*+*dat*.

belief *n* (*faith*) ве́ра; (*confidence*) убежде́ние. **believable** *adj* правдоподо́бный. **believe** *vt* ве́рить *impf*, по~ *pf* +*dat*; **~ in** ве́рить *impf* в+*acc*. **believer** *n* ве́рующий *sb*.

belittle *vt* умаля́ть *impf*, умали́ть *pf*.

bell *n* ко́локол; (*doorbell*) звоно́к; **~ tower** колоко́льня.

bellicose *adj* войнственный. **belligerence** *n* войнственность. **belligerent** *adj* вою́ющий; (*aggressive*) войнственный.

bellow *vt* & *i* реве́ть *impf*.

bellows *n pl* мехи́ *m pl.*

belly *n* живо́т.

belong *vi* принадлежа́ть *impf* (**to** (к)+*dat*). **belongings** *n pl* пожи́тки (-ков) *pl.*

Belorussian *n* белору́с, ~ка; *adj* белору́сский.

beloved *adj* & *sb* возлю́бленный.

below *adv* (*position*) вниз, (*place*) внизу́, ни́же; *prep* ни́же+*gen*.

belt *n* (*strap*) по́яс, (*also tech*) реме́нь; (*zone*) зо́на, полоса́.

bench *n* скаме́йка; (*for work*) стано́к.

bend *n* изги́б; *vt* (& *i*, *also* **~ down**) сгиба́ть(ся) *impf*, согну́ть(ся) *pf*; **~ over** склоня́ться *impf*, склони́ться *pf* над+*instr*.

beneath *prep* под+*instr.*

benediction *n* благослове́ние.

benefactor *n* благоде́тель *m*. **benefactress** *n* благоде́тельница

beneficial *adj* поле́зный. **beneficiary** *n* получа́тель *m*; (*law*) насле́дник.

benefit *n* по́льза; (*allowance*) посо́бие; (*theat*) бенефи́с; *vt* приноси́ть *impf*, принести́ *pf* по́льзу +*dat*; *vi* извлека́ть *impf*, извле́чь *pf* вы́году.

benevolence *n* благожела́тельность. **benevolent** *adj* благожела́тельный.

benign *adj* до́брый, мя́гкий; (*tumour*) доброка́чественный.

bent *adj* скло́нность.

bequeath *vt* завеща́ть *impf* & *pf* (**to**+*dat*). **bequest** *n* посме́ртный дар.

berate *vt* руга́ть *impf*, вы́~ *pf*.

bereave *vt* лиша́ть *impf*, лиши́ть *pf* (**of** +*gen*). **bereavement** *n* тяжёлая утра́та.

berry *n* я́года.

berserk *adj*: **go ~** взбеси́ться *pf*.

berth *n* (*bunk*) ко́йка; (*naut*) стоя́нка; *vi* прича́ливать *impf*, прича́лить *pf*.

beseech *vt* умоля́ть *impf*, умоли́ть *pf*.

beset *vt* осажда́ть *impf*, осади́ть *pf*.

beside *prep* о́коло+*gen*, ря́дом с+*instr*; **~ the point** некста́ти; **~ o.s.** вне себя́. **besides** *adv* кро́ме того́; *prep* кро́ме+*gen*.

besiege vt осаждать impf, осадить pf.

besotted adj одурманенный.

bespoke adj сделанный на заказ.

best adj лучший, самый лучший; adv лучше всего, больше всего; all the ~! всего наилучшего! at ~ в лучшем случае; do one's ~ делать impf, с~ pf всё возможное; ~ man шафер.

bestial adj зверский. **bestiality** n зверство.

bestow vt даровать impf & pf.

bestseller n бестселлер.

bet n пари neut indecl; (stake) ставка; vi держать impf пари (on на+acc); vt (stake) ставить impf, по~ pf; he bet me £5 он поспорил со мной 5 фунтов.

betray vt изменять impf, изменить pf+dat. **betrayal** n измена.

better adj лучший; adv лучше; (more) больше; vt улучшать impf, улучшить pf; all the ~ тем лучше; ~ off более состоятельный; ~ o.s. выдвигаться impf, выдвинуться pf; get ~ (health) поправляться impf, поправиться pf; get the ~ of брать impf, взять pf верх над+instr; had ~: you had ~ go вам (dat) лучше бы пойти; think ~ of передумывать impf, передумать pf. **betterment** n улучшение.

between prep между+instr.

bevel vt скашивать impf, скосить pf.

beverage n напиток.

bevy n стайка.

beware vi остерегаться impf, остеречься pf (of +gen).

bewilder vt сбивать impf, сбить pf с толку. **bewildered** adj озадаченный. **bewilderment** n замешательство.

bewitch vt заколдовывать impf, заколдовать pf; (fig) очаровывать impf, очаровать pf. **bewitching** adj очаровательный.

beyond prep за+acc & instr; по ту сторону+gen; (above) сверх+gen; (outside) вне+gen; the back of ~ край света.

bias n (inclination) уклон; (prejudice) предупреждение. **biased** adj предупреждённый.

bib n нагрудник.

Bible n Библия. **biblical** adj библейский.

bibliographical n библиографический. **bibliography** n библиография.

bicarbonate (of soda) n питьевая сода.

biceps n бицепс.

bicker vi пререкаться impf.

bicycle n велосипед.

bid n предложение цены; (attempt) попытка; vt & i предлагать impf, предложить pf (цену) (for за+acc); vt (command) приказывать impf, приказать pf +dat. **bidding** n предложение цены; (command) приказание.

bide vt: ~ one's time ожидать impf благоприятного случая.

biennial adj двухлетний; n двухлетник.

bier n катафалк.

bifocals n pl бифокальные очки pl.

big adj большой; (also important) крупный.

bigamist n (man) двоеженец; (woman) двумужница. **bigamy** n двубрачие.

bigwig n шишка.

bike n велосипед. **biker** n мотоциклист.

bikini n бикини neut indecl.

bilateral adj двусторонний.

bilberry n черника (no pl; usu collect).

bile n жёлчь. **bilious** adj жёлчный.

bilingual adj двуязычный.

bill[1] n счёт; (parl) законопроект; (~ of exchange) вексель; (poster) афиша; vt (announce) объявлять impf, объявить pf в афишах; (charge) присылать impf, прислать pf счёт +dat.

bill[2] n (beak) клюв.

billet vt расквартировывать impf, расквартировать pf.

billiards n бильярд.

billion n биллион.

billow n вал; vi вздыматься impf.

bin n мусорное ведро; (corn) закром.

bind vt (tie) связывать impf, связать pf; (oblige) обязывать impf, обязать pf; (book) переплетать impf, переплести pf. **binder** n (person) переплётчик; (agric) вязáльщик; (for papers) пáпка. **binding** n переплёт.

binge n кутёж.

binoculars n pl бинóкль m.

biochemistry n биохимия. **biographer** n биóграф. **biographical** adj биографический. **biography** n биогрáфия. **biological** adj биологический. **biologist** n биóлог. **biology** n биолóгия.

bipartisan adj двухпартийный.

birch n берёза; (rod) рóзга.

bird n птица; ~ of prey хищная птица.

birth n рождéние; (descent) происхождéние; ~ certificate мéтрика; ~ control противозачáточные мéры f pl. **birthday** n день m рождéния; fourth ~ четырёхлéтие. **birthplace** n мéсто рождéния. **birthright** n прáво по рождéнию.

biscuit n печéнье.

bisect vt разрезáть impf, разрéзать pf пополáм.

bisexual adj бисексуáльный.

bishop n епископ; (chess) слон.

bit[1] n (piece) кусóчек; a ~ немнóго; not a ~ ничýть.

bit[2] n (tech) сверлó; (bridle) удилá (-л) pl.

bitch n (coll) стéрва. **bitchy** adj стервóзный.

bite n укýс; (snack) закýска; (fishing) клёв; vt кусáть impf, укусить pf; vi (fish) клевáть impf, клюнуть pf. **biting** adj éдкий.

bitter adj гóрький. **bitterness** n гóречь.

bitumen n битýм.

bivouac n бивáк.

bizarre adj стрáнный.

black adj чёрный; ~ eye подбитый глаз; ~ market чёрный рынок; v: ~ out (vt) затемнять impf, затемнить pf; (vi) терять impf, по~ pf сознáние; n (colour) чёрный цвет; (~ person) негр, ~итя́нка; (mourning) трáур. **blackberry** n ежевика (no pl; usu collect). **blackbird** n чёрный дрозд. **blackboard** n доскá. **blackcurrant** n чёрная сморóдина (no pl; usu collect). **blacken** vt (fig) чернить impf, о~ pf. **blackleg** n штрейкбрéхер. **blacklist** n вносить

impf, внести pf в чёрный список. **blackmail** n шантáж; vt шантажировать impf. **blackout** n затемнéние; (faint) потéря сознáния. **blacksmith** n кузнéц.

bladder n пузырь m.

blade n (knife) лéзвие; (oar) лóпасть; (grass) былинка.

blame n винá, порицáние; vt винить impf (for в+prep); be to ~ быть виновáтым. **blameless** adj безупрéчный.

blanch vt (vegetables) ошпáривать impf, ошпáрить pf; vi бледнéть impf, по~ pf.

bland adj мягкий; (dull) прéсный.

blandishments n pl лесть.

blank adj (look) отсýтствующий; (paper) чистый; n (space) прóпуск; (form) бланк; (cartridge) холостóй патрóн; ~ cheque незапóлненный чек.

blanket n одеáло.

blare vi трубить impf, про~ pf.

blasé adj пресыщенный.

blasphemous adj богохýльный. **blasphemy** n богохýльство.

blast n (wind) порыв вéтра; (explosion) взрыв; vt взрывáть impf, взорвáть pf; ~ off стартовáть impf & pf. **blast-furnace** n дóмна.

blatant adj явный.

blaze n (flame) плáмя neut; (fire) пожáр; vi пылáть impf.

blazer n лёгкий пиджáк.

bleach n хлóрка, отбéливатель m; vt отбéливать impf, отбелить pf.

bleak adj пустынный; (dreary) унылый.

bleary-eyed adj с затумáненными глазáми.

bleat vi блéять impf.

bleed vi кровоточить impf.

bleeper n персонáльный сигнализáтор.

blemish n пятнó.

blend n смесь; vt смéшивать impf, смешáть pf; vi гармонировать impf. **blender** n миксер.

bless vt благословлять impf, благословить pf. **blessed** adj благословéнный. **blessing** n (action) благословéние; (object) блáго.

blight vt губить impf, по~ pf.

blind adj слепóй; ~ alley тупик; n

штóра; vt ослепля́ть impf, ослепи́ть pf. **blindfold** vt завя́зывать impf, завяза́ть pf глаза́+dat. **blindness** n слепота́.

blink vi мига́ть impf, мигну́ть pf. **blinkers** n pl шо́ры (-p) pl.

bliss n блаже́нство. **blissful** adj блаже́нный.

blister n пузы́рь m, волды́рь m.

blithe adj весёлый; (carefree) беспе́чный.

blitz n бомбёжка.

blizzard n мете́ль.

bloated adj вздутый.

blob n (liquid) ка́пля; (colour) кля́кса.

bloc n блок.

block n (wood) чурба́н; (stone) глы́ба; (flats) жило́й дом; vt прегражда́ть impf, прегради́ть pf; ~ **up** забива́ть impf, заби́ть pf.

blockade n блока́да; vt блоки́ровать impf & pf.

blockage n зато́р.

bloke n па́рень m.

blond n блонди́н, ~ка; adj белоку́рый.

blood n кровь; ~ **donor** до́нор; ~ **poisoning** n зараже́ние кро́ви; ~ **pressure** кровяно́е давле́ние; ~ **relation** бли́зкий ро́дственник, -ая ро́дственница; ~ **transfusion** перелива́ние кро́ви. **bloodhound** n ище́йка. **bloodshed** n кровопроли́тие. **bloodshot** adj нали́тый кро́вью. **bloodthirsty** adj кровожа́дный. **bloody** adj крова́вый.

bloom n расцве́т; vi цвести́ pf.

blossom n цвет; **in** ~ в цвету́.

blot n кля́кса; пятно́; vt (dry) промока́ть impf, промокну́ть pf; (smudge) па́чкать impf, за~ pf.

blotch n пятно́.

blotting-paper n промока́тельная бума́га.

blouse n ко́фточка, блу́зка.

blow¹ n уда́р.

blow² vt & i дуть impf; ~ **away** сноси́ть impf, снести́ pf; ~ **down** вали́ть impf, по~ pf; ~ **one's nose** сморка́ться impf, сморкну́ться pf; ~ **out** задува́ть impf, заду́ть pf; ~ **over** (fig) проходи́ть impf, пройти́ pf; ~ **up** взрыва́ть impf, взорва́ть pf; (inflate) надува́ть impf, наду́ть pf. **blow-lamp** n пая́льная ла́мпа.

blubber¹ n во́рвань.

blubber² vi реве́ть impf.

bludgeon n дуби́нка; vt (compel) вынужда́ть impf, вы́нудить pf.

blue adj (dark) си́ний; (light) голубо́й; n си́ний, голубо́й, цвет. **bluebell** n колоко́льчик. **bluebottle** n си́няя му́ха. **blueprint** n си́нька, светоко́пия; (fig) прое́кт.

bluff n блеф; vi блефова́ть impf.

blunder n опло́шность; vi оплоша́ть pf.

blunt adj тупо́й; (person) прямо́й; vt тупи́ть impf, за~, ис~ pf.

blur vt затума́нивать impf, затума́нить pf. **blurred** adj расплы́вчатый.

blurt vt: ~ **out** выба́лтывать impf, вы́болтать pf.

blush vi красне́ть impf, по~ pf.

bluster vi бушева́ть impf; n пусты́е слова́ neut pl.

boar n бо́ров; (wild) каба́н.

board n доска́; (committee) правле́ние, сове́т; **on** ~ на борт(у́); vt сади́ться impf, сесть pf (на кора́бль, в по́езд и т.д.); ~ **up** забива́ть impf, заби́ть pf. **boarder** n пансионе́р. **boarding-house** n пансио́н. **boarding-school** n интерна́т.

boast vi хва́статься impf, по~ pf; vt горди́ться impf +instr. **boaster** n хвасту́н. **boastful** adj хвастли́вый.

boat n (small) ло́дка; (large) кора́бль m.

bob vi подпры́гивать impf, подпры́гнуть pf.

bobbin n кату́шка.

bobsleigh n бо́бслей.

bode vt: ~**well/ill** предвеща́ть impf хоро́шее/недо́брое.

bodice n лиф, корса́ж.

bodily adv целико́м; adj теле́сный.

body n те́ло, ту́ловище; (corpse) труп; (group) о́рган; (main part) основна́я часть. **bodyguard** n телохрани́тель m. **bodywork** n ку́зов.

bog n боло́та; **get** ~**ged down** увяза́ть impf, увя́знуть pf. **boggy** adj боло́тистый.

bogus adj подде́льный.

boil¹ n (med) furру́нкул.

boil² vi кипе́ть impf, вс~ pf; vt кипяти́ть impf, с~ pf; (cook) вари́ть *impf*, c~ *pf*; ~ **down to** сходи́ться *impf*, сойти́сь *pf* к тому́, что; ~**over** выкипа́ть *impf*, вы́кипеть *pf*; *n* кипе́ние; **bring to the** ~ доводи́ть *impf*, довести́ *pf* до кипе́ния. **boiled** *adj* варёный. **boiler** *n* котёл; ~ **suit** комбинезо́н. **boiling** *adj* кипя́щий; ~ **point** то́чка кипе́ния; ~ **water** кипято́к.

boisterous *adj* шумли́вый.

bold *adj* сме́лый; (*type*) жи́рный.

bollard *n* (*in road*) столб; (*on quay*) пал.

bolster *n* ва́лик; *vt*: ~ **up** подпира́ть *impf*, подпере́ть *pf*.

bolt *n* засо́в; (*tech*) болт; *vt* запира́ть *impf*, запере́ть *pf* на засо́в; скрепля́ть *impf*, скрепи́ть *pf* болта́ми; *vi* (*flee*) удира́ть *impf*, удра́ть *pf*; (*horse*) понести́ *pf*.

bomb *n* бо́мба; *vt* бомби́ть *impf*. **bombard** *vt* бомбарди́ровать *impf*. **bombardment** *n* бомбардиро́вка. **bomber** *n* бомбардиро́вщик.

bombastic *adj* напы́щенный.

bond *n* (*econ*) облига́ция; (*link*) связь; *pl* око́вы (-в) *pl*, (*fig*) у́зы (уз) *pl*.

bone *n* кость.

bonfire *n* костёр.

bonnet *n* ка́пор; (*car*) капо́т.

bonus *n* пре́мия.

bony *adj* кости́стый.

boo *vt* осви́стывать *impf*, освиста́ть *pf*; *vi* улюлю́кать *impf*.

booby trap *n* лову́шка.

book *n* кни́га; *vt* (*order*) зака́зывать *impf*, заказа́ть *pf*; (*reserve*) брони́ровать *impf*, за~ *pf*. **bookbinder** *n* переплётчик. **bookcase** *n* кни́жный шкаф. **booking** *n* зака́з; ~ **office** ка́сса. **bookkeeper** *n* бухга́лтер. **bookmaker** *n* букме́кер. **bookshop** *n* кни́жный магази́н.

boom[1] *n* (*barrier*) бон.

boom[2] *n* (*sound*) гул; (*econ*) бум; *vi* гуде́ть *impf*; (*fig*) процвета́ть *impf*.

boon *n* бла́го.

boor *n* хам. **boorish** *adj* ха́мский.

boost *n* соде́йствие; *vt* увели́чивать *impf*, увели́чить *pf*.

boot *n* боти́нок; (*high*) сапо́г; (*football*) бу́тса; (*car*) бага́жник.

booth *n* кио́ск, бу́дка; (*polling*) каби́на.

booty *n* добы́ча.

booze *n* вы́пивка; *vi* выпива́ть *impf*.

border *n* (*frontier*) грани́ца; (*trim*) кайма́; (*gardening*) бордю́р; *vi* грани́чить *impf* (**on** с+*instr*). **borderline** *n* грани́ца.

bore[1] *n* (*calibre*) кана́л (ствола́); *vt* сверли́ть *impf*, про~ *pf*.

bore[2] *n* (*thing*) ску́ка; (*person*) ску́чный челове́к; *vt* надоеда́ть *impf*, надое́сть *pf*. **boredom** *n* ску́ка. **boring** *adj* ску́чный.

born *adj* прирождённый; **be** ~ роди́ться *impf* & *pf*.

borough *n* райо́н.

borrow *vt* одолжа́ть *impf*, одолжи́ть *pf* (**from** y+*gen*).

Bosnia *n* Бо́сния. **Bosnian** *n* босни́ец, -и́йка; *adj* босни́йский.

bosom *n* грудь.

boss *n* нача́льник; *vt* кома́ндовать *impf*, c~ *pf* +*instr*. **bossy** *adj* кома́ндирский.

botanical *adj* ботани́ческий. **botanist** *n* бота́ник. **botany** *n* бота́ника.

botch *vt* зала́тывать *impf*, зала́тать *pf*.

both *adj* & *pron* о́ба *m* & *neut*, о́бе *f*; ~ **... and** и... и.

bother *n* доса́да; *vt* беспоко́ить *impf*.

bottle *n* буты́лка; ~**neck** суже́ние; *vt* разлива́ть *impf*, разли́ть *pf* по буты́лкам; ~ **up** сде́рживать *impf*, сдержа́ть *pf*.

bottom *n* ни́жняя часть; (*of river etc.*) дно; (*buttocks*) зад; **at the** ~ **of** (*stairs*) внизу́+*gen*; **get to the** ~ **of** добира́ться *impf*, добра́ться *pf* до су́ти +*gen*; *adj* са́мый ни́жний. **bottomless** *adj* бездо́нный.

bough *n* сук.

boulder *n* валу́н.

bounce *vi* подпры́гивать *impf*, подпры́гнуть *pf*; (*cheque*) верну́ться *pf*.

bound[1] *n* (*limit*) преде́л; *vt* ограни́чивать *impf*, ограни́чить *pf*.

bound[2] *n* (*spring*) прыжо́к; *vi* пры́гать *impf*, пры́гнуть *pf*.

bound[3] *adj*: **he is** ~ **to be there** он обяза́тельно там бу́дет.

bound[4] *adj*: **to be** ~ **for** направля́ться *impf*, напра́виться *pf* в+*acc*.

boundary *n* грани́ца.

boundless *adj* безграни́чный.

bountiful *adj* (*generous*) ще́дрый;

(*ample*) оби́льный. **bounty** *n* щéд-рость; (*reward*) прéмия.

bouquet *n* букéт.

bourgeois *adj* буржуáзный. **bourgeoisie** *n* буржуази́я.

bout *n* (*med*) при́ступ; (*sport*) схвáтка.

bow¹ *n* (*weapon*) лук; (*knot*) бант; (*mus*) смычóк.

bow² *n* (*obeisance*) поклóн; *vi* клáняться *impf*, поклони́ться *pf*; *vt* склоня́ть *impf*, склони́ть *pf*.

bow³ *n* (*naut*) нос.

bowel *n* кишкá; (*depths*) нéдра (-р) *pl*.

bowl¹ *n* ми́ска.

bowl² *n* (*ball*) шар; *vi* подавáть *impf*, подáть *pf* мяч. **bowler** *n* подаю́щий *sb* мяч; (*hat*) котелóк. **bowling-alley** *n* кегельбáн. **bowls** *n* игрá в шары́.

box¹ *n* корóбка, я́щик; (*theat*) лóжа; ~ **office** кáсса.

box² *vi* бокси́ровать *impf*. **boxer** *n* боксёр. **boxing** *n* бокс. **Boxing Day** *n* второ́й день Рождествá.

boy *n* мáльчик. **boyfriend** *n* молодóй человéк. **boyhood** *n* óтрочество. **boyish** *adj* мальчи́шеский.

boycott *n* бойкóт; *vt* бойкоти́ровать *impf* & *pf*.

bra *n* ли́фчик.

brace *n* (*clamp*) скрéпа; *pl* подтя́жки *f pl*; (*dental*) ши́на; *vt* скрепля́ть *impf*, скрепи́ть *pf*; ~ **o.s.** собирáться *impf*, собрáться *pf* с си́лами.

bracelet *n* браслéт.

bracing *adj* бодря́щий.

bracket *n* (*support*) кронштéйн; *pl* скóбки *f pl*; (*category*) категóрия.

brag *vi* хвáстаться *impf*, по~ *pf*.

braid *n* тесьмá.

braille *n* шрифт Брáйля.

brain *n* мозг. **brainstorm** *n* припáдок безýмия. **brainwash** *vt* промывáть *impf*, промы́ть *pf* мозги́+*dat*. **brainwave** *n* блестя́щая идéя.

braise *vt* туши́ть *impf*, с~ *pf*.

brake *n* тóрмоз; *vt* тормози́ть *impf*, за~ *pf*.

bramble *n* ежеви́ка.

bran *n* óтруби (-бéй) *pl*.

branch *n* вéтка; (*fig*) óтрасль; (*comm*) филиáл; *vi* разветвля́ться *impf*, разветви́ться *pf*; ~ **out** (*fig*)

расширя́ть *impf*, расши́рить *pf* дéятельность.

brand *n* (*mark*) клеймó; (*make*) мáрка; (*sort*) сорт; *vt* клейми́ть *impf*, за~ *pf*.

brandish *vt* размáхивать *impf*+*instr*.

brandy *n* коньяк.

brash *adj* нахáльный.

brass *n* латýнь, жёлтая медь; (*mus*) мéдные инструмéнты *m pl*; *adj* латýнный, мéдный; ~ **band** мéдный духовóй оркéстр; **top** ~ вы́сшее начáльство.

brassière *n* бюстгáлтер.

brat *n* чертёнок.

bravado *n* бравáда.

brave *adj* хрáбрый; *vt* покоря́ть *impf*, покори́ть *pf*. **bravery** *n* хрáбрость.

bravo *int* брáво.

brawl *n* скандáл; *vi* дрáться *impf*, по~ *pf*.

brawny *adj* мýскулистый.

bray *n* крик ослá; *vi* кричáть *impf*.

brazen *adj* бессты́дный.

brazier *n* жарóвня.

breach *n* нарушéние; (*break*) пролóм; (*mil*) брешь; *vt* проламывать *impf*, проломи́ть *pf*; (*rule*) нарушáть *impf*, нару́шить *pf*.

bread *n* хлеб; (*white*) бýлка. **breadcrumb** *n* крóшка. **breadwinner** *n* корми́лец.

breadth *n* ширинá; (*fig*) широтá.

break *n* пролóм, разры́в; (*pause*) переры́в, пáуза; *vt* разбивáть(ся) *impf*, с~ *pf*; разбивáть(ся) *impf*, разби́ть(ся) *pf*; *vt* (*violate*) нарушáть *impf*, нару́шить *pf*; ~ **away** вырывáться *impf*, вы́рваться *pf*; ~ **down** (*vi*) (*tech*) ломáться *impf*, с~ *pf*; (*talks*) срывáться *impf*, сорвáться *pf*; (*vt*) (*door*) выламывать *impf*, вы́ломать *pf*; ~ **in/to** вламываться *impf*, вломи́ться *pf* в+*acc*; ~ **off** (*vt* & *i*) отламывать(ся) *impf*, отломи́ть(ся) *pf*; (*vi*) (*speaking*) замолчáть *pf*; (*vt*) (*relations*) порывáть *impf*, порвáть *pf*; ~ **out** вырывáться *impf*, вы́рваться *pf*; (*fire*, *war*) вспы́хнуть *pf*; ~ **through** пробивáться *impf*, проби́ться *pf*; ~ **up** (*vi*) (*marriage*) распадáться *impf*, распáсться *pf*; (*meeting*) прерывáться *impf*, прервáться *pf*; (*vt*) (*disperse*) разгоня́ть *impf*, разогна́ть *pf*; (*vt & i*) разбива́ть(ся) *impf*, разби́ть(ся) *pf*; ~ **with** порыва́ть *impf*, порва́ть *pf* с+*instr*. **breakage** *n* поло́мка. **breakdown** *n* поло́мка; (*med*) не́рвный срыв. **breaker** *n* бурýн. **breakfast** *n* за́втрак; *vi* за́втракать *impf*, по~ *pf*. **breakneck** *adj*: at ~ **speed** сломя́ го́лову. **breakthrough** *n* проры́в. **breakwater** *n* волноре́з.

breast *n* грудь; ~**-feeding** *n* кормле́ние гру́дью; ~ **stroke** *n* брасс. **breath** *n* дыха́ние; be out of ~ запыха́ться *impf & pf*. **breathe** *vi* дыша́ть *impf*; ~ **in** вдыха́ть *impf*, вдохну́ть *pf*; ~ **out** выдыха́ть *impf*, вы́дохнуть *pf*. **breather** *n* передышка. **breathless** *adj* запыха́вшийся.

breeches *n pl* бри́джи (-жей) *pl*.

breed *n* поро́да; *vi* размножа́ться *impf*, размно́житься *pf*; *vt* разводи́ть *impf*, развести́ *pf*. **breeder** *n* -во́д: cattle ~ скотово́д. **breeding** *n* разведе́ние, -во́дство; (*upbringing*) воспи́танность.

breeze *n* ветеро́к; (*naut*) бриз. **breezy** *adj* све́жий.

brevity *n* кра́ткость.

brew *vt* (*beer*) вари́ть *impf*, с~ *pf*; (*tea*) зава́ривать *impf*, завари́ть *pf*; (*beer*) ва́рка; (*tea*) зава́рка. **brewer** *n* пивова́р. **brewery** *n* пивова́ренный заво́д.

bribe *n* взя́тка; *vt* подкупа́ть *impf*, подкупи́ть *pf*. **bribery** *n* по́дкуп.

brick *n* кирпи́ч; *adj* кирпи́чный. **bricklayer** *n* ка́менщик.

bridal *adj* сва́дебный. **bride** *n* неве́ста. **bridegroom** *n* жени́х. **bridesmaid** *n* подру́жка неве́сты.

bridge[1] *n* мост; (*of nose*) перено́сица; *vt* (*gap*) заполня́ть *impf*, запо́лнить *pf*; (*overcome*) преодолева́ть *impf*, преодоле́ть *pf*.

bridge[2] *n* (*game*) бридж.

bridle *n* узда́; *vi* возмуща́ться *impf*, возмути́ться *pf*.

brief *adj* недо́лгий; (*concise*) кра́ткий; *n* инстру́кция; *vt* инструкти́ровать *impf & pf*. **briefcase** *n* портфе́ль *m*. **briefing** *n* инструкта́ж. **briefly** *adv* кра́тко. **briefs** *n pl* трусы́ (-со́в) *pl*.

brigade *n* брига́да. **brigadier** *n* генера́л-майо́р.

bright *adj* я́ркий. **brighten** (*also* ~ **up**) *vi* проясня́ться *impf*, проясни́ться *pf*; *vt* оживля́ть *impf*, оживи́ть *pf* & я́ркость. **brightness** *n* я́ркость.

brilliant *adj* блестя́щий.

brim *n* край; (*hat*) поля́ (-ле́й) *pl*.

brine *n* рассо́л.

bring *vt* (*carry*) приноси́ть *impf*, принести́ *pf*; (*lead*) приводи́ть *impf*, привести́ *pf*; (*transport*) привози́ть *impf*, привезти́ *pf*; ~ **about** приноси́ть *impf*, принести́ *pf*; ~ **back** возвраща́ть *impf*, возврати́ть *pf*; ~ **down** сва́ливать *impf*, свали́ть *pf*; ~ **round** (*unconscious person*) приводи́ть *impf*, привести́ *pf* в себя́; (*deliver*) привози́ть *impf*, привезти́ *pf*; ~ **up** (*educate*) воспи́тывать *impf*, воспита́ть *pf*; (*question*) поднима́ть *impf*, подня́ть *pf*.

brink *n* край.

brisk *adj* (*lively*) оживлённый; (*air etc.*) све́жий; (*quick*) бы́стрый.

bristle *n* щети́на; *vi* щети́ниться *impf*, о~ *pf*.

Britain *n* Великобрита́ния, А́нглия. **British** *adj* брита́нский, англи́йский; ~ **Isles** Брита́нские острова́ *m pl*. **Briton** *n* брита́нец, -нка; англича́нин, -а́нка.

brittle *adj* хру́пкий.

broach *vt* затра́гивать *impf*, затро́нуть *pf*.

broad *adj* широ́кий; in ~ **daylight** средь бе́ла дня; in ~ **outline** в о́бщих черта́х. **broad-minded** *adj* с широ́кими взгля́дами. **broadly** *adv*: ~ **speaking** вообще́ говоря́.

broadcast *n* переда́ча; *vt* передава́ть *impf*, переда́ть *pf* по ра́дио, по телеви́дению; (*seed*) се́ять *impf*, по~ *pf* вразбро́с. **broadcaster** *n* ди́ктор. **broadcasting** *n* радио-, теле-, веща́ние.

brocade *n* парча́.

broccoli *n* бро́кколи *neut indecl*.

brochure *n* брошю́ра.

broke *predic* без гроша́. **broken** *adj* сло́манный; ~**-hearted** с разби́тым се́рдцем.

broker *n* комиссионе́р.

bronchitis *n* бронхи́т.

bronze *n* бро́нза; *adj* бро́нзовый.

brooch *n* брошь, бро́шка.

brood n вы́водок; vi мра́чно размышля́ть impf.

brook[1] n ручей.

brook[2] vt терпе́ть impf.

broom n метла́. **broomstick** n (witches') помело́.

broth n бульо́н.

brothel n публи́чный дом.

brother n брат; ~-in-law n (sister's husband) зять; (husband's brother) де́верь; (wife's brother) шу́рин; (wife's sister's husband) своя́к. **brotherhood** n бра́тство. **brotherly** adj бра́тский.

brow n (eyebrow) бровь; (forehead) лоб; (of hill) гребень m. **brow-beaten** adj запу́ганный.

brown adj кори́чневый; (eyes) ка́рий; n кори́чневый цвет; vt (cul) подрумя́нивать impf, подрумя́нить pf.

browse vi (look around) осма́триваться impf, осмотре́ться pf; (in book) просма́тривать impf просмотре́ть pf кни́гу.

bruise n синя́к; vt ушиба́ть impf, ушиби́ть pf.

brunette n брюне́тка.

brunt n основна́я тя́жесть.

brush n щётка; (paint) кисть; vt (clean) чи́стить impf, вы́~, по~ pf (щёткой); (touch) легко́ каса́ться impf, косну́ться pf +gen; (hair) расчёсывать impf, расчеса́ть pf щёткой; ~ aside, off отма́хиваться impf, отмахну́ться pf от+gen; ~ up сме́тать impf, смести́ pf; (renew) подчища́ть impf, подчи́стить pf.

brushwood n хво́рост.

Brussels sprouts n pl брюссе́льская капу́ста.

brutal adj жесто́кий. **brutality** n жесто́кость. **brutalize** vt ожесточа́ть impf, ожесточи́ть pf. **brute** n живо́тное sb; (person) ското́на. **brutish** adj ха́мский.

B.Sc. abbr бакала́вр нау́к.

bubble n пузы́рь m; vi пузы́риться impf; кипе́ть impf, вс~ pf.

buck n саме́ц оле́ня, кро́лика etc.; vi брыка́ться impf.

bucket n ведро́.

buckle n пря́жка; vt застёгивать impf, застегну́ть pf (пря́жкой); vi (warp) коро́биться impf, по~, с~ pf.

bud n по́чка.

Buddhism n будди́зм. **Buddhist** n будди́ст; adj будди́йский.

budge vt & i шевели́ть(ся) impf, по~ pf.

budget n бюдже́т; vi: ~ for предусма́тривать impf, предусмотре́ть pf в бюдже́те.

buff adj све́тло-кори́чневый.

buffalo n бу́йвол.

buffet[1] n буфе́т.

buffet[2] vt броса́ть impf (impers).

buffoon n шут.

bug n (insect) бука́шка; (germ) инфе́кция; (in computer) оши́бка в програ́мме; (microphone) потайно́й микрофо́н; vt (install ~) устана́вливать impf, установи́ть pf аппарату́ру для подслу́шивания в+prep; (listen) подслу́шивать impf.

bugle n горн.

build n (of person) телосложе́ние; vt стро́ить impf, по~ pf; ~ on пристра́ивать impf, пристро́ить pf (to к+dat); ~ up (vt) создава́ть impf, созда́ть pf; (vi) накопля́ться impf, накопи́ться pf. **builder** n строи́тель m. **building** n (edifice) зда́ние; (action) строи́тельство; ~ site строи́тельная площа́дка; ~ society жили́щно-строи́тельный кооперати́в.

built-up area n застро́енный райо́н.

bulb n лу́ковица; (electric) ла́мпочка. **bulbous** adj лу́ковичный.

Bulgaria n Болга́рия. **Bulgarian** n болга́рин, -га́рка; adj болга́рский.

bulge n вы́пуклость; vi выпя́чиваться impf, выпира́ть impf. **bulging** adj разбу́хший, оттопы́ривающийся.

bulk n (size) объём; (greater part) бо́льшая часть; in ~ гурто́м. **bulky** adj громо́здкий.

bull n бык; (male) саме́ц. **bulldog** n бульдо́г. **bulldoze** vt расчища́ть impf, расчи́стить pf бульдо́зером. **bulldozer** n бульдо́зер. **bullfinch** n снеги́рь m. **bullock** n вол. **bull's-eye** n я́блоко.

bullet n пу́ля. **bullet-proof** adj пуленепроница́емый, пуленепробива́емый... пулесто́йкий.

bulletin n бюллете́нь m.

bullion n: gold ~ зо́лото в сли́тках.

bully n задира m & f; vt запу́гивать impf, запуга́ть pf.

bum n зад.

bumble-bee n шмель m.

bump n (blow) уда́р, толчо́к; (swelling) ши́шка; (in road) уха́б; vi ударя́ться impf, уда́риться pf; ~ into ната́лкиваться impf, натолкну́ться pf на+acc. **bumper** n ба́мпер.

bumpkin n дереве́нщина m & f.

bumptious adj самоуве́ренный.

bumpy adj уха́бистый.

bun n сдо́бная бу́лка; (hair) пучо́к.

bunch n (of flowers) буке́т; (grapes) гроздь; (keys) свя́зка.

bundle n у́зел; vt свя́зывать impf, связа́ть pf в у́зел; ~ off спрова́живать impf, спрова́дить pf.

bungalow n бу́нгало neut indecl.

bungle vt по́ртить impf, ис~ pf.

bunk n ко́йка.

bunker n бу́нкер.

buoy n буй. **buoyancy** n плаву́честь; (fig) бо́дрость. **buoyant** adj плаву́чий; (fig) бо́дрый.

burden n бре́мя neut; vt обременя́ть impf, обремени́ть pf.

bureau n бюро́ neut indecl. **bureaucracy** n бюрокра́тия. **bureaucrat** n бюрокра́т. **bureaucratic** adj бюрократи́ческий.

burger n котле́та.

burglar n взло́мщик. **burglary** n кра́жа со взло́мом. **burgle** vt гра́бить impf, о~ pf.

burial n погребе́ние.

burlesque n бурле́ск.

burly adj здорове́нный.

burn vt жечь impf, с~ pf; vt & i (injure) обжига́ть(ся) impf, обже́чь(ся) pf; vi горе́ть impf, с~ pf; (by sun) загора́ть impf, загоре́ть pf; n ожо́г. **burner** n горе́лка.

burnish vt полирова́ть impf, от~ pf.

burp vi рыга́ть impf, рыгну́ть pf.

burrow n нора́; vi рыть impf, вы́~ pf нору; (fig) ры́ться impf.

bursar n казначе́й. **bursary** n стипе́ндия.

burst n разры́в, вспы́шка; vi разрыва́ться impf, разорва́ться pf; (bubble) ло́паться impf, ло́пнуть pf; vt разрыва́ть impf, разорва́ть pf; ~ into tears распла́каться pf.

bury vt (dead) хорони́ть impf, по~ pf; (hide) зарыва́ть impf, зары́ть pf.

bus n авто́бус.

bush n куст. **bushy** adj густо́й.

busily adv энерги́чно.

business n (affair, dealings) де́ло; (firm) предприя́тие; mind your own ~ не ва́ше де́ло; on ~ по де́лу. **businesslike** adj делово́й. **businessman** n бизнесме́н.

busker n у́личный музыка́нт.

bust n бюст; (bosom) грудь.

bustle n суета́; vi суети́ться impf.

busy adj за́нятый; vt: ~ o.s. занима́ться impf, заня́ться pf (with +instr). **busybody** n назо́йливый челове́к.

but conj но, а; ~ then зато́; prep кро́ме+gen.

butcher n мясни́к; vt ре́зать impf, за~ pf; ~'s shop мясна́я sb.

butler n дворе́цкий sb.

butt[1] n (cask) бо́чка.

butt[2] n (of gun) прикла́д; (cigarette) оку́рок.

butt[3] n (target) мише́нь.

butt[4] vt бода́ть impf, за~ pf; ~ in вме́шиваться impf, вмеша́ться pf.

butter n (сли́вочное) ма́сло; vt нама́зывать impf, нама́зать pf ма́слом; ~ up льсти́ть impf, по~ pf. **buttercup** n лю́тик. **butterfly** n ба́бочка.

buttock n я́годица.

button n пу́говица; (knob) кно́пка; vt застёгивать impf, застегну́ть pf. **buttonhole** n пе́тля.

buttress n контрфо́рс; vt подпира́ть impf, подпере́ть pf.

buxom adj полногру́дая.

buy n поку́пка; vt покупа́ть impf, купи́ть pf. **buyer** n покупа́тель m.

buzz n жужжа́ние; vi жужжа́ть impf.

buzzard n каню́к.

buzzer n зу́ммер.

by adv ми́мо; prep (near) о́коло+gen, у+gen; (beside) ря́дом с+instr; (past) ми́мо+gen; (time) к+dat; (means) instr without prep; ~ and large в це́лом.

bye int пока́!

by-election n дополни́тельные вы́боры m pl.

Byelorussian see Belorussian

bygone adj мину́вший; let ~s be ~s что прошло́, то прошло́. **by-law** n постановле́ние. **bypass** n обхо́д; vt обходи́ть impf, обойти́ pf. **by-product** n побо́чный проду́кт. **byroad** n небольша́я доро́га. **bystander** *n* свиде́тель *m*. **byway** *n* просёлоч-ная доро́га. **byword** *n* олицетво-ре́ние (for +gen).

Byzantine *adj* византи́йский.

C

cab *n* (*taxi*) такси́ *neut indecl*; (*of lorry*) каби́на.
cabaret *n* кабаре́ *neut indecl*.
cabbage *n* капу́ста.
cabin *n* (*hut*) хи́жина; (*aeron*) каби́на; (*naut*) каю́та.
cabinet *n* шкаф; (*Cabinet*) кабине́т; ~**maker** краснодере́вец; ~**minister** мини́стр-член кабине́та.
cable *n* (*rope*) кана́т; (*electric*) ка́бель *m*; (*cablegram*) телегра́мма; *vt & i* телеграфи́ровать *impf & pf*.
cache *n* потайно́й склад.
cackle *vi* гогота́ть *impf*.
cactus *n* ка́ктус.
caddy *n* (*box*) ча́йница.
cadet *n* новобра́нец.
cadge *vt* стреля́ть *impf*, стрельну́ть *pf*.
cadres *n pl* ка́дры *m pl*.
Caesarean (section) *n* ке́сарево-сече́ние.
cafe *n* кафе́ *neut indecl*. **cafeteria** *n* кафете́рий.
caffeine *n* кофеи́н.
cage *n* кле́тка.
cajole *vt* зада́бривать *impf*, задо́-брить *pf*.
cake *n* (*large*) торт, (*small*) пиро́ж-ное *sb*; (*fruit~*) кекс; *vt*: ~**d** об-ле́пленный (in +*instr*).
calamitous *adj* бе́дственный. **calam-ity** *n* бе́дствие.
calcium *n* ка́льций.
calculate *vt* вычисля́ть *impf*, вы́-числить *pf*; *vi* рассчи́тывать *impf*, рассчита́ть *pf* (on на+*acc*). **calcula-tion** *n* вычисле́ние, расчёт. **calcu-lator** *n* калькуля́тор.
calendar *n* календа́рь *m*.
calf[1] *n* (*cow*) телёнок.
calf[2] *n* (*leg*) икра́.
calibrate *vt* калиброва́ть *impf*. **cali-bre** *n* кали́бр.
call *v* звать *impf*, по~ *pf*; (*name*) называ́ть *impf*, назва́ть *pf*; (*cry*)

крича́ть *impf*, кри́кнуть *pf*; (*wake*) буди́ть *impf*, раз~ *pf*; (*visit*) захо-ди́ть *impf*, зайти́ *pf* (on к+*dat*; at в+*acc*); (*stop at*) остана́вливаться *impf*, останови́ться *pf* (at в, на, +*prep*); (*summon*) вызыва́ть *impf*, вы́звать *pf*; (*ring up*) звони́ть *impf*, по~ *pf* +*dat*; ~ **for** (*require*) тре́-бовать *impf*, по~ *pf* +*gen*; (*fetch*) заходи́ть *impf*, зайти́ *pf* за+*instr*; ~ **off** отменя́ть *impf*, отмени́ть *pf*; ~ **out** вскри́кивать *impf*, вскри́кнуть *pf*; ~ **up** призыва́ть *impf*, призва́ть *pf*; *n* (*cry*) крик; (*summons*) зов, призы́в; (*telephone*) (телефо́нный) вы́зов, разгово́р; (*visit*) визи́т; (*sig-nal*) сигна́л; ~**box** телефо́н-авто-ма́т; ~**up** призы́в. **caller** *n* посети́-тель *m*, ~ница, *(tel)* позвони́вший *sb*. **calling** *n* (*vocation*) призва́ние.
callous *adj* (*person*) чёрствый.
callus *n* мозо́ль.
calm *adj* споко́йный; *n* споко́йствие; *vt & i* (~ *down*) успока́ивать(ся) *impf*, успоко́ить(ся) *pf*.
calorie *n* кало́рия.
camber *n* скат.
camcorder *n* камко́рдер.
camel *n* верблю́д.
camera *n* фотоаппара́т. **cameraman** *n* киноопера́тор.
camouflage *n* камуфля́ж; *vt* маски-рова́ть *impf*, за~ *pf*.
camp *n* ла́герь *m*; *vi* (*set up* ~) рас-полага́ться *impf*, расположи́ться *pf* ла́герем; (*go camping*) жить *impf* в пала́тках; ~**bed** раскладу́шка; ~**fire** костёр.
campaign *n* кампа́ния; *vi* проводи́ть *impf*, провести́ *pf* кампа́нию.
campsite *n* ла́герь *m*, ке́мпинг.
campus *n* университе́тский городо́к.
can[1] *n* ба́нка; *vt* консерви́ровать *impf*, за~ *pf*.
can[2] *v aux* (*be able*) мочь *impf*, с~ *pf* +*inf*; (*know how*) уме́ть *impf*, с~ *pf* +*inf*.
Canada *n* Кана́да. **Canadian** *n* кана́-дец, -дка; *adj* кана́дский.
canal *n* кана́л.
canary *n* канаре́йка.
cancel *vt* (*make void*) аннули́ровать *impf & pf*; (*call off*) отменя́ть *impf*, отмени́ть *pf*; (*stamp*) гаси́ть *impf*, по~ *pf*. **cancellation** *n* аннули́рова-

ние; отме́на.

cancer *n* рак; (C~) Рак. **cancerous** *adj* ра́ковый.

candelabrum *n* канделя́бр.

candid *adj* открове́нный.

candidate *n* кандида́т.

candied *adj* заса́харенный.

candle *n* свеча́. **candlestick** *n* подсве́чник.

candour *n* открове́нность.

candy *n* сла́дости *f pl*.

cane *n* (*plant*) тростни́к; (*stick*) трость, па́лка; *vt* бить *impf*, по~ *pf* па́лкой.

canine *adj* соба́чий; *n* (*tooth*) клык.

canister *n* ба́нка, коро́бка.

canker *n* рак.

cannabis *n* гаши́ш.

cannibal *n* людое́д. **cannibalism** *n* людое́дство.

cannon *n* пу́шка; **~-ball** пу́шечное ядро́.

canoe *n* кано́э *neut indecl*; *vi* пла́вать *indet*, плыть *det* на кано́э.

canon *n* кано́н; (*person*) кано́ник. **canonize** *vt* канонизова́ть *impf* & *pf*.

canopy *n* балдахи́н.

cant *n* (*hypocrisy*) ха́нжество; (*jargon*) жарго́н.

cantankerous *adj* сварли́вый.

cantata *n* канта́та.

canteen *n* столо́вая *sb*.

canter *n* лёгкий гало́п; *vi* (*rider*) е́здить *indet*, е́хать *det* лёгким гало́пом; (*horse*) ходи́ть *indet*, идти́ *det* лёгким гало́пом.

canvas *n* (*art*) холст; (*naut*) паруси́на; (*tent material*) брезе́нт.

canvass *vi* агити́ровать *impf*, с~ *pf* (**for** за+*acc*); *n* собира́ние голосо́в; агита́ция. **canvasser** *n* собира́тель *m* голосо́в.

canyon *n* каньо́н.

cap *n* (*of uniform*) фура́жка; (*cloth*) ке́пка; (*woman's*) чепе́ц; (*lid*) кры́шка; *vt* превосходи́ть *impf*, превзойти́ *pf*.

capability *n* спосо́бность. **capable** *adj* спосо́бный (**of** на+*acc*).

capacious *adj* вмести́тельный. **capacity** *n* ёмкость; (*ability*) спосо́бность; **in the ~ of** в ка́честве +*gen*.

cape¹ *n* (*geog*) мыс.

cape² *n* (*cloak*) наки́дка.

caper *vi* скака́ть *impf*.

capers¹ *n pl* (*cul*) ка́персы *m pl*.

capillary *adj* капилля́рный.

capital *adj* (*letter*) прописно́й; **~ punishment** сме́ртная казнь; *n* (*town*) столи́ца; (*letter*) прописна́я бу́ква; (*econ*) капита́л. **capitalism** *n* капитали́зм. **capitalist** *n* капитали́ст; *adj* капиталисти́ческий. **capitalize** *vt* извлека́ть *impf*, извле́чь *pf* вы́году (**on** из+*gen*).

capitulate *vi* капитули́ровать *impf* & *pf*. **capitulation** *n* капитуля́ция.

caprice *n* капри́з. **capricious** *adj* капри́зный.

Capricorn *n* Козеро́г.

capsize *vt* & *i* опроки́дывать(ся) *impf*, опроки́нуть(ся) *pf*.

capsule *n* ка́псула.

captain *n* капита́н; *vt* быть капита́ном +*gen*.

caption *n* по́дпись; (*cin*) титр.

captious *adj* приди́рчивый.

captivate *vt* пленя́ть *impf*, плени́ть *pf*. **captivating** *adj* плени́тельный. **captive** *adj* & *n* пле́нный. **captivity** *n* нево́ля; (*esp mil*) плен. **capture** *n* взя́тие, захва́т, пои́мка; *vt* (*person*) брать *impf*, взять *pf* в плен; (*seize*) захва́тывать *impf*, захвати́ть *pf*.

car *n* маши́на; автомоби́ль *m*; **~ park** стоя́нка.

carafe *n* графи́н.

caramel(s) *n* караме́ль.

carat *n* кара́т.

caravan *n* фурго́н; (*convoy*) карава́н.

caraway (seeds) *n* тмин.

carbohydrate *n* углево́д. **carbon** *n* углеро́д; **~ copy** ко́пия; **~ dioxide** углекислота́; **~ monoxide** о́кись углеро́да; **~ paper** копирова́льная бума́га.

carburettor *n* карбюра́тор.

carcass *n* ту́ша.

card *n* (*stiff paper*) карто́н; (*visiting* ~) ка́рточка; (*playing* ~) ка́рта; (*greetings* ~) откры́тка; (*ticket*) биле́т. **cardboard** *n* карто́н; *adj* карто́нный.

cardiac *adj* серде́чный.

cardigan *n* кардига́н.

cardinal *adj* кардина́льный; **~ number** коли́чественное числи́тельное *sb*; *n* кардина́л.

care n (*trouble*) забóта; (*caution*) осторóжность; (*tending*) ухóд; **in the ~ of** на попечéнии +*gen*; **take ~** осторóжно!; смотри́(те)!; **take ~ of** заботиться *impf*, по~ *pf* o+*prep*; *vi*: **I don't ~** мне всё равнó; **~ for** (*look after*) ухáживать *impf* за+*instr*; (*like*) нрáвиться *impf*, по~ *pf impers* +*dat*.

career n карьéра.

carefree adj беззабóтный. **careful** adj (*cautious*) осторóжный; (*thorough*) тщáтельный. **careless** adj (*negligent*) небрéжный; (*incautious*) неосторóжный.

caress n лáска; *vt* ласкáть *impf*.

caretaker n смотри́тель m, ~ница; *attrib* врéменный.

cargo n груз.

caricature n карикатýра; *vt* изображáть *impf*, изобрази́ть *pf* в карикатýрном ви́де.

carnage n резня́.

carnal adj плóтский.

carnation n гвозди́ка.

carnival n карнавáл.

carnivorous adj плотоя́дный.

carol n (*рождéственский*) гимн.

carouse vi кути́ть *impf*, кутнýть *pf*.

carp[1] n карп.

carp[2] vi придирáться *impf*, придрáться *pf* (at к+*dat*).

carpenter n плóтник. **carpentry** n плóтничество.

carpet n ковёр; *vt* покрывáть *impf*, покры́ть *pf* коврóм.

carping adj приди́рчивый.

carriage n (*vehicle*) карéта; (*rly*) вагóн; (*conveyance*) перевóзка; (*bearing*) осáнка. **carriageway** n проéзжая часть дорóги. **carrier** n (*on bike*) багáжник; (*firm*) транспóртная кампáния; (*med*) бациллоноси́тель m.

carrot n морквóка; *pl* морквóвь (*collect*).

carry vt (*by hand*) носи́ть *indet*, нести́ *det*; переноси́ть *impf*, перенести́ *pf*; (*in vehicle*) вози́ть *indet*, везти́ *det*; (*sound*) передавáть *impf*, передáть *pf*; *vi* (*sound*) быть слы́шен; **be carried away** увлекáться *impf*, увлéчься *pf*; **~ on** (*continue*) продолжáть *impf*; **~ out** выполня́ть *impf*, вы́полнить *pf*; **~ over** пере

носи́ть *impf*, перенести́ *pf*.

cart n телéга; *vt* (*lug*) тащи́ть *impf*.

cartilage n хрящ.

carton n картóнка.

cartoon n карикатýра; (*cin*) мультфи́льм. **cartoonist** n карикатури́ст, ~ка.

cartridge n патрóн; (*of record player*) звукоснимáтель m.

carve vt рéзать *impf* по+*dat*; (*in wood*) вырезáть *impf*, вы́резать *pf*; (*in stone*) высекáть *impf*, вы́сечь; (*slice*) нарезáть *impf*, нарéзать *pf*. **carving** n резьбá; **~ knife** нож для нарезáния мя́са.

cascade n каскáд; *vi* пáдать *impf*.

case[1] n (*instance*) слýчай; (*law*) дéло; (*med*) больнóй sb; (*gram*) падéж; **in ~** (*в слýчае*) éсли; **in any ~** во вся́ком слýчае; **in no ~** не в кóем слýчае; **just in ~** на вся́кий слýчай.

case[2] n (*box*) я́щик; (*suitcase*) чемодáн; (*small box*) корóбка; (*cover*) чехóл; (*display ~*) витри́на.

cash n нали́чные sb; (*money*) дéньги pl; **~ on delivery** налóженным платежóм; **~ desk, register** кáсса; *vt*: **~ a cheque** получáть *impf*, получи́ть *pf* дéньги по чéку. **cashier** n касси́р.

casing n (*tech*) кожýх.

casino n кази́но *neut indecl*.

cask n бóчка.

casket n шкатýлка.

casserole n (*pot*) лáтка; (*stew*) рагý *neut indecl*.

cassette n кассéта; **~ recorder** кассéтный магнитофóн.

cassock n ря́са.

cast vt (*throw*) бросáть *impf*, брóсить *pf*; (*shed*) сбрáсывать *impf*, сбрóсить *pf*; (*theat*) распределя́ть *impf*, распредели́ть *pf* рóли +*dat*; (*found*) лить *impf*, с~ *pf*; **~ off** (*knitting*) спускáть *impf*, спусти́ть *pf* пéтли; (*naut*) отплывáть *impf*, отплы́ть *pf*; **~ on** (*knitting*) набирáть *impf*, набрáть *pf* пéтли; n (*of mind etc.*) склад; (*mould*) фóрма; (*moulded object*) слéпок; (*med*) ги́псовая повя́зка; (*theat*) дéйствующие ли́ца (-ц) *pl*. **castaway** n потерпéвший sb кораблекрушéние. **cast iron** n чугýн. **cast-iron** adj чугýнный. **cast-offs** n pl нóшеное плáтье.

castanet *n* кастанье́та.

caste *n* ка́ста.

castigate *vt* бичева́ть *impf*.

castle *n* за́мок; (*chess*) ладья́.

castor *n* (*wheel*) ро́лик; ~ sugar са́харная пу́дра.

castrate *vt* кастри́ровать *impf & pf*. **castration** *n* кастра́ция.

casual *adj* (*chance*) случа́йный; (*offhand*) небре́жный; (*clothes*) бу́дничный; (*unofficial*) неофициа́льный; (*informal*) лёгкий; (*labour*) подённый; ~ **labourer** подёнщик, -ица.

casualty *n* (*wounded*) ра́неный *sb*; (*killed*) уби́тый *sb*; *pl* поте́ри (-рь) *pl*; ~ **ward** пала́та ско́рой по́мощи.

cat *n* ко́шка; (*tom*) кот; ~'s-eye (*on road*) (доро́жный) рефле́ктор.

catalogue *n* катало́г; (*price list*) прейскура́нт; *vt* каталогизи́ровать *impf & pf*.

catalyst *n* катализа́тор. **catalytic** *adj* каталити́ческий.

catapult *n* (*toy*) рога́тка; (*hist, aeron*) катапу́льта; *vt & i* катапульти́ровать(ся) *impf & pf*.

cataract *n* (*med*) катара́кта.

catarrh *n* катар.

catastrophe *n* катастро́фа. **catastrophic** *adj* катастрофи́ческий.

catch *vt* (*ball, fish, thief*) лови́ть *impf*, пойма́ть *pf*; (*surprise*) застава́ть *impf*, заста́ть *pf*; (*disease*) заража́ться *impf*, зарази́ться *pf* +*instr*; (*be in time for*) успева́ть *impf*, успе́ть *pf* на+*acc*; *vt & i* (*snag*) зацепля́ть(ся) *impf*, зацепи́ть(ся) *pf* (*on* за+*acc*); ~ **on** (*become popular*) привива́ться *impf*, приви́ться *pf*; ~ **up with** догоня́ть *impf*, догна́ть *pf*; *n* (*of fish*) уло́в; (*trick*) уло́вка; (*on door etc.*) задвижка. **catching** *adj* зара́зный. **catchword** *n* мо́дное словечко. **catchy** *adj* прили́пчивый.

categorical *adj* категори́ческий. **category** *n* катего́рия.

cater *vi*: ~ **for** поставля́ть *impf*, поста́вить *pf* прови́зию для+*gen*; (*satisfy*) удовлетворя́ть *impf*, удовлетвори́ть *pf*. **caterer** *n* поставщи́к (прови́зии).

caterpillar *n* гу́сеница.

cathedral *n* собо́р.

catheter *n* кате́тер.

Catholic *adj* католи́ческий; *n* като-

лик, -и́чка. **Catholicism** *n* католи́чество.

cattle *n* скот.

Caucasus *n* Кавка́з.

cauldron *n* коте́л.

cauliflower *n* цветна́я капу́ста.

cause *n* причи́на, по́вод; (*law etc.*) де́ло; *vt* причиня́ть *impf*, причини́ть *pf*; вызыва́ть *impf*, вы́звать *pf*; (*induce*) заставля́ть *impf*, заста́вить *pf*.

caustic *adj* е́дкий.

cauterize *vt* прижига́ть *impf*, приже́чь *pf*.

caution *n* осторо́жность; (*warning*) предостереже́ние; *vt* предостерега́ть *impf*, предостере́чь *pf*. **cautious** *adj* осторо́жный. **cautionary** *adj* предостерега́ющий.

cavalcade *n* кавалька́да. **cavalier** *adj* бесцеремо́нный. **cavalry** *n* кавале́рия.

cave *n* пеще́ра; *vi*: ~ **in** обва́ливаться *impf*, обвали́ться *pf*; (*yield*) сдава́ться *impf*, сда́ться *pf*. **caveman** *n* пеще́рный челове́к. **cavern** *n* пеще́ра. **cavernous** *adj* пещери́стый.

caviare *n* икра́.

cavity *n* впа́дина, по́лость; (*in tooth*) дупло́.

cavort *vi* скака́ть *impf*.

caw *vi* ка́ркать *impf*, ка́ркнуть *pf*.

CD *abbr* (*of compact disc*) компа́кт-ди́ск; ~ **player** прои́грыватель *m* компа́кт-ди́сков.

cease *vt & i* прекраща́ть(ся) *impf*, прекрати́ть(ся) *pf*; *vt* перестава́ть *impf*, переста́ть *pf* (+*inf*); ~**fire** прекраще́ние огня́. **ceaseless** *adj* непреста́нный.

cedar *n* кедр.

cede *vt* уступа́ть *impf*, уступи́ть *pf*.

ceiling *n* потоло́к; (*fig*) макси́ма́льный у́ровень *m*.

celebrate *vt & i* пра́здновать *impf*, от~ *pf*; (*extol*) прославля́ть *impf*, просла́вить *pf*. **celebrated** *adj* знамени́тый. **celebration** *n* пра́зднование. **celebrity** *n* знамени́тость.

celery *n* сельдере́й.

celestial *adj* небе́сный.

celibacy *n* безбра́чие. **celibate** *adj* холосто́й; *n* холостя́к.

cell *n* (*prison*) ка́мера; (*biol*) кле́тка.

cellar *n* подва́л.

cello *n* виолонче́ль.

cellophane *n* целлофа́н. **cellular** *adj* кле́точный. **celluloid** *n* целлуло́ид.

Celt *n* кельт. **Celtic** *adj* ке́льтский.

cement *n* цеме́нт; *vt* цементи́ровать *impf*, за~ *pf*.

cemetery *n* кла́дбище.

censor *n* це́нзор; *vt* подверга́ть *impf*, подве́ргнуть *pf* цензу́ре. **censorious** *adj* сверхкрити́ческий. **censorship** *n* цензу́ра. **censure** *n* порица́ние; *vt* порица́ть *impf*.

census *n* пе́репись.

cent *n* цент; **per ~** проце́нт.

centenary *n* столе́тие. **centennial** *adj* столе́тний. **centigrade** *adj*: 10° ~ 10° по Це́льсию. **centimetre** *n* сантиме́тр. **centipede** *n* сороконо́жка.

central *adj* центра́льный; ~ **heating** центра́льное отопле́ние. **centralization** *n* централиза́ция. **centralize** *vt* централизова́ть *impf* & *pf*. **centre** *n* центр; середи́на; ~**forward** центр нападе́ния; *vi* & *i*: ~ **on** сосредото́чивать(ся) *impf*, сосредото́чить(ся) *pf* на+*prep*. **centrifugal** *adj* центробе́жный.

century *n* столе́тие, век.

ceramic *adj* керами́ческий. **ceramics** *n pl* кера́мика.

cereals *n pl* хле́бные зла́ки *m pl*; **breakfast ~** зерновы́е хло́пья (-ев) *pl*.

cerebral *adj* мозгово́й.

ceremonial *adj* церемониа́льный; *n* церемониа́л. **ceremonious** *adj* церемо́нный. **ceremony** *n* церемо́ния.

certain *adj* (*confident*) уве́рен (-нна); (*undoubted*) несомне́нный; (*unspecified*) изве́стный; (*inevitable*) ве́рный; **for ~** наверняка́. **certainly** *adv* (*of course*) коне́чно, безусло́вно; (*without doubt*) несомне́нно; ~ **not!** ни в ко́ем слу́чае. **certainty** *n* (*conviction*) уве́ренность; (*fact*) несомне́нный факт.

certificate *n* свиде́тельство; сертифика́т. **certify** *vt* удостоверя́ть *impf*, удостове́рить *pf*.

cervical *adj* ше́йный. **cervix** *n* ше́йка ма́тки.

cessation *n* прекраще́ние.

cf. *abbr* ср., сравни́.

CFCs *abbr* (*of* chlorofluorocarbons) хлори́рованные фторуглеро́ды *m pl*.

chafe *vt* (*rub*) тере́ть *impf*; (*rub sore*) натира́ть *impf*, натере́ть *pf*.

chaff *n* (*husks*) мяки́на; (*straw*) се́чка.

chaffinch *n* за́блик.

chagrin *n* огорче́ние.

chain *n* цепь; ~ **reaction** цепна́я реа́кция; ~ **smoker** за́ядлый кури́льщик.

chair *n* стул, (*armchair*) кре́сло; (*univ*) ка́федра; *vt* (*preside*) председа́тельствовать *impf* на+*prep*. **chairman, -woman** *n* председа́тель *m*, ~ница.

chalice *n* ча́ша.

chalk *n* мел. **chalky** *adj* мелово́й.

challenge *n* (*summons*, *fig*) вы́зов; (*sentry's*) о́клик; (*law*) отво́д; *vt* вызыва́ть *impf*, вы́звать *pf*; (*sentry*) оклика́ть *impf*, окли́кнуть *pf*; (*law*) отводи́ть *impf*, отвести́ *pf*. **challenger** *n* претенде́нт. **challenging** *adj* интригу́ющий.

chamber *n* (*cavity*) ка́мера; (*hall*) зал; (*polit*) пала́та; *pl* (*law*) адвока́тская конто́ра, (*judge's*) кабине́т (судьи́); ~ **music** ка́мерная му́зыка; ~ **pot** ночно́й горшо́к. **chambermaid** *n* го́рничная *sb*.

chameleon *n* хамелео́н.

chamois *n* (*animal*) се́рна; (~*leather*) за́мша.

champagne *n* шампа́нское *sb*.

champion *n* чемпио́н, ~ка; (*upholder*) побо́рник, -ица; *vt* боро́ться *impf* за +*acc*. **championship** *n* пе́рвенство, чемпиона́т.

chance *n* случа́йность; (*opportunity*) возмо́жность, (*favourable*) слу́чай; (*likelihood*) шанс (*usu pl*); **by ~** случа́йно; *adj* случа́йный; *vi*: ~ **it** рискну́ть *pf*.

chancellery *n* канцеля́рия. **chancellor** *n* ка́нцлер; (*univ*) ре́ктор; **C~ of the Exchequer** ка́нцлер казначе́йства.

chancy *adj* риско́ванный.

chandelier *n* лю́стра.

change *n* переме́на; измене́ние; (*of clothes etc.*) сме́на; (*money*) сда́ча; (*of trains etc.*) переса́дка; **for a ~** для разнообра́зия; *vt* & *i* меня́ть(ся) *impf*; изменя́ть(ся) *impf*, изменить(ся) *pf*; *vi* (*one's clothes*) переодева́ться *impf*, переоде́ться *pf*; (*trains etc.*) переса́живаться *impf*, пересе́сть *pf*; *vt* (*a baby*) перепелёнывать *impf*, перепелена́ть *pf*; (*money*) обме́нивать *impf*, обменя́ть *pf*; (*give ~ for*) разме́нивать *impf*, разменя́ть *pf*; ~ **into** превраща́ться *impf*, преврати́ться *pf* в+*acc*; ~ **over to** переходи́ть *impf*, перейти́ *pf* на+*acc*. **changeable** *adj* изме́нчивый.

channel *n* (*water*) проли́в; (*also TV*) кана́л; (*fig*) путь *m*; **the (English) C~** Ла-Ма́нш; *vt* (*fig*) направля́ть *impf*.

chant *n* (*eccl*) песнопе́ние; *vt & i* петь *impf*; (*slogans*) сканди́ровать *impf & pf*.

chaos *n* ха́ос. **chaotic** *adj* хаоти́чный.

chap *n* (*person*) па́рень *m*.

chapel *n* часо́вня; (*Catholic*) капе́лла.

chaperone *n* компаньо́нка.

chaplain *n* капелла́н.

chapped *adj* потреска́вшийся.

chapter *n* глава́.

char *vt & i* обу́гливать(ся) *impf*, обу́глить(ся) *pf*.

character *n* хара́ктер; (*theat*) де́йствующее лицо́; (*letter*) бу́ква; (*Chinese etc.*) иеро́глиф. **characteristic** *adj* характе́рный; *n* сво́йство; (*of person*) черта́ хара́ктера. **characterize** *vt* характеризова́ть *impf & pf*.

charade *n* шара́да.

charcoal *n* древе́сный у́голь *m*.

charge *n* (*for gun; electr*) заря́д; (*fee*) пла́та; (*person*) пито́мец, -мица; (*accusation*) обвине́ние; (*mil*) ата́ка; **be in ~ of** заве́довать *impf* +*instr*; **in the ~ of** на попече́нии +*gen*; *vt* (*gun; electr*) заряжа́ть *impf*, заряди́ть *pf*; (*accuse*) обвиня́ть *impf*, обвини́ть *pf* (**with** в+*prep*); (*mil*) атакова́ть *impf & pf*; *vi* броса́ться *impf*, бро́ситься *pf* в ата́ку; ~ **for** брать *impf*, взять *pf* (за+*acc*); ~ **to (the account of)** запи́сывать *impf*, записа́ть *pf* на счёт+*gen*.

chariot *n* колесни́ца.

charisma *n* обая́ние. **charismatic** *adj* обая́тельный.

charitable *adj* благотвори́тельный; (*kind, merciful*) милосе́рдный. **char-**

ity *n* (*kindness*) милосе́рдие; (*organization*) благотвори́тельная организа́ция.

charlatan *n* шарлата́н.

charm *n* очарова́ние; пре́лесть; (*spell*) за́говор; *pl* ча́ры (чар) *pl*; (*amulet*) талисма́н; (*trinket*) брело́к; *vt* очаро́вывать *impf*, очарова́ть *pf*. **charming** *adj* очарова́тельный, преле́стный.

chart *n* (*naut*) морска́я ка́рта; (*table*) гра́фик; *vt* наноси́ть *impf*, нанести́ *pf* на гра́фик. **charter** *n* (*document*) ха́ртия; (*statutes*) уста́в; *vt* нанима́ть *impf*, наня́ть *pf*.

charwoman *n* приходя́щая убо́рщица.

chase *vt* гоня́ться *indet*, гна́ться *det* за+*instr*; *n* пого́ня; (*hunting*) охо́та.

chasm *n* (*abyss*) бе́здна.

chassis *n* шасси́ *neut indecl*.

chaste *adj* целому́дренный.

chastise *vt* кара́ть *impf*, по~ *pf*.

chastity *n* целому́дрие.

chat *n* бесе́да; *vi* бесе́довать *impf*; ~ **show** телевизио́нная бесе́да-интервью́ *f*.

chatter *n* болтовня́; *vi* болта́ть *impf*; (*teeth*) стуча́ть *impf*. **chatterbox** *n* болту́н. **chatty** *adj* разгово́рчивый.

chauffeur *n* шофёр.

chauvinism *n* шовини́зм. **chauvinist** *n* шовини́ст; *adj* шовинисти́ческий.

cheap *adj* дешёвый. **cheapen** *vt* (*fig*) опошля́ть *impf*, опошли́ть *pf*. **cheaply** *adv* дёшево.

cheat *vt* обма́нывать *impf*, обману́ть *pf*; *vi* плутова́ть *impf*, на~, с~ *pf*; *n* (*person*) обма́нщик, -ица; плут; (*act*) обма́н.

check[1] *n* контро́ль *m*, прове́рка; (*chess*) шах; ~**mate** шах и мат; *vt* (*examine*) проверя́ть *impf*, прове́рить *pf*; контроли́ровать *impf*, про~ *pf*; (*restrain*) сде́рживать *impf*, сдержа́ть *pf*; ~ **in** регистри́роваться *impf*, за~ *pf*; ~ **out** выпи́сываться *impf*, вы́писаться *pf*; ~**out** ка́сса; ~**up** осмо́тр.

check[2] *n* (*pattern*) кле́тка. **check(ed)** *adj* кле́тчатый.

cheek *n* щека́; (*impertinence*) на́глость. **cheeky** *adj* на́глый.

cheep *vi* пища́ть *impf*, пи́скнуть *pf*.

cheer n ободря́ющий во́зглас; ~s! за (ва́ше) здоро́вье!; vt (applaud) приве́тствовать impf & pf; ~ up ободря́ть(ся) impf, ободри́ть(ся) pf. **cheerful** adj весёлый. **cheerio** int пока́. **cheerless** adj уны́лый.

cheese n сыр; ~-cake ватру́шка.

cheetah n хи́мина.

chef n (шеф-)по́вар.

chemical adj хими́ческий; n химика́т. **chemist** n хи́мик; (druggist) апте́карь m; ~'s (shop) апте́ка. **chemistry** n хи́мия.

cheque n чек; ~-book че́ковая кни́жка.

cherish vt (foster) леле́ять impf; (hold dear) дорожи́ть impf +instr; (love) нежно люби́ть impf.

cherry n ви́шня; adj вишнёвый.

cherub n херуви́м.

chess n ша́хматы (-т) pl; ~-board ша́хматная доска́; ~-men n ша́хматы (-т) pl.

chest n сунду́к; (anat) грудь; ~ of drawers комо́д.

chestnut n кашта́н; (horse) гнеда́я sb.

chew vt жева́ть impf. **chewing-gum** n жева́тельная рези́нка.

chic adj элега́нтный.

chick n цыплёнок. **chicken** n ку́рица; цыплёнок; adj трусли́вый; ~ out тру́сить impf, c~ pf. **chicken-pox** n ветря́нка.

chicory n цико́рий.

chief n глава́ m & f; (boss) нача́льник; (of tribe) вождь m; adj гла́вный. **chiefly** adv гла́вным о́бразом. **chieftain** n вождь m.

chiffon n шифо́н.

child n ребёнок; ~-birth ро́ды (-дов) pl. **childhood** n де́тство. **childish** adj де́тский. **childless** adj безде́тный. **childlike** adj де́тский. **childrens'** adj де́тский.

chili n стручко́вый пе́рец.

chill n хо́лод; (ailment) просту́да; vt охлажда́ть impf, охлади́ть pf. **chilly** adj прохла́дный.

chime n (set of bells) набо́р колоколо́в; pl (sound) перезво́н; (of clock) бой; vt & i (clock) бить impf, про~ pf; vi (bell) звони́ть impf, по~ pf.

chimney n труба́; ~-sweep трубочи́ст.

chimpanzee n шимпанзе́ m indecl.

chin n подборо́док.

china n фарфо́р. **China** n Кита́й. **Chinese** n кита́ец, -а́нка; adj кита́йский.

chink¹ n (sound) звон; vi звене́ть impf, про~ pf.

chink² n (crack) щель.

chintz n си́тец.

chip vt & i отка́лывать(ся) impf, отколо́ть(ся) pf; n (of wood) ще́пка; (in cup) щерби́на; (in games) фи́шка; pl карто́фель-соло́мка (collect); (electron) чип, микросхе́ма.

chiropodist n челове́к, занима́ющийся педикю́ром. **chiropody** n педикю́р.

chirp vi чири́кать impf.

chisel n (wood) стаме́ска; (masonry) зуби́ло; vt высека́ть impf, вы́сечь pf.

chit n (note) запи́ска.

chivalrous adj ры́царский. **chivalry** n ры́царство.

chlorine n хлор. **chloroform** n хлорофо́рм. **chlorophyll** n хлорофи́лл.

chock-full adj битко́м наби́тый.

chocolate n шокола́д; (sweet) шокола́дка.

choice n вы́бор; adj отбо́рный.

choir n хор m; ~-boy пе́вчий sb.

choke n (valve) дро́ссель m; vi дави́ться impf, по~ pf; (with anger etc.) задыха́ться impf, задохну́ться pf (with от+gen); vt (suffocate) души́ть impf, за~ pf; (of plants) заглуша́ть, глуши́ть impf, заглуши́ть pf.

cholera n холе́ра.

cholesterol n холестери́н.

choose vt (select) выбира́ть impf, вы́брать pf; (decide) реша́ть impf, реши́ть pf. **choosy** adj разбо́рчивый.

chop vt (also ~ down) руби́ть impf, рубну́ть, рубану́ть pf; ~ off отруба́ть impf, отруби́ть pf; n (cul) отбивна́я котле́та.

chopper n топо́р. **choppy** adj бурли́вый.

chop-sticks n па́лочки f pl для еды́.

choral adj хорово́й. **chorale** n хора́л.

chord n (mus) акко́рд.

chore n обя́занность.

choreographer n хорео́граф. **chore-**

ography n хореогра́фия.
chorister n пе́вчий sb.
chortle vi фы́ркать impf, фы́ркнуть pf.
chorus n хор; (refrain) припе́в.
christen vt крести́ть impf & pf. Christian n христиани́н, -а́нка; adj христиа́нский; ~ name и́мя neut. Christianity n христиа́нство. Christmas n Рождество́; ~ Day пе́рвый день Рождества́; ~ Eve соче́льник; ~ tree ёлка.
chromatic adj хромати́ческий. chrome n хром. chromium n хром. chromosome n хромосо́ма.
chronic adj хрони́ческий.
chronicle n хро́ника, ле́топись.
chronological adj хронологи́ческий.
chrysalis n ку́колка.
chrysanthemum n хризанте́ма.
chubby adj пу́хлый.
chuck vt броса́ть impf, бро́сить pf; ~ out вышиба́ть impf, вы́шибить pf.
chuckle vi посме́иваться impf.
chum n това́рищ.
chunk n ломо́ть m.
church n це́рковь. churchyard n кла́дбище.
churlish adj грубы́й.
churn n маслобо́йка; vt сбива́ть impf, сбить pf; vi (foam) пе́ниться impf, вс~ pf; (stomach) крути́ть impf; ~ out выпека́ть impf, вы́печь pf; ~ up взбить pf.
chute n жёлоб.
cider n сидр.
cigar n сига́ра. cigarette n сигаре́та; папиро́са; ~ lighter зажига́лка.
cinder n шлак; pl зола́.
cine-camera n киноаппара́т. cinema n кино́ neut indecl.
cinnamon n кори́ца.
cipher n нуль m; (code) шифр.
circle n круг; (theatre) я́рус; vi кружи́ться impf; vt (walking) обходи́ть impf, обойти́ pf; (flying) облета́ть impf, облете́ть pf. circuit n кругооборо́т; объе́зд, обхо́д; (electron) схе́ма; (electr) цепь. circuitous adj окружно́й. circular adj кру́глый; (moving in a circle) кругово́й; n циркуля́р. circulate vi циркули́ровать impf; vt распространя́ть impf, распространи́ть pf. circulation n (air)

циркуля́ция; (distribution) распростране́ние; (of newspaper) тира́ж; (med) кровообраще́ние.
circumcise vt обреза́ть impf, обре́зать pf. circumcision n обреза́ние.
circumference n окру́жность.
circumspect adj осмотри́тельный.
circumstance n обстоя́тельство; under the ~s при да́нных обстоя́тельствах, в тако́м слу́чае; under no ~s ни при каки́х обстоя́тельствах, ни в ко́ем слу́чае.
circumvent vt обходи́ть impf, обойти́ pf.
circus n цирк.
cirrhosis n цирро́з.
CIS abbr (of Commonwealth of Independent States) СНГ.
cistern n бачо́к.
citadel n цитаде́ль.
cite vt ссыла́ться impf, сосла́ться pf на+acc.
citizen n граждани́н, -а́нка. citizenship n гражда́нство.
citrus n ци́трус; adj ци́трусовый.
city n го́род.
civic adj гражда́нский. civil adj гражда́нский; (polite) ве́жливый; ~ engineer гражда́нский инжене́р; ~ engineering гражда́нское строи́тельство; C~ Servant госуда́рственный слу́жащий sb; чино́вник; C~ Service госуда́рственная слу́жба. civilian n шта́тский sb; adj шта́тский. civility n ве́жливость. civilization n цивилиза́ция. civilize vt цивилизова́ть impf & pf. civilized adj цивилизо́ванный.
clad adj оде́тый.
claim n (demand) тре́бование, притяза́ние; (assertion) утвержде́ние; vt (demand) тре́бовать impf +gen; (assert) утвержда́ть impf, утверди́ть pf. claimant n претенде́нт.
clairvoyant n яснови́дец, -дица; adj яснови́дящий.
clam n моллю́ск; vi: ~ up отка́зываться impf, отказа́ться pf разгова́ривать.
clamber vi кара́бкаться impf, вс~ pf.
clammy adj вла́жный.
clamour n шум; vi: ~ for шу́мно тре́бовать impf, по~ pf +gen.
clamp n зажи́м; vt скрепля́ть impf, скрепи́ть pf; ~ down on прижа́ть pf.

clan n клан.

clandestine adj тáйный.

clang, clank n лязг; vt & i ля́згать impf, ля́згнуть pf (+instr).

clap vt & i хло́пать impf, хло́пнуть pf +dat; n хлопо́к; (thunder) удáр.

claret n бордó neut indecl.

clarification n (explanation) разъясне́ние. **clarify** vt разъясня́ть impf, разъясни́ть pf.

clarinet n кларне́т.

clarity n я́сность.

clash n (conflict) столкнове́ние; (disharmony) дисгармóния; vi стáлкиваться impf, столкну́ться pf; (coincide) совпадáть impf, совпáсть pf; не гармони́ровать impf.

clasp n застёжка; (embrace) объя́тие; vt обхвáтывать impf, обхвати́ть pf; ~ one's hands сплести́ pf пáльцы рук.

class n класс; ~-room класс; vt классифици́ровать impf & pf.

classic adj класси́ческий; n клáссик; pl (literature) клáссика; (Latin and Greek) класси́ческие языки́ m pl. **classical** adj класси́ческий.

classification n классификáция. **classified** adj засекре́ченный. **classify** vt классифици́ровать impf & pf.

classy adj клáссный.

clatter n стук; vi стучáть impf, по~ pf.

clause n статья́; (gram) предложе́ние.

claustrophobia n клаустрофóбия.

claw n кóготь; vt царáпать impf когтя́ми.

clay n гли́на; adj гли́няный.

clean adj чи́стый; adv (fully) совершéнно; ~-shaven глáдко вы́бритый; vt чи́стить impf, вы́~, по~ pf. **cleaner** n убóрщик, -ица. **cleaner's** n химчи́стка. **clean(li)ness** n чистотá. **cleanse** vt очищáть impf, очи́стить pf.

clear adj я́сный; (transparent) прозрáчный; (distinct) отчётливый; (free) свобóдный (of от+gen); (pure) чи́стый; vt & i очищáть(ся) impf, очи́стить(ся) pf; vt (jump over) перепры́гивать impf, перепры́гнуть pf; (acquit) опрáвдывать impf, оправдáть pf; ~ away убирáть impf,

убрáть pf со столá; ~ off (go away) убирáться impf, убрáться pf; ~ out (vt) вычищáть impf, вы́чистить pf; (vi) (make off) убирáться impf, убрáться pf; ~ up (tidy (away)) убирáть impf, убрáть pf; (weather) проясня́ться impf, проясни́ться pf; (explain) выясня́ть impf, вы́яснить pf. **clearance** n расчи́стка; (permission) разреше́ние. **clearing** n (glade) поля́на. **clearly** adv я́сно.

cleavage n разре́з груди́.

clef n (mus) ключ.

cleft n тре́щина.

clemency n милосе́рдие.

clench vt (fist) сжимáть impf, сжáть pf; (teeth) сти́скивать impf, сти́снуть pf.

clergy n духове́нство. **clergyman** n свяще́нник. **clerical** adj (eccl) духóвный; (of clerk) канцеля́рский. **clerk** n контóрский служащий sb.

clever adj у́мный. **cleverness** n уме́ние.

cliche n клише́ neut indecl.

click vt щёлкать impf, щёлкнуть pf +instr.

client n клие́нт. **clientele** n клиенту́ра.

cliff n утёс.

climate n кли́мат. **climatic** adj климати́ческий.

climax n кульминáция.

climb vt & i лáзить indet, лезть det на+acc; влезáть impf, влезть pf на+acc; поднимáться impf, подня́ться pf на+acc; ~ down (tree) слезáть impf, слезть pf (с+gen); (mountain) спускáться impf, спусти́ться pf (с+gen); (give in) отступáть impf, отступи́ть pf; n подъём. **climber** n альпини́ст, ~ка; (plant) вью́щееся расте́ние. **climbing** n альпини́зм.

clinch vt: ~ a deal закрепи́ть pf сде́лку.

cling vi (stick) прилипáть impf, прили́пнуть pf (to к+dat); (grasp) цепля́ться impf, цепи́ться pf (to за+acc).

clinic n кли́ника. **clinical** adj клини́ческий.

clink vt & i звене́ть impf, про~ pf (+instr); ~ glasses чóкаться impf, чóкнуться pf; n звон.

clip[1] n скре́пка; зажи́м; vt скрепля́ть

impf, скрепи́ть *pf*.

clip² *vt* (*cut*) подстрига́ть *impf*, подстри́чь *pf*. clippers *n pl* но́жницы *f pl*. clipping *n* (*extract*) вы́резка.

clique *n* кли́ка.

cloak *n* плащ. cloakroom *n* гардеро́б; (*lavatory*) убо́рная *sb*.

clock *n* часы́ *m pl*; ~-wise по часово́й стре́лке; ~-work часово́й механи́зм; *vi*: ~ in, out отмеча́ться *impf*, отме́титься *pf* приходя́ на рабо́ту/ уходя́ с рабо́ты.

clod *n* ком.

clog *vt*: ~ up засоря́ть *impf*, засори́ть *pf*.

cloister *n* арка́да.

close *adj* (*near*) бли́зкий; (*stuffy*) ду́шный; *vt & i* (*also* ~ down) закрыва́ть(ся) *impf*, закры́ть(ся) *pf*; (*conclude*) зака́нчивать *impf*, зако́нчить *pf*; *adv* бли́зко (to от+*gen*). closed *adj* закры́тый. closeted *adj*: be ~ together совеща́ться *impf* наедине́. close-up *n* фотогра́фия сня́тая кру́пным пла́ном. closing *n* закры́тие; *adj* заключи́тельный. closure *n* закры́тие.

clot *n* сгу́сток; *vi* сгуща́ться *impf*, сгусти́ться *pf*.

cloth *n* ткань; (*duster*) тря́пка; (*table*-~) ска́терть.

clothe *vt* одева́ть *impf*, оде́ть (in +*instr*, в+*acc*) *pf*. clothes *n pl* оде́жда, пла́тье.

cloud *n* о́блако; (*rain* ~) ту́ча; *vt* затемня́ть *impf*, затемни́ть *pf*; омрача́ть *impf*, омрачи́ть *pf*; ~ over покрыва́ться *impf*, покры́ться *pf* облака́ми, ту́чами. cloudy *adj* о́блачный; (*liquid*) му́тный.

clout *vt* ударя́ть *impf*, уда́рить *pf*; *n* затре́щина; (*fig*) влия́ние.

clove *n* гвозди́ка; (*of garlic*) зубо́к.

cloven *adj* раздво́енный.

clover *n* кле́вер.

clown *n* кло́ун.

club *n* (*stick*) дуби́нка; *pl* (*cards*) тре́фы (треф) *pl*; (*association*) клуб; *vt* колоти́ть *impf*, по~ *pf* дуби́нкой; *vi*: ~ together скла́дываться *impf*, сложи́ться *pf*.

cluck *vi* куда́хтать *impf*.

clue *n* (*evidence*) ули́ка; (*to puzzle*) ключ; (*hint*) намёк.

clump *n* гру́ппа.

clumsiness *n* неуклю́жесть. clumsy *adj* неуклю́жий.

cluster *n* гру́ппа; *vi* собира́ться *impf*, собра́ться *pf* гру́ппами.

clutch *n* (*grasp*) хва́тка; ко́гти *m pl*; (*tech*) сцепле́ние; *vt* зажима́ть *impf*, зажа́ть *pf*, *vi*: ~ at хвата́ться *impf*, хвати́ться *pf* за+*acc*.

clutter *n* беспоря́док; *vt* загроможда́ть *impf*, загромозди́ть *pf*.

c/o *abbr* (*of care of*) по а́дресу +*gen*; че́рез+*acc*.

coach *n* (*horse-drawn*) каре́та; (*rly*) ваго́н; (*bus*) авто́бус; (*tutor*) репети́тор; (*sport*) тре́нер; *vt* репети́ровать *impf*; тренирова́ть *impf*, на~ *pf*.

coagulate *vi* сгуща́ться *impf*, сгусти́ться *pf*.

coal *n* у́голь *m*; ~mine у́гольная ша́хта.

coalition *n* коали́ция.

coarse *adj* гру́бый.

coast *n* побере́жье, бе́рег; ~ guard береговая охра́на; *vi* (*move without power*) дви́гаться *impf*, дви́нуться *pf* по ине́рции. coastal *adj* берегово́й, прибре́жный.

coat *n* пальто́ *neut indecl*; (*layer*) слой; (*animal*) шерсть, мех; ~ of arms герб; *vt* покрыва́ть *impf*, покры́ть *pf*.

coax *vt* угова́ривать *impf*, уговори́ть *pf*.

cob *n* (*corn-*~) поча́ток кукуру́зы.

cobble *n* булы́жник (*also collect*). cobbled *adj* булы́жный.

cobbler *n* сапо́жник.

cobweb *n* паути́на.

Coca-Cola *n* (*propr*) ко́ка-ко́ла.

cocaine *n* кокаи́н.

cock *n* (*bird*) пету́х; (*tap*) кран; (*of gun*) куро́к; *vt* (*gun*) взводи́ть *impf*, взвести́ *pf* куро́к+*gen*.

cockerel *n* петушо́к.

cockle *n* сердцеви́дка.

cockpit *n* (*aeron*) каби́на.

cockroach *n* тарака́н.

cocktail *n* кокте́йль *m*.

cocky *adj* чва́нный.

cocoa *n* кака́о *neut indecl*.

coco(a)nut *n* коко́с.

cocoon *n* ко́кон.

cod *n* треска́.

code *n* (*of laws*) ко́декс; (*cipher*) код;

vt шифрова́ть *impf*, за~ *pf*. **codify** *vt* кодифици́ровать *impf & pf*.

co-education *n* совме́стное обуче́ние.

coefficient *n* коэффицие́нт.

coerce *vt* принужда́ть *impf*, прину́дить *pf*. **coercion** *n* принужде́ние.

coexist *vi* сосуществова́ть *impf*. **coexistence** *n* сосуществова́ние.

coffee *n* ко́фе *m indecl*; ~**mill** *n* кофе́йница; ~**pot** *n* кофе́йник.

coffer *n pl* казна́.

coffin *n* гроб.

cog *n* зубе́ц. **cogwheel** *n* зубча́тое колесо́.

cogent *adj* убеди́тельный.

cohabit *vi* сожи́тельствовать *impf*.

coherent *adj* свя́зный. **cohesion** *n* сплочённость. **cohesive** *adj* сплочённый.

coil *vt & i* свёртывать(ся) *impf*, сверну́ть(ся) *pf* кольцо́м; *n* кольцо́; (*electr*) кату́шка.

coin *n* моне́та; *vt* чека́нить *impf*, от~ *pf*.

coincide *vi* совпада́ть *impf*, совпа́сть *pf*. **coincidence** *n* совпаде́ние. **coincidental** *adj* случа́йный.

coke *n* кокс.

colander *n* дуршла́г.

cold *n* хо́лод; (*med*) просту́да, на́сморк; *adj* холо́дный; ~**blooded** *adj* жесто́кий; (*zool*) холоднокро́вный.

colic *n* ко́лики *f pl*.

collaborate *vi* сотру́дничать *impf*. **collaboration** *n* сотру́дничество. **collaborator** *n* сотру́дник, -ица; (*traitor*) коллаборациони́ст, -и́стка.

collapse *vi* ру́хнуть *pf*; *n* паде́ние, круше́ние.

collar *n* воротни́к; (*dog's*) оше́йник; ~**bone** *n* ключи́ца.

colleague *n* колле́га *m & f*.

collect *vt* собира́ть *impf*, собра́ть *pf*; (*as hobby*) коллекциони́ровать *impf*; (*fetch*) забира́ть *impf*, забра́ть *pf*. **collected** *adj* (*calm*) собранный; ~ **works** собра́ние сочине́ний. **collection** *n* (*stamps etc.*) колле́кция; (*church etc.*) сбор; (*post*) вы́емка. **collective** *n* коллекти́в; *adj* коллекти́вный; ~ **farm** колхо́з; ~ **noun** собира́тельное существи́тельное *sb*. **collectivization** *n* коллективиза́ция. **collector** *n* сбо́рщик; коллекционе́р.

college *n* колле́дж, учи́лище.

collide *vi* ста́лкиваться *impf*, столкну́ться *pf*. **collision** *n* столкнове́ние.

colliery *n* каменноуго́льная ша́хта.

colloquial *adj* разгово́рный. **colloquialism** *n* разгово́рное выраже́ние.

collusion *n* та́йный сго́вор.

colon[1] *n* (*anat*) то́лстая кишка́.

colon[2] *n* (*gram*) двоето́чие.

colonel *n* полко́вник.

colonial *adj* колониа́льный. **colonialism** *n* колониали́зм. **colonize** *vt* колонизова́ть *impf & pf*. **colony** *n* коло́ния.

colossal *adj* колосса́льный.

colour *n* цвет, кра́ска; (*pl*) (*flag*) знамя *neut*; ~**blind** страда́ющий дальтони́змом; ~ **film** цветна́я плёнка; *vt* раскра́шивать *impf*, раскра́сить *pf*; *vi* красне́ть *impf*, по~ *pf*. **coloured** *adj* цветно́й. **colourful** *adj* я́ркий. **colourless** *adj* бесцве́тный.

colt *n* жеребёнок.

column *n* (*archit, mil*) коло́нна; (*of smoke etc.*) столб; (*of print*) столбе́ц. **columnist** *n* журнали́ст.

coma *n* ко́ма.

comb *n* гребёнка; *vt* причёсывать *impf*, причеса́ть *pf*.

combat *n* бой; *vt* боро́ться *impf* с+*instr*, про́тив+*gen*.

combination *n* сочета́ние; комбина́ция. **combine** *n* комбина́т; (~*harvester*) комба́йн; *vt & i* совмеща́ть(ся) *impf*, совмести́ть(ся) *pf*. **combined** *adj* совме́стный.

combustion *n* горе́ние.

come *vi* (*on foot*) приходи́ть *impf*, прийти́ *pf*; (*by transport*) приезжа́ть *impf*, прие́хать *pf*; ~ **about** случа́ться *impf*, случи́ться *pf*; ~ **across** натолкну́ться *pf* на+*acc*; ~ **back** возвраща́ться *impf*, возврати́ться *pf*; ~ **in** входи́ть *impf*, войти́ *pf*; ~ **out** выходи́ть *impf*, вы́йти *pf*; ~ **round** (*revive*) приходи́ть *impf*, прийти́ *pf* в себя́; (*visit*) заходи́ть *impf*, зайти́ *pf*; (*agree*) соглаша́ться *impf*, согласи́ться *pf*; ~ **up to** (*approach*) подходи́ть *impf*, подойти́ *pf* к+*dat*;

(reach) доходи́ть *impf*, дойти́ *pf* до+*gen*. **come-back** *n* возвраще́ние. **come-down** *n* униже́ние.

comedian *n* комедиа́нт. **comedy** *n* коме́дия.

comet *n* коме́та.

comfort *n* комфо́рт; *(convenience)* удо́бство; *(consolation)* утеше́ние; *vt* утеша́ть *impf*, уте́шить *pf*. **comfortable** *adj* удо́бный.

comic *adj* коми́ческий; *n* ко́мик; *(magazine)* ко́микс. **comical** *adj* смешно́й.

coming *adj* сле́дующий.

comma *n* запята́я *sb*.

command *n* *(order)* прика́з; *(order, authority)* кома́нда; **have ~ of** *(master)* владе́ть *impf* +*instr*; *vt* прика́зывать *impf*, приказа́ть *pf* +*dat*; *(mil)* кома́ндовать *impf*, **c~** *pf* +*instr*. **commandant** *n* коменда́нт. **commandeer** *vt* реквизи́ровать *impf* & *pf*. **commander** *n* команди́р; **~ in-chief** главнокома́ндующий *sb*. **commandment** *n* за́поведь. **commando** *n* деса́нтник.

commemorate *vt* ознамено́вывать *impf*, ознаменова́ть *pf*. **commemoration** *n* ознаменова́ние. **commemorative** *adj* па́мятный.

commence *vt* & *i* начина́ть(ся) *impf*, нача́ть(ся) *pf*. **commencement** *n* нача́ло.

commend *vt* хвали́ть *impf*, по~ *pf*; *(recommend)* рекомендова́ть *impf* & *pf*. **commendable** *adj* похва́льный. **commendation** *n* похвала́.

commensurate *adj* соразме́рный.

comment *n* замеча́ние; *vi* де́лать *impf*, **c~** *pf* замеча́ния; **~ on** комменти́ровать *impf* & *pf*, про~ *pf*. **commentary** *n* коммента́рий. **commentator** *n* коммента́тор.

commerce *n* комме́рция. **commercial** *adj* торго́вый; *n* рекла́ма.

commiserate *vi*: **~ with** соболе́зновать *impf* +*dat*. **commiseration** *n* соболе́знование.

commission *n* *(order for work)* зака́з; *(agent's fee)* комиссио́нные *sb*; *(of inquiry etc.)* коми́ссия; *(mil)* офице́рское зва́ние; *vt* зака́зывать *impf*, заказа́ть *pf*. **commissionaire** *n* швейца́р. **commissioner** *n* комисса́р.

commit *vt* соверша́ть *impf*, соверши́ть *pf*; **~ o.s.** обя́зываться *impf*, обяза́ться *pf*. **commitment** *n* обяза́тельство.

committee *n* комите́т.

commodity *n* това́р.

commodore *n* *(officer)* коммодо́р.

common *adj* о́бщий; *(ordinary)* просто́й; *n* общи́нная земля́; **~ sense** здра́вый смысл. **commonly** *adv* обы́чно. **commonplace** *adj* бана́льный. **commonwealth** *n* содру́жество.

commotion *n* сумато́ха.

communal *adj* общи́нный, коммуна́льный. **commune** *n* комму́на; *vi* обща́ться *impf*.

communicate *vt* передава́ть *impf*, переда́ть *pf*; сообща́ть *impf*, сообщи́ть *pf*. **communication** *n* сообще́ние; связь. **communicative** *adj* разгово́рчивый.

communion *n* *(eccl)* прича́стие.

communiqué *n* коммюнике́ *neut indecl*.

Communism *n* коммуни́зм. **Communist** *n* коммуни́ст, **~ка**; *adj* коммунисти́ческий.

community *n* общи́на.

commute *vt* заменя́ть *impf*, замени́ть *pf*; *(travel)* добира́ться *impf*, добра́ться *pf* тра́нспортом. **commuter** *n* регуля́рный пассажи́р.

compact[1] *n* *(agreement)* соглаше́ние. **compact**[2] *adj* компа́ктный; **~ disc** компа́кт-ди́ск; *n* пу́дреница.

companion *n* това́рищ; *(handbook)* спра́вочник. **companionable** *adj* общи́тельный. **companionship** *n* дру́жеское обще́ние. **company** *n* о́бщество, *(also firm)* компа́ния; *(theat)* тру́ппа; *(mil)* ро́та.

comparable *adj* сравни́мый. **comparative** *adj* сравни́тельный; *n* сравни́тельная сте́пень. **compare** *vt* & *i* сра́внивать(ся) *impf*, сравни́ть(ся) *pf* (**to, with** c+*instr*). **comparison** *n* сравне́ние.

compartment *n* отделе́ние; *(rly)* купе́ *neut indecl*.

compass *n* ко́мпас; *pl* ци́ркуль *m*.

compassion *n* сострада́ние. **compassionate** *adj* сострада́тельный.

compatibility *n* совмести́мость. **compatible** *adj* совмести́мый.

compatriot *n* соотече́ственник, -ица.

compel vt заставля́ть impf, заста́-
вить pf.

compensate vt компенси́ровать
impf & pf (for за+acc). **compensation** n компенса́ция.

compete vi конкури́ровать impf;
соревнова́ться impf.

competence n компете́нтность. **competent** adj компете́нтный.

competition n (contest) соревно-
ва́ние, состяза́ние; (rivalry) конку-
ре́нция. **competitive** adj (comm)
конкурентоспосо́бный. **competitor**
n конкуре́нт, ~ка.

compilation n (result) компиля́ция;
(act) составле́ние. **compile** vt соста-
вля́ть impf, соста́вить pf. **compiler**
n составитель m, ~ница.

complacency n самодово́льство.
complacent adj самодово́льный.

complain vi жа́ловаться impf, по-
pf. **complaint** n жа́лоба.

complement n дополне́ние; (full
number) (ли́чный) соста́в; vt допол-
ня́ть impf, допо́лнить pf. **comple-
mentary** adj дополни́тельный.

complete vt заверша́ть impf, за-
верши́ть pf; adj (entire, thorough)
по́лный; (finished) зако́нченный.
completion n заверше́ние.

complex adj сло́жный; n ко́мплекс.
complexity n сло́жность.

complexion n цвет лица́.

compliance n усту́пчивость. **compliant** adj усту́пчивый.

complicate vt осложня́ть impf, осло-
жни́ть pf. **complicated** adj сло́ж-
ный. **complication** n осложне́ние.

complicity n соуча́стие.

compliment n комплиме́нт; pl при-
ве́т; vt говори́ть impf компли-
ме́нт(ы) +dat; хвали́ть impf, по-
pf. **complimentary** adj ле́стный; (free)
беспла́тный.

comply vi: ~ with (fulfil) исполня́ть
impf, испо́лнить pf; (submit to)
подчиня́ться impf, подчини́ться pf
+dat.

component n дета́ль; adj составно́й.

compose vt (music etc.) сочиня́ть
impf, сочини́ть pf; (draft; constitute)
составля́ть impf, соста́вить pf.
composed adj споко́йный; be ~ of
состоя́ть impf из+gen. **composer** n
компози́тор. **composition** n сочи-

не́ние; (make-up) соста́в.

compost n компо́ст.

composure n самооблада́ние.

compound[1] n (chem) соедине́ние;
adj сло́жный.

compound[2] n (enclosure) огоро́жен-
ное ме́сто.

comprehend vt понима́ть impf, по-
ня́ть pf. **comprehensible** adj поня́т-
ный. **comprehension** n понима́ние.

comprehensive adj всеобъе́млю-
щий; ~ school общеобразова́тель-
ная шко́ла.

compress vt сжима́ть impf, сжать
pf. **compressed** adj сжа́тый. **compression** n сжа́тие. **compressor** n
компре́ссор.

comprise vt состоя́ть impf из+gen.

compromise n компроми́сс; vt
проклямети́ровать impf, ~ pf; vi идти́
impf, пойти́ pf на компроми́сс.

compulsion n принужде́ние. **compulsory** adj обяза́тельный.

compunction n угрызе́ние со́вести.

computer n компью́тер.

comrade n това́рищ. **comradeship**
n това́рищество.

con[1] see pro[1]

con[2] vt надува́ть impf, наду́ть pf.

concave adj вогну́тый.

conceal vt скрыва́ть impf, скрыть pf.

concede vt уступа́ть impf, уступи́ть
pf; (admit) признава́ть impf, при-
зна́ть pf; (goal) пропуска́ть impf,
пропусти́ть pf.

conceit n самомне́ние. **conceited**
adj самовлюблённый.

conceivable adj мы́слимый. **conceive** vt (plan, imagine) заду́мывать
impf, заду́мать pf; (biol) зачина́ть
impf зача́ть pf; vi забере́менеть pf.

concentrate vt & i сосредото́чи-
вать(ся) impf, сосредото́чить(ся) pf
(on на+prep); vt (also chem)
концентри́ровать impf, с~ pf. **concentration** n сосредото́ченность,
концентра́ция.

concept n поня́тие. **conception** n
поня́тие; (biol) зача́тие.

concern n (worry) забо́та; (comm)
предприя́тие; vt каса́ться impf +gen;
~ o.s. with занима́ться impf, за-
ня́ться pf +instr. **concerned** adj
озабо́ченный; as far as I'm ~ что
каса́ется меня́. **concerning** prep

относи́тельно+*gen.*

concert *n* конце́рт. **concerted** *adj* согласо́ванный.

concertina *n* гармо́ника.

concession *n* усту́пка; (*econ*) конце́ссия. **concessionary** *adj* концессио́нный.

conciliation *n* примире́ние. **conciliatory** *adj* примири́тельный.

concise *adj* кра́ткий. **conciseness** *n* сжа́тость, кра́ткость.

conclude *vt* заключа́ть *impf*, заключи́ть *pf*. **concluding** *adj* заключи́тельный. **conclusion** *n* заключе́ние; (*deduction*) вы́вод. **conclusive** *adj* реша́ющий.

concoct *vt* стря́пать *impf*, co~ *pf*. **concoction** *n* стряпня́.

concourse *n* зал.

concrete *n* бето́н; *adj* бето́нный; (*fig*) конкре́тный.

concur *vi* соглаша́ться *impf*, согласи́ться *pf*. **concurrent** *adj* одновре́менный.

concussion *n* сотрясе́ние.

condemn *vt* осужда́ть *impf*, осуди́ть *pf*; (*as unfit for use*) бракова́ть *impf*, за~ *pf*. **condemnation** *n* осужде́ние.

condensation *n* конденса́ция. **condense** *vt* (*liquid etc.*) конденси́ровать *impf* & *pf*; (*text etc.*) сокраща́ть *impf*, сократи́ть *pf*. **condensed** *adj* сжа́тый; (*milk*) сгущённый. **condenser** *n* конденса́тор.

condescend *vi* снисходи́ть *impf*, снизойти́ *pf*. **condescending** *adj* снисходи́тельный. **condescension** *n* снисхожде́ние.

condiment *n* припра́ва.

condition *n* усло́вие; (*state*) состоя́ние; *vt* (*determine*) обусло́вливать *impf*, обусло́вить *pf*; (*psych*) приуча́ть *impf*, приучи́ть *pf*. **conditional** *adj* усло́вный.

condolence *n*: *pl* соболе́знование.

condom *n* презервати́в.

condone *vt* закрыва́ть *impf*, закры́ть *pf* глаза́ на+*acc*.

conducive *adj* спосо́бствующий (to +*dat.*)

conduct *n* (*behaviour*) поведе́ние; *vt* вести́ *impf*, по~, про~ *pf*; (*mus*) дирижи́ровать *impf* +*instr*; (*phys*) проводи́ть *impf*. **conduction** *n* прово-

води́мость. **conductor** *n* (*bus*) конду́ктор; (*phys*) проводни́к; (*mus*) дирижёр.

conduit *n* трубопрово́д.

cone *n* ко́нус; (*bot*) ши́шка.

confectioner *n* конди́тер; ~'s (*shop*) конди́терская *sb*. **confectionery** *n* конди́терские изде́лия *neut pl*.

confederation *n* конфедера́ция.

confer *vt* присужда́ть *impf*, присуди́ть (on +*dat*) *pf*; *vi* совеща́ться *impf*. **conference** *n* совеща́ние; конфере́нция.

confess *vt* & *i* (*acknowledge*) признава́ть(ся) *impf*, призна́ть(ся) *pf* (to в+*prep*); (*eccl*) испове́довать(ся) *impf* & *pf*. **confession** *n* призна́ние; и́споведь. **confessor** *n* духовни́к.

confidant(e) *n* бли́зкий собесе́дник.

confide *vt* доверя́ть *impf*, дове́рить *pf*; ~ in дели́ться *impf*, по~ *pf* c+*instr*. **confidence** *n* (*trust*) дове́рие; (*certainty*) уве́ренность; (*self-*~) самоуве́ренность. **confident** *adj* уве́ренный. **confidential** *adj* секре́тный.

confine *vt* ограни́чивать *impf*, ограни́чить *pf*; (*shut in*) заключа́ть *impf*, заключи́ть *pf*. **confinement** *n* заключе́ние. **confines** *n pl* преде́лы *m pl*.

confirm *vt* подтвержда́ть *impf*, подтверди́ть *pf*. **confirmation** *n* подтвержде́ние; (*eccl*) конфирма́ция. **confirmed** *adj* закоренéлый.

confiscate *vt* конфискова́ть *impf* & *pf*. **confiscation** *n* конфиска́ция.

conflict *n* конфли́кт; противоре́чие; *vi*: ~ with противоре́чить *impf* +*dat*. **conflicting** *adj* противоречи́вый.

conform *vi*: ~ to подчиня́ться *impf*, подчини́ться *pf* +*dat*. **conformity** *n* соотве́тствие; (*compliance*) подчине́ние.

confound *vt* сбива́ть *impf*, сбить *pf* c то́лку. **confounded** *adj* прокля́тый.

confront *vt* стоя́ть *impf* лицо́м к лицу́ c+*instr*; ~ (*person*) with ста́вить *impf*, по~ *pf* лицо́м к лицу́ c+*instr*. **confrontation** *n* конфронта́ция.

confuse *vt* смуща́ть *impf*, смути́ть *pf*; (*also mix up*) пу́тать *impf*, за~, c~ *pf*. **confusion** *n* смуще́ние;

путаница.

congeal vt густе́ть impf, за~ pf; (blood) свёртываться impf, сверну́ться pf.

congenial adj прия́тный.

congenital adj врождённый.

congested adj перепо́лненный. **congestion** n (traffic) зато́р.

congratulate vt поздравля́ть impf, поздра́вить pf (on c+instr). **congratulation** n поздравле́ние; ~s! поздравля́ю!

congregate vi собира́ться impf, собра́ться pf. **congregation** n (eccl) прихожа́не (-н) pl.

congress n съезд. **Congressman** n конгрессме́н.

conic(al) adj кони́ческий.

conifer n хво́йное де́рево. **coniferous** adj хво́йный.

conjecture n дога́дка; vt гада́ть impf.

conjugal adj супру́жеский.

conjugate vt спряга́ть impf, про~ pf. **conjugation** n спряже́ние.

conjunction n (gram) сою́з; in ~ with совме́стно c+instr.

conjure vi: ~ up (in mind) вызыва́ть impf, вы́звать pf в воображе́нии. **conjurer** n фо́кусник. **conjuring trick** n фо́кус.

connect vt & i свя́зывать(ся) impf, связа́ть(ся) pf; соединя́ть(ся) impf, соедини́ть(ся) pf. **connected** adj свя́занный. **connection, -exion** n связь; (rly etc.) переса́дка.

connivance n попусти́тельство. **connive** vi: ~ at попусти́тельствовать impf +dat.

connoisseur n знато́к.

conquer vt (country) завоёвывать impf, завоева́ть pf; (enemy) побежда́ть impf, победи́ть pf; (habit) преодолева́ть impf, преодоле́ть pf. **conqueror** n завоева́тель m. **conquest** n завоева́ние.

conscience n со́весть. **conscientious** adj добросо́вестный. **conscious** adj созна́тельный; predic в созна́нии; be ~ of сознава́ть impf +acc. **consciousness** n созна́ние.

conscript vt призыва́ть impf, призва́ть pf на вое́нную слу́жбу; n призывни́к. **conscription** n во́инская пови́нность.

consecrate vt освяща́ть impf, освя-

ти́ть pf. **consecration** n освяще́ние.

consecutive adj после́довательный.

consensus n согла́сие.

consent vi соглаша́ться impf, согласи́ться pf (to +inf, на+acc); n согла́сие.

consequence n после́дствие; of great ~ большо́го значе́ния, of some ~ дово́льно ва́жный. **consequent** adj вытека́ющий. **consequential** adj ва́жный. **consequently** adv сле́довательно.

conservation n сохране́ние; (of nature) охра́на приро́ды. **conservative** adj консервати́вный; n консерва́тор. **conservatory** n оранжере́я. **conserve** vt сохраня́ть impf, сохрани́ть pf.

consider vt (think over) обду́мывать impf, обду́мать pf; (examine) рассма́тривать impf, рассмотре́ть pf; (regard as, be of opinion that) счита́ть impf, счесть pf +instr, за+acc, что; (take into account) счита́ться impf c+instr. **considerable** adj значи́тельный. **considerate** adj внима́тельный. **consideration** n рассмотре́ние; внима́ние; (factor) фа́ктор; take into ~ принима́ть impf, приня́ть pf во внима́ние. **considering** prep принима́я +acc во внима́ние.

consign vt передава́ть impf, переда́ть pf. **consignment** n (goods) па́ртия; (consigning) отпра́вка това́ров.

consist vi: ~ of состоя́ть impf из +gen. **consistency** n после́довательность; (density) консисте́нция. **consistent** adj после́довательный; ~ with совмести́мый c+instr.

consolation n утеше́ние. **console**[1] vt утеша́ть impf, уте́шить pf.

console[2] n (control panel) пульт управле́ния.

consolidate vt укрепля́ть impf, укрепи́ть pf. **consolidation** n укрепле́ние.

consonant n согла́сный sb.

consort n супру́г, ~a.

conspicuous adj заме́тный.

conspiracy n за́говор. **conspirator** n заговбрщик, -ица. **conspiratorial** adj заговбрщицкий. **conspire** vi устра́ивать impf, устро́ить pf за́говор.

constable *n* полицейский *sb*.

constancy *n* постоянство. **constant** *adj* постоянный. **constantly** *adv* постоянно.

constellation *n* созвездие.

consternation *n* тревога.

constipation *n* запор.

constituency *n* избирательный округ. **constituent** *n* (*component*) составная часть; (*voter*) избиратель *m*; *adj* составной. **constitute** *vt* составлять *impf*, составить *pf*. **constitution** *n* (*polit*, *med*) конституция; (*composition*) составление. **constitutional** *adj* (*polit*) конституционный.

constrain *vt* принуждать *impf*, принудить *pf*. **constrained** *adj* (*inhibited*) стеснённый. **constraint** *n* принуждение; (*inhibition*) стеснение.

constrict *vt* (*compress*) сжимать *impf*, сжать *pf*; (*narrow*) суживать *impf*, сузить *pf*. **constriction** *n* сжатие; сужение.

construct *vt* строить *impf*, по~ *pf*. **construction** *n* строительство; (*also gram*) конструкция; (*interpretation*) истолкование; ~ site стройка. **constructive** *adj* конструктивный.

construe *vt* истолковывать *impf*, истолковать *pf*.

consul *n* консул. **consulate** *n* консульство.

consult *vt* советоваться *impf*, по~ *pf* c+*instr*. **consultant** *n* консультант. **consultation** *n* консультация.

consume *vt* потреблять *impf*, потребить *pf*; (*eat or drink*) съедать *impf*, съесть *pf*. **consumer** *n* потребитель *m*; ~ **goods** товары *m pl* широкого потребления.

consummate *vt* завершать *impf*, завершить *pf*; ~ **a marriage** осуществлять *impf*, осуществить *pf* брачные отношения. **consummation** *n* завершение; (*of marriage*) осуществление.

consumption *n* потребление.

contact *n* контакт; (*person*) связь; ~ **lens** контактная линза; *vt* связываться *impf*, связаться *pf* c+*instr*.

contagious *adj* заразный.

contain *vt* содержать *impf*; (*restrain*) сдерживать *impf*, сдержать *pf*. **con-**

tainer *n* (*vessel*) сосуд; (*transport*) контейнер.

contaminate *vt* загрязнять *impf*, загрязнить *pf*. **contamination** *n* загрязнение.

contemplate *vt* (*gaze*) созерцать *impf*; размышлять *impf*; (*consider*) предполагать *impf*, предположить *pf*. **contemplation** *n* созерцание; размышление. **contemplative** *adj* созерцательный.

contemporary *n* современник; *adj* современный.

contempt *n* презрение; ~ **of court** неуважение к суду; **hold in** ~ презирать *impf*. **contemptible** *adj* презренный. **contemptuous** *adj* презрительный.

contend *vi* (*compete*) состязаться *impf*; ~ **for** оспаривать *impf*; ~ **with** справляться *impf*, справиться *pf* c+*instr*; *vt* утверждать *impf*. **contender** *n* претендент.

content[1] *n* содержание; *pl* содержимое *sb*; (*table of*) ~**s** содержание.

content[2] *predic* доволен (-льна); *vt*: ~ **o.s. with** довольствоваться *impf*, y~ *pf* +*instr*. **contented** *adj* довольный.

contention *n* (*claim*) утверждение. **contentious** *adj* спорный.

contest *n* состязание; *vt* (*dispute*) оспаривать *impf*, оспорить *pf*. **contestant** *n* участник, -ица, состязания.

context *n* контекст.

continent *n* материк. **continental** *adj* материковый.

contingency *n* возможный случай; ~ **plan** вариант плана. **contingent** *adj* случайный; *n* контингент.

continual *adj* непрестанный. **continuation** *n* продолжение. **continue** *vt & i* продолжать(ся) *impf*, продолжить(ся) *pf*. **continuous** *adj* непрерывный.

contort *vt* искажать *impf*, исказить *pf*. **contortion** *n* искажение.

contour *n* контур; ~ **line** горизонталь.

contraband *n* контрабанда.

contraception *n* предупреждение зачатия. **contraceptive** *n* противозачаточное средство; *adj* противозачаточный.

contract n контра́кт, до́говор; vi (make a ~) заключа́ть impf, заключи́ть pf контра́кт; vt & i (shorten, reduce) сокраща́ть(ся) impf, сократи́ть(ся) pf; vt (illness) заболева́ть impf, заболе́ть pf +instr. **contraction** n сокраще́ние; pl (med) схва́тки f pl. **contractor** n подря́дчик.

contradict vt противоре́чить impf +dat. **contradiction** n противоре́чие. **contradictory** adj противоре́чивый.

contraflow n встре́чное движе́ние.

contralto n контра́льто (voice) neut & (person) f indecl.

contraption n приспособле́ние.

contrary adj (opposite) противополо́жный; (perverse) капри́зный; ~ to вопреки́+dat; n: on the ~ наоборо́т.

contrast n контра́ст, противополо́жность; vt противопоставля́ть impf, противопоста́вить pf (with +dat); vi контрасти́ровать impf.

contravene vt наруша́ть impf, нару́шить pf. **contravention** n наруше́ние.

contribute vt (to fund etc.) же́ртвовать impf, по~ pf (to в+acc); ~ to (further) соде́йствовать impf & pf, по~ pf +dat; (write for) сотру́дничать impf в+prep. **contribution** n (money) поже́ртвование; (fig) вклад. **contributor** n (donor) же́ртвователь m; (writer) сотру́дник.

contrite adj ка́ющийся.

contrivance n приспособле́ние. **contrive** vt ухитря́ться impf, ухитри́ться pf +inf.

control n (mastery) контро́ль m; (operation) управле́ние; pl управле́ния pl; vt (dominate, verify) контроли́ровать impf, про~ pf; (regulate) управля́ть impf +instr; ~ o.s. сде́рживаться impf, сдержа́ться pf.

controversial adj спо́рный. **controversy** n спор.

convalesce vi выздора́вливать impf. **convalescence** n выздоровле́ние. **convection** n конве́кция. **convector** n конве́ктор.

convene vt созыва́ть impf, созва́ть pf.

convenience n удо́бство; (public ~)

убо́рная sb. **convenient** adj удо́бный.

convent n же́нский монасты́рь m.

convention n (assembly) съезд; (agreement) конве́нция; (custom) обы́чай; (conventionality) усло́вность. **conventional** adj общепри́нятый; (also mil) обы́чный.

converge vi сходи́ться impf, сойти́сь pf. **convergence** n схо́димость.

conversant predic: ~ with знако́м c+instr.

conversation n разгово́р. **conversational** adj разгово́рный. **converse**[1] vi разгова́ривать impf.

converse[2] n обра́тное sb. **conversely** adv наоборо́т. **conversion** n (change) превраще́ние; (of faith) обраще́ние; (of building) перестро́йка. **convert** vt (change) превраща́ть impf, преврати́ть pf (into в+acc); (to faith) обраща́ть impf, обрати́ть pf (to в+acc); (a building) перестра́ивать impf, перестро́ить pf. **convertible** adj обрати́мый; n автомоби́ль m со снима́ющейся кры́шей.

convex adj вы́пуклый.

convey vt (transport) перевози́ть impf, перевезти́ pf; (communicate) передава́ть impf, переда́ть pf. **conveyance** n перево́зка; переда́ча. **conveyancing** n нотариа́льная переда́ча. **conveyor belt** n транспортёрная ле́нта.

convict n осуждённый sb; vt осужда́ть impf, осуди́ть pf. **conviction** n (law) осужде́ние; (belief) убежде́ние. **convince** vt убежда́ть impf, убеди́ть pf. **convincing** adj убеди́тельный.

convivial adj весёлый.

convoluted adj изви́листый; (fig) запу́танный.

convoy n конво́й.

convulse vt: be ~d with содрога́ться impf, содрогну́ться pf от+gen. **convulsion** n (med) конву́льсия.

cook n куха́рка, по́вар; vt гото́вить impf; vi вари́ться impf; c~ pf. **cooker** n плита́, печь. **cookery** n кулина́рия.

cool adj прохла́дный; (calm) хладнокро́вный; (unfriendly) холо́дный; vt охлажда́ть impf, охлади́ть pf; ~

down, off остывать *impf*, остыть (*ну*)ть *pf*. **coolness** *n* прохлада; (*calm*) хладнокровие; (*manner*) холодок.

coop *n* курятник; *vt*: ~ **up** держать *impf* взаперти.

cooperate *vi* сотрудничать *impf*. **cooperation** *n* сотрудничество. **cooperative** *n* кооператив; *adj* кооперативный; (*helpful*) услужливый.

co-opt *vt* кооптировать *impf* & *pf*.

coordinate *vt* координировать *impf* & *pf*; *n* координата. **coordination** *n* координация.

cope *vi*: ~ **with** справляться *impf*, справиться *pf* c+*instr*.

copious *adj* обильный.

copper *n* (*metal*) медь; *adj* медный.

coppice, copse *n* рощица.

copulate *vi* совокупляться *impf*, совокупиться *pf*.

copy *n* копия; (*book*) экземпляр; *vt* (*reproduce*) копировать *impf*, c~ *pf*; (*transcribe*) переписывать *impf*, переписать *pf*; (*imitate*) подражать *impf* +*dat*. **copyright** *n* авторское право.

coral *n* коралл.

cord *n* (*string*) верёвка; (*electr*) шнур.

cordial *adj* сердечный.

corduroy *n* рубчатый вельвет.

core *n* сердцевина; (*fig*) суть.

cork *n* (*material*; *stopper*) пробка; (*float*) поплавок. **corkscrew** *n* штопор.

corn[1] *n* зерно; (*wheat*) пшеница; (*maize*) кукуруза. **cornflakes** *n pl* кукурузные хлопья (-пьев) *pl*. **cornflour** *n* кукурузная мука. **corny** *adj* (*coll*) банальный.

corn[2] *n* (*med*) мозоль.

cornea *n* роговая оболочка.

corner *n* угол; ~**stone** *n* краеугольный камень *m*; *vt* загонять *impf*, загнать *pf* в угол.

cornet *n* (*mus*) корнет; (*ice-cream*) рожок.

cornice *n* карниз.

coronary (thrombosis) *n* коронаротромбоз. **coronation** *n* коронация. **coroner** *n* медик судебной экспертизы.

corporal[1] *n* капрал.

corporal[2] *adj* телесный; ~ **punishment** телесное наказание.

corporate *adj* корпоративный. **corporation** *n* корпорация.

corps *n* корпус.

corpse *n* труп.

corpulent *adj* тучный.

corpuscle *n* кровяной шарик.

correct *adj* правильный; (*conduct*) корректный; *vt* исправлять *impf*, исправить *pf*. **correction** *n* исправление.

correlation *n* соотношение.

correspond *vi* соответствовать *impf* (**to, with** +*dat*); (*by letter*) переписываться *impf*. **correspondence** *n* соответствие; (*letters*) корреспонденция. **correspondent** *n* корреспондент. **corresponding** *adj* соответствующий (**to** +*dat*).

corridor *n* коридор.

corroborate *vt* подтверждать *impf*, подтвердить *pf*.

corrode *vt* разъедать *impf*, разъесть *pf*. **corrosion** *n* коррозия. **corrosive** *adj* едкий.

corrugated iron *n* рифлёное железо.

corrupt *adj* (*person*) развращённый; (*government*) продажный; *vt* развращать *impf*, развратить *pf*. **corruption** *n* развращение; коррупция.

corset *n* корсет.

cortège *n* кортеж.

cortex *n* кора.

corundum *n* корунд.

cosmetic *adj* косметический. **cosmetics** *n pl* косметика.

cosmic *adj* космический. **cosmonaut** *n* космонавт.

cosmopolitan *adj* космополитический.

cosmos *n* космос.

Cossack *n* казак, -ачка.

cosset *vt* нежить *impf*.

cost *n* стоимость, цена; *vt* стоить *impf*.

costly *adj* дорогой.

costume *n* костюм.

cosy *adj* уютный.

cot *n* детская кроватка.

cottage *n* коттедж; ~ **cheese** творог.

cotton *n* хлопок; (*cloth*) хлопчатобумажная ткань; (*thread*) нитка; ~ **wool** вата; *adj* хлопковый; хлопчатобумажный.

couch *n* диван.

couchette n спа́льное ме́сто.

cough n ка́шель m; vi ка́шлять impf.

council n сове́т; ~ **tax** ме́стный нало́г; ~ **house** жильё из обще́ственного фо́нда. **councillor** n член сове́та.

counsel n (advice) сове́т; (lawyer) адвока́т; vt сове́товать impf, по~ pf +dat.

count[1] vt счита́ть impf, со~, сочть pf; ~ **on** рассчи́тывать impf на+acc; n счёт. **countdown** n отсчёт вре́мени.

count[2] n (title) граф.

countenance n лицо́; vt одобря́ть impf, одо́брить pf.

counter n прила́вок; (token) фи́шка; adv: **run** ~ **to** идти́ impf вразре́з с+instr; vt пари́ровать impf, от~ pf. **counteract** vt противоде́йствовать impf +dat. **counterbalance** n противове́с; vt уравнове́шивать impf, уравнове́сить pf. **counterfeit** adj подде́льный. **counterpart** n соотве́тственная часть. **counterpoint** n контрапу́нкт. **counter-revolutionary** n контрреволюционе́р; adj контрреволюцио́нный. **countersign** vt ста́вить impf, по~ pf втору́ю по́дпись на+prep.

countess n графи́ня.

countless adj бесчи́сленный.

country n (nation) страна́; (native land) ро́дина; (rural areas) дере́вня; adj дереве́нский, се́льский. **countryman** n (compatriot) соoте́чественник; се́льский жи́тель m. **countryside** n приро́дный ландша́фт.

county n гра́фство.

coup n (polit) переворо́т.

couple n па́ра; (a few) не́сколько +gen; vt сцепля́ть impf, сцепи́ть pf.

coupon n купо́н; тало́н; ва́учер.

courage n хра́брость. **courageous** adj хра́брый.

courier n (messenger) курье́р; (guide) гид.

course n курс; (process) ход, тече́ние; (of meal) блю́до; **of** ~ коне́чно.

court n двор; (sport) корт, площа́дка; (law) суд; ~ **martial** вое́нный суд; vt уха́живать impf за+instr.

courteous adj ве́жливый. **courtesy** n ве́жливость. **courtier** n придво́рный sb. **courtyard** n двор.

cousin n двою́родный брат, -ная сестра́.

cove n бу́хточка.

covenant n догово́р.

cover n (covering; lid) покры́шка; (shelter) укры́тие; (chair ~; soft case) чехо́л; (bed) покрыва́ло; (book) переплёт, обло́жка; under separate ~ в отде́льном конве́рте; vt покрыва́ть impf, покры́ть pf; (hide, protect) закрыва́ть impf, закры́ть pf. **coverage** n освеще́ние. **covert** adj скры́тый.

covet vt пожела́ть pf +gen.

cow[1] n коро́ва. **cowboy** n ковбо́й. **cowshed** n хлев.

cow[2] vt запу́гивать impf, запуга́ть pf.

coward n трус. **cowardice** n тру́сость. **cowardly** adj трусли́вый.

cower vi съёживаться impf, съёжиться pf.

cox(swain) n рулево́й m.

coy adj жема́нно стыдли́вый.

crab n краб.

crack n (in cup, ice) тре́щина; (in wall) щель; (noise) треск; adj первокла́ссный; vt (break) коло́ть impf, рас~ pf; (china) бить impf, с~ pf тре́щину в+acc; vi тре́снуть pf. **crackle** vi потре́скивать impf.

cradle n колыбе́ль.

craft n (trade) ремесло́; (boat) су́дно. **craftiness** n хи́трость. **craftsman** n реме́сленник. **crafty** adj хи́трый.

crag n утёс. **craggy** adj скали́стый.

cram vt (fill) набива́ть impf, наби́ть pf; (stuff in) впи́хивать impf, впихну́ть pf; vi (study) зубри́ть impf.

cramp[1] n (med) су́дорога.

cramp[2] vt стесня́ть impf, стесни́ть pf. **cramped** adj те́сный.

cranberry n клю́ква.

crane n (bird) жура́вль m; (machine) кран; vt (one's neck) вытя́гивать impf, вы́тянуть pf (ше́ю).

crank[1] n заводна́я ру́чка; ~-**shaft** коле́нчатый вал; vt заводи́ть impf, завести́ pf.

crank[2] n (eccentric) чуда́к. **cranky** adj чуда́ческий.

cranny n щель.

crash n (noise) гро́хот, треск; (accident) ава́рия; (financial) крах; ~ **course** уско́ренный курс; ~ **helmet**

защи́тный шлем; ~ landing ава-
ри́йная поса́дка; vi (~ into) вреза́ть-
ся impf, вреза́ться pf в+acc; (aeron)
разбива́ть impf, разби́ться pf;
(fall with ~) гро́хнуться pf; vt (bang
down) гро́хнуть pf.

crass adj гру́бый.

crate n я́щик.

crater n кра́тер.

crave vi: ~ for жа́ждать impf +gen.
craving n стра́стное жела́ние.

crawl vi по́лзать indet, ползти́ det;
~ with кише́ть+instr; (sport)
кроль m.

crayon n цветно́й каранда́ш.

craze n ма́ния. crazy adj поме́-
шанный (about на+prep).

creak n скрип; vi скрипе́ть impf.

cream n сли́вки (-вок) pl; (cosmetic;
cul) крем; ~ cheese сли́вочный
сыр; soured ~ смета́на; vt сбива́ть
impf, сбить pf; adj (of cream)
сли́вочный; (colour) кре́мовый.
creamy adj сли́вочный, кре́мовый.

crease n скла́дка; vt мять impf, из~,
с~ pf. creased adj мя́тый.

create vt создава́ть impf, созда́ть pf.
creation n созда́ние. creative adj
тво́рческий. creator n созда́тель m.
creature n созда́ние.

crèche n (де́тские) я́сли (-лей) pl.

credence n ве́ра; give ~ ве́рить impf
(to +dat). credentials n pl удосто-
вере́ние; (diplomacy) вери́тельные
гра́моты f pl. credibility n правдо-
подо́бие; (of person) спосо́бность
вызыва́ть дове́рие. credible adj (of
thing) правдоподо́бный; (of person)
заслу́живающий дове́рия.

credit n дове́рие; (comm) креди́т;
(honour) честь; give ~ кредитова́ть
impf & pf +acc; отдава́ть impf,
отда́ть pf до́лжное+dat; ~ card кре-
ди́тная ка́рточка; vt: ~ with припи́-
сывать impf, приписа́ть pf +dat.
creditable adj похва́льный. cred-
itor n кредито́р.

credulity n легкове́рие. credulous
adj легкове́рный.

creed n убежде́ния neut pl; (eccl)
вероиспове́дание.

creep vi по́лзать indet, ползти́ det.
creeper n (plant) по́лзу́чее расте́-
ние.

cremate vt креми́ровать impf & pf.

cremation n крема́ция. crematorium n кремато́рий.

crêpe n креп.

crescendo adv, adj, & n креще́ндо
indecl.

crescent n полуме́сяц.

crest n гре́бень m; (heraldry) герб.

crevasse, crevice n расще́лина, рас-
се́лина.

crew n брига́да; (of ship, plane)
экипа́ж.

crib n (bed) де́тская крова́тка; vi
спи́сывать impf, списа́ть pf.

crick n растяже́ние мышц.

cricket[1] n (insect) сверчо́к.

cricket[2] n (sport) кри́кет; ~ bat бита́.

crime n преступле́ние.

Crimea n Крым. Crimean adj кры́м-
ский.

criminal n престу́пник; adj престу́п-
ный; (of crime) уголо́вный.

crimson adj мали́новый.

cringe vi (cower) съёживаться impf,
съёжиться pf.

crinkle n морщи́на; vt & i мо́р-
щить(ся) impf, на~, с~ pf.

cripple n кале́ка m & f; vt кале́чить
impf, ис~ pf; (fig) расша́тывать
impf, расшата́ть pf.

crisis n кри́зис.

crisp adj (brittle) хрустя́щий; (fresh)
све́жий. crisps pl pl хрустя́щий кар-
то́фель m.

criss-cross adv крест-на́крест.

criterion n крите́рий.

critic n кри́тик. critical adj крити́че-
ский. critically adv (ill) тяжело́.
criticism n кри́тика. criticize vt
критикова́ть impf. critique n кри́-
тика.

croak vi ква́кать impf, ква́кнуть pf;
хрипе́ть impf.

Croat n хорва́т, ~ка. Croatia n
Хорва́тия. Croatian adj хорва́т-
ский.

crochet n вяза́ние крючко́м; vt
вяза́ть impf, с~ pf (крючко́м).

crockery n посу́да.

crocodile n крокоди́л.

crocus n кро́кус.

crony n закады́чный друг.

crook n (staff) по́сох; (swindler)
моше́нник. crooked adj криво́й;
(dishonest) нече́стный.

crop n (yield) урожа́й; pl культу́ры

f pl; (*bird's*) зоб; *vt* (*cut*) подстрига́ть *impf*, подстри́чь *pf*; ~ up возника́ть *impf*, возни́кнуть *pf*.

croquet *n* кроке́т.

cross *n* крест; (*biol*) по́месь; *adj* (*angry*) злой; *vt* пересека́ть *impf*, пересе́чь *pf*; (*biol*) скре́щивать *impf*, скрести́ть *pf*; ~ off, out вычёркивать *impf*, вы́черкнуть *pf*; ~ o.s. крести́ться *impf*, пере~ *pf*; ~ over переходи́ть *impf*, перейти́ *pf* (че́рез) +*acc*. ~bar попере́чина. ~breed по́месь; ~country race кросс; ~examination перекрёстный допро́с; ~examine, ~question подверга́ть *impf*, подве́ргнуть *pf* перекрёстному допро́су; ~eyed косогла́зый; ~legged: sit ~ сиде́ть *impf* по-туре́цки; ~reference перекрёстная ссы́лка; ~road(s) перекрёсток; (*fig*) распу́тье; ~section перекрёстное сече́ние; ~wise *adv* крест-на́крест; ~word (puzzle) кроссво́рд. **crossing** *n* (*intersection*) перекрёсток; (*foot*) перехо́д; (*transport; rly*) перее́зд.

crotch *n* (*anat*) проме́жность.

crotchet *n* (*mus*) четвертна́я но́та.

crotchety *adj* раздражи́тельный.

crouch *vi* приседа́ть *impf*, присе́сть *pf*.

crow *n* воро́на; as the ~ flies по прямо́й ли́нии; *vi* кукаре́кать *impf*. **crowbar** *n* лом.

crowd *n* толпа́; *vi* тесни́ться *impf*, с~ *pf*; ~ into вти́скиваться *impf*, вти́снуться *pf*. **crowded** *adj* перепо́лненный.

crown *n* коро́на; (*tooth*) коро́нка; (*head*) те́мя; (*hat*) тулья́; *vt* коронова́ть *impf & pf*.

crucial *adj* (*important*) о́чень ва́жный; (*decisive*) реша́ющий; (*critical*) крити́ческий.

crucifix, crucifixion *n* распя́тие. **crucify** *vt* распина́ть *impf*, распя́ть *pf*.

crude *adj* (*rude*) грубый; (*raw*) сыро́й. **crudeness, crudity** *n* гру́бость.

cruel *adj* жесто́кий. **cruelty** *n* жесто́кость.

cruise *n* круи́з; *vi* крейси́ровать *impf*. **cruiser** *n* кре́йсер.

crumb *n* кро́шка.

crumble *vt* кроши́ть *impf*, рас~ *pf*; *vi* обва́ливаться *impf*, обвали́ться *pf*. **crumbly** *adj* рассы́пчатый.

crumple *vt* мять *impf*, с~ *pf*; (*intentionally*) ко́мкать *impf*, с~ *pf*.

crunch *n* (*fig*) реша́ющий моме́нт; *vt* грызть *impf*, раз~ *pf*; *vi* хрусте́ть *impf*, хру́стнуть *pf*.

crusade *n* кресто́вый похо́д; (*fig*) кампа́ния. **crusader** *n* крестоно́сец; (*fig*) боре́ц (for за+*acc*).

crush *n* да́вка; (*infatuation*) си́льное увлече́ние; *vt* дави́ть *impf*, за~, раз~ *pf*; (*crease*) мять *impf*, с~ *pf*; (*fig*) подавля́ть *impf*, подави́ть *pf*.

crust *n* (*of earth*) кора́; (*bread etc.*) ко́рка.

crutch *n* косты́ль *m*.

crux *n*: ~ of the matter суть де́ла.

cry *n* крик; a far ~ from далеко́ от+*gen*; *vi* (*weep*) пла́кать *impf*; (*shout*) крича́ть *impf*.

crypt *n* склеп. **cryptic** *adj* загадо́чный.

crystal *n* криста́лл; (*glass*) хруста́ль *m*. **crystallize** *vt & i* кристаллизова́ть(ся) *impf & pf*.

cub *n* детёныш; bear ~ медвежо́нок, fox ~ лисёнок; lion ~ львёнок; wolf ~ волчо́нок.

cube *n* куб. **cubic** *adj* куби́ческий.

cubicle *n* каби́на.

cuckoo *n* куку́шка.

cucumber *n* огуре́ц.

cuddle *vt* обнима́ть *impf*, обня́ть *pf*; *vi* обнима́ться *impf*, обня́ться *pf*; ~ up прижима́ться *impf*, прижа́ться *pf* (to к+*dat*).

cudgel *n* дуби́нка.

cue[1] *n* (*theat*) ре́плика.

cue[2] *n* (*billiards*) кий.

cuff[1] *n* манже́та; off the ~ экспро́мтом; ~link за́понка.

cuff[2] *vt* (*hit*) шлёпать *impf*, шлёпнуть *pf*.

cul-de-sac *n* тупи́к.

culinary *adj* кулина́рный.

cull *vt* (*select*) отбира́ть *impf*, отобра́ть *pf*; (*slaughter*) бить *impf*.

culminate *vi* конча́ться *impf*, ко́нчиться *pf* (in +*instr*). **culmination** *n* кульминацио́нный пункт.

culpability *n* вино́вность. **culpable** *adj* вино́вный. **culprit** *n* вино́вник.

cult *n* культ.

cultivate *vt* (*land*) обраба́тывать *impf*, обрабо́тать *pf*; (*crops*) выра́щивать

impf; вы́растить *impf*; (*develop*) развива́ть *impf*, разви́ть *pf*.
cultural *adj* культу́рный. **culture** *n* культу́ра. **cultured** *adj* культу́рный.
cumbersome *adj* громо́здкий.
cumulative *adj* кумуляти́вный.
cunning *n* хи́трость; *adj* хи́трый.
cup *n* ча́шка; (*prize*) ку́бок.
cupboard *n* шкаф.
cupola *n* ку́пол.
curable *adj* излечи́мый.
curative *adj* целе́бный.
curator *n* храни́тель *m*.
curb *vt* обу́здывать *impf*, обузда́ть *pf*.
curd (*cheese*) *n* творо́г. **curdle** *vt & i* свёртывать(ся) *impf*, сверну́ть(ся) *pf*.
cure *n* сре́дство (for про́тив+*gen*); *vt* выле́чивать *impf*, вы́лечить *pf*; (*smoke*) копти́ть *impf*, за~ *pf*; (*salt*) соли́ть *impf*, по~ *pf*.
curfew *n* коменда́нтский час.
curiosity *n* любопы́тство. **curious** *adj* любопы́тный.
curl *n* ло́кон; *vt* завива́ть *impf*, зави́ть *pf*; ~ up свёртываться *impf*, сверну́ться *pf*. **curly** *adj* кудря́вый.
currants *n pl* (*dried*) изю́м (*collect*).
currency *n* валю́та; (*prevalence*) хожде́ние. **current** *adj* теку́щий; *n* тече́ние; (*air*) струя́; (*water*; *electr*) ток.
curriculum *n* курс обуче́ния; ~ vitae автобиогра́фия.
curry[1] *n* кэ́рри *neut indecl*.
curry[2] *vt*: ~ favour with заи́скивать *impf* пе́ред+*instr*, y+*gen*.
curse *n* прокля́тие; (*oath*) руга́тельство; *vt* проклина́ть *impf*, прокля́сть *pf*; *vi* руга́ться *impf*, по~ *pf*.
cursory *adj* бе́глый.
curt *adj* ре́зкий.
curtail *vt* сокраща́ть *impf*, сократи́ть *pf*.
curtain *n* занаве́ска.
curts(e)y *n* револа́нс; *vi* де́лать *impf*, с~ *pf* револа́нс.
curve *n* изги́б; (*line*) крива́я *sb*; *vi* изгиба́ться *impf*, изогну́ться *pf*.
cushion *n* поду́шка; *vt* смягча́ть *impf*, смягчи́ть *pf*.
custard *n* сла́дкий зава́рной крем.
custodian *n* храни́тель *m*. **custody** *n* опе́ка; (*of police*) аре́ст; to take

into ~ арестова́ть *pf*.
custom *n* обы́чай; (*comm*) клиенту́ра; *pl* (*duty*) тамо́женные по́шлины *f pl*; go through ~s проходи́ть *impf*, пройти́ *pf* тамо́женный осмо́тр; ~-house тамо́жня; ~ officer тамо́женник. **customary** *adj* обы́чный. **customer** *n* клие́нт; покупа́тель *m*.
cut *vt* ре́зать *impf*, по~ *pf*; (*hair*) стричь *impf*, о~ *pf*; (*mow*) коси́ть *impf*, с~ *pf*; (*price*) снижа́ть *impf*, сни́зить *pf*; (*cards*) снима́ть *impf*, снять *pf* коло́ду; ~ back (*prune*) подреза́ть *impf*, подре́зать *pf*; (*reduce*) сокраща́ть *impf*, сократи́ть *pf*; ~ down сруба́ть *impf*, сруби́ть *pf*; ~ off отреза́ть *impf*, отре́зать *pf*; (*interrupt*) прерыва́ть *impf*, пре-рва́ть *pf*; (*disconnect*) отключа́ть *impf*, отключи́ть *pf*; ~ out выре́-зывать *impf*, вы́резать *pf*; ~ out for со́зданный для+*gen*; ~ up разреза́ть *impf*, разре́зать *pf*; *n* (*gash*) поре́з; (*clothes*) покро́й; (*reduction*) сниже́ние; ~ glass хруста́ль *m*.
cute *adj* симпати́чный.
cutlery *n* ножи́, ви́лки и ло́жки *pl*.
cutlet *n* отбивна́я котле́та.
cutting *n* (*press*) вы́резка; (*plant*) черено́к; *adj* ре́зкий.
CV *abbr* (*of curriculum vitae*) автобиогра́фия.
cycle *n* цикл; (*bicycle*) велосипе́д; *vi* е́здить *impf* на велосипе́де. **cyclic(al)** *adj* цикли́ческий. **cyclist** *n* велосипеди́ст.
cylinder *n* цили́ндр. **cylindrical** *adj* цилиндри́ческий.
cymbals *n pl* таре́лки *f pl*.
cynic *n* ци́ник. **cynical** *adj* цини́чный. **cynicism** *n* цини́зм.
cypress *n* кипари́с.
Cyrillic *n* кири́ллица.
cyst *n* киста́.
Czech *n* чех, че́шка; *adj* че́шский; ~ Republic Че́шская Респу́блика.

D

dab *n* мазо́к; *vt* (*eyes etc.*) прикла́дывать *impf* плато́к к+*dat*; ~ on накла́дывать *impf*, наложи́ть *pf* мазка́ми.

dabble *vi*: ~ in поверхностно заниматься *impf*, заняться *pf* +*instr*.

dachshund *n* такса.

dad, daddy *n* папа; ~long-legs *n* долгоножка.

daffodil *n* жёлтый нарцисс.

daft *adj* глупый.

dagger *n* кинжал.

dahlia *n* георгин.

daily *adv* ежедневно; *adj* ежедневный; *n* (*charwoman*) приходящая уборщица; (*newspaper*) ежедневная газета.

dainty *adj* изящный.

dairy *n* маслобойня; (*shop*) молочная *sb*; *adj* молочный.

dais *n* помост.

daisy *n* маргаритка.

dale *n* долина.

dally *vi* (*dawdle*) мешкать *impf*; (*toy*) играть *impf* +*instr*; (*flirt*) флиртовать *impf*.

dam *n* (*barrier*) плотина; *vt* запруживать *impf*, запрудить *pf*.

damage *n* повреждение; *pl* убытки *m pl*; *vt* повреждать *impf*, повредить *pf*.

damn *vt* (*curse*) проклинать *impf*, проклясть *pf*; (*censure*) осуждать *impf*, осудить *pf*; *int* чёрт возьми!; **I don't give a** ~ мне наплевать. **damnation** *n* проклятие. **damned** *adj* проклятый.

damp *n* сырость; *adj* сырой; *vt* (*also* **dampen**) смачивать *impf*, смочить *pf*; (*fig*) охлаждать *impf*, охладить *pf*.

dance *vi* танцевать *impf*; *n* танец; (*party*) танцевальный вечер. **dancer** *n* танцор, ~ка; (*ballet*) танцовщик, -ица; балерина.

dandelion *n* одуванчик.

dandruff *n* перхоть.

Dane *n* датчанин, -анка; **Great** ~ дог. **Danish** *adj* датский.

danger *n* опасность. **dangerous** *adj* опасный.

dangle *vt &i* покачивать(ся) *impf*.

dank *adj* промозглый.

dapper *adj* выхоленный.

dare *vi* (*have courage*) осмеливаться *impf*, осмелиться *pf*; (*have impudence*) сметь *impf*, по~ *pf*; *vt* вызывать *impf*, вызвать *pf* *n* вызов. **daredevil** *n* лихач; *adj* отчаянный.

daring *n* отвага; *adj* отчаянный.

dark *adj* тёмный; ~ **blue** тёмносиний; *n* темнота. **darken** *vt* затемнять *impf*, затемнить *pf*; *vi* темнеть *impf*, по~ *pf*. **darkly** *adv* мрачно. **darkness** *n* темнота.

darling *n* дорогой *sb*, милый *sb*; *adj* дорогой.

darn *vt* штопать *impf*, за~ *pf*.

dart *n* стрела; (*for game*) метательная стрела; (*tuck*) вытачка; *vi* броситься *pf*.

dash *n* (*hyphen*) тире *neut indecl*; (*admixture*) примесь; *vt* швырять *impf*, швырнуть *pf*; *vi* бросаться *impf*, броситься *pf*. **dashboard** *n* приборная доска. **dashing** *adj* лихой.

data *n pl* данные *sb pl*. **database** *n* база данных.

date[1] *n* (*fruit*) финик.

date[2] *n* число, дата; (*engagement*) свидание; **out of** ~ устарелый; **up to** ~ современный; **in** ~ **course** дела; *vt* датировать *impf &pf*; (*go out with*) встречаться *impf* c+*instr*; *vi* (*originate*) относиться *impf* (*from* к+*instr*).

dative *adj* (*n*) дательный (падеж).

daub *vt* мазать *impf*, на~ *pf* (*with* +*instr*).

daughter *n* дочь; ~-**in-law** невестка (*in relation to mother*), сноха (*in relation to father*).

daunting *adj* угрожающий.

dawdle *vi* мешкать *impf*.

dawn *n* рассвет; (*also fig*) заря; *vi* (*day*) рассветать *impf*, рассвести *pf* *impers*; ~ (**up**)**on** осенять *impf*, осенить *pf*; **it** ~**ed on me** меня осенило.

day *n* день *m*; (*24 hours*) сутки *pl*; (*period*) период, время *neut*; ~ **after** ~ изо дня в день; **the** ~ **after tomorrow** послезавтра; **the** ~ **before** накануне; **the** ~ **before yesterday** позавчера; **the other** ~ на днях; **by** ~ днём; **every other** ~ через день; ~ **off** выходной день *m*; **one** ~ однажды; **these** ~**s** в наши дни. **daybreak** *n* рассвет. **day-dreams** *n pl* мечты *f pl*. **daylight** *n* дневной свет; **in broad** ~ средь бела дня. **daytime** *n*: **in the** ~ днём.

daze *n*: **in a** ~, **dazed** *adj* оглушён (-ена).

dazzle vt ослепля́ть impf, ослепи́ть pf.
deacon n дья́кон.

dead adj (of body) мёртвый; (animals) до́хлый; (plants) увя́дший; (numb) онеме́вший; n: the ~ мёртвые sb pl; at ~ of night глубо́кой но́чью; adv (completely) соверше́нно; ~ end тупи́к; ~ heat одновре́менный фи́ниш; ~line преде́льный срок; ~lock тупи́к.
deaden vt заглуша́ть impf, заглуши́ть pf.
deadly adj смерте́льный.
deaf adj глухо́й; ~ and dumb глухонемо́й. **deafen** vt оглуша́ть impf, оглуши́ть pf. **deafness** n глухота́.
deal[1] n: a great, good, ~ мно́го (+gen); (with comp) гора́здо.
deal[2] n (bargain) сде́лка; (cards) сда́ча; vt (cards) сдава́ть impf, сдать pf; (blow) наноси́ть impf, нанести́ pf; ~ in торгова́ть impf +instr; ~ out распределя́ть impf, распредели́ть pf; ~ with (take care of) занима́ться impf, заня́ться pf +instr; (handle a person) поступа́ть impf, поступи́ть pf c+instr; (treat a subject) рассма́тривать impf, рассмотре́ть pf; (cope with) справля́ться impf, спра́виться pf c+instr. **dealer** n торго́вец (in +instr).
dean n дека́н.
dear adj дорого́й; (also n) ми́лый (sb).
dearth n недоста́ток.
death n смерть; put to ~ казни́ть impf & pf; ~bed n сме́ртное ло́же; ~ certificate свиде́тельство о сме́рти; ~ penalty сме́ртная казнь. **deathly** adj смерте́льный.
debar vt: ~ from не допуска́ть impf до+gen.
debase vt унижа́ть impf, уни́зить pf; (coinage) понижа́ть impf, пони́зить pf ка́чество +gen.
debatable adj спо́рный. **debate** n пре́ния (-ий) pl; vt обсужда́ть impf, обсуди́ть pf.
debauched adj развращённый. **debauchery** n разврат.
debilitate vt ослабля́ть impf, осла́бить pf. **debility** n сла́бость.
debit n де́бет; vt дебетова́ть impf & pf.
debris n обло́мки m pl.
debt n долг. **debtor** n должни́к.

début n дебю́т; make one's ~ дебюти́ровать impf & pf.
decade n десятиле́тие.
decadence n декаде́нтство. **decadent** adj декаде́нтский.
decaffeinated adj без кофеи́на.
decant vt перелива́ть impf, перели́ть pf. **decanter** n графи́н.
decapitate vt обезгла́вливать impf, обезгла́вить pf.
decay vi гнить impf, c~ pf; (tooth) разруша́ться impf, разру́шиться pf; n гние́ние; (tooth) разруше́ние.
decease n кончи́на. **deceased** adj поко́йный; n поко́йник, -ица.
deceit n обма́н. **deceitful** adj лжи́вый. **deceive** vt обма́нывать impf, обману́ть pf.
deceleration n замедле́ние.
December n дека́брь m; adj дека́брьский.
decency n прили́чие. **decent** adj прили́чный.
decentralization n децентрализа́ция. **decentralize** vt децентрализова́ть impf & pf.
deception n обма́н. **deceptive** adj обма́нчивый.
decibel n дециба́л.
decide vt реша́ть impf, реши́ть pf. **decided** adj реши́тельный.
deciduous adj листопа́дный.
decimal n десяти́чная дробь; adj десяти́чный; ~ point запята́я sb.
decimate vt (fig) коси́ть impf, c~ pf.
decipher vt расшифро́вывать impf, расшифрова́ть pf.
decision n реше́ние. **decisive** adj (firm) реши́тельный, (deciding) реша́ющий.
deck n па́луба; (bus etc.) эта́ж; ~chair n шезло́нг; vt: ~ out украша́ть impf, укра́сить pf.
declaim vt деклами́ровать impf, про~ pf.
declaration n объявле́ние; (document) деклара́ция. **declare** vt (proclaim) объявля́ть impf, объяви́ть pf; (assert) заявля́ть impf, заяви́ть pf.
declension n склоне́ние. **decline** n упа́док; vi приходи́ть impf, прийти́ pf в упа́док; vt отклоня́ть impf, отклони́ть pf; (gram) склоня́ть impf, про~ pf.

decode vt расшифро́вывать impf, расшифрова́ть pf.

decompose vi разлага́ться impf, разложи́ться pf.

décor n эстети́ческое оформле́ние.

decorate vt украша́ть impf, укра́сить pf; (room) ремонти́ровать impf, от~ pf; (with medal etc.) награжда́ть impf, награди́ть pf. **decoration** n украше́ние; (medal) о́рден. **decorative** adj декорати́вный. **decorator** n маля́р.

decorous adj прили́чный. **decorum** n прили́чие.

decoy n (bait) прима́нка; vt зама́нивать impf, замани́ть pf.

decrease vt & i уменьша́ть(ся) impf, уме́ньшить(ся) pf; n уменьше́ние.

decree n ука́з; vt постановля́ть impf, постанови́ть pf.

decrepit adj дря́хлый.

dedicate vt посвяща́ть impf, посвяти́ть pf. **dedication** n посвяще́ние.

deduce vt заключа́ть impf, заключи́ть pf.

deduct vt вычита́ть impf, вы́честь pf. **deduction** n (subtraction) вы́чет; (inference) вы́вод.

deed n посту́пок; (heroic) по́двиг; (law) акт.

deem vt счита́ть impf, счесть pf +acc & instr.

deep adj глубо́кий; (colour) тёмный; (sound) ни́зкий; ~ freeze морози́льник. **deepen** vt & i углубля́ть(ся) impf, углуби́ть(ся) pf.

deer n оле́нь m.

deface vt обезобра́живать impf, обезобра́зить pf.

defamation n диффама́ция. **defamatory** adj клеветни́ческий.

default n (failure to pay) неупла́та; (failure to appear) нея́вка; (comput) автомати́ческий вы́бор; vi не выполня́ть impf обяза́тельств.

defeat n пораже́ние; vt побежда́ть impf, победи́ть pf. **defeatism** n пораже́нчество. **defeatist** n пораже́нец; adj пораже́нческий.

defecate vi испражня́ться impf, испражни́ться pf.

defect n дефе́кт; vi перебега́ть impf, перебежа́ть pf. **defective** adj неиспра́вный. **defector** n перебе́жчик.

defence n защи́та. **defenceless** adj беззащи́тный. **defend** vt защища́ть impf, защити́ть pf. **defendant** n подсуди́мый sb. **defender** n защи́тник. **defensive** adj оборони́тельный.

defer[1] vt (postpone) отсро́чивать impf, отсро́чить pf.

defer[2] vi: ~ to подчиня́ться impf +dat. **deference** n уваже́ние. **deferential** adj почти́тельный.

defiance n неповинове́ние; in ~ of вопреки́+dat. **defiant** adj вызыва́ющий.

deficiency n недоста́ток. **deficient** adj недоста́точный. **deficit** n дефици́т.

defile vt оскверня́ть impf, оскверни́ть pf.

define vt определя́ть impf, определи́ть pf. **definite** adj определённый. **definitely** adv несомне́нно. **definition** n определе́ние. **definitive** adj оконча́тельный.

deflate vt & i спуска́ть impf, спусти́ть pf; vt (person) сбива́ть impf, сбить pf спесь с+gen. **deflation** n дефля́ция.

deflect vt отклоня́ть impf, отклони́ть pf.

deforestation n обезле́сение.

deformed adj уро́дливый. **deformity** n уро́дство.

defraud vt обма́нывать impf, обману́ть pf; ~ of выма́нивать impf, вы́манить pf +acc & y+gen (of person).

defray vt опла́чивать impf, оплати́ть pf.

defrost vt размора́живать impf, разморо́зить pf.

deft adj ло́вкий.

defunct adj бо́льше не существу́ющий.

defy vt (challenge) вызыва́ть impf, вы́звать pf; (disobey) не подчиня́ться impf, не подчини́ться pf +dat.

defy vt (challenge) вызыва́ть impf, вы́звать pf; (disobey) не подчиня́ться impf, по~ pf про́тив+acc; (fig) не подда́ваться impf +dat.

degenerate vi вырожда́ться impf, вы́родиться pf; adj вы́родившийся.

degradation n униже́ние. **degrade** vt унижа́ть impf, уни́зить pf. **degrading** adj унизи́тельный.

degree n сте́пень; (math etc.) гра́дус; (univ) учёная сте́пень.

dehydrate vt обезво́живать impf,

обезво́дить *pf.* dehydration *n* обез-
во́живание.

deign *vi* снисходи́ть *impf*, снизойти́
pf.

deity *n* божество́.

dejected *adj* удручённый.

delay *n* заде́ржка; without ~ неме́д-
ленно; *vt* заде́рживать *impf*, задер-
жа́ть *pf.*

delegate *n* делега́т; *vt* делеги́ровать
impf & pf. delegation *n* делега́ция.

delete *vt* вычёркивать *impf*, вы́-
черкнуть *pf.*

deliberate *adj* (*intentional*) предна-
ме́ренный; (*careful*) осторо́жный;
vt & i размышля́ть *impf*, раз-
мы́слить *pf* (о+*prep*); (*discuss*) сове-
ща́ться *impf* (о+*prep*). deliberation
n размышле́ние; (*discussion*) сове-
ща́ние.

delicacy *n* (*tact*) делика́тность;
(*dainty*) ла́комство. delicate *adj*
то́нкий; (*tactful, needing tact*) делика́т-
ка́тный; (*health*) боле́зненный.

delicatessen *n* гастроно́м.

delicious *adj* о́чень вку́сный.

delight *n* наслажде́ние; (*delightful
thing*) пре́лесть. delightful *adj* пре-
ле́стный.

delinquency *n* престу́пность. delinquent *n* правонаруши́тель *m*,
~ница; *adj* вино́вный.

delirious *adj*: be ~ бре́дить *impf*. delirium *n* бред.

deliver *vt* (*goods*) доставля́ть *impf*,
доста́вить *pf*; (*save*) избавля́ть *impf*,
изба́вить *pf* (from от+*gen*); (*lecture*)
прочита́ть *impf*, проче́сть *pf*; (*letters*) разноси́ть *impf*, разнести́ *pf*;
(*speech*) произноси́ть *impf*, произ-
нести́ *pf*; (*blow*) наноси́ть *impf*,
нанести́ *pf*. deliverance *n* изба-
вле́ние. delivery *n* доста́вка.

delta *n* де́льта.

delude *vt* вводи́ть *impf*, ввести́ *pf* в
заблужде́ние.

deluge *n* (*flood*) пото́п; (*rain*) ли́-
вень *m*; (*fig*) пото́к.

delusion *n* заблужде́ние; ~s of grandeur ма́ния вели́чия.

de luxe *adj* -люкс (*added to noun*).

delve *vi* углубля́ться *impf*, углу-
би́ться *pf* (into в+*acc*).

demand *n* тре́бование; (*econ*) спрос
(for на+*acc*); *vt* тре́бовать *impf*, по~

pf +*gen*. demanding *adj* тре́бова-
тельный.

demarcation *n* демарка́ция.

demean *vt*: ~ o.s. унижа́ться *impf*,
уни́зиться *pf.*

demeanour *n* мане́ра вести́ себя́.

demented *adj* сумасше́дший. de-
mentia *n* слабоу́мие.

demise *n* кончи́на.

demobilize *vt* демобилизова́ть *impf
& pf.*

democracy *n* демокра́тия. democrat
n демокра́т. democratic *adj* демо-
крати́ческий. democratization *n*
демократиза́ция.

demolish *vt* (*destroy*) разруша́ть
impf, разру́шить *pf*; (*building*) сно-
си́ть *impf*, снести́ *pf*; (*refute*)
опроверга́ть *impf*, опрове́ргнуть *pf.*
demolition *n* разруше́ние; снос.

demon *n* де́мон.

demonstrable *adj* доказу́емый. de-
monstrably *adv* нагля́дно. demonstrate *vt* демонстри́ровать *impf &
pf*; *vi* уча́ствовать *impf* в демон-
стра́ции. demonstration *n* демон-
стра́ция. demonstrative *adj* экспан-
си́вный; (*gram*) указа́тельный. dem-
onstrator *n* демонстра́тор; (*polit*)
демонстра́нт.

demoralize *vt* деморализова́ть *impf
& pf.*

demote *vt* понижа́ть *impf*, пони́зить
pf в до́лжности.

demure *adj* скро́мный.

den *n* берло́га.

denial *n* отрица́ние; (*refusal*) отка́з.

denigrate *vt* черни́ть *impf*, о~ *pf.*

denim *adj* джинсо́вый; *n* джинсо́вая
ткань.

Denmark *n* Да́ния.

denomination *n* (*money*) досто́ин-
ство; (*relig*) вероисповеда́ние. denominator *n* знамена́тель *m*.

denote *vt* означа́ть *impf*, озна́чить
pf.

denounce *vt* (*condemn*) осужда́ть
impf, осуди́ть *pf*; (*inform on*) до-
носи́ть *impf*, донести́ *pf* на+*acc*.

dense *adj* густо́й; (*stupid*) тупо́й.

density *n* пло́тность.

dent *n* вмя́тина; *vt* де́лать *impf*, с~
pf вмя́тину в+*prep*.

dental *adj* зубно́й. dentist *n* зубно́й
врач. dentures *n pl* зубно́й проте́з.

denunciation n (*condemnation*) осуждéние; (*informing*) донóс.

deny vt отрицáть *impf*; (*refuse*) откáзывать *impf*, отказáть *pf* +dat (*person*) в+prep.

deodorant n дезодорáнт.

depart vi отбывáть *impf*, отбы́ть *pf*; (*deviate*) отклоня́ться *impf*, отклони́ться *pf* (from от+gen).

department n отдéл; (*univ*) кáфедра; ~ store универмáг.

departure n отбы́тие; (*deviation*) отклонéние.

depend vi зави́сеть *impf* (on от+gen); (*rely*) полагáться *impf*, положи́ться *pf* (on на+acc). **dependable** adj надёжный. **dependant** n иждивéнец. **dependence** n зави́симость. **dependent** adj зави́симый.

depict vt изображáть *impf*, изобрази́ть *pf*.

deplete vt истощáть *impf*, истощи́ть *pf*. **depleted** adj истощённый. **depletion** n истощéние.

deplorable adj плачéвный. **deplore** vt сожалéть *impf* o+prep.

deploy vt развёртывать *impf*, разверну́ть *pf*. **deployment** n развёртывание.

deport vt депорти́ровать *impf & pf*; высылáть *impf*, вы́слать *pf*. **deportation** n депортáция; вы́сылка.

deportment n осáнка.

depose vt свергáть *impf*, свéргнуть *pf*. **deposit** n (*econ*) вклад; (*advance*) задáток; (*sediment*) осáдок; (*coal etc.*) месторождéние; vt (*econ*) вноси́ть *impf*, внести́ *pf*.

depot n (*transport*) депó *neut indecl*; (*store*) склад.

deprave vt развращáть *impf*, разврати́ть *pf*. **depraved** adj развращённый. **depravity** n разврáт.

deprecate vt осуждáть *impf*, осуди́ть *pf*.

depreciate vt & i (*econ*) обесцéнивать(ся) *impf*, обесцéнить(ся) *pf*. **depreciation** n обесцéнивание.

depress vt (*dispirit*) удручáть *impf*, удручи́ть *pf*. **depressed** adj удручённый. **depressing** adj угнетáющий. **depression** n (*hollow*) впáдина; (*econ, med, meteorol, etc.*) депрéссия.

deprivation n лишéние. **deprive** vt

лишáть *impf*, лиши́ть *pf* (of +gen).

depth n глубинá; in the ~ of winter в разгáре зимы́.

deputation n депутáция. **deputize** vi замещáть *impf*, замести́ть *pf* (for +acc). **deputy** n замести́тель m; (*parl*) депутáт.

derail vt: be derailed сходи́ть *impf*, сойти́ *pf* с рéльсов. **derailment** n сход с рéльсов.

deranged adj сумасшéдший.

derelict adj забрóшенный.

deride vt высмéивать *impf*, вы́смеять *pf*. **derision** n высмéивание. **derisive** adj (*mocking*) насмéшливый. **derisory** adj (*ridiculous*) смехотвóрный.

derivation n происхождéние. **derivative** n произвóдное sb; adj произвóдный. **derive** vt извлекáть *impf*, извлéчь *pf*; vi: ~ from происходи́ть *impf*, произойти́ *pf* от+gen.

derogatory adj отрицáтельный.

descend vi (& t) (*go down*) спускáться *impf*, спусти́ться *pf* (c+gen); be descended from происходи́ть *impf*, произойти́ *pf* из, от, +gen. **descendant** n потóмок. **descent** n спуск; (*lineage*) происхождéние.

describe vt опи́сывать *impf*, описáть *pf*. **description** n описáние. **descriptive** adj описáтельный.

desecrate vt осквернять *impf*, оскверни́ть *pf*. **desecration** n осквернéние.

desert[1] n (*waste*) пусты́ня.

desert[2] vt покидáть *impf*, поки́нуть *pf*; (*mil*) дезерти́ровать *impf & pf*. **deserter** n дезерти́р. **desertion** n дезерти́рство.

deserts n pl заслýги f pl. **deserve** vt заслýживать *impf*, заслужи́ть *pf*. **deserving** adj достóйный (of +gen).

design n (*pattern*) узóр; (*of car etc.*) констрýкция, проéкт; (*industrial*) дизáйн; (*aim*) ýмысел; vt проекти́ровать *impf*, c~ *pf*; (*intend*) предназначáть *impf*, предназнáчить *pf*.

designate vt (*indicate*) обозначáть *impf*, обознáчить *pf*; (*appoint*) назначáть *impf*, назнáчить *pf*.

designer n (*tech*) констрýктор; (*industrial*) дизáйнер; (*of clothes*) модельéр.

desirable adj желáтельный. **desire**

n жела́ние; *vt* жела́ть *impf*, по~ *pf* +*gen*.

desist *vi* (*refrain*) возде́рживаться *impf*, воздержа́ться *pf* (from от+*gen*).

desk *n* пи́сьменный стол; (*school*) па́рта.

desolate *adj* забро́шенный. **desolation** *n* забро́шенность.

despair *n* отча́яние; *vi* отча́иваться *impf*, отча́яться *pf*. **desperate** *adj* отча́янный. **desperation** *n* отча́яние.

despicable *adj* презре́нный. **despise** *vt* презира́ть *impf*, презре́ть *pf*.

despite *prep* несмотря́ на+*acc*.

despondency *n* уны́ние. **despondent** *adj* уны́лый.

despot *n* де́спот.

dessert *n* десе́рт.

destination *n* (*of goods*) ме́сто назначе́ния; (*of journey*) цель. **destiny** *n* судьба́.

destitute *adj* без вся́ких средств.

destroy *vt* разруша́ть *impf*, разру́шить *pf*. **destroyer** *n* (*naut*) эсми́нец. **destruction** *n* разруше́ние. **destructive** *adj* разруши́тельный.

detach *vt* отделя́ть *impf*, отдели́ть *pf*. **detached** *adj* отде́льный; (*objective*) беспристра́стный; ~ **house** особня́к. **detachment** *n* (*objectivity*) беспристра́стие; (*mil*) отря́д.

detail *n* дета́ль, подро́бность; **in detail** подро́бно; *vt* подро́бно расска́зывать *impf*, рассказа́ть *pf*. **detailed** *adj* подро́бный.

detain *vt* заде́рживать *impf*, задержа́ть *pf*. **detainee** *n* заде́ржанный *sb*.

detect *vt* обнару́живать *impf*, обнару́жить *pf*. **detection** *n* обнаруже́ние; (*crime*) рассле́дование. **detective** *n* детекти́в; ~ **film, story, etc.** детекти́в. **detector** *n* дете́ктор.

detention *n* задержа́ние; (*school*) заде́ржка в наказа́ние.

deter *vt* уде́рживать *impf*, удержа́ть *pf* (from от+*gen*).

detergent *n* мо́ющее сре́дство.

deteriorate *vi* ухудша́ться *impf*, уху́дшиться *pf*. **deterioration** *n* ухудше́ние.

determination *n* реши́мость. **determine** *vt* (*ascertain*) устана́вливать *impf*, установи́ть *pf*; (*be decisive factor*) определя́ть *impf*, определи́ть *pf*; (*decide*) реша́ть *impf*, реши́ть *pf*. **determined** *adj* реши́тельный.

deterrent *n* сре́дство устраше́ния.

detest *vt* ненави́деть *impf*. **detestable** *adj* отврати́тельный.

detonate *vt & i* взрыва́ть(ся) *impf*, взорва́ть(ся) *pf*. **detonator** *n* детона́тор.

detour *n* объе́зд.

detract *vi*: ~ **from** умаля́ть *impf*, умали́ть *pf* +*acc*.

detriment *n* уще́рб. **detrimental** *adj* вре́дный.

deuce *n* (*tennis*) ра́вный счёт.

devaluation *n* девальва́ция. **devalue** *vt* девальви́ровать *impf & pf*.

devastate *vt* опустоша́ть *impf*, опусто́шить *pf*. **devastated** *adj* потрясённый. **devastating** *adj* уничтожа́ющий. **devastation** *n* опустоше́ние.

develop *vt & i* развива́ть(ся) *impf*, разви́ть(ся) *pf*; *vt* (*phot*) проявля́ть *impf*, прояви́ть *pf*. **developer** *n* (*of land etc.*) застро́йщик. **development** *n* разви́тие.

deviant *adj* ненорма́льный. **deviate** *vi* отклоня́ться *impf*, отклони́ться *pf* (from от+*gen*). **deviation** *n* отклоне́ние.

device *n* прибо́р.

devil *n* чёрт. **devilish** *adj* чёртовский.

devious *adj* (*circuitous*) окружно́й; (*person*) непоря́дочный.

devise *vt* приду́мывать *impf*, приду́мать *pf*.

devoid *adj* лишённый (of +*gen*).

devolution *n* переда́ча (вла́сти).

devote *vt* посвяща́ть *impf*, посвяти́ть *pf*. **devoted** *adj* пре́данный. **devotee** *n* покло́нник. **devotion** *n* пре́данность.

devour *vt* пожира́ть *impf*, пожра́ть *pf*.

devout *adj* на́божный.

dew *n* роса́.

dexterity *n* ло́вкость. **dext(e)rous** *adj* ло́вкий.

diabetes *n* диабе́т. **diabetic** *n* диабе́тик; *adj* диабети́ческий.

diabolic(al) *adj* дья́вольский.

diagnose *vt* диагности́ровать *impf & pf*. **diagnosis** *n* диа́гноз.

diagonal n диагона́ль; adj диаго-
на́льный. **diagonally** adv по диа-
гона́ли.

diagram n диагра́мма.

dial n (clock) цифербла́т; (tech) шка-
ла́; vt набира́ть impf, набра́ть pf.

dialect n диале́кт.

dialogue n диало́г.

diameter n диа́метр. **diametric(al)**
adj диаметра́льный; ~ly opposed
диаметра́льно противополо́жный.

diamond n алма́з; (shape) ромб; pl
(cards) бу́бны (-бён, -бна́м) pl.

diaper n пелёнка.

diaphragm n диафра́гма.

diarrhoea n поно́с.

diary n дневни́к.

dice see **die**[1]

dicey adj риско́ванный.

dictate vt диктова́ть impf, про~ pf.
dictation n дикто́вка. **dictator** n
дикта́тор. **dictatorial** adj дикта́тор-
ский. **dictatorship** n диктату́ра.

diction n ди́кция.

dictionary n слова́рь m.

didactic adj дидакти́ческий.

die[1] n (pl **dice**) игра́льная кость; (pl
dies) (stamp) штамп.

die[2] vi (person) умира́ть impf, уме-
ре́ть pf; (animal) до́хнуть impf, из~,
по~ pf; (plant) вя́нуть impf, за~ pf;
be dying to о́чень хоте́ть impf; ~
down (fire, sound) угаса́ть impf,
уга́снуть pf; ~ out вымира́ть impf,
вы́мереть pf.

diesel n (engine) ди́зель m; attrib
ди́зельный.

diet n дие́та; (habitual food) пи́ща;
vi быть на дие́те. **dietary** adj диети́-
ческий.

differ vi отлича́ться impf; разли-
ча́ться impf; (disagree) расходи́ться
impf, разойти́сь pf. **difference** n
ра́зница; (disagreement) разногла́-
сие. **different** adj разли́чный; ра́з-
ный. **differential** n (math, tech)
дифференциа́л; (difference) ра́зни-
ца. **differentiate** vt различа́ть impf,
различи́ть pf.

difficult adj тру́дный. **difficulty** n
тру́дность; (difficult situation) за-
трудне́ние; without ~ без труда́.

diffidence n неуве́ренность в себе́.
diffident adj неуве́ренный в себе́.

diffused adj рассе́янный.

dig n (archaeol) раско́пки f pl; (poke)
тычо́к; (gibe) шпи́лька; pl (lodg-
ings) кварти́ра; give a ~ in the ribs
ткнуть pf ло́ктем под ребро́; vt ко-
па́ть impf, вы́~ pf; рыть impf, вы́~
pf; ~ up (bone) выка́пывать impf,
вы́копать pf; (land) вска́пывать
impf, вскопа́ть pf.

digest vt перева́ривать impf, перева-
ри́ть pf. **digestible** adj удобова-
ри́мый. **digestion** n пищеваре́ние.

digger n (tech) экскава́тор.

digit n (math) знак.

dignified adj велича́вый. **dignitary**
n сано́вник. **dignity** n досто́инство.

digress vi отклоня́ться impf, откло-
ни́ться pf. **digression** n отклоне́-
ние.

dike n да́мба; (ditch) ров.

dilapidated adj ве́тхий.

dilate vt & i расширя́ть(ся) impf,
расши́рить(ся) pf.

dilemma n диле́мма.

dilettante n дилета́нт.

diligence n прилежа́ние. **diligent** adj
приле́жный.

dilute vt разбавля́ть impf, разба́вить
pf.

dim adj (not bright) ту́склый; (vague)
сму́тный; (stupid) тупо́й.

dimension n (pl) разме́ры m pl;
(math) измере́ние. **-dimensional** in
comb -ме́рный; three-~ трёхме́р-
ный.

diminish vt & i уменьша́ть(ся) impf,
уме́ньшить(ся) pf. **diminutive** adj
ма́ленький; n уменьши́тельное sb.

dimness n ту́склость.

dimple n я́мочка.

din n гро́хот; (voices) гам.

dine vi обе́дать impf, по~ pf. **diner**
n обе́дающий sb.

dinghy n шлю́пка; (rubber ~) на-
дувна́я ло́дка.

dingy adj (drab) ту́склый; (dirty)
гря́зный.

dining-car n ваго́н-рестора́н. **dining-
room** n столо́вая sb. **dinner** n обе́д;
~-jacket смо́кинг.

dinosaur n диноза́вр.

diocese n епа́рхия.

dip vt (immerse) окуна́ть impf, оку-
ну́ть pf; (partially) обма́кивать impf,
обмакну́ть pf; vi (slope) понижа́ть-
ся impf, пони́зиться pf; n (depres-

sion) впа́дина; (slope) укло́н; have a ~ (bathe) купа́ться impf, вы́~ pf.

diphtheria n дифтери́я.

diphthong n дифто́нг.

diploma n дипло́м. **diplomacy** n дипло́ма́тия. **diplomat** n диплома́т. **diplomatic** adj дипломати́ческий.

dire adj стра́шный; (ominous) злове́щий.

direct adj прямо́й; ~ **current** постоя́нный ток; vt направля́ть impf, напра́вить pf; (guide, manage) руководи́ть impf +instr; (film) режисси́ровать impf. **direction** n направле́ние; (guidance) руково́дство; (instruction) указа́ние; (film) режиссу́ра; **stage** ~ рема́рка. **directive** n директи́ва. **directly** adv пря́мо; (at once) сра́зу. **director** n дире́ктор; (film etc.) режиссёр(-постано́вщик). **directory** n спра́вочник, указа́тель m; (tel) телефо́нная кни́га.

dirt n грязь. **dirty** adj гря́зный; vt па́чкать impf, за~ pf.

disability n физи́ческий/психи́ческий недоста́ток; (disablement) инвали́дность. **disabled** adj: he is ~ он инвали́д.

disadvantage n невы́годное положе́ние; (defect) недоста́ток. **disadvantageous** adj невы́годный.

disaffected adj недово́льный.

disagree vi не соглаша́ться impf, согласи́ться pf; (not correspond) не соотве́тствовать impf +dat. **disagreeable** adj неприя́тный. **disagreement** n разногла́сие; (quarrel) ссо́ра.

disappear vi исчеза́ть impf, исче́знуть pf. **disappearance** n исчезнове́ние.

disappoint vt разочаро́вывать impf, разочарова́ть pf. **disappointed** adj разочаро́ванный. **disappointing** adj разочаро́вывающий. **disappointment** n разочарова́ние.

disapproval n неодобре́ние. **disapprove** vt & i не одобря́ть impf.

disarm vt (mil) разоружа́ть impf, разоружи́ть pf; (criminal; also fig) обезору́живать impf, обезору́жить pf. **disarmament** n разоруже́ние.

disarray n беспоря́док.

disaster n бе́дствие. **disastrous** adj катастрофи́ческий.

disband vt распуска́ть impf, распусти́ть pf; vi расходи́ться impf, разойти́сь pf.

disbelief n неве́рие.

disc, disk n диск; ~ **jockey** веду́щий sb переда́чу.

discard vt отбра́сывать impf, отбро́сить pf.

discern vt различа́ть impf, различи́ть pf. **discernible** adj различи́мый. **discerning** adj проница́тельный.

discharge vt (ship etc.) разгружа́ть impf, разгрузи́ть pf (gun; electr) разряжа́ть impf, разряди́ть pf; (dismiss) увольня́ть impf, уво́лить pf; (prisoner) освобожда́ть impf, освободи́ть pf; (debt; duty) выполня́ть impf, вы́полнить pf; (from hospital) выпи́сывать impf, вы́писать pf; n разгру́зка; (electr) разря́д; увольне́ние; освобожде́ние; выполне́ние; (matter discharged) выделе́ния neut pl.

disciple n учени́к.

disciplinarian n сторо́нник дисципли́ны. **disciplinary** adj дисциплина́рный. **discipline** n дисципли́на; vt дисциплини́ровать impf & pf.

disclaim vt (deny) отрица́ть impf; ~ **responsibility** слага́ть impf, сложи́ть pf с себя́ отве́тственность.

disclose vt обнару́живать impf, обнару́жить pf. **disclosure** n обнаруже́ние.

discoloured adj обесцве́ченный.

discomfit vt смуща́ть impf, смути́ть pf. **discomfiture** n смуще́ние.

discomfort n неудо́бство.

disconcert vt смуща́ть impf, смути́ть pf.

disconnect vt разъединя́ть impf, разъедини́ть pf; (switch off) выключа́ть impf, вы́ключить pf. **disconnected** adj (incoherent) бессвя́зный.

disconsolate adj неуте́шный.

discontent n недово́льство. **discontented** adj недово́льный.

discontinue vt прекраща́ть impf, прекрати́ть pf.

discord n разногла́сие; (mus) диссона́нс. **discordant** adj несогласу́ющийся; диссони́рующий.

discotheque n дискоте́ка.

discount n скидка; vt (*disregard*) не принимать *impf*, принять *pf* в расчёт.

discourage vt обескураживать *impf*, обескуражить *pf*; (*dissuade*) отговаривать *impf*, отговорить *pf*.

discourse n речь.

discourteous adj невежливый.

discover vt открывать *impf*, открыть *pf*; (*find out*) обнаруживать *impf*, обнаружить *pf*. **discovery** n открытие.

discredit n позор; vt дискредитировать *impf & pf*.

discreet adj тактичный. **discretion** n (*judgement*) усмотрение; (*prudence*) благоразумие; at one's ~ по своему усмотрению.

discrepancy n несоответствие.

discriminate vt различать *impf*, различить *pf*; ~ **against** дискриминировать *impf & pf*. **discrimination** n (*taste*) разборчивость; (*bias*) дискриминация.

discus n диск.

discuss vt обсуждать *impf*, обсудить *pf*. **discussion** n обсуждение.

disdain n презрение. **disdainful** adj презрительный.

disease n болезнь. **diseased** adj больной.

disembark vi высаживаться *impf*, высадиться *pf*.

disenchantment n разочарование.

disengage vt освобождать *impf*, освободить *pf*; (*clutch*) отпускать *impf*, отпустить *pf*.

disentangle vt распутывать *impf*, распутать *pf*.

disfavour n немилость.

disfigure vt уродовать *impf*, из~ *pf*.

disgrace n позор; (*disfavour*) немилость; vt позорить *impf*, о~ *pf*. **disgraceful** adj позорный.

disgruntled adj недовольный.

disguise n маскировка; vt маскировать *impf*, за~ *pf*; (*conceal*) скрывать *impf*, скрыть *pf*. **disguised** adj замаскированный.

disgust n отвращение; vt внушать *impf*, внушить *pf*. отвращение +dat. **disgusting** adj отвратительный.

dish n блюдо; pl посуда collect; ~-washer (посудо)мо́ечная маши́на; vt: ~ **up** подавать *impf*, подать *pf*.

dishearten vt обескураживать *impf*, обескуражить *pf*.

dishevelled adj растрёпанный.

dishonest adj нечестный. **dishonesty** n нечестность. **dishonour** n бесчестье; vt бесчестить *impf*, о~ *pf*. **dishonourable** adj бесчестный.

disillusion vt разочаровывать *impf*, разочаровать *pf*. **disillusionment** n разочарованность.

disinclination n несклонность, неохота. **disinclined** adj be ~ не хотеться *impers+dat*.

disinfect vt дезинфицировать *impf & pf*. **disinfectant** n дезинфицирующее средство.

disingenuous adj неискренний.

disinherit vt лишать *impf*, лишить *pf* наследства.

disintegrate vi распадаться *impf*, распасться *pf*. **disintegration** n распад.

disinterested adj бескорыстный.

disjointed adj бессвязный.

disk *see* disc

dislike n нелюбовь (for к+dat); vt не любить *impf*.

dislocate vt (*med*) вывихнуть *pf*.

dislodge vt смещать *impf*, сместить *pf*.

disloyal adj нелояльный. **disloyalty** n нелояльность.

dismal adj мрачный.

dismantle vt разбирать *impf*, разобрать *pf*.

dismay vt смущать *impf*, смутить *pf*; n смущение.

dismiss vt (*sack*) увольнять *impf*, уволить *pf*; (*disband*) распускать *impf*, распустить *pf*. **dismissal** n увольнение; роспуск.

dismount vi спешиваться *impf*, спешиться *pf*.

disobedience n непослушание. **disobedient** adj непослушный. **disobey** vt не слушаться *impf +gen*.

disorder n беспорядок. **disorderly** adj (*untidy*) беспорядочный; (*unruly*) буйный.

disorganized adj неорганизованный.

disorientation n дезориентация. **disoriented** adj: I am/was ~ я потеря́л(а) направление.

disown vt отказываться *impf*, отказаться *pf* от+gen.

disparaging adj оскорби́тельный.

disparity n нера́венство.

dispassionate adj беспристра́стный.

dispatch vt (send) отправля́ть impf, отпра́вить pf; (deal with) расправля́ться impf, распра́виться pf c+instr; n отпра́вка; (message) донесе́ние; (rapidity) быстрота́; ~-rider мотоцикли́ст свя́зи.

dispel vt рассе́ивать impf, рассе́ять pf.

dispensable adj необяза́тельный.

dispensary n апте́ка.

dispensation n (exemption) освобожде́ние (от обяза́тельства). **dispense** vt (distribute) раздава́ть impf, разда́ть pf; ~ with обходи́ться impf, обойти́сь pf без+gen.

dispersal n распростране́ние. **disperse** vt (drive away) разгоня́ть impf, разогна́ть pf; (scatter) рассе́ивать impf, рассе́ять pf; vi расходи́ться impf, разойти́сь pf.

dispirited adj удручённый.

displaced adj: ~ persons переме-щённые ли́ца neut pl.

display n пока́з; vt пока́зывать impf, показа́ть pf.

displeased predic недово́лен (-льна).

displeasure n недово́льство.

disposable adj однора́зовый. **disposal** n удале́ние; at your ~ в ва́шем распоряже́нии. **dispose** vi: ~ of избавля́ться impf, изба́виться pf от+gen. **disposed** predic: ~ to располо́жен (-ена) к+dat or +inf. **disposition** n расположе́ние; (temperament) нрав.

disproportionate adj непропорцио-на́льный.

disprove vt опроверга́ть impf, опрове́ргнуть pf.

dispute n (debate) спор; (quarrel) ссо́ра; vt оспа́ривать impf, оспо́рить pf.

disqualification n дисквалифика́ция. **disqualify** vt дисквалифици́ровать impf & pf.

disquieting adj трево́жный.

disregard n пренебреже́ние +instr; vt игнори́ровать impf & pf; пренебрега́ть impf, пренебре́чь pf +instr.

disrepair n неиспра́вность.

disreputable adj по́льзующийся дурно́й сла́вой. **disrepute** n дурна́я сла́ва.

disrespect n неуваже́ние. **disrespectful** adj непочти́тельный.

disrupt vt срыва́ть impf, сорва́ть pf. **disruptive** adj подрывно́й.

dissatisfaction n недово́льство. **dissatisfied** adj недово́льный.

dissect vt разреза́ть impf, разре́зать pf; (med) вскрыва́ть impf, вскрыть pf.

disseminate vt распространя́ть impf, распространи́ть pf; **dissemination** n распростране́ние.

dissension n раздо́р. **dissent** n расхожде́ние; (eccl) раско́л.

dissertation n диссерта́ция.

disservice n плоха́я услу́га.

dissident n диссиде́нт.

dissimilar adj несхо́дный.

dissipate vt (dispel) рассе́ивать impf, рассе́ять pf; (squander) прома́тывать impf, промота́ть pf. **dissipated** adj распу́тный.

dissociate vt: ~ o.s. отмежёвываться impf, отмежева́ться pf (from от+gen).

dissolute adj распу́тный. **dissolution** n расторже́ние; (parl) ро́спуск. **dissolve** vt & i (in liquid) раствори́ть(ся) impf, раствори́ть(ся) pf; vt (annul) расторга́ть impf, расто́ргнуть pf; (parl) распуска́ть impf, распусти́ть pf.

dissonance n диссона́нс. **dissonant** adj диссони́рующий.

dissuade vt отгова́ривать impf, отговори́ть pf.

distance n расстоя́ние; from a ~ и́здали; in the ~ вдалеке́. **distant** adj далёкий, (also of relative) да́льний; (reserved) сде́ржанный.

distaste n отвраще́ние. **distasteful** adj проти́вный.

distended adj наду́тый.

distil vt (whisky) перегоня́ть impf, перегна́ть pf; (water) дистилли́ровать impf & pf. **distillation** n перего́нка; дистилля́ция. **distillery** n перего́нный заво́д.

distinct adj (different) отли́чный; (clear) отчётливый; (evident) заме́тный. **distinction** n (difference; excellence) отли́чие; (discrimination) разли́чие. **distinctive** adj отличи́тельный. **distinctly** adv я́сно.

distinguish vt различа́ть impf,

различи́ть *pf*; ~ o.s. отлича́ться *impf*, отличи́ться *pf*. **distinguished** *adj* выдаю́щийся.

distort *vt* искажа́ть *impf*, искази́ть *pf*; (*misrepresent*) извраща́ть *impf*, изврати́ть *pf*. **distortion** *n* искаже́ние; извраще́ние.

distract *vt* отвлека́ть *impf*, отвле́чь *pf*. **distraction** *n* (*amusement*) развлече́ние; (*madness*) безу́мие.

distraught *adj* обезу́мевший.

distress *n* (*suffering*) огорче́ние; (*danger*) бе́дствие; *vt* огорча́ть *impf*, огорчи́ть *pf*.

distribute *vt* распределя́ть *impf*, распредели́ть *pf*. **distribution** *n* распределе́ние. **distributor** *n* распредели́тель *m*.

district *n* райо́н.

distrust *n* недове́рие; *vt* не доверя́ть *impf*. **distrustful** *adj* недове́рчивый.

disturb *vt* беспоко́ить *impf*, о~ *pf*. **disturbance** *n* наруше́ние поко́я; *pl* (*polit etc.*) беспоря́дки *m pl*.

disuse *n* неупотребле́ние; fall into ~ выходи́ть *impf*, вы́йти *pf* из употребле́ния. **disused** *adj* вы́шедший из употребле́ния.

ditch *n* кана́ва, ров.

dither *vi* колеба́ться *impf*.

ditto *n* то же са́мое; *adv* так же.

divan *n* дива́н.

dive *vi* ныря́ть *impf*, нырну́ть *pf*; (*aeron*) пики́ровать *impf* & *pf*; *n* ныро́к, прыжо́к в во́ду. **diver** *n* водола́з.

diverge *vi* расходи́ться *impf*, разойти́сь *pf*. **divergent** *adj* расходя́щийся.

diverse *adj* разнообра́зный. **diversification** *n* расшире́ние ассорти́мента. **diversify** *vt* разнообра́зить *impf*. **diversion** *n* (*detour*) объе́зд; (*amusement*) развлече́ние. **diversity** *n* разнообра́зие. **divert** *vt* отклоня́ть *impf*, отклони́ть *pf*; (*amuse*) развлека́ть *impf*, развле́чь *pf*. **diverting** *adj* заба́вный.

divest *vt* (*deprive*) лиша́ть *impf*, лиши́ть *pf* (of +*gen*); ~ o.s. отка́зываться *impf*, отказа́ться *pf* (of от+*gen*).

divide *vt* (*share*; *math*) дели́ть *impf*, по~ *pf*; (*separate*) разделя́ть *impf*, раздели́ть *pf*. **dividend** *n* дивиде́нд.

divine *adj* боже́ственный.

diving *n* ныря́ние; ~-**board** трампли́н.

divinity *n* (*quality*) боже́ственность; (*deity*) божество́; (*theology*) богосло́вие.

divisible *adj* дели́мый. **division** *n* (*dividing*) деле́ние, разделе́ние; (*section*) отде́л; (*mil*) диви́зия.

divorce *n* разво́д; *vi* разводи́ться *impf*, развести́сь *pf*. **divorced** *adj* разведённый.

divulge *vt* разглаша́ть *impf*, разгласи́ть *pf*.

DIY *abbr* (*of* do-it-yourself): he is good at ~ у него́ золоты́е ру́ки; ~ shop магази́н «сде́лай сам».

dizziness *n* головокруже́ние. **dizzy** *adj* (*causing dizziness*) головокружи́тельный; I am ~ у меня́ кру́жится голова́.

DNA *abbr* (*of* deoxyribonucleic acid) ДНК.

do *vt* де́лать *impf*, с~ *pf*; *vi* (*be suitable*) годи́ться *impf*; (*suffice*) быть доста́точным; ~-it-yourself *see* DIY; that will ~ хва́тит!; how ~ you ~? здра́вствуйте!; как вы пожива́ете?; ~ away with (*abolish*) уничтожа́ть *impf*, уничто́жить *pf*; ~ in (*kill*) убива́ть *impf*, уби́ть *pf*; ~ up (*restore*) ремонти́ровать *impf*, от~ *pf*; (*wrap up*) завёртывать *impf*, заверну́ть *pf*; (*fasten*) застёгивать *impf*, застегну́ть *pf*; ~ without обходи́ться *impf*, обойти́сь *pf* без+*gen*.

docile *adj* поко́рный. **docility** *n* поко́рность.

dock¹ *n* (*naut*) док; *vt* ста́вить *impf*, по~ *pf* в док; *vi* входи́ть *impf*, войти́ *pf* в док; *vi* (*spacecraft*) стыкова́ться *impf*, со~ *pf*. **docker** *n* до́кер. **dockyard** *n* верфь.

dock² *n* (*law*) скамья́ подсуди́мых.

docket *n* квита́нция; (*label*) ярлы́к.

doctor *n* врач; (*also univ*) до́ктор; *vt* (*castrate*) кастри́ровать *impf* & *pf*; (*spay*) удаля́ть *impf*, удали́ть *pf* я́ичники у+*gen*; (*falsify*) фальсифици́ровать *impf* & *pf*. **doctorate** *n* сте́пень до́ктора.

doctrine *n* доктри́на.

document *n* докуме́нт; *vt* документи́ровать *impf* & *pf*. **documentary** *n* документа́льный фильм. documentation n документа́ция.

doddery adj дря́хлый.

dodge n уве́ртка; vt уклоня́ться impf, уклони́ться pf от+gen; (jump to avoid) отска́кивать impf, отскочи́ть pf (от+gen). dodgy adj ка́верзный.

doe n са́мка.

dog n соба́ка, пёс; (fig) пресле́довать impf. dog-eared adj захва́танный.

dogged adj упо́рный.

dogma n до́гма. dogmatic adj догмати́ческий.

doings n pl дела́ neut pl.

doldrums n: be in the ~ хандри́ть impf.

dole n посо́бие по безрабо́тице; vt (~ out) выдава́ть impf, вы́дать pf. doleful adj ско́рбный.

doll n ку́кла.

dollar n до́ллар.

dollop n соли́дная по́рция.

dolphin n дельфи́н.

domain n (estate) владе́ние; (field) о́бласть.

dome n ку́пол.

domestic adj (of household; animals) дома́шний; (of family) семе́йный; (polit) вну́тренний; n прислу́га. domesticate vt прируча́ть impf, приручи́ть pf. domesticity n дома́шняя, семе́йная, жизнь.

domicile n местожи́тельство.

dominance n госпо́дство. dominant adj преоблада́ющий; госпо́дствующий. dominate vt госпо́дствовать impf над+instr. domineering adj вла́стный.

dominion n влады́чество; (realm) владе́ние.

domino n кость домино́; pl (game) домино́ neut indecl.

don vt надева́ть impf, наде́ть pf.

donate vt же́ртвовать impf, по~ pf. donation n поже́ртвование.

donkey n осёл.

donor n же́ртвователь m; (med) до́нор.

doom n (ruin) ги́бель; vt обрека́ть impf, обре́чь pf.

door n дверь. doorbell n (дверно́й) звоно́к. doorman n швейца́р. doormat n полови́к. doorstep n поро́г. doorway n дверно́й проём.

dope n (drug) нарко́тик; vt дурма́нить impf, о~ pf.

dormant adj (sleeping) спя́щий; (inactive) безде́йствующий.

dormer window n слухово́е окно́.

dormitory n о́бщая спа́льня.

dormouse n со́ня.

dorsal adj спинно́й.

dosage n дозиро́вка. dose n до́за.

dossier n досье́ neut indecl.

dot n то́чка; vt ста́вить impf, по~ pf то́чки на+acc; (scatter) усе́ивать impf, усе́ять pf (with +instr); ~ted line пункти́р.

dote vi: ~ on обожа́ть impf.

double adj двойно́й; (doubled) удво́енный; ~-bass контраба́с; ~ bed двуспа́льная крова́ть; ~-breasted двубо́ртный; ~-cross обма́нывать impf, обману́ть pf; ~-dealer двуру́шник; ~-dealing двуру́шничество; ~-decker двухэта́жный авто́бус; ~-edged обоюдоо́стрый; ~ glazing двойны́е ра́мы f pl; ~ room ко́мната на двои́х; adv вдво́е; (two together) вдвоём; n двойно́е коли́чество; (person's) двойни́к; pl (sport) па́рная игра́; vt & i удва́ивать(ся) impf, удво́ить(ся) pf; ~ back враща́ться impf, верну́ться pf наза́д; ~ up (in pain) скрю́чиваться impf, скрю́читься pf; (share a room) помеща́ться impf, помести́ться pf вдвоём в одно́й ко́мнате; (~ up as) рабо́тать impf + instr по совмести́тельству.

doubt n сомне́ние; vt сомнева́ться impf в+prep. doubtful adj сомни́тельный. doubtless adv несомне́нно.

dough n те́сто. doughnut n по́нчик.

douse vt (drench) залива́ть impf, зали́ть pf.

dove n го́лубь m. dovetail n ла́сточкин хвост.

dowdy adj неэлега́нтный.

down¹ n (fluff) пух.

down² adv (motion) вниз; (position) внизу́; be ~ with (ill) боле́ть impf +instr; prep вниз c+gen, по+dat; (along) (вдоль) по+dat; vt: (gulp) опроки́дывать impf, опроки́нуть pf; ~-and-out бродя́га m; ~cast, ~hearted уны́лый. downfall n ги́бель. downhill adv под го́ру. downpour *n* ли́вень *m*. **downright** *adj* я́вный; *adv* совершённо. **downstairs** *adv* (*motion*) вниз; (*position*) внизу́. **downstream** *adv* вниз по тече́нию. **down-to-earth** *adj* реалисти́ческий. **downtrodden** *adj* угнетённый.

dowry *n* прида́ное *sb*.

doze *vi* дрема́ть *impf*.

dozen *n* дю́жина.

drab *adj* бесцве́тный; (*boring*) ску́чный.

draft *n* (*outline, rough copy*) набро́сок; (*document*) прое́кт; (*econ*) тра́тта; *see also* **draught**; *vt* составля́ть *impf*, соста́вить *pf* план, прое́кт, +*gen*.

drag *vt* тащи́ть *impf*; (*river etc.*) драги́ровать *impf & pf*; ~ **on** (*vi*) затя́гиваться *impf*, затяну́ться *pf*; *n* (*burden*) обу́за; (*on cigarette*) затя́жка; **in** ~ в же́нской оде́жде.

dragon *n* драко́н. **dragonfly** *n* стрекоза́.

drain *n* водосто́к; (*leakage; fig*) уте́чка; *vt* осуша́ть *impf*, осуши́ть *pf*; *vi* спуска́ться *impf*, спусти́ться *pf*.

drainage *n* дрена́ж; (*system*) канализа́ция.

drake *n* селе́зень *m*.

drama *n* дра́ма; (*quality*) драмати́зм. **dramatic** *adj* драмати́ческий. **dramatist** *n* драмату́рг. **dramatize** *vt* драматизи́ровать *impf & pf*.

drape *vt* драпирова́ть *impf*, за~ *pf*; *n* драпиро́вка.

drastic *adj* радика́льный.

draught *n* (*air*) сквозня́к; (*traction*) тя́га; *pl* (*game*) ша́шки *f pl*; *see also* **draft**; **there is a** ~ сквози́т; ~ **beer** пи́во из бо́чки. **draughtsman** *n* черте́жник. **draughty** *adj*: **it is** ~ **here** здесь ду́ет.

draw *n* (*in lottery*) ро́зыгрыш; (*attraction*) прима́нка; (*drawn game*) ничья́; *vt* (*pull*) тяну́ть *impf*, по~ *pf*; таска́ть *indet*, тащи́ть *det*; (*curtains*) заде́ргивать *impf*, задёрнуть *pf* (*занаве́ски*); (*attract*) привлека́ть *impf*, привле́чь *pf*; (*pull out*) выта́скивать *impf*, вы́тащить *pf*; (*sword*) обнажа́ть *impf*, обнажи́ть *pf*; (*lots*) броса́ть *impf*, бро́сить *pf* (*жре́бий*); (*water, inspiration*) че́рпать *impf*, черпну́ть *pf*; (*evoke*) вызыва́ть *impf*, вы́звать *pf*; (*conclusion*) выводи́ть

impf, вы́вести *pf* (*заключе́ние*); (*diagram*) черти́ть *impf*, на~ *pf*; (*picture*) рисова́ть *impf*, на~ *pf*; *vi* (*sport*) сыгра́ть *pf* вничью́; ~ **aside** отводи́ть *impf*, отвести́ *pf* в сто́рону; ~ **back** (*withdraw*) отступа́ть *impf*, отступи́ть *pf*; ~ **in** втя́гивать *impf*, втяну́ть *pf*; (*train*) входи́ть *impf*, войти́ *pf* в ста́нцию; (*car*) подходи́ть *impf*, подойти́ *pf* (**to** к + *dat*); (*days*) станови́ться *impf* коро́че; ~ **out** выта́гивать *impf*, вы́тянуть *pf*; (*money*) выпи́сывать *impf*, вы́писать *pf*; (*train/car*) выходи́ть *impf*, вы́йти *pf* (*со ста́нции*/ *на доро́гу*); ~ **up** (*car*) подходи́ть *impf*, подойти́ *pf* (**to** к + *dat*); (*document*) составля́ть *impf*, соста́вить *pf*. **drawback** *n* недоста́ток. **drawbridge** *n* подъёмный мост. **drawer** *n* я́щик. **drawing** *n* (*action*) рисова́ние, черче́ние; (*object*) рису́нок, чертёж; ~**board** чертёжная доска́; ~**pin** кно́пка; ~**room** гости́ная *sb*.

drawl *n* протя́жное произноше́ние.

dread *n* страх; *vt* боя́ться *impf* +*gen*. **dreadful** *adj* ужа́сный.

dream *n* сон; (*fantasy*) мечта́; *vi* ви́деть *impf*, у~ *pf* сон; ~ **of** ви́деть *impf*, у~ *pf* во сне́; (*fig*) мечта́ть *impf* o+*prep*.

dreary *adj* (*weather*) па́смурный; (*boring*) ску́чный.

dredge *vt* (*river etc.*) драги́ровать *impf & pf*. **dredger** *n* дра́га.

dregs *n pl* оса́дки (-ков) *pl*.

drench *vt* прома́чивать *impf*, промочи́ть *pf*; **get** ~**ed** промока́ть *impf*, промо́кнуть *pf*.

dress *n* пла́тье; (*apparel*) оде́жда; ~ **circle** бельэта́ж; ~**maker** портни́ха; ~ **rehearsal** генера́льная репети́ция; *vt & i* одева́ть(ся) *impf*, оде́ть(ся) *pf*; *vt* (*cul*) приправля́ть *impf*, припра́вить *pf*; (*med*) перевя́зывать *impf*, перевяза́ть *pf*; ~ **up** наряжа́ться *impf*, наряди́ться *pf* (**as** + *instr*).

dresser *n* ку́хонный шкаф.

dressing *n* (*cul*) припра́ва; (*med*) перевя́зка; ~**gown** хала́т; ~**room** убо́рная *sb*; ~**table** туале́тный сто́лик.

dribble *vi* (*person*) пуска́ть *impf*, пусти́ть *pf* слю́ни; (*sport*) вести́ *impf* мяч.

dried adj сушёный. **drier** n сушилка.

drift n (meaning) смысл; (snow) сугроб; (naut) дрейфовать impf по течению; (snow etc.) скопляться impf, скопиться pf; ~ **apart** расходиться impf, разойтись pf.

drill[1] n сверло; (dentist's) бур; vt сверлить impf, про~ pf.

drill[2] vt (mil) обучать impf, обучить pf строю; vi проходить impf, пройти pf строевую подготовку; n строевая подготовка.

drink n напиток; vt пить impf, вы́~ pf; ~**driving** вождение в нетрезвом состоянии. **drinking-water** n питьевая вода.

drip n (action) ка́панье; (drop) капля; vi капать impf, капнуть pf.

drive n (journey) езда́; (excursion) прогу́лка; (campaign) похо́д, кампа́ния; (energy) эне́ргия; (tech) приво́д; (driveway) подъездна́я доро́га; vt (urge; chase) вводить impf, вгнать det; (vehicle) водить indet, вести det; управлять impf +instr; (convey) возить indet, везти det, по~ pf; vi (travel) ездить indet, ехать det, по~ pf; vi доводить impf, довести pf (to до+gen); (nail etc.) вбивать impf, вбить pf (into в+acc); ~ **away** vt прогонять impf, прогнать pf; vi уезжать impf, уехать pf; ~ **up** подъезжать impf, подъехать pf (to к+dat).

driver n (of vehicle) водитель m, шофёр; **driving** adj (force) дви́жущий; (rain) проливно́й; ~-**licence** води́тельские права́ neut pl; ~-**test** экза́мен на получе́ние води́тельских прав; ~-**wheel** веду́щее колесо́.

drizzle n ме́лкий дождь m; vi моросить impf.

drone n (bee; idler) тру́тень m; (of voice) жужжа́ние; (of engine) гул; vi (buzz) жужжа́ть impf; (~ **on**) бубни́ть impf.

drool vi пуска́ть impf, пусти́ть pf слю́ни.

droop vi поника́ть impf, пони́кнуть pf.

drop n (of liquid) ка́пля; (fall) паде́ние, пониже́ние; vt & i (price) снижа́ть(ся) impf, сни́зить(ся) pf; vt (fall) па́дать impf, упа́сть pf; vt (let fall) роня́ть impf, урони́ть pf; (aban-

don) броса́ть impf, бро́сить pf; ~ **behind** отстава́ть impf, отста́ть pf; ~ **in** заходи́ть impf, зайти́ pf (on к+dat); ~ **off** (fall asleep) засыпа́ть impf, засну́ть pf; (from car) выса́живать impf, вы́садить pf; ~ **out** выбыва́ть impf, вы́быть pf (of из+gen). **droppings** n pl помёт.

drought n за́суха.

droves n pl: **in** ~ толпа́ми.

drown vt топи́ть impf, у~ pf; (sound) заглуша́ть impf, заглуши́ть pf; vi тону́ть impf, у~ pf.

drowsy adj со́нливый.

drudgery n ну́дная рабо́та.

drug n медикаме́нт; (narcotic) нарко́тик; ~ **addict** наркома́н, ~ка; vt дава́ть impf, дать pf нарко́тик+dat.

drum n бараба́н; vi бить impf в бараба́н; бараба́нить impf; ~ **sth into s.o.** вда́лбливать impf, вдолби́ть pf + dat of person в го́лову. **drummer** n бараба́нщик.

drunk adj пья́ный. **drunkard** n пья́ница m & f. **drunken** adj пья́ный; ~ **driving** вожде́ние в нетре́звом состоя́нии. **drunkenness** n пья́нство.

dry adj сухо́й; ~ **land** су́ша; vt суши́ть impf, вы́~ pf; (wipe dry) вытира́ть impf, вы́тереть pf; vi со́хнуть impf, вы́~, про~ pf. **dry-cleaning** n химчи́стка. **dryness** n су́хость.

dual adj двойно́й; (joint) совме́стный; ~-**purpose** двойно́го назначе́ния.

dub[1] vt (nickname) прозыва́ть impf, прозва́ть pf.

dub[2] vt (cin) дубли́ровать impf & pf.

dubious adj сомни́тельный.

duchess n герцоги́ня. **duchy** n ге́рцогство.

duck[1] n (bird) у́тка.

duck[2] vt (immerse) окуна́ть impf, окуну́ть pf; (one's head) нагну́ть pf; (evade) увёртываться impf, уверну́ться pf от+gen; vi (~ **down**) наклоня́ться impf, наклони́ться pf.

duckling n утёнок.

duct n прохо́д; (anat) прото́к.

dud n (forgery) подде́лка; (shell) неразорва́вшийся снаря́д; adj подде́льный; (worthless) него́дный.

due n (credit) до́лжное sb; pl взно́сы m pl; adj (proper) до́лжный, надлежа́щий; predic (expected) до́лжен

(-жна); in ~ course со временем; ~ south прямо на юг; ~ to благодаря +dat.

duel n дуэль.

duet n дуэт.

duke n герцог.

dull adj (tedious) скучный; (colour) тусклый, (weather) пасмурный; (not sharp; stupid) тупой; vt притуплять impf, притупить pf.

duly adv надлежащим образом; (punctually) своевременно.

dumb adj немой. **dumbfounded** adj ошарашенный.

dummy n (tailor's) манекен; (baby's) соска; ~ run испытательный рейс.

dump n свалка; vt сваливать impf, свалить pf.

dumpling n клёцка.

dumpy adj приземистый.

dune n дюна.

dung n навоз.

dungarees n pl комбинезон.

dungeon n темница.

dunk vt макать impf, макнуть pf.

duo n пара; (mus) дуэт.

dupe vt надувать impf, надуть pf; n простофиля m & f.

duplicate n копия; in ~ в двух экземплярах; adj (double) двойной; (identical) идентичный; vt размножать impf, размножить pf **duplicity** n двуличность.

durability n прочность. **durable** adj прочный. **duration** n продолжительность.

duress n принуждение; under ~ под давлением.

during prep во время +gen; (throughout) в течение +gen.

dusk n сумерки (-рек) pl.

dust n пыль; ~bin мусорный ящик; ~-jacket суперобложка; ~man мусорщик; ~pan совок; vt & i (clean) стирать impf, стереть pf пыль (c+gen); (sprinkle) посыпать impf, посыпать pf sth +acc, with +instr. **duster** n пыльная тряпка. **dusty** adj пыльный.

Dutch adj голландский; n: the ~ голландцы m pl. **Dutchman** n голландец. **Dutchwoman** n голландка.

dutiful adj послушный. **duty** n (obligation) долг; обязанность; (office) дежурство; (tax) пошлина; be on ~

дежурить impf; ~-free adj беспошлинный.

dwarf n карлик; vt (tower above) возвышаться impf, возвыситься pf над +instr.

dwell vi обитать impf; ~ upon останавливаться impf на+prep. **dweller** n житель m. **dwelling** n жилище.

dwindle vi убывать impf, убыть pf.

dye n краситель m; vt окрашивать impf, окрасить pf.

dynamic adj динамический. **dynamics** n pl динамика.

dynamite n динамит.

dynamo n динамо neut indecl.

dynasty n династия.

dysentery n дизентерия.

dyslexia n дислексия. **dyslexic** adj: he is ~ он дислектик.

E

each adj & pron каждый; ~ other друг друга (dat -гу, etc.).

eager adj (pupil) усердный; I am ~ to мне не терпится +inf; очень желаю +inf. **eagerly** adv с нетерпением; жадно. **eagerness** n сильное желание.

eagle n орёл.

ear[1] n (corn) колос.

ear[2] n (anat) ухо; (sense) слух; ~-ache боль в ухе; ~drum барабанная перепонка; ~-mark (assign) предназначать impf, предназначить pf; ~phone наушник; ~ring серьга; (clip-on) клипс; ~shot: within ~ в пределах слышимости; out of ~ вне пределов слышимости.

earl n граф.

early adj ранний; adv рано.

earn vt зарабатывать impf, заработать pf; (deserve) заслуживать impf, заслужить pf. **earnings** n pl заработок.

earnest adj серьёзный; n: in ~ всерьёз.

earth n земля; (soil) почва; vt заземлять impf, заземлить pf. **earthenware** adj глиняный. **earthly** adj земной. **earthquake** n землетрясение. **earthy** adj землистый; (coarse) грубый.

earwig n уховёртка.

ease n (*facility*) лёгкость; (*unconstraint*) непринуждённость; with ~ легко; vt облегча́ть *impf*, облегчи́ть *pf*; vi успока́иваться *impf*, успоко́иться *pf*.

easel n мольбе́рт.

east n восто́к; (*naut*) ост; adj восто́чный. **easterly** adj восто́чный. **eastern** adj восто́чный. **eastward(s)** adv на восто́к, к восто́ку.

Easter n Па́сха.

easy adj лёгкий; (*unconstrained*) непринуждённый; ~-going ужи́вчивый.

eat vt есть *impf*, с~ *pf*; ку́шать *impf*, по~, с~ *pf*; ~ away разъеда́ть *impf*, разъе́сть *pf*; ~ into въеда́ться *impf*, въе́сться *pf* в+*acc*; ~ up доеда́ть *impf*, дое́сть *pf*. **eatable** adj съедо́бный.

eaves n pl стреха́. **eavesdrop** vi подслу́шивать *impf*.

ebb n (*tide*) отли́в; (*fig*) упа́док.

ebony n чёрное де́рево.

ebullient adj кипу́чий.

EC abbr (*of European Community*) Европе́йское соо́бщество.

eccentric n чуда́к; adj эксцентри́чный.

ecclesiastical adj церко́вный.

echo n э́хо; vi (*resound*) отража́ться *impf*, отрази́ться *pf*; vt (*repeat*) повторя́ть *impf*, повтори́ть *pf*.

eclipse n затме́ние; vt затмева́ть *impf*, затми́ть *pf*.

ecological adj экологи́ческий. **ecology** n эколо́гия.

economic adj экономи́ческий. **economical** adj эконо́мный. **economist** n экономи́ст. **economize** vt & i эконо́мить *impf*, с~ *pf*. **economy** n эконо́мика; (*saving*) эконо́мия.

ecstasy n экста́з. **ecstatic** adj экстати́ческий.

eddy n водоворо́т.

edge n край; (*blade*) ле́звие; on ~ в не́рвном состоя́нии; have the ~ on име́ть *impf* преиму́щество над+*instr*; vt (*border*) окаймля́ть *impf*, окайми́ть *pf*; vi пробира́ться *impf*, пробра́ться *pf*. **edging** n кайма́. **edgy** adj раздражи́тельный.

edible adj съедо́бный.

edict n ука́з.

edifice n зда́ние. **edifying** adj назида́тельный.

edit vt редакти́ровать *impf*, от~ *pf*; (*cin*) монти́ровать *impf*, с~ *pf*. **edition** n изда́ние; (*number of copies*) тира́ж. **editor** n реда́ктор. **editorial** n передова́я статья́; adj реда́кторский, редакцио́нный.

educate vt дава́ть *impf*, дать *pf* образова́ние +*dat*; where was he educated? где он получи́л образова́ние? **educated** adj образо́ванный. **education** n образова́ние. **educational** adj образова́тельный; (*instructive*) уче́бный.

eel n у́горь m.

eerie adj жу́ткий.

effect n (*result*) сле́дствие; (*validity*; *influence*) де́йствие; (*impression*; *theat*) эффе́кт; in ~ факти́чески; take ~ вступа́ть *impf*, вступи́ть *pf* в си́лу; (*medicine*) начина́ть *impf*, нача́ть *pf* де́йствовать; vt произво́дить *impf*, произвести́ *pf*. **effective** adj эффекти́вный; (*striking*) эффе́ктный; (*actual*) факти́ческий. **effectiveness** n эффекти́вность.

effeminate adj женоподо́бный.

effervesce vi пузы́риться *impf*. **effervescent** adj (*fig*) и́скря́щийся.

efficiency n эффекти́вность. **efficient** adj эффекти́вный; (*person*) организо́ванный.

effigy n изображе́ние.

effort n уси́лие.

effrontery n на́глость.

effusive adj экспанси́вный.

e.g. abbr напр.

egalitarian adj эгалита́рный.

egg[1] n яйцо́; ~cup рю́мка для яйца́; ~shell яи́чная скорлупа́.

egg[2] vt: ~ on подстрека́ть *impf*, подстрекну́ть *pf*.

ego n «Я». **egocentric** adj эгоцентри́ческий. **egoism** n эгои́зм. **ego(t)ist** n эгои́ст; ~ка. **ego(t)istical** adj эгоцентри́ческий. **egotism** n эготи́зм.

Egypt n Еги́пет. **Egyptian** n египтя́нин, -я́нка; adj еги́петский.

eiderdown n пухово́е одея́ло.

eight adj & n во́семь; (*number 8*) восьмёрка. **eighteen** adj & n восемна́дцать. **eighteenth** adj & n восемна́дцатый. **eighth** adj & n восьмо́й; (*fraction*) восьма́я sb. **eightieth** adj & n восьмидеся́тый.

eighty *adj* & *n* во́семьдесят; *pl (decade)* восьмидеся́тые го́ды (-до́в) *m pl.*

either *adj* & *pron (one of two)* оди́н из двух, тот и́ли друго́й; *(both)* и тот, и друго́й; о́ба; *(one or other)* любо́й; *adv* & *conj*: ~ ... и́ли... и́ли, ли́бо... ли́бо.

eject *vt* выбра́сывать *impf*, вы́бросить *pf*; *vi (pilot)* катапульти́роваться *impf* & *pf.*

eke *vt*: ~ out a living перебива́ться *impf*, переби́ться *pf* ко́е-ка́к.

elaborate *adj (ornate)* витиева́тый; *(detailed)* подро́бный; *vt* разраба́тывать *impf*, разрабо́тать *pf*; *(detail)* уточня́ть *impf*, уточни́ть *pf.*

elapse *vi* проходи́ть *impf*, пройти́ *pf*; *(expire)* истека́ть *impf*, исте́чь *pf.*

elastic *n* рези́нка; *adj* эласти́чный; ~ band рези́нка. elasticity *n* эласти́чность.

elated *adj* в восто́рге. elation *n* восто́рг.

elbow *n* ло́коть *m*; *vt*: ~ (one's way) through прота́лкиваться *impf*, протолкну́ться *pf* че́рез+*acc.*

elder¹ *n (tree)* бузина́.

elder² *n (person)* ста́рец; *pl* ста́ршие *sb*; *adj* ста́рший. elderly *adj* пожило́й. eldest *adj* ста́рший.

elect *adj* и́збранный; *vt* избира́ть *impf*, избра́ть *pf.* election *n* вы́боры *m pl.* elector *n* избира́тель *m.* electoral *adj* избира́тельный. electorate *n* избира́тели *m pl.*

electric(al) *adj* электри́ческий; ~ shock уда́р электри́ческим то́ком. electrician *n* эле́ктрик. electricity *n* электри́чество. electrify *vt (convert to electricity)* электрифици́ровать *impf* & *pf*; *(charge with electricity; fig)* электризова́ть *impf*, на-*pf.* electrode *n* электро́д. electron *n* электро́н. electronic *adj* электро́нный. electronics *n* электро́ника.

electrocute *vt* убива́ть *impf*, уби́ть *pf* электри́ческим то́ком; *(execute)* казни́ть *impf* & *pf* на электри́ческом сту́ле. electrolysis *n* электро́лиз.

elegance *n* элега́нтность. elegant *adj* элега́нтный.

elegy *n* эле́гия.

element *n* элеме́нт; *(earth, wind, etc.)* стихия́; be in one's ~ быть в свое́й стихи́и. elemental *adj* стихи́йный. elementary *adj* элемента́рный; *(school etc.)* нача́льный.

elephant *n* слон.

elevate *vt* поднима́ть *impf*, подня́ть *pf.* elevated *adj* возвы́шенный. elevation *n (height)* высота́. elevator *n (lift)* лифт.

eleven *adj* & *n* оди́ннадцать. eleventh *adj* & *n* оди́ннадцатый; at the ~ hour в после́днюю мину́ту.

elf *n* эльф.

elicit *vt (obtain)* выявля́ть *impf*, вы́явить *pf*; *(evoke)* вызыва́ть *impf*, вы́звать *pf.*

eligible *adj* име́ющий пра́во (for на+*acc*); *(bachelor)* подходя́щий.

eliminate *vt (do away with)* устраня́ть *impf*, устрани́ть *pf*; *(rule out)* исключа́ть *impf*, исключи́ть *pf.*

élite *n* эли́та.

ellipse *n* э́ллипс. elliptic(al) *adj* эллипти́ческий.

elm *n* вяз.

elocution *n* ора́торское иску́сство.

elongate *vt* удлиня́ть *impf*, удлини́ть *pf.*

elope *vi* бежа́ть *det* (с возлю́бленным).

eloquence *n* красноре́чие. eloquent *adj* красноречи́вый.

else *adv (besides)* ещё; *(instead)* друго́й; *(with neg)* бо́льше; nobody ~ никто́ бо́льше; or ~ и́наче; a (не) то; и́ли же; s.o. ~ кто́-нибудь друго́й; something ~? ещё что́-нибудь? elsewhere *adv (place)* в друго́м ме́сте; *(direction)* в друго́е ме́сто.

elucidate *vt* разъясня́ть *impf*, разъясни́ть *pf.*

elude *vt* избега́ть *impf* +*gen.* elusive *adj* неулови́мый.

emaciated *adj* истощённый.

emanate *vi* исходи́ть *impf* (from из, от, +*gen*).

emancipate *vt* эмансипи́ровать *impf* & *pf.* emancipation *n* эмансипа́ция.

embankment *n (river)* набережная *sb*; *(rly)* на́сыпь.

embargo *n* эмба́рго *neut indecl.*

embark *vi* сади́ться *impf*, сесть *pf* на кора́бль; ~ upon предпринима́ть *impf*, предприня́ть *pf.* embarkation *n* посáдка (на корáбль).

embarrass *vt* смущáть *impf*, смутúть *pf*; be ~ed чýвствовать *impf* себя́ неудóбно. **embarrassing** *adj* неудóбный. **embarrassment** *n* смущéние.

embassy *n* посóльство.

embedded *adj* врéзанный.

embellish *vt* (*adorn*) украшáть *impf*, укрáсить *pf*; (*story*) прикрáшивать *impf*, прикрáсить *pf*. **embellishment** *n* украшéние.

embers *n pl* тлéющие уголькú *m pl*.

embezzle *vt* растрáчивать *impf*, растрáтить *pf*. **embezzlement** *n* растрáта.

embitter *vt* ожесточáть *impf*, ожесточúть *pf*.

emblem *n* эмблéма.

embodiment *n* воплощéние. **embody** *vt* воплощáть *impf*, воплотúть *pf*.

emboss *vt* чекáнить *impf*, вы́~, от~ *pf*.

embrace *n* объя́тие; *vi* обнимáться *impf*, обня́ться *pf*; *vt* обнимáть *impf*, обня́ть *pf*; (*accept*) принимáть *impf*, приня́ть *pf*; (*include*) охвáтывать *impf*, охватúть *pf*.

embroider *vt* вышивáть *impf*, вы́шить *pf*; (*story*) прикрáшивать *impf*, прикрáсить *pf*. **embroidery** *n* вы́шивка.

embroil *vt* впу́тывать *impf*, впу́тать *pf*.

embryo *n* эмбриóн.

emerald *n* изумру́д.

emerge *vi* появля́ться *impf*, появúться *pf*. **emergence** *n* появлéние. **emergency** *n* крáйняя необходúмость; state of ~ чрезвычáйное положéние; ~ exit запаснóй вы́ход.

emery paper *n* наждáчная бумáга.

emigrant *n* эмигрáнт, ~ка. **emigrate** *vi* эмигрúровать *impf & pf*. **emigration** *n* эмигрáция.

eminence *n* (*fame*) знаменúтость. **eminent** *adj* выдаю́щийся. **eminently** *adv* чрезвычáйно.

emission *n* испускáние. **emit** *vt* испускáть *impf*, испустúть *pf*; (*light*) излучáть *impf*, излучúть *pf*; (*sound*) издавáть *impf*, издáть *pf*.

emotion *n* эмóция, чýвство. **emotional** *adj* эмоционáльный.

empathize *vt* сопережавáть *impf*, сопережúть *pf*. **empathy** *n* эмпáтия.

emperor *n* императóр.

emphasis *n* ударéние. **emphasize** *vt* подчёркивать *impf*, подчеркну́ть *pf*. **emphatic** *adj* вырáзительный; категорúческий.

empire *n* импéрия.

empirical *adj* эмпирúческий.

employ *vt* (*use*) пóльзоваться *impf* +*instr*; (*person*) нанимáть *impf*, наня́ть *pf*. **employee** *n* сотрýдник, рабóчий *sb.* **employer** *n* работодáтель *m.* **employment** *n* рабóта, слýжба; (*use*) испóльзование.

empower *vt* уполномóчивать *impf*, уполномóчить *pf* (to на+*acc*).

empress *n* императрúца.

emptiness *n* пустотá. **empty** *adj* пустóй; ~-headed пустоголóвый; *vt* (*container*) опорожня́ть *impf*, опорóжнúть *pf*; (*solid*) высыпáть *impf*, вы́сыпать *pf*; (*liquid*) выливáть *impf*, вы́лить *pf*; *vi* пустéть *impf*, о~ *pf*.

emulate *vt* достигáть *impf*, достúгнуть, достúчь *pf* +*gen*; (*copy*) подражáть *impf* +*dat*.

emulsion *n* эмýльсия.

enable *vt* давáть *impf*, дать *pf* возмóжность +*dat & inf*.

enact *vt* (*law*) принимáть *impf*, приня́ть *pf*; (*theat*) разы́грывать *impf*, разыгрáть *pf*. **enactment** *n* (*law*) постановлéние; (*theat*) игрá.

enamel *n* эмáль; *adj* эмáлевый; *vt* эмалировáть *impf & pf*.

encampment *n* лáгерь *m.*

enchant *vt* очарóвывать *impf*, очаровáть *pf*. **enchanting** *adj* очаровáтельный. **enchantment** *n* очаровáние.

encircle *vt* окружáть *impf*, окружúть *pf*.

enclave *n* анклáв.

enclose *vt* огорáживать *impf*, огородúть *pf*; (*in letter*) приклáдывать *impf*, приложúть *pf*; please find ~d прилагáется (-áются) +*nom*. **enclosure** *n* огорóженное мéсто; (*in letter*) приложéние.

encode *vt* шифровáть *impf*, за~ *pf*.

encompass *vt* (*encircle*) окружáть *impf*, окружúть *pf*; (*contain*) заключáть *impf*, заключúть *pf*.

encore *int* бис!; *n* вы́зов на бис.

encounter *n* встре́ча; (*in combat*) столкнове́ние; *vt* встреча́ть *impf*, встре́тить *pf*; (*fig*) ста́лкиваться *impf*, столкну́ться *pf* c+*instr*.

encourage *vt* ободря́ть *impf*, ободри́ть *pf*. **encouragement** *n* ободре́ние. **encouraging** *adj* ободри́тельный.

encroach *vi* вторга́ться *impf*, вто́ргнуться *pf* (**on** в+*acc*). **encroachment** *n* вторже́ние.

encumber *vt* обременя́ть *impf*, обремени́ть *pf*. **encumbrance** *n* обу́за.

encyclopaedia *n* энциклопе́дия. **encyclopaedic** *adj* энциклопеди́ческий.

end *n* коне́ц; (*death*) смерть; (*purpose*) цель; **an ~ in itself** самоце́ль; **in the ~** в конце́ концо́в; **make ~s meet** своди́ть *impf*, свести́ *pf* концы́ с конца́ми; **no ~ of** ма́сса+*gen*; **on ~** (*upright*) стоймя́, дыбо́м; (*continuously*) подря́д; **put an ~ to** класть *impf*, положи́ть *pf* коне́ц +*dat*; *vt* конча́ть *impf*, ко́нчить *pf*; (*halt*) прекраща́ть *impf*, прекрати́ть *pf*; *vi* конча́ться *impf*, ко́нчиться *pf*.

endanger *vt* подверга́ть *impf*, подве́ргнуть *pf* опа́сности.

endearing *adj* привлека́тельный. **endearment** *n* ла́ска.

endeavour *n* попы́тка; (*exertion*) уси́лие; (*undertaking*) де́ло; *vi* стара́ться *impf*, по~ *pf*.

endemic *adj* энеми́ческий.

ending *n* оконча́ние. **endless** *adj* бесконе́чный.

endorse *vt* (*document*) подпи́сывать *impf*, подписа́ть *pf*; (*support*) подде́рживать *impf*, поддержа́ть *pf*. **endorsement** *n* по́дпись; подде́ржка; (*on driving licence*) проко́л.

endow *vt* обеспе́чивать *impf*, обеспе́чить *pf* постоя́нным дохо́дом; (*fig*) одаря́ть *impf*, одари́ть *pf*. **endowment** *n* поже́ртвование; (*talent*) дарова́ние.

endurance *n* (*of person*) выно́сливость; (*of object*) про́чность. **endure** *vt* выноси́ть *impf*, вы́нести *pf*; терпе́ть *impf*, по~ *pf*; *vi* продолжа́ться *impf*, продо́лжиться *pf*.

enemy *n* враг; *adj* вра́жеский.

energetic *adj* энерги́чный. **energy** *n*

эне́ргия; *pl* си́лы *f pl*.

enforce *vt* (*law etc.*) следи́ть *impf* за выполне́нием +*gen*. **enforcement** *n* наблюде́ние за выполне́нием +*gen*.

engage *vt* (*hire*) нанима́ть *impf*, наня́ть *pf*; (*tech*) зацепля́ть *impf*, зацепи́ть *pf*. **engaged** *adj* (*occupied*) за́нятый; **be ~ in** занима́ться *impf*, заня́ться *pf* +*instr*; **become ~** обруча́ться *impf*, обручи́ться *pf* (**to** c+*instr*). **engagement** *n* (*appointment*) свида́ние; (*betrothal*) обруче́ние; (*battle*) бой; **~ ring** обруча́льное кольцо́. **engaging** *adj* привлека́тельный.

engender *vt* порожда́ть *impf*, породи́ть *pf*.

engine *n* дви́гатель *m*; (*rly*) локомоти́в; **~-driver** *n* (*rly*) машини́ст. **engineer** *n* инжене́р; *vt* (*fig*) организова́ть *impf & pf*. **engineering** *n* инжене́рное де́ло, те́хника.

England *n* А́нглия. **English** *adj* англи́йский; *n*: **the ~** *pl* англича́не (-н) *pl*. **Englishman**, **-woman** *n* англича́нин, -а́нка.

engrave *vt* гравирова́ть *impf*, вы́~ *pf*; (*fig*) вреза́ть *impf*, вре́зать *pf*. **engraver** *n* гравёр. **engraving** *n* гравю́ра.

engross *vt* поглоща́ть *impf*, поглоти́ть *pf*; **be ~ed in** быть поглощённым +*instr*.

engulf *vt* поглоща́ть *impf*, поглоти́ть *pf*.

enhance *vt* увели́чивать *impf*, увели́чить *pf*.

enigma *n* зага́дка. **enigmatic** *adj* зага́дочный.

enjoy *vt* получа́ть *impf*, получи́ть *pf* удово́льствие от+*gen*; наслажда́ться *impf*, наслади́ться *pf* +*instr*; (*health etc.*) облада́ть *impf* +*instr*; **~ o.s.** хорошо́ проводи́ть *impf*, провести́ *pf* вре́мя. **enjoyable** *adj* прия́тный. **enjoyment** *n* удово́льствие.

enlarge *vt* увели́чивать *impf*, увели́чить *pf*; **~ upon** распространя́ться *impf*, распространи́ться *pf* o+*prep*. **enlargement** *n* увеличе́ние.

enlighten *vt* просвеща́ть *impf*, просвети́ть *pf*. **enlightenment** *n* просвеще́ние.

enlist *vi* поступа́ть *impf*, поступи́ть *pf* на вое́нную слу́жбу; *vt* (*mil*) вербова́ть *impf*, за~ *pf*; (*support etc.*) заруча́ться *impf*, заручи́ться *pf* +*instr*.

enliven *vt* оживля́ть *impf*, оживи́ть *pf*.

enmity *n* вражда́.

ennoble *vt* облагора́живать *impf*, облагоро́дить *pf*.

ennui *n* тоска́.

enormity *n* чудо́вищность. **enormous** *adj* огро́мный. **enormously** *adv* чрезвыча́йно.

enough *adj* доста́точно +*gen*; *adv* доста́точно, дово́льно; be ~ хвата́ть *impf*, хвати́ть *pf impers*+*gen*.

enquire, enquiry *see* inquire, inquiry

enrage *vt* беси́ть *impf*, вз~ *pf*.

enrapture *vt* восхища́ть *impf*, восхити́ть *pf*.

enrich *vt* обогаща́ть *impf*, обогати́ть *pf*.

enrol *vt* & *i* запи́сывать(ся) *impf*, записа́ть(ся) *pf*. **enrolment** *n* за́пись.

en route *adv* по пути́ (to, for в+*acc*).

ensconce *vt*: ~ o.s. заса́живаться *impf*, засе́сть *pf* (with за+*acc*).

ensemble *n* (*mus*) анса́мбль *m*.

enshrine *vt* (*fig*) охраня́ть *impf*, охрани́ть *pf*.

ensign *n* (*flag*) флаг.

enslave *vt* порабоща́ть *impf*, поработи́ть *pf*.

ensue *vi* сле́довать *impf*. **ensuing** *adj* после́дующий.

ensure *vt* обеспе́чивать *impf*, обеспе́чить *pf*.

entail *vt* (*necessitate*) влечь *impf* за собо́й.

entangle *vt* запу́тывать *impf*, запу́тать *pf*.

enter *vt* & *i* входи́ть *impf*, войти́ *pf* в+*acc*; (*by transport*) въезжа́ть *impf*, въе́хать *pf* в+*acc*; *vt* (*join*) поступа́ть *impf*, поступи́ть *pf* в, на, +*acc*; (*competition*) вступа́ть *impf*, вступи́ть *pf* в+*acc*; (*in list*) вноси́ть *impf*, внести́ *pf* в+*acc*.

enterprise *n* (*undertaking*) предприя́тие; (*initiative*) предприи́мчивость. **enterprising** *adj* предприи́мчивый.

entertain *vt* (*amuse*) развлека́ть *impf*, развле́чь *pf*; (*guests*) принима́ть *impf*, приня́ть *pf*; угоща́ть *impf*, угости́ть *pf* (to +*instr*); (*hopes*) пита́ть *impf*. **entertaining** *adj* зани-

ма́тельный. **entertainment** *n* развлече́ние; (*show*) представле́ние.

enthral *vt* порабоща́ть *impf*, порабо́тить *pf*.

enthusiasm *n* энтузиа́зм. **enthusiast** *n* энтузиа́ст, ~ка. **enthusiastic** *adj* восто́рженный; по́лный энтузиа́зма.

entice *vt* зама́нивать *impf*, замани́ть *pf*. **enticement** *n* прима́нка. **enticing** *adj* зама́нчивый.

entire *adj* по́лный, це́лый, весь. **entirely** *adv* вполне́, соверше́нно; (*solely*) исключи́тельно. **entirety** *n*: in its ~ по́лностью.

entitle *vt* (*authorize*) дава́ть *impf*, дать *pf* пра́во+*dat* (to на+*acc*); be ~d (*book*) называ́ться *impf*; be ~ to име́ть *impf* пра́во на+*acc*.

entity *n* объе́кт; феноме́н.

entomology *n* энтомоло́гия.

entourage *n* сви́та.

entrails *n pl* вну́тренности (-тей) *pl*.

entrance[1] *n* вход, въезд; (*theat*) вы́ход; ~ exam вступи́тельный экза́мен; ~ hall вестибю́ль *m*.

entrance[2] *vt* (*charm*) очаро́вывать *impf*, очарова́ть *pf*. **entrancing** *adj* очарова́тельный.

entrant *n* уча́стник (for +*gen*).

entreat *vt* умоля́ть *impf*, умоли́ть *pf*. **entreaty** *n* мольба́.

entrench *vt* be, become ~ed (*fig*) укореня́ться *impf*, укорени́ться *pf*.

entrepreneur *n* предпринима́тель *m*.

entrust *vt* (*secret*) вверя́ть *impf*, вве́рить *pf* (to +*dat*); (*object*; *person*) поруча́ть *impf*, поручи́ть *pf* (to +*dat*).

entry *n* вход, въезд; вступле́ние; (*theat*) вы́ход; (*note*) за́пись; (*in reference book*) статья́.

entwine *vt* (*interweave*) сплета́ть *impf*, сплести́ *pf*; (*wreathe*) обвива́ть *impf*, обви́ть *pf*.

enumerate *vt* перечисля́ть *impf*, перечи́слить *pf*.

enunciate *vt* (*express*) излага́ть *impf*, изложи́ть *pf*; (*pronounce*) произноси́ть *impf*, произнести́ *pf*. **enunciation** *n* изложе́ние; произноше́ние.

envelop *vt* оку́тывать *impf*, оку́тать *pf*. **envelope** *n* конве́рт.

enviable *adj* зави́дный. **envious** *adj* зави́стливый.

environment n среда; (the ~) окружа́ющая среда́. **environs** n pl окре́стности f pl.

envisage vt предусма́тривать impf, предусмотре́ть pf.

envoy n посла́нник, аге́нт.

envy n за́висть; vt зави́довать impf, по~ pf +dat.

enzyme n энзи́м.

ephemeral adj эфеме́рный.

epic n эпопе́я; adj эпи́ческий.

epidemic n эпиде́мия.

epilepsy n эпиле́псия. **epileptic** n эпиле́птик; adj эпилепти́ческий.

epilogue n эпило́г.

episode n эпизо́д. **episodic** adj эпизоди́ческий.

epistle n посла́ние.

epitaph n эпита́фия.

epithet n эпи́тет.

epitome n воплоще́ние. **epitomize** vt воплоща́ть impf, воплоти́ть pf.

epoch n эпо́ха.

equal adj ра́вный, одина́ковый; (capable of) спосо́бный (to на+acc, +inf); n ра́вный sb; vt равня́ться impf +dat. **equality** n ра́венство. **equalize** vt ура́внивать impf, уравня́ть pf; vi (sport) равня́ть impf, с~ pf счёт. **equally** adv равно́, ра́вным о́бразом.

equanimity n хладнокро́вие.

equate vt прира́внивать impf, приравня́ть pf (with к+dat).

equation n (math) уравне́ние.

equator n эква́тор. **equatorial** adj экваториа́льный.

equestrian adj ко́нный.

equidistant adj равностоя́щий. **equilibrium** n равнове́сие.

equip vt обору́довать impf & pf; (person) снаряжа́ть impf, снаряди́ть pf; (fig) вооружа́ть impf, вооружи́ть pf. **equipment** n обору́дование, снаряже́ние.

equitable adj справедли́вый. **equity** n справедли́вость; pl (econ) обыкнове́нные а́кции f pl.

equivalent adj эквивале́нтный; n эквивале́нт.

equivocal adj двусмы́сленный.

era n э́ра.

eradicate vt искореня́ть impf, искорени́ть pf.

erase vt стира́ть impf, стере́ть pf; (from memory) вычёркивать impf, вы́черкнуть pf (из па́мяти). **eraser** n ла́стик.

erect adj прямо́й; vt сооружа́ть impf, сооруди́ть pf. **erection** n сооруже́ние; (biol) эре́кция.

erode vt разруша́ть impf, разру́шить pf. **erosion** n эро́зия; (fig) разруше́ние.

erotic adj эроти́ческий.

err vi ошиба́ться impf, ошиби́ться pf; (sin) греши́ть impf, со~ pf.

errand n поруче́ние; run ~s быть на посы́лках (for y+gen).

erratic adj неро́вный.

erroneous adj оши́бочный. **error** n оши́бка.

erudite adj учёный. **erudition** n эруди́ция.

erupt vi взрыва́ться impf, взорва́ться pf; (volcano) изверга́ться impf, изве́ргнуться pf. **eruption** n изверже́ние.

escalate vi возраста́ть impf, возрасти́ pf; vt интенсифици́ровать impf & pf.

escalator n эскала́тор.

escapade n вы́ходка. **escape** n (from prison) побе́г; (from danger) спасе́ние; (leak) уте́чка; have a narrow ~ едва́ спасти́сь; vi (flee) бежа́ть impf & pf; убега́ть impf, убежа́ть pf; (save o.s.) спаса́ться impf, спасти́сь pf; (leak) утека́ть impf, уте́чь pf; vt избега́ть impf, избежа́ть pf +gen; (groan) вырыва́ться impf, вы́рваться pf из, у, +gen.

escort n (mil) эско́рт; (of lady) кавале́р; vt сопровожда́ть impf, сопроводи́ть pf; (mil) эскорти́ровать impf & pf.

Eskimo n эскимо́с, ~ка.

esoteric adj эзотери́ческий.

especially adv осо́бенно.

espionage n шпиона́ж.

espousal n подде́ржка. **espouse** vt (fig) подде́рживать impf, поддержа́ть pf.

essay n о́черк.

essence n (philos) су́щность; (gist) суть; (extract) эссе́нция. **essential** adj (fundamental) суще́ственный; (necessary) необходи́мый; n pl (necessities) необходи́мое sb; (crux) суть; (fundamentals) осно́вы f pl.

essentially adv по существу́.

establish vt (set up) учрежда́ть impf, учреди́ть pf; (fact etc.) устана́вливать impf, установи́ть pf. **establishment** n (action) учрежде́ние, установле́ние; (institution) учрежде́ние.

estate n (property) име́ние; (after death) насле́дство; (housing ~) жило́й масси́в; ~ agent аге́нт по прода́же недви́жимости; ~ car автомоби́ль m с ку́зовом «универса́л».

esteem n уваже́ние; vt уважа́ть impf. **estimate** n (of quality) оце́нка; (of cost) сме́та; vt оце́нивать impf, оцени́ть pf. **estimation** n оце́нка, мне́ние.

Estonia n Эсто́ния. **Estonian** n эсто́нец, -нка; adj эсто́нский.

estranged adj отчуждённый. **estrangement** n отчужде́ние.

estuary n у́стье.

etc. abbr и т.д. etcetera и так да́лее.

etch vt трави́ть impf, вы́- pf. **etching** n (action) травле́ние; (object) офо́рт.

eternal adj ве́чный. **eternity** n ве́чность.

ether n эфи́р. **ethereal** adj эфи́рный.

ethical adj эти́ческий, эти́чный. **ethics** n э́тика.

ethnic adj этни́ческий.

etiquette n этике́т.

etymology n этимоло́гия.

EU abbr (of European Union) ЕС.

eucalyptus n эвкали́пт.

Eucharist n прича́стие.

eulogy n похвала́.

euphemism n эвфеми́зм. **euphemistic** adj эвфемисти́ческий.

Europe n Евро́па. **European** n европе́ец; adj европе́йский; ~ **Community** Европе́йское соо́бщество; ~ **Union** Европе́йский сою́з.

evacuate vt (person, place) эвакуи́ровать impf & pf. **evacuation** n эвакуа́ция.

evade vt уклоня́ться impf, уклони́ться pf от+gen.

evaluate vt оце́нивать impf, оцени́ть pf. **evaluation** n оце́нка.

evangelical adj ева́нгельский. **evangelist** n евангели́ст.

evaporate vt & i испаря́ть(ся) impf, испари́ть(ся) pf. **evaporation** n испаре́ние.

evasion n уклоне́ние (of от+gen). **evasive** adj укло́нчивый.

eve n кану́н; on the ~ накану́не.

even adj ро́вный; (number) чётный; **get** ~ расквита́ться pf (with с+instr); adv да́же; (just) как раз; (with comp) ещё; ~ **if** да́же е́сли; ~ **though** хотя́; ~ **so** всё-таки; **not** ~ да́же не; vt выра́внивать impf, вы́ровнять pf.

evening n ве́чер; adj вече́рний; ~ **class** вече́рние ку́рсы m pl.

evenly adv по́ровну, ро́вно. **evenness** n ро́вность.

event n собы́тие, происше́ствие; **in the** ~ в слу́чае+gen; **in any** ~ во вся́ком слу́чае; **in the** ~ в коне́чном счёте. **eventful** adj по́лный собы́тий. **eventual** adj коне́чный. **eventuality** n возмо́жность. **eventually** adv в конце́ концо́в.

ever adv (at any time) когда́-либо, когда́-нибудь; (always) всегда́; (emph) же; ~ **since** с тех пор (как); ~ **so** о́чень; **for** ~ навсегда́; **hardly** ~ почти́ никогда́. **evergreen** adj вечнозелёный; n вечнозелёное расте́ние. **everlasting** adj ве́чный.

evermore adv: **for** ~ навсегда́.

every adj ка́ждый, вся́кий, все (pl); ~ **now and then** вре́мя от вре́мени; ~ **other** ка́ждый второ́й; ~ **other day** че́рез день. **everybody**, **everyone** pron ка́ждый, все (pl). **everyday** adj (daily) ежедне́вный; (commonplace) повседне́вный. **everything** pron всё. **everywhere** adv всю́ду, везде́.

evict vt выселя́ть impf, вы́селить pf. **eviction** n выселе́ние.

evidence n свиде́тельство, доказа́тельство; **give** ~ свиде́тельствовать impf (о+prep; +acc; +что). **evident** adj очеви́дный.

evil n зло; adj злой.

evoke vt вызыва́ть impf, вы́звать pf.

evolution n эволю́ция. **evolutionary** adj эволюцио́нный. **evolve** vt & i развива́ть(ся) impf, разви́ть(ся) pf.

ewe n овца́.

ex- in comb бы́вший.

exacerbate vt обостря́ть impf, обостри́ть pf.

exact adj то́чный; vt взы́скивать

impf, взыска́ть *pf* (from, of с+*gen*).
exacting *adj* тре́бовательный. **exactitude, exactness** *n* то́чность.
exactly *adv* то́чно; (*just*) как раз; (*precisely*) и́менно.

exaggerate *vt* преувели́чивать *impf*, преувели́чить *pf*. **exaggeration** *n* преувеличе́ние.

exalt *vt* возвыша́ть *impf*, возвы́сить *pf*; (*extol*) превозноси́ть *impf*, превознести́ *pf*.

examination *n* (*inspection*) осмо́тр; (*exam*) экза́мен; (*law*) допро́с. **examine** *vt* (*inspect*) осма́тривать *impf*, осмотре́ть *pf*; (*test*) экзаменова́ть *impf*, про~ *pf*; (*law*) допра́шивать *impf*, допроси́ть *pf*. **examiner** *n* экзамена́тор.

example *n* приме́р; for ~ наприме́р.

exasperate *vt* раздража́ть *impf*, раздражи́ть *pf*. **exasperation** *n* раздраже́ние.

excavate *vt* раска́пывать *impf*, раскопа́ть *pf*. **excavations** *n pl* раско́пки *f pl*. **excavator** *n* экскава́тор.

exceed *vt* превыша́ть *impf*, превы́сить *pf*. **exceedingly** *adv* чрезвыча́йно.

excel *vt* превосходи́ть *impf*, превзойти́ *pf*; *vi* отлича́ться *impf*, отличи́ться *pf* (at, in в+*prep*). **excellence** *n* превосхо́дство. **excellency** *n* превосходи́тельство. **excellent** *adj* отли́чный.

except *vt* исключа́ть *impf*, исключи́ть *pf*; *prep* кро́ме+*gen*. **exception** *n* исключе́ние; take ~ to возража́ть *impf*, возрази́ть *pf* про́тив+*gen*. **exceptional** *adj* исключи́тельный.

excerpt *n* отры́вок.

excess *n* избы́ток. **excessive** *adj* чрезме́рный.

exchange *n* обме́н (of +*instr*); (of currency) разме́н; (building) би́ржа; (telephone) центра́льная телефо́нная ста́нция; ~ rate курс; *vt* обме́нивать *impf*, обменя́ть *pf* (for на+*acc*) обме́нивать́ся *impf*, обменя́ться *pf* +*instr*.

Exchequer *n* казначе́йство.

excise[1] *n* (duty) акци́з(ный сбор).

excise[2] *vt* (cut out) выреза́ть *impf*, вы́резать *pf*.

excitable *adj* возбуди́мый. **excite** *vt* (cause, arouse) возбужда́ть *impf*,

возбуди́ть *pf*; (thrill, agitate) волнова́ть *impf*, вз~ *pf*. **excitement** *n* возбужде́ние; волне́ние.

exclaim *vi* восклица́ть *impf*, воскли́кнуть *pf*. **exclamation** *n* восклица́ние; ~ mark восклица́тельный знак.

exclude *vt* исключа́ть *impf*, исключи́ть *pf*. **exclusion** *n* исключе́ние. **exclusive** *adj* исключи́тельный.

excommunicate *vt* отлуча́ть *impf*, отлучи́ть *pf* (от це́ркви).

excrement *n* экскреме́нты (-тов) *pl*.

excrete *vt* выделя́ть *impf*, вы́делить *pf*. **excretion** *n* выделе́ние.

excruciating *adj* мучи́тельный.

excursion *n* экску́рсия.

excusable *adj* прости́тельный. **excuse** *n* оправда́ние; (pretext) отгово́рка; *vt* (forgive) извиня́ть *impf*, извини́ть *pf*; (justify) опра́вдывать *impf*, оправда́ть *pf*; (release) освобожда́ть *impf*, освободи́ть *pf* (from от+*gen*); ~ me! извини́те!; прости́те!

execute *vt* исполня́ть *impf*, испо́лнить *pf*; (criminal) казни́ть *impf* & *pf*. **execution** *n* исполне́ние; казнь. **executioner** *n* пала́ч. **executive** *n* исполни́тельный о́рган; (person) руководи́тель *m*; *adj* исполни́тельный.

exemplary *adj* приме́рный. **exemplify** *vt* (illustrate by example) приводи́ть *impf*, привести́ *pf* приме́р +*gen*; (serve as example) служи́ть *impf*, по~ *pf* приме́ром +*gen*.

exempt *vt* освобожда́ть *impf*, освободи́ть *pf* (from от+*gen*). **exemption** *n* освобожде́ние.

exercise *n* (use) примене́ние; (physical ~; task) упражне́ние; take ~ упражня́ться *impf*; ~ book тетра́дь; *vt* (use) применя́ть *impf*, примени́ть *pf*; (dog) прогу́ливать *impf*; (train) упражня́ть *impf*.

exert *vt* ока́зывать *impf*, оказа́ть *pf*; ~ o.s. стара́ться *impf*, по~ *pf*. **exertion** *n* напряже́ние.

exhale *vt* выдыха́ть *impf*, вы́дохнуть *pf*.

exhaust *n* вы́хлоп; ~ fumes выхлопны́е га́зы *m pl*; ~ pipe выхлопна́я труба́; *vt* (use up) истоща́ть *impf*, exhibit 323 export

истощи́ть *pf*; (*person*) изнуря́ть *impf*, изнури́ть *pf*; (*subject*) исче́рпывать *impf*, исче́рпать *pf*. exhausted *adj*: be ~ (*person*) быть измождённым. exhausting *adj* изнури́тельный. exhaustion *n* изнуре́ние; (*depletion*) истоще́ние. exhaustive *adj* исче́рпывающий.

exhibit *n* экспона́т; (*law*) веще́ственное доказа́тельство; *vt* (*manifest*) проявля́ть *impf*, прояви́ть *pf*; (*publicly*) выставля́ть *impf*, вы́ставить *pf*. exhibition *n* проявле́ние; (*public ~*) вы́ставка. exhibitor *n* экспоне́нт.

exhilarated *adj* в приподнятом настрое́нии. exhilarating *adj* возбужда́ющий. exhilaration *n* возбужде́ние.

exhort *vt* увещева́ть *impf*. exhortation *n* увещева́ние.

exhume *vt* выка́пывать *impf*, вы́копать *pf*.

exile *n* изгна́ние; (*person*) изгна́нник; *vt* изгоня́ть *impf*, изгна́ть *pf*.

exist *vi* существова́ть *impf*. existence *n* существова́ние. existing *adj* существу́ющий.

exit *n* вы́ход; (*theat*) ухо́д (со сце́ны); ~ visa выездна́я ви́за; *vi* уходи́ть *impf*, уйти́ *pf*.

exonerate *vt* опра́вдывать *impf*, оправда́ть *pf*.

exorbitant *adj* непоме́рный.

exorcize *vt* (*spirits*) изгоня́ть *impf*, изгна́ть *pf*.

exotic *adj* экзоти́ческий.

expand *vt* & *i* расширя́ть(ся) *impf*, расши́рить(ся) *pf*; ~ on распространя́ться *impf*, распространи́ться *pf* о+*prep*. expanse *n* простра́нство. expansion *n* расшире́ние. expansive *adj* экспанси́вный.

expatriate *n* экспатриа́нт, ~ка.

expect *vt* (*await*) ожида́ть *impf* +*gen*; ждать *impf* +*gen*, что; (*suppose*) полага́ть *impf* +*gen*, чтобы. expectant *adj* выжида́тельный; ~ mother бере́менная же́нщина. expectation *n* ожида́ние.

expediency *n* целесообра́зность. expedient *n* приём; *adj* целесообра́зный. expedite *vt* ускоря́ть *impf*, уско́рить *pf*. expedition *n* экспе

ди́ция. expeditionary *adj* экспедицио́нный.

expel *vt* (*drive out*) выгоня́ть *impf*, вы́гнать *pf*; (*from school etc.*) исключа́ть *impf*, исключи́ть *pf*; (*from country etc.*) изгоня́ть *impf*, изгна́ть *pf*.

expend *vt* тра́тить *impf*, ис~, по~ *pf*. expendable *adj* необяза́тельный. expenditure *n* расхо́д. expense *n* расхо́д; *pl* расхо́ды *m pl*, at the ~ of за счёт+*gen*; (*fig*) цено́ю+*gen*. expensive *adj* дорого́й.

experience *n* о́пыт; (*incident*) пережива́ние; *vt* испы́тывать *impf*, испыта́ть *pf*; (*undergo*) пережива́ть *impf*, пережи́ть *pf*. experienced *adj* о́пытный.

experiment *n* экспериме́нт; *vi* эксперименти́ровать *impf* (on, with над, с+*instr*). experimental эксперимента́льный.

expert *n* экспе́рт; *adj* о́пытный. expertise *n* специа́льные зна́ния *neut pl*.

expire *vi* (*period*) истека́ть *impf*, исте́чь *pf*. expiry *n* истече́ние.

explain *vt* объясня́ть *impf*, объясни́ть *pf*. explanation *n* объясне́ние. explanatory *adj* объясни́тельный.

expletive *n* (*oath*) бра́нное сло́во.

explicit *adj* я́вный; (*of person*) прямо́й.

explode *vt* & *i* взрыва́ть(ся) *impf*, взорва́ть(ся) *pf*; *vt* (*discredit*) опроверга́ть *impf*, опрове́ргнуть *pf*; *vi* (*with anger etc.*) разража́ться *impf*, разрази́ться *pf*.

exploit *n* по́двиг; *vt* эксплуати́ровать *impf*; (*use to advantage*) испо́льзовать *impf* & *pf*. exploitation *n* эксплуата́ция. exploiter *n* эксплуата́тор.

exploration *n* иссле́дование. exploratory *adj* иссле́довательский. explore *vt* иссле́довать *impf* & *pf*. explorer *n* иссле́дователь *m*.

explosion *n* взрыв. explosive *n* взры́вчатое вещество́; *adj* взры́вчатый; (*fig*) взрывно́й.

exponent *n* (*interpreter*) истолкова́тель *m*; (*advocate*) сторо́нник.

export *n* вы́воз, э́кспорт; *vt* вывози́ть *impf*, вы́везти *pf*; экспорти́ровать *impf* & *pf*. exporter *n* экспортёр.

expose vt (*bare*) раскрыва́ть *impf*, раскры́ть *pf*; (*subject*) подверга́ть *impf*, подве́ргнуть *pf* (to +*dat*); (*discredit*) разоблача́ть *impf*, разоблачи́ть *pf*; (*phot*) экспони́ровать *impf & pf*.

exposition n изложе́ние.

exposure n подверга́ние (to +*dat*); (*phot*) вы́держка; (*unmasking*) разоблаче́ние; (*med*) хо́лод.

expound vt излага́ть *impf*, изложи́ть *pf*.

express n (*train*) экспре́сс; adj (*clear*) то́чный; (*purpose*) специа́льный; (*urgent*) сро́чный; vt выража́ть *impf*, вы́разить *pf*. **expression** n выраже́ние; (*expressiveness*) вырази́тельность. **expressive** adj вырази́тельный. **expressly** adv (*clearly*) я́сно; (*specifically*) специа́льно.

expropriate vt экспроприи́ровать *impf & pf*. **expropriation** n экспроприа́ция.

expulsion n (*from school etc.*) исключе́ние; (*from country etc.*) изгна́ние.

exquisite adj утончённый.

extant adj сохрани́вшийся.

extempore adv экспро́мптом. **extemporize** vt & i импровизи́ровать *impf*, сымпровизи́ровать *pf*.

extend vt (*stretch out*) протя́гивать *impf*, протяну́ть *pf*; (*enlarge*) расширя́ть *impf*, расши́рить *pf*; (*prolong*) продлева́ть *impf*, продли́ть *pf*; vi простира́ться *impf*, простере́ться *pf*. **extension** n (*enlarging*) расшире́ние; (*time*) продле́ние; (*to house*) пристро́йка; (*tel*) доба́вочный. **extensive** adj обши́рный. **extent** n (*degree*) сте́пень.

extenuating adj: ~ circumstances смягча́ющие вину́ обстоя́тельства *neut pl*.

exterior n вне́шность; adj вне́шний.

exterminate vt истребля́ть *impf*, истреби́ть *pf*. **extermination** n истребле́ние.

external adj вне́шний.

extinct adj (*volcano*) поту́хший; (*species*) вы́мерший; become ~ вымира́ть *impf*, вы́мереть *pf*. **extinction** n вымира́ние.

extinguish vt гаси́ть *impf*, по~ *pf*. **extinguisher** n огнетуши́тель *m*.

extol vt превозноси́ть *impf*, превознести́ *pf*.

extort vt вымога́ть *impf* (from y+*gen*). **extortion** n вымога́тельство. **extortionate** adj вымога́тельский.

extra n (*theat*) стати́ст, ~ка; (*payment*) припла́та; adj дополни́тельный; (*special*) осо́бый; adv осо́бенно.

extract n экстра́кт; (*from book etc.*) вы́держка; vt извлека́ть *impf*, извле́чь *pf*. **extraction** n извлече́ние; (*origin*) происхожде́ние. **extradite** vt выдава́ть *impf*, вы́дать *pf*. **extradition** n вы́дача.

extramarital adj внебра́чный.

extraneous adj посторо́нний.

extraordinary adj чрезвыча́йный.

extrapolate vt & i экстраполи́ровать *impf & pf*.

extravagance n расточи́тельность. **extravagant** adj расточи́тельный; (*fantastic*) сумасбро́дный.

extreme n кра́йность; adj кра́йний. **extremity** n (*end*) край; (*adversity*) кра́йность; pl (*hands & feet*) коне́чности *f pl*.

extricate vt выпу́тывать *impf*, вы́путать *pf*.

exuberance n жизнера́достность. **exuberant** adj жизнера́достный.

exude vt & i выделя́ть(ся) *impf*, вы́делить(ся) *pf*; (*fig*) излуча́ть(ся) *impf*, излучи́ть(ся) *pf*.

exult vi ликова́ть *impf*. **exultant** adj лику́ющий. **exultation** n ликова́ние.

eye n глаз; (*needle etc.*) ушко́; vt разгля́дывать *impf*, разгляде́ть *pf*. **eyeball** n глазно́е я́блоко. **eyebrow** n бровь. **eyelash** n ресни́ца. **eyelid** n ве́ко. **eyeshadow** n те́ни *f pl* для век. **eyesight** n зре́ние. **eyewitness** n очеви́дец.

F

fable n ба́сня.

fabric n (*structure*) структу́ра; (*cloth*) ткань. **fabricate** vt (*invent*) выду́мывать *impf*, вы́думать *pf*. **fabrication** n вы́думка.

fabulous adj ска́зочный.

façade n фаса́д.

face n лицо́; (*expression*) выраже́ние;

(*grimace*) грима́са; (*side*) сторона́; (*surface*) пове́рхность; (*clock etc.*) цифербла́т; make ~в ко́рчить *impf* ро́жи; ~ down лицо́м вниз; ~ to ~ лицо́м к лицу́; in the ~ of пе́ред лицо́м+*gen*, вопреки́+*dat*; on the ~ of it на пе́рвый взгляд; *vt* (*be turned towards*) быть обращённым к+*dat*; (*of person*) стоя́ть *impf* лицо́м к+*dat*; (*meet firmly*) смотре́ть *impf* в лицо́+*dat*; (*cover*) облицева́ть *impf*, облицева́ть *pf*; I can't ~ it я да́же ду́мать об э́том не могу́. faceless *adj* безли́чный.

facet *n* грань; (*fig*) аспе́кт.

facetious *adj* шутли́вый.

facial *adj* лицево́й.

facile *adj* пове́рхностный. **facilitate** *vt* облегча́ть *impf*, облегчи́ть *pf*. **facility** *n* (*ease*) лёгкость; (*ability*) спосо́бность; *pl* (*conveniences*) удо́бства *neut pl*, (*opportunities*) возмо́жности *f pl*.

facing *n* облицо́вка; (*of garment*) отде́лка.

facsimile *n* факси́миле *neut indecl*.

fact *n* факт; the ~ is that ... де́ло в том, что...; as a matter of ~ со́бственно говоря́; in ~ на са́мом де́ле.

faction *n* фра́кция.

factor *n* фа́ктор.

factory *n* фа́брика, заво́д.

factual *adj* факти́ческий.

faculty *n* спосо́бность; (*univ*) факульте́т.

fade *vi* (*wither*) вя́нуть *impf*, за~ *pf*; (*colour*) выцвета́ть *impf*, вы́цвести *pf*; (*sound*) замира́ть *impf*, замере́ть *pf*.

faeces *n pl* кал.

fag *n* (*cigarette*) сигаре́тка.

fail *n*: without ~ обяза́тельно; *vi* (*weaken*) слабе́ть *impf*; (*break down*) отка́зывать *impf*, отказа́ть *pf*; (*not succeed*) терпе́ть *impf*, по~ *pf* неуда́чу; не удава́ться *impf*, уда́ться *pf impers*+*dat*; *vt* & *i* (*exam*) прова́ливать(ся) *impf*, провали́ть(ся) *pf*; *vt* (*disappoint*) подводи́ть *impf*, подвести́ *pf*. failing *n* недоста́ток; *prep* за неиме́нием +*gen*. failure *n* неуда́ча; (*person*) неуда́чник, -ица.

faint *n* обморок; *adj* (*weak*) сла́бый; (*pale*) бле́дный; I feel ~ мне ду́рно;

~-hearted малоду́шный; *vi* па́дать *impf*, упа́сть *pf* в о́бморок

fair[1] *n* я́рмарка.

fair[2] *adj* (*hair, skin*) све́тлый; (*weather*) я́сный; (*just*) справедли́вый; (*average*) сно́сный; a ~ amount дово́льно мно́го +*gen*. fairly *adv* дово́льно.

fairy *n* фе́я; ~-tale ска́зка.

faith *n* ве́ра; (*trust*) дове́рие. faithful *adj* ве́рный; yours ~ly с уваже́нием.

fake *n* подде́лка; *vt* подде́лывать *impf*, подде́лать *pf*.

falcon *n* со́кол.

fall *n* паде́ние; *vi* па́дать *impf*, (у)па́сть *pf*; ~ apart распада́ться *impf*, распа́сться *pf*; ~ asleep засыпа́ть *impf*, засну́ть *pf*; ~ back on прибега́ть *impf*, прибе́гнуть *pf* к+*dat*; ~ down упа́сть *pf*; (*building*) разва́ливаться *impf*, разва́ли́ться *pf*; ~ in ру́хнуть *pf*; ~ in love with влюбля́ться *impf*, влюби́ться *pf* в+*acc*; ~ off отпада́ть *impf*, отпа́сть *pf*; ~ out выпада́ть *impf*, вы́пасть *pf*; (*quarrel*) поссо́риться *pf*; ~ over опроки́дываться *impf*, опроки́нуться *pf*; ~ through прова́ливаться *impf*, провали́ться *pf*; ~-out радиоакти́вные оса́дки (-ков) *pl*.

fallacy *n* оши́бка.

fallible *adj* подве́рженный оши́бкам.

fallow *n*: lie ~ лежа́ть *impf* под па́ром.

false *adj* ло́жный; (*teeth*) иску́сственный; ~ start неве́рный старт. falsehood *n* ложь. falsification *n* фальсифика́ция. falsify *vt* фальсифици́ровать *impf* & *pf*. falsity *n* ло́жность.

falter *vi* спотыка́ться *impf*, споткну́ться *pf*; (*stammer*) запина́ться *impf*, запну́ться *pf*.

fame *n* сла́ва. famed *adj* изве́стный.

familiar *adj* (*well known*) знако́мый; (*usual*) обы́чный; (*informal*) фамилья́рный. familiarity *n* знако́мство; фамилья́рность. familiarize *vt* ознакомля́ть *impf*, ознако́мить *pf* (with c+*instr*).

family *n* семья́; *attrib* семе́йный; ~-tree родосло́вная *sb*.

famine *n* го́лод. famished *adj*: be ~ голода́ть *impf*.

famous *adj* знамени́тый.

fan[1] *n* ве́ер; (*ventilator*) вентиля́тор;

~-belt ремень *m* вентилятора; *vt* обмахивать *impf*, обмахнуть *pf*; (*flame*) раздувать *impf*, раздуть *pf*.
fan² *n* поклонник, -ица; (*sport*) болельщик. fanatic *n* фанатик. fanatical *adj* фанатический.

fanciful *adj* причудливый. fancy *n* фантазия; (*whim*) причуда; take a ~ to увлекаться *impf*, увлечься *pf* +*instr*; *adj* витиеватый; *vt* (*imagine*) представлять *impf*, представить *pf* себе; (*suppose*) полагать *impf*; (*like*) нравиться *impf*, по~ *pf impers*+*dat*; ~ dress маскарадный костюм; ~-dress костюмированный.

fanfare *n* фанфара.

fang *n* клык; (*serpent's*) ядовитый зуб.

fantasize *vi* фантазировать *impf*. fantastic *adj* фантастический. fantasy *n* фантазия.

far *adj* дальний; Russia is ~ away Россия очень далеко; *adv* далеко; (*fig*) намного; as ~ as (*prep*) до +*gen*; (*conj*) поскольку; by ~ намного; (in) so ~ as поскольку; so ~ до сих пор; ~-fetched притянутый за волосы; ~-reaching далеко идущий; ~-sighted дальновидный.
farce *n* фарс. farcical *adj* смехотворный.

fare *n* (*price*) проездная плата; (*food*) пища; *vi* поживать *impf*. farewell *int* прощай(те)!; *n* прощание; *attrib* прощальный; bid ~ прощаться *impf*, проститься *pf* (to c+*instr*).
farm *n* ферма. farmer *n* фермер. farming *n* сельское хозяйство.
fart *n* (*vulg*) пукание; *vi* пукать *impf*, пукнуть *pf*.
farther *see* further. farthest *see* furthest.
fascinate *vt* очаровывать *impf*, очаровать *pf*. fascinating *adj* очаровательный. fascination *n* очарование.
Fascism *n* фашизм. Fascist *n* фашист, ~ка; *adj* фашистский.
fashion *n* мода; (*manner*) манера; after a ~ некоторым образом; *vt* придавать *impf*, придать *pf* форму +*dat*. fashionable *adj* модный.
fast¹ *n* пост; *vi* поститься *impf*.
fast² *adj* (*rapid*) скорый, быстрый;

(*colour*) стойкий; (*shut*) плотно закрытый; be ~ (*timepiece*) спешить *impf*.
fasten *vt* (*attach*) прикреплять *impf*, прикрепить *pf* (to к+*dat*); (*tie*) привязывать *impf*, привязать *pf* (to к+*dat*); (*garment*) застёгивать *impf*, застегнуть *pf*. fastener, fastening *n* запор, задвижка; (*on garment*) застёжка.
fastidious *adj* брезгливый.
fat *n* жир; *adj* (*greasy*) жирный; (*plump*) толстый; get ~ толстеть *impf*, по~ *pf*.
fatal *adj* роковой; (*deadly*) смертельный. fatalism *n* фатализм. fatality *n* (*death*) смертельный случай. fate *n* судьба. fateful *adj* роковой.
father *n* отец; ~-in-law (*husband's* ~) свёкор; (*wife's* ~) тесть *m*. fatherhood *n* отцовство. fatherland *n* отечество. fatherly *adj* отеческий.
fathom *n* морская сажень; *vt* (*fig*) понимать *impf*, понять *pf*.
fatigue *n* утомление; *vt* утомлять *impf*, утомить *pf*.
fatten *vt* откармливать *impf*, откормить *pf*; *vi* толстеть *impf*, по~ *pf*. fatty *adj* жирный.
fatuous *adj* глупый.
fault *n* недостаток; (*blame*) вина; (*geol*) сброс. faultless *adj* безупречный. faulty *adj* дефектный.
fauna *n* фауна.
favour *n* (*kind act*) любезность; (*goodwill*) благосклонность; in (s.o.'s) ~ в пользу +*gen*; be in ~ of быть за+*acc*; *vt* (*support*) благоприятствовать *impf* +*dat*; (*treat with partiality*) оказывать *impf*, оказать *pf* предпочтение +*dat*. favourable *adj* (*propitious*) благоприятный; (*approving*) благосклонный. favourite *n* любимец, -мица; (*also sport*) фаворит, ~ка; *adj* любимый.
fawn¹ *n* оленёнок; *adj* желтовато-коричневый.
fawn² *vi* подлизываться *impf*, подлизаться *pf* (on к+*dat*).
fax *n* факс; *vt* посылать *impf*, послать *pf* по факсу.
fear *n* страх, боязнь, опасение; *vt* & *i* бояться *impf* +*gen*; опасаться *impf* +*gen*. fearful *adj* (*terrible*) страш-

ный; (*timid*) пугли́вый. **fearless** *adj* бесстра́шный. **fearsome** *adj* гро́зный.

feasibility *n* осуществи́мость. **feasible** *adj* осуществи́мый.

feast *n* (*meal*) пир; (*festival*) пра́здник; *vi* пирова́ть *impf*.

feat *n* по́двиг.

feather *n* перо́.

feature *n* черта́; (*newspaper*) (*темати́ческая*) статья́; ~ **film** худо́жественный фильм; *vt* помеща́ть *impf*, помести́ть *pf* на ви́дном ме́сте; (*in film*) пока́зывать *impf*, показа́ть *pf*; *vi* игра́ть *impf* сыгра́ть *pf* роль.

February *n* февра́ль *m*; *adj* февра́льский.

feckless *adj* безала́берный.

federal *adj* федера́льный. **federation** *n* федера́ция.

fee *n* гонора́р; (*entrance* ~ *etc.*) взнос; *pl* (*regular payment, school, etc.*) пла́та.

feeble *adj* сла́бый.

feed *n* корм; *vt* корми́ть *impf*, на~, по~ *pf*; *vi* корми́ться *impf*, по~ *pf*; ~ **up** отка́рмливать *impf*, откорми́ть *pf*; **I am fed up with** мне надое́л (-а, -о; -и) +*nom*. **feedback** *n* обра́тная связь.

feel *vt* чу́вствовать *impf*, по~ *pf*; (*think*) счита́ть *impf*, счесть *pf*; *vi* (~ *bad etc.*) чу́вствовать *impf*, по~ *pf* себя́ +*adv*, +*instr*; ~ **like** хоте́ться *impf* *impers*+*dat*. **feeling** *n* (*sense*) ощуще́ние; (*emotion*) чу́вство; (*impression*) впечатле́ние; (*mood*) настрое́ние.

feign *vt* притворя́ться *impf*, притвори́ться *pf* +*instr*. **feigned** *adj* притво́рный.

feline *adj* коша́чий.

fell *vt* (*tree*) сруба́ть *impf*, сруби́ть *pf*; (*person*) сбива́ть *impf*, сбить *pf* с ног.

fellow *n* па́рень *m*; (*of society etc.*) член; ~ **countryman** соотéчественник. **fellowship** *n* това́рищество.

felt *n* фетр; *adj* фе́тровый; ~**-tip pen** флома́стер.

female *n* (*animal*) са́мка; (*person*) же́нщина; *adj* же́нский. **feminine** *adj* же́нский, же́нственный; (*gram*) же́нского ро́да. **femininity** *n* же́нст-

венность. **feminism** *n* феминѝзм. **feminist** *n* фемини́ст, ~ка; *adj* фемини́стский.

fence *n* забо́р; *vt*: ~ **in** огора́живать *impf*, огороди́ть *pf*; ~ **off** отгора́живать *impf*, отгороди́ть *pf*; *vi* (*sport*) фехтова́ть *impf*. **fencer** *n* фехтова́льщик, -ица. **fencing** *n* (*enclosure*) забо́р; (*sport*) фехтова́ние.

fend *vt*: ~ **off** отража́ть *impf*, отрази́ть *pf*; *vi*: ~ **for o.s.** забо́титься *impf*, по~ *pf* о себе́. **fender** *n* решётка.

fennel *n* фе́нхель *m*.

ferment *n* броже́ние; *vi* броди́ть *impf*; *vt* ква́сить *impf*, за~ *pf*; (*excite*) возбужда́ть *impf*, возбуди́ть *pf*. **fermentation** *n* броже́ние; (*excitement*) возбужде́ние.

fern *n* па́поротник.

ferocious *adj* свире́пый. **ferocity** *n* свире́пость.

ferret *n* хорёк; *vt*: ~ **out** (*search out*) разню́хивать *impf*, разню́хать *pf*; *vi*: ~ **about** (*rummage*) ры́ться *impf*.

ferry *n* паро́м; *vt* перевози́ть *impf*, перевезти́ *pf*.

fertile *adj* плодоро́дный. **fertility** *n* плодоро́дие. **fertilize** *vt* (*soil*) удобря́ть *impf*, удо́брить *pf*; (*egg*) оплодотворя́ть *impf*, оплодотвори́ть *pf* **fertilizer** *n* удобре́ние.

fervent *adj* горя́чий. **fervour** *n* жар.

fester *vi* гнои́ться *impf*.

festival *n* пра́здник, (*music etc.*) фестива́ль *m*. **festive** *adj* пра́здничный. **festivities** *n pl* торжества́ *neut pl*.

festoon *vt* украша́ть *impf*, укра́сить *pf*.

fetch *vt* (*carrying*) приноси́ть *impf*, принести́ *pf*; (*leading*) приводи́ть *impf*, привести́ *pf*; (*go and come back with*) (*on foot*) идти́ *impf*, по~ *pf* за+*instr*; (*by vehicle*) заезжа́ть *impf*, зае́хать *pf* за+*instr*; (*price*) выруча́ть *impf*, вы́ручить *pf*. **fetching** *adj* привлека́тельный.

fetid *adj* злово́нный.

fetish *n* фети́ш.

fetter *vt* ско́вывать *impf*, скова́ть *pf*; *n*: *pl* кандалы́ (-ло́в) *pl*; (*fig*) око́вы (-в) *pl*.

fettle *n* состоя́ние.

feud *n* кро́вная месть.

feudal *adj* феода́льный. **feudalism** *n* феодали́зм.

fever *n* лихора́дка. **feverish** *adj* лихора́дочный.

few *adj* & *pron* немно́гие *pl*; ма́ло +*gen*; а ~ не́сколько +*gen*; quite a ~ нема́ло +*gen*.

fiancé *n* жени́х. **fiancée** *n* неве́ста.

fiasco *n* прова́л.

fib *n* враньё; *vi* привира́ть *impf*, привра́ть *pf*.

fibre *n* волокно́. **fibreglass** *n* стекловолокно́. **fibrous** *adj* волокни́стый.

fickle *adj* непостоя́нный.

fiction *n* худо́жественная литерату́ра; (*invention*) вы́думка. **fictional** *adj* беллетристи́ческий. **fictitious** *adj* вы́мышленный.

fiddle *n* (*violin*) скри́пка; (*swindle*) обма́н; *vi*: ~ about безде́льничать *impf*; ~ with верте́ть *impf*; *vt* (*falsify*) подде́лывать *impf*, подде́лать *pf*; (*cheat*) жи́лить *impf*, у~ *pf*.

fidelity *n* ве́рность.

fidget *n* непосе́да *m* & *f*; *vi* ёрзать *impf*; не́рвничать *impf*. **fidgety** *adj* непосе́дливый.

field *n* по́ле; (*sport*) площа́дка; (*sphere*) о́бласть; ~-glasses полево́й бино́кль *m*. ~work полевы́е рабо́ты *f pl*.

fiend *n* дья́вол. **fiendish** *adj* дья́вольский.

fierce *adj* свире́пый; (*strong*) си́льный.

fiery *adj* о́гненный.

fifteen *adj* & *n* пятна́дцать. **fifteenth** *adj* & *n* пятна́дцатый. **fifth** *adj* & *n* пя́тый; (*fraction*) пя́тая *sb*. **fiftieth** *adj* & *n* пятидеся́тый. **fifty** *adj* & *n* пятьдеся́т; *pl* (*decade*) пятидеся́тые го́ды (-до́в) *m pl*.

fig *n* инжи́р.

fight *n* дра́ка; (*battle*) бой; (*fig*) борьба́; *vt* боро́ться *impf* с+*instr*; *vi* дра́ться *impf*; *vt* & *i* (*wage war*) воева́ть *impf* с+*instr*. **fighter** *n* бое́ц; (*aeron*) истреби́тель *m*. **fighting** *n* бой *m pl*.

figment *n* плод воображе́ния.

figurative *adj* перено́сный. **figure** *n* (*form, body, person*) фигу́ра; (*number*) ци́фра; (*diagram*) рису́нок; (*image*) изображе́ние; (*of speech*)

оборо́т ре́чи; ~-head (*naut*) носово́е украше́ние; (*person*) номина́льная глава́; *impf*; *vi* фигури́ровать *impf*; ~ out вычисля́ть *impf*, вы́числить *pf*.

filament *n* волокно́; (*electr*) нить.

file[1] *n* (*tool*) напи́льник; *vt* подпи́ливать *impf*, подпили́ть *pf*.

file[2] *n* (*folder*) па́пка; (*comput*) файл; *vt* подшива́ть *impf*, подши́ть *pf*; (*complaint*) подава́ть *impf*, пода́ть *pf*.

file[3] *n* (*row*) ряд; in (*single*) ~ гусько́м.

filigree *n* филигра́нь; *adj* филигра́нный.

fill *vt* & *i* (*also* ~ up) наполня́ть(ся) *impf*, напо́лнить(ся) *pf*; *vt* заполня́ть *impf*, запо́лнить *pf*; (*tooth*) пломбирова́ть *impf*, за~ *pf*; (*occupy*) занима́ть *impf*, заня́ть *pf*; (*satiate*) насыща́ть *impf*, насы́тить *pf*; ~ in (*vt*) заполня́ть *impf*, запо́лнить *pf*; (*vi*) замеща́ть *impf*, замести́ть *pf*.

fillet *n* (*cul*) филе́ *neut indecl*.

filling *n* (*tooth*) пло́мба; (*cul*) начи́нка.

filly *n* кобы́лка.

film *n* (*layer*; *phot*) плёнка; (*cin*) фильм; ~ star кинозвезда́; *vt* снима́ть *impf*, снять *pf*.

filter *n* фильтр; *vt* фильтрова́ть *impf*, про~ *pf*; ~ through, out проса́чиваться *impf*, просочи́ться *pf*.

filth *n* грязь. **filthy** *adj* гря́зный.

fin *n* плавни́к.

final *n* фина́л; *pl* выпускны́е экза́мены *m pl*; *adj* после́дний; (*decisive*) оконча́тельный. **finale** *n* фина́л. **finalist** *n* финали́ст. **finality** *n* зако́нченность. **finalize** *vt* (*complete*) заверша́ть *impf*, заверши́ть *pf*; (*settle*) ула́живать *impf*, ула́дить *pf*. **finally** *adv* наконе́ц.

finance *n* фина́нсы (-сов) *pl*; *vt* финанси́ровать *impf* & *pf*. **financial** *adj* фина́нсовый. **financier** *n* финанси́ст.

finch *n see comb, e.g.* bullfinch

find *n* нахо́дка; *vt* находи́ть *impf*, найти́ *pf*; (*person*) застава́ть *impf*, заста́ть *pf*; ~ out узнава́ть *impf*, узна́ть *pf*; ~ fault with придира́ться *impf*, придра́ться *pf* к+*dat*. **finding**

n pl (*of inquiry*) вы́воды *m pl*.

fine[1] *n* (*penalty*) штраф; *vt* штрафова́ть *impf*, о~ *pf*.

fine[2] *adj* (*weather*) я́сный; (*excellent*) прекра́сный; (*delicate*) то́нкий; (*of sand etc.*) ме́лкий; ~ **arts** изобрази́тельные иску́сства *neut pl*; *adv* хорошо́. **finery** *n* наря́д. **finesse** *n* то́нкость.

finger *n* па́лец; ~**nail** но́готь; ~**print** отпеча́ток па́льца; ~**tip** ко́нчик па́льца; **have at** (**one's**) ~**s** знать *impf* как свои́ пять па́льцев; *vt* щу́пать *impf*, по~ *pf*.

finish *n* коне́ц; (*polish*) отде́лка; (*sport*) фи́ниш; *vt & i* конча́ть(ся) *impf*, ко́нчить(ся) *pf*; *vt* ока́нчивать *impf*, око́нчить *pf*.

finite *adj* коне́чный.

Finland *n* Финля́ндия. **Finn** *n* финн, фи́нка. **Finnish** *adj* фи́нский.

fir *n* ель, пи́хта.

fire *vt* (*bake*) обжига́ть *impf*, обже́чь *pf*; (*excite*) воспламеня́ть *impf*, воспламени́ть *pf*; (*gun*) стреля́ть *impf* из+*gen* (**at** в+*acc*, по+*dat*); (*dismiss*) увольня́ть *impf*, уво́лить *pf*; *n* ого́нь *m*; (*grate*) ками́н; (*conflagration*) пожа́р; (*bonfire*) костёр; (*fervour*) пыл; **be on** ~ горе́ть *impf*; **catch** ~ загора́ться *impf*, загоре́ться *pf*; **set** ~ **to, set on** ~ поджига́ть *impf*, подже́чь *pf*; ~**alarm** пожа́рная трево́га; ~**arm(s)** огнестре́льное ору́жие; ~ **brigade** пожа́рная кома́нда; ~**engine** пожа́рная маши́на; ~**escape** пожа́рная ле́стница; ~ **extinguisher** огнетуши́тель *m*; ~**guard** ками́нная решётка; ~**man** пожа́рный *sb*; ~ **place** ками́н; ~**side** ме́сто у ками́на; ~ **station** пожа́рное депо́ *neut indecl*; ~**wood** дрова́ (-в) *pl*; ~**work** фейерве́рк. **firing** *n* (*shooting*) стрельба́.

firm[1] *n* (*business*) фи́рма.

firm[2] *adj* твёрдый. **firmness** *n* твёрдость.

first *adj* пе́рвый; *n* пе́рвый *sb*; *adv* снерва́, снача́ла; (*for the* ~ *time*) впервы́е; **in the** ~ **place** во-пе́рвых; ~ **of all** пре́жде всего́; **at** ~ **sight** на пе́рвый взгляд; ~ **aid** пе́рвая по́мощь; ~**class** первокла́ссный; ~**hand** из пе́рвых рук; ~**rate** первокла́ссный.

fiscal *adj* фина́нсовый.

fish *n* ры́ба; *adj* ры́бный; *vi* лови́ть *impf* ры́бу; ~ **for** (*compliments etc.*) напра́шиваться *impf*, напроси́ться *pf* на+*acc*; ~ **out** выта́скивать *impf*, вы́таскать *pf*. **fisherman** *n* рыба́к. **fishery** *n* ры́бный про́мысел. **fishing** *n* ры́бная ло́вля; ~ **boat** рыболо́вное су́дно; ~ **line** леса́; ~ **rod** у́дочка. **fishmonger** *n* торго́вец ры́бой. **fishy** *adj* ры́бный; (*dubious*) подозри́тельный.

fissure *n* тре́щина.

fist *n* кула́к.

fit[1] *n*: **be a good** ~ хорошо́ сиде́ть *impf*; *adj* (*suitable*) подходя́щий, го́дный; (*healthy*) здоро́вый; *vt* (*be suitable*) годи́ться *impf* +*dat*, на+*acc*, для+*gen*; *vt & i* (*be the right size* (*for*)) подходи́ть *impf*, подойти́ *pf* (+*dat*); (*adjust*) прила́живать *impf*, прила́дить *pf* (**to** к+*dat*); (*be small enough for*) входи́ть *impf*, войти́ *pf* в+*acc*; ~ **out** снабжа́ть *impf*, снабди́ть *pf*.

fit[2] *n* (*attack*) припа́док; (*fig*) поры́в. **fitful** *adj* поры́вистый.

fitter *n* монтёр. **fitting** *n* (*of clothes*) приме́рка; *pl* армату́ра; *adj* подходя́щий.

five *adj & n* пять; (*number 5*) пятёрка; ~**year plan** пятиле́тка.

fix *n* (*dilemma*) переде́лка; (*drugs*) уко́л; *vt* (*repair*) чини́ть *impf*, по~ *pf*; (*settle*) назнача́ть *impf*, назна́чить *pf*; (*fasten*) укрепля́ть *impf*, укрепи́ть *pf*; ~ **up** (*organize*) организова́ть *impf & pf*; (*install*) устана́вливать *impf*, установи́ть *pf*. **fixation** *n* фикса́ция. **fixed** *adj* устано́вленный. **fixture** *n* (*sport*) предсто́ящее спорти́вное мероприя́тие; (*fitting*) приспособле́ние.

fizz, fizzle *vi* шипе́ть *impf*; **fizzle out** выдыха́ться *impf*, вы́дохнуться *pf*. **fizzy** *adj* шипу́чий.

flabbergasted *adj* ошеломлённый.

flabby *adj* дря́блый.

flag[1] *n* флаг, зна́мя *neut*; *vt*: ~ **down** остана́вливать *impf*, останови́ть *pf*.

flag[2] *vi* (*weaken*) ослабева́ть *impf*, ослабе́ть *pf*.

flagon *n* кувши́н.

flagrant *adj* вопию́щий.

flagship *n* фла́гман.

flagstone *n* плита́.

flair *n* чутьё.

flake *n* слой; *pl* хло́пья (-ьев) *pl*; *vi* шелуши́ться *impf*. **flaky** *adj* слои́стый.

flamboyant *adj* цвети́стый.

flame *n* пла́мя *neut*, ого́нь *m*; *vi* пыла́ть *impf*.

flange *n* фла́нец.

flank *n* (*of body*) бок; (*mil*) фланг; *vt* быть сбо́ку +*gen*.

flannel *n* флане́ль; (*for face*) моча́лка для лица́.

flap *n* (*board*) откидна́я доска́; (*pocket, tent* ~) кла́пан; (*panic*) па́ника; *vt* взма́хивать *impf*, взмахну́ть *pf* +*instr*; *vi* развева́ться *impf*.

flare *n* вспы́шка; (*signal*) сигна́льная раке́та; *vi* вспы́хивать *impf*, вспы́хнуть *pf*; ~ **up** (*fire*) возгора́ться *impf*, возгоре́ться *pf*; (*fig*) вспыли́ть *pf*.

flash *n* вспы́шка; in a ~ ми́гом; *vi* сверка́ть *impf*, сверкну́ть *pf*. **flash-back** *n* ретроспе́кция. **flashy** *adj* показно́й.

flask *n* фля́жка.

flat¹ *n* (*dwelling*) кварти́ра.

flat² *n* (*mus*) бемо́ль *m*; (*tyre*) спу́щенная ши́на; on the ~ на пло́скости; *adj* пло́ский; ~**-fish** ка́мбала. **flatly** *adv* наотре́з. **flatten** *vt & i* выра́внивать(ся) *impf*, вы́ровнять(ся) *pf*.

flatmate *n* сосе́д, ~ка по кварти́ре.

flatter *vt* льстить *impf*, по~ *pf* +*dat*. **flattering** *adj* льсти́вый. **flattery** *n* лесть.

flaunt *vt* щеголя́ть *impf*, щегольну́ть *pf* +*instr*.

flautist *n* флейти́ст.

flavour *n* вкус; (*fig*) при́вкус; *vt* приправля́ть *impf*, припра́вить *pf*.

flaw *n* изъя́н.

flax *n* лён. **flaxen** *adj* (*colour*) соло́менный.

flea *n* блоха́; ~ market барахо́лка.

fleck *n* кра́пинка.

flee *vi* бежа́ть *impf & pf* (from от+*gen*); *vt* бежа́ть *impf & pf* +*gen*.

fleece *n* руно́; *vt* (*fig*) обдира́ть *impf*, ободра́ть *pf*. **fleecy** *adj* шерсти́стый.

fleet *n* флот; (*vehicles*) парк.

fleeting *adj* мимолётный.

flesh *n* (*as opposed to mind*) плоть; (*meat*) мя́со; in the ~ во плоти́. **fleshy** *adj* мяси́стый.

flex *n* шнур; *vt* сгиба́ть *impf*, согну́ть *pf*. **flexibility** *adj* ги́бкость. **flexible** *adj* ги́бкий.

flick *vt & i* щёлкать *impf*, щёлкнуть *pf* (+*instr*); ~ **through** пролиста́ть *pf*.

flicker *n* мерца́ние; *vi* мерца́ть *impf*.

flier *see* flyer

flight¹ *n* (*fleeing*) бе́гство; put (take) to ~ обраща́ть(ся) *impf*, обрати́ть(ся) *pf* в бе́гство.

flight² *n* (*flying*) полёт; (*trip*) рейс; ~ **of stairs** ле́стничный марш. **flighty** *adj* ве́треный.

flimsy *adj* (*fragile*) непро́чный; (*dress*) лёгкий; (*excuse*) сла́бый.

flinch *vi* (*recoil*) отпря́дывать *impf*, отпря́нуть *pf*; (*fig*) уклоня́ться *impf*, уклони́ться *pf* (from от+*gen*).

fling *vt* швыря́ть *impf*, швырну́ть *pf*; *vi* (*also* ~ *o.s.*) броса́ться *impf*, бро́ситься *pf*.

flint *n* креме́нь *m*.

flip *vt* щёлкать *impf*, щёлкнуть *pf* +*instr*.

flippant *adj* легкомы́сленный.

flipper *n* ласт.

flirt *n* коке́тка; *vi* флиртова́ть *impf* (with с+*instr*). **flirtation** *n* флирт.

flit *vi* порха́ть *impf*, порхну́ть *pf*.

float *n* поплаво́к; *vi* пла́вать *indet*, плыть *det*; *vt* (*company*) пуска́ть *impf*, пусти́ть *pf* в ход.

flock *n* (*animals*) ста́до; (*birds*) ста́я; *vi* стека́ться *impf*, сте́чься *pf*.

flog *vt* сечь *impf*, вы́~ *pf*.

flood *n* наводне́ние; (*bibl*) пото́п; (*fig*) пото́к; *vi* (*river etc.*) выступа́ть *impf*, вы́ступить *pf* из берего́в; *vt* затопля́ть *impf*, затопи́ть *pf*. **floodgate** *n* шлюз. **floodlight** *n* проже́ктор.

floor *n* пол; (*storey*) эта́ж; ~**board** полови́ца; *vt* (*confound*) ста́вить *impf*, по~ *pf* в тупи́к.

flop *vi* (*fall*) плю́хаться *impf*, плю́хнуться *pf*; (*fail*) прова́ливаться *impf*, провали́ться *pf*.

flora *n* фло́ра. **floral** *adj* цвето́чный.

florid *adj* цвети́стый; (*ruddy*) румя́ный. **florist** *n* торго́вец цвета́ми.

flounce¹ *vi* броса́ться *impf*, бро́ситься *pf*.

flounce² n (of skirt) оборка.
flounder¹ n (fish) камбала.
flounder² vi барахтаться impf.
flour n мука.
flourish n (movement) размахивание (+instr); (of pen) росчерк; vi (thrive) процветать impf; vt (wave) размахивать impf, размахнуть pf +instr.
flout vt попирать impf, попрать pf.
flow vi течь impf; литься impf; n течение.
flower n цветок; ~-bed клумба; ~pot цветочный горшок; vi цвести impf. **flowery** adj цветистый.
fluctuate vi колебаться impf, по~ pf. **fluctuation** n колебание.
flue n дымоход.
fluent adj беглый. **fluently** adv свободно.
fluff n пух. **fluffy** adj пушистый.
fluid n жидкость; adj жидкий.
fluke n случайная удача.
fluorescent adj флюоресцентный.
fluoride n фторид.
flurry n (squall) шквал; (fig) волна.
flush n (redness) румянец; vi (redden) краснеть impf, по~ pf; vt спускать impf, спустить pf воду в+acc.
flustered adj сконфуженный.
flute n флейта.
flutter vi (flit) порхать impf, порхнуть pf; (wave) развеваться impf. **flux** n: in a state of ~ в состоянии изменения.
fly¹ n (insect) муха.
fly² vi летать indet, лететь det, по~ pf; (flag) развеваться impf; (hasten) нестись impf, по~ pf; vt (aircraft) управлять impf +instr; (transport) перевозить impf, перевезти pf (самолётом); (flag) поднимать impf, поднять pf. **flyer, flier** n лётчик. **flying** n полёт.
foal n (horse) жеребёнок.
foam n пена; ~ plastic пенопласт; ~ rubber пенорезина; vi пениться impf, вс~ pf. **foamy** adj пенистый.
focal adj фокусный. **focus** n фокус; (fig) центр; vt фокусировать impf, с~ pf; (concentrate) сосредоточивать impf, сосредоточить pf.
fodder n корм.
foe n враг.
foetus n зародыш.
fog n туман. **foggy** adj туманный.

foible n слабость.
foil¹ n (metal) фольга; (contrast) контраст.
foil² vt (thwart) расстраивать impf, расстроить pf.
foil³ n (sword) рапира.
foist vt навязывать impf, навязать pf (on +dat).
fold¹ n (sheep-~) овчарня.
fold² n складка, сгиб; vt складывать impf, сложить pf. **folder** n папка. **folding** adj складной.
foliage n листва.
folk n народ, люди pl; pl (relatives) родня collect; attrib народный. **folklore** n фольклор.
follow vt следовать impf, по~ pf +dat; (walk behind) идти det за+instr; (fig) следить impf за+instr. **follower** n последователь m. **following** adj следующий.
folly n глупость.
fond adj нежный; be ~ of любить impf +acc.
fondle vt ласкать impf.
fondness n любовь.
font n (eccl) купель.
food n пища, еда. **foodstuff** n пищевой продукт.
fool n дурак; vt дурачить impf, о~ pf; vi: ~ about дурачиться impf. **foolhardy** adj безрассудно храбрый. **foolish** adj глупый. **foolishness** n глупость. **foolproof** adj абсолютно надёжный.
foot n нога; (measure) фут; (of hill etc.) подножие; on ~ пешком; put one's ~ in it сесть pf в лужу. **football** n футбол; attrib футбольный. **footballer** n футболист. **foothills** n pl предгорье. **footing** n (fig) базис; lose one's ~ оступиться pf; on an equal ~ на равной ноге. **footlights** n pl рампа. **footman** n лакей. **footnote** n сноска. **footpath** n тропинка; (pavement) тротуар. **footprint** n след. **footstep** n (sound) шаг; (footprint) след. **footwear** n обувь.
for prep (of time) в течение +gen, на +acc; (of purpose) для+gen, за+acc, +instr; (price) за+acc; (on account of) из-за+gen; (in place of) вместо+gen; ~ the sake of ради+gen; as ~ что касается+gen; conj так как.

forage *n* фура́ж; *vi*: ~ for разы́скивать *impf*.

foray *n* набе́г.

forbearance *n* возде́ржанность.

forbid *vt* запреща́ть *impf*, запрети́ть *pf* (+*dat* (*person*) & *acc* (*thing*)). **forbidding** *adj* гро́зный.

force *n* (*strength, validity*) си́ла; (*meaning*) смысл; *pl* (*armed* ~) вооружённые си́лы *f pl*; by ~ си́лой; *vt* (*compel*) заставля́ть *impf*, заста́вить *pf*; (*lock etc.*) взла́мывать *impf*, взлома́ть *pf*. **forceful** *adj* си́льный; (*speech*) убеди́тельный. **forcible** *adj* наси́льственный.

forceps *n* щипцы́ (-цо́в) *pl*.

ford *n* брод; *vt* переходи́ть *impf*, перейти́ *pf* вброд+*acc*.

fore *n*: come to the ~ выдвига́ться *impf*, вы́двинуться *pf* на пере́дний план.

forearm *n* предпле́чье. **foreboding** *n* предчу́вствие. **forecast** *n* предсказа́ние; (*of weather*) прогно́з; *vt* предска́зывать *impf*, предсказа́ть *pf*. **forecourt** *n* пере́дний двор. **forefather** *n* пре́док. **forefinger** *n* указа́тельный па́лец. **forefront** *n* (*foreground*) пере́дний план; (*leading position*) аванга́рд. **foregone** *adj*: ~ conclusion предрешённый исхо́д. **foreground** *n* пере́дний план. **forehead** *n* лоб.

foreign *adj* (*from abroad*) иностра́нный; (*alien*) чу́ждый; (*external*) вне́шний; ~ body иноро́дное те́ло; ~ currency валю́та. **foreigner** *n* иностра́нец, -нка. **foreman** *n* ма́стер.

foremost *adj* выдаю́щийся; first and ~ пре́жде всего́.

forename *n* и́мя.

forensic *adj* суде́бный.

forerunner *n* предве́стник. **foresee** *vt* предви́деть *impf*. **foreshadow** *vt* предвеща́ть *impf*. **foresight** *n* предви́дение; (*caution*) предусмотри́тельность.

forest *n* лес.

forestall *vt* предупрежда́ть *impf*, предупреди́ть *pf*.

forester *n* лесни́чий *sb*. **forestry** *n* лесово́дство.

foretaste *n* предвкуше́ние; *vt* предвкуша́ть *impf*, предвкуси́ть *pf*. **fore-**

tell *vt* предска́зывать *impf*, предсказа́ть *pf*. **forethought** *n* предусмотри́тельность. **forewarn** *vt* предостерега́ть *impf*, предостере́чь *pf*. **foreword** *n* предисло́вие.

forfeit *n* (*in game*) фант; *vt* лиша́ться *impf*, лиши́ться *pf* +*gen*.

forge[1] *n* (*smithy*) ку́зница; (*furnace*) горн; *vt* кова́ть *impf*, вы́~ *pf*; (*fabricate*) подде́лывать *impf*, подде́лать *pf*.

forge[2] *vi*: ~ ahead продвига́ться *impf*, продви́нуться *pf* вперёд.

forger *n* фальшивомоне́тчик. **forgery** *n* подде́лка.

forget *vt* забыва́ть *impf*, забы́ть *pf*. **forgetful** *adj* забы́вчивый.

forgive *vt* проща́ть *impf*, прости́ть *pf*. **forgiveness** *n* проще́ние.

forgo *vt* возде́рживаться *impf*, воздержа́ться *pf* от+*gen*.

fork *n* (*eating*) ви́лка; (*digging*) ви́лы (-л) *pl*; (*in road*) разветвле́ние; *vi* (*road*) разветвля́ться *impf*, разветви́ться *pf*.

forlorn *adj* жа́лкий.

form *n* (*shape, kind*) фо́рма; (*class*) класс; (*document*) анке́та; *vt* (*make, create*) образо́вывать *impf*, образова́ть *pf*; (*develop; make up*) составля́ть *impf*, соста́вить *pf*; *vi* образо́вываться *impf*, образова́ться *pf*. **formal** *adj* форма́льный; (*official*) официа́льный. **formality** *n* форма́льность. **format** *n* форма́т. **formation** *n* образова́ние. **formative** *adj*: ~ years молоды́е го́ды (-до́в) *m pl*.

former *adj* (*earlier*) пре́жний; (*ex*) бы́вший; the ~ (*of two*) пе́рвый. **formerly** *adv* пре́жде.

formidable *adj* (*dread*) гро́зный; (*arduous*) тру́дный.

formless *adj* бесфо́рменный.

formula *n* фо́рмула. **formulate** *vt* формули́ровать *impf*, с~ *pf*. **formulation** *n* формулиро́вка.

forsake *vt* (*desert*) покида́ть *impf*, поки́нуть *pf*; (*renounce*) отка́зываться *impf*, отказа́ться *pf* от+*gen*.

fort *n* форт.

forth *adv* вперёд, да́льше; back and ~ взад и вперёд; and so ~ и так да́лее. **forthcoming** *adj* предстоя́щий; be ~ (*available*) поступа́ть

impf, поступи́ть *pf*. **forthwith** *adv*
неме́дленно.

fortieth *adj & n* сороково́й.

fortification *n* укрепле́ние. **fortify** *vt*
укрепля́ть *impf*, укрепи́ть *pf*; (*fig*)
подкрепля́ть *impf*, подкрепи́ть *pf*.
fortitude *n* сто́йкость.

fortnight *n* две неде́ли *f pl*. **fort-
nightly** *adj* двухнеде́льный; *adv* раз
в две неде́ли.

fortress *n* кре́пость.

fortuitous *adj* случа́йный.

fortunate *adj* счастли́вый. **fortu-
nately** *adv* к сча́стью. **fortune** *n*
(*destiny*) судьба́; (*good* ~) сча́стье;
(*wealth*) состоя́ние.

forty *adj & n* со́рок; *pl* (*decade*) соро-
кове́ го́ды (-до́в) *m pl*.

forward *adj* пере́дний; (*presumptuous*) развя́зный; *n* (*sport*) напада́-
ющий *sb*; *adv* вперёд; *vt* (*letter*)
пересыла́ть *impf*, пересла́ть *pf*.

fossil *n* ископа́емое *sb*; *adj* ископа́-
емый. **fossilized** *adj* ископа́емый.

foster *vt* (*child*) приюти́ть *pf*; (*idea*)
вына́шивать *impf*, вы́носить *pf*;
(*create*) создава́ть *impf*, созда́ть *pf*;
(*cherish*) леле́ять *impf*; ~-**child** при-
ёмыш.

foul *adj* (*dirty*) гря́зный; (*repulsive*)
отврати́тельный; (*obscene*) непри-
сто́йный; *n* (*sport*) наруше́ние
пра́вил; *vt* (*dirty*) па́чкать *impf*,
за~, ис~ *pf*; (*entangle*) запу́тывать
impf, запу́тать *pf*.

found *vt* осно́вывать *impf*, основа́ть
pf.

foundation *n* (*of building*) фунда́-
мент; (*basis*) осно́ва; (*institution*)
учрежде́ние; (*fund*) фонд. **founder**[1]
n основа́тель *m*.

founder[2] *vi* (*naut*, *fig*) тону́ть *impf*,
по~ *pf*.

foundry *n* лите́йная *sb*.

fountain *n* фонта́н; ~-**pen** авторуч-
ка.

four *adj & n* четы́ре; (*number 4*)
четвёрка; **on all** ~**s** на четвере́нь-
ках. **fourteen** *adj & n* четы́рнад-
цать. **fourteenth** *adj & n* четы́р-
надцатый. **fourth** *adj & n* четвёр-
тый; (*quarter*) че́тверть.

fowl *n* (*domestic*) дома́шняя пти́ца;
(*wild*) дичь *collect*.

fox *n* лиса́, лиси́ца; *vt* озада́чивать

impf, озада́чить *pf*.

foyer *n* фойе́ *neut indecl*.

fraction *n* (*math*) дробь; (*portion*) ча-
сти́ца.

fractious *adj* раздражи́тельный.

fracture *n* перело́м; *vt & i* лома́ть-
(ся) *impf*, с~ *pf*.

fragile *adj* ло́мкий.

fragment *n* обло́мок; (*of conversation*) отры́вок; (*of writing*) фрагме́нт.
fragmentary *adj* отры́вочный.

fragrance *n* арома́т. **fragrant** *adj*
арома́тный, души́стый.

frail *adj* хру́пкий.

frame *n* о́стов; (*build*) телосло-
же́ние; (*picture*) ра́ма; (*cin*) кадр; ~
of mind настро́ение; *vt* (*devise*)
создава́ть *impf*, созда́ть *pf*; (*formulate*) формули́ровать *impf*, с~ *pf*;
(*picture*) вставля́ть *impf*, вста́вить
pf в ра́му; (*incriminate*) фабрико-
ва́ть *impf*, с~ *pf* обвине́ние про́-
тив+*gen*. **framework** *n* о́стов; (*fig*)
ра́мки *f pl*.

franc *n* франк.

France *n* Фра́нция.

franchise *n* (*comm*) привиле́гия;
(*polit*) пра́во го́лоса.

frank[1] *adj* открове́нный.

frank[2] *vt* (*letter*) франки́ровать *impf*
& *pf*.

frantic *adj* неи́стовый.

fraternal *adj* бра́тский. **fraternity** *n*
бра́тство.

fraud *n* обма́н; (*person*) обма́нщик.
fraudulent *adj* обма́нный.

fraught *adj*: ~ **with** чрева́тый +*instr*.

fray[1] *vt & i* обтрёпывать(ся) *impf*,
обтрепа́ть(ся) *pf*.

fray[2] *n* бой.

freak *n* уро́д; *attrib* необы́чный.

freckle *n* весну́шка. **freckled** *adj*
весну́шчатый.

free *adj* свобо́дный; (*gratis*) бес-
пла́тный; ~ **kick** штрафно́й уда́р;
~ **speech** свобо́да сло́ва; *vt* осво-
божда́ть *impf*, освободи́ть *pf*. **freedom** *n* свобо́да. **freehold** *n* неогра-
ни́ченное пра́во со́бственности на
недви́жимость. **freelance** *adj* вне-
шта́тный. **Freemason** *n* франкма-
со́н.

freeze *vi* замерза́ть *impf*, мёрзнуть
impf, замёрзнуть *pf*; *vt* заморо́жи-
вать *impf*, заморо́зить *pf*. **freezer** *n*

морозильник; (*compartment*) морозилка. **freezing** *adj* морозный; **below** ~ ниже нуля.

freight *n* фрахт. **freighter** *n* (*ship*) грузовое судно.

French *adj* французский; ~ **bean** фасоль; ~ **horn** валторна; ~ **windows** двустворчатое окно до пола. **Frenchman** *n* француз. **Frenchwoman** *n* француженка.

frenetic *adj* неистовый.

frenzied *adj* неистовый. **frenzy** *n* неистовство.

frequency *n* частота. **frequent** *adj* частый; *vt* часто посещать *impf*.

fresco *n* фреска.

fresh *adj* свежий; (*new*) новый; ~ **water** пресная вода. **freshen** *vt* освежать *impf*, освежить *pf*; *vi* свежеть *impf*, по~ *pf*. **freshly** *adv* свежо; (*recently*) недавно. **freshness** *n* свежесть. **freshwater** *adj* пресноводный.

fret¹ *vi* мучиться *impf*. **fretful** *adj* раздражительный.

fret² *n* (*mus*) лад.

fretsaw *n* лобзик.

friar *n* монах.

friction *n* трение; (*fig*) трения *neut pl*.

Friday *n* пятница.

fridge *n* холодильник.

fried *adj*: ~ **egg** яичница.

friend *n* друг, подруга; приятель *m*, ~ница. **friendly** *adj* дружеский. **friendship** *n* дружба.

frieze *n* фриз.

frigate *n* фрегат.

fright *n* испуг. **frighten** *vt* пугать *impf*, ис~, на~ *pf*. **frightful** *adj* страшный.

frigid *adj* холодный.

frill *n* оборка.

fringe *n* бахрома; (*of hair*) чёлка; (*edge*) край.

frisk *vi* (*frolic*) резвиться *impf*; *vt* (*search*) шмонать *impf*. **frisky** *adj* резвый.

fritter *vt*: ~ **away** растрачивать *impf*, растратить *pf*.

frivolity *n* легкомысленность. **frivolous** *adj* легкомысленный.

fro *adv*: **to** and ~ взад и вперёд.

frock *n* платье.

frog *n* лягушка.

frolic *vi* резвиться *impf*.

from *prep* от+gen; (~ *off, down* ~; *in time*) с+gen; (*out of*) из+gen; (*according to*) по+dat; (*because of*) из-за+gen; ~ **above** сверху; ~ **abroad** из-за границы; ~ **afar** издали; ~ **among** из числа+gen; ~ **behind** из-за+gen; ~ **day to day** изо дня в день; ~ **everywhere** отовсюду; ~ **here** отсюда; ~ **memory** по памяти; ~ **now on** отныне; ~ **there** оттуда; ~ **time to time** время от времени; ~ **under** из-под+gen.

front *n* фасад, передняя сторона; (*mil*) фронт; **in** ~ **of** впереди+gen, перед+instr; *adj* передний; (*first*) первый.

frontier *n* граница.

frost *n* мороз; ~**-bite** отморожение; ~**-bitten** отмороженный. **frosted** *adj*: ~ **glass** матовое стекло. **frosty** *adj* морозный; (*fig*) ледяной.

froth *n* пена; *vi* пениться *impf*, вс~ *pf*. **frothy** *adj* пенистый.

frown *n* хмурый взгляд; *vi* хмуриться *impf*, на~ *pf*.

frugal *adj* (*careful*) бережливый; (*scanty*) скудный.

fruit *n* плод; *collect* фрукты *m pl*; *adj* фруктовый. **fruitful** *adj* плодотворный. **fruition** *n*: **come to** ~ осуществиться *pf*. **fruitless** *adj* бесплодный.

frustrate *vt* фрустрировать *impf* & *pf*. **frustrating** *adj* фрустрирующий. **frustration** *n* фрустрация.

fry¹ *n*: **small** ~ мелюзга.

fry² *vt* & *i* жарить(ся) *impf*, за~, из~ *pf*. **frying-pan** *n* сковорода.

fuel *n* топливо.

fugitive *n* беглец.

fulcrum *n* точка опоры.

fulfil *vt* (*perform*) выполнять *impf*, выполнить *pf*; (*dreams*) осуществлять *impf*, осуществить *pf*. **fulfilling** *adj* удовлетворяющий. **fulfilment** *n* выполнение; осуществление; удовлетворение.

full *adj* полный (of +gen, instr); (*replete*) сытый; ~ **stop** точка; ~ **time**: **I work** ~ **time** я работаю на полную ставку; *n*: **in** ~ полностью; **to the** ~ в полной мере. **fullness** *n* полнота. **fully** *adv* вполне.

fulsome *adj* чрезмерный.

fumble *vi*: ~ for нащу́пывать *impf* +*acc*; ~ with вози́ться *impf* c+*instr*.

fume *vi* (*with anger*) кипе́ть *impf*, вс~ *pf* гне́вом. fumes *n pl* испаре́ния *neut pl*. fumigate *vt* окури́вать *impf*, окури́ть *pf*.

fun *n* заба́ва; it was ~ бы́ло заба́вно; have ~ забавля́ться *impf*; make ~ of смея́ться *impf*, по~ *pf* над+*instr*.

function *n* фу́нкция; (*event*) ве́чер; *vi* функциони́ровать *impf*; де́йствовать *impf*. functional *adj* функциона́льный. functionary *n* чино́вник.

fund *n* фонд; (*store*) запа́с.

fundamental *adj* основно́й; *n*: *pl* осно́вы *f pl*.

funeral *n* по́хороны (-о́н, -она́м) *pl*.

fungus *n* гриб.

funnel *n* воро́нка; (*chimney*) дымова́я труба́.

funny *adj* смешно́й; (*odd*) стра́нный.

fur *n* мех; ~ coat шу́ба.

furious *adj* бе́шеный.

furnace *n* горн, печь.

furnish *vt* (*provide*) снабжа́ть *impf*, снабди́ть *pf* (with c+*instr*); (*house*) обставля́ть *impf*, обста́вить *pf*. furniture *n* ме́бель.

furrow *n* борозда́.

furry *adj* пуши́стый.

further, farther *comp adj* дальне́йший; *adv* да́льше; *vt* продвига́ть *impf*, продви́нуть *pf*. furthermore *adv* к тому́ же. furthest, farthest *superl adj* са́мый да́льний.

furtive *adj* скры́тый, та́йный.

fury *n* я́рость.

fuse[1] *vt* & *i* (*of metal*) сплавля́ть(ся) *impf*, спла́вить(ся) *pf*.

fuse[2] *n* (*in bomb*) запа́л; (*detonating device*) взрыва́тель *m*.

fuse[3] *n* (*electr*) про́бка; *vi* перегора́ть *impf*, перегоре́ть *pf*.

fuselage *n* фюзеля́ж.

fusion *n* пла́вка, слия́ние.

fuss *n* суета́; *vi* суети́ться *impf*. fussy *adj* суетли́вый; (*fastidious*) разбо́рчивый.

futile *adj* тще́тный. futility *n* тще́тность.

future *n* бу́дущее *sb*; (*gram*) бу́дущее вре́мя *neut*; *adj* бу́дущий. futuristic *adj* футури́стический.

fuzzy *adj* (*hair*) пуши́стый; (*blurred*) расплы́вчатый.

G

gabble *vi* тарато́рить *impf*.

gable *n* щипе́ц.

gad *vi*: ~ about шата́ться *impf*.

gadget *n* приспособле́ние.

gaffe *n* опло́шность.

gag *n* кляп; *vt* засо́вывать *impf*, засу́нуть *pf* кляп в рот+*dat*.

gaiety *n* весёлость. gaily *adv* ве́село.

gain *n* при́быль; *pl* дохо́ды *m pl*; (*increase*) приро́ст; *vt* (*acquire*) получа́ть *impf*, получи́ть *pf*; ~ on нагоня́ть *impf*, нагна́ть *pf*.

gait *n* похо́дка.

gala *n* пра́зднество; *adj* пра́здничный.

galaxy *n* гала́ктика; (*fig*) плея́да.

gale *n* бу́ря, шторм.

gall[1] *n* (*bile*) жёлчь; (*cheek*) на́глость; ~-bladder жёлчный пузы́рь *m*.

gall[2] *vt* (*vex*) раздража́ть *impf*, раздражи́ть *pf*.

gallant *adj* (*brave*) хра́брый; (*courtly*) гала́нтный. gallantry *n* хра́брость; гала́нтность.

gallery *n* галере́я.

galley *n* (*ship*) гале́ра; (*kitchen*) ка́мбуз.

gallon *n* галло́н.

gallop *n* гало́п; *vi* галопи́ровать *impf*.

gallows *n pl* ви́селица.

gallstone *n* жёлчный ка́мень *m*.

galore *adv* в изоби́лии.

galvanize *vt* гальванизи́ровать *impf* & *pf*.

gambit *n* гамби́т.

gamble *n* (*undertaking*) риско́ванное предприя́тие; *vi* игра́ть *impf* в аза́ртные и́гры; (*fig*) рискова́ть *impf* (with +*instr*); ~ away прои́грывать *impf*, проигра́ть *pf*. gambler *n* игро́к. gambling *n* аза́ртные и́гры *f pl*.

game *n* игра́; (*single* ~) па́ртия; (*collect, animals*) дичь; *adj* (*ready*) гото́вый. gamekeeper *n* лесни́к.

gammon *n* о́корок.

gamut *n* га́мма.

gang *n* ба́нда; (*workmen*) брига́да.

gangrene *n* гангре́на.

gangster *n* га́нгстер.

gangway *n* (*passage*) прохо́д; (*naut*) схо́дни (-ней) *pl*.

gaol n тюрьма; vt заключать impf, заключить pf в тюрьму. **gaoler** n тюремщик.

gap n (empty space; deficiency) пробел; (in wall etc.) брешь; (fig) разрыв.

gape vi (person) зевать impf (at на +acc); (chasm) зиять impf.

garage n гараж.

garb n одеяние.

garbage n мусор.

garbled adj искажённый.

garden n сад; attrib садовый. **gardener** n садовник. **gardening** n садоводство.

gargle vi полоскать impf, про~ pf горло.

gargoyle n горгулья.

garish adj кричащий.

garland n гирлянда.

garlic n чеснок.

garment n предмет одежды.

garnish n гарнир; vt гарнировать impf & pf.

garret n мансарда.

garrison n гарнизон.

garrulous adj болтливый.

gas n газ; attrib газовый; vt отравлять impf, отравить pf газом. **gaseous** adj газообразный.

gash n порез; vt порезать pf.

gasket n прокладка.

gasp vi задыхаться impf, задохнуться pf.

gastric adj желудочный.

gate n (large) ворота (-т) pl; (small) калитка. **gateway** n (gate) ворота (-т) pl; (entrance) вход.

gather vt & i собирать(ся) impf, собрать(ся) pf; vt заключать impf, заключить pf. **gathering** n (assembly) собрание.

gaudy adj кричащий.

gauge n (measure) мера; (instrument) калибр, измерительный прибор; (rly) колея; (criterion) критерий; vt измерять impf, измерить pf; (estimate) оценивать impf, оценить pf.

gaunt adj тощий.

gauntlet n рукавица.

gauze n марля.

gay adj весёлый; (bright) пёстрый; (homosexual) гомосексуальный.

gaze n пристальный взгляд; vi пристально глядеть impf (at на+acc).

gazelle n газель.

GCSE abbr (of General Certificate of Secondary Education) аттестат о среднем образовании.

gear n (equipment) принадлежности f pl; (in car) скорость; ~ lever рычаг; vt приспособлять impf, приспособить pf (to к+dat). **gearbox** n коробка передач.

gel n косметическое желе neut indecl. **gelatine** n желатин.

gelding n мерин.

gelignite n гелигнит.

gem n драгоценный камень m.

Gemini n Близнецы m pl.

gender n род.

gene n ген.

genealogy n генеалогия.

general n генерал; adj общий; (nationwide) всеобщий; in ~ вообще. **generalization** n обобщение. **generalize** vi обобщать impf, обобщить pf. **generally** adv (usually) обычно; (in general) вообще.

generate vt порождать impf, породить pf. **generation** n (in descent) поколение. **generator** n генератор.

generic adj родовой; (general) общий.

generosity n (magnanimity) великодушие; (munificence) щедрость. **generous** adj великодушный; щедрый.

genesis n происхождение; (G~) Книга Бытия.

genetic adj генетический. **genetics** n генетика.

genial adj (of person) добродушный.

genital adj половой. **genitals** n pl половые органы m pl.

genitive adj (n) родительный (падеж).

genius n (person) гений; (ability) гениальность.

genocide n геноцид.

genre n жанр.

genteel adj благовоспитанный.

gentile adj нееврейский; n нееврей, ~ка.

gentility n благовоспитанность.

gentle adj (mild) мягкий; (quiet) тихий; (light) лёгкий. **gentleman** n джентльмен. **gentleness** n мягкость. **gents** n pl мужская уборная sb.

genuine adj (authentic) подлинный;

(*sincere*) и́скренний.

genus *n* род.

geographical *adj* географи́ческий. geography *n* геогра́фия. geological *adj* геологи́ческий. geologist *n* гео́лог. geology *n* геоло́гия. geometric(al) *adj* геометри́ческий. geometry *n* геоме́трия.

Georgia *n* Гру́зия. Georgian *n* грузи́н, ~ка; *adj* грузи́нский.

geranium *n* гера́нь.

geriatric *adj* гериатри́ческий.

germ *m* микро́б.

German *n* не́мец, не́мка; *adj* неме́цкий; ~ measles красну́ха.

germane *adj* уме́стный.

Germanic *adj* герма́нский.

Germany *n* Герма́ния.

germinate *vi* прораста́ть *impf*, прорасти́ *pf*.

gesticulate *vi* жестикули́ровать *impf*. gesture *n* жест.

get *vt* (*obtain*) достава́ть *impf*, доста́ть *pf*; (*receive*) получа́ть *impf*, получи́ть *pf*; (*understand*) понима́ть *impf*, поня́ть *pf*; (*disease*) зара-жа́ться *impf*, зарази́ться *pf* +*instr*; (*induce*) угова́ривать *impf*, уговори́ть *pf* (*to do* +*inf*); (*fetch*) приноси́ть *impf*, принести́ *pf*; *vi* (*become*) станови́ться *impf*, стать *pf* +*instr*; have got (*have*) име́ть *impf*; have got to быть до́лжен (-жна́) +*inf*; ~ about (*spread*) распро-страня́ться *impf*, распространи́ться *pf*; (*move around*) передвига́ться *impf*; (*travel*) разъезжа́ть *impf*; ~ at (*mean*) хоте́ть *impf* сказа́ть; ~ away (*slip off*) ускольза́ть *impf*, ускользну́ть *pf*; (*escape*) убега́ть *impf*, убежа́ть *pf*; (*leave*) уезжа́ть *impf*, уе́хать *pf*; ~ away with *vi* избега́ть *impf*, избежа́ть *pf* отве́т-ственности за+*acc*; ~ back (*recover*) получа́ть *impf*, получи́ть *pf* обра́т-но; (*return*) возвраща́ться *impf*, верну́ться *pf*; ~ by (*manage*) справля́ться *impf*, спра́виться *pf*; ~ down сходи́ть *impf*, сойти́ *pf*; ~ down to принима́ться *impf*, при-ня́ться *pf* за+*acc*; ~ off слеза́ть *impf*, слезть *pf* с+*gen*; ~ on са-ди́ться *impf*, сесть *pf* в, на, +*acc*; (*prosper*) преуспева́ть *impf*, пре-успе́ть *pf*; ~ on with (*person*) ужи-

ва́ться *impf*, ужи́ться *pf* с+*instr*; ~ out of (*avoid*) избавля́ться *impf*, изба́виться *pf* от+*gen*; (*car*) выхо-ди́ть *impf*, вы́йти *pf* из+*gen*; ~ round to успева́ть *impf*, успе́ть *pf*; ~ to (*reach*) достига́ть *impf*, до-сти́гнуть & дости́чь *pf* +*gen*; ~ up (*from bed*) встава́ть *impf*, встать *pf*.

geyser *n* (*spring*) ге́йзер; (*water-heater*) коло́нка.

ghastly *adj* ужа́сный.

gherkin *n* огуре́ц.

ghetto *n* ге́тто *neut indecl*.

ghost *n* привиде́ние. ghostly *adj* при́зрачный.

giant *n* гига́нт; *adj* гига́нтский.

gibberish *n* тараба́рщина.

gibbet *n* ви́селица.

gibe *n* насме́шка; *vi* насмеха́ться *impf* (at над+*instr*).

giblets *n pl* потроха́ (-хо́в) *pl*.

giddiness *n* головокруже́ние. giddy *predic*: I feel ~ у меня́ кру́жится голова́.

gift *n* (*present*) пода́рок; (*donation*; *ability*) дар. gifted *adj* одарённый.

gig *n* (*theat*) выступле́ние.

gigantic *adj* гига́нтский.

giggle *n* хихи́канье; *vi* хихи́кать *impf*, хихи́кнуть *pf*.

gild *vt* золоти́ть *impf*, вы́~, по~ *pf*.

gill *n* (*of fish*) жа́бра.

gilt *n* позоло́та; *adj* золочённый.

gimmick *n* трюк.

gin *n* (*spirit*) джин.

ginger *n* имби́рь *m*; *adj* (*colour*) ры́-жий.

gingerly *adv* осторо́жно.

gipsy *n* цыга́н, ~ка.

giraffe *n* жира́ф.

girder *n* ба́лка. girdle *n* по́яс.

girl *n* (*child*) де́вочка; (*young woman*) де́вушка. girlfriend *n* подру́га. girlish *adj* де́вичий.

girth *n* обхва́т; (*on saddle*) подпру́га.

gist *n* суть.

give *vt* дава́ть *impf*, дать *pf*; ~ away выдава́ть *impf*, вы́дать *pf*; ~ back возвраща́ть *impf*, возврати́ть *pf*; ~ in (*yield*, *vi*) уступа́ть *impf*, усту-пи́ть *pf* (to +*dat*); (*hand in*, *vt*) вру-ча́ть *impf*, вручи́ть *pf*; ~ out (*emit*) издава́ть *impf*, изда́ть *pf*; (*distrib-ute*) раздава́ть *impf*, разда́ть *pf*; ~ up отка́зываться *impf*, отказа́ться *pf* от+*gen*; (*habit etc.*) броса́ть *impf*, бро́сить *pf*; ~ o.s. up сдава́ться *impf*, сда́ться *pf*. given *predic* (*inclined*) скло́нен (-онна́, -о́нно) (to к+*dat*).

glacier *n* ледни́к.

glad *adj* ра́достный; *predic* рад. gladden *vt* ра́довать *impf*, об~ *pf*.

glade *n* поля́на.

gladly *adv* охо́тно.

glamorous *adj* я́ркий; (*attractive*) привлека́тельный.

glamour *n* я́ркость; привлека́тельность.

glance *n* (*look*) бе́глый взгляд; *vi*: ~ at взгля́дывать *impf*, взгляну́ть *pf* на+*acc*.

gland *n* железа́. glandular *adj* желе́зистый.

glare *n* (*light*) ослепи́тельный блеск; (*look*) свире́пый взгляд; *vi* свире́по смотре́ть *impf* (at на+*acc*). glaring *adj* (*dazzling*) ослепи́тельный; (*mistake*) грубый.

glasnost *n* гла́сность.

glass *n* (*substance*) стекло́; (*drinking vessel*) стака́н; (*wine* ~) рю́мка; (*mirror*) зе́ркало; *pl* (*spectacles*) очки́ (-ко́в) *pl*; *attrib* стекля́нный. glassy *adj* (*look*) ту́склый.

glaze *vt* глазу́рь; *vt* (*with glass*) застекля́ть *impf*, застекли́ть *pf*; (*pottery*) глазурова́ть *impf* & *pf*; (*cul*) глази́ровать *impf* & *pf*. glazier *n* стеко́льщик.

gleam *n* про́блеск; *vi* свети́ться *impf*.

glean *vt* собира́ть *impf*, собра́ть *pf* по крупи́цам.

glee *n* весе́лье. gleeful *adj* лику́ющий.

glib *adj* бо́йкий.

glide *vi* скользи́ть *impf*; (*aeron*) плани́ровать *impf*, с~ *pf*. glider *n* планёр.

glimmer *n* мерца́ние; *vi* мерца́ть *impf*.

glimpse *vt* мелько́м ви́деть *impf*, у~ *pf*.

glint *n* блеск; *vi* блесте́ть *impf*.

glisten, glitter *vi* блесте́ть *impf*.

gloat *vi* злора́дствовать *impf*.

global *adj* (*world-wide*) мирово́й; (*total*) всео́бщий. globe *n* (*sphere*) шар; (*the earth*) земно́й шар; (*chart*) гло́бус. globule *n* ша́рик.

gloom *n* мрак. gloomy *adj* мра́чный.

glorify *vt* прославля́ть *impf*, просла́вить *pf*. glorious *adj* сла́вный; (*splendid*) великоле́пный. glory *n* сла́ва; *vi* торжествова́ть *impf*.

gloss *n* лоск; *vi*: ~ over зама́зывать *impf*, зама́зать *pf*.

glossary *n* глосса́рий.

glove *n* перча́тка.

glow *n* за́рево; (*of cheeks*) румя́нец; *vi* (*incandesce*) накаля́ться *impf*, накали́ться *pf*; (*shine*) сия́ть *impf*.

glucose *n* глюко́за.

glue *n* клей; *vt* прикле́ивать *impf*, прикле́ить *pf* (to к+*dat*).

glum *adj* угрю́мый.

glut *n* избы́ток.

glutton *n* обжо́ра *m* & *f*. gluttonous *adj* обжо́рливый. gluttony *n* обжо́рство.

gnarled *adj* (*hands*) шишкова́тый; (*tree*) сучкова́тый.

gnash *vt* скрежета́ть *impf* +*instr*.

gnat *n* кома́р.

gnaw *vt* грызть *impf*.

gnome *n* гном.

go *n* (*energy*) эне́ргия; (*attempt*) попы́тка; be on the ~ быть в движе́нии; have a ~ пыта́ться *impf*, по~ *pf*; *vi* (on foot) ходи́ть *impf*, идти́ *det*, пойти́ *pf*; (*by transport*) е́здить *indet*, е́хать *det*, по~ *pf*; (*work*) рабо́тать *impf*; (*become*) станови́ться *impf*, стать *pf* +*instr*; (*belong*) идти́ *impf*; be ~ing (to do) собира́ться *impf*, собра́ться *pf* (+*inf*); ~ about (*set to work at*) бра́ться *impf*, взя́ться *pf* за+*acc*; (*wander*) броди́ть *indet*; ~ away (on foot) уходи́ть *impf*, уйти́ *pf*; (*by transport*) уезжа́ть *impf*, уе́хать *pf*; ~ down спуска́ться *impf*, спусти́ться *pf* (с+*gen*); ~ in(to) (*enter*) входи́ть *impf*, войти́ *pf* (в+*acc*); (*investigate*) рассле́довать *impf* & *pf*; ~ off (*go away*) уходи́ть *impf*, уйти́ *pf*; (*deteriorate*) по́ртиться *impf*, ис~ *pf*; ~ on (*continue*) продолжа́ть(ся) *impf*, продо́лжить(ся) *pf*; ~ out выходи́ть *impf*, вы́йти *pf*; (*flame etc.*) га́снуть *impf*, по~ *pf*; ~ over (*inspect*) пересма́тривать *impf*, пересмотре́ть *pf*; (*rehearse*) повторя́ть *impf*, повтори́ть *pf*; (*change allegiance etc.*) переходи́ть *impf*, перейти́ *pf* (to в, на, +*acc*, к+*dat*);

~ **through** (*scrutinize*) разбира́ть *impf*, разобра́ть *pf*; ~ **through with** доводи́ть *impf*, довести́ *pf* до конца́; ~ **without** обходи́ться *impf*, обойти́сь *pf* без+*gen*; ~**ahead** предприи́мчивый; ~**between** посре́дник.

goad *vt* (*instigate*) подстрека́ть *impf*, подстрекну́ть *pf* (**into** к+*dat*); (*taunt*) раздража́ть *impf*.

goal *n* (*aim*) цель; (*sport*) воро́та (-т) *pl*; (*point won*) гол. **goalkeeper** *n* врата́рь *m*.

goat *n* коза́; (*male*) козёл.

gobble *vt* (*eat*) жрать *impf*; ~ **up** пожира́ть *impf*, пожра́ть *pf*.

goblet *n* бока́л, ку́бок.

god *n* бог; (G~) Бог. **godchild** *n* кре́стник, -ица. **god-daughter** *n* кре́стница. **goddess** *n* боги́ня. **godfather** *n* кре́стный *sb*. **God-fearing** *adj* богобоя́зненный. **godless** *adj* безбо́жный. **godly** *adj* на́божный. **godmother** *n* кре́стная *sb*. **godparent** *n* кре́стный *sb*. **godsend** *n* бо́жий дар. **godson** *n* кре́стник.

goggle *vi* тара́щить *impf* глаза́ (at на+*acc*); *n: pl* защи́тные очки́ (-ко́в) *pl*.

going *adj* де́йствующий. **goings-on** *n pl* дела́ *neut pl*.

gold *n* зо́лото; *adj* золото́й; ~**plated** накладно́го зо́лота; ~**smith** золоты́х дел ма́стер. **golden** *adj* золото́й; ~ **eagle** бе́ркут. **goldfish** *n* золота́я ры́бка.

golf *n* гольф; ~ **club** (*implement*) клю́шка; ~ **course** площа́дка для го́льфа. **golfer** *n* игро́к в гольф.

gondola *n* гондо́ла.

gong *n* гонг.

gonorrhoea *n* три́ппер.

good *n* добро́; *pl* (*wares*) това́р(ы); **do** ~ (*benefit*) идти́ *impf*, пойти́ *pf* на по́льзу +*dat*; *adj* хоро́ший, до́брый; ~**humoured** доброду́шный; ~**looking** краси́вый; ~ **morning** до́брое у́тро!; ~ **night** споко́йной но́чи! **goodbye** *int* проща́й(те)!; до свида́ния! **goodness** *n* доброта́.

goose *n* гусь *m*; ~**flesh** гуси́ная ко́жа.

gooseberry *n* крыжо́вник.

gore[1] *n* (*blood*) запёкшаяся кровь.

gore[2] *vt* (*pierce*) бода́ть *impf*, за~ *pf*.

gorge *n* (*geog*) уще́лье; *vi & t* объ-

еда́ться *impf*, объе́сться *pf* (on +*instr*).

gorgeous *adj* великоле́пный.

gorilla *n* гори́лла.

gorse *n* утёсник.

gory *adj* крова́вый.

gosh *int* бо́же мой!

Gospel *n* Ева́нгелие.

gossip *n* спле́тня; (*person*) спле́тник, -ица; *vi* спле́тничать *impf*, на~ *pf*.

Gothic готи́ческий.

gouge *vt*: ~ **out** выда́лбливать *impf*, вы́долбить *pf*; (*eyes*) выка́лывать *impf*, вы́колоть *pf*.

goulash *n* гуля́ш.

gourmet *n* гурма́н.

gout *n* пода́гра.

govern *vt* пра́вить *impf* +*instr*; (*determine*) определя́ть *impf*, определи́ть *pf* **governess** *n* гуверна́нтка. **government** *n* прави́тельство. **governmental** *adj* прави́тельственный. **governor** *n* губерна́тор; (*of school etc.*) член правле́ния.

gown *n* пла́тье; (*official's*) ма́нтия.

grab *vt* захва́тывать *impf*, захвати́ть *pf*.

grace *n* (*gracefulness*) гра́ция; (*refinement*) изя́щество; (*favour*) ми́лость; (*at meal*) моли́тва; **have the** ~ **to** быть насто́лько такти́чен, что; **with bad** ~ нелюбе́зно; **with good** ~ с досто́инством; *vt* (*adorn*) украша́ть *impf*, укра́сить *pf*; (*favour*) удоста́ивать *impf*, удосто́ить *pf* (**with** +*gen*). **graceful** *adj* грацио́зный.

gracious *adj* ми́лостивый.

gradation *n* града́ция.

grade *n* (*level*) сте́пень; (*quality*) сорт; *vt* сортирова́ть *impf*, рас~ *pf*.

gradient *n* укло́н.

gradual *adj* постепе́нный.

graduate *n* око́нчивший *sb* университе́т, вуз; *vi* конча́ть *impf*, око́нчить *pf* (университе́т, вуз); *vt* градуи́ровать *impf & pf*.

graffiti *n* на́дписи *f pl*.

graft *n* (*bot*) черено́к; (*med*) переса́дка (живо́й тка́ни); *vt* (*bot*) привива́ть *impf*, приви́ть *pf* (**to** +*dat*); (*med*) переса́живать *impf*, переса́дить *pf*.

grain *n* (*seed*; *collect*) зерно́; (*particle*)

крупи́нка; (*of sand*) песчи́нка; (*of wood*) (дре́весное) волокно́; **against the ~** не по нутру́.

gram(me) *n* грамм.

grammar *n* грамма́тика; **~ school** гимна́зия. **grammatical** *adj* граммати́ческий.

gramophone *n* прои́грыватель *m*; **~ record** граммпласти́нка.

granary *n* амба́р.

grand *adj* великоле́пный; **~ piano** роя́ль *m*. **grandchild** *n* внук, вну́чка. **granddaughter** *n* вну́чка. **grandfather** *n* де́душка *m*. **grandmother** *n* ба́бушка. **grandparents** *n* ба́бушка и де́душка. **grandson** *n* внук. **grandstand** *n* трибу́на.

grandeur *n* вели́чие.

grandiose *adj* грандио́зный.

granite *n* грани́т.

granny *n* ба́бушка.

grant *n* (*financial*) дота́ция; (*univ*) стипе́ндия; *vt* дарова́ть *impf & pf*; (*concede*) допуска́ть *impf*, допусти́ть *pf*; **take for ~ed** (*assume*) счита́ть *impf*, счесть *pf* само́ собо́й разуме́ющимся; (*not appreciate*) принима́ть *impf* как до́лжное.

granular *adj* зерни́стый.

granulated *adj*: **~ sugar** са́харный песо́к.

granule *n* зёрнышко.

grape *n* виногра́д. **grapefruit** *n* гре́йпфрут.

graph *n* гра́фик.

graphic *adj* графи́ческий; (*vivid*) я́ркий.

graphite *n* графи́т.

grapple *vi* (*struggle*) боро́ться *impf* (**with** *c+instr*).

grasp *n* (*grip*) хва́тка; (*comprehension*) понима́ние; *vt* (*clutch*) хвата́ть *impf*, схвати́ть *pf*; (*comprehend*) понима́ть *impf*, поня́ть *pf*. **grasping** *adj* жа́дный.

grass *n* трава́. **grasshopper** *n* кузне́чик. **grassy** *adj* травяни́стый.

grate[1] *n* (*in fireplace*) решётка.

grate[2] *vt* (*rub*) тере́ть *impf*, на~ *pf*; *vi* (*sound*) скрипе́ть *impf*; **~ (up)on** (*irritate*) раздража́ть *impf*, раздражи́ть *pf*.

grateful *adj* благода́рный.

grater *n* тёрка.

gratify *vt* удовлетворя́ть *impf*, удо-

влетвори́ть *pf*.

grating *n* решётка.

gratis *adv* беспла́тно.

gratitude *n* благода́рность.

gratuitous *adj* (*free*) дарово́й; (*motiveless*) беспричи́нный.

gratuity *n* (*tip*) чаевы́е *sb pl*.

grave[1] *n* моги́ла. **gravedigger** *n* моги́льщик. **gravestone** *n* надгро́бный ка́мень *m*. **graveyard** *n* кла́дбище.

grave[2] *adj* серьёзный.

gravel *n* гра́вий.

gravitate *vi* тяготе́ть *impf* (**towards** к+*dat*). **gravitational** *adj* гравитацио́нный. **gravity** *n* (*seriousness*) серьёзность; (*force*) тя́жесть.

gravy *n* (*мясна́я*) подли́вка.

graze[1] *vi* (*feed*) пасти́сь *impf*.

graze[2] *n* (*abrasion*) цара́пина; *vt* (*touch*) задева́ть *impf*, заде́ть *pf*; (*abrade*) цара́пать *impf*, о~ *pf*.

grease *n* жир; (*lubricant*) сма́зка; **~-paint** грим; *vt* сма́зывать *impf*, сма́зать *pf*. **greasy** *adj* жи́рный.

great *adj* (*large*) большо́й; (*eminent*) вели́кий; (*splendid*) замеча́тельный; **to a ~ extent** в большо́й сте́пени; **a ~ deal** мно́го (+*gen*); **a ~ many** мно́гие; **~-aunt** двою́родная ба́бушка; **~-granddaughter** пра́внучка; **~-grandfather** пра́дед; **~-grandmother** праба́бка; **~-grandson** пра́внук; **~-uncle** двою́родный де́душка *m*. **greatly** *adv* о́чень.

Great Britain *n* Великобрита́ния.

Greece *n* Гре́ция.

greed *n* жа́дность (**for** к+*dat*). **greedy** *adj* жа́дный (**for** к+*dat*).

Greek *n* грек, греча́нка; *adj* гре́ческий.

green *n* (*colour*) зелёный цвет; (*piece of land*) лужо́к; *pl* зе́лень *collect*; *adj* зелёный; (*inexperienced*) нео́пытный. **greenery** *n* зе́лень. **greenfly** *n* тля. **greengrocer** *n* зеленщи́к. **greenhouse** *n* тепли́ца; **~ effect** парнико́вый эффе́кт.

greet *vt* здоро́ваться *impf*, по~ *pf* с +*instr*; (*meet*) встреча́ть *impf*, встре́тить *pf*. **greeting** *n* приве́т(ствие).

gregarious *adj* общи́тельный.

grenade *n* грана́та.

grey *adj* се́рый; (*hair*) седо́й.

greyhound *n* борза́я *sb*.

grid n (grating) решётка; (electr) сеть; (map) координа́тная се́тка.

grief n го́ре; **come to** ~ терпе́ть impf, по~ pf неуда́чу.

grievance n жа́лоба, оби́да.

grieve vt огорча́ть impf, огорчи́ть pf; vi горева́ть impf (for о+prep).

grievous adj тя́жкий.

grill n ра́шпер; vt (cook) жа́рить impf, за~, из~ pf (на ра́шпере); (question) допра́шивать impf, допроси́ть pf.

grille n (grating) решётка.

grim adj (stern) суро́вый; (unpleasant) неприя́тный.

grimace n грима́са; vi грима́сничать impf.

grime n грязь. **grimy** adj гря́зный.

grin n усме́шка; vi усмеха́ться impf, усмехну́ться pf.

grind vt (flour etc.) моло́ть impf, с~ pf; (axe) точи́ть impf, на~ pf; ~ one's teeth скрежета́ть impf зуба́ми.

grip n хва́тка; vt схва́тывать impf, схвати́ть pf.

gripe vi ворча́ть impf.

gripping adj захва́тывающий.

grisly adj жу́ткий.

gristle n хрящ.

grit n песо́к; (for building) гра́вий; (firmness) вы́держка.

grizzle vi хны́кать impf.

groan n стон; vi стона́ть impf.

grocer n бакале́йщик; ~'s (shop) бакале́йная ла́вка, гастроно́м. **groceries** n pl бакале́я collect.

groggy adj разби́тый.

groin n (anat) пах.

groom n ко́нюх; (bridegroom) жени́х; vt (horse) чи́стить impf, по~ pf; (prepare) гото́вить impf, под~ pf (for к+dat); **well-groomed** хорошо́ вы́глядящий.

groove n желобо́к.

grope vi нащу́пывать impf (for, after +acc).

gross[1] n (12 dozen) гросс.

gross[2] adj (fat) ту́чный; (coarse) гру́бый; (total) валово́й; ~ **weight** вес бру́тто.

grotesque adj гроте́скный.

grotto n грот.

ground n земля́; (earth) по́чва; pl (dregs) гу́ща; (sport) площа́дка; pl (of house) парк; (reason) основа́ние; ~ **floor** пе́рвый эта́ж; vt (instruct) обуча́ть impf, обучи́ть pf основа́м (in +gen); (aeron) запреща́ть impf, запрети́ть pf полёты +gen; vi (naut) сади́ться impf, сесть pf на мель.

groundless adj необосно́ванный.

groundwork n фунда́мент.

group n гру́ппа; vt & i группирова́ть(ся) impf, с~ pf.

grouse[1] n шотла́ндская куропа́тка.

grouse[2] vi (grumble) ворча́ть impf.

grove n ро́ща.

grovel vi пресмыка́ться impf (before пе́ред+instr).

grow vi расти́ impf; (become) станови́ться impf, стать pf +instr; vt (cultivate) выра́щивать impf, вы́растить pf; (hair) отра́щивать impf, отрасти́ть pf; ~ **up** (person) выраста́ть impf, вы́расти pf; (custom) возника́ть impf, возни́кнуть pf.

growl n ворча́ние; vi ворча́ть impf (at на+acc).

grown-up adj взро́слый sb.

growth n рост; (med) о́пухоль.

grub n (larva) личи́нка; (food) жратва́; vi: ~ **about** ры́ться impf. **grubby** adj запа́чканный.

grudge n зло́ба; **have a** ~ **against** име́ть impf зуб про́тив+gen; vt жале́ть impf, по~ pf +acc, +gen.

grudgingly adv неохо́тно.

gruelling adj изнури́тельный.

gruesome adj жу́ткий.

gruff adj (surly) грубова́тый; (voice) хри́плый.

grumble vi ворча́ть impf (at на+acc).

grumpy adj брюзгли́вый.

grunt n хрю́канье; vi хрю́кать impf, хрю́кнуть pf.

guarantee n гара́нтия; vt гаранти́ровать impf & pf (against от+gen). **guarantor** n поручи́тель m.

guard n (device) предохрани́тель; (watch; soldiers) карау́л; (sentry) часово́й sb; (watchman) сто́рож; (rly) конду́ктор; pl (prison) надзира́тель m; vt охраня́ть impf, охрани́ть pf; vi: ~ **against** остерега́ться impf, остере́чься pf +gen, inf.

guardian n храни́тель m; (law) опеку́н.

guer(r)illa n партиза́н; ~ **warfare** партиза́нская война́.

guess n дога́дка; vt & i дога́дываться

impf, догада́ться pf (o+prep); vt (~ correctly) уга́дывать impf, угада́ть pf. **guesswork** n дога́дки f pl.

guest n гость m; ~ house ма́ленькая гости́ница.

guffaw n хо́хот; vi хохота́ть impf.

guidance n руково́дство. **guide** n проводни́к, гид; (guidebook) путеводи́тель m; vt води́ть indet, вести́ det; (direct) руководи́ть impf +instr; ~ed missile управля́емая раке́та. **guidelines** n pl инстру́кции f pl; (advice) сове́т.

guild n ги́льдия, цех.

guile n кова́рство. **guileless** adj простоду́шный.

guillotine n гильоти́на.

guilt n вина́; (guiltiness) вино́вность. **guilty** adj (of crime) вино́вный (of в+prep); (of wrong) винова́тый.

guinea-pig n морска́я сви́нка; (fig) подо́пытный кро́лик.

guise n: under the ~ of под ви́дом +gen.

guitar n гита́ра. **guitarist** n гитари́ст.

gulf n (geog) зали́в; (chasm) про́пасть.

gull n ча́йка.

gullet n (oesophagus) пищево́д; (throat) го́рло.

gullible adj легкове́рный.

gully n (ravine) овра́г.

gulp n глото́к; vt жа́дно глота́ть impf.

gum¹ n (anat) десна́.

gum² n каме́дь; (glue) клей; vt скле́ивать impf, скле́ить pf.

gumption n инициати́ва.

gun n (piece of ordnance) ору́дие, пу́шка; (rifle etc.) ружьё; (pistol) пистоле́т; vt: ~ down расстре́ливать impf, расстреля́ть pf. **gunner** n артиллери́ст. **gunpowder** n по́рох.

gurgle vi бу́лькать impf.

gush vi хлы́нуть pf.

gusset n клин.

gust n поры́в. **gusty** adj поры́вистый.

gusto n смак.

gut n кишка́; pl (entrails) кишки́ f pl; pl (bravery) му́жество; vt потроши́ть impf, вы́~ pf; (devastate) опустоша́ть impf, опустоши́ть pf.

gutter n (of roof) (водосто́чный) жёлоб; (of road) сто́чная кана́ва.

guttural adj горта́нный.

guy¹ n (rope) отта́жка.

guy² n (fellow) па́рень m.

guzzle vt (food) пожира́ть impf, пожра́ть pf; (liquid) хлеба́ть impf, хлебну́ть pf.

gym n (gymnasium) гимнасти́ческий зал; (gymnastics) гимна́стика. **gymnasium** n гимнасти́ческий зал. **gymnast** n гимна́ст. **gymnastic** adj гимнасти́ческий. **gymnastics** n гимна́стика.

gynaecologist n гинеко́лог. **gynaecology** n гинеколо́гия.

gyrate vi враща́ться impf.

H

haberdashery n галантере́я; (shop) галантере́йный магази́н.

habit n привы́чка; (monk's) ря́са.

habitable adj приго́дный для жилья́. **habitat** n есте́ственная среда́. **habitation** n: unfit for ~ неприго́дный для жилья́.

habitual adj привы́чный.

hack¹ vt руби́ть impf; ~saw ножо́вка.

hack² n (hired horse) наёмная ло́шадь; (writer) халту́рщик. **hackneyed** adj изби́тый.

haddock n пи́кша.

haemophilia n гемофили́я. **haemorrhage** n кровотече́ние. **haemorrhoids** n pl геморро́й collect.

hag n карга́.

haggard adj изможде́нный.

haggle vi торгова́ться impf, с~ pf.

hail¹ n град; vi it is ~ing идёт град. **hailstone** n гра́дина.

hail² vt (greet) приве́тствовать impf (& pf in past); (taxi) подзыва́ть impf, подозва́ть pf.

hair n (single ~) во́лос; collect (human) во́лосы (-о́с, -оса́м) pl; (animal) шерсть. **hairbrush** n щётка для воло́с. **haircut** n стри́жка; have a ~ постри́чься pf. **hair-do** n причёска. **hairdresser** n парикма́хер. **hairdresser's** n парикма́херская sb. **hair-dryer** n фен. **hairstyle** n причёска. **hairy** adj волоса́тый.

hale adj: ~ and hearty здоро́вый и бо́дрый.

half n полови́на; (sport) тайм; adj

полови́нный; in ~ попола́м; one and a ~ полтора́; ~ past (one etc.) полови́на (второ́го и т.д.); ~-**hearted** равноду́шный; ~ an hour полчаса́; ~-**time** переры́в ме́жду та́ймами; ~**way** на полпути́; ~-**witted** слабоу́мный.

hall n (large room) зал; (entrance ~) холл, вестибю́ль m; (~ of residence) общежи́тие. **hallmark** n пробо́рное клеймо́; (fig) при́знак.

hallo int здра́сте, приве́т; (on telephone) алло́.

hallucination n галлюцина́ция.

halo n (around Saint) нимб; (fig) орео́л.

halt n остано́вка; vt & i остана́вливать(ся) impf, останови́ть(ся) pf; int (mil) стой(те)! **halting** adj запина́ющий.

halve vt дели́ть impf, раз~ pf попола́м.

ham n (cul) ветчина́.

hamlet n деревушка.

hammer n молото́к; vt бить impf молотко́м.

hammock n гама́к.

hamper[1] n (basket) корзи́на с кры́шкой.

hamper[2] vt (hinder) меша́ть impf, по~ pf +dat.

hamster n хомя́к.

hand n рука́; (worker) рабо́чий sb; (writing) по́черк; (clock ~) стре́лка; at ~ под руко́й; on ~s and knees на четвере́ньках; vt передава́ть impf, переда́ть pf; ~ in подава́ть impf, пода́ть pf; ~ out раздава́ть impf, разда́ть pf. **handbag** n су́мка. **handbook** n руково́дство. **handcuffs** n pl нару́чники m pl. **handful** n горсть.

handicap n (sport) гандика́п; (hindrance) поме́ха. **handicapped** adj: ~ person инвали́д.

handicraft n ремесло́.

handiwork n ручна́я рабо́та.

handkerchief n носово́й плато́к.

handle n ру́чка, рукоя́тка; vt (people) обраща́ться impf c+instr; (situations) справля́ться impf, спра́виться pf c+instr; (touch) тро́гать impf, тро́нуть pf руко́й, рука́ми. **handlebar(s)** n руль m.

handmade adj ручно́й рабо́ты.

handout n пода́чка; (document) лифле́т.

handrail n пери́ла (-л) pl.

handshake n рукопожа́тие.

handsome adj краси́вый; (generous) ще́дрый.

handwriting n по́черк.

handy adj (convenient) удо́бный; (skilful) ло́вкий; come in ~ пригоди́ться pf.

hang vt ве́шать impf, пове́сить pf; vi висе́ть impf; ~ about слоня́ться impf; ~ on (cling) держа́ться impf; (tel) не ве́шать impf тру́бку; (persist) упо́рствовать impf; ~ out выве́шивать impf, вы́весить pf; (spend time) болта́ться impf; ~ up ве́шать impf, пове́сить pf; (tel) ве́шать impf, пове́сить pf тру́бку. **hanger** n ве́шалка. **hanger-on** n прилипа́ла m & f. **hangman** n пала́ч.

hangar n анга́р.

hangover n похме́лье.

hang-up n ко́мплекс.

hanker vi: ~ after мечта́ть impf о+prep.

haphazard adj случа́йный.

happen vi (occur) случа́ться impf, случи́ться pf; происходи́ть impf, произойти́ pf; (~ to be somewhere) ока́зываться impf, оказа́ться pf; ~ upon натолка́ться impf, натолкну́ться pf на+acc.

happiness n сча́стье. **happy** adj счастли́вый; ~-**go-lucky** беззабо́тный.

harass vt (pester) дёргать impf; (persecute) пресле́довать impf. **harassment** n тра́вля; пресле́дование.

harbinger n предве́стник.

harbour n га́вань, порт; vt (person) укрыва́ть impf, укры́ть pf; (thoughts) зата́ивать impf, затаи́ть pf.

hard adj твёрдый; (difficult) тру́дный; (difficult to bear) тяжёлый; (severe) суро́вый; ~-**boiled egg** яйцо́ вкруту́ю; ~-**headed** практи́чный; ~-**hearted** жестокосе́рдный; ~-**up** стеснённый в сре́дствах; ~-**working** трудолюби́вый. **hardboard** n строи́тельный карто́н.

harden vi затвердева́ть impf, затверде́ть pf; (fig) ожесточа́ться impf, ожесточи́ться pf.

hardly adv едва́ (ли).

hardship n (privation) нужда́.

hardware n скобяны́е изде́лия neut pl; (comput) аппарату́ра.

hardy adj (robust) выно́сливый; (plant) морозостойкий.

hare n за́яц.

hark vi: ~ back to возвраща́ться impf, верну́ться pf к+dat; int слу́шай(те)!

harm n вред; vt вреди́ть impf, по~ pf +dat. **harmful** adj вре́дный. **harmless** adj безвре́дный.

harmonic adj гармони́ческий. **harmonica** n губна́я гармо́ника. **harmonious** adj гармони́чный. **harmonize** vi гармони́ровать impf (with c+instr). **harmony** n гармо́ния.

harness n у́пряжь; vt запряга́ть impf, запря́чь pf; (fig) испо́льзовать impf & pf.

harp n а́рфа; vi: ~ on тверди́ть impf o+prep.

harpoon n гарпу́н.

harpsichord n клавеси́н.

harrow n борона́. **harrowing** adj душераздира́ющий.

harsh adj (sound, colour) ре́зкий; (cruel) суро́вый.

harvest n жа́тва, сбор (плодо́в); (yield) урожа́й; (fig) плоды́ m pl; vt & abs собира́ть impf, собра́ть pf (урожа́й).

hash n: make a ~ of напу́тать pf +acc, в+prep.

hashish n гаши́ш.

hassle n беспоко́йство.

hassock n поду́шечка.

haste n спе́шка. **hasten** vi спеши́ть impf, по~ pf; vt & i торопи́ть(ся) impf, по~ pf; vt ускоря́ть impf, уско́рить pf. **hasty** adj (hurried) поспе́шный; (quick-tempered) вспы́льчивый.

hat n ша́пка; (stylish) шля́па.

hatch[1] n люк; ~-back маши́на-пика́п.

hatch[2] vi вылу́пливаться, вылупля́ться impf, вы́лупиться pf.

hatchet n топо́рик.

hate n не́нависть; vt ненави́деть impf. **hateful** adj ненави́стный. **hatred** n не́нависть.

haughty adj надме́нный.

haul n (fish) уло́в; (loot) добы́ча; (distance) езда́; vt (drag) тяну́ть impf; таска́ть indet, тащи́ть det. **haulage** n перево́зка.

haunt n люби́мое ме́сто; vt (ghost) обита́ть impf; (memory) пресле́довать impf. **haunted** adj: ~ house дом с привиде́ниями. **haunting** adj навя́зчивый.

have vt име́ть impf; I ~ (possess) у меня́ (есть; был, -á, -о) +nom; I ~ not у меня́ нет (past не́ было) +gen; I ~ (got) to я до́лжен +inf; you had better вам лу́чше бы +inf; ~ on (wear) быть оде́тым в +prep; (be engaged in) быть за́нятым +instr.

haven n (refuge) убе́жище.

haversack n рюкза́к.

havoc n (devastation) опустоше́ние; (disorder) беспоря́док.

hawk[1] n (bird) я́стреб.

hawk[2] vt (trade) торгова́ть impf вразно́с+instr. **hawker** n разно́счик.

hawser n трос.

hawthorn n боя́рышник.

hay n се́но; make ~ коси́ть impf, с~ pf се́но; ~ fever се́нная лихора́дка. **haystack** n стог.

hazard n риск; vt рискова́ть impf +instr. **hazardous** adj риско́ванный.

haze n ды́мка.

hazel n лещи́на. **hazelnut** n лесно́й оре́х.

hazy adj тума́нный; (vague) сму́тный.

he pron он.

head n голова́; (mind) ум; (~ of coin) лицева́я сторона́ моне́ты; ~s or tails? орёл и́ли ре́шка?; (chief) глава́ m, нача́льник; attrib гла́вный; (lead) возглавля́ть impf, возгла́вить pf; (ball) забива́ть impf, заби́ть pf голово́й; vi: ~ for направля́ться impf, напра́виться pf в, на, +acc, к+dat. **headache** n головна́я боль. **head-dress** n головно́й убо́р. **header** n уда́р голово́й. **heading** n (title) заголо́вок. **headland** n мыс. **headlight** n фа́ра. **headline** n заголо́вок. **headlong** adv стремгла́в. **headmaster, -mistress** n дире́ктор шко́лы. **head-on** adj головно́й; adv в лоб. **headphone** n нау́шник. **headquarters** n штаб-кварти́ра. **headscarf** n косы́нка. **headstone** n надгро́бный ка́мень m. **headstrong** adj своево́льный. **headway** n движе́ние вперёд. **heady** adj опьяня́ющий.

heal vt изле́чивать impf, излечи́ть

pf; *vi* зажива́ть *impf*, зажи́ть *pf*.
healing *adj* целе́бный.
health *n* здоро́вье; ~ **care** здраво-
охране́ние. **healthy** *adj* здоро́вый;
(*beneficial*) поле́зный.

heap *n* ку́ча; *vt* нагроможда́ть *impf*,
нагромозди́ть *pf*.

hear *vt* слы́шать *impf*, y~ *pf*; (*listen
to*) слу́шать *impf*, по~ *pf*; ~ **out**
выслу́шивать *impf*, вы́слушать *pf*.
hearing *n* слух; (*law*) слу́шание.
hearsay *n* слух.

hearse *n* катафа́лк.

heart *n* се́рдце; (*essence*) суть; *pl
(cards)* че́рви (-ве́й) *pl*; **by** ~ на-
изу́сть; ~ **attack** серде́чный при́-
ступ. **heartburn** *n* изжо́га. **hearten**
vt ободря́ть *impf*, ободри́ть *pf*.
heartfelt *adj* серде́чный. **heartless**
adj бессерде́чный. **heart-rending**
adj душераздира́ющий. **hearty** *adj
(cordial)* серде́чный; (*vigorous*)
здоро́вый.

hearth *n* оча́г.

heat *n* жара́; (*phys*) теплота́; (*of feeling*) пыл; (*sport*) забе́г, зае́зд; *vt
& i (heat up)* нагрева́ть(ся) *impf*,
нагре́ть(ся) *pf*; *vt (house)* топи́ть
impf. **heater** *n* нагрева́тель *m*. **heating** *n* отопле́ние.

heath *n* пу́стошь.

heathen *n* язы́чник; *adj* язы́ческий.
heather *n* ве́реск.

heave *vt (lift)* поднима́ть *impf*, под-
ня́ть *pf*; (*pull*) тяну́ть *impf*, по~ *pf*.

heaven *n (sky)* не́бо; (*paradise*) рай;
pl небеса́ *neut pl*. **heavenly** *adj*
небе́сный; (*divine*) боже́ственный.

heavy *adj* тяжёлый; (*strong, intense*)
си́льный. **heavyweight** *n* тяжело-
ве́с.

Hebrew *adj (древне)евре́йский*.

heckle *vt* пререка́ться *impf* c+*instr*.

hectic *adj* лихора́дочный.

hedge *n* живая и́згородь. **hedgerow**
n шпале́ра.

hedgehog *n* ёж.

heed *vt* обраща́ть *impf*, обрати́ть *pf*
внима́ние на+*acc*. **heedless** *adj* не-
бре́жный.

heel[1] *n (of foot)* пята́; (*of foot, sock*)
пя́тка; (*of shoe*) каблу́к.

heel[2] *vi* крени́ться *impf*, на~ *pf*.

hefty *adj* дю́жий.

heifer *n* тёлка.

height *n* высота́; (*of person*) рост.
heighten *vt (strengthen)* уси́ливать
impf, уси́лить *pf*.

heinous *adj* гну́сный.

heir *n* насле́дник. **heiress** *n* насле́д-
ница. **heirloom** *n* фами́льная вещь.

helicopter *n* вертолёт.

helium *n* ге́лий.

hell *n* ад. **hellish** *adj* а́дский.

hello *see* hallo

helm *n* руль.

helmet *n* шлем.

help *n* по́мощь; *vt* помога́ть *impf*,
помо́чь *pf* +*dat*; (*can't* ~) не мочь
impf не +*inf*; ~ **o.s.** брать *impf*,
взять *pf* себе́; ~ **yourself!** бери́те!
helpful *adj* поле́зный; (*obliging*)
услу́жливый. **helping** *n (of food)*
по́рция. **helpless** *adj* беспо́мощ-
ный.

helter-skelter *adv* как попа́ло.

hem *n* рубе́ц; *vt* подруба́ть *impf*,
подруби́ть *pf*; ~ **in** окружа́ть *impf*,
окружи́ть *pf*.

hemisphere *n* полуша́рие.

hemp *n (plant)* коно́пля; (*fibre*)
пенька́.

hen *n (female bird)* са́мка; (*domestic
fowl*) ку́рица.

hence *adv (from here)* отсю́да; (*as a
result*) сле́довательно; **3 years** ~
че́рез три го́да. **henceforth** *adv*
отны́не.

henchman *n* приспе́шник.

henna *n* хна.

hepatitis *n* гепати́т.

her *poss pron* её; свой.

herald *n* ве́стник; *vt* возвеща́ть *impf*,
возвести́ть *pf*.

herb *n* трава́. **herbaceous** *adj* травя-
но́й; ~ **border** цвето́чный бордю́р.
herbal *adj* травяно́й.

herd *n* ста́до; (*people*) толпи́ться
impf, c~ *pf*; *vt (tend)* пасти́ *impf*;
(*drive*) загоня́ть *impf*, загна́ть *pf* в
ста́до.

here *adv (position)* здесь, тут; (*direction*) сюда́; ~ **is ... вот** (+*nom*);
~ **and there** там и сям; ~ **you are!**
пожа́луйста. **hereabout(s)** *adv* по-
бли́зости. **hereafter** *adv* в бу́дущем.
hereby *adv* э́тим. **hereupon** *adv (in
consequence*) всле́дствие э́того; (*after*) по́сле э́того. **herewith** *adv* при
сём.

hereditary adj насле́дственный. **heredity** n насле́дственность.

heresy n е́ресь. **heretic** n ерети́к. **heretical** adj ерети́ческий.

heritage n насле́дие.

hermetic adj гермети́ческий.

hermit n отше́льник.

hernia n гры́жа.

hero n геро́й. **heroic** adj герои́ческий.

heroin n герои́н.

heroine n геро́иня. **heroism** n геро́изм.

heron n ца́пля.

herpes n лиша́й.

herring n сельдь; (food) селёдка.

hers poss pron её; свой.

herself pron (emph) (она́) сама́; (refl) себя́.

hertz n герц.

hesitant adj нереши́тельный. **hesitate** vi колеба́ться impf, по~ pf; (in speech) запина́ться impf, запну́ться pf. **hesitation** n колеба́ние.

hessian n мешкови́на.

heterogeneous adj разноро́дный.

heterosexual adj гетеросексуа́льный.

hew vt руби́ть impf.

hexagon n шестиуго́льник.

hey int эй!

heyday n расцве́т.

hi int приве́т!

hiatus n пробе́л.

hibernate vi быть impf в спя́чке; впада́ть impf, впасть pf в спя́чку. **hibernation** n спя́чка.

hiccup vi ика́ть impf, икну́ть pf; n: pl ико́та.

hide¹ n (skin) шку́ра.

hide² vt & i (conceal) пря́тать(ся) impf, с~ pf; скрыва́ть(ся) impf, скры́ть(ся) pf.

hideous adj отврати́тельный.

hideout n укры́тие.

hiding n (flogging) по́рка.

hierarchy n иера́рхия.

hieroglyphics n pl иеро́глифы m pl.

hi-fi n прои́грыватель m с высококаче́ственным воспроизведе́нием зву́ка за́писи.

higgledy-piggledy adv как придётся.

high adj высо́кий; (wind) си́льный; (on drugs) в наркоти́ческом дурма́не; ~er education вы́сшее образова́ние; ~-handed своево́льный;

~-heeled на высо́ких каблука́х; ~jump прыжо́к в высоту́; ~-minded благоро́дный; иде́йный; ~-pitched высо́кий; ~-rise высо́тный. **highbrow** adj интеллектуа́льный. **highland(s)** n го́рная страна́. **highlight** n (fig) вы́сшая то́чка; vt обраща́ть impf, обрати́ть pf внима́ние на+acc.

highly adv весьма́; ~-strung легко́ возбужда́емый. **highness** n (title) высо́чество. **highstreet** n гла́вная у́лица. **highway** n магистра́ль.

hijack vt похища́ть impf, похи́тить pf. **hijacker** n похити́тель m.

hike n похо́д.

hilarious adj умори́тельный. **hilarity** n весе́лье.

hill n холм. **hillock** n хо́лмик. **hillside** n склон холма́. **hilly** adj холми́стый.

hilt n рукоя́тка.

himself pron (emph) (он) сам; (refl) себя́.

hind adj (rear) за́дний.

hinder vt меша́ть impf, по~ pf +dat. **hindrance** n поме́ха.

Hindu n инду́с; adj инду́сский.

hinge n шарни́р; vi (fig) зави́сеть impf от+gen.

hint n намёк; vi намека́ть impf, намекну́ть pf (at на+acc)

hip n (anat) бедро́.

hippie n хи́ппи neut indecl.

hippopotamus n гиппопота́м.

hire n наём, прока́т; ~-purchase поку́пка в рассро́чку; vt нанима́ть impf, наня́ть pf; ~ out сдава́ть impf, сдать pf напрока́т.

his poss pron его́; свой.

hiss n шипе́ние; vi шипе́ть impf; vt (performer) осви́стывать impf, освиста́ть pf.

historian n исто́рик. **historic(al)** adj истори́ческий. **history** n исто́рия.

histrionic adj театра́льный.

hit n (blow) уда́р; (on target) попада́ние (в цель); (success) успе́х; vt (strike) ударя́ть impf, уда́рить pf; (target) попада́ть impf, попа́сть pf (в цель); ~ (up)on находи́ть impf, найти́ pf.

hitch n (stoppage) заде́ржка; vt (fasten) привя́зывать impf, привяза́ть pf; ~ up подтя́гивать impf, подтяну́ть pf; ~-hike е́здить indet, е́хать

det, по~ *pf* автостопом.
hither *adv* сюда. hitherto *adv* до сих пор.
HIV *abbr (of human immunodeficiency virus)* ВИЧ.
hive *n* улей.
hoard *n* запас; *vt* скапливать *impf*, скопить *pf*.
hoarding *n* рекламный щит.
hoarse *adj* хриплый.
hoax *n* надувательство.
hobble *vi* ковылять *impf*.
hobby *n* хобби *neut indecl*.
hock *n (wine)* рейнвейн.
hockey *n* хоккей.
hoe *n* мотыга; *vt* мотыжить *impf*.
hog *n* боров.
hoist *n* подъёмник; *vt* поднимать *impf*, поднять *pf*.
hold¹ *n (naut)* трюм.
hold² *n (grasp)* захват; *(influence)* влияние (on на+*acc*); catch ~ of ухватиться *pf* за+*acc*; *vt (grasp)* держать *impf*; *(contain)* вмещать *impf*, вместить *pf*; *(possess)* владеть *impf* +*instr*; *(conduct)* проводить *impf*, провести *pf*; *(consider)* считать *impf*, счесть *pf* (+*acc* & *instr*, за+*acc*); *vi* держаться *impf*; *(weather)* продержаться *impf*, продержаться *pf*; ~ back сдерживать(ся) *impf*, сдержать(ся) *pf*; ~ forth разглагольствовать *impf*; ~ on *(wait)* подождать *pf*; *(tel)* не вешать трубку; *(grip)* держаться *impf* (to за+*acc*); ~ out *(stretch out)* протягивать *impf*, протянуть *pf*; *(resist)* не сдаваться *impf*; ~ up *(support)* поддерживать *impf*, поддержать *pf*; *(impede)* задерживать *impf*, задержать *pf*. holdall *n* сумка. hold-up *n (robbery)* налёт; *(delay)* задержка.
hole *n* дыра; *(animal's)* нора; *(golf)* лунка.
holiday *n (day off)* выходной день; *(festival)* праздник; *(annual leave)* отпуск; *pl (school)* каникулы (-л) *pl*; ~maker турист; on ~ в отпуске.
holiness *n* святость.
Holland *n* Голландия.
hollow *n* впадина; *(valley)* лощина; *adj* пустой; *(sunken)* впалый; *(sound)* глухой; *vt (~ out)* выдалбливать *impf*, выдолбить *pf*.
holly *n* остролист.

holocaust *n* массовое уничтожение.
holster *n* кобура.
holy *adj* святой, священный.
homage *n* почтение; pay ~ to преклоняться *impf*, преклониться *pf* перед+*instr*.
home *n* дом; *(native land)* родина; at ~ дома; feel at ~ чувствовать *impf* себя как дома; *adj* домашний; *(native)* родной; H~ Affairs внутренние дела *neut pl*; *adv (direction)* домой; *(position)* дома. homeland *n* родина. homeless *adj* бездомный. homemade *adj (food)* домашний; *(object)* самодельный. homesick *adj*: be ~ скучать *impf* по дому. homewards *adv* домой, восвояси.
homely *adj* простой.
homicide *n (action)* убийство.
homogeneous *adj* однородный.
homosexual *n* гомосексуалист; *adj* гомосексуальный.
honest *n* честный. honesty *n* честность.
honey *n* мёд. honeymoon *n* медовый месяц. honeysuckle *n* жимолость.
honk *vi* гудеть *impf*.
honorary *adj* почётный.
honour *n* честь; *vt (respect)* почитать *impf*; *(confer)* удостаивать *impf*, удостоить *pf* (with +*gen*); *(fulfil)* выполнять *impf*, выполнить *pf*. honourable *adj* честный.
hood *n* капюшон; *(tech)* капот.
hoodwink *vt* обманывать *impf*, обмануть *pf*.
hoof *n* копыто.
hook *n* крючок; *vt (hitch)* зацеплять *impf*, зацепить *pf*; *(fasten)* застёгивать *impf*, застегнуть *pf*.
hooligan *n* хулиган.
hoop *n* обруч.
hoot *vi (owl)* ухать *impf*, ухнуть *pf*; *(horn)* гудеть *impf*. hooter *n* гудок.
hop¹ *n (plant; collect)* хмель *m*.
hop² *n (jump)* прыжок; *vi* прыгать *impf*, прыгнуть *pf* (на одной ноге).
hope *n* надежда; *vi* надеяться *impf*, по~ *pf (for* на+*acc)*. hopeful *adj (promising)* обнадёживающий; I am ~ я надеюсь. hopefully *adv* с надеждой; *(it is hoped)* надо надеяться. hopeless *adj* безнадёжный.
horde *n (hist, fig)* орда.

horizon n горизо́нт. horizontal adj горизонта́льный.

hormone n гормо́н.

horn n рог; (French horn) валто́рна; (car) гудо́к.

hornet n ше́ршень m.

horny adj (calloused) мозо́листый.

horoscope n гороско́п.

horrible, horrid adj ужа́сный. horrify vt ужаса́ть impf, ужасну́ть pf. horror n у́жас.

hors-d'oeuvre n заку́ска.

horse n ло́шадь. horse-chestnut n ко́нский кашта́н. horseman, -woman n вса́дник, -ица. horseplay n возня́. horsepower n лошади́ная си́ла. horse-racing n ска́чки (-чек) pl. horse-radish n хрен. horseshoe n подко́ва.

horticulture n садово́дство.

hose n (~-pipe) шланг.

hosiery n чуло́чные изде́лия neut pl.

hospitable adj гостеприи́мный.

hospital n больни́ца.

hospitality n гостеприи́мство.

host¹ n (multitude) мно́жество.

host² n (entertaining) хозя́ин.

hostage n зало́жник.

hostel n общежи́тие.

hostess n хозя́йка; (air ~) стюарде́сса.

hostile adj вражде́бный. hostility n вражде́бность; pl вое́нные де́йствия neut pl.

hot adj горя́чий, жа́ркий; (pungent) о́стрый; ~-headed вспы́льчивый; ~-water bottle гре́лка. hotbed n (fig) оча́г. hothouse n тепли́ца. hotplate n пли́тка.

hotel n гости́ница.

hound n охо́тничья соба́ка; vt трави́ть impf, за~ pf.

hour n час. hourly adj ежеча́сный.

house n дом; (parl) пала́та; attrib дома́шний; vt помеща́ть impf, помести́ть pf. household n семья́; adj хозя́йственный; дома́шний. housekeeper n эконо́мка. house-warming n новосе́лье. housewife n хозя́йка. housework n дома́шняя рабо́та. housing n (accommodation) жильё; (casing) кожу́х; ~ estate жило́й масси́в.

hovel n лачу́га.

hover vi (bird) пари́ть impf; (heli-copter) висе́ть impf; (person) мая́чить impf. hovercraft n су́дно на возду́шной поду́шке, СВП.

how adv как, каки́м о́бразом: ~ do you do? здра́вствуйте!; ~ many, ~ much ско́лько (+gen). however adv как бы ни (+past); conj одна́ко, тем не ме́нее; ~ much ско́лько бы ни (+gen & past).

howl n вой; vi выть impf. howler n гру́бейшая оши́бка.

hub n (of wheel) ступи́ца; (fig) центр, средото́чие.

hubbub n шум, гам.

huddle vi: ~ together прижима́ться impf, прижа́ться pf друг к дру́гу.

hue n (tint) отте́нок.

huff n: in a ~ оскорблённый.

hug n объя́тие; vt (embrace) обнима́ть impf, обня́ть pf.

huge adj огро́мный.

hulk n ко́рпус (корабля́). hulking adj (bulky) грома́дный; (clumsy) неуклю́жий.

hull n (of ship) ко́рпус.

hum n жужжа́ние; vi (buzz) жужжа́ть impf; vt & i (person) напева́ть impf.

human adj челове́ческий, людско́й; n челове́к. humane, humanitarian adj челове́чный. humanity n (human race) челове́чество; (humaneness) гума́нность; the Humanities гуманита́рные нау́ки f pl.

humble adj (person) смире́нный; (abode) скро́мный; vt унижа́ть impf, уни́зить pf.

humdrum adj однообра́зный.

humid adj вла́жный. humidity n вла́жность.

humiliate vt унижа́ть impf, уни́зить pf. humiliation n униже́ние.

humility n смире́ние.

humorous adj юмористи́ческий. humour n ю́мор; (mood) настрое́ние; vt потака́ть impf +dat.

hump n горб; (of earth) буго́р.

humus n перегно́й.

hunch n (idea) предчу́вствие; vt го́рбить impf, с~ pf. hunchback n (person) горбу́н, ~ья. hunchbacked adj горба́тый.

hundred adj & n сто; ~s of со́тни f pl +gen; two ~ две́сти; three ~ три́ста; four ~ четы́реста; five ~ пятьсо́т. hundredth adj & n со́тый.

Hungarian n венгр, венгéрка; adj венгéрский. **Hungary** n Вéнгрия.

hunger n гóлод; (fig) жáжда (for +gen); ~ **strike** голодóвка; vi голодáть impf; ~ **for** жáждать impf +gen. **hungry** adj голóдный.

hunk n ломóть m.

hunt n охóта; (fig) пóиски m pl (for +gen); vt охóтиться impf на+acc, за+instr; (persecute) травить impf, за~ pf; ~ **down** выследить pf; ~ **for** искáть impf +acc or gen; ~ **out** отыскáть pf. **hunter** n охóтник. **hunting** n охóта.

hurdle n (sport; fig) барьéр. **hurdler** n барьерúст. **hurdles** n pl (sport) барьéрный бег.

hurl vt швырять impf, швырнуть pf. **hurly-burly** n суматóха.

hurrah, hurray int урá!

hurricane n урагáн.

hurried adj торопливый. **hurry** n спéшка; **be in a** ~ спешить impf; vt & i торопить(ся) impf, по~ pf; vi спешить impf, по~ pf.

hurt n ущéрб; vi болéть impf; vt повреждáть impf, повредить pf; (offend) обижáть impf, обидеть pf.

hurtle vi нестись impf, по~ pf.

husband n муж.

hush n тишинá; vt: ~ **up** заминáть impf, замять pf; int тише!

husk n шелухá.

husky adj (voice) хриплый.

hustle n толкотня; vt (push) заталкáть impf, затолкнуть pf; (herd people) загонять impf, загнáть pf; vt & i (hurry) торопить(ся) impf, по~ pf.

hut n хижина.

hutch n клéтка.

hyacinth n гиацинт.

hybrid n гибрид; adj гибридный.

hydrangea n гортéнзия.

hydrant n гидрáнт.

hydraulic adj гидравлический.

hydrochloric acid n соляная кислотá. **hydroelectric** adj гидроэлектрический; ~ **power station** гидроэлектростáнция, ГЭС f indecl. **hydrofoil** n сýдно на подвóдных крыльях, СПК.

hydrogen n водорóд.

hyena n гиéна.

hygiene n гигиéна. **hygienic** adj гигиенический.

hymn n гимн.

hyperbole n гипéрбола.

hyphen n дефис. **hyphen(ate)** vt писáть impf, на~ pf чéрез дефис.

hypnosis n гипнóз. **hypnotic** adj гипнотический. **hypnotism** n гипнотизм. **hypnotist** n гипнотизёр. **hypnotize** vt гипнотизировать impf, за~ pf.

hypochondria n ипохóндрия. **hypochondriac** n ипохóндрик.

hypocrisy n лицемéрие. **hypocrite** n лицемéр. **hypocritical** adj лицемéрный.

hypodermic adj подкóжный.

hypothesis n гипóтеза. **hypothesize** vi строить impf, по~ pf гипотéзу. **hypothetical** adj гипотетический.

hysterectomy n гистерэктомия, удалéние мáтки.

hysteria n истéрия. **hysterical** adj истерический. **hysterics** n pl истéрика.

I

I pron я.

ibid(em) adv там же.

ice n лёд; ~**age** ледникóвый перúод; ~**axe** ледорýб; ~**cream** морóженое sb; ~ **hockey** хоккéй (с шáйбой); ~ **rink** катóк; ~ **skate** конёк; vi катáться impf на конькáх; vt (chill) заморáживать impf, морóзить pf; (cul) глазировáть impf & pf; vi: ~ **over, up** обледеневáть impf, обледенéть pf. **iceberg** n áйсберг. **icicle** n сосýлька. **icing** n (cul) глазýрь. **icy** adj ледянóй.

icon n икóна.

ID abbr (of identification) удостоверéние лúчности.

idea n идéя, мысль; (conception) понятие.

ideal n идеáл; adj идеáльный. **idealism** n идеализм. **idealist** n идеалист. **idealize** vt идеализировать impf & pf.

identical adj тождéственный, одинáковый. **identification** n (recognition) опознáние; (of person) установлéние лúчности. **identify** vt опознавáть impf, опознáть pf. **identity** n (*of person*) ли́чность; ~ **card** удостовере́ние ли́чности.

ideological *adj* идеологи́ческий. **ideology** *n* идеоло́гия.

idiom *n* идио́ма. **idiomatic** *adj* идиомати́ческий.

idiosyncrasy *n* идиосинкрази́я.

idiot *n* идио́т. **idiotic** *adj* идио́тский.

idle *adj* (*unoccupied; lazy; purposeless*) пра́здный; (*vain*) тще́тный; (*empty*) пусто́й; (*machine*) неде́йствующий; *vi* безде́льничать *impf*; (*engine*) рабо́тать *impf* вхолосту́ю; *vt*: ~ **away** пра́здно проводи́ть *impf*, провести́ *pf*. **idleness** *n* пра́здность.

idol *n* и́дол. **idolatry** *n* идолопокло́нство; (*fig*) обожа́ние. **idolize** *vt* боготвори́ть *impf*.

idyll *n* иди́ллия. **idyllic** *adj* идилли́ческий.

i.e. *abbr* т.е., то есть.

if *conj* е́сли, е́сли бы; (*whether*) ли; **as** ~ как бу́дто; **even** ~ да́же е́сли; ~ **only** е́сли бы то́лько.

ignite *vt* зажига́ть *impf*, заже́чь *pf*; *vi* загора́ться *impf*, загоре́ться *pf*. **ignition** *n* зажига́ние.

ignoble *adj* ни́зкий.

ignominious *adj* позо́рный.

ignoramus *n* неве́жда *m*. **ignorance** *n* неве́жество, (*of certain facts*) неве́дение. **ignorant** *adj* неве́жественный; (*uninformed*) несве́дущий (*of* в+*prep*).

ignore *vt* не обраща́ть *impf* внима́ния на+*acc*; игнори́ровать *impf* & *pf*.

ilk *n*: **of that** ~ тако́го ро́да.

ill *n* (*evil*) зло; (*harm*) вред; *pl* (*misfortunes*) несча́стья (-тий) *pl*; *adj* (*sick*) больно́й; (*bad*) дурно́й; *adv* пло́хо, ду́рно; **fall** ~ заболева́ть *impf*, заболе́ть *pf*; ~-**advised** неблагоразу́мный; ~-**mannered** неве́жливый; ~-**treat** *vt* пло́хо обраща́ться *impf* c+*instr*.

illegal *adj* нелега́льный. **illegality** *n* незако́нность.

illegible *adj* неразбо́рчивый.

illegitimacy *n* незако́нность; (*of child*) незаконнорождённость. **illegitimate** *adj* незако́нный; незаконнорождённый.

illicit *adj* незако́нный, недозво́ленный.

illiteracy *n* негра́мотность. **illiterate** *adj* негра́мотный.

illness *n* боле́знь.

illogical *adj* нелоги́чный.

illuminate *vt* освеща́ть *impf*, освети́ть *pf*. **illumination** *n* освеще́ние.

illusion *n* иллю́зия. **illusory** *adj* иллюзо́рный.

illustrate *vt* иллюстри́ровать *impf* & *pf*, про~ *pf*. **illustration** *n* иллюстра́ция. **illustrative** *adj* иллюстрати́вный.

illustrious *adj* знамени́тый.

image *n* (*phys; statue etc.*) изображе́ние; (*optical* ~) отраже́ние; (*likeness*) ко́пия; (*metaphor; conception*) о́браз; (*reputation*) репута́ция. **imagery** *n* о́бразность.

imaginable *adj* вообрази́мый. **imaginary** *adj* вообража́емый. **imagination** *n* воображе́ние. **imagine** *vt* вообража́ть *impf*, вообрази́ть *pf*; (*conceive*) представля́ть *impf*, предста́вить *pf* себе́.

imbecile *n* слабоу́мный *sb*; (*fool*) глупе́ц.

imbibe *vt* (*absorb*) впи́тывать *impf*, впита́ть *pf*.

imbue *vt* внуша́ть *impf*, внуши́ть *pf* +*dat* (*with* +*acc*).

imitate *vt* подража́ть *impf* +*dat*. **imitation** *n* подража́ние (*of* +*dat*); *attrib* иску́сственный. **imitative** *adj* подража́тельный.

immaculate *adj* безупре́чный.

immaterial *adj* (*unimportant*) несуще́ственный.

immature *adj* незре́лый.

immeasurable *adj* неизмери́мый.

immediate *adj* (*direct*) непосре́дственный; (*swift*) неме́дленный. **immediately** *adv* то́тчас, сра́зу.

immemorial *adj*: **from time** ~ с незапа́мятных времён.

immense *adj* огро́мный.

immerse *vt* погружа́ть *impf*, погрузи́ть *pf*. **immersion** *n* погруже́ние.

immigrant *n* иммигра́нт, ~ка. **immigration** *n* иммигра́ция.

imminent *adj* надвига́ющийся; (*danger*) грозя́щий.

immobile *adj* неподви́жный. **immobilize** *vt* парализова́ть *impf* & *pf*.

immoderate *adj* неуме́ренный.

immodest *adj* нескро́мный.

immoral *adj* безнра́вственный. **immorality** *n* безнра́вственность.

immortal *adj* бессме́ртный. **immortality** *n* бессме́ртие. **immortalize** *vt* обессме́ртить *pf*.

immovable *adj* неподви́жный; (*fig*) непоколеби́мый.

immune *adj* (*to illness*) невоспри́мчивый (*to* к+*dat*); (*free from*) свобо́дный (*from* от+*gen*). **immunity** *n* иммуните́т (*from* к+*dat*); освобожде́ние (*from* от+*gen*). **immunize** *vt* иммунизи́ровать *impf* & *pf*.

immutable *adj* неизме́нный.

imp *n* бесёнок.

impact *n* уда́р; (*fig*) влия́ние.

impair *vt* вреди́ть *impf*, по~ *pf*.

impale *vt* протыка́ть *impf*, проткну́ть *pf*.

impart *vt* дели́ться *impf*, по~ *pf* +*instr* (*to* с+*instr*).

impartial *adj* беспристра́стный.

impassable *adj* непроходи́мый; (*for vehicles*) непроезжа́й.

impasse *n* тупи́к.

impassioned *adj* стра́стный.

impassive *adj* бесстра́стный.

impatience *n* нетерпе́ние. **impatient** *adj* нетерпели́вый.

impeach *vt* обвиня́ть *impf*, обвини́ть *pf* (*for* в+*prep*).

impeccable *adj* безупре́чный.

impecunious *adj* безде́нежный.

impedance *n* по́лное сопротивле́ние. **impede** *vt* препя́тствовать *impf*, вос~ *pf* +*dat*. **impediment** *n* препя́тствие; (*in speech*) заика́ние.

impel *vt* побужда́ть *impf*, побуди́ть *pf* (*to* +*inf*, к+*dat*).

impending *adj* предстоя́щий.

impenetrable *adj* непроница́емый.

imperative *adj* необходи́мый; *n* (*gram*) повели́тельное наклоне́ние.

imperceptible *adj* незаме́тный.

imperfect *n* имперфе́кт; *adj* несоверше́нный. **imperfection** *n* несоверше́нство; (*fault*) недоста́ток. **imperfective** *adj* (*n*) несоверше́нный (вид).

imperial *adj* импе́рский. **imperialism** *n* империали́зм. **imperialist** *n* империали́ст; *attrib* империалисти́ческий.

imperil *vt* подверга́ть *impf*, подве́ргнуть *pf* опа́сности.

imperious *adj* вла́стный.

impersonal *adj* безли́чный.

impersonate *vt* (*imitate*) подража́ть *impf*; (*pretend to be*) выдава́ть *impf*, вы́дать *pf* себя́ за+*acc*. **impersonation** *n* подража́ние.

impertinence *n* де́рзость. **impertinent** *adj* де́рзкий.

imperturbable *adj* невозмути́мый.

impervious *adj* (*fig*) глухо́й (*to* к +*dat*).

impetuous *adj* стреми́тельный.

impetus *n* дви́жущая си́ла.

impinge *vi*: ~ (up)on ока́зывать *impf*, оказа́ть *pf* (отрица́тельный) эффе́кт на+*acc*.

implacable *adj* неумоли́мый.

implant *vt* вводи́ть *impf*, ввести́ *pf*; (*fig*) се́ять *impf*, по~ *pf*.

implement[1] *n* ору́дие, инструме́нт.

implement[2] *vt* (*fulfil*) выполня́ть *impf*, вы́полнить *pf*.

implicate *vt* впу́тывать *impf*, впу́тать *pf*. **implication** *n* (*inference*) намёк; *pl* значе́ние.

implicit *adj* подразумева́емый; (*absolute*) безоговоро́чный.

implore *vt* умоля́ть *impf*.

imply *vt* подразумева́ть *impf*.

impolite *adj* неве́жливый.

imponderable *adj* неопределённый.

import *n* (*meaning*) значе́ние; (*of goods*) и́мпорт; *vt* импорти́ровать *impf* & *pf*. **importer** *n* импортёр.

importance *n* ва́жность. **important** *adj* ва́жный.

impose *vt* (*tax*) облага́ть *impf*, обложи́ть *pf* +*instr* (*on* +*acc*); (*obligation*) налага́ть *impf*, наложи́ть *pf* (*on* на+*acc*); ~ (*o.s.*) on налега́ть *impf* на+*acc*. **imposing** *adj* внуши́тельный. **imposition** *n* обложе́ние, наложе́ние.

impossibility *n* невозмо́жность. **impossible** *adj* невозмо́жный.

impostor *n* самозва́нец.

impotence *n* бесси́лие; (*med*) импоте́нция. **impotent** *adj* бесси́льный; (*med*) импоте́нтный.

impound *vt* (*confiscate*) конфискова́ть *impf* & *pf*.

impoverished *adj* обедне́вший.

impracticable *adj* невыполни́мый.

imprecise *n* нето́чный.

impregnable *adj* непристу́пный.

impregnate vt (fertilize) оплодотворять impf, оплодотворить pf; (saturate) пропитывать impf, пропитать pf.

impresario n агент.

impress vt производить impf, произвести pf (какое-либо) впечатление на+acc; ~ upon (s.o.) внушать impf, внушить pf (+dat). impression n впечатление; (imprint) отпечаток; (reprint) (стереотипное) издание. impressionism n импрессионизм. impressionist n импрессионист. impressive adj впечатляющий.

imprint n отпечаток; vt отпечатывать impf, отпечатать pf; (on memory) запечатлевать impf, запечатлеть pf.

imprison vt заключать impf, заключить pf (в тюрьму). imprisonment n тюремное заключение.

improbable adj невероятный.

impromptu adj импровизированный; adv без подготовки, экспромтом.

improper adj (incorrect) неправильный; (indecent) неприличный. impropriety n неуместность.

improve vt & i улучшать(ся) impf, улучшить(ся) pf. improvement n улучшение.

improvisation n импровизация. improvise vt импровизировать impf, сымпровизировать pf.

imprudent adj неосторожный.

impudence n наглость. impudent adj наглый.

impulse n толчок, импульс; (sudden tendency) порыв. impulsive adj импульсивный.

impunity n: with ~ безнаказанно.

impure adj нечистый.

impute vt приписывать impf, приписать pf (to +dat).

in prep (place) в+prep, на+prep; (into) в+acc, на+acc; (point in time) в+prep, на+prep; in the morning (etc.) утром (instr); in spring (etc.) весной (instr); (at some stage in; throughout) во время +gen; (duration) за+acc; (after interval of) через+acc; (during course of) в течение+gen; (circumstance) при+prep; adv (place) внутри; (motion) внутрь; (at home) дома; (in

fashion) в моде; in here, there (place) здесь, там; (motion) сюда, туда; adj внутренний; (fashionable) модный; n: the ins and outs все ходы и выходы.

inability n неспособность.

inaccessible adj недоступный.

inaccurate adj неточный.

inaction n бездействие. inactive adj бездейственный. inactivity n бездейственность.

inadequate adj недостаточный.

inadmissible adj недопустимый.

inadvertent adj нечаянный.

inalienable adj неотъемлемый.

inane adj глупый.

inanimate adj неодушевлённый.

inappropriate adj неуместный.

inarticulate adj (person) косноязычный; (indistinct) невнятный.

inasmuch adv: ~ as так как; ввиду того, что.

inattentive adj невнимательный.

inaudible adj неслышимый.

inaugural adj вступительный. inaugurate vt (admit to office) торжественно вводить impf, ввести pf в должность; (open) открывать impf, открыть pf; (introduce) вводить impf, ввести pf. inauguration n введение в должность; открытие; начало.

inauspicious adj неблагоприятный.

inborn, inbred adj врождённый.

incalculable adj неисчислимый.

incandescent adj накалённый.

incantation n заклинание.

incapability n неспособность. incapable adj неспособный (of к+dat, на+acc).

incapacitate vt делать impf, с~ pf неспособным incapacity n неспособность.

incarcerate vt заключать impf, заключить pf (в тюрьму). incarceration n заключение (в тюрьму).

incarnate adj воплощённый. incarnation n воплощение.

incendiary adj зажигательный.

incense¹ n фимиам, ладан.

incense² vt разгневать pf.

incentive n побуждение.

inception n начало.

incessant adj непрестанный.

incest n кровосмешение.

inch n дюйм; ~ **by** ~ ма́ло-пома́лу; vi ползти́ impf.

incidence n (phys) паде́ние; (prevalence) распростране́ние. **incident** n слу́чай, инциде́нт. **incidental** adj (casual) случа́йный; (inessential) несуще́ственный. **incidentally** adv ме́жду про́чим.

incinerate vt испепеля́ть impf, испепели́ть pf. **incinerator** n мусоросжига́тельная печь.

incipient adj начина́ющийся.

incision n надре́з (на+acc). **incisive** adj (fig) о́стрый. **incisor** n резе́ц.

incite vt подстрека́ть impf, подстрекну́ть pf (to к+dat). **incitement** n подстрека́тельство.

inclement adj суро́вый.

inclination n (slope) накло́н; (propensity) скло́нность (for, to к+dat). **incline** n накло́н; vt & i склоня́ть(ся) impf, склони́ть(ся) pf. **inclined** predic (disposed) скло́нен (-онна́, -о́нно) (to к+dat).

include vt включа́ть impf, включи́ть pf (**in** в+acc); (contain) заключа́ть impf, заключи́ть pf в себе́. **including** prep включа́я+acc. **inclusion** n включе́ние. **inclusive** adj включа́ющий (в себе́); adv включи́тельно.

incognito adv инко́гнито.

incoherent adj бессвя́зный.

income n дохо́д; ~ **tax** подохо́дный нало́г.

incommensurate adj несоразме́рный.

incomparable adj несравни́мый (to, with c+instr); (matchless) несравне́нный.

incompatible adj несовмести́мый.

incompetence n некомпете́нтность. **incompetent** adj некомпете́нтный.

incomplete adj непо́лный, незако́нченный.

incomprehensible adj непоня́тный.

inconceivable adj невообрази́мый.

inconclusive adj (evidence) недоста́точный; (results) неопределённый.

incongruity n несоотве́тствие. **incongruous** adj несоотве́тствующий.

inconsequential adj незначи́тельный.

inconsiderable adj незначи́тельный. **inconsiderate** adj невнима́тельный.

inconsistency n непосле́довательность. **inconsistent** adj непосле́довательный.

inconsolable adj безуте́шный.

inconspicuous adj незаме́тный.

incontinence n (med) недержа́ние. **incontinent** adj: **be** ~ страда́ть impf недержа́нием.

incontrovertible adj неопроверж́мый.

inconvenience n неудо́бство; vt затрудня́ть impf, затрудни́ть pf. **inconvenient** adj неудо́бный.

incorporate vt (include) включа́ть impf, включи́ть pf; (unite) объединя́ть impf, объедини́ть pf.

incorrect adj непра́вильный.

incorrigible adj неисправи́мый.

incorruptible adj неподку́пный.

increase n рост, увеличе́ние; (in pay etc.) приба́вка; vt & i увели́чивать(ся) impf, увели́чить(ся) pf.

incredible adj невероя́тный.

incredulous adj недове́рчивый.

increment n приба́вка.

incriminate vt изоблича́ть impf, изобличи́ть pf.

incubate vt (eggs) выводи́ть impf, вы́вести pf (в инкуба́торе). **incubator** n инкуба́тор.

inculcate vt внедря́ть impf, внедри́ть pf.

incumbent adj (in office) стоя́щий у вла́сти; **it is** ~ (up)on **you** вы обя́заны.

incur vt навлека́ть impf, навле́чь pf на себя́.

incurable adj неизлечи́мый.

incursion n (invasion) вторже́ние; (attack) набе́г.

indebted predic в долгу́ (to у+gen).

indecency n неприли́чие. **indecent** adj неприли́чный.

indecision n нереши́тельность. **indecisive** adj нереши́тельный.

indeclinable adj несклоня́емый.

indeed adv в са́мом де́ле, действи́тельно; (interrog) неуже́ли?

indefatigable adj неутоми́мый.

indefensible adj не име́ющий оправда́ния.

indefinable adj неопредели́мый. **indefinite** adj неопределённый.

indelible adj несмыва́емый.

indemnify vt: ~ **against** страхова́ть

impf, за~ *pf* от+*gen*; ~ **for** (*compensate*) компенси́ровать *impf* & *pf.*

indemnity *n* (*against loss*) гара́нтия от убы́тков; (*compensation*) компенса́ция.

indent *vt* (*printing*) писа́ть *impf*, с~ *pf* с о́тступом. **indentation** *n* (*notch*) зубе́ц; (*printing*) о́тступ.

independence *n* незави́симость, самостоя́тельность. **independent** *adj* незави́симый, самостоя́тельный.

indescribable *adj* неопису́емый.

indestructible *adj* неразруши́мый.

indeterminate *adj* неопределённый.

index *n* (*alphabetical*) указа́тель *m*; (*econ*) и́ндекс; (*pointer*) стре́лка; ~ **finger** указа́тельный па́лец.

India *n* И́ндия. **Indian** *n* инди́ец, индиа́нка; (*American*) инде́ец, индиа́нка; *adj* инди́йский; (*American*) инде́йский; ~ **summer** ба́бье ле́то.

indicate *vt* ука́зывать *impf*, указа́ть *pf*; (*be a sign of*) свиде́тельствовать *impf* о+*prep*. **indication** *n* указа́ние; (*sign*) при́знак. **indicative** *adj* ука́зывающий; (*gram*) изъяви́тельный; *n* изъяви́тельное наклоне́ние. **indicator** *n* указа́тель *m*.

indict *vt* обвиня́ть *impf*, обвини́ть *pf* (**for** в+*prep*).

indifference *n* равноду́шие. **indifferent** *adj* равноду́шный; (*mediocre*) посре́дственный.

indigenous *adj* тузе́мный.

indigestible *adj* неудобовари́мый.

indigestion *n* несваре́ние желу́дка.

indignant *adj* негоду́ющий; **be** ~ негодова́ть *impf* (**with** на+*acc*). **indignation** *n* негодова́ние.

indignity *n* оскорбле́ние.

indirect *adj* непрямо́й; (*econ*; *gram*) ко́свенный.

indiscreet *adj* нескро́мный. **indiscretion** *n* нескро́мность.

indiscriminate *adj* неразбо́рчивый. **indiscriminately** *adv* без разбо́ра.

indispensable *adj* необходи́мый.

indisposed *predic* (*unwell*) нездоро́в.

indisputable *adj* бесспо́рный.

indistinct *adj* нея́сный.

indistinguishable *adj* неразличи́мый.

individual *n* ли́чность; *adj* индивидуа́льный. **individualism** *n* индивидуали́зм. **individualist** *n* индивидуали́ст. **individualistic** *adj* индивиду-

алисти́ческий. **individuality** *n* индивидуа́льность.

indivisible *adj* недели́мый.

indoctrinate *vt* внуша́ть *impf*, внуши́ть *pf* +*dat* (**with** +*acc*).

indolence *n* ле́ность. **indolent** *adj* лени́вый.

indomitable *adj* неукроти́мый.

Indonesia *n* Индоне́зия.

indoor *adj* ко́мнатный. **indoors** *adv* (*position*) в до́ме; (*motion*) в дом.

induce *vt* (*prevail on*) убежда́ть *impf*, убеди́ть *pf*; (*bring about*) вызыва́ть *impf*, вы́звать *pf*. **inducement** *n* побужде́ние.

induction *n* (*logic, electr*) инду́кция; (*in post*) введе́ние в до́лжность.

indulge *vt* потво́рствовать *impf* +*dat*; *vi* предава́ться *impf*, преда́ться *pf* (**in** +*dat*). **indulgence** *n* потво́рство; (*tolerance*) снисходи́тельность. **indulgent** *adj* снисходи́тельный.

industrial *adj* промы́шленный. **industrialist** *n* промы́шленник. **industrious** *adj* трудолюби́вый. **industry** *n* промы́шленность; (*zeal*) трудолю́бие.

inebriated *adj* пья́ный.

inedible *adj* несъедо́бный.

ineffective, ineffectual *adj* безрезульта́тный; (*person*) неспосо́бный.

inefficiency *n* неэффекти́вность. **inefficient** *adj* неэффекти́вный.

ineligible *adj* не име́ющий пра́ва (**for** на+*acc*).

inept *adj* неуме́лый.

inequality *n* нера́венство.

inert *adj* ине́ртный. **inertia** *n* (*phys*) ине́рция; (*sluggishness*) ине́ртность.

inescapable *adj* неизбе́жный.

inevitability *n* неизбе́жность. **inevitable** *adj* неизбе́жный.

inexact *adj* нето́чный.

inexcusable *adj* непрости́тельный.

inexhaustible *adj* неистощи́мый.

inexorable *adj* неумоли́мый.

inexpensive *adj* недорого́й.

inexperience *n* нео́пытность. **inexperienced** *adj* нео́пытный.

inexplicable *adj* необъясни́мый.

infallible *adj* непогреши́мый.

infamous *adj* позо́рный. **infamy** *n* позо́р.

infancy *n* младе́нчество. **infant** *n* младе́нец. **infantile** *adj* де́тский.

infantry n пехо́та.

infatuate vt вскружи́ть pf го́лову +dat. **infatuation** n увлече́ние.

infect vt заража́ть impf, зарази́ть pf (with +instr). **infection** n зара́за, инфе́кция. **infectious** adj зара́зный; (fig) зарази́тельный.

infer vt заключа́ть impf, заключи́ть pf. **inference** n заключе́ние.

inferior adj (in rank) ни́зший; (in quality) ху́дший, плохо́й; n подчинённый sb. **inferiority** n бо́лее ни́зкое ка́чество; ~ **complex** ко́мплекс неполноце́нности.

infernal adj а́дский. **inferno** n ад.

infertile adj неплодоро́дный.

infested adj: **be** ~ **with** кише́ть impf +instr.

infidelity n неве́рность.

infiltrate vt постепе́нно проника́ть impf, прони́кнуть pf в+acc.

infinite adj бесконе́чный. **infinitesimal** adj бесконе́чно ма́лый. **infinitive** n инфинити́в. **infinity** n бесконе́чность.

infirm adj не́мощный. **infirmary** n больни́ца. **infirmity** n не́мощь.

inflame vt & i (excite) возбужда́ть(ся) impf, возбуди́ть(ся) pf; (med) воспаля́ть(ся) impf, воспали́ть(ся) pf. **inflammable** adj огнеопа́сный. **inflammation** n воспале́ние. **inflammatory** adj подстрека́тельский.

inflate vt надува́ть impf, наду́ть pf. **inflation** n (econ) инфля́ция.

inflection n (gram) фле́ксия.

inflexible adj неги́бкий; (fig) непреклонный.

inflict vt (blow) наноси́ть impf, нанести́ pf ((up)on +dat); (suffering) причиня́ть impf, причини́ть pf ((up)on +dat); (penalty) налага́ть impf, наложи́ть pf ((up)on на+acc); ~ **o.s.** (up)on навя́зываться impf, навяза́ться pf +dat.

inflow n втека́ние, прито́к.

influence n влия́ние; vt влия́ть impf, по~ pf на+acc. **influential** adj влия́тельный.

influenza n грипп.

influx n (fig) наплы́в.

inform vt сообща́ть impf, сообщи́ть pf +dat (of, about +acc, о+prep); vi доноси́ть impf, донести́ pf (against на+acc).

informal adj (unofficial) неофициа́льный; (casual) обы́денный.

informant n осведоми́тель m. **information** n информа́ция. **informative** adj поучи́тельный. **informer** n доно́счик.

infra-red adj инфракра́сный.

infrequent adj ре́дкий.

infringe vt (violate) наруша́ть impf, нару́шить pf; vi: ~ (up)on посяга́ть impf, посягну́ть pf на+acc. **infringement** n наруше́ние; посяга́тельство.

infuriate vt разъяря́ть impf, разъяри́ть pf.

infuse vt (fig) внуша́ть impf, внуши́ть pf (into +dat). **infusion** n (fig) внуше́ние; (herbs etc) насто́й.

ingenious adj изобрета́тельный. **ingenuity** n изобрета́тельность.

ingenuous adj бесхи́тростный.

ingot n сли́ток.

ingrained adj закоренелый.

ingratiate vt ~ **o.s.** вкра́дываться impf, вкра́сться pf в ми́лость (with +dat).

ingratitude n неблагода́рность.

ingredient n ингредие́нт, составля́ющее sb.

inhabit vt жить impf в, на, +prep; обита́ть impf в, на, +prep. **inhabitant** n жи́тель m, ~ница.

inhalation n вдыха́ние. **inhale** vt вдыха́ть impf, вдохну́ть pf.

inherent adj прису́щий (in +dat).

inherit vt насле́довать impf & pf, у~ pf. **inheritance** n насле́дство.

initiative n инициати́ва.

inhibit vt стесня́ть impf, стесни́ть pf. **inhibited** adj стесни́тельный. **inhibition** n стесне́ние.

inhospitable adj негостеприи́мный; (fig) недружелю́бный.

inhuman(e) adj бесчелове́чный.

inimical adj вражде́бный; (harmful) вре́дный.

inimitable adj неподража́емый.

iniquity n несправедли́вость.

initial adj (перво)нача́льный; n нача́льная бу́ква; pl инициа́лы m pl; vt ста́вить impf, по~ pf инициа́лы на+acc. **initially** adv в нача́ле.

initiate vt вводи́ть impf, ввести́ pf (into в+acc). **initiation** n введе́ние.

initiative n инициати́ва.

inject vt вводи́ть impf, ввести́ pf (person +dat, substance +acc). **injection** n уко́л; (fig) инъе́кция.

injunction n (law) суде́бный запре́т.

injure vt повреждáть impf, повреди́ть pf. injury n ра́на.

injustice n несправедли́вость.

ink n черни́ла (-л).

inkling n представле́ние.

inland adj вну́тренний; adv (motion) внутрь страны́; (place) внутри́ страны́; I~ Revenue управле́ние нало́говых сбо́ров.

in-laws n pl ро́дственники m pl супру́га, -ги.

inlay n инкруста́ция; vt инкрусти́ровать impf & pf.

inlet n (of sea) у́зкий зали́в.

inmate n (prison) заключённый sb; (hospital) больно́й sb.

inn n гости́ница.

innate adj врождённый.

inner adj вну́тренний; innermost adj глубоча́йший; (fig) сокрове́ннейший.

innocence n неви́нность; (guiltlessness) невино́вность. innocent adj неви́нный; (not guilty) невино́вный (of в+prep).

innocuous adj безвре́дный.

innovate vi вводи́ть impf, ввести́ pf но́вшества. innovation n нововведе́ние. innovative adj нова́торский. innovator n нова́тор.

innuendo n намёк, инсинуа́ция.

innumerable adj бесчи́сленный.

inoculate vt привива́ть impf, приви́ть pf +dat (against +acc). inoculation n приви́вка.

inoffensive adj безоби́дный.

inopportune adj несвоевре́менный.

inordinate adj чрезме́рный.

inorganic adj неоргани́ческий.

in-patient n стациона́рный больно́й sb.

input n ввод.

inquest n суде́бное сле́дствие, дозна́ние.

inquire vt спра́шивать impf, спроси́ть pf; vi справля́ться impf, спра́виться pf (about о+prep); рассле́довать impf & pf (into +acc). inquiry n вопро́с, спра́вка; (investigation) рассле́дование.

inquisition n инквизи́ция. inquisitive adj пытли́вый, любозна́тельный.

inroad n (attack) набе́г; (fig) посяга́тельство (on, into на+acc).

insane adj безу́мный. insanity n безу́мие.

insatiable adj ненасы́тный.

inscribe vt надпи́сывать impf, надписа́ть pf; (engrave) выреза́ть impf, вы́резать pf. inscription n на́дпись.

inscrutable adj непостижи́мый, непроница́емый.

insect n насеко́мое sb. insecticide n инсектици́д.

insecure adj (unsafe) небезопа́сный; (not confident) неуве́ренный (в себе́).

insemination n оплодотворе́ние.

insensible adj (unconscious) потеря́вший созна́ние.

insensitive adj нечувстви́тельный.

inseparable adj неотдели́мый; (people) неразлу́чный.

insert vt вставля́ть impf, вста́вить pf; вкла́дывать impf, вложи́ть pf; (coin) опуска́ть impf, опусти́ть pf. insertion n (inserting) вставле́ние, вкла́дывание; (thing inserted) вста́вка.

inshore adj прибре́жный; adv бли́зко к бе́регу.

inside n вну́тренняя часть; pl (anat) вну́тренности f pl; turn ~ out вывёртывать impf, вы́вернуть pf наизна́нку; adj вну́тренний; adv (place) внутри́; (motion) внутрь; prep (place) внутри́+gen, в+prep; (motion) внутрь+gen, в+acc.

insidious adj кова́рный.

insight n проница́тельность.

insignia n зна́ки m pl разли́чия.

insignificant adj незначи́тельный.

insincere adj неи́скренний.

insinuate vt (hint) намека́ть impf, намекну́ть pf на+acc. insinuation n инсинуа́ция.

insipid adj пре́сный.

insist vt & i наста́ивать impf, настоя́ть pf (on на+prep). insistence n насто́йчивость. insistent adj насто́йчивый.

insolence n на́глость. insolent adj на́глый.

insoluble adj (problem) неразреши́мый; (in liquid) нераствори́мый.

insolvent adj несостоя́тельный.

insomnia n бессо́нница.

inspect vt инспекти́ровать impf,

про~ pf. **inspection** n инспе́кция.
inspector n инспе́ктор; (ticket ~) контролёр.
inspiration n вдохнове́ние. **inspire** vt вдохновля́ть impf, вдохнови́ть pf; внуша́ть impf, внуши́ть pf +dat (with +acc).
instability n неусто́йчивость; (of character) неуравнове́шенность.
install vt (person in office) вводи́ть impf, ввести́ pf в до́лжность; (apparatus) устана́вливать impf, установи́ть pf. **installation** n введе́ние в до́лжность; устано́вка; pl сооруже́ния neut pl.
instalment n (comm) взнос; (publication) вы́пуск; часть; by ~s в рассро́чку.
instance n (example) приме́р; (case) слу́чай; for ~ наприме́р.
instant n мгнове́ние, моме́нт; adj неме́дленный; (coffee etc.) раствори́мый. **instantaneous** adj мгнове́нный. **instantly** adv . неме́дленно, то́тчас.
instead adv вме́сто (of +gen); ~ of going вме́сто того́, что́бы пойти́.
instep n подъём.
instigate vt подстрека́ть impf, подстрекну́ть pf (to к+dat). **instigation** n подстрека́тельство. **instigator** n подстрека́тель m, ~ница.
instil vt (ideas etc.) внуша́ть impf, внуши́ть pf (into +dat).
instinct n инсти́нкт. **instinctive** adj инстинкти́вный.
institute n институ́т; vt (establish) устана́вливать impf, установи́ть pf; (introduce) вводи́ть impf, ввести́ pf; (reforms) проводи́ть impf, провести́ pf. **institution** n учрежде́ние.
instruct vt (teach) обуча́ть impf, обучи́ть pf (in +dat); (inform) сообща́ть impf, сообщи́ть pf +dat; (command) прика́зывать impf, приказа́ть pf +dat. **instruction** n (in pl) инстру́кция; (teaching) обуче́ние. **instructive** adj поучи́тельный. **instructor** n инстру́ктор.
instrument n ору́дие, инструме́нт. **instrumental** adj (mus) инструмента́льный; (gram) твори́тельный; be ~ in спосо́бствовать impf, по~ pf +dat; n (gram) твори́тельный паде́ж. **instrumentation** n

(mus) инструменто́вка.
insubordinate adj неподчиня́ющийся.
insufferable adj невыноси́мый.
insular adj (fig) ограни́ченный.
insulate vt изоли́ровать impf & pf. **insulation** n изоля́ция. **insulator** n изоля́тор.
insulin n инсули́н.
insult n оскорбле́ние; vt оскорбля́ть impf, оскорби́ть pf. **insulting** adj оскорби́тельный.
insuperable adj непреодоли́мый.
insurance n страхова́ние; attrib страхово́й. **insure** vt страхова́ть impf, за~ pf (against от+gen).
insurgent n повста́нец.
insurmountable adj непреодоли́мый.
insurrection n восста́ние.
intact adj це́лый.
intake n (of persons) набо́р; (consumption) потребле́ние.
intangible adj неосяза́емый.
integral adj неотъе́млемый. **integrate** vt & i интегри́роваться impf & pf. **integration** n интегра́ция.
integrity n (honesty) че́стность.
intellect n интелле́кт. **intellectual** n интеллиге́нт; adj интеллектуа́льный.
intelligence n (intellect) ум; (information) све́дения neut pl; (~ service) разве́дка. **intelligent** adj у́мный. **intelligentsia** n интеллиге́нция. **intelligible** adj поня́тный.
intemperate adj невозде́ржанный.
intend vt собира́ться impf, собра́ться pf; (design) предназнача́ть impf, предназна́чить pf (for для +gen, на+acc).
intense adj си́льный. **intensify** vt & i уси́ливать(ся) impf, уси́лить(ся) pf. **intensity** n интенси́вность, си́ла. **intensive** adj интенси́вный.
intent n наме́рение; adj (resolved) стремя́щийся (on к+dat); (occupied) погружённый (on в+acc); (earnest) внима́тельный. **intention** n наме́рение. **intentional** adj наме́ренный.
inter vt хорони́ть impf, по~ pf.
interact vi взаимоде́йствовать impf. **interaction** n взаимоде́йствие.
intercede vi хода́тайствовать impf, по~ pf (for за+acc; with пе́ред+instr).
intercept vt перехва́тывать impf,

перехвати́ть pf. **interception** n перехва́т.

interchange n обме́н (of +instr); (junction) тра́нспортная развя́зка; vt обме́ниваться impf, обменя́ться pf +instr. **interchangeable** adj взаимозаменя́емый.

inter-city adj междугоро́дный.

intercom n вну́тренняя телефо́нная связь.

interconnected adj взаимосвя́занный. **interconnection** n взаимосвя́зь.

intercourse n (social) обще́ние; (trade; sexual) сноше́ния neut pl.

interdisciplinary adj межотраслево́й.

interest n интере́с (in к+dat); (econ) проце́нты m pl; vt интересова́ть impf; (~ person in) заинтересо́вывать impf, заинтересова́ть pf (in +instr); be ~ed in интересова́ться impf +instr. **interesting** adj интере́сный.

interfere vi вме́шиваться impf, вмеша́ться pf (in в+acc). **interference** n вмеша́тельство; (radio) поме́хи f pl.

interim n: in the ~ тем вре́менем; adj промежу́точный; (temporary) вре́менный.

interior n вну́тренность; adj вну́тренний.

interjection n восклица́ние; (gram) междоме́тие.

interlock vt & i сцепля́ть(ся) impf, сцепи́ть(ся) pf.

interloper n незва́ный гость m.

interlude n (theat) антра́кт; (mus, fig) интерлю́дия.

intermediary n посре́дник.

intermediate adj промежу́точный.

interminable adj бесконе́чный.

intermission n переры́в; (theat) антра́кт.

intermittent adj преры́вистый.

intern vt интерни́ровать impf & pf.

internal adj вну́тренний; ~ combustion engine дви́гатель m вну́треннего сгора́ния.

international adj междунаро́дный; n (contest) междунаро́дные состяза́ния neut pl.

internment n интерни́рование.

interplay n взаимоде́йствие.

interpret vt (explain) толкова́ть impf; (understand) истолко́вывать impf, истолкова́ть pf; vt переводи́ть impf, перевести́ pf. **interpretation** n толкова́ние. **interpreter** n перево́дчик, -ица.

interrelated adj взаимосвя́занный. **interrelationship** n взаи́мная связь.

interrogate vt допра́шивать impf, допроси́ть pf. **interrogation** n допро́с. **interrogative** adj вопроси́тельный.

interrupt vt прерыва́ть impf, прерва́ть pf. **interruption** n переры́в.

intersect vt & i пересека́ть(ся) impf, пересе́чь(ся) pf. **intersection** n пересече́ние.

intersperse vt (scatter) рассыпа́ть impf, рассы́пать pf (between, among ме́жду+instr, среди́+gen).

intertwine vt & i переплета́ть(ся) impf, переплести́(сь) pf.

interval n интерва́л; (theat) антра́кт.

intervene vi (occur) происходи́ть impf, произойти́ pf; ~ in вме́шиваться impf, вмеша́ться pf в+acc. **intervention** n вмеша́тельство; (polit) интерве́нция.

interview n интервью́ neut indecl; vt интервью́ировать impf & pf, про~ pf. **interviewer** n интервью́ер.

interweave vt votkáть pf.

intestate adj без завеща́ния.

intestine n кишка́; pl кише́чник.

intimacy n инти́мность. **intimate**[1] adj инти́мный.

intimate[2] vt (hint) намека́ть impf, намекну́ть pf на+acc. **intimation** n намёк.

intimidate vt запу́гивать impf, запуга́ть pf.

into prep в, во+acc, на+acc.

intolerable adj невыноси́мый. **intolerance** n нетерпи́мость. **intolerant** adj нетерпи́мый.

intonation n интона́ция.

intoxicated adj пья́ный. **intoxication** n опьяне́ние.

intractable adj неподатливый.

intransigent adj н~примири́мый.

intransitive adj непереходный.

intrepid adj неустраши́мый.

intricacy n запу́танность. **intricate** adj запу́танный.

intrigue n интри́га; vi интригова́ть impf; vt интригова́ть impf, за~ pf.

intrinsic adj прису́щий; (value) вну́тренний.

introduce vt вводи́ть impf, ввести́ pf; (person) представля́ть impf, предста́вить pf. **introduction** n введе́ние; представле́ние; (to book) предисло́вие. **introductory** adj вступи́тельный.

introspection n интроспе́кция.

intrude vi вторга́ться impf, вто́ргнуться pf (into в+acc); (disturb) меша́ть impf, по~ pf. **intruder** n (burglar) граби́тель m. **intrusion** n вторже́ние.

intuition n интуи́ция. **intuitive** adj интуити́вный.

inundate vt наводня́ть impf, наводни́ть pf (with +instr). **inundation** n наводне́ние.

invade vt вторга́ться impf, вто́ргнуться pf в+acc. **invader** n захва́тчик.

invalid[1] n (person) инвали́д.

invalid[2] adj недействи́тельный. **invalidate** vt де́лать impf, с~ pf неде́йствительным.

invaluable adj неоцени́мый.

invariable adj неизме́нный.

invasion n вторже́ние.

invective n брань.

invent vt изобрета́ть impf, изобрести́ pf; (think up) выду́мывать impf, вы́думать pf. **invention** n изобрете́ние; вы́думка. **inventive** adj изобрета́тельный. **inventor** n изобрета́тель m.

inventory n инвента́рь m.

inverse adj обра́тный; n противополо́жность. **invert** vt перевора́чивать impf, переверну́ть pf. **inverted commas** n pl кавы́чки f pl.

invest vt & i (econ) вкла́дывать impf, вложи́ть pf (де́ньги) (in в+acc).

investigate vt иссле́довать impf & pf; (law) рассле́довать impf & pf. **investigation** n иссле́дование; рассле́дование.

investment n (econ) вклад. **investor** n вкла́дчик.

inveterate adj закорене́лый.

invidious adj оскорби́тельный.

invigorate vt оживля́ть impf, оживи́ть pf.

invincible adj непобеди́мый.

inviolable adj неруши́мый.

invisible adj неви́димый.

invitation n приглаше́ние. **invite** vt приглаша́ть impf, пригласи́ть pf. **inviting** adj привлека́тельный.

invoice n факту́ра.

invoke vt обраща́ться impf, обрати́ться pf к+dat.

involuntary adj нево́льный.

involve vt (entangle) вовлека́ть impf, вовле́чь pf; (entail) влечь impf за собо́й. **involved** adj сло́жный.

invulnerable adj неуязви́мый.

inward adj вну́тренний. **inwardly** adv внутри́. **inwards** adv внутрь.

iodine n йод.

iota n: not an ~ ни на йо́ту.

IOU n долгова́я распи́ска.

Iran n Ира́н. **Iranian** n ира́нец, -нка; adj ира́нский.

Iraq n Ира́к. **Iraqi** n ира́кец; жи́тель m, ~ница Ира́ка; adj ира́кский.

irascible adj раздражи́тельный.

irate adj гне́вный.

Ireland n Ирла́ндия.

iris n (anat) ра́дужная оболо́чка; (bot) каса́тик.

Irish adj ирла́ндский. **Irishman** n ирла́ндец. **Irishwoman** n ирла́ндка.

irk vt раздража́ть impf, раздражи́ть pf +dat. **irksome** adj раздражи́тельный.

iron n желе́зо; (for clothes) утю́г; adj желе́зный; vt гла́дить impf, вы́~ pf. **ironic(al)** adj ирони́ческий. **irony** n иро́ния.

irradiate vt (subject to radiation) облуча́ть impf, облучи́ть pf. **irradiation** n облуче́ние.

irrational adj неразу́мный.

irreconcilable adj непримири́мый.

irrefutable adj неопроверж́мый.

irregular adj нерегуля́рный; (gram) непра́вильный; (not even) неро́вный.

irrelevant adj неуме́стный.

irreparable adj непоправи́мый.

irreplaceable adj незамени́мый.

irrepressible adj неудержи́мый.

irreproachable adj безупре́чный.

irresistible adj неотрази́мый.

irresolute adj нереши́тельный.

irrespective adj: ~ of несмотря́ на +acc.

irresponsible adj безотве́тственный.

irretrievable adj непоправи́мый.

irreverent adj непочти́тельный.

irreversible adj необрати́мый.
irrevocable adj неотменя́емый.
irrigate vt ороша́ть impf, ороси́ть pf.
irrigation n ороше́ние.
irritable adj раздражи́тельный. **irritate** vt раздража́ть impf, раздражи́ть pf. **irritation** n раздраже́ние.
Islam n исла́м. **Islamic** adj мусульма́нский.
island, isle n о́стров. **islander** n островитя́нин, -я́нка.
isolate vt изоли́ровать impf & pf. **isolation** n изоля́ция.
Israel n Изра́иль m. **Israeli** n изра-ильтя́нин, -я́нка; adj изра́ильский.
issue n (question) (спо́рный) вопро́с; (of bonds etc.) вы́пуск; (of magazine) но́мер; vi выходи́ть impf, вы́йти pf; (flow) вытека́ть impf, вы́течь pf; vt выпуска́ть impf, вы́пустить pf; (give out) выдава́ть impf, вы́дать pf.
isthmus n переше́ек.
it pron он, она́, оно́; demonstrative э́то.
Italian n италья́нец, -нка; adj италья́нский.
italics n pl курси́в; in ~ курси́вом. **italicize** vt выделя́ть impf, вы́делить pf курси́вом.
Italy n Ита́лия.
ITAR-Tass abbr ИТА́Р-ТА́СС.
itch n зуд; vi чеса́ться impf.
item n (on list) предме́т; (in account) статья́; (on agenda) пункт; (in programme) но́мер. **itemize** vt перечисля́ть impf, перечи́слить pf.
itinerant adj стра́нствующий. **itinerary** n маршру́т.
its poss pron его́, её; свой.
itself pron (emph) (он(о́)) сам(о́), (она́) сама́; (refl) себя́; -ся (suffixed to vt).
ivory n слоно́вая кость.
ivy n плющ.

J

jab n толчо́к; (injection) уко́л; vt ты́-кать impf, ткнуть pf.
jabber vi тарато́рить impf.
jack n (cards) вале́т; (lifting device) домкра́т; vt (~ up) поднима́ть impf, подня́ть pf домкра́том.

jackdaw n га́лка.
jacket n (tailored) пиджа́к; (anorak) ку́ртка; (on book) (су́пер)обло́жка.
jackpot n банк.
jade n (mineral) нефри́т.
jaded adj утомлённый.
jagged adj зазу́бренный.
jaguar n ягуа́р.
jail see **gaol**
jam[1] n (crush) да́вка; (in traffic) про́бка; vt (thrust) впи́хивать impf, впихну́ть pf (into в+acc); (wedge open; block) закли́нивать impf, закли́нить pf; (radio) заглуша́ть impf, заглуши́ть pf; vi (machine) закли́ниваться impf, закли́ниться pf impers+acc).
jam[2] n (conserve) варе́нье, джем.
jangle vi (& t) звяка́ть (+instr).
janitor n привра́тник.
January n янва́рь; adj янва́рский.
Japan n Япо́ния. **Japanese** n япо́нец, -нка; adj япо́нский.
jar[1] n (container) ба́нка.
jar[2] vi (irritate) раздража́ть impf, раздражи́ть pf (upon +acc).
jargon n жарго́н.
jasmin(e) n жасми́н.
jaundice n желту́ха. **jaundiced** adj (fig) цини́чный.
jaunt n прогу́лка. **jaunty** adj бо́дрый.
javelin n копьё.
jaw n че́люсть; pl пасть, рот.
jay n со́йка.
jazz n джаз; adj джа́зовый.
jealous adj ревни́вый; (envious) зави́стливый; be ~ of (person) ревнова́ть impf; (thing) зави́довать impf, по~ pf +dat; (rights) ревни́во обере-га́ть impf, обере́чь pf. **jealousy** n ре́вность; за́висть.
jeans n pl джи́нсы (-сов) pl.
jeer n насме́шка; vt & i насмеха́ться impf (at над+instr).
jelly n (sweet) желе́ neut indecl; (aspic) студе́нь m. **jellyfish** n меду́за.
jeopardize vt подверга́ть impf, подве́ргнуть pf опа́сности. **jeopardy** n опа́сность.
jerk n рыво́к; vt дёргать impf +instr; vi (twitch) дёргаться impf, дёр-нуться pf. **jerky** adj неро́вный.
jersey n (garment) джéмпер; (fabric) джéрси neut indecl.
jest n шу́тка; in ~ в шу́тку; vi шути́ть

impf, по~ *pf*. **jester** *n* шут.

jet¹ *n* (*stream*) струя́; (*nozzle*) со́пло; ~ **engine** реакти́вный дви́гатель *m*; ~ **plane** реакти́вный самолёт.

jet² *n* (*mineralogy*) гага́т; ~-**black** чёрный как смоль.

jettison *vt* выбра́сывать *impf*, вы́бросить *pf* за борт.

jetty *n* при́стань.

Jew *n* евре́й, евре́йка. **Jewish** *adj* евре́йский.

jewel *n* драгоце́нность, драгоце́нный ка́мень *m*. **jeweller** *n* ювели́р. **jewellery** *n* драгоце́нности *f pl*.

jib *n* (*naut*) кли́вер; *vi*: ~ **at** уклоня́ться *impf* от+*gen*.

jigsaw *n* (*puzzle*) моза́ика.

jingle *n* зня́канье; *vi* (& *t*) зня́кать *impf*, зня́кнуть *pf* (+*instr*).

job *n* (*work*) рабо́та; (*task*) зада́ние; (*position*) ме́сто. **jobless** *adj* безрабо́тный.

jockey *n* жоке́й; *vi* оттира́ть *impf* друг дру́га.

jocular *adj* шутли́вый.

jog *n* (*push*) толчо́к; *vt* подта́лкивать *impf*, подтолкну́ть *pf*; *vi* бе́гать *impf* трусцо́й. **jogger** *n* занима́ющийся оздорови́тельным бе́гом. **jogging** *n* оздорови́тельный бег.

join *vt* & *i* соединя́ть(ся) *impf*, соедини́ть(ся) *pf*; *vt* (*a group of people*) присоединя́ться *impf*, присоедини́ться *pf* к+*dat*; (*as member*) вступа́ть *impf*, вступи́ть *pf* в+*acc*; *vi*: ~ **in** принима́ть *impf*, приня́ть *pf* уча́стие (в+*prep*); ~ **up** вступа́ть *impf*, вступи́ть *pf* в а́рмию.

joiner *n* столя́р.

joint *n* соедине́ние; (*anat*) суста́в; (*meat*) кусо́к; *adj* совме́стный; (*common*) о́бщий.

joist *n* перекла́дина.

joke *n* шу́тка; *vi* шути́ть *impf*, по~ *pf*. **joker** *n* шутни́к; (*cards*) джо́кер.

jollity *n* весе́лье. **jolly** *adj* весёлый; *adv* о́чень.

jolt *n* толчо́к; *vt* & *i* трясти́(сь) *impf*.

jostle *vt* & *i* толка́ть(ся) *impf*, толкну́ть(ся) *pf*.

jot *n* йо́та; **not a** ~ ни на йо́ту; *vt* (~ **down**) запи́сывать *impf*, записа́ть *pf*.

journal *n* журна́л; (*diary*) дневни́к.

journalese *n* газе́тный язы́к. **journalism** *n* журнали́стика. **journalist** *n* журнали́ст.

journey *n* путеше́ствие; *vi* путеше́ствовать *impf*.

jovial *adj* весёлый.

joy *n* ра́дость. **joyful, joyous** *adj* ра́достный. **joyless** *adj* безра́достный. **joystick** *n* рыча́г управле́ния; (*comput*) джо́йстик.

jubilant *adj* лику́ющий; **be** ~ ликова́ть *impf*. **jubilation** *n* ликова́ние.

jubilee *n* юбиле́й.

Judaism *n* юдаи́зм.

judge *n* судья́ *m*; (*connoisseur*) цени́тель *m*; *vt* & *i* суди́ть *impf*. **judgement** *n* (*legal decision*) реше́ние; (*opinion*) мне́ние; (*discernment*) рассуди́тельность.

judicial *adj* суде́бный. **judiciary** *n* судьи́ *m pl*. **judicious** *adj* здравомы́слящий.

judo *n* дзюдо́ *neut indecl*.

jug *n* кувши́н.

juggernaut *n* (*lorry*) многото́нный грузови́к; (*fig*) неумоли́мая си́ла.

juggle *vi* жонгли́ровать *impf*. **juggler** *n* жонглёр.

jugular *n* яре́мная ве́на.

juice *n* сок. **juicy** *adj* со́чный.

July *n* ию́ль *m*; *adj* ию́льский.

jumble *n* (*disorder*) беспоря́док; (*articles*) барахло́; *vt* перепу́тывать *impf*, перепу́тать *pf*.

jump *n* прыжо́к, скачо́к; *vi* пры́гать *impf*, пры́гнуть *pf*; скака́ть *impf*; (*from shock*) вздра́гивать *impf*, вздро́гнуть *pf*; *vt* (~ **over**) перепры́гивать *impf*, перепры́гнуть *pf*; ~ **at** (*offer*) хвата́ться *impf*, ухвати́ться *pf* за+*acc*; ~ **up** вска́кивать *impf*, вскочи́ть *pf*.

jumper *n* дже́мпер.

jumpy *adj* не́рвный.

junction *n* (*rly*) у́зел; (*roads*) перекрёсток.

juncture *n*: **at this** ~ в э́тот моме́нт.

June *n* ию́нь *m*; *adj* ию́ньский.

jungle *n* джу́нгли (-лей) *pl*.

junior *adj* мла́дший; ~ **school** нача́льная шко́ла.

juniper *n* можжеве́льник.

junk *n* (*rubbish*) барахло́.

jurisdiction *n* юрисди́кция.

jurisprudence *n* юриспруде́нция.

juror *n* прися́жный *sb.* **jury** *n* прися́жные *sb*; (*in competition*) жюри́ *neut indecl.*

just *adj* (*fair*) справедли́вый; (*deserved*) заслу́женный; *adv* (*exactly*) как раз, и́менно; (*simply*) про́сто; (*barely*) едва́; (*very recently*) то́лько что; ~ **in case** на вся́кий слу́чай.

justice *n* (*proceedings*) правосу́дие; (*fairness*) справедли́вость; **do ~ to** отдава́ть *impf*, отда́ть *pf* до́лжное +*dat.*

justify *vt* опра́вдывать *impf*, оправда́ть *pf.* **justification** *n* оправда́ние.

jut *vi* (~ *out*) выдава́ться *impf*; выступа́ть *impf.*

juvenile *n* & *adj* несовершенноле́тний *sb* & *adj.*

juxtapose *vt* помеща́ть *impf*, помести́ть *pf* ря́дом; (*for comparison*) сопоставля́ть *impf*, сопоста́вить *pf* (*with* с+*instr*).

K

kaleidoscope *n* калейдоско́п.
kangaroo *n* кенгуру́ *m indecl.*
Kazakhstan *n* Казахста́н.
keel *n* киль *m*; *vi*: ~ **over** опроки́дываться *impf*, опроки́нуться *pf.*
keen *adj* (*enthusiastic*) по́лный энтузиа́зма; (*sharp*) о́стрый; (*strong*) си́льный; **be ~ on** увлека́ться *impf*, увле́чься *pf* +*instr*; (*want to do*) о́чень хоте́ть *impf* +*inf.*
keep[1] *n* (*tower*) гла́вная ба́шня; (*maintenance*) содержа́ние.
keep[2] *vt* (*possess, maintain*) держа́ть *impf*; храни́ть *impf*; (*observe*) соблюда́ть *impf*, соблюсти́ *pf* (*the law*); сде́рживать *impf*, сдержа́ть *pf* (*one's word*); (*family*) содержа́ть *impf*; (*diary*) вести́ *impf*; (*detain*) заде́рживать *impf*, задержа́ть *pf*; (*retain, reserve*) сохраня́ть *impf*, сохрани́ть *pf*; *vi* (*remain*) остава́ться *impf*, оста́ться *pf*; (*of food*) не по́ртиться *impf*; ~ **back** (*vt*) (*hold back*) уде́рживать *impf*, удержа́ть *pf*; (*vi*) держа́ться *impf* сза́ди; ~ **do- ing sth** всё +*verb*: **she ~s giggling** она́ всё хихи́кает; ~ **from** уде́рживаться *impf*, удержа́ться *pf* от+*gen*; ~ **on** продолжа́ть *impf*; продол-

жить *pf* (+*inf*); ~ **up** (**with**) (*vi*) не отстава́ть *impf* (от+*gen*).
keepsake *n* пода́рок на па́мять.
keg *n* бочо́нок.
kennel *n* конура́.
kerb *n* край тротуа́ра.
kernel *n* (*nut*) ядро́; (*grain*) зерно́; (*fig*) суть.
kerosene *n* кероси́н.
kettle *n* ча́йник.
key *n* ключ; (*piano, typewriter*) кла́виш(а); (*mus*) тона́льность; *attrib* веду́щий, ключево́й. **keyboard** *n* клавиату́ра. **keyhole** *n* замо́чная сква́жина.
KGB *abbr* КГБ.
khaki *n* & *adj* ха́ки *neut, adj indecl.*
kick *n* уда́р ного́й, пино́к; *vt* ударя́ть *impf*, уда́рить *pf* ного́й; пина́ть *impf*, пнуть *pf*; *vi* (*of horse etc.*) ляга́ться *impf.* **kick-off** *n* нача́ло (игры́).
kid[1] *n* (*goat*) козлёнок; (*child*) малы́ш.
kid[2] *vt* (*deceive*) обма́нывать *impf*, обману́ть *pf*; *vi* (*joke*) шути́ть *impf*, по~ *pf.*
kidnap *vt* похища́ть *impf*, похи́тить *pf.*
kidney *n* по́чка.
kill *vt* убива́ть *impf*, уби́ть *pf.* **killer** *n* уби́йца *m* & *f.* **killing** *n* уби́йство; *adj* (*murderous, fig*) уби́йственный; (*amusing*) умори́тельный.
kiln *n* обжи́говая печь.
kilo *n* кило́ *neut indecl.* **kilohertz** *n* килоге́рц. **kilogram(me)** *n* килогра́мм. **kilometre** *n* киломе́тр. **kilowatt** *n* килова́тт.
kilt *n* шотла́ндская ю́бка.
kimono *n* кимоно́ *neut indecl.*
kin *n* (*family*) семья́; (*collect, relatives*) родня́.
kind[1] *n* сорт, род; **a ~ of** что́-то вро́де+*gen*; **this ~ of** тако́й; **what ~ of** что (э́то, он, *etc.*) за +*nom*; **~ of** (*adv*) как бу́дто, ка́к-то.
kind[2] *adj* до́брый.
kindergarten *n* де́тский сад.
kindle *vt* зажига́ть *impf*, заже́чь *pf.* **kindling** *n* расто́пка.
kindly *adj* до́брый; *adv* любе́зно; (*with imper*) (*request*) бу́дьте добры́, +*imper.* **kindness** *n* доброта́.
kindred *adj*: ~ **spirit** родна́я душа́.

kinetic adj кинети́ческий.

king n коро́ль m (also chess, cards, fig); (draughts) да́мка. **kingdom** n короле́вство; (fig) ца́рство. **kingfisher** n зиморо́док.

kink n переги́б.

kinship n родство́; (similarity) схо́дство. **kinsman, -woman** n ро́дственник, -ица.

kiosk n кио́ск; (telephone) бу́дка.

kip n сон; vi дрыхну́ть impf.

kipper n копчёная селёдка.

Kirghizia n Кирги́зия.

kiss n поцелу́й; vt & i целова́ть(ся) impf, по~ pf.

kit n (clothing) снаряже́ние; (tools) набо́р, компле́кт; vt: ~ out снаряжа́ть impf, снаряди́ть pf. **kitbag** n вещево́й мешо́к.

kitchen n ку́хня; attrib ку́хонный; ~ garden огоро́д.

kite n (toy) змей.

kitsch n дешёвка.

kitten n котёнок.

knack n сноро́вка.

knapsack n рюкза́к.

knead vt меси́ть impf, c~ pf.

knee n коле́но. **kneecap** n коле́нная ча́шка.

kneel vi стоя́ть impf на коле́нях; (~ down) станови́ться impf, стать pf на коле́ни.

knickers n pl тру́сики (-ов) pl.

knick-knack n безделу́шка.

knife n нож; vt коло́ть impf, за~ pf ножо́м.

knight n (hist) ры́царь m; (holder of order) кавале́р; (chess) конь m. **knighthood** n ры́царское зва́ние.

knit vt (garment) вяза́ть impf, c~ pf; vi (bones) сраста́ться impf, срасти́сь pf; ~ one's brows хму́рить impf, на~ pf бро́ви. **knitting** n (action) вяза́ние; (object) вяза́нье; ~-needle спи́ца. **knitwear** n трикота́ж.

knob n ши́шка, кно́пка; (door handle) ру́чка. **knobb(l)y** adj ши́шкова́тый.

knock n (noise) стук; (blow) уда́р; vt & i (strike) ударя́ть impf, уда́рить pf; (strike door etc.) стуча́ть impf, по~ pf (at в+acc); ~ about (treat roughly) колоти́ть impf, по~ pf; (wander) шата́ться impf; ~ down (person) сбива́ть impf, сбить pf с

ног; (building) сноси́ть impf, снести́ pf; ~ off сбива́ть impf, сбить pf; (stop work) шаба́шить impf (рабо́ту); (deduct) сбавля́ть impf, сба́вить pf; ~ out выбива́ть impf, вы́бить pf; (sport) нокаути́ровать impf & pf; ~-out нока́ут; ~ over опроки́дывать impf, опроки́нуть impf. **knocker** n дверно́й молото́к.

knoll n буго́р.

knot n у́зел; vt завя́зывать impf, завяза́ть pf узло́м. **knotty** adj (fig) запу́танный.

know vt знать impf; (~ how to) уме́ть impf, c~ pf +inf; ~-how уме́ние. **knowing** adj многозначи́тельный. **knowingly** adv созна́тельно. **knowledge** n зна́ние; to my ~ наско́лько мне изве́стно.

knuckle n суста́в па́льца; vi: ~ down to впряга́ться impf, впря́чься pf в+acc; ~ under уступа́ть impf, уступи́ть pf (to +dat).

Korea n Коре́я.

ko(w)tow vi (fig) раболе́пствовать impf (to пе́ред+instr).

Kremlin n Кремль m.

kudos n сла́ва.

L

label n этике́тка, ярлы́к; vt прикле́ивать impf, прикле́ить pf ярлы́к к+dat.

laboratory n лаборато́рия.

laborious adj кропотли́вый.

labour n труд; (med) ро́ды (-дов) pl; attrib трудово́й; ~ force рабо́чая си́ла; ~-intensive трудоёмкий; L~ Party лейбори́стская па́ртия; vi труди́ться impf; vt: ~ a point входи́ть impf, войти́ pf в изли́шние подро́бности. **laboured** adj затруднённый; (style) вы́мученный. **labourer** n чернорабо́чий sb. **labourite** n лейбори́ст.

labyrinth n лабири́нт.

lace n (fabric) кру́жево; (cord) шнуро́к; vt (~ up) шнурова́ть impf, за~ pf.

lacerate vt (also fig) терза́ть impf, ис~ pf. **laceration** n (wound) рва́ная ра́на.

lack n недоста́ток (of +gen, в+prep),

отсу́тствие; *vt* & *i* не хвата́ть *impf*, хвати́ть *pf* impers +dat (person), +gen (object).

lackadaisical *adj* то́мный.

laconic *adj* лакони́чный.

lacquer *n* лак; *vt* лакирова́ть *impf*, от~ *pf.*

lad *n* па́рень *m.*

ladder *n* ле́стница.

laden *adj* нагру́женный.

ladle *n* (spoon) поло́вник; *vt* че́рпать *impf*, черпну́ть *pf.*

lady *n* да́ма, ле́ди *f indecl.* **ladybird** *n* бо́жья коро́вка.

lag[1] *vi*: ~ behind отстава́ть *impf*, отста́ть *pf* (от+gen).

lag[2] *vt* (insulate) изоли́ровать *impf* & *pf.*

lagoon *n* лагу́на.

lair *n* ло́говище.

laity *n* (in religion) миря́не (-н) *pl.*

lake *n* о́зеро.

lamb *n* ягнёнок.

lame *adj* хромо́й; be ~ хрома́ть *impf*; go ~ хроме́ть *impf*, о~ *pf*; *vt* кале́чить *impf*, о~ *pf.*

lament *n* плач; *vt* сожале́ть *impf* о+prep. **lamentable** *adj* приско́рбный.

laminated *adj* слои́стый.

lamp *n* ла́мпа; (in street) фона́рь *m.* **lamp-post** *n* фона́рный столб. **lampshade** *n* абажу́р.

lance *n* пи́ка; *vt* (med) вскрыва́ть *impf*, вскрыть *pf* (ланце́том).

land *n* земля́; (dry ~) су́ша; (country) страна́; *vi* (naut) прича́ливать *impf*, прича́лить *pf*; *vt* & *i* (aeron) приземля́ть(ся) *impf*, приземли́ть(ся) *pf*; (find o.s.) попада́ть *impf*, попа́сть *pf*. **landing** *n* (aeron) поса́дка; (on stairs) площа́дка; ~-stage при́стань *n.* **landlady** *n* хозя́йка. **landlord** *n* хозя́ин. **landmark** *n* (conspicuous object) ориенти́р; (fig) ве́ха. **landowner** *n* землевладе́лец. **landscape** *n* ландша́фт; (also picture) пейза́ж. **landslide** *n* о́ползень *m.*

lane *n* (in country) доро́жка; (street) переу́лок; (passage) прохо́д; (on road) ряд; (in race) доро́жка.

language *n* язы́к; (style, speech) речь.

languid *adj* то́мный.

languish *vi* томи́ться *impf.*

languor *n* то́мность.

lank *adj* (hair) гла́дкий. **lanky** *adj* долговя́зый.

lantern *n* фона́рь *m.*

lap[1] *n* (of person) коле́ни (-ней) *pl*; (sport) круг.

lap[2] *vt* (drink) лака́ть *impf*, вы́~ *pf*; *vi* (water) плеска́ться *impf.*

lapel *n* отворо́т.

lapse *n* (mistake) оши́бка; (interval) промежу́ток; (expiry) истече́ние; *vi* впада́ть *impf*, впасть *pf* (into в+acc); (expire) истека́ть *impf*, исте́чь *pf.*

lapwing *n* чи́бис.

larch *n* ли́ственница.

lard *n* свино́е са́ло.

larder *n* кладова́я sb.

large *adj* большо́й; *n*: at ~ (free) на свобо́де; by and ~ вообще́ говоря́; **largely** *adj* в значи́тельной сте́пени.

largesse *n* ще́дрость.

lark[1] *n* (bird) жа́воронок.

lark[2] *n* прока́за; *vi* (~ about) резви́ться *impf.*

larva *n* личи́нка.

laryngitis *n* ларинги́т. **larynx** *n* горта́нь.

lascivious *adj* похотли́вый.

laser *n* ла́зер.

lash *n* (blow) уда́р плётью; (eyelash) ресни́ца; *vt* (beat) хлеста́ть *impf*, хлестну́ть *pf*; (tie) привя́зывать *impf*, привяза́ть *pf* (to к+dat).

last[1] *n* (cobbler's) коло́дка.

last[2] *adj* (final) после́дний; (most recent) про́шлый; the year (etc.) before ~ позапро́шлый год (и т.д.); ~ but one предпосле́дний; ~ night вчера́ ве́чером; at ~ наконе́ц; *adv* (after all others) по́сле всех; (on the last occasion) в после́дний раз; (lastly) наконе́ц.

last[3] *vi* (go on) продолжа́ться *impf*, продо́лжиться *pf*; дли́ться *impf*, про~ *pf*; (be preserved) сохраня́ться *impf*, сохрани́ться *pf*; (suffice) хвата́ть *impf*, хвати́ть *pf*. **lasting** *adj* (permanent) постоя́нный; (durable) про́чный.

lastly *adv* в заключе́ние; наконе́ц.

latch *n* щеко́лда.

late *adj* по́здний; (recent) неда́вний; (dead) поко́йный; be ~ for опа́здывать *impf*, опозда́ть *pf* на+acc; *adv* по́здно; *n*: of ~ за после́днее вре́мя. **lately** *adv* за после́днее вре́мя.

latent adj скры́тый.

lateral adj боково́й.

lath n ре́йка, дра́нка (also collect).

lathe n тока́рный стано́к.

lather n (мы́льная) пе́на; vt & i мы́лить(ся) impf, на~ pf.

Latin adj лати́нский; n лати́нский язы́к; ~-**American** латиноамерика́нский.

latitude n свобо́да; (geog) широта́.

latter adj после́дний; ~-**day** совреме́нный. **latterly** adv за после́днее вре́мя.

lattice n решётка.

Latvia n Ла́твия. **Latvian** n латви́ец, -и́йка; латы́ш, ~ка; adj латви́йский, латы́шский.

laud vt хвали́ть impf, по~ pf. **laudable** adj похва́льный.

laugh n смех; vi смея́ться impf (at над+instr); ~ **it off** отшу́чиваться impf, отшути́ться pf; ~**ing-stock** посме́шище. **laughable** adj смешно́й. **laughter** n смех.

launch[1] vt (ship) спуска́ть impf, спусти́ть pf на́ воду; (rocket) запуска́ть impf, запусти́ть pf; (undertake) начина́ть impf, нача́ть pf; n спуск на́ воду; за́пуск. **launcher** n (for rocket) пускова́я устано́вка. **launching pad** n пускова́я площа́дка.

launch[2] n (naut) ка́тер.

launder vt стира́ть impf, вы́~ pf. **laund(e)rette** n пра́чечная sb самообслу́живания. **laundry** n (place) пра́чечная sb; (articles) бельё.

laurel n ла́вр(овое де́рево).

lava n ла́ва.

lavatory n убо́рная sb.

lavender n лава́нда.

lavish adj ще́дрый; (abundant) оби́льный; vt расточа́ть impf (upon +dat).

law n зако́н; (system) пра́во; ~ **and order** правопоря́док. **law-court** n суд. **lawful** adj зако́нный. **lawless** adj беззако́нный.

lawn n газо́н; ~-**mower** газонокоси́лка.

lawsuit n проце́сс.

lawyer n адвока́т, юри́ст.

lax adj сла́бый. **laxative** n слаби́тельное sb. **laxity** n сла́бость.

lay[1] adj (non-clerical) све́тский.

lay[2] vt (place) класть impf, положи́ть pf; (cable, pipes) прокла́дывать impf, проложи́ть pf; (carpet) стлать impf, по~ pf; (trap etc.) устра́ивать impf, устро́ить pf; (eggs) класть impf, положи́ть pf; v abs (lay eggs) нести́сь impf, с~ pf; ~ **aside** откла́дывать impf, отложи́ть pf; ~ **bare** раскрыва́ть impf, раскры́ть pf; ~ **a bet** держа́ть пари́ (on на+acc); ~ **down** (relinquish) отка́зываться impf, отказа́ться pf от +gen; (rule etc.) устана́вливать impf, установи́ть pf; ~ **off** (workmen) увольня́ть impf, уво́лить pf; ~ **out** (spread) выкла́дывать impf, вы́ложить pf; (garden) разбива́ть impf, разби́ть pf; ~ **the table** накрыва́ть impf, накры́ть pf стол (for (meal) к+dat); ~ **up** запаса́ть impf, запасти́ pf +acc, +gen; **be laid up** быть прико́ванным к посте́ли. **layabout** n безде́льник.

layer n слой, пласт.

layman n миря́нин; (non-expert) неспециали́ст.

laze vi безде́льничать impf. **laziness** n лень. **lazy** adj лени́вый; ~-**bones** n лентя́й, ~ка.

lead[1] n (example) приме́р; (leadership) руково́дство; (position) пе́рвое ме́сто; (theat) гла́вная роль; (electr) про́вод; (dog's) поводо́к; vt води́ть indet, вести́ det; (be in charge of) руководи́ть impf +instr; (induce) побужда́ть impf, побуди́ть pf; vt & i (cards) ходи́ть impf (с+gen); vi (sport) занима́ть impf, заня́ть pf пе́рвое ме́сто; ~ **away** уводи́ть impf, увести́ pf; ~ **to** (result in) приводи́ть impf, привести́ pf к+dat.

lead[2] n (metal) свине́ц. **leaden** adj свинцо́вый.

leader n руководи́тель m, ~ница, ли́дер; (mus) пе́рвая скри́пка; (editorial) передова́я статья́. **leadership** n руково́дство.

leading adj веду́щий, выдаю́щийся; ~ **article** передова́я статья́.

leaf n лист; (of table) откидна́я доска́; vi: ~ **through** перели́стывать impf, перелиста́ть pf. **leaflet** n листо́вка.

league n ли́га; **in** ~ **with** в сою́зе с +instr.

leak n течь, уте́чка; vi (escape) течь impf; (allow water to ~) пропуска́ть *impf* во́ду; ~ out проса́чиваться *impf*, просочи́ться *pf*.

lean[1] *adj* (*thin*) худо́й; (*meat*) по́стный.

lean[2] *vt* & *i* прислоня́ть(ся) *impf*, прислони́ть(ся) *pf* (against к+*dat*); *vi* (~ on, rely on) опира́ться *impf*, опере́ться *pf* (on на+*acc*); (*be inclined*) быть скло́нным (to(wards) к+*dat*); ~ back отки́дываться *impf*, отки́нуться *pf*; ~ out of высо́вываться *impf*, вы́сунуться *pf* в +*acc*. **leaning** *n* скло́нность.

leap *n* прыжо́к, скачо́к; *vi* пры́гать *impf*, пры́гнуть *pf*; скака́ть *impf*; ~ year високо́сный год.

learn *vt* учи́ться *impf*, об~ *pf* +*dat*; (*find out*) узнава́ть *impf*, узна́ть *pf*. **learned** *adj* учёный. **learner** *n* учени́к, -и́ца. **learning** *n* (*studies*) уче́ние; (*erudition*) учёность.

lease *n* аре́нда; *vt* (*of owner*) сдава́ть *impf*, сдать *pf* в аре́нду; (*of tenant*) брать *impf*, взять *pf* в аре́нду. **leaseholder** *n* аренда́тор.

leash *n* при́вязь.

least *adj* наиме́ньший, мале́йший; *adv* ме́нее всего́; at ~ по кра́йней ме́ре; not in the ~ ничу́ть.

leather *n* ко́жа; *attrib* ко́жаный.

leave[1] *n* (*permission*) разреше́ние; (*holiday*) о́тпуск; on ~ в о́тпуске; take (one's) ~ проща́ться *impf*, прости́ться *pf* (of с+*instr*).

leave[2] *vt* & *i* оставля́ть *impf*, оста́вить *pf*; (*abandon*) покида́ть *impf*, поки́нуть *pf*; (*go away*) уходи́ть *impf*, уйти́ *pf* (from от+*gen*); уезжа́ть *impf*, уе́хать *pf* (from от+*gen*); (*go out of*) выходи́ть *impf*, вы́йти *pf* из+*gen*; (*entrust*) предоставля́ть *impf*, предоста́вить *pf* (to +*dat*); ~ out пропуска́ть *impf*, пропусти́ть *pf*.

lecherous *adj* развра́тный.

lectern *n* анало́й; (*in lecture room*) пюпи́тр.

lecture *n* (*discourse*) ле́кция; (*reproof*) нота́ция; *vi* (*deliver* ~(s)) чита́ть *impf*, про~ ле́кцию (-ии) (on по+*dat*); *vt* (*admonish*) чита́ть *impf*, про~ нота́цию+*dat*; ~ room аудито́рия. **lecturer** *n* ле́ктор; (*univ*) преподава́тель *m*, ~ница.

ledge *n* вы́ступ; (*shelf*) по́лочка.

ledger *n* гла́вная кни́га.

lee *n* защи́та; *adj* подве́тренный.

leech *n* (*worm*) пия́вка.

leek *n* лук-поре́й.

leer *vi* криви́ться *impf*, с~ *pf*.

leeward *n* подве́тренная сторона́; *adj* подве́тренный.

leeway *n* (*fig*) свобо́да де́йствий.

left *n* ле́вая сторона́; (the L~; *polit*) ле́вые *sb pl*; *adj* ле́вый; *adv* нале́во, сле́ва (of от+*gen*); ~-hander левша́ *m* & *f*; ~-wing ле́вый.

left-luggage office *n* ка́мера хране́ния.

leftovers *n pl* оста́тки *m pl*; (*food*) объе́дки (-ков) *pl*.

leg *n* нога́; (*of furniture etc.*) но́жка; (*of journey etc.*) эта́п.

legacy *n* насле́дство.

legal *adj* (*of the law*) правово́й; (*lawful*) лега́льный. **legality** *n* лега́льность. **legalize** *vt* легализи́ровать *impf* & *pf*.

legend *n* леге́нда. **legendary** *adj* легенда́рный.

leggings *n pl* вя́заные рейту́зы (-з) *pl*.

legible *adj* разбо́рчивый.

legion *n* легио́н.

legislate *vi* издава́ть *impf*, изда́ть *pf* зако́ны. **legislation** *n* законода́тельство. **legislative** *adj* законода́тельный. **legislator** *n* законода́тель *m*. **legislature** *n* законода́тельные учрежде́ния *neut pl*.

legitimacy *n* зако́нность; (*of child*) законнорождённость. **legitimate** *adj* зако́нный; (*child*) законнорождённый. **legitimize** *vt* узако́нивать *impf*, узако́нить *pf*.

leisure *n* свобо́дное вре́мя, досу́г; at ~ на досу́ге. **leisurely** *adj* неторопли́вый.

lemon *n* лимо́н. **lemonade** *n* лимона́д.

lend *vt* дава́ть *impf*, дать *pf* взаймы́ (to +*dat*); ода́лживать *impf*, одолжи́ть *pf* (to +*dat*).

length *n* длина́; (*of time*) продолжи́тельность; (*of cloth*) отре́з; at ~ подро́бно. **lengthen** *vt* & *i* удлиня́ть(ся) *impf*, удлини́ть(ся) *pf*. **lengthways** *adv* в длину́, вдоль. **lengthy** *adj* дли́нный.

leniency *n* снисходи́тельность. **lenient** *adj* снисходи́тельный.

lens n линза; (*phot*) объектив; (*anat*) хрусталик.

Lent n великий пост.

lentil n чечевица.

Leo n Лев.

leopard n леопард.

leotard n трико *neut indecl*.

leper n прокажённый *sb*. **leprosy** n проказа.

lesbian n лесбиянка; *adj* лесбийский.

lesion n повреждение.

less *adj* меньший; *adv* меньше, менее; *prep* за вычетом +*gen*.

lessee n арендатор.

lessen *vt & i* уменьшать(ся) *impf*, уменьшить(ся) *pf*.

lesser *adj* меньший.

lesson n урок.

lest *conj* (*in order that not*) чтобы не; (*that*) как бы не.

let n (*lease*) сдача в наём; *vt* (*allow*) позволять *impf*, позволить *pf* +*dat*; разрешать *impf*, разрешить *pf* +*dat*; (*rent out*) сдавать *impf*, сдать *pf* внаём (to +*dat*); *v aux* (*imperative*) (*1st person*) давай(те); (*3rd person*) пусть; ~ **alone** не говоря уже о+*prep*; ~ **down** (*lower*) опускать *impf*, опустить *pf*; (*fail*) подводить *impf*, подвести *pf*; (*disappoint*) разочаровывать *impf*, разочаровать *pf*; ~ **go** выпускать *impf*, выпустить *pf*; ~'s go пойдёмте!; пошли!; поехали!; ~ **in(to)** (*admit*) впускать *impf*, впустить *pf* в+*acc*; (*into secret*) посвящать *impf*, посвятить *pf* в+*acc*; ~ **know** давать *impf*, дать *pf* знать +*dat*; ~ **off** (*gun*) выстрелить *pf* из+*gen*; (*not punish*) отпускать *impf*, отпустить *pf* без наказания; ~ **out** (*release, loosen*) выпускать *impf*, выпустить *pf*; ~ **through** пропускать *impf*, пропустить *pf*; ~ **up** затихать *impf*, затихнуть *pf*.

lethal *adj* (*fatal*) смертельный; (*weapon*) смертоносный.

lethargic *adj* летаргический. **lethargy** n летаргия.

letter n письмо; (*symbol*) буква; (*printing*) литера; ~-**box** почтовый ящик. **lettering** n шрифт.

lettuce n салат.

leukaemia n лейкемия.

level n уровень; *adj* ровный; ~ **crossing** (железнодорожный) переезд; ~-**headed** уравновешенный; *vt* (*make* ~) выравнивать *impf*, выровнять *pf*; (*sport*) сравнивать *impf*, сравнять *pf*; (*gun*) наводить *impf*, навести *pf* (at в, на, +*acc*); (*criticism*) направлять *impf*, направить *pf* (at против+*gen*).

lever n рычаг. **leverage** n действие рычага; (*influence*) влияние.

levity n легкомыслие.

levy n (*tax*) сбор; *vt* (*tax*) взимать *impf* (from c+*gen*).

lewd *adj* (*lascivious*) похотливый; (*indecent*) сальный.

lexicon n словарь m.

liability n (*responsibility*) ответственность (for за+*acc*); (*burden*) обуза. **liable** *adj* ответственный (for за+*acc*); (*susceptible*) подверженный (to +*dat*).

liaise *vi* поддерживать *impf* связь (c+*instr*). **liaison** n связь; (*affair*) любовная связь.

liar n лгун, ~ья.

libel n клевета; *vt* клеветать *impf*, на~ *pf* на+*acc*. **libellous** *adj* клеветнический.

liberal n либерал; *adj* либеральный; (*generous*) щедрый.

liberate *vt* освобождать *impf*, освободить *pf*. **liberation** n освобождение. **liberator** n освободитель m.

libertine n распутник.

liberty n свобода; at ~ на свободе.

Libra n Весы (-сов) *pl*.

librarian n библиотекарь m. **library** n библиотека.

libretto n либретто *neut indecl*.

licence[1] n (*permission, permit*) разрешение, лицензия; (*liberty*) излишняя) вольность. **license, -ce**[2] *vt* (*allow*) разрешать *impf*, разрешить *pf* +*dat*; давать *impf*, дать *pf* право +*dat*.

licentious *adj* распущенный.

lichen n лишайник.

lick n лизание; *vt* лизать *impf*, лизнуть *pf*.

lid n крышка; (*eyelid*) веко.

lie[1] n (*untruth*) ложь; *vi* лгать *impf*, со~ *pf*.

lie[2] n: ~ **of the land** (*fig*) положение вещей; *vi* лежать *impf*; (*be situated*) находи́ться *impf*; ~ down ложи́ться *impf*, лечь *pf*; ~ in оставáться *impf* в постéли.

lieu *n*: in ~ of вмéсто+*gen*.

lieutenant *n* лейтенáнт.

life *n* жизнь; (*way of* ~) óбраз жи́зни; (*energy*) жи́вость. **lifebelt** *n* спасáтельный пóяс. **lifeboat** *n* спасáтельная лóдка. **lifebuoy** *n* спасáтельный круг. **lifeguard** *n* спасáтель *m*, -ница. **life-jacket** *n* спасáтельный жилéт. **lifeless** *adj* безжи́зненный. **lifelike** *adj* реалисти́чный. **lifeline** *n* спасáтельный конéц. **lifelong** *adj* пожи́зненный. **life-size(d)** *adj* в натурáльную величину́. **lifetime** *n* жизнь.

lift *n* (*machine*) лифт, подъёмник; (*force*) подъёмная си́ла; can I have a ~ подвози́ть *impf*, подвезти́ *pf*; *vt & i* поднимáть(ся) *impf*, подня́ть(ся) *pf*.

ligament *n* свя́зка.

light[1] *n* свет, освещéние; (*source of* ~) огóнь *m*, лáмпа, фонáрь *m*; *pl* (*traffic* ~) светофóр; can I have a ~? мóжно прикури́ть?; ~-bulb лáмпочка; *adj* (*bright*) свéтлый; (*pale*) блéдный; *vt & i* (*ignite*) зажигáть(ся) *impf*, зажéчь(ся) *pf*; *vt* (*illuminate*) освещáть *impf*, освети́ть *pf*; ~ up освещáть(ся) *impf*, освети́ть(ся) *pf*; (*begin to smoke*) закури́ть *pf*.

light[2] *adj* (*not heavy*) лёгкий; ~-hearted беззабóтный.

lighten[1] *vt* (*make lighter*) облегчáть *impf*, облегчи́ть *pf*; (*mitigate*) смягчáть *impf*, смягчи́ть *pf*.

lighten[2] *vt* (*illuminate*) освещáть *impf*, освети́ть *pf*; *vi* (*grow bright*) светлéть *impf*, по-~ *pf*.

lighter *n* зажигáлка.

lighthouse *n* мая́к.

lighting *n* освещéние.

lightning *n* мóлния.

lightweight *n* (*sport*) легковéс; *adj* легковéсный.

like[1] *adj* (*similar*) похóжий (на+*acc*); what is he ~? что он за человéк?

like[2] *vt* нрáвиться *impf*, по-~ *pf* *impers*+*dat*: I ~ him он мне нрáвится; люби́ть *impf*; *vi* (*wish*) хотéть *impf*; if you ~ éсли хоти́те; I should ~ я хотéл бы; мне хотéлось

бы. **likeable** *adj* симпати́чный.

likelihood *n* вероя́тность. **likely** *adj* (*probable*) вероя́тный; (*suitable*) подходя́щий.

liken *vt* уподобля́ть *impf*, уподóбить *pf* (to +*dat*).

likeness *n* (*resemblance*) схóдство; (*portrait*) портрéт.

likewise *adv* (*similarly*) подóбно; (*also*) тóже, тáкже.

liking *n* вкус (for к+*dat*).

lilac *n* сирéнь; *adj* сирéневый.

lily *n* ли́лия; ~ of the valley лáндыш.

limb *n* член.

limber *vi*: ~ up разминáться *impf*, размя́ться *pf*.

limbo *n* (*fig*) состоя́ние неопределённости.

lime[1] *n* (*mineralogy*) и́звесть. **limelight** *n*: in the ~ (*fig*) в цéнтре внимáния. **limestone** *n* известня́к.

lime[2] *n* (*fruit*) лайм.

lime[3] *n* (~-*tree*) ли́па.

limit *n* грани́ца, предéл; *vt* ограни́чивать *impf*, ограни́чить *pf*. **limitation** *n* ограничéние. **limitless** *adj* безграни́чный.

limousine *n* лимузи́н.

limp[1] *n* хромотá; *vi* хромáть *impf*.

limp[2] *adj* мя́гкий; (*fig*) вя́лый.

limpid *adj* прозрáчный.

linchpin *n* чекá.

line[1] *n* (*long mark*) ли́ния, чертá; (*transport*, *tel*) ли́ния; (*cord*) верёвка; (*wrinkle*) морщи́на; (*limit*) грани́ца; (*row*) ряд; (*of words*) строкá; (*of verse*) стих; *vt* (*paper*) линовáть *impf*, раз-~ *pf*; *vt & i* (~ up) выстрáивать(ся) *impf*, вы́строить(ся) *pf* в ряд.

line[2] *vt* (*clothes*) класть *impf*, положи́ть *pf* на подклáдку.

lineage *n* происхождéние.

linear *adj* линéйный.

lined[1] *adj* (*paper*) линóванный; (*face*) морщи́нистый.

lined[2] *adj* (*garment*) на подклáдке.

linen *n* полотнó; *collect* бельё.

liner *n* лáйнер.

linesman *n* боковóй судья́ *m*.

linger *vi* задéрживаться *impf*, задержáться *pf*.

lingerie *n* дáмское бельё.

lingering *adj* (*illness*) затяжнóй.

lingo *n* жаргóн.

linguist n лингви́ст. **linguistic** adj лингвисти́ческий. **linguistics** n лингви́стика.

lining n (clothing etc.) подкла́дка; (tech) облицо́вка.

link n (of chain) звено́; (connection) связь; vt соединя́ть impf, соедини́ть pf; свя́зывать impf, связа́ть pf.

lino(leum) n линоле́ум.

lintel n переми́чка.

lion n лев. **lioness** n льви́ца.

lip n губа́; (of vessel) край. **lipstick** n губна́я пома́да.

liquefy vt & i превраща́ть(ся) impf, преврати́ть(ся) pf в жи́дкое состоя́ние.

liqueur n ликёр.

liquid n жи́дкость; adj жи́дкий.

liquidate vt ликвиди́ровать impf & pf. **liquidation** n ликвида́ция; go into ~ ликвиди́роваться impf & pf.

liquor n (спиртно́й) напи́ток.

liquorice n лакри́ца.

list[1] n спи́сок; vt составля́ть impf, соста́вить pf спи́сок +gen; (enumerate) перечисля́ть impf, перечи́слить pf.

list[2] vi (naut) накреня́ться impf, крени́ться impf, накрени́ться pf.

listen vi слу́шать impf, по~ pf (to +acc). **listener** n слу́шатель m.

listless adj апати́чный.

litany n лита́ния.

literacy n гра́мотность.

literal adj буква́льный.

literary adj литерату́рный.

literate adj гра́мотный.

literature n литерату́ра.

lithe adj ги́бкий.

lithograph n литогра́фия.

Lithuania n Литва́. **Lithuanian** n лито́вец, -вка; adj лито́вский.

litigation n тя́жба.

litre n литр.

litter n (rubbish) сор; (brood) помёт; vt (make untidy) сори́ть impf, на~ pf (with +instr).

little n немно́гое; ~ by ~ ма́ло-пома́лу; a ~ немно́го +gen; adj ма́ленький, небольшо́й; (in height) небольшо́го ро́ста; (in distance, time) коро́ткий; adv ма́ло, немно́го.

liturgy n литурги́я.

live[1] adj живо́й; (coals) горя́щий; (mil) боево́й; (electr) под напряже́нием; (broadcast) прямо́й.

live[2] vi жить impf; ~ **down** загла́живать impf, загла́дить pf; ~ **on** (feed on) пита́ться impf +instr; ~ **through** пережива́ть impf, пережи́ть pf; ~ **until, to see** дожива́ть impf, дожи́ть pf до+gen; ~ **up to** жить impf согла́сно +dat.

livelihood n сре́дства neut pl к жи́зни.

lively adj живо́й.

liven (up) vt & i оживля́ть(ся) impf, ожиби́ть(ся) pf.

liver n пе́чень; (cul) печёнка.

livery n ливре́я.

livestock n скот.

livid adj (angry) взбешённый.

living n сре́дства neut pl к жи́зни; **earn a** ~ зараба́тывать impf, зараба́тать pf на жизнь; adj живо́й; ~ **room** гости́ная sb.

lizard n я́щерица.

load n груз; (also fig) бре́мя neut; (electr) нагру́зка; pl (lots) ку́ча; vt (goods) грузи́ть impf, по~ pf; (vehicle) грузи́ть impf, на~ pf; (fig) обременя́ть impf, обремени́ть pf; (gun, camera) заряжа́ть impf, заряди́ть pf.

loaf[1] n буха́нка.

loaf[2] vi безде́льничать impf. **loafer** n безде́льник.

loan n заём; vt дава́ть impf, дать pf взаймы́.

loath, loth predic: be ~ to не хоте́ть impf +inf.

loathe vt ненави́деть impf. **loathing** n отвраще́ние. **loathsome** adj отврати́тельный.

lob vt высоко́ подбра́сывать impf, подбро́сить pf.

lobby n вестибю́ль m; (parl) кулуа́ры (-ров) pl.

lobe n (of ear) мо́чка.

lobster n ома́р.

local adj ме́стный.

locality n ме́стность.

localized adj локализо́ванный.

locate vt (place) помеща́ть impf, помести́ть pf; (find) находи́ть impf, найти́ pf; be ~d находи́ться impf.

location n (position) местонахожде́ние; **on** ~ (cin) на нату́ре.

locative adj (n) ме́стный (паде́ж).

lock[1] n (of hair) ло́кон; pl во́лосы (-о́с, -оса́м) pl.

lock² n замо́к; (canal) шлюз; vt & i запира́ть(ся) impf, запере́ть(ся) pf; ~ out не впуска́ть impf; ~ up (imprison) сажа́ть impf, посади́ть pf; (close) закрыва́ть(ся) impf, закры́ть(ся) pf.

locker n шка́фчик.

locket n медальо́н.

locksmith n сле́сарь m.

locomotion n передвиже́ние. **locomotive** n локомоти́в.

lodge n (hunting) (охо́тничий) до́мик; (porter's) сторо́жка; (Masonic) ло́жа; vt (accommodate) помеща́ть impf, помести́ть pf; (complaint) подава́ть impf, пода́ть pf; vi (reside) жить impf (with у+gen); (stick) заса́живать impf, засе́сть pf. **lodger** n жиле́ц, жили́ца. **lodging** n (also pl) кварти́ра, (снима́емая) ко́мната.

loft n (attic) черда́к.

lofty adj о́чень высо́кий; (elevated) возвы́шенный.

log n бревно́; (for fire) поле́но; ~-**book** (naut) ва́хтенный журна́л.

logarithm n логари́фм.

loggerhead n: be at ~s быть в ссо́ре.

logic n ло́гика. **logical** adj (of logic) логи́ческий; (consistent) логи́чный.

logistics n pl материа́льно-техни́ческое обеспе́чение; (fig) пробле́мы f pl организа́ции.

logo n эмбле́ма.

loin n (pl) поясни́ца; (cul) филе́йная часть.

loiter vi слоня́ться impf.

lone, lonely adj одино́кий. **loneliness** n одино́чество.

long¹ vi (want) стра́стно жела́ть impf, по~ pf (for +gen); (miss) тоскова́ть impf (for по+dat).

long² adj (space) дли́нный; (time) до́лгий; (in measurements) длино́й в+acc; in the ~ run в коне́чном счёте; ~-**sighted** дальнозо́ркий; ~-**suffering** долготерпели́вый; ~-**term** долгосро́чный; ~-**winded** многоречи́вый; adv до́лго; ~ ago (long) давно́; as ~ as пока́; ~ before задо́лго до+gen.

longevity n долгове́чность.

longing n стра́стное жела́ние (for +gen); тоска́ (for по+dat); adj тоску́ющий.

longitude n долгота́.

longways adv в длину́.

look n (glance) взгляд; (appearance) вид; (expression) выраже́ние; vi смотре́ть impf, по~ pf (at на, в, +acc); (appear) вы́глядеть impf +instr; (face) выходи́ть impf (towards, onto на+acc); ~ **about** осма́триваться impf, осмотре́ться pf; ~ **after** (attend to) присма́тривать impf, присмотре́ть pf за+instr; ~ **down** on презира́ть impf; ~ **for** иска́ть impf +acc, +gen; ~ **forward** to предвкуша́ть impf, предвкуси́ть pf; ~ **in on** загля́дывать impf, загляну́ть pf к+dat; ~ **into** (investigate) рассма́тривать impf, рассмотре́ть pf; ~ **like** быть похо́жим на+acc; it ~s like rain похо́же на (то, что бу́дет) дождь; ~ **on** (regard) счита́ть impf, счесть pf (as +instr, за+instr); ~ **out** выгля́дывать impf, вы́глянуть pf (в окно́); быть насторо́же; imper осторо́жно!; ~ **over, through** просма́тривать impf, просмотре́ть pf; ~ **round** (inspect) осма́тривать impf, осмотре́ть pf; ~ **up** (raise eyes) поднима́ть impf, подня́ть pf глаза́; (in dictionary etc.) иска́ть impf; (improve) улучша́ться impf, улу́чшиться pf; ~ **up to** уважа́ть impf.

loom¹ n тка́цкий стано́к.

loom² vi вырисо́вываться impf, вы́рисоваться; (fig) надвига́ться impf.

loop n пе́тля; vi образо́вывать impf, образова́ть pf пе́тлю; (fasten with loop) закрепля́ть impf, закрепи́ть pf пе́тлей; (wind) обма́тывать impf, обмота́ть pf (around вокру́г+gen). **loophole** n бойни́ца; (fig) лазе́йка.

loose adj (free; not tight) свобо́дный; (not fixed) неприкреплённый; (connection, screw) сла́бый; (lax) распу́щенный; at a ~ end без де́ла. **loosen** vt & i ослабля́ть(ся) impf, осла́бить(ся) pf.

loot n добы́ча; vt гра́бить impf, о~ pf.

lop vt (tree) подреза́ть impf, подре́зать pf; (~ off) отруба́ть impf, отруби́ть pf.

lope vi бе́гать indet, бежа́ть det вприпры́жку.

lopsided adj кривобо́кий.

loquacious adj болтли́вый.

lord n (*master*) господи́н; (*eccl*) Госпо́дь; (*peer*; *title*) лорд; vt: ~ it over помыка́ть *impf* +*instr*. **lordship** n (*title*) све́тлость.

lore n зна́ния *neut pl*.

lorry n грузови́к.

lose vt теря́ть *impf*, по~ *pf*; vt & i (*game etc.*) прои́грывать *impf*, проигра́ть *pf*; vi (*clock*) отстава́ть *impf*, отста́ть *pf*. **loss** n поте́ря; (*monetary*) убы́ток; (*in game*) про́игрыш.

lot n жре́бий; (*destiny*) уча́сть; (*of goods*) па́ртия; a ~, ~s мно́го; the ~ всё, все *pl*.

loth see **loath**

lotion n лосьо́н.

lottery n лотере́я.

loud adj (*sound*) гро́мкий; (*noisy*) шу́мный; (*colour*) крича́щий; out ~ вслух. **loudspeaker** n громкоговори́тель *m*.

lounge n гости́ная *sb*; vi сиде́ть *impf* развали́сь; (*idle*) безде́льничать *impf*.

louse n вошь. **lousy** adj (*coll*) парши́вый.

lout n балбе́с, у́вален *m*.

lovable adj ми́лый. **love** n любо́вь (of, for к+*dat*); in ~ with влюблённый в+*acc*; vt люби́ть *impf*. **lovely** adj прекра́сный; (*delightful*) преле́стный. **lover** n любо́вник, -ица.

low[1] adj ни́зкий, невысо́кий; (*quiet*) ти́хий.

lower[1] vt опуска́ть *impf*, опусти́ть *pf*; (*price*, *voice*, *standard*) понижа́ть *impf*, пони́зить *pf*.

lower[2] adj ни́жний.

lowland n ни́зменность.

lowly adj скро́мный.

loyal adj ве́рный. **loyalty** n ве́рность.

LP abbr (of **long-playing record**) долгоигра́ющая пласти́нка.

Ltd. abbr (of **Limited**) с ограни́ченной отве́тственностью.

lubricant n сма́зка. **lubricate** vt сма́зывать *impf*, сма́зать *pf*. **lubrication** n сма́зка.

lucid adj я́сный. **lucidity** n я́сность.

luck n (*chance*) случа́й; (*good* ~) сча́стье, уда́ча; (*bad* ~) неуда́ча. **luckily** adv к сча́стью. **lucky** adj счастли́вый; be ~ везти́ *imp*, по~ *pf* *impers* +*dat*: I was ~ мне повезло́.

lucrative adj при́быльный.

ludicrous adj смехотво́рный.

lug vt (*drag*) таска́ть *indet*, тащи́ть *det*.

luggage n бага́ж.

lugubrious adj печа́льный.

lukewarm adj теплова́тый; (*fig*) прохла́дный.

lull n (*in storm*) зати́шье; (*interval*) переры́в; vt (*to sleep*) убаю́кивать *impf*, убаю́кать *pf*; (*suspicions*) усыпля́ть *impf*, усыпи́ть *pf*.

lullaby n колыбе́льная пе́сня.

lumbar adj поясни́чный.

lumber[1] vi (*move*) брести́ *impf*.

lumber[2] n (*domestic*) ру́хлядь; vt обременя́ть *impf*, обремени́ть *pf*. **lumberjack** n лесору́б.

luminary n свети́ло.

luminous adj светя́щийся.

lump n ком; (*swelling*) о́пухоль; vt: ~ together сме́шивать *impf*, смеша́ть *pf* (в одно́).

lunacy n безу́мие.

lunar adj лу́нный.

lunatic n (n) сумасше́дший (sb).

lunch n обе́д; ~-hour, ~-time обе́денный переры́в; vi обе́дать *impf*, по~ *pf*.

lung n лёгкое *sb*.

lunge n де́лать *impf*, с~ *pf* вы́пад (at про́тив+*gen*).

lurch[1] n: leave in the ~ покида́ть *impf*, поки́нуть *pf* в беде́.

lurch[2] vi (*stagger*) ходи́ть *indet*, идти́ *det* шата́ясь.

lure n прима́нка; vt прима́нивать *impf*, примани́ть *pf*.

lurid adj (*gaudy*) крича́щий; (*details*) жу́ткий.

lurk vi зата́иваться *impf*, затаи́ться *pf*.

luscious adj со́чный.

lush adj пы́шный, со́чный.

lust n по́хоть (of, for к+*dat*); vi стра́стно жела́ть *impf*, по~ *pf* (for +*gen*). **lustful** adj похотли́вый.

lustre n гля́нец. **lustrous** adj гля́нцеви́тый.

lusty adj (*healthy*) здоро́вый; (*lively*) живо́й.

lute n (*mus*) лю́тня.

luxuriant adj пы́шный.

luxuriate vi наслажда́ться *impf*, насладиться *pf* (in +*instr*).

luxurious adj роско́шный. **luxury** n ро́скошь.

lymph *attrib* лимфати́ческий.
lynch *vt* линчева́ть *impf & pf.*
lyric *n* ли́рика; *pl* слова́ *neut pl* пе́сни. lyrical *adj* лири́ческий.

M

MA *abbr* (*of* Master of Arts) маги́стр гуманита́рных нау́к.
macabre *adj* жу́ткий.
macaroni *n* макаро́ны (-н) *pl.*
mace *n* (*of office*) жезл.
machination *n* махина́ция.
machine *n* маши́на; (*state ~*) аппара́т; (*tool ~*) станок; *vt* обраба́тывать *impf*, обрабо́тать *pf* на станке; (*sew*) шить *impf*, с~ *pf* (на маши́не). machinery *n* (*machines*) маши́ны *f pl*; (*of state*) аппара́т. machinist *n* машини́ст; (*sewing*) швейни́к, -и́ца, швея́.
mackerel *n* ску́мбрия, макре́ль.
mackintosh *n* плащ.
mad *adj* сумасше́дший. madden *vt* беси́ть *impf*, вз~ *pf.* madhouse *n* сумасше́дший дом. madly *adv* безу́мно. madman *n* сумасше́дший *sb.* madness *n* сумасше́ствие. madwoman *n* сумасше́дшая *sb.*
madrigal *n* мадрига́л.
maestro *n* маэ́стро *m indecl.*
Mafia *n* ма́фия.
magazine *n* журна́л; (*of gun*) магази́н.
maggot *n* личи́нка.
magic *n* ма́гия, волшебство́; *adj* (*also* magical) волше́бный. magician *n* волше́бник; (*conjurer*) фо́кусник.
magisterial *adj* авторите́тный.
magistrate *n* судья́ *m.*
magnanimity *n* великоду́шие. magnanimous *adj* великоду́шный.
magnate *n* магна́т.
magnesium *n* ма́гний.
magnet *n* магни́т. magnetic *adj* магни́тный; (*attractive*) притяга́тельный. magnetism *n* магнети́зм; притяга́тельность. magnetize *vt* намагни́чивать *impf*, намагни́тить *pf.*
magnification *n* увеличе́ние.
magnificence *n* великоле́пие. magnificent *adj* великоле́пный.

magnify *vt* увели́чивать *impf*, увели́чить *pf*; (*exaggerate*) преувели́чивать *impf*, преувели́чить *pf.* magnifying glass *n* увеличи́тельное стекло́.
magnitude *n* величина́; (*importance*) ва́жность.
magpie *n* соро́ка.
mahogany *n* кра́сное де́рево.
maid *n* прислу́га. maiden *adj* (*aunt etc.*) незаму́жняя; (*first*) пе́рвый; ~ name де́вичья фами́лия.
mail *n* (*letters*) по́чта; ~ order почто́вый зака́з; *vt* посыла́ть *impf*, посла́ть *pf* по по́чте.
maim *vt* кале́чить *impf*, ис~ *pf.*
main *n* (*gas* ~; *pl*) магистра́ль; in the ~ в основно́м; *adj* основно́й, гла́вный; (*road*) магистра́льный. mainland *n* матери́к. mainly *adv* в основно́м. mainstay *n* (*fig*) гла́вная опо́ра.
maintain *vt* (*keep up*) подде́рживать *impf*, поддержа́ть *pf*; (*family*) содержа́ть *impf*; (*machine*) обслу́живать *impf*, обслужи́ть *pf*; (*assert*) утвержда́ть *impf.* maintenance *n* подде́ржка; содержа́ние; обслу́живание.
maize *n* кукуру́за.
majestic *adj* вели́чественный. majesty *n* вели́чественность; (*title*) вели́чество.
major[1] *n* (*mil*) майо́р.
major[2] *adj* (*greater*) бо́льший; (*more important*) бо́лее ва́жный; (*main*) гла́вный; (*mus*) мажо́рный; ~ key мажо́р. majority *n* большинство́; (*full age*) совершенноле́тие.
make *vt* де́лать *impf*, с~ *pf*; (*produce*) производи́ть *impf*, произвести́ *pf*; (*prepare*) гото́вить *impf*, при~ *pf*; (*amount to*) равня́ться *impf* +*dat*; (*earn*) зараба́тывать *impf*, зарабо́тать *pf*; (*compel*) заставля́ть *impf*, заста́вить *pf*; (*reach*) добира́ться *impf*, добра́ться *pf* до+*gen*; (*be in time for*) успева́ть *impf*, успе́ть *pf* на+*acc*; be made of состоя́ть *impf* из+*gen*; ~ as if, though де́лать *impf*, с~ *pf* вид, что; ~ a bed стели́ть *impf*, по~ *pf* посте́ль; ~believe притворя́ться *impf*, притвори́ться *pf*; ~believe притво́рство; ~ do with дово́льство-

ваться *impf*, у~ *pf* +*instr*; ~ off
удира́ть *impf*, удра́ть *pf*; ~ out
(*cheque*) выпи́сывать *impf*, вы́писать *pf*; (*assert*) утвержда́ть *impf*,
утверди́ть *pf*; (*understand*) разбира́ть *impf*, разобра́ть *pf*; ~ over
передава́ть *impf*, переда́ть *pf*; ~ up
(*form, compose, complete*) составля́ть *impf*, соста́вить *pf*; (*invent*)
выду́мывать *impf*, вы́думать *pf*;
(*theat*) гримирова́ть(ся) *impf*, за~
pf; ~-up (*theat*) грим; (*cosmetics*)
косме́тика; (*composition*) соста́в; ~
it up мири́ться *impf*, по~ *pf* (with
c+*instr*); ~ up for возмеща́ть *impf*,
возмести́ть *pf*; ~ up one's mind
реша́ться *impf*, реши́ться *pf*. make
n ма́рка. makeshift *adj* вре́менный.
malady *n* боле́знь.
malaise *n* (*fig*) беспоко́йство.
malaria *n* маля́рия.
male *n* (*animal*) саме́ц; (*person*)
мужчи́на *m*; *adj* мужско́й.
malevolence *n* недоброжела́тельность. **malevolent** *adj* недоброжела́тельный.
malice *n* зло́ба. **malicious** *adj* зло́бный.
malign *vt* клевета́ть *impf*, на~ *pf*
на+*acc*. **malignant** *adj* (*harmful*)
зловре́дный; (*malicious*) зло́бный;
(*med*) злока́чественный.
malinger *vi* притворя́ться *impf*, притвори́ться *pf* больны́м. **malingerer**
n симуля́нт.
mallard *n* кря́ква.
malleable *adj* ко́вкий; (*fig*) пода́тливый.
mallet *n* (деревя́нный) молото́к.
malnutrition *n* недоеда́ние.
malpractice *n* престу́пная небре́жность.
malt *n* со́лод.
maltreat *vt* пло́хо обраща́ться *impf*
c+*instr*.
mammal *n* млекопита́ющее *sb*.
mammoth *adj* грома́дный.
man *n* (*human, person*) челове́к;
(*human race*) челове́чество; (*male*)
мужчи́на *m*; (*labourer*) рабо́чий *m*;
pl (*soldiers*) солда́ты *m pl*; *vt* (*furnish with men*) укомплекто́вывать
impf, укомплектова́ть *pf* ли́чным
соста́вом; ста́вить *impf*, по~ *pf*
люде́й к+*dat*; (*stall etc.*) обслужи-

вать *impf*, обслужи́ть *pf*; (*gate,
checkpoint*) стоя́ть *impf* на+*prep*.
manacle *n* нару́чник; *vt* надева́ть
impf, наде́ть *pf* нару́чники на+*acc*.
manage *vt* (*control*) управля́ть *impf*
+*instr*; *vi*(&*t*) (*cope*) справля́ться
impf, спра́виться *pf* (c+*instr*); (*succeed*) суме́ть *pf*. **management** *n*
управле́ние (of +*instr*); (*the* ~) администра́ция. **manager** *n* управля́ющий *sb* (of +*instr*); ме́неджер.
managerial *adj* администрати́вный.
managing director *n* дире́ктор-распоряди́тель *m*.
mandarin *n* мандари́н.
mandate *n* манда́т. **mandated** *adj*
подманда́тный. **mandatory** *adj* обяза́тельный.
mane *n* гри́ва.
manful *adj* му́жественный.
manganese *n* ма́рганец.
manger *n* я́сли (-лей) *pl*; dog in the
~ соба́ка на се́не.
mangle *vt* (*mutilate*) кале́чить *impf*,
ис~ *pf*.
mango *n* ма́нго *neut indecl*.
manhandle *vt* гру́бо обраща́ться
impf c+*instr*.
manhole *n* смотрово́й коло́дец.
manhood *n* возмужа́лость.
mania *n* ма́ния. **maniac** *n* манья́к,
-я́чка. **manic** *adj* маниака́льный.
manicure *n* маникю́р; *vt* де́лать
impf, c~ *pf* маникю́р +*dat*. **manicurist** *n* маникю́рша.
manifest *adj* очеви́дный; *vt* (*display*)
проявля́ть *impf*, прояви́ть *pf*; *n*
манифе́ст. **manifestation** *n* проявле́ние. **manifesto** *n* манифе́ст.
manifold *adj* разнообра́зный.
manipulate *vt* манипули́ровать *impf*
+*instr*. **manipulation** *n* манипуля́ция.
manly *adj* му́жественный.
mankind *n* челове́чество.
manner *n* (*way*) о́браз; (*behaviour*)
мане́ра; *pl* мане́ры *f pl*. **mannerism**
n мане́ра.
mannish *adj* мужеподо́бный.
manoeuvrable *adj* манёвренный.
manoeuvre *n* манёвр; *vt* & *i* маневри́ровать *impf*.
manor *n* поме́стье; (*house*) поме́щичий дом.
manpower *n* челове́ческие ресу́рсы
m pl.

manservant n слуга́ m.

mansion n особня́к.

manslaughter n непредумы́шленное уби́йство.

mantelpiece n ками́нная доска́.

manual adj ручно́й; n руково́дство. **manually** adv вручну́ю.

manufacture n произво́дство; vt производи́ть impf, произвести́ pf. **manufacturer** n фабрика́нт.

manure n наво́з.

manuscript n ру́копись.

many adj & n мно́го +gen, мно́гие pl; how ~ ско́лько +gen.

map n ка́рта; (of town) план; vt: ~ out намеча́ть impf, наме́тить pf.

maple n клён.

mar vt по́ртить impf, ис~ pf.

marathon n марафо́н.

marauder n мароде́р. **marauding** adj мароде́рский.

marble n мра́мор; (toy) ша́рик; attrib мра́морный.

March n март; adj ма́ртовский. **march** vi маршировать impf, про~ pf; n марш.

mare n кобы́ла.

margarine n маргари́н.

margin n (on page) по́ле; (edge) край; profit ~ при́быль; safety ~ запа́с про́чности.

marigold n ноготки́ (-ко́в) pl.

marijuana n марихуа́на.

marina n мари́на.

marinade n марина́д; vt маринова́ть impf, за~ pf.

marine adj морско́й; n (soldier) солда́т морско́й пехо́ты; pl морска́я пехо́та. **mariner** n моря́к.

marionette n марионе́тка.

marital adj супру́жеский, бра́чный.

maritime adj морско́й; (near sea) примо́рский.

mark¹ n (coin) ма́рка.

mark² n (for distinguishing) ме́тка; (sign) знак; (school) отме́тка; (trace) след; on your ~s на старт!; vt (indicate; celebrate) отмеча́ть impf, отме́тить pf; (school etc.) проверя́ть impf, прове́рить pf; (stain) па́чкать impf, за~ pf; (sport) закрыва́ть impf, закры́ть pf; ~ my words по-мни(те) мои́ слова́!; ~ out размеча́ть impf, разме́тить pf. **marker** n знак; (in book) закла́дка.

market n ры́нок; ~ garden огоро́д; ~-place база́рная пло́щадь; vt продава́ть impf, прода́ть pf.

marksman n стрело́к.

marmalade n апельси́новый джем.

maroon¹ adj (n) (colour) тёмно-бордо́вый (цвет).

maroon² vt (put ashore) выса́живать impf, вы́садить pf (на необита́емом о́строве); (cut off) отреза́ть impf, отре́зать pf.

marquee n тэнт.

marquis n марки́з.

marriage n брак; (wedding) сва́дьба; attrib бра́чный. **marriageable** adj; ~ age бра́чный во́зраст. **married** adj (man) жена́тый; (woman) заму́жняя, за́мужем; (to each other) жена́ты; (of ~ persons) супру́жеский.

marrow n ко́стный мозг; (vegetable) кабачо́к.

marry vt (of man) жени́ться impf & pf на +prep; (of woman) выходи́ть impf, вы́йти pf за́муж за +acc; vi (of couple) пожени́ться pf.

marsh n боло́то. **marshy** adj боло́тистый.

marshal n ма́ршал; vt выстра́ивать impf, вы́строить pf; (fig) собира́ть impf, собра́ть pf.

marsupial n су́мчатое живо́тное sb.

martial adj вое́нный; ~ law вое́нное положе́ние.

martyr n му́ченик, -ица; vt му́чить impf, за~ pf. **martyrdom** n му́ченичество.

marvel n чу́до; vi изумля́ться impf, изуми́ться pf. **marvellous** adj чуде́сный.

Marxist n маркси́ст; adj маркси́стский. **Marxism** n маркси́зм.

marzipan n марципа́н.

mascara n тушь.

mascot n талисма́н.

masculine adj мужско́й; (gram) мужско́го ро́да; (of woman) муже-подо́бный.

mash n карто́фельное пюре́ neut indecl; vt размина́ть impf, размя́ть pf.

mask n ма́ска; vt маскирова́ть impf, за~ pf.

masochism n мазохи́зм. **masochist** n мазохи́ст. **masochistic** adj мазохи́стский.

mason n ка́менщик; (M~) масо́н. **Masonic** adj масо́нский. **masonry** n ка́менная кла́дка.

masquerade n маскара́д; vi: ~ as выдава́ть impf, вы́дать pf себя́ за +acc.

Mass n (eccl) ме́сса.

mass n ма́сса; (majority) большинство́; attrib ма́ссовый; ~ media сре́дства neut pl ма́ссовой информа́ции; ~-produced ма́ссового произво́дства; ~ production ма́ссовое произво́дство; vt масси́ровать impf & pf.

massacre n резня́; vt выреза́ть impf, вы́резать pf.

massage n масса́ж; vt масси́ровать impf & pf. **masseur, -euse** n массажи́ст, ~ка.

massive adj масси́вный.

mast n ма́чта.

master n (owner) хозя́ин; (of ship) капита́н; (teacher) учи́тель m; (M~, univ) маги́стр; (workman; artist) ма́стер; (original) по́длинник, оригина́л; be ~ of владе́ть impf +instr; ~-key отмы́чка; vt (overcome) преодолева́ть impf, преодоле́ть pf; справля́ться impf, спра́виться pf c+instr; (a subject) овладева́ть impf, овладе́ть pf +instr. **masterful** adj вла́стный. **masterly** adj мастерско́й. **masterpiece** n шеде́вр. **mastery** n (of a subject) владе́ние (of +instr).

masturbate vi мастурби́ровать impf.

mat n ко́врик, (at door) полови́к; (on table) подста́вка.

match[1] n спи́чка. **matchbox** n спи́чечная коро́бка.

match[2] n (equal) ро́вня m & f; (contest) матч, состяза́ние; (marriage) па́ртия; vi & t (go well (with)) гармони́ровать impf (c+instr); подходи́ть impf, подойти́ pf (к+dat).

mate[1] n (chess) мат.

mate[2] n (one of pair) саме́ц, са́мка; (fellow worker) това́рищ; (naut) по́мощник капита́на; vi (of animals) спа́риваться impf, спа́риться pf.

material n материа́л; (cloth) мате́рия; pl (necessary articles) принадле́жности f pl. **materialism** n материали́зм. **materialistic** adj материалисти́ческий. **materialize** vi осуществ-

вля́ться impf, осуществи́ться pf.

maternal adj матери́нский; ~ grand-father де́душка с матери́нской стороны́. **maternity** n матери́нство; ~ leave декре́тный о́тпуск; ~ ward роди́льное отделе́ние.

mathematical adj математи́ческий. **mathematician** n матема́тик. **mathematics, maths** n матема́тика.

matinée n дневно́й спекта́кль m.

matriarchal adj матриарха́льный. **matriarchy** n матриарха́т.

matriculate vi быть при́нятым в вуз. **matriculation** n зачисле́ние в вуз.

matrimonial adj супру́жеский. **matrimony** n брак.

matrix n ма́трица.

matron n (hospital) ста́ршая сестра́.

matt adj ма́товый.

matted adj спу́танный.

matter n (affair) де́ло; (question) вопро́с; (substance) вещество́; (philos; med) мате́рия; (printed) материа́л; a ~ of life and death вопро́с жи́зни и сме́рти; a ~ of opinion спо́рное де́ло; a ~ of taste де́ло вку́са; as a ~ of fact факти́чески; со́бственно говоря́; what's the ~? в чём де́ло?; what's the ~ with him? что с ним?; ~-of-fact прозаи́чный; vi име́ть impf значе́ние; it doesn't ~ э́то не име́ет значе́ния; it ~s a lot to me для меня́ э́то о́чень ва́жно.

matting n рого́жа.

mattress n матра́с.

mature adj зре́лый; vi зреть impf, со~ pf. **maturity** n зре́лость.

maul vt терза́ть impf.

mausoleum n мавзоле́й.

mauve adj (n) розова́то-лило́вый (цвет).

maxim n сенте́нция.

maximum n ма́ксимум; adj максима́льный.

may v aux (possibility, permission) мочь impf, с~ pf; (possibility) возмо́жно, что +indicative; (wish) пусть +indicative.

May n (month) май; adj ма́йский ~ Day Пе́рвое sb ма́я.

maybe adv мо́жет быть.

mayonnaise n майоне́з.

mayor n мэр. **mayoress** n жена́ мэ́ра; же́нщина-мэр.

maze n лабири́нт.

meadow *n* луг.

meagre *adj* скудный.

meal¹ *n* еда; at ~times во время еды.

meal² *n* (*grain*) мука. mealy *adj*: ~-mouthed сладкоречивый.

mean¹ *adj* (*average*) средний; *n* (*middle point*) середина; *pl* (*method*) средство, способ; *pl* (*resources*) средства *neut pl*; by all ~s конечно, пожалуйста; by ~s of при помощи +*gen*, посредством +*gen*; by no ~s совсем не; ~s test проверка нуждаемости.

mean² *adj* (*ignoble*) подлый; (*miserly*) скупой; (*poor*) убогий.

mean³ *vt* (*have in mind*) иметь *impf* в виду; (*intend*) намереваться *impf* +*inf*; (*signify*) значить *impf*.

meander *vi* (*stream*) извиваться *impf*; (*person*) бродить *impf*. meandering *adj* извилистый.

meaning *n* значение. meaningful *adj* (много)значительный. meaningless *adj* бессмысленный.

meantime, meanwhile *adv* между тем.

measles *n* корь. measly *adj* ничтожный.

measurable *adj* измеримый. measure *n* мера; made to ~ сшитый по мерке; сделанный на заказ; *vt* измерять *impf*, измерить *pf*; (*for clothes*) снимать *impf*, снять *pf* мерку с+*gen*; *vi* иметь *impf* +*acc*: the room ~s 30 feet in length комната имеет тридцать футов в длину; ~ off, out отмерять *impf*, отмерить *pf*; ~ up to соответствовать *impf* +*dat*. measured *adj* (*rhythmical*) мерный. measurement *n* (*action*) измерение; *pl* (*dimensions*) размеры *m pl*.

meat *n* мясо. meatball *n* котлета. meaty *adj* мясистый; (*fig*) содержательный.

mechanic *n* механик. mechanical *adj* механический; (*fig*; *automatic*) машинальный; ~ engineer инженер-механик; ~ engineering машиностроение. mechanics *n* механика. mechanism *n* механизм. mechanization *n* механизация. mechanize *vt* механизировать *impf* & *pf*.

medal *n* медаль. medallion *n* медальон. medallist *n* медалист.

meddle *vi* вмешиваться *impf*, вме-

шаться *pf* (in, with в+*acc*).

media *pl of* medium

mediate *vi* посредничать *impf*. mediation *n* посредничество. mediator *n* посредник.

medical *adj* медицинский; ~ student медик, -ичка. medicated *adj* (*impregnated*) пропитанный лекарством. medicinal *adj* (*of medicine*) лекарственный; (*healing*) целебный. medicine *n* медицина; (*substance*) лекарство.

medieval *adj* средневековый.

mediocre *adj* посредственный. mediocrity *n* посредственность.

meditate *vi* размышлять *impf*. meditation *n* размышление. meditative *adj* задумчивый.

Mediterranean *adj* средиземноморский; *n* Средиземное море.

medium *n* (*means*) средство; (*phys*) среда; (*person*) медиум; *pl* (*mass media*) средства *neut pl* массовой информации; *adj* средний; happy ~ золотая середина.

medley *n* смесь; (*mus*) попурри *neut indecl*.

meek *adj* кроткий.

meet *vt* & *i* встречать(ся) *impf*, встретить(ся) *pf*; *vt* (*make acquaintance*) знакомиться *impf*, по~ *pf* с+*instr*; *vi* (*assemble*) собираться *impf*, собраться *pf*. meeting *n* встреча; (*of committee*) заседание, митинг.

megalomania *n* мегаломания.

megaphone *n* мегафон.

melancholic *adj* меланхолический. melancholy *n* грусть; *adj* унылый, грустный.

mellow *adj* (*colour*, *sound*) сочный; (*person*) добродушный; *vi* смягчаться *impf*, смягчиться *pf*.

melodic *adj* мелодический. melodious *adj* мелодичный. melody *n* мелодия.

melodrama *n* мелодрама. melodramatic *adj* мелодраматический.

melon *n* дыня; (*water-~*) арбуз.

melt *vt* & *i* растапливать(ся) *impf*, растопить(ся) *pf*; (*smelt*) плавить(ся) *impf*, рас~ *pf*; (*dissolve*) растворять(ся) *impf*, растворить(ся) *pf*; *vi* (*thaw*) таять *impf*, рас~ *pf*; ~ing point точка плавления.

member n член. **membership** n членство; (number of ~) количество членов; attrib членский.

membrane n перепонка.

memento n сувенир. **memoir** n pl мемуары (-ров) pl; воспоминания neut pl. **memorable** adj достопамятный. **memorandum** n записка. **memorial** adj мемориальный; n памятник. **memorize** vt запоминать impf, запомнить pf. **memory** n память; (recollection) воспоминание.

menace n угроза; vt угрожать impf +dat. **menacing** adj угрожающий.

menagerie n зверинец.

mend vt чинить impf, по~ pf; (clothes) штопать impf, за~ pf; ~ one's ways исправляться impf, исправиться pf.

menial adj низкий, чёрный.

meningitis n менингит.

menopause n климакс.

menstrual adj менструальный. **menstruation** n менструация.

mental adj умственный; (of ~ illness) психический; ~ arithmetic счёт в уме. **mentality** n ум; (character) склад ума.

mention vt упоминать impf, упомянуть pf; don't ~ it не за что!; not to ~ не говоря уже о+prep.

menu n меню neut indecl.

mercantile adj торговый.

mercenary adj корыстный; (hired) наёмный; n наёмник.

merchandise n товары m pl. **merchant** n купец; торговец; ~ navy торговый флот.

merciful adj милосердный. **mercifully** adv к счастью. **merciless** adj беспощадный.

mercurial adj (person) изменчивый. **mercury** n ртуть.

mercy n милосердие; at the ~ of во власти +gen.

mere adj простой; a ~ £40 всего лишь сорок фунтов. **merely** adv только, просто.

merge vt & i сливать(ся) impf, слить(ся) pf. **merger** n объединение.

meridian n меридиан.

meringue n меренга.

merit n заслуга, достоинство; vt за-

служивать impf, заслужить pf +gen.

mermaid n русалка.

merrily adv весело. **merriment** n веселье. **merry** adj весёлый; ~-go-round карусель; ~-making веселье.

mesh n сеть; vi сцепляться impf, сцепиться pf.

mesmerize vt гипнотизировать impf, за~ pf.

mess n (disorder) беспорядок; (trouble) беда; (eating-place) столовая sb; vi: ~ about возиться impf; ~ up портить impf, ис~ pf.

message n сообщение. **messenger** n курьер.

Messiah n мессия m. **Messianic** adj мессианский.

Messrs abbr господа (gen -д) m pl.

messy adj (untidy) беспорядочный; (dirty) грязный.

metabolism n обмен веществ.

metal n металл; adj металлический. **metallic** adj металлический. **metallurgy** n металлургия.

metamorphosis n метаморфоза.

metaphor n метафора. **metaphorical** adj метафорический.

metaphysical adj метафизический. **metaphysics** n метафизика.

meteor n метеор. **meteoric** adj метеорический. **meteorite** n метеорит. **meteorological** adj метеорологический. **meteorology** n метеорология.

meter n счётчик; vt измерять impf, измерить pf.

methane n метан.

method n метод. **methodical** adj методичный.

Methodist n методист; adj методистский.

methodology n методология.

methylated adj: ~ spirit(s) денатурат.

meticulous adj тщательный.

metre n метр. **metric(al)** adj метрический.

metronome n метроном.

metropolis n столица. **metropolitan** adj столичный; n (eccl) митрополит.

mettle n характер.

Mexican adj мексиканский; n мексиканец, -анка. **Mexico** n Мексика.

mezzanine n антресоли f pl.

miaow int мя́у; n мя́уканье; vi мяу́кать impf, мяу́кнуть pf.

mica n слюда́.

microbe n микро́б. microchip n чип, микросхе́ма. microcomputer n микрокомпью́тер. microcosm n микроко́см. microfilm n микрофи́льм. micro-organism n микрооргани́зм. microphone n микрофо́н. microscope n микроско́п. microscopic adj микроскопи́ческий. microwave n микроволна́; ~ oven микровол́новая печь.

mid adj; ~ May середи́на ма́я. midday n по́лдень m; attrib полуд́енный. middle n середи́на; adj сре́дний; ~-aged сре́дних лет; M~ Ages сре́дние века́ m pl; ~-class буржуа́зный; ~man посре́дник; ~sized сре́днего разме́ра. middleweight n сре́дний вес.

midge n мо́шка.

midget n ка́рлик, -ица.

midnight n по́лночь; attrib полуно́чный. midriff n диафра́гма. midst n середи́на. midsummer n середи́на ле́та. midway adv на полпути́. midweek n середи́на неде́ли. midwinter n середи́на зимы́.

midwife n акуше́рка. midwifery n акуше́рство.

might n мощь; with all one's ~ изо всех сил. mighty adj мо́щный.

migraine n мигре́нь.

migrant adj кочу́ющий; (bird) перелётный; n (person) переселе́нец; (bird) перелётная пти́ца. migrate vi мигри́ровать impf & pf. migration n мигра́ция. migratory adj кочу́ющий; (bird) перелётный.

mike n микрофо́н.

mild adj мя́гкий.

mildew n пле́сень.

mile n ми́ля. mileage n расстоя́ние в ми́лях; (of car) пробе́г. milestone n верстово́й столб; (fig) ве́ха.

militancy n вои́нственность. militant adj вои́нствующий; n активи́ст. military adj вое́нный; n вое́нные sb pl. militate vi: ~ against говори́ть impf про́тив+gen. militia n мили́ция. militiaman n милиционе́р.

milk n молоко́; attrib моло́чный; vt до́ить impf, по~ pf. milkman n продаве́ц молока́. milky adj моло́чный;

M~ Way Мле́чный Путь m.

mill n ме́льница; (factory) фа́брика; vt (grain etc.) моло́ть impf, с~ pf; (metal) фрезерова́ть impf, от~ pf; (coin) гурти́ть impf; vi: ~ around толпи́ться impf. miller n ме́льник.

millennium n тысячеле́тие.

millet n (plant) про́со; (grain) пшено́.

milligram(me) n миллигра́мм. millimetre n миллиме́тр.

million n миллио́н. millionaire n миллионе́р. millionth adj миллио́нный.

millstone n жёрнов; (fig) ка́мень m на ше́е.

mime n мим; (dumb-show) панто́-ми́ма; vt изобража́ть impf, изобрази́ть pf мими́чески. mimic n ми́мист; vt передра́знивать impf, передразни́ть pf. mimicry n имита́ция.

minaret n минаре́т.

mince n (meat) фарш; vt руби́ть impf; (in machine) пропуска́ть impf, пропусти́ть pf че́рез мясору́бку; vi (walk) семени́ть impf; not ~ matters говори́ть impf без обиняко́в. mincemeat n начи́нка из изю́ма, минда́ля и т.п.

mind n ум; bear in ~ име́ть impf в виду́; change one's ~ переду́мывать impf, переду́мать pf; make up one's ~ реша́ться impf, реши́ться pf; you're out of your ~ вы с ума́ сошли́; vt (give heed to) обраща́ть impf, обрати́ть pf внима́ние на+acc; (look after) присма́тривать impf, присмотре́ть pf за+instr; I don't ~ я ничего́ не име́ю про́тив; don't ~ me не обраща́й(те) внима́ния на меня́!; ~ you don't forget смотри́ не забу́дь!; ~ your own business не вме́шивайтесь в чужи́е дела́!; never ~ ничего́! mindful adj по́мнящий. mindless adj бессмы́сленный.

mine[1] poss pron мой; свой.

mine[2] n ша́хта, копь; (fig) исто́чник; (mil) ми́на; vt (obtain from ~) добыва́ть impf, добы́ть pf; (mil) мини́ровать impf & pf. minefield n ми́нное по́ле. miner n шахтёр.

mineral n минера́л; adj минера́льный; ~ water минера́льная вода́. mineralogy n минерало́гия.

mingle vt & i сме́шивать(ся) impf, смеша́ть(ся) pf.

miniature n миниатюра; adj миниатюрный.

minibus n микроавтобус.

minim n (mus) половинная нота.

minimal adj минимальный. minimize vt (reduce) доводить impf, довести pf до минимума. minimum n минимум; adj минимальный.

mining n горное дело.

minister n министр; (eccl) священник. ministerial adj министерский. ministration n помощь. ministry n (polit) министерство; (eccl) духовенство.

mink n норка; attrib норковый.

minor adj (unimportant) незначительный; (less important) второстепенный; (mus) минорный; n (person under age) несовершеннолетний n; (mus) минор. minority n меньшинство; (age) несовершеннолетие.

minstrel n менестрель m.

mint¹ n (plant) мята; (peppermint) перечная мята.

mint² n (econ) монетный двор; in ~ condition новенький; vt чеканить impf, от~, вы~ pf.

minuet n менуэт.

minus prep минус+acc; без+gen; n минус.

minuscule adj малюсенький.

minute¹ n минута; pl протокол.

minute² adj мелкий. minutiae n pl мелочи (-чей) f pl.

miracle n чудо. miraculous adj чудесный.

mirage n мираж.

mire n (mud) грязь; (swamp) болото.

mirror n зеркало; vt отражать impf, отразить pf.

mirth n веселье.

misadventure n несчастный случай.

misapprehension n недопонимание.

misappropriate vt незаконно присваивать impf, присвоить pf. misbehave vi дурно вести impf себя. misbehaviour n дурное поведение.

miscalculate vt неправильно рассчитывать impf, рассчитать pf; (fig, abs) просчитываться impf, просчитаться pf. miscalculation n просчёт. miscarriage n (med) выкидыш; ~ of justice судебная ошибка. miscarry vi (med) иметь impf выкидыш.

miscellaneous adj разный, разнообразный. miscellany n смесь.

mischief n (harm) вред; (naughtiness) озорство. mischievous adj озорной. misconception n неправильное представление. misconduct n дурное поведение. misconstrue vt неправильно истолковывать impf, истолковать pf.

misdeed, misdemeanour n проступок. misdirect vt неправильно направлять impf, направить pf; (letter) неправильно адресовать impf & pf. miser n скупец. miserable adj (unhappy, wretched) несчастный, жалкий; (weather) скверный. miserly adj скупой. misery n страдание.

misfire vi давать impf, дать pf осечку. misfit n (person) неудачник. misfortune n несчастье. misgiving n опасение. misguided adj обманутый.

mishap n неприятность. misinform vt неправильно информировать impf & pf. misinterpret vt неверно истолковывать impf, истолковать pf. misjudge vt неверно оценивать impf, оценить pf. misjudgement n неверная оценка. mislay vt затерять pf. mislead vt вводить impf, ввести pf в заблуждение. mismanage vt плохо управлять impf +instr. mismanagement n плохое управление. misnomer n неправильное название.

misogynist n женоненавистник. misogyny n женоненавистничество.

misplaced adj неуместный. misprint n опечатка. misquote vt неправильно цитировать impf, про~ pf. misread vt (fig) неправильно истолковывать impf, истолковать pf. misrepresent vt искажать impf, исказить pf. misrepresentation n искажение.

Miss n (title) мисс.

miss n промах; vi промахиваться impf, промахнуться pf; vt (fail to hit, see, hear) пропускать impf, пропустить pf; (train) опаздывать impf, опоздать pf на+acc; (regret absence of) скучать impf по+dat; ~ out пропускать impf, пропустить pf; ~ the point не понимать impf, понять pf сути.

misshapen *adj* уро́дливый.

missile *n* снаря́д, раке́та.

missing *adj* отсу́тствующий, недоста́ющий; (*person*) пропа́вший бе́з ве́сти.

mission *n* ми́ссия; командиро́вка. **missionary** *n* миссионе́р. **missive** *n* посла́ние.

misspell *vt* непра́вильно писа́ть *impf*, на~ *pf*. **misspelling** *n* непра́вильное написа́ние.

mist *n* тума́н; *vt & i* затума́нивать(ся) *impf*, затума́нить(ся) *pf*.

mistake *vt* непра́вильно понима́ть *impf*, поня́ть *pf*; ~ **for** принима́ть *impf*, приня́ть *pf* за+*acc*; *n* оши́бка; **make a** ~ ошиба́ться *impf*, ошиби́ться *pf*. **mistaken** *adj* оши́бочный; **be** ~ ошиба́ться *impf*, ошиби́ться *pf*.

mister *n* ми́стер, господи́н.

mistletoe *n* оме́ла.

mistress *n* хозя́йка; (*teacher*) учи́тельница; (*lover*) любо́вница.

mistrust *vt* не доверя́ть *impf* +*dat*; *n* недове́рие. **mistrustful** *adj* недове́рчивый.

misty *adj* тума́нный.

misunderstand *vt* непра́вильно понима́ть *impf*, поня́ть *pf*. **misunderstanding** *n* недоразуме́ние.

misuse *vt* непра́вильно употребля́ть *impf*, употреби́ть *pf*; (*ill treat*) ду́рно обраща́ться *impf* с+*instr*; *n* непра́вильное употребле́ние.

mite *n* (*insect*) клещ; (*child*) кро́шка; **widow's** ~ ле́пта вдови́цы; **not a** ~ ничу́ть.

mitigate *vt* смягча́ть *impf*, смягчи́ть *pf*. **mitigation** *n* смягче́ние.

mitre *n* ми́тра.

mitten *n* рукави́ца.

mix *vt* меша́ть *impf*, с~ *pf*; *vi* сме́шиваться *impf*, смеша́ться *pf*; (*associate*) обща́ться *impf*; ~ **up** (*confuse*) пу́тать *impf*, с~ *pf*; **get** ~**ed up in** заме́шиваться *impf*, замеша́ться *pf* в+*acc*; *n* смесь. **mixer** *n* смеси́тель *m*; (*cul*) ми́ксер. **mixture** *n* смесь; (*medicine*) миксту́ра.

moan *n* стон; *vi* стона́ть *impf*, про~ *pf*.

moat *n* (крепостно́й) ров.

mob *n* толпа́; *vt* (*attack*) напада́ть *impf*, напа́сть *pf* толпо́й на+*acc*.

mobster *n* банди́т.

mobile *adj* подвижно́й, передвижно́й. **mobility** *n* подви́жность. **mobilization** *n* мобилиза́ция. **mobilize** *vt & i* мобилизова́ть(ся) *impf & pf*.

moccasin *n* мокаси́н (*gen pl* -н).

mock *vt & i* издева́ться *impf* над +*instr*; *adj* (*sham*) подде́льный; (*pretended*) мни́мый; ~**-up** *n* маке́т. **mockery** *n* издева́тельство; (*travesty*) паро́дия.

mode *n* (*manner*) о́браз; (*method*) ме́тод.

model *n* (*representation*) моде́ль; (*pattern*, *ideal*) образе́ц; (*artist's*) нату́рщик, -ица; (*fashion*) манеке́нщик, -ица; (*make*) моде́ль; *adj* образцо́вый; *vt* лепи́ть *impf*, вы́~, с~ *pf*; (*clothes*) демонстри́ровать *impf & pf*; *vi* (*act as* ~) быть нату́рщиком, -ицей; (*be* ~) быть манеке́нщиком, -ицей; ~ **after**, **on** создава́ть *impf*, созда́ть *pf* по образцу́ +*gen*.

moderate *adj* (*various senses*; *polit*) уме́ренный; (*medium*) сре́дний; *vt* умеря́ть *impf*, уме́рить *pf*; *vi* стиха́ть *impf*, сти́хнуть *pf*. **moderation** *n* уме́ренность; **in** ~ уме́ренно.

modern *adj* совреме́нный; (*language*, *history*) но́вый. **modernization** *n* модерниза́ция. **modernize** *vt* модернизи́ровать *impf & pf*.

modest *adj* скро́мный. **modesty** *n* скро́мность.

modification *n* модифика́ция. **modify** *vt* модифици́ровать *impf & pf*.

modish *adj* мо́дный.

modular *adj* мо́дульный. **modulate** *vt* модули́ровать *impf*. **modulation** *n* модуля́ция. **module** *n* мо́дуль *m*.

mohair *n* мохе́р.

moist *adj* вла́жный. **moisten** *vt & i* увлажня́ть(ся) *impf*, увлажни́ть(ся) *pf*. **moisture** *n* вла́га.

molar *n* (*tooth*) коренно́й зуб.

mole¹ *n* (*on skin*) роди́нка.

mole² *n* (*animal*; *agent*) крот.

molecular *adj* молекуля́рный. **molecule** *n* моле́кула.

molest *vt* пристава́ть *impf*, приста́ть *pf* к+*dat*.

mollify *vt* смягча́ть *impf*, смягчи́ть *pf*.

mollusc *n* моллю́ск.

molten *adj* распла́вленный.

moment *n* моме́нт, миг; **at the** ~

сейча́с; at the last ~ в после́днюю мину́ту; just a ~ сейча́с! **momentarily** adv на мгнове́ние. **momentary** adj мгнове́нный. **momentous** adj ва́жный. **momentum** n коли́чество движе́ния; (impetus) дви́жущая си́ла; gather ~ набира́ть impf, набра́ть pf ско́рость.

monarch n мона́рх. **monarchy** n мона́рхия.

monastery n монасты́рь m. **monastic** adj мона́шеский.

Monday n понеде́льник.

monetary adj де́нежный. **money** n де́ньги (-нег, -ньга́м) pl; ~-lender ростовщи́к.

mongrel n дворня́жка.

monitor n (naut; TV) монито́р; vt проверя́ть impf, прове́рить pf.

monk n мона́х.

monkey n обезья́на.

mono n мо́но neut indecl. **monochrome** adj одноцве́тный. **monogamous** adj единобра́чный. **monogamy** n единобра́чие. **monogram** n моногра́мма. **monograph** n моногра́фия. **monolith** n моноли́т. **monolithic** adj моноли́тный. **monologue** n моноло́г. **monopolize** vt монополизи́ровать impf & pf. **monopoly** n монопо́лия. **monosyllabic** adj односло́жный. **monosyllable** n односло́жное сло́во. **monotone** n моното́нность; in a ~ моното́нно. **monotonous** adj моното́нный. **monotony** n моното́нность.

monsoon n (wind) муссо́н; (rainy season) дождли́вый сезо́н.

monster n чудо́вище. **monstrosity** n чудо́вище. **monstrous** adj чудо́вищный; (huge) грома́дный.

montage n монта́ж.

month n ме́сяц. **monthly** adj ме́сячный; n ежеме́сячник; adv ежеме́сячно.

monument n па́мятник. **monumental** adj монумента́льный.

moo vi мыча́ть impf.

mood¹ n (gram) наклоне́ние.

mood² n настрое́ние. **moody** adj капри́зный.

moon n луна́. **moonlight** n лу́нный свет; vi халту́рить impf. **moonlit** adj лу́нный.

moor¹ n ме́стность, поро́сшая ве́ре-

ском. **moorland** n ве́ресковая пу́стошь.

moor² vt & i швартова́ть(ся) impf, при~ pf. **mooring** n (place) прича́л; pl (cables) швартóвы pl m.

Moorish adj маврита́нский.

moose n америка́нский лось m.

moot adj спо́рный.

mop n шва́бра; vt протира́ть impf, протере́ть pf (шва́брой); ~ one's brow вытира́ть impf, вы́тереть pf лоб; ~ up вытира́ть impf, вы́тереть pf.

mope vi хандри́ть impf.

moped n мопе́д.

moraine n море́на.

moral adj мора́льный; n мора́ль; pl нра́вы m pl. **morale** n мора́льное состоя́ние. **morality** n нра́вственность, мора́ль. **moralize** vi морализи́ровать impf.

morass n боло́то.

moratorium n морато́рий.

morbid adj боле́зненный.

more adj (greater quantity) бо́льше +gen; (additional) ещё; adv бо́льше; (forming comp) бо́лее; and what is ~ и бо́льше того́; ~ or less бо́лее и́ли ме́нее; once ~ ещё раз. **moreover** adv сверх того́; кро́ме того́.

morgue n морг.

moribund adj умира́ющий.

morning n у́тро; in the ~ у́тром; in the ~s по утра́м; attrib у́тренний.

moron n слабоу́мный sb.

morose adj угрю́мый.

morphine n мо́рфий.

Morse (code) n а́збука Мо́рзе.

morsel n кусо́чек.

mortal adj сме́ртный; (fatal) смерте́льный; n сме́ртный sb. **mortality** n сме́ртность.

mortar n (vessel) сту́п(к)а; (cannon) миноме́т; (cement) (известко́вый) раство́р.

mortgage n ссу́да на поку́пку до́ма; vt закла́дывать impf, заложи́ть pf.

mortify vt унижа́ть impf, уни́зить pf.

mortuary n морг.

mosaic n моза́ика; adj моза́ичный.

mosque n мече́ть.

mosquito n кома́р.

moss n мох. **mossy** adj мши́стый.

most adj наибо́льший; n наибо́льшее коли́чество; adj & n (majority) большинство +gen; бо́льшая часть +gen; adv бо́льше всего́, наибо́лее; (forming superl) са́мый. mostly adv гла́вным о́бразом.

MOT (test) n техосмо́тр.

motel n моте́ль m.

moth n мотылёк; (clothes-~) моль.

mother n мать; vt относи́ться impf по-матери́нски к +dat; ~-in-law (wife's ~) тёща; (husband's ~) свекро́вь; ~-of-pearl перламу́тр; adj перламу́тровый; ~ tongue родно́й язы́к. motherhood n матери́нство. motherland n ро́дина. motherly adj матери́нский.

motif n моти́в.

motion n движе́ние; (gesture) жест; (proposal) предложе́ние; vt пока́зывать impf, показа́ть pf жёстом, чтобы +past. motionless adj неподви́жный. motivate vt побужда́ть impf, побуди́ть pf. motivation n побужде́ние. motive n моти́в; adj дви́жущий.

motley adj пёстрый.

motor n дви́гатель m, мото́р; ~ bike мотоци́кл; ~ boat мото́рная ло́дка; ~ car автомоби́ль m; ~ cycle мотоци́кл; ~-cyclist мотоцикли́ст; ~ racing автомоби́льные го́нки f pl; ~ scooter мотороллер; ~ vehicle автомаши́на. motoring n автомоби́лизм. motorist n автомобили́ст, ~ка. motorize vt моторизова́ть impf & pf. motorway n автостра́да.

mottled adj кра́пчатый.

motto n деви́з.

mould¹ n (shape) фо́рма, фо́рмочка; vt формова́ть impf, с~ pf. moulding n (archit) лепно́е украше́ние.

mould² n (fungi) пле́сень. mouldy adj заплесневе́лый.

moulder vi разлага́ться impf, разложи́ться pf.

moult vi линя́ть impf, вы́~ pf.

mound n холм; (heap) на́сыпь.

Mount n (in names) гора́.

mount vt (ascend) поднима́ться impf, подня́ться pf на+acc; (~ a horse etc.) сади́ться impf, сесть pf на+acc; (picture) накле́ивать impf, накле́ить pf на карто́н; (gun) устана́вливать impf, установи́ть pf; ~ up (accumulate) нака́пливаться impf, накопи́ться pf; n (for picture) карто́н;

(horse) верхова́я ло́шадь.

mountain n гора́; attrib го́рный. mountaineer n альпини́ст, ~ка. mountaineering n альпини́зм. mountainous adj гори́стый.

mourn vt опла́кивать impf, опла́кать pf; vi скорбе́ть impf (over o+prep). mournful adj ско́рбный. mourning n тра́ур.

mouse n мышь.

mousse n мусс.

moustache n усы́ (усо́в) pl.

mousy adj мыши́ный; (timid) ро́бкий.

mouth n рот; (poetical) уста́ (-т) pl; (entrance) вход; (of river) у́стье; vt говори́ть impf, сказа́ть pf одни́ми губа́ми. mouthful n глото́к. mouthorgan n губна́я гармо́ника. mouthpiece n мундшту́к; (person) ру́пор.

movable adj подви́жной.

move n (in game) ход; (change of residence) перее́зд; (movement) движе́ние; (step) шаг; vt & i дви́гать(ся) impf, дви́нуться pf; vt (affect) тро́гать impf, тро́нуть pf; (propose) вноси́ть impf, внести́ pf; (develop) развива́ться impf, разви́ться pf; (~ house) переезжа́ть impf, перее́хать pf; ~ away (vt & i) удаля́ть(ся) impf, удали́ть(ся) pf; (vi) уезжа́ть impf, уе́хать pf; ~ in въезжа́ть impf, въе́хать pf; ~ on идти́ impf, пойти́ pf да́льше; ~ out съезжа́ть impf, съе́хать pf (of c+gen). movement n движе́ние; (mus) часть. moving adj дви́жущийся; (touching) тро́гательный.

mow vt (also ~ down) коси́ть impf, с~ pf. mower n коси́лка.

MP abbr (of Member of Parliament) член парла́мента.

Mr abbr ми́стер, господи́н. Mrs abbr ми́ссис f indecl, госпожа́.

Ms n миз, госпожа́.

much adj & n мно́го +gen; мно́гое sb; adv о́чень; (with comp adj) гора́здо.

muck n (dung) наво́з; (dirt) грязь; ~ about вози́ться impf; ~ out чи́стить impf, вы́~ pf; ~ up изга́живать impf, изга́дить pf.

mucous adj сли́зистый. mucus n слизь.

mud n грязь. mudguard n крыло́.

muddle vt пу́тать impf, c~ pf; vi: ~ **through** ко́е-ка́к справля́ться impf, спра́виться pf; n беспоря́док.

muddy adj гря́зный; vt обры́згивать impf, обры́згать pf гря́зью.

muff n му́фта.

muffle vt (for warmth) заку́тывать impf, заку́тать pf; (sound) глуши́ть impf, за~ pf.

mug n (vessel) кру́жка; (face) мо́рда.

muggy adj сыро́й и тёплый.

mulch n му́льча; vt мульчи́ровать impf & pf.

mule n мул.

mull vt: ~ **over** обду́мывать impf, обду́мать pf. **mulled** adj: ~ **wine** глинтве́йн.

mullet n (grey ~) кефа́ль; (red ~) бараку́лька.

multicoloured adj многокра́сочный.

multifarious adj разнообра́зный.

multilateral adj многосторо́нний.

multimillionaire n мультимиллионе́р. **multinational** adj многонациона́льный.

multiple adj составно́й; (numerous) многочи́сленный; ~ **sclerosis** рассе́янный склеро́з; n кра́тное число́; **least common** ~ о́бщее наиме́ньшее кра́тное sb. **multiplication** n умноже́ние. **multiplicity** n многочи́сленность. **multiply** vt (math) умножа́ть impf, умно́жить pf; vi размножа́ться impf, размно́житься pf.

multi-storey adj многоэта́жный.

multitude n мно́жество; (crowd) толпа́.

mum[1] adj: keep ~ молча́ть impf.

mum[2] n (mother) ма́ма.

mumble vt & i бормота́ть impf, про~ pf.

mummy[1] n (archaeol) му́мия.

mummy[2] n (mother) ма́ма, ма́мочка.

mumps n сви́нка.

munch vt жева́ть impf.

mundane adj земно́й.

municipal adj муниципа́льный. **municipality** n муниципалите́т.

munitions n pl вое́нное иму́щество.

mural n стенна́я ро́спись.

murder n уби́йство; vt убива́ть impf, уби́ть pf; (language) коверка́ть impf, ис~ pf. **murderer**, **murderess** n уби́йца m & f. **murderous** adj уби́йственный.

murky adj тёмный, мра́чный.

murmur n шёпот; vt & i шепта́ть impf, шепну́ть pf.

muscle n му́скул. **muscular** adj мы́шечный; (person) мускули́стый.

Muscovite n москви́ч, ~ка.

muse vi размышля́ть impf.

museum n музе́й.

mush n ка́ша.

mushroom n гриб.

music n му́зыка; (sheet ~) но́ты f pl; ~-**hall** мю́зик-хо́лл; ~ **stand** пюпи́тр. **musical** adj музыка́льный; n опере́тта. **musician** n музыка́нт.

musk n му́скус.

musket n мушке́т.

Muslim n мусульма́нин, -а́нка; adj мусульма́нский.

muslin n мусли́н.

mussel n ми́дия.

must v aux (obligation) до́лжен (-жна́) predic+inf; на́до impers+dat & inf; (necessity) ну́жно impers+dat & inf; ~ **not** (prohibition) нельзя́ impers +dat & inf.

mustard n горчи́ца.

muster vt собира́ть impf, собра́ть pf; (courage etc.) собира́ться impf, собра́ться pf c+instr.

musty adj за́тхлый.

mutation n мута́ция.

mute adj немо́й; n немо́й sb; (mus) сурди́нка. **muted** adj приглушён-ный.

mutilate vt уве́чить impf, из~ pf. **mutilation** n уве́чье.

mutineer n мяте́жник. **mutinous** adj мяте́жный. **mutiny** n мяте́ж; vi бунтова́ть impf, взбунтова́ться pf.

mutter vt & i бормота́ть impf; impf; n бормота́ние.

mutton n бара́нина.

mutual adj взаи́мный; (common) о́бщий.

muzzle n (animal's) мо́рда; (on animal) намо́рдник; (of gun) ду́ло; vt надева́ть impf, наде́ть pf намо́рдник на+acc; (fig) заставля́ть impf, заста́вить pf молча́ть.

my poss pron мой; свой.

myopia n близору́кость. **myopic** adj близору́кий.

myriad n мириа́ды (-д) pl; adj бесчи́сленный.

myrtle n мирт; attrib ми́ртовый.

myself *pron* (*emph*) (я) сам, сама;
(*refl*) себя; -ся (*suffixed to vt*).

mysterious *adj* тайнственный. **mystery** *n* тайна.

mystic(al) *adj* мистический. **mystic** *n* мистик. **mysticism** *n* мистицизм. **mystification** *n* озадаченность. **mystify** *vt* озадачивать *impf*, озадачить *pf*.

myth *n* миф. **mythical** *adj* мифический. **mythological** *adj* мифологический. **mythology** *n* мифология.

N

nag[1] *n* (*horse*) лошадь.

nag[2] *vt* (*also* ~ *at*) пилить *impf* +*acc*; *vi* (*of pain*) ныть *impf*.

nail *n* (*finger-*, *toe-~*) ноготь *m*; (*metal spike*) гвоздь *m*; ~ **varnish** лак для ногтей; *vt* прибивать *impf*, прибить *pf* (гвоздями).

naive *adj* наивный. **naivety** *n* наивность.

naked *adj* голый; ~ **eye** невооружённый глаз. **nakedness** *n* нагота.

name *n* название; (*forename*) имя *neut*; (*surname*) фамилия; (*reputation*) репутация: **what is his ~?** как его зовут?; ~**-plate** дощечка с фамилией; ~**sake** тёзка *m* & *f*; *vt* называть *impf*, назвать *pf* (*appoint*) назначать *impf*, назначить *pf*. **nameless** *adj* безымянный. **namely** *adv* (а) именно; то есть.

nanny *n* няня.

nap *n* короткий сон; *vi* вздремнуть *pf*.

nape *n* загривок.

napkin *n* салфетка.

nappy *n* пелёнка.

narcissus *n* нарцисс.

narcotic *adj* наркотический; *n* наркотик.

narrate *vt* рассказывать *impf*, рассказать *pf*. **narration** *n* рассказ. **narrative** *n* рассказ; *adj* повествовательный. **narrator** *n* рассказчик.

narrow *adj* узкий; *vt* & *i* суживать(ся) *impf*, сузить(ся) *pf*. **narrowly** *adv* (*hardly*) чуть, еле-еле; he ~ **escaped drowning** он чуть не утонул. **narrow-minded** *adj* ограниченный. **narrowness** *n* узость.

nasal *adj* носовой; (*voice*) гнусавый.

nasturtium *n* настурция.

nasty *adj* неприятный, противный; (*person*) злой.

nation *n* (*people*) народ; (*country*) страна. **national** *adj* национальный, народный; (*of the state*) государственный; *n* подданный *sb*. **nationalism** *n* национализм. **nationalist** *n* националист, ~ка. **nationalistic** *adj* националистический. **nationality** *n* национальность; (*citizenship*) гражданство, подданство. **nationalization** *n* национализация. **nationalize** *vt* национализировать *impf* & *pf*.

native *n* (~ *of*) уроженец, -нка (+*gen*); (*aborigine*) туземец, -мка; *adj* (*innate*) природный; (*of one's birth*) родной; (*indigenous*) туземный; ~ **land** родина; ~ **language** родной язык; ~ **speaker** носитель *m* языка.

nativity *n* Рождество (Христово).

natter *vi* болтать *impf*.

natural *adj* естественный, природный; ~ **resources** природные богатства *neut pl*; ~ **selection** естественный отбор; *n* (*mus*) бекар. **naturalism** *n* натурализм. **naturalist** *n* натуралист. **naturalistic** *adj* натуралистический. **naturalization** *n* натурализация. **naturalize** *vt* натурализировать *impf* & *pf*. **naturally** *adv* естественно. **nature** *n* природа; (*character*) характер; **by ~** по природе.

naught *n*: **come to ~** сводиться *impf*, свестись *pf* к нулю.

naughty *adj* шаловливый.

nausea *n* тошнота. **nauseate** *vt* тошнить *impf impers* от +*gen*. **nauseating** *adj* тошнотворный. **nauseous** *adj*: **I feel ~** меня тошнит.

nautical *n* морской.

naval *adj* (военно-)морской.

nave *n* неф.

navel *n* пупок.

navigable *adj* судоходный. **navigate** *vt* (*ship*) вести *impf*; (*sea*) плавать *impf* по+*dat*. **navigation** *n* навигация. **navigator** *n* штурман.

navvy *n* землекоп.

navy *n* военно-морской флот; ~ **blue** тёмно-синий.

Nazi *n* нацист, ~ка; *adj* нацистский. **Nazism** *n* нацизм.

NB *abbr* нотабе́не.

near *adv* бли́зко; ~ at hand под ру-
ко́й; ~ by ря́дом; *prep* во́зле+*gen*,
о́коло+*gen*, у+*gen*; *adj* бли́зкий; ~-
sighted близору́кий; *vt* & *i* прибли-
жа́ться *impf*, прибли́зиться *pf* к
+*dat*. **nearly** *adv* почти́.

neat *adj* (*tidy*) опря́тный, аккура́т-
ный; (*clear*) чёткий; (*undiluted*)
неразба́вленный.

nebulous *adj* нея́сный.

necessarily *adv* обяза́тельно. **necessary** *adj* необходи́мый; (*inevitable*) неизбе́жный. **necessitate** *vt*
де́лать *impf*, с~ *pf* необходи́мым.
necessity *n* необходи́мость; неиз-
бе́жность; (*object*) предме́т пе́рвой
необходи́мости.

neck *n* ше́я; (*of garment*) вы́рез; ~
and ~ голова́ в го́лову. **necklace** *n*
ожере́лье. **neckline** *n* вы́рез.

nectar *n* некта́р.

née adj урождённая.

need *n* нужда́; *vt* нужда́ться *impf*
в+*prep*; I (*etc.*) ~ мне (*dat*) ну́жен (
-жна́, -жно, -жны́) +*nom*; I ~ five
roubles мне ну́жно пять рубле́й.

needle *n* игла́, иго́лка; (*knitting*)
спи́ца; (*pointer*) стре́лка; *vt* приди-
ра́ться *impf*, придра́ться *pf* к+*dat*.

needless *adj* нену́жный; ~ to say
разуме́ется. **needy** *adj* нужда́ю-
щийся.

negation *n* отрица́ние. **negative** *adj*
отрица́тельный; *n* отрица́ние;
(*phot*) негати́в.

neglect *vt* пренебрега́ть *impf*, пре-
небре́чь *pf* +*instr*; не забо́титься
impf о+*prep*; *n* пренебреже́ние;
(*condition*) забро́шенность. **neg-
lectful** *adj* небре́жный, невнима́-
тельный (**of** к+*dat*). **negligence** *n*
небре́жность. **negligent** *adj* небре́ж-
ный. **negligible** *adj* незначи́тель-
ный.

negotiate *vi* вести́ *impf* перегово́ры;
vt (*arrange*) заключа́ть *impf*, за-
ключи́ть *pf*; (*overcome*) преодоле-
ва́ть *impf*, преодоле́ть *pf*. **negoti-
ation** *n* (*discussion*) перегово́ры *m
pl*.

Negro *n* негр; *adj* негритя́нский.

neigh *n* ржа́ние; *vi* ржать *impf*.

neighbour *n* сосе́д, ~ка. **neighbourhood** *n* ме́стность; **in the** ~ **of**

о́коло+*gen*. **neighbouring** *adj* со-
се́дний. **neighbourly** *adj* добросо-
се́дский.

neither *adv* та́кже не, то́же не; *pron*
ни тот, ни друго́й; ~ ... nor ни... ни.

neon *n* нео́н; *attrib* нео́новый.

nephew *n* племя́нник.

nepotism *n* кумовство́.

nerve *n* нерв; (*courage*) сме́лость;
(*impudence*) на́глость; **get on the** ~s
of де́йствовать *impf*, по~ *pf* +*dat*
на не́рвы. **nervous** *adj* не́рвный; ~
breakdown не́рвное расстро́йство.
nervy *adj* нерво́зный.

nest *n* гнездо́; ~ **egg** сбереже́ния
neut pl; *vi* гнезди́ться *impf*. **nestle**
vi льнуть *impf*, при~ *pf*.

net[1] *n* сеть, се́тка; *vt* (*catch*) лови́ть
impf, пойма́ть *pf* сетя́ми.

net[2], **nett** *adj* чи́стый; *vt* получа́ть
impf, получи́ть *pf* ... чи́стого до-
хо́да.

Netherlands *n* Нидерла́нды (-ов) *pl*.

nettle *n* крапи́ва.

network *n* сеть.

neurologist *n* невро́лог. **neurology**
n невроло́гия. **neurosis** *n* невро́з.
neurotic *adj* невроти́ческий.

neuter *adj* сре́дний, сре́днего ро́да;
n сре́дний род; *vt* кастри́ровать
impf & *pf*. **neutral** *adj* нейтра́льный;
n (*gear*) нейтра́льная ско́рость.
neutrality *n* нейтралите́т. **neutralize** *vt* нейтрализова́ть *impf* & *pf*.
neutron *n* нейтро́н.

never *adv* никогда́; ~ **again** никогда́
бо́льше; ~ **mind** ничего́!; всё рав-
но́!; ~ **once** ни ра́зу. **nevertheless**
conj, adv тем не ме́нее.

new *adj* но́вый; (*moon, potatoes*)
молодо́й. **new-born** *adj* новорож-
дённый. **newcomer** *n* прише́лец.
newfangled *adj* новомо́дный. **newly**
adv то́лько что, неда́вно. **newness**
n новизна́.

news *n* но́вость, -ти *pl*, изве́стие, -ия
pl. **newsagent** *n* продаве́ц газе́т.
newsletter *n* информацио́нный
бюллете́нь *m*. **newspaper** *n* газе́та.
newsprint *n* газе́тная бума́га. **news-
reel** *n* кинохро́ника.

newt *n* трито́н.

New Zealand *n* Но́вая Зела́ндия; *adj*
новозела́ндский.

next *adj* сле́дующий, бу́дущий; *adv*

(~ *time*) в сле́дующий раз; (*then*) пото́м, зате́м; ~ door (*house*) в сосе́днем до́ме; (*flat*) в сосе́дней кварти́ре; ~ of kin ближа́йший ро́дственник; ~ to ря́дом с+*instr*; (*fig*) почти́. **next-door** *adj* сосе́дний; ~ **neighbour** ближа́йший сосе́д.

nib *n* перо́.

nibble *vt & i* грызть *impf*; *vt* обгрыза́ть *impf*, обгры́зть *pf*; (*grass*) щипа́ть *impf*; (*fish*) клева́ть *impf*.

nice *adj* (*pleasant*) прия́тный, хоро́ший; (*person*) ми́лый. **nicety** *n* то́нкость.

niche *n* ни́ша; (*fig*) своё ме́сто.

nick *n* (*scratch*) цара́пина; (*notch*) зару́бка; in the ~ of time в са́мый после́дний моме́нт; *vt* (*scratch*) цара́пать *impf*, о-~ *pf*; (*steal*) сти́брить *pf*.

nickel *n* ни́кель *m*.

nickname *n* про́звище; *vt* прозыва́ть *impf*, прозва́ть *pf*.

nicotine *n* никоти́н.

niece *n* племя́нница.

niggardly *adj* скупо́й.

niggling *adj* ме́лочный.

night *n* ночь; (*evening*) ве́чер; at ~ но́чью; last ~ вчера́ ве́чером; ночно́й; ~-club ночно́й клуб. **night-cap** *n* ночно́й колпа́к; (*drink*) стака́нчик спиртно́го на ночь. **night-dress** *n* ночна́я руба́шка. **nightfall** *n* наступле́ние но́чи. **nightingale** *n* солове́й. **nightly** *adj* ежено́щный; *adv* ежено́щно. **nightmare** *n* кошма́р. **nightmarish** *adj* кошма́рный.

nil *n* нуль *m*.

nimble *adj* прово́рный.

nine *adj & n* де́вять; (*number 9*) девя́тка. **nineteen** *adj & n* девятна́дцать. **nineteenth** *adj & n* девятна́дцатый. **ninetieth** *adj & n* девяно́стый. **ninety** *adj & n* девяно́сто; *pl* (*decade*) девяно́стые го́ды (-до́в) *m pl*. **ninth** *adj & n* девя́тый.

nip *vt* (*pinch*) щипа́ть *impf*, щипну́ть *pf*; (*bite*) куса́ть *impf*, укуси́ть *pf*; ~ in the bud пресека́ть *impf*, пресе́чь *pf* в заро́дыше; *n* щипо́к; уку́с; there's a ~ in the air во́здух па́хнет моро́зцем.

nipple *n* сосо́к.

nirvana *n* нирва́на.

nit *n* гни́да.

nitrate *n* нитра́т. **nitrogen** *n* азо́т.

no *adj* (*not any*) никако́й, не оди́н; (*not a fool etc.*) (совсе́м) не; нет; (ниско́лько) не+*comp*; *n* отрица́ние, отка́з; (*in vote*) го́лос „про́тив"; ~ doubt коне́чно, несомне́нно; ~ longer уже́ не, бо́льше не; no one никто́; ~ wonder не удиви́тельно.

Noah's ark *n* Но́ев ковче́г.

nobility *n* (*class*) дворя́нство; (*quality*) благоро́дство. **noble** *adj* дворя́нский; благоро́дный. **nobleman** *n* дворяни́н.

nobody *pron* никто́; *n* ничто́жество.

nocturnal *adj* ночно́й.

nod *vi* кива́ть *impf*, кивну́ть *pf* голово́й; *n* кивко́к.

nodule *n* узело́к.

noise *n* шум. **noiseless** *adj* бесшу́мный. **noisy** *adj* шу́мный.

nomad *n* коче́вник. **nomadic** *adj* кочево́й.

nomenclature *n* номенклату́ра. **nominal** *adj* номина́льный. **nominate** *vt* (*propose*) выдвига́ть *impf*, вы́двинуть *pf*; (*appoint*) назнача́ть *impf*, назна́чить *pf*. **nomination** *n* выдвиже́ние; назначе́ние. **nominative** *adj* (*n*) имени́тельный (паде́ж). **nominee** *n* кандида́т.

non-alcoholic *adj* безалкого́льный. **non-aligned** *adj* неприсоедини́вшийся.

nonchalance *n* беззабо́тность. **nonchalant** *adj* беззабо́тный.

non-commissioned *adj*: ~ officer у́нтер-офице́р. **non-committal** *adj* укло́нчивый.

non-conformist *n* нонконформи́ст; *adj* нонконформи́стский.

nondescript *adj* неопределённый.

none *pron* (*no one*) никто́; (*nothing*) ничто́; (*not one*) не оди́н; *adv* ниско́лько не; ~ the less тем не ме́нее.

nonentity *n* ничто́жество.

non-existent *adj* несуществу́ющий. **non-fiction** *adj* документа́льный. **non-intervention** *n* невмеша́тельство. **non-party** *adj* беспарти́йный. **non-payment** *n* неплатёж.

nonplus *vt* ста́вить *impf*, по-~ *pf* в тупи́к.

non-productive *adj* непроизводи́тельный. **non-resident** *adj* не прожива́ющий (где-нибудь).

nonsense n ерунда́. **nonsensical** adj бессмы́сленный.

non-smoker n (person) некуря́щий sb; (compartment) купе́ neut indecl, для некуря́щих. **non-stop** adj безостано́вочный; (flight) беспоса́дочный; adv без остано́вок; без посáдок. **non-violent** adj ненаси́льственный.

noodles n pl лапша́.

nook n уголо́к.

noon n по́лдень m.

no one see no

noose n пе́тля.

nor conj и не; то́же; **neither ... ~** ни... ни.

norm n но́рма. **normal** adj норма́льный. **normality** n норма́льность. **normalize** vt нормализова́ть impf & pf.

north n се́вер; (naut) норд; adj се́верный; adv к се́веру, на се́вер; **~-east** се́веро-восто́к; **~-easterly, -eastern** се́веро-восто́чный; **~-west** се́веро-за́пад; **~-westerly, -western** се́веро-за́падный. **northerly** adj се́верный. **northern** adj се́верный. **northerner** n северя́нин, -я́нка. **northward(s)** adv на се́вер, к се́веру.

Norway n Норве́гия. **Norwegian** adj норве́жский; n норве́жец, -жка.

nose n нос; vt: **~ about, out** разню́хивать impf, разню́хать pf. **nosebleed** n кровотече́ние из носу. **nosedive** n пике́ neut indecl.

nostalgia n ностальги́я. **nostalgic** adj ностальги́ческий.

nostril n ноздря́.

not adv не; нет; ни; **~ at all** ниско́лько, ничу́ть; (reply to thanks) не сто́ит (благода́рности); **~ once** ни ра́зу; **~ that** не то, что́бы; **~ too** дово́льно +neg; **~ to say** что́бы не сказа́ть; **~ to speak of** не говоря́ уже о+prep.

notable adj заме́тный; (remarkable) замеча́тельный. **notably** adv (especially) осо́бенно; (perceptibly) заме́тно.

notary (public) n нота́риус.

notation n нота́ция; (mus) но́тное письмо́.

notch n зару́бка; vt: **~ up** вы́игры-

вать impf, вы́играть pf.

note n (record) заме́тка, за́пись; (annotation) примеча́ние; (letter) запи́ска; (banknote) банкно́т; (mus) но́та; (tone) тон; (attention) внима́ние; vt отмеча́ть impf, отме́тить pf; **~ down** запи́сывать impf, записа́ть pf. **notebook** n записна́я кни́жка. **noted** adj знамени́тый; изве́стный (for +instr). **notepaper** n почто́вая бума́га. **noteworthy** adj досто́йный внима́ния.

nothing n ничто́, ничего́; **~ but** ничего́ кро́ме+gen, то́лько; **~ of the kind** ничего́ подо́бного; **come to ~** конча́ться impf, ко́нчиться pf ниче́м; **for ~** (free) да́ром; (in vain) зря, напра́сно; **have ~ to do with** не име́ть impf никако́го отноше́ния к+dat; **there is (was) ~ for it** (but to) ничего́ друго́го не оста́ётся (оста́валось) (как); **to say ~ of** не говоря́ уже о+prep.

notice n (sign) объявле́ние; (warning) предупрежде́ние; (attention) внима́ние; (review) о́тзыв; **give (in) one's ~** подава́ть impf, пода́ть pf заявле́ние об ухо́де с рабо́ты; **give s.o. ~** предупрежда́ть impf, предупреди́ть pf об увольне́нии; **take ~ of** обраща́ть impf, обрати́ть pf внима́ние на+acc; **~-board** доска́ для объявле́ний; vt замеча́ть impf, заме́тить pf. **noticeable** adj заме́тный. **notification** n извеще́ние. **notify** vt извеща́ть impf, извести́ть pf (of o+prep).

notion n поня́тие.

notoriety n дурна́я сла́ва. **notorious** adj пресловутый.

notwithstanding prep несмотря́ на+acc; adv тем не ме́нее.

nought n (nothing) see **naught**; (zero) нуль m; (figure 0) ноль m.

noun n (им) neut) существи́тельное sb.

nourish vt пита́ть impf, на~ pf. **nourishing** adj пита́тельный. **nourishment** n пита́ние.

novel adj но́вый; (unusual) необыкнове́нный; n рома́н. **novelist** n романи́ст. **novelty** n (newness) новизна́; (new thing) нови́нка.

November n ноя́брь m; adj ноя́брьский.

novice n (eccl) послушник, -ица; (beginner) новичо́к.

now adv тепе́рь, сейча́с; (immediately) то́тчас же; (next) тогда́; conj: ~ (that) раз, когда́; (every) ~ and again, then вре́мя от вре́мени; by ~ уже́; from ~ on впредь. nowadays adv в на́ше вре́мя.

nowhere adv (place) нигде́; (direction) никуда́; pron: I have ~ to go мне не́куда пойти́.

noxious adj вре́дный.

nozzle n сопло́.

nuance n нюа́нс.

nuclear adj я́дерный. nucleus n ядро́.

nude adj обнажённый, наго́й; n обнажённая фигу́ра.

nudge vt подта́лкивать impf, подтолкну́ть pf ло́ктем; n толчо́к ло́ктем.

nudity n нагота́.

nugget n саморо́док.

nuisance n доса́да; (person) раздража́ющий челове́к.

null adj: ~ and void недействи́тельный. nullify vt аннули́ровать impf & pf nullity n недействи́тельность.

numb adj онеме́лый, (from cold) окочене́лый; v ~ онеме́ть pf; (from cold) окочене́ть pf.

number n (total) коли́чество; (total; symbol; math; gram) число́; (identifying numeral; item) но́мер; ~plate номерна́я доще́чка; vt (assign ~ to) нумерова́ть impf, за~, про~ pf; (contain) насчи́тывать impf; ~ among причисля́ть impf, причи́слить pf к+dat; his days are ~ed его́ дни сочтены́.

numeral n ци́фра; (gram) (и́мя neut) числи́тельное sb. numerical adj числово́й. numerous adj многочи́сленный; (many) мно́го +gen pl.

nun n мона́хиня. nunnery n (же́нский) монасты́рь m.

nuptial adj сва́дебный; n: pl сва́дьба.

nurse n (child's) ня́ня; (medical) медсестра́; vt (suckle) корми́ть impf, на~, по~ pf; (tend sick) уха́живать impf за+instr; nursing home сана́торий; дом престаре́лых. nursery n (room) де́тская sb; (day) ~ я́сли (-лей) pl; (for plants) пито́мник; ~ rhyme де́тские прибау́тки f pl; ~ school де́тский сад.

nut n оре́х; (for bolt etc.) га́йка. nutshell n: in a ~ в двух слова́х.

nutmeg n муска́тный оре́х.

nutrient n пита́тельное вещество́. nutrition n пита́ние. nutritious adj пита́тельный.

nylon n нейло́н; pl нейло́новые чулки́ (-ло́к) pl.

nymph n ни́мфа.

O

O int о!; ах!

oaf n неуклю́жий челове́к.

oak n дуб; attrib дубо́вый.

oar n весло́. oarsman n гребе́ц.

oasis n оа́зис.

oath n прися́га; (expletive) руга́тельство.

oatmeal n овся́нка. oats n pl овёс (овса́) collect.

obdurate adj упря́мый.

obedience n послуша́ние. obedient adj послу́шный.

obese n ту́чный. obesity n ту́чность.

obey vt слу́шаться impf, по~ pf +gen; (law, order) подчиня́ться impf, подчини́ться pf +dat.

obituary n некроло́г.

object n (thing) предме́т; (aim) цель; (gram) дополне́ние; vi возража́ть impf, возрази́ть pf (to про́тив+gen); I don't ~ я не про́тив. objection n возраже́ние; I have no ~ я не возража́ю. objectionable adj неприя́тный. objective adj объекти́вный; n цель. objectivity n объекти́вность. objector n возража́ющий sb.

obligation n обяза́тельство; I am under an ~ я обя́зан(а). obligatory adj обяза́тельный. oblige vt обя́зывать impf, обяза́ть pf; be ~d to (grateful) быть обя́занным+dat. obliging adj услу́жливый.

oblique adj косо́й; (fig; gram) ко́свенный.

obliterate vt (efface) стира́ть impf, стере́ть pf; (destroy) уничтожа́ть impf, уничто́жить pf. obliteration n стира́ние; уничтоже́ние.

oblivion n забве́ние. oblivious adj (forgetful) забы́вчивый; to be ~ of не замеча́ть impf +gen.

oblong adj продолгова́тый.

obnoxious adj проти́вный.

oboe n гобо́й.

obscene adj непристо́йный. **obscenity** n непристо́йность.

obscure adj (unclear) нея́сный; (little known) малоизве́стный; vt затемня́ть impf, затемни́ть pf; де́лать impf, c~ pf нея́сным. **obscurity** n нея́сность; неизве́стность.

obsequious adj подобостра́стный.

observance n соблюде́ние; (rite) обря́д. **observant** adj наблюда́тельный. **observation** n наблюде́ние; (remark) замеча́ние. **observatory** n обсервато́рия. **observe** vt (law etc.) соблюда́ть impf, соблюсти́ pf; (watch) наблюда́ть impf; (remark) замеча́ть impf, заме́тить pf. **observer** n наблюда́тель m.

obsess vt пресле́довать impf; **obsessed by** одержи́мый +instr. **obsession** n одержи́мость; (idea) навя́зчивая иде́я. **obsessive** adj навя́зчивый.

obsolete adj устаре́лый, вы́шедший из употребле́ния.

obstacle n препя́тствие.

obstetrician n акуше́р. **obstetrics** n акуше́рство.

obstinacy n упря́мство. **obstinate** adj упря́мый.

obstreperous adj бу́йный.

obstruct vt загражда́ть impf, загради́ть pf; (hinder) препя́тствовать impf, вос~ pf +dat. **obstruction** n загражде́ние; (obstacle) препя́тствие. **obstructive** adj загражда́ющий; препя́тствующий.

obtain vt получа́ть impf, получи́ть pf; достава́ть impf, доста́ть pf.

obtrusive adj навя́зчивый; (thing) броса́ющийся в глаза́.

obtuse adj тупо́й.

obviate vt устраня́ть impf, устрани́ть pf.

obvious adj очеви́дный.

occasion n слу́чай; (cause) по́вод; (occurrence) собы́тие; vt причиня́ть impf, причини́ть pf. **occasional** adj ре́дкий. **occasionally** adv иногда́, вре́мя от вре́мени.

occult adj окку́льтный; n: **the** ~ окку́льт.

occupancy n заня́тие. **occupant** n жи́тель m, ~ница. **occupation** n заня́тие; (military ~) оккупа́ция; (profession) профе́ссия. **occupational** adj профессиона́льный; ~ **therapy** трудотерапи́я. **occupy** vt занима́ть impf, заня́ть pf; (mil) оккупи́ровать impf & pf.

occur vi (happen) случа́ться impf, случи́ться pf; (be found) встреча́ться impf; ~ **to** приходи́ть impf, прийти́ pf в го́лову+dat. **occurrence** n слу́чай, происше́ствие.

ocean n океа́н. **oceanic** adj океа́нский.

o'clock adv: (at) **six** ~ (в) шесть часо́в.

octagonal adj восьмиуго́льный.

octave n (mus) окта́ва.

October n октя́брь m; adj октя́брьский.

octopus n осьмино́г.

odd adj (strange) стра́нный; (not in a set) разро́зненный; (number) нечётный; (not paired) непа́рный; (casual) случа́йный; **five hundred** ~ пятьсо́т с ли́шним; ~ **job** случа́йная рабо́та. **oddity** n стра́нность; (person) чуда́к, -а́чка. **oddly** adv стра́нно; ~ **enough** как э́то ни стра́нно. **oddment** n оста́ток. **odds** n pl ша́нсы m pl; **be at** ~ **with** (person) не ла́дить с+instr; (things) не соотве́тствовать impf +dat; **long** (short) ~ нера́вные (почти́ ра́вные) ша́нсы m pl; **the** ~ **are that** вероя́тнее всего́, что; ~ **and ends** обры́вки m pl.

ode n о́да.

odious adj ненави́стный.

odour n за́пах.

oesophagus n пищево́д.

of prep expressing 1. origin: из+gen: **he comes** ~ **a working-class family** он из рабо́чей семьи́; 2. cause: от +gen: **he died** ~ **hunger** он у́мер от го́лода; 3. authorship: gen: **the works** ~ **Pushkin** сочине́ния Пу́шкина; 4. material: из+gen: **made** ~ **wood** сде́ланный из де́рева; 5. reference: о+prep: **he talked** ~ **Lenin** он говори́л о Ле́нине; 6. partition: gen (often in -у́(-ю)): **a glass** ~ **milk, tea** стака́н молока́, ча́ю; из+gen: **one** ~ **them** оди́н из них; 7. belonging: gen: **the capital** ~ **England** столи́ца А́нглии.

off adv: in phrasal vv, see v, e.g. clear ~ убира́ться; prep (from surface of) c+gen; (away from) от+gen; ~ and on вре́мя от вре́мени; ~-white не совсе́м бе́лый.

offal n требуха́.

offence n (insult) оби́да; (against law) просту́пок, преступле́ние; take ~ обижа́ться impf, оби́деться pf (at на+acc). offend vt обижа́ть impf, оби́деть pf; ~ against наруша́ть impf, нару́шить pf. offender n правонаруши́тель m, ~ница. offensive adj (attacking) наступа́тельный; (insulting) оскорби́тельный; (repulsive) проти́вный; n нападе́ние.

offer vt предлага́ть impf, предложи́ть pf; n предложе́ние; on ~ в прода́же.

offhand adj бесцеремо́нный.

office n (position) до́лжность; (place, room etc.) бюро́ neut indecl, конто́ра, канцеля́рия. officer n до́лжностное лицо́; (mil) офице́р. official adj служе́бный; (authorized) официа́льный; n до́лжностно́е лицо́. officiate vi (eccl) соверша́ть impf, соверши́ть pf богослуже́ние. officious adj (intrusive) навя́зчивый.

offing n: be in the ~ предстоя́ть impf.

off-licence n ви́нный магази́н. offload vt разгружа́ть impf, разгрузи́ть pf. off-putting adj отт́алкивающий. offset vt возмеща́ть impf, возмести́ть pf. offshoot n о́тпрыск. offshore adj прибре́жный. offside adv вне игры́. offspring n пото́мок; (collect) пото́мки m pl.

often adv ча́сто.

ogle vt & i смотре́ть impf с вожделе́нием на+acc.

ogre n велика́н-людое́д.

oh int o!; ax!

ohm n ом.

oil n ма́сло; (petroleum) нефть; (paint) ма́сло, ма́сляные кра́ски f pl; vt сма́зывать impf, сма́зать pf; ~-painting карти́на, напи́санная ма́сляными кра́сками; ~ rig нефтяна́я вы́шка; ~-tanker та́нкер; ~-well нефтяна́я сква́жина. oilfield n месторожде́ние нефти. oilskin n клеёнка; pl непромока́емый костю́м.

oily adj масляни́стый.

ointment n мазь.

OK adv & adj хорошо́, норма́льно; int ла́дно!; vt одобря́ть impf, одо́брить pf.

old adj ста́рый; (ancient; of long standing) стари́нный; (former) бы́вший; how ~ are you? ско́лько тебе́, вам, (dat) лет?; ~ age ста́рость; ~-age pension пе́нсия по ста́рости; old-fashioned старомо́дный; ~ maid ста́рая де́ва; ~ man (also father, husband) стари́к; ~-time стари́нный; ~ woman стару́ха; (coll) стару́шка.

olive n (fruit) оли́вка; (colour) оли́вковый цвет; adj оли́вковый; ~ oil оли́вковое ма́сло.

Olympic adj олимпи́йский; ~ games Олимпи́йские и́гры f pl.

omelette n омле́т.

omen n предзнаменова́ние. ominous adj злове́щий.

omission n про́пуск; (neglect) упуще́ние. omit vt (leave out) пропуска́ть impf, пропусти́ть pf; (neglect) упуска́ть impf, упусти́ть pf.

omnibus n (bus) авто́бус; (collection) колле́кция.

omnipotence n всемогу́щество. omnipotent adj всемогу́щий. omnipresent adj вездесу́щий. omniscient adj всеве́дущий.

on prep (position) на+prep; (direction) на+acc; (time) в+acc; ~ the next day на сле́дующий день; ~ Mondays (repeated action) по понеде́льникам (dat pl); ~ the first of June пе́рвого ию́ня (gen); (concerning) по+prep, o+prep, на+acc; adv да́льше, вперёд; in phrasal vv, see vv, e.g. move ~ идти́ да́льше; and so ~ и так да́лее, и т.д.; be ~ (film etc.) идти́ impf; further ~ да́льше; later ~ по́зже.

once n & adv (оди́н) раз; (on past occasion) одна́жды; (formerly) не́когда; all at ~ неожи́данно; at ~ сра́зу, неме́дленно; (if, when) ~ как то́лько; ~ again, more ещё раз; ~ and for all раз и навсегда́; ~ or twice не́сколько раз; ~ upon a time there lived …жил-был….

oncoming adj: ~ traffic встре́чное движе́ние.

one adj оди́н (одна́, -но́); (only, sin-

gle) еди́нственный; *n* оди́н; *pron*:
not usu translated; *v translated in 2nd
pers sg or by impers construction*: ~
never knows никогда́ не зна́ешь; ~
where can ~ buy this book? где
мо́жно купи́ть э́ту кни́гу?; ~ after
another оди́н за други́м; ~ and all
все до одного́; все как оди́н; ~ and
only еди́нственный; ~ and the same
оди́н и тот же; ~ another друг дру́га
(*dat* -гу, *etc.*); ~ fine day в оди́н
прекра́сный день; ~ o'clock час; ~
parent family семья́ с одни́м роди́-
телем; ~-sided, -track, -way односто-
сторо́нний; ~-time бы́вший; ~-way
street у́лица односторо́ннего движе́-
же́ния.

onerous *adj* тя́гостный.
oneself *pron* себя́; -ся (*suffixed to vt*).
onion *n* (*plant; pl collect*) лук; (*single* ~) лу́ковица.
onlooker *n* наблюда́тель *m*.
only *adj* еди́нственный; *adv* то́лько;
if ~ е́сли бы то́лько; ~ just то́лько
что; *conj* но.
onset *n* нача́ло.
onslaught *n* на́тиск.
onus *n* отве́тственность.
onward(s) *adv* вперёд.
ooze *vt & i* сочи́ться *impf*.
opal *n* опа́л.
opaque *adj* непрозра́чный.
open *adj* откры́тый; (*frank*) откро-
ве́нный; in the ~ air на откры́том
во́здухе; ~-minded *adj* непредупре-
ждённый; *vt & i* открыва́ть(ся)
impf, откры́ть(ся) *pf*; *vi* (*begin*) на-
чина́ться *impf*, нача́ться *pf*; (*flowers*) распуска́ться *impf*, распусти́ть-
ся *pf*. **opening** *n* откры́тие; (*aperture*) отве́рстие; (*beginning*) нача́ло;
adj нача́льный, пе́рвый; (*introductory*) вступи́тельный.
opera *n* о́пера; *attrib* о́перный; ~-
house *n* о́перный теа́тр.
operate *vi* де́йствовать *impf* (upon
на+*acc*); (*med*) опери́ровать *impf* &
pf (on +*acc*); *vt* управля́ть *impf*
+*instr*.
operatic *adj* о́перный.
operating-theatre *n* операцио́нная
sb. **operation** *n* де́йствие; (*med; mil*)
опера́ция. **operational** *adj* (*in use*)
де́йствующий; (*mil*) операти́вный.
operative *adj* де́йствующий. **oper-**

ator *n* опера́тор; (*telephone* ~)
телефони́ст, ~ка.
operetta *n* опере́тта.
ophthalmic *adj* глазно́й.
opinion *n* мне́ние; in my ~ по-
мо́ему; ~ poll опро́с обще́ствен-
ного мне́ния. **opinionated** *adj* дог-
мати́чный.
opium *n* о́пиум.
opponent *n* проти́вник.
opportune *adj* своевре́менный. **opportunism** *n* оппортуни́зм. **oppor-
tunist** *n* оппортуни́ст. **opportunis-
tic** *n* оппортунисти́ческий. **opportunity** *n* слу́чай, возмо́жность.
oppose *vt* (*resist*) проти́виться *impf*,
вос~ *pf* +*dat*; (*speak etc. against*)
выступа́ть *impf*, вы́ступить *pf* про-
тив+*gen*. **opposed** *adj* про́тив (to
+*gen*); as ~ to в противополо́ж-
ность+*dat*. **opposing** *adj* проти́в-
ный; (*opposite*) противополо́жный.
opposite *adj* противополо́жный;
(*reverse*) обра́тный; *n* противопо-
ло́жность; just the ~ как раз на-
оборо́т; *adv* напро́тив; *prep* (на)-
про́тив+*gen*. **opposition** *n* (*resistance*) сопротивле́ние; (*polit*) оппо-
зи́ция.
oppress *vt* угнета́ть *impf*. **oppression** *n* угнете́ние. **oppressive** *adj*
угнета́ющий. **oppressor** *n* угнета́-
тель *m*.
opt *vi* выбира́ть *impf*, вы́брать *pf*
(for +*acc*); ~ out не принима́ть *impf*
уча́стия (of в+*prep*).
optic *adj* зри́тельный. **optical** *adj*
опти́ческий. **optician** *n* о́птик. **optics** *n* о́птика.
optimism *n* оптими́зм. **optimist** *n*
оптими́ст. **optimistic** *adj* оптими-
сти́ческий. **optimum** *adj* оптима́ль-
ный.
option *n* вы́бор. **optional** *adj* необя-
за́тельный.
opulence *n* бога́тство. **opulent** *adj*
бога́тый.
opus *n* о́пус.
or *conj* и́ли; ~ else ина́че; ~ so при-
близи́тельно.
oracle *n* ора́кул.
oral *adj* у́стный; *n* у́стный экза́мен.
orange *n* (*fruit*) апельси́н; (*colour*)
ора́нжевый цвет; *attrib* апельси́но-
вый; *adj* ора́нжевый.

oration *n* речь. **orator** *n* ора́тор.

oratorio *n* орато́рия.

oratory *n* (*speech*) красноре́чие.

orbit *n* орби́та; *vt* враща́ться *impf* по орби́те вокру́г+*gen*. **orbital** *adj* орбита́льный.

orchard *n* фрукто́вый сад.

orchestra *n* орке́стр. **orchestral** *adj* орке́стровый. **orchestrate** *vt* оркестрова́ть *impf* & *pf*. **orchestration** *n* оркестро́вка.

orchid *n* орхиде́я.

ordain *vt* предпи́сывать *impf*, предписа́ть *pf*; (*eccl*) посвяща́ть *impf*, посвяти́ть *pf* (в духо́вный сан).

ordeal *n* тяжёлое испыта́ние.

order *n* поря́док; (*command*) прика́з; (*for goods*) зака́з; (*insignia, medal; fraternity*) о́рден; (*archit*) о́рдер; *pl* (*holy* ~) духо́вный сан; in ~ to (для того́) чтобы +*inf*; *vt* (*command*) прика́зывать *impf*, приказа́ть *pf* +*dat*; (*goods etc.*) зака́зывать *impf*, заказа́ть *pf*. **orderly** *adj* аккура́тный; (*quiet*) ти́хий; *n* (*med*) санита́р; (*mil*) ордина́рец.

ordinance *n* декре́т.

ordinary *adj* обыкнове́нный, обы́чный.

ordination *n* посвяще́ние.

ore *n* руда́.

organ *n* о́рган; (*mus*) орга́н. **organic** *adj* органи́ческий. **organism** *n* органи́зм. **organist** *n* органи́ст. **organization** *n* организа́ция. **organize** *vt* организо́вывать *impf* (*pres not used*), организова́ть *impf* (*in pres*) & *pf*; устра́ивать *impf*, устро́ить *pf*. **organizer** *n* организа́тор.

orgy *n* о́ргия.

Orient *n* Восто́к. **oriental** *adj* восто́чный.

orient, orientate *vt* ориенти́ровать *impf* &*pf* (o.s. -ся). **orientation** *n* ориента́ция.

orifice *n* отве́рстие.

origin *n* происхожде́ние, нача́ло. **original** *adj* оригина́льный; (*initial*) первонача́льный; (*genuine*) по́длинный; *n* оригина́л. **originality** *n* оригина́льность. **originate** *vt* порожда́ть *impf*, породи́ть *pf*; *vi* брать *impf*, взять *pf* нача́ло (from, in в+*prep*, от+*gen*); (*arise*) возника́ть *impf*, возни́кнуть *pf*. **originator** *n*

а́втор, инициа́тор.

ornament *n* украше́ние; *vt* украша́ть *impf*, укра́сить *pf*. **ornamental** *adj* декорати́вный.

ornate *adj* витиева́тый.

ornithologist *n* орнито́лог. **ornithology** *n* орнитоло́гия.

orphan *n* сирота́ *m* & *f*; *vt*: be ~ed сироте́ть *impf*, o~ *pf*. **orphanage** *n* сиро́тский дом. **orphaned** *adj* осироте́лый.

orthodox *adj* ортодокса́льный; (*eccl*, O~) правосла́вный. **orthodoxy** *n* ортодо́ксия; (O~) правосла́вие.

orthopaedic *adj* ортопеди́ческий.

oscillate *vi* колеба́ться *impf*, по~ *pf*. **oscillation** *n* колеба́ние.

osmosis *n* о́смос.

ostensible *adj* мни́мый. **ostensibly** *adv* я́кобы.

ostentation *n* выставле́ние напока́з. **ostentatious** *adj* показно́й.

osteopath *n* остеопа́т. **osteopathy** *n* остеопа́тия.

ostracize *vt* подверга́ть *impf*, подве́ргнуть *pf* остраки́зму.

ostrich *n* стра́ус.

other *adj* друго́й, ино́й; тот; every ~ ка́ждый второ́й; every ~ day че́рез день; on the ~ hand с друго́й стороны́; on the ~ side на той стороне́, по ту сто́рону; one or the ~ тот и́ли ино́й; the ~ day на днях, неда́вно; the ~ way round наоборо́т; the ~s остальны́е *sb pl*. **otherwise** *adv* & *conj* и́на́че, а то.

otter *n* вы́дра.

ouch *int* ой!, ай!

ought *v aux* до́лжен (-жна́) (бы) +*inf*.

ounce *n* у́нция.

our, ours *poss pron* наш; свой. **ourselves** *pron* (*emph*) (мы) са́ми; (*refl*) себя́; -ся (*suffixed to vt*).

oust *vt* вытесня́ть *impf*, вы́теснить *pf*.

out *adv* 1. *in phrasal vv often rendered by pref* вы-; 2.: to be ~ *in various senses*: he is ~ (*not at home*) его́ нет до́ма; (*not in office etc.*) он вы́шел; (*sport*) выходи́ть *impf*, вы́йти *pf* из игры́; (*of fashion*) вы́йти *pf* из мо́ды; (*be published*) вы́йти *pf* из печа́ти; (*of candle etc.*) поту́хнуть *pf*; (*of flower*) распусти́ться *pf*; (*be unconscious*) потеря́ть *pf*

сознáние; 3.: ~-and-~ отъя́влен-
ный; 4.: ~ of из+gen, вне+gen; ~ of
date устарéлый, старомóдный; ~ of
doors на откры́том вóздухе; ~ of
work безрабóтный.

outbid vt предлагáть impf, пред-
ложи́ть pf бóлее высóкую цéну,
чем+nom. **outboard** adj: ~ **motor**
подвеснóй мотóр m. **outbreak** n (of
anger, disease) вспы́шка; (of war)
начáло. **outbuilding** n надвóрная
пострóйка. **outburst** n взрыв. **outcast** n изгнáнник. **outcome** n ре-
зультáт. **outcry** n (шýмные) про-
тéсты m pl. **outdated** adj устарéлый. **outdo** vt превосходи́ть impf,
превзойти́ pf.
outdoor adj, **outdoors** adv на от-
кры́том вóздухе, на у́лице.
outer adj (external) внéшний, нарýжный; (far from centre) дáльний. **out-
ermost** adj сáмый дáльний.
outfit n (equipment) снаряжéние; (set
of things) набóр; (clothes) наря́д.
outgoing adj (person) n издéржки f pl. **outgrow** vt вырастáть
impf, вы́расти pf из+gen. **outhouse**
n надвóрная пострóйка.
outing n прогýлка, экскýрсия.
outlandish adj дикови́нный. **outlaw**
n лицó вне закóна; банди́т; vt объ-
явля́ть impf, объяви́ть pf вне закóна. **outlay** n издéржки f pl. **outlet** n
выходнóе отвéрстие; (fig) вы́ход;
(market) ры́нок; (shop) торгóвая
тóчка. **outline** n очертáние, кóнтур;
vt очéрчивать impf, очерти́ть pf;
(plans etc.) набрáсывать impf, на-
бросáть pf. **outlive** vt пережи́ть pf.
outlook n перспекти́вы f pl; (attitude) кругозóр. **outlying** adj пери-
фери́йный. **outmoded** adj старомóдный. **outnumber** vt чи́сленно
превосходи́ть impf, превзойти́ pf.
out-patient n амбулатóрный больнóй sb. **outpost** n форпóст. **output**
n вы́пуск, продýкция.
outrage n безобрáзие; (indignation)
возмущéние; vt оскорбля́ть impf,
оскорби́ть pf. **outrageous** adj воз-
мути́тельный.
outright adv (entirely) вполнé; (once
for all) раз (и) навсегдá; (openly)

откры́то; adj прямóй. **outset** n
начáло; at the ~ вначáле; from the
~ с сáмого начáла.
outside n нарýжная сторонá; at the
~ сáмое бóльшее; from the ~ снарýжи;
on the ~ снарýжи; adj нарýжный,
внéшний; (sport) крáйний; adv (on
the ~) снарýжи; (to the ~) нарýжу;
(out of doors) на откры́том вóздухе,
на ýлице; prep вне+gen; за предé-
лами+gen. **outsider** n посторóнний
sb; (sport) аутсáйдер.
outsize adj бóльше стандáртного
размéра. **outskirts** n pl окрáина.
outspoken adj прямóй. **outstanding** adj (remarkable) выдаю́щийся;
(unpaid) неуплáченный. **outstay** vt:
~ one's welcome заси́живаться impf,
засидéться pf. **outstretched** adj распростёртый. **outstrip** vt обгоня́ть
impf, обогнáть pf.
outward adj (external) внéшний, нарýжный. **outwardly** adv внéшне, на
вид. **outwards** adv нарýжу.
outweigh vt перевéшивать impf, перевéсить pf. **outwit** vt перехитри́ть
pf.
oval adj овáльный; n овáл.
ovary n яи́чник.
ovation n овáция.
oven n (industrial) печь; (domestic)
духóвка.
over adv & prep with vv: see vv; prep
(above) над+instr; (through; covering) по+dat; (concerning) о+prep;
(across) чéрез+acc; (on the other side
of) по ту стóрону+gen; (more than)
свы́ше+gen; бóлее+gen; (with age)
за+acc; all ~ (finished) всё кóнчено;
(everywhere) повсю́ду; all ~ the
country по всей странé; ~ again
ещё раз; ~ against по сравнéнию
с+instr; ~ and above не говоря́ ужé
о+prep; ~ the telephone по теле-
фóну; ~ there вон там.
overall n халáт; pl комбинезóн; adj
óбщий. **overawe** vt внушáть impf,
внуши́ть pf благоговéйный страх
+dat. **overbalance** vi теря́ть impf,
по~ pf равновéсие. **overbearing** adj
влáстный. **overboard** adv (motion)
зá борт; (position) за бóртом. **overcast** adj óблачный. **overcoat** n
пальтó neut indecl. **overcome** vt
преодолевáть impf, преодолéть pf;

adj охва́ченный. **overcrowded** *adj* перепо́лненный. **overcrowding** *n* переполне́ние. **overdo** *vt* (*cook*) пережа́ривать *impf*, пережа́рить *pf*; ~ **it, things** (*work too hard*) переутомля́ться *impf*, переутоми́ться *pf*; (*go too far*) переба́рщивать *impf*, переборщи́ть *pf*.

overdose *n* чрезме́рная до́за. **overdraft** *n* превыше́ние креди́та; (*amount*) долг ба́нку. **overdraw** *vi* превыша́ть *impf*, превы́сить *pf* креди́т (в ба́нке). **overdue** *adj* просро́ченный; **be** ~ (*late*) запа́здывать *impf*, запозда́ть *pf*. **overestimate** *vt* переоце́нивать *impf*, переоцени́ть *pf*. **overflow** *vi* перелива́ться *impf*, перели́ться *pf*; (*river etc.*) разлива́ться *impf*, разли́ться *pf*; (*outlet*) перели́в. **overgrown** *adj* заро́сший. **overhang** *vt* & *i* выступа́ть *impf* над+*instr*; *n* свес, вы́ступ.

overhaul *vt* ремонти́ровать *impf* & *pf*; *n*: ремо́нт. **overhead** *adv* наверху́, над голово́й; *adj* возду́шный, подвесно́й; *n*: *pl* накладны́е расхо́ды *m pl*. **overhear** *vt* неча́янно слы́шать *impf*, y~ *pf*. **overheat** *vt* & *i* перегрева́ть(ся) *impf*, перегре́ть(ся) *pf*. **overjoyed** быть в восто́рге (**at** от+*gen*). **overland** *adj* сухопу́тный; *adv* по су́ше. **overlap** *vt* части́чно покрыва́ть *impf*, покры́ть *pf*; *vi* части́чно совпада́ть *impf*, совпа́сть *pf*.

overleaf *adv* на оборо́те. **overload** *vt* перегружа́ть *impf*, перегрузи́ть *pf*. **overlook** *vt* (*look down on*) смотре́ть *impf* све́рху на+*acc*; (*of window*) выходи́ть *impf* на, в, +*acc*; (*not notice*) не замеча́ть *impf*, заме́тить *pf* +*gen*; (~ *offence etc.*) проща́ть *impf*, прости́ть *pf*.

overly *adv* сли́шком.

overnight *adv* (*during the night*) за́ ночь; (*suddenly*) неожи́данно; **stay** ~ ночева́ть *impf*, пере~ *pf*; *adj* ночно́й. **overpay** *vt* перепла́чивать *impf*, переплати́ть *pf*.

over-populated *adj* перенаселённый. **over-population** *n* перенаселённость. **overpower** *vt* одолева́ть *impf*, одоле́ть *pf*. **overpriced** *adj* завы́шенный в цене́. **over-production** *n* перепроизво́дство. **overrate**

vt переоце́нивать *impf*, переоцени́ть *pf*. **override** *vt* (*fig*) отверга́ть *impf*, отве́ргнуть *pf*. **overriding** *adj* гла́вный, реша́ющий. **overrule** *vt* отверга́ть *impf*, отве́ргнуть *pf*. **overrun** *vt* (*conquer*) завоёвывать *impf*, завоева́ть *pf*; **be** ~ **with** кише́ть *impf* +*instr*.

overseas *adv* за мо́рем, че́рез мо́ре; *adj* замо́рский. **oversee** *vt* надзира́ть *impf* за+*instr*. **overseer** *n* надзира́тель *m*, ~ница. **overshadow** *vt* затмева́ть *impf*, затми́ть *pf*. **overshoot** *vt* переходи́ть *impf*, перейти́ *pf* грани́цу. **oversight** *n* случа́йный недосмо́тр. **oversleep** *vi* просыпа́ть *impf*, проспа́ть *pf*. **overspend** *vi* тра́тить *impf* сли́шком мно́го. **overstate** *vt* преувели́чивать *impf*, преувели́чить *pf*. **overstep** *vt* переступа́ть *impf*, переступи́ть *pf* +*acc*, че́рез+*acc*.

overt *adj* я́вный, откры́тый.

overtake *vt* обгоня́ть *impf*, обогна́ть *pf*. **overthrow** *vt* сверга́ть *impf*, све́ргнуть *pf*. **overtime** *n* (*work*) сверхуро́чная рабо́та; (*payment*) сверхуро́чное *sb*; *adv* сверхуро́чно. **overtone** *n* скры́тый намёк.

overture *n* предложе́ние; (*mus*) увертю́ра.

overturn *vt* & *i* опроки́дывать(ся) *impf*, опроки́нуть(ся) *pf*. **overwhelm** *vt* подавля́ть *impf*, подави́ть *pf*. **overwhelming** *adj* подавля́ющий. **overwork** *vt* & *i* переутомля́ть(ся) *impf*, переутоми́ть(ся) *pf*; *n* переутомле́ние.

owe *vt* (~ *money*) быть до́лжным +*acc* & *dat*; (*be indebted*) быть обя́занным +*instr* & *dat*; **he, she, ~s me three roubles** он до́лжен, она́ должна́, мне три рубля́; **she ~s him her life** она́ обя́зана ему́ жи́знью.

owing *adj*: **be** ~ причита́ться *impf* (**to** +*dat*); ~ **to** из-за+*gen*, по причи́не+*gen*.

owl *n* сова́.

own *adj* свой; (свой) со́бственный; **on one's** ~ самостоя́тельно; (*alone*) оди́н; *vt* (*possess*) владе́ть *impf* +*instr*; (*admit*) признава́ть *impf*, призна́ть *pf*; ~ **up** признава́ться *impf*, призна́ться *pf*. **owner** *n* владе́лец. **ownership** *n* владе́ние (of +*instr*), cóбственность.

ox *n* вол.

oxidation *n* окисление. **oxide** *n* óкись. **oxidize** *vt* & *i* окисля́ть(ся) *impf*, окислить(ся) *pf*. **oxygen** *n* кислоро́д.

oyster *n* у́стрица.

ozone *n* озо́н.

P

pace *n* шаг; (*fig*) темп; keep ~ with идти́ *impf* в но́гу с+*instr*; set the ~ задава́ть *impf*, зада́ть *pf* темп; *vi*: ~ up and down ходи́ть *indet* взад и вперёд. **pacemaker** *n* (*med*) электро́нный стимуля́тор.

pacifism *n* пацифи́зм. **pacifist** *n* пацифи́ст. **pacify** *vt* усмиря́ть *impf*, усмири́ть *pf*.

pack *n* у́зел, вьюк; (*soldier's*) ра́нец; (*hounds*) сво́ра; (*wolves*) ста́я; (*cards*) коло́да; *vt* (& *i*) упако́вывать(ся) *impf*, упакова́ть(ся) *pf*; (*cram*) набива́ть *impf*, наби́ть *pf*. **package** *n* посы́лка, паке́т; ~ holiday организо́ванная тури́стическая пое́здка. **packaging** *n* упако́вка. **packet** *n* паке́т; па́чка; (*large sum of money*) ку́ча де́нег. **packing-case** *n* я́щик.

pact *n* пакт.

pad[1] *n* (*cushion*) поду́шечка; (*shin- etc.*) щито́к; (*of paper*) блокно́т; *vt* подбива́ть *impf*, подби́ть *pf*. **padding** *n* наби́вка.

paddle[1] *n* (*oar*) весло́; *vi* (*row*) грести́ *impf*.

paddle[2] *n* (*wade*) ходи́ть *indet*, идти́ *det*, пойти́ *pf* босико́м по воде́.

paddock *n* вы́гон.

padlock *n* вися́чий замо́к; *vt* запира́ть *impf*, запере́ть *pf* на вися́чий замо́к.

paediatric *adj* педиатри́ческий. **paediatrician** *n* педиа́тор.

pagan *n* язы́чник, -ица; *adj* язы́ческий. **paganism** *n* язы́чество.

page[1] *n* (~-*boy*) паж; *vt* (*summon*) вызыва́ть *impf*, вы́звать *pf*.

page[2] *n* (*of book*) страни́ца.

pageant *n* пы́шная проце́ссия. **pageantry** *n* пы́шность.

pail *n* ведро́.

pain *n* боль; *pl* (*efforts*) уси́лия *neut pl*; ~-killer болеутоля́ющее сре́дство; *vt* (*fig*) огорча́ть *impf*, огорчи́ть *pf*; be ~ (*part of body*) боле́ть *impf*. **painless** *adj* безболе́зненный. **painstaking** *adj* стара́тельный.

paint *n* кра́ска; *vt* кра́сить *impf*, по~ *pf*; (*portray*) писа́ть *impf*, на~ *pf* кра́сками. **paintbrush** *n* кисть. **painter** *n* (*artist*) худо́жник, -ица; (*decorator*) маля́р; **painting** *n* (*art*) жи́вопись; (*picture*) карти́на.

pair *n* па́ра; *often not translated with nn denoting a single object, e.g.* a ~ of scissors но́жницы (-ц) *pl*; a ~ of trousers па́ра брюк; *vt* спа́ривать *impf*, спа́рить *pf*; ~ off разделя́ться *impf*, раздели́ться *pf* по па́рам.

Pakistan *n* Пакиста́н. **Pakistani** *n* пакиста́нец, -а́нка; *adj* пакиста́нский.

pal *n* прия́тель *m*, ~ница.

palace *n* дворе́ц.

palatable *adj* вку́сный; (*fig*) прия́тный. **palate** *n* нёбо; (*fig*) вкус. **palatial** *adj* великоле́пный.

palaver *n* (*trouble*) беспоко́йство; (*nonsense*) чепуха́.

pale[1] *n* (*stake*) кол; beyond the ~ невообрази́мый.

pale[2] *adj* бле́дный; *vi* бледне́ть *impf*, по~ *pf*.

palette *n* пали́тра.

pall[1] *n* покро́в.

pall[2] *vi*: ~ on надоеда́ть *impf*, надое́сть *pf* +*dat*.

palliative *adj* паллиати́вный; *n* паллиати́в.

pallid *adj* бле́дный. **pallor** *n* бле́дность.

palm[1] *n* (*tree*) па́льма; P~ Sunday Ве́рбное воскресе́нье.

palm[2] *n* (*of hand*) ладо́нь; *vt*: ~ off всу́чивать *impf*, всучи́ть *pf* (on +*dat*). **palpable** *adj* ося́заемый.

palpitations *n pl* сердцебие́ние.

paltry *adj* ничто́жный.

pamper *vt* балова́ть *impf*, из~ *pf*.

pamphlet *n* брошю́ра.

pan[1] *n* (*saucepan*) кастрю́ля; (*frying-*~) сковорода́; (*of scales*) ча́шка; *vt*: ~ out промыва́ть *impf*, промы́ть *pf*; (*fig*) выходи́ть *impf*, вы́йти *pf*.

pan[2] *vi* (*cin*) панорами́ровать *impf* & *pf*.

panacea n панацея.

panache n рисовка.

pancake n блин.

pancreas n поджелудочная железа.

panda n панда.

pandemonium n гвалт.

pander vi: ~ to потворствовать impf +dat.

pane n оконное стекло.

panel n панель; (control-~) щит управления; (of experts) группа специалистов; (of judges) жюри neut indecl. panelling n панельная обшивка.

pang n pl муки (-к) pl.

panic n паника; ~-stricken охваченный паникой; vi впадать impf, впасть pf в панику. panicky adj панический.

pannier n корзинка.

panorama n панорама. panoramic adj панорамный.

pansy n анютины глазки (-зок) pl.

pant vi дышать impf с одышкой.

panther n пантера.

panties n pl трусики (-ков) pl.

pantomime n рождественское представление; (dumb show) пантомима.

pantry n кладовая sb.

pants n pl трусы (-сов) pl; (trousers) брюки (-к) pl.

papal adj папский.

paper n бумага; pl документы m pl; (newspaper) газета; (wallpaper) обои (-оев) pl; (treatise) доклад; adj бумажный; vt оклеивать impf, оклеить pf обоями. paperback n книга в бумажной обложке. paperclip n скрепка. paperwork n канцелярская работа.

par n: feel below ~ чувствовать impf себя неважно; on a ~ with наравне с+instr.

parable n притча.

parabola n парабола.

parachute n парашют; vi спускаться impf, спуститься pf с парашютом. parachutist n парашютист.

parade n парад; vi шествовать impf; vt (show off) выставлять impf, выставить pf напоказ.

paradigm n парадигма.

paradise n рай.

paradox n парадокс. paradoxical adj парадоксальный.

paraffin n (~ oil) керосин.

paragon n образец.

paragraph n абзац.

parallel adj параллельный; n параллель; vt соответствовать impf +dat.

paralyse vt парализовать impf & pf. paralysis n паралич.

parameter n параметр.

paramilitary adj полувоенный.

paramount adj первостепенный.

paranoia n паранойя paranoid adj: he is ~ он параноик.

parapet n (mil) бруствер.

paraphernalia n принадлежности f pl.

paraphrase n пересказ; vt пересказывать impf, пересказать pf.

parasite n паразит. parasitic adj паразитический.

parasol n зонтик.

paratrooper n парашютист-десантник.

parcel n пакет, посылка.

parch vt иссушать impf, иссушить pf; become ~ed пересыхать impf, пересохнуть pf.

parchment n пергамент.

pardon n прощение; (law) помилование; vt прощать impf, простить pf; (law) помиловать pf.

pare vt (fruit) чистить impf, о~ pf; ~ away, down урезать impf, урезать pf.

parent n родитель m, ~ница. parentage n происхождение. parental adj родительский.

parentheses n pl (brackets) скобки f pl.

parish n приход. parishioner n прихожанин, -анка.

parity n равенство.

park n парк; (for cars etc.) стоянка; vt & abs ставить impf, по~ pf (машину). parking n стоянка.

parliament n парламент. parliamentarian n парламентарий. parliamentary adj парламентский.

parlour n гостиная sb.

parochial adj приходский; (fig) ограниченный. parochialism n ограниченность.

parody n пародия; vt пародировать impf & pf.

parole n честное слово: on ~ освобождённый под честное слово.

paroxysm *n* парокси́зм.

parquet *n* парке́т; *attrib* парке́тный.

parrot *n* попуга́й.

parry *vt* пари́ровать *impf & pf*, от~ *pf*.

parsimonious *adj* скупо́й.

parsley *n* петру́шка.

parsnip *n* пастерна́к.

parson *n* свяще́нник.

part *n* часть; (*in play*) роль; (*mus*) па́ртия; **for the most ~** бо́льшей ча́стью; **in ~** ча́стью; **for my ~** что каса́ется меня́; **take ~ in** уча́ствовать *impf* в+*prep*; **~-time** (за́нятый) непо́лный рабо́чий день; *vt & i* (*divide*) разделя́ть(ся) *impf*, раздели́ть(ся) *pf*; *vi* (*leave*) расстава́ться *impf*, расста́ться *pf* (**from, with** с+*instr*); **~ one's hair** де́лать *impf*, с~ *pf* себе́ пробо́р.

partake *vi* принима́ть *impf*, приня́ть *pf* уча́стие (**in, of** в+*prep*); (*eat*) есть *impf*, съ~ *pf* (**of** +*acc*).

partial *adj* части́чный; (*biased*) пристра́стный; **~ to** неравноду́шный к+*dat*. **partiality** *n* (*bias*) пристра́стность. **partially** *adv* части́чно.

participant *n* уча́стник, -ица (*in* +*gen*). **participate** *vi* уча́ствовать *impf* (*in* в+*prep*). **participation** *n* уча́стие.

participle *n* прича́стие.

particle *n* части́ца.

particular *adj* осо́бый, осо́бенный; (*fussy*) разбо́рчивый; *n* подро́бность; **in ~** в ча́стности.

parting *n* (*leave-taking*) проща́ние; (*of hair*) пробо́р.

partisan *n* (*adherent*) сторо́нник; (*mil*) партиза́н; *attrib* (*biased*) пристра́стный; партиза́нский.

partition *n* (*wall*) перегоро́дка; (*polit*) разде́л; *vt* разделя́ть *impf*, раздели́ть *pf*; **~ off** отгора́живать *impf*, отгороди́ть *pf*.

partly *adv* части́чно.

partner *n* (*in business*) компаньо́н; (*in dance, game*) партнёр, ~ша. **partnership** *n* това́рищество.

partridge *n* куропа́тка.

party *n* (*polit*) па́ртия; (*group*) гру́ппа; (*social gathering*) вечери́нка; (*law*) сторона́; **be a ~ to** принима́ть *impf*, приня́ть *pf* уча́стие в+*prep*; *attrib* парти́йный; **~ line** (*polit*)

ли́ния па́ртии; (*telephone*) о́бщий телефо́нный про́вод; **~ wall** о́бщая стена́.

pass *vt & i* (*go past; of time*) проходи́ть *impf*, пройти́ *pf* (**by** ми́мо +*gen*); (*travel past*) проезжа́ть *impf*, прое́хать *pf* (**by** ми́мо+*gen*); (**~ examination**) сдава́ть *impf*, сдать *pf* (экза́мен); *vt* (*sport*) пасова́ть *impf*, пасну́ть *pf*; (*overtake*) обгоня́ть *impf*, обогна́ть *pf*; (*time*) проводи́ть *impf*, провести́ *pf*; (*hand on*) передава́ть *impf*, переда́ть *pf*; (*law, resolution*) утвержда́ть *impf*, утверди́ть *pf*; (*sentence*) выноси́ть *impf*, вы́нести *pf* (**upon** +*dat*); ~ **as, for** слыть *impf*, про~ *pf* +*instr*, за+*acc*; ~ **away** (*die*) сконча́ться *pf*; ~ **off as** выдава́ть *impf*, вы́дать *pf* себя́ за+*acc*; ~ **out** теря́ть *impf*, по~ *pf* созна́ние; ~ **over** (*in silence*) обходи́ть *impf*, обойти́ *pf* молча́нием; ~ **round** передава́ть *impf*, переда́ть *pf*; ~ **up** подава́ть *impf*, пода́ть *pf*; (*miss*) пропуска́ть *impf*, пропусти́ть *pf*; *n* (*permit*) про́пуск; (*sport*) пас; (*geog*) перева́л; **come to** ~ случа́ться *impf*, случи́ться *pf*; **make a** ~ **at** пристава́ть *impf*, приста́ть *pf* к+*dat*.

passable *adj* проходи́мый, прое́зжий; (*not bad*) неплохо́й.

passage *n* прохо́д; (*of time*) тече́ние; (*sea trip*) рейс; (*in house*) коридо́р; (*in book*) отры́вок; (*mus*) пасса́ж.

passenger *n* пассажи́р.

passer-by *n* прохо́жий *sb*.

passing *adj* (*transient*) мимолётный; *n*: **in** ~ мимохо́дом.

passion *n* страсть (**for** к+*dat*) **passionate** *adj* стра́стный.

passive *adj* пасси́вный; (*gram*) страда́тельный; *n* страда́тельный зало́г. **passivity** *n* пасси́вность.

Passover *n* евре́йская Па́сха.

passport *n* па́спорт.

password *n* паро́ль *m*.

past *adj* про́шлый; (*gram*) проше́дший; *n* про́шлое *sb*; (*gram*) проше́дшее вре́мя *neut*; *prep* ми́мо +*gen*; (*beyond*) за+*instr*; *adv* ми́мо.

pasta *n* макаро́нные изде́лия *neut pl*.

paste *n* (*of flour*) те́сто; (*creamy mixture*) па́ста; (*glue*) клей; (*jewellery*) страз; *vt* накле́ивать *impf*, накле́ить *pf*.

pastel *n* (*crayon*) пасте́ль; (*drawing*) рису́нок пасте́лью; *attrib* пасте́льный.

pasteurize *vt* пастеризова́ть *impf* & *pf*.

pastime *n* времяпрепровожде́ние.

pastor *n* па́стор. **pastoral** *adj* (*bucolic*) пастора́льный; (*of pastor*) па́сторский.

pastry *n* (*dough*) те́сто; (*cake*) пиро́жное *sb*.

pasture *n* (*land*) па́стбище.

pasty¹ *n* пирожо́к.

pasty² *adj* (~-*faced*) бле́дный.

pat *n* шлепо́к; (*of butter etc.*) кусо́к; *vt* хлопа́ть *impf*, по~ *pf*.

patch *n* запла́та; (*over eye*) повя́зка (на глазу́); (*spot*) пятно́; (*of land*) уча́сток земли́; *vt* ста́вить *impf*, по~ *pf* запла́ту на+*acc*; ~ up (*fig*) ула́живать *impf*, ула́дить *pf*. **patchwork** *n* лоску́тная рабо́та; *attrib* лоску́тный **patchy** *adj* неро́вный.

pâté *n* паште́т.

patent *adj* я́вный; ~ leather лаки́рованная ко́жа; *n* пате́нт; *vt* патентова́ть *impf*, за~ *pf*.

paternal *adj* отцо́вский. **paternity** *n* отцо́вство.

path *n* тропи́нка, тропа́; (*way*) путь *m*.

pathetic *adj* жа́лкий.

pathological *adj* патологи́ческий. **pathologist** *n* пато́лог.

pathos *n* па́фос.

pathway *n* тропи́нка, тропа́.

patience *n* терпе́ние; (*cards*) пасья́нс. **patient** *adj* терпели́вый; *n* больно́й *sb*, пацие́нт, ~ка.

patio *n* терра́са.

patriarch *n* патриа́рх. **patriarchal** *adj* патриарха́льный.

patriot *n* патрио́т, ~ка. **patriotic** *adj* патриоти́ческий. **patriotism** *n* патриоти́зм.

patrol *n* патру́ль *m*; on ~ на дозо́ре; *vt* & *i* патрули́ровать *impf*.

patron *n* покрови́тель *m*; (*of shop*) клие́нт **patronage** *n* покрови́тельство. **patroness** *n* покрови́тельница. **patronize** *vt* (*treat condescendingly*) снисходи́тельно относи́ться *impf*, к+*dat*. **patronizing** *adj* покрови́тельственный.

patronymic *n* о́тчество.

patter¹ *vi* (*sound*) бараба́нить *impf*; *n* посту́кивание.

patter² *n* (*speech*) скорогово́рка.

pattern *n* (*design*) узо́р; (*model*) образе́ц; (*sewing*) вы́кройка.

paunch *n* брюшко́.

pauper *n* бедня́к.

pause *n* па́уза, переры́в; (*mus*) ферма́та; *vi* остана́вливаться *impf*, останови́ться *pf*.

pave *vt* мости́ть *impf*, вы́~ *pf*; ~ the way подготовля́ть *impf*, подгото́вить *pf* по́чву (for для+*gen*). **pavement** *n* тротуа́р.

pavilion *n* павильо́н.

paw *n* ла́па; *vt* тро́гать *impf* ла́пой; (*horse*) бить *impf* копы́том.

pawn¹ *n* (*chess*) пе́шка.

pawn² *n*: in ~ в закла́де; *vt* закла́дывать *impf*, заложи́ть *pf*. **pawnbroker** *n* ростовщи́к. **pawnshop** *n* ломба́рд.

pay *vt* плати́ть *impf*, за~, у~ *pf* (for за+*acc*); (*bill etc.*) опла́чивать *impf*, оплати́ть *pf*; *vi* (*be profitable*) окупа́ться *impf*, окупи́ться *pf*; *n* жа́лованье, зарпла́та; ~ packet полу́чка; ~-roll платёжная ве́домость. **payable** *adj* подлежа́щий упла́те. **payee** *n* получа́тель *m*. **payload** *n* поле́зная нагру́зка. **payment** *n* упла́та, платёж.

pea *n* (*also pl, collect*) горо́х.

peace *n* мир; in ~ в поко́е; ~ and quiet мир и тишина́. **peaceable**, **peaceful** *adj* ми́рный.

peach *n* пе́рсик.

peacock *n* павли́н.

peak *n* (*of cap*) козырёк; (*summit*, *fig*) верши́на; ~ hour часы́ *m pl* пик.

peal *n* (*sound*) звон, трезво́н; (*of laughter*) взрыв.

peanut *n* ара́хис.

pear *n* гру́ша.

pearl *n* (*also fig*) жемчу́жина; *pl* (*collect*) же́мчуг.

peasant *n* крестья́нин, -я́нка; *attrib* крестья́нский.

peat *n* торф.

pebble *n* га́лька.

peck *vt* & *i* клева́ть *impf*, клю́нуть *pf*; *n* клево́к.

pectoral *adj* грудно́й.

peculiar adj (distinctive) своеобра́зный; (strange) стра́нный; ~ to сво́йственный +dat. **peculiarity** n осо́бенность; стра́нность.

pecuniary adj де́нежный.

pedagogical adj педагоги́ческий.

pedal n педа́ль; vi нажима́ть impf, нажа́ть pf педа́ль; (ride bicycle) е́хать impf, по~ pf на велосипе́де.

pedant n педа́нт. **pedantic** adj педанти́чный.

peddle vt торгова́ть impf вразно́с +instr.

pedestal n пьедеста́л.

pedestrian adj пешехо́дный; (prosaic) прозаи́ческий; n пешехо́д; ~ crossing перехо́д.

pedigree n родосло́вная sb; adj поро́дистый.

pedlar n разно́счик.

pee n пи-пи́ neut indecl; vi мочи́ться impf, по~ pf.

peek vi (~ in) загля́дывать impf, загляну́ть pf; (~ out) выгля́дывать impf, вы́глянуть pf.

peel n кожура́; vt очища́ть impf, очи́стить pf; vi (skin) шелуши́ться impf; (paint, ~ off) сходи́ть impf, сойти́ pf. **peelings** n pl очи́стки (-ков) pl.

peep vi (~ in) загля́дывать impf, загляну́ть pf; (~ out) выгля́дывать impf, вы́глянуть pf; n (glance) бы́стрый взгляд; ~hole глазо́к.

peer[1] vi всма́триваться impf, всмотре́ться pf (at в+acc).

peer[2] n (noble) пэр; (person one's age) све́рстник.

peeved adj раздражённый. **peevish** adj раздражи́тельный.

peg n ко́лышек; (clothes ~) крючо́к; (for hat etc.) ве́шалка; off the ~ гото́вый; vt прикрепля́ть impf, прикрепи́ть pf ко́лышком, -ками.

pejorative adj уничижи́тельный.

pelican n пелика́н.

pellet n ша́рик; (shot) дроби́на.

pelt[1] n (skin) шку́ра.

pelt[2] vt забра́сывать impf, заброса́ть pf; vi (rain) бараба́нить impf.

pelvis n таз.

pen[1] n (for writing) ру́чка; ~-friend друг по перепи́ске.

pen[2] n (enclosure) заго́н.

penal adj уголо́вный. **penalize** vt штрафова́ть impf, o~ pf. **penalty** n наказа́ние; (sport) штраф; ~ area штрафна́я площа́дка; ~ kick штрафно́й уда́р. **penance** n епитимья́.

penchant n скло́нность (for к+dat).

pencil n каранда́ш; ~-sharpener точи́лка.

pendant n подве́ска.

pending adj (awaiting decision) ожида́ющий реше́ния; prep (until) в ожида́нии +gen, до+gen.

pendulum n ма́ятник.

penetrate vt проника́ть impf, прони́кнуть pf в+acc. **penetrating** adj проница́тельный; (sound) пронзи́тельный. **penetration** n проникнове́ние; (insight) проница́тельность.

penguin n пингви́н.

penicillin n пеницилли́н.

peninsula n полуо́стров.

penis n пе́нис.

penitence n раска́яние. **penitent** adj раска́ивающийся; n ка́ющийся гре́шник.

penknife n перочи́нный нож.

pennant n вы́мпел.

penniless adj без гроша́.

penny n пе́нни neut indecl, пенс.

pension n пе́нсия; vt: ~ off увольня́ть impf, уво́лить pf на пе́нсию. **pensionable** adj (age) пенсио́нный. **pensioner** n пенсионе́р, ~ка.

pensive adj заду́мчивый.

pentagon n пятиуго́льник; the P~ Пентаго́н.

Pentecost n Пятидеся́тница.

penthouse n шика́рная кварти́ра на ве́рхнем этаже́.

pent-up adj (anger etc.) сде́рживаемый.

penultimate adj предпосле́дний.

penury n нужда́.

peony n пио́н.

people n pl (persons) лю́ди pl; sg (nation) наро́д; vt населя́ть impf, насели́ть pf.

pepper n пе́рец; vt пе́рчить impf, на~, по~ pf. **peppercorn** n пе́рчинка.

peppermint n пе́речная мя́та; (sweet) мя́тная конфе́та.

per prep (for each) (person) на+acc; as ~ согла́сно+dat; ~ annum в год; ~ capita на челове́ка; ~ hour в час; ~ se сам по себе́.

perceive vt воспринимать impf, воспринять pf.

per cent adv & n процент. **percentage** n процент; (part) часть.

perceptible adj заметный. **perception** n восприятие; (quality) понимание. **perceptive** adj тонкий.

perch[1] n (fish) óкунь m.

perch[2] n (roost) насест m; vi садиться impf, сесть pf. **perched** adj высоко сидящий, расположенный.

percussion n (~ instruments) ударные инструменты m pl.

peremptory adj повелительный.

perennial adj (enduring) вечный; n (bot) многолетнее растение.

perestroika n перестройка.

perfect adj совершенный; (gram) перфектный; n перфект; ~ совершенствовать impf, y~ pf. **perfection** n совершенство. **perfective** adj (n) совершенный (вид).

perforate vt перфорировать impf & pf. **perforation** n перфорация.

perform vt (carry out) исполнять impf, исполнить pf; (theat, mus) играть impf, сыграть pf; vi выступать impf, выступить pf; (function) работать impf. **performance** n исполнение; (of person, device) действие; (of play etc.) представление, спектакль m; (of engine etc.) эксплуатационные качества neut pl. **performer** n исполнитель m.

perfume n духи (-хов) pl; (smell) аромат.

perfunctory adj поверхностный.

perhaps adv может быть.

peril n опасность, риск. **perilous** adj опасный, рискованный.

perimeter n внешняя граница; (geom) периметр.

period n период; (epoch) эпоха; (menstrual) месячные sb pl. **periodic** adj периодический. **periodical** adj периодический; n периодическое издание.

peripheral adj периферийный. **periphery** n периферия.

periscope n перископ.

perish vi погибать impf, погибнуть pf; (spoil) портиться impf, ис~ pf. **perishable** adj скоропортящийся.

perjure v: ~ o.s. нарушать impf, нарушить pf клятву. **perjury** n лже-

свидетельство.

perk[1] n льгота.

perk[2] vi: ~ up оживляться impf, оживиться pf. **perky** adj бойкий.

perm n перманент. **permanence** n постоянство. **permanent** adj постоянный.

permeable adj проницаемый. **permeate** vt проникать impf, проникнуть pf в+acc.

permissible adj допустимый. **permission** n разрешение. **permissive** adj (слишком) либеральный; ~ society общество вседозволенности. **permissiveness** n вседозволенность. **permit** vt разрешать impf, разрешить pf +dat; n пропуск.

permutation n перестановка.

pernicious adj пагубный.

perpendicular adj перпендикулярный; n перпендикуляр.

perpetrate vt совершать impf, совершить pf. **perpetrator** n виновник.

perpetual adj вечный. **perpetuate** vt увековечивать impf, увековечить pf. **perpetuity** n вечность; in ~ навсегда, навечно.

perplex vt озадачивать impf, озадачить pf. **perplexity** n озадаченность.

persecute vt преследовать impf. **persecution** n преследование.

perseverance n настойчивость. **persevere** vi настойчиво, продолжать impf (in, at etc. +acc, inf).

Persian n перс, ~иянка; adj персидский.

persist vi упорствовать impf (in в+prep); настойчиво продолжать impf (in +acc, inf). **persistence** n упорство. **persistent** adj упорный.

person n человек; (in play; gram) лицо; in ~ лично. **personable** adj привлекательный. **personage** n личность. **personal** adj личный. **personality** n личность. **personally** adv лично. **personification** n олицетворение. **personify** vt олицетворять impf, олицетворить pf.

personnel n кадры (-ров) pl, персонал; ~ department отдел кадров.

perspective n перспектива.

perspiration n пот. **perspire** vi потеть impf, вс~ pf.

persuade vt (convince) убеждать impf, убедить pf (of в+prep); (in-

duce) угова́ривать *impf*, уговори́ть *pf*. **persuasion** *n* убежде́ние. **persuasive** *adj* убеди́тельный.

pertain *vi*: ~ **to** относи́ться *impf* отнести́сь *pf* к+*dat*.

pertinent *adj* уме́стный.

perturb *vt* трево́жить *impf*, вс~ *pf*.

peruse *vt* (*read*) внима́тельно чита́ть *impf*, про~ *pf*; (*fig*) рассма́тривать *impf*, рассмотре́ть *pf*.

pervade *vt* наполня́ть *impf*. **pervasive** *adj* распространённый.

perverse *adj* капри́зный. **perversion** *n* извраще́ние. **pervert** *vt* извраща́ть *impf*, изврати́ть *pf*; *n* извращённый челове́к.

pessimism *n* пессими́зм. **pessimist** *n* пессими́ст. **pessimistic** *adj* пессимисти́ческий.

pest *n* вреди́тель *m*; (*fig*) зану́да. **pester** *vt* пристава́ть *impf*, приста́ть *pf* к+*dat*. **pesticide** *n* пестици́д.

pet *n* (*animal*) дома́шнее живо́тное *sb*; (*favourite*) люби́мец, -мица; ~ **shop** зоомагази́н; *vt* ласка́ть *impf*.

petal *n* лепесто́к.

peter *vi*: ~ **out** (*road*) исчеза́ть *impf*, исче́знуть *pf*; (*stream*; *enthusiasm*) иссяка́ть *impf*, исся́кнуть *pf*.

petite *adj* ма́ленькая.

petition *n* пети́ция; *vt* подава́ть *impf*, пода́ть *pf* проше́ние +*dat*. **petitioner** *n* проси́тель *m*.

petrified *adj* окамене́лый; **be** ~ (*fig*) оцепене́ть *pf* (**with** от+*gen*).

petrol *n* бензи́н; ~ **pump** бензоколо́нка; ~ **station** бензозапра́вочная ста́нция; ~ **tank** бензоба́к. **petroleum** *n* нефть.

petticoat *n* ни́жняя ю́бка.

petty *adj* ме́лкий; ~ **cash** де́ньги (де́нег, -ньга́м) *pl* на ме́лкие расхо́ды.

petulant *adj* раздражи́тельный.

pew *n* (церко́вная) скамья́.

phallic *adj* фалли́ческий. **phallus** *n* фа́ллос.

phantom *n* фанто́м.

pharmaceutical *adj* фармацевти́ческий. **pharmacist** *n* фармаце́вт. **pharmacy** *n* фарма́ция; (*shop*) апте́ка.

phase *n* фа́за; *vt*: ~ **in, out** постепе́нно вводи́ть *impf*, упраздня́ть *impf*.

Ph.D. *abbr* (*of* **Doctor of Philosophy**)

кандида́т нау́к.

pheasant *n* фаза́н.

phenomenal *adj* феномена́льный. **phenomenon** *n* фено́мен.

phial *n* пузырёк.

philanderer *n* волоки́та *m*.

philanthropic *adj* филантропи́ческий. **philanthropist** *n* филантро́п. **philanthropy** *n* филантро́пия.

philately *n* филатели́я.

philharmonic *adj* филармони́ческий.

Philistine *n* (*fig*) фили́стер.

philosopher *n* фило́соф. **philosophical** *adj* филосо́фский. **philosophize** *vi* филосо́фствовать *impf*. **philosophy** *n* филосо́фия.

phlegm *n* мокрота́. **phlegmatic** *adj* флегмати́ческий.

phobia *n* фо́бия.

phone *n* телефо́н; *vt* & *i* звони́ть *impf*, по~ *pf*+*dat*. *See also* **telephone**

phonetic *adj* фонети́ческий. **phonetics** *n* фоне́тика.

phoney *adj* подде́льный.

phosphorus *n* фо́сфор.

photo *n* фо́то *neut indecl*. **photocopier** *n* копирова́льная маши́на. **photocopy** *n* фотоко́пия; *vt* де́лать *impf*, с~ *pf* фотоко́пию +*gen*. **photogenic** *adj* фотогени́чный. **photograph** *n* фотогра́фия; *vt* фотографи́ровать *impf*, с~ *pf*. **photographer** *n* фото́граф. **photographic** *adj* фотографи́ческий. **photography** *n* фотогра́фия.

phrase *n* фра́за; *vt* формули́ровать *impf*, с~ *pf*.

physical *adj* физи́ческий; ~ **education** физкульту́ра; ~ **exercises** заря́дка. **physician** *n* врач. **physicist** *n* фи́зик. **physics** *n* фи́зика.

physiological *adj* физиологи́ческий. **physiologist** *n* физио́лог. **physiology** *n* физиоло́гия. **physiotherapist** *n* физиотерапе́вт. **physiotherapy** *n* физиотерапи́я.

physique *n* телосложе́ние.

pianist *n* пиани́ст, ~ка. **piano** *n* фортепья́но *neut indecl*; (*grand*) роя́ль *m*; (*upright*) пиани́но *neut indecl*.

pick[1] *vt* (*flower*) срыва́ть *impf*, сорва́ть *pf*; (*gather*) собира́ть *impf*, собра́ть *pf*; (*select*) выбира́ть *impf*, вы́брать *pf*; ~ **one's nose, teeth** ковыря́ть *impf*, ковырну́ть *pf* в носу́, в зуба́х; ~ a quarrel иска́ть *impf* ссо́ры (with c+*instr*); ~ one's way выбира́ть *impf*, вы́брать *pf* доро́гу; ~ on (nag) придира́ться *impf* к+*dat*; ~ out отбира́ть *impf*, отобра́ть *pf*; ~ up (lift) поднима́ть *impf*, подня́ть *pf*; (acquire) приобрета́ть *impf*, приобрести́ *pf*; (fetch) (on foot) заходи́ть *impf*, зайти́ *pf* за+*instr*; (in vehicle) заезжа́ть *impf*, зае́хать *pf* за+*instr*; (a cold; a girl) подцепля́ть *impf*, подцепи́ть *pf*; ~ o.s. up поднима́ться *impf*, подня́ться *pf*; ~up (truck) пика́п; (electron) звукосни-ма́тель *m*.

pick[2] *n* вы́бор; (best part) лу́чшая часть; take your ~ выбира́й(те)!

pick[3], pickaxe *n* кирка́.

picket *n* (person) пике́тчик, -ица; (collect) пике́т; *vt* пикети́ровать *impf*.

pickle *n* соле́нье; *vt* соли́ть *impf*, по~ *pf*. pickled *adj* солёный.

pickpocket *n* карма́нник.

picnic *n* пикни́к.

pictorial *adj* изобрази́тельный; (illustrated) иллюстри́рованный. picture *n* карти́на; (of health etc.) воплоще́ние; (film) фильм; the ~s кино́ *neut indecl*; *vt* (to o.s.) представля́ть *impf*, предста́вить *pf* себе́.

picturesque *adj* живопи́сный.

pie *n* пиро́г.

piece *n* кусо́к, часть; (one of set) шту́ка; (of paper) листо́к; (mus, literature) произведе́ние; (chess) фигу́ра; (coin) моне́та; take to ~s разбира́ть *impf*, разобра́ть *pf* (на ча́сти); ~ of advice сове́т; ~ of information све́дение; ~ of news но́вость; ~work сде́льщина; ~worker сде́ль-щик; ~ together воссоздава́ть *impf*, воссозда́ть *pf* карти́ну +*gen*.

piecemeal *adv* по частя́м.

pier *n* (mole) мол; (projecting into sea) пирс; (of bridge) бык; (between windows etc.) простёнок.

pierce *vt* пронза́ть *impf*, пронзи́ть *pf*; (ears) прока́лывать *impf*, проколо́ть *pf*. piercing *adj* пронзи́тель-ный.

piety *n* на́божность.

pig *n* свинья́. pigheaded *adj* упря́-мый. piglet *n* поросёнок. pigsty *n* свина́рник. pigtail *n* коси́чка.

pigeon *n* го́лубь; ~hole отделе́ние для бума́г.

pigment *n* пигме́нт. pigmentation *n* пигмента́ция.

pike *n* (fish) щу́ка.

pilchard *n* сарди́н(к)а.

pile[1] *n* (heap) ку́ча, ки́па; *vt*: ~ up сва́ливать *impf*, свали́ть *pf* в ку́чу; (load) нагружа́ть *impf*, нагрузи́ть *pf* (with +*instr*); *vi*: ~ in(to), on забира́ться *impf*, забра́ться *pf* в+*acc*; ~ up накопля́ться, нака́пливаться *impf*, накопи́ться *pf*.

pile[2] *n* (on cloth etc.) ворс.

piles *n pl* геморро́й collect.

pilfer *vt* ворова́ть *impf*.

pilgrim *n* пилигри́м. pilgrimage *n* пало́мничество.

pill *n* пилю́ля; the ~ противозача́-точная пилю́ля.

pillage *n* грабить *impf*, o~ *pf*; *v abs* мародёрствовать *impf*.

pillar *n* столб; ~box стоя́чий почто́вый я́щик.

pillion *n* за́днее сиде́нье (мотоци́-кла).

pillory *n* позо́рный столб; *vt* (fig) пригвожда́ть *impf*, пригвозди́ть *pf* к позо́рному столбу́.

pillow *n* поду́шка. pillowcase *n* на́-волочка.

pilot *n* (naut) ло́цман; (aeron) пило́т; *adj* о́пытный, про́бный; *vt* пилоти́-ровать *impf*.

pimp *n* сво́дник.

pimple *n* прыщ.

pin *n* була́вка; (peg) па́лец; ~point то́чно определя́ть *impf*, определи́ть *pf*; ~stripe то́нкая поло́ска; *vt* прика́лывать *impf*, приколо́ть *pf*; (press) прижима́ть *impf*, прижа́ть *pf* (against к+*dat*).

pinafore *n* пере́дник.

pincers *n pl* (tool) кле́щи (-ще́й) *pl*, пинце́т; (claw) клешня́ *f pl*.

pinch *vt* щипа́ть *impf*, (у)щипну́ть *pf*; (finger in door etc.) прищемля́ть *impf*, прищеми́ть *pf*; (of shoe) жать *impf*; (steal) стяну́ть *pf*; *n* щипо́к; (of salt) щепо́тка; at a ~ в кра́йнем слу́чае.

pine[1] *vi* томи́ться *impf*; ~ for тоскова́ть *impf* по+*dat*, *prep*.

pine[2] *n* (tree) сосна́.

pineapple *n* анана́с.

ping-pong n пинг-по́нг.

pink n (colour) ро́зовый цвет; adj ро́зовый.

pinnacle n верши́на.

pint n пи́нта.

pioneer n пионе́р, ~ка; vt прокла́дывать impf, проложи́ть pf путь к+dat.

pious adj набо́жный.

pip[1] n (seed) зёрнышко.

pip[2] n (sound) бип.

pipe n труба́; (mus) ду́дка; (for smoking) тру́бка; ~-dream пуста́я мечта́; vt пуска́ть impf, пусти́ть pf по труба́м; vi ~ down затиха́ть impf, зати́хнуть pf. **pipeline** n трубопрово́д; (oil) нефтепрово́д. **piper** n волы́нщик. **piping** adj: ~ hot с пы́лу.

piquant adj пика́нтный.

pique n: in a fit of ~ в поры́ве раздраже́ния.

pirate n пира́т.

pirouette n пируэ́т; vi де́лать impf, с~ pf пируэ́т(ы).

Pisces n Ры́бы f pl.

pistol n пистоле́т.

piston n по́ршень m.

pit n я́ма; (mine) ша́хта; (orchestra ~) орке́стр; (motor-racing) запра́вочно-ремо́нтный пункт; vt: ~ against выставля́ть impf, вы́ставить pf про́тив +gen.

pitch[1] n (resin) смола́; ~-black чёрный как смоль; ~-dark о́чень тёмный.

pitch[2] vt (camp, tent) разбива́ть impf, разби́ть pf; (throw) броса́ть impf, бро́сить pf; vi (fall) па́дать impf, (у)па́сть pf; (ship) кача́ть impf, n (football ~ etc.) площа́дка; (degree) у́ровень m; (mus) высота́; (slope) укло́н.

pitcher n (vessel) кувши́н.

pitchfork n ви́лы (-л) pl.

piteous adj жа́лкий.

pitfall n западня́.

pith n сердцеви́на; (essence) суть. **pithy** adj содержа́тельный.

pitiful adj жа́лкий. **pitiless** adj безжа́лостный.

pittance n жа́лкие гроши́ (-ше́й) pl.

pity n жа́лость; it's a ~ жа́лко, жаль; take ~ on сжа́литься pf над+instr; what a ~! как жа́лко!; vt жале́ть impf, по~ pf; I ~ you мне жаль тебя́.

pivot n сте́ржень m; (fig) центр; vi враща́ться impf.

pixie n эльф.

pizza n пи́цца.

placard n афи́ша, плака́т.

placate vt умиротворя́ть impf, умиротвори́ть pf.

place n ме́сто; in ~ of вме́сто+gen; in the first, second, ~ во-пе́рвых, во-вторы́х; out of ~ не на ме́сте; (unsuitable) неуме́стный; take ~ случа́ться impf, случи́ться pf; (prearranged event) состоя́ться pf; take the ~ of заменя́ть impf, замени́ть pf; vt (stand) ста́вить impf, по~ pf; (lay) класть impf, положи́ть pf; (an order etc.) помеща́ть impf, помести́ть pf.

placenta n плаце́нта.

placid adj споко́йный.

plagiarism n плагиа́т. **plagiarize** vt займствовать impf & pf.

plague n чума́; vt му́чить impf, за~, из~ pf.

plaice n ка́мбала.

plain n равни́на; adj (clear) я́сный; (simple) просто́й; (ugly) некраси́вый; ~-clothes policeman переоде́тый полице́йский sb.

plaintiff n исте́ц, исти́ца.

plaintive adj жа́лобный.

plait n коса́; vt плести́ impf, с~ pf.

plan n план; vt плани́ровать impf, за~, с~ pf; (intend) намерева́ться impf +inf.

plane[1] n (tree) плата́н.

plane[2] n (tool) руба́нок; vt строга́ть impf, вы́~ pf.

plane[3] n (surface) пло́скость; (level) у́ровень m; (aeroplane) самолёт.

planet n плане́та.

plank n доска́.

plant n расте́ние; (factory) заво́д; vt сажа́ть impf, посади́ть pf; (fix firmly) про́чно ста́вить impf, по~ pf; (garden etc.) заса́живать impf, засади́ть pf (with +instr).

plantation n (of trees) (лесо)насажде́ние; (of cotton etc.) планта́ция.

plaque n до́щечка.

plasma n пла́зма.

plaster n пла́стырь m; (for walls etc.) штукату́рка; (of Paris) гипс; vt (wall) штукату́рить impf, от~, о~ pf; (cover) облепля́ть impf, облепи́ть *pf.* **plasterboard** *n* сухая штукатурка. **plasterer** *n* штукатур.

plastic *n* пластмасса; *adj (malleable)* пластичный; *(made of ~)* пластмассовый; ~ **surgery** пластическая хирургия.

plate *n* тарелка; *(metal sheet)* лист; *(in book)* (вкладная) иллюстрация; *(name ~ etc.)* дощечка.

plateau *n* плато *neut indecl.*

platform *n* платформа; *(rly)* перрон.

platinum *n* платина.

platitude *n* банальность.

platoon *n* взвод.

plausible *adj* правдоподобный.

play *vt & i* играть *impf*, сыграть *pf (game)* в+*acc*, *(instrument)* на+*prep*, *(record)* ставить *impf*, по~ *pf*; ~ **down** преуменьшать *impf*, преуменьшить *pf*; ~ **a joke, trick, on** подшучивать *impf*, подшутить *pf* над +*instr*; ~ **off** играть *impf*, сыграть *pf* решающую партию; ~**off** решающая встреча; ~ **safe** действовать *impf* наверняка; *n* игра; *(theat)* пьеса. **player** *n* игрок; *(actor)* актёр, актриса; *(musician)* музыкант. **playful** *adj* игривый. **playground** *n* площадка для игр. **playgroup, playschool** *n* детский сад. **playing** *n*: ~**card** игральная карта; ~**field** игровая площадка. **playmate** *n* друг детства. **plaything** *n* игрушка. **playwright** *n* драматург.

plea *n (entreaty)* мольба; *(law)* заявление. **plead** *vi* умолять *impf (with +acc*; for о+*prep)*; *vt (offer as excuse)* ссылаться *impf*, сослаться *pf* на+*acc*; ~ **(not) guilty** (не) признавать *impf*, признать *pf* себя виновным.

pleasant *adj* приятный. **pleasantry** *n* любезность. **please** *vt* нравиться *impf*, по~ *pf* +*dat*; *imper* пожалуйста; будьте добры. **pleased** *adj* довольный; *predic* рад. **pleasing, pleasurable** *adj* приятный. **pleasure** *n* удовольствие.

pleat *n* складка; *vt* плиссировать *impf.*

plebiscite *n* плебисцит.

plectrum *n* плектр.

pledge *n (security)* залог; *(promise)* зарок, обещание; *vt* отдавать *impf*, отдать *pf* в залог; ~ **o.s.** обязываться *impf*, обязаться *pf*; ~ **one's**

word давать *impf*, дать *pf* слово.

plentiful *adj* обильный. **plenty** *n* изобилие; ~ **of** много+*gen.*

plethora *n (fig)* изобилие.

pleurisy *n* плеврит.

pliable *adj* гибкий.

pliers *n pl* плоскогубцы (-цев) *pl.*

plight *n* незавидное положение.

plimsolls *n pl* спортивные тапочки *f pl.*

plinth *n* плинтус.

plod *vi* тащиться *impf.*

plonk *vt* плюхнуть *pf.*

plot *n (of land)* участок; *(of book etc.)* фабула; *(conspiracy)* заговор; *vt (on graph, map, etc.)* наносить *impf*, нанести на график, на карту; *v abs (conspire)* составлять *impf*, составить *pf* заговор.

plough *n* плуг; *vt* пахать *impf*, вс~ *pf*; *vi*: ~ **through** пробиваться *impf*, пробиться *pf* сквозь+*acc.*

ploy *n* уловка.

pluck *n (courage)* смелость; *vt (chicken)* щипать *impf*, об~ *pf*; *(mus)* щипать *impf*; *(flower)* срывать *impf*, сорвать *pf*; ~ **up courage** собираться *impf*, собраться *pf* с духом; *vi*: ~ **at** дёргать *impf*, дёрнуть *pf.* **plucky** *adj* смелый.

plug *n (stopper)* пробка; *(electr)* вилка; *(electr socket)* розетка; *vt (~ up)* затыкать *impf*, заткнуть *pf*; ~ **in** включать *impf*, включить *pf.*

plum *n* слива.

plumage *n* оперение.

plumb *n* лот; *adv* вертикально; *(fig)* точно; *vt* измерять *impf*, измерить *pf* глубину+*gen*; *(fig)* проникать *impf*, проникнуть *pf* в+*acc*; ~ **in** подключать *impf*, подключить *pf.*

plumber *n* водопроводчик. **plumbing** *n* водопровод.

plume *n (feather)* перо; *(on hat etc.)* султан.

plummet *vi* падать *impf*, (у)пасть *pf.*

plump[1] *adj* пухлый.

plump[2] *vi*: ~ **for** выбирать *impf*, выбрать *pf.*

plunder *vt* грабить *impf*, о~ *pf*; *n* добыча.

plunge *vt & i (immerse)* погружать(ся) *impf*, погрузить(ся) *pf (into* в+*acc)*; *vi (dive)* нырять *impf*, нырнуть *pf*; *(rush)* бросаться *impf*, бро-

pluperfect *n* давнопрошéдшее врéмя *neut.*

plural *n* мнóжественное числó.

pluralism *n* плюрали́зм. **pluralistic** *adj* плюралисти́ческий.

plus *prep* плюс+*acc*; *n* (знак) плюс.

plushy *adj* шика́рный.

plutonium *n* плутóний.

ply *vt* (*tool*) рабóтать *impf* +*instr*; (*task*) занима́ться *impf* +*instr*; (*keep supplied*) пóтчевать *impf* (*with* +*instr*); ~ **with questions** засыпáть *impf*, засы́пать *pf* вопрóсами.

plywood *n* фанéра.

p.m. *adv* пóсле полу́дня.

pneumatic *adj* пневмати́ческий; ~ **drill** отбóйный молотóк.

pneumonia *n* воспалéние лёгких.

poach[1] *vt* (*cook*) вари́ть *impf*; ~ed **egg** яйцó-пашóт.

poach[2] *vi* браконьéрствовать *impf*. **poacher** *n* браконьéр.

pocket *n* карма́н; **out of** ~ в убы́тке; ~ **money** карма́нные дéньги (-нег, -ньга́м) *pl*; *vt* класть *impf*, положи́ть *pf* в карма́н.

pock-marked *adj* рябóй.

pod *n* стручóк.

podgy *adj* тóлстенький.

podium *n* трибу́на; (*conductor's*) пульт.

poem *n* стихотворéние; (*longer* ~) поэ́ма. **poet** *n* поэ́т. **poetess** *n* поэтéсса. **poetic(al)** *adj* поэти́ческий. **poetry** *n* поэ́зия, стихи́ *m pl*.

pogrom *n* погрóм.

poignancy *n* острота́. **poignant** *adj* óстрый.

point[1] *n* тóчка; (*place*; *in list*) пункт; (*in score*) очкó; (*in time*) момéнт; (*in space*) мéсто; (*essence*) суть; (*sense*) смысл; (*sharp* ~) острие́; (*tip*) кóнчик; (*power* ~) штéпсель *m*; *pl* (*rly*) стрéлка. **be on the** ~ **of** (*doing*) собира́ться *impf*, собра́ться *pf* +*inf*; **beside, off, the** ~ нектáти; **that is the** ~ в э́том и дéло; **the** ~ **is that** дéло в том, что; **there is no** ~ (*in doing*) не имéет смы́сла (+*inf*); **to the** ~ кста́ти; ~**blank** прямóй; ~ **of view** тóчка зрéния.

point[2] *vt* (*wall*) расши́вать *impf*, расши́ть *pf* швы+*gen*; (*gun etc.*) наводи́ть *impf*, навести́ *pf* (**at** на+*acc*);

vi по-, у-, ка́зывать *impf* по-, у-, каза́ть *pf* (**to** на+*acc*). **pointed** *adj* (*sharp*) óстрый. **pointer** *n* указáтель *m*, стрéлка. **pointless** *adj* бессмы́сленный.

poise *n* уравновéшенность. **poised** *adj* (*composed*) уравновéшенный; (*ready*) готóвый (**to** к+*dat*).

poison *n*-яд; *vt* отравля́ть *impf*, отрави́ть *pf* **poisonous** *adj* ядови́тый.

poke *vt* (*prod*) ты́кать *impf*, ткнуть *pf*; ~ **fun at** подшу́чивать *impf*, подшути́ть *pf* над+*instr*; (*thrust*) совáть *impf*, су́нуть *pf*; ~ **the fire** мешáть *impf*, по~ *pf* у́гли в ками́не; *n* тычóк. **poker**[1] *n* (*rod*) кочергá.

poker[2] *n* (*cards*) пóкер.

poky *adj* тéсный.

Poland *n* Пóльша.

polar *adj* поля́рный; ~ **bear** бéлый медвéдь *m*. **polarity** *n* поля́рность. **polarize** *vt* поляризовáть *impf* & *pf*.

pole[1] *n* (*geog*; *phys*) пóлюс; ~**-star** Поля́рная звездá.

pole[2] *n* (*rod*) столб, шест; ~**-vaulting** прыжóк с шестóм.

Pole *n* поля́к, пóлька.

polemic *adj* полеми́ческий; *n* полéмика.

police *n* поли́ция; (*as pl*) полицéйские *sb*; (*in Russia*) мили́ция; ~ **station** полицéйский учáсток. **policeman** *n* полицéйский *sb*, полисмéн; (*in Russia*) милиционéр. **policewoman** *n* жéнщина-полицéйский *sb*; (*in Russia*) жéнщина-милиционéр.

policy[1] *n* поли́тика.

policy[2] *n* (*insurance*) пóлис.

polio *n* полиомиели́т.

Polish *adj* пóльский.

polish *n* (*gloss*, *process*) полирóвка; (*substance*) политу́ра; (*fig*) лоск; *vt* полировáть *impf*, от~ *pf*; ~ **off** расправля́ться *impf*, распрáвиться *pf* с+*instr*. **polished** *adj* оттóченный.

polite *adj* вéжливый. **politeness** *n* вéжливость.

politic *adj* полити́чный. **political** *adj* полити́ческий; ~ **economy** полит-экóномика; ~ **prisoner** политзаключённый *sb*. **politician** *n* поли́тик. **politics** *n* поли́тика.

poll *n* (*voting*) голосовáние; (*opinion* ~) опрóс; **go to the** ~**s** голосовáть *impf*, про~ *pf*; *vt* получа́ть *impf*, получи́ть *pf*.

pollen *n* пыльца́. **pollinate** *vt* опыля́ть *impf*, опыли́ть *pf*.

polling *attrib*: ~ **booth** каби́на для голосова́ния; ~ **station** избира́тельный уча́сток.

pollutant *n* загрязни́тель *m*. **pollute** *vt* загрязня́ть *impf*, загрязни́ть *pf*. **pollution** *n* загрязне́ние.

polo *n* по́ло *neut indecl*; ~**neck sweater** водола́зка.

polyester *n* полиэфи́р. **polyethylene** *n* полиэтиле́н. **polyglot** *n* полигло́т; *adj* многоязы́чный. **polygon** *n* многоуго́льник. **polymer** *n* полиме́р. **polystyrene** *n* полистиро́л. **polytechnic** *n* техни́ческий вуз. **polythene** *n* полиэтиле́н. **polyunsaturated** *adj*: ~ **fats** полиненасы́щенные жиры́ *m pl*. **polyurethane** *n* полиурета́н.

pomp *n* пы́шность. **pomposity** *n* напы́щенность. **pompous** *adj* напы́щенный.

pond *n* пруд.

ponder *vt* обду́мывать *impf*, обду́мать *pf*; *vi* размышля́ть *impf*, размы́слить *pf*.

ponderous *adj* тяжелове́сный.

pony *n* по́ни *m indecl*.

poodle *n* пу́дель *m*.

pool¹ *n* (*of water*) прудо́к; (*puddle*) лу́жа; (*swimming* ~) бассе́йн.

pool² *n* (*collective stakes*) совоку́пность ста́вок; (*common fund*) о́бщий фонд; *vt* объединя́ть *impf*, объедини́ть *pf*.

poor *adj* бе́дный; (*bad*) плохо́й; *n*: **the** ~ бедняки́ *m pl*. **poorly** *predic* нездоро́в.

pop¹ *n* хло́пать *impf*, хло́пнуть *pf*; *vt* (*put*) бы́стро всу́нуть *pf* (**into** в+*acc*); ~ **in** забега́ть *impf*, забежа́ть *pf* к+*dat*; *n* хлопо́к

pop² *adj* поп-; ~ **concert** поп-конце́рт; ~ **music** поп-му́зыка.

pope *n* Па́па *m*.

poplar *n* то́поль *m*.

poppy *n* мак.

populace *n* просто́й наро́д. **popular** *adj* наро́дный; (*liked*) популя́рный. **popularity** *n* популя́рность. **popularize** *vt* популяризи́ровать *impf* & *pf*. **populate** *vt* населя́ть *impf*, насе-

ли́ть *pf*. **population** *n* населе́ние. **populous** *adj* (мно́го)лю́дный.

porcelain *n* фарфо́р.

porch *n* крыльцо́.

porcupine *n* дикобра́з.

pore¹ *n* по́ра.

pore² *vi*: ~ **over** погружа́ться *impf*, погрузи́ться *pf* в+*acc*.

pork *n* свини́на.

pornographic *adj* порнографи́ческий. **pornography** *n* порногра́фия.

porous *adj* пори́стый.

porpoise *n* морска́я свинья́.

porridge *n* овся́ная ка́ша.

port¹ *n* (*harbour*) порт; (*town*) порто́вый го́род.

port² *n* (*naut*) ле́вый борт.

port³ *n* (*wine*) портве́йн.

portable *adj* портати́вный.

portend *vt* предвеща́ть *impf*. **portent** *n* предзнаменова́ние. **portentous** *adj* злове́щий.

porter¹ *n* (*at door*) швейца́р.

porter² *n* (*carrier*) носи́льщик.

portfolio *n* портфе́ль *m*; (*artist's*) па́пка.

porthole *n* иллюмина́тор.

portion *n* часть, до́ля; (*of food*) по́рция.

portly *adj* доро́дный.

portrait *n* портре́т. **portray** *vt* изобража́ть *impf*, изобрази́ть *pf*. **portrayal** *n* изображе́ние.

Portugal *n* Португа́лия. **Portuguese** *n* португа́лец, -лка; *adj* португа́льский.

pose *n* по́за; *vt* (*question*) ста́вить *impf*, по~ *pf*; (*a problem*) представля́ть *impf*, предста́вить *pf*; *vi* пози́ровать *impf*; ~ **as** выдава́ть *impf*, вы́дать *pf* себя́ за+*acc*.

posh *adj* шика́рный.

posit *vt* постули́ровать *impf* & *pf*.

position *n* положе́ние, пози́ция; **in a** ~ **to** в состоя́нии +*inf*; *vt* ста́вить *impf*, по~ *pf*.

positive *adj* положи́тельный; (*convinced*) уве́ренный; (*proof*) несомне́нный; *n* (*phot*) позити́в.

possess *vt* облада́ть *impf* +*instr*; владе́ть *impf* +*instr*; (*of feeling etc.*) овладева́ть *impf*, овладе́ть *pf* +*instr*. **possessed** *adj* одержи́мый. **possession** *n* владе́ние (*of* +*instr*); *pl* со́бственность. **possessive** *adj* со́бственнический. **possessor** n обладатель m.

possibility n возможность. **possible** adj возможный; as much as ~ сколько возможно; as soon as ~ как можно скорее. **possibly** adv возможно, может (быть).

post[1] n (pole) столб; vt (~ up) вывешивать impf, вывесить pf.

post[2] n (station) пост, (job) должность; vt (station) расставлять impf, расставить pf; (appoint) назначать impf, назначить pf.

post[3] n (letters, ~ office) почта; by ~ почтой; attrib почтовый; ~-box почтовый ящик; ~-code почтовый индекс; ~ office почта; vt (send by ~) отправлять impf, отправить pf по почте; (put in ~-box) опускать impf, опустить pf в почтовый ящик.

postage n почтовый сбор, почтовые расходы m pl; ~ stamp почтовая марка. **postal** adj почтовый; ~-order почтовый перевод. **postcard** n открытка.

poster n афиша, плакат.

poste restante n до востребования.

posterior adj задний; n зад.

posterity n потомство.

post-graduate n аспирант.

posthumous adj посмертный.

postman n почтальон. **postmark** n почтовый штемпель m.

post-mortem n вскрытие трупа.

postpone vt отсрочивать impf, отсрочить pf. **postponement** n отсрочка.

postscript n постскриптум.

postulate vt постулировать impf & pf.

posture n поза, положение.

post-war adj послевоенный.

posy n букетик.

pot n горшок; (cooking ~) кастрюля; ~-shot выстрел наугад; vt (food) консервировать impf, за~ pf; (plant) сажать impf, посадить pf в горшок; (billiards) загонять impf, загнать pf в лузу.

potash n поташ. **potassium** n калий.

potato n (also collect) картошка (no pl); (plant; also collect) картофель m (no pl).

potency n сила. **potent** adj сильный. **potential** adj потенциальный; n потенциал. **potentiality** n потенци-

альность.

pot-hole n (in road) выбоина.

potion n зелье.

potter[1] vi: ~ about возиться impf.

potter[2] n гончар. **pottery** n (goods) гончарные изделия neut pl; (place) гончарная sb.

potty[1] adj (crazy) помешанный (about на+prep).

potty[2] n ночной горшок.

pouch n сумка.

poultry n домашняя птица.

pounce vi: ~ (up)on набрасываться impf, наброситься pf на+acc.

pound[1] n (measure) фунт; ~ sterling фунт стерлингов.

pound[2] vt (strike) колотить impf, по~ pf n+dat, в+acc; vi (heart) колотиться impf; ~ along (run) мчаться impf с грохотом.

pour vt лить impf; ~ out наливать impf, налить pf; vi литься impf; it is ~ing (with rain) дождь льёт как из ведра.

pout vi дуть(ся) impf, на~ pf.

poverty n бедность; ~-stricken убогий.

POW abbr военнопленный sb.

powder n порошок; (cosmetic) пудра; vt пудрить impf, на~ pf. **powdery** adj порошкообразный.

power n (vigour) сила; (might) могущество; (ability) способность; (control) власть; (authorization) полномочие; (State) держава; ~ cut перерыв электропитания; ~ point розетка; ~ station электростанция. **powerful** adj сильный. **powerless** adj бессильный.

practicable adj осуществимый. **practical** adj практический. **practically** adv практически. **practice** n практика; (custom) обычай; (mus) занятия neut pl; in ~ на практике; put into ~ осуществлять impf, осуществить pf. **practise** vt (also abs of doctor etc.) практиковать impf; упражняться impf в+prep; (mus) заниматься impf, заняться pf на +prep.

practised adj опытный. **practitioner** n (doctor) практикующий врач; general ~ врач общей практики.

pragmatic adj прагматический. **pragmatism** n прагматизм. **pragmatist** n прагматик.

prairie 408 premier

prairie n пре́рия.

praise vt хвали́ть impf, по~ pf; n похвала́. **praiseworthy** adj похва́льный.

pram n де́тская коля́ска.

prance vi (horse) гарцева́ть impf; (fig) задава́ться impf.

prank n вы́ходка.

prattle vi лепета́ть; n ле́пет.

prawn n креве́тка.

pray vi моли́ться impf, по~ pf (to +dat; for o+prep). **prayer** n моли́тва.

preach vt & i пропове́дывать impf. **preacher** n пропове́дник.

preamble n преа́мбула.

pre-arrange vt зара́нее организо́вывать impf, организова́ть pf.

precarious adj ненадёжный; опа́сный.

precaution n предосторо́жность. **precautionary** adj: ~ measures ме́ры предосторо́жности.

precede vt предше́ствовать impf +dat. **precedence** n предпочте́ние. **precedent** n прецеде́нт. **preceding** adj предыду́щий.

precept n наставле́ние.

precinct n двор; pl окре́стности f pl.

pedestrian ~ уча́сток для пешехо́дов; **shopping** ~ торго́вый пасса́ж.

precious adj драгоце́нный; (style) мане́рный; adv о́чень.

precipice n обры́в. **precipitate** adj (person) опроме́тчивый; vt (throw down) низверга́ть impf, низве́ргнуть pf; (hurry) ускоря́ть impf, уско́рить pf. **precipitation** n (meteorol) оса́дки m pl. **precipitous** adj обры́вистый.

précis n конспе́кт.

precise adj то́чный. **precisely** adv то́чно; (in answer) и́менно. **precision** n то́чность.

preclude vt предотвраща́ть impf, предотврати́ть pf.

precocious adj ра́но разви́вшийся.

preconceived adj предвзя́тый. **preconception** n предвзя́тое мне́ние.

pre-condition n предпосы́лка.

precursor n предше́ственник.

predator n хи́щник. **predatory** adj хи́щный.

predecessor n предше́ственник.

predestination n предопределе́ние.

predetermine vt предреша́ть impf, предреши́ть pf.

predicament n затрудни́тельное положе́ние.

predicate n (gram) сказу́емое sb. **predicative** adj предикати́вный.

predict vt предска́зывать impf, предсказа́ть pf. **predictable** adj предсказу́емый. **prediction** n предсказа́ние.

predilection n пристра́стие (for к +dat).

predispose vt предрасполага́ть impf, предрасположи́ть pf (to к+dat). **predisposition** n предрасположе́ние (to к+dat).

predominance n преоблада́ние. **predominant** adj преоблада́ющий. **predominate** vi преоблада́ть impf.

pre-eminence n превосхо́дство. **pre-eminent** adj выдаю́щийся.

pre-empt vt (fig) завладева́ть impf, завладе́ть pf +instr пре́жде други́х. **pre-emptive** adj (mil) упрежда́ющий.

preen vt (of bird) чи́стить impf, по~ pf клю́вом; ~ o.s. (be proud) горди́ться impf собо́й.

pre-fab n сбо́рный дом. **pre-fabricated** adj сбо́рный.

preface n предисло́вие.

prefect n префе́кт; (school) ста́роста m.

prefer vt предпочита́ть impf, предпоче́сть pf. **preferable** adj предпочти́тельный. **preference** n предпочте́ние. **preferential** adj предпочти́тельный.

prefix n приста́вка.

pregnancy n бере́менность. **pregnant** adj бере́менная.

prehistoric adj доистори́ческий.

prejudice n предубежде́ние; (detriment) уще́рб; vt наноси́ть impf, нанести́ pf уще́рб+dat; ~ against предубежда́ть impf, предубеди́ть pf про́тив+gen; be ~d against име́ть impf предубежде́ние про́тив +gen.

preliminary adj предвари́тельный.

prelude n прелю́дия.

premarital adj добра́чный.

premature adj преждевре́менный.

premeditated adj преднаме́ренный.

premier adj пе́рвый; n премье́р-мини́стр. **première** n премье́ра.

premise, premiss n (logic) (пред)-посы́лка. premises n pl помеще́-ние.

premium n пре́мия.

premonition n предчу́вствие.

preoccupation n озабо́ченность; (absorbing subject) забо́та. preoccupied adj озабо́ченный. preoccupy vt поглоща́ть impf, поглоти́ть pf.

preparation n приготовле́ние; pl подгото́вка (for к+dat); (substance) препара́т. preparatory adj подготови́тельный. prepare vt & i при-, под-, гота́вливать(ся) impf, при-, под-, гото́вить(ся) pf (for к+dat). prepared adj гото́вый.

preponderance n переве́с.

preposition n предло́г.

prepossessing adj привлека́тельный.

preposterous adj неле́пый.

prerequisite n предпосы́лка.

prerogative n прерогати́ва.

presage vt предвеща́ть impf.

Presbyterian n пресвитериа́нин, -а́нка; adj пресвитериа́нский.

prescribe vt предпи́сывать impf, предписа́ть pf; (med) пропи́сывать impf, прописа́ть pf. prescription n (med) реце́пт.

presence n прису́тствие; ~ of mind прису́тствие ду́ха. present adj прису́тствующий; (being dealt with) да́нный; (existing now) ны́нешний; (also gram) настоя́щий; predic нали́цо; be ~ прису́тствовать impf (at на+prep); ~-day ны́нешний; n: the настоя́щее sb; (gram) настоя́щее вре́мя neut; (gift) пода́рок; at ~ в настоя́щее вре́мя neut; for the ~ пока́; vt (introduce) представля́ть impf, предста́вить pf (to +dat); (award) вруча́ть impf, вручи́ть pf; (a play) ста́вить impf, по~ pf; (a gift) преподноси́ть impf, преподнести́ pf +dat (with +acc); ~ o.s. явля́ться impf, яви́ться pf. presentable adj прили́чный. presentation n (introducing) представле́ние; (awarding) подноше́ние.

presentiment n предчу́вствие.

presently adv вско́ре.

preservation n сохране́ние. preservative n консерва́нт. preserve vt (keep safe) сохраня́ть impf, сохрани́ть pf; (maintain) храни́ть impf; (food) консерви́ровать impf, за~ pf; n (for game etc) запове́дник; (jam) варе́нье.

preside vi председа́тельствовать impf (at на+prep). presidency n президе́нтство. president n президе́нт. presidential adj президе́нтский. presidium n прези́диум.

press n (machine) пресс; (printing firm) типогра́фия; (publishing house) изда́тельство; (the ~) пре́сса, печа́ть; ~ conference пресс-конфере́нция; vt (button etc) нажима́ть impf, нажа́ть pf; (clasp) прижима́ть impf, прижа́ть pf (to к+dat); (iron) гла́дить impf, вы́~ pf; (insist on) наста́ивать impf, настоя́ть pf на +prep; (urge) угова́ривать impf; ~ on (make haste) потора́пливаться impf.

pressing adj неотло́жный. pressure n давле́ние; ~-cooker скорова́рка; ~ group инициати́вная гру́ппа. pressurize vt (fig) ока́зывать impf, оказа́ть pf давле́ние на+acc. pressurized adj гермети́ческий.

prestige n прести́ж. prestigious adj прести́жный.

presumably adv предположи́тельно. presume vt полага́ть impf; (venture) позволя́ть impf, позво́лить pf себе́. presumption n предположе́ние; (arrogance) самонаде́янность. presumptuous adj самонаде́янный.

presuppose vt предполага́ть impf.

pretence n притво́рство. pretend vt притворя́ться impf, притвори́ться pf (to be +instr); де́лать impf, с~ pf вид (что); vi: ~ to претендова́ть impf на+acc. pretender n претенде́нт. pretension n прете́нзия. pretentious adj претенцио́зный.

pretext n предло́г.

prettiness n милови́дность. pretty adj хоро́шенький; adv дово́льно.

prevail vi (predominate) преоблада́ть impf; ~ (up)on угова́ривать impf, уговори́ть pf. prevalence n распростране́ние. prevalent adj распространённый.

prevaricate vi ува́ливать impf увильну́ть pf.

prevent vt (stop from happening)

предупрежда́ть *impf*, предупреди́ть *pf*; (*stop from doing*) меша́ть *impf*, по~ *pf* +*dat*. **prevention** *n* предупрежде́ние. **preventive** *adj* предупреди́тельный.

preview *n* предвари́тельный просмо́тр.

previous *adj* предыду́щий; *adv*: ~ to до+*gen*; пре́жде чем +*inf*. **previously** *adv* ра́ньше.

pre-war *adj* довое́нный.

prey *n* (*animal*) добы́ча; (*victim*) же́ртва (to +*gen*); bird of ~ хи́щная пти́ца; *vi*: ~ (up)on (*emotion etc.*) му́чить *impf*.

price *n* цена́; ~-list прейскура́нт; *vt* назнача́ть *impf*, назна́чить *pf* це́ну +*gen*. **priceless** *adj* бесце́нный.

prick *vt* коло́ть *impf*, у~ *pf*; (*conscience*) му́чить *impf*; ~ up one's ears навостри́ть *pf* у́ши; *n* уко́л. **prickle** *n* (*thorn*) колю́чка; (*spine*) игла́. **prickly** *adj* колю́чий.

pride *n* го́рдость; ~ o.s. on гор-ди́ться *impf* +*instr*.

priest *n* свяще́нник; (*non-Christian*) жрец.

prig *n* педа́нт.

prim *adj* чо́порный.

primarily *adv* первонача́льно; (*above all*) пре́жде всего́. **primary** *adj* основно́й; ~ school нача́льная шко́ла. **prime** *n*: in one's ~ в расцве́те сил; *adj* (*chief*) гла́вный; ~ minister премье́р-мини́стр; *vt* (*engine*) заправля́ть *impf*, запра́вить *pf*; (*bomb*) активизи́ровать *impf* & *pf*; (*with facts*) инструкти́ровать *impf* & *pf*; (*with paint etc.*) грунтова́ть *impf*, за~ *pf*. **primer** *n* (*paint etc.*) грунт. **prim(a)eval** *adj* первобы́тный. **primitive** *adj* первобы́тный; (*crude*) примити́вный. **primordial** *adj* иско́нный.

primrose *n* первоцве́т; (*colour*) бле́дно-жёлтый цвет.

prince *n* принц; (*in Russia*) князь. **princely** *adj* кня́жеский; (*sum*) огро́мный. **princess** *n* принце́сса; (*wife*) княги́ня; (*daughter*) княжна́.

principal *n* гла́вный; *n* дире́ктор. **principality** *n* кня́жество. **principally** *adv* гла́вным о́бразом.

principle *n* при́нцип; in ~ в при́нципе; on ~ принципиа́льно. **prin-**

cipled *adj* принципиа́льный.

print *n* (*mark*) след; (*also phot*) отпеча́ток; (*printing*) печа́ть; (*picture*) о́ттиск; in ~ в прода́же; out of ~ распро́данный; *vt* (*impress*) запечатлева́ть *impf*, запечатле́ть *pf*; (*book etc.*) печа́тать *impf*, на~ *pf*; (*write*) писа́ть *impf*, на~ *pf* печа́тными бу́квами; (*phot*; ~ out, off) отпеча́тывать *impf*, отпеча́тать *pf*; ~ out (*of computer etc.*) распеча́тывать *impf*, распеча́тать *pf*; ~-out распеча́тка. **printer** *n* (*person*) печа́тник, типо́граф; (*of computer*) при́нтер. **printing** *n* печа́тание; ~-press печа́тный стано́к.

prior *adj* пре́жний; *adv*: ~ to до+*gen*. **priority** *n* приорите́т. **priory** *n* монасты́рь *m*.

prise *vt*: ~ open взла́мывать *impf*, взлома́ть *pf*.

prism *n* при́зма.

prison *n* тюрьма́; *attrib* тюре́мный; ~ camp ла́герь *m*. **prisoner** *n* заключённый *sb*; (~ of war) (вое́нно)пле́нный *sb*.

pristine *adj* нетро́нутый.

privacy *n* уедине́ние; (*private life*) ча́стная жизнь. **private** *adj* (*personal*) ча́стный, ли́чный; (*confidential*) конфиденциа́льный; in ~ наедине́; в ча́стной жи́зни; *n* рядово́й *sb*.

privation *n* лише́ние.

privilege *n* привиле́гия. **privileged** *adj* привилегиро́ванный.

privy *adj*: ~ to посвящённый в+*acc*.

prize *n* пре́мия, приз; ~-winner призёр; *vt* высоко́ цени́ть *impf*.

pro¹ *n*: ~s and cons до́воды *m pl* за и про́тив.

pro² *adj* (*professional*) профессиона́л.

probability *n* вероя́тность. **probable** *adj* вероя́тный. **probably** *adv* вероя́тно.

probate *n* утвержде́ние завеща́ния. **probation** *n* испыта́тельный срок; (*law*) усло́вный пригово́р; got two years ~ получи́л два го́да усло́вно. **probationary** *adj* испыта́тельный.

probe *n* (*med*) зонд; (*fig*) рассле́дование; *vt* зонди́ровать *impf*; (*fig*) рассле́довать *impf* & *pf*.

probity *n* че́стность.

problem *n* пробле́ма, вопро́с; (*math*)

зада́ча. problematic adj проблема-
ти́чный.

procedural adj процеду́рный. procedure n процеду́ра. proceed vi (go
further) идти́ impf, пойти́ pf да́ль-
ше; (act) поступа́ть impf, поступи́ть
pf; (abs, ~ to say; continue) про-
должа́ть impf, продо́лжить pf; (of
action) продолжа́ться impf, продо́л-
житься pf; ~ from исходи́ть impf
из, от+gen; ~ to (begin to) при-
нима́ться impf, приня́ться pf +inf.
proceedings n pl (activity) де́ятель-
ность; (legal ~) судопроизво́дство;
(published report) труды́ m pl, за-
пи́ски f pl. proceeds n pl вы́руч-
ка. process n проце́сс; vt обраба́-
тывать impf, обрабо́тать pf. procession n проце́ссия, ше́ствие.
proclaim vt провозглаша́ть impf,
провозгласи́ть pf. proclamation n
провозглаше́ние.
procure vt достава́ть impf, доста́ть pf.
prod vt ты́кать impf, ткнуть pf; n
тычо́к.
prodigal adj расточи́тельный.
prodigious adj огро́мный. prodigy
n: child ~ вундерки́нд.
produce vt (evidence etc.) представ-
ля́ть impf, предста́вить pf; (ticket
etc.) предъявля́ть impf, предъяви́ть
pf; (play etc.) ста́вить impf, по~ pf;
(manufacture; cause) производи́ть
impf, произвести́ pf; n (collect)
проду́кты m pl. producer n (econ)
производи́тель m; (of play etc.) режиссёр. product n проду́кт; (result)
результа́т. production n произво́д-
ство; (of play etc.) постано́вка. productive adj продукти́вный; (fruitful) плодотво́рный. productivity n
производи́тельность.
profane adj све́тский; (blasphemous)
богоху́льный. profanity n бого-
ху́льство.
profess vt (pretend) притворя́ться
impf, притвори́ться pf (to be +instr);
(declare) заявля́ть impf, заяви́ть pf;
(faith) испове́довать impf. profession n (job) профе́ссия. professional
adj профессиона́льный; n профес-
сиона́л. professor n профе́ссор.
proffer vt предлага́ть impf, пред-
ложи́ть pf.
proficiency n уме́ние. proficient adj

уме́лый.
profile n про́филь m.
profit n (benefit) по́льза; (monetary)
при́быль; vt приноси́ть impf, при-
нести́ pf по́льзу +dat; vi: ~ from
по́льзоваться impf, вос~ pf +instr
(financially) получа́ть impf, полу-
чи́ть pf при́быль на+prep. profitable adj (lucrative) при́быльный;
(beneficial) поле́зный. profiteering
n спекуля́ция.
profligate adj распу́тный.
profound adj глубо́кий.
profuse adj оби́льный. profusion n
изоби́лие.
progeny n пото́мство.
prognosis n прогно́з.
program(m)e n програ́мма; vt про-
грамми́ровать impf, за~ pf. pro-
grammer n программи́ст.
progress n прогре́сс; (success) успе́-
хи m pl; make ~ де́лать impf, с~ pf
успе́хи; vi продвига́ться impf, про-
дви́нуться pf вперёд. progression
n продвиже́ние. progressive adj
прогресси́вный.
prohibit vt запреща́ть impf, запре-
ти́ть pf. prohibition n запреще́ние;
(on alcohol) сухо́й зако́н. prohibi-
tive adj запрети́тельный; (price) не-
досту́пный.
project vt (plan) проекти́ровать
impf, с~ pf; (a film) демонстри́-
ровать impf, про~ pf; vi (jut out)
выступа́ть impf; n прое́кт. projectile n снаря́д. projection n (cin)
прое́кция; (protrusion) вы́ступ; (forecast) прогно́з. projector n прое́к-
тор.
proletarian adj пролета́рский. proletariat n пролетариа́т.
proliferate vi распространя́ться
impf, распространи́ться pf. prolif-
eration n распростране́ние.
prolific adj плодови́тый.
prologue n проло́г.
prolong vt продлева́ть impf, про-
дли́ть pf.
promenade n ме́сто для гуля́нья; (at
seaside) на́бережная sb; vi прогу́-
ливаться impf, прогуля́ться pf.
prominence n изве́стность. prominent adj выступа́ющий; (distinguished) выдаю́щийся.
promiscuity n лёгкое поведе́ние.

promiscuous adj лёгкого поведе́ния.

promise n обеща́ние; vt обеща́ть impf & pf. **promising** adj многообеща́ющий.

promontory n мыс.

promote vt (in rank) продвига́ть impf, продви́нуть pf; (assist) спосо́бствовать impf & pf +dat; (publicize) реклами́ровать impf. **promoter** n (of event etc.) аге́нт. **promotion** n (in rank) продвиже́ние; (comm) рекла́ма.

prompt adj бы́стрый, неме́дленный; adv ро́вно; vt (incite) побужда́ть impf, побуди́ть pf к+dat; +inf); (speaker; also fig) подска́зывать impf, подсказа́ть pf +dat; (theat) суфли́ровать impf +dat; n подска́зка. **prompter** n суфлёр.

prone adj (лежа́щий) ничко́м; predic: ~ to скло́нен (-онна́, -о́нно) к+dat.

prong n зубе́ц.

pronoun n местоиме́ние.

pronounce vt (declare) объявля́ть impf, объяви́ть pf; (articulate) произноси́ть impf, произнести́ pf. **pronounced** adj я́вный; заме́тный. **pronouncement** n заявле́ние. **pronunciation** n произноше́ние.

proof n доказа́тельство; (printing) корректу́ра; ~-reader корре́ктор; adj (impenetrable) непроница́емый (against для+gen); (not yielding) не-поддаю́щийся (against +dat).

prop[1] n (support) подпо́рка; (fig) опо́ра; vt (~ open, up) подпира́ть impf, подпере́ть pf; (fig) подде́рживать impf, поддержа́ть pf.

prop[2] n (theat) see props

propaganda n пропага́нда.

propagate vt & i размножа́ть(ся) impf, размно́жить(ся) pf; (disseminate) распространя́ть(ся) impf, рас-простра́ни́ть(ся) pf. **propagation** n размноже́ние; распростране́ние.

propel vt приводи́ть impf, привести́ pf в движе́ние. **propeller** n винт.

propensity n накло́нность (to к+dat; +inf).

proper adj (correct) пра́вильный; (suitable) подходя́щий; (decent) присто́йный; ~ noun и́мя со́бственное. **properly** adv как сле́дует.

property n (possessions) со́бствен-ность, иму́щество; (attribute) сво́йство; pl (theat) реквизи́т.

prophecy n проро́чество. **prophesy** vt проро́чить impf, на~ pf. **prophet** n проро́к. **prophetic** adj проро́-ческий.

propitious adj благоприя́тный.

proponent n сторо́нник.

proportion n пропо́рция; (due relation) соразме́рность; pl разме́ры m pl. **proportional** adj пропорци-она́льный. **proportionate** adj соразме́рный (to +dat; с+instr).

proposal n предложе́ние. **propose** vt предлага́ть impf, предложи́ть pf; (intend) предполага́ть impf; vi (~ marriage) де́лать impf, с~ pf пред-ложе́ние (to +dat). **proposition** n предложе́ние.

propound vt предлага́ть impf, пред-ложи́ть pf на обсужде́ние.

proprietor n со́бственник, хозя́ин.

propriety n прили́чие.

props n pl (theat) реквизи́т.

propulsion n движе́ние вперёд.

prosaic adj прозаи́ческий.

proscribe vt (forbid) запреща́ть impf, запрети́ть pf.

prose n про́за.

prosecute vt пресле́довать impf. **prosecution** n суде́бное пресле́до-вание; (prosecuting party) обвине́-ние. **prosecutor** n обвини́тель m.

prospect n вид; (fig) перспекти́ва; vi: ~ for иска́ть impf. **prospective** adj бу́дущий. **prospector** n развед-чик. **prospectus** n проспе́кт.

prosper vi процвета́ть impf. **pros-perity** n процвета́ние. **prosperous** adj процвета́ющий; (wealthy) зажи́-точный.

prostate (gland) n проста́та.

prostitute n проститу́тка. **prostitu-tion** n проститу́ция.

prostrate adj распростёртый, (лежа́-щий) ничко́м; (exhausted) обесси́-ленный; (with grief) уби́тый (with +instr).

protagonist n гла́вный геро́й; (in contest) протагони́ст.

protect vt защища́ть impf, защи-ти́ть pf. **protection** n защи́та. **protect-ive** adj защи́тный. **protector** n за-щи́тник.

protégé(e) n протеже́ m & f indecl.

protein n бело́к.

protest n проте́ст; vi протестова́ть impf & pf; vt (affirm) утвержда́ть impf.

Protestant n протеста́нт, ~ка; adj протеста́нтский.

protestation n (торже́ственное) заявле́ние (o+prep; что); (protest) проте́ст.

protocol n протоко́л.

proton n прото́н.

prototype n прототи́п.

protract vt тяну́ть impf. protracted adj дли́тельный.

protrude vi выдава́ться impf, вы́даться pf.

proud adj го́рдый; be ~ of горди́ться impf +instr.

prove vt дока́зывать impf, доказа́ть pf; vi ока́зываться impf, оказа́ться pf (to be +instr). proven adj дока́занный.

provenance n происхожде́ние.

proverb n посло́вица. proverbial adj вошедший в погово́рку; (well-known) общеизве́стный.

provide vt (supply person) снабжа́ть impf, снабди́ть pf (with +instr); (supply thing) предоставля́ть impf, предоста́вить pf (to, for +dat); дава́ть impf, дать pf (to, for +dat); vi: ~ for предусма́тривать impf, предусмотре́ть pf +acc; (~ for family etc.) содержа́ть impf +acc. provided (that) conj при усло́вии, что; е́сли то́лько.

providence n провиде́ние; (foresight) предусмотри́тельность. provident adj предусмотри́тельный. providential adj счастли́вый.

providing see provided (that)

province n о́бласть; pl (the ~) провинция. provincial adj провинциа́льный.

provision n снабже́ние; pl (food) прови́зия; (in agreement etc.) положе́ние; make ~ against принима́ть impf, приня́ть pf ме́ры проти́в+gen. provisional adj вре́менный. proviso n усло́вие.

provocation n провока́ция. provocative adj провокацио́нный. provoke vt провоци́ровать impf, с~ pf; (call forth, cause) вызыва́ть impf, вы́звать pf.

prow n нос.

prowess n уме́ние.

prowl vi ры́скать impf.

proximity n бли́зость.

proxy n полномо́чие; (person) уполномо́ченный sb, замести́тель m; by ~ по дове́ренности; stand ~ for быть impf замести́телем +gen.

prudence n благоразу́мие. prudent adj благоразу́мный.

prudery n притво́рная стыдли́вость. prudish adj ни в ме́ру стыдли́вый.

prune¹ n (plum) черносли́в.

prune² vt (trim) об-, под-, реза́ть impf, об-, под-, ре́зать pf.

pry vi сова́ть impf нос (into в+acc).

PS abbr (of postscript) постскри́птум.

psalm n псало́м.

pseudonym n псевдони́м.

psyche n пси́хика. psychiatric adj психиатри́ческий. psychiatrist n психиа́тр. psychiatry n психиатри́я. psychic adj яснови́дящий. psychoanalysis n психоана́лиз. psychoanalyst n психоанали́тик. psychoanalytic(al) adj психоаналити́ческий. psychological adj психологи́ческий. psychologist n психо́лог. psychology n психоло́гия. psychopath n психопа́т. psychopathic adj психопати́ческий. psychosis n психо́з. psychotherapy n психотерапи́я.

PTO abbr (of please turn over) см. на об., смотри́ на оборо́те.

pub n пивна́я sb.

puberty n полова́я зре́лость.

public adj обще́ственный; (open) публи́чный, откры́тый; ~ school ча́стная сре́дняя шко́ла; n пу́блика, обще́ственность; in ~ откры́то, публи́чно. publication n изда́ние. publicity n рекла́ма. publicize vt реклами́ровать impf & pf. publicly adv публи́чно, откры́то. publish vt публикова́ть impf, o~ pf; (book) издава́ть impf, изда́ть pf. publisher n изда́тель m. publishing n (business) изда́тельское де́ло; ~ house изда́тельство.

pucker vt & i мо́рщить(ся) impf, с~ pf.

pudding n пу́динг, запека́нка; (dessert) сла́дкое sb.

puddle n лу́жа.

puff n (of wind) поры́в; (of smoke) дымо́к; ~ pastry слоёное те́сто; vi пыхте́ть impf; ~ at (pipe etc.) попы́хивать impf +instr; vt: ~ up, out (inflate) надува́ть impf, наду́ть pf.

pugnacious adj драчли́вый.

puke vi рвать impf, вы~ pf impers +acc.

pull vt тяну́ть impf, по~ pf; таска́ть indet, тащи́ть det, по~ pf; (a muscle) растя́гивать impf, растяну́ть pf; vt & i дёргать impf, дёрнуть pf (at (за)+acc); ~ s.o.'s leg разы́грывать impf, разыгра́ть pf; ~ the trigger спуска́ть impf, спусти́ть pf курόк; ~ apart, to pieces разрыва́ть impf, разорва́ть pf; (fig) раскри́тиковать pf; ~ down (demolish) сноси́ть impf, снести́ pf; ~ in (of train) прибыва́ть impf, прибы́ть pf; ~ off (garment) стя́гивать impf, стяну́ть pf; (achieve) успе́шно заверша́ть impf, заверши́ть pf; ~ on (garment) натя́гивать impf, натяну́ть pf; ~ out (vt) (remove) выта́скивать impf, вы́тащить pf; (vi) (withdraw) отка́зываться impf, отказа́ться pf от уча́стия (of в+prep); (of vehicle) отъезжа́ть impf, отъе́хать pf от обо́чины (доро́ги); (of train) отходи́ть impf, отойти́ pf (от ста́нции); ~ through выжива́ть impf, вы́жить pf; ~ o.s. together брать impf, взять pf себя́ в ру́ки; ~ up (vt) подтя́гивать impf, подтяну́ть pf; (vt & i) (stop) остана́вливать(ся) impf, останови́ть(ся) pf; n тя́га; (fig) блат.

pulley n блок.

pullover n пуло́вер.

pulp n пу́льпа.

pulpit n ка́федра.

pulsate vi пульси́ровать impf. **pulse** n пульс.

pulses n pl (food) бобо́вые sb.

pulverize vt размельча́ть impf, размельчи́ть pf.

pummel vt колоти́ть impf, по~ pf.

pump n насо́с; vt кача́ть impf; ~ in(to) вка́чивать impf, вкача́ть pf; ~ out выка́чивать impf, вы́качать pf; ~ up нака́чивать impf, накача́ть pf.

pumpkin n ты́ква.

pun n каламбу́р.

punch¹ vt (with fist) ударя́ть impf, уда́рить pf кулако́м; (hole) пробива́ть impf, проби́ть pf; (a ticket) компости́ровать impf, про~ pf; ~ up дра́ка; n (blow) уда́р кулако́м; (for tickets) компо́стер; (for piercing) перфора́тор.

punch² n (drink) пунш.

punctilious adj щепети́льный.

punctual adj пунктуа́льный. **punctuality** n пунктуа́льность.

punctuate vt ста́вить impf, по~ pf зна́ки препина́ния в+acc; (fig) прерыва́ть impf, прерва́ть pf. **punctuation** n пунктуа́ция; ~ marks зна́ки m pl препина́ния.

puncture n проко́л; vt прока́лывать impf, проколо́ть pf.

pundit n (fig) знато́к.

pungent adj е́дкий.

punish vt нака́зывать impf, наказа́ть pf. **punishable** adj наказу́емый. **punishment** n наказа́ние.

punitive adj кара́тельный.

punter n (gambler) игро́к; (client) клие́нт.

puny adj хи́лый.

pupil n учени́к, -и́ца; (of eye) зрачо́к.

puppet n марионе́тка, ку́кла.

puppy n щено́к.

purchase n поку́пка; (leverage) то́чка опо́ры; vt покупа́ть impf, купи́ть pf. **purchaser** n покупа́тель m.

pure adj чи́стый.

purée n пюре́ neut indecl.

purely adv чи́сто.

purgatory n чисти́лище; (fig) ад. **purge** vt очища́ть impf, очи́стить pf; n очище́ние; (polit) чи́стка.

purification n очи́стка. **purify** vt очища́ть impf, очи́стить pf.

purist n пури́ст.

puritan, P., n пурита́нин, -а́нка. **puritanical** adj пурита́нский.

purity n чистота́.

purple adj (n) пу́рпу́рный, фиоле́товый (цвет).

purport vt претендова́ть impf.

purpose n цель, намере́ние; on ~ наро́чно; to no ~ напра́сно. **purposeful** adj целеустремлённый. **purposeless** adj бесце́льный. **purposely** adv наро́чно.

purr *vi* мурлы́кать *impf*.

purse *n* кошелёк; *vt* поджима́ть *impf*, поджа́ть *pf*.

pursue *vt* пресле́довать *impf*. **pursuit** *n* пресле́дование; (*pastime*) заня́тие.

purveyor *n* поставщи́к.

pus *n* гной.

push *vt* толка́ть *impf*, толкну́ть *pf*; (*press*) нажима́ть *impf*, нажа́ть *pf*; (*urge*) подта́лкивать *impf*, подтолкну́ть *pf*; *vi* толка́ться *impf*; be ~ed for име́ть *impf* ма́ло+*gen*; he is ~ing fifty ему́ ско́ро сту́кнет пятьдеся́т; ~ one's way проти́скиваться *impf*, проти́снуться *pf*; ~ around (*person*) помыка́ть *impf* +*instr*; ~ aside (*also fig*) отстраня́ть *impf*, отстрани́ть *pf*; ~ away отта́лкивать *impf*, оттолкну́ть *pf*; ~ off (*vi*) (*in boat*) отта́лкиваться *impf*, оттолкну́ться *pf* (от бе́рега); (*go away*) убира́ться *impf*, убра́ться *pf*; ~ on (*vi*) продолжа́ть *impf* путь; *n* толчо́к; (*energy*) эне́ргия. **pushchair** *n* коля́ска. **pusher** *n* (*drugs*) продаве́ц нарко́тиков. **pushy** *adj* напо́ристый.

puss, pussy(-cat) *n* ки́ска.

put *vt* класть *impf*, положи́ть *pf*; (*upright*) ста́вить *impf*, по~ *pf*; помеща́ть *impf*, помести́ть *pf*; (*into specified place*) приводи́ть *impf*, привести́ *pf*; (*express*) выража́ть *impf*, вы́разить *pf*; (*a question*) задава́ть *impf*, зада́ть *pf*; ~ an end, a stop, to класть *impf*, положи́ть *pf* коне́ц +*dat*; ~ o.s. in another's place ста́вить *impf*, по~ *pf* себя́ на ме́сто +*gen*; ~ about (*rumour etc.*) распространя́ть *impf*, распространи́ть *pf*; ~ away (*tidy*) убира́ть *impf*, убра́ть *pf*; (*save*) откла́дывать *impf*, отложи́ть *pf*; ~ back (*in place*) ста́вить *impf*, по~ *pf* на ме́сто; (*clock*) переводи́ть *impf*, перевести́ *pf* наза́д; ~ by (*money*) откла́дывать *impf*, отложи́ть *pf*; ~ down класть *impf*, положи́ть *pf*; (*suppress*) подавля́ть *impf*, подави́ть *pf*; (*write down*) запи́сывать *impf*, записа́ть *pf*; (*passengers*) выса́живать *impf*, вы́садить *pf*; (*attribute*) припи́сывать *impf*, приписа́ть *pf* (to +*dat*); ~ forward (*proposal*) предлага́ть *impf*, предложи́ть *pf*; (*clock*) переводи́ть

impf, перевести́ *pf* вперёд; ~ in (*install*) устана́вливать *impf*, установи́ть *pf*; (*a claim*) предъявля́ть *impf*, предъяви́ть *pf*; (*interpose*) вставля́ть *impf*, вста́вить *pf*; ~ in an appearance появля́ться *impf*, появи́ться *pf*; ~ off (*postpone*) откла́дывать *impf*, отложи́ть *pf*; (*repel*) отта́лкивать *impf*, оттолкну́ть *pf*; (*dissuade*) отгова́ривать *impf*, отговори́ть *pf* от+*gen*, +*inf*; ~ on (*clothes*) надева́ть *impf*, наде́ть *pf*; (*kettle, a record, a play*) ста́вить *impf*, по~ *pf*; (*turn on*) включа́ть *impf*, включи́ть *pf*; (*add to*) прибавля́ть *impf*, приба́вить *pf*; ~ on airs ва́жничать *impf*; ~ on weight толсте́ть *impf*, по~ *pf*; ~ out (*vex*) обижа́ть *impf*, оби́деть *pf*; (*inconvenience*) затрудня́ть *impf*, затрудни́ть *pf*; (*a fire etc.*) туши́ть *impf*, по~ *pf*; ~ through (*tel*) соединя́ть *impf*, соедини́ть *pf* по телефо́ну; ~ up (*building*) стро́ить *impf*, по~ *pf*; (*hang up*) ве́шать *impf*, пове́сить *pf*; (*price*) повыша́ть *impf*, повы́сить *pf*; (*a guest*) дава́ть *impf*, дать *pf* ночле́г +*dat*; (*as guest*) ночева́ть *impf*, пере~ *pf*; ~ up to (*instigate*) подбива́ть *impf*, подби́ть *pf* на+*acc*; ~ up with терпе́ть *impf*.

putative *adj* предполага́емый.

putrefy *vi* гнить *impf*, с~ *pf*. **putrid** *adj* гнило́й.

putty *n* зама́зка.

puzzle *n* (*enigma*) зага́дка; (*toy etc.*) головоло́мка; (*jigsaw*) моза́ика; *vt* озада́чивать *impf*, озада́чить *pf*; ~ out разгада́ть *pf*; *vi*: ~ over лома́ть *impf* себе́ го́лову над+*instr*.

pygmy *n* пигме́й.

pyjamas *n pl* пижа́ма.

pylon *n* пило́н.

pyramid *n* пирами́да.

pyre *n* погреба́льный костёр.

python *n* пито́н.

Q

quack[1] *n* (*sound*) кря́канье; *vi* кря́кать *impf*, кря́кнуть *pf*.

quack[2] *n* шарлата́н.

quad *n* (*court*) четырёхуго́льный двор; *pl* (*quadruplets*) че́тверо близнецо́в. **quadrangle** *n* (*figure*) четырёхуго́льник; (*court*) четырёх-уго́льный двор. **quadrant** *n* квадра́нт.

quadruped *n* четвероно́гое живо́тное *sb*. **quadruple** *adj* четверно́й; *vt & i* учетверя́ть *impf*, учетвери́ть(ся) *pf*. **quadruplets** *n pl* че́тверо близнецо́в.

quagmire *n* боло́то.

quail *n* (*bird*) пе́репел.

quaint *adj* причу́дливый.

quake *vi* дрожа́ть *impf* (with от +*gen*).

Quaker *n* ква́кер, ~ка.

qualification *n* (*for post etc.*) квалифика́ция; (*reservation*) огово́рка. **qualified** *adj* компете́нтный; (*limited*) ограни́ченный. **qualify** *vt & i* (*prepare for job*) гото́вить(ся) *impf* (for к+*dat*; +*inf*); *vt* (*render fit*) де́лать *impf*, с~ *pf* приго́дным; (*entitle*) дава́ть *impf*, дать *pf* пра́во +*dat* (to на+*acc*); (*limit*): ~ what one says сде́лать *pf* огово́рку; *vi* получа́ть *impf*, получи́ть *pf* дипло́м; ~ for (*be entitled to*) име́ть *impf* пра́во на+*acc*.

qualitative *adj* ка́чественный. **quality** *n* ка́чество.

qualm *n* сомне́ние; (*of conscience*) угрызе́ние со́вести.

quandary *n* затрудни́тельное положе́ние.

quantify *vt* определя́ть *impf*, определи́ть *pf* коли́чество +*gen*. **quantitative** *adj* коли́чественный. **quantity** *n* коли́чество.

quarantine *n* каранти́н.

quarrel *n* ссо́ра; *vi* ссо́риться *impf*, по~ *pf* (with c+*instr*; about, for из-за+*gen*). **quarrelsome** *adj* вздо́рный.

quarry[1] *n* (*for stone etc.*) каменоло́мня; *vt* добыва́ть *impf*, добы́ть *pf*.

quarry[2] *n* (*prey*) добы́ча.

quart *n* ква́рта. **quarter** *n* че́тверть; (*of year; of town*) кварта́л; *pl* кварти́ры *f pl*; a ~ to one без че́тверти час; ~-final четверть-фина́л; *vt* (*divide*) дели́ть *impf*, раз~ *pf* на четы́ре ча́сти; (*lodge*) расквартиро́вывать *impf*, расквартирова́ть *pf*. **quarterly** *adj* кварта́льный; *adv* раз в кварта́л. **quartet** *n* кварте́т. **quartz** *n* кварц.

quash *vt* (*annul*) аннули́ровать *impf* & *pf*; (*crush*) подавля́ть *impf*, подави́ть *pf*.

quasi- *in comb* ква́зи-.

quaver *vi* дрожа́ть *impf*; *n* (*mus*) восьма́я *sb* но́ты.

quay *n* на́бережная *sb*.

queasy *adj*: I feel ~ меня́ тошни́т.

queen *n* короле́ва; (*cards*) да́ма; (*chess*) ферзь *m*.

queer *adj* стра́нный.

quell *vt* подавля́ть *impf*, подави́ть *pf*.

quench *vt* (*thirst*) утоля́ть *impf*, утоли́ть *pf*; (*fire, desire*) туши́ть *impf*, по~ *pf*.

query *n* вопро́с; *vt* (*express doubt*) выража́ть *impf* вы́разить *pf* сомне́ние в+*prep*. **quest** *n* по́иски *m pl*; in ~ of в по́исках+*gen*. **question** *n* вопро́с; beyond ~ вне сомне́ния; it is a ~ of э́то вопро́с+*gen*; it is out of the ~ об э́том не мо́жет быть и ре́чи; the person in ~ челове́к, о кото́ром идёт речь; the ~ is this де́ло в э́том; ~ mark вопроси́тельный знак; *vt* расспра́шивать *impf*, расспроси́ть *pf*; (*interrogate*) допра́шивать *impf* допроси́ть *pf*; (*doubt*) сомнева́ться *impf* в+*prep*. **questionable** *adj* сомни́тельный. **questionnaire** *n* вопро́сник.

queue *n* о́чередь; *vi* стоя́ть *impf* в о́череди.

quibble *n* софи́зм; (*minor criticism*) приди́рка; *vi* придира́ться *impf*; (*argue*) спо́рить *impf*.

quick *adj* ско́рый, бы́стрый; ~-tempered вспы́льчивый; ~-witted нахо́дчивый; *n*: to the ~ за живо́е; *adv* ско́ро, бы́стро; ~er as *imper* скоре́е! **quicken** *vt & i* ускоря́ть(ся), уско́рить(ся) *pf*. **quickness** *n* быстрота́. **quicksand** *n* зыбу́чий песо́к. **quicksilver** *n* ртуть.

quid *n* (*money*) фунт.

quiet *n* (*silence*) тишина́; (*calm*) споко́йствие; *adj* ти́хий; споко́йный; *int* ти́ше!; *vt & i* успока́ивать(ся) *impf*, успоко́ить(ся) *pf*.

quill *n* перо́; (*spine*) игла́.

quilt *n* (*stégaное*) одея́ло; *vt* стега́ть *impf*, вы́~ *pf*. **quilted** *adj* стёганый.

quintessential *adj* наибо́лее суще́ственный.

quintet *n* квинте́т. **quins, quintuplets**

n pl пять близнецо́в.

quip *n* острота́; остри́ть *impf*, c~ *pf*.

quirk *n* причу́да. **quirky** *adj* с причу́дами.

quit *vt* (*leave*) покида́ть *impf*, покину́ть *pf*; (*stop*) перестава́ть *impf*, переста́ть *pf*; (*give up*) броса́ть *impf*, бро́сить *pf*; (*resign*) уходи́ть *impf*, уйти́ *pf* c+*gen*.

quite *adv* (*wholly*) совсе́м; (*rather*) дово́льно; ~ a few дово́льно мно́го.

quits *predic*: we are ~ мы с тобо́й кви́ты; I am ~ with him я расквита́лся (*past*) с ним.

quiver *vi* (*tremble*) трепета́ть *impf*; *n* тре́пет.

quiz *n* виктори́на. **quizzical** *adj* насме́шливый.

quorum *n* кво́рум.

quota *n* но́рма.

quotation *n* цита́та; (*of price*) цена́; ~ marks кавы́чки (-чек) *pl*. **quote** *vt* цити́ровать *impf*, про~ *pf*; ссыла́ться *impf*, сосла́ться *pf* на+*acc*; (*price*) назнача́ть *impf*, назна́чить *pf*.

R

rabbi *n* равви́н.

rabbit *n* кро́лик.

rabble *n* сброд.

rabid *adj* бе́шеный. **rabies** *n* бе́шенство.

race[1] *n* (*ethnic* ~) ра́са; род.

race[2] *n* (*contest*) (*on foot*) бег; (*of cars etc.*; *fig*) го́нка, го́нки *f pl*; (*of horses*) ска́чки *f pl*; ~-**track** трек; (*for horse* ~) скакова́я доро́жка; *vi* (*compete*) состяза́ться *impf* в ско́рости; (*rush*) мча́ться *impf*, *vt* бежа́ть *impf* наперегонки́ c+*instr*. **racecourse** *n* ипподро́м. **racehorse** *n* скакова́я ло́шадь.

racial *adj* ра́совый. **rac(ial)ism** *n* раси́зм. **rac(ial)ist** *n* раси́ст, ~ка; *adj* раси́стский.

racing *n* (*horses*) ска́чки *f pl*; (*cars*) го́нки *f pl*; ~ car го́ночный автомоби́ль *m*; ~ **driver** го́нщик.

rack *n* (*for hats etc.*) ве́шалка; (*for plates etc.*) стелла́ж; (*in train etc.*) се́тка; *vt*: ~ **one's brains** лома́ть *impf* себе́ го́лову.

racket[1] *n* (*bat*) раке́тка.

racket[2] *n* (*uproar*) шум; (*illegal activity*) рэ́кет. **racketeer** *n* рэкети́р.

racy *adj* колори́тный.

radar *n* (*system*) радиолока́ция; (*apparatus*) радиолока́тор, рада́р; *attrib* рада́рный.

radiance *n* сия́ние. **radiant** *adj* сия́ющий. **radiate** *vt* & *i* излуча́ть(ся) *impf*, излучи́ться *pf*. **radiation** *n* излуче́ние. **radiator** *n* батаре́я; (*in car*) радиа́тор.

radical *adj* радика́льный; *n* радика́л.

radio *n* ра́дио *neut indecl*; (*set*) радиоприёмник; *vt* ради́ровать *impf* & *pf* +*dat*.

radioactive *adj* радиоакти́вный. **radioactivity** *n* радиоакти́вность. **radiologist** *n* радио́лог; рентгено́лог. **radiotherapy** *n* радиотерапи́я.

radish *n* реди́ска.

radius *n* ра́диус.

raffle *n* лотере́я; *vt* разы́грывать *impf*, разыгра́ть *pf* в лотере́е.

raft *n* плот.

rafter *n* (*beam*) стропи́ло.

rag *n* тря́пка; *pl* (*clothes*) лохмо́тья (-ьев) *pl*.

rage *n* я́рость; all the ~ после́дний крик мо́ды; *vi* беси́ться *impf*; (*storm etc.*) бушева́ть *impf*.

ragged *adj* (*jagged*) зазу́бренный; (*of clothes*) рва́ный.

raid *n* налёт; (*by police*) обла́ва; *vt* де́лать *impf*, c~ *pf* налёт на+*acc*.

rail *n* пери́ла (-л) *pl*; (*rly*) рельс; by ~ по́ездом. **railing** *n* пери́ла (-л) *pl*.

railway *n* желе́зная доро́га; *attrib* железнодоро́жный. **railwayman** *n* железнодоро́жник.

rain *n* дождь *m*; *v impers*: it is (was) ~ing идёт (шёл) дождь; *vt* осыпа́ть *impf*, осы́пать *pf* +*instr* (upon +*acc*); *vi* осыпа́ться *impf*, осы́паться *pf*. **rainbow** *n* ра́дуга. **raincoat** *n* плащ. **raindrop** *n* дождева́я ка́пля. **rainfall** *n* (*amount of rain*) коли́чество оса́дков. **rainy** *adj* дождли́вый; ~ **day** чёрный день *m*.

raise *vt* (*lift*) поднима́ть *impf*, подня́ть *pf*; (*heighten*) повыша́ть *impf*, повы́сить *pf*; (*provoke*) вызыва́ть *impf*, вы́звать *pf*; (*money*) собира́ть *impf*, собра́ть *pf*; (*children*) расти́ть *impf*.

raisin *n* изю́минка; *pl* (*collect*) изю́м.

rake n (*tool*) гра́бли (-бель & -блей) pl; vt грести́ *impf*; (~ *together, up*) сгреба́ть *impf*, сгрести́ *pf*.

rally vt & i спла́чивать(ся) *impf*, сплоти́ть(ся) *pf*; vi (*after illness etc.*) оправля́ться *impf*, опра́виться *pf*; n (*meeting*) слёт; ми́тинг; (*motoring* ~) (а́вто)ра́лли *neut indecl*; (*tennis*) обме́н уда́рами.

ram n (*sheep*) бара́н; vt (*beat down*) трамбова́ть *impf*, у~ *pf*; (*drive in*) вбива́ть *impf*, вбить *pf*.

ramble vi (*walk*) прогу́ливаться *impf*, прогуля́ться *pf*; (*speak*) бубни́ть *impf*; n прогу́лка. **rambling** adj (*incoherent*) бессвя́зный.

ramification n (*fig*) после́дствие.

ramp n скат.

rampage vi бу́йствовать *impf*.

rampant adj (*plant*) бу́йный; (*unchecked*) безуде́ржный.

rampart n вал.

ramshackle adj ве́тхий.

ranch n ра́нчо *neut indecl*.

rancid adj прого́рклый.

rancour n зло́ба.

random adj случа́йный; at ~ науда́чу.

range n (*of mountains*) цепь; (*artillery* ~) полиго́н; (*of voice*) диапазо́н; (*scope*) круг, преде́лы m pl; (*operating distance*) да́льность; vi (*vary*) колеба́ться *impf*, по~ *pf*; (*wander*) броди́ть *impf*; ~ over (*include*) охва́тывать *impf*, охвати́ть *pf*.

rank[1] n (*row*) ряд; (*taxi*) стоя́нка такси́; (*grade*) зва́ние, чин, ранг; vt (*classify*) классифици́ровать *impf* & *pf*; (*consider*) счита́ть *impf* (as +*instr*); vi: ~ with быть в числе́+*gen*.

rank[2] adj (*luxuriant*) бу́йный; (*in smell*) злово́нный; (*gross*) я́вный.

rankle vi боле́ть *impf*.

ransack vt (*search*) обша́ривать *impf*, обша́рить *pf*; (*plunder*) гра́бить *impf*, о~ *pf*.

ransom n вы́куп; vt выкупа́ть *impf*, вы́купить *pf*.

rant vi вопи́ть *impf*.

rap n стук; vt (*réзко*) ударя́ть *impf*, уда́рить *pf*; vi стуча́ть *impf*, сту́кнуть *pf*.

rape[1] vt наси́ловать *impf*, из~ *pf*; n изнаси́лование.

rape[2] n (*plant*) рапс.

rapid adj бы́стрый; n: pl поро́г, быстрина́. **rapidity** n быстрота́.

rapt adj восхищённый; (*absorbed*) поглощённый. **rapture** n восто́рг. **rapturous** adj восто́рженный.

rare[1] adj (*of meat*) недожа́ренный.

rare[2] adj ре́дкий. **rarity** n ре́дкость.

rascal n плут.

rash[1] n сыпь.

rash[2] adj опроме́тчивый.

rasher n ло́мтик (беко́на).

rasp n (*file*) ра́шпиль m; (*sound*) скре́жет; vt: ~ out га́ркнуть *pf*.

raspberry n мали́на (*no pl; usu collect*).

rasping adj (*sound*) скрипу́чий.

rat n кры́са; ~ race го́нка за успе́хом.

ratchet n храпови́к.

rate n но́рма, ста́вка; (*speed*) ско́рость; pl ме́стные нало́ги m pl; at any ~ во вся́ком слу́чае; vt оце́нивать *impf*, оцени́ть *pf*; (*consider*) счита́ть *impf*; vi счита́ться *impf* (as +*instr*).

rather adv скоре́е; (*somewhat*) дово́льно; he (she) had (would) ~ он (она́) предпочёл (-чла́) бы+*inf*.

ratification n ратифика́ция. **ratify** vt ратифици́ровать *impf* & *pf*.

rating n оце́нка.

ratio n пропо́рция.

ration n паёк, рацио́н; vt норми́ровать *impf* & *pf*; be ~ed выдава́ться *impf*, выда́ться *pf* по ка́рточкам.

rational adj разу́мный. **rationalism** n рационали́зм. **rationality** n разу́мность. **rationalize** vt обосно́вывать *impf*, обоснова́ть *pf*; (*industry etc.*) рационализи́ровать *impf* & *pf*.

rattle vi & t (*sound*) греме́ть *impf* (+*instr*); ~ along (*move*) грохота́ть *impf*; ~ off (*utter*) отбараба́нить *pf*; n (*sound*) треск, гро́хот; (*toy*) погрему́шка. **rattlesnake** n грему́чая змея́.

raucous adj ре́зкий.

ravage vt опустоша́ть *impf*, опустоши́ть *pf*; n: pl разруши́тельное де́йствие.

rave vi бре́дить *impf*; ~ about быть в восто́рге от+*gen*.

raven n во́рон.

ravenous adj голо́дный как волк.

ravine n уще́лье.

ravishing adj восхити́тельный.

raw adj сыро́й; (inexperienced) нео́пытный; ~ material(s) сырьё (no pl).

ray n луч.

raze vt: ~ to the ground ровня́ть impf, с~ pf с землёй.

razor n бри́тва; ~-blade ле́звие.

reach vt (attain, extend to, arrive at) достига́ть impf, дости́чь & дости́гнуть pf +gen, до+gen; доходи́ть impf, дойти́ pf до+gen; (with hand) дотя́гиваться impf, дотяну́ться pf до+gen; vi (extend) простира́ться impf; n досяга́емость; (pl, of river) тече́ние.

react vi реаги́ровать impf, от~, про~ pf (to на+acc). **reaction** n реа́кция.

reactionary adj реакцио́нный; n реакционе́р. **reactor** n реа́ктор.

read vt чита́ть impf, про~, проче́сть pf; (mus) разбира́ть impf, разобра́ть pf; (~ a meter etc.) снима́ть impf, снять pf показа́ния +gen; (univ) изуча́ть impf; (interpret) толкова́ть impf. **readable** adj интере́сный. **reader** n чита́тель m, ~ница; (book) хрестома́тия.

readily adv (willingly) охо́тно; (easily) легко́. **readiness** n гото́вность.

reading n чте́ние; (on meter) показа́ние.

ready adj гото́вый (for к+dat, на+acc); get ~ гото́виться impf; ~-made гото́вый; ~ money нали́чные де́ньги (-нег, -ньга́м) pl.

real adj настоя́щий, реа́льный; ~ estate недви́жимость. **realism** n реали́зм. **realist** n реали́ст. **realistic** adj реалисти́чный, -и́ческий. **reality** n действи́тельность; in ~ действи́тельно. **realization** n (of plan etc.) осуществле́ние; (of assets) реализа́ция; (understanding) осозна́ние. **realize** vt (plan etc.) осуществля́ть impf, осуществи́ть pf; (assets) реализова́ть impf & pf; (apprehend) осознава́ть impf, осозна́ть pf. **really** adv действи́тельно, в са́мом де́ле.

realm n (kingdom) короле́вство; (sphere) о́бласть.

reap vt жать impf, сжать pf; (fig) пожина́ть impf, пожа́ть pf.

rear[1] vt (lift) поднима́ть impf, подня́ть pf; (children) воспи́тывать impf, воспита́ть pf; vi (of horse) станови́ться impf, стать pf на дыбы́.

rear[2] n за́дняя часть; (mil) тыл; bring up the ~ замыка́ть impf, замкну́ть pf ше́ствие; (also mil) ты́льный. **rearguard** n арьерга́рд; ~ action арьерга́рдный бой.

rearmament n перевооруже́ние.

rearrange vt меня́ть impf.

reason n (cause) причи́на, основа́ние; (intellect) ра́зум, рассу́док; vi рассужда́ть impf; ~ with (person) угова́ривать impf +acc. **reasonable** adj разу́мный; (inexpensive) недорого́й.

reassurance n успока́ивание. **reassure** vt успока́ивать impf, успоко́ить pf.

rebate n ски́дка.

rebel n повста́нец; vi восстава́ть impf, восста́ть pf. **rebellion** n восста́ние. **rebellious** adj мяте́жный.

rebound vi отска́кивать impf, отскочи́ть pf; n рикоше́т.

rebuff n отпо́р; vt дава́ть impf, дать pf +dat отпо́р.

rebuild vt перестра́ивать impf, перестро́ить pf.

rebuke vt упрека́ть impf, упрекну́ть pf; n упрёк.

rebuttal n опроверже́ние.

recalcitrant adj непоко́рный.

recall vt (an official) отзыва́ть impf, отозва́ть pf; (remember) вспомина́ть impf, вспо́мнить pf; n о́тзыв; (memory) па́мять.

recant vi отрека́ться impf, отре́чься pf.

recapitulate vt резюми́ровать impf & pf.

recast vt переде́лывать impf, переде́лать pf.

recede vi отходи́ть impf, отойти́ pf.

receipt n (receiving) получе́ние; pl (amount) вы́ручка; (written ~) квита́нция. **receive** vt (admit, entertain) принима́ть impf, приня́ть pf; (get, be given) получа́ть impf, получи́ть pf. **receiver** n (radio, television) приёмник; (tel) тру́бка.

recent adj неда́вний; (new) но́вый. **recently** adv неда́вно.

receptacle n вмести́лище. **reception** n приём; ~ room приёмная sb. **receptionist** n секрета́рь m, -рша, в приёмной. **receptive** *adj* восприи́мчивый.

recess *n* (*parl*) кани́кулы (-л) *pl*; (*niche*) ни́ша. **recession** *n* спад.

recipe *n* реце́пт.

recipient *n* получа́тель *m*.

reciprocal *adj* взаи́мный. **reciprocate** *vt* отвеча́ть *impf* (взаи́мностью) на+*acc*.

recital *n* (со́льный) конце́рт. **recitation** *n* публи́чное чте́ние. **recite** *vt* деклами́ровать *impf*, про~ *pf*; (*list*) перечисля́ть *impf*, перечи́слить *pf*.

reckless *adj* (*rash*) опроме́тчивый; (*careless*) неосторо́жный.

reckon *vt* подсчи́тывать *impf*, подсчита́ть *pf*; (*also regard as*) счита́ть *impf*, счесть *pf* (to be +*instr*); *vi*: ~ on рассчи́тывать *impf*, рассчита́ть *pf* на+*acc*; ~ with счита́ться *impf* c+*instr*. **reckoning** *n* счёт; day of ~ час распла́ты.

reclaim *vt* тре́бовать *impf*, по~ *pf* обра́тно; (*land*) осва́ивать *impf*, осво́ить *pf*.

recline *vi* полулежа́ть *impf*.

recluse *n* затво́рник.

recognition *n* узнава́ние; (*acknowledgement*) призна́ние. **recognize** *vt* узнава́ть *impf*, узна́ть *pf*; (*acknowledge*) признава́ть *impf*, призна́ть *pf*.

recoil *vi* отпря́дывать *impf*, отпря́нуть *pf*.

recollect *vt* вспомина́ть *impf*, вспо́мнить *pf*. **recollection** *n* воспомина́ние.

recommend *vt* рекомендова́ть *impf* & *pf*. **recommendation** *n* рекоменда́ция.

recompense *n* вознагражде́ние; *vt* вознагражда́ть *impf*, вознаград́ить *pf*.

reconcile *vt* примиря́ть *impf*, примири́ть *pf*; ~ o.s. примиря́ться *impf*, примири́ться *pf* c+*instr*). **reconciliation** *n* примире́ние.

reconnaissance *n* разве́дка. **reconnoitre** *vt* разве́дывать *impf*, разве́дать *pf*.

reconstruct *vt* перестра́ивать *impf*, перестро́ить *pf*. **reconstruction** *n* перестро́йка.

record *vt* запи́сывать *impf*, записа́ть *pf*; *n* за́пись; (*minutes*) протоко́л; (*gramophone* ~) граммпласти́нка;

(*sport etc.*) реко́рд; off the ~ неофициа́льно; *adj* реко́рдный; ~-breaker, -holder рекордсме́н, ~ка; ~-player прои́грыватель *m*. **recorder** *n* (*mus*) блок-фле́йта. **recording** *n* за́пись.

recount[1] *vt* (*narrate*) переска́зывать *impf*, пересказа́ть *pf*.

re-count[2] *vt* (*count again*) пересчи́тывать *impf*, пересчита́ть *pf*; *n* пересчёт.

recoup *vt* возвраща́ть *impf*, верну́ть *pf* (*losses* потеря́нное).

recourse *n*: have ~ to прибега́ть *impf*, прибе́гнуть *pf* к+*dat*.

recover *vt* (*regain possession*) получа́ть *impf*, получи́ть *pf* обра́тно; возвраща́ть *impf*, верну́ть *pf*; *vi* (~ *health*) поправля́ться *impf*, попра́виться *pf* (*from* по́сле+*gen*). **recovery** *n* возвраще́ние; выздоровле́ние.

recreate *vt* воссоздава́ть *impf*, воссозда́ть *pf*.

recreation *n* развлече́ние, о́тдых.

recrimination *n* взаи́мное обвине́ние.

recruit *n* новобра́нец; *vt* вербова́ть *impf*, за~ *pf*. **recruitment** *n* вербо́вка.

rectangle *n* прямоуго́льник. **rectangular** *adj* прямоуго́льный.

rectify *vt* исправля́ть *impf*, испра́вить *pf*.

rector *n* (*priest*) прихо́дский свяще́нник; (*univ*) ре́ктор. **rectory** *n* дом прихо́дского свяще́нника.

rectum *n* пряма́я кишка́.

recuperate *vi* поправля́ться *impf*, попра́виться *pf*. **recuperation** *n* выздоровле́ние.

recur *vi* повторя́ться *impf*, повтори́ться *pf*. **recurrence** *n* повторе́ние. **recurrent** *adj* повторя́ющийся.

recycle *vt* перераба́тывать *impf*, перерабо́тать *pf*.

red *adj* кра́сный; (*of hair*) ры́жий; *n* кра́сный цвет; (*polit*) кра́сный; in the ~ в долгу́; ~-handed с поли́чным; ~ herring ло́жный след; ~-hot раскалённый докрасна́; R~ Indian инде́ец, индиа́нка; ~ tape волоки́та. **redcurrant** *n* кра́сная сморо́дина (*no pl*; *usu collect*). **redden** *vt* окра́шивать *impf*, окра́сить *pf* в кра́сный цвет; *vi* красне́ть *impf*, по~ *pf*. **reddish** *adj* краснова́тый; *(hair)* рыжева́тый.

redecorate *vt* отде́лывать *impf*, отде́лать *pf*.

redeem *vt* *(buy back)* выкупа́ть *impf*, вы́купить *pf*; *(from sin)* искупа́ть *impf*, искупи́ть *pf*. **redeemer** *n* искупи́тель *m*. **redemption** *n* вы́куп; искупле́ние.

redeploy *vt* передислоци́ровать *impf* & *pf*.

redo *vt* переде́лывать *impf*, переде́лать *pf*.

redouble *vt* удва́ивать *impf*, удво́ить *pf*.

redress *vt* исправля́ть *impf*, испра́вить *pf*; ~ **the balance** восстана́вливать *impf*, восстанови́ть *pf* равнове́сие; *n* возмеще́ние.

reduce *vt* *(decrease)* уменьша́ть *impf*, уме́ньшить *pf*; *(lower)* снижа́ть *impf*, сни́зить *pf*; *(shorten)* сокраща́ть *impf*, сократи́ть *pf*; *(bring to)* доводи́ть *impf*, довести́ *pf* (**to** в+*acc*). **reduction** *n* уменьше́ние, сниже́ние, сокраще́ние; *(discount)* ски́дка.

redundancy *n* *(dismissal)* увольне́ние. **redundant** *adj* изли́шний; **make** ~ увольня́ть *impf*, уво́лить *pf*.

reed *n* *(plant)* тростни́к; *(in oboe etc.)* язычо́к.

reef *n* риф.

reek *n* вонь; *vi*: ~ *(of)* воня́ть *impf* (+*instr*).

reel[1] *n* кату́шка; *vt*: ~ **off** *(story etc.)* отбараба́нить *pf*.

reel[2] *vi* *(stagger)* пошатываться *impf*, пошатну́ться *pf*.

refectory *n* *(monastery)* тра́пезная *sb*; *(univ)* столо́вая *sb*.

refer *vt* *(direct)* отсыла́ть *impf*, отосла́ть *pf* (**to** к+*dat*); *vi*: ~ **to** *(cite)* ссыла́ться *impf*, сосла́ться *pf* на +*acc*; *(mention)* упомина́ть *impf*, упомяну́ть *pf* +*acc*. **referee** *n* судья́ *m*; *vt* суди́ть *impf*. **reference** *n* *(to book etc.)* ссы́лка; *(mention)* упомина́ние; *(testimonial)* характери́стика; ~ **book** спра́вочник. **referendum** *n* рефере́ндум.

refine *vt* очища́ть *impf*, очи́стить *pf*. **refined** *adj* *(in style etc.)* утончённый; *(in manners)* культу́рный. **re-**

finement *n* утончённость. **refinery** *n* *(oil* ~*)* нефтеочисти́тельный заво́д.

refit *vt* переобору́довать *impf* & *pf*.

reflect *vt* отража́ть *impf*, отрази́ть *pf*; *vi* размышля́ть *impf*, размы́слить *pf* (**on** о+*prep*). **reflection** *n* отраже́ние; размышле́ние; **on** ~ поду́мав. **reflective** *adj* *(thoughtful)* серьёзный. **reflector** *n* рефле́ктор. **reflex** *n* рефле́кс; *adj* рефле́кторный. **reflexive** *adj* *(gram)* возвра́тный.

reform *vt* реформи́ровать *impf* & *pf*; *vt* & *i* *(of people)* исправля́ть(ся) *impf*, испра́вить(ся) *pf*; *n* рефо́рма; исправле́ние. **Reformation** *n* Реформа́ция.

refract *vt* преломля́ть *impf*, преломи́ть *pf*.

refrain[1] *n* припе́в.

refrain[2] *vi* возде́рживаться *impf*, воздержа́ться *pf* (**from** от+*gen*).

refresh *vt* освежа́ть *impf*, освежи́ть *pf*. **refreshments** *n pl* напи́тки *m pl*.

refrigerate *vt* охлажда́ть *impf*, охлади́ть *pf*. **refrigeration** *n* охлажде́ние. **refrigerator** *n* холоди́льник.

refuge *n* убе́жище; take ~ находи́ть *impf*, найти́ *pf* убе́жище. **refugee** *n* бе́женец, -нка.

refund *vt* возвраща́ть *impf*, возврати́ть *pf*; *(expenses)* возмеща́ть *impf*, возмести́ть *pf*; *n* возвраще́ние (де́нег); возмеще́ние.

refusal *n* отка́з. **refuse**[1] *vt* отка́зывать *impf*, отказа́ть *pf*.

refuse[2] *n* му́сор.

refute *vt* опроверга́ть *impf*, опрове́ргнуть *pf*.

regain *vt* возвраща́ть *impf*, верну́ть *pf*.

regal *adj* короле́вский.

regale *vt* угоща́ть *impf*, угости́ть *pf* (**with** +*instr*).

regalia *n pl* рега́лии *f pl*.

regard *vt* смотре́ть *impf*, по~ *pf* на+*acc*; *(take into account)* счита́ться *impf* с+*instr*; ~ **as** счита́ть *impf* +*instr*, за+*acc*; **as** ~**s** что каса́ется+*gen*; *n* *(esteem)* уваже́ние; *(attention)* внима́ние; *pl* приве́т. **regarding** *prep* относи́тельно+*gen*. **regardless** *adv* не обраща́я внима́ния; ~ **of** не счита́ясь с+*instr*.

regatta n регáта.
regenerate vt перерождáть impf, перероди́ть pf. **regeneration** n перерождéние.
regent n péгент.
régime n режи́м.
regiment n полк. **regimental** adj полковóй. **regimentation** n регламентáция.
region n регио́н. **regional** adj региона́льный.
register n реéстр; (also mus) реги́стр; vt регистри́ровать impf, за~ pf; (a letter) отправля́ть impf, отпра́вить pf заказны́м. **registered** adj (letter) заказнóй. **registrar** n регистра́тор. **registration** n регистра́ция; ~ number нóмер маши́ны. **registry** n регистрату́ра; ~ office загс.
regression n регрéсс. **regressive** adj регресси́вный.
regret vt сожалéть impf о+prep; n сожалéние. **regretful** adj пóлный сожалéния. **regrettable** adj приско́рбный. **regrettably** adv к сожалéнию.
regular adj регуля́рный; (also gram) пра́вильный; n (coll) завсегда́тай. **regularity** n регуля́рность. **regulate** vt регули́ровать impf, у~ pf. **regulation** n регули́рование; pl пра́вила neut pl.
rehabilitate vt реабилити́ровать impf & pf. **rehabilitation** n реабилитáция.
rehearsal n репети́ция. **rehearse** vt репети́ровать impf, от~ pf.
reign n цáрствование; vi цáрствовать impf; (fig) цари́ть impf.
reimburse vt возмещáть impf, возмести́ть pf (+dat of person). **reimbursement** n возмещéние.
rein n по́вод.
reincarnation n перевоплощéние.
reindeer n сéверный олéнь m.
reinforce vt подкрепля́ть impf, подкрепи́ть pf. **reinforcement** n (also pl) подкреплéние.
reinstate vt восстанáвливать impf, восстанови́ть pf. **reinstatement** n восстановлéние.
reiterate vt повторя́ть impf, повтори́ть pf.
reject vt отвергáть impf, отвéргнуть

pf; (as defective) браковáть impf, за~ pf; n брак. **rejection** n откáз (of от+gen).
rejoice vi ра́доваться impf, об~ pf (in, at +dat). **rejoicing** n рáдость.
rejoin vt (вновь) присоединя́ться impf, присоедини́ться pf к+dat.
rejuvenate vt омолáживать impf, омолоди́ть pf.
relapse n рецеди́в; vi снóва впадáть impf, впасть pf (into в+acc); (into illness) снóва заболевáть impf, заболéть pf.
relate vt (tell) рассказывать impf, рассказáть pf; (connect) связывать impf, связáть pf; vi относи́ться impf (to к+dat). **related** adj ро́дственный.
relation n отношéние; (person) рóдственник, -ица. **relationship** n (connection; liaison) связь; (kinship) родствó. **relative** adj относи́тельный; n рóдственник, -ица. **relativity** n относи́тельность.
relax vt ослабля́ть impf, осла́бить pf; vi (rest) расслабля́ться impf, расслáбиться pf. **relaxation** n ослаблéние; (rest) óтдых.
relay n (shift) смéна; (sport) эстафéта; (electr) релé neut indecl; vt передавáть impf, передáть pf.
release vt (set free) освобождáть impf, освободи́ть pf; (unfasten, let go) отпускáть impf, отпусти́ть pf; (film etc.) выпускáть impf, выпустить pf; n освобождéние; выпуск.
relegate vt переводи́ть impf, перевести́ pf (в ни́зшую гру́ппу). **relegation** n перевóд (в ни́зшую гру́ппу).
relent vi смягчáться impf, смягчи́ться pf. **relentless** adj непрестáнный.
relevance n умéстность. **relevant** adj относя́щийся к дéлу; умéстный.
reliability n надёжность. **reliable** adj надёжный. **reliance** n довéрие. **reliant** adj: be ~ upon зави́сеть impf от+gen.
relic n остáток, рели́квия.
relief[1] n (art, geol) рельéф.
relief[2] n (alleviation) облегчéние; (assistance) пóмощь; (in duty) смéна. **relieve** vt (alleviate) облегчáть impf, облегчи́ть pf; (replace) сменя́ть impf, смени́ть pf; (unburden) освобождáть impf, освободи́ть pf (of от+gen).

religion *n* рели́гия. **religious** *adj* религио́зный.

relinquish *vt* оставля́ть *impf*, оста́вить *pf*; (*right etc.*) отка́зываться *impf*, отказа́ться *pf* от+*gen*.

relish *n* (*enjoyment*) смак; (*cul*) припра́ва; *vt* смакова́ть *impf*.

relocate *vt* & *i* перемеща́ть(ся) *impf*, перемести́ть(ся) *pf*.

reluctance *n* неохо́та. **reluctant** *adj* неохо́тный; be ~ to не жела́ть *impf* +*inf*.

rely *vi* полага́ться *impf*, положи́ться *pf* (on на+*acc*).

remain *vi* остава́ться *impf*, оста́ться *pf*. **remainder** *n* оста́ток. **remains** *n pl* оста́тки *m pl*; (*human* ~) оста́нки (-ков) *pl*.

remand *vt* содержа́ть *impf* под стра́жей; be on ~ содержа́ться *impf* под стра́жей.

remark *vt* замеча́ть *impf*, заме́тить *pf*; *n* замеча́ние. **remarkable** *adj* замеча́тельный.

remarry *vi* вступа́ть *impf*, вступи́ть *pf* в но́вый брак.

remedial *adj* лече́бный. **remedy** *n* сре́дство (for от, про́тив+*gen*); *vt* исправля́ть *impf*, испра́вить *pf*.

remember *vt* по́мнить *impf*, вспомина́ть *impf*, вспо́мнить *pf*; (*greet*) передава́ть *impf*, переда́ть *pf* приве́т от+*gen* (to +*dat*). **remembrance** *n* па́мять.

remind *vt* напомина́ть *impf*, напо́мнить *pf* +*dat* (of +*acc*, o+*prep*). **reminder** *n* напомина́ние.

reminiscence *n* воспомина́ние. **reminiscent** *adj* напомина́ющий.

remiss *predic* небре́жный. **remission** *n* (*pardon*) отпуще́ние; (*med*) реми́ссия. **remit** *vt* пересыла́ть *impf*, пересла́ть *pf*. **remittance** *n* перево́д де́нег; (*money*) де́нежный перево́д.

remnant *n* оста́ток.

remonstrate *vi*: ~ with увещева́ть *impf* +*acc*.

remorse *n* угрызе́ния *neut pl* со́вести. **remorseful** *adj* по́лный раска́яния. **remorseless** *adj* безжа́лостный.

remote *adj* отдалённый; ~ control дистанцио́нное управле́ние.

removal *n* (*taking away*) удале́ние;

(*of obstacles*) устране́ние. **remove** *vt* (*take away*) убира́ть *impf*, убра́ть *pf*; (*get rid of*) устраня́ть *impf*, устрани́ть *pf*.

remuneration *n* вознагражде́ние. **remunerative** *adj* вы́годный.

renaissance *n* возрожде́ние; the R~ Возрожде́ние.

render *vt* воздава́ть *impf*, возда́ть *pf*; (*help etc.*) ока́зывать *impf*, оказа́ть *pf*; (*role etc.*) исполня́ть *impf*, испо́лнить *pf*; (*stone*) штукату́рить *impf*, o~, от~ *pf*. **rendering** *n* исполне́ние.

rendezvous *n* (*meeting*) свида́ние.

renegade *n* ренега́т, ~ка.

renew *vt* (*extend; continue*) возобновля́ть *impf*, возобнови́ть *pf*; (*replace*) обновля́ть *impf*, обнови́ть *pf*. **renewal** *n* (воз)обновле́ние.

renounce *vt* отверга́ть *impf*, отве́ргнуть *pf*; (*claim*) отка́зываться *impf*, отказа́ться *pf* от+*gen*.

renovate *vt* ремонти́ровать *impf*, от~ *pf*. **renovation** *n* ремо́нт.

renown *n* сла́ва. **renowned** *adj* изве́стный; be ~ for сла́виться *impf* +*instr*.

rent *n* (*for home*) квартпла́та; (*for premises*) (аре́ндная) пла́та; *vt* (*of tenant*) аре́ндовать *impf* & *pf*; (*of owner*) сдава́ть *impf*, сдать *pf*.

renunciation *n* (*repudiation*) отрица́ние; (*of claim*) отка́з.

rep *n* (*comm*) аге́нт.

repair *vt* ремонти́ровать *impf*, от~ *pf*; *n* (*also pl*) ремо́нт (*only sg*); почи́нка; in good/bad ~ в хоро́шем/ плохо́м состоя́нии.

reparations *n pl* репара́ции *f pl*.

repatriate *vt* репатрии́ровать *impf* & *pf*. **repatriation** *n* репатриа́ция.

repay *vt* отпла́чивать *impf*, отплати́ть *pf* (*person* +*dat*). **repayment** *n* отпла́та.

repeal *vt* отменя́ть *impf*, отмени́ть *pf*; *n* отме́на.

repeat *vt* & *i* повторя́ть(ся) *impf*, повтори́ть(ся) *pf*; *n* повторе́ние. **repeatedly** *adv* неоднокра́тно.

repel *vt* отта́лкивать *impf*, оттолкну́ть *pf*; (*enemy*) отража́ть *impf*, отрази́ть *pf*.

repent *vi* раска́иваться *impf*, раска́яться *pf*. **repentance** *n* раска́яние.

repentant *adj* раска́ивающийся.

repercussion *n* после́дствие.

repertoire *n* репертуа́р. **repertory** *n* (*store*) запа́с; (*repertoire*) репертуа́р; ~ **company** постоя́нная тру́ппа.

repetition *n* повторе́ние. **repetitious**, **repetitive** *adj* повторя́ющийся.

replace *vt* (*put back*) класть *impf*, положи́ть *pf* обра́тно; (*substitute*) заменя́ть *impf*, замени́ть *pf* (**by** +*instr*). **replacement** *n* заме́на.

replay *n* переигро́вка.

replenish *vt* пополня́ть *impf*, попо́лнить *pf*.

replete *adj* насы́щенный; (*sated*) сы́тый.

replica *n* ко́пия.

reply *vt & i* отвеча́ть *impf*, отве́тить *pf* (**to** на+*acc*); *n* отве́т.

report *vt* сообща́ть *impf*, сообщи́ть *pf*; *vi* докла́дывать *impf*, доложи́ть *pf*; (*present o.s.*) явля́ться *impf*, яви́ться *pf*; *n* сообще́ние; докла́д; (*school*) та́бель *m*; (*sound*) звук взры́ва, вы́стрела. **reporter** *n* корреспонде́нт.

repose *n* (*rest*) о́тдых; (*peace*) поко́й.

repository *n* храни́лище.

repossess *vt* изыма́ть *impf*, изъя́ть *pf* за непла́тёж.

reprehensible *adj* предосуди́тельный.

represent *vt* представля́ть *impf*; (*portray*) изобража́ть *impf*, изобрази́ть *pf*. **representation** *n* (*being represented*) представи́тельство; (*statement of case*) представле́ние; (*portrayal*) изображе́ние. **representative** *adj* изобража́ющий (**of** +*acc*); (*typical*) типи́чный; *n* представи́тель *m*.

repress *vt* подавля́ть *impf*, подави́ть *pf*. **repression** *n* подавле́ние, репре́ссия. **repressive** *adj* репресси́вный.

reprieve *vt* отсро́чивать *impf*, отсро́чить *pf* +*dat* приведе́ние в исполне́ние (сме́ртного) пригово́ра; *n* отсро́чка приведе́ния в исполне́ние (сме́ртного) пригово́ра; (*fig*) переды́шка.

reprimand *n* вы́говор; *vt* де́лать *impf*, с~ *pf* вы́говор +*dat*.

reprint *vt* переиздава́ть *impf*, переизда́ть *pf*; *n* переизда́ние.

reprisal *n* отве́тная ме́ра.

reproach *vt* упрека́ть *impf*, упрекну́ть *pf* (**with** в+*prep*). **reproachful** *adj* укори́зненный.

reproduce *vt* воспроизводи́ть *impf*, воспроизвести́ *pf*; *vi* размножа́ться *impf*, размно́житься *pf*. **reproduction** *n* (*action*) воспроизведе́ние; (*object*) репроду́кция; (*of offspring*) размноже́ние. **reproductive** *adj* воспроизводи́тельный.

reproof *n* вы́говор. **reprove** *vt* де́лать *impf* с~ *pf* вы́говор +*dat*.

reptile *n* пресмыка́ющееся *sb*.

republic *n* респу́блика. **republican** *adj* республика́нский; *n* республика́нец, -нка.

repudiate *vt* (*renounce*) отка́зываться *impf*, отказа́ться *pf* от+*gen*; (*reject*) отверга́ть *impf*, отве́ргнуть *pf*. **repudiation** *n* отка́з (**of** от+*gen*).

repugnance *n* отвраще́ние. **repugnant** *adj* проти́вный.

repulse *vt* отража́ть *impf*, отрази́ть *pf*. **repulsion** *n* отвраще́ние. **repulsive** *adj* отврати́тельный.

reputable *adj* по́льзующийся хоро́шей репута́цией. **reputation**, **repute** *n* репута́ция. **reputed** *adj* предполага́емый. **reputedly** *adv* по о́бщему мне́нию.

request *n* про́сьба; **by**, **on**, ~ по про́сьбе; *vt* проси́ть *impf*, по~ *pf* +*acc*, +*gen* (*person* +*acc*).

requiem *n* ре́квием.

require *vt* (*demand*; *need*) тре́бовать *impf*, по~ *pf* +*gen*; (*need*) нужда́ться *impf* в+*prep*. **requirement** *n* тре́бование; (*necessity*) потре́бность. **requisite** *adj* необходи́мый; *n* необходи́мая вещь. **requisition** *n* реквизи́ция; *vt* реквизи́ровать *impf* & *pf*.

resale *n* перепрода́жа.

rescind *vt* отменя́ть *impf*, отмени́ть *pf*.

rescue *vt* спаса́ть *impf*, спасти́ *pf*; *n* спасе́ние. **rescuer** *n* спаси́тель *m*.

research *n* иссле́дование (+*gen*); (*occupation*) иссле́довательская рабо́та; *vi*: ~ **into** иссле́довать *impf* & *pf* +*acc*. **researcher** *n* иссле́дователь *m*.

resemblance *n* схо́дство. **resemble**

vt походи́ть *impf* на+*acc.*

resent *vt* возмуща́ться *impf*, возмути́ться *pf.* **resentful** *adj* возмущённый. **resentment** *n* возмуще́ние.

reservation *n* (*doubt*) огово́рка; (*booking*) предвари́тельный зака́з; (*land*) резерва́ция. **reserve** *vt* (*keep*) резерви́ровать *impf* & *pf*; (*book*) зака́зывать *impf*, заказа́ть *pf*; *n* (*stock; mil*) запа́с, резе́рв; (*sport*) запасно́й игро́к; (*nature* ~ *etc.*) заповéдник; (*proviso*) огово́рка; (*self-restraint*) сде́ржанность; *attrib* запасно́й. **reserved** *adj* (*person*) сде́ржанный. **reservist** *n* резерви́ст. **reservoir** *n* (*for water*) водохрани́лище; (*for other fluids*) резервуа́р.

resettle *vt* переселя́ть *impf*, пересели́ть *pf*. **resettlement** *n* переселе́ние.

reshape *vt* видоизменя́ть *impf*, видоизмени́ть *pf*.

reshuffle *n* перестано́вка.

reside *vi* прожива́ть *impf*. **residence** *n* (*residing*) прожива́ние; (*abode*) местожи́тельство; (*official* ~ *etc.*) резиде́нция. **resident** *n* (*постоя́нный*) жи́тель *m*, ~ница; *adj* прожива́ющий; (*population*) постоя́нный. **residential** *adj* жило́й.

residual *adj* оста́точный. **residue** *n* оста́ток.

resign *vi* отка́зываться *impf*, отказа́ться *pf* от+*gen*; *vi* уходи́ть, уйти́ *pf* в отста́вку; ~ *o.s.* to покоря́ться *impf*, покори́ться *pf* +*dat.* **resignation** *n* отста́вка, заявле́ние об отста́вке; (*being resigned*) поко́рность. **resigned** *adj* поко́рный.

resilient *adj* выно́сливый.

resin *n* смола́.

resist *vt* сопротивля́ться *impf* +*dat*; (*temptation*) устоя́ть *pf* пе́ред+*instr.* **resistance** *n* сопротивле́ние. **resistant** *adj* сто́йкий.

resolute *adj* реши́тельный. **resolution** *n* (*character*) реши́тельность; (*vow*) заро́к; (*at meeting etc.*) резолю́ция; (*of problem*) разреше́ние. **resolve** *vt* (*decide*) реша́ть *impf*, реши́ть *pf*; (*settle*) разреша́ть *impf*, разреши́ть *pf*; *n* реши́тельность; (*decision*) реше́ние.

resonance *n* резона́нс. **resonant** *adj*

зву́чный.

resort *vi*: ~ to прибега́ть *impf*, прибе́гнуть *pf* к+*dat*; *n* (*place*) куро́рт; in the last ~ в кра́йнем слу́чае.

resound *vi* (*of sound etc.*) раздава́ться *impf*, разда́ться *pf*; (*of place*) оглаша́ться *impf*, огласи́ться *pf* (with +*instr*).

resource *n* (*usu pl*) ресу́рс. **resourceful** *adj* нахо́дчивый.

respect *n* (*relation*) отноше́ние; (*esteem*) уваже́ние; with ~ to что каса́ется+*gen*; *vt* уважа́ть *impf*. **respectability** *n* респекта́бельность. **respectable** *adj* прили́чный. **respectful** *adj* почти́тельный. **respective** *adj* свой. **respectively** *adv* соотве́тственно.

respiration *n* дыха́ние. **respirator** *n* респира́тор. **respiratory** *adj* дыха́тельный.

respite *n* переды́шка.

resplendent *adj* блиста́тельный.

respond *vi*: ~ to отвеча́ть *impf*, отве́тить *pf* на+*acc*; (*react*) реаги́ровать *impf*, про~, от~ *pf* на+*acc*. **response** *n* отве́т; (*reaction*) о́тклик. **responsibility** *n* отве́тственность; (*duty*) обя́занность. **responsible** *adj* отве́тственный (to пе́ред +*instr*, for за+*acc*); (*reliable*) надёжный. **responsive** *adj* отзы́вчивый.

rest[1] *vi* отдыха́ть *impf*, отдохну́ть *pf*; *vt* (*place*) класть *impf*, положи́ть *pf*; (*allow to* ~) дава́ть *impf*, дать *pf* о́тдых+*dat*; *n* (*repose*) о́тдых; (*peace*) поко́й; (*mus*) па́уза; (*support*) опо́ра.

rest[2] *n* (*remainder*) оста́ток; (*the others*) остальны́е *sb pl.*

restaurant *n* рестора́н.

restful *adj* успока́ивающий.

restitution *n* возвраще́ние.

restive *adj* беспоко́йный.

restless *adj* беспоко́йный.

restoration *n* реставра́ция; (*return*) восстановле́ние. **restore** *vt* реставри́ровать *impf* & *pf*; (*return*) восстана́вливать *impf*, восстанови́ть *pf*.

restrain *vt* уде́рживать *impf*, удержа́ть *pf* (from от+*gen*). **restraint** *n* сде́ржанность.

restrict *vt* ограни́чивать *impf*, ограни́чить *pf*. **restriction** *n* ограниче́ние. **restrictive** *adj* ограничи́тельный.

result vi сле́довать impf; происходи́ть impf (from из+gen); ~ in конча́ться impf, ко́нчиться pf +instr; n результа́т; as a ~ в результа́те (of +gen).

resume vt & i возобновля́ть(ся) impf, возобнови́ть(ся) pf. **résumé** n резюме́ neut indecl. **resumption** n возобновле́ние.

resurrect vt (fig) воскреша́ть impf, воскреси́ть pf. **resurrection** n (of the dead) воскресе́ние; (fig) воскреше́ние.

resuscitate vt приводи́ть impf, привести́ pf в созна́ние.

retail n ро́зничная прода́жа; attrib ро́зничный; adv в ро́зницу; vt продава́ть impf, прода́ть pf в ро́зницу; vi продава́ться impf в ро́зницу. **retailer** n ро́зничный торго́вец.

retain vt уде́рживать impf, удержа́ть pf.

retaliate vi отпла́чивать impf, отплати́ть pf тем же. **retaliation** n отпла́та, возме́здие.

retard vt замедля́ть impf, заме́длить pf. **retarded** adj отста́лый.

retention n удержа́ние. **retentive** adj (memory) хоро́ший.

reticence n сде́ржанность. **reticent** adj сде́ржанный.

retina n сетча́тка.

retinue n сви́та.

retire vi (withdraw) удаля́ться impf, удали́ться pf; (from office etc.) уходи́ть impf, уйти́ pf в отста́вку. **retired** adj в отста́вке. **retirement** n отста́вка. **retiring** adj скро́мный.

retort[1] vt отвеча́ть impf, отве́тить pf ре́зко; n возраже́ние.

retort[2] n (vessel) рето́рта.

retrace vt: ~ one's steps возвраща́ться impf, возврати́ться pf.

retract vt (draw in) втя́гивать impf, втяну́ть pf; (take back) брать impf, взять pf назад.

retreat vi отступа́ть impf, отступи́ть pf; n отступле́ние; (withdrawal) уедине́ние; (place) убе́жище.

retrenchment n сокраще́ние расхо́дов.

retrial n повто́рное слу́шание де́ла.

retribution n возме́здие.

retrieval n возвраще́ние; (comput) по́иск (информа́ции); vt брать impf,

взять pf обра́тно.

retrograde adj (fig) реакцио́нный.

retrospect n: in ~ ретроспекти́вно.

retrospective adj (law) име́ющий обра́тную си́лу.

return vt & i (give back; come back) возвраща́ть(ся) impf, возврати́ть(ся) impf, верну́ть(ся) pf; vt (elect) избира́ть impf, избра́ть pf; n возвраще́ние; возвра́т; (profit) при́быль; by ~ обра́тной по́чтой; in ~ взаме́н (for +gen); many happy ~s! с днём рожде́ния!; ~ match встре́тный матч; ~ ticket обра́тный биле́т.

reunion n встре́ча (друзе́й и т. п.); family ~ сбор всей семьи́. **reunite** vt воссоединя́ть impf, воссоедини́ть pf.

reuse vt сно́ва испо́льзовать impf & pf.

rev n оборо́т; vt & i: ~ up рвану́ть(ся) pf.

reveal vt обнару́живать impf, обнару́жить pf. **revealing** adj показа́тельный.

revel vi пирова́ть impf; ~ in наслажда́ться impf +instr.

revelation n открове́ние.

revenge vt: ~ o.s. мстить impf, отомсти́ть pf (for за+acc; on +dat); n месть.

revenue n дохо́д.

reverberate vi отража́ться impf. **reverberation** n отраже́ние; (fig) о́тзвук.

revere vt почита́ть impf. **reverence** n почте́ние. **Reverend** adj (in title) (его́) преподо́бие. **reverent(ial)** adj почти́тельный.

reverie n мечта́ние.

reversal n (change) измене́ние; (of decision) отме́на. **reverse** adj обра́тный; ~ gear за́дний ход; vt (change) изменя́ть impf, измени́ть pf; (decision) отменя́ть impf, отмени́ть pf; vi дава́ть impf, дать pf за́дний ход; n (the ~) обра́тное sb, противополо́жное sb; (~ gear) за́дний ход; (~ side) обра́тная сторона́. **reversible** adj обрати́мый; (cloth) двусторо́нний. **reversion** n возвраще́ние. **revert** vi возвраща́ться impf (to в+acc, к+dat); (law) переходи́ть impf, перейти́ pf (to к+dat).

review n (re-examination) пересмо́тр; (mil) пара́д; (survey) обзо́р;

(*criticism*) реце́нзия; *vt* (*re-examine*) пересма́тривать *impf*, пересмотре́ть *pf*; (*survey*) обозрева́ть *impf*, обозре́ть *pf*; (*troops etc.*) принима́ть *impf*, приня́ть *pf* пара́д+*gen*; (*book etc.*) реценз́ировать *impf*, про~ *pf*. **reviewer** *n* реценз́ент.

revise *vt* пересма́тривать *impf*, пересмотре́ть *pf*; исправля́ть *impf*, испра́вить *pf*; *vi* (*for exam*) гото́виться *impf* (for к+*dat*). **revision** *n* пересмо́тр, исправле́ние.

revival *n* возрожде́ние; (*to life etc.*) оживле́ние. **revive** *vt* возрожда́ть *impf*, возроди́ть *pf*; (*resuscitate*) оживля́ть *impf*, оживи́ть *pf*; *vi* ожива́ть *impf*, ожи́ть *pf*.

revoke *vt* отменя́ть *impf*, отмени́ть *pf*.

revolt *n* бунт; *vt* вызыва́ть *impf*, вы́звать *pf* отвраще́ние у+*gen*; *vi* бунтова́ть *impf*, взбунтова́ться *pf*. **revolting** *adj* отврати́тельный.

revolution *n* (*single turn*) оборо́т; (*polit*) револю́ция. **revolutionary** *adj* революцио́нный; *n* революцион́ер. **revolutionize** *vt* революциониз́ировать *impf* & *pf*. **revolve** *vt* & *i* враща́ть(ся) *impf*. **revolver** *n* револьве́р.

revue *n* ревю́ *neut indecl*.

revulsion *n* отвраще́ние.

reward *n* вознагражде́ние; *vt* (воз)награжда́ть *impf*, (воз)награди́ть *pf*.

rewrite *vt* перепи́сывать *impf*, переписа́ть *pf*; (*recast*) переде́лывать *impf*, переде́лать *pf*.

rhapsody *n* рапсо́дия.

rhetoric *n* рито́рика. **rhetorical** *adj* ритори́ческий.

rheumatic *adj* ревмати́ческий. **rheumatism** *n* ревмати́зм.

rhinoceros *n* носоро́г.

rhododendron *n* рододе́ндрон.

rhubarb *n* реве́нь *m*.

rhyme *n* ри́фма; *pl* (*verse*) стихи́ *m pl*; *vi* & *t* рифмова́ть(ся) *impf*.

rhythm *n* ритм. **rhythmic(al)** *adj* ритми́ческий, -чный.

rib *n* ребро́.

ribald *adj* непристо́йный.

ribbon *n* ле́нта.

rice *n* рис.

rich *adj* бога́тый; (*soil*) ту́чный;

(*food*) жи́рный. **riches** *n pl* бога́тство. **richly** *adv* (*fully*) вполне́.

rickety *adj* (*shaky*) расша́танный.

ricochet *vi* рикошети́ровать *impf* & *pf*.

rid *vt* освобожда́ть *impf*, освободи́ть *pf* (of от+*gen*); get ~ of избавля́ться *impf*, изба́виться *pf* от+*gen*. **riddance** *n*: good ~! ска́тертью доро́га!

riddle *n* (*enigma*) зага́дка.

riddled *adj*: ~ with изрешечённый; (*fig*) прони́занный.

ride *vi* е́здить *indet*, е́хать *det*, по~ *pf* (on horseback верхо́м); *vt* е́здить *indet*, е́хать *det*, по~ *pf* в, на+*prep*; *n* пое́здка, езда́. **rider** *n* вса́дник, -ица; (*clause*) дополне́ние.

ridge *n* хребе́т; (on cloth) ру́бчик; (of roof) конёк.

ridicule *n* насме́шка; *vt* осме́ивать *impf*, осмея́ть *pf*. **ridiculous** *adj* смешно́й.

riding *n* (horse-~) (верхова́я) езда́.

rife *predic* распространённый.

riff-raff *n* подо́нки (-ков) *pl*.

rifle *n* винто́вка; *vt* (*search*) обы́скивать *impf*, обыска́ть *pf*.

rift *n* тре́щина (also *fig*).

rig *vt* оснаща́ть *impf*, оснасти́ть *pf*; ~ out наряжа́ть *impf*, наряди́ть *pf*; ~ up скола́чивать *impf*, сколоти́ть *pf*; *n* бурова́я устано́вка. **rigging** *n* такела́ж.

right *adj* (*position*; *justified*; *polit*) пра́вый; (*correct*) пра́вильный; (the one wanted) тот; (*suitable*) подходя́щий; ~ angle прямо́й у́гол; *vt* исправля́ть *impf*, испра́вить *pf*; *n* пра́во; (what is just) справедли́вость; (~ side) пра́вая сторона́; (the R~; *polit*) пра́вые *sb pl*; be in the ~ быть пра́вым; by ~s по пра́ву; ~ of way пра́во прохо́да, прое́зда; *adv* (*straight*) пря́мо; (*exactly*) то́чно, как раз; (to the full) соверше́нно; (*correctly*) пра́вильно; как сле́дует; (on the ~) спра́ва от+*gen*; (to the ~) напра́во; ~ away сейча́с.

righteous *adj* (*person*) пра́ведный; (action) справедли́вый.

rightful *adj* зако́нный.

rigid *adj* жёсткий; (*strict*) стро́гий. **rigidity** *n* жёсткость; стро́гость.

rigmarole *n* канитель.

rigorous adj стро́гий. **rigour** n стро́гость.

rim n (of wheel) о́бод; (spectacles) опра́ва. **rimless** adj без опра́вы.

rind n кожура́.

ring[1] n кольцо́; (circle) круг; (boxing) ринг; (circus) (циркова́я) аре́на; ~ **road** кольцева́я доро́га; vt (encircle) окружа́ть impf, окружи́ть pf.

ring[2] vi (sound) звони́ть impf, по~ pf; (ring out, of shot etc.) раздава́ться impf, разда́ться pf; (of place) оглаша́ться impf, огласи́ться pf (with +instr); vt звони́ть impf, по~ pf в+acc; ~ **back** перезва́нивать impf, перезвони́ть pf; ~ **off** пове́сить pf тру́бку; ~ **up** звони́ть impf, по~ pf +dat; n звон, звоно́к.

ringleader n глава́рь m.

rink n като́к.

rinse vt полоска́ть impf, вы́~ pf; n полоска́ние.

riot n бунт; run ~ бу́йствовать impf; (of plants) бу́йно разраста́ться impf, разрасти́сь pf; vi бунтова́ть impf, взбунтова́ться pf. **riotous** adj бу́йный.

rip vt & i рва́ть(ся) impf; разо~ pf; ~ **up** разрыва́ть impf, разорва́ть pf; n проре́ха, разре́з.

ripe adj зре́лый, спе́лый. **ripen** v де́лать impf, с~ pf зре́лым; vi созрева́ть impf, созре́ть pf. **ripeness** n зре́лость.

ripple n рябь; vt & i покрыва́ть(ся) impf, покры́ть(ся) pf ря́бью.

rise vi поднима́ться impf, подня́ться pf; повыша́ться impf, повы́ситься pf; (get up) встава́ть impf, встать pf; (rebel) восстава́ть impf, восста́ть pf; (sun etc.) в(о)сходи́ть impf, взойти́; n подъём, возвыше́ние; (in pay) приба́вка; (of sun etc.) восхо́д. **riser** n: he is an early ~ он ра́но встаёт. **rising** n (revolt) восста́ние.

risk n риск; vt рискова́ть impf, рискну́ть pf +instr. **risky** adj риско́ванный. **risqué** adj непристо́йный.

rite n обря́д. **ritual** n ритуа́л; adj ритуа́льный.

rival n сопе́рник, -ица; adj сопе́рничающий; vt сопе́рничать impf с+instr. **rivalry** n сопе́рничество.

river n река́. **riverside** attrib прибре́жный.

rivet n заклёпка; vt заклёпывать impf, заклепа́ть pf; (fig) прико́вывать impf, прикова́ть pf (on k+dat).

road n доро́га; (street) у́лица; ~**block** загражде́ние на доро́ге; ~**map** (доро́жная) ка́рта; ~ **sign** доро́жный знак. **roadside** n обо́чина; attrib придоро́жный. **roadway** n мостова́я sb.

roam vt & i броди́ть impf (по+dat).

roar n (animal's) рёв; vi реве́ть impf.

roast n & i жа́рить(ся) impf, за~, из~ pf; adj жа́реный; ~ **beef** ро́стбиф; n жарко́е sb.

rob vt гра́бить impf, о~ pf; красть impf, y~ pf y+gen (of +acc); (deprive) лиша́ть impf, лиши́ть pf (of +gen). **robber** n граби́тель m. **robbery** n грабёж.

robe n (also pl) ма́нтия.

robin n мали́новка.

robot n ро́бот.

robust adj кре́пкий.

rock[1] n (geol) (го́рная) поро́да; (cliff etc.) скала́; (large stone) большо́й ка́мень m; on the ~s (in difficulty) на мели́; (drink) со льдом.

rock[2] vt & i кача́ть(ся) impf, качну́ть(ся) pf; n (mus) рок; ~**ing-chair** кача́лка; ~ **and roll** рок-н-ро́лл.

rockery n альпина́рий.

rocket n раке́та; vi подска́кивать impf, подскочи́ть pf.

rocky adj скали́стый; (shaky) ша́ткий.

rod n (stick) прут; (bar) сте́ржень m; (fishing-~) у́дочка.

rodent n грызу́н.

roe[1] n икра́; (soft) моло́ки (-о́к) pl.

roe[2] (-deer) n косу́ля.

rogue n плут.

role n роль.

roll[1] n (cylinder) руло́н; (register) рее́стр; (bread) бу́лочка; ~**-call** перекли́чка.

roll[2] vt & i ката́ть(ся) indet, кати́ть(ся) det, по~ pf; (~ up) свёртывать(ся) impf, сверну́ть(ся) pf; vt (~ out) dough) раска́тывать impf, раската́ть pf; vi (sound) греме́ть impf; ~ **over** перевора́чиваться impf, переверну́ться pf; n (of drums) бараба́нная дробь; (of thunder) раска́т.

roller n (small) ро́лик; (large) като́к.

(*for hair*) бигуди́ neut indecl; ~-skates коньки́ m pl на ро́ликах.

rolling adj (*of land*) холми́стый; ~-pin ска́лка. ~-stock подвижно́й соста́в.

Roman n ри́млянин, -я́нка; adj ри́мский; ~ **Catholic** (n) като́лик, -и́чка; (adj) ри́мско-католи́ческий.

romance n (*tale; love affair*) рома́н; (*quality*) рома́нтика.

Romanesque adj рома́нский.

Romania n Румы́ния. **Romanian** n румы́н, -ка; adj румы́нский.

romantic adj романти́чный, -ческий. **romanticism** n романти́зм.

romp vi вози́ться impf.

roof n кры́ша; ~ **of the mouth** нёбо; vt крыть impf, покры́ть pf.

rook[1] n (*chess*) ладья́.

rook[2] n (*bird*) грач.

room n ко́мната; (*in hotel*) но́мер; (*space*) ме́сто. **roomy** adj просто́рный.

roost n насе́ст.

root[1] n ко́рень m; **take** ~ укореня́ться impf, укорени́ться pf; vi пуска́ть impf, пусти́ть pf ко́рни; ~ **out** выры́вать impf, вы́рвать pf с ко́рнем; **rooted to the spot** прико́ванный к ме́сту.

root[2] vi (*rummage*) ры́ться impf; ~ **for** боле́ть impf за +acc.

rope n верёвка; ~-ladder верёвочная ле́стница; vt: ~ **in** (*enlist*) втя́гивать impf, втяну́ть pf; ~ **off** о(т)гора́живать impf, о(т)городи́ть pf верёвкой.

rosary n чётки (-ток) pl.

rose n ро́за; (*nozzle*) се́тка.

rosemary n розмари́н.

rosette n розе́тка.

rosewood n ро́зовое де́рево.

roster n расписа́ние дежу́рств.

rostrum n трибу́на.

rosy adj ро́зовый; (*cheeks*) румя́ный.

rot n гниль; (*nonsense*) вздор; vi гнить impf, c~ pf; vt гнои́ть impf, c~ pf.

rota n расписа́ние дежу́рств. **rotary** adj враща́тельный, ротацио́нный. **rotate** vt & i враща́ть(ся) impf. **rotation** n враще́ние; **in** ~ по о́череди.

rote n: **by** ~ наизу́сть.

rotten adj гнило́й; (*fig*) отврати́тельный.

rotund adj (*round*) кру́глый; (*plump*) по́лный.

rouble n рубль m.

rough adj (*uneven*) неро́вный; (*coarse*) гру́бый; (*sea*) бу́рный; (*approximate*) приблизи́тельный; ~ **copy** чернови́к; n: **the** ~ тру́дности f pl; vt: ~ **it** жить impf без удо́бств. **roughage** n гру́бая пи́ща. **roughly** adv гру́бо; (*approximately*) приблизи́тельно.

roulette n руле́тка.

round adj кру́глый; ~-shouldered суту́лый; n (~ *object*) круг; (*circuit; also pl*) обхо́д; (*sport*) тур, ра́унд; (*series*) ряд; (*ammunition*) патро́н; (*of applause*) взрыв; adv вокру́г; (*in a circle*) по кру́гу; **all** ~ круго́м; **all the year** ~ кру́глый год; prep вокру́г+gen; круго́м+gen; по+dat; ~ **the corner** (*motion*) за́ угол, (*position*) за угло́м; vt (*go* ~) огиба́ть impf, обогну́ть pf; ~ **off** (*complete*) заверша́ть impf, заверши́ть pf; ~ **up** сгоня́ть impf, согна́ть pf; ~-**up** заго́н; (*raid*) обла́ва. **roundabout** n (*merry-go-round*) карусе́ль; (*road junction*) кольцева́я тра́нспортная развя́зка; adj око́льный.

rouse vt буди́ть impf, раз~ pf; (*to action etc.*) побужда́ть impf, побуди́ть pf (**to** к+dat). **rousing** adj восто́рженный.

rout n (*defeat*) разгро́м.

route n маршру́т, путь m.

routine n заведённый поря́док, режи́м; adj устано́вленный; очередно́й.

rove vi скита́ться impf.

row[1] n (*line*) ряд.

row[2] n (*in boat*) гресть impf.

row[3] n (*dispute*) ссо́ра; (*noise*) шум; vi ссо́риться impf, по~ pf.

rowdy adj бу́йный.

royal adj короле́вский; (*majestic*) великоле́пный. **royalist** n рояли́ст; adj рояли́стский. **royalty** n член, чле́ны pl, короле́вской семьи́; (*fee*) а́вторский гонора́р.

rub vt & i тере́ть(ся) impf; vt (*polish; chafe*) натира́ть impf, натере́ть pf; (~ *dry*) вытира́ть impf, вы́тереть pf; ~ **in, on** втира́ть impf, втере́ть pf; ~ **out** стира́ть impf, стере́ть pf; ~ **it in** растравля́ть impf, растрави́ть pf ра́ну.

rubber n рези́на; (*eraser, also ~ band*) рези́нка; *attrib* рези́новый; ~**stamp** (*fig*) штампова́ть *impf*.
rubbish n му́сор; (*nonsense*) чепуха́.
rubble n ще́бень m.
rubella n красну́ха.
ruby n руби́н.
ruck vt (~ *up*) мять *impf*, из~, с~ *pf*.
rucksack n рюкза́к.
rudder n руль m.
ruddy adj (*face*) румя́ный; (*damned*) прокля́тый.
rude adj грубый. **rudeness** n гру́бость.
rudimentary adj рудимента́рный. **rudiments** n pl осно́вы f pl.
rueful adj печа́льный.
ruff n (*frill*) брыжи (-жей) pl; (*of feathers, hair*) кольцо́ (пе́рьев, ше́рсти) вокру́г ше́и.
ruffian n хулига́н.
ruffle n обо́рка; vt (*hair*) еро́шить *impf*, взъ~ pf; (*water*) ряби́ть *impf*; (*person*) смуща́ть *impf*, смути́ть pf.
rug n (*mat*) ковёр; (*wrap*) плед.
rugby n ре́гби neut indecl.
rugged adj (*rocky*) скали́стый.
ruin n (*downfall*) ги́бель; (*building, ruins*) разва́лины f pl, руи́ны f pl; vt губи́ть *impf*, по~ pf. **ruinous** adj губи́тельный.
rule n пра́вило; (*for measuring*) лине́йка; (*government*) правле́ние; as a ~ как пра́вило; vt & i пра́вить *impf* (+*instr*); (*decree*) постановля́ть *impf*, постанови́ть pf; ~ **out** исключа́ть *impf*, исключи́ть pf. **ruled** adj лино́ванный. **ruler** n (*person*) прави́тель m, ~ница; (*object*) лине́йка. **ruling** n (*of court etc.*) постановле́ние.
rum n (*drink*) ром.
Rumania(n) see Romania(n)
rumble vi громыха́ть *impf*; n громыха́ние.
ruminant n жва́чное (живо́тное) sb.
ruminate vi (*fig*) размышля́ть *impf* (over, on o+*prep*).
rummage vi ры́ться *impf*.
rumour n слух; vt: it is ~ed that хо́дят слу́хи (pl), что.
rump n крестец; ~ **steak** ромште́кс.
rumple vt мять *impf*, из~, с~ pf; (*hair*) еро́шить *impf*, взъ~ pf.

run vi бе́гать indet, бежа́ть det, по~ pf; (*work, of machines*) рабо́тать *impf*; (*ply, of bus etc.*) ходи́ть det, идти́ det; (*seek election*) выставля́ть *impf*, вы́ставить pf свою́ кандидату́ру; (*of play etc.*) идти́ *impf*; (*of ink, dye*) расплыва́ться *impf*, расплы́ться pf; (*flow*) течь *impf*; (*of document*) гласи́ть *impf*; vt (*manage; operate*) управля́ть *impf* +*instr*; (*a business etc.*) вести́ *impf*; (*of low*) иссяка́ть *impf*, исся́кнуть pf; ~ **risks** рискова́ть *impf*; ~ **across, into** (*meet*) встреча́ться *impf*, встре́титься pf c+*instr*; ~ **away** (*flee*) убега́ть *impf*, убежа́ть pf; ~ **down** (*knock down*) задави́ть pf; (*disparage*) принижа́ть *impf*, прини́зить pf; be ~ **down** (*of person*) переутоми́ться pf (*in past tense*); ~**down** (*decayed*) запу́щенный; ~ **in** (*engine*) обка́тывать *impf*, обката́ть pf; ~ **into** see ~ **across**; ~ **out** конча́ться *impf*, ко́нчиться pf; ~ **out of** истощáть *impf*, истощи́ть pf свой запа́с +*gen*; ~ **over** (*glance over*) бе́гло просма́тривать *impf*, просмотре́ть pf; (*injure*) задави́ть pf; ~ **through** (*pierce*) прока́лывать *impf*, проколо́ть pf; (*money*) прома́тывать *impf*, промота́ть pf; (*review*) повторя́ть *impf*, повтори́ть pf; ~ **to** (*reach*) (*of money*) хвата́ть *impf*, хвати́ть pf impers+gen на+acc; the money won't ~ to a car э́тих де́нег не хва́тит на маши́ну; ~ **up against** ната́лкиваться *impf*, натолкну́ться pf на +acc; n бег; (*sport*) перебе́жка; (*journey*) пое́здка; (*period*) полоса́; at a ~ бего́м; on the ~ в бега́х; ~ **on** большо́й спрос на+*acc*; in the long ~ в конце́ концо́в.
rung n ступе́нька.
runner n (*also tech*) бегу́н; (*of sledge*) по́лоз; (*bot*) побе́г; ~ **bean** фасо́ль; ~**-up** уча́стник, заня́вший второ́е ме́сто. **running** n бег; (*management*) управле́ние (*of +instr*); be in the ~ име́ть *impf* ша́нсы; adj бегу́щий; (*of* ~) бегово́й; (*after* pl n, *in succession*) подря́д; ~ **commentary** репорта́ж; ~ **water** водопрово́д. **runway** n взлётно-поса́дочная полоса́.
rupee n ру́пия.
rupture n разры́в; vt & i прорыь-

ва́ть(ся) *impf*, прорва́ть(ся) *pf*.
rural *adj* се́льский.
ruse *n* уло́вка.
rush[1] *n* (*bot*) тростни́к.
rush[2] *vt & i* (*hurry*) торопи́ть(ся) *impf*, по~ *pf*; *vi* (*dash*) броса́ться *impf*, бро́ситься *pf*; (*of water*) нести́сь *impf*; по~ *pf*; *vt* (*to hospital etc.*) умча́ть *pf*; *n* (*of blood etc.*) прили́в; (*hurry*) спе́шка; be in a ~ торопи́ться *impf*; ~-hour(s) часы́ *m pl* пик.
Russia *n* Росси́я. **Russian** *n* ру́сский *sb*; *adj* (*of ~ nationality, culture*) ру́сский; (*of ~ State*) росси́йский.
rust *n* ржа́вчина; *vi* ржа́веть *impf*, за~, по~ *pf*.
rustic *adj* дереве́нский.
rustle *n* ше́лест, шо́рох, шуршанье; *vi & t* шелесте́ть *impf* (+*instr*); ~ up раздобыва́ть *impf*; раздобы́ть *pf*.
rusty *adj* ржа́вый.
rut *n* колея́.
ruthless *adj* безжа́лостный.
rye *n* рожь; *attrib* ржано́й.

S

Sabbath *n* (*Jewish*) суббо́та; (*Christian*) воскресе́нье. **sabbatical** *n* годи́чный о́тпуск.
sable *n* со́боль.
sabotage *n* диве́рсия; *vt* саботи́ровать *impf & pf*. **saboteur** *n* диверса́нт.
sabre *n* са́бля.
sachet *n* упако́вка.
sack[1] *vt* (*plunder*) разгра́бить *pf*.
sack[2] *n* мешо́к; (*dismissal*): be the ~ быть уво́ленным; *vt* увольня́ть *impf*, уво́лить *pf*. **sacking** *n* (*hessian*) мешкови́на.
sacrament *n* та́инство; (*Eucharist*) прича́стие. **sacred** *adj* свяще́нный, свято́й. **sacrifice** *n* же́ртва; *vt & i* же́ртвовать *impf*, по~ *pf* +*instr*. **sacrilege** *n* святота́тство. **sacrosanct** *adj* свяще́нный.
sad *adj* печа́льный, гру́стный. **sadden** *vt* печа́лить *impf*, о~ *pf*.
saddle *n* седло́; *vt* седла́ть *impf*, о~ *pf*; (*burden*) обременя́ть *impf*, обремени́ть *pf* (with +*instr*).
sadism *n* сади́зм. **sadist** *n* сади́ст.

sadistic *adj* сади́стский.
sadness *n* печа́ль, грусть.
safe *n* сейф; *adj* (*unharmed*) невреди́мый; (*out of danger*) в безопа́сности; (*secure*) безопа́сный; (*reliable*) надёжный; ~ and sound цел и невреди́м. **safeguard** *n* предохрани́тельная ме́ра; *vt* предохраня́ть *impf*, предохрани́ть *pf*. **safety** *n* безопа́сность; ~-belt реме́нь *m* безопа́сности; ~ pin англи́йская була́вка; ~-valve предохрани́тельный кла́пан.
sag *vi* (*of rope, curtain*) провиса́ть *impf*, прови́снуть *pf*; (*of ceiling*) прогиба́ться *impf*, прогну́ться *pf*.
saga *n* са́га.
sage[1] *n* (*herb*) шалфе́й.
sage[2] *n* (*person*) мудре́ц; *adj* му́дрый.
Sagittarius *n* Стреле́ц.
sail *n* па́рус; *vt* (*a ship*) управля́ть *impf* +*instr*; *vi* пла́вать *indet*, плыть *det*; (*depart*) отплыва́ть *impf*, отплы́ть *pf*. **sailing** *n* (*sport*) па́русный спорт; ~-ship па́русное су́дно. **sailor** *n* матро́с, моря́к.
saint *n* свято́й *sb*. **saintly** *adj* свято́й.
sake *n*: for the ~ of ра́ди+*gen*.
salad *n* сала́т; ~-dressing припра́ва к сала́ту.
salami *n* саля́ми *f indecl*.
salary *n* жа́лованье.
sale *n* прода́жа; (*also amount sold*) сбыт (*no pl*); (*with reduced prices*) распрода́жа; be for ~ продава́ться *impf*. **saleable** *adj* хо́дкий. **salesman** *n* продаве́ц. **saleswoman** *n* продавщи́ца.
salient *adj* основно́й.
saliva *n* слюна́.
sallow *adj* желтова́тый.
salmon *n* лосо́сь *m*.
salon *n* сало́н. **saloon** *n* (*on ship*) сало́н; (*car*) седа́н; (*bar*) бар.
salt *n* соль; ~-cellar соло́нка; ~ water морска́я вода́; ~-water морско́й; *adj* солёный; *vt* соли́ть *impf*, по~ *pf*. **salty** *adj* солёный.
salutary *adj* благотво́рный. **salute** *n* отда́ча че́сти; (*with guns*) салю́т; *vt & i* отдава́ть *impf*, отда́ть *pf* честь (+*dat*).
salvage *n* спасе́ние; *vt* спаса́ть *impf*, спасти́ *pf*.

salvation *n* спасе́ние; S~ Army А́рмия спасе́ния.

salve *n* мазь; *vt*: ~ one's conscience успока́ивать *impf*, успоко́ить *pf* со́весть.

salvo *n* залп.

same *adj*: the ~ тот же (са́мый); (*applying to both or all*) оди́н; (*identical*) одина́ковый; *pron*: the ~ одно́ и то́ же, то же са́мое; *adv*: the ~ таки́м же о́бразом, так же; all the ~ всё-таки, тем не ме́нее. **sameness** *n* однообра́зие.

samovar *n* самова́р.

sample *n* образе́ц; *vt* про́бовать *impf*, по~ *pf*.

sanatorium *n* санато́рий.

sanctify *vt* освяща́ть *impf*, освяти́ть *pf*. **sanctimonious** *adj* ха́нжеский.

sanction *n* са́нкция; *vt* санкциони́ровать *impf* & *pf*. **sanctity** *n* (*holiness*) свя́тость; (*sacredness*) свяще́нность. **sanctuary** *n* святи́лище; (*refuge*) убе́жище; (*for wild life*) запове́дник.

sand *n* песо́к; *vt* (~ *down*) шку́рить *impf*, по~ *pf*; ~dune дюна.

sandal *n* санда́лия.

sandalwood *n* санда́ловое де́рево.

sandbank *n* о́тмель.

sandpaper *n* шку́рка; *vt* шлифова́ть *impf*, от~ *pf* шку́ркой.

sandstone *n* песча́ник.

sandwich *n* бутербро́д; *vt*: ~ between втискивать *impf*, вти́снуть *pf* ме́жду+*instr*.

sandy *adj* (*of sand*) песча́ный; (*like sand*) песо́чный; (*hair*) рыжева́тый.

sane *adj* норма́льный; (*sensible*) разу́мный.

sang-froid *n* самооблада́ние.

sanguine *adj* оптимисти́ческий.

sanitary *adj* санита́рный; гигиени́ческий; ~ towel гигиени́ческая поду́шка. **sanitation** *n* (*conditions*) санита́рные усло́вия *neut pl*; (*system*) водопрово́д и канализа́ция. **sanity** *n* психи́ческое здоро́вье; (*good sense*) здра́вый смысл.

sap *n* (*bot*) сок; *vt* (*exhaust*) истоща́ть *impf*, истощи́ть *pf*.

sapling *n* са́женец.

sapphire *n* сапфи́р.

sarcasm *n* сарка́зм. **sarcastic** *adj* сарка́стический.

sardine *n* сарди́на.

sardonic *adj* сардони́ческий.

sash[1] *n* (*scarf*) куша́к.

sash[2] *n* (*frame*) скользя́щая ра́ма; ~-window подъёмное окно́.

satanic *adj* сатани́нский.

satchel *n* ра́нец, су́мка.

satellite *n* спу́тник, сателли́т (*also fig*); ~ dish параболи́ческая анте́нна; таре́лка (*coll*); ~ TV спу́тниковое телеви́дение.

satiate *vt* насыща́ть *impf*, насы́тить *pf*.

satin *n* атла́с.

satire *n* сати́ра. **satirical** *adj* сатири́ческий. **satirist** *n* сати́рик. **satirize** *vt* высме́ивать *impf*, вы́смеять *pf*.

satisfaction *n* удовлетворе́ние. **satisfactory** *adj* удовлетвори́тельный. **satisfy** *vt* удовлетворя́ть *impf*, удовлетвори́ть *pf*; (*hunger, curiosity*) утоля́ть *impf*, утоли́ть *pf*.

saturate *vt* насыща́ть *impf*, насы́тить *pf*; I got ~d (*by rain*) я промо́к до ни́тки. **saturation** *n* насыще́ние.

Saturday *n* суббо́та.

sauce *n* со́ус; (*cheek*) на́глость. **saucepan** *n* кастрю́ля. **saucer** *n* блю́дце. **saucy** *adj* на́глый.

Saudi *n* сау́довец, -вка; *adj* сау́довский. **Saudi Arabia** *n* Сау́довская Ара́вия.

sauna *n* фи́нская ба́ня.

saunter *vi* прогу́ливаться *impf*.

sausage *n* соси́ска; (*salami-type*) колбаса́.

savage *adj* ди́кий; (*fierce*) свире́пый; (*cruel*) жесто́кий; *n* дика́рь *m*; *vt* искуса́ть *pf*. **savagery** *n* ди́кость; жесто́кость.

save *vt* (*rescue*) спаса́ть *impf*, спасти́ *pf*; (*money*) копи́ть *impf*, на~ *pf*; (*put aside, keep*) бере́чь *impf*; (*avoid using*) эконо́мить *impf*, с~ *pf*; *vi*: ~ up копи́ть *impf*, на~ *pf* де́ньги. **savings** *n pl* сбереже́ния *neut pl*; ~ bank сберега́тельная ка́сса. **saviour** *n* спаси́тель *m*.

savour *vt* смакова́ть *impf*.

savoury *adj* пика́нтный; (*fig*) поря́дочный.

saw *n* пила́; *vt* пили́ть *impf*; ~ up распи́ливать *impf*, распили́ть *pf*. **sawdust** *n* опи́лки (-лок) *pl*.

saxophone *n* саксофо́н.

say vt говори́ть impf, сказа́ть pf; to
~ nothing of не говоря́ уже́ о+prep;
that is to ~ то есть; (let us) ска́-
жем; it is said (that) говоря́т (что);
n (opinion) мне́ние; (influence) влия́-
ние; have one's ~ вы́сказаться pf.
saying n погово́рка.

scab n (on wound) струп; (polit)
штрейкбре́хер.

scabbard n но́жны (gen -жен) pl.

scaffold n эшафо́т. scaffolding n
леса́ (-со́в) pl.

scald vt обва́ривать impf, обвари́ть
pf.

scale n (ratio) масшта́б; (grading)
шкала́; (mus) га́мма; vt (climb)
взбира́ться impf, взобра́ться pf
на+acc; ~ down понижа́ть impf,
пони́зить pf.

scales¹ n pl (of fish) чешуя́ (collect).

scales² n pl весы́ (-со́в) pl.

scallop n гребешо́к; (decoration)
фесто́н.

scalp n ко́жа головы́.

scalpel n ска́льпель m.

scaly adj чешу́йчатый; (of boiler
etc.) покры́тый на́кипью.

scamper vi бы́стро бе́гать impf;
(frolic) резви́ться impf.

scan vt & i (verse) сканди́ровать(ся)
impf; vt (intently) рассма́тривать
impf, (quickly) просма́тривать impf,
просмотре́ть pf; (med) просве́чи-
вать impf, просвети́ть pf; n просве́-
чивание.

scandal n сканда́л; (gossip) спле́тни
(-тен) pl. scandalize vt шоки́ровать
impf & pf. scandalous adj сканда́-
льный.

Scandinavia n Сканди́навия. Scandinavian adj скандина́вский.

scanty adj ску́дный.

scapegoat n козёл отпуще́ния.

scar n шрам; vt оставля́ть impf,
оста́вить pf шрам на+prep.

scarce adj дефици́тный; (rare)
ре́дкий. scarcely adv едва́. scarcity
n дефици́т; ре́дкость.

scare vt пуга́ть impf, ис~, на~ pf; ~
away, off отпу́гивать impf, отпуг-
ну́ть pf; n па́ника. scarecrow n пу́-
гало.

scarf n шарф.

scarlet adj (n) а́лый (цвет).

scathing adj уничтожа́ющий.

scatter vt & i рассыпа́ть(ся) impf,
рассы́пать(ся) pf; (disperse) рассé-
ивать(ся) impf, рассе́ять(ся) pf; ~
brained ветреный. scattered adj раз-
бро́санный; (sporadic) отде́льный.

scavenge vi ры́ться impf в отбро́-
сах. scavenger n (person) мусорщик; (animal) живо́тное sb, пита́-
ющееся па́далью.

scenario n сцена́рий. scene n (place
of disaster etc.) ме́сто; (place of action) ме́сто де́йствия; (view) вид,
пейза́ж; (picture) карти́на; (theat)
сце́на, явле́ние; (incident) сце́на;
behind the ~s за кули́сами; make a
~ устра́ивать impf, устро́ить pf
сце́ну. scenery n (theat) декора́ция;
(landscape) пейза́ж. scenic adj жи-
вопи́сный.

scent n (smell) арома́т; (perfume)
духи́ (-хо́в) pl; (trail) след. scented
adj души́стый.

sceptic n ске́птик. sceptical adj скеп-
ти́ческий. scepticism n скептици́зм.

schedule n (timetable) расписа́ние;
vt составля́ть impf, соста́вить pf
расписа́ние +gen.

schematic adj схемати́ческий.
scheme n (plan) прое́кт; (intrigue)
махина́ция; vi интригова́ть impf.

schism n раско́л.

schizophrenia n шизофрени́я. schizo-
phrenic adj шизофрени́ческий; n
шизофре́ник.

scholar n учёный sb: scholarly adj
учёный. scholarship n учёность;
(payment) стипе́ндия.

school n шко́ла; attrib шко́льный;
vt (train) приуча́ть impf, приучи́ть
pf (to к+dat, +inf). school-book n
уче́бник. schoolboy n шко́льник.
schoolgirl n шко́льница. schooling
n обуче́ние. school-leaver n вы-
пускни́к, -и́ца. school teacher n
учи́тель m, -ница.

schooner n шху́на.

sciatica n и́шиас.

science n нау́ка; ~ fiction нау́чная
фанта́стика. scientific adj нау́ч-
ный. scientist n учёный sb.

scintillating adj блиста́тельный.

scissors n pl но́жницы (-ц) pl.

scoff vi (mock) смея́ться impf (at
над+instr).

scold vt брани́ть impf, вы́~ pf.

scoop n (large) черпа́к; (ice-cream ~) ло́жка для моро́женого; vt (~ out, up) вычёрпывать impf, вы́черпать pf.

scooter n (motor ~) мотоpólep.

scope n (range) преде́лы m pl; (chance) возмо́жность.

scorch vt (fingers) обжига́ть impf, обже́чь pf; (clothes) сжига́ть impf, сжечь pf.

score n (of points etc.) счёт; (mus) партиту́ра; pl (great numbers) мно́жество; vt (notch) де́лать impf, c~ pf зару́бки на+prep; (points etc.) получа́ть impf, получи́ть pf; (mus) оркестрова́ть impf & pf; vi (keep ~) вести́ impf, c~ pf счёт. **scorer** n счётчик.

scorn n презре́ние; vt презира́ть impf презре́ть pf. **scornful** adj презри́тельный.

Scorpio n Скорпио́н.

scorpion n скорпио́н.

Scot n шотла́ндец, -дка. **Scotch** n (whisky) шотла́ндское ви́ски neut indecl. **Scotland** n Шотла́ндия. **Scots, Scottish** adj шотла́ндский.

scoundrel n подле́ц.

scour[1] vt (cleanse) отчища́ть impf, отчи́стить pf.

scour[2] vt & i (rove) ры́скать impf (по+dat).

scourge n бич.

scout n разве́дчик; (S~) бойска́ут; vi: ~ about разы́скивать impf (for +acc).

scowl vi хму́риться impf, на~ pf; n хму́рый взгляд.

scrabble vi: ~ about ры́ться impf.

scramble vi кара́бкаться impf, вс~ pf; (struggle) дра́ться impf (for за +acc); ~d eggs яи́чница-болту́нья.

scrap[1] n (fragment etc.) кусо́чек; pl оста́тки m pl; pl (of food) объе́дки (-ков) pl; ~ metal металлоло́м; vt сдава́ть impf, сдать pf в утиль.

scrap[2] n (fight) дра́ка; vi дра́ться impf.

scrape vt скрести́ impf; (graze) цара́пать impf, o~ pf; ~ off отскреба́ть impf, отскрести́ pf; ~ through (exam) с трудо́м выде́рживать impf, вы́держать pf; ~ together наскреба́ть impf, наскрести́ pf.

scratch vt цара́пать impf, o~ pf; vt & i (when itching) чеса́ть(ся) impf, по~ pf; n цара́пина.

scrawl n кара́кули f pl; vt писа́ть impf, на~ pf кара́кулями.

scrawny adj сухопа́рый.

scream n крик; vi крича́ть impf, кри́кнуть pf.

screech n визг; vi визжа́ть impf.

screen n ши́рма; (cin, TV) экра́н; ~ play сцена́рий; vt (protect) защища́ть impf, защити́ть pf; (hide) укрыва́ть impf, укры́ть pf; (show film etc.) демонстри́ровать impf & pf; (check on) проверя́ть impf, прове́рить pf; ~ off отгора́живать impf, отгороди́ть pf ши́рмой.

screw n винт; vt (~ on) приви́нчивать impf, привинти́ть pf; (~ up) зави́нчивать impf, завинти́ть pf; (crumple) ко́мкать impf, c~ pf; ~ up one's eyes щу́риться impf, co~ pf. **screwdriver** n отвёртка.

scribble vt строчи́ть impf, на~ pf; n кара́кули f pl.

script n (of film etc.) сцена́рий; (of speech etc.) текст; (writing system) письмо́; ~-writer сценари́ст.

Scripture n свяще́нное писа́ние.

scroll n сви́ток; (design) завито́к.

scrounge vt (cadge) стреля́ть impf, стрельну́ть pf; vi попроша́йничать impf.

scrub[1] n (brushwood) куста́рник; (area) за́росли f pl.

scrub[2] vt мыть impf, вы́~ pf щёткой.

scruff n: by the ~ of the neck за ши́ворот.

scruffy adj обо́дранный.

scrum n схва́тка вокру́г мяча́.

scruple n (also pl) колеба́ния neut pl; угрызе́ния neut pl со́вести. **scrupulous** adj скрупулёзный.

scrutinize vt рассма́тривать impf. **scrutiny** n рассмотре́ние.

scuffed adj поцара́панный.

scuffle n потасо́вка.

sculpt vt вая́ть impf, из~ pf. **sculptor** n ску́льптор. **sculpture** n скульпту́ра.

scum n на́кипь.

scurrilous adj непристо́йный.

scurry vi поспе́шно бе́гать indet, бежа́ть det.

scuttle[1] n (coal ~) ведёрко для угля.

scuttle[2] vi (run away) удирать impf, удрать pf.

scythe n коса.

sea n море; attrib морской; ~ front набережная sb; ~-gull чайка; ~-level уровень m моря; ~-lion морской лев; ~-shore побережье. **sea-board** n побережье. **seafood** n продукты m pl моря.

seal[1] n (on document etc.) печать; vt скреплять impf, скрепить pf печатью; (close) запечатывать impf, запечатать pf; ~ up заделывать impf, заделать pf

seal[2] n (zool) тюлень m; (fur-~) котик.

seam n шов; (geol) пласт.

seaman n моряк, матрос.

seamless adj без шва.

seamstress n швея.

seance n спиритический сеанс.

seaplane n гидросамолёт.

searing adj палящий.

search vt обыскивать impf, обыскать pf; vi искать impf (for +acc); n поиски m pl; обыск; ~-party поисковая группа. **searching** adj (look) испытующий. **searchlight** n прожектор.

seasick adj: I was ~ меня укачало. **seaside** n берег моря.

season n сезон; (one of four) время neut года; ~ ticket сезонный билет; vt (flavour) приправлять impf, приправить pf. **seasonable** adj по сезону; (timely) своевременный. **seasonal** adj сезонный. **seasoning** n приправа.

seat n (place) место; (of chair) сиденье; (chair) стул; (bench) скамейка; (of trousers) зад; ~ belt привязной ремень m; vt сажать impf, посадить pf; (of room etc.) вмещать impf, вместить pf; be ~ed садиться impf, сесть pf.

seaweed n морская водоросль.

secateurs n pl секатор.

secede vi откалываться impf, отколоться pf. **secession** n откол.

secluded adj укромный. **seclusion** n укромность.

second[1] adj второй; ~-class второклассный; ~-hand подержанный; (of information) из вторых рук; ~-

rate второразрядный; ~ sight ясновидение; on ~ thoughts взвесив всё ещё раз; have ~ thoughts передумывать impf, передумать pf (about +acc); n второй sb; (date) второе (число) sb; (time) секунда; pl (comm) товар второго сорта; ~ hand (of clock) секундная стрелка; vt (support) поддерживать impf, поддержать pf; (transfer) откомандировывать impf откомандировать pf. **secondary** adj вторичный, второстепенный; (education) средний. **secondly** adv во-вторых.

secrecy n секретность. **secret** n тайна, секрет; adj тайный, секретный; (hidden) потайной.

secretarial adj секретарский. **secretariat** n секретариат. **secretary** n секретарь m, -рша; (minister) министр.

secrete vt (conceal) укрывать impf, укрыть pf; (med) выделять impf, выделить pf. **secretion** n укрывание; (med) выделение. **secretive** adj скрытный.

sect n секта. **sectarian** adj сектантский.

section n секция; (of book) раздел; (geom) сечение. **sector** n сектор.

secular adj светский. **secularization** n секуляризация.

secure adj (safe) безопасный; (firm) надёжный; (emotionally) уверенный; vt (fasten) закреплять impf, закрепить pf; (guarantee) обеспечивать impf, обеспечить pf; (obtain) доставать impf, достать pf. **security** n безопасность; (guarantee) залог; pl ценные бумаги f pl.

sedate adj степенный.

sedation n успокоение. **sedative** n успокаивающее средство.

sedentary adj сидячий.

sediment n осадок.

seduce vt соблазнять impf, соблазнить pf. **seduction** n обольщение. **seductive** adj соблазнительный.

see vt & i видеть impf, у~ pf; vt (watch, look) смотреть impf, по~ pf; (find out) узнавать impf, узнать pf; (understand) понимать impf, понять pf; (meet) видеться impf, у~ pf c+instr; (imagine) представлять impf, представить pf себе; (escort,

~ *off*) провожа́ть *impf*, проводи́ть *pf*; ~ **about** (*attend to*) забо́титься *impf*, по~ *pf* o+*prep*; ~ **through** (*fig*) ви́деть *impf*, наскво́зь+*acc*.

seed *n* се́мя *neut*. **seedling** *n* се́янец; *pl* расса́да. **seedy** *adj* (*shabby*) потрёпанный.

seeing (**that**) *conj* ввиду́ того́, что.

seek *vt* иска́ть *impf* +*acc*, *gen*.

seem *vi* каза́ться *impf*, по~ *pf* (+*instr*). **seemingly** *adv* по-ви́димому.

seemly *adj* прили́чный.

seep *vi* проса́чиваться *impf*, просочи́ться *pf*.

seethe *vi* кипе́ть *impf*, вс~ *pf*.

segment *n* отре́зок; (*of orange etc.*) до́лька; (*geom*) сегме́нт.

segregate *vt* отделя́ть *impf*, отдели́ть *pf*. **segregation** *n* сегрега́ция.

seismic *adj* сейсми́ческий.

seize *vt* хвата́ть *impf*, схвати́ть *pf*; *vi*: ~ **up** заеда́ть *impf*, зае́сть *pf impers*+*acc*; ~ **upon** ухва́тываться *impf*, ухвати́ться за+*acc*. **seizure** *n* захва́т; (*med*) припа́док.

seldom *adv* ре́дко.

select *adj* и́збранный; *vt* отбира́ть *impf*, отобра́ть *pf*. **selection** *n* (*choice*) вы́бор. **selective** *adj* разбо́рчивый.

self *n* со́бственное «я» *neut indecl*.

self- *in comb* само-; ~**absorbed** эгоцентри́чный; ~**assured** самоуве́ренный; ~**catering** (**accommodation**) жильё с ку́хней; ~**centred** эгоцентри́чный; ~**confessed** открове́нный; ~**confidence** самоуве́ренность; ~**confident** самоуве́ренный; ~**conscious** засте́нчивый; ~**contained** (*person*) незави́симый; (*flat etc.*) отде́льный; ~**control** самооблада́ние; ~**defence** самозащи́та; ~**denial** самоотрече́ние; ~**determination** самоопределе́ние; ~**effacing** скро́мный; ~**employed person** незави́симый предпринима́тель *m*; ~**esteem** самоуваже́ние; ~**evident** очеви́дный; ~**governing** самоуправля́ющий; ~**help** самопо́мощь; ~**importance** самомне́ние; ~**imposed** доброво́льный; ~**indulgent** изба́лованный; ~**interest** со́бственный интере́с; ~**pity** жа́лость к себе́; ~**portrait** автопортре́т; ~**preservation** самосохране́ние; ~**reliance** само-

стоя́тельность; ~**respect** самоуваже́ние; ~**righteous** *adj* ха́нжеский; ~**sacrifice** самопоже́ртвование; ~**satisfied** самодово́льный; ~**service** самообслу́живание (*attrib*: *in gen after n*); ~**styled** самозва́нный; ~**sufficient** самостоя́тельный.

selfish *adj* эгоисти́чный. **selfless** *adj* самоотве́рженный.

sell *vt* & *i* продава́ть(ся) *impf*, прода́ть(ся) *pf*; *vt* (*deal in*) торгова́ть *impf* +*instr*; ~ **out** распродава́ть *impf*, распрода́ть *pf*. **seller** *n* продаве́ц. **selling** *n* прода́жа. **sell-out** *n*: the play was a ~ пье́са прошла́ с аншла́гом.

Sellotape *n* (*propr*) ли́пкая ле́нта.

semantic *adj* семанти́ческий. **semantics** *n* сема́нтика.

semblance *n* ви́димость.

semen *n* се́мя *neut*.

semi- *in comb* полу-; ~**detached house** дом, разделённый о́бщей стено́й. **semibreve** *n* це́лая но́та. **semicircle** *n* полукру́г. **semicircular** *adj* полукру́глый. **semicolon** *n* то́чка с запято́й. **semiconductor** *n* полупроводни́к. **semifinal** *n* полуфина́л.

seminar *n* семина́р. **seminary** *n* семина́рия.

semiquaver *n* шестна́дцатая но́та.

semitone *n* полуто́н.

senate *n* сена́т; (*univ*) сове́т. **senator** *n* сена́тор.

send *vt* посыла́ть *impf*, посла́ть *pf* (**for** за+*instr*); ~ **off** отправля́ть *impf*, отпра́вить *pf*; ~**off** про́воды (-дов) *pl*. **sender** *n* отправи́тель *m*.

senile *adj* ста́рческий. **senility** *n* ста́рческое слабоу́мие.

senior *adj* (*n*) ста́рший (*sb*); ~ **citizen** стари́к, стару́ха. **seniority** *n* старшинство́.

sensation *n* сенса́ция; (*feeling*) ощуще́ние. **sensational** *adj* сенсацио́нный.

sense *n* чу́вство; (*good* ~) здра́вый смысл; (*meaning*) смысл; *pl* (*sanity*) ум; *vt* чу́вствовать *impf*. **senseless** *adj* бессмы́сленный.

sensibility *n* чувстви́тельность; *pl* самолю́бие. **sensible** *adj* благоразу́мный. **sensitive** *adj* чувстви́тельный; (*touchy*) оби́дчивый. **sensitiv-**

ity *n* чувстви́тельность.

sensory *adj* чувстви́тельный.

sensual, sensuous *adj* чу́вственный.

sentence *n* (*gram*) предложе́ние; (*law*) пригово́р; *vt* пригова́ривать *impf*, приговори́ть *pf* (to к+*dat*).

sentiment *n* (*feeling*) чу́вство; (*opinion*) мне́ние. **sentimental** *adj* сентимента́льный. **sentimentality** *n* сентимента́льность.

sentry *n* часово́й *sb*.

separable *adj* отдели́мый. **separate** *adj* отде́льный; *vt* & *i* отделя́ть(ся) *impf*, отдели́ть(ся) *pf*. **separation** *n* отделе́ние. **separatism** *n* сепарати́зм. **separatist** *n* сепарати́ст.

September *n* сентя́брь *m*; *adj* сентя́брьский.

septic *adj* септи́ческий.

sepulchre *n* моги́ла.

sequel *n* (*result*) после́дствие; (*continuation*) продолже́ние. **sequence** *n* после́довательность; ~ of events ход собы́тий.

sequester *vt* секвестрова́ть *impf* & *pf*.

sequin *n* блёстка.

Serb(ian) *adj* се́рбский; *n* серб, ~ка. **Serbia** *n* Се́рбия. **Serbo-Croat(ian)** *adj* сербскохорва́тский.

serenade *n* серена́да.

serene *adj* споко́йный. **serenity** *n* споко́йствие.

serf *n* крепостно́й *sb*. **serfdom** *n* крепостно́е пра́во.

sergeant *n* сержа́нт.

serial *adj*: ~ **number** сери́йный но́мер; *n* (*story*) рома́н с продолже́нием; (*broadcast*) сери́йная постано́вка. **serialize** *vt* ста́вить *impf*, по~ *pf* в не́скольких частя́х. **series** *n* (*succession*) ряд; (*broadcast*) се́рия переда́ч.

serious *adj* серьёзный. **seriousness** *n* серьёзность.

sermon *n* про́поведь.

serpent *n* змея́.

serrated *adj* зазу́бренный.

serum *n* сы́воротка.

servant *n* слуга́ *m*, служа́нка. **serve** *vt* служи́ть *impf*, по~ *pf* +*dat* (as, for +*instr*); (*attend to*) обслу́живать *impf*, обслужи́ть *pf*; (*food; ball*) подава́ть *impf*, пода́ть *pf*; (*sentence*) отбыва́ть *impf*, отбы́ть *pf*; (*writ etc.*) вруча́ть *impf*, вручи́ть *pf* (on +*dat*); *vi* (*be suitable*) годи́ться (for на+*acc*, для+*gen*); (*sport*) подава́ть *impf*, пода́ть *pf* мяч; it ~s him right поде́лом ему́ (*dat*). **service** *n* (*act of serving; branch of public work; eccl*) слу́жба; (*quality of* ~) обслу́живание; (*of car etc.*) техобслу́живание; (*set of dishes*) серви́з; (*sport*) пода́ча; (*transport*) сообще́ние; at your ~ к ва́шим услу́гам; *vt* (*car*) проводи́ть *impf*, провести́ *pf* техобслу́живание +*gen*; ~ **charge** пла́та за обслу́живание; ~ **station** ста́нция обслу́живания. **serviceable** *n* (*useful*) поле́зный; (*durable*) про́чный. **serviceman** *n* военнослу́жащий *sb*.

serviette *n* салфе́тка.

servile *adj* рабо́лепный.

session *n* заседа́ние, се́ссия.

set[1] *vt* (*put*; ~ **clock, trap**) ста́вить *impf*, по~ *pf*; (*table*) накрыва́ть *impf*, накры́ть *pf*; (*bone*) вправля́ть *impf*, впра́вить *pf*; (*hair*) укла́дывать *impf*, уложи́ть *pf*; (*gem*) оправля́ть *impf*, опра́вить *pf*; (*bring into state*) приводи́ть *impf*, привести́ *pf* (in, to в+*acc*); (*example*) подава́ть *impf*, пода́ть *pf*; (*task*) задава́ть *impf*, зада́ть *pf*; *vi* (*solidify*) тверде́ть *impf*, за~ *pf*; застыва́ть *impf*, засты́(ну)ть *pf*; (*sun etc.*) заходи́ть *impf*, зайти́ *pf*; сади́ться *impf*, сесть *pf*; ~ **about** (*begin*) начина́ть *impf*, нача́ть *pf*; (*attack*) напада́ть *impf*, напа́сть *pf* на+*acc*; ~ **back** (*impede*) препя́тствовать *impf*, вос~ *pf* +*dat*; ~**back** (*enhance*) неуда́ча; ~ **in** наступа́ть *impf*, наступи́ть *pf*: ~ **off** (*on journey*) отправля́ться *impf*, отпра́виться *pf*; (*enhance*) оттеня́ть *impf*, оттени́ть *pf*; ~ **out** (*state*) излага́ть *impf*, изложи́ть *pf*; (*on journey*) see ~ **off**; ~ **up** (*business*) осно́вывать *impf*, основа́ть *pf*.

set[2] *n* набо́р, компле́кт; (*of dishes*) серви́з; (*radio*) приёмник; (*television*) телеви́зор; (*tennis*) сет; (*theat*) декора́ция; (*cin*) съёмочная площа́дка.

set[3] *adj* (*established*) устано́вленный.

settee *n* дива́н.

setting n (*frame*) опра́ва; (*surroundings*) обстано́вка; (*of mechanism etc.*) устано́вка; (*of sun etc.*) захо́д.

settle vt (*decide*) реша́ть impf, реши́ть pf; (*reconcile*) ула́живать impf, ула́дить pf; (*a bill etc.*) опла́чивать impf, оплати́ть pf; (*calm*) успока́ивать impf, успоко́ить pf; vi поселя́ться impf, посели́ться pf; (*subside*) оседа́ть impf, осе́сть pf; ~ **down** уса́живаться impf, усе́сться pf (*to* за+*acc*). **settlement** n поселе́ние; (*agreement*) соглаше́ние; (*payment*) упла́та. **settler** n поселе́нец.

seven adj & n семь; (*number 7*) семёрка. **seventeen** adj & n семна́дцать. **seventeenth** adj & n семна́дцатый. **seventh** adj & n седьмо́й; (*fraction*) седьма́я sb. **seventieth** adj & n семидеся́тый. **seventy** adj & n се́мьдесят; pl (*decade*) семидеся́тые го́ды (-до́в) m pl.

several pron (*adj*) не́сколько (+*gen*).

severance n разры́в; ~ **pay** выходно́е посо́бие.

severe adj стро́гий, суро́вый; (*pain, frost*) си́льный; (*illness*) тяжёлый. **severity** n стро́гость, суро́вость.

sew vt шить impf, с~ pf; ~ **on** приши́ва́ть impf, приши́ть pf; ~ **up** заши́ва́ть impf, заши́ть pf.

sewage n сто́чные во́ды f pl; ~-**farm** поля́ neut pl ороше́ния. **sewer** n сто́чная труба́. **sewerage** n канализа́ция.

sewing n шитьё; ~-**machine** шве́йная маши́на.

sex n (*gender*) пол; (*sexual activity*) секс; have ~ име́ть impf сноше́ние. **sexual** adj полово́й, сексуа́льный; ~ **intercourse** полово́е сноше́ние. **sexuality** n сексуа́льность. **sexy** adj эроти́ческий.

sh int ти́ше!; тсс!

shabby adj ве́тхий.

shack n лачу́га.

shackles n pl око́вы (-в) pl.

shade n тень; (*of colour, meaning*) отте́нок; (*lamp-~*) абажу́р; а ~ чуть-чу́ть; vt затеня́ть impf, затени́ть pf; (*eyes etc.*) заслоня́ть impf заслони́ть pf; (*drawing*) тушева́ть

impf, за~ pf. **shadow** n тень; vt (*follow*) та́йно следи́ть impf за+instr. **shadowy** adj тёмный. **shady** adj тени́стый; (*suspicious*) подозри́тельный.

shaft n (*of spear*) дре́вко; (*arrow; fig*) стрела́; (*of light*) луч; (*of cart*) огло́бля; (*axle*) вал; (*mine, lift*) ша́хта.

shaggy adj лохма́тый.

shake vt & i трясти́(сь) impf; vi (*tremble*) дрожа́ть impf; vt (*weaken*) колеба́ть impf, по~ pf; (*shock*) потряса́ть impf потрясти́ pf; ~ **hands** пожима́ть impf, пожа́ть pf ру́ку (*with* +dat); ~ **one's head** пока́чать pf голово́й; ~ **off** стря́хивать impf, стряхну́ть pf; (*fig*) избавля́ться impf, изба́виться pf от+gen. **shaky** adj ша́ткий.

shallow adj ме́лкий; (*fig*) пове́рхностный.

sham vt & i притворя́ться impf, притвори́ться pf +instr; n притво́рство; (*person*) притво́рщик, -ица; adj притво́рный.

shambles n хао́с.

shame n (*guilt*) стыд; (*disgrace*) позо́р; what a ~! как жаль!; vt стыди́ть impf, при~ pf. **shameful** adj позо́рный. **shameless** adj бессты́дный.

shampoo n шампу́нь m.

shanty[1] n (*hut*) хиба́рка; ~ **town** трущо́ба.

shanty[2] n (*song*) матро́сская пе́сня.

shape n фо́рма; vt придава́ть impf, прида́ть pf фо́рму+dat; vi: ~ **up** скла́дываться impf, сложи́ться pf. **shapeless** adj бесфо́рменный. **shapely** adj стро́йный.

share n до́ля; (*econ*) а́кция; vt дели́ть impf, по~ pf; (*opinion etc.*; ~ **out**) разделя́ть impf, раздели́ть pf. **shareholder** n акционе́р.

shark n аку́ла.

sharp adj о́стрый; (*steep*) круто́й; (*sudden; harsh*) ре́зкий; n (*mus*) дие́з; adv (*with time*) ро́вно; (*of angle*) кру́то. **sharpen** vt точи́ть impf, на~ pf.

shatter vt & i разбива́ть(ся) impf, разби́ть(ся) pf вдре́безги; vt (*hopes etc.*) разруша́ть impf, разру́шить pf.

shave vt & i бри́ть(ся) impf, по~ pf; n бритьё. **shaver** n электри́ческая бри́тва.

shawl n шаль.

she pron она́.

sheaf n сноп; (of papers) свя́зка.

shear vt стричь impf, о~ pf. **shears** n pl но́жницы (-ц) pl.

sheath n но́жны (gen -жен) pl.

shed¹ n сара́й.

shed² vt (tears, blood, light) пролива́ть impf, проли́ть pf; (skin, clothes) сбра́сывать impf, сбро́сить pf.

sheen n блеск.

sheep n овца́. **sheepish** adj сконфу́женный. **sheepskin** n овчи́на; ~ coat дублёнка.

sheer adj (utter) су́щий; (textile) прозра́чный; (rock etc.) отве́сный.

sheet n (on bed) простыня́; (of glass, paper, etc.) лист.

sheikh n шейх.

shelf n по́лка.

shell n (of mollusc etc.) ра́ковина; (of tortoise) щит; (of egg, nut) скорлупа́; (of building etc.) о́стов; (explosive ~) снаря́д; vt (peas etc.) лущи́ть impf, об~ pf; (bombard) обстре́ливать impf, обстреля́ть pf. **shellfish** n (mollusc) моллю́ск; (crustacean) ракообра́зное sb.

shelter n убе́жище; vt (provide with refuge) приюти́ть pf; vt & i укрыва́ть(ся) impf, укры́ть(ся) pf.

shelve¹ vt (defer) откла́дывать impf, отложи́ть pf.

shelve² vi (slope) отло́го спуска́ться impf.

shelving n (shelves) стелла́ж.

shepherd n пасту́х; vt проводи́ть impf, провести́ pf.

sherry n хе́рес.

shield n щит; vt защища́ть impf, защити́ть pf.

shift vt & i (change position) перемеща́ть(ся) impf, перемести́ть(ся) pf; (change) меня́ть(ся) impf; n перемеще́ние; переме́на; (of workers) сме́на; ~ work сме́нная рабо́та. **shifty** adj ско́льзкий.

shimmer vi мерца́ть impf; n мерца́ние.

shin n го́лень.

shine vi свети́ть(ся) impf; (glitter) блесте́ть impf; (excel) блиста́ть impf; (sun, eyes) сия́ть impf; vt (a light) освеща́ть impf, освети́ть pf

фонарём (on +acc); n гля́нец.

shingle n (pebbles) га́лька.

shingles n опоя́сывающий лиша́й.

shiny adj блестя́щий.

ship n кора́бль m; су́дно; vt (transport) перевози́ть impf, перевезти́ pf; (dispatch) отправля́ть impf, отпра́вить pf. **shipbuilding** n судострои́тельство. **shipment** n (dispatch) отпра́вка; (goods) па́ртия. **shipping** n суда́ (-до́в) pl. **shipshape** adv в по́лном поря́дке. **shipwreck** n кораблекруше́ние; be ~ed терпе́ть impf, по~ pf кораблекруше́ние. **shipyard** n верфь.

shirk vt ув́иливать impf, увильну́ть pf от+gen.

shirt n руба́шка.

shit n (vulg) говно́; vi срать impf, по~ pf.

shiver vi (tremble) дрожа́ть impf; n дрожь.

shoal n (of fish) ста́я.

shock n (emotional) потрясе́ние; (impact) уда́р, толчо́к; (electr) уда́р то́ком; (med) шок; vt шоки́ровать impf. **shocking** adj (outrageous) сканда́льный; (awful) ужа́сный.

shoddy adj халту́рный.

shoe n ту́фля; vt подко́вывать impf, подкова́ть pf. **shoe-lace** n шнуро́к. **shoemaker** n сапо́жник. **shoe-string** n: on a ~ с небольши́ми сре́дствами.

shoo int кш!; vt прогоня́ть impf, прогна́ть pf.

shoot vt & i (discharge) стреля́ть impf (a gun из+gen; at в+acc, по +dat); (arrow) пуска́ть impf, пусти́ть pf; (kill) застре́ливать impf, застрели́ть pf; (execute) расстре́ливать impf, расстреля́ть pf; (hunt) охо́титься impf на+acc; (football) бить impf (по воро́там); (cin) снима́ть impf, снять pf (фильм); vi (go swiftly) проноси́ться impf, пронести́сь pf; ~ down (aircraft) сбива́ть impf, сбить pf; ~ up (grow) бы́стро расти́ impf, по~ pf; (prices) подска́кивать impf, подскочи́ть pf; n (branch) росто́к, побе́г; (hunt) охо́та. **shooting** n стрельба́; (hunting) охо́та; ~-gallery тир.

shop n магази́н; (workshop) мастерска́я sb, цех; ~ assistant продаве́ц,

-вщи́ца; ~-lifter магази́нный вор; ~-lifting воровство́ в магази́нах; ~ steward цехово́й ста́роста m; ~-window витри́на; vi де́лать impf, с~ pf поку́пки (f pl). shopkeeper n ла́вочник. shopper n покупа́тель m, ~ница. shopping n поку́пки f pl; go, do one's ~ де́лать impf, с~ pf поку́пки; ~-centre торго́вый центр.

shore¹ n бе́рег.

shore² vt: ~ up подпира́ть impf, подпере́ть pf.

short adj коро́ткий; (not tall) ни́зкого ро́ста; (deficient) недоста́точный; be ~ of испы́тывать impf, испыта́ть pf недоста́ток в+prep; (curt) ре́зкий; in ~ одни́м сло́вом; ~-change обсчи́тывать impf, обсчита́ть pf; ~ circuit коро́ткое замыка́ние; ~ cut коро́ткий путь m; ~-list оконча́тельный спи́сок; ~-list включа́ть impf, включи́ть pf в оконча́тельный спи́сок; ~-lived недолгове́чный; ~-sighted близору́кий; (fig) недальнови́дный; ~ story расска́з; in ~ supply дефици́тный; ~-tempered вспы́льчивый; ~-term краткосро́чный; ~-wave коротково́лновый. shortage n недоста́ток. shortcoming n недоста́ток. shorten vt & i укора́чивать(ся) impf, укороти́ть(ся) pf. shortfall n дефици́т. shorthand n стеногра́фия; ~ typist машини́стка-стенографи́стка. shortly adv: ~ after вско́ре (по́сле +gen); ~ before незадо́лго (до+gen). shorts n pl шо́рты (-т) pl.

shot n (discharge of gun) вы́стрел; (pellets) дробь; (person) стрело́к; (attempt) попы́тка; (phot) сни́мок; (cin) кадр; (sport) (stroke) уда́р; (throw) бросо́к; like a ~ неме́дленно; ~-gun дробови́к.

should v aux (ought) до́лжен (бы) +inf; you ~ know that вы должны́ э́то знать; he ~ be here soon он до́лжен бы быть тут ско́ро; (conditional) бы ~+past: I ~ say я бы сказа́л(а); I ~ like я бы хоте́л(а).

shoulder n плечо́; ~-blade лопа́тка; ~-strap брете́лька; взва́ливать impf, взвали́ть pf на пле́чи; (fig) брать impf, взять pf на себя́.

shout n крик; vi крича́ть impf, кри́кнуть pf; ~ down перекри́кивать

impf, перекрича́ть pf.

shove n толчо́к; vt & i толка́ть(ся) impf, толкну́ть pf; ~ off (coll) убира́ться impf, убра́ться pf.

shovel n лопа́та; vt (~ up) сгреба́ть impf, сгрести́ pf.

show vt пока́зывать impf, показа́ть pf; (exhibit) выставля́ть impf, вы́ставить pf; (film etc.) демонстри́ровать impf, про~ pf; vi (also ~ up) быть ви́дным, заме́тным; ~ off (vi) привлека́ть impf; привле́чь pf к себе́ внима́ние; ~ up see vi; (appear) появля́ться impf; появи́ться pf; n (exhibition) вы́ставка; (theat) спекта́кль m; (effect) ви́димость; ~ of hands голосова́ние подня́тием руки́; ~-case витри́на; ~-jumping соревнова́ние по ска́чкам; ~-room сало́н. showdown n развя́зка.

shower n (rain) до́ждик; (hail; fig) град; (~-bath) душ; (fig) осыпа́ть impf, осы́пать pf +instr (on +acc); vi принима́ть impf, приня́ть pf душ. showery adj дождли́вый. showpiece n образе́ц. showy adj показно́й.

shrapnel n шрапне́ль.

shred n клочо́к; not a ~ ни ка́пли; vt мельчи́ть impf, из~ pf.

shrewd adj проница́тельный.

shriek n визжа́ть impf; взви́гнуть pf.

shrill adj пронзи́тельный.

shrimp n креве́тка.

shrine n святы́ня.

shrink vi сади́ться impf, сесть pf; (recoil) отпря́нуть pf; vt вызыва́ть impf, вы́звать pf уса́дку у+gen; ~ from избега́ть impf +gen. shrinkage n уса́дка.

shrivel vi смо́рщиваться impf, смо́рщиться pf.

shroud n са́ван; vt (fig) оку́тывать impf, оку́тать pf (in +instr).

Shrove Tuesday вто́рник на ма́сленой неде́ле.

shrub n куст. shrubbery n куста́рник.

shrug vt & i пожима́ть impf, пожа́ть pf (плеча́ми).

shudder n содрога́ние; vi содрога́ться impf, содрогну́ться pf.

shuffle vt & i (one's feet) ша́ркать impf (нога́ми); (cards) тасова́ть impf, с~ pf; n тасо́вка.

shun vt избега́ть impf +gen.

shunt vi (rly) маневри́ровать impf, с~ pf; vt (rly) переводи́ть impf, перевести́ pf на запасно́й путь.

shut vt & i (also ~ down) закрыва́ть(ся) impf, закры́ть(ся) pf; ~ out (exclude) исключа́ть impf, исключи́ть pf; (fence off) загора́живать impf, загороди́ть pf; (keep out) не пуска́ть impf, пусти́ть pf; ~ up (vi) замолча́ть pf; (imper) заткни́сь!

shutter n ста́вень m; (phot) затво́р.

shuttle n челно́к.

shy[1] adj засте́нчивый.

shy[2] vi (in alarm) отпря́дывать impf, отпря́нуть pf.

Siberia n Сиби́рь. **Siberian** adj сиби́рский; n сибиря́к, -я́чка.

sick adj больно́й; be ~ (vomit) рвать impf, вы́~ pf impers +acc: he was ~ его́ вы́рвало; feel ~ тошни́ть impf impers +acc: be ~ of надоеда́ть impf, надое́сть pf +nom (object) & dat (subject): I'm ~ of her она́ мне надое́ла; ~-leave о́тпуск по боле́зни. **sicken** vi вызыва́ть impf, вы́звать pf тошноту́, (disgust) отвраще́ние, y+gen; vi заболева́ть impf, заболе́ть pf. **sickening** adj отврати́тельный.

sickle n серп.

sickly adj боле́зненный; (nauseating) тошнотво́рный. **sickness** n боле́знь; (vomiting) тошнота́.

side n сторона́; (of body) бок; ~ by ~ ря́дом (with c+instr); on the ~ на стороне́; vi: ~ with встава́ть impf, встать pf на сто́рону+gen; ~-effect побо́чное де́йствие; ~-step (fig) уклоня́ться impf, уклони́ться pf от+gen; ~-track (distract) отвлека́ть impf, отвле́чь pf. **sideboard** n буфе́т; pl ба́ки (-к) pl. **sidelight** n боково́й фона́рь m. **sideline** n (work) побо́чная рабо́та.

sidelong adj (glance) косо́й.

sideways adv бо́ком.

siding n запасно́й путь m.

sidle vi: ~ up to подходи́ть impf, подойти́ pf к (+dat) бочко́м.

siege n оса́да; lay ~ to осажда́ть impf, осади́ть pf; raise the ~ of снима́ть, снять pf оса́ду c+gen.

sieve n си́то; vt просе́ивать impf, просе́ять pf.

sift vt просе́ивать impf, просе́ять pf; (fig) тща́тельно рассма́тривать impf, рассмотре́ть pf.

sigh vi вздыха́ть impf, вздохну́ть pf; n вздох.

sight n (faculty) зре́ние; (view) вид; (spectacle) зре́лище; pl достопримеча́тельности f pl; (on gun) прице́л; at first ~ с пе́рвого взгля́да; catch ~ of уви́деть pf; know by ~ знать impf в лицо́; lose ~ of теря́ть impf, по~ pf из виду; (fig) упуска́ть impf, упусти́ть pf из виду.

sign n знак; (indication) при́знак; (~board) вы́веска; vt & abs подпи́сывать(ся) impf, подписа́ть(ся) pf; vi (give) подава́ть impf, пода́ть pf знак; ~ on (as unemployed) запи́сываться impf, записа́ться pf в спи́ски безрабо́тных; (~ up) нанима́ться impf, наня́ться pf.

signal n сигна́л; vt & i сигнализи́ровать impf & pf. **signal-box** n сигна́льная бу́дка. **signalman** n сигна́льщик.

signatory n подписа́вший sb; (of treaty) сторона́, подписа́вшая догово́р.

signature n по́дпись.

significance n значе́ние. **significant** adj значи́тельный. **signify** vt означа́ть impf.

signpost n указа́тельный столб.

silage n си́лос.

silence n молча́ние, тишина́; vt заста́вить pf замолча́ть. **silencer** n глуши́тель m. **silent** adj (not speaking) безмо́лвный; (of film) немо́й; (without noise) ти́хий; be ~ молча́ть impf.

silhouette n силуэ́т; vt: be ~d вырисо́вываться impf, вырисова́ться pf (against на фо́не+gen).

silicon n кре́мний. **silicone** n силико́н.

silk n шёлк; attrib шёлковый. **silky** adj шелкови́стый.

sill n подоко́нник.

silly adj глу́пый.

silo n си́лос.

silt n ил.

silver n серебро́; (cutlery) столо́вое серебро́; adj (of ~) сере́бряный; (silvery) серебри́стый; ~-plated посере́бренный. **silversmith** n сере́бряных дел ма́стер. **silverware** n столо́вое серебро́. **silvery** adj серебри́стый.

similar adj подо́бный (to +dat). **similarity** n схо́дство. **similarly** adv подо́бным о́бразом.

simile n сравне́ние.

simmer vt кипяти́ть impf на ме́дленном огне́; vi кипе́ть impf на ме́дленном огне́; ~ **down** успока́иваться impf, успоко́иться pf.

simper vi жема́нно улыба́ться impf, улыбну́ться pf.

simple adj просто́й; ~-**minded** тупова́тый. **simplicity** n простота́. **simplify** vt упроща́ть impf, упрости́ть pf. **simply** adv про́сто.

simulate vt притворя́ться impf, притвори́ться pf +instr; (conditions etc.) модели́ровать impf & pf. **simulated** adj (pearls etc.) иску́сственный.

simultaneous adj одновре́ме́нный.

sin n грех; vi греши́ть impf, со~ pf.

since adv с тех пор; prep c+gen; conj с тех пор как; (reason) так как.

sincere adj и́скренний. **sincerely** adv и́скренне; yours ~ и́скренне Ваш. **sincerity** n и́скренность.

sinew n сухожи́лие.

sinful adj гре́шный.

sing vt & i петь impf, про~, с~ pf.

singe vt пали́ть impf, о~ pf.

singer n певе́ц, -ви́ца.

single adj оди́н; (unmarried) (of man) нежена́тый; (of woman) незаму́жняя; (bed) односпа́льный; ~-**handed** без посторо́нней по́мощи; ~-**minded** целеустремлённый; ~ **parent** мать/оте́ц-одино́чка; ~ **room** ко́мната на одного́; n (ticket) биле́т в оди́н коне́ц; pl (tennis etc.) одино́чная игра́ vt: ~ **out** выделя́ть impf, вы́делить pf. **singly** adv по-одному́.

singular n еди́нственное число́; adj еди́нственный; (unusual) необыча́йный. **singularly** adv необыча́йно.

sinister adj злове́щий.

sink vi (descend slowly) опуска́ться impf, опусти́ться pf; (in mud etc.) погружа́ться impf, погрузи́ться pf; (in water) тону́ть impf, по~ pf; vt (ship) топи́ть impf, по~ pf; (pipe, post) вка́пывать impf, вкопа́ть pf; n ра́ковина.

sinner n гре́шник, -ица.

sinus n па́зуха.

sip vt пить impf, ма́ленькими глотка́ми; n ма́ленький глото́к.

siphon n сифо́н; ~ **off** (also fig) перека́чивать impf, перекача́ть pf.

sir n сэр.

siren n сире́на.

sister n сестра́; ~-**in-law** (husband's sister) золо́вка; (wife's sister) своя́ченица; (brother's wife) неве́стка.

sit vi (be sitting) сиде́ть impf; (~ **down**) сади́ться impf, сесть pf; (parl, law) заседа́ть impf; vt уса́живать impf, усади́ть pf; (exam) сдава́ть impf; ~ **back** отки́дываться impf, отки́нуться pf; ~ **down** сади́ться impf, сесть pf; ~ **up** приподнима́ться impf, приподня́ться pf; (not go to bed) не ложи́ться impf спать.

site n (where a thing takes place) ме́сто; (where a thing is) местоположе́ние.

sitting n (parl etc.) заседа́ние; (for meal) сме́на; ~-**room** гости́ная sb.

situated adj: be ~ находи́ться impf. **situation** n местоположе́ние; (circumstances) положе́ние; (job) ме́сто.

six adj & n шесть; (number 6) шестёрка. **sixteen** adj & n шестна́дцать. **sixteenth** adj & n шестна́дцатый. **sixth** adj & n шесто́й; (fraction) ше́стая sb. **sixtieth** adj & n шестидеся́тый. **sixty** adj & n шестьдеся́т; pl (decade) шестидеся́тые го́ды (-до́в) m pl.

size n разме́р; vt: ~ **up** оце́нивать impf, оцени́ть pf. **sizeable** adj значи́тельный.

sizzle vi шипе́ть impf.

skate[1] n (fish) скат.

skate[2] n (ice-~) конёк; (roller-~) конёк на ро́ликах; vi ката́ться impf на конька́х; **skating-rink** като́к.

skeleton n скеле́т.

sketch n зарисо́вка; (theat) скетч; vt & i зарисо́вывать impf, зарисова́ть pf. **sketchy** adj схемати́ческий; (superficial) пове́рхностный.

skew adj косо́й; on the ~ ко́со.

skewer n ве́ртел.

ski n лы́жа; ~-**jump** трампли́н; vi ходи́ть impf на лы́жах.

skid n зано́с; vi заноси́ть impf, занести́ pf impers+acc.

skier n лы́жник. **skiing** n лы́жный спорт.

skilful *adj* иску́сный. **skill** *n* мастер-
ство́; (*countable*) поле́зный на́вык.
skilled *adj* иску́сный; (*trained*) ква-
лифици́рованный.

skim *vt* снима́ть *impf*, снять *pf*
(*cream* сли́вки *pl, scum* на́кипь)
c+*gen*; *vi* скользи́ть *impf* (over,
along по+*dat*); ~ through бе́гло
просма́тривать *impf*, просмотре́ть
pf; *adj*: ~ milk снято́е молоко́.

skimp *vt & i* скупи́ться *impf* (на+*acc*).
skimpy *adj* ску́дный.

skin *n* ко́жа; (*of fruit
etc.*) кожура́; (*on milk*) пе́нка; *vt*
сдира́ть *impf*, содра́ть *pf* ко́жу,
шку́ру, c+*gen*; (*fruit*) снима́ть *impf*,
снять *pf* кожуру́ c+*gen*. **skinny** *adj*
то́щий.

skip[1] *vi* скака́ть *impf*; (*with rope*)
пры́гать *impf* че́рез скака́лку; *vt*
(*omit*) пропуска́ть *impf*, пропусти́ть
pf.

skip[2] *n* (*container*) скип.

skipper *n* (*naut*) шки́пер.

skirmish *n* схва́тка.

skirt *n* ю́бка; *vt* обходи́ть *impf*, обо-
йти́ *pf* стороно́й; ~ing-board плинтус.

skittle *n* ке́гля; *pl* ке́гли *f pl*.

skulk *vi* (*hide*) скрыва́ться *impf*;
(*creep*) кра́сться *impf*.

skull *n* че́реп.

skunk *n* скунс.

sky *n* не́бо. **skylark** *n* жа́воронок.
skylight *n* окно́ в кры́ше. **skyline**
n горизо́нт. **skyscraper** *n* небоскрёб.

slab *n* плита́; (*of cake etc.*) кусо́к.

slack *adj* (*loose*) сла́бый; (*sluggish*)
вя́лый; (*negligent*) небре́жный; *n* (*of
rope*) слабина́; *pl* брю́ки (-к) *pl*.
slacken *vt* ослабля́ть *impf*, осла́-
бить *pf*; *vt & i* (*slow down*) замед-
ля́ть(ся) *impf*, заме́длить(ся) *pf*; *vi*
ослабева́ть *impf*, ослабе́ть *pf*.

slag *n* шлак.

slam *vt & i* захло́пывать(ся) *impf*,
захло́пнуть(ся) *pf*.

slander *n* клевета́; *vt* клевета́ть
impf, на~ *pf* на+*acc*. **slanderous** *adj*
клеветни́ческий.

slang *n* жарго́н. **slangy** *adj* жарго́н-
ный.

slant *vt & i* наклоня́ть(ся) *impf*, на-
клони́ть(ся) *pf*; *n* укло́н. **slanting**
adj косо́й.

slap *vt* шлёпать *impf*, шлёпнуть *pf*;
n шлепо́к; *adv* пря́мо. **slapdash** *adj*
небре́жный. **slapstick** *n* фарс.

slash *vt* (*cut*) поро́ть *impf*, рас~ *pf*;
(*fig*) уре́зывать *impf*, уре́зать *pf*; *n*
разре́з; (*sign*) дробь.

slat *n* пла́нка.

slate[1] *n* сла́нец; (*for roofing*) (кро-
ве́льная) пли́тка.

slate[2] *vt* (*criticize*) разноси́ть *impf*,
разнести́ *pf*.

slaughter *n* (*of animals*) убо́й; (*massacre*) резня́; *vt* (*animals*) ре́зать
impf, за~ *pf*; (*people*) убива́ть *impf*,
уби́ть *pf*. **slaughterhouse** *n* бо́йня.

Slav *n* славяни́н, -я́нка; *adj* славя́н-
ский.

slave *n* раб, рабы́ня; *vi* рабо́тать
impf как раб. **slavery** *n* ра́бство.
Slavic *adj* славя́нский.

slavish *adj* ра́бский.

Slavonic *adj* славя́нский.

slay *vt* убива́ть *impf*, уби́ть *pf*.

sleazy *adj* убо́гий.

sledge *n* са́ни (-не́й) *pl*.

sledge-hammer *n* кува́лда.

sleek *adj* гла́дкий.

sleep *n* сон; go to ~ засыпа́ть *impf*,
засну́ть *pf*; *vi* спать *impf*; (*spend the
night*) ночева́ть *impf*, пере~ *pf*.
sleeper *n* спя́щий *sb*; (*on track*)
шпа́ла; (*sleeping-car*) спа́льный ва-
го́н. **sleeping** *adj* спя́щий; ~-bag
спа́льный мешо́к; ~-car спа́льный
ваго́н; ~-pill снотво́рная табле́тка.
sleepless *adj* бессо́нный. **sleepy**
adj со́нный.

sleet *n* мо́крый снег.

sleeve *n* рука́в; (*of record*) конве́рт.

sleigh *n* са́ни (-не́й) *pl*.

sleight-of-hand *n* ло́вкость рук.

slender *adj* (*slim*) то́нкий; (*meagre*)
ску́дный; (*of hope etc.*) сла́бый.

sleuth *n* сыщик.

slice *n* кусо́к; *vt* (~ up) нареза́ть
impf, наре́зать *pf*.

slick *adj* (*dextrous*) ло́вкий; (*crafty*)
хи́трый; *n* нефтяна́я плёнка.

slide *vi* скользи́ть *impf*; *vt* (*drawer
etc.*) задвига́ть *impf*, задви́нуть *pf*;
n (*children's* ~) го́рка; (*microscope
*~) предме́тное стекло́; (*phot*) диа-
позити́в, слайд; (*for hair*) зако́лка.
sliding *adj* (*door*) задвижно́й.

slight[1] *adj* (*slender*) тóнкий; (*inconsiderable*) небольшóй; (*light*) лёгкий; not the ~est ни малéйшего, -шей (*gen*); not in the ~est ничýть.

slight[2] *vt* пренебрегáть *impf*, пренебрéчь *pf* +*instr*; *n* обúда.

slightly *adv* слегкá, немнóго.

slim *adj* тóнкий; (*chance etc.*) слáбый; *vi* худéть *impf*, по~ *pf*.

slime *n* слизь. **slimy** *adj* слúзистый; (*person*) скóльзкий.

sling *vt* (*throw*) швырять *impf*, швырнýть *pf*; (*suspend*) подвéшивать *impf*, подвéсить *pf*; *n* (*med*) пéревязь.

slink *vi* крáсться *impf*.

slip *n* (*mistake*) ошúбка; (*garment*) комбинáция; (*pillowcase*) нáволочка; (*paper*) листóчек; ~ of the tongue обмóлвка; give the ~ ускользнýть *pf* от+*gen*; *vi* скользúть *impf*, скользнýть *pf*; (*fall over*) поскользнýться *pf*; (*from hands etc.*) выскáльзывать *impf*, выскользнуть *pf*; *vt* (*insert*) совáть *impf*, сýнуть *pf*; ~ off (*depart*) ускользáть *impf*, ускользнýть *pf*; ~ up (*make mistake*) ошибáться *impf*, ошибúться *pf*. **slipper** *n* тáпка. **slippery** *adj* скóльзкий.

slit *vt* разрезáть *impf*, разрéзать *pf*; (*throat*) перерéзать *pf*; *n* щель; (*cut*) разрéз.

slither *vi* скользúть *impf*.

sliver *n* щéпка.

slob *n* неряха *m & f*.

slobber *vi* пускáть *impf*, пустúть *pf* слюни.

slog *vt* (*hit*) сúльно ударять *impf*, удáрить *pf*; (*work*) упóрно рабóтать *impf*.

slogan *n* лóзунг.

slop *n*: *pl* помóи (-óев) *pl*; *vt & i* выплéскивать(ся) *impf*, выплескать(ся) *pf*.

slope *n* (*artificial*) наклóн; (*geog*) склон; *vi* имéть *impf* наклóн. **sloping** *adj* наклóнный.

sloppy *adj* (*work*) неряшливый; (*sentimental*) сентиментáльный.

slot *n* отвéрстие; ~-machine автомáт; *vt*: ~ in вставлять *impf*, встáвить *pf*.

sloth *n* лень.

slouch *vi* (*stoop*) сутýлиться *impf*.

slovenly *adj* неряшливый.

slow *adj* мéдленный; (*tardy*) медлúтельный; (*stupid*) тупóй; (*business*) вялый; be ~ (*clock*) отставáть *impf*, отстáть *pf*; *adv* мéдленно; *vt & i* (~ down, up) замедлять(ся) *impf*, замéдлить(ся) *pf*.

sludge *n* (*mud*) грязь; (*sediment*) отстóй.

slug *n* (*zool*) слизняк.

sluggish *adj* вялый.

sluice *n* шлюз.

slum *n* трущóба.

slumber *n* сон; *vi* спать *impf*.

slump *n* спад; *vi* рéзко пáдать *impf*, (у)пáсть *pf*; (*of person*) свáливаться *impf*, свалúться *pf*.

slur *vt* говорúть *impf* невнятно; *n* (*stigma*) пятнó.

slush *n* слякоть.

slut *n* (*sloven*) неряха; (*trollop*) потаскýха.

sly *adj* хúтрый; on the ~ тайкóм.

smack[1] *vi*: ~ of пáхнуть *impf* +*instr*.

smack[2] *n* (*slap*) шлепóк; *vt* шлёпать *impf*, шлёпнуть *pf*.

small *adj* мáленький, небольшóй, мáлый; (*of agent, particles; petty*) мéлкий; ~ change мéлочь; ~-scale мелкомасштáбный; ~ talk свéтская бесéда.

smart[1] *vi* сáднить *impf impers*.

smart[2] *adj* элегáнтный; (*brisk*) быстрый; (*cunning*) лóвкий; (*sharp*) смекáлистый (*coll*).

smash *vt & i* разбивáть(ся) *impf*, разбúть(ся) *pf*; *vi*: ~ into врезáться *impf*, врéзаться *pf* в+*acc*; *n* (*crash*) грóхот; (*collision*) столкновéние; (*blow*) сúльный удáр.

smattering *n* поверхностное знáние.

smear *vt* смáзывать *impf*, смáзать *pf*; (*dirty*) пáчкать *impf*, за~, ис~ *pf*; (*discredit*) порóчить *impf*, о~ *pf*; *n* (*spot*) пятнó; (*slander*) клеветá; (*med*) мазóк.

smell *n* (*sense*) обоняние; (*odour*) зáпах; *vt* чýвствовать *impf* зáпах+*gen*; (*sniff*) нюхать *impf*, по~ *pf*; ~ of пáхнуть *impf* +*instr*. **smelly** *adj* вонючий.

smelt *vt* (*ore*) плáвить *impf*; (*metal*) выплавлять *impf*, выплавить *pf*.

smile *vi* улыбáться *impf*, улыбнýться *pf*; *n* улыбка.

smirk vi ухмыля́ться impf, ухмыль-
ну́ться pf; n ухмы́лка.
smith n кузне́ц.
smithereens n: (in)to ~ вдре́безги.
smithy n ку́зница.
smock n блу́за.
smog n тума́н (с ды́мом).
smoke n дым; ~screen дымова́я за-
ве́са; vt & i (cigarette etc.) кури́ть
impf, по~ pf; vt (cure; colour) коп-
ти́ть impf, за~ pf; vi (abnormally)
дыми́ть impf; (of fire) дыми́ться
impf. **smoker** n кури́льщик, -ица,
куря́щий sb. **smoky** adj ды́мный.
smooth adj (surface etc.) гла́дкий;
(movement etc.) пла́вный; vt при-
гла́живать impf, пригла́дить pf; ~
over сгла́живать impf, сгла́дить pf.
smother vt (stifle, also fig) души́ть
impf, за~ pf; (cover) покрыва́ть
impf, покры́ть pf.
smoulder vi тлеть impf.
smudge n пятно́; vt сма́зывать impf,
сма́зать pf.
smug adj самодово́льный.
smuggle vt провози́ть impf, про-
везти́ pf контраба́ндой; (convey secretly) проноси́ть impf, пронести́ pf.
smuggler n контрабанди́ст. **smug-
gling** n контраба́нда.
smut n са́жа; (indecency) непристо́й-
ность. **smutty** adj гря́зный; непри-
сто́йный.
snack n заку́ска; ~ bar закусочная
sb, (within institution) буфе́т.
snag n (fig) загво́здка; vt зацепля́ть
impf, зацепи́ть pf.
snail n ули́тка.
snake n змея́.
snap n (of dog or person) огрыза́ть-
ся impf, огрызну́ться pf (at на+acc);
vt & i (break) обрыва́ть(ся) impf,
оборва́ть(ся) pf; vt (make sound)
щёлкать impf, щёлкнуть pf +instr;
~ up (buy) расхва́тывать impf, рас-
хвата́ть pf; n (sound) щёлк; (photo)
сни́мок; adj (decision) скоропали́-
тельный. **snappy** adj (brisk) живо́й;
(stylish) шика́рный. **snapshot** n
сни́мок.
snare n лову́шка.
snarl vi рыча́ть impf, за~ pf; n рыча́-
ние.
snatch vt хвата́ть impf, (с)хвати́ть
pf; vi: ~ at хвата́ться impf, (с)хва-

ти́ться pf за+acc; n (fragment)
обры́вок.
sneak vi (slink) кра́сться impf; vt
(steal) стащи́ть pf; n я́бедник, -ица
(coll). **sneaking** adj та́йный. **sneaky**
adj лука́вый.
sneer vi насмеха́ться impf (at над
+instr).
sneeze vi чиха́ть impf, чихну́ть pf;
n чиха́нье.
snide adj еха́дный.
sniff vi шмы́гать impf, шмыгну́ть pf
но́сом; vt нюхать impf, по~ pf.
snigger vi хихи́кать impf, хихи́кнуть
pf; n хихи́канье.
snip vt ре́зать impf (но́жницами); ~
off среза́ть impf, сре́зать pf.
snipe vi стреля́ть impf из укры́тия
(at в+acc); (fig) напада́ть impf, на-
па́сть pf на+acc. **sniper** n сна́йпер.
snippet n отре́зок; pl (of news etc.)
обры́вки m pl.
snivel vi (run at nose) распуска́ть
impf, распусти́ть pf со́пли; (whimper) хны́кать impf.
snob n сноб. **snobbery** n сноби́зм.
snobbish adj сноби́стский.
snoop vi шпио́нить impf; ~ about
разню́хивать impf, разню́хать pf.
snooty adj чва́нный.
snooze vi вздремну́ть pf; n коро́т-
кий сон.
snore vi храпе́ть impf.
snorkel n шно́ркель m.
snort vi фы́ркать impf, фы́ркнуть pf.
snot n со́пли (-лей) pl.
snout n ры́ло, мо́рда.
snow n снег; ~white белосне́жный;
vi: it is ~ing, it snows идёт снег;
~ed under зава́ленный рабо́той; we
were ~ed up, в нас занесло́ сне́гом.
snowball n снежо́к. **snowdrop** n
подсне́жник. **snowflake** n снежи́нка.
snowman n снежная ба́ба. **snow-
storm** n мете́ль. **snowy** adj сне́ж-
ный; (snow-white) белосне́жный.
snub vt игнори́ровать impf & pf.
snuff[1] n (tobacco) нюхательный
таба́к.
snuff[2] vt: ~ out туши́ть impf, по~
pf.
snuffle vi сопе́ть impf.
snug adj ую́тный.
snuggle vi: ~ up to прижима́ться
impf, прижа́ться pf к+dat.

so adv так; (*in this way*) так, таки́м о́бразом; (*thus, at beginning of sentence*) (*also*) та́кже, то́же; conj (*therefore*) поэ́тому; and ~ on и так да́лее; if ~ в тако́м слу́чае; ~ ... as так(о́й)... как; ~ as to с тем что́бы; ~-called так называ́емый; (in) ~ far as насто́лько; ~ long! пока́!; ~ long as поско́льку; ~ much насто́лько; ~ much ~ до тако́й сте́пени; ~ much the better тем лу́чше; ~ that что́бы; ~... that так... что; ~ to say, speak так сказа́ть; ~ what? ну и что?

soak vt мочи́ть impf, на~ pf; (*drench*) прома́чивать impf, промочи́ть pf; ~ up впи́тывать impf, впита́ть pf; vi: ~ through проса́чиваться impf, просочи́ться pf; get ~ed промока́ть impf, промо́кнуть pf.

soap n мы́ло; vt мы́лить impf, на~ pf; ~ opera многосери́йная переда́ча; ~ powder стира́льный порошо́к. **soapy** adj мы́льный.

soar vi пари́ть impf; (*prices*) подска́кивать impf, подскочи́ть pf.

sob vi рыда́ть impf; n рыда́ние.

sober adj тре́звый; vt & i: ~ up отрезвля́ть(ся) impf, отрезви́ть(ся) pf. **sobriety** n тре́звость.

soccer n футбо́л.

sociable adj общи́тельный. **social** adj обще́ственный, социа́льный; S~ Democrat социа́л-демокра́т; ~ sciences обще́ственные нау́ки f pl; ~ security социа́льное обеспе́чение. **socialism** n социали́зм. **socialist** n социали́ст; adj социалисти́ческий. **socialize** vt обща́ться impf. **society** n о́бщество. **sociological** adj социологи́ческий **sociologist** n социо́лог. **sociology** n социоло́гия.

sock n носо́к.

socket n (*eye*) впа́дина; (*electr*) штепсель m; (*for bulb*) патро́н.

soda n со́да; ~-water со́довая вода́.

sodden adj промо́кший.

sodium n на́трий.

sodomy n педера́стия.

sofa n дива́н.

soft adj мя́гкий; (*sound*) ти́хий; (*colour*) нея́ркий; (*malleable*) ко́вкий; (*tender*) не́жный; ~ drink безалкого́льный напи́ток. **soften** vt & i

смягча́ть(ся) impf, смягчи́ть(ся) pf. **softness** n мя́гкость. **software** n програ́ммное обеспе́чение.

soggy adj сыро́й.

soil[1] n по́чва.

soil[2] vt па́чкать impf, за~, ис~ pf.

solace n утеше́ние.

solar adj со́лнечный.

solder n припо́й; vt пая́ть impf; (~ together) спа́ивать impf, спая́ть pf. **soldering iron** n пая́льник.

soldier n солда́т.

sole[1] n (*of foot, shoe*) подо́шва.

sole[2] n (*fish*) морско́й язы́к.

sole[3] adj еди́нственный.

solemn adj торже́ственный. **solemnity** n торже́ственность.

solicit vt проси́ть impf, по~ pf +acc, gen, o+prep; vi (*of prostitute*) пристава́ть impf к мужчи́нам. **solicitor** n адвока́т. **solicitous** adj забо́тливый.

solid adj (*not liquid*) твёрдый; (*not hollow; continuous*) сплошно́й; (*firm*) про́чный; (*pure*) чи́стый; n твёрдое те́ло; pl твёрдая пи́ща. **solidarity** n солида́рность. **solidify** vi затвердева́ть impf, затверде́ть pf. **solidity** n твёрдость; про́чность.

soliloquy n моноло́г.

solitary adj одино́кий, уединённый; ~ confinement одино́чное заключе́ние. **solitude** n одино́чество, уедине́ние.

solo n со́ло neut indecl; adj со́льный; adv со́ло. **soloist** n соли́ст, ~ка.

solstice n солнцестоя́ние.

soluble adj раствори́мый. **solution** n раство́р; (*of puzzle etc.*) реше́ние.

solve vt реша́ть impf, реши́ть pf. **solvent** adj растворя́ющий; (*financially*) платёжеспосо́бный; n раствори́тель m.

sombre adj мра́чный.

some adj & pron (*any*) како́й-нибудь; (*a certain*) како́й-то; (*a certain amount or number of*) не́который, *or often expressed by noun in* (*partitive*) gen; (*several*) не́сколько+gen; (~ people, things) не́которые pl; ~ day когда́-нибудь; ~ more ещё; ~ ... others одни́... други́е. **somebody, someone** n, pron (*def*) кто́-то; (*indef*) кто́-нибудь. **somehow** adv ка́к-то; ка́к-нибудь; (*for* *some reason*) почему-то; ~ or other так или иначе.

somersault *n* сальто *neut indecl*; *vi* кувыркаться *impf*, кувыр(к)нуться *pf*.

something *n & pron* (*def*) что-то; (*indef*) что-нибудь; ~ like (*approximately*) приблизительно; (*a thing like*) что-то вроде+*gen*. **sometime** *adv* некогда; *adj* бывший. **sometimes** *adv* иногда. **somewhat** *adv* несколько, довольно. **somewhere** *adv* (*position*) (*def*) где-то; (*indef*) где-нибудь; (*motion*) куда-то; куда-нибудь.

son *n* сын; ~-in-law зять *m*.

sonata *n* соната.

song *n* песня.

sonic *adj* звуковой.

sonnet *n* сонет.

soon *adv* скоро; (*early*) рано; as ~ as как только; as ~ as possible как можно скорее; ~er or later рано или поздно; the ~er the better чем раньше, тем лучше.

soot *n* сажа, копоть.

soothe *vt* успокаивать *impf*, успокоить *pf*; (*pain*) облегчать *impf*, облегчить *pf*.

sophisticated *adj* (*person*) искушённый; (*equipment*) сложный.

soporific *adj* снотворный.

soprano *n* сопрано (*voice*) *neut &* (*person*) *indecl*.

sorcerer *n* колдун. **sorcery** *n* колдовство.

sordid *adj* грязный.

sore *n* болячка; *adj* больной; my throat is ~ у меня болит горло.

sorrow *n* печаль. **sorrowful** *adj* печальный. **sorry** *adj* жалкий; *predic*: be ~ жалеть *impf* (*about* o+*prep*); жаль *impers*+*dat* (*for* +*gen*); ~! извини(те)!

sort *n* род, вид, сорт; *vt* (*also* ~ out) сортировать *impf*, рас~ *pf*; (*also fig*) разбирать *impf*, разобрать *pf*.

sortie *n* вылазка.

SOS *n* (радио)сигнал бедствия.

soul *n* душа.

sound[1] *adj* (*healthy, thorough*) здоровый; (*in good condition*) исправный; (*logical*) здравый, разумный; (*of sleep*) крепкий.

sound[2] *n* (*noise*) звук, шум; *attrib*

звуковой; ~ effects звуковые эффекты *m pl*; *vi* звучать *impf*, про~ *pf*.

sound[3] *vt* (*naut*) измерять *impf*, измерить *pf* глубину +*gen*; (*fig*) зондировать *impf*, по~ *pf*; *n* зонд.

sound[4] *n* (*strait*) пролив.

soup *n* суп; *vt*: ~ed up форсированный.

sour *adj* кислый; ~ cream сметана; *vt & i* (*fig*) озлоблять(ся) *impf*, озлобить(ся) *pf*.

source *n* источник; (*of river*) исток.

south *n* юг; (*naut*) зюйд; *adj* южный; *adv* к югу, на юг; ~-east юго-восток; ~-west юго-запад. **southerly** *adj* южный. **southern** *adj* южный. **southerner** *n* южанин, -анка. **southward(s)** *adv* на юг, к югу.

souvenir *n* сувенир.

sovereign *adj* суверенный; *n* монарх. **sovereignty** *n* суверенитет.

soviet *n* совет; S~ Union Советский Союз; *adj* (S~) советский.

sow[1] *n* свинья.

sow[2] *vt* (*seed*) сеять *impf*, по~ *pf*; (*field*) засевать *impf*, засеять *pf*.

soya *n*: ~ bean соевый боб.

spa *n* курорт.

space *n* (*place, room*) место; (*expanse*) пространство; (*interval*) промежуток; (*outer* ~) космос; *attrib* космический; *vt* расставлять *impf*, расставить *pf* с промежутками. **spacecraft, -ship** *n* космический корабль *m*. **spacious** *adj* просторный.

spade *n* (*tool*) лопата; *pl* (*cards*) пики (пик) *pl*.

spaghetti *n* спагетти *neut indecl*.

Spain *n* Испания.

span *n* (*of bridge*) пролёт; (*aeron*) размах; *vt* (*of bridge*) соединять *impf*, соединить *pf* стороны +*gen*; (*river*) берега +*gen*; (*fig*) охватывать *impf*, охватить *pf*.

Spaniard *n* испанец, -нка. **Spanish** *adj* испанский.

spank *vt* шлёпать *impf*, шлёпнуть *pf*.

spanner *n* гаечный ключ.

spar[1] *n* (*aeron*) лонжерон.

spar[2] *vi* боксировать *impf*; (*fig*) препираться *impf*.

spare *adj* (*in reserve*) запасной; (*extra, to* ~) лишний; (*of seat, time*) свобо́дный; ~ parts запасны́е ча́сти f pl; ~ room ко́мната для госте́й; n: pl запча́сти f pl; vt (grudge) жале́ть impf, по~ pf +acc, gen; he ~d no pains он не жале́л трудо́в; (do without) обходи́ться impf, обойти́сь pf без+gen; (time) уделя́ть impf, удели́ть pf; (show mercy towards) щади́ть impf, по~ pf; (save from) избавля́ть impf, изба́вить pf от+gen: ~ me the details изба́вьте меня́ от подро́бностей.

spark n и́скра; ~-plug запа́льная свеча́; vt (~ off) вызыва́ть impf, вы́звать pf.

sparkle vi сверка́ть impf.

sparrow n воробе́й.

sparse adj ре́дкий.

Spartan adj спарта́нский.

spasm n спазм. **spasmodic** adj спазмоди́ческий.

spastic n парали́тик.

spate n разли́в; (fig) пото́к.

spatial adj простра́нственный.

spatter, splatter vt (liquid) бры́згать impf +instr; (person etc.) забры́згивать impf, забры́згать pf (with +instr); vi плеска́ть(ся) impf, плесну́ть pf.

spatula n шпа́тель m.

spawn n & i мета́ть impf (икру́); (fig) порожда́ть impf, породи́ть pf.

speak vt & i говори́ть impf, сказа́ть pf; vi (make speech) выступа́ть impf, вы́ступить pf (с ре́чью); (~ out) выска́зываться impf, вы́сказаться pf (for за+acc; against про́тив+gen). **speaker** n говоря́щий sb; (giving speech) выступа́ющий sb; (orator) ора́тор; (S~, parl) спи́кер; (loud-~) громкоговори́тель m.

spear n копьё; vt пронза́ть impf, пронзи́ть pf копьём. **spearhead** vt возглавля́ть impf, возгла́вить pf.

special adj осо́бый, специа́льный. **specialist** n специали́ст, ~ка. **speciality** n специа́льность. **specialization** n специализа́ция. **specialize** vt & i специализи́ровать(ся) impf & pf. **specially** adv осо́бенно.

species n вид.

specific adj осо́бенный. **specification(s)** n специфика́ция. **specify** vt уточня́ть impf, уточни́ть pf.

specimen n образе́ц, экземпля́р.

speck n кра́пинка, пя́тнышко. **speckled** adj кра́пчатый.

spectacle n зре́лище; pl очки́ (-ко́в) pl.

spectacular adj эффе́ктный; (amazing) потряса́ющий.

spectator n зри́тель m.

spectre n при́зрак.

spectrum n спектр.

speculate vi (meditate) размышля́ть impf, размы́слить pf (on o+prep); (conjecture) гада́ть impf; (comm) спекули́ровать impf. **speculation** n (conjecture) дога́дка; (comm) спекуля́ция. **speculative** adj гипотети́ческий; спекуляти́вный. **speculator** n спекуля́нт.

speech n речь. **speechless** adj (fig) онеме́вший.

speed n ско́рость; vi мча́ться impf, про~ pf; (illegally) превыша́ть, превы́сить pf ско́рость; vt: ~ up ускоря́ть impf, ускори́ть pf. **speedboat** n быстрохо́дный ка́тер. **speedometer** n спидо́метр. **speedy** adj бы́стрый, ско́рый.

spell[1] n (charm) заговор.

spell[2] vt (say) произноси́ть impf, произнести́ pf по бу́квам; (write) пра́вильно писа́ть impf, на~ pf; how do you ~ that word? как пи́шется э́то сло́во?

spell[3] n (period) пери́од.

spellbound adj зачаро́ванный.

spelling n правописа́ние.

spend vt (money; effort) тра́тить impf, ис~, по~ pf; (time) проводи́ть impf, провести́ pf.

sperm n спе́рма.

sphere n сфе́ра; (ball) шар. **spherical** adj сфери́ческий.

spice n пря́ность; vt приправля́ть impf, припра́вить pf. **spicy** adj пря́ный; (fig) пика́нтный.

spider n пау́к.

spike n (point) острие́; (on fence) зубе́ц; (on shoes) шип.

spill vt & i (liquid) пролива́ть(ся) impf, проли́ть(ся) pf; (dry substance) рассыпа́ть(ся) impf, рассы́пать(ся) pf.

spin vt (thread etc.) прясть impf, с~ pf; (coin) подбра́сывать impf, подбро́сить pf; vt & i (turn) кружи́ть(ся) impf; ~ out (prolong) затяги-

вать *impf*, затяну́ть *pf*.
spinach *n* шпина́т.
spinal *adj* спинно́й; ~ column спинно́й хребе́т; ~ cord спинно́й мозг.
spindle *n* ось *m*. **spindly** *adj* дли́нный и то́нкий.
spine *n* (*anat*) позвоно́чник, хребе́т; (*prickle*) игла́; (*of book*) корешо́к.
spineless *adj* (*fig*) бесхара́ктерный.
spinning *n* пряде́ние; ~-wheel пря́лка.
spinster *n* незаму́жняя же́нщина.
spiral *adj* спира́льный; (*staircase*) винтово́й; *n* спира́ль; *vi* (*rise sharply*) ре́зко возраста́ть *impf*, возрасти́ *pf*.
spire *n* шпиль *m*.
spirit *n* дух, душа́; *pl* (*mood*) настрое́ние; *pl* (*drinks*) спиртно́е *sb*; ~-level ватерпа́с; *vt*: ~ away та́йно уноси́ть *impf*, унести́ *pf*. **spirited** *adj* живо́й. **spiritual** *adj* духо́вный. **spiritualism** *n* спирити́зм. **spiritualist** *n* спири́т.
spit[1] *n* (*skewer*) ве́ртел.
spit[2] *vi* плева́ть *impf*, плю́нуть *pf*; (*of rain*) мороси́ть *impf*; (*of fire*) разбры́згивать *impf*, разбры́згать *pf* и́скры; (*sizzle*) шипе́ть *impf*; *vt*: ~ out выплёвывать *impf*, вы́плюнуть *pf*; ~ing image то́чная ко́пия; *n* слюна́.
spite *n* зло́ба; in ~ of несмотря́ на +*acc*. **spiteful** *adj* зло́бный.
spittle *n* слюна́.
splash *vt* (*person*) забры́згивать *impf*, забры́згать *pf* (with +*instr*); (~ liquid) бры́згать *impf* +*instr*; *vi* пле́ска́ть(ся) *impf*, плесну́ть *pf* (*move*) шлёпать *impf*, шлёпнуть *pf* (through по+*dat*); *n* (*act, sound*) плеск; (*mark made*) пятно́.
splatter *see* spatter
spleen *n* селезёнка.
splendid *adj* великоле́пный. **splendour** *n* великоле́пие.
splice *vt* (*ropes etc.*) сра́щивать *impf*, срасти́ть *pf*; (*film, tape*) скле́ивать *impf*, скле́ить *pf* концы́+*gen*.
splint *n* ши́на.
splinter *n* оско́лок; (*in skin*) зано́за; *vt & i* расщепля́ть(ся) *impf*, расще́пи́ть(ся) *pf*.
split *n* расще́лина, расще́п; (*schism*) раско́л; *pl* шпага́т; *vt & i* расщепля́ть(ся) *impf*, расщепи́ть(ся) *pf*;

раска́лывать(ся) *impf*, расколо́ть(ся) *pf*; *vt* (*divide*) дели́ть *impf*, раз~ *pf*; ~ second мгнове́ние о́ка; ~ up (*part company*) расходи́ться *impf*, разойти́сь *pf*.
splutter *vi* бры́згать *impf* слюно́й; *vt* (*utter*) говори́ть *impf* захлёбываясь.
spoil *n* (*booty*) добы́ча; *vt & i* (*damage; decay*) по́ртить(ся) *impf*, ис~ *pf*; *vt* (*indulge*) балова́ть *impf*, из~ *pf*.
spoke *n* спи́ца.
spokesman, -woman *n* представи́тель *m*, ~ница.
sponge *n* гу́бка; ~ cake бискви́т; *vt* (*wash*) мыть *impf*, вы́~, по~ *pf* гу́бкой; *vi*: ~ on жить *impf* за счёт+*gen*. **sponger** *n* прижива́льщик. **spongy** *adj* гу́бчатый.
sponsor *n* спо́нсор; *vt* финанси́ровать *impf & pf*.
spontaneity *n* спонта́нность. **spontaneous** *adj* спонта́нный.
spoof *n* паро́дия.
spooky *adj* жу́ткий.
spool *n* кату́шка.
spoon *n* ло́жка; *vt* че́рпать *impf*, черпну́ть *pf* ло́жкой. **spoonful** *n* ло́жка.
sporadic *adj* спора́дический.
sport *n* спорт; ~s car спорти́вный автомоби́ль *m*; *vt* щеголя́ть *impf*, щегольну́ть *pf* +*instr*. **sportsman** *n* спортсме́н. **sporty** *adj* спорти́вный.
spot *n* (*place*) ме́сто; (*mark*) пятно́; (*pimple*) пры́щик; on the ~ на ме́сте; (*at once*) сра́зу; *vt* ~ check вы́борочная прове́рка; *vt* (*notice*) замеча́ть *impf*, заме́тить *pf*. **spotless** *adj* абсолю́тно чи́стый. **spotlight** *n* проже́ктор; (*fig*) внима́ние. **spotty** *adj* прыщева́тый.
spouse *n* супру́г, ~а.
spout *vi* бить *impf* струёй; хлы́нуть *pf*; (*pontificate*) ора́торствовать *impf*; *vt* изверга́ть *impf*, изве́ргнуть *pf*; (*verses etc.*) деклами́ровать *impf*, про~ *pf*; *n* (*tube*) но́сик; (*jet*) струя́.
sprain *vt* растя́гивать *impf*, растяну́ть *pf*; *n* растяже́ние.
sprawl *vi* (*of person*) разва́ливаться *impf*, развали́ться *pf*; (*of town*) раски́дываться *impf*, раски́нуться *pf*.

spray[1] *n* (*flowers*) вет(оч)ка.

spray[2] *n* брызги (-г) *pl*; (*atomizer*) пульвериза́тор; *vt* опры́скивать *impf*, опры́скать *pf* (*with* +*instr*); (*cause to scatter*) распыля́ть *impf*, распыли́ть *pf*.

spread *vt & i* (*news, disease, etc.*) распространя́ть(ся) *impf*, распространи́ть(ся) *pf*; *vt* (~ *out*) расстила́ть *impf*, разостла́ть *pf*; (*unfurl, unroll*) развёртывать *impf*, разверну́ть *pf*; (*bread etc.* +*acc*; *butter etc.* +*instr*) нама́зывать *impf*, нама́зать *pf*; *n* (*expansion*) распростране́ние; (*span*) разма́х; (*feast*) пир; (*paste*) па́ста.

spree *n* кутёж; go on a ~ кути́ть *impf*, кутну́ть *pf*.

sprig *n* ве́точка.

sprightly *adj* бо́дрый.

spring *vi* (*jump*) пры́гать *impf*, пры́гнуть *pf*; *vt* (*tell unexpectedly*) неожи́данно сообща́ть *impf*, сообщи́ть *pf* (on +*dat*); ~ a leak дава́ть *impf*, дать *pf* течь; ~ from (*originate*) происходи́ть *impf*, произойти́ *pf* из+*gen*; *n* (*jump*) прыжо́к; (*season*) весна́, *attrib* весе́нний; (*water*) исто́чник; (*elasticity*) упру́гость; (*coil*) пружи́на; ~-clean генера́льная убо́рка. springboard *n* трампли́н.

sprinkle *vt* (*with liquid*) опры́скивать *impf*, опры́скать *pf* (*with* +*instr*); (*with solid*) посыпа́ть *impf*, посы́пать *pf* (*with* +*instr*). sprinkler *n* разбры́згиватель *m*.

sprint *vi* бежа́ть *impf* на коро́ткую диста́нцию; (*rush*) рвану́ться *pf*; *n* спринт. sprinter *n* спри́нтер.

sprout *vi* пуска́ть *impf*, пусти́ть *pf* ростки́; *n* росто́к; *pl* брюссе́льская капу́ста.

spruce[1] *adj* наря́дный, элега́нтный; *vt*: ~ o.s. up приводи́ть *impf*, привести́ *pf* себя́ в поря́док.

spruce[2] *n* ель.

spur *n* шпо́ра; (*fig*) сти́мул; on the ~ of the moment под влия́нием мину́ты; *vt*: ~ on подхлёстывать *impf*, подхлестну́ть *pf*.

spurious *adj* подде́льный.

spurn *vt* отверга́ть *impf*, отве́ргнуть *pf*.

spurt *n* (*jet*) струя́; (*effort*) рыво́к; *vi* бить *impf* струёй; (*make an effort*) де́лать *impf*, с~ *pf* рыво́к.

spy *n* шпио́н; *vi* шпио́нить *impf* (on за+*instr*). spying *n* шпиона́ж.

squabble *n* перебра́нка; *vi* вздо́рить *impf*, по~ *pf*.

squad *n* кома́нда, гру́ппа.

squadron *n* (*mil*) эскадро́н; (*naut*) эска́дра; (*aeron*) эскадри́лья.

squalid *adj* убо́гий.

squall *n* шквал.

squalor *n* убо́жество.

squander *vt* растра́чивать *impf*, растра́тить *pf*.

square *n* (*shape*) квадра́т; (*in town*) пло́щадь; (*on paper, material*) кле́тка; (*instrument*) науго́льник; *adj* квадра́тный; (*meal*) пло́тный; ~ root квадра́тный ко́рень *m*; *vt* (*accounts*) своди́ть *impf*, свести́ *pf*; (*math*) возводи́ть *impf*, возвести́ *pf* в квадра́т; *vi* (*correspond*) соотве́тствовать *impf* (*with* +*dat*).

squash *n* (*crowd*) толку́чка; (*drink*) сок; *vt* разда́вливать *impf*, разда́вить *pf*; (*suppress*) подавля́ть *impf*, подави́ть *pf*; *vi* вти́скиваться *impf*, вти́снуться *pf*.

squat *adj* призе́мистый; *vi* сиде́ть *impf* на ко́рточках; ~ down сади́ться *impf*, сесть *pf* на ко́рточки.

squatter *n* незако́нный жиле́ц.

squawk *n* клёкот; *vi* клекота́ть *impf*.

squeak *n* писк; (*of object*) скрип; *vi* пища́ть *impf*, пи́скнуть *pf*; (*of object*) скрипе́ть *impf*, скри́пнуть *pf*. squeaky *adj* пискли́вый, скрипу́чий.

squeal *n* визг; *vi* визжа́ть *impf*, ви́згнуть *pf*.

squeamish *adj* брезгли́вый.

squeeze *n* (*crush*) да́вка; (*pressure*) сжа́тие; (*hand*) пожа́тие; *vt* дави́ть *impf*; сжима́ть *impf*, сжать *pf*; ~ in впи́хивать(ся) *impf*, впихну́ть(ся) *pf*; вти́скивать(ся) *impf*, вти́снуть(ся) *pf*; ~ out выжима́ть *impf*, вы́жать *pf*; ~ through проти́скивать(ся) *impf*, проти́снуть(ся) *pf*.

squelch *vi* хлю́пать *impf*, хлю́пнуть *pf*.

squid *n* кальма́р.

squint *n* косогла́зие; *vi* коси́ть *impf*; (*screw up eyes*) щу́риться *impf*.

squire *n* сквайр, поме́щик.

squirm *vi* (*wriggle*) извива́ться *impf*, изви́ться *pf*.

squirrel n бе́лка.

squirt n струя́; vi бить impf струёй; vt пуска́ть impf, пусти́ть pf струю́ (substance +gen; at na+acc).

St. abbr (of Street) ул., у́лица; (of Saint) св., Свято́й, -а́я.

stab n уда́р (ножо́м etc.); (pain) внеза́пная о́страя боль; vt наноси́ть impf, нанести́ pf уда́р (ножо́м etc.) (person +dat).

stability n усто́йчивость, стаби́льность. **stabilize** vt стабилизи́ровать impf & pf.

stable adj усто́йчивый, стаби́льный; (psych) уравнове́шенный; n коню́шня.

staccato n стакка́то neut indecl; adv стакка́то; adj отры́вистый.

stack n ку́ча; vt скла́дывать impf, сложи́ть pf в ку́чу.

stadium n стадио́н.

staff n (personnel) штат, сотру́дники m pl; (stick) по́сох, жезл; adj шта́тный; (mil) штабно́й.

stag n саме́ц-оле́нь m.

stage n (theat) сце́на; (period) ста́дия; vt (theat) ста́вить impf, по~ pf; (organize) организова́ть impf & pf; ~-manager режиссёр.

stagger vi шата́ться impf, шатну́ться pf; vt (hours of work etc.) распределя́ть impf, распредели́ть pf. **be staggered** vi поража́ться impf, порази́ться pf. **staggering** adj потряса́ющий.

stagnant adj (water) стоя́чий; (fig) засто́йный. **stagnate** vi заста́иваться impf, застоя́ться pf; (fig) косне́ть impf, за~ pf.

staid adj степе́нный.

stain n пятно́; (dye) кра́ска; vt па́чкать impf, за~, ис~ pf; (dye) окра́шивать impf, окра́сить pf; ~ed glass цветно́е стекло́. **stainless** adj: ~ steel нержаве́ющая сталь.

stair n ступе́нька. **staircase, stairs** n pl ле́стница.

stake n (stick) кол; (bet) ста́вка; (comm) до́ля; be at ~ быть поста́вленным на ка́рту; vt (mark out) огора́живать impf, огороди́ть pf ко́льями; (support) укрепля́ть impf, укрепи́ть pf ко́лом; (risk) ста́вить impf, по~ pf на ка́рту.

stale adj несве́жий; (musty, damp)

за́тхлый; (hackneyed) изби́тый.

stalemate n пат; (fig) тупи́к.

stalk n сте́бель m; vt высле́живать impf; vi (& t) (stride) ше́ствовать impf (no+dat).

stall n сто́йло; (booth) ларёк; pl (theat) парте́р; vi (of engine) гло́хнуть impf, за~ pf; (play for time) оття́гивать impf, оттяну́ть pf вре́мя; vt (engine) неча́янно заглуша́ть impf, заглуши́ть pf.

stallion n жеребе́ц.

stalwart adj сто́йкий; n сто́йкий приве́рженец.

stamina n выно́сливость.

stammer vi заика́ться impf; n заика́ние.

stamp n печа́ть; (postage) (почто́вая) ма́рка; vt штампова́ть impf, vi то́пать impf, то́пнуть pf (нога́ми); ~ out поборо́ть pf.

stampede n пани́ческое бе́гство; vi обраща́ться impf в пани́ческое бе́гство.

stance n пози́ция.

stand n (hat, coat) ве́шалка; (music) пюпи́тр; (umbrella, support) подста́вка; (booth) ларёк; (taxi) стоя́нка; (at stadium) трибу́на; (position) пози́ция; (resistance) сопротивле́ние; vi стоя́ть impf; (~ up) встава́ть impf, встать pf; (remain in force) остава́ться impf, оста́ться в си́ле; vt (put) ста́вить impf, по~ pf; (endure) терпе́ть impf, по~ pf; ~ back отходи́ть impf, отойти́ pf (from от+gen); (not go forward) держа́ться impf позади́; ~ by (vi) (not interfere) не вме́шиваться impf, вмеша́ться pf; (be ready) быть impf на гото́ве; (vt) (support) подде́рживать impf, поддержа́ть pf; (stick to) приде́рживаться impf +gen; ~ down (resign) уходи́ть impf, уйти́ pf с по́ста (as +gen); ~ for (signify) означа́ть impf; (tolerate) I shall not ~ for it я не потерплю́; ~-in замести́тель m; ~ in (for) замеща́ть impf, замести́ть pf; ~ out выделя́ться impf, вы́делиться pf; ~ up встава́ть impf, встать pf; ~ up for (defend) отста́ивать impf, отстоя́ть pf; ~ up to (endure) выде́рживать impf, вы́держать pf; (not give in to) противостоя́ть impf +dat.

standard n (*norm*) станда́рт, норм; (*flag*) зна́мя neut; ~ of living жи́зненный у́ровень m; adj норма́льный, станда́ртный. **standardization** n нормализа́ция, стандартиза́ция. **standardize** vt стандартизи́ровать impf & pf; нормализова́ть impf & pf.

standing n положе́ние; adj (*upright*) сто́йчий; (*permanent*) постоя́нный.

standpoint n то́чка зре́ния.

standstill n остано́вка, засто́й, па́уза; be at a ~ стоя́ть impf на мёртвой то́чке; bring (come) to a ~ остана́вливать(ся) impf, останови́ть(ся) pf.

stanza n строфа́.

staple[1] n (*metal bar*) скоба́; (*for paper*) скре́пка; vt скрепля́ть impf, скрепи́ть pf.

staple[2] n (*product*) гла́вный проду́кт; adj основно́й.

star n звезда́; (*asterisk*) звёздочка; vi игра́ть impf, сыгра́ть pf гла́вную роль. **starfish** n морска́я звезда́.

starboard n пра́вый борт.

starch n крахма́л; vt крахма́лить impf, на~ pf. **starchy** adj крахма́листый; (*prim*) чо́порный.

stare n при́стальный взгляд; vi при́стально смотре́ть impf (at на+acc).

stark adj (*bare*) го́лый; (*desolate*) пусты́нный; (*sharp*) ре́зкий; adv соверше́нно.

starling n скворе́ц.

starry adj звёздный.

start n нача́ло; (*sport*) старт; vi начина́ться impf, нача́ться pf; (*engine*) заводи́ться impf, завести́сь pf; (*set out*) отправля́ться impf, отпра́виться pf; (*shudder*) вздра́гивать impf, вздро́гнуть pf; (*sport*) старто́ва́ть impf & pf; vt начина́ть impf, нача́ть pf (gerund, inf, +inf by, +gerund с того́, что...; with +instr, с +gen); (*car, engine*) заводи́ть impf, завести́ pf; (*fire, rumour*) пуска́ть impf, пусти́ть pf; (*found*) осно́вывать impf, основа́ть pf. **starter** n (*tech*) ста́ртёр; (*cul*) заку́ска. **starting-point** n отправно́й пункт.

startle vt испуга́ть pf.

starvation n го́лод. **starve** vi голода́ть impf; (*to death*) умира́ть impf, умере́ть с го́лоду; vt мори́ть impf,

по~, у~ pf го́лодом. **starving** adj голода́ющий; (*hungry*) о́чень голо́дный.

state n (*condition*) состоя́ние; (*polit*) госуда́рство, штат; adj (*ceremonial*) торже́ственный; пара́дный; (*polit*) госуда́рственный; vt (*announce*) заявля́ть impf, заяви́ть pf; (*expound*) излага́ть impf, изложи́ть pf. **stateless** adj не име́ющий гражда́нства. **stately** adj вели́чественный. **statement** n заявле́ние; (*comm*) отчёт. **statesman** n госуда́рственный де́ятель m.

static adj неподви́жный.

station n (*rly*) вокза́л, ста́нция; (*social*) обще́ственное положе́ние; (*meteorological, hydro-electric power, radio etc.*) ста́нция; (*post*) пост; vt размеща́ть impf, размести́ть pf. **stationary** adj неподви́жный.

stationery n канцеля́рские принадле́жности f pl; (*writing-paper*) почто́вая бума́га; ~ shop канцеля́рский магази́н.

statistic n статисти́ческое да́нное. **statistical** adj статисти́ческий. **statistician** n стати́стик. **statistics** n стати́стика.

statue n ста́туя. **statuette** n статуэ́тка.

stature n рост; (*merit*) кали́бр.

status n ста́тус. **status quo** n ста́тус-кво́ neut indecl.

statute n стату́т. **statutory** adj устано́вленный зако́ном.

staunch adj ве́рный.

stave vt: ~ off предотвраща́ть impf, предотврати́ть pf.

stay n (*time spent*) пребыва́ние; vi (*remain*) остава́ться impf, оста́ться pf (to dinner обе́дать); (*put up*) остана́вливаться impf, останови́ться pf (at place) в+prep; at (friends' etc.) y+gen); (*live*) жить; ~ behind остава́ться impf, оста́ться pf; ~ in остава́ться impf, оста́ться pf до́ма; ~ up не ложи́ться impf спать; (*trousers*) держа́ться impf. **staying-power** n вы́носливость.

stead n: stand s.o. in good ~ ока́зываться impf, оказа́ться pf поле́зным кому́-л.

steadfast adj сто́йкий, непоколеби́мый.

steady adj (firm) усто́йчивый; (continuous) непреры́вный; (wind, temperature) ро́вный; (speed) постоя́нный; (unshakeable) непоколеби́мый; vt (boat etc.) приводи́ть impf, привести́ pf в равнове́сие.

steak n бифште́кс.

steal vt & abs ворова́ть impf, с~ pf; красть impf, у~ pf; vi (creep) кра́сться impf; подкра́дываться impf, подкра́сться pf. **stealth** n: by ~ укра́дкой. **stealthy** adj ворова́тый, та́йный, скры́тый.

steam n пар; at full ~ на всех пара́х; let off ~ (fig) дава́ть impf, дать pf вы́ход свои́м чу́вствам; vt па́рить impf; vi па́риться impf, по~ pf; (vessel) ~ up (mist over) запотева́ть impf, запоте́ть pf; поте́ть impf, за~, от~ pf; ~ engine парова́я маши́на. **steamer**, **steamship** n парохо́д. **steamy** adj напо́лненный па́ром; (passionate) горя́чий.

steed n конь m.

steel n сталь; adj стально́й; vt: ~ o.s. ожесточа́ться impf, ожесточи́ться pf; ~ works сталелите́йный заво́д. **steely** adj стально́й.

steep¹ adj круто́й; (excessive) чрезме́рный.

steep² vt (immerse) погружа́ть impf, погрузи́ть pf (in в+acc); (saturate) пропи́тывать impf, пропита́ть pf (in +instr).

steeple n шпиль m. **steeplechase** n ска́чки f pl с препя́тствиями.

steer vt управля́ть impf, пра́вить impf +instr; vi abs рули́ть impf; ~ clear of избега́ть impf, избежа́ть pf +gen. **steering-wheel** n руль m.

stem¹ n сте́бель m; (of wine-glass) но́жка; (ling) осно́ва; vi: ~ from происходи́ть impf, произойти́ pf от+gen.

stem² vt (stop) остана́вливать impf, останови́ть pf.

stench n злово́ние.

stencil n трафаре́т; (tech) шабло́н; vt наноси́ть impf, нанести́ pf по трафаре́ту. **stencilled** adj трафаре́тный.

step n (pace, action) шаг; (dance) па neut indecl; (of stairs, ladder) ступе́нь; ~ by ~ шаг за ша́гом; in ~ в но́гу; out of ~ не в но́гу; take ~s

принима́ть impf, приня́ть pf ме́ры vi шага́ть impf, шагну́ть pf; ступа́ть impf, ступи́ть pf; ~ **aside** сторони́ться impf, по~ pf; ~ **back** отступа́ть impf, отступи́ть pf; ~ **down** (resign) уходи́ть impf, уйти́ pf в отста́вку; ~ **forward** выступа́ть impf, вы́ступить pf; ~ **in** (intervene) вме́шиваться impf, вмеша́ться pf; ~ **on** наступа́ть impf, наступи́ть pf на +acc (s.o.'s foot кому́-л. на́ ногу); ~ **over** перешага́ивать impf, перешагну́ть pf +acc, че́рез+acc; ~ **up** (increase) повыша́ть impf, повы́сить pf. **step-ladder** n стремя́нка. **stepping-stone** n ка́мень m для перехо́да; (fig) сре́дство. **steps** n pl ле́стница.

stepbrother n сво́дный брат. **stepdaughter** n па́дчерица. **stepfather** n о́тчим. **stepmother** n ма́чеха. **stepsister** n сво́дная сестра́. **stepson** n па́сынок.

steppe n степь.

stereo n (system) стереофони́ческая систе́ма; (stereophony) стереофо́ния; adj (recorded in ~) сте́рео indecl. **stereophonic** adj стереофони́ческий. **stereotype** n стереоти́п. **stereotyped** adj стереоти́пный.

sterile adj стери́льный. **sterility** n стери́льность. **sterilization** n стерилиза́ция. **sterilize** vt стерилизова́ть impf & pf.

sterling n сте́рлинг; pound ~ фунт сте́рлингов; adj сте́рлинговый.

stern¹ n корма́.

stern² adj суро́вый, стро́гий.

stethoscope n стетоско́п.

stew n (cul) мя́со тушёное вме́сте с овоща́ми; vt & i (cul) туши́ть(ся) impf, с~ pf; (fig) томи́ть(ся) impf.

steward n бортпроводни́к. **stewardess** n стюарде́сса.

stick¹ n па́лка; (of chalk etc.) па́лочка; (hockey) клю́шка.

stick² vt (spear) зака́лывать impf, заколо́ть pf; (make adhere) прикле́ивать impf, прикле́ить pf (to к+dat); (coll) (put) ста́вить impf, по~ pf; (lay) класть impf, положи́ть pf; (endure) терпе́ть impf, вы́~ pf; vi (adhere) ли́пнуть impf (to к+dat); прилипа́ть impf, прили́пнуть pf (to к+dat); ~ **in** (thrust in)

втыка́ть *impf*, воткну́ть *pf*; (*into opening*) всо́вывать *impf*, всу́нуть *pf*; ~ on (*glue on*) накле́ивать *impf*, накле́ить *pf*; ~ out (*thrust out*) высо́вывать *impf*, вы́сунуть *pf* (*from* из+*gen*); (*project*) торча́ть *impf*; ~ to (*keep to*) приде́рживаться *impf*, придержа́ться *pf* +*gen*; (*remain at*) не отвлека́ться *impf* от+*gen*; ~ together держа́ться *impf* вме́сте; ~ up for защища́ть *impf*, защити́ть *pf*; be, get, stuck застрева́ть *impf*, застря́ть *pf*. **sticker** *n* накле́йка.
sticky *adj* ли́пкий.
stiff *adj* жёсткий, неги́бкий; (*prim*) чо́порный; (*difficult*) тру́дный; (*penalty*) суро́вый; be ~ (*ache*) боле́ть *impf*. **stiffen** *vt* де́лать *impf*, с~ *pf* жёстким; *vi* станови́ться *impf*, стать *pf* жёстким. **stiffness** *n* жёсткость; (*primness*) чо́порность.
stifle *vt* души́ть *impf*, за~ *pf*; (*suppress*) подавля́ть *impf*, подави́ть *pf*; (*sound*) заглуша́ть *impf*, заглуши́ть *pf*; *vi* задыха́ться *impf*, задохну́ться *pf*. **stifling** *adj* уду́шливый.
stigma *n* клеймо́.
stile *n* перела́з (*coll*).
stilettos *n pl* ту́фли *f pl* на шпи́льках.
still *adv* (всё) ещё; (*nevertheless*) тем не ме́нее; (*motionless*) неподви́жно; stand ~ не дви́гаться *impf*, дви́нуться *pf*; *n* (*quiet*) тишина́; *adj* ти́хий; (*immobile*) неподви́жный. **still-born** *adj* мертворождённый. **still life** *n* натюрмо́рт. **stillness** *n* тишина́.
stilted *adj* ходу́льный.
stimulant *n* возбужда́ющее сре́дство. **stimulate** *vt* возбужда́ть *impf*, возбуди́ть *pf*. **stimulating** *adj* возбуди́тельный. **stimulation** *n* возбужде́ние. **stimulus** *n* сти́мул.
sting *n* (*wound*) уку́с; (*stinger*; *fig*) жа́ло; *vt* жа́лить *impf*, у~ *pf*; *vi* (*burn*) жечь *impf*. **stinging** *adj* (*caustic*) язви́тельный.
stingy *adj* скупо́й.
stink *n* вонь; *vi* воня́ть *impf* (of +*instr*). **stinking** *adj* воню́чий.
stint *n* срок; *vi*: ~on скупи́ться *impf*, по~ *pf* на+*acc*.
stipend *n* (*salary*) жа́лование; (*grant*) стипе́ндия.

stipulate *vt* обусло́вливать *impf*, обусло́вить *pf*. **stipulation** *n* усло́вие.
stir *n* (*commotion*) шум; *vt* (*mix*) меша́ть *impf*, по~ *pf*; (*excite*) волнова́ть *impf*, вз~ *pf*; *vi* (*move*) шевели́ться *impf*, шевельну́ться *pf*; ~ up возбужда́ть *impf*, возбуди́ть *pf*. **stirring** *adj* волну́ющий.
stirrup *n* стре́мя *neut*.
stitch *n* стежо́к; (*knitting*) пе́тля; (*med*) шов; (*pain*) ко́лики *f pl*; *vt* (*embroider, make line of*) стро́чить *impf*, про~ *pf*; (*join by sewing, make, suture*) сшива́ть *impf*, сшить *pf*; ~ up зашива́ть *impf*, заши́ть *pf*. **stitching** *n* (*stitches*) стро́чка.
stoat *n* горноста́й.
stock *n* (*store*) запа́с; (*of shop*) ассортиме́нт; (*live~*) скот; (*cul*) бульо́н; (*lineage*) семья́; (*fin*) а́кции *f pl*; in ~ в нали́чии; out of ~ распро́дан; take ~ of крити́чески оце́нивать *impf*, оцени́ть *pf*; *adj* станда́ртный; *vt* име́ть в нали́чии; ~ up запаса́ться *impf*, запасти́сь *pf* (with +*instr*). **stockbroker** *n* биржево́й ма́клер. **stock-exchange** *n* би́ржа. **stockpile** *n* запа́с; *vt* нака́пливать *impf*, накопи́ть *pf*. **stock-taking** *n* переучёт.
stocking *n* чуло́к.
stocky *adj* призе́мистый.
stodgy *adj* тяжёлый.
stoic(al) *adj* стои́ческий. **stoicism** *n* стоици́зм.
stoke *vt* топи́ть *impf*.
stolid *adj* флегмати́чный.
stomach *n* желу́док, (*also surface of body*) живо́т; *vt* терпе́ть *impf*, по~ *pf*. **stomach ache** *n* боль в животе́.
stone *n* ка́мень *m*; (*of fruit*) ко́сточка; *adj* ка́менный; *vt* побива́ть *impf*, поби́ть *pf* камня́ми; (*fruit*) вынима́ть *impf*, вы́нуть *pf* ко́сточки из+*gen*. **Stone Age** *n* ка́менный век. **stone-deaf** *adj* соверше́нно глухо́й. **stone-mason** *n* ка́менщик. **stonily** *adv* с ка́менным выраже́нием, хо́лодно. **stony** *adj* камени́стый; (*fig*) ка́менный.
stool *n* табуре́т, табуре́тка.
stoop *n* суту́лость; *vt & i* суту́лить(ся) *impf*, с~ *pf*; (*bend down*) наклоня́ть(ся) *impf*, наклони́ть(ся)

pf; ~ to (*abase o.s.*) унижа́ться *impf*, уни́зиться *pf* до+*gen*; (*condescend*) снисходи́ть *impf*, снизойти́ *pf* до +*gen*. **stooped, stooping** *adj* суту́лый.

stop *n* остано́вка; put a ~ to положи́ть *pf* коне́ц +*dat*; *vt* остана́вливать *impf*, останови́ть *pf*; (*discontinue*) прекраща́ть *impf*, прекрати́ть *pf*; (*restrain*) уде́рживать *impf*, удержа́ть *pf* (*from* от+*gen*); *vi* остана́вливаться *impf*, останови́ться *pf*; (*discontinue*) прекраща́ться *impf*, прекрати́ться *pf*; (*cease*) переставать *impf*, переста́ть *pf* (+*inf*); ~ up заты́кать *impf*, заткну́ть *pf*. **stoppage** *n* остано́вка; (*strike*) забасто́вка. **stopper** *n* про́бка. **stop-press** *n* э́кстренное сообще́ние в газе́те. **stop-watch** *n* секундоме́р.

storage *n* хране́ние. **store** *n* запа́с; (*storehouse*) склад; (*shop*) магази́н; set ~ by цени́ть *impf*; what is in ~ for me? что ждёт меня́ впереди́?; *vt* запаса́ть *impf*, запасти́ *pf*; (*put into storage*) сдава́ть *impf*, сдать *pf* на хране́ние. **storehouse** *n* склад. **store-room** кладова́я *sb*.

storey *n* эта́ж.

stork *n* а́ист.

storm *n* бу́ря, (*thunder* ~) гроза́; *vt* (*mil*) штурмова́ть *impf*; *vi* бушева́ть *impf*. **stormy** *adj* бу́рный.

story *n* расска́з, по́весть; (*anecdote*) анекдо́т; (*plot*) фа́була; ~-teller расска́зчик.

stout *adj* (*strong*) кре́пкий, (*staunch*) сто́йкий; (*portly*) доро́дный.

stove *n* (*with fire inside*) печь; (*cooker*) плита́.

stow *vt* укла́дывать *impf*, уложи́ть *pf*. **stowaway** *n* безбиле́тный пассажи́р.

straddle *vt* (*sit astride*) сиде́ть *impf* верхо́м на+*prep*; (*stand astride*) стоя́ть *impf*, расста́вив но́ги над+*instr*.

straggle *vi* отстава́ть *impf*, отста́ть *pf*. **straggler** *n* отста́вший *sb*. **straggling** *adj* разбро́санный. **straggly** *adj* растрёпанный.

straight *adj* прямо́й; (*undiluted*) неразба́вленный; *predic* (*in order*) в поря́дке; *adv* пря́мо; ~ away сра́зу. **straighten** *vt & i* выпрямля́ть(ся) *impf*, вы́прямить(ся) *pf*; *vt* (*put in*

order) поправля́ть *impf*, попра́вить *pf*. **straightforward** *adj* прямо́й; (*simple*) просто́й.

strain[1] *n* (*tension*) натяже́ние; (*sprain*) растяже́ние; (*effort, exertion*) напряже́ние; (*tendency*) скло́нность; (*sound*) звук; *vt* (*stretch*) натя́гивать *impf*, натяну́ть *pf*; (*sprain*) растя́гивать *impf*, растяну́ть *pf*; (*exert*) напряга́ть *impf*, напря́чь *pf*; (*filter*) проце́живать *impf*, процеди́ть *pf*; *vi* (*also exert o.s.*) напряга́ться *impf*, напря́чься *pf*. **strained** *adj* натя́нутый. **strainer** *n* (*tea*) си́течко; (*sieve*) си́то.

strain[2] *n* (*breed*) поро́да.

strait(s) *n* (*geog*) проли́в. **strait-jacket** *n* смири́тельная руба́шка. **straits** *n pl* (*difficulties*) затрудни́тельное положе́ние.

strand[1] *n* (*hair, rope*) прядь; (*thread, also fig*) нить.

strand[2] *vt* сажа́ть *impf*, посади́ть *pf* на мель. **stranded** *adj* на мели́.

strange *adj* стра́нный; (*unfamiliar*) незнако́мый; (*alien*) чужо́й. **strangely** *adv* стра́нно. **strangeness** *n* стра́нность. **stranger** *n* незнако́мец.

strangle *vt* души́ть *impf*, за~ *pf*. **stranglehold** *n* мёртвая хва́тка. **strangulation** *n* удуше́ние.

strap *n* реме́нь *m*; *vt* (*tie up*) стя́гивать *impf*, стяну́ть *pf* ремнём. **strapping** *adj* ро́слый.

stratagem *n* хи́трость. **strategic** *adj* стратеги́ческий. **strategist** *n* страте́г. **strategy** *n* страте́гия.

stratum *n* слой.

straw *n* соло́ма; (*drinking*) соло́минка; the last ~ после́дняя ка́пля; *adj* соло́менный.

strawberry *n* клубни́ка (*no pl; usu collect*); (*wild* ~) земляни́ка (*no pl; usu collect*).

stray *vi* сбива́ться *impf*, сби́ться *pf*; (*digress*) отклоня́ться *impf*, отклони́ться *pf*; *adj* (*lost*) заблуди́вшийся; (*homeless*) бездо́мный; *n* (*from flock*) отби́вшееся от ста́да живо́тное *sb*; ~ **bullet** шальна́я пу́ля.

streak *n* полоса́ (*of luck* везе́ния); (*tendency*) жи́лка; *vi* (*rush*) проноси́ться *impf*, пронести́сь *pf*. **streaked** *adj* с поло́сами (*with*

+gen). **streaky** adj полоса́тый; (meat) с просло́йками жи́ра.

stream n (brook, tears) руче́й; (brook, flood, tears, people etc.) пото́к; (current) тече́ние; ~ вверх/вниз по тече́нию; vi течь impf; струи́ться impf; (rush) проноси́ться impf, пронести́сь pf; (blow) развева́ться impf. **streamer** n вы́мпел. **stream-lined** adj обтека́емый; (fig) хорошо́ нала́женный.

street n у́лица; adj у́личный: ~ lamp у́личный фона́рь m.

strength n си́ла; (numbers) чи́сленность; on the ~ of в си́лу+gen. **strengthen** vt уси́ливать impf, уси́лить pf.

strenuous adj (work) тру́дный; (effort) напряжённый.

stress n напряже́ние; (mental) стресс; (emphasis) ударе́ние; vt (accent) ста́вить impf, по~ pf ударе́ние на+acc; (emphasize) подчёркивать impf подчеркну́ть pf. **stressful** adj стре́ссовый.

stretch n (expanse) отре́зок; at a ~ (in succession) подря́д; vt & i (widen, spread out) растя́гивать(ся) impf, растяну́ть(ся) pf; (in length, ~ out limbs) вытя́гивать(ся) impf, вы́тянуть(ся) pf; (tauten) натя́гивать(ся) impf, натяну́ть(ся) pf; (extend, e.g. rope, ~ forth limbs) протя́гивать(ся) impf, протяну́ть(ся) pf; vi (material, land) тяну́ться impf; ~ one's legs (coll) размина́ть impf, размя́ть pf но́ги. **stretcher** n носи́лки (-лок) pl.

strew vt разбра́сывать impf, разброса́ть pf; ~ with посыпа́ть impf, посы́пать pf +instr.

stricken adj поражённый.

strict adj стро́гий. **stricture(s)** n (стро́гая) кри́тика.

stride n (большо́й) шаг; pl (fig) успе́хи m pl; to take sth in one's ~ преодолева́ть impf, преодоле́ть pf что-л. без уси́лий; vi шага́ть impf.

strident adj ре́зкий.

strife n раздо́р.

strike n (refusal to work) забасто́вка; (mil) уда́р; vi (be on ~) бастова́ть impf; (go on ~) забастова́ть pf (attack) ударя́ть impf, уда́рить pf; (the hour) бить impf, про~ pf; vt (hit)

ударя́ть impf, уда́рить pf; (impress) поража́ть impf, порази́ть pf; (discover) открыва́ть impf, откры́ть pf; (match) зажига́ть impf, заже́чь pf; (the hour) бить impf, про~ pf; (occur to) приходи́ть impf, прийти́ pf в го́лову+dat; ~ off вычёркивать impf, вы́черкнуть pf; ~ up начина́ть impf, нача́ть pf. **striker** n забасто́вщик. **striking** adj порази́тельный.

string n бечёвка; (mus) струна́; (series) ряд; pl (mus) стру́нные инструме́нты m pl; ~ bag, ~ vest се́тка; vt (thread) низа́ть impf, на~ pf; ~ along (coll) води́ть за нос; ~ out (prolong) растя́гивать impf, растяну́ть pf; **strung up** (tense) напряжённый. **stringed** adj стру́нный. **stringy** adj (fibrous) волокни́стый; (meat) жи́листый.

stringent adj стро́гий.

strip¹ n полоса́, поло́ска.

strip² vt (undress) раздева́ть impf, разде́ть pf; (deprive) лиша́ть impf, лиши́ть pf (of +gen); ~ off (tear off) сдира́ть impf, содра́ть pf; vi раздева́ться impf, разде́ться pf. **striptease** n стрипти́з.

stripe n полоса́. **striped** adj полоса́тый.

strive vi (endeavour) стреми́ться impf (for к+dat); (struggle) боро́ться impf (for за+acc; against про́тив +gen).

stroke n (blow, med) уда́р; (of oar) взмах; (swimming) стиль m; (of pen etc.) штрих; (piston) ход; vt гла́дить impf, по~ pf.

stroll n прогу́лка; vi прогу́ливаться impf, прогуля́ться pf.

strong adj си́льный; (stout, of drinks) кре́пкий; (healthy) здоро́вый; (opinion etc.) твёрдый. **stronghold** n кре́пость. **strong-minded, strong-willed** adj реши́тельный.

structural adj структу́рный. **structure** n структу́ра; (building) сооруже́ние; vt организова́ть impf & pf.

struggle n борьба́; vi боро́ться impf (for за+acc; against про́тив+gen); (writhe, ~ with (fig)) би́ться (with над+instr).

strum vi бренча́ть impf (on на +prep).

strut[1] *n* (*vertical*) стойка; (*horizontal*) распорка.

strut[2] *vi* ходить indet, идти det го́голем.

stub *n* огры́зок; (*cigarette*) оку́рок; (*counterfoil*) корешо́к; *vt*: ~ one's toe ударя́ться *impf*, уда́риться *pf* ного́й (on на+*acc*); ~ out гаси́ть *impf*, по~ *pf*.

stubble *n* жнивьё; (*hair*) щети́на.

stubborn *adj* упря́мый. **stubbornness** *n* упря́мство.

stucco *n* штукату́рка.

stud[1] *n* (*collar*, *cuff*) за́понка; (*nail*) гвоздь *m* с большо́й шля́пкой; *vt* (*bestrew*) усе́ивать *impf*, усе́ять *pf* (with +*instr*).

stud[2] *n* (*horses*) ко́нный заво́д.

student *n* студе́нт, ~ка.

studied *adj* напускно́й.

studio *n* сту́дия.

studious *adj* лю́бящий нау́ку; (*diligent*) стара́тельный.

study *n* изуче́ние; *pl* заня́тия *neut pl*; (*investigation*) иссле́дование; (*art*, *mus*) этю́д; (*room*) кабине́т; *vt* изуча́ть *impf*, изучи́ть *pf*; учи́ться *impf*, об~ *pf* +*dat*; (*scrutinize*) рассма́тривать *impf*, рассмотре́ть *pf*; *vi* (*take lessons*) учи́ться *impf*, об~ *pf*; (*do one's studies*) занима́ться *impf*.

stuff *n* (*material*) материа́л; (*things*) ве́щи *f pl*; *vt* набива́ть *impf*, наби́ть *pf*; (*cul*) начиня́ть *impf*, начини́ть *pf*; (*cram into*) запи́хивать *impf*, запиха́ть *pf* (into в+*acc*); (*shove into*) сова́ть *impf*, су́нуть *pf* (into в+*acc*); *vi* (*overeat*) объеда́ться *impf*, объе́сться *pf*. **stuffiness** *n* духота́. **stuffing** *n* наби́вка; (*cul*) начи́нка. **stuffy** *adj* ду́шный.

stumble *vi* (*also fig*) спотыка́ться *impf*, споткну́ться *pf* (over о+*acc*); ~ upon натыка́ться *impf*, наткну́ться *pf* на+*acc*. **stumbling-block** *n* ка́мень *m* преткнове́ния.

stump *n* (*tree*) пень *m*; (*pencil*) огры́зок; (*limb*) культя́; *vt* (*perplex*) ста́вить *impf*, по~ *pf* в тупи́к.

stun *vt* (*also fig*) оглуша́ть *impf*, оглуши́ть *pf*. **stunning** *adj* потряса́ющий.

stunt[1] *n* трюк.

stunt[2] *vt* заде́рживать *impf*, заде́ржать *pf* рост+*gen*. **stunted** *adj* низкоро́слый.

stupefy *vt* оглуша́ть *impf*, оглуши́ть *pf*. **stupendous** *adj* колосса́льный. **stupid** *adj* глу́пый. **stupidity** *n* глу́пость. **stupor** *n* оцепене́ние.

sturdy *adj* кре́пкий.

stutter *n* заика́ние; *vi* заика́ться *impf*.

sty[1] *n* (*pig*~) свина́рник.

sty[2] *n* (*on eye*) ячме́нь *m*.

style *n* стиль *m*; (*taste*) вкус; (*fashion*) мо́да; (*sort*) род; (*of hair*) причёска. **stylish** *adj* мо́дный. **stylist** *n* (*of hair*) парикма́хер. **stylistic** *adj* стилисти́ческий. **stylize** *vt* стилизова́ть *impf* & *pf*.

stylus *n* игла́ звукоснима́теля.

suave *adj* обходи́тельный.

subconscious *adj* подсозна́тельный; *n* подсозна́ние. **subcontract** *vt* дава́ть *impf*, дать *pf* подря́дчику. **subcontractor** *n* подря́дчик. **subdivide** *vt* подразделя́ть *impf*, подраздели́ть *pf*. **subdivision** *n* подразделе́ние. **subdue** *vt* покоря́ть *impf*, покори́ть *pf*. **subdued** *adj* (*suppressed*, *dispirited*) пода́вленный; (*soft*) мя́гкий; (*indistinct*) приглушённый. **sub-editor** *n* помо́щник реда́ктора.

subject *n* (*theme*) те́ма; (*discipline*, *theme*) предме́т; (*question*) вопро́с; (*thing on to which action is directed*) объе́кт; (*gram*) подлежа́щее *sb*; (*national*) по́дданный *sb*; *adj*: ~ to (*susceptible to*) подве́рженный+*dat*; (*on condition that*) при усло́вии, что...; е́сли; be ~ to (*change etc.*) подлежа́ть *impf* +*dat*; *vt*: ~ to подверга́ть *impf*, подве́ргнуть *pf* +*dat*. **subjection** *n* подчине́ние. **subjective** *adj* субъекти́вный. **subjectivity** *n* субъекти́вность. **subject-matter** *n* (*of book*, *lecture*) содержа́ние, те́ма; (*of discussion*) предме́т.

subjugate *vt* покоря́ть *impf*, покори́ть *pf*. **subjugation** *n* покоре́ние. **subjunctive** (**mood**) *n* сослага́тельное наклоне́ние.

sublet *vt* передава́ть *impf*, переда́ть *pf* в суба́ренду.

sublimate *vt* сублими́ровать *impf* & *pf*. **sublimation** *n* сублима́ция. **sublime** *adj* возвы́шенный.

subliminal *adj* подсозна́тельный.

sub-machine-gun n автома́т. **submarine** n подво́дная ло́дка. **submerge** vt погружа́ть impf, погрузи́ть pf. **submission** n подчине́ние; (for inspection) представле́ние. **submissive** adj поко́рный. **submit** vi подчиня́ться impf, подчини́ться pf (to +dat); vt представля́ть impf, предста́вить pf. **subordinate** n подчинённый sb; adj подчинённый; (secondary) второстепе́нный; (gram) прида́точный; vt подчиня́ть impf, подчини́ть pf. **subscribe** vi подпи́сываться impf, подписа́ться pf (to на+acc); ~ to (opinion) присоединя́ться impf, присоедини́ться pf к+dat. **subscriber** n подпи́счик; абоне́нт. **subscription** n подпи́ска, абонеме́нт; (fee) взнос. **subsection** n подразде́л. **subsequent** adj после́дующий. **subsequently** adv впосле́дствии. **subservient** adj рабо́лепный. **subside** vi убыва́ть impf, убы́ть pf; (soil) оседа́ть impf, осе́сть pf. **subsidence** n (soil) оседа́ние. **subsidiary** adj вспомога́тельный; (secondary) второстепе́нный; n филиа́л. **subsidize** vt субсиди́ровать impf & pf. **subsidy** n субси́дия. **subsist** vi (live) жить impf (on +instr). **substance** n вещество́; (essence) су́щность, суть; (content) содержа́ние. **substantial** adj (durable) про́чный; (considerable) значи́тельный; (food) пло́тный. **substantially** adv (basically) в основно́м; (considerably) значи́тельно. **substantiate** vt обосно́вывать impf, обоснова́ть pf. **substitute** n (person) замести́тель m; (thing) заме́на; vt заменя́ть impf, замени́ть pf +instr (for +acc); I ~ water for milk заменя́ю молоко́ водо́й. **substitution** n заме́на. **subsume** vt относи́ть impf, отнести́ pf к како́й-л. катего́рии. **subterfuge** n уве́ртка. **subterranean** adj подзе́мный. **subtitle** n подзаголо́вок; (cin) субти́тр. **subtle** adj то́нкий. **subtlety** n то́нкость. **subtract** vt вычита́ть impf, вы́честь pf. **subtraction** n вычита́ние. **suburb** n при́город. **suburban** adj при́городный. **subversion** n подрывна́я де́ятельность. **subversive** adj

подрывно́й. **subway** n подзе́мный перехо́д.

succeed vi удава́ться impf, уда́ться pf; the plan will ~ план уда́стся; he ~ed in buying the book ему́ удало́сь купи́ть кни́гу; (be successful) преуспева́ть impf, преуспе́ть pf (in в+prep); (follow) сменя́ть impf, смени́ть pf; (be heir) насле́довать impf & pf (to +dat). **succeeding** adj после́дующий. **success** n успе́х. **successful** adj успе́шный. **succession** n (series) ряд; (to throne) престолонасле́дие; right of ~ пра́во насле́дования; in ~ подря́д, оди́н за други́м. **successive** adj (consecutive) последова́тельный. **successor** n прее́мник.

succinct adj сжа́тый.

succulent adj со́чный.

succumb vi (to pressure) уступа́ть impf, уступи́ть pf (to +dat); (to temptation) поддава́ться impf, подда́ться pf (to +dat).

such adj тако́й; ~ people таки́е лю́ди; ~ as (for example) так наприме́р; (of ~ a kind as) тако́й как; ~ beauty as yours така́я красота́ как ва́ша; (that which) тот, кото́рый; I shall read ~ books as I like я бу́ду чита́ть те кни́ги, кото́рые мне нра́вятся; ~ as to тако́й, что́бы; his illness was not ~ as to cause anxiety его́ боле́знь была́ не тако́й (серьёзной), что́бы вы́звать беспоко́йство; ~ and ~ тако́й-то; pron тако́в; ~ was his character тако́в был его́ хара́ктер; as ~ сам по себе́; ~ is not the case э́то не так. **suchlike** pron (inanimate) тому́ подо́бное; (people) таки́е лю́ди pl.

suck vt соса́ть impf; ~ in вса́сывать impf, всоса́ть pf; (engulf) заса́сывать impf, засоса́ть pf; ~ out выса́сывать impf, вы́сосать pf; ~ up to (coll) подли́зываться impf, подлиза́ться pf к+dat. **sucker** n (biol, rubber device) приско́ска; (bot) корнево́й побе́г. **suckle** vt корми́ть impf, на~ pf гру́дью. **suction** n вса́сывание.

sudden adj внеза́пный. **suddenly** adv вдруг. **suddenness** n внеза́пность.

sue vt & i подава́ть impf, пода́ть pf

в суд (на+*acc*); ~ s.o. for damages предъявля́ть *impf*, предъяви́ть *pf* (к) кому́-л. иск о возмеще́нии уще́рба.

suede *n* за́мша; *adj* за́мшевый.

suet *n* нутряно́е са́ло.

suffer *vt* страда́ть *impf*, по~ *pf* +*instr*; от+*gen*; (*loss, defeat*) терпе́ть *impf*, по~ *pf*; (*tolerate*) терпе́ть *impf*; *vi* страда́ть *impf*, по~ *pf* (from +*instr*, от+*gen*). sufferance *n*: he is here on ~ его́ здесь те́рпят. suffering *n* страда́ние.

suffice *vi* & *t* быть доста́точным (для+*gen*); хвата́ть *impf*, хвати́ть *pf* *impers*+*gen* (+*dat*). sufficient *adj* доста́точный.

suffix *n* су́ффикс.

suffocate *vt* удуша́ть *impf*, удуши́ть *pf*; *vi* задыха́ться *impf*, задохну́ться *pf*. suffocating *adj* уду́шливый. suffocation *n* удуше́ние.

suffrage *n* избира́тельное пра́во.

suffuse *vt* залива́ть *impf*, зали́ть *pf* (with +*instr*).

sugar *n* са́хар; *adj* са́харный; ~ sláщивать *impf*, подсласти́ть *pf*; ~ basin са́харница; ~ beet са́харная свёкла; ~ cane са́харный тро́стник. sugary *adj* са́харный; (*fig*) сла́щавый.

suggest *vt* предлага́ть *impf*, предложи́ть *pf*; (*evoke*) напомина́ть *impf*, напо́мнить *pf*; (*indicate*) намека́ть *impf*, намекну́ть *pf* на+*acc*; (*indicate*) говори́ть *impf* o+*prep*. suggestion *n* предложе́ние; (*psych*) внуше́ние. suggestive *adj* вызыва́ющий мы́сли (of o+*prep*); (*indecent*) соблазни́тельный.

suicidal *adj* самоуби́йственный; (*fig*) губи́тельный. suicide *n* самоуби́йство; commit ~ соверша́ть *impf*, соверши́ть *pf* самоуби́йство.

suit *n* (*clothing*) костю́м; (*law*) иск; (*cards*) масть; follow ~ (*fig*) сле́довать *impf*, по~ *pf* приме́ру; *vt* (*be convenient for*) устра́ивать *impf*, устро́ить *pf*; (*adapt*) приспоса́бливать *impf*, приспособи́ть *pf*; (*be ~able for, match*) подходи́ть *impf*, подойти́ *pf* (+*dat*); (*look attractive on*) идти́ *impf* +*dat*. suitability *n* приго́дность. suitable *adj* (*fitting*) подходя́щий; (*convenient*) удо́бный.

suitably *adv* соотве́тственно. suitcase *n* чемода́н.

suite *n* (*retinue*) сви́та; (*furniture*) гарниту́р; (*rooms*) апарта́менты *m pl*; (*mus*) сюи́та.

suitor *n* покло́нник.

sulk *vi* ду́ться *impf*. sulky *adj* наду́тый.

sullen *adj* угрю́мый.

sully *vt* пятна́ть *impf*, за~ *pf*.

sulphur *n* се́ра. sulphuric *adj*: ~ acid се́рная кислота́.

sultana *n* (*raisin*) изю́минка; *pl* кишми́ш (*collect*).

sultry *adj* зно́йный.

sum *n* су́мма; (*arithmetical problem*) арифмети́ческая зада́ча; *pl* арифме́тика; *v*: ~ up *vi* & *t* (*summarize*) подводи́ть *impf*, подвести́ *pf* ито́ги (+*gen*); *vt* (*appraise*) оце́нивать *impf*, оцени́ть *pf*.

summarize *vt* сумми́ровать *impf* & *pf*. summary *n* резюме́ *neut indecl*, сво́дка; *adj* сумма́рный; (*dismissal*) бесцеремо́нный.

summer *n* ле́то; *attrib* ле́тний. summer-house *n* бесе́дка.

summit *n* верши́на; ~ meeting встре́ча на верха́х.

summon *vt* вызыва́ть *impf*, вы́звать *pf*; ~ up one's courage собира́ться *impf*, собра́ться *pf* с ду́хом. summons *n* вы́зов; (*law*) пове́стка в суд; *vt* вызыва́ть *impf*, вы́звать *pf* в суд.

sumptuous *adj* роско́шный.

sun *n* со́лнце; in the ~ на со́лнце. sunbathe *vi* загора́ть *impf*. sunbeam *n* со́лнечный луч. sunburn *n* зага́р; (*inflammation*) со́лнечный ожо́г. sunburnt *adj* загоре́лый; become ~ загора́ть *impf*, загоре́ть *pf*. Sunday *n* воскресе́нье.

sundry *adj* ра́зный; all and ~ всё и вся.

sunflower *n* подсо́лнечник. sunglasses *n pl* очки́ (-ко́в) *pl* от со́лнца.

sunken *adj* (*cheeks, eyes*) впа́лый; (*submerged*) погружённый; (*ship*) зато́пленный; (*below certain level*) ни́же (како́го-л. у́ровня).

sunlight *n* со́лнечный свет. sunny *adj* со́лнечный. sunrise *n* восхо́д со́лнца. sunset *n* зака́т. sunshade *n* (*parasol*) зо́нтик; (*awning*) наве́с. **sunshine** *n* со́лнечный свет. **sunstroke** *n* со́лнечный уда́р. **suntan** *n* зага́р. **sun-tanned** *adj* загоре́лый. **super** *adj* замеча́тельный. **superb** *adj* превосхо́дный. **supercilious** *adj* высокоме́рный. **superficial** *adj* пове́рхностный. **superficiality** *n* пове́рхностность. **superfluous** *adj* ли́шний. **superhuman** *adj* сверхчелове́ческий. **superintendent** *n* заве́дующий *sb* (*of* +*instr*); (*police*) ста́рший полице́йский офице́р. **superior** *n* ста́рший *sb*; *adj* (*better*) превосхо́дный; (*in rank*) ста́рший; (*haughty*) высокоме́рный. **superiority** *n* превосхо́дство. **superlative** *adj* превосхо́дный; *n* (*gram*) превосхо́дная сте́пень. **superman** *n* сверхчелове́к. **supermarket** *n* универса́м. **supernatural** *adj* сверхъесте́ственный. **superpower** *n* сверхдержа́ва. **supersede** *vt* заменя́ть *impf*, замени́ть *pf*. **supersonic** *adj* сверхзвуково́й. **superstition** *n* суеве́рие. **superstitious** *adj* суеве́рный. **superstructure** *n* надстро́йка. **supervise** *vt* наблюда́ть *impf* за+*instr*. **supervision** *n* надзо́р. **supervisor** *n* нача́льник; (*of studies*) руководи́тель *m*.

supper *n* у́жин; **have ~** у́жинать *impf*, по~ *pf*.

supple *adj* ги́бкий. **suppleness** *n* ги́бкость.

supplement *n* (*to book*) дополне́ние; (*to periodical*) приложе́ние; *vt* дополня́ть *impf*, дополнить *pf*. **supplementary** *adj* дополни́тельный.

supplier *n* поставщи́к. **supply** *n* (*stock*) запа́с; (*econ*) предложе́ние; *pl* (*mil*) припа́сы (-ов) *pl*, *vt* снабжа́ть *impf*, снабди́ть *pf* (*with* +*instr*.

support *n* подде́ржка; *vt* подде́рживать *impf*, поддержа́ть *pf*; (*family*) содержа́ть *impf*. **supporter** *n* сторо́нник; (*sport*) боле́льщик. **supportive** *adj* уча́стливый.

suppose *vt* (*think*) полага́ть *impf*; (*presuppose*) предполага́ть *impf*, предположи́ть *pf*; (*assume*) допуска́ть *impf*, допусти́ть *pf*. **supposed** *adj* (*assumed*) предполага́емый. **supposition** *n* предположе́ние.

suppress *vt* подавля́ть *impf*, пода-

ви́ть *pf*. **suppression** *n* подавле́ние.
supremacy *n* госпо́дство. **supreme** *adj* верхо́вный.
surcharge *n* наце́нка.
sure *adj* уве́ренный (*of* в+*prep*; *that* что); (*reliable*) ве́рный; **~ enough** действи́тельно; **he is ~ to come** он обяза́тельно придёт; **make ~ of** (*convince o.s.*) убежда́ться *impf*, убеди́ться *pf* в+*prep*; **make ~ that** (*check up*) проверя́ть *impf*, прове́рить *pf* что. **surely** *adv* наверняка́.
surety *n* пору́ка; **stand ~ for** руча́ться *impf*, поручи́ться *pf* за+*acc*.
surf *n* прибо́й; *vi* занима́ться *impf*, заня́ться *pf* сёрфингом.
surface *n* пове́рхность; (*exterior*) вне́шность; **on the ~** (*fig*) вне́шне; **under the ~** (*fig*) по существу́; *adj* пове́рхностный; *vi* всплыва́ть *impf*, всплыть *pf*.
surfeit *n* (*surplus*) изли́шек.
surge *n* волна́; *vi* (*rise, heave*) вздыма́ться *impf*; (*emotions*) нахлы́нуть *pf*; **~ forward** ри́нуться *pf* вперёд.
surgeon *n* хиру́рг. **surgery** *n* (*treatment*) хирурги́я; (*place*) кабине́т; (*~ hours*) приёмные часы́ *m pl* (врача́). **surgical** *adj* хирурги́ческий.
surly *adj* (*morose*) угрю́мый; (*rude*) гру́бый.
surmise *vt & i* предполага́ть *impf*, предположи́ть *pf*.
surmount *vt* преодолева́ть *impf*, преодоле́ть *pf*.
surname *n* фами́лия.
surpass *vt* превосходи́ть *impf*, превзойти́ *pf*.
surplus *n* изли́шек; *adj* изли́шний.
surprise *n* (*astonishment*) удивле́ние; (*surprising thing*) сюрпри́з; *vt* удивля́ть *impf*, удиви́ть *pf*; (*come upon suddenly*) застава́ть *impf*, заста́ть *pf* враспло́х; **be ~d** (*at*) удивля́ться *impf*, удиви́ться *pf* (+*dat*). **surprising** *adj* удиви́тельный.
surreal *adj* сюрреалисти́ческий. **surrealism** *n* сюрреали́зм. **surrealist** *n* сюрреали́ст; *adj* сюрреалисти́ческий.
surrender *n* сда́ча; (*renunciation*) отка́з; *vt* сдава́ть *impf*, сдать *pf*; (*give up*) отка́зываться *impf*, отказа́ться *pf* от+*gen*; *vi* сдава́ться *impf*, сда́ться *pf*; **~ o.s. to** предава́ться *impf*,

преда́ться pf +dat.

surreptitious adj та́йный.

surrogate n замени́тель m.

surround vt окружа́ть impf, окружи́ть pf (with +instr). **surrounding** adj окружа́ющий. **surroundings** n (environs) окре́стности f pl; (milieu) среда́.

surveillance n надзо́р.

survey n (review) обзо́р; (inspection) инспе́кция; (poll) опро́с; vt (review) обозрева́ть impf, обозре́ть pf; (inspect) инспекти́ровать impf, про~ pf; (poll) опра́шивать impf, опроси́ть pf. **surveyor** n инспе́ктор.

survival n (surviving) выжива́ние; (relic) пережи́ток. **survive** vt пережива́ть impf, пережи́ть pf; vi выжива́ть impf, вы́жить pf. **survivor** n уцеле́вший sb; (fig) боре́ц.

susceptible adj подве́рженный (to влия́нию +gen); (sensitive) чувстви́тельный (to к+dat); (impressionable) впечатли́тельный.

suspect n подозрева́емый sb; adj подозри́тельный; vt подозрева́ть impf (of в+prep); (assume) полага́ть impf (that что).

suspend vt (hang up) подве́шивать impf, подве́сить pf; приостана́вливать impf, приостанови́ть pf; (debar temporarily) вре́менно отстраня́ть impf, отстрани́ть pf; ~ed sentence усло́вный пригово́р. **suspender** n (stocking) подвя́зка. **suspense** n неизве́стность. **suspension** n (halt) приостано́вка; (of car) рессо́ры f pl; ~ bridge вися́чий мост.

suspicion n подозре́ние; on ~ по подозре́нию (of в+loc); (trace) отте́нок. **suspicious** adj подозри́тельный.

sustain vt (support) подде́рживать impf, поддержа́ть pf; (suffer) претерпе́ть pf. **sustained** adj (uninterrupted) непреры́вный. **sustenance** n пи́ща.

swab n (mop) шва́бра; (med) тампо́н; (specimen) мазо́к.

swagger vi раска́чивать impf с ва́жным ви́дом.

swallow[1] n глото́к; vt про備та́тывать impf, проглота́ть pf; ~ up поглоща́ть impf, поглоти́ть pf.

swallow[2] n (bird) ла́сточка.

swamp n боло́та; vt залива́ть impf, зали́ть pf; (fig) зава́ливать impf, завали́ть pf (with +instr). **swampy** adj боло́тистый.

swan n ле́бедь m.

swap n обме́н; vt (for different thing) меня́ть impf, об~, по~ pf (for на +acc); (for similar thing) обме́ниваться impf, обменя́ться pf +instr.

swarm n рой; (crowd) толпа́; vi рои́ться impf; толпи́ться impf; (teem) кише́ть impf (with +instr).

swarthy adj сму́глый.

swastika n сва́стика.

swat n прихло́пывать impf, прихло́пнуть pf.

swathe n (expanse) простра́нство; vt (wrap) заку́тывать impf, заку́тать pf.

sway n (influence) влия́ние; (power) власть vt & i кача́ть(ся) impf, качну́ть(ся) pf; vt (influence) име́ть impf влия́ние на+acc.

swear vi (vow) кля́сться impf, по~ pf; (curse) руга́ться impf, ругну́ться pf; ~-word руга́тельство.

sweat n пот; vi поте́ть impf, вс~ pf. **sweater** n сви́тер. **sweaty** adj по́тный.

swede n брю́ква.

Swede n швед, ~дка. **Sweden** n Шве́ция. **Swedish** adj шве́дский.

sweep n (span) разма́х; (chimney-~) трубочи́ст; vt подмета́ть impf, подмести́ pf; vi (go majestically) ходи́ть indet, идти́ det, пойти́ pf велича́во; (move swiftly) мча́ться impf; ~ away смета́ть impf, смести́ pf. **sweeping** adj (changes) радика́льный; (statement) огу́льный.

sweet n (sweetmeat) конфе́та; (dessert) сла́дкое sb; adj сла́дкий; (fragrant) души́стый; (dear) ми́лый. **sweeten** vt подсла́щивать impf, подсласти́ть pf. **sweetheart** n возлю́бленный, -нная sb. **sweetness** n сла́дость.

swell vi (up) опуха́ть impf, опу́хнуть pf; vt & i (a sail) надува́ть(ся) impf, наду́ть(ся) pf; vt (increase) увели́чивать impf, увели́чить pf; n (of sea) зыбь. **swelling** n о́пухоль.

swelter vi изнемога́ть impf от жары́. **sweltering** adj зно́йный.

swerve vi ре́зко свёртывать, свора́чивать impf, сверну́ть pf.

swift *adj* бы́стрый.

swig *n* глото́к; *vt* хлеба́ть *impf*.

swill *n* по́йло; *vt* (*rinse*) полоска́ть *impf*, вы́~ *pf*.

swim *vi* пла́вать *indet*, плыть *det*; *vt* (*across*) переплыва́ть *impf*, переплы́ть *pf* +*acc*, че́рез+*acc*. swimmer *n* плове́ц, пловчи́ха. swimming *n* пла́вание. swimming-pool *n* бассе́йн для пла́вания. swim-suit *n* купа́льный костю́м.

swindle *vt* обма́нывать *impf*, обману́ть *pf*; *n* обма́н. swindler *n* моше́нник.

swine *n* свинья́.

swing *vi* кача́ться *impf*, качну́ться *pf*; *vt* кача́ть *impf*, качну́ть *pf* +*acc*, *instr*; (*arms*) разма́хивать *impf* +*instr*; *n* кача́ние; (*shift*) крен; (*seat*) каче́ли (-лей) *pl*; in full ~ в по́лном разга́ре.

swingeing *adj* (*huge*) грома́дный; (*forcible*) си́льный.

swipe *n* си́льный уда́р; *vt* с си́лой ударя́ть *impf*, уда́рить *pf*.

swirl *vi* крути́ться *impf*; *n* (*of snow*) вихрь *m*.

swish *n* (*cut the air*) рассека́ть *impf*, рассе́чь *pf* во́здух со сви́стом; (*rustle*) шелесте́ть *impf*; *vt* (*tail*) взма́хивать *impf*, взмахну́ть *pf* +*instr*; (*brandish*) разма́хивать *impf* +*instr*; *n* (*of whip*) свист; (*rustle*) ше́лест.

Swiss *n* швейца́рец, -ца́рка; *adj* швейца́рский.

switch *n* (*electr*) выключа́тель *m*; (*change*) измене́ние; *vt* & *i* (*also ~ over*) переключа́ть(ся) *impf*, переключи́ть(ся) *pf*; *vt* (*swap*) меня́ться *impf*, об~, по~ *pf* +*instr*; ~ off выключа́ть *impf*, вы́ключить *pf*; ~ on включа́ть *impf*, включи́ть *pf*. switchboard *n* коммута́тор.

Switzerland *n* Швейца́рия.

swivel *vt* & *i* враща́ть(ся) *impf*.

swollen *adj* взду́тый.

swoon *n* о́бморок; *vi* па́дать *impf*, упа́сть *pf* в о́бморок.

swoop *vi*: ~ down налета́ть *impf*, налете́ть *pf* (on на+*acc*); *n* налёт; at one fell ~ одни́м уда́ром.

sword *n* меч.

sycophantic *adj* льсти́вый.

syllable *n* слог.

syllabus *n* програ́мма.

symbol *n* си́мвол. symbolic(al) *adj* символи́ческий. symbolism *n* симво́лизм. symbolize *vt* символизи́ровать *impf*.

symmetrical *adj* симметри́ческий. symmetry *n* симме́трия.

sympathetic *adj* сочу́вственный. sympathize *vi* сочу́вствовать *impf* (with +*dat*). sympathizer *n* сторо́нник. sympathy *n* сочу́вствие.

symphony *n* симфо́ния.

symposium *n* симпо́зиум.

symptom *n* симпто́м. symptomatic *adj* симтомати́чный.

synagogue *n* синаго́га.

synchronization *n* синхрониза́ция. synchronize *vt* синхронизи́ровать *impf* & *pf*.

syndicate *n* синдика́т.

syndrome *n* синдро́м.

synonym *n* сино́ним. synonymous *adj* синоними́ческий.

synopsis *n* конспе́кт.

syntax *n* си́нтаксис.

synthesis *n* си́нтез. synthetic *adj* синтети́ческий.

syphilis *n* си́филис.

Syria *n* Си́рия. Syrian *n* сири́ец, сири́йка; *adj* сири́йский.

syringe *n* шприц; *vt* спринцева́ть *impf*.

syrup *n* сиро́п; (*treacle*) па́тока.

system *n* систе́ма; (*network*) сеть; (*organism*) органи́зм. systematic *adj* системати́ческий. systematize *vt* систематизи́ровать *impf* & *pf*.

T

tab *n* (*loop*) пе́телька; (*on uniform*) петли́ца; (*of boot*) ушко́; keep ~s on следи́ть *impf* за+*instr*.

table *n* стол; (*chart*) табли́ца; ~cloth ска́терть; ~spoon столо́вая ло́жка; ~ tennis насто́льный те́ннис; *vt* (*for discussion*) предлага́ть *impf*, предложи́ть *pf* на обсужде́ние.

tableau *n* жива́я карти́на.

tablet *n* (*pill*) табле́тка; (*of stone*) плита́; (*memorial* ~) мемориа́льная доска́; (*name plate*) доще́чка.

tabloid *n* (*newspaper*) малоформа́тная газе́та; (*derog*) бульва́рная газе́та.

taboo *n* табу́ *neut indecl*; *adj* запрещённый.

tacit *adj* молчали́вый. **taciturn** *adj* неразгово́рчивый.

tack[1] *n* (*nail*) гво́здик; (*stitch*) намётка; (*naut*) галс; (*fig*) курс; *vt* (*fasten*) прикрепля́ть *impf*, прикрепи́ть *pf* гво́здиками; (*stitch*) смётывать *impf*, смета́ть *pf* на живу́ю ни́тку; (*fig*) добавля́ть *impf*, доба́вить *pf* ((on)to +*dat*); *vi* (*naut*; *fig*) лави́ровать *impf*.

tack[2] *n* (*riding*) сбру́я (*collect*).

tackle *n* (*requisites*) снасть (*collect*); (*sport*) блокиро́вка; *vt* (*problem*) бра́ться *impf*, взя́ться *pf* за+*acc*; (*sport*) блоки́ровать *impf* & *pf*.

tacky *adj* ли́пкий.

tact *n* такт(и́чность). **tactful** *adj* такти́чный.

tactical *adj* такти́ческий. **tactics** *n pl* та́ктика.

tactless *adj* беста́ктный.

tadpole *n* голова́стик.

Tadzhikistan *n* Таджикиста́н.

tag *n* (*label*) ярлы́к; (*of lace*) наконе́чник; *vt* (*label*) прикрепля́ть *impf*, прикрепи́ть *pf* ярлы́к на+*acc*; *vi*: ~ along (*follow*) тащи́ться *impf* сза́ди; may I ~ along? мо́жно с ва́ми?

tail *n* хвост; (*of shirt*) ни́жний коне́ц; (*of coat*) фа́лда; (*of coin*) обра́тная сторона́ моне́ты; heads or ~s? орёл и́ли ре́шка?; *pl* (*coat*) фрак; *vt* (*shadow*) высле́живать *impf*; *vi*: ~ away, off постепе́нно уменьша́ться *impf*; (*grow silent, abate*) затиха́ть *impf*. **tailback** *n* хвост. **tailcoat** *n* фрак.

tailor *n* портно́й *sb*; ~-made сши́тый на зака́з; (*fig*) сде́ланный индивидуа́льно.

taint *vi* по́ртить *impf*, ис~ *pf*.

Taiwan *n* Тайва́нь *m*.

take *vt* (*various senses*) брать *impf*, взять *pf*; (*also seize, capture*) захва́тывать *impf*, захвати́ть *pf*; (*receive, accept*) ~ breakfast; ~ medicine; ~ steps) принима́ть *impf*, приня́ть *pf*; (*convey, escort*) провожа́ть *impf*, проводи́ть *pf*; (*public transport*) е́здить *indet*, е́хать *det*, по~ *pf* +*instr*, на+*prep*; (*photograph*) снима́ть *impf*, снять *pf*; (*occupy*) ~

time) занима́ть *impf*, заня́ть *pf*; (*impers*) how long does it ~? ско́лько вре́мени ну́жно?; (*size in clothing*) носи́ть *impf*; (*exam*) сдава́ть *impf*; *vi* (*be successful*) име́ть *impf* успе́х (*of injection*) привива́ться *impf*, приви́ться *pf*; ~ after походи́ть *impf* на+*acc*; ~ away (*remove*) убира́ть *impf*, убра́ть *pf*; (*subtract*) вычита́ть *impf*, вы́честь *pf*; ~-away магази́н, где продаю́т на вы́нос; ~ back (*return*) возвраща́ть *impf*, возврати́ть *pf*; (*retrieve, retract*) брать *impf*, взять *pf* наза́д; ~ down (*in writing*) запи́сывать *impf*, записа́ть *pf*; (*remove*) снима́ть *impf*, снять *pf*; ~ s.o., sth for, to be принима́ть *impf*, приня́ть *pf* за+*acc*; ~ from отнима́ть *impf*, отня́ть *pf* у, от+*gen*; ~ in (*carry in*) вноси́ть *impf*, внести́ *pf*; (*lodgers*; *work*) брать *impf*, взять *pf*; (*clothing*) ушива́ть *impf*, уши́ть *pf*; (*understand*) понима́ть *impf*, поня́ть *pf*; (*deceive*) обма́нывать *impf*, обману́ть *pf*; ~ off (*clothing*) снима́ть *impf*, снять *pf*; (*mimic*) передра́знивать *impf*, передразни́ть *pf*; (*aeroplane*) взлета́ть *impf*, взлете́ть *pf*; ~-off (*imitation*) подража́ние; (*aeron*) взлёт; ~ on (*undertake, hire*) брать *impf*, взять *pf* на себя́; (*acquire*) приобрета́ть *impf*, приобрести́ *pf*; (*at game*) сража́ться *impf*, срази́ться *pf* с+*instr* (at в+*acc*); ~ out вынима́ть *impf*, вы́нуть *pf*; (*dog*) выводи́ть *impf*, вы́вести *pf* (for a walk на прогу́лку); (*to theatre, restaurant etc.*) приглаша́ть *impf*, пригласи́ть *pf* (to в+*acc*); we took them out every night мы приглаша́ли их куда́-нибудь ка́ждый ве́чер; ~ it out on срыва́ть *impf*, сорва́ть *pf* всё на+*prep*; ~ over принима́ть *impf*, приня́ть *pf* руково́дство +*instr*; ~ to (*thing*) пристрасти́ться *pf* к+*dat*; (*person*) привя́зываться *impf*, привяза́ться *pf* к +*dat*; (*begin*) станови́ться *impf*, стать *pf* +*inf*; ~ up (*interest oneself in*) занима́ться *impf*, заня́ться *pf* (*with an official etc.*) обраща́ться *impf*, обрати́ться *pf* с+*instr*, к+*dat*; (*challenge*) принима́ть *impf*, приня́ть *pf*; (*time, space*) занима́ть *impf*, заня́ть *pf*; ~ up with (*person*) свя́зываться *impf*, связа́ться *pf* c+*instr*; *n* (*cin*) дубль *m*.

taking *adj* привлека́тельный.

takings *n pl* сбор.

talcum powder *n* тальк.

tale *n* расска́з.

talent *n* тала́нт. **talented** *adj* тала́нтливый.

talk *vi* разгова́ривать *impf* (to, with c+*instr*); (*gossip*) спле́тничать *impf*, на~ *pf*; *vt & i* говори́ть *impf*, по~ *pf*; ~ down to говори́ть свысока́ c+*instr*; ~ into угова́ривать *impf*, уговори́ть *pf* +*inf*; ~ out of отгова́ривать *impf*, отговори́ть *pf* +*inf*, от+*gen*; ~ over (*discuss*) обсужда́ть *impf*, обсуди́ть *pf*; ~ round (*persuade*) переубежда́ть *impf*, переубеди́ть *pf*; *n* (*conversation*) разгово́р; (*lecture*) бесе́да; *pl* перегово́ры (-ров) *pl*. **talkative** *adj* разгово́рчивый; (*derog*) болтли́вый. **talker** *n* говоря́щий *sb*; (*chatterer*) болту́н (*coll*); (*orator*) ора́тор. **talking-to** *n* (*coll*) вы́говор.

tall *adj* высо́кий; (*in measurements*) ро́стом в+*acc*.

tally *n* (*score*) счёт; *vi* соотве́тствовать (with +*dat*).

talon *n* ко́готь *m*.

tambourine *n* бу́бен.

tame *adj* ручно́й; (*insipid*) пре́сный; *vt* прируча́ть *impf*, приручи́ть *pf*. **tamer** *n* укроти́тель *m*.

tamper *vi*: ~ with (*meddle*) тро́гать *impf*, тро́нуть *pf*; (*forge*) подде́лывать *impf*, подде́лать *pf*.

tampon *n* тампо́н.

tan *n* (*sun*) зага́р; *adj* желтова́токори́чневый; *vt* (*hide*) дуби́ть *impf*, вы́~ *pf*; (*beat*) (*coll*) дубаси́ть *impf*, от~ *pf*; *vi* загора́ть *impf*, загоре́ть *pf*; (*of sun*): tanned загоре́лый.

tang *n* (*taste*) ре́зкий при́вкус; (*smell*) о́стрый за́пах.

tangent *n* (*math*) каса́тельная *sb*; (*trigonometry*) та́нгенс; go off at a ~ отклоня́ться *impf*, отклони́ться *pf* от те́мы.

tangerine *n* мандари́н.

tangible *adj* ощути́мый.

tangle *vt & i* запу́тывать(ся) *impf*, запу́таться *pf*; *n* пу́таница.

tango *n* та́нго *neut indecl*.

tangy *adj* о́стрый; ре́зкий.

tank *n* бак; (*mil*) танк.

tankard *n* кру́жка.

tanker *n* (*sea*) та́нкер; (*road*) автоцисте́рна.

tantalize *vt* дразни́ть *impf*.

tantamount *predic* равноси́лен (-льна) (to +*dat*).

tantrum *n* при́ступ раздраже́ния.

tap[1] *n* кран; *vt* (*resources*) испо́льзовать *impf & pf*; (*telephone conversation*) подслу́шивать *impf*.

tap[2] *n* (*knock*) стук; *vt* стуча́ть *impf*, по~ *pf* в+*acc*, по+*dat*; **~-dance** (*vi*) отбива́ть *impf*, отби́ть *pf* чечётку; (*n*) чечётка; **~-dancer** чечёточник, -ица.

tape *n* (*cotton strip*) тесьма́; (*adhesive, magnetic, measuring, etc.*) ле́нта; **~-measure** руле́тка; ~ recorder магнитофо́н; ~ recording за́пись; *vt* (*seal*) закле́ивать *impf*, закле́ить *pf*; (*record*) запи́сывать *impf*, записа́ть *pf* на ле́нту.

taper *vt & i* су́живать(ся) *impf*, су́зить(ся) *pf*.

tapestry *n* гобеле́н.

tar *n* дёготь *m*.

tardy *adj* (*slow*) медли́тельный; (*late*) запозда́лый.

target *n* мише́нь, цель.

tariff *n* тари́ф.

tarmac *n* (*material*) гудро́н; (*road*) гудрони́рованное шоссе́ *neut indecl*; (*runway*) бетони́рованная площа́дка; *vt* гудрони́ровать *impf & pf*.

tarnish *vt* де́лать *impf*, с~ *pf* ту́склым; (*fig*) пятна́ть *impf*, за~ *pf*; *vi* тускне́ть *impf*, по~ *pf*.

tarpaulin *n* брезе́нт.

tarragon *n* эстраго́н.

tart[1] *adj* (*taste*) ки́слый; (*fig*) ко́лкий.

tart[2] *n* (*pie*) сла́дкий пиро́г.

tart[3] *n* (*prostitute*) шлю́ха.

tartan *n* шотла́ндка.

tartar *n* ви́нный ка́мень *m*.

task *n* зада́ча; take to ~ де́лать *impf*, с~ *pf* вы́говор+*dat*; ~ force операти́вная гру́ппа.

Tass *abbr* ТАСС, Телегра́фное аге́нтство Сове́тского Сою́за.

tassel *n* ки́сточка.

taste *n* (*also fig*) вкус; take a ~ of про́бовать *impf*, по~ *pf*; *vt* чу́вствовать *impf*, по~ *pf* вкус+*gen*;

(*sample*) про́бовать *impf*, по~ *pf*; (*fig*) вкуша́ть *impf*, вкуси́ть *pf*; (*wine etc.*) дегусти́ровать *impf* & *pf*; *vi* име́ть *impf* вкус, при́вкус (of +*gen*). **tasteful** *adj* (сде́ланный) со вку́сом. **tasteless** *adj* безвку́сный. **tasting** *n* дегуста́ция. **tasty** *adj* вку́сный.

tatter *n pl* лохмо́тья (-ьев) *pl.* **tattered** *adj* обо́рванный.

tattoo *n* (*design*) татуиро́вка; *vt* татуи́ровать *impf* & *pf*.

taunt *n* насме́шка; *vt* насмеха́ться *impf* над+*instr*.

Taurus *n* Теле́ц.

taut *adj* ту́го натя́нутый; туго́й.

tavern *n* таве́рна.

tawdry *adj* мишу́рный.

tawny *adj* рыжева́то-кори́чневый.

tax *n* нало́г; ~-**free** освобождённый от нало́га; *vt* облага́ть *impf*, обло-жи́ть *pf* нало́гом; (*strain*) напряга́ть *impf*, напря́чь *pf*; (*patience*) испы́-тывать *impf*, испыта́ть *pf*. **taxable** *adj* подлежа́щий обложе́нию нало́-гом. **taxation** *n* обложе́ние нало́-гом. **taxing** *adj* утоми́тельный. **tax-payer** *n* налогоплате́льщик.

taxi *n* такси́ *neut indecl*; ~-**driver** води́тель *m* такси́; ~ **rank** стоя́нка такси́; *vi* (*aeron*) рули́ть *impf*.

tea *n* чай; ~ **bag** паке́тик с сухи́м ча́ем; ~ **cloth**, ~ **towel** полоте́нце для посу́ды; ~ **cosy** чехо́льщик (для ча́йника); ~-**cup** ча́йная ча́шка; ~-**leaf** ча́йный лист; ~-**pot** ча́йник; ~-**spoon** ча́йная ло́жка; ~ **strainer** ча́йное си́течко.

teach *vt* учи́ть *impf*, на~ *pf* (*person* +*acc*; *subject* +*dat*, *inf*); преподава́ть *impf* (*subject* +*acc*); (*coll*) проу́чи-вать *impf*, проучи́ть *pf*. **teacher** *n* учи́тель *m*, ~ница; преподава́тель *m*, ~ница; ~-**training college** педаго-ги́ческий институ́т. **teaching** *n* (*instruction*) обуче́ние; (*doctrine*) уче́ние.

teak *n* тик; *attrib* ти́ковый.

team *n* (*sport*) кома́нда; (*of people*) брига́да; (*of horses etc.*) упря́жка; ~-**mate** член той же кома́нды; ~-**work** сотру́дничество; *vi* (~ *up*) объ-едина́ться *impf*, объедини́ться *pf*.

tear[1] *n* (*rent*) проре́ха; *vt* (*also* ~ *up*) рвать *impf*; (*also* ~ *up*) разрыва́ть

impf, разорва́ть *pf*; *vi* рва́ться *impf*; (*rush*) мча́ться *impf*; ~ **down, off** срыва́ть *impf*, сорва́ть *pf*; ~ **out** вы-рыва́ть *impf*, вы́рвать *pf*.

tear[2] *n* (~-*drop*) слеза́; ~-**gas** слезо-точи́вый газ. **tearful** *adj* слезли́вый.

tease *vt* дразни́ть *impf*.

teat *n* сосо́к.

technical *adj* техни́ческий; ~ **college** техни́ческое учи́лище. **technicality** *n* форма́льность. **technically** *adv* (*strictly*) форма́льно. **technician** *n* те́хник. **technique** *n* те́хника. (*method*) ме́тод. **technology** *n* тех-ноло́гия, те́хника. **technological** *adj* технологи́ческий. **technologist** *n* техно́лог.

teddy-bear *n* медвежо́нок.

tedious *adj* ску́чный. **tedium** *n* ску́ка.

teem[1] *vi* (*swarm*) кише́ть *impf* (with +*instr*).

teem[2] *vi*: it is ~ing (with rain) дождь льёт как из ведра́.

teenage *adj* ю́ношеский. **teenager** *n* подро́сток. **teens** *n pl* во́зраст от трина́дцати до девятна́дцати лет.

teeter *vi* кача́ться *impf*, качну́ться *pf*.

teethe *vi*: the child is teething у ре-бёнка прорезы́ваются зу́бы; **teeth-ing troubles** (*fig*) нача́льные проб-ле́мы *f pl*.

teetotal *adj* тре́звый. **teetotaller** *n* тре́звенник.

telecommunication(s) *n* да́льняя связь. **telegram** *n* телегра́мма. **tele-graph** *n* телегра́ф; ~ **pole** теле-гра́фный столб. **telepathic** *adj* телепати́ческий. **telepathy** *n* теле-па́тия. **telephone** *n* телефо́н; *vt* (*message*) телефони́ровать *impf* & *pf* +*acc*, о+*prep*; (*person*) звони́ть *impf*, по~ *pf* (по телефо́ну) +*dat*; ~ **box** телефо́нная бу́дка; ~ **direc-tory** телефо́нная кни́га; ~ **exchange** телефо́нная ста́нция; ~ **number** но́мер телефо́на. **telephonist** *n* те-лефони́ст, ~ка. **telephoto lens** *n* телеобъекти́в. **telescope** *n* теле-ско́п. **telescopic** *adj* телескопи́че-ский. **televise** *vt* пока́зывать *impf*, показа́ть *pf* по телеви́дению. **tele-vision** *n* телеви́дение; (*set*) телеви́-зор; *attrib* телевизио́нный. **telex** *n* те́лекс.

tell *vt* & *i* (*relate*) расска́зывать *impf*,

рассказа́ть *pf* (*thing told* +*acc*, o+*prep*; *person told* +*dat*); *vt* (*utter, inform*) говори́ть *impf*, сказа́ть *pf* (*thing uttered* +*acc*; *thing informed about* o+*prep*; *person informed* +*dat*); (*order*) веле́ть *impf* & *pf* +*dat*; ~ one thing from another отлича́ть *impf*, отличи́ть *pf* +*acc* от+*gen*; *vi* (*have an effect*) ска́зываться *impf*, сказа́ться *pf* (*on* на+*prep*); ~ off отчи́тывать *impf*, отчита́ть *pf*; ~ on, ~ tales about я́бедничать *impf*, на- *pf* на+*acc*. **teller** *n* (*of story*) рассказ-чик; (*of votes*) счётчик; (*in bank*) касси́р. **telling** *adj* (*effective*) эффек-ти́вный; (*significant*) многозначи́-тельный. **telltale** *n* спле́тник; *adj* преда́тельский.

temerity *n* де́рзость.

temp *n* рабо́тающий *sb* вре́менно; *vi* рабо́тать *impf* вре́менно.

temper *n* (*character*) нрав; (*mood*) настрое́ние; (*anger*) гнев; lose one's ~ выходи́ть *impf*, вы́йти *pf* из себя́; *vt* (*fig*) смягча́ть *impf*, смягчи́ть *pf*.

temperament *n* темпера́мент. **temperamental** *adj* темпера́ментный.

temperance *n* (*moderation*) уме́рен-ность; (*sobriety*) тре́звенность.

temperate *adj* уме́ренный.

temperature *n* температу́ра; (*high* ~) повы́шенная температу́ра; take s.o.'s ~ измеря́ть *impf*, изме́рить *pf* температу́ру +*dat*.

tempest *n* бу́ря. **tempestuous** *adj* бу́рный.

template *n* шабло́н.

temple[1] *n* (*religion*) храм.

temple[2] *n* (*anat*) висо́к.

tempo *n* темп.

temporal *adj* (*of time*) временно́й; (*secular*) мирско́й.

temporary *adj* вре́менный.

tempt *vt* соблазня́ть *impf*, соблаз-ни́ть *pf*; ~ fate испы́тывать *impf*, испыта́ть *pf* судьбу́. **temptation** *n* собла́зн. **tempting** *adj* соблазни́-тельный.

ten *adj* & *n* де́сять; (*number 10*) деся́тка. **tenth** *adj* & *n* деся́тый.

tenable *adj* (*logical*) разу́мный.

tenacious *adj* це́пкий. **tenacity** *n* це́пкость.

tenancy *n* (*renting*) наём помеще́-ния; (*period*) срок аре́нды. **tenant** *n* аренда́тор.

tend[1] *vi* (*be apt*) име́ть скло́нность (*to* к+*dat*, +*inf*).

tend[2] *vt* (*look after*) уха́живать *impf* за+*instr*.

tendency *n* тенде́нция. **tendentious** *adj* тенденцио́зный.

tender[1] *vt* (*offer*) предлага́ть *impf*, предложи́ть *pf*; *vi* (*make* ~ *for*) подава́ть *impf*, пода́ть *pf* зая́вку (*на* торга́х); *n* предложе́ние; legal ~ зако́нное платёжное сре́дство.

tender[2] *adj* (*delicate, affectionate*) не́жный. **tenderness** *n* не́жность.

tendon *n* сухожи́лие.

tendril *n* у́сик.

tenement *n* (*dwelling-house*) жило́й дом; ~-house многокварти́рный дом.

tenet *n* до́гмат, при́нцип.

tennis *n* те́ннис.

tenor *n* (*direction*) направле́ние; (*purport*) смысл; (*mus*) те́нор.

tense[1] *n* вре́мя *neut*.

tense[2] *vt* напряга́ть *impf*, напря́чь *pf*; *adj* напряжённый. **tension** *n* напряже́ние.

tent *n* пала́тка.

tentacle *n* щу́пальце.

tentative *adj* (*experimental*) про́бный; (*preliminary*) предвари́тельный.

tenterhooks *n pl*: be on ~ сиде́ть *impf* как на иго́лках.

tenth see **ten**

tenuous *adj* (*fig*) неубеди́тельный.

tenure *n* (*of property*) владе́ние; (*of office*) пребыва́ние в до́лжности; (*period*) срок; (*guaranteed employment*) несменя́емость.

tepid *adj* теплова́тый.

term *n* (*period*) срок; (*univ*) семе́стр; (*school*) че́тверть; (*technical word*) те́рмин; (*expression*) выраже́ние; *pl* (*conditions*) усло́вия *neut pl*; (*relations*) отноше́ния *neut pl*; on good ~s в хоро́ших отноше́ниях; come to ~s with (*resign o.s. to*) покоря́ться *impf*, покори́ться *pf* к+*dat*; *vt* называ́ть *impf*, назва́ть *pf*.

terminal *adj* коне́чный; (*med*) смер-те́льный; *n* (*electr*) зажи́м; (*computer, aeron*) термина́л; (*terminus*) коне́чная остано́вка.

terminate *vt* & *i* конча́ть(ся) *impf*, ко́нчить(ся) *pf* (*in* +*instr*). **termination** *n* прекраще́ние.

terminology n терминоло́гия.

terminus n коне́чная остано́вка.

termite n терми́т.

terrace n терра́са; (*houses*) ряд домо́в.

terracotta n терракóта.

terrain n ме́стность.

terrestrial adj земно́й.

terrible adj ужа́сный. **terribly** adv ужа́сно.

terrier n терье́р.

terrific adj (*huge*) огро́мный; (*splendid*) потряса́ющий. **terrify** vt ужаса́ть impf, ужасну́ть pf.

territorial adj территориа́льный. **territory** n террито́рия.

terror n у́жас; (*person; polit*) терро́р. **terrorism** n террори́зм. **terrorist** n террори́ст, ~ка. **terrorize** vt терроризи́ровать impf & pf.

terse adj кра́ткий.

tertiary adj тре́тичный; (*education*) вы́сший.

test n испыта́ние, про́ба; (*exam*) экза́мен; контро́льная рабо́та; (*analysis*) ана́лиз; ~-tube проби́рка; vt (*try out*) испы́тывать impf, испыта́ть pf; (*check up on*) проверя́ть impf, прове́рить pf; (*give exam to*) экзаменова́ть impf, про~ pf.

testament n завеща́ние; Old, New T~ Ве́тхий, Но́вый заве́т.

testicle n яи́чко.

testify vi свиде́тельствовать impf (to в по́льзу+gen; against про́тив+gen); vt (*declare*) заявля́ть impf, заяви́ть pf; (*be evidence of*) свиде́тельствовать о+prep.

testimonial n рекоменда́ция, характери́стика. **testimony** n свиде́тельство.

tetanus n столбня́к.

tetchy adj раздражи́тельный.

tête-à-tête n & adv тет-а-те́т.

tether n: be at, come to the end of one's ~ дойти́ pf до то́чки; vt привя́зывать impf, привяза́ть pf.

text n текст. **textbook** n уче́бник.

textile adj тексти́льный; n ткань; pl тексти́ль m (*collect*).

textual adj текстово́й.

texture n тексту́ра.

than conj (*comparison*) чем; other ~ (*except*) кро́ме+gen.

thank vt благодари́ть impf, по~ pf (for за+acc); ~ God сла́ва Бо́гу; ~

you спаси́бо; благодарю́ вас; n pl благода́рность; ~s to (*good result*) благодаря́ +dat; (*bad result*) из-за+gen. **thankful** adj благода́рный. **thankless** adj неблагода́рный. **thanksgiving** n благодаре́ние.

that *demonstrative* adj & pron тот; ~ which тот кото́рый; rel pron кото́рый; conj что; (*purpose*) что́бы; ~ так, до тако́й сте́пени.

thatched adj соло́менный.

thaw vt раста́пливать impf, растопи́ть pf; vi та́ять impf, рас~ pf.

the def article, not translated; adv тем; the ... the ... чем...тем; ~ more ~ better чем бо́льше, тем лу́чше.

theatre n теа́тр; (*lecture* ~) аудито́рия; (*operating* ~) операцио́нная sb; ~-goer театра́л. **theatrical** adj театра́льный.

theft n кра́жа.

their, **theirs** poss pron их; свой.

theme n те́ма.

themselves pron (*emph*) (они́) са́ми; (*refl*) себя́; -ся (suffixed to vt).

then adv (at that time) тогда́; (*after that*) пото́м; now and ~ вре́мя от вре́мени; conj в тако́м слу́чае, тогда́; adj тогда́шний; by ~ к тому́ вре́мени; since ~ с тех пор.

thence adv отту́да. **thenceforth**, **-forward** adv с того́/э́того вре́мени.

theologian n тео́лог. **theological** adj теологи́ческий. **theology** n теоло́гия.

theorem n теоре́ма. **theoretical** adj теорети́ческий. **theorize** vi теоретизи́ровать impf. **theory** n тео́рия.

therapeutic adj терапевти́ческий. **therapist** n (*psychotherapist*) психотерапе́вт. **therapy** n терапи́я.

there adv (*place*) там; (*direction*) туда́; int вот!; ну!; ~ is, are есть, име́ется (-е́ются); ~ you are (*on giving sth*) пожа́луйста. **thereabouts** adv (*near*) поблизости; (*approximately*) приблизи́тельно. **thereafter** adv по́сле э́того. **thereby** adv таки́м о́бразом. **therefore** adv поэ́тому. **therein** adv в э́том. **thereupon** adv зате́м.

thermal adj теплово́й, терми́ческий; (*underwear*) тёплый.

thermometer n термо́метр, гра́дусник. **thermos** n те́рмос. **thermostat**

n термоста́т.

thesis *n* (*proposition*) те́зис; (*dissertation*) диссерта́ция.

they *pron* они́.

thick *adj* то́лстый, (*in measurements*) толщино́й в+*acc*; (*dense*) густо́й; (*stupid*) тупо́й; **~-skinned** толстоко́жий. **thicken** *vt & i* утолща́ть(ся) *impf*, утолсти́ть(ся) *pf*; (*make, become denser*) сгуща́ть(ся) *impf*, сгусти́ть(ся) *pf*; *vi* (*become more intricate*) усложня́ться *impf*, усложни́ться *pf*. **thicket** *n* ча́ща. **thickness** *n* (*also dimension*) толщина́; (*density*) густота́; (*layer*) слой. **thickset** *adj* корена́стый.

thief *n* вор. **thieve** *vi* ворова́ть *impf*. **thievery** *n* воровство́.

thigh *n* бедро́.

thimble *n* напёрсток.

thin *adj* (*slender; not thick*) то́нкий; (*lean*) худо́й; (*too liquid*) жи́дкий; (*sparse*) ре́дкий; *vt & i* де́лать(ся) *impf*, с~ *pf* то́нким, жи́дким, *vi*: (*also ~ out*) реде́ть *impf*, по~ *pf*; *vt*: ~ out проре́живать *impf*, проре́дить *pf*.

thing *n* вещь; (*object*) предме́т; (*matter*) де́ло.

think *vt & i* ду́мать *impf*, по~ *pf* (*about, of* о+*prep*); (*consider*) счита́ть *impf*, счесть *pf* (*that* что); *vi* (*reflect, reason*) мы́слить *impf*; (*intend*) намерева́ться *impf* (*of doing* +*inf*); ~ out проду́мывать *impf*, проду́мать *pf*; ~ over обду́мывать *impf*, обду́мать *pf*; ~ up, of приду́мывать *impf*, приду́мать *pf*. **thinker** *n* мысли́тель *m*. **thinking** *adj* мы́слящий; *n* (*reflection*) размышле́ние; **to my way of** ~ по моему́ мне́нию.

third *adj & n* тре́тий; (*fraction*) треть; T~ **World** стра́ны *f pl* тре́тьего ми́ра.

thirst *n* жа́жда (*for* +*gen* (*fig*)); *vi* (*fig*) жа́ждать *impf* (*for* +*gen*). **thirsty** *adj*: be ~ хоте́ть *impf* пить.

thirteen *adj & n* трина́дцать. **thirteenth** *adj & n* трина́дцатый.

thirtieth *adj & n* тридца́тый. **thirty** *adj & n* три́дцать; *pl* (*decade*) тридца́тые го́ды (-до́в) *m pl*.

this *demonstrative adj & pron* э́тот; like ~ вот так; ~ **morning** сего́дня у́тром.

thistle *n* чертополо́х.

thither *adv* туда́.

thorn *n* шип. **thorny** *adj* колю́чий; (*fig*) терни́стый.

thorough *adj* основа́тельный; (*complete*) соверше́нный. **thoroughbred** *adj* чистокро́вный. **thoroughfare** *n* прое́зд; (*walking*) прохо́д. **thoroughgoing** *adj* радика́льный. **thoroughly** *adv* (*completely*) соверше́нно. **thoroughness** *n* основа́тельность.

though *conj* хотя́; несмотря́ на то, что; as ~ как бу́дто; *adv* одна́ко.

thought *n* мысль; (*meditation*) размышле́ние; (*intention*) наме́рение; *pl* (*opinion*) мне́ние. **thoughtful** *adj* заду́мчивый; (*considerate*) внима́тельный. **thoughtless** *adj* необду́манный; (*inconsiderate*) невнима́тельный.

thousand *adj & n* ты́сяча. **thousandth** *adj & n* ты́сячный.

thrash *vt* бить *impf*, по~ *pf*; ~ out (*discuss*) обстоя́тельно обсужда́ть *impf*, обсуди́ть *pf*; *vi*: ~ about мета́ться *impf*. **thrashing** *n* (*beating*) взбу́чка (*coll*).

thread *n* ни́тка, нить (*also fig*); (*of screw etc.*) резьба́; *vt* (*needle*) продева́ть *impf*, проде́ть *pf* ни́тку в +*acc*; (*beads*) нани́зывать *impf*, наниза́ть *pf*; ~ one's way пробира́ться *impf*, пробра́ться *pf* (*through* че́рез+*acc*). **threadbare** *adj* потёртый.

threat *n* угро́за. **threaten** *vt* угрожа́ть *impf*, грози́ть *impf*, при~ *pf* (*person* +*dat*; *with* +*instr*; *to do* +*inf*).

three *adj & n* три; (*number 3*) тро́йка; **~-dimensional** adj трёхме́рный; **~-quarters** три че́тверти. **threefold** *adj* тройно́й; *adv* втройне́. **threesome** *n* тро́йка.

thresh *vt* молоти́ть *impf*.

threshold *n* поро́г.

thrice *adv* три́жды.

thrift *n* бережли́вость. **thrifty** *adj* бережли́вый.

thrill *n* тре́пет; *vt* восхища́ть *impf*, восхити́ть *pf*; be thrilled быть в восто́рге. **thriller** *n* приключе́нческий, детекти́вный (*novel*) рома́н, (*film*) фильм. **thrilling** *adj* захва́тывающий.

thrive *vi* процвета́ть *impf*.

throat n го́рло.

throb vi (heart) си́льно би́ться impf; пульси́ровать impf; n бие́ние; пульса́ция.

throes n pl: in the ~ в мучи́тельных попы́тках.

thrombosis n тромбо́з.

throne n трон, престо́л; come to the ~ вступа́ть impf, вступи́ть pf на престо́л.

throng n толпа́; vi толпи́ться impf; vt заполня́ть impf, запо́лнить pf.

throttle n (tech) дро́ссель m; vt (strangle) души́ть impf, за~ pf; (tech) дроссели́ровать impf & pf; ~ down сба́вить impf, сба́вить pf газ.

through prep (across, via, ~ opening) че́рез+acc; (esp ~ thick of) сквозь+acc; (air, streets etc.) по+dat; (agency) посре́дством+gen; (reason) из-за+gen; (from beginning to end) до конца́; be ~ with (sth) ока́нчивать impf, око́нчить pf; (s.o.) порыва́ть impf, порва́ть pf с+instr; put ~ (on telephone) соединя́ть impf, соедини́ть pf; ~ and ~ соверше́нно; adj (train) прямо́й; (traffic) сквозно́й. **throughout** adv повсю́ду, во всех отноше́ниях; prep по всему́ (всей, всему́; pl всем)+dat; (from beginning to end) с нача́ла до конца́+gen.

throw n бросо́к; vt броса́ть impf, бро́сить pf; (confuse) смуща́ть impf, смути́ть pf; (rider) сбра́сывать impf, сбро́сить pf; (party) устра́ивать impf, устро́ить pf; ~ o.s. into броса́ться impf, бро́ситься pf в+acc; ~ away, out выбра́сывать impf, вы́бросить pf; ~ down сбра́сывать impf, сбро́сить pf; ~ in (add) доба́вить impf, доба́вить pf; (sport) вбра́сывать impf, вбро́сить pf; ~ in вбра́сывание мяча́; ~ off сбра́сывать impf, сбро́сить pf; ~ open распа́хивать impf, распахну́ть pf; ~ out (see also ~ away) (expel) выгоня́ть impf, вы́гнать pf; (reject) отверга́ть impf, отве́ргнуть pf; ~ over, ~ up (abandon) броса́ть impf, бро́сить pf; ~ up подбра́сывать impf, подбро́сить pf; (vomit) рвать impf, вы́~ pf impers; he threw up его́ вы́рвало.

thrush n (bird) дрозд.

thrust n (shove) толчо́к; (tech) тя́га; vt (shove) толка́ть impf, толкну́ть pf; (~ into, out of; give quickly, carelessly) сова́ть impf, су́нуть pf.

thud n глухо́й звук; vi па́дать impf, pf с глухи́м сту́ком.

thug n головоре́з (coll).

thumb n большо́й па́лец; under the ~ of под башмако́м у+gen; vt: ~ through перели́стывать impf, перелиста́ть pf; ~ a lift голосова́ть impf, про~ pf.

thump n (blow) тяжёлый уда́р; (thud) глухо́й звук, стук; vt колоти́ть impf, по~ pf в+acc, по+dat; vi колоти́ть impf.

thunder n гром; vi греме́ть impf; it thunders гром греми́т. **thunderbolt** n уда́р мо́лнии. **thunderous** adj громово́й. **thunderstorm** n гроза́. **thundery** adj грозово́й.

Thursday n четве́рг.

thus adv так, таки́м о́бразом.

thwart vt меша́ть impf, по~ pf +dat; (plans) расстра́ивать impf, расстро́ить pf.

thyme n тимья́н.

thyroid n (~ gland) щитови́дная железа́.

tiara n тиа́ра.

tick n (noise) ти́канье; (mark) пти́чка; vi ти́кать impf, ти́кнуть pf; vt отмеча́ть impf, отме́тить pf пти́чкой; ~ off (scold) отде́лывать impf, отде́лать pf.

ticket n биле́т; (label) ярлы́к; (season ~) ка́рточка; (cloakroom ~) номеро́к; (receipt) квита́нция; ~ collector контролёр; ~ office (биле́тная) ка́сса.

tickle n щеко́тка; vt щекота́ть impf, по~ pf; (amuse) весели́ть impf, по~, раз~ pf; vi щекота́ть impf, по~ pf impers; my throat ~s у меня́ щеко́чет в го́рле. **ticklish** adj (fig) щекотли́вый; to be ~ боя́ться impf щеко́тки.

tidal adj прили́во-отли́вный; ~ wave прили́вная волна́.

tide n прили́в и отли́в; high ~ прили́в; low ~ отли́в; (current, tendency) тече́ние; the ~ turns (fig) собы́тия принима́ют друго́й оборо́т; vt: ~ over помога́ть impf, помо́чь pf +dat of person спра́виться (*difficulty* c+*instr*); will this money ~ you over? вы протя́нете с э́тими деньга́ми?

tidiness *n* аккура́тность. **tidy** *adj* аккура́тный; (*considerable*) поря́дочный; *vt* убира́ть *impf*, убра́ть *pf*; приводи́ть *impf*, привести́ *pf* в поря́док.

tie *n* (*garment*) га́лстук; (*cord*) завя́зка; (*link*, *tech*) связь; (*equal points etc.*) ра́вный счёт; end in a ~ зака́нчиваться *impf*, зако́нчиться *pf* вничью́; (*burden*) обу́за; *pl* (*bonds*) у́зы (уз) *pl*; *vt* свя́зывать *impf*, связа́ть *pf* (*also fig*); (~ *up*) завя́зывать *impf*, завяза́ть *pf*; (*restrict*) ограни́чивать *impf*, ограни́чить *pf*; ~ down (*fasten*) привя́зывать *impf*, привяза́ть *pf*; ~ up (*tether*) привя́зывать *impf*, привяза́ть *pf*; (*parcel*) перевя́зывать *impf*, перевяза́ть *pf*; *vi* (*be ~d*) завя́зываться *impf*, завяза́ться *pf*; (*sport*) сыгра́ть *pf* вничью́; ~ in, up, with совпада́ть *impf*, совпа́сть *pf* c+*instr*.

tier *n* ряд, я́рус.

tiff *n* размо́лвка.

tiger *n* тигр.

tight *adj* (*cramped*) те́сный; у́зкий; (*strict*) стро́гий; (*taut*) туго́й; ~ corner (*fig*) тру́дное положе́ние. **tighten** *vt & i* натя́гиваться *impf*, натяну́ться *pf*; (*clench*, *contract*) сжима́ть(ся) *impf*, сжа́ться *pf*; ~ one's belt потуже затя́гивать *impf*, затяну́ть *pf* по́яс (*also fig*); ~ up (*discipline etc.*) подтя́гивать *impf*, подтяну́ть *pf* (*coll*). **tightly** *adv* (*strongly*) про́чно; (*closely*, *cramped*) те́сно. **tightrope** *n* натя́нутый кана́т. **tights** *n pl* колго́тки (-ток) *pl*.

tile *n* (*roof*) черепи́ца (*also collect*); (*decorative*) ка́фель *m* (*also collect*); *vt* крыть *impf*, по~ *pf* черепи́цей, ка́фелем. **tiled** *adj* (*roof*) черепи́чный; (*floor*) ка́фельный.

till[1] *prep* до+*gen*; not ~ то́лько (Friday в пя́тницу; the next day на сле́дующий день); *conj* пока́ не; ~ то́лько когда́.

till[2] *n* ка́сса.

till[3] *vt* возде́лывать *impf*, возде́лать *pf*.

tiller *n* (*naut*) ру́мпель *m*.

tilt *n* накло́н; at full ~ по́лным хо́дом;

vt & i наклоня́ть(ся) *impf*, наклони́ть(ся) *pf*; (*heel* (*over*)) крени́ть(ся) *impf*, на~ *pf*.

timber *n* лесоматериа́л.

time *n* вре́мя *neut*; (*occasion*) раз; (*mus*) такт; (*sport*) тайм; *pl* (*period*) времена́ *pl*; (*in comparison*) раз; five ~s as big в пять раз бо́льше; (*multiplication*) four ~s four четы́режды четы́ре; ~ and ~ again, ~ after ~ не раз, ты́сячу раз; at a ~ ра́зом, одновре́менно; at the ~ в э́то вре́мя; at ~s времена́ми; at the same ~ в то же вре́мя; before my ~ до меня́; for a long ~ до́лго; (*up to now*) давно́; for the ~ being пока́; from ~ to ~ вре́мя от вре́мени; in ~ (*early enough*) во́-время; (*with* ~) со вре́менем; in good ~ заблаговре́менно; in ~ with в такт +*dat*; in no ~ момента́льно; on ~ во́-время; one at a ~ по одному́; be in ~ успева́ть *impf*, успе́ть *pf* (for к+*dat*, на+*acc*); have ~ to (*manage*) успева́ть *impf*, успе́ть *pf* +*inf*; have a good ~ хорошо́ проводи́ть *impf*, провести́ *pf* вре́мя; it is ~ пора́ (to +*inf*); what is the ~? кото́рый час?; ~ bomb бо́мба заме́дленного де́йствия; ~-consuming отнима́ющий мно́го вре́мени; ~ difference ра́зница во вре́мени; ~ lag отстава́ние во вре́мени; ~ zone часово́й по́яс; *vt* (*choose*) выбира́ть *impf*, вы́брать *pf* вре́мя +*gen*; (*ascertain* ~ *of*) измеря́ть *impf*, изме́рить *pf* вре́мя +*gen*. **timeless** *adj* ве́чный. **timely** *adj* своевре́менный. **timetable** *n* расписа́ние; гра́фик.

timid *adj* ро́бкий.

tin *n* (*metal*) о́лово; (*container*) ба́нка; (*cake-*~) фо́рма; (*baking* ~) противень *m*; ~ foil оловя́нная фольга́; ~-opener консе́рвный нож; ~ned food консе́рвы (-вов) *pl*.

tinge *n* отте́нок; *vt* (*also fig*) слегка́ окра́шивать *impf*, окра́сить *pf*.

tingle *vi* (*sting*) коло́ть *impf impers*; my fingers ~ у меня́ ко́лет па́льцы; his nose ~d with the cold моро́з пощи́пывал ему́ нос; (*burn*) горе́ть *impf*.

tinker *vi*: ~ with вози́ться *impf* c+*instr*.

tinkle *n* звон, звя́канье; *vi* (& *t*) звене́ть *impf* (+*instr*).

tinsel n мишура́.

tint n отте́нок; vt подкра́шивать impf, подкра́сить pf.

tiny adj кро́шечный.

tip¹ n (end) ко́нчик.

tip² n (money) чаевы́е (-ы́х) pl; (advice) сове́т; (dump) сва́лка; vt & i (tilt) наклоня́ть(ся) impf, наклони́ть(ся) pf; (give ~) дава́ть impf, дать pf (person +dat; money де́ньги на чай, information ча́стную информа́цию); ~ out выва́ливать impf, вы́валить pf; ~ over, up (vt & i) опроки́дывать(ся) impf, опроки́нуть(ся) pf.

Tippex n (propr) бели́ла.

tipple n напи́ток.

tipsy adj подвы́пивший.

tiptoe n: on ~ на цы́почках.

tip-top adj превосхо́дный.

tirade n тира́да.

tire vt (weary) утомля́ть impf, утоми́ть pf; vi утомля́ться impf, утоми́ться pf. **tired** adj уста́лый; be ~ of: I am ~ of him он мне надое́л; I am ~ of playing мне надое́ло игра́ть; ~ out изму́ченный. **tiredness** n уста́лость. **tireless** adj неутоми́мый. **tiresome** adj надое́дливый. **tiring** adj утоми́тельный.

tissue n ткань; (handkerchief) бума́жная салфе́тка. **tissue-paper** n папиро́сная бума́га.

tit¹ n (bird) сини́ца.

tit² n: ~ for tat зуб за́ зуб.

titbit n ла́комый кусо́к; (news) пика́нтная но́вость.

titillate vt щекота́ть impf, по~ pf.

title n (of book etc.) загла́вие; (rank) зва́ние; (sport) зва́ние чемпио́на; ~-holder чемпио́н; ~-page ти́тульный лист; ~ role загла́вная роль. **titled** adj титуло́ванный.

titter n хихи́канье; vi хихи́кать impf, хихи́кнуть pf.

to prep (town, a country, theatre, school, etc.) в+acc; (the sea, the moon, the ground, post-office, meeting, concert, north, etc.) на+acc; (the doctor; towards, up ~, one's surprise etc.) к+dat; (with accompaniment of) под+acc; (in toast) за+acc; (time): ten minutes ~ three без десяти́ три; (compared with) в сравне́нии c+instr; it is ten ~ one that

де́вять из десяти́ за то, что; ~ the left (right) нале́во (напра́во); (in order to) чтобы+inf; adv: shut the door ~ закро́йте дверь; come ~ приходи́ть impf, прийти́ pf в созна́ние; ~ and fro взад и вперёд.

toad n жа́ба. **toadstool** n пога́нка.

toast n (bread) поджа́ренный хлеб; (drink) тост; vt (bread) поджа́ривать impf, поджа́рить pf; (drink) пить impf, вы́~ pf за здоро́вье +gen. **toaster** n то́стер.

tobacco n таба́к. **tobacconist's** n (shop) таба́чный магази́н.

toboggan n са́ни (-не́й) pl; vi ката́ться impf на саня́х.

today adv сего́дня; (nowadays) в на́ши дни; n сего́дняшний день m; ~'s newspaper сего́дняшняя газе́та.

toddler n малы́ш.

toe n па́лец ноги́; (of sock etc.) носо́к; vt: ~ the line (fig) ходи́ть indet по стру́нке.

toffee n (substance) ири́с; (a single ~) ири́ска.

together adv вме́сте; (simultaneously) одновреме́нно.

toil n тяжёлый труд; vi труди́ться impf.

toilet n туале́т; ~ paper туале́тная бума́га. **toiletries** n pl туале́тные принадле́жности f pl.

token n (sign) знак; (coin substitute) жето́н; as a ~ of в знак +gen; attrib символи́ческий.

tolerable adj терпи́мый; (satisfactory) удовлетвори́тельный. **tolerance** n терпи́мость. **tolerant** adj терпи́мый. **tolerate** vt терпе́ть impf, по~ pf; (allow) допуска́ть impf, допусти́ть pf. **toleration** n терпи́мость.

toll¹ n (duty) по́шлина; take its ~ ска́зываться impf, сказа́ться pf (on на+prep).

toll² vi звони́ть impf, по~ pf.

tom(-cat) n кот.

tomato n помидо́р; attrib тома́тный.

tomb n моги́ла. **tombstone** n надгро́бный ка́мень m.

tomboy n сорване́ц.

tome n том.

tomorrow adv за́втра; n за́втрашний день m; ~ morning за́втра у́тром; the day after ~ послеза́втра; see you

~ до за́втра.

ton n то́нна; (pl, lots) ма́сса.

tone n тон; vt: ~ **down** смягча́ть impf, смягчи́ть pf; ~ **up** тонизи́ровать impf & pf.

tongs n щипцы́ (-цо́в) pl.

tongue n язы́к; ~-**in-cheek** с насме́шкой, ирони́чески; ~-**tied** косноязы́чный; ~-**twister** скорогово́рка.

tonic n (med) тонизи́рующее сре́дство; (mus) то́ника; (drink) напи́ток «то́ник».

tonight adv сего́дня ве́чером.

tonnage n тонна́ж.

tonsil n минда́лина. **tonsillitis** n тонзилли́т.

too adv сли́шком; (also) та́кже, то́же; (very) о́чень; (moreover) к тому́ же; none ~ не сли́шком.

tool n инструме́нт; (fig) ору́дие.

toot n гудо́к; vi гуде́ть impf.

tooth n зуб; (tech) зубе́ц; attrib зубно́й; ~-**brush** зубна́я щётка. **toothache** n зубна́я боль. **toothless** adj беззу́бый; (fig) зубна́я па́ста. **toothpick** n зубочи́стка. **toothy** adj зуба́стый (coll).

top¹ n (toy) волчо́к.

top² n (of object; fig) верх; (of hill etc.) верши́на; (of tree) верху́шка; (of head) маку́шка; (lid) кры́шка; (upper part) ве́рхняя часть; ~ **hat** цили́ндр; ~-**heavy** переве́шивающий в свое́й ве́рхней ча́сти; ~-**secret** соверше́нно секре́тный; on ~ of (position) на+prep, сверх+gen; (on to) на+acc; on ~ of everything сверх всего́; from ~ to bottom све́рху до́низу; at the ~ of one's voice во весь го́лос; at ~ speed во весь опо́р; adj ве́рхний, вы́сший, са́мый высо́кий; (foremost) пе́рвый; vt (cover) покрыва́ть impf, покры́ть pf; (exceed) превосходи́ть impf, превзойти́ pf; (cut ~ off) обреза́ть impf, обре́зать pf верху́шку +gen; ~ **up** (with liquid) долива́ть impf, доли́ть pf.

topic n те́ма, предме́т. **topical** adj актуа́льный.

topless adj с обнажённой гру́дью.

topmost adj са́мый ве́рхний; са́мый ва́жный.

topographical adj топографи́ческий. **topography** n топогра́фия.

topple vt & i опроки́дывать(ся) impf, опроки́нуть(ся) pf.

topsy-turvy adj повёрнутый вверх дном; (disorderly) беспоря́дочный; adv вверх дном.

torch n электри́ческий фона́рь m; (flaming) фа́кел.

torment n муче́ние, му́ка; vt му́чить impf, за~, из~ pf.

tornado n торна́до neut indecl.

torpedo n торпе́да; vt торпеди́ровать impf & pf.

torrent n пото́к. **torrential** adj (rain) проливно́й.

torso n ту́ловище; (art) торс.

tortoise n черепа́ха. **tortoise-shell** n черепа́ха.

tortuous adj изви́листый.

torture n пы́тка; (fig) му́ка; vt пыта́ть impf; (torment) му́чить impf, за~, из~ pf.

toss n бросо́к; win (lose) the ~ (не) выпада́ть impf, вы́пасть pf жре́бий impers (I won the ~ мне вы́пал жре́бий); vt броса́ть impf, бро́сить pf; (coin) подбра́сывать impf, подбро́сить pf; (head) вски́дывать impf, вски́нуть pf; (salad) переме́шивать impf, перемеша́ть pf; vi (in bed) мета́ться impf; ~ **aside, away** отбра́сывать impf, отбро́сить pf; ~ **up** броса́ть impf, бро́сить pf жре́бий.

tot¹ n (child) малы́ш; (of liquor) глото́к.

tot²: ~ **up** (vt) скла́дывать impf, сложи́ть pf; (vi) равня́ться impf (to +dat).

total n ито́г, су́мма; adj о́бщий; (complete) по́лный; in ~ в це́лом, вме́сте; vt подсчи́тывать impf, подсчита́ть pf; vi равня́ться impf +dat. **totalitarian** adj тоталита́рный. **totality** n вся су́мма целико́м; the ~ of всего. **totally** adv соверше́нно.

totter vi шата́ться impf.

touch n прикоснове́ние; (sense) осяза́ние; (shade) отте́нок; (taste) при́вкус; (small amount) чу́точка; (of illness) лёгкий при́ступ; get in ~ **with** свя́зываться impf, связа́ться pf c+instr; keep in (lose) ~ **with** подде́рживать impf, поддержа́ть pf (теря́ть impf, по~ pf) связь, конта́кт c+instr; put the finishing

~es to отде́лывать *impf*, отде́лать *pf*; *vt* (*lightly*) прикаса́ться *impf*, прикосну́ться *pf* к+dat; каса́ться *impf*, косну́ться *pf* +gen; (*also disturb*; *affect*) тро́гать *impf*, тро́нуть *pf*; (*be comparable with*) идти́ *impf* в сравне́нии с+instr; *vi* (*be contiguous*; *come into contact*) соприкаса́ться *impf*, соприкосну́ться *pf*; ~ **down** приземля́ться *impf*, приземли́ться *pf*; ~down поса́дка; ~ (up)on (*fig*) каса́ться *impf*, косну́ться *pf* +gen; ~ up поправля́ть *impf*, попра́вить *pf*. touched *adj* тро́нутый. touchiness *n* оби́дчивость. touching *adj* тро́гательный. touchstone *n* про́бный ка́мень *m*. touchy *adj* оби́дчивый.

tough *adj* жёсткий; (*durable*) про́чный; (*difficult*) тру́дный; (*hardy*) выно́сливый. toughen *vt & i* де́лать(ся) *impf*, с~ *pf* жёстким.

tour *n* (*journey*) путеше́ствие, пое́здка; (*excursion*) экску́рсия; (*of artistes*) гастро́ли *f pl*; (*of duty*) объе́зд; *vi* (*& t*) путеше́ствовать *impf* (по+dat); (*theat*) гастроли́ровать *impf*. tourism *n* тури́зм. tourist *n* тури́ст, ~ка.

tournament *n* турни́р.

tousle *vt* взъеро́шивать *impf*, взъеро́шить *pf* (*coll*).

tout *n* зазыва́ла *m*; (*ticket* ~) жучо́к.

tow *vt* букси́ровать *impf*; *n*: on ~ на букси́ре.

towards *prep* к+dat.

towel *n* полоте́нце.

tower *n* ба́шня; *vi* вы́ситься *impf*, возвыша́ться *impf* (above над+instr).

town *n* го́род; *attrib* городско́й; ~ hall ра́туша. townsman *n* горожа́нин.

toxic *adj* токси́ческий.

toy *n* игру́шка; *vi*: ~ with (*sth in hands*) верте́ть *impf* в рука́х; (*trifle with*) игра́ть *impf* (с)+instr.

trace *n* след; *vt* (*track down*) высле́живать *impf*, вы́следить *pf*; (*copy*) кальки́ровать *impf*, с~ *pf*; ~ out (*plan*) набра́сывать *impf*, наброса́ть *impf*; (*map, diagram*) черти́ть *impf*, на~ *pf*.

tracing-paper *n* ка́лька.

track *n* (*path*) доро́жка; (*mark*) след; (*rly*) путь *m*, (*sport, on tape*) доро́ж-

ка; (*on record*) за́пись; ~ suit трениро́вочный костю́м; off the beaten ~ в глуши́; go off the ~ (*fig*) отклоня́ться *impf*, отклони́ться *pf* от те́мы; keep ~ of следи́ть *impf* за +instr; lose ~ of теря́ть *impf*, по~ *pf* след+gen; *vt* просле́живать *impf*, проследи́ть *pf*; ~ down высле́живать *impf*, вы́следить *pf*.

tract[1] *n* (*land*) простра́нство.

tract[2] *n* (*pamphlet*) брошю́ра.

tractor *n* тра́ктор.

trade *n* торго́вля; (*occupation*) профе́ссия, ремесло́; ~ mark фабри́чная ма́рка; ~ union профсою́з; ~unionist член профсою́за; *vi* торгова́ть *impf* (in +instr); *vt* (*swap like things*) обме́ниваться *impf*, обменя́ться *pf* +instr; (~ for sth different) обме́нивать *impf*, обменя́ть *pf* (for на+acc); (~ in) сдава́ть *impf*, сдать *pf* в счёт поку́пки но́вого. trader, tradesman *n* торго́вец. trading *n* торго́вля.

tradition *n* тради́ция. traditional *adj* традицио́нный. traditionally *adv* по тради́ции.

traffic *n* движе́ние; (*trade*) торго́вля; ~ jam про́бка; *vi* торгова́ть *impf* (in +instr). trafficker *n* торго́вец (in +instr). traffic-lights *n pl* светофо́р.

tragedy *n* траге́дия. tragic *adj* траги́ческий.

trail *n* (*trace, track*) след; (*path*) тропи́нка; *vt* (*track*) высле́живать *impf*, вы́следить *pf*; *vt & i* (*drag*) таска́ть(ся) *indet*, тащи́ть(ся) *det*. trailer *n* (*on vehicle*) прице́п; (*cin*) (кино)ро́лик.

train *n* по́езд; (*of dress*) шлейф; *vt* (*instruct*) обуча́ть *impf*, обучи́ть *pf* (in +dat); (*prepare*) гото́вить *impf* (for к+dat); (*sport*) трениро́вать *impf*, на~ *pf*; (*animals*) дрессирова́ть *impf*, вы́~ *pf*; (*aim*) наводи́ть *impf*, навести́ *pf*; (*plant*) направля́ть *impf*, напра́вить *pf* рост+gen; *vi* приготовля́ться *impf*, пригото́виться *pf* (for к+dat); (*sport*) трениров́аться *impf*, на~ *pf*. trainee *n* стажёр, практика́нт. trainer *n* (*sport*) тре́нер; (*of animals*) дрессиро́вщик; (*shoe*) кроссо́вка. training *n* обуче́ние; (*sport*) трениро́вка; (*of animals*) дрессиро́вка; ~-college (*teachers'*) педагоги́ческий институ́т.

traipse vi таска́ться indet, тащи́ться det.

trait n черта́.

traitor n преда́тель m, ~ница.

trajectory n траекто́рия.

tram n трамва́й.

tramp n (vagrant) бродя́га m; vi (walk heavily) то́пать impf. **trample** vt топта́ть impf, по~, ис~ pf; ~ down выта́птывать impf, вы́топтать pf; ~ on (fig) попира́ть impf, попра́ть pf.

trampoline n бату́т.

trance n транс.

tranquil adj споко́йный. **tranquillity** n споко́йствие. **tranquillize** vt успока́ивать impf, успоко́ить pf. **tranquillizer** n транквилиза́тор.

transact vt (business) вести́ impf; (a deal) заключа́ть impf, заключи́ть pf. **transaction** n де́ло, сде́лка; pl (publications) труды́ m pl.

transatlantic adj трансатланти́ческий.

transcend vt превосходи́ть impf, превзойти́ pf. **transcendental** adj (philos.) трансцендента́льный.

transcribe vt (copy out) перепи́сывать impf, переписа́ть pf. **transcript** n ко́пия. **transcription** n (copy) ко́пия.

transfer n (of objects) перено́с, перемеще́ние; (of money; of people) перево́д; (of property) переда́ча; (design) переводна́я карти́нка; vt (objects) переноси́ть impf, перенести́ pf; перемеща́ть impf, перемести́ть pf; (money; people; design) переводи́ть impf, перевести́ pf; (property) передава́ть impf, переда́ть pf; vi (to different job) переходи́ть impf, перейти́ pf; (change trains etc.) переса́живаться impf, пересе́сть pf. **transferable** adj допуска́ющий переда́чу.

transfix vt (fig) прико́вывать impf, прикова́ть pf к ме́сту.

transform vt & i преобразо́вывать(ся) impf, преобразова́ть(ся) pf; ~ into vt (i) превраща́ть(ся) impf, преврати́ть(ся) pf в+acc. **transformation** n преобразова́ние; превраще́ние. **transformer** n трансформа́тор.

transfusion n перелива́ние (кро́ви).

transgress vt наруша́ть impf, нару́шить pf; vi (sin) греши́ть impf, за~ pf. **transgression** n наруше́ние; (sin) грех.

transience n мимолётность. **transient** adj мимолётный.

transistor n транзи́стор; ~ radio транзи́сторный приёмник.

transit n транзи́т; in ~ (goods) при перево́зке; (person) по пути́; ~ camp транзи́тный ла́герь m. **transition** n перехо́д. **transitional** adj перехо́дный. **transitive** adj перехо́дный. **transitory** adj мимолётный.

translate vt переводи́ть impf, перевести́ pf. **translation** n перево́д. **translator** n перево́дчик.

translucent adj полупрозра́чный.

transmission n переда́ча. **transmit** vt передава́ть impf, переда́ть pf. **transmitter** n (радио)переда́тчик.

transparency n (phot) диапозити́в. **transparent** adj прозра́чный.

transpire vi (become known) обнару́живаться impf, обнару́житься pf; (occur) случа́ться impf, случи́ться pf.

transplant vt переса́живать impf, пересади́ть pf; (med) де́лать impf, с~ pf переса́дку+gen; n (med) переса́дка.

transport n (various senses) тра́нспорт; (conveyance) перево́зка; attrib тра́нспортный; vt перевози́ть impf, перевезти́ pf. **transportation** n тра́нспорт, перево́зка.

transpose vt переставля́ть impf, переста́вить pf; (mus) транспони́ровать impf & pf. **transposition** n перестано́вка; (mus) транспониро́вка.

transverse adj попере́чный.

transvestite n трансвести́т.

trap n лову́шка (also fig), западня́; vt (catch) лови́ть impf, пойма́ть pf (в лову́шку); (jam) защемля́ть impf, защеми́ть pf. **trapdoor** n люк.

trapeze n трапе́ция.

trapper n зверолов.

trappings n pl (fig) (exterior attributes) вне́шние атрибу́ты m pl; (adornments) украше́ния neut pl.

trash n дрянь (coll). **trashy** adj дрянно́й.

trauma *n* тра́вма. **traumatic** *adj* травмати́ческий.

travel *n* путеше́ствие; ~ **agency** бюро́ *neut indecl* путеше́ствий; ~ **sick**: be ~**sick** укача́ть *impf*; укача́ть *pf impers* +*acc*; I am ~**sick** in cars меня́ в маши́не ука́чивает; *vi* путеше́ствовать *impf*; *vt* объеха́ть *impf*, объе́хать *pf*. **traveller** *n* путеше́ственник; (*salesman*) коммивояжёр; ~'s **cheque** тури́стский чек.

traverse *vt* пересека́ть *impf*, пересе́чь *pf*.

travesty *n* паро́дия.

trawler *n* тра́улер.

tray *n* подно́с; **in-** (**out-**)~ корзи́нка для входя́щих (исходя́щих) бума́г.

treacherous *adj* преда́тельский; (*unsafe*) ненадёжный. **treachery** *n* преда́тельство.

treacle *n* па́тока.

tread *n* похо́дка; (*stair*) ступе́нька; (*of tyre*) проте́ктор; *vi* ступа́ть *impf*, ступи́ть *pf*; ~ **on** наступа́ть *impf*, наступи́ть *pf* на+*acc*; *vt* топта́ть *impf*.

treason *n* изме́на.

treasure *n* сокро́вище; *vt* высоко́ цени́ть *impf*. **treasurer** *n* казначе́й. **treasury** *n* (*also fig*) сокро́вищница; the T~ госуда́рственное казначе́йство.

treat *n* (*pleasure*) удово́льствие; (*entertainment*) угоще́ние; *vt* (*have as guest*) угоща́ть *impf*, угости́ть *pf* (to +*instr*); (*med*) лечи́ть *impf* (for от +*gen*; with +*instr*); (*behave towards*) обраща́ться *impf* с+*instr*; (*process*) обраба́тывать *impf*, обрабо́тать *pf* (with +*instr*); (*discuss*) трактова́ть *impf* о+*prep*; (*regard*) относи́ться *impf*, отнести́сь *pf* к+*dat* (as как к+*dat*). **treatise** *n* тракта́т. **treatment** *n* (*behaviour*) обраще́ние; (*med*) лече́ние; (*processing*) обрабо́тка; (*discussion*) тракто́вка. **treaty** *n* догово́р.

treble *adj* тройно́й; (*trebled*) утро́енный; *adv* втро́е; *n* (*mus*) диска́нт; *vt* & *i* утра́ивать(ся) *impf*, утро́ить(ся) *pf*.

tree *n* де́рево.

trek *n* (*migration*) переселе́ние; (*journey*) путеше́ствие; *vi* (*migrate*) переселя́ться *impf*, пересели́ться *pf*;

(*journey*) путеше́ствовать *impf*.

trellis *n* шпале́ра; (*for creepers*) решётка.

tremble *vi* дрожа́ть *impf* (with от +*gen*). **trembling** *n* дрожь; in fear and ~ трепеща́.

tremendous *adj* (*huge*) огро́мный; (*excellent*) потряса́ющий.

tremor *n* дрожь; (*earthquake*) толчо́к. **tremulous** *adj* дрожа́щий.

trench *n* кана́ва, ров; (*mil*) око́п.

trend *n* направле́ние, тенде́нция. **trendy** *adj* мо́дный.

trepidation *n* тре́пет.

trespass *n* (*on property*) наруше́ние грани́ц; *vi* наруша́ть *impf*, нару́шить *pf* грани́цу (on +*gen*); (*fig*) вторга́ться *impf*, вто́ргнуться *pf* (on в+*acc*). **trespasser** *n* наруши́тель *m*.

trestle *n* ко́злы (-зел, -злам) *pl*; ~ **table** стол на ко́злах.

trial *n* (*test*) испыта́ние (*also ordeal*), про́ба; (*law*) проце́сс, суд; (*sport*) попы́тка; on ~ (*probation*) на испыта́нии; (*of objects*) взя́тый на про́бу; (*law*) под судо́м; ~ **and error** ме́тод проб и оши́бок.

triangle *n* треуго́льник. **triangular** *adj* треуго́льный.

tribal *adj* племенно́й. **tribe** *n* пле́мя *neut*.

tribulation *n* го́ре, несча́стье.

tribunal *n* трибуна́л.

tributary *n* прито́к. **tribute** *n* дань; pay ~ (*fig*) отдава́ть *impf*, отда́ть *pf* дань (уваже́ния) (to +*dat*).

trice *n*: in a ~ мгнове́нно.

trick *n* (*ruse*) хи́трость; (*deception*) обма́н; (*conjuring* ~) фо́кус; (*stunt*) трюк; (*joke*) шу́тка; (*habit*) привы́чка; (*cards*) взя́тка; play a ~ on игра́ть *impf*, сыгра́ть *pf* шу́тку с +*instr*; *vt* обма́нывать *impf*, обману́ть *pf*. **trickery** *n* обма́н.

trickle *vi* сочи́ться *impf*.

trickster *n* обма́нщик. **tricky** *adj* сло́жный.

tricycle *n* трёхколёсный велосипе́д.

trifle *n* пустя́к; a ~ (*adv*) немно́го +*gen*; *vi* шути́ть *impf*, по~ *pf* (with c+*instr*). **trifling** *adj* пустяко́вый.

trigger *n* (*of gun*) куро́к; *vt*: ~ **off** вызыва́ть *impf*, вы́звать *pf*.

trill *n* трель.

trilogy n трило́гия.

trim n поря́док, гото́вность; in fighting ~ в боево́й гото́вности; in good ~ (sport) в хоро́шей фо́рме; (haircut) подстри́жка; adj опря́тный; vt (cut, clip, cut off) подреза́ть impf, подре́зать pf; (hair) подстрига́ть impf, подстри́чь pf; (a dress etc.) отде́лывать impf, отде́лать pf. **trimming** n (on dress) отде́лка; (to food) гарни́р.

Trinity n Тро́ица.

trinket n безделу́шка.

trio n три́о neut indecl; (of people) тро́йка.

trip n пое́здка, путеше́ствие, экску́рсия; (business ~) командиро́вка; vi (stumble) спотыка́ться impf, споткну́ться pf (over o+acc); vt (also ~ up) подставля́ть impf, подста́вить pf но́жку +dat (also fig); (confuse) запу́тывать impf, запу́тать pf.

triple adj тройно́й; (tripled) утро́енный; vt & i утра́ивать(ся) impf, утро́ить(ся) pf. **triplet** n (mus) трио́ль; (one of ~s) близне́ц (из тро́йни); pl тро́йня.

tripod n трено́жник.

trite adj бана́льный.

triumph n торжество́, побе́да; vi торжествова́ть impf, вос~ pf (over над+instr). **triumphal** adj триумфа́льный. **triumphant** adj (exultant) торжеству́ющий; (victorious) победоно́сный.

trivia n pl ме́лочи (-че́й) pl. **trivial** adj незначи́тельный. **triviality** n тривиа́льность. **trivialize** vt опошля́ть impf, опо́шлить pf.

trolley n теле́жка; (table on wheels) сто́лик на колёсиках. **trolley-bus** n тролле́йбус.

trombone n тромбо́н.

troop n гру́ппа, отря́д; pl (mil) войска́ neut pl; vi идти́ impf, по~ pf стро́ем.

trophy n трофе́й; (prize) приз.

tropic n тро́пик. **tropical** adj тропи́ческий.

trot n рысь; vi рыси́ть impf; (rider) е́здить indet, е́хать det, по~ pf ры́сью; (horse) ходи́ть indet, идти́ det, пойти́ pf ры́сью.

trouble n (worry) беспоко́йство, трево́га; (misfortune) беда́; (unpleasantness) неприя́тности f pl; (effort, pains) труд; (care) забо́та; (disrepair) неиспра́вность (with в+prep); (illness) боле́знь; heart ~ больно́е се́рдце; ~-maker наруши́тель m, ~ница споко́йствия; ask for ~ напра́шиваться impf, напроси́ться pf на неприя́тности; be in ~ име́ть impf неприя́тности; get into ~ попа́сть pf в беду́; take ~ стара́ться impf, по~ pf; take the ~ труди́ться impf, по~ pf (to +inf); the ~ is (that) беда́ в том, что; vt (make anxious, disturb, give pain) беспоко́ить impf; may I ~ you for ...? мо́жно попроси́ть у вас +acc?; vi (take the ~) труди́ться impf. **troubled** adj беспоко́йный. **troublesome** adj (restless, fidgety) беспоко́йный; (capricious) капри́зный; (difficult) тру́дный.

trough n (for food) корму́шка.

trounce vt (beat) поро́ть impf, вы́~ pf; (defeat) разбива́ть impf, разби́ть pf.

troupe n тру́ппа.

trouser-leg n штани́на (coll). **trousers** n pl брю́ки (-к) pl, штаны́ (-но́в) pl.

trout n форе́ль.

trowel n (for building) мастеро́к; (garden ~) садо́вый сово́к.

truancy n прогу́л. **truant** n прогу́льщик; play ~ прогу́ливать impf, прогуля́ть pf.

truce n переми́рие.

truck[1] n: have no ~ with не име́ть impf никаки́х дел с+instr.

truck[2] n (lorry) грузови́к; (rly) ваго́н-платфо́рма.

truculent adj свире́пый.

trudge vi уста́ло тащи́ться impf.

true adj (faithful, correct) ве́рный; (correct) пра́вильный; (story) правди́вый; (real) настоя́щий; come ~ сбыва́ться impf, сбы́ться pf.

truism n трюи́зм. **truly** adv (sincerely) и́скренне; (really, indeed) действи́тельно; yours ~ пре́данный Вам.

trump n ко́зырь m; vt бить impf, по~ pf ко́зырем; ~ up фабрикова́ть impf, c~ pf.

trumpet n труба́; vt (proclaim) труби́ть impf o+prep. **trumpeter** n труба́ч.

truncate vt усека́ть impf, усе́чь pf.

truncheon n дуби́нка.

trundle vt & i ката́ть(ся) indet, кати́ть(ся) det, по~ pf.

trunk n (stem) ствол; (anat) ту́ловище; (elephant's) хо́бот; (box) сунду́к; pl (swimming) пла́вки (-вок) pl; (boxing etc.) трусы́ (-со́в) pl; ~ **call** вы́зов по междугоро́дному телефо́ну; ~ **road** магистра́льная доро́га.

truss n (girder) фе́рма; (med) гры́жевóй банда́ж; vt (tie (up), bird) свя́зывать impf, связа́ть pf; (reinforce) укрепля́ть impf, укрепи́ть pf.

trust n дове́рие; (body of trustees) опе́ка; (property held in ~) довери́тельная со́бственность; (econ) трест; take on ~ принима́ть impf, приня́ть pf на ве́ру; vt доверя́ть impf, дове́рить pf +dat (with +acc; to +inf); vi (hope) наде́яться impf, по~ pf. **trustee** n опеку́н. **trustful, trusting** adj дове́рчивый. **trustworthy, trusty** adj надёжный, ве́рный.

truth n пра́вда; tell the ~ говори́ть impf, сказа́ть pf пра́вду; to tell you the ~ по пра́вде говоря́. **truthful** adj правди́вый.

try n (attempt) попы́тка; (test, trial) испыта́ние, про́ба; vt (taste; sample) про́бовать impf, по~ pf; (patience) испы́тывать impf, испыта́ть pf; (law) суди́ть impf (for за+acc); vi (endeavour) стара́ться impf, по~ pf; ~ **on** (clothes) примеря́ть impf, приме́рить pf. **trying** adj тру́дный.

tsar n царь m. **tsarina** n цари́ца.

tub n ка́дка; (bath) ва́нна; (of margarine etc.) упако́вка.

tubby adj то́лстенький.

tube n тру́бка, труба́; (toothpaste etc.) тю́бик; (underground) метро́ neut indecl.

tuber n клубень m. **tuberculosis** n туберкулёз.

tubing n трубы́ m pl. **tubular** adj тру́бчатый.

tuck n (in garment) скла́дка; vt (thrust into, ~ away) засо́вывать impf, засу́нуть pf; (hide away) пря́тать impf, с~ pf; ~ **in** (shirt etc.) заправля́ть impf, запра́вить pf; ~ **in, up** (blanket, skirt) подтыка́ть impf, подоткну́ть pf; ~ **up** (sleeves) засу́чивать impf, засучи́ть pf; (in bed) укрыва́ть impf, укры́ть pf.

Tuesday n вто́рник.

tuft n пучо́к.

tug vt тяну́ть impf, по~ pf; vi (sharply) дёргать impf, дёрнуть pf (at за+acc); n рыво́к; (tugboat) букси́р.

tuition n обуче́ние (in +dat).

tulip n тюльпа́н.

tumble vi (fall) па́дать impf, (у)па́сть pf; n паде́ние. **tumbledown** adj полуразру́шенный. **tumbler** n стака́н.

tumour n о́пухоль.

tumult n (uproar) сумато́ха; (agitation) волне́ние. **tumultuous** adj шу́мный.

tuna n туне́ц.

tundra n ту́ндра.

tune n мело́дия; in ~ в тон, (of instrument) настро́енный; out of ~ не в тон, фальши́вый, (of instrument) расстро́енный; change one's ~ (пере)меня́ть impf, переменя́ть pf тон; vt (instrument; radio) настра́ивать impf, настро́ить pf; (engine etc.) регули́ровать impf, от~ pf; ~ **in** настра́ивать impf, настро́ить (radio) ра́дио (to на+acc); vi: ~ **up** настра́ивать impf, настро́ить pf инструме́нт(ы). **tuneful** adj мелоди́чный. **tuner** n (mus) настро́йщик; (receiver) приёмник.

tunic n туни́ка; (of uniform) ки́тель m.

tuning n настро́йка; (of engine) регулиро́вка; ~-**fork** камерто́н.

tunnel n тунне́ль m; vi прокла́дывать impf, проложи́ть pf тунне́ль m.

turban n тюрба́н.

turbine n турби́на.

turbulence n бу́рность; (aeron) турбуле́нтность. **turbulent** adj бу́рный.

tureen n су́пник.

turf n дёрн.

turgid adj (pompous) напы́щенный.

Turk n ту́рок, турча́нка. **Turkey** n Ту́рция.

turkey n индю́к, f инде́йка; (dish) индю́шка.

Turkish adj туре́цкий. **Turkmenistan** n Туркмениста́н.

turmoil n (disorder) беспоря́док; (uproar) сумато́ха.

turn n (change of direction) поворо́т;

(*revolution*) оборо́т; (*service*) услу́га; (*change*) измене́ние; (*one's ~ to do sth*) о́чередь; (*theat*) но́мер; ~ of phrase оборо́т ре́чи; at every ~ на ка́ждом шагу́; by, in turn(s) по о́череди; *vt* (*handle, key, car around, etc.*) повора́чивать *impf*, поверну́ть *pf*; (*revolve, rotate*) враща́ть *impf*; (*page, on its face*) перевёртывать *impf*, переверну́ть *pf*; (*direct*) направля́ть *impf*, напра́вить *pf*; (*cause to become*) де́лать *impf*, с~ *pf* +*instr*; (*on lathe*) точи́ть *impf*; *vi* (*change direction*) повора́чивать *impf*, поверну́ть *pf*; (*rotate*) враща́ться *impf*; (~ round) повора́чиваться *impf*, поверну́ться *pf*; (*become*) станови́ться *impf*, стать *pf* +*instr*; ~ against ополча́ться *impf*, ополчи́ться *pf* на +*acc*, про́тив+*gen*; ~ around see ~ round; ~ away (*vt & i*) отвора́чивать(ся) *impf*, отверну́ть(ся) *pf*; (*refuse admittance*) прогоня́ть *impf*, прогна́ть *pf*; ~ back (*vi*) повора́чивать *impf*, поверну́ть *pf* наза́д; (*vt*) (*bend back*) отгиба́ть *impf*, отогну́ть *pf*; ~ down (*refuse*) отклоня́ть *impf*, отклони́ть *pf*; (*collar*) отгиба́ть *impf*, отогну́ть *pf*; (*make quieter*) де́лать *impf*, с~ *pf* ти́ше; ~ grey (*vi*) седе́ть *impf*, по~ *pf*; ~ in (*so as to face inwards*) повора́чивать *impf*, поверну́ть *pf* вовну́трь; ~ inside out вывора́чивать *impf*, вы́вернуть *pf* наизна́нку; ~ into (*change into*) (*vt & i*) превраща́ть(ся) *impf*, преврати́ть(ся) *pf* в+*acc*; (*street*) свора́чивать *impf*, сверну́ть *pf* на +*acc*; ~ off (*light, radio etc.*) выключа́ть *impf*, вы́ключить *pf*; (*tap*) закрыва́ть *impf*, закры́ть *pf*; (*vi*) (*branch off*) свора́чивать *impf*, сверну́ть *pf*; ~ on (*light, radio etc.*) включа́ть *impf*, включи́ть *pf*; (*tap*) открыва́ть *impf*, откры́ть *pf*; (*attack*) напада́ть *impf*, напа́сть *pf* на +*acc*; ~ out (*light etc.*): see ~ off; (*prove to be*) ока́зываться *impf*, оказа́ться *pf* (to be +*instr*); (*drive out*) выгоня́ть *impf*, вы́гнать *pf*; (*pockets*) вывёртывать *impf*, вы́вернуть *pf*; (*be present*) приходи́ть *impf*, прийти́ *pf*; (*product*) выпуска́ть *impf*, вы́пустить *pf*; ~ over (*page, on its face, roll over*) (*vt & i*)

перевёртывать(ся) *impf*, переверну́ть(ся) *pf*; (*hand over*) передава́ть *impf*, переда́ть *pf*; (*think about*) обду́мывать *impf*, обду́мать *pf*; (*overturn*) (*vt & i*) опроки́дывать(ся) *impf*, опроки́нуть(ся) *pf*; ~ pale бледне́ть *impf*, по~ *pf*; ~ red красне́ть *impf*, по~ *pf*; ~ round (*vi*) (*rotate*; ~ one's back; ~ to face sth*) повора́чиваться *impf*, поверну́ться *pf*; (~ to face) обора́чиваться *impf*, обёрну́ться *pf*; (*vt*) повёртывать *impf*, поверну́ть *pf*; ~ sour скиса́ть *impf*, ски́снуть *pf*; ~ to обраща́ться *impf*, обрати́ться *pf* к+*dat* (for за +*instr*); ~ up (*appear*) появля́ться *impf*, появи́ться *pf*; (*be found*) находи́ться *impf*, найти́сь *pf*; (*shorten garment*) подшива́ть *impf*, подши́ть *pf*; (*crop up*) подвёртываться *impf*, подверну́ться *pf*; (*bend up; stick up*) (*vt & i*) загиба́ть(ся) *impf*, загну́ть(ся) *pf*; (*make louder*) де́лать *impf*, с~ *pf* гро́мче; ~ up one's nose воро́тить *impf* нос (at от+*gen*) (*coll*); ~ upside down перевора́чивать *impf*, переверну́ть *pf* вверх дном. turn-out *n* коли́чество приходя́щих. turn-up *n* (*on trousers*) обшла́г.

turner *n* то́карь *m*.

turning *n* (*road*) поворо́т. turning-point *n* поворо́тный пункт.

turnip *n* ре́па.

turnover *n* (*econ*) оборо́т; (*of staff*) теку́честь рабо́чей си́лы.

turnpike *n* доро́жная заста́ва.

turnstile *n* турнике́т.

turntable *n* (*rly*) поворо́тный круг; (*gramophone*) диск.

turpentine *n* скипида́р.

turquoise *n* (*material, stone*) бирюза́; *adj* бирюзо́вый.

turret *n* ба́шенка.

turtle *n* черепа́ха.

turtle-dove *n* го́рлица.

tusk *n* би́вень *m*, клык.

tussle *n* дра́ка; *vi* дра́ться *impf* (for за+*acc*).

tutor *n* (*private teacher*) ча́стный дома́шний учи́тель *m*, ~ница; (*univ*) преподава́тель *m*, ~ница; (*primer*) уче́бник; *vt* (*instruct*) обуча́ть *impf*, обучи́ть *pf* (in +*dat*); (*give lessons to*) дава́ть *impf*, дать *pf* уро́ки+*dat*; (*guide*) руководи́ть *impf* +*instr*.

tutorial *n* консультáция.

tutu *n* (*ballet*) пáчка.

TV *abbr* (*of television*) ТВ, телеви́дение; (*set*) телеви́зор.

twang *n* (*of string*) рéзкий звук (натя́нутой струны́); (*voice*) гнуса́вый го́лос.

tweak *n* щипо́к; *vt* щипáть *impf*, (у)щипну́ть *pf*.

tweed *n* твид.

tweezers *n pl* пинцéт.

twelfth *adj & n* двенáдцатый. twelve *adj & n* двенáдцать.

twentieth *adj & n* двадцáтый. twenty *adj & n* двáдцать; *pl* (*decade*) двадцáтые го́ды (-до́в) *m pl*.

twice *adv* двáжды; ~ as вдво́е, в два рáза +*comp*.

twiddle *vt* (*turn*) вертéть *impf* +*acc*, *instr*; (*toy with*) игрáть *impf* +*instr*; ~ one's thumbs (*fig*) бездéльничать *impf*.

twig *n* вéточка, прут.

twilight *n* су́мерки (-рек) *pl*.

twin *n* близнéц; *pl* (*Gemini*) Близнецы́ *m pl*; ~ beds пáра односпáльных кровáтей; ~ brother братблизнéц; ~ town го́род-побрáтим.

twine *n* бечёвка, шпагáт; *vt* (*twist, weave*) вить *impf*, с~ *pf*; *vt & i* (~ *round*) обвивáть(ся) *impf*, обви́ть(ся) *pf*.

twinge *n* при́ступ (бóли); (*of conscience*) угрызéние.

twinkle *n* мерцáние; (*of eyes*) огонёк; *vi* мерцáть *impf*, сверкáть *impf*. twinkling *n* мерцáние; in the ~ of an eye в мгновéние óка.

twirl *vt & i* (*twist, turn*) вертéть(ся) *impf*; (*whirl, spin*) кружи́ть(ся) *impf*.

twist *vt* (*bend*) изги́б, поворóт; (~*ing*) кручéние; (*in story*) поворóт фáбулы; *vt* скру́чивать *impf*, крути́ть *impf*, с~ *pf*; (*distort*) искажáть *impf*, искази́ть *pf*; (*sprain*) подвёртывать *impf*, подверну́ть *pf*; *vi* (*climb, meander, twine*) ви́ться *impf*. twisted *adj* искривлённый (*also fig*).

twit *n* дурáк.

twitch *n* подёргивание; *vt & i* дёргать(ся) *impf*, дёрнуть(ся) *pf* (at за +*acc*).

twitter *n* щёбет; *vi* щебетáть *impf*, чири́кать *impf*.

two *adj & n* два, две (*f*); (*collect*; 2

pairs*) двóе; (*number 2*) двóйка; in ~ (*in half*) нáдвое, пополáм; ~seater двухмéстный (автомоби́ль); ~-way двусторо́нний. twofold *adj* двойнóй; *adv* вдвойнé. twosome *n* пáра.

tycoon *n* магнáт.

type *n* тип, род; (*printing*) шрифт; *vt* писáть *impf*, на~ *pf* на маши́нке. typescript *n* маши́нопись. typewriter *n* пи́шущая маши́нка. typewritten *adj* машинопи́сный.

typhoid *n* брюшнóй тиф.

typical *adj* типи́чный. typify *vt* служи́ть *impf*, по~ *pf* типи́чным примéром +*gen*.

typist *n* машини́стка.

typography *n* книгопечáтание; (*style*) оформлéние.

tyrannical *adj* тирани́ческий. tyrant *n* тирáн.

tyre *n* ши́на.

U

ubiquitous *adj* вездесу́щий.

udder *n* вы́мя *neut*.

UFO *abbr* (*of unidentified flying object*) НЛО, неопóзнанный летáющий объéкт.

ugh *int* тьфу!

ugliness *n* урóдство. ugly *adj* некраси́вый, урóдливый; (*unpleasant*) неприя́тный.

UK *abbr* (*of United Kingdom*) Соединённое Королéвство.

Ukraine *n* Украи́на. Ukrainian *n* украи́нец, -нка; *adj* украи́нский.

ulcer *n* я́зва.

ulterior *adj* скры́тый.

ultimate *adj* (*final*) послéдний, окончáтельный; (*purpose*) конéчный. ultimately *adv* в конéчном счёте, в концé концóв. ultimatum *n* ультимáтум.

ultrasound *n* ультразву́к. ultra-violet *adj* ультрафиолéтовый.

umbilical *adj*: ~ cord пуповина.

umbrella *n* зóнтик, зонт.

umpire *n* судья́ *m*; *vt & i* суди́ть *impf*.

umpteenth *adj*: for the ~ time в котóрый раз.

unabashed *adj* без вся́кого смущéния. unabated *adj* неослáбленный.

unable adj: be ~ to не мочь impf, с~ pf; быть не в состоянии; (not know how to) не уметь impf, с~ pf. **unabridged** adj несокращённый. **unaccompanied** adj без сопровождения; (mus) без аккомпанемента. **unaccountable** adj необъяснимый. **unaccustomed** adj (not accustomed) непривыкший (to k+dat); (unusual) непривычный. **unadulterated** adj настоящий; (utter) чистейший. **unaffected** adj непринуждённый. **unaided** adj без помощи, самостоятельный. **unambiguous** adj недвусмысленный. **unanimity** n единодушие. **unanimous** adj единодушный. **unanswerable** adj (irrefutable) неопровержимый. **unarmed** adj невооружённый. **unashamed** adj бессовестный. **unassailable** adj неприступный; (irrefutable) неопровержимый. **unassuming** adj скромный. **unattainable** adj недосягаемый. **unattended** adj без присмотра. **unattractive** adj непривлекательный. **unauthorized** adj неразрешённый. **unavailable** adj не имеющийся в наличии, недоступный. **unavoidable** adj неизбежный. **unaware** predic: be ~ of не сознавать impf +acc; не знать impf o+prep. **unawares** adv врасплох.

unbalanced adj (psych) неуравновешенный. **unbearable** adj невыносимый. **unbeatable** adj (unsurpassable) не могущий быть превзойдённым; (invincible) непобедимый. **unbeaten** adj (undefeated) непокорённый; (unsurpassed) непревзойдённый. **unbelief** n неверие. **unbelievable** adj невероятный. **unbeliever** n неверующий sb. **unbiased** adj беспристрастный. **unblemished** adj незапятнанный. **unblock** vt прочищать impf, прочистить pf. **unbolt** vt отпирать impf, отпереть pf. **unborn** adj ещё не рождённый. **unbounded** adj неограниченный. **unbreakable** adj небьющийся. **unbridled** adj разнузданный. **unbroken** adj (intact) неразбитый, целый; (continuous) непрерывный; (unsurpassed) непобитый; (horse) необъезженный. **unbuckle** vt расстёгивать impf, расстегнуть pf. **unburden** vt:

~ o.s. отводить impf, отвести pf душу. **unbutton** vt расстёгивать impf, расстегнуть pf.

uncalled-for adj неуместный. **uncanny** adj жуткий, сверхъестественный. **unceasing** adj непрерывный. **unceremonious** adj бесцеремонный. **uncertain** adj (not sure, hesitating) неуверенный; (indeterminate) неопределённый, неясный; be ~ (not know for certain) точно не знать impf; in no ~ terms недвусмысленно. **uncertainty** n неизвестность; неопределённость. **unchallenged** adj не вызывающий возражений. **unchanged** adj неизменившийся. **unchanging** adj неизменяющийся. **uncharacteristic** adj нетипичный. **uncharitable** adj немилосердный, жестокий. **uncharted** adj неисследованный. **unchecked** adj (unrestrained) необузданный. **uncivilized** adj нецивилизованный. **unclaimed** adj невостребованный.

uncle n дядя m.

unclean adj нечистый. **unclear** adj неясный. **uncomfortable** adj неудобный. **uncommon** adj необыкновенный; (rare) редкий. **uncommunicative** adj неразговорчивый, сдержанный. **uncomplaining** adj безропотный. **uncomplicated** adj несложный. **uncompromising** adj бескомпромиссный. **unconcealed** adj нескрываемый. **unconcerned** adj (unworried) беззаботный; (indifferent) равнодушный. **unconditional** adj безоговорочный, безусловный. **unconfirmed** adj неподтверждённый. **unconnected** adj: ~ with не связанный с+instr. **unconscious** adj (also unintentional) бессознательный; (predic) без сознания; be ~ of не сознавать impf +gen; n подсознательное sb. **unconsciousness** n бессознательное состояние. **unconstitutional** adj неконституционный. **uncontrollable** adj неудержимый. **uncontrolled** adj бесконтрольный. **unconventional** adj небычный; оригинальный. **unconvincing** adj неубедительный. **uncooked** adj сырой. **uncooperative** adj неотзывчивый. **uncouth** adj грубый. **uncover** vt раскрывать *impf*, раскры́ть *pf*. **uncritical** *adj* некрити́чный.

unctuous *adj* еле́йный.

uncut *adj* неразре́занный; (*unabridged*) несокращённый.

undamaged *adj* неповреждённый.

undaunted *adj* бесстра́шный. **undecided** *adj* (*not settled*) нерешённый; (*irresolute*) нереши́тельный.

undefeated *adj* непокорённый. **undemanding** *adj* нетре́бовательный.

undemocratic *adj* недемократи́ческий. **undeniable** *adj* неоспори́мый.

under *prep* (*position*) под+*instr*; (*direction*) под+*acc*; (*fig*) под +*instr*; (*less than*) ме́ньше+*gen*; (*in view of, in the reign, time of*) при+*prep*; ∼-**age** несовершенноле́тний; ∼**way** на ходу́; *adv* (*position*) внизу́; (*direction*) вниз; (*less*) ме́ньше.

undercarriage *n* шасси́ *neut indecl*. **underclothes** *n pl* ни́жнее бельё. **undercoat** *n* (*of paint*) грунто́вка. **undercover** *adj* та́йный. **undercurrent** *n* подво́дное тече́ние; (*fig*) скры́тая тенде́нция. **undercut** *vt* (*price*) назнача́ть *impf*, назна́чить *pf* бо́лее ни́зкую це́ну чем+*nom*. **underdeveloped** *adj* слаборазви́тый. **underdog** *n* неуда́чник.

underdone *adj* недожа́ренный. **underemployment** *n* непо́лная за́нятость. **underestimate** *vt* недооце́нивать *impf*, недооцени́ть *pf*; *n* недооце́нка. **underfoot** *adv* под нога́ми.

undergo *vt* подверга́ться *impf*, подве́ргнуться *pf* +*dat*; (*endure*) переноси́ть *impf*, перенести́ *pf* **undergraduate** *n* студе́нт, ∼ка. **underground** *n* (*rly*) метро́ *neut indecl*; (*fig*) подпо́лье; *adj* подзе́мный; (*fig*) подпо́льный; *adv* под землёй; (*fig*) подпо́льно. **undergrowth** *n* подле́сок. **underhand** *adj* закули́сный.

underlie *vt* (*fig*) лежа́ть *impf* в осно́ве +*gen*. **underline** *vt* подчёркивать *impf*, подчеркну́ть *pf*. **underlying** *adj* лежа́щий в осно́ве. **underling** *n* подчинённый *sb*.

undermine *vt* (*authority*) подрыва́ть *impf*, подорва́ть *pf*; (*health*) разруша́ть *impf*, разру́шить *pf*.

underneath *adv* (*position*) внизу́; (*direction*) вниз; *prep* (*position*) под

+*instr*; (*direction*) под+*acc*; *n* ни́жняя часть; *adj* ни́жний.

undernourished *adj* исхуда́лый; be ∼ недоеда́ть *impf*.

underpaid *adj* низкоопла́чиваемый. **underpants** *n pl* трусы́ (-со́в) *pl*. **underpass** *n* прое́зд под полотно́м доро́ги; тонне́ль *m*. **underpin** *vt* подводи́ть *impf*, подвести́ *pf* фунда́мент под+*acc*; (*fig*) подде́рживать *impf*, поддержа́ть *pf*. **underprivileged** *adj* обделённый; (*poor*) бе́дный. **underrate** *vt* недооце́нивать *impf*, недооцени́ть *pf*.

underscore *vt* подчёркивать *impf*, подчеркну́ть *pf*. **under-secretary** *n* замести́тель *m* мини́стра. **underside** *n* ни́жняя сторона́, низ. **undersized** *adj* малоро́слый. **understaffed** *adj* неукомплекто́ванный.

understand *vt* понима́ть *impf*, поня́ть *pf*; (*have heard say*) слы́шать *impf*. **understandable** *adj* поня́тный. **understanding** *n* понима́ние; (*agreement*) соглаше́ние; *adj* (*sympathetic*) отзы́вчивый.

understate *vt* преуменьша́ть *impf*, преуме́ньшить *pf*. **understatement** *n* преуменьше́ние.

understudy *n* дублёр.

undertake *vt* (*enter upon*) предпринима́ть *impf*, предприня́ть *pf*; (*responsibility*) брать *impf*, взять *pf* на себя́; (+*inf*) обя́зываться *impf*, обяза́ться *pf*. **undertaker** *n* гробовщи́к. **undertaking** *n* предприя́тие; (*pledge*) гара́нтия.

undertone *n* (*fig*) подте́кст; in an ∼ вполго́лоса. **underwater** *adj* подво́дный. **underwear** *n* ни́жнее бельё. **underweight** *adj* исхуда́лый. **underworld** *n* (*mythology*) преиспо́дняя *sb*; (*criminals*) престу́пный мир. **underwrite** *vt* (*guarantee*) гаранти́ровать *impf* & *pf*. **underwriter** *n* страхо́вщик.

undeserved *adj* незаслу́женный. **undesirable** *adj* нежела́тельный; *n* нежела́тельное лицо́. **undeveloped** *adj* нера́звитый; (*land*) незастро́енный. **undignified** *adj* недосто́йный. **undiluted** *adj* неразба́вленный. **undisciplined** *adj* недисциплини́рованный. **undiscovered** *adj* неоткры́тый. **undisguised** *adj* я́вный.

undisputed adj бесспо́рный. undistinguished adj заура́дный. undisturbed adj (untouched) нетро́нутый; (peaceful) споко́йный. undivided adj: ~ attention по́лное внима́ние undo vt (open) открыва́ть impf, откры́ть pf; (untie) развя́зывать impf, развяза́ть pf; (unbutton, unhook, unbuckle) расстёгивать impf, расстегну́ть pf; (destroy, cancel) уничтожа́ть impf, уничто́жить pf. undoubted adj несомне́нный. undoubtedly adv несомне́нно. undress vt & i раздева́ть(ся) impf, разде́ть(ся) pf. undue adj чрезме́рный. unduly adv чрезме́рно.

undulating adj волни́стый; (landscape) холми́стый.

undying adj (eternal) ве́чный.

unearth vt (dig up) выка́пывать impf, вы́копать pf из земли́; (fig) раска́пывать impf, раскопа́ть pf. uneasiness n (anxiety) беспоко́йство; (awkwardness) нело́вкость. uneasy adj беспоко́йный; нело́вкий. uneconomic adj нерента́бельный. uneconomical adj (car etc.) неэкономи́чный; (person) неэконо́мный. uneducated adj необразо́ванный. unemployed adj безрабо́тный. unemployment n безрабо́тица; ~ benefit посо́бие по безрабо́тице. unending adj бесконе́чный. unenviable adj незави́дный. unequal adj нера́вный. unequalled adj непревзойдённый. unequivocal adj недвусмы́сленный. unerring adj безоши́бочный.

uneven adj неро́вный. uneventful adj непримеча́тельный. unexceptional adj обы́чный. unexpected adj неожи́данный. unexplored adj неиссле́дованный.

unfailing adj неизме́нный; (inexhaustible) неисчерпа́емый. unfair adj несправедли́вый. unfaithful adj неве́рный. unfamiliar adj незнако́мый; (unknown) неве́домый. unfashionable adj немо́дный. unfasten vt (detach, untie) открепля́ть impf, открепи́ть pf; (undo, unbutton, unhook) расстёгивать impf, расстегну́ть pf; (open) открыва́ть impf, откры́ть pf. unfavourable adj неблагоприя́тный. unfeeling adj

бесчу́вственный. unfinished adj незако́нченный. unfit adj него́дный; (unhealthy) нездоро́вый. unflagging adj неослабева́ющий. unflattering adj неле́стный. unflinching adj непоколеби́мый. unfold vt & i развёртывать(ся) impf, разверну́ть(ся) pf; vi (fig) раскрыва́ться impf, раскры́ться pf. unforeseen adj непредви́денный. unforgettable adj незабыва́емый. unforgivable adj непрости́тельный. unforgiving adj непроща́ющий. unfortunate adj несча́стный; (regrettable) неуда́чный; n неуда́чник. unfortunately adv к сожале́нию. unfounded adj необосно́ванный. unfriendly adj недружелю́бный. unfulfilled adj (hopes etc.) неосуществлённый; (person) неудовлетворённый. unfurl vt & i развёртывать(ся) impf, разверну́ть(ся) pf. unfurnished adj немебли́рованный.

ungainly adj неуклю́жий. ungovernable adj неуправля́емый. ungracious adj нелюбе́зный. ungrateful adj неблагода́рный. unguarded adj (incautious) неосторо́жный.

unhappiness n несча́стье. unhappy adj несчастли́вый. unharmed adj невреди́мый. unhealthy adj нездоро́вый; (harmful) вре́дный. unheard-of adj неслы́ханный. unheeded adj незаме́ченный. unheeding adj невнима́тельный. unhelpful adj бесполе́зный; (person) неотзы́вчивый. unhesitating adj реши́тельный. unhesitatingly adv без колеба́ния. unhindered adj беспрепя́тственный. unhinge vt (fig) расстра́ивать impf, расстро́ить pf. unholy adj (impious) нечести́вый; (awful) ужа́сный. unhook vt (undo hooks of) расстёгивать impf, расстегну́ть pf; (uncouple) расцепля́ть impf, расцепи́ть pf. unhurt adj невреди́мый.

unicorn n единоро́г.

unification n объедине́ние.

uniform n фо́рма; adj единообра́зный; (unchanging) постоя́нный. uniformity n единообра́зие.

unify vt объединя́ть impf, объедини́ть pf.

unilateral adj односторо́нний.

unimaginable adj невообрази́мый. **unimaginative** adj лишённый воображе́ния, прозаи́чный. **unimportant** adj нева́жный. **uninformed** adj (ignorant) несве́дущий (about о +prep); (ill-informed) неосведомлённый. **uninhabited** adj необита́емый. **uninhibited** adj нестеснённый. **uninspired** adj бана́льный. **unintelligible** adj непоня́тный. **unintentional** adj неча́янный. **unintentionally** adv неча́янно. **uninterested** adj незаинтересо́ванный. **uninteresting** adj неинтере́сный. **uninterrupted** adj непреры́вный.

union n (alliance) сою́з; (joining together, alliance) объедине́ние; (trade ~) профсою́з. **unionist** n член профсою́за; (polit) униони́ст.

unique adj уника́льный.

unison n: in ~ (mus) в унисо́н; (fig) в согла́сии.

unit n едини́ца; (mil) часть.

unite vt & i соединя́ть(ся) impf, соедини́ть(ся) pf; объединя́ть(ся) impf, объедини́ть(ся) pf. **united** adj соединённый, объединённый; U~ Kingdom Соединённое Короле́вство; U~ Nations Организа́ция Объединённых На́ций; U~ States Соединённые Шта́ты m pl Аме́рики. **unity** n еди́нство.

universal adj всео́бщий; (many-sided) универса́льный. **universe** n вселе́нная sb; (world) мир.

university n университе́т; attrib университе́тский.

unjust adj несправедли́вый. **unjustifiable** adj непрости́тельный. **unjustified** adj неопра́вданный.

unkempt adj нечёсаный. **unkind** adj недо́брый, злой. **unknown** adj неизве́стный.

unlawful adj незако́нный. **unleaded** adj неэтили́рованный. **unleash** vt (also fig) развя́зывать impf, развяза́ть pf.

unless conj е́сли... не.

unlike adj непохо́жий (на+acc); (in contradistinction to) в отли́чие от +gen. **unlikely** adj малове-роя́тный; it is ~ that вряд ли. **unlimited** adj неограни́ченный. **unlit** adj неосвещённый. **unload** vt (vehicle etc.) разгружа́ть impf, разгрузи́ть pf;

(goods etc.) выгружа́ть impf, вы́грузить pf. **unlock** vt отпира́ть impf, отпере́ть pf; открыва́ть impf, откры́ть pf. **unlucky** adj (number etc.) несчастли́вый; (unsuccessful) неуда́чный.

unmanageable adj тру́дный, непоко́рный. **unmanned** adj автомати́ческий. **unmarried** adj холосто́й; (of man) жена́тый; (of woman) незаму́жняя. **unmask** vt (fig) разоблача́ть impf, разоблачи́ть pf. **unmentionable** adj неупомина́емый. **unmistakable** adj несомне́нный, я́сный. **unmitigated** adj (thorough) отъя́вленный; be ~ остава́ться impf, оста́ться pf равноду́шен, -шна.

unnatural adj неесте́ственный. **unnecessary** adj нену́жный. **unnerve** vt лиша́ть impf, лиши́ть pf му́жества; (upset) расстра́ивать impf, расстро́ить pf. **unnoticed** adj незаме́ченный.

unobserved adj незаме́ченный. **unobtainable** adj недосту́пный. **unobtrusive** adj скро́мный, ненавя́зчивый. **unoccupied** adj незаня́тый, свобо́дный; (house) пусто́й. **unofficial** adj неофициа́льный. **unopposed** adj не встре́тивший сопротивле́ния. **unorthodox** adj неортодокса́льный.

unpack vt распако́вывать impf, распакова́ть pf. **unpaid** adj (bill) неупла́ченный; (person) не получа́ющий пла́ты; (work) беспла́тный. **unpalatable** adj невку́сный; (unpleasant) неприя́тный. **unparalleled** adj несравни́мый. **unpleasant** adj неприя́тный. **unpleasantness** n неприя́тность. **unpopular** adj непопуля́рный. **unprecedented** adj беспреце́дентный. **unpredictable** adj непредска́зуемый. **unprejudiced** adj беспристра́стный. **unprepared** adj неподгото́вленный, него́товый. **unprepossessing** adj непривлека́тельный. **unpretentious** adj просто́й, без прете́нзий. **unprincipled** adj беспринци́пный. **unproductive** adj непродукти́вный. **unprofitable** adj невы́годный. **unpromising** adj малообеща́ющий. **unprotected** adj незащищённый. **unproven** adj недока́занный. **unprovoked** adj непровоци́рованный. **unpublished** adj неопублико́ванный, неи́зданный. **unpunished** adj безнака́занный.

unqualified adj неквалифици́рованный; (unconditional) безогово́рочный. **unquestionable** adj несомне́нный, неоспори́мый. **unquestionably** adv несомне́нно, бесспо́рно.

unravel vt & i распу́тывать(ся) impf, распута́ть(ся) pf, vt (solve) разга́дывать impf, разгада́ть pf. **unread** adj (book etc.) непрочи́танный. **unreadable** adj (illegible) неразбо́рчивый; (boring) нечитабе́льный. **unreal** adj нереа́льный. **unrealistic** adj нереа́льный. **unreasonable** adj (person) неразу́мный; (behaviour, demand, price) необосно́ванный. **unrecognizable** adj неузнава́емый. **unrecognized** adj непри́знанный. **unrefined** adj неочи́щенный; (manners etc.) грубый. **unrelated** adj не име́ющий отноше́ния (to к+dat), несвя́занный (to с+instr); we are ~ мы не ро́дственники. **unrelenting** adj (ruthless) безжа́лостный; (unremitting) неосла́бный. **unreliable** adj ненадёжный. **unremarkable** adj невыдаю́щийся. **unremitting** adj неосла́бный; (incessant) беспреста́нный. **unrepentant** adj нераска́явшийся. **unrepresentative** adj нетипи́чный. **unrequited** adj: ~ love неразделённая любо́вь. **unreserved** adj (full) по́лный; (open) открове́нный; (unconditional) безогово́рочный; (seat) незаброни́рованный. **unresolved** adj нерешённый. **unrest** n беспоко́йство; (polit) волне́ния neut pl. **unrestrained** adj несде́ржанный. **unrestricted** adj неограни́ченный. **unripe** adj незре́лый. **unrivalled** adj беспадо́бный. **unroll** vt & i развёртывать(ся) impf, разверну́ть(ся) pf. **unruffled** adj (smooth) гла́дкий; (calm) споко́йный. **unruly** adj непоко́рный.

unsafe adj опа́сный; (insecure) ненадёжный. **unsaid** adj: leave ~ молча́ть impf о+prep. **unsaleable** adj нехо́дкий. **unsalted** adj несолёный. **unsatisfactory** adj неудовлетвори́тельный. **unsatisfied** adj неудовлетворённый. **unsavoury** adj

(unpleasant) неприя́тный; (disreputable) сомни́тельный. **unscathed** adj невреди́мый; (predic) цел и невреди́м. **unscheduled** adj (transport) внеочередно́й; (event) незаплани́рованный. **unscientific** adj ненау́чный. **unscrew** vt & i отви́нчивать(ся) impf, отвинти́ть(ся) pf. **unscrupulous** adj беспринци́пный. **unseat** vt (of horse) сбра́сывать impf, сбро́сить pf с седла́; (parl) лиша́ть impf, лиши́ть pf парла́ментского манда́та.

unseemly adj неподоба́ющий. **unseen** adj неви́димый. **unselfconscious** adj непосре́дственный. **unselfish** adj бескоры́стный. **unsettle** vt выбива́ть impf, вы́бить pf из коле́й; (upset) расстра́ивать impf, расстро́ить pf. **unsettled** adj (weather) неусто́йчивый; (unresolved) нерешённый. **unsettling** adj волну́ющий. **unshakeable** adj непоколеби́мый. **unshaven** adj небри́тый. **unsightly** adj непригля́дный, уро́дливый. **unsigned** adj неподпи́санный. **unskilful** adj неуме́лый. **unskilled** adj неквалифици́рованный. **unsociable** adj необщи́тельный. **unsold** adj непро́данный. **unsolicited** adj непро́шенный. **unsolved** adj нерешённый. **unsophisticated** adj просто́й. **unsound** adj (unhealthy, unwholesome) нездоро́вый; (not solid) непро́чный; (unfounded) необосно́ванный; of ~ mind душевнобольно́й. **unspeakable** adj (inexpressible) невырази́мый; (very bad) отврати́тельный. **unspecified** adj то́чно не ука́занный, неопределённый. **unspoilt** adj неиспо́рченный. **unspoken** adj невы́сказанный. **unstable** adj неусто́йчивый; (mentally) неуравнове́шенный. **unsteady** adj неусто́йчивый. **unstuck** adj: come ~ откле́иваться impf, откле́иться pf; (fig) прова́ливаться impf, провали́ться pf. **unsuccessful** adj неуда́чный, безуспе́шный. **unsuitable** adj неподходя́щий. **unsuited** adj неприго́дный. **unsung** adj невоспе́тый. **unsupported** adj неподде́ржанный. **unsure** adj неуве́ренный (of o.s. в себе́). **unsurpassed** adj непревзойдённый. **unsurprising** adj неудиви́-

тельный. **unsuspected** adj (*unforeseen*) непредви́денный. **unsuspecting** adj недозрева́ющий. **unsweetened** adj неподсла́щенный. **unswerving** adj непоколеби́мый. **unsympathetic** adj несочу́вствующий. **unsystematic** adj несистемати́чный.

untainted adj неиспо́рченный. **untangle** vt распу́тывать *impf*, распу́тать *pf*. **untapped** adj: ~ **resources** неиспо́льзованные ресу́рсы *m pl*. **untenable** adj несостоя́тельный. **untested** adj неиспы́танный. **unthinkable** adj невообрази́мый. **unthinking** adj безду́мный. **untidiness** *n* неопря́тность; (*disorder*) беспоря́док. **untidy** adj неопря́тный; (*in disorder*) в беспоря́дке. **untie** vt развя́зывать *impf*, развяза́ть *pf*; (*set free*) освобожда́ть *impf*, освободи́ть *pf*.

until prep до+gen; not ~ не ра́ньше +gen; ~ **then** до тех пор; *conj* пока́, пока́… не; *not* ~ то́лько когда́.

untimely adj (*premature*) безвре́менный; (*inappropriate*) неуме́стный. **untiring** adj неутоми́мый. **untold** adj (*incalculable*) бесчётный, несме́тный; (*inexpressible*) невырази́мый; (*indifferent*) равноду́шный. **untoward** adj неблагоприя́тный. **untrained** adj необу́ченный. **untried** adj неиспы́танный. **untroubled** adj споко́йный. **untrue** adj неве́рный. **untrustworthy** adj ненадёжный. **untruth** *n* непра́вда, ложь. **untruthful** adj лжи́вый.

unusable adj неприго́дный. **unused** adj неиспо́льзованный; (*unaccustomed*) непривы́кший (to к+dat); I am ~ to this я к э́тому не привы́к. **unusual** adj необыкнове́нный, необы́чный. **unusually** adv необыкнове́нно. **unutterable** adj невырази́мый.

unveil vt (*statue*) торже́ственно открыва́ть *impf*, откры́ть *pf*; (*disclose*) обнаро́довать *impf & pf*.

unwanted adj нежела́нный. **unwarranted** adj неоправ́данный. **unwary** adj неосторо́жный. **unwavering** adj непоколеби́мый. **unwelcome** adj нежела́тельный; (*unpleasant*) неприя́тный. **unwell** adj нездоро́вый. **unwieldy** adj громо́здкий. **unwilling**

adj несклонный; be ~ не хоте́ть *impf*, за~ *pf* (to +inf). **unwillingly** adv неохо́тно. **unwillingness** *n* неохо́та. **unwind** vt & i разма́тывать(ся) *impf*, размота́ть(ся) *pf*; (*rest*) отдыха́ть *impf*, отдохну́ть *pf*. **unwise** adj не(благо)разу́мный. **unwitting** adj нево́льный. **unwittingly** adv нево́льно. **unworkable** adj неприменимый. **unworldly** adj не от ми́ра сего́. **unworthy** adj недосто́йный. **unwrap** vt развёртывать *impf*, разверну́ть *pf*. **unwritten** adj: ~ **law** непи́саный зако́н.

unyielding adj упо́рный, неподатли́вый.

unzip vt расстёгивать *impf*, расстегну́ть *pf* (мо́лнию+gen).

up adv (*motion*) вверх, вверх; (*position*) наверху́, вверху́; ~ **and down** вверх и вниз; (*back and forth*) взад и вперёд; ~ **to** (*towards*) к+dat; (*as far as, until*) до+gen; ~ **to now** до сих пор; be ~ **against** what+*instr*; it is ~ **to you**+*inf*, это вам+*inf*, вы должны́+*inf*; what's ~? что случи́лось?; в чём де́ло?; **your time is** ~ ва́ше вре́мя истекло́; **and about на ногах; he isn't ~ yet** он ещё не встал; **he isn't ~ to this job** он не годи́тся для э́той рабо́ты; *prep* вверх по+dat; (*along*) (вдоль) по+dat; *vt* повыша́ть *impf*, повы́сить; *vi* (*leap up*) взять *pf*; *adj*: ~-**to-date** совреме́нный; (*fashionable*) мо́дный; ~-**and-coming** многообеща́ющий; *n*: ~**s and downs** (*fig*) превра́тности *f pl* судьбы́.

upbringing *n* воспита́ние.

update vt модернизи́ровать *impf & pf*; (*a book etc.*) дополня́ть *impf*, допо́лнить *pf*.

upgrade vt повыша́ть *impf*, повы́сить *pf* (по слу́жбе).

upheaval *n* потрясе́ние.

uphill adj (*fig*) тяжёлый; *adv* в го́ру.

uphold vt подде́рживать *impf*, подержа́ть *pf*.

upholster vt обива́ть *impf*, оби́ть *pf*. **upholsterer** *n* обо́йщик. **upholstery** *n* оби́вка.

upkeep *n* содержа́ние.

upland *n* гори́стая часть страны́; *adj* наго́рный.

uplift vt поднима́ть *impf*, подня́ть *pf*.

up-market *adj* дорого́й.

upon *prep* (*position*) на+*prep*, (*motion*) на+*acc*; *see* on

upper *adj* ве́рхний; (*socially, in rank*) вы́сший; **gain the** ~ **hand** одержа́ть *impf*, одержа́ть *pf* верх (*over* над+*instr*); *n* передо́к. **uppermost** *adj* са́мый ве́рхний, вы́сший; **be** ~ **in person's mind** бо́льше всего́ занима́ть *impf*, заня́ть *pf* мы́сли кого́-л.

upright *n* сто́йка; *adj* вертика́льный; (*honest*) че́стный; ~ **piano** пиани́но *neut indecl*.

uprising *n* восста́ние.

uproar *n* шум, гам.

uproot *vt* вырыва́ть *impf*, вы́рвать *pf* с ко́рнем; (*people*) выселя́ть *impf*, вы́селить *pf*.

upset *n* расстро́йство; *vt* расстра́ивать *impf*, расстро́ить *pf*; (*overturn*) опроки́дывать *impf*, опроки́нуть *pf*; *adj* (*miserable*) расстро́енный; ~ **stomach** расстро́йство желу́дка.

upshot *n* развя́зка, результа́т.

upside-down *adj* перевёрнутый вверх дном; *adv* вверх дном; (*in disorder*) в беспоря́дке.

upstairs *adv* (*position*) наверху́; (*motion*) наве́рх; *n* ве́рхний эта́ж; *adj* находя́щийся в ве́рхнем этаже́.

upstart *n* вы́скочка *m & f*.

upstream *adv* про́тив тече́ния; (*situation*) вверх по тече́нию.

upsurge *n* подъём, волна́.

uptake *n*: **be quick on the** ~ бы́стро сообража́ть *impf*, сообрази́ть *pf*.

upturn *n* (*fig*) улучше́ние. **upturned** *adj* (*face etc.*) по́днятый кве́рху; (*inverted*) перевёрнутый.

upward *adj* напра́вленный вверх. **upwards** *adv* вверх; ~ **of** свы́ше +*gen*.

uranium *n* ура́н.

urban *adj* городско́й.

urbane *adj* ве́жливый.

urchin *n* мальчи́шка *m*.

urge *n* (*incitement*) побужде́ние; (*desire*) жела́ние; *vt* (*impel*, ~ **on**) гоня́ть *impf*, подогна́ть *pf*; (*warn*) предупрежда́ть *impf*, предупреди́ть *pf*; (*try to persuade*) убежда́ть *impf*. **urgency** *n* сро́чность, ва́жность; **a matter of great** ~ сро́чное де́ло. **urgent** *adj* сро́чный; (*insistent*) наста́ятельный. **urgently** *adv* сро́чно.

urinate *vi* мочи́ться *impf*, по~ *pf*. **urine** *n* моча́.

urn *n* у́рна.

US(A) *abbr* (*of United States of America*) США, Соединённые Шта́ты Аме́рики.

usable *adj* го́дный к употребле́нию.

usage *n* употребле́ние; (*treatment*) обраще́ние. **use** *n* (*utilization*) употребле́ние, по́льзование; (*benefit*) по́льза; (*application*) примене́ние; **it is no** ~ (-ing) бесполе́зно (+*inf*); **make** ~ **of** испо́льзовать *impf & pf*; по́льзоваться *impf* +*instr*; *vt* употребля́ть *impf*, употреби́ть *pf*; по́льзоваться *impf* +*instr*; (*apply*) применя́ть *impf*, примени́ть *pf*; (*treat*) обраща́ться *impf* c+*instr*; **I** ~**d to see him often** я ча́сто его́ встреча́л; **be, get** ~**d to** привыка́ть *impf*, привы́кнуть *pf* (**to** к+*dat*); ~ **up** расхо́довать *impf*, из~ *pf*. **used** *adj* (*second-hand*) ста́рый. **useful** *adj* поле́зный; **come in** ~, **prove** ~ пригоди́ться *pf* (**to** +*dat*). **useless** *adj* бесполе́зный. **user** *n* потреби́тель *m*.

usher *n* (*theat*) биле́тер; *vt* (*lead in*) вводи́ть *impf*, ввести́ *pf*; (*proclaim*, ~ **in**) возвеща́ть *impf*, возвести́ть *pf*. **usherette** *n* билетёрша.

USSR *abbr* (*of Union of Soviet Socialist Republics*) СССР, Сою́з Сове́тских Социалисти́ческих Респу́блик.

usual *adj* обыкнове́нный, обы́чный; **as** ~ как обы́чно. **usually** *adv* обыкнове́нно, обы́чно.

usurp *vt* узурпи́ровать *impf & pf*. **usurper** *n* узурпа́тор.

usury *n* ростовщи́чество.

utensil *n* инструме́нт; *pl* у́тварь, посу́да.

uterus *n* ма́тка.

utilitarian *adj* утилита́рный. **utilitarianism** *n* утилитари́зм. **utility** *n* поле́зность; *pl*: **public utilities** комму́нальные услу́ги *f pl*. **utilize** *vt* испо́льзовать *impf & pf*.

utmost *adj* (*extreme*) кра́йний; **this is of the** ~ **importance to me** э́то для меня́ кра́йне ва́жно; *n*: **do one's** ~ де́лать *impf*, с~ *pf* всё возмо́жное.

Utopia *n* уто́пия. **utopian** *adj* утопи́ческий.

utter *attrib* по́лный, абсолю́тный;
(*out-and-out*) отъя́вленный (*coll*); *vt*
произноси́ть *impf*, произнести́ *pf*;
(*let out*) издава́ть *impf*, изда́ть *pf*.
utterance *n* (*uttering*) произнесе́-
ние; (*pronouncement*) выска́зыва-
ние. **utterly** *adv* соверше́нно.
Uzbek *n* узбе́к, -е́чка. **Uzbekistan** *n*
Узбекиста́н.

V

vacancy *n* (*for job*) вака́нсия, сво-
бо́дное ме́сто; (*at hotel*) свобо́дный
но́мер. **vacant** *adj* (*post*) вака́нт-
ный; (*post; not engaged, free*) сво-
бо́дный; (*empty*) пусто́й; (*look*) от-
су́тствующий. **vacate** *vt* освобож-
да́ть *impf*, освободи́ть *pf*. **vacation** *n* кани́кулы (-л) *pl*; (*leave*) о́т-
пуск.
vaccinate *vt* вакцини́ровать *impf* &
pf. **vaccination** *n* приви́вка (*against*
от, про́тив+*gen*). **vaccine** *n* вакци́-
на.
vacillate *vi* колеба́ться *impf*. **vacil-
lation** *n* колеба́ние.
vacuous *adj* пусто́й. **vacuum** *n* ва́ку-
ум; (*fig*) пустота́; ~-clean чи́стить
impf, вы́-, по~ *pf* пылесо́сом; ~
cleaner пылесо́с; ~ flask те́рмос.
vagabond *n* бродя́га *m*.
vagary *n* капри́з.
vagina *n* влага́лище.
vagrant *n* бродя́га *m*.
vague *adj* (*indeterminate, uncertain*)
неопределённый; (*unclear*) нея́сный;
(*dim*) сму́тный; (*absent-minded*)
рассе́янный. **vagueness** *n* неопределённость, нея́сность; (*absent-
mindedness*) рассе́янность.
vain *adj* (*futile*) тще́тный, напра́с-
ный; (*empty*) пусто́й; (*conceited*)
тщесла́вный; in ~ напра́сно.
vale *n* дол, доли́на.
valentine *n* (*card*) поздрави́тельная
ка́рточка с днём свято́го Валенти́-
на.
valet *n* камерди́нер.
valiant *adj* хра́брый.
valid *adj* действи́тельный; (*weighty*)
ве́ский. **validate** *vt* (*ratify*) утверж-
да́ть *impf*, утверди́ть *pf*. **validity**
n действи́тельность; (*weightiness*)

ве́скость.
valley *n* доли́на.
valour *n* до́блесть.
valuable *adj* це́нный; *n pl* це́нности
f pl. **valuation** *n* оце́нка. **value** *n*
це́нность; (*math*) величина́; *pl* це́н-
ности *f pl*; ~-added tax нало́г на
доба́вленную сто́имость; ~ judgement субъекти́вная оце́нка; *vt* (*estimate*) оце́нивать *impf*, оцени́ть *pf*;
(*hold dear*) цени́ть *impf*.
valve *n* (*tech, med, mus*) кла́пан;
(*tech*) ве́нтиль *m*; (*radio*) электро́н-
ная ла́мпа.
vampire *n* вампи́р.
van *n* фурго́н.
vandal *n* ванда́л. **vandalism** *n* ванда-
ли́зм. **vandalize** *vt* разруша́ть *impf*,
разру́шить *pf*.
vanguard *n* аванга́рд.
vanilla *n* вани́ль.
vanish *vi* исчеза́ть *impf*, исче́знуть
pf.
vanity *n* (*futility*) тщета́; (*conceit*)
тщесла́вие.
vanquish *vt* побежда́ть *impf*, побе-
ди́ть *pf*.
vantage-point *n* (*mil*) наблюда́тель-
ный пункт; (*fig*) вы́годная пози́ция.
vapour *n* пар.
variable *adj* изме́нчивый; (*weather*)
неусто́йчивый, переме́нный; *n*
(*math*) переме́нная (величина́).
variance *n*: be at ~ with (*contradict*)
противоре́чить *impf*+*dat*; (*disagree*)
расходи́ться *impf*, разойти́сь *pf* во
мне́ниях c+*instr*. **variant** *n* вариа́нт.
variation *n* (*varying*) измене́ние;
(*variant*) вариа́нт; (*variety*) разно-
ви́дность; (*mus*) вариа́ция.
varicose *adj*: ~ veins расшире́ние
вен.
varied *adj* разнообра́зный. **variegated** *adj* разноцве́тный. **variety** *n*
разнообра́зие; (*sort*) разнови́д-
ность; (*a number*) ряд; ~ show
варьете́ *neut indecl*. **various** *adj*
ра́зный.
varnish *n* лак; *vt* лакирова́ть *impf*,
от~ *pf*.
vary *vt* разнообра́зить *impf*, меня́ть
impf; *vi* (*change*) меня́ться *impf*;
(*differ*) рази́ться *impf*.
vase *n* ва́за.
Vaseline *n* (*propr*) вазели́н.

vast adj громáдный. **vastly** adv значи́тельно.

VAT abbr (of value-added tax) налóг на добáвленную стóимость.

vat n чан, бак.

vaudeville n водеви́ль m.

vault¹ n (leap) прыжóк; vt перепры́гивать impf, перепры́гнуть pf; vi пры́гать impf, пры́гнуть pf.

vault² n (arch, covering) свод; (cellar) пóгреб; (tomb) склеп. **vaulted** adj свóдчатый.

VDU abbr (of visual display unit) монитóр.

veal n теля́тина.

vector n (math) вéктор.

veer vi (change direction) изменя́ть impf, измени́ть pf направлéние; (turn) повора́чивать impf, повороти́ть pf.

vegetable n óвощ; adj овощнóй. **vegetarian** n вегетариáнец, -нка; attrib вегетариáнский. **vegetate** vi (fig) прозябáть impf. **vegetation** n расти́тельность.

vehemence n (force) си́ла; (passion) стрáстность. **vehement** adj (forceful) си́льный; (passionate) стрáстный.

vehicle n трáнспортное срéдство; (motor ~) автомоби́ль m; (medium) срéдство.

veil n вуáль; (fig) завéса. **veiled** adj скры́тый.

vein n вéна; (of leaf, streak) жи́лка; in the same ~ в том же дýхе.

velocity n скóрость.

velvet n бáрхат; adj бáрхатный. **velvety** adj бархати́стый.

vending-machine n торгóвый автомáт. **vendor** n продавéц, -вщи́ца.

vendetta n вендéтта.

veneer n фанéра; (fig) лоск.

venerable adj почтéнный. **venerate** vt благоговéть impf пéред+instr. **veneration** n благоговéние.

venereal adj венери́ческий.

venetian blind n жалюзи́ neut indecl.

vengeance n месть; take ~ мстить impf, ото~ pf (on +dat; for +acc); with a ~ вовсю́. **vengeful** adj мсти́тельный.

venison n олéнина.

venom n яд. **venomous** adj ядови́тый.

vent¹ n (opening) вы́ход (also fig), отвéрстие; vt (feelings) давáть impf, дать pf вы́ход+dat; излива́ть impf, изли́ть pf (on на+acc).

vent² n (slit) разрéз.

ventilate vt провéтривать impf, провéтрить pf. **ventilation** n вентиля́ция. **ventilator** n вентиля́тор.

ventriloquist n чревовещáтель m.

venture n предприя́тие; v (dare) осмéливаться impf, осмéлиться pf; vt (risk) рисковáть impf +instr.

venue n мéсто.

veranda n верáнда.

verb n глагóл. **verbal** adj (oral) ýстный; (relating to words) словéсный; (gram) отглагóльный. **verbatim** adj дословный; adv дослóвно. **verbose** adj многослóвный.

verdict n приговóр.

verge n (also fig) край; (of road) обóчина; (fig) грань; on the ~ of на грáни+gen; he was on the ~ of telling all он чуть не рассказáл всё; vi: ~ on грани́чить impf с+instr.

verification n провéрка; (confirmation) подтверждéние. **verify** vt проверя́ть impf, провéрить pf; (confirm) подтверждáть impf, подтверди́ть pf.

vermin n вреди́тели m pl.

vernacular n роднóй язы́к; мéстный диалéкт; (homely language) разговóрный язы́к.

versatile adj многосторóнний.

verse n (also bibl) стих; (stanza) строфá; (poetry) стихи́ m pl. **versed** adj óпытный, свéдущий (in в+prep).

version n (variant) вариáнт; (interpretation) вéрсия; (text) текст.

versus prep прóтив+gen.

vertebra n позвонóк; pl позвонóчник. **vertebrate** n позвонóчное живóтное sb.

vertical adj вертикáльный; n вертикáль.

vertigo n головокружéние.

verve n жи́вость, энтузиáзм.

very adj (that ~ same) тот сáмый; (this ~ same) э́тот сáмый; at that ~ moment в тот сáмый момéнт; (precisely) как раз; you are the ~ person I was looking for как раз вас искáл; the ~ (even the) дáже, оди́н; the ~ thought frightens me однá, да́же, мысль об э́том меня́ пуга́ет; (the extreme) са́мый; at the ~ end в са́мом конце́; adv о́чень; ~ much о́чень; ~ much +comp гора́здо +comp; ~+superl, superl; ~ first са́мый пе́рвый; ~ well (agreement) хорошо́, ла́дно; not ~ не о́чень, дово́льно +neg.

vessel n сосу́д; (ship) су́дно.

vest[1] n ма́йка; (waistcoat) жиле́т.

vest[2] vt (with power) облека́ть impf, обле́чь pf (with +instr). **vested** adj: ~ **interest** ли́чная заинтересо́ванность; ~ **interests** (entrepreneurs) кру́пные предпринима́тели m pl.

vestibule n вестибю́ль m.

vestige n (trace) след; (sign) при́знак.

vestments n pl (eccl) облаче́ние.

vestry n ри́зница.

vet n ветерина́р; vt (fig) проверя́ть impf, прове́рить pf.

veteran n ветера́н; adj ста́рый.

veterinary adj ветерина́рный; n ветерина́р.

veto n ве́то neut indecl; vt налага́ть impf, наложи́ть pf ве́то на+acc.

vex vt досажда́ть impf, досади́ть pf +dat. **vexation** n доса́да. **vexed** adj (annoyed) серди́тый; (question) спо́рный. **vexatious, vexing** adj доса́дный.

via prep че́рез+acc.

viable adj (able to survive) жизнеспосо́бный; (feasible) осуществи́мый.

viaduct n виаду́к.

vibrant adj (lively) живо́й. **vibrate** vi вибри́ровать impf; vt (make ~) заставля́ть impf, заста́вить pf вибри́ровать. **vibration** n вибра́ция. **vibrato** n вибра́то neut indecl.

vicar n прихо́дский свяще́нник. **vicarage** n дом свяще́нника.

vicarious adj чужо́й.

vice[1] n (evil) поро́к.

vice[2] n (tech) тиски́ (-ко́в) pl.

vice- in comb ви́це-, замести́тель m; ~-**chairman** замести́тель m председа́теля; ~-**chancellor** (univ) проре́ктор; ~-**president** ви́це-президе́нт. **viceroy** n ви́це-коро́ль m.

vice versa adv наоборо́т.

vicinity n окре́стность; in the ~ побли́зости (of от+gen).

vicious adj зло́бный; ~ **circle** поро́чный круг.

vicissitude n превра́тность.

victim n же́ртва; (of accident) пострада́вший sb. **victimization** n пресле́дование. **victimize** vt пресле́довать impf.

victor n победи́тель m, ~ница.

Victorian adj викториа́нский.

victorious adj победоно́сный. **victory** n побе́да.

video n (~ recorder, ~ cassette, ~ film) ви́део neut indecl; ~ **camera** видеока́мера; ~ **cassette** видеокассе́та; ~ (**cassette**) **recorder** видеомагнитофо́н; ~ **game** видеоигра́; vt запи́сывать impf, записа́ть pf на ви́део.

vie vi сопе́рничать impf (with с+instr; for в+prep).

Vietnam n Вьетна́м. **Vietnamese** n вьетна́мец, -мка; adj вьетна́мский.

view n (prospect, picture) вид; (opinion) взгляд; (viewing) просмо́тр; (inspection) осмо́тр; in ~ of ввиду́ +gen; on ~ вы́ставленный для обозре́ния; with a ~ to с це́лью+gen, +inf; vt (pictures etc.) рассма́тривать impf; (inspect) осма́тривать impf, осмотре́ть pf; (mentally) смотре́ть impf на+acc. **viewer** n зри́тель m, ~ница. **viewfinder** n видоиска́тель m. **viewpoint** n то́чка зре́ния.

vigil n бо́дрствование; **keep** ~ бо́дрствовать impf, дежу́рить impf. **vigilance** n бди́тельность. **vigilant** adj бди́тельный. **vigilante** n дружи́нник.

vigorous adj си́льный, энерги́чный. **vigour** n си́ла, эне́ргия.

vile adj гну́сный. **vilify** vt черни́ть impf, о~ pf.

villa n ви́лла.

village n дере́вня; attrib дереве́нский. **villager** n жи́тель m дере́вни.

villain n злоде́й.

vinaigrette n припра́ва из у́ксуса и оли́вкового ма́сла.

vindicate vt опра́вдывать impf, оправда́ть pf. **vindication** n оправда́ние.

vindictive adj мсти́тельный.

vine n виногра́дная лоза́.

vinegar n у́ксус.

vineyard n виногра́дник.

vintage n (year) год; (fig) вы́пуск; attrib (wine) ма́рочный; (car) архаи́ческий.

viola n (mus) альт.

violate vt (treaty, privacy) нарушать impf, нарушить pf; (grave) осквернять impf, осквернить pf. violation n нарушение; осквернение.

violence n (physical coercion, force) насилие; (strength, force) сила. violent adj (person, storm, argument) свирепый; (pain) сильный; (death) насильственный. violently adv сильно, очень.

violet n (bot) фиалка; (colour) фиолетовый цвет; adj фиолетовый.

violin n скрипка. violinist n скрипач, ~ка.

VIP abbr (of very important person) очень важное лицо.

viper n гадюка.

virgin n девственница, (male) девственник; V~ Mary дева Мария. virginal adj девственный. virginity n девственность. Virgo n Дева.

virile adj мужественный. virility n мужество.

virtual adj фактический. virtually adv фактически. virtue n (excellence) добродетель; (merit) достоинство; by ~ of на основании+gen. virtuosity n виртуозность. virtuoso n виртуоз. virtuous adj добродетельный.

virulent adj (med) вирулентный; (fig) злобный.

virus n вирус.

visa n виза.

vis-à-vis prep (with regard to) по отношению к+dat.

viscount n виконт. viscountess n виконтесса.

viscous adj вязкий.

visibility n видимость. visible adj видимый. visibly adv явно, заметно.

vision n (sense) зрение; (apparition) видение; (dream) мечта; (insight) проницательность. visionary adj (unreal) призрачный; (impracticable) неосуществимый; (insightful) проницательный; n (dreamer) мечтатель m.

visit n посещение, визит; vt посещать impf, посетить pf; (call on) заходить impf, зайти pf к+dat. visitation n официальное посещение. visitor n гость m, посетитель m.

visor n (of cap) козырёк; (in car)

солнцезащитный щиток; (of helmet) забрало.

vista n перспектива, вид.

visual adj (of vision) зрительный; (graphic) наглядный; ~ aids наглядные пособия neut pl. visualize vt представлять impf, представить pf себе.

vital adj абсолютно необходимый (to, for для+gen); (essential to life) жизненный; of ~ importance первостепенной важности. vitality n (liveliness) энергия. vitally adv жизненно.

vitamin n витамин.

vitreous adj стеклянный.

vitriolic adj (fig) едкий.

vivacious adj живой. vivacity n живость.

viva (voce) n устный экзамен.

vivid adj (bright) яркий; (lively) живой. vividness n яркость; живость.

vivisection n вивисекция.

vixen n лисица-самка.

viz. adv то есть, а именно.

vocabulary n (range, list, of words) словарь m; (range of words) запас слов; (of a language) словарный состав.

vocal adj голосовой; (mus) вокальный; (noisy) шумный; ~ chord голосовая связка. vocalist n певец, -вица.

vocation n призвание. vocational adj профессиональный.

vociferous adj шумный.

vodka n водка.

vogue n мода; in ~ в моде.

voice n голос; vt выражать impf, выразить pf.

void n пустота; adj пустой; (invalid) недействительный; ~ of лишённый +gen.

volatile adj (chem) летучий; (person) непостоянный, неустойчивый.

volcanic adj вулканический. volcano n вулкан.

vole n (zool) полёвка.

volition n воля; by one's own ~ по своей воле.

volley n (missiles) залп; (fig) град; (sport) удар с лёта; vt (sport) ударять impf, ударить pf с лёта. volleyball n волейбол.

volt n вольт. voltage n напряжение.

voluble adj говорли́вый.

volume n (book) том; (capacity, size) объём; (loudness) гро́мкость. **voluminous** adj обши́рный.

voluntary adj доброво́льный. **volunteer** n доброво́лец; vt предлага́ть impf, предложи́ть pf; vi (offer) вызыва́ться impf, вы́зваться pf (inf, +inf; for в+acc); (mil) идти́ impf, пойти́ pf доброво́льцем.

voluptuous adj сластолюби́вый.

vomit n рво́та; vt (& i) рвать impf, вы́рвать pf impers (+instr); he was ~ing blood его́ рва́ло кро́вью.

voracious adj прожо́рливый; (fig) ненасы́тный.

vortex n (also fig) водоворо́т, вихрь m.

vote n (poll) голосова́ние; (individual ~) го́лос; the ~ (suffrage) пра́во го́лоса; (resolution) во́тум no pl; ~ of no confidence во́тум недове́рия (in +dat); ~ of thanks выраже́ние благода́рности; vi голосова́ть impf, про~ pf (for за+acc; against про́тив+gen); vt (allocate by ~) ассигнова́ть impf & pf; (deem) признава́ть impf, призна́ть pf; the film was ~d a failure фильм был при́знан неуда́чным; ~ in избира́ть impf, избра́ть pf голосова́нием. **voter** n избира́тель m.

vouch vi: ~ for руча́ться impf, поручи́ться pf за+acc. **voucher** n (receipt) распи́ска; (coupon) тало́н.

vow n обе́т; vt кля́сться impf, по~ pf в+prep.

vowel n гла́сный sb.

voyage n путеше́ствие.

vulgar adj вульга́рный, гру́бый, по́шлый. **vulgarity** n вульга́рность, по́шлость.

vulnerable adj уязви́мый.

vulture n гриф; (fig) хи́щник.

W

wad n комо́к; (bundle) па́чка. **wadding** ва́та; (padding) наби́вка.

waddle vi ходи́ть indet, идти́ det, пойти́ pf вперева́лку (coll).

wade vt & i (river) переходи́ть impf, перейти́ pf вброд; vi: ~ through (mud etc.) пробира́ться impf, про-

бра́ться pf по+dat; (sth boring etc.) одолева́ть impf, одоле́ть pf.

wafer n ва́фля.

waffle[1] n (dish) ва́фля.

waffle[2] vi трепа́ться impf.

waft vt & i нести́(сь) impf, по~ pf.

wag vt & i (tail) виля́ть impf, вильну́ть pf (+instr); vt (finger) грози́ть impf, по~ pf +instr.

wage[1] n (pay) see wages

wage[2] vt: ~ war вести́ impf, про~ pf войну́.

wager n пари́ neut indecl; vi держа́ть impf пари́ (that что); vt ста́вить impf по~ pf.

wages n pl зарабо́тная пла́та.

waggle vt & i пома́хивать impf, помаха́ть pf (+instr).

wag(g)on n (carriage) повозка; (cart) теле́га; (rly) ваго́н-платфо́рма.

wail n вопль m; vi вопи́ть impf.

waist n та́лия; (level of ~) по́яс; ~-deep, high (adv) по по́яс. **waistband** n по́яс. **waistcoat** n жиле́т. **waistline** n та́лия.

wait n ожида́ние; lie in ~ (for) подстерега́ть impf, подсте́речь pf; vi (& i) (also ~ for) ждать impf (+gen); vi (be a waiter, waitress) быть официа́нтом, -ткой; ~ on обслу́живать impf, обслужи́ть pf. **waiter** n официа́нт. **waiting** n: ~-list спи́сок; ~-room приёмная sb; (rly) зал ожида́ния. **waitress** n официа́нтка.

waive vt отка́зываться impf, отказа́ться pf от+gen.

wake[1] n (at funeral) поми́нки (-нок) pl.

wake[2] n (naut) кильва́тер; in the ~ of по сле́ду +gen, за+instr.

wake[3] vt (also ~ up) буди́ть impf, раз~ pf; vi (also ~ up) просыпа́ться impf, просну́ться pf.

Wales n Уэ́льс.

walk n (walking) ходьба́; (gait) похо́дка; (stroll) прогу́лка; (path) тропа́; ~-out (strike) забасто́вка; (as protest) демонстрати́вный ухо́д; ~-over лёгкая побе́да; ten minutes' ~ from here де́сять мину́т ходьбы́ отсю́да; go for a ~ идти́ impf, пойти́ pf гуля́ть; from all ~s of life всех слоёв о́бщества; vi ходи́ть indet, идти́ det, пойти́ pf; гуля́ть impf, по~ pf; ~ away, off уходи́ть impf, уйти́

pf; ~ **in** входи́ть impf, войти́ pf; ~
out выходи́ть impf, вы́йти pf; ~ **out**
on броса́ть impf, бро́сить pf; vt
(traverse) обходи́ть impf, обойти́ pf;
(take for ~) выводи́ть impf, вы́-
вести pf гуля́ть. **walker** n ходо́к.
walkie-talkie n ра́ция. **walking** n
ходьба́; ~-**stick** трость.
Walkman n (propr) во́кмен.
wall n стена́; vt обноси́ть impf, обне-
сти́ pf стено́й; ~ **up** (door, window) заде́лывать impf, заде́лать pf;
(brick up) замуро́вывать impf, за-
муро́вать pf.
wallet n бума́жник.
wallflower n желтофио́ль.
wallop n си́льный уда́р; vt си́льно
ударя́ть impf, уда́рить pf.
wallow vi валя́ться impf; ~ **in** (give
o.s. up to) погружа́ться impf, погру-
зи́ться pf в+acc.
wallpaper n обо́и (обо́ев) pl.
walnut n гре́цкий оре́х; (wood, tree)
оре́ховое де́рево, оре́х.
walrus n морж.
waltz n вальс; vi вальси́ровать impf.
wan adj бле́дный.
wand n па́лочка.
wander vi броди́ть impf; (also of
thoughts etc.) блужда́ть impf; ~ **from**
the point отклоня́ться impf, откло-
ни́ться pf от те́мы. **wanderer** n стра́н-
ник.
wane n: be on the ~ убыва́ть impf;
vi убыва́ть impf, убы́ть pf; (weaken)
ослабева́ть impf, ослабе́ть pf.
wangle vt заполуча́ть impf, заполу-
чи́ть pf.
want n (lack) недоста́ток; (requirement) потре́бность; (desire) жела́-
ние; for ~ of за недоста́тком +gen;
vt хоте́ть impf, за~ pf +gen, acc;
(need) нужда́ться impf в+prep; I ~
you to come at six я хочу́, чтобы
ты пришёл в шесть. **wanting** adj:
be ~ недостава́ть impf (impers
+gen); **experience is** ~ недостаёт
о́пыта.
wanton adj (licentious) распу́тный;
(senseless) бессмы́сленный.
war n война́; (attrib) вое́нный; **at** ~
в состоя́нии войны́; ~ **memorial**
па́мятник па́вшим в войне́.
ward n (hospital) пала́та; (child etc.)
подопе́чный sb; (district) райо́н; vt:

~ **off** отража́ть impf, отрази́ть pf.
warden n (prison) нача́льник; (college) ре́ктор; (hostel) коменда́нт.
warder n тюре́мщик.
wardrobe n гардеро́б.
warehouse n склад. **wares** n pl
изде́лия neut pl, това́ры m pl.
warfare n война́.
warhead n боева́я голо́вка.
warily adv осторо́жно.
warlike adj вои́нственный.
warm n тепло́; adj (also fig) тёплый;
~-**hearted** серде́чный; vt & i греть-
(ся) impf; согрева́ть(ся) impf, со-
гре́ть(ся) pf; ~ **up** (food etc.) подо-
грева́ть(ся) impf, подогре́ть(ся) pf;
(liven up) оживля́ть(ся) impf, ожи-
ви́ть(ся) pf; (sport) размина́ться
impf, размя́ться pf; (mus) разы́-
грываться impf, разыгра́ться pf.
warmth n тепло́; (cordiality) сер-
де́чность.
warn vt предупрежда́ть impf, пре-
дупреди́ть pf (about о+prep). **warn-**
ing n предупрежде́ние.
warp vt & i (wood) коро́бить(ся)
impf, по~, с~ pf; vt (pervert) из-
враща́ть impf, изврати́ть pf.
warrant n (for arrest etc.) о́рдер; vt
(justify) опра́вдывать impf, оправ-
да́ть pf; (guarantee) гаранти́ровать
impf & pf. **warranty** n гара́нтия.
warrior n во́ин.
warship n вое́нный кора́бль m.
wart n борода́вка.
wartime n: **in** ~ во вре́мя войны́.
wary adj осторо́жный.
wash n мытьё; (thin layer) то́нкий
слой; (lotion) примо́чка; (surf) при-
бо́й; (backwash) попу́тная волна́; **at**
the ~ в сти́рке; **have a** ~ мы́ться
impf, по~ pf; ~-**basin** умыва́льник;
~-**out** (fiasco) прова́л; ~-**room** умы-
ва́льная sb; vt & i мы́ть(ся) impf,
вы́~, по~ pf; vt (clothes) стира́ть
impf, вы́~ pf; (of sea) омыва́ть
impf; ~ **away, off, out** смыва́ть(ся)
impf, смы́ть(ся) pf; (carry away)
сноси́ть impf, снести́ pf; ~ **out** (rinse)
спола́скивать impf, сполосну́ть pf;
~ **up** (dishes) мыть impf, вы́~, по~
pf (посу́ду); ~ **one's hands** (of it)
умыва́ть impf, умы́ть pf ру́ки.
washed-out adj (exhausted) утомлённый. **washer** n (tech) ша́йба.

washing n (of clothes) стирка; (clothes) бельё; ~**machine** стиральная машина; ~**powder** стиральный порошок; ~-**up** (action) мытьё посуды; (dishes) грязная посуда; ~-**up liquid** жидкое мыло для мытья посуды.

wasp n оса.

wastage n утечка. **waste** n (desert) пустыня; (refuse) отбросы m pl; (of time, money, etc.) растрата; **go to** ~ пропадать impf, пропасть pf даром; adj (desert) пустынный; (superfluous) невозделанный; **lay** ~ опустошать impf, опустошить pf; ~**land** пустырь m; ~ **paper** ненужная бумаги f pl; (for recycling) макулатура; ~ **products** отходы (-дов) pl; ~-**paper basket** корзина для бумаги; vt тратить impf, по~, ис~ pf; (time) терять impf, по~ pf; vi: ~ **away** чахнуть impf, за~ pf. **wasteful** adj расточительный.

watch n (timepiece) часы (-сов) pl; (duty) дежурство; (naut) вахта; **keep** ~ **over** наблюдать impf за+instr; ~-**dog** сторожевой пёс; ~-**tower** сторожевая башня; vt (observe) наблюдать impf; (keep an eye on) следить impf за+instr; (look after) смотреть impf, по~ pf за+instr; ~ **television, a film** смотреть impf, по~ pf телевизор, фильм; vi смотреть impf; ~ **out** (be careful) беречься impf (for +gen); ~ **out for** ждать impf +gen; ~ **out!** осторожно! **watchful** adj бдительный. **watchman** n (ночной) сторож. **watchword** n лозунг.

water n вода; ~-**colour** акварель; ~-**heater** кипятильник; ~-**main** водопроводная магистраль; ~-**melon** арбуз; ~-**pipe** водопроводная труба; ~-**ski** (n) водная лыжа; ~-**skiing** водолыжный спорт; ~-**supply** водоснабжение; ~-**way** водный путь m; vt (flowers etc.) поливать impf, полить pf; (animals) поить impf, на~ pf; (irrigate) орошать impf, оросить pf; vi (eyes) слезиться impf; (mouth): **my mouth** ~**s** у меня слюнки текут; ~ **down** разбавлять impf, разбавить pf. **watercourse** n русло. **watercress** n кресс водяной.

waterfall n водопад. **waterfront** n часть города примыкающая к берегу. **watering-can** n лейка. **waterlogged** adj заболоченный. **watermark** n водяной знак. **waterproof** adj непромокаемый; n непромокаемый плащ. **watershed** n водораздел. **waterside** n берег. **watertight** adj водонепроницаемый; (fig) неопровержимый. **waterworks** n pl водопроводные сооружения neut pl. **watery** adj водянистый.

watt n ватт.

wave vt (hand etc.) махать impf, махнуть pf +instr; (flag) размахивать impf +instr; vi (~ hand) махать impf, по~ pf (at +dat); (flutter) развеваться impf; ~ **aside** отмахиваться impf, отмахнуться pf от+gen; ~ **down** останавливать impf, остановить pf; n (in various senses) волна; (of hand) взмах; (in hair) завивка. **wavelength** n длина волны. **waver** vi колебаться impf. **wavy** adj волнистый.

wax n воск; (in ear) сера; vt вощить impf, на~ pf. **waxwork** n восковая фигура; pl музей восковых фигур.

way n (road, path, route; fig) дорога, путь m; (direction) сторона; (manner) образ; (method) способ; (respect) отношение; (habit) привычка; **by the** ~ (fig) кстати, между прочим; **on the** ~ по дороге, по пути; **this** ~ (direction) сюда; (in this ~) таким образом; **the other** ~ **round** наоборот; **under** ~ на ходу; **be in the** ~ мешать impf; **get out of the** ~ уходить impf, уйти pf с дороги; **give** ~ (yield) поддаваться impf, поддаться pf (to +dat); (collapse) обрушиваться impf, обрушиться pf; **go out of one's** ~ стараться impf, по~ pf изо всех сил +inf; **get, have, one's own** ~ добиваться impf, добиться pf своего; **make** ~ уступать impf, уступить pf дорогу (for +dat). **waylay** v (lie in wait for) подстерегать impf, подстеречь pf; (stop) перехватывать impf, перехватить pf по пути. **wayside** adj придорожный; n: **fall by the** ~ выбывать impf, выбыть pf из строя.

wayward adj своенравый.

WC *abbr* (*of* water-closet) уборная *sb*. **we** *pron* мы.

weak *adj* слабый. **weaken** *vt* ослаблять *impf*, ослабить *pf*; *vi* слабеть *impf*, о~ *pf*. **weakling** *n* (*person*) слабый человек; (*plant*) слабое растение. **weakness** *n* слабость.

weal *n* (*mark*) рубец.

wealth *n* богатство; (*abundance*) изобилие. **wealthy** *adj* богатый.

wean *vt* отнимать *impf*, отнять *pf* от груди; (*fig*) отучать *impf*, отучить *pf* (of, from от+*gen*).

weapon *n* оружие. **weaponry** *n* вооружение.

wear *n* (*wearing*) носка; (*clothing*) одежда; (~ *and tear*) износ; *vt* носить *impf*; быть в+*prep*; what shall I ~? что мне надеть?; *vi* носиться *impf*; ~ off (*pain, novelty*) проходить *impf*, пройти *pf*; (*cease to have effect*) переставать *impf*, перестать *pf* действовать; ~ out (*clothes*) изнашивать(ся) *impf*, износить(ся) *pf*; (*exhaust*) измучивать *impf*, измучить *pf*.

weariness *n* усталость. **wearing**, **wearisome** *adj* утомительный. **weary** *adj* усталый; *vt* & *i* утомлять(ся) *impf*, утомить(ся) *pf*.

weasel *n* ласка.

weather *n* погода; be under the ~ неважно себя чувствовать *impf*; ~-beaten обветренный; ~ forecast прогноз погоды; *vt* (*storm etc.*) выдерживать *impf*, выдержать *pf*; (*expose to atmosphere*) подвергать *impf*, подвергнуть *pf* атмосферному влиянию. **weather-cock**, **weather-vane** *n* флюгер. **weatherman** *n* метеоролог.

weave[1] *vt* & *i* (*fabric*) ткать *impf*, со~ *pf*; *vt* (*fig*; *also wreath etc.*) плести *impf*, с~ *pf*. **weaver** *n* ткач, ~иха.

weave[2] *vi* (*wind*) виться *impf*.

web *n* (*cobweb*; *fig*) паутина; (*fig*) сплетение. **webbed** *adj* перепончатый. **webbing** *n* тканая лента.

wed *vt* (*of man*) жениться *impf* & *pf* на+*prep*; (*of woman*) выходить *impf*, выйти *pf* замуж за+*acc*; (*unite*) сочетать *impf* & *pf*; *vi* пожениться *impf* & *pf*. **wedded** *adj* супружеский; ~ to (*fig*) преданный +*dat*. **wedding** *n* свадьба,

бракосочетание; ~-cake свадебный торт; ~-day день *m* свадьбы; ~-dress подвенечное платье; ~-ring обручальное кольцо.

wedge *n* клин; *vt* (~ *open*) заклинивать *impf*, заклинить *pf*; *vt* & ~ in(to) вклинивать(ся) *impf*, вклинить(ся) *pf* (в+*acc*).

wedlock *n* брак; born out of ~ рождённый вне брака, внебрачный.

Wednesday *n* среда.

weed *n* сорняк; ~-killer гербицид; *vt* полоть *impf*, вы~ *pf*; ~ out удалять *impf*, удалить *pf*. **weedy** *adj* (*person*) тощий.

week *n* неделя; ~-end суббота и воскресенье, выходные *sb pl*. **weekday** *n* будний день *m*. **weekly** *adj* еженедельный; (*wage*) недельный; *adv* еженедельно; *n* еженедельник.

weep *vi* плакать *impf*. **weeping willow** *n* плакучая ива.

weigh *vt* (*also fig*) взвешивать *impf*, взвесить *pf*; (*consider*) обдумывать *impf*, обдумать *pf*; *vt* & *i* (*so much*) весить *impf*; ~ down отягощать *impf*, отяготить *pf*; ~ on тяготить *impf*; ~ out отвешивать *impf*, отвесить *pf*; ~ up (*appraise*) оценивать *impf*, оценить *pf*. **weight** *n* (*also authority*) вес; (*load, also fig*) тяжесть; (*sport*) штанга; (*influence*) влияние; lose ~ худеть *impf*, по~ *pf*; put on ~ толстеть *impf*, по~ *pf*; ~-lifter штангист; ~-lifting поднятие тяжестей; *vt* (*make heavier*) утяжелять *impf*, утяжелить *pf*. **weightless** *adj* невесомый. **weighty** *adj* веский.

weir *n* плотина.

weird *adj* (*strange*) странный.

welcome *n* приём; *adj* желанный; (*pleasant*) приятный; you are ~ (*don't mention it*) пожалуйста; you are ~ to use my bicycle мой велосипед к вашим услугам; you are ~ to stay the night вы можете переночевать у меня/нас; *vt* приветствовать *impf* (& *pf* in past tense); *int* добро пожаловать!

weld *vt* сваривать *impf*, сварить *pf*. **welder** *n* сварщик.

welfare *n* благосостояние; W~ State государство всеобщего благосостояния.

well[1] *n* колодец; (*for stairs*) лестничная клетка.

well² vi: ~ up (anger etc.) вскипать impf, вскипеть pf; tears ~ed up глаза наполнились слезами.

well³ adj (healthy) здоровый; feel ~ чувствовать impf, по~ pf себя хорошо, здоровым; get ~ поправляться impf, поправиться pf; look ~ хорошо выглядеть impf; all is ~ всё в порядке; int ну(!); adv хорошо; (very much) очень; as ~ how; as ~ as (in addition to) кроме+gen; it may ~ be true вполне возможно, что это так; very ~! хорошо!; ~ done! молодец!; ~-balanced уравновешенный; ~-behaved (благо)воспитанный; ~-being благополучие; ~-bred благовоспитанный; ~-built крепкий; ~-defined чёткий; ~-disposed благосклонный; ~ done (cooked) (хорошо) прожаренный; ~-fed откормленный; ~-founded обоснованный; ~-groomed (person) холёный; ~-heeled состоятельный; ~-informed (хорошо) осведомлённый (about в+prep); ~-known известный; ~-meaning действующий из лучших побуждений; ~-nigh почти; ~-off состоятельный; ~-paid хорошо оплачиваемый; ~-preserved хорошо сохранившийся; ~-to-do состоятельный; ~-wisher доброжелатель m.

wellington (boot) n резиновый сапог. Welsh adj уэльский. Welshman n валлиец. Welshwoman n валлийка.

welter n путаница.

wend vt: ~ one's way держать impf путь.

west n запад; (naut) вест; adj западный; adv на запад, к западу. westerly adj западный. western adj западный; n (film) вестерн. westward(s) adv на запад, к западу.

wet adj мокрый; (paint) непросохший; (rainy) дождливый; ~ through промокший до нитки; n (dampness) влажность; (rain) дождь m; vt мочить impf, на~ pf.

whack n (blow) удар; vt колотить impf, по~ pf. whacked adj разбитый.

whale n кит.

wharf n пристань.

what pron (interrog, int) что; (how much) сколько; (rel) (то,) что; ~ (...)

for зачем; ~ if a что если; ~ is your name как вас зовут?; adj (interrog, int) какой; ~ kind of какой. whatever, whatsoever pron что бы ни +past (~ you think что бы вы ни думали); всё, что (take ~ you want возьмите всё, что хотите); adj какой бы ни+past (~ books he read(s) какие бы книги он ни прочитал); (at all): there is no chance ~ нет никакой возможности; is there any chance ~? есть ли хоть какая-нибудь возможность?

wheat n пшеница.

wheedle vt (coax into doing) уговаривать impf, уговорить pf с помощью лести; ~ out of выманивать impf, выманить pf у+gen.

wheel n колесо; (steering ~, helm) руль m; (potter's) гончарный круг; vt (push) катать indet, катить det, по~ pf; vt & i (turn) повёртывать(ся) impf, повернуть(ся) pf; vi (circle) кружиться impf. wheelbarrow n тачка. wheelchair n инвалидное кресло.

wheeze vi сопеть impf.

when adv когда; conj когда, в то время как; (whereas) тогда как; (if) если; (although) хотя. whence adv откуда. whenever adv когда же; conj (every time) всякий раз когда; (at any time) когда; (no matter when) когда бы ни+past; we shall have dinner ~ you arrive во сколько бы вы ни приехали, мы пообедаем.

where adv & conj (place) где; (whither) куда; from ~ откуда. whereabouts adv где; n местонахождение. whereas conj тогда как; хотя. whereby adv & conj посредством чего. wherein adv & conj в чём. wherever adv & conj (place) где; (whither) куда бы ни+past; ~ he goes куда бы он ни пошёл; ~ you like где/куда хотите. wherewithal n средства neut pl.

whet vt точить impf, на~ pf; (fig) возбуждать impf, возбудить pf.

whether conj ли; I don't know ~ he will come я не знаю, придёт ли он; ~ he comes or not придёт (ли) он или нет.

which adj (interrog, rel) какой; pron (interrog) какой; (person) кто; (rel) кото́рый; (*rel to whole statement*) что; ~ **is** ~? (*persons*) кто из них кто?; (*things*) что-что? **whichever** *adj & pron* како́й бы ни+*past*; **book you choose** каку́ю бы кни́гу ты ни вы́брал; любо́й (**take** ~ **book you want** возьми́те любу́ю кни́гу).

whiff *n* за́пах.

while *n* вре́мя *neut*; **a little** ~ недо́лго; **a long** ~ до́лго; **for a long** ~ (*up to now*) давно́; **for a** ~ на вре́мя; **in a little** ~ ско́ро; **it is worth** ~ сто́ит э́то сде́лать; *vt*: ~ **away** проводи́ть *impf*, провести́ *pf*; *conj* пока́; **in the** ~ в то вре́мя как; (*although*) хотя́; (*contrast*) a; **we went to the cinema** ~ **they went to the theatre** мы ходи́ли в кино́, а они́ в теа́тр. **whilst** *see* **while**

whim *n* при́хоть, капри́з.

whimper *vi* хны́кать *impf*; (*dog*) скули́ть *impf*.

whimsical *adj* капри́зный; (*odd*) причу́дливый.

whine *n* (*wail*) вой; (*whimper*) хны́канье; *vi* (*dog*) скули́ть *impf*; (*wail*) выть; (*whimper*) хны́кать *impf*.

whinny *vi* ти́хо ржать *impf*.

whip *n* кнут, хлыст; *vt* (*lash*) хлеста́ть *impf*, хлестну́ть *pf*; (*cream*) сбива́ть *impf*, сбить *pf*; ~ **off** скиды́вать *impf*, ски́нуть *pf*; ~ **out** выха́тывать *impf*, вы́хватить *pf*; ~ **round** бы́стро повёртываться *impf*, поверну́ться *pf*; ~**round** сбор де́нег; ~ **up** (*stir up*) разжига́ть *impf*, разже́чь *pf*.

whirl *n* круже́ние; (*of dust, fig*) вихрь *m*; (*turmoil*) сумато́ха; *vt & i* кружи́ть(ся) *impf*, за~ *pf*. **whirlpool** *n* водоворо́т. **whirlwind** *n* вихрь *m*.

whirr *vi* жужжа́ть *impf*.

whisk *n* (*of twigs etc.*) ве́ничек; (*utensil*) муто́вка; (*movement*) пома́хивание; *vt* (*cream etc.*) сбива́ть *impf*, сбить *pf*; ~ **away, off** (*brush off*) сма́хивать *impf*, смахну́ть *pf*; (*take away*) бы́стро уноси́ть *impf*, унести́ *pf*.

whisker *n* (*human*) во́лос на лице́; (*animal*) ус; *pl* (*human*) бакенба́рды *f pl*.

whisky *n* ви́ски *neut indecl*.

whisper *n* шёпот; *vt & i* шепта́ть *impf*, шепну́ть *pf*.

whistle *n* (*sound*) свист; (*instrument*) свисто́к; *vi* свисте́ть *impf*, свист-

нуть *pf*; *vt* насви́стывать *impf*.

white *adj* бе́лый; (*hair*) седо́й; (*pale*) бле́дный; (*with milk*) с молоко́м; **paint** ~ кра́сить *impf*, по~ *pf* в бе́лый цвет; ~**collar worker** слу́жащий *sb*; ~ **lie** неви́нная ложь; *n* (*colour*) бе́лый цвет; (*egg, eye*) бело́к; (~ *person*) бе́лый *sb*. **whiten** *vt* бели́ть *impf*, на~, по~, вы́~ *pf*; *vi* беле́ть *impf*, по~ *pf*. **whiteness** *n* белизна́. **whitewash** *n* побе́лка; *vt* бели́ть *impf*, по~ *pf*; (*fig*) обеля́ть *impf*, обели́ть *pf*.

whither *adv & conj* куда́.

Whitsun *n* Тро́ица.

whittle *vt*: ~ **down** уменьша́ть *impf*, уме́ньшить *pf*.

whiz(z) *vi*: ~ **past** просвисте́ть *pf*.

who *pron* (*interrog*) кто; (*rel*) кото́рый.

whoever *pron* кто бы ни+*past*; (*he who*) тот, кто.

whole *adj* (*entire*) весь, це́лый; (*intact, of number*) це́лый; *n* (*thing complete*) це́лое *sb*; (*all there is*) весь *sb*; (*sum*) су́мма; **on the** ~ в о́бщем. **wholehearted** *adj* беззаве́тный. **whole-heartedly** *adv* от всего́ се́рдца. **wholemeal** *adj* из непросе́янной муки́. **wholesale** *adj* опто́вый; (*fig*) ма́ссовый; *adv* о́птом. **wholesaler** *n* опто́вый торго́вец. **wholesome** *adj* здоро́вый. **wholly** *adv* по́лностью.

whom *pron* (*interrog*) кого́ *etc.*; (*rel*) кото́рого *etc.*

whoop *n* крик; *vi* крича́ть *impf*, кри́кнуть *pf*; ~ **it up** бу́рно весели́ться *impf*; ~**ing cough** коклю́ш.

whore *n* проститу́тка.

whose *pron* (*interrog, rel*) чей; (*rel*) кото́рого.

why *adv* почему́; *int* да ведь!

wick *n* фити́ль *m*.

wicked *adj* ди́кий. **wickedness** *n* ди́кость.

wicker *attrib* плетёный.

wicket *n* (*cricket*) воро́тца.

wide *adj* широ́кий; (*extensive*) обши́рный; (*in measurements*) в ширину́; ~ **open** широко́ откры́тый; *adv* (*off target*) ми́мо це́ли. **widely** *adv* широко́. **widen** *vt & i* расширя́ть(ся) *impf*, расши́рить(ся) *pf*. **widespread** *adj* распространённый.

widow *n* вдова́. **widowed** *adj* овдовевший. **widower** n вдове́ц.

width n ширина́; (*fig*) широта́; (*of cloth*) полотни́ще.

wield vt (*brandish*) разма́хивать *impf* +instr; (*power*) по́льзоваться *impf* +instr.

wife n жена́.

wig n пари́к.

wiggle vt & i (*move*) шевели́ть(ся) *impf*, по~, шевельну́ть(ся) *pf* (+instr).

wigwam n вигва́м.

wild adj ди́кий; (*flower*) полево́й; (*uncultivated*) невозде́ланный; (*tempestuous*) бу́йный; (*furious*) неи́стовый; (*ill-considered*) необду́манный; be ~ about быть без ума́ от+gen; ~-goose chase сумасбро́дная зате́я; n: pl дебри́ (-рей) pl. **wildcat** adj (*unofficial*) неофициа́льный. **wilderness** n пусты́ня. **wildfire** n. spread like ~ распространя́ться *impf*, распространи́ться *pf* с молниено́сной быстрото́й. **wildlife** n жива́я приро́да. **wildness** n ди́кость.

wile n хи́трость.

wilful adj (*obstinate*) упря́мый; (*deliberate*) преднаме́ренный.

will n во́ля; (~-power) си́ла во́ли; (*at death*) завеща́ние; against one's ~ про́тив во́ли; of one's own free ~ доброво́льно; with a ~ с энтузиа́змом; good ~ до́брая во́ля; make one's ~ писа́ть *impf*, на~ *pf* завеща́ние; vt (*want*) хоте́ть *impf*, за~ *pf* +gen, acc; v aux: he ~ be president он бу́дет президе́нтом; he ~ return tomorrow он верне́тся за́втра; ~ you open the window? откро́йте окно́, пожа́луйста. **willing** adj гото́вый; (*eager*) стара́тельный. **willingly** adv охо́тно. **willingness** n гото́вность.

willow n и́ва.

willy-nilly adv во́лей-нево́лей.

wilt vi поника́ть *impf*, пони́кнуть *pf*.

wily adj хи́трый.

win n побе́да; vt & i выи́грывать *impf*, вы́играть *pf*; vt (*obtain*) добива́ться *impf*, доби́ться *pf* +gen; ~ over угова́ривать *impf*, уговори́ть *pf*; (*charm*) располага́ть *impf*, расположи́ть *pf* к себе́.

wince vi вздра́гивать *impf*, вздро́гнуть *pf*.

winch n лебёдка; поднима́ть *impf*, подня́ть *pf* с по́мощью лебёдки.

wind[1] n (*air*) ве́тер; (*breath*) дыха́ние; (*flatulence*) ве́тры m pl; ~ instrument духово́й инструме́нт; ~-swept откры́тый ветра́м; get ~ of пронюхивать *impf*, проню́хать *pf*; vt (*make gasp*) заставля́ть *impf*, заста́вить *pf* задохну́ться.

wind[2] vi (*meander*) ви́ться *impf*; изви́ва́ться *impf*; vt (*coil*) нама́тывать *impf*, намота́ть *pf*; (*watch*) заводи́ть *impf*, завести́ *pf*; (*wrap*) уку́тывать *impf*, уку́тать *pf*; ~ up (vt) (*reel*) сма́тывать *impf*, смота́ть *pf*; (*watch*) see wind[2]; (vt & i) (*end*) конча́ть(ся) *impf*, ко́нчить(ся) *pf*. **winding** adj (*meandering*) изви́листый; (*staircase*) винтово́й.

windfall n па́далица; (*fig*) золото́й дождь.

windmill n ветряна́я ме́льница.

window n окно́; (*of shop*) витри́на; ~-box нару́жный я́щик для цвето́в; ~-cleaner мо́йщик о́кон; ~-dressing оформле́ние витри́н; (*fig*) показу́ха; ~-frame око́нная ра́ма; ~-ledge подоко́нник; ~-pane око́нное стекло́; ~-shopping рассма́тривание витри́н; ~-sill подоко́нник.

windpipe n дыха́тельное го́рло. **windscreen** n ветрово́е стекло́; ~ wiper дво́рник. **windsurfer** n виндсёрфинги́ст. **windsurfing** n виндсёрфинг. **windward** adj наве́тренный. **windy** adj ве́треный.

wine n вино́; ~ bar ви́нный погребо́к; ~ bottle ви́нная буты́лка; ~-list ка́рта вин; ~-tasting дегуста́ция вин. **wineglass** n рю́мка. **winery** n ви́нный заво́д. **winy** adj ви́нный.

wing n (*also polit*) крыло́; (*archit*) фли́гель m; (*sport*) фланг; pl (*theat*) кули́сы f pl. **winged** adj крыла́тый.

wink vt: ~ (*blink*) морга́ние; (*as sign*) подми́гивание; vi мига́ть *impf*, мигну́ть *pf*; ~ at подми́гивать *impf*, подмигну́ть *pf* +dat; (*fig*) смотре́ть *impf*, по~ *pf* сквозь па́льцы на+acc.

winkle vt: ~ out выко́вы́ривать *impf*, вы́ковырять *pf*.

winner n победи́тель m, ~ница. **winning** adj (*victorious*) вы́игравший; (*shot etc.*) реша́ющий; (*charming*) обая́тельный; n: pl вы́игрыш; ~-post фи́нишный столб.

winter n зима́; attrib зи́мний. **wintry**

adj зи́мний; (*cold*) холо́дный.

wipe *vt* (*also* ~ *out inside of*) вытира́ть *impf*, вы́тереть *pf*; ~ **away**, **off** стира́ть *impf*, стере́ть *pf*; ~ **out** (*exterminate*) уничтожа́ть *impf*, уничто́жить *pf*; (*cancel*) смыва́ть *impf*, смыть *pf*.

wire *n* про́волока; (*carrying current*) про́вод; ~ **netting** про́волочная се́тка. **wireless** *n* ра́дио *neut indecl*. **wiring** *n* электропрово́дка. **wiry** *adj* жи́листый.

wisdom *n* му́дрость; ~ **tooth** зуб му́дрости. **wise** *adj* му́дрый; (*prudent*) благоразу́мный.

wish *n* жела́ние; **with best** ~**es** хоро́шего, с наилу́чшими пожела́ниями; *vt* хоте́ть *impf*, за~ *pf* (I ~ I could see him мне хоте́лось бы его́ ви́деть; I ~ to go я хочу́ пойти́; I ~ you to come early я хочу́, чтобы вы ра́но пришли́; I ~ the day were over хорошо́ бы день уже́ ко́нчился); жела́ть +*gen* (I ~ you luck жела́ю вам уда́чи); (*congratulate on*) поздравля́ть *impf*, поздра́вить *pf* (I ~ you a happy birthday поздравля́ю тебя́ с днём рожде́ния); *vi*: ~ **for** жела́ть *impf* +*gen*; мечта́ть *impf* о+*prep*. **wishful** *adj*: ~ **thinking** самообольще́ние; приня́тие жела́емого за действи́тельное.

wisp *n* (*of straw*) пучо́к; (*hair*) клочо́к; (*smoke*) стру́йка.

wisteria *n* глици́ния.

wistful *adj* тоскли́вый.

wit *n* (*mind*) ум; (*wittiness*) остроу́мие; (*person*) остря́к; **be at one's** ~**'s end** не знать *impf* что де́лать.

witch *n* ве́дьма; ~-**hunt** охо́та за ве́дьмами. **witchcraft** *n* колдовство́.

with *prep* (*in company of, together* ~) (вме́сте) с+*instr*; (*as a result of*) от+*gen*; (*at house of, in keeping of*) y+*gen*; (*by means of*) +*instr*; (*in spite of*) несмотря́ на+*acc*; (*including*) включа́я+*acc*; ~ **each/one another** друг с дру́гом.

withdraw *vt* (*retract*) брать *impf*, взять *pf* наза́д; (*hand*) отдёргивать *impf*, отдёрнуть *pf*; (*cancel*) снима́ть *impf*, снять *pf*; (*mil*) выводи́ть *impf*, вы́вести *pf*; (*money from circulation*) изыма́ть *impf*, изъя́ть из обраще́ния; (*diplomat etc.*) отзы-

ва́ть *impf*, отозва́ть *pf*; (*from bank*) брать *impf*, взять *pf*; *vi* удаля́ться *impf*, удали́ться *pf*; (*drop out*) выбыва́ть *impf*, вы́быть *pf*; (*mil*) отходи́ть *impf*, отойти́ *pf*. **withdrawal** *n* (*retraction*) взя́тие наза́д; (*cancellation*) сня́тие; (*mil*) отхо́д; (*money from circulation*) изъя́тие; (*departure*) ухо́д. **withdrawn** *adj* за́мкнутый.

wither *vi* вя́нуть *impf*, за~ *pf*. **withering** *adj* (*fig*) уничтожа́ющий.

withhold *vt* (*refuse to grant*) не дава́ть *impf*, дать *pf* +*gen*; (*payment*) уде́рживать *impf*, удержа́ть *pf*; (*information*) ута́ивать *impf*, утаи́ть *pf*.

within *prep* (*inside*) внутри́+*gen*, в+*prep*; (~ *the limits of*) в преде́лах +*gen*; (*time*) в тече́ние +*gen*; *adv* внутри́; **from** ~ изнутри́.

without *prep* без+*gen*; ~ **saying good-bye** не проща́ясь; **do** ~ обходи́ться *impf*, обойти́сь *pf* без+*gen*.

withstand *vt* выде́рживать *impf*, вы́держать *pf*.

witness *n* (*person*) свиде́тель *m*; (*eye*-~) очеви́дец; (*to signature etc.*) завери́тель *m*; **bear** ~ **to** свиде́тельствовать *impf*, за~ *pf*; ~-**box** ме́сто для свиде́тельских показа́ний; *vt* быть свиде́телем+*gen*; (*document etc.*) заверя́ть *impf*, заве́рить *pf*.

witticism *n* остро́та. **witty** *adj* остроу́мный.

wizard *n* волше́бник, колду́н.

wizened *adj* морщи́нистый.

wobble *vt* & *i* шата́ть(ся) *impf*, шатну́ть(ся) *pf*; *vi* (*voice*) дрожа́ть *impf*. **wobbly** *adj* ша́ткий.

woe *n* го́ре; ~ **is me!** го́ре мне! **woeful** *adj* жа́лкий.

wolf *n* волк; *vt* пожира́ть *impf*, пожра́ть *pf*.

woman *n* же́нщина. **womanizer** *n* волоки́та. **womanly** *adj* же́нственный.

womb *n* ма́тка.

wonder *n* чу́до; (*amazement*) изумле́ние; (*it's*) **no** ~ неудиви́тельно; *vt* интересова́ться *impf* (I ~ who will come интере́сно, кто придёт); *vi*: **I shouldn't** ~ **if** неудиви́тельно бу́дет, е́сли; I ~ **if you could help me** не могли́ бы вы мне помо́чь; ~ **at** удивля́ться *impf*, удиви́ться *pf* +*dat*. **wonderful, wondrous** *adj* замеча́тельный.

wont *n*: as is his ~ по своему́ обыкнове́нию; *predic*: be ~ to име́ть привы́чку+*inf*.

woo *vt* уха́живать *impf* за+*instr*.

wood *n* (*forest*) лес; (*material*) де́рево; (*firewood*) дрова́ *pl*. **woodcut** *n* гравю́ра на де́реве. **wooded** *adj* леси́стый. **wooden** *adj* (*also fig*) деревя́нный. **woodland** *n* леси́стая ме́стность; *attrib* лесно́й. **woodpecker** *n* дя́тел. **woodwind** *n* деревя́нные духовы́е инструме́нты *m pl*. **woodwork** *n* столя́рная рабо́та; (*wooden parts*) деревя́нные ча́сти (-те́й) *pl*. **woodworm** *n* жучо́к. **woody** *adj* (*plant etc*.) деревяни́стый; (*wooded*) леси́стый.

wool *n* шерсть. **woollen** *adj* шерстяно́й. **woolly** *adj* шерсти́стый; (*indistinct*) нея́сный.

word *n* сло́во; (*news*) изве́стие; by ~ of mouth у́стно; have a ~ with поговори́ть *pf* с+*instr*; in a ~ одни́м сло́вом; in other ~s други́ми слова́ми; ~ for ~ сло́во в сло́во; ~ processor компью́тер(-изда́тель) *m*; *vt* выража́ть *impf*, вы́разить *pf*; формули́ровать *impf*, с~ *pf*. **wording** *n* формулиро́вка.

work *n* рабо́та; (*labour; toil; scholarly* ~) труд; (*occupation*) заня́тие; (*studies*) заня́тия *neut pl*; (*of art*) произведе́ние; (*book*) сочине́ние; *pl* (*factory*) заво́д; (*mechanism*) механи́зм; at ~ (*doing*~) за рабо́той; (*at place of* ~) на рабо́те; out of ~ безрабо́тный; ~force рабо́чая си́ла; ~load нагру́зка; *vi* (*also function*) рабо́тать *impf* (at, on над+*instr*); (*study*) занима́ться *impf*, заня́ться *pf*; (*also toil, labour*) труди́ться *impf*; (*have effect, function*) де́йствовать *impf*; (*succeed*) удава́ться *impf*, уда́ться *pf*; *vt* (*operate*) управля́ть *impf* +*instr*; обраща́ться *impf* с+*instr*; (*wonders*) твори́ть *impf*, со~ *pf*; (*soil*) обраба́тывать *impf*, обрабо́тать *pf*; (*compel to* ~) заставля́ть *impf*, заста́вить *pf* рабо́тать; ~ **in** вставля́ть *impf*, вста́вить *pf*; ~ **off** (*debt*) отраба́тывать *impf*, отрабо́тать *pf*; (*weight*) сгоня́ть *impf*, согна́ть *pf*; (*energy*) дава́ть *impf*, дать *pf* вы́ход +*dat*; ~ **out** (*solve*) находи́ть *impf*, найти́ *pf* реше́ние +*gen*; (*plans etc*.)

разраба́тывать *impf*, разрабо́тать *pf*; (*sport*) тренирова́ться *impf*; everything ~ed out well всё ко́нчилось хорошо́; ~ out at (*amount to*) составля́ть *impf*, соста́вить *pf*; ~ up (*perfect*) выраба́тывать *impf*, вы́работать *pf*; (*excite*) возбужда́ть *impf*, возбуди́ть *pf*; (*appetite*) нагу́ливать *impf*, нагуля́ть *pf*. **workable** *adj* осуществи́мый, реа́льный. **workaday** *adj* бу́дничный. **workaholic** *n* трудого́лик. **worker** *n* рабо́тник; (*manual*) рабо́чий *sb*. **working** *adj*: ~ class рабо́чий класс; ~ hours рабо́чее вре́мя *neut*; ~ party коми́ссия. **workman** *n* рабо́тник. **workmanlike** *adj* иску́сный. **workmanship** *n* иску́сство, мастерство́. **workshop** *n* мастерска́я *sb*.

world *n* мир, свет; *attrib* мирово́й; ~-famous всеми́рно изве́стный; ~ war мирова́я война́; ~-wide всеми́рный. **worldly** *adj* мирско́й; (*person*) о́пытный.

worm *n* червь *m*; (*intestinal*) глист; *vt*: ~ o.s. into вкра́дываться *impf*, вкра́сться *pf* в+*acc*; ~ out выве́дывать *impf*, вы́ведать *pf* (of y+*gen*); ~ one's way пробира́ться *impf*, пробра́ться *pf*.

worry *n* (*anxiety*) беспоко́йство; (*care*) забо́та; *vt* беспоко́ить *impf*, о~ *pf*; *vi* беспоко́иться *impf*, о~ *pf* (about о+*prep*).

worse *adj* ху́дший; *adv* ху́же; *n*: from bad to ~ всё ху́же и ху́же. **worsen** *vt & i* ухудша́ть(ся) *impf*, ухудши́ть(ся) *pf*.

worship *n* поклоне́ние (of +*dat*); (*service*) богослуже́ние; *vt* поклоня́ться *impf* +*dat*; (*adore*) обожа́ть *impf*. **worshipper** *n* покло́нник, -ица.

worst *adj* наиху́дший, са́мый плохо́й; *adv* ху́же всего́; *n* са́мое плохо́е.

worth *n* (*value*) цена́, це́нность; (*merit*) досто́инство; give me a pound's ~ of petrol да́йте мне бензи́на на фунт; *adj*: be ~ (*of equal value to*) сто́ить *impf* (what is it ~? ско́лько э́то сто́ит?); (*deserve*) сто́ить *impf* +*gen* (is this film ~ seeing? сто́ит посмотре́ть э́тот фильм?). **worthless** *adj* ничего́ не сто́ящий; (*useless*) бесполе́зный. **worthwhile** *adj* сто́ящий. **worthy** *adj* досто́йный.

would *v aux* (*conditional*): he ~ be angry if he found out он бы рассерди́лся, е́сли бы узна́л; (*expressing wish*) she ~ like to know она́ бы хоте́ла знать; I ~ rather я бы предпочёл; (*expressing indirect speech*): he said he ~ be late он сказа́л, что придёт по́здно.

would-be *adj*: ~ actor челове́к мечта́ющий стать актёром.

wound *n* ра́на; *vt* ра́нить *impf & pf*. **wounded** *adj* ра́неный.

wrangle *n* препира́ние; *vi* препира́ться *impf*.

wrap *n* (*shawl*) шаль; *vt* (*also* ~ up) завёртывать *impf*, заверну́ть *pf*; ~ up (*in wraps*) заку́тывать(ся) *impf*, заку́тать(ся) *pf*; ~ped up in (*fig*) поглощённый +*instr*. **wrapper** *n* обёртка. **wrapping** *n* обёртка; ~ paper обёрточная бума́га.

wrath *n* гнев.

wreak *vt*: ~ havoc on разоря́ть *impf*, разори́ть *pf*.

wreath *n* вено́к.

wreck *n* (*ship*) оста́нки (-ов) корабля́; (*vehicle, person, building, etc.*) разва́лина; *vt* (*destroy, also fig*) разруша́ть *impf*, разру́шить *pf*; be ~ed терпе́ть *impf*, по~ *pf* круше́ние; (*of plans etc.*) ру́хнуть *pf*. **wreckage** *n* обло́мки *m pl* круше́ния.

wren *n* крапи́вник.

wrench *n* (*jerk*) дёрганье; (*tech*) га́ечный ключ; (*fig*) боль; *vt* (*snatch, pull out*) вырыва́ть *impf*, вы́рвать *pf* (from y+gen); ~ open взла́мывать *impf*, взлома́ть *pf*.

wrest *vt* (*wrench*) вырыва́ть *impf*, вы́рвать *pf* (from y+gen).

wrestle *vi* боро́ться *impf*. **wrestler** *n* боре́ц. **wrestling** *n* борьба́.

wretch *n* несча́стный *sb*; (*scoundrel*) негодя́й. **wretched** *adj* жа́лкий; (*unpleasant*) скве́рный.

wriggle *vi* извива́ться *impf*, изви́ться *pf*; (*fidget*) ёрзать *impf*; ~ out of увиливать *impf*, увильну́ть от+gen.

wring *vt* (*also* ~ out) выжима́ть *impf*, вы́жать *pf*; (*extort*) исторга́ть *impf*, исто́ргнуть *pf* (from y+gen); (*neck*) свёртывать *impf*, сверну́ть *pf* (+*dat*); ~ one's hands лома́ть *impf*, с~ *pf* ру́ки.

wrinkle *n* морщи́на; *vt & i* мо́рщить-

(ся) *impf*, с~ *pf*.

wrist *n* запя́стье; ~-watch нару́чные часы́ (-со́в) *pl*.

writ *n* пове́стка.

write *vt & i* писа́ть *impf*, на~ *pf*; ~ down запи́сывать *impf*, записа́ть *pf*; ~ off (*cancel*) спи́сывать *impf*, списа́ть *pf*; the car was a ~-off маши́на была́ соверше́нно испо́рчена; ~ out выпи́сывать *impf*, вы́писать *pf* (in full по́лностью); (*account of*) подро́бно опи́сывать *impf*, описа́ть *pf*; (*notes*) перепи́сывать *impf*, переписа́ть *pf*; ~-up (*report*) отчёт. **writer** *n* писа́тель *m*, ~ница.

writhe *vi* ко́рчиться *impf*, с~ *pf*.

writing *n* (*handwriting*) по́черк; (*work*) произведе́ние; in ~ в пи́сьменной фо́рме; ~-paper почто́вая бума́га.

wrong *adj* (*incorrect*) непра́вильный, неве́рный; (*the wrong* ...) не тот (I have bought the ~ book я купи́л не ту кни́гу; you've got the ~ number (*tel*) вы не туда́ попа́ли); (*mistaken*) непра́вый (you are ~ ты непра́в); (*unjust*) несправедли́вый; (*sinful*) дурно́й; (*out of order*) нела́дный; (*side of cloth*) ле́вый; ~ side out наизна́нку; ~ way round наоборо́т; *n* зло; (*injustice*) несправедли́вость; be in the ~ быть непра́вым; do ~ греши́ть *impf*, со~ *pf*; *adv* непра́вильно, неве́рно; go ~ не получа́ться *impf*, получи́ться *pf*; v обижа́ть *impf*, оби́деть *pf*; (*be unjust to*) быть несправедли́вым к+dat. **wrongdoer** *n* престу́пник, гре́шник, -ица. **wrongful** *adj* несправедли́вый. **wrongly** *adv* непра́вильно; (*unjustly*) справедли́во.

wrought *adj*: ~ iron сва́рочное желе́зо.

wry *adj* (*smile*) криво́й; (*humour*) сухо́й, ирони́ческий.

X

xenophobia *n* ксенофо́бия.

X-ray *n* (*picture*) рентге́н(овский сни́мок); *pl* (*radiation*) рентге́новы лучи́ *m pl*; *vt* (*photograph*) де́лать *impf*, с~ *pf* рентге́н +gen.

Y

yacht n я́хта. yachting n па́русный спорт. yachtsman n яхтсме́н.

yank vt рвану́ть pf.

yap vi тя́вкать impf, тя́вкнуть pf.

yard¹ n (piece of ground) двор.

yard² n (measure) ярд. yardstick n (fig) мери́ло.

yarn n пря́жа; (story) расска́з.

yawn n зево́к; vi зева́ть impf, зевну́ть pf; (chasm etc.) зия́ть impf.

year n год; ~ in, ~ out из го́да в год. yearbook n ежего́дник. yearly adj ежего́дный, годово́й; adv ежего́дно.

yearn vi тоскова́ть impf (for по+dat). yearning n тоска́ (for по+dat).

yeast n дро́жжи (-же́й) pl.

yell n крик; vi крича́ть impf, кри́кнуть pf.

yellow adj жёлтый; n жёлтый цвет. yellowish adj желтова́тый.

yelp n визг; vi визжа́ть impf, ви́згнуть pf.

yes adv да; n утвержде́ние, согла́сие; (in vote) го́лос «за».

yesterday adv вчера́; n вчера́шний день m; ~ morning вчера́ у́тром; the day before ~ позавчера́; ~'s newspaper вчера́шняя газе́та.

yet adv (still) ещё; (so far) до сих пор; (in questions) уже́; (nevertheless) тем не ме́нее; as ~ пока́, до сих пор; not ~ ещё не; conj одна́ко, но.

yew n тис.

Yiddish n и́диш.

yield n (harvest) урожа́й; (econ) дохо́д; vt (fruit, revenue, etc.) приноси́ть impf, принести́ pf; дава́ть impf, дать pf; (give up) сдава́ть impf, сдать pf; vi (give in) (to enemy etc.) уступа́ть impf, уступи́ть pf (to +dat); (give way) поддава́ться impf, подда́ться pf (to +dat).

yoga n йо́га.

yoghurt n кефи́р.

yoke n (also fig) ярмо́; (fig) и́го; (of dress) коке́тка; vt впряга́ть impf, впрячь pf в ярмо́.

yolk n желто́к.

yonder adv вон там; adj вон тот.

you pron (familiar sg) ты; (familiar pl, polite sg & pl) вы; (one) not usu

translated; v translated in 2nd pers sg or by impers construction: ~ never know никогда́ не зна́ешь.

young adj молодо́й; the ~ молодёжь; n (collect) детёныши m pl.

youngster n ма́льчик, де́вочка.

your(s) poss pron (familiar sg; also in letter) твой; (familiar pl, polite sg & pl; also in letter) ваш; свой. yourself pron (emph) (familiar sg) (ты) сам (m), сама́ (f); (familiar pl, polite sg & pl) (вы) са́ми; (refl) себя́; -ся (suffixed to vt); by ~ (independently) самостоя́тельно, сам; (alone) оди́н.

youth n (age) мо́лодость; (young man) ю́ноша m; (collect, as pl) молодёжь; ~ club молодёжный клуб; ~ hostel молодёжная турба́за. youthful adj ю́ношеский.

Yugoslavia n Югосла́вия.

Z

zany adj смешно́й.

zeal n рве́ние, усе́рдие. zealot n фана́тик. zealous adj ре́вностный, усе́рдный.

zebra n зе́бра.

zenith n зени́т.

zero n нуль m, ноль m.

zest n (piquancy) пика́нтность; (ardour) энтузиа́зм; ~ for life жизнера́достность.

zigzag n зигза́г; adj зигзагообра́зный; vi де́лать impf, с~ pf зигза́ги; идти́ де́т зигза́гами.

zinc n цинк.

Zionism n сиони́зм. Zionist n сиони́ст.

zip n (~ fastener) (застёжка-)мо́лния; vt & i: ~ up застёгивать(ся) impf, застегну́ть(ся) pf на мо́лнию.

zodiac n зодиа́к; sign of the ~ знак зодиа́ка.

zombie n челове́к спя́щий на ходу́.

zone n зо́на; (geog) по́яс.

zoo n зоопа́рк. zoological adj зоологи́ческий; ~ garden(s) зоологи́ческий сад. zoologist n зоо́лог. zoology n зооло́гия.

zoom vi (rush) мча́ться impf; ~ in (phot) де́лать impf, с~ pf наплы́в; ~ lens объекти́в с переме́нным фо́кусным расстоя́нием.

Zulu adj зулу́сский; n зулу́с, ~ка.

Appendix I **Spelling Rules**

It is assumed that the user is acquainted with the following spelling rules which affect Russian declension and conjugation.

1. ы, ю, and я do not follow г, к, х, ж, ч, ш, and щ; instead, и, у, and а are used, e.g. ма́льчикив, кричу́, лежа́т, ноча́ми; similarly, ю and я do not follow ц; instead, у or а are used.

2. Unstressed о does not follow ж, ц, ч, ш, or щ; instead, е is used, e.g. му́жем, ме́сяцев, хоро́шее.

Appendix II **Declension of Russian Nouns**

The following patterns are regarded as regular and are not shown in the dictionary entries. Forms marked * should be particularly noted.

1 *Masculine*

Singular	nom	acc	gen	dat	instr	prep
	обе́д	~	~а	~у	~ом	~е
	слу́ча|й	~й	~я	~ю	~ем	~е
	марш	~	~а	~у	~ем	~е
	каранда́ш	~	~а́	~у́	~о́м*	~е́
	сцена́ри|й	~й	~я	~ю	~ем	~и*
	портфе́л|ь	~ь	~я	~ю	~ем	~е

Plural	nom	acc	gen	dat	instr	prep
	обе́д|ы	~ы	~ов	~ам	~ами	~ах
	слу́ча|и	~и	~ев	~ям	~ями	~ях
	ма́рш|и	~и	~ей*	~ам	~ами	~ах
	каранда́ш|и́	~и́	~е́й*	~а́м	~а́ми	~а́х
	сцена́ри|и	~и	~ев*	~ям	~ями ,	~ях
	портфе́л|и	~и	~ей*	~ям	~ями	~ях

2 *Feminine*

Singular	nom	acc	gen	dat	instr	prep
	газе́т|а	~у	~ы	~е	~ой	~е
	ба́н|я	~ю	~и	~е	~ей	~е
	ли́ни|я	~ю	~и	~и*	~ей	~и*
	ста́ту|я	~ю	~и	~е*	~ей	~е*
	бол|ь	~ь	~и	~и*	~ью*	~и*

Plural	nom	acc	gen	dat	instr	prep
	газе́т|ы	~ы	~	~ам	~ами	~ах
	ба́н|и	~и	~ь*	~ям	~ями	~ях
	ли́ни|и	~и	~й*	~ям	~ями	~ях
	ста́ту|и	~и	~й*	~ям	~ями	~ях
	бо́л|и	~и	~ей*	~ям	~ями	~ях

3 Neuter

Singular	nom	acc	gen	dat	instr	prep
	чу́вств|о	~о	~а	~у	~ом	~е
	учи́лищ|е	~е	~а	~у	~ем	~е
	зда́ни|е	~е	~я	~ю	~ем	~и*
	уще́л|ье	~ье	~ья	~ью	~ьем	~ье

Plural	nom	acc	gen	dat	instr	prep
	чу́вств|а	~а	~	~ам	~ами	~ах
	учи́лищ|а	~а	~	~ам	~ами	~ах
	зда́ни|я	~я	~й*	~ям	~ями	~ях
	уще́л|ья	~ья	~ий*	~ьям	~ьями	~ьях

Appendix III Declension of Russian Adjectives

The following patterns are regarded as regular and are not shown in the dictionary entries.

Singular	nom	acc	gen	dat	instr	prep
Masculine	тёпл|ый	~ый	~ого	~ому	~ым	~ом
Feminine	тёпл|ая	~ую	~ой	~ой	~ой	~ой
Neuter	тёпл|ое	~ое	~ого	~ому	~ым	~ом

Plural	nom	acc	gen	dat	instr	prep
Masculine	тёпл|ые	~ые	~ых	~ым	~ыми	~ых
Feminine	тёпл|ые	~ые	~ых	~ым	~ыми	~ых
Neuter	тёпл|ые	~ые	~ых	~ым	~ыми	~ых

Appendix IV **Conjugation of Russian Verbs**

The following patterns are regarded as regular and are not shown in the dictionary entries.

1. -e- conjugation

(a) **чита́|ть**	~ю	~ешь	~ет	~ем	~ете	~ют
(b) **сия́|ть**	~ю	~ешь	~ет	~ем	~ете	~ют
(c) **про́б|овать**	~ую	~уешь	~ует	~уем	~уете	~уют
(d) **рис|ова́ть**	~у́ю	~у́ешь	~у́ет	~у́ем	~у́ете	~у́ют

2. -и- conjugation

(a) **говор|и́ть**	~ю́	~и́шь	~и́т	~и́м	~и́те	~я́т
(b) **стро́|ить**	~ю	~ишь	~ит	~им	~ите	~ят

Notes

1. Also belonging to the **-e-** conjugation are:

   i) most other verbs in **-ать** (but see Note 2(v) below), e.g. **жа́ждать** (жа́жду, -ждешь); **пря́тать** (пря́чу, -чешь), **колеба́ть** (коле́блю, -блешь).

   ii) verbs in **-еть** for which the 1st pers sing **-ею** is given, e.g. **жале́ть**.

   iii) verbs in **-нуть** for which the 1st pers sing **-ну** is given (e.g. **вя́нуть**), ю becoming у in the 1st pers sing and 3rd pers pl.

   iv) verbs in **-ять** which drop the я in conjugation, e.g. **ла́ять** (ла́ю, ла́ешь); **се́ять** (се́ю, се́ешь).

2. Also belonging to the **-и-** conjugation are:

   i) verbs in consonant + **-ить** which change the consonant in the first person singular, e.g. **досади́ть** (-ажу́, -ади́шь), or insert an **-л-**, e.g. **доба́-вить** (доба́влю, -вишь).

   ii) other verbs in vowel + **-ить**, e.g. **затаи́ть**, **кле́ить** (as 2b above).

   iii) verbs in **-еть** for which the 1st pers sing is given as consonant + **ю** or **у**, e.g. **звене́ть** (-ню́, -ни́шь), **ви́деть** (ви́жу, ви́дишь).

   iv) two verbs in **-ять** (**стоя́ть**, **боя́ться**).

   v) verbs in **-ать** whose stem ends in ч, ж, щ, or ш, not changing between the infinitive and conjugation, e.g. **крича́ть** (-чу́, -чи́шь). Cf. Note 1(i).

Key to the Russian Alphabet

Capital	Lower-case	Approximate English Sound
А	а	a
Б	б	b
В	в	v
Г	г	g
Д	д	d
Е	е	ye
Ё	ё	yo
Ж	ж	zh (as in measure)
З	з	z
И	и	i
Й	й	y
К	к	k
Л	л	l
М	м	m
Н	н	n
О	о	o
П	п	p
Р	р	r
С	с	s
Т	т	t
У	у	oo
Ф	ф	f
Х	х	kh (as in lo*ch*)
Ц	ц	ts
Ч	ч	ch
Ш	ш	sh
Щ	щ	shch
Ъ	ъ	″ ("hard sign"; not pronounced as separate sound)
Ы	ы	y
Ь	ь	′ ("soft sign"; not pronounced as separate sound)
Э	э	e
Ю	ю	yu
Я	я	ya